COLONIAL AMERICA

Essays in Politics and Social Development

Fourth Edition

Edited by
Stanley N. Katz
American Council of Learned Societies

John M. Murrin
Princeton University

Douglas Greenberg
American Council of Learned Societies

McGraw-Hill, Inc.
New York St. Louis San Francisco Auckland Bogotá
Caracas Lisbon London Madrid Mexico City Milan
Montreal New Delhi San Juan Singapore
Sydney Tokyo Toronto

COLONIAL AMERICA
Essays in Politics and Social Development

This book is printed on acid-free paper.

7 8 9 0 DOC DOC 9 0 9 8 7

ISBN 0-07-033748-9

This book was set in Janson by Arcata Graphics/Kingsport.
The editors were Peter Labella, Niels Aaboe, and Peggy Rehberger; the production supervisor was Al Rihner.
The cover was designed by Carla Bauer.
R. R. Donnelley & Sons Company was printer and binder.

Library of Congress Cataloging-in-Publication Data

Colonial America: essays in politics and social development/edited by
    Stanley N. Katz, John M. Murrin, Douglas Greenberg.—4th ed.
    p.   cm.
    ISBN 0-07-033748-9
    1. United States—Social conditions—To 1865.   2. United
States—Politics and government—Colonial period, ca. 1600-1775.
I. Katz, Stanley Nider.   II. Murrin, John M.   III. Greenberg,
Douglas.
HN57.C584   1993
306'.0973—dc20   92-16316

About the Editors

Stanley N. Katz was born in 1934 and received his education at Harvard University. He has taught in the history departments at Harvard University, the University of Wisconsin at Madison, the University of Chicago, and Princeton University, and in law schools at the University of Chicago and the University of Pennsylvania. His research has been in colonial political and legal history. Among his publications are *Newcastle's New York: Anglo-American Politics, 1732–1753*, *New Perspectives on the American Past* (with Stanley I. Kutler), and an edition of *The Case and Tryal of John Peter Zenger*. He is editor of the *Oliver Wendell Holmes Devise History of the United States Supreme Court*, the co-editor of *Reviews in American History* and member of the editorial boards of *Journal of Interdisciplinary History*, *American Journal of Legal History*, and *Pennsylvania Magazine of History and Biography*. He is currently President of the American Council of Learned Societies and Senior Fellow at the Woodrow Wilson School of Public and International Affairs, Princeton University.

John M. Murrin was born in Minneapolis in 1935 and received his degrees from the College of St. Thomas, the University of Notre Dame, and Yale University. He taught for ten years at Washington University, St. Louis, before moving to Princeton in 1973 where he is now professor of history. Active in both the Columbia Seminar in Early American History and the Philadelphia Center for Early American Studies, he has published articles in several journals and in *Essays on the American Revolution*, edited by Stephen G. Kurtz and James H. Hutson (1973), *Three British Revolutions*, edited by J. G. A. Pocock (1980), and *Saints and Revolutionaries*, which he co-edited with David D. Hall and Thad W. Tate (1983).

Douglas Greenberg was born in Jersey City, New Jersey in 1947. He received his B.A. with Highest Distinction in History from Rutgers University and his M.A. and Ph.D. degrees from Cornell University. He taught history at Lawrence University and Princeton University, where he was also Assistant Dean of the Faculty. He is the author of *Crime and Law Enforcement in the Colony of New York, 1691–1776* and coauthor of *The American People: A History*. In addition, he has written widely on the humanities and higher education in both scholarly and popular journals. He is currently Vice President of the American Council of Learned Societies, and teaches American legal and constitutional history, as well as early American history, at Rutgers University. In addition, he has served since 1985 as the Chairman of the New Jersey Historical Commission.

iii

*This volume is dedicated
to the many students we shared
at Princeton University
between 1978 and 1987
and
to the memory of our colleague
Wesley Frank Craven*

Contents

v

Preface to the Fourth Edition

This edition has reduced the number of selections from twenty-five to twenty-four and has retained ten essays from the third edition. The other fifteen are new to this edition. Only three of the essays that appeared in the first two editions have been included. The field of early American history remains one of the most active and rapidly changing sub-specialties in the discipline. Those changes are reflected in the selections for this edition. If there is one characteristic of the field that we noted above all others as we were making editorial decisions, it was that politics as they were understood twenty years ago have assumed a much less significant role in the literature. The rise of social history, which in some sense inspired this collection when it first appeared, has now been joined by a congeries of hybrid methods that link social phenomena to culture, religion, and politics in quite innovative ways. Many of the new essays added to this collection have been chosen because they embody these new approaches.

While it is difficult to codify principles of selection for an anthology like this one, some basic assumptions have guided us. In general, we have retained in this edition only articles whose scholarly significance remains as great as it was when the essay first appeared *and* that have proven to be unusually well-adapted to teaching. In selecting new essays, we have leaned in the direction of including the work of younger scholars wherever possible in order to reflect not only where the field has been but also where, in our judgment, it is going. Finally, while we have tried to include more material from the still emerging fields of Women's history, African American history, and Native American history, we have tried to be quite self-conscious about not ghettoizing these fields in our organization of the volume.

In all of these tasks of selection, we have been greatly assisted by the advice of several readers who examined our first attempt to select items for this fourth edition. We remain indebted to them and to our many scholarly colleagues in early American history whose work could not be included here but that continues to inspire our interest and our admiration.

The editors welcome comments and suggestions from teachers who use this volume, if only to help guide us in planning any subsequent edition.

Stanley N. Katz
John M. Murrin
Douglas Greenberg

Preface to the Third Edition

This edition has expanded the number of selections from twenty-two to twenty-five and has retained seven essays from the second edition while restoring one from the first. The other seventeen are new to this edition, but only about half have actually been published since 1974. We have tried to take account of shifting emphases within a field that remains as dynamic and innovative as ever. Items that once seemed to stand in lonely isolation but now fit into broader patterns of interpretation have been incorporated, even though several of them were written before 1970. While we have sought a reasonable balance, both chronological and regional, we have generally preferred scholarly imagination and creativity to the simple coverage of a topic, however central.

Although this collection is now a rather long book, it represents only a fraction of recent labors by numerous scholars. Indeed our greatest difficulty has been deciding which pieces of high quality to omit. Where merit seemed about even between potential choices, as it often did, we have selected what we believe is more suitable for undergraduate teaching. Other editors would have produced a different list, of course, but we hope that the quality of our entries speaks for itself.

The editors welcome comments and suggestions from teachers who use this volume, if only to help guide us in planning any subsequent edition.

Stanley N. Katz
John M. Murrin

Preface to the Second Edition

Ten of the original twenty-one essays have been replaced in this edition. Not all of the new essays have been written since 1971, however, since my aim in revising has been to change the focus of the volume rather than to bring it "up to date." In response to a survey of the users of the first edition, I have tried to eliminate those essays which did not "teach" well, and to incorporate some previously neglected subject matter. My enthusiasm for the original set of essays persists, but I believe that the present edition may prove more widely useful.

The essays new to this volume add especially to the coverage of the several races and ethnic groups who occupied and developed the North American mainland. They also cover urban and economic history more adequately, and give some special attention to the problems of the less fortunate members of early American society.

The new edition requires the same caveat as the first: it covers colonial history in a most idiosyncratic and personal fashion. I continue to believe that the field as a whole is the most vibrant in American history, but its richness is so remarkable that it simply cannot be sampled in a slim volume. I find these essays exciting and representative of the best working in the field. That seems justification enough.

Preface to the First Edition

This volume of essays is designed as supplementary reading for the colonial history survey course, although I hope instructors may find it useful in social history courses and graduate proseminars in colonial history. The essays are reprinted in full, with all charts and footnotes.

The essays are distributed over the full time period covered in the colonial course, but no essays on the Revolutionary era are included, since the Revolution is generally given a semester to itself and requires a more intensive selection than could be included in this volume. I have not reprinted essays on "European background" or "comparative colonization," although I am fully persuaded of their place in American history, since both fields are now so extensive that it is impossible to represent them fairly in a volume of this sort.

The colonial period is currently the subject of some of the most exciting substantive and methodological work in American history, and it seems important to me to convey a sense of the new discoveries and techniques to students. My selection is also slightly weighted in favor of the eighteenth century, since it has been my experience that paperback monographs for the earlier century are more readily available.

The essays are mostly concerned with colonial socio-political development. In justification I will plead only that this seems to be the most promising area of recent research, and it is the area in which I am most interested. The essays are, in addition, mostly by younger scholars, although no slight is intended to established historians. Rather, I assume that instructors will assign works by leading scholars in addition to these articles. The book is intended to do no more than to make a series of provocative and enlightening essays accessible to undergraduates and to provide a selection of readings out of which the instructor can choose those that suit his own lectures and reading list.

PROLOGUE:
THE CONTACT
OF CULTURES

I

Virgin Soil Epidemics as a Factor in the Aboriginal Depopulation in America

ALFRED W. CROSBY

The voyages of Columbus initiated the first sustained contact be-tween Europeans and Africans on the one hand and natives of the Americas on the other. Historians have long known that the main immediate effect of this contact was a demographic catas-trophe of terrifying proportions, probably the greatest such disas-ter in world history. Throughout the Americas native popula-tions plummeted from the effects of epidemic disease. Even Europeans with no particular sympathy for the Indians were horrified by what they saw. As one Spaniard put it, "the bare look and smell of a European" was enough to wipe out a whole village.

Estimates of the precise extent of this vast human tragedy vary both in absolute numbers and proportionally. It now seems certain, however, that no less than 85 percent of the native popu-lation of the Valley of Mexico, for example, died within a century of contact with Europeans, and the loss may have exceeded 95 percent. The pace and extent of demographic decline was similar everywhere in the hemisphere. Alfred Crosby is one of the most perceptive and original historians to confront the consequences of contact between the two biological and cultural worlds in the af-termath of 1492.

In this article Crosby attempts to analyze the role of epidemic disease in a new way, arguing that despite what some other scholars have argued, Amerindians had no special susceptibility to European and African diseases. Rejecting the thrust of much earlier scholarship, Crosby conceives epidemics as social as well as biological events. Note the importance that the age of disease vic-tims plays in Crosby's interpretation. What role does he assign to the varying ways in which different cultures interpret epidemics? To what extent does his interpretation emphasize the social and cultural consequences and significance of "virgin soil epidemics" over the biological ones?

Reprinted by permission from Alfred W. Crosby, "Virgin Soil Epidemics as a Factor in the Aboriginal Depopulation in America," *William and Mary Quarterly*, 3rd ser., XXXIII (1976), 289–299.

During the last few decades historians have demonstrated increasing concern with the influence of disease in history, particularly the history of the New World. For example, the latest generation of Americanists chiefly blames diseases imported from the Old World for the disparity between the number of American aborigines in 1492—new estimates of which soar as high as one hundred million or approximately one-sixth of the human race at that time—and the few million pure Indians and Eskimos alive at the end of the nineteenth century. There is no doubt that chronic disease was an important factor in the precipitous decline, and it is highly probable that the greatest killer was epidemic disease, especially as manifested in virgin soil epidemics.[1]

Virgin soil epidemics are those in which the populations at risk have had no previous contact with the diseases that strike them and are therefore immunologically almost defenseless. The importance of virgin soil epidemics in American history is strongly indicated by evidence that a number of dangerous maladies—smallpox, measles, malaria, yellow fever, and undoubtedly several more—were unknown in the pre-Columbian New World.[2] In theory the initial appearance of these diseases is as certain to have set off deadly epidemics as dropping lighted matches into tinder is certain to cause fires.

The thesis that epidemics have been chiefly responsible for the awesome diminution in the number of native Americans is based on more than theory. The early chronicles of America are full of reports of horrendous epidemics and steep population declines, confirmed in many cases by recent quantitative analyses of Spanish tribute records and other sources.[3] The evidence provided by the documents of British and French America is not as definitely supportive of the thesis because the conquerors of those areas did not establish permanent set-

---

[1] Henry F. Dobyns, "Estimating Aboriginal American Population: An Appraisal of Techniques with a New Hemispheric Estimate," *Current Anthropology*, VII (1966), 395–449, is an excellent place to begin an examination of this theory.

[2] Percy M. Ashburn, *The Ranks of Death: A Medical History of the Conquest of America*, ed. Frank D. Ashburn (New York, 1947); Sherburne F. Cook, "The Significance of Disease in the Extinction of the New England Indians," *Human Biology*, XLV (1973), 485–508; Alfred W. Crosby, Jr., *The Columbian Exchange: Biological and Cultural Consequences of 1492* (Westport, Conn., 1972), 31–63; Henry F. Dobyns, "An Outline of Andean Epidemic History to 1720," *Bulletin of the History of Medicine*, XXXVII (1963), 493–515; Frederick L. Dunn, "On the Antiquity of Malaria in the Western Hemisphere," *Hum. Bio.*, XXXVII (1965), 385–393; Robert F. Fortuine, "The Health of the Eskimos, as Portrayed in the Earliest Written Accounts," *Bull. Hist. Med.*, XLV (1971), 98–114.

[3] Wilbur R. Jacobs, "The Tip of an Iceberg: Pre-Columbian Indian Demography and Some Implications for Revisionism," *William and Mary Quarterly*, 3d Ser., XXXI (1974), 123–132, is a good brief introduction to the subject which cites most of the recent works.

tlements and begin to keep continuous records until the seventeenth century, by which time at least some of the worst epidemics of imported diseases had probably already taken place. Furthermore, the British tended to drive the Indians away, rather than ensnaring them as slaves and peons, as the Spaniards did, with the result that many of the most important events of aboriginal history in British America occurred beyond the range of direct observation by literate witnesses.

Even so, the surviving records for North America do contain references—brief, vague, but plentiful—to deadly epidemics among the Indians, of which we shall cite a few of the allegedly worst. In 1616–1619 an epidemic, possibly of bubonic or pneumonic plague, swept coastal New England from Cape Cod to Maine, killing as many as nine out of every ten it touched.[4] During the 1630s and into the next decade, smallpox, the most fatal of all the recurrent Indian killers, whipsawed back and forth through the St. Lawrence-Great Lakes region, eliminating half the people of the Huron and Iroquois confederations.[5] In 1738 smallpox destroyed half the Cherokees, and in 1759 nearly half the Catawbas.[6] During the American Revolution it attacked the Piegan tribe and killed half its members.[7] It ravaged the plains tribes shortly before they were taken under United States jurisdiction by the Louisiana Purchase, killing two-thirds of the Omahas and perhaps half the population between the Missouri River and New Mexico.[8] In the 1820s fever devastated the people of the Columbia River area, erasing perhaps four-fifths of them.[9] In 1837 smallpox returned to the plains and destroyed about half of the aborigines there.[10]

Unfortunately, the documentation of these epidemics, as of the many others of the period, is slight, usually hearsay, sometimes dated years after the events described, and often colored by emotion. Skepticism is eminently justified and is unlikely to be dispelled by the discovery of great quantities of first-hand reports on epidemics among the North American Indians. We must depend on analysis of what lit-

---

[4] Cook, "The Significance of Disease," *Hum. Bio.*, XLV (1973), 487–491, 497.

[5] John Duffy, "Smallpox and the Indians of the American Colonies," *Bull. Hist. Med.*, XXV (1951), 328; Wilcomb E. Washburn, *The Indian in America* (New York, 1975), 105.

[6] Duffy, "Smallpox and the Indians of the American Colonies," *Bull. Hist. Med.*, XXV (1951), 335, 338.

[7] Washburn, *Indian in America*, 105.

[8] E. Wagner Stearn and Allen E. Stearn, *The Effect of Smallpox on the Destiny of the Amerindian* (Boston, 1945), 74–76.

[9] James Mooney, *The Aboriginal Population of America North of Mexico*, Smithsonian Miscellaneous Collections, LXXX, No. 7 (Washington, D. C., 1928), 14.

[10] Stearn and Stearn, *Effect of Smallpox*, 81–85; Henry R. Schoolcraft, *Information Respecting the History, Condition and Prospects of the Indian Tribes of the United States*, Pt. III (Philadelphia, 1853), 254.

tle we now know, and we must supplement that little by examination of recent epidemics among native Americans.

Let us begin by asking why the American aborigines offered so little resistance to imported epidemic diseases. Their susceptibility has long been attributed to special weakness on their part, an explanation that dates from the period of colonization, received the stamp of authority from such natural historians as the Comte de Buffon, and today acquires the color of authenticity from the science of genetics.[11] In its latest version, the hypothesis of genetic weakness holds that during the pre-Columbian millennia the New World Indians had no occasion to build up immunities to such diseases as smallpox and measles. Those aborigines who were especially lacking in defenses against these maladies were not winnowed out before they passed on their vulnerabilities to their offspring. Although there is no way to test this hypothesis for pre-Columbian times, medical data on living American aborigines do not sustain it, and the scientific community inclines toward the view that native Americans have no special susceptibility to Old World diseases that cannot be attributed to environmental influences, and probably never did have.[12]

The genetic weakness hypothesis may have some validity, but it is unproven and probably unprovable, and is therefore a weak reed to lean upon. What is more, we have no need of it. The death rate among white United States soldiers in the Civil War who contracted smallpox, a disease to which their ancestors had been exposed for many generations, was 38.5 percent, probably about the percentage of Aztecs who died of that disease in 1520.[13] The difference between the Union troops and the Aztec population is, of course, that most of the former had been vaccinated or exposed to the disease as children, while the latter was a completely virgin soil population.

It should also be asked why the decline in numbers of the American aborigines went on as long as it did, 400 years or so, in contrast to the

[11] Henry Steele Commager and Elmo Giordanetti, eds., *Was America a Mistake: An Eighteenth-Century Controversy* (New York, 1967), *passim*.

[12] John F. Marchand, "Tribal Epidemics in the Yukon," *Journal of the American Medical Association*, CXXIII (1943), 1020; Maurice L. Sievers, "Disease Patterns Among Southwestern Indians," *Public Health Reports*, LXXXI (1966), 1075–1083; Jacob A. Brody *et al.*, "Measles Vaccine Field Trials in Alaska," *Jour. Amer. Med. Assoc.*, CLXXXIX (1964), 339–342; Willard R. Centerwall, "A Recent Experience with Measles in a 'Virgin-Soil' Population," in *Biomedical Challenges Presented by the American Indian*, Pan-American Sanitary Bureau, *Scientific Publication*, No. 165 (Washington, D. C., 1968), 77–79; James V. Neel *et al.*, "Notes on the Effect of Measles and Measles Vaccine in a Virgin-Soil Population of South American Indians," *American Journal of Epidemiology*, XCI (1970), 418–429; interviews with Dr. Frederick L. Dunn of the George Williams Hooper Foundation, University of California at San Francisco.

[13] Surgeon General, U. S. Army, *The Medical and Surgical History of the War of the Rebellion*, I, pt. iii (Washington, D. C., 1888), 625; Crosby, *Columbian Exchange*, 52.

decline caused by Europe's most famous virgin soil epidemic, the Black Death, which lasted no more than 100 to 200 years.[14] The answer is that the Indians and Eskimos did not experience the onslaught of Old World diseases all at the same time and that other factors were also responsible for depressing their population levels. As far as we can say now, Old World diseases were the chief determinants in the demographic histories of particular tribes for 100 to 150 years after each tribe's first full exposure to them. In addition, the newcomers, whose dire influence on native Americans must not be underestimated just because it has been overestimated, reduced the aboriginal populations by warfare, murder, dispossession, and interbreeding. Thereafter the Indians began a slow, at first nearly imperceptible, recovery. The greatest exceptions were the peoples of the tropical lowlands and islands who, under the extra heavy burden of insect-borne fevers, mostly of African provenance, held the downward course to oblivion.[15]

The Indians of Mexico's central highlands perfectly fit this pattern of sharp decline for four to six generations followed by gradual recovery. Appalling depopulation began with the nearly simultaneous arrival of Cortés and smallpox; the nadir occurred sometime in the seventeenth century; and then Indian numbers slowly rose. The pattern of European population history was approximately the same in the two centuries following the Black Death.[16] The recovery in numbers of the Indians of the United States in the twentieth century is probably part of a similar phenomenon.

But why did Europeans lose one-third or so to the Black Death, imported from Asia, while the American aborigines lost perhaps as much as 90 percent to the diseases imported from the Old World? The answers are probably related to the factors that have caused many fatalities in recent virgin soil epidemics among native Americans, not of such deadly diseases as smallpox and plague, which are tightly controlled in our era, but of such relatively mild maladies as measles and influenza. In 1952 the Indians and Eskimos of Ungava Bay, in Northern Quebec, had an epidemic of measles: 99 percent became sick and about 7 percent died, even though some had the benefit of modern medicine. In 1954 an epidemic of measles broke out among the abo-

---

[14] William McNeill, "Plagues and Peoples: A Natural History of Human Infections," chaps. 4, 5. Mr. McNeill allowed me to read the typed manuscript of his forthcoming book.

[15] Dobyns, "Estimating Aboriginal Population," *Current Anthro.*, VII (1966), 415; Joseph de Acosta, *The Natural and Moral History of the Indies*, trans. Edward Grimston, I (New York, n.d.), 160.

[16] Charles Gibson, *The Aztecs Under Spanish Rule: A History of the Indians of the Valley of Mexico, 1519–1810* (Stanford, Calif., 1964), 139, 141. McNeill, "Plagues and Peoples," chaps. 4, 5.

rigines of Brazil's remote Xingu National Park: the death rate was 9.6 percent for those of the afflicted who had modern medical treatment and 26.8 percent for those who did not. In 1968 when the Yanomamas of the Brazilian-Venezuelan borderlands were struck by measles, 8 or 9 percent died despite the availability of some modern medicines and treatment. The Kreen-Akorores of the Amazon Basin, recently contacted for the first time by outsiders, lost at least 15 percent of their people in a single brush with common influenza.[17]

The reasons for the massive losses to epidemics in the last four hundred years and the considerable losses to the epidemics just cited can be grouped conveniently in two categories, the first relating to the nature of the disease or diseases, and the second having to do with how individuals and societies react to the threat of epidemic death.

First, we must recognize that the reputations of measles and influenza as mild diseases are not entirely justified. Contemporary native Americans who contract them are not cured by "miracle drugs," even when modern medical treatment is available, because there are no such drugs. Modern physicians do not *cure* measles, influenza, and such other viral maladies as smallpox, chicken pox, and mumps, but try, usually successfully, to keep off other infections until the normal functioning of undistracted immune systems kills off the invading viruses. If doctors fail in this task or are not available, the death rate will be "abnormally high." Measles killed more than 6 percent of all the white Union soldiers and almost 11 percent of all the black Union soldiers it infected during the Civil War, even though the waves of this disease that swept the army were not virgin soil epidemics.[18]

Virgin soil epidemics are different from others in the age incidence of those they kill, as well as in the quantity of their victims. Evidence from around the world suggests that such epidemics of a number of diseases with reputations as Indian killers—smallpox, measles, influenza, tuberculosis, and others—carry off disproportionately large percentages of people aged about fifteen to forty—men and women of the prime years of life who are largely responsible for the vital functions of food procurement, defense, and procreation.[19] Unfortunately little evidence exists to support or deny the hypothesis that native American virgin soil epidemics have been especially lethal to young

---

[17] A. F. W. Peart and F. P. Nagler, "Measles in the Canadian Arctic, 1952," *Canadian Journal of Public Health*, XLV (1954), 155; Noel Nutels, "Medical Problems of Newly Contacted Indian Groups," in *Biomedical Pan-Am. Challenges*, San. Bur., *Sci. Pub.*, No. 165 (1968), 70. Neel *et al.*, "Notes on the Effect of Measles," *Am. Jour. Epidemiology*, XCI (1970), 426; W. Jesco von Puttkamer, "Brazil's Kreen-Akarores, Requiem for a Tribe," *National Geographic*, CXLVII (1975), 254.

[18] Surgeon General, *Medical and Surgical History*, I, pt. iii, 649.

[19] Macfarlane Burnet and David O. White, *Natural History of Infectious Disease*, 4th ed. (Cambridge, 1972), 97–100.

adults. There is no doubt, however, that they have been extremely deadly for the very young. Infants are normally protected against infectious diseases common in the area of their births by antibodies passed on to them before birth by their immunologically experienced mothers, antibodies which remain strong enough to fend off disease during the first precarious months of life. This first line of defense does not exist in virgin soil epidemics. The threat to young children is more than just bacteriological: they are often neglected by ailing adults during such epidemics and often die when their ailing mother's milk fails. Infants in traditional aboriginal American societies are commonly two years of age or even older before weaning, so the failure of mothers' milk can boost the death rate during epidemics to a greater extent than modern urbanites would estimate on the basis of their own child-care practices.[20]

Mortality rates rise sharply when several virgin soil epidemics strike simultaneously. When the advance of the Alaska Highway in 1943 exposed the Indians of Teslin Lake to fuller contact with the outside world than they had ever had before, they underwent in one year waves of measles, German measles, dysentery, catarrhal jaundice, whooping cough, mumps, tonsillitis, and miningococcic meningitis. This pulverizing experience must have been common among aborigines in the early post-Columbian generations, although the chroniclers, we may guess, often put the blame on only the most spectacular of the diseases, usually smallpox. A report from Española in 1520 attributed the depopulation there to smallpox, measles, respiratory infection, and other diseases unnamed. Simultaneous epidemics of diseases, including smallpox and at least one other, possibly influenza, occurred in Meso-America in the early 1520s.[21] The action of other diseases than the one most apparently in epidemic stage will often cause dangerous complications, even if they have been long in common circulation among the victims. In the Ungava Bay and Yanomama epidemics the final executioner was usually bronchopneumonia, which advanced when measles leveled the defenses of aborigines weakened by diseases already present—malaria and pneumonia among the South Americans, and tuberculosis and influenza among the North Americans.[22]

[20] Frederick W. Hodge, ed., *Handbook of American Indians North of Mexico*, Pt. I (Washington, D. C., 1912), 265.

[21] Marchand, "Tribal Epidemics in the Yukon," *Jour. Am. Med. Assoc.*, CXXII (1943), 1019–1020; *Colección de Documentos Inéditos, Relativos al Descubrimiento, Conquista y Organización de las Antiguas Posesiones Españolas de América y Oceania* (Madrid, 1864–1868), I, 397–398, 428–429; Crosby, *Columbian Exchange*, 49, 58.

[22] Peart and Nagler, "Measles in the Canadian Arctic, 1952," *Can. Jour. Pub. Health*, XLV (1954), 147, 152; Neel *et al.*, "Notes on the Effect of Measles," *Am. Jour. Epidemiology*, XCI (1970), 422, 425.

Successive epidemics may take longer to dismantle societies than simultaneous attacks by several diseases, but they can be as thorough.
The documentation of American Indians' experience of successive epidemics is slim and not expressed as statistics, but the records are
nonetheless suggestive. The Dakotas kept annual chronicles on
leather or cloth showing by a single picture the most important event
of each year. These records indicate that all or part of this people suffered significantly in the epidemics listed below, at least one of which,
cholera, and possibly several others were virgin soil. It should be
noted that the considerable lapses of time between the smallpox epidemics meant that whole new generations of susceptibles were subject
to infection upon the return of the disease and that the repeated or-
deals must have had much of the deadliness of virgin soil epidemics.

Epidemics among the Dakota Indians, 1780–1851.[23]

1780–1781	Smallpox.
1801–1802	Smallpox ("all sick winter").
1810	Smallpox.
1813–1814	Whooping cough.
1818–1819	Measles ("little smallpox winter").
1837	Smallpox.
1845–1846	Disease or diseases not identified ("many sick win-ter").
1849–1850	Cholera ("many people had the cramps winter").
1850–1851	Smallpox ("all the time sick with the big smallpox winter").

Virgin soil epidemics tend to be especially deadly because no one is
immune in the afflicted population and so nearly everyone gets sick at
once. During a period of only a few days in the 1960s every member
of the Tchikao tribe of Xingu Park fell ill with influenza, and only the
presence of outside medical personnel prevented a general disaster.
Witnesses to the Ungava Bay and Yanomama epidemics noted the
murderous effect of nearly universal illness, however brief in duration.
The scientists with the Yanomamas found that when both parents and
children became sick, "there was a drastic breakdown of both the will
and the means for necessary nursing." The observers saw several families in which grandparents, parents, and their children were simultaneously ill.[24]

[23] Garrick Mallery, "Pictographs of the North American Indian: A Preliminary Paper," *Fourth Annual Report of the Bureau of Ethnology: 1882–1883*, IV (Washington, D. C.,
1886), 103–125, 131–142; Alexis A. Praus, *The Sioux, 1798–1922: A Dakota Winter
Count*, Cranbrook Institute of Science, Bulletin 44 (Bloomfield Hills, Mich., 1962), 15.

[24] Orlando Boas and Claudio Villas Boas, "Saving Brazil's Stone Age Tribes from Extinction," *Nat. Geog.*, CXXXIV (1968), 444; Peart and Nagler, "Measles in the Canadian
Arctic, 1952," *Can. Jour. Pub. Health*, XLV (1954), 153; Neel *et al.*, "Notes on the Effects
of Measles," *Am. Jour. Epidemiology*, XCI (1970), 427; Centerwall, "A Recent Experience
with Measles," Pan-Am. San. Bur., *Sci. Pub.* No. 165 (1968), 80–81.

The fire goes out and the cold creeps in; the sick, whom a bit of food and a cup of water might save, die of hunger and the dehydration of fever; the seed remains above the ground as the best season for planting passes, or there is no one well enough to harvest the crop before the frost. In the 1630s smallpox swept through New England, and William Bradford wrote of a group of Indians who lived near a Plymouth colony trading post that "they fell down so generally of this disease as they were in the end not able to help one another, no not to make a fire nor to fetch a little water to drink, nor any to bury the dead. But would strive as long as they could, and when they could procure no other means to make fire, they would burn the wooden trays and dishes they ate their meat in, and their very bows and arrows. And some would crawl out on all fours to get a little water, and sometimes die by the way and not to be able to get in again." [25]

The second category of factors—those which pertain to the ways native Americans reacted to epidemic diseases—often had as decisive an influence on the death rate as did the virulency of the disease. American aborigines were subjected to an immense barrage of disease, and their customs and religions provided little to help them through the ordeal. Traditional treatments, though perhaps effective against pre-Columbian diseases, were rarely so against acute infections from abroad, and they were often dangerous, as in the swift transfer of a patient from broiling sweathouse to frigid lake.[26] Thus, to take a modern example, when smallpox broke out among the Moqui Indians in Arizona in 1898, 632 fell ill but only 412 accepted treatment from a physician trained in modern medical practice. Although he had no medicines to cure smallpox or even to prevent secondary bacterial infections, only 24 of his patients died. By contrast, 163 of the 220 who refused his help and presumably, put their faith in traditional Indian therapy, died.[27]

Native Americans had no conception of contagion and did not practice quarantine of the sick in pre-Columbian times, nor did they accept the new theory or practice until taught to do so by successive disasters. The Relation of 1640 of the Jesuit missionaries in New France contains the complaint that during epidemics of the most contagious and deadly maladies the Hurons continued to live among the sick "in the same indifference, and community of all things, as if they were in perfect health." The result, of course, was that nearly everyone contracted the infections, "the evil spread from house to house, from vil-

[25] William Bradford, *Of Plymouth Plantation*, ed. Samuel Eliot Morison (New York, 1952), 271.

[26] Harold E. Driver, *Indians of North America* (Chicago, 1961), 396–430.

[27] *Report of the Commissioner of Indian Affairs*, Pt. I, in *Annual Reports of the Department of Interior for the Fiscal Year Ended June 30, 1899* (Washington, D. C., 1899), 158–159.

lage to village, and finally became scattered throughout the country."[28]

Such ignorance of the danger of infection can be fatal, but so can
knowledge when it creates terror, leading to fatalism or to frenzied,
destructive behavior.[29] A large proportion of those who fall acutely ill
in an epidemic will die, even if the disease is a usually mild one, like
influenza or whooping cough, unless they are provided with drink,
food, shelter, and competent nursing. These will be provided if their
kin and friends fulfill the obligations of kinship and friendship, but
will they do so? Will the sense of these obligations be stronger than
fear, which can kill by paralyzing all action to help the sick or by gal-
vanizing the healthy into flight?

If we may rely on negative evidence, we may say that aboriginal kin
and tribal loyalties remained stronger than the fear of disease for a remarkably long time after the coming of the micro-organisms from the
Old World. We will never be able to pinpoint chronologically any
change as subtle as the failure of these ties, but whenever it happened
for a given group in a given epidemic the death rate almost certainly
rose. In most epidemics, contagious disease operating in crowded wig-
wams and long houses would spread so fast before terror took hold
that panicky flight would serve more to spread the infection than to
rob it of fresh victims, and any decline in the number of new cases,
and consequently of deaths that might result from flight, would at the
very least be cancelled by the rise in the number of sick who died of
neglect. Observers of the Ungava Bay epidemic reported that a fatalis-
tic attitude toward the disease caused the loss of several entire families, whose members would not help each other or themselves. Scientists with the Yanomamas during their battle with measles recorded
that fatalism killed some and panic killed more: the healthy abandoned
the sick and fled to other villages, carrying the disease with them.[30]

---

[28] Reuben Gold Thwaites, ed., *The Jesuit Relations and Allied Documents: Travels and
Explorations of the Jesuit Missionaries in New France, 1610–1791* . . . , XIX (Cleveland,
Ohio, 1898), 89.

[29] The fear of epidemic disease and the psychic stress created by the advance of European and African invaders doubtless had a direct effect on disease and death rates. Extreme anxiety decreases the organism's ability to resist attack. See J. E. Nardini, "Survival Factors in American Prisoners of War of the Japanese," *American Journal of
Psychiatry*, CXC (1952), 241-248; Henry Krystal and William G. Niederland, *Psychic
Traumatization, Afteraffects in Individuals and Communities* (Boston, 1971); Robert Jay
Lifton, *Death in Life: Survivors of Hiroshima* (New York, 1967).

[30] Peart and Nagler, "Measles in the Canadian Arctic, 1952," *Can. Jour. Pub. Health*,
XLV (1954), 153; Centerwall, "Recent Experience with Measles," Pan-Am. San. Bur.,
Sci. Pub., No. 165 (1968), 81. We must not regard such behavior as typical only of Indians and other pre-literate peoples. The classic description of this kind of pathological individualism is contained in the first pages of *The Decameron*, in which Giovanni Boccac-
cio depicts how medieval Florentines reacted to the Black Death.

When a killing epidemic strikes a society that accepts violence as a way of reacting to crises and believes in life after death—characteristics of many Christian and many Indian societies—the results can be truly hideous. Many fourteenth-century Europeans reacted to the Black Death by joining the Flagellants or by killing Jews. Some Indians similarly turned on the whites whom they blamed for the epidemics, but most were obliged by their circumstances to direct their fear and rage against themselves. During the epidemic of 1738 many Cherokees killed themselves in horror of permanent disfigurement, according to their contemporary, James Adair. Members of the Lewis and Clark expedition were told that in the 1802 smallpox epidemic the Omahas "carried their franzey to verry extrodinary length, not only burning their Village, but they put their *wives* and children to *Death* with a view of their all going to some better Countrey." In 1837 smallpox killed so many of the Blackfeet and so terrified those left alive after the first days of the epidemic that many committed suicide when they saw the initial signs of the disease in themselves. It is estimated that about 6,000, two-thirds of all the Blackfeet, died during the epidemic.[31]

The story of that same epidemic among the Mandans, as George Catlin received it, cannot be exceeded in its horror:

> It seems that the Mandans were surrounded by several war-parties of their most powerful enemies the Sioux, at that unlucky time, and they could not therefore disperse upon the plains, by which many of them could have been saved; and they were necessarily inclosed within the piquets of their village, where the disease in a few days became so very malignant that death ensued in a few hours after its attacks; and so slight were their hopes when they were attacked, that nearly half of them destroyed themselves with their knives, with their guns, and by dashing their brains out by leaping head-foremost from a thirty foot ledge of rocks in front of their village. The first symptoms of the disease was a rapid swelling of the body, and so very virulent had it become, that very many died in two or three hours after their attack, and in many cases without the appearance of disease upon their skin. Utter dismay seemed to possess all classes and ages and they gave themselves up in despair as entirely lost. There was but one continual crying and howling and praying to the Great Spirit for his protection during the nights and days; and there being but few living, and those in too appalling despair, nobody thought of burying the dead, whose bodies, whole families together, were

[31] Samuel Williams, ed., *Adair's History of the American Indians* (Johnson City, Tenn., 1930), 245; Bernard DeVoto, ed., *The Journals of Lewis and Clark* (Boston, 1953), 18–19; John C. Ewers, *The Blackfeet: Raiders on the Northwestern Plains* (Norman, Okla., 1958), 65–66.

> left in horrid and loathsome piles in their own wigwams, with a
> few buffalo robes, etc. thrown over them, there to decay, and be
> devoured by their own dogs.[32]

During that epidemic the number of Mandans shrank from about
1,600 to between 125 and 145.[33]

Whether the Europeans and Africans came to the native Americans
in war or peace, they always brought death with them, and the final
comment may be left to the Superior of the Jesuit Missions to the Indians of New France, who wrote in confusion and dejection in the
1640s, that "since the Faith has come to dwell among these people, all
things that make men die have been found in these countries."[34]

---

[32] George Catlin, *Letters and Notes on the Manners, Customs, and Condition of the North
American Indians*, II (Minneapolis, 1965 [orig. publ. London, 1841]), 257. For corrobora-
tion see M. M. Quaife, ed., "The Smallpox Epidemic on the Upper Missouri," *Mississippi
Valley Historical Review*, XVII (1930), 278–299.

[33] Hodge, ed., *Handbook of American Indians*, 797–798.

[34] Thwaites, ed., *Jesuit Relations*, XXXII, 253.

THE FIRST
SETTLEMENTS

II

Politics and Social Structure in Virginia

BERNARD BAILYN

Colonial political history has traditionally been studied from an institutional viewpoint. The powers of governors, the role of councils, and the rise of representative assemblies have preoccupied historians who assumed that colonial political systems were sufficient unto themselves and that their development demonstrated the steady growth of democracy in America.

In the following essay, however, Bernard Bailyn defines "politics" very broadly. He argues that there existed in the seventeenth century a correspondence between state and society, and that there was, consequently, a virtual identity between colonial political and social leadership. Bailyn accordingly surveys the history of politics in Virginia to show that patterns of leadership in the highest level of society changed several times in the course of the seventeenth century and that, in response, the structure of politics also changed. He suggests that colonial Virginia's major political upheaval, Bacon's Rebellion, was in reality the birthpang of a new ruling elite, the climax to the emergence of a new social structure.

The factors that shape the contours of political life thus become, for Bailyn, family structure, provisions for the inheritance of wealth, and the labor system, rather than the prerogatives of the governor and the assembly's power of the purse.

By the end of the seventeenth century the American colonists faced an array of disturbing problems in the conduct of public affairs. Settlers from England and Holland, reconstructing familiar institutions on American shores, had become participants in what would appear to have been a wave of civil disobedience. Constituted authority was confronted with repeated challenges. Indeed, a veritable anarchy seems to have prevailed at the center of colonial society, erupting in a series of insurrections that began as early as 1635 with the "thrusting out" of Governor Harvey in Virginia. Culpeper's Rebellion in Carolina, the Protestant Association in Maryland, Bacon's Rebellion in Virginia, Leisler's seizure of power in New York, the resistance to and finally the overthrow of Andros in New England—every colony was affected.

Reprinted, by permission of the author and publisher, from *Seventeenth-Century America: Essays in Colonial History*, edited by James Morton Smith. Published for the Institute of Early American History and Culture, Williamsburg, Virginia. © 1959, 1987 The University of North Carolina Press.

These outbursts were not merely isolated local affairs. Although their immediate causes were rooted in the particular circumstances of the separate colonies, they nevertheless had common characteristics. They were, in fact, symptomatic of a profound disorganization of European society in its American setting. Seen in a broad view, they reveal a new configuration of forces which shaped the origins of American politics.

In a letter written from Virginia in 1632, George Sandys, the resident treasurer, reported despondently on the character and condition of the leading settlers. Some of the councilors were "no more then Ciphers," he wrote; others were "miserablie poore"; and the few substantial planters lived apart, taking no responsibility for public concerns. There was, in fact, among all those "worthie the mencioninge" only one person deserving of full approval. Lieutenant William Peirce "refuses no labour, nor sticks at anie expences that may aduantage the publique." Indeed, Sandys added, Peirce was "of a Capacitie that is not to bee expected in a man of his breedinge." [1]

The afterthought was penetrating. It cut below the usual complaints of the time that many of the settlers were lazy malcontents hardly to be preferred to the Italian glassworkers, than whom, Sandys wrote, "a more damned crew hell never vomited." [2] What lay behind Sandys' remark was not so much that wretched specimens were arriving in the shipments of servants nor even that the quality of public leadership was declining but that the social foundations of political power were being strangely altered.

All of the settlers in whatever colony presumed a fundamental relationship between social structure and political authority. Drawing on a common medieval heritage, continuing to conceive of society as a hierarchical unit, its parts justly and naturally separated into inferior and superior levels, they assumed that superiority was indivisible; there was not one hierarchy for political matters, another for social purposes. John Winthrop's famous explanation of God's intent that "in all times some must be rich some poore, some highe and eminent in power and dignitie; others meane and in subieccion" could not have been more carefully worded. Riches, dignity, and power were properly placed in apposition; they pertained to the same individuals. [3]

So closely related were social leadership and political leadership that experience if not theory justified an identification between state and society. To the average English colonist the state was not an abstrac-

[1] Sandys to John Ferrar, April 11, 1623, Susan M. Kingsbury, ed., *The Records of the Virginia Company of London* (4 vols.; Washington, D.C., 1906–35), IV, 110–11.

[2] Sandys to "Mr. Farrer," March 1622/23, *ibid.*, 23.

[3] John Winthrop, "Modell of Christian Charity," *Winthrop Papers* (5 vols.; Boston, 1929–47), II, 282.

tion existing above men's lives, justifying itself in its own terms, taking occasional human embodiment. However glorified in monarchy, the state in ordinary form was indistinguishable from a more general social authority; it was woven into the texture of everyday life. It was the same squire or manorial lord who in his various capacities collated to the benefice, set the rents, and enforced the statutes of Parliament and the royal decrees. Nothing could have been more alien to the settlers than the idea that competition for political leadership should be open to all levels of society or that obscure social origins or technical skills should be considered valuable qualifications for office. The proper response to new technical demands on public servants was not to give power to the skilled but to give skills to the powerful.[4] The English gentry and landed aristocracy remained politically adaptable and hence politically competent, assuming when necessary new public functions, eliminating the need for a professional state bureaucracy. By their amateur competence they made possible a continuing identification between political and social authority.

In the first years of settlement no one had reason to expect that this characteristic of public life would fail to transfer itself to the colonies. For at least a decade and a half after its founding there had been in the Jamestown settlement a small group of leaders drawn from the higher echelons of English society. Besides well-born soldiers of fortune like George Percy, son of the Earl of Northumberland, there were among them four sons of the West family—children of Lord de la Warr and his wife, a second cousin of Queen Elizabeth. In Virginia the West brothers held appropriately high positions; three of them served as governors.[5] Christopher Davison, the colony's secretary, was the son of Queen Elizabeth's secretary, William Davison, M.P. and Privy Councilor.[6] The troublesome John Martin, of Martin's Brandon, was the son of Sir Richard Martin, twice Lord Mayor of London, and also the brother-in-law of Sir Julius Caesar, Master of the Rolls and Privy Councilor.[7] Sir Francis and Haute Wyatt were sons of substantial Kent gentry and grandsons of the Sir Thomas Wyatt who led the rebellion of 1554 against Queen Mary.[8] George Sandys' father was the Archbishop of York; of his three older brothers, all knights and M.P.'s, two were eminent country gentlemen, and the third, Edwin, of Vir-

[4] Cf. J. H. Hexter, "The Education of the Aristocracy in the Renaissance," *Jour. of Modern Hist.*, 22 (1950), 1–20.

[5] *Dictionary of National Biography*, 1908–9 edn. (New York), XV, 836–37; Annie L. Jester and Martha W. Hiden, comps. and eds., *Adventurers of Purse and Person: Virginia 1607–1625* ([Princeton, N.J.], 1956), 349–50.

[6] *D.N.B.*, V, 632; Richard B. Davis, *George Sandys: Poet-Adventurer* (London, 1955), 112–13n.

[7] Alexander Brown, *Genesis of the United States* (Boston, 1890), II, 943–44.

[8] Jester and Hiden, comps., *Adventurers*, 372; *D.N.B.*, XXI, 1092–93, 1102–4.

ginia Company fame, was a man of great influence in the city.[9] George
Thorpe was a former M.P. and Gentleman of the Privy Chamber.[10]

More impressive than such positions and relationships was the cultural level represented. For until the very end of the Company period,
Virginia remained to the literary and scientific an exotic attraction, its
settlement an important moment in Christian history.[11] Its original
magnetism for those in touch with intellectual currents affected the
early immigration. Of the twenty councilors of 1621, eight had been
educated at Oxford, Cambridge, or the Inns of Court. Davison, like
Martin trained in the law, was a poet in a family of poets. Thorpe was
a "student of Indian views on religion and astronomy." Francis Wyatt
wrote verses and was something of a student of political theory.
Alexander Whitaker, M.A., author of *Good Newes from Virginia*, was
the worthy heir "of a good part of the learning of his renowned father," the master of St. John's College and Regius Professor of Divinity at Cambridge. John Pory, known to history mainly as the speaker
of the first representative assembly in America, was a Master of Arts,
"protege and disciple of Hakluyt," diplomat, scholar, and traveler,
whose writings from and about America have a rightful place in literary history. Above all there was George Sandys, "poet, traveller, and
scholar," a member of Lord Falkland's literary circle; while in
Jamestown he continued as a matter of course to work on his notable
translation of Ovid's *Metamorphoses.*[12]

There was, in other words, during the first years of settlement a direct transference to Virginia of the upper levels of the English social
hierarchy as well as of the lower. If the great majority of the settlers
were recruited from the yeoman class and below, there was nevertheless a reasonable representation from those upper groups acknowledged to be the rightful rulers of society.

It is a fact of some importance, however, that this governing elite
did not survive a single generation, at least in its original form. By the
thirties their number had declined to insignificance. Percy, for example, left in 1612. Whitaker drowned in 1617. Sandys and Francis Wyatt arrived only in 1621, but their enthusiasm cooled quickly; they
were both gone by 1626. Of the Wests, only John was alive and resident in the colony a decade after the collapse of the Company. Davison, who returned to England in 1622 after only a year's stay, was sent
back in 1623 but died within a year of his return. Thorpe was one of
the six councilors slain in the massacre of 1622. Pory left for England

[9] Davis, *Sandys*, Chap. I.
[10] Brown, *Genesis*, II, 1031.
[11] Perry Miller, *Errand into the Wilderness* (Cambridge, Mass., 1956), 99–140; Howard
Mumford Jones, *The Literature of Virginia in the Seventeenth Century* (*Memoirs of the
American Academy of Arts and Sciences*, XIX, Part 2, Boston, 1946), 3–7.
[12] Davis, *Sandys*, especially 190–92; Harry C. Porter, "Alexander Whitaker," *Wm. and
Mary Qtly.*, 3rd ser., 14 (1957), 336; Jones, *Literature of Virginia*, 14n, 5–6, 26–28.

in 1622; his return as investigating commissioner in 1624 was temporary, lasting only a few months. And the cantankerous Martin graced the Virginia scene by his absence after 1625; he is last heard from in the early 1630's petitioning for release from a London debtor's prison.[13]

To be sure, a few representatives of important English families, like John West and Edmund Scarborough, remained. There were also one or two additions from the same social level.[14] But there were few indeed of such individuals, and the basis of their authority had changed. The group of gentlemen and illuminati that had dominated the scene during the Company era had been dispersed. Their disappearance created a political void which was filled soon enough, but from a different area of recruitment, from below, from the toughest and most fortunate of the surviving planters whose eminence by the end of the thirties had very little to do with the transplantation of social status.[15]

The position of the new leaders rested on their ability to wring material gain from the wilderness. Some, like Samuel Mathews, started with large initial advantages,[16] but more typical were George Menefie and John Utie, who began as independent landowners by right of

[13] Davis, *Sandys*, 195–97, 112–13n; Jester and Hiden, comps., *Adventurers*, 350–51; Brown, *Genesis*, II, 1031, 970; *Va. Mag. of Hist. and Biog.*, 54 (1946), 60–61; Jones, *Literature of Virginia*, 14n.

[14] Scarborough was a well-educated younger son of an armigerous Norfolk family. Among the additions were Charles Harmar (who died in 1640), nephew of the warden of Winchester College and brother of the Greek Reader, later the Greek Professor, at Oxford; and Nathaniel Littleton, whose father was Chief Justice of North Wales, two of whose brothers were Fellows of All Souls and a third Chief Justice of Common Pleas and Lord Keeper of the Great Seal. Susie M. Ames, ed., *County Court Records of Accomack-Northampton, Virginia, 1632–1640* (Washington, D.C., 1954), xxvii, xxix–xxx, xxxv.

[15] The difficulty of maintaining in Virginia the traditional relationship between social and political authority became in 1620 the basis of an attack by a group of "ancient planters," including Francis West, on the newly appointed governor, Sir George Yeardley. Although Yeardley had been knighted two years earlier in an effort to enhance his personal authority, the petitioners argued that his lack of eminence was discouraging settlement. "Great Actions," they wrote, "are carryed with best successe by such Comanders who haue personall Aucthoritye & greatness answerable to the Action, Sithence itt is nott easye to swaye a vulgar and seruile Nature by vulgar & seruile Spiritts." Leadership should devolve on commanders whose "Eminence or Nobillitye" is such that "euerye man subordinate is ready to yeild a willing submission wthowt contempt or repyning." The ordinary settlers, they said, would not obey the same authority "conferrd vpon a meane man . . . no bettar than selected owt of their owne Ranke." If, therefore, the Company hoped to attract and hold colonists, especially of "the bettar sorte," it should select as leaders in Virginia "some eythar Noble or little lesse in Honor or Dower . . . to maintayne & hold vp the dignitye of so Great and good a cawse." Kingsbury, ed., *Records of the Virginia Company*, III, 231–32.

[16] For Mathews' twenty-three servants and his "Denbigh" plantation, described in 1649 as a self-sufficient village, see John C. Hotten, ed., *Original List of Persons of Quality* . . . (London, 1874), 233–34; Jester and Hiden, comps., *Adventurers*, 244–45; *A Perfect Description of Virginia* . . . , in Peter Force, comp., *Tracts and Other Papers Relating Principally to the Origin, Settlement, and Progress of the Colonies in North America* (4 vols., Washington, D.C., 1836–46), II, no. 8, 14–15.

transporting themselves and only one or two servants. Abraham Wood, famous for his explorations and like Menefie and Utie the future possessor of large estates and important offices, appears first as a servant boy on Mathews' plantation. Adam Thoroughgood, the son of a country vicar, also started in Virginia as a servant, aged fourteen. William Spencer is first recorded as a yeoman farmer without servants.[17]

Such men as these—Spencer, Wood, Menefie, Utie, Mathews— were the most important figures in Virginia politics up to the Restoration, engrossing large tracts of land, dominating the Council, unseating Sir John Harvey from the governorship. But in no traditional sense were they a ruling class. They lacked the attributes of social authority, and their political dominance was a continuous achievement. Only with the greatest difficulty, if at all, could distinction be expressed in a genteel style of life, for existence in this generation was necessarily crude. Mathews may have created a flourishing estate and Menefie had splendid fruit gardens, but the great tracts of land such men claimed were almost entirely raw wilderness. They had risen to their positions, with few exceptions, by brute labor and shrewd manipulation; they had personally shared the burdens of settlement. They succeeded not because of, but despite, whatever gentility they may have had. William Claiborne may have been educated at the Middle Temple; Peirce could not sign his name; but what counted was their common capacity to survive and flourish in frontier settlements.[18] They were tough, unsentimental, quick-tempered, crudely ambitious men concerned with profits and increased landholdings, not the grace of life. They roared curses, drank exuberantly, and gambled (at least according to deVries) for their servants when other commodities were lacking.[19] If the worst of Governor Harvey's offenses had been to knock out the teeth of an offending councilor with a cudgel, as he did on one occasion, no one would have questioned his right to the governorship.[20] Rank had its privileges, and these men were the first to claim them, but rank itself was unstable and the lines of class or status

[17] Jester and Hiden, comps., *Adventurers*, 248–49, 321, 329, 339–40; Hotten, ed., *Persons of Quality*, 226, 237, 233, 253, 228; Clarence W. Alvord and Lee Bidgood, *The First Explorations of the Trans-Alleghany Region . . . 1650–1674* (Cleveland, 1912), 34ff.

[18] *Wm. and Mary Qtly.*, 2nd ser., 19 (1939), 475n; Davis, *Sandys*, 158n.

[19] Ames, ed., *Accomack-Northampton Recs.*, xxxiv, xxxix–xl; Susie M. Ames, *Studies of the Virginia Eastern Shore in the Seventeenth Century* (Richmond, Va., 1940), 181, 183. De-Vries wrote of his astonishment at seeing servants gambled away: "I told them that I had never seen such work in Turk or Barbarian, and that it was not becoming Christians." David P. deVries, *Short Historical . . . Notes of Several Voyages . . .* (Hoorn, 1655), reprinted in the New York Hist. Soc., *Collections*, 2nd ser., 3 (1857), 36, 125.

[20] Harvey readily confessed to the deed, offering as an official justification the fact that it had all taken place outside the Council chamber, and anyhow the fellow had "assailed him with ill language." *The Aspinwall Papers*, Mass. Hist. Soc., *Collections*, 4th ser., 9 (1871), 133n.

were fluid. There was no insulation for even the most elevated from the rude impact of frontier life.

As in style of life so in politics, these leaders of the first permanently settled generation did not re-create the characteristics of a stable gentry. They had had little opportunity to acquire the sense of public responsibility that rests on deep identification with the land and its people. They performed in some manner the duties expected of leaders, but often public office was found simply burdensome. Reports such as Sandys' that Yeardley, the councilor and former governor, was wholly absorbed in his private affairs and scarcely glanced at public matters and that Mathews "will rather hazard the payment of fforfeitures then performe our Injunctions" were echoed by Harvey throughout his tenure of office. Charles Harmar, justice of the peace on the Eastern Shore, attended the court once in eight years, and Claiborne's record was only slightly better. Attendance to public duties had to be specifically enjoined, and privileges were of necessity accorded provincial officeholders. The members of the Council were particularly favored by the gift of tax exemption.[21]

The private interests of this group, which had assumed control of public office by virtue not of inherited status but of newly achieved and strenuously maintained economic eminence, were pursued with little interference from the traditional restraints imposed on a responsible ruling class. Engaged in an effort to establish themselves in the land, they sought as specific ends: autonomous local jurisdiction, an aggressive expansion of settlement and trading enterprises, unrestricted access to land, and, at every stage, the legal endorsement of acquisitions. Most of the major public events for thirty years after the dissolution of the Company—and especially the overthrow of Harvey—were incidents in the pursuit of these goals.

From his first appearance in Virginia, Sir John Harvey threatened the interests of this emerging planter group. While still in England he had identified himself with the faction that had successfully sought the collapse of the Company, and thus his mere presence in Virginia was a threat to the legal basis of land grants made under the Company's charter. His demands for the return as public property of goods that had once belonged to the Company specifically jeopardized the planters' holdings. His insistence that the governorship was more than a mere chairmanship of the Council tended to undermine local autonomy. His conservative Indian policy not only weakened the settlers' hand in what already seemed an irreconcilable enmity with the natives but also restricted the expansion of settlement. His opposition to Clai-

---

[21] Kingsbury, ed., *Records of the Virginia Company*, IV, 110–11; *Va. Mag. of Hist. and Biog.*, 8 (1900–1), 30; Ames, ed., *Accomack-Northampton Recs.*, xxv, xxix; William W. Hening, ed., *The Statutes-at-Large . . . of Virginia (1619–1792)* (New York, 1823), I, 350, 454; Philip A. Bruce, *Institutional History of Virginia in the Seventeenth Century* (2 vols.; New York, 1910), II, Chaps. XV, XXIX.

borne's claim to Kent Island threatened to kill off the lucrative Chesapeake Bay trade, and his attempt to ban the Dutch ships from the colony endangered commerce more generally. His support of the official policy of economic diversification, together with his endorsement of the English schemes of tobacco monopoly, alienated him finally and completely from the Council group.[22]

Within a few months of his assuming the governorship, Harvey wrote home with indignation of the "waywardness and oppositions" of the councilors and condemned them for factiously seeking "rather for their owne endes then either seekinge the generall good or doinge right to particular men." Before a year was out the antagonisms had become so intense that a formal peace treaty had to be drawn up between Harvey and the Council. But both sides were adamant, and conflict was inescapable. It exploded in 1635 amid comic opera scenes of "extreame coller and passion" complete with dark references to Richard the Third and musketeers "running with their peices presented." The conclusion was Harvey's enraged arrest of George Menefie "of suspicion of Treason to his Majestie"; Utie's response, "And wee the like to you sir"; and the governor's forced return to England.[23]

Behind these richly heroic "passings and repassings to and fro" lies not a victory of democracy or representative institutions or anything of the sort. Democracy, in fact, was identified in the Virginians' minds with the "popular and tumultuary government" that had prevailed in the old Company's quarter courts, and they wanted none of it; the Assembly as a representative institution was neither greatly sought after nor hotly resisted.[24] The victory of 1635 was that of resolute leaders of settlement stubbornly fighting for individual establishment. With the reappointment of Sir Francis Wyatt as governor, their victory was assured and in the Commonwealth period it was completely realized. By 1658, when Mathews was elected governor, effective interference from outside had disappeared and the supreme authority had been assumed by an Assembly which was in effect a league of local magnates secure in their control of county institutions.[25]

One might at that point have projected the situation forward into a

---

[22] The charges and countercharges are summarized, together with supporting documents, in the profuse footnotes of *Aspinwall Papers*, 131–52.

[23] *Va. Mag. of Hist. and Biog.*, 8 (1900–1), 30, 43–45; I (1893–94), 418, 419, 427, 420.

[24] *Ibid.*, I (1893–94), 418; Hening, ed., *Va. Stat. at L.*, I, 232–33. For a balanced statement of the importance attached by contemporaries to Virginia's representative Assembly, see Wesley Frank Craven, *Dissolution of the Virginia Company* (New York, 1932), 71 ff., 330 ff. Cf. Charles M. Andrews, *The Colonial Period of American History* (4 vols.; New Haven, Conn., 1934–38), I, 181 ff., and Davis, " 'Liberalism' in the Virginia Company and Colony," *Sandys*, Appendix G.

[25] Wesley Frank Craven, *The Southern Colonies in the Seventeenth Century, 1607–1689* (Baton Rouge, La., 1949), 288–94.

picture of dominant county families dating from the 1620's and 1630's, growing in identification with the land and people, ruling with increasing responsibility from increasingly eminent positions. But such a projection would be false. The fact is that with a few notable exceptions like the Scarboroughs and the Wormeleys, these struggling planters of the first generation failed to perpetuate their leadership into the second generation. Such families as the Woods, the Uties, the Mathews, and the Peirces faded from dominant positions of authority after the deaths of their founders. To some extent this was the result of the general insecurity of life that created odds against the physical survival in the male line of any given family. But even if male heirs had remained in these families after the death of the first generation, undisputed eminence would not. For a new emigration had begun in the forties, continuing for close to thirty years, from which was drawn a new ruling group that had greater possibilities for permanent dominance than Harvey's opponents had had. These newcomers absorbed and subordinated the older group, forming the basis of the most celebrated oligarchy in American history.

Most of Virginia's great eighteenth-century names, such as Bland, Burwell, Byrd, Carter, Digges, Ludwell, and Mason, appear in the colony for the first time within ten years either side of 1655. These progenitors of the eighteenth-century aristocracy arrived in remarkably similar circumstances. The most important of these immigrants were younger sons of substantial families well connected in London business and governmental circles and long associated with Virginia; family claims to land in the colony or inherited shares of the original Company stock were now brought forward as a basis for establishment in the New World.

Thus the Bland family interests in Virginia date from a 1618 investment in the Virginia Company by the London merchant John Bland, supplemented in 1622 by another in Martin's Hundred. The merchant never touched foot in America, but three of his sons did come to Virginia in the forties and fifties to exploit these investments. The Burwell fortunes derive from the early subscription to the Company of Edward Burwell, which was inherited in the late forties by his son, Lewis I. The first William Byrd arrived about 1670 to assume the Virginia properties of his mother's family, the Steggs, which dated back to the early days of the Company. The Digges's interests in Virginia stem from the original investments of Sir Dudley Digges and two of his sons in the Company, but it was a third son, Edward, who emigrated in 1650 and established the American branch of the family. Similarly, the Masons had been financially interested in Virginia thirty-two years before 1652, when the first immigrant of that family appeared in the colony. The Culpeper clan, whose private affairs enclose much of the history of the South in the second half of the seventeenth century, was first represented in Virginia by Thomas Culpeper, who arrived in 1649; but the family interests in Virginia had been established a full generation earlier. Thomas' father, uncle, and cousin had all been members of the original Virginia Company and their shares had descended in the family. Even Governor Berkeley fits the pattern. There is no mystery about his sudden exchange in 1642 of the life of a dilettante courtier for that of a colonial administrator and estate manager. He was a younger son without prospects, and his family's interests in Virginia, dating from investments in the Company made twenty years earlier, as well as his appointment held out the promise of an independent establishment in America.[26]

Claims on the colony such as these were only one, though the most important, of a variety of forms of capital that might provide the basis for secure family fortunes. One might simply bring over enough of a merchant family's resources to begin immediately building up an imposing estate, as, presumably, did that ambitious draper's son, William Fitzhugh. The benefits that accrued from such advantages were quickly translated into landholdings in the development of which these settlers were favored by the chronology of their arrival. For though they extended the area of cultivation in developing their landholdings, they were not obliged to initiate settlement. They fell heirs to large areas of the tidewater region that had already been brought under cultivation. "Westover" was not the creation of William Byrd; it had originally been part of the De la Warr estate, passing, with improvements, to Captain Thomas Pawlett, thence to Theodorick Bland, and finally to Byrd. Lewis Burwell inherited not only his father's land, but also the developed estate of his stepfather, Wingate. Some of the Carters' lands may be traced back through John Utie to a John Jefferson, who left Virginia as early as 1628. Abraham Wood's entire Fort Henry property ended in the hands of the Jones family. The Blands' estate in Charles City County, which later became the Harrisons' "Berkeley" plantation, was cleared for settlement in 1619 by servants of the "particular" plantation of Berkeley's Hundred.[27]

Favored thus by circumstance, a small group within the second generation migration moved toward setting itself off in a permanent way as a ruling landed gentry. That they succeeded was due not only to

[26] Nell M. Nugent, *Cavaliers and Pioneers* (Richmond, Va., 1934), I, 160; Jester and Hiden, comps., *Adventurers*, 97, 108, 154–55, 288; Louis B. Wright, *The First Gentlemen of Virginia* (San Marino, Calif., 1940), 312–13; *Va. Mag. of Hist. and Biog.*, 35 (1927), 227–28; Helen Hill, *George Mason, Constitutionalist* (Cambridge, Mass., 1938), 3–4; Fairfax Harrison, "A Key Chart of the . . . Culpepers . . . ," *Va. Mag. of Hist. and Biog.*, 33 (1925), f. 113, 339, 344; *D.N.B.*, II, 368; Kingsbury, ed., *Records of the Virginia Company*, II, 75, 90, 391.

[27] Wright, *First Gentlemen*, 155 ff.; Jester and Hiden, comps., *Adventurers*, 98, 108, 339–41, 363–64, 97, 99.

their material advantages but also to the force of their motivation. For these individuals were in social origins just close enough to establishment in gentility to feel the pangs of deprivation most acutely. It is not the totally but the partially dispossessed who build up the most propulsive aspirations, and behind the zestful lunging at propriety and status of a William Fitzhugh lay not the narcotic yearnings of the disinherited but the pent-up ambitions of the gentleman *manqué*. These were neither hardhanded pioneers nor dilettante romantics, but ambitious younger sons of middle-class families who knew well enough what gentility was and sought it as a specific objective.[28]

The establishment of this group was rapid. Within a decade of their arrival they could claim, together with a fortunate few of the first generation, a marked social eminence and full political authority at the county level. But their rise was not uniform. Indeed, by the seventies a new circumstance had introduced an effective principle of social differentiation among the colony's leaders. A hierarchy of position within the newly risen gentry was created by the Restoration government's efforts to extend its control more effectively over its mercantile empire. Demanding of its colonial executives and their advisors closer supervision over the external aspects of the economy, it offered a measure of patronage necessary for enforcement. Public offices dealing with matters that profoundly affected the basis of economic life—tax collection, customs regulation, and the bestowal of land grants—fell within the gift of the governor and tended to form an inner circle of privilege. One can note in Berkeley's administration the growing importance of this barrier of officialdom. Around its privileges there formed the "Green Spring" faction, named after Berkeley's plantation near Jamestown, a group bound to the governor not by royalist sympathies so much as by ties of kinship and patronage.

Thus Colonel Henry Norwood, related to Berkeley by a "near affinity in blood," was given the treasurership of the colony in 1650, which he held for more than two decades. During this time Thomas Ludwell, a cousin and Somerset neighbor of the governor, was secretary of state, in which post he was succeeded in 1678 by his brother Philip, who shortly thereafter married Berkeley's widow. This Lady Berkeley, it should be noted, was the daughter of Thomas Culpeper, the immigrant of 1649 and a cousin of Thomas Lord Culpeper who became governor in 1680. Immediately after her marriage to Berkeley, her brother Alexander requested and received from the governor the nomination to the surveyor-generalship of Virginia, a post he filled for twenty-three years while resident in England, appointing as successive deputies the brothers Ludwell, to whom by 1680 he was twice related

---

[28] Fitzhugh's letters, scattered through the *Va. Mag. of Hist. and Biog.*, I–VI, cannot be equalled as sources for the motivation of this group.

by marriage. Lady Berkeley was also related through her mother to William Byrd's wife, a fact that explains much about Byrd's prolific office-holding.[29]

The growing distinctiveness of provincial officialdom within the landed gentry may also be traced in the transformation of the Council. Originally, this body had been expected to comprise the entire effective government, central and local; councilors were to serve, individually or in committees, as local magistrates. But the spread of settlement upset this expectation, and at the same time as the local offices were falling into the hands of autonomous local powers representing leading county families, the Council, appointed by the governor and hence associated with official patronage, increasingly realized the separate, lucrative privileges available to it.[30]

As the distinction between local and central authority became clear, the county magistrates sought their own distinct voice in the management of the colony, and they found it in developing the possibilities of burgess representation. In the beginning there was no House of Burgesses; representation from the burghs and hundreds was conceived of not as a branch of government separate from the Council but as a periodic supplement to it.[31] Until the fifties the burgesses, meeting in the Assemblies with the councilors, felt little need to form themselves into a separate house, for until that decade there was little

---

[29] Colonel [Henry] Norwood, *A Voyage to Virginia* (1649), in Force, ed., *Tracts*, III, 49, 50; *Va. Mag. of Hist. and Biog.*, 33 (1925), 5, 8; Harrison, "Key Chart," *ibid.*, 351–55, 348; *Wm. and Mary Qtly.*, 1st ser., 19 (1910–11), 209–10. It was after Culpeper's appointment to the governorship that Byrd was elevated to the Council and acquired the auditor- and receiver-generalships. William G. and Mary N. Stanard, comps., *The Colonial Virginia Register* (Albany, N.Y., 1902), 22–23.

The Berkeley-Norwood connection may be followed out in other directions. Thus the Colonel Francis Moryson mentioned by Norwood as his friend and traveling companion and whom he introduced to the governor was given command of the fort at Point Comfort upon his arrival in 1649, replacing his brother, Major Richard Moryson, whose son Charles was given the same post in the 1660's. Francis, who found the command of the fort "profitable to him," was elevated by Berkeley to the Council and temporarily to the deputy-governorship, "wherein he got a competent estate"; he finally returned to England in the position of colony agent. Norwood, *Voyage*, 50; *Va. Mag. of Hist. and Biog.*, 9 (1900–1), 122–23; Ella Lonn, *The Colonial Agents of the Southern Colonies* (Chapel Hill, 1945), 21 ff.

The inner kinship core of the group enclosed the major provincial positions mentioned above. But the wider reaches of the clique extended over the Council, the collectorships, and the naval offices as well as minor positions within the influence of the governor. On these posts and their holders, see Stanard and Stanard, comps., *Va. Register*, 38–40; Bruce, *Institutional History*, II, Chaps. XXXVIII–XLII. On the limitations of the gubernatorial influence after 1660, see Craven, *Southern Colonies*, 293.

[30] Craven, *Southern Colonies*, 167–69; 270, 288; Bruce, *Institutional History*, II, Chap. XV.

[31] For the Assembly as "the other Counsell," see the "Ordinance and Constitution" of 1621 in Kingsbury, ed., *Records of the Virginia Company*, III, 483–84.

evidence of a conflict of interests between the two groups. But when, after the Restoration, the privileged status of the Council became unmistakable and the county magnates found control of the increasingly important provincial administration preempted by this body, the burgess part of the Assembly took on a new meaning in contrast to that of the Council. Burgess representation now became vital to the county leaders if they were to share in any consistent way in affairs larger than those of the counties. They looked to the franchise, hitherto broad not by design but by neglect, introducing qualifications that would ensure their control of the Assembly. Their interest in provincial government could no longer be expressed in the conglomerate Assembly, and at least by 1663 the House of Burgesses began to meet separately as a distinct body voicing interests potentially in conflict with those of the Council.[32]

Thus by the eighth decade the ruling class in Virginia was broadly based on leading county families and dominated at the provincial level by a privileged officialdom. But this social and political structure was too new, too lacking in the sanctions of time and custom, its leaders too close to humbler origins and as yet too undistinguished in style of life, to be accepted without a struggle. A period of adjustment was necessary, of which Bacon's Rebellion was the climactic episode.

Bacon's Rebellion began as an unauthorized frontier war against the Indians and ended as an upheaval that threatened the entire basis of social and political authority. Its immediate causes have to do with race relations and settlement policy, but behind these issues lay deeper elements related to resistance against the maturing shape of a new social order. These elements explain the dimensions the conflict reached.

There was, first, resistance by substantial planters to the privileges and policies of the inner provincial clique led by Berkeley and composed of those directly dependent on his patronage. These dissidents, among whom were the leaders of the Rebellion, represented neither the downtrodden masses nor a principle of opposition to privilege as such. Their discontent stemmed to a large extent from their own exclusion from privileges they sought. Most often their grievances were based on personal rebuffs they had received as they reached for entry into provincial officialdom. Thus—to speak of the leaders of the Rebellion—Giles Bland arrived in Virginia in 1671 to take over the agency of his late uncle in the management of his father's extensive landholdings, assuming at the same time the lucrative position of customs collector which he had obtained in London. But, amid angry cries of *"pittyfull fellow, puppy* and *Sonn of a Whore,"* he fell out first with Berkeley's cousin and favorite, Thomas Ludwell, and finally with the governor himself; for his "Barbarous and Insolent Behaviors"

---

[32] Andrews, *Colonial Period,* I, 184–85; Craven, *Southern Colonies,* 289 ff.

Bland was fined, arrested, and finally removed from the collector-ship.[33] Of the two "chiefe Incendiarys," William Drummond and Richard Lawrence, the former had been quarreling with Berkeley since 1664, first over land claims in Carolina, then over a contract for build-ing a fort near James City, and repeatedly over lesser issues in the General Court; Lawrence "some Years before . . . had been partially treated at Law, for a considerable Estate on behalfe of a Corrupt fa-vorite." Giles Brent, for his depredations against the Indians in viola-tion of official policy, had not only been severely fined but barred from public office.[34] Bacon himself could not have appeared under more fa-vorable circumstances. A cousin both of Lady Berkeley and of the councilor Nathaniel Bacon, Sr., and by general agreement "a Gent:man of a Liberall education" if of a somewhat tarnished reputa-tion, he had quickly staked out land for himself and had been elevated, for reasons "best known to the Governour," to the Council. But being "of a most imperious and dangerous hidden Pride of heart . . . very ambitious and arrogant," he wanted more, and quickly. His alienation from and violent opposition to Berkeley were wound in among the an-imosities created by the Indian problem and were further complicated by his own unstable personality; they were related also to the fact that Berkeley finally turned down the secret offer Bacon and Byrd made in 1675 for the purchase from the governor of a monopoly of the Indian trade.[35]

These specific disputes have a more general aspect. It was three decades since Berkeley had assumed the governorship and begun rally-ing a favored group, and it was over a decade since the Restoration had given this group unconfined sway over the provincial government. In those years much of the choice tidewater land as well as the choice of-fices had been spoken for, and the tendency of the highly placed was to hold firm. Berkeley's Indian policy—one of stabilizing the borders be-tween Indians and whites and protecting the natives from depredation by land-hungry settlers—although a sincere attempt to deal with an

[33] Jester and Hiden, comps., *Adventurers*, 98–99; R. H. McIlwaine, ed., *Minutes of the Council and General Court . . . 1622–1632, 1670–1676* (Richmond, Va., 1924), 399, 423.

[34] Charles M. Andrews, ed., *Narratives of the Insurrections, 1675–1690* (New York, 1915), 96, 27; Wilcomb E. Washburn, "The Humble Petition of Sarah Drummond," *Wm. and Mary Qtly.*, 3rd ser., 13 (1956), 368–69; H. R. McIlwaine, ed., *Journals of the House of Burgesses of Virginia 1659/60–1693* (Richmond, Va., 1914), 14.

[35] Wilcomb E. Washburn, *The Governor and the Rebel, A History of Bacon's Rebellion in Virginia* (Chapel Hill, 1957), 17–19; Andrews, ed., *Narratives*, 74, 100. For the offer to buy the monopoly and Berkeley's initial interest in it, see Bacon to Berkeley, September 18, 1675, and William and Frances Berkeley to Bacon, September 21, 1675, Coventry Papers, Longleat Library of the Marquises of Bath, LXXVII, 6, 8 (microfilm copy, Li-brary of Congress); for the refusal, see *Aspinwall Papers*, 166. Mr. Washburn, who first called attention to these Bacon letters at Longleat, is editing them for publication by the Virginia Historical Society.

extremely difficult problem, was also conservative, favoring the established. Newcomers like Bacon and Bland and particularly landholders on the frontiers felt victimized by a stabilization of the situation or by a controlled expansion that maintained on an extended basis the existing power structure. They were logically drawn to aggressive positions. In an atmosphere charged with violence, their interests constituted a challenge to provincial authority. Bacon's primary appeal in his "Manifesto" played up the threat of this challenge:

> Let us trace these men in Authority and Favour to whose hands the dispensation of the Countries wealth had been commited; let us observe the sudden Rise of their Estates [compared] with the Quality in wch they first entered this Country. . . . And lett us see wither their extractions and Education have not bin vile, And by what pretence of learning and vertue they could [enter] soe soon into Imployments of so great Trust and consequence, let us . . . see what spounges have suckt up the Publique Treasure and wither it hath not bin privately contrived away by unworthy Favourites and juggling Parasites whose tottering Fortunes have bin repaired and supported at the Publique chardg.

Such a threat to the basis of authority was not lost on Berkeley or his followers. Bacon's merits, a contemporary wrote, "thretned an eclips to there riseing gloryes. . . . (if he should continue in the Governours favour) of Seniours they might becom juniours, while there younger Brother . . . might steale away that blessing, which they accounted there owne by birthright." [36]

But these challengers were themselves challenged, for another main element in the upheaval was the discontent among the ordinary settlers at the local privileges of the same newly risen county magnates who assailed the privileges of the Green Spring faction. The specific Charles City County grievances were directed as much at the locally dominant family, the Hills, as they were at Berkeley and his clique. Similarly, Surry County complained of its county court's highhanded and secretive manner of levying taxes on "the poore people" and of setting the sheriffs' and clerks' fees; they petitioned for the removal of these abuses and for the right to elect the vestry and to limit the tenure of the sheriffs. At all levels the Rebellion challenged the stability of newly secured authority. [37]

It is this double aspect of discontent behind the violence of the Rebellion that explains the legislation passed in June, 1676, by the so-

---

[36] Craven, *Southern Colonies*, 362–73; *Va. Mag. of Hist. and Biog.*, 1 (1893–94), 56–57; Andrews, ed., *Narratives*, 53.

[37] *Va. Mag. of Hist. and Biog.*, 3 (1895–96), 132 ff. (esp. 142–46), 239–52, 341–49; IV, 1–15; II, 172.

called "Bacon's Assembly." At first glance these laws seem difficult to interpret because they express disparate if not contradictory interests. But they yield readily to analysis if they are seen not as the reforms of a single group but as efforts to express the desires of two levels of discontent with the way the political and social hierarchy was becoming stabilized. On the one hand, the laws include measures designed by the numerically predominant ordinary settlers throughout the colony as protests against the recently acquired superiority of the leading county families. These were popular protests and they relate not to provincial affairs but to the situation within the local areas of jurisdiction. Thus the statute restricting the franchise to freeholders was repealed; freemen were given the right to elect the parish vestrymen; and the county courts were supplemented by elected freemen to serve with the regularly appointed county magistrates.

On the other hand, there was a large number of measures expressing the dissatisfactions not so much of the ordinary planter but of the local leaders against the prerogatives recently acquired by the provincial elite, prerogatives linked to officialdom and centered in the Council. Thus the law barring office-holding to newcomers of less than three years' residence struck at the arbitrary elevation of the governor's favorites, including Bacon; and the acts forbidding councilors to join the county courts, outlawing the governor's appointment of sheriffs and tax collectors, and nullifying tax exemption for councilors all voiced objections of the local chieftains to privileges enjoyed by others. From both levels there was objection to profiteering in public office.[38]

Thus the wave of rebellion broke and spread. But why did it subside? One might have expected that the momentary flood would have become a steady tide, its rhythms governed by a fixed political constellation. But in fact it did not; stable political alignments did not result. The conclusion to this controversy was characteristic of all the insurrections. The attempted purges and counterpurges by the leaders of the two sides were followed by a rapid submerging of factional identity. Occasional references were later made to the episode, and there were individuals who found an interest in keeping its memory alive. Also, the specific grievances behind certain of the attempted legal reforms of 1676 were later revived. But of stable parties or factions around these issues there were none.

It was not merely that in the late years of the century no more than in the early was there to be found a justification for permanently organized political opposition or party machinery, that persistent, organized dissent was still indistinguishable from sedition; more impor-

<hr>

[38] Hening, ed., *Va. Stat. at L.*, II, 341–65.

tant was the fact that at the end of the century as in 1630 there was agreement that some must be "highe and eminent in power and dignitie; others meane and in subieccion."[39] Protests and upheaval had resulted from the discomforts of discovering who was, in fact, which, and what the particular consequences of "power and dignitie" were.

But by the end of the century the most difficult period of adjustment had passed and there was an acceptance of the fact that certain families were distinguished from others in riches, in dignity, and in access to political authority. The establishment of these families marks the emergence of Virginia's colonial aristocracy.

It was a remarkable governing group. Its members were soberly responsible, alive to the implications of power; they performed their public obligations with notable skill.[40] Indeed, the glare of their accomplishments is so bright as occasionally to blind us to the conditions that limited them. As a ruling class the Virginian aristocracy of the eighteenth century was unlike other contemporary nobilities or aristocracies, including the English. The differences, bound up with the special characteristics of the society it ruled, had become clear at the turn of the seventeenth century.

Certain of these characteristics are elusive, difficult to grasp and analyze. The leaders of early eighteenth-century Virginia were, for example, in a particular sense, cultural provincials. They were provincial not in the way of Polish *szlachta* isolated on their estate by poverty and impassable roads, nor in the way of sunken *seigneurs* grown rustic and oldfashioned in lonely Norman chateaux. The Virginians were far from uninformed or unaware of the greater world; they were in fact deeply and continuously involved in the cultural life of the Atlantic community. But they knew themselves to be provincials in the sense that their culture was not self-contained; its sources and superior expressions were to be found elsewhere than in their own land. They must seek it from afar; it must be acquired, and once acquired be maintained according to standards externally imposed, in the creation of which they had not participated. The most cultivated of them read much, purposefully, with a diligence the opposite of that essential requisite of aristocracy, uncontending ease. William Byrd's diary with its daily records of stints of study is a stolid testimonial to the virtues of

---

[39] Thus the Burgesses, proposing in 1706 that the vestries be made elective, did not dispute the Council's assertion that the "men of Note & Estates" should have authority and assured them that the people would voluntarily elect the "best" men in the parish. H. R. McIlwaine, ed., *Legislative Journals of the Council of Colonial Virginia* (Richmond, Va., 1918 19), I, 168.

[40] Charles S. Sydnor, *Gentlemen Freeholders: Political Practices in Washington's Virginia* (Chapel Hill, 1952), Chaps. I, VI–IX.

regularity and effort in maintaining standards of civilization set abroad.[41]

In more evident ways also the Virginia planters were denied an uncontending ease of life. They were not *rentiers*. Tenancy, when it appeared late in the colonial period, was useful to the landowners mainly as a cheap way of improving lands held in reserve for future development. The Virginia aristocrat was an active manager of his estate, drawn continuously into the most intimate contacts with the soil and its cultivation. This circumstance limited his ease, one might even say bound him to the soil, but it also strengthened his identity with the land and its problems and saved him from the temptation to create of his privileges an artificial world of self-indulgence.[42]

But more important in distinguishing the emerging aristocracy of Virginia from other contemporary social and political elites were two very specific circumstances. The first concerns the relationship between the integrity of the family unit and the descent of real property. "The English political family," Sir Lewis Namier writes with particular reference to the eighteenth-century aristocracy,

> is a compound of "blood," name, and estate, this last . . . being the most important of the three. . . . The name is a weighty symbol, but liable to variations. . . . the estate . . . is, in the long run, the most potent factor in securing continuity through identification. . . . Primogeniture and entails psychically preserve the family in that they tend to fix its position through the successive generations, and thereby favour conscious identification.

The descent of landed estates in eighteenth-century England was controlled by the complicated device known as the strict settlement which provided that the heir at his marriage received the estate as a life tenant, entailing its descent to his unborn eldest son and specifying the limitations of the encumbrances upon the land that might be made in behalf of his daughters and younger sons.[43]

It was the strict settlement, in which in the eighteenth century perhaps half the land of England was bound, that provided continuity over generations for the landed aristocracy. This permanent identifica-

[41] Albert Goodwin, ed., *The European Nobility in the Eighteenth Century* (London, 1953), *passim*; John Clive and Bernard Bailyn, "England's Cultural Provinces: Scotland and America," *Wm. and Mary Qtly.*, 3rd ser., 9 (1954), 200–13; Louis B. Wright and Marion Tinling, eds., *The Secret Diary of William Byrd of Westover 1709–1712* (Richmond, Va., 1941).

[42] Willard F. Bliss, "The Rise of Tenancy in Virginia," *Va. Mag. of Hist. and Biog.*, 58 (1950), 427 ff.; Louis B. Wright, *Cultural Life of the American Colonies, 1607–1763* (New York, 1957), 5–11.

[43] Lewis B. Namier, *England in the Age of the American Revolution* (London, 1930), 22–23; H. J. Habakkuk, "Marriage Settlements in the Eighteenth Century," Royal Hist. Soc., *Transactions*, 4th ser., 32 (1950), 15–30.

tion of the family with a specific estate and with the status and offices that pertained to it was achieved at the cost of sacrificing the young sons. It was a single stem of the family only that retained its superiority; it alone controlled the material basis for political dominance.

This basic condition of aristocratic governance in England was never present in the American colonies, and not for lack of familiarity with legal forms. The economic necessity that had prompted the widespread adoption of the strict settlement in England was absent in the colonies. Land was cheap and easily available, the more so as one rose on the social and political ladder. There was no need to deprive the younger sons or even daughters of landed inheritances in order to keep the original family estate intact. Provision could be made for endowing each of them with plantations, and they in turn could provide similarly for their children. Moreover, to confine the stem family's fortune to a single plot of land, however extensive, was in the Virginia economy to condemn it to swift decline. Since the land was quickly worn out and since it was cheaper to acquire new land than to rejuvenate the worked soil by careful husbandry, geographical mobility, not stability, was the key to prosperity. Finally, since land was only as valuable as the labor available to work it, a great estate was worth passing intact from generation to generation only if it had annexed to it a sufficient population of slaves. Yet this condition imposed severe rigidities in a plantation's economy—for a labor force bound to a particular plot was immobilized—besides creating bewildering confusions in law.

The result, evident before the end of the seventeenth century, was a particular relationship between the family and the descent of property. There was in the beginning no intent on the part of the Virginians to alter the traditional forms; the continued vitality of the ancient statutes specifying primogeniture in certain cases was assumed.[44] The first clear indication of a new trend came in the third quarter of the century, when the leading gentry, rapidly accumulating large estates, faced for the first time the problem of the transfer of property. The result was the subdivision of the great holdings and the multiplication of smaller plots while the net amount of land held by the leading families continued to rise.[45]

This trend continued. Primogeniture neither at the end of the seventeenth century nor after prevailed in Virginia. It was never popular even among the most heavily endowed of the tidewater families. The most common form of bequest was a grant to the eldest son of the undivided home plantation and gifts of other tracts outside the home county to the younger sons and daughters. Thus by his will of 1686 Robert Beverley, Sr., bequeathed to his eldest son, Peter, all his land in

---

[44] Clarence R. Keim, Influence of Primogeniture and Entail in the Development of Virginia (unpublished Ph.D. dissertation, University of Chicago, 1926), Chap. 1.

[45] E.g., Ames, Eastern Shore, 29–32.

Gloucester County lying between "Chiescake" and "Hoccadey's" creeks (an unspecified acreage); to Robert, the second son, another portion of the Gloucester lands amounting to 920 acres; to Harry, 1,600 acres in Rappahannock County; to John, 3,000 acres in the same county; to William, two plantations in Middlesex County; to Thomas, 3,000 acres in Rappahannock and New Kent counties; to his wife, three plantations including those "whereon I now live" for use during her lifetime, after which they were to descend to his daughter Catherine, who was also to receive £200 sterling; to his daughter Mary, £150 sterling; to "the childe that my wife goeth with, be it male or female," all the rest of his real property; and the residue of his personal property was "to be divided and disposed in equall part & portion betwix my wife and children." Among the bequests of Ralph Wormeley, Jr., in 1700 was an estate of 1,500 acres to his daughter Judith as well as separate plantations to his two sons.

Entail proved no more popular than primogeniture. Only a small minority of estates, even in the tidewater region, were ever entailed. In fact, despite the extension of developed land in the course of the eighteenth century, more tidewater estates were docked of entails than were newly entailed.[46]

Every indication points to continuous and increasing difficulty in reproducing even pale replicas of the strict settlement. In 1705 a law was passed requiring a special act of the Assembly to break an entail; the law stood, but between 1711 and 1776 no fewer than 125 such private acts were passed, and in 1734 estates of under £200 were exempted from the law altogether. The labor problem alone was an insuperable barrier to perpetuating the traditional forms. A statute of 1727, clarifying the confused legislation of earlier years, had attempted to ensure a labor force on entailed land by classifying slaves as real property and permitting them to be bound together with land into bequests. But by 1748 this stipulation had resulted in such bewildering "doubts, variety of opinions, and confusions" that it was repealed. The repeal was disallowed in London, and in the course of a defense of its action the Assembly made vividly clear the utter impracticality of entailment in Virginia's economy. Slaves, the Assembly explained, were essential to the success of a plantation, but "slaves could not be kept on the lands to which they were annexed without manifest prejudice to the tenant in

<hr/>

[46] Keim, Primogeniture and Entail, 44 ff., 113–14. Keim found that only 1 of a sample of 72 wills in Westmoreland (1653–72) contained provisions for entailing; by 1756–61 the proportions had risen to 14 out of 39, but these entails covered only small parts of the total estates. Typical of his other tidewater samples are Middlesex, 1698–1703, 16 out of 65, and 1759–72, 7 out of 48; Henrico, 1677–87, 2 out of 29, and no increase for the later periods. The piedmont samples show even smaller proportions; *ibid.*, 54–62. The Beverley will is printed in *Va. Mag. of Hist. and Biog.*, 3 (1895–96), 47–51; on Wormeley, see *ibid.*, 36 (1928), 101.

tail . . . often the tenant was the proprietor of fee simple land much fitter for cultivation than his intailed lands, where he could work his slaves to a much greater advantage." On the other hand, if a plantation owner did send entailed slaves where they might be employed most economically the result was equally disastrous:

> the frequent removing and settling them on other lands in other counties and parts of the colony far distant from the county court where the deeds or wills which annexed them were recorded and the intail lands lay; the confusion occasioned by their mixture with fee simple slaves of the same name and sex and belonging to the same owner; the uncertainty of distinguishing one from another after several generations, no register of their genealogy being kept and none of them having surnames, were great mischiefs to purchasers, strangers, and creditors, who were often unavoidably deceived in their purchases and hindered in the recovery of their just debts. It also lessened the credit of the country; it being dangerous for the merchants of Great Britain to trust possessors of many slaves for fear the slaves might be intailed.[47]

A mobile labor force free from legal entanglements and a rapid turnover of lands, not a permanent hereditary estate, were prerequisites of family prosperity. This condition greatly influenced social and political life. Since younger sons and even daughters inherited extensive landed properties, equal often to those of the eldest son, concentration of authority in the stem family was precluded. Third generation collateral descendants of the original immigrant were as important in their own right as the eldest son's eldest son. Great clans like the Carters and the Lees, though they may have acknowledged a central family seat, were scattered throughout the province on estates of equal influence. The four male Carters of the third generation were identified by contemporaries by the names of their separate estates, and, indistinguishable in style of life, they had an equal access to political power.[48]

Since material wealth was the basis of the status which made one eligible for public office, there was a notable diffusion of political influence throughout a broadening group of leading families. No one son was predestined to represent the family interest in politics, but as many as birth and temperament might provide. In the 1750's there were no

---

[47] Hening, ed., *Va. Stat. at L.*, III, 320, IV, 399–400, 222 ff., V, 441–42n (quoted). In 1765 the legal rigors of entailment were permanently relaxed by a law permitting the leasing of entailed land for up to three lives, a move made necessary, the Assembly said, because "many large tracts of entailed lands remain uncultivated, the owners not having slaves to work them. . . ." *ibid.*, VIII, 183. For a striking example of the difficulties of maintaining entailed lands, see *ibid.*, VI, 297–99; Keim, Primogeniture and Entail, 108.

[48] Louis Morton, *Robert Carter of Nomini Hall* (Williamsburg, 1941), 11.

fewer than seven Lees of the same generation sitting together in the Virginia Assembly; in the Burgesses they spoke for five separate counties. To the eldest, Philip Ludwell Lee, they conceded a certain social superiority that made it natural for him to sit in the Council. But he did not speak alone for the family; by virtue of inheritance he had no unique authority over his brothers and cousins.

The leveling at the top of the social and political hierarchy, creating an evenness of status and influence, was intensified by continuous intermarriage within the group. The unpruned branches of these flourishing family trees, growing freely, met and intertwined until by the Revolution the aristocracy appeared to be one great tangled cousinry.[49]

As political power became increasingly diffused throughout the upper stratum of society, the Council, still at the end of the seventeenth century a repository of unique privileges, lost its effective superiority. Increasingly through the successive decades its authority had to be exerted through alignments with the Burgesses—alignments made easier as well as more necessary by the criss-crossing network of kinship that united the two houses. Increasingly the Council's distinctions became social and ceremonial.[50]

The contours of Virginia's political hierarchy were also affected by a second main conditioning element, besides the manner of descent of family property. Not only was the structure unusually level and broad at the top, but it was incomplete in itself. Its apex, the ultimate source of legal decision and control, lay in the quite different society of England, amid the distant embroilments of London, the court, and Parliament. The levers of control in that realm were for the most part hidden from the planters; yet the powers that ruled this remote region could impose an arbitrary authority directly into the midst of Virginia's affairs.

One consequence was the introduction of instabilities in the tenure and transfer of the highest offices. Tenure could be arbitrarily interrupted, and the transfer to kin of such positions at death or resignation—uncertain in any case because of the diffusion of family authority—could be quite difficult or even impossible. Thus William Byrd II returned from England at the death of his father in 1704 to take over the family properties, but though he was the sole heir he did not automatically or completely succeed to the elder Byrd's provincial offices. He did, indeed, become auditor of Virginia after his father, but only because he had carefully arranged for the succession while still in London; his father's Council seat went to someone else, and it took three years of patient maneuvering through his main London contact, Mica-

---

[49] Burton J. Hendrick, *The Lees of Virginia* (Boston, 1935), 97.
[50] Percy S. Flippin, *The Royal Government in Virginia, 1624–1775* (New York, 1919), 166–67, 169; Herbert L. Osgood, *The American Colonies in the Eighteenth Century* (4 vols.; New York, 1924–25), IV, 231–32.

jah Jerry, to secure another; he never did take over the receivership. Even such a power as "King" Carter, the reputed owner at his death of 300,000 acres and 1,000 slaves, was rebuffed by the resident deputy governor and had to deploy forces in England in order to transfer a Virginia naval office post from one of his sons to another. There was family continuity in public office, but at the highest level it was uncertain, the result of place-hunting rather than of the absolute prerogative of birth.[51]

Instability resulted not only from the difficulty of securing and transferring high appointive positions but also and more immediately from the presence in Virginia of total strangers to the scene, particularly governors and their deputies, armed with extensive jurisdiction and powers of enforcement. The dangers of this element in public life became clear only after Berkeley's return to England in 1677, for after thirty-five years of residence in the colony Sir William had become a leader in the land independent of his royal authority. But Howard, Andros, and Nicholson were governors with full legal powers but with at best only slight connections with local society. In them, social leadership and political leadership had ceased to be identical.

In the generation that followed Berkeley's departure, this separation between the two spheres created the bitterest of political controversies. Firmly entrenched behind their control of the colony's government, the leading families battled with every weapon available to reduce the power of the executives and thus to eliminate what appeared to be an external and arbitrary authority. Repeated complaints by the governors of the intractable opposition of a league of local oligarchs marked the Virginians' success. Efforts by the executives to discipline the indigenous leaders could only be mildly successful. Patronage was a useful weapon, but its effectiveness diminished steadily, ground down between a resistant Assembly and an office-hungry bureaucracy in England. The possibility of exploiting divisions among the resident powers also declined as kinship lines bound the leading families closer together and as group interests became clearer with the passage of time. No faction built around the gubernatorial power could survive independently; ultimately its adherents would fall away and it would weaken. It was a clear logic of the situation that led the same individuals who had promoted Nicholson as a replacement for Andros to work against him once he assumed office.[52]

[51] John S. Bassett, ed., *The Writings of "Colonel William Byrd of Westover in Virginia Esqr"* (New York, 1901), *xlviii–ix*; Morton, *Carter*, 28n.

[52] For the classic outcry against "the party of Malecontents," see Spotswood's letter to the Board of Trade, March 25, 1719, in R. A. Brock, ed., *The Official Letters of Alexander Spotswood* (Richmond, Va., 1882–85), II, 308 ff.; cf. 285. On patronage, see Flippin, *Royal Government*, 208–214; Leonard W. Labaree, *Royal Government in America* (New Haven, Conn., 1930), 102; Worthington C. Ford, "A Sketch of Sir Francis Nicholson," *Mag. of Amer. His.*, 29 (1893), 508–12.

Stability could be reached only by the complete identification of external and internal authority through permanent commitment by the appointees to local interests. Commissary Blair's extraordinary success in Virginia politics was based not only on his excellent connections in England but also on his marriage into the Harrison family, which gave him support of an influential kinship faction. There was more than hurt pride and thwarted affection behind Nicholson's reported insane rage at being spurned by the highly marriageable Lucy Burwell; and later the astute Spotswood, for all his success in imposing official policy, fully quieted the controversies of his administration only by succumbing completely and joining as a resident Virginia landowner the powers aligned against him.[53]

But there was more involved than instability and conflict in the discontinuity between social and political organization at the topmost level. The state itself had changed its meaning. To a Virginia planter of the early eighteenth century the highest public authority was no longer merely one expression of a general social authority. It had become something abstract, external to his life and society, an ultimate power whose purposes were obscure, whose direction could neither be consistently influenced nor accurately plotted, and whose human embodiments were alien and antagonistic.

The native gentry of the early eighteenth century had neither the need nor the ability to fashion a new political theory to comprehend their experience, but their successors would find in the writings of John Locke on state and society not merely a reasonable theoretical position but a statement of self-evident fact.

I have spoken exclusively of Virginia, but though the histories of each of the colonies in the seventeenth century are different, they exhibit common characteristics. These features one might least have expected to find present in Virginia, and their presence there is, consequently, most worth indicating.

In all of the colonies the original transference of an ordered European society was succeeded by the rise to authority of resident settlers whose influence was rooted in their ability to deal with the problems of life in wilderness settlements. These individuals attempted to stabilize their positions, but in each case they were challenged by others arriving after the initial settlements, seeking to exploit certain advantages of position, wealth, or influence. These newcomers, securing after the

---

[53] Peter Laslett, "John Locke. . . ," *Wm. and Mary Qtly.*, 3rd ser., 14 (1957), 398; Daniel E. Motley, *Life of Commissary James Blair* . . . (Baltimore, 1901), 10, 43 ff.; William S. Perry, ed., *Historical Collections Relating to the . . . Church* ([Hartford], 1870–78), 1, 69, 72–73, 88, 90, 102, 135; Leonidas Dodson, *Alexander Spotswood* (Philadelphia, 1932), 251ff.

Restoration governmental appointments in the colonies and drawn together by personal ties, especially those of kinship and patronage,
came to constitute colonial officialdom. This group introduced a new
principle of social organization; it also gave rise to new instabilities in a
society in which the traditional forms of authority were already being
subjected to severe pressures. By the eighth decade of the seventeenth
century the social basis of public life had become uncertain and insecure, its stability delicate and sensitive to disturbance. Indian warfare,
personal quarrels, and particularly the temporary confusion in external
control caused by the Glorious Revolution became the occasions for
violent challenges to constituted authority.

By the end of the century a degree of harmony had been achieved,
but the divergence between political and social leadership at the topmost level created an area of permanent conflict. The political and social structures that emerged were by European standards strangely
shaped. Everywhere as the bonds of empire drew tighter the meaning
of the state was changing. Herein lay the origins of a new political system.

From Servant to Freeholder:
Status Mobility and Property Accumulation
in Seventeenth-Century Maryland

RUSSELL R. MENARD

*We tend to think of Southern colonial history as the story of plan-
tation society, the history of plantation owners and Negro slaves.
We have always known, of course, that not all whites were slave
owners, nor were all blacks slaves. The group least prominent in
the historical record has been poorer whites, since they have not
left behind the rich literary evidence that has familiarized us
with their "betters." Russell Menard and his co-workers in the
Chesapeake school of colonial historians have mined the quantitative evidence available in Maryland and Virginia, and have
thereby begun to build up a picture of the totality of colonial soci-*

Reprinted by permission from Russell R. Menard, "From Servant to Freeholder: Status Mobility and Property Accumulation in Seventeenth-Century Maryland," *William
and Mary Quarterly*, 3rd ser., XXX (1973), 37–64.

ety. Their results have been particularly revealing for the seven-teenth century, which has been much more difficult to analyze by traditional historical methods. The results are important and surprising.

In this essay, Menard analyzes that majority of immigrants to seventeenth-century Maryland who came as servants in order to pay their passage to the New World. It has always been tempting to look backward from the vantage point of eighteenth-century plantation life to the origins of that "mature" form of Southern colonial life, but Menard suggests that we will understand plantation society better if we begin from the beginning.

He finds two phases in the social history of the servant class in seventeenth-century Maryland. In the first, from about 1640 to 1660, immigrants approximated the general American myth of socio-economic mobility. Servants were treated well, worked out their indentures, moved from renting to landowning, and frequently rose to positions of wealth and power. In the second, however, during the last decades of the century, the story of servant life history was not so happy. These men tended to remain servants. They were rather less likely than earlier immigrants to become landowners, even if they successfully worked out their indentures. Nor did they come to play significant roles in political society.

Why were the sons less upwardly mobile than their fathers? Menard believes that the key was a dramatic rise in Maryland population after 1660, which increased the numbers of those competing for land and power. This demographic revolution was accompanied by rising land prices and falling tobacco prices, both of which made it difficult for small farmers to achieve yeoman status. Thus a combination of physical and economic forces dramatically altered the prospects for success of servants and petty farmers during the course of the seventeenth century, and altered the nature of indentured servitude as a labor system to the disadvantage of immigrants and the native poor and to the advantage of landowners.

Menard thus reasons from a painstaking analysis of local records to a systematic interpretation of Maryland social and economic life. Can these records tell us, however, how clear this pattern was to contemporaries? Were servants and petty farmers conscious of the fact that their chances were declining? How would we expect poor whites in the seventeenth century to react to such a perception? Was such a development inevitable, given the economic environment of Maryland, or can it be attributed to political decisions consciously taken? How aware were Marylanders of the existence of a labor "system"? Whatever your answers to these questions, it should be clear that Menard and his colleagues are providing us with powerful tools and critically important information for understanding how colonists actually lived.

Miles Gibson, Stephen Sealus, and William Scot all arrived in Maryland as indentured servants in the 1660s. They completed their terms and soon accumulated enough capital to purchase land. Thereafter, their careers diverged sharply. Gibson, aided by two good marriages, gained a place among the local gentry and served his county as justice of the peace, burgess, and sheriff. At his death in 1692, he owned more than two thousand acres of land and a personal estate appraised at over six hundred pounds sterling, including nine slaves.[1] Sealus's career offers a sharp contrast to that of his highly successful contemporary. He lost a costly court case in the mid-1670s and apparently was forced to sell his plantation to cover the expenses. He spent the rest of his days working other men's land. By 1691, Sealus was reduced to petitioning the county court for relief. He was "both weake and lame," he pleaded, "and not able to worke whereby to maintaine himselfe nor his wife." His petition was granted, but the Sealus family remained poor. Stephen died in 1696, leaving an estate appraised at £18 6s.[2] William Scot did not approach Gibson's success, but he did manage to avoid the dismal failure of Sealus. He lived on his small plantation for nearly forty years, served his community in minor offices, and slowly accumulated property. In his will, Scot gave all seven of his sons land of their own and provided his three daughters with small dowries.[3] Although interesting in themselves, these brief case histories do not reveal very much about the life chances of servants in the seventeenth century. They do suggest a range of accomplishment, but how are we to tell whether Scot, Sealus, or Gibson is most typical, or even if any one of them represents the position that most servants attained? Did servitude offer any hard-working Englishman without capital a good chance of becoming, like Miles Gibson, a man of means and position in a new community? Or did servitude only offer, as it finally offered Stephen Sealus, a chance to live in poverty in another place? Perhaps

---

[1] Baltimore County Land Records, IR#PP, 64 (all manuscript sources cited in this essay are in the Maryland Hall of Records, Annapolis, Md.); Patents, XII, 269, 283; IB&IL#C, 22, 29, 44, 63, 65; Testamentary Proceedings, 15C, 51; Kenneth L. Carroll, "Thomas Thurston, Renegade Maryland Quaker," *Maryland Historical Magazine*, LXII (1967), 189; William Hand Browne *et al.*, eds., *Archives of Maryland . . .* (Baltimore, 1883–), VII, 349; XV, 253; XVII, 142; Inventories and Accounts, XII, 152–153; XIIIA, 53–58; XX, 208–209.

[2] Patents, XI, 334, 573; XII, 342, 427; *Md. Arch.*, LXVI, 18–19, 138–139; Dorchester County Land Records, Old#3, 101–103; Old#4½, 121; Inventories and Accounts, XIV, 67.

[3] Somerset County Judicials, DT7, 146; SC, 134; Somerset County Land Records, L, 22; Patents, XXII, 59, 77; XIX, 562; Rent Roll, IX, 15; Somerset Wills, Box 2, folder 50; Inventories and Accounts, XXXIV, 159–160; XXXV, 280.

Scot was more typical. Did servitude promise poor men a chance to obtain moderate prosperity and respectability for themselves and their families? How much property and status mobility did most servants manage to achieve in the seventeenth century? This essay examines the careers of a group of men who immigrated to Maryland in the seventeenth century in order to provide some of the data needed for answers to such questions.[4]

The study of mobility requires an assessment of a man's position in society for at least two points in his career, a task that the general absence of census materials, tax lists, and assessment records makes difficult. Nevertheless, a study of mobility among servants is possible because we know their place in the social structure at the beginning of their careers in the New World. Servants started at the bottom of white society: they entered the colonies with neither freedom nor capital. Since we can define their position on arrival, measuring the degree of success they achieved is a fairly simple task. We can, as the capsule biographies of Gibson, Sealus, and Scot demonstrate, describe their progress in the New World. A study of the fortunes of indentured servants and the way those fortunes changed over time provides a sensitive indicator of the opportunities available within colonial society.

The broadest group under study in this essay consists of 275 men who entered Maryland as servants before the end of 1642, although the main concern is with 158 for whom proof exists that they survived to be freemen.[5] Not all the men who came into Maryland as servants by 1642 are included in the 275. No doubt a few servants escape any recorded mention, while others appear who are not positively identified as servants. One large group falling into this latter category included 66 men, not specifically called servants, who were listed in the proofs of headrights as having been transported into the colony at the expense of someone else to whom they were not related. It is probable that all of these men emigrated under indentures, but since proof was lacking they have been excluded from the study.[6]

---

[4] Useful studies of indentured servants in colonial history include Thomas J. Wertenbaker, *The Planters of Colonial Virginia* (Princeton, 1922); Richard B. Morris, *Government and Labor in Early America* (New York, 1946); Abbot Emerson Smith, *Colonists in Bondage: White Servitude and Convict Labor in America, 1607–1776* (Chapel Hill, 1947); Marcus Wilson Jernegan, *Laboring and Dependent Classes in Colonial America, 1607–1783* (Chicago, 1931); Mildred Campbell, "Social Origins of Some Early Americans," in James Morton Smith, ed., *Seventeenth-Century America: Essays in Colonial History* (Chapel Hill, 1959), 63–89.

[5] The period could have been extended to include those arriving as late as 1644 or 1645, but this seemed pointless. It was only necessary to have a group large enough so that an occasional error would not alter percentages drastically; 158 seemed adequate for that purpose.

[6] The terms servant and servitude covered a wide variety of men and situations in the 17th century and the terms of the contracts the men in this sample served under are not

The mortality rate among these servants was probably high. One hundred and seventeen of the 275—more than 40 percent—did not appear in the records as freemen. The deaths of 14 of the missing are mentioned,[7] but we can only speculate on the fate of most of the servants who disappeared. Some may have been sold out of the province before their terms were completed, and some may have run away, while others may have left Maryland immediately after becoming freemen. A majority probably died while still servants, victims of the unusual climate, poor food, ill housing, hard work, or an occasional cruel master, before they had a chance to discover for themselves if America was a land of opportunity.

For the 158 who definitely survived the rigors of servitude, opportunity was abundant. Seventy-nine to 81 (identification is uncertain in two cases) of the survivors, about 50 percent, eventually acquired land in Maryland. To be properly interpreted, however, this figure must be understood within the context of the careers of those who failed to acquire land. Fourteen of those who survived servitude but did not acquire land in Maryland died within a decade of completing their terms. Another 25 left before they had lived in the colony for ten years as freemen. These figures are conservative, for they include only those for whom death or migration can be proven. Twenty-five of the 158 survivors appear only briefly in the records and then vanish without a trace, presumably among the early casualties or emigrants. Furthermore, there is no reason to believe that those who left were any less successful than those who remained. At least 11 of the 25 known emigrants became landowners in Virginia. Only 13 to 15 of the 158 servants who appeared in the records as freemen (less than 10 percent) lived for more than a decade in Maryland as freemen without becoming landowners.[8]

Those who acquired land did so rapidly. The interval between achieving freedom and acquiring land, which was discovered in forty-six cases, ranged from two years for Richard Nevill and Phillip West to twelve for John Norman and Walter Walterlin. Francis Pope, for

---

known. However, I am confident that the men under study shared three characteristics: first, they did not pay their own passage; second, they arrived in Maryland without capital; third, they were bound in service for a term of years. As a means of determining whether the selection process contained any significant bias, the careers of the 66 transportees were also studied. Including them would have slightly strengthened the argument presented in this essay.

[7] *Md. Arch.*, I, 17; IV, 22–23, 49, 52–53; V, 192, 197; Raphael Semmes, "Claiborne vs. Clobery et als. in the High Court of Admiralty," *Md. Hist. Mag.*, XXVII (1933), 181, 185–186.

[8] The figure of 10% may be too high. A few of the men who do not appear as landowners may have held freeholds on one of the private manors for which we do not have records.

whom the interval was seven years, and John Maunsell, who took eight, came closer to the median of seven and one-half years.

The holdings of the vast majority of those who acquired land were small. Most lived as small planters on tracts ranging in size from fifty acres to four hundred acres, although fourteen former servants managed to become large landowners, possessing at least one thousand acres at one time in their lives. Zachary Wade, who owned over four thousand acres at his death in 1678 and about five thousand acres in the early 1670s, ranked with the largest landowners in Maryland.[9]

Inventories of personal estates, taken at death, have survived for 31 of the 158 former servants. Analysis of the inventories reinforces the conclusion that most of these men became small planters. About 60 percent of the inventories show personal property appraised at less than one hundred pounds sterling.[10] Men whose estates fell into this range led very simple lives. In most cases, livestock accounted for more than half the total value of their personal possessions. At best their clothing and household furnishings were meager. They either worked their plantations themselves or with the help of their wives and children, for few of these small planters owned servants and even fewer owned slaves. In Aubrey Land's apt phrase, they led lives of "rude sufficiency."[11] But they fared no better than if they had remained in England.

Not all former servants remained small planters. Twelve of the thirty-one left estates appraised at more than one hundred pounds. Men such as John Halfhead, Francis Pope, and James Walker could be described as substantial planters. Their life style was not luxurious, but their economic position was secure and their assets usually included a servant or two and perhaps even a slave.[12] Two men, Zachary Wade and Henry Adams, gained entry into the group of planter-merchants who dominated the local economy in the seventeenth century. Wade,

----

[9] For a list of Wade's land at his death, see his will in Charles County Wills, 1665–1708, 54–56.

[10] The use of £100 as a cutoff point is derived from Aubrey Land, "Economic Base and Social Structure: The Northern Chesapeake in the Eighteenth Century," *Journal of Economic History*, XXV (1965), 642. There is no way of determining whether these inventories constitute a representative sample. My impression is that they are biased in favor of the wealthiest and that a more complete series would show 75 to 80% of the estates worth less than £100. Prior to the early 1680s, estates were appraised in tobacco. I have translated them into sterling according to the average price of tobacco in the year the inventory was taken. See Russell R. Menard, "Farm Prices of Maryland Tobacco, 1659–1710," *Md. Hist. Mag.*, forthcoming, for details.

[11] Land, "Northern Chesapeake," *Journal Econ. Hist.*, XXV (1965), 642.

[12] Testamentary Proceedings, V, 363–365; Inventories and Accounts, I, 394–397, 500–503; III, 63–65.

whose estate was appraised at just over four hundred pounds, was wealthier than 95 percent of his contemporaries, while Adams left an estate valued at £569 15s. ld. when he died in 1686.[13]

There are still other measures of mobility which confirm the picture of abundant opportunity for ex-servants that the study of property accumulation has indicated. Abbot E. Smith has estimated that only two of every ten servants brought to America in the seventeenth century became stable and useful members of colonial society, but if we take participation in government as indicative of stability and usefulness, the careers of the 158 men who survived servitude demonstrate that Smith's estimates are much too low, at least for the earlier part of the century.[14]

Former servants participated in the government of Maryland as jurors, minor office holders, justices of the peace, sheriffs, burgesses, and officers in the militia. Many also attended the Assembly as freemen at those sessions at which they were permitted. The frequency with which responsible positions were given to ex-servants testifies to the impressive status mobility they achieved in the mid-seventeenth century. Seventy-five or seventy-six of the survivors—just under 50 percent—sat on a jury, attended an Assembly session, or filled an office in Maryland. As was the case with landholding, this figure must be understood in light of the careers of those who failed to participate. Fourteen of the nonparticipants died within a decade of becoming freemen; another twenty-seven left the province within ten years of completing their terms. There is no reason to assume that those who left did not participate in their new homes—two of the twenty-seven, John Tue and Mathew Rhodan, became justices of the peace in Virginia, while two others, Thomas Yewell and Robert Sedgrave, served as militia officer and clerk of a county court respectively.[15] If we eliminate the twenty-five who appeared but fleetingly in the records, only sixteen or seventeen (slightly more than 10 percent) lived for more

---

[13] Inventories and Accounts, V, 197–203; VIII, 389; IX, 239–244. The statement on Wade's relative wealth is based on an analysis of all inventories filed in the 1670s.

[14] Smith, *Colonists in Bondage*, 299–300. In an earlier essay Smith used an estimate of 8% and explained this low figure by reference to the "at best irresponsible, lazy, and ungoverned, and at worst frankly criminal" character of the typical servant! "The Indentured Servant and Land Speculation in Seventeenth Century Maryland," *American Historical Review*, XL (1934–1935), 467–472.

[15] Lyon G. Tyler, "Washington and His Neighbors," *William and Mary Quarterly*, 1st Scr., IV (1895–1896), 41, 75; Charles Arthur Hoppin, "The Good Name and Fame of the Washingtons," *Tylers Quarterly Historical and Genealogical Magazine*, IV (1922–1923), 350; *Md. Arch.*, IV, 540–541.

than a decade in the province as freemen without leaving any record of contribution to the community's government.[16]

For most former servants participation was limited to occasional service as a juror, an appointment as constable, or service as a sergeant in the militia. Some compiled remarkable records in these minor positions. William Edwin, who was brought into the province in 1634 by Richard Gerard and served his time with the Jesuits, sat on nine provincial court juries and served a term as constable.[17] Richard Nevill, who also entered Maryland in 1634, served on six provincial court juries and was a sergeant in the militia.[18] A former servant of Gov. Leonard Calvert, John Halfhead, served on eleven juries and attended two sessions of the Assembly.[19] John Robinson managed, in five years before his death in 1643, to attend two Assemblies, sit on three provincial court juries, and serve as constable and coroner of St. Clement's Hundred.[20]

A high percentage of the 158 survivors went beyond service in these minor posts to positions of authority in the community. Twenty-two of them served the province as justice of the peace, burgess, sheriff, councillor, or officer in the militia. They accounted for four of Maryland's militia officers, twelve burgesses, sixteen justices, seven sheriffs, and two members of the Council.

For nine of the twenty-two former servants who came to hold major office in Maryland, tenure was brief. They served for a few years as an officer in the militia or as a county justice, or sat as burgess in a single session of the Assembly. During most of John Maunsell's twenty years in Maryland, participation was limited to occasional service as a juror. In 1649, he was returned as burgess from St. Mary's County.[21] Daniel Clocker, who started out in Maryland as a servant to Thomas Cornwallis, compiled an impressive record of minor office holding. He sat on numerous provincial court juries, served St. Mary's County as overseer of the highways, and was named to the Common Council of St. Mary's City in 1671. In 1655, when many more qualified men (Clocker was illiterate) were barred from office because of their Catholicism or suspect loyalty, he was appointed justice in St. Mary's County, a post

[16] The figure of 10% is probably too high. The absence of county court records for St. Mary's and Calvert counties and the partial loss of those for Kent—three of the four counties in which most of the men lived—make a complete study of participation impossible. Undoubtedly some of the men counted as nonparticipants sat on juries for which the records are lost.

[17] Patents, I, 20, 38; AB&H, 5; *Md. Arch.*, IV, 33, 260, 403; X, 74, 134, 143, 273, 295; XLI, 119, 340.

[18] Patents, I, 20, 38; AB&H, 244; II, 79; *Md. Arch.*, IV, 238, 240, 444; X, 54, 116, 525; XLI, 340.

[19] Patents, I, 121; II, 579; *Md. Arch.*, I, 72, 116; IV, 9, 21, 180, 237, 240, 349, 409, 447; LVII, 309.

[20] *Md. Arch.*, I, 120; III, 89; IV, 9, 21, 176.

[21] *Ibid.*, I, 237.

he held for three years at most. Clocker was appointed militia officer by the rebellious Governor Josias Fendall in 1660, but again his taste of power was brief.[22] John Cage, also a former servant to Cornwallis, was appointed to the Charles County bench in April 1660, but sat for only six months. Although Cage lived in Maryland for eighteen years after his brief term as justice, his participation was limited to infrequent jury duty.[23] James Walker sat as justice in Charles County for a little more than two years. He lived in Maryland for more than thirty years, but this is the only recorded instance of his holding office.[24]

Thirteen of the twenty-two men who acquired office could count themselves among Maryland's rulers in the first few decades following the founding of the province. Two even reached the Council, although neither became a major figure in the provincial government. John Hatch first participated as a provincial court juror in February 1643. By December 1647, he had been appointed sheriff of St. Mary's County. He was elected to the Assembly from St. George's Hundred in 1650 and from Charles County in 1658 and 1660. Hatch also sat as justice in Charles County from 1658 to 1661. He was appointed to the Council in 1654 and served until 1658. His son-in-law, Governor Fendall, again elevated him to the Council in 1660 during the rebellion against Lord Baltimore. Although after 1661 he was excluded from major office because his loyalty to the proprietor was suspect, he did manage to compile an impressive record of accomplishment for a man who entered Maryland as a servant.[25] Robert Vaughan also entered Maryland as a servant, probably to Lord Baltimore. Vaughan attended the 1638 session of the Assembly as a freeman. He must have been an able man, for he was already both a sergeant in the militia and constable of St. George's Hundred. In 1640, he was returned as burgess from St. Clement's Hundred. He moved to Kent Island in 1642, probably at the urging of Governor Calvert, who sorely needed loyal supporters on the island which was a hotbed of opposition to his interests. Vaughan sat as justice of Kent for twenty-six years before he died in 1668 and served as an officer in the militia for at least that long. He was a member of the Council in 1648.[26]

Although Hatch and Vaughan were the only former servants to reach positions of importance in the provincial government, eleven others became men of real weight in their counties of residence. These eleven averaged more than ten years on the bench, more than three sessions as burgess, and just under two years as sheriff. Zachary Wade,

[22] Patents, AB&H, 36, 244; *Md. Arch.*, IV, 230, 539; X, 295, 413; XLI, 427; XLIX, 29, 206; LI, 387; LVII, 597.

[23] Patents, II, 570; AB&H, 244; *Md. Arch.*, IV, 213; LIII, 69, 92, 363, 502, 543.

[24] *Md. Arch.*, XLI, 87–88.

[25] *Ibid.*, I, 249–261, 380; III, 311–314; IV, 181, 349; XLI, 62, 87–88; LIII, 76.

[26] Patents, I, 99; *Md. Arch.*, 1, 2, 85, 125, 259–261, 426; III, 124–127, 211–213.

formerly a servant to Margaret Brent, was returned to the Assembly from St. Mary's County in 1658 and from Charles County from 1660 to 1666. He sat as justice of Charles County in 1660 and was reappointed in 1663. Wade served on the bench for a year and then stepped down to take a term as sheriff. He returned to the bench in 1667 and sat until his death in 1678.[27] Henry Adams was brought into Maryland in 1638 and served his time with Thomas Greene, who later became governor. He was first appointed to the Charles County bench in 1658 and served continuously as justice until his death in 1686, with the exception of one year, 1665–1666, during which he was sheriff. Adams also represented Charles County in the Assembly in 1661, 1663–1664, and in every session from 1671 to 1684, when illness prevented him from assuming his seat.[28] Nicholas Gwyther started out in Maryland as a servant to Thomas Cornwallis. Although he was never appointed justice and sat only once in the Assembly, his seven years as sheriff of St. Mary's County and three years as sheriff of Charles County made him one of the mainstays of Maryland's county government.[29]

The significant role played by former servants in Maryland's government in the mid-seventeenth century and the opportunities available to industrious men can also be seen in an examination of the officials of Charles County in the years immediately following its establishment in 1658. Six justices were appointed to the Charles County bench by a commission dated May 10, 1658. Four of them—John Hatch, James Lindsey, Henry Adams, and James Walker—began their careers in Maryland as servants. In the next three years, four more ex-servants—John Cage, James Langworth, Francis Pope, and Zachary Wade—were appointed justices. Hatch, Wade, and Adams also represented the county in the Assembly in this period. Nicholas Gwyther, another former servant, was Charles County's first sheriff; four of the five men who immediately succeeded Gwyther were former servants. In the late 1650s and early 1660s, Charles County was governed by men who had entered the province under indentures.[30]

The accomplishments of those former servants who were especially successful were recognized by the community through the use of titles of distinction. At least 19 of the 158 survivors acquired the title of mister, gentleman, or esquire and retained it until they died. The 13 men who achieved positions of importance in the colony's government were all honored in this fashion. Office was not, however, the only path to a title. John Courts, for example, rode to distinction on his son's coat-

[27] Patents, II, 575; *Md. Arch.*, I, 380–383, 426; II, 8; III, 492; V, 21; XLI, 62; LIII, 76.
[28] Patents, I, 18; AB&H, 377; *Md. Arch.*, I, 396; III, 424, 519; XIII, 54; XLI, 87–88.
[29] Patents, AB&H, 60; *Md. Arch.*, I, 369, 460; X, 124; XLI, 88.
[30] *Md. Arch.*, I, 380–383, 396, 426, 451, 460; II, 8; III, 481, 492, 519; XLI, 87–88; LIII, 69, 76.

tails. Although his father acquired a substantial landed estate, John Courts, Jr., started from humble beginnings, nevertheless married well, and, perhaps as a result of his father-in-law's influence, gained appointment to the Charles County bench in 1685. He represented the county in the Associator's Assembly and was appointed to the Council in 1692, a position he held until he died ten years later as one of Maryland's wealthiest men, leaving an estate worth over £1,800, including thirty slaves and six servants. John Courts, Sr., was regularly addressed as mister after his more illustrious son was appointed to the Council.[31] A few other men were honored with titles for part of their lives, but lost them before they died, as in the case of John Cage, who was only called mister during his brief tenure as justice.[32]

Although the personal history of each of these 158 men is unique, common patterns may be discerned. We can construct a career model for indentured servants in Maryland in the middle of the seventeenth century which should reveal something about the way opportunity was structured and what options were open to men at various stages in their lives. We can also identify some of the components necessary for constructing a successful career in Maryland.

As a group, the indentured servants were young when they emigrated. While they ranged in age from mere boys such as Ralph Hasleton to the "old and decripit" Original Browne, the great majority were in their late teens and early twenties. Age on arrival was determined in thirty-six cases with a median of nineteen.[33] Probably most were from English families of the "middling sort," yeomen, husbandmen, and artisans, men whose expectations might well include the acquisition of a freehold or participation in local government.[34]

The careers of these men suggest that a few had formal education. Robert Vaughan and Robert Sedgrave both served as clerks in county court, a position requiring record-keeping skills.[35] Cuthbert Fenwick was attorney to Thomas Cornwallis, who was probably the wealthiest man in Maryland in the 1630s and 1640s. It seems unlikely that Cornwallis would have allowed a man without education to manage his estate during his frequent absences from the province.[36] These men

[31] *Ibid.*, XVII, 380; Charles County Inventories, 1673–1717, 143–148, 311; Charles County Accounts, 1708–1735, 47–49, 51–54, 72–73; David W. Jordan, "The Royal Period of Colonial Maryland, 1689–1715" (Ph.D. diss., Princeton University, 1966), 351, 352.

[32] *Md. Arch.*, X, 160; LIII, 69, 92, 318.

[33] Patents, AB&H, 151; *Md. Arch.*, X, 192; Semmes, "Claiborne vs. Clobery," *Md. Hist. Mag.*, XXVIII (1933), 184.

[34] Campbell, "Social Origins," in Smith, ed., *Seventeenth-Century America*, 63–89.

[35] *Md. Arch.*, IV, 540–541; Donnell MacClure Owings, *His Lordship's Patronage: Offices of Profit in Colonial Maryland* (Baltimore, 1953), 146.

[36] *Md. Arch.*, I, 85.

were, however, not at all typical, for most of the 158 survivors were without education. Total illiterates outnumbered those who could write their names by about three to two, and it is probable that many who could sign their names could do little more.[37]

A servant's life was not easy, even by seventeenth-century standards. Probably they worked the ten to fourteen hours a day, six days a week, specified in the famous Elizabethan Statute of Artificers. Servants could be sold, and there were severe penalties for running away. They were subject to the discipline of their masters, including corporal punishment within reason. On the other hand, servants had rights to adequate food, clothing, shelter, and a Sunday free from hard labor. Servants could not sue at common law, but they could protest ill-treatment and receive a hearing in the courts. Cases in this period are few, but the provincial court seems to have taken seriously its obligation to enforce the terms of indentures and protect servants' rights.[38] No instances of serious mistreatment of servants appear in the records in the late 1630s and early 1640s. Servants were worked long and hard, but they were seldom abused. Moreover, the servant who escaped premature death soon found himself a free man in a society that offered great opportunities for advancement.[39]

None of the indentures signed by these servants has survived, but it is possible to offer some reasonable conjecture concerning the terms of their service. John Lewger and Jerome Hawley, in their *Relation of Maryland*, offered some advice to men thinking of transporting servants into the province and they also printed a model indenture. A servant was to work at whatever his master "shall there imploy him, according to the custome of the Countrey." In return, the master was to

---

[37] Determining literacy was difficult because there are few original papers. It was assumed that if a clerk recorded a man's mark, that man was illiterate, and that if a clerk recorded a signature when transcribing a document that also contained the mark of another man, the man whose signature was recorded could sign his name. This method is not foolproof, but it seems the best available given the limitations of the data. There were 37 illiterates and 24 who could write their names.

[38] A bill considered but not passed by the 1639 Assembly describes rules governing master-servant relations that were probably followed in practice. *Ibid.*, I, 52–54. For a revealing example of the provincial court's concern for the rights of servants, see *ibid.*, IV, 35–39. For discussions of the legal status of indentured servants, see Lois Green Carr, "County Government in Maryland, 1689–1709" (Ph.D. diss., Harvard University, 1968), 315–319, 583–584; and Morris, *Government and Labor*, 390–512.

[39] Edmund S. Morgan presents an understanding of the treatment of servants in Virginia just before the settlement of Maryland that differs sharply from the one offered here in "The First American Boom: Virginia 1618 to 1630," *WMQ*, 3d Ser., XXVIII (1971), 195–198. Even if servants were as abused and degraded as Morgan suspects, consideration of the opportunities available to ex-servants in Virginia in the 1620s and 1630s might alter his perspective on the institution. For evidence of extensive mobility among former servants in early Virginia, see Wertenbaker, *Planters of Colonial Virginia*, 60–83.

pay his passage and provide food, lodging, clothing, and other "necessaries" during the servant's term "and at the end of the said term, to give him one whole yeeres provision of Corne, and fifty acres of Land, according to the order of the countrey." [40] The order or custom of the country was specified in an act passed by the October 1640 session of the Assembly. Upon completion of his term the servant was to receive "one good Cloth Suite of Keirsey or Broadcloth a Shift of white linen one new pair of Stockins and Shoes two hoes one axe 3 barrels of Corne and fifty acres of land five whereof at least to be plantable." The land records make it clear that the requirement that masters give their former servants fifty acres of land cannot be taken literally. In practice, custom demanded only that a master provide a servant with the rights for fifty acres, an obligation assumed by the proprietor in 1648. If a servant wished to take advantage of this right and actually acquire a tract, he had to locate some vacant land and pay surveyor's and clerk's fees himself.[41]

The usual term of service, according to Lewger and Hawley, was five years. However, they suggested, "for any artificer, or one that shall deserve more than ordinary, the Adventurer shall doe well to shorten that time . . . rather then to want such usefull men." [42] A bill considered but not passed by the 1639 Assembly would have required servants arriving in Maryland without indentures to serve for four years if they were eighteen years old or over and until the age of twenty-four if they were under eighteen.[43] The gap between time of arrival and first appearance in the records as freemen for the men under study suggests that the terms specified in this rejected bill were often followed in practice.

Servants were occasionally able to work out arrangements with their masters which allowed them to become freemen before their terms were completed. John Courts and Francis Pope purchased their remaining time from Fulke Brent, probably arranging to pay him out of whatever money they could earn by working as freemen. Thomas Todd, a glover, was released from servitude early by his master, John Lewger. In return, Todd was to dress a specified number of skins and also to make breeches and gloves for Lewger. George Evelin released three of his servants, Philip West, William Williamson, and John Hopson, for one year, during which they were to provide food, cloth-

[40] *A Relation of Maryland* . . . (1635), in Clayton Colman Hall, ed., *Narratives of Early Maryland, 1633–1684*, Original Narratives of Early American History (New York, 1910), 99. On the authorship of this pamphlet, see L. Leon Bernard, "Some New Light on the Early Years of the Baltimore Plantation," *Md. Hist. Mag.*, XLIV (1947), 100.

[41] *Md. Arch.*, I, 97; III, 226; Patents, I, 27, 99; AB&H, 101, 102. A 50-acre warrant could be purchased for 100 pounds of tobacco or less. *Md. Arch.*, IV, 319, 328.

[42] *Relation of Maryland*, in Hall, ed., *Narratives of Early Maryland*, 100.

[43] *Md. Arch.*, I, 80.

ing, and lodging for themselves and also pay Evelin one thousand pounds of tobacco each.[44] Such opportunities were not available to all servants, however, and most probably served full terms.

On achieving freedom there were three options open to the former servant: he could either hire out for wages, lease land and raise tobacco on his own, or work on another man's plantation as a sharecropper. Although custom demanded that servants be granted the rights to fifty acres of land on completing their terms, actual acquisition of a tract during the first year of freedom was simply impracticable, and all former servants who eventually became freeholders were free for at least two years before they did so. To acquire land, one had to either pay surveyor's and clerk's fees for a patent or pay a purchase price to a landholder. The land then had to be cleared and housing erected. Provisions had to be obtained in some way until the crop was harvested, for a man could not survive a growing season on a mere three barrels of corn. Tools, seed, and livestock were also necessary. All this required capital, and capital was precisely what servants did not have.[45] Wage labor, sharecropping, and leaseholding all offered men a chance to accumulate enough capital to get started on their own plantations and to sustain themselves in the meantime.

Wages were high in mid-seventeenth-century Maryland, usually fifteen to twenty pounds of tobacco per day for unskilled agricultural labor and even higher for those with much needed skills. These were remarkable rates given the fact that a man working alone could harvest, on the average, no more than fifteen hundred to two thousand pounds of tobacco a year.[46] Thirty-two of the 158 survivors were designated artisans in the records: 11 carpenters, 4 blacksmiths, 5 tailors, 4 sawyers, 2 millwrights, a brickmason, mariner, cooper, glover, and barber-surgeon. These men probably had little trouble marketing their skills. At a time when labor was scarce, even men who had nothing but a strong back and willing hands must have found all the work they wanted. However, few of the 158 men devoted themselves to full time wage labor for extended periods. Instead, most worked their own crop and only hired out occasionally to supplement their planting income.

[44] *Ibid.*, IV, 27, 283; V, 183; Patents, II, 509.

[45] According to John Hammond, some masters did permit their servants to accumulate capital while still under indenture. *Leah and Rachel, or, the Two Fruitfull Sisters Virginia and Mary-land* (1656), in Hall, ed., *Narratives of Early Maryland*, 292. However, there is no evidence to support Hammond's assertion that this practice was extensive.

[46] Manfred Jonas, "Wages in Early Colonial Maryland," *Md. Hist. Mag.*, LI (1956), 27–38. For the amount of tobacco a man could produce in a year, see Lewis Cecil Gray, *History of Agriculture in the Southern United States to 1860*, I (Washington, D.C., 1932), 218–219; Carr, "County Government in Maryland," appendix IV, 94–96; Arthur Pierce Middleton, *Tobacco Coast: A Maritime History of Chesapeake Bay in the Colonial Era* (Newport News, Va., 1953), 103.

Nevertheless, some men did sign contracts or enter into verbal agreements for long-term wage labor. There were some differences between their status and that of indentured servants. They probably could not be sold, they could sue at common law for breach of covenant, and they may have possessed some political privileges.[47] There were severe restrictions on their personal freedom, however, and their daily life must have been similar to a servant's. Wages ranged from eleven hundred to fifteen hundred pounds of tobacco a year plus shelter, food, and clothing. Ex-servants occasionally hired out for long terms, perhaps because of heavy indebtedness or lack of alternative opportunities, or perhaps because of the security such contracts afforded. Recently freed servants may have found long-term wage contracts an attractive means of making the transition from indentured laborer to free colonist.[48] While long-term wage labor was, in a sense, a prolongation of servitude, it could also serve as a means of capital accumulation and an avenue of mobility.

The records reveal little of the extent or conditions of sharecropping in the 1640s, but it is clear that several of the 158 former servants did work on another man's plantation for a share of the crop.[49] By the 1660s—and there seems no reason to assume that this was not also the case in the earlier period—working for a "share" meant that a man joined other workers on a plantation in making a crop, the size of his share to be determined by dividing the total crop by the number of laborers. Contracts often required the plantation owner to pay the cropper's taxes and provide diet, lodging, and washing, while obliging the cropper to work at other tasks around the plantation.[50] The status of such sharecroppers seems indistinguishable from that of wage laborers on long-term contracts.

Most of the 158 former servants established themselves as small planters on leased land immediately after they had completed their terms. There were two types of leases available to ex-servants, leaseholds for life or for a long term of years and short-term leaseholds or tenancies at will. Although these forms of leaseholding differed in several important respects, both allowed the tenant to become the head of

---

[47] For an exception to the general rule that men with long-term wage contracts could not be sold, see *Md. Arch.*, IV, 173–174. For purposes of taxation, wage laborers were considered freemen, but it is not certain that for political purposes they were counted among the freemen of the province. See *ibid.*, I, 123. Biographical studies suggest that, in general, political participation was limited to heads of households.

[48] *Ibid.*, I, 166, 173–174, 201, 286, 468. John Hammond recommended that immigrants without capital sign year-long wage contracts when they arrived in the colonies. *Leah and Rachel*, in Hall, ed., *Narratives of Early Maryland*, 293.

[49] Patents, III, 18; *Md. Arch.*, X, 208.

[50] For examples of sharecropping arrangements, see Talbot County Court Proceedings, 1685–1689, 287; Charles County Court and Land Records, H#1, 160–162; *Md. Arch.*, XLIX, 326–327.

a household. As householders, former bondsmen achieved a degree of independence and a measure of responsibility denied to servants, wage laborers, and sharecroppers. Heads of households were masters in their own families, responsible for the discipline, education, and maintenance of their subordinates. They formed the backbone of the political community, serving on juries, sitting in Assembly, and filling the minor offices. The favorable man/land ratio in early Maryland made the formation of new households a fairly easy task and servants usually became householders soon after completing their terms.[51]

In many ways there was little difference between land held in fee simple and a lease for life or for a long term of years. Such leases were inheritable and could be sold; they were usually purchased for a lump sum and yearly rents were often nominal. Terms varied considerably, but all long-term leaseholds provided the tenant a secure tenure and a chance to build up equity in his property. Such leases were not common in seventeenth-century Maryland, although a few appear on the private manors in St. Mary's County in the 1640s. Probably men were reluctant to purchase a lease when they could acquire land in fee simple for little additional outlay.[52]

Tenancies at will or short-term leaseholds, usually running for no more than six or seven years, were undoubtedly the most common form of tenure for recently freed servants. In contrast to long-term leases, short-term leaseholds offered little security, could not be sold or inherited, and terminated at the death of either party to the contract. Their great advantage was the absence of an entry fee, a feature particularly attractive to men without capital. Since land was plentiful and labor scarce, rents must have been low, certainly no higher than five hundred pounds of tobacco a year for a plantation and perhaps as low as two hundred pounds. Rent for the first year, furthermore, was probably not demanded until after the crop was in. No contracts for the 1640s have survived, but later in the century tenants were often required to make extensive improvements on the plantation. Although tenure was insecure, short-term leaseholding afforded ample opportunity for mobility as long as tobacco prices remained high. In the 1640s and 1650s, leaseholding benefited both landlord and tenant. Landlords had their land cleared, housing erected, and orchards planted and fenced while receiving a small rental income. Tenants were able to accumulate the capital necessary to acquire a tract of their own.[53]

---

[51] For some indication of the status of heads of households in early Maryland, see *Md. Arch.*, I, 123, 197.

[52] For examples of long-term leases, see *ibid.*, LIII, 127; LX, 51–52; Baltimore County Deeds, RM#HS, 218–219.

[53] For examples of short-term leases, see *Md. Arch.*, LX, 305; LIV, 12–13, 79–80, 244–245; Charles County Court and Land Records, I#1, 41; K#1, 33–34.

Prior to 1660, small planters, whether leaseholders or landowners, frequently worked in partnership with another man when attempting to carve new plantations out of the wilderness. Much hard work was involved in clearing land, building shelter, and getting in a crop; men who could not afford to buy servants or pay wages often joined with a mate. Partners Joseph Edlow and Christopher Martin, John Courts and Francis Pope, John Shirtcliffe and Henry Spinke, and William Brown and John Thimbelly were all former servants who arrived in Maryland before the end of 1642. They must have found their "mateships" mutually beneficial, since, except for Martin who died in 1641, all eventually became landowners.[54]

Some men—about 10 percent of those former servants who lived in Maryland for more than a decade as freemen—did not manage to escape tenancy. Rowland Mace, for example, was still a leaseholder on St. Clement's Manor in 1659, after which he disappeared from the records.[55] The inventory of the estate of Charles Steward, who lived on Kent Island as a freeman for more than forty years and was frequently called planter, indicates that he was operating a plantation when he died in 1685, but Steward failed to acquire freehold title to a tract of his own.[56] A few others acquired land, held it briefly, and then returned to leaseholding arrangements. John Maunsell had some prosperous years in Maryland. He arrived in the province in 1638 as a servant to William Bretton and served about four years. He patented one hundred acres in 1649 and added five hundred more in 1651, but he could not hold the land and in 1653 sold it all to William Whittle. He then moved to St. Clement's Manor, where he took up a leasehold, and was still a tenant on the manor when he died in 1660.[57] John Shanks, although he too suffered fluctuations in prosperity, ended his career on a more positive note. Entering Maryland in 1640 as a servant to Thomas Gerard, he must have been quite young when he arrived, for he did not gain his freedom until 1648. In 1652 he patented two hundred acres and also purchased the freedom of one Abigail, a servant to Robert Brooke, whom he soon married. He sold his land in 1654, and, following Maunsell's path, took up a leasehold on St. Clement's Manor. Shanks, however, managed to attain the status of a freeholder again, owning three hundred acres in St. Mary's County when he died in 1684. His inventory—the estate was appraised at just under one hundred pounds—indicates that Shanks ended life in Maryland as a fairly prosperous small planter.[58]

[54] Patents, II, 534, 550; III, 6–7; *Md. Arch.*, IV, 92–93.
[55] *Md. Arch.*, LIII, 627.
[56] Inventories and Accounts, VIII, 373.
[57] Patents, I, 68–69; II, 438; AB&H, 373, 380, 421; *Md. Arch.*, LIII, 627, 630.
[58] Patents, AB&H, 15, 78, 101, 232, 319–320, 411; *Md. Arch.*, LIII, 627, 633, 635; Wills, IV, 91; Inventories and Accounts, VIII, 373–375; IX, 83.

Most of the 158 former servants, if they lived in Maryland for more than ten years as freemen, acquired land and held it for as long as they remained in the province. Almost any healthy man in Maryland in the 1640s and 1650s, if he worked hard, practiced thrift, avoided expensive lawsuits, and did not suffer from plain bad luck, could become a landowner in a short time. Tobacco prices were relatively high, and, while living costs may also have been high, land was not expensive. Even at the highest rates a one hundred-acre tract could be patented for less than five hundred pounds of tobacco, and even the lowest estimates indicate that a man could harvest twelve hundred pounds in a year.[59] Again barring ill-health and misfortune, retaining land once acquired must not have been too difficult a task, at least before tobacco prices fell after the Restoration.

Hard work and thrift were, of course, not the only paths to landownership. For some the fruits of office cleared the way. William Empson, for example, was still a tenant to Thomas Baker in 1658, after ten years of freedom. In 1659, Nicholas Gwyther employed him as deputy sheriff, and in the next year Empson was able to purchase a plantation from his former landlord.[60] Others charmed their way to the status of freeholder. Henry Adams married Mary Cockshott, daughter of John Cockshott and stepdaughter of Nicholas Causine, both of whom were substantial Maryland planters. To the historian, though perhaps not to Adams, Miss Cockshott's most obvious asset was twelve hundred acres of land which her mother had taken up for her and her sister Jane in 1649.[61]

For most former servants progress stopped with the acquisition of a small plantation. Others managed to go beyond small planter status to become men of wealth and power. What was it that distinguished the 13 former servants who became men of importance in Maryland politics from the other 145 who survived servitude?

Education was one factor. We have already seen that a few of the 158 probably possessed some formal training. Early colonial Maryland did not have enough educated men to serve as justices or sheriffs, perform clerical and surveying functions, or work as attorneys in the courts. Under such conditions, a man proficient with the pen could do quite well for himself. Men such as Cuthbert Fenwick, Robert Vaughan, and Robert Sedgrave found their education valuable in making the transition from servant to man of consequence. While approximately 60 percent of the 158 who survived servitude were totally illiterate, only 2 of the 13 who came to exercise real power in Maryland

[59] *Md. Arch.*, I, 163.
[60] *Ibid.*, XLI, 344; LIII, 26, 74–75.
[61] Patents, II, 535; *Md. Arch.*, XLI, 169–174.

and only 7 of the 22 who held major office were unable to write their names.

Marriage played a role in some of the most impressive success stories. Henry Adams's marriage has already been mentioned. Zachary Wade married a niece of Thomas Hatton, principal secretary of Maryland in the 1650s.[62] James Langsworth married a Gardiner, thereby allying himself with a very prominent southern Maryland family.[63] Cuthbert Fenwick married at least twice. We know nothing of his first wife, but Fenwick found fame and fortune by marrying in 1649 Jane Moryson, widow of a prominent Virginian, a niece of Edward Eltonhead, one of the masters of chancery, and a sister of William Eltonhead, who sat on the Maryland Council in the 1650s.[64]

It would be a mistake, however, to overestimate the significance of education and marriage in the building of a successful career. Certainly they helped, but they were not essential ingredients. Nicholas Gwyther became a man of consequence in Maryland, but married a former servant.[65] John Warren served as justice of St. Mary's County for nine years, but could not write his name.[66] Daniel Clocker and John Maunsell both held major office in Maryland. Both were illiterate and both married former servants.[67] Clearly, Maryland in the middle of the seventeenth century was open enough to allow a man who started at the bottom without special advantages to acquire a substantial estate and a responsible position.

It seems probable that Maryland continued to offer ambitious immigrants without capital a good prospect of advancement throughout the 1640s and 1650s. But there is evidence to suggest that opportunities declined sharply after 1660. True, the society did not become completely closed and some men who started life among the servants were still able to end life among the masters. Miles Gibson is a case in point, and there were others. Philip Lynes emigrated as a servant in the late 1660s and later became a member of the Council and a man of considerable wealth.[68] Christopher Goodhand, who also entered Maryland as a servant in the late 1660s, later served as justice of Kent County and

---

[62] Carr, "County Government in Maryland," appendix IV, 371–373.

[63] Wills, I, 133–141.

[64] Harry Wright Newman, *The Flowering of the Maryland Palatinate* . . . (Washington, D.C., 1961), 280–290; Patents, III, 413–414.

[65] *Md. Arch.*, X, 32.

[66] *Ibid.*, V, 33; LXVI, 5.

[67] Patents, II, 581; AB&H, 35, 150; *Md. Arch.*, XLIX, 29, 290.

[68] Patents, XVI, 411; XVIII, 110; *Md. Arch.*, XXVII, 181; Inventories and Accounts, XXX, 280; XXXIIB, 128; Wills, XII, 151A.

TABLE 1   *Servant Officer Holders, 1634–1689*
(Former servants serving as burgess, justice of the peace, and sheriff in Charles, Kent, and St. Mary's counties, Maryland, 1634–1689, by date of first appointment.)

	New officials	*Servants*	
		NUMBER	PERCENT
1634–1649	57	11–12	19.3–22.8
1650–1659	39	12	30.8
1660–1669	64	9	14.1
1670–1679	44	4–5	9.1–11.4
1680–1689	46	4	8.7

left an estate appraised at nearly six hundred pounds.[69] However, in the latter part of the century men such as Gibson, Goodhand, and Lynes were unusual; at mid-century they were not. As Table 1 illustrates, the chances that a former servant would attain an office of power in Maryland diminished sharply as the century progressed.[70]

This reduction in the proportion of former servants among Maryland's rulers is directly related to basic demographic processes that worked fundamental changes in the colony's political structure. The rapid growth in the population of the province during the seventeenth century affected the life chances of former servants in at least two ways. First, there was a reduction in the number of offices available in proportion to the number of freemen, resulting in increased competition for positions of power and profit. Secondly, there was an increase in the number of men of wealth and status available to fill positions of authority. In the decades immediately following the founding of the province there were simply not enough men who conformed to the standards people expected their rulers to meet. As a consequence, many uneducated small planters of humble origins were called upon to rule. Among the immigrants to Maryland after the Restoration were a number of younger sons of English gentry families and an even larger

[69] Patents, XV, 379; XVII, 65; *Md. Arch.*, XVII, 379; Inventories and Accounts, WB#3, 542; XXVI, 326.

[70] This is not intended to exclude the possibility of cyclical fluctuations similar to those identified by P. M. G. Harris in "The Social Origins of American Leaders: The Demographic Foundations," *Perspectives in American History*, III (1969), 159–344. Biographies of the men who held major office in Maryland from 1634 to 1692 do not reveal any obvious cyclical patterns, but this is not a long enough period to provide a fair test for Harris's hypotheses. It may be that further research will reveal cyclical changes within this long-term decline. This issue is discussed more fully in my dissertation, "Politics and Social Structure in Seventeenth Century Maryland," to be submitted to the University of Iowa.

TABLE 2   *Illiterate Office Holders, 1634–1689*
(Illiterates serving as burgess, justice of the peace, and sheriff in
Charles, Kent, and St. Mary's counties, Maryland, 1634–1689, by
date of first appointment.)

| | New officials | Illiterates | |
		NUMBER	PERCENT
1634–1649	57	16	28.1
1650–1659	39	9	23.1
1660–1669	64	17	26.6
1670–1679	44	1	2.3
1680–1689	46	4	8.7

number of merchants, many of whom were attracted to the Chesapeake as a result of their engagement in the tobacco trade. By the late
seventeenth century, these new arrivals, together with a steadily growing number of native gentlemen, had created a ruling group with more
wealth, higher status, and better education than the men who had
ruled earlier in the century. As this group grew in size, poor illiterate
planters were gradually excluded from office. Table 2, which focuses
on the educational levels of all major office holders by measuring literacy, demonstrates the degree and rate of change.[71]

Former servants also found that their chances of acquiring land and
of serving as jurors and minor office holders were decreasing. Probably
the movement of prices for tobacco and land was the most important
factor responsible for this decline of opportunity. During the 1640s
and 1650s, the available evidence—which, it must be admitted, is not
entirely satisfactory—indicates that farm prices for Chesapeake tobacco fluctuated between one and one-half and three pence per
pound.[72] After 1660, prices declined due to overproduction, mercan-
tilist restrictions, and a poorly developed marketing system that allowed farm prices to sink far below those justified by European price
levels.[73] By using crop appraisals and other data from estate inventories, it is possible to construct a fairly dependable series for farm prices
of Maryland tobacco from 1659 to 1710. In the 1660s, prices averaged
1.3d. per pound. For the 1670s, the average was just over a penny.

[71] The argument in this paragraph is a major theme of my dissertation. See also Jordan, "Royal Period of Colonial Maryland," and Bernard Bailyn, "Politics and Social
Structure in Virginia," in Smith, ed., *Seventeenth-Century America*, 90–115.

[72] Gray, *History of Agriculture*, I, 262–263; Wertenbaker, *Planters of Colonial Virginia*,
66.

[73] Jacob M. Price, "The Tobacco Adventure to Russia: Enterprise, Politics, and
Diplomacy in the Quest for a Northern Market for English Colonial Tobacco,
1676–1722," American Philosophical Society, *Transactions*, N.S., LI (1961), 5–6; Wertenbaker, *Planters of Colonial Virginia*, 88–96.

During each of the next three decades the average price was less than a penny per pound.[74] Falling tobacco prices were not, however, the only obstacle to land acquisition, for while tobacco prices were going down, land prices were going up. V. J. Wyckoff has argued that the purchase price of land increased by 135 percent from 1663 to 1700.[75]

One consequence of these price changes was a change in the nature and dimensions of short-term leaseholding. In the 1640s and 1650s, tenancy was a typical step taken by a man without capital on the road to land acquisition. However, falling tobacco prices and rising land prices made it increasingly difficult to accumulate the capital necessary to purchase a freehold. In the 1660s fragmentary results suggest that only 10 percent of the householders in Maryland were established on land they did not own. By the end of the century the proportion of tenants had nearly tripled. Tenancy was no longer a transitory status; for many it had become a permanent fate.[76]

A gradual constriction of the political community paralleled the rise in tenancy. In years immediately following settlement, all freemen, whether or not they owned land, regularly participated in government as voters, jurors, and minor office holders.[77] At the beginning of the eighteenth century a very different situation prevailed. In a proclamation of 1670, Lord Baltimore disfranchised all freemen who possessed neither fifty acres of land nor a visible estate worth forty pounds sterling. This meant, in effect, that short-term leaseholders could no longer vote, since few could meet the forty pounds requirement.[78] Furthermore, by the early eighteenth century landowners virtually monopolized jury duty and the minor offices.[79] In the middle of the seventeenth century, most freemen in Maryland had an ample oppor-

[74] Menard, "Farm Prices of Maryland Tobacco," *Md. Hist. Mag.*, forthcoming.

[75] "Land Prices in Seventeenth-Century Maryland," *American Economic Review*, XXVIII (1938), 81–88. It seems reasonable to assume that rents rose with land prices.

[76] These assertions concerning tenancy are based on Carr's work on Prince George's County in the early 18th century (see "County Government in Maryland," 605), on Carville Earle's work on Anne Arundel, and on my research on Charles, St. Mary's, and Somerset counties. The work on Charles and St. Mary's is summarized in Menard, "Population Growth and Land Distribution in St. Mary's County, 1634–1710" (unpubl. report prepared for the St. Mary's City Commission, 1971). A copy of this report is available at the Maryland Hall of Records.

[77] For example, 34 men sat on the first three juries convened in the provincial court in 1643. Twenty-three of them did not own land, and nonlandowners were a majority on all three. *Md. Arch.*, IV, 176–177, 180, 191.

[78] Charles M. Andrews, *The Colonial Period of American History*, II (New Haven, 1936), 339–340; Carr, "County Government in Maryland," 608. Inventories were found for 17 nonlandowners who died in Somerset County in the period 1670–1690. Only three had estates worth more than £40, and two of those three had sources of income other than planting.

[79] Carr, "County Government in Maryland," 606. My research in Somerset County confirms Carr's findings.

tunity to acquire land and participate in community government; by the end of the century a substantial portion of the free male heads of households were excluded from the political process and unable to become landowners.

Evidence for this general constriction of opportunity can be seen in the careers of the children of the 158 survivors. No attempt was made at a systematic survey of the fortunes of the second generation, but enough information was gathered in the course of research to support some generalizations. In only one family did the children clearly outdistance the accomplishments of their father. John Courts's sone, John Jr., became a member of the Council, while his daughter, Elizabeth, married James Keech, later a provincial court justice.[80] Of the 22 former servants who came to hold major office in Maryland, only 6 either left sons who also held major office or daughters who married men who did so. The great leap upward in the histories of these families took place in the first generation. If the immigrants managed to become small, landowning planters, their children maintained that position but seldom moved beyond it. If the immigrants were somewhat more successful and obtained offices of power, their children sometimes were able to maintain the family station but often experienced downward mobility into small planter status.

In order to provide more direct evidence that opportunities for men who entered Maryland without capital were declining, an effort was made to study the careers of a group of servants who arrived in the 1660s and 1670s. The problems encountered were formidable. The increase in population and the fact that by this time servants could end up in any one of ten counties in Maryland made simple name correlation from headright entries unreliable. To surmount this difficulty an alternative approach was developed. In 1661, in order to regulate the length of service for those servants brought into the colony without indentures, the Assembly passed an act requiring that masters bring their servants into the county courts to have their ages judged and registered.[81] Using a list of names from this source simplified the problem of identification by placing the servants geographically and providing precise information about their age and length of service. Even with these additional aids, career-line study of obscure men proved difficult and the sample disappointingly small. However, the results did confirm inferences drawn from data about price changes and tenancy and offered support for the argument that as the century progressed, servants found it increasingly difficult to acquire land and participate in government.

From 1662 to 1672, 179 servants were brought into the Charles

[80] Wills, XII, 215–217. See also n. 31 above.
[81] *Md. Arch.*, I, 409–419.

County Court to have their ages judged.[82] Only 58 of the 179 definitely appeared in the records as freemen, a fact which in itself suggests declining opportunities, since there does seem to be a relationship between a man's importance in the community and the frequency of his appearance in the public records.[83] Of the 58 of whom something could be learned, only 13 to 17—22 to 29 percent—eventually became landowners. Furthermore, none acquired great wealth. Mark Lampton, who owned 649 acres in the early 1690s, was the largest landowner in the group and the only one who owned more than 500 acres. Robert Benson, whose estate was appraised at just over two hundred pounds, left the largest inventory. Lampton was the only other one of the 58 whose estate was valued at more than one hundred pounds.[84]

A study of the participation of these men in local government indicates that opportunities in this field were also declining. Only twenty-three to twenty-five of the fifty-eight sat on a jury or filled an office, and the level at which they participated was low. Only one, Henry Hardy, who was appointed to the Charles County bench in 1696, held major office.[85] A few others compiled impressive records as minor office holders. Mathew Dike, for example, sat on eight juries and served as overseer of the highways and constable, while Robert Benson was twice a constable and fourteen times a juryman.[86] For most of these men, however, occasional service as a juror was the limit of their participation. Five of the twenty-three known participants served only once as a juror, while another six only sat twice.

The contrast between the careers of these 58 men and the 158 who entered Maryland before 1642 is stark. At least 46 of the 58 lived in the province as freemen for over a decade. In other words, 50 to 57 percent lived in Maryland as freemen for more than ten years and did

---

[82] Charles County was chosen for two reasons. First, many of the servants who arrived by 1642 settled there, so it provides geographical continuity; second, there are exceptionally good 17th-century records for the county.

[83] In this connection, in a similar study of 116 servants brought into Prince George's County from 1696 to 1706, only 5 to 8 appeared as heads of households on a nearly complete tax list of 1719, so the project was abandoned.

[84] Patents, NS#2, 34; Charles County Court and Land Records, Q#1, 120–121; S#1, 343–344; Wills, XI, 200; Inventories and Accounts, 19½B, 136–138; XXI, 292–293.

[85] Hardy was also the only one of the 58 to acquire a title of distinction. Charles County Court and Land Records, V#1, 20–21. It is probable that the Richard Gwin who was appointed justice in Baltimore County in 1685 is identical with the Richard Gwin brought into Charles County Court to have his age judged by Francis Pope in 1664. Gwin was "living in Adultry" and was not allowed to sit on the bench. *Md. Arch.*, V, 524–525; XVII, 380; LIII, 451; Baltimore County Court Proceedings, 1682–1686, 358.

[86] Charles County Court and Land Records, H#1, 338; I#1, 176; K#1, 384; M#1, 208, 223; N#1, 166, 323; P#1, 7; Q#1, 27; R#1, 136, 237, 369, 482; S#1, 2, 28, 247, 275, 279; V#1, 62, 133, 210, 241, 333, 351.

not acquire land, while 36 to 40 percent did not participate in government. Only about 10 percent of the 158 who arrived in the earlier period and lived in the colony for a decade as freemen failed to become landowners and participants.[87]

How successful, then, in the light of these data, was the institution of servitude in seventeenth-century Maryland? The answer depends on perspective and chronology. Servitude had two primary functions. From the master's viewpoint its function was to supply labor. From the point of view of the prospective immigrant without capital, servitude was a means of mobility, both geographic and social; that is, it was a way of getting to the New World and, once there, of building a life with more prosperity and standing than one could reasonably expect to attain at home. Its success in performing these two quite different functions varied inversely as the century progressed. Prior to 1660, servitude served both purposes well. It provided large planters with an inexpensive and capable work force and allowed poor men entry into a society offering great opportunities for advancement. This situation in which the two purposes complemented each other did not last, and the institution gradually became more successful at supplying labor as it became less so at providing new opportunities. Some men were always able to use servitude as an avenue of mobility, but, over the course of the century, more and more found that providing labor for larger planters, first as servants and later as tenants, was their permanent fate.

---

[87] There are two possible objections to this comparison. Although I do not think either is valid, both are difficult to refute. First, it could be argued that the quality of servants declined over the course of the century. Mildred Campbell, however, noticed no such change in the status of servants leaving Bristol from 1654 to 1685. "Social Origins," in Smith, ed., *Seventeenth-Century America*, 63–89. Secondly, although the first group includes servants in general and the second only redemptioners, it does not follow that there are significant differences between the two categories. Both groups consisted largely of poor, illiterate farmers and artisans; both also included a few poor but educated men. Henry Hardy, for example, seems to have had some education, while the three Dulany brothers arrived in Maryland as redemptioners. Aubrey C. Land, *The Dulanys of Maryland: A Biographical Study of Daniel Dulany, the Elder (1685–1753), and Daniel Dulany, the Younger (1722–1797)* (Baltimore, 1955), 3.

The Planter's Wife:
The Experience of White Women in Seventeenth-Century Maryland

LOIS G. CARR
AND LORENA S. WALSH

For about a decade beginning in the mid-1960s, most studies of colonial families concentrated on New England with a strong emphasis on males—fathers and sons. This essay by Lois Carr and Lorena Walsh reminds us how much we miss through such an approach. The role and behavior of women underscore some of the most significant social differences between the early Chesapeake colonies and New England. While most Puritan females traveled as part of organized families, a great majority of the women who reached Virginia and Maryland arrived as unmarried servants, not wives or daughters of other settlers. About half of them either bore bastard children or were pregnant at marriage, but these rates then fell dramatically for their native-born daughters. Because life expectancy was much shorter than in New England, the family was brittle, orphanhood became the eventual experience of most surviving children, and the larger society somehow had to adjust to these realities.

Some important questions remain unanswered. What kinds of women were likely to accept indentured bondage thousands of miles from home and family? How desperate did they have to be to venture alone into the terrifying world of an oceanic vessel with its crew of irreverent and salacious sailors? In short, did the women of the early Chesapeake colonies probably come from farther down the social scale than their male counterparts? If so, did they have better chances than men for dramatic upward mobility? Finally, did removal to America enhance a woman's chances to achieve social respectability for herself and her daughters? Ought we perhaps to seek social idealism in the early South more among its women than its men?

Four facts were basic to all human experience in seventeenth-century Maryland. First, for most of the period the great majority of inhabitants had been born in what we now call Britain. Population increase

Reprinted by permission from Lois G. Carr and Lorena S. Walsh, "The Planter's Wife: The Experience of White Women in Seventeenth-Century Maryland," *William and Mary Quarterly*, 3rd ser., XXXIV (1977), 542–571.

in Maryland did not result primarily from births in the colony before the late 1680s and did not produce a predominantly native population of adults before the first decade of the eighteenth century. Second, immigrant men could not expect to live beyond age forty-three, and 70 percent would die before age fifty. Women may have had even shorter lives. Third, perhaps 85 percent of the immigrants, and practically all the unmarried immigrant women, arrived as indentured servants and consequently married late. Family groups were never predominant in the immigration to Maryland and were a significant part for only a brief time at mid-century. Fourth, many more men than women immigrated during the whole period.[1] These facts—immigrant predominance, early death, late marriage, and sexual imbalance—created circumstances of social and demographic disruption that deeply affected family and community life.

We need to assess the effects of this disruption on the experience of women in seventeenth-century Maryland. Were women degraded by the hazards of servitude in a society in which everyone had left community and kin behind and in which women were in short supply? Were traditional restraints on social conduct weakened? If so, were women more exploited or more independent and powerful than women who remained in England? Did any differences from English experience which we can observe in the experience of Maryland women survive the transformation from an immigrant to a predominantly native-born society with its own kinship networks and community traditions? The tentative argument put forward here is that the answer to all these questions is Yes. There were degrading aspects of servitude, although these probably did not characterize the lot of most women; there were fewer restraints on social conduct, especially in courtship, than in England; women were less protected but also more powerful than those who remained at home; and at least some of these changes survived the appearance in Maryland of New World creole communities. However, these issues are far from settled, and we shall offer some suggestions as to how they might be further pursued.

Maryland was settled in 1634, but in 1650 there were probably no more than six hundred persons and fewer than two hundred adult

---

[1] Russell R. Menard, "Economy and Society in Early Colonial Maryland" (Ph.D. diss., University of Iowa, 1975), 153–212, and "Immigrants and Their Increase: The Process of Population Growth in Early Colonial Maryland," in Aubrey C. Land, Lois Green Carr, and Edward C. Papenfuse, eds., *Law, Society, and Politics in Early Maryland* (Baltimore, 1977), 88–110, hereafter cited as Menard, "Immigrants and Their Increase"; Lorena S. Walsh and Russell R. Menard, "Death in the Chesapeake: Two Life Tables for Men in Early Colonial Maryland," *Maryland Historical Magazine*, LXIX (1974), 211–227. In a sample of 806 headrights Menard found only two unmarried women who paid their own passage ("Economy and Society," 187).

women in the province. After that time population growth was steady; in 1704 a census listed 30,437 white persons, of whom 7,163 were adult women.[2] Thus in discussing the experience of white women in seventeenth-century Maryland we are dealing basically with the second half of the century.

Marylanders of that period did not leave letters and diaries to record their New World experience or their relationships to one another. Nevertheless, they left trails in the public records that give us clues. Immigrant lists kept in England and documents of the Maryland courts offer quantifiable evidence about the kinds of people who came and some of the problems they faced in making a new life. Especially valuable are the probate court records. Estate inventories reveal the kinds of activities carried on in the house and on the farm, and wills, which are usually the only personal statements that remain for any man or woman, show something of personal attitudes. This essay relies on the most useful of the immigrant lists and all surviving Maryland court records, but concentrates especially on the surviving records of the lower Western Shore, an early-settled area highly suitable for tobacco. Most of this region comprised four counties: St. Mary's, Calvert, Charles, and Prince George's (formed in 1696 from Calvert and Charles). Inventories from all four counties, wills from St. Mary's and Charles, and court proceedings from Charles and Prince George's provide the major data.[3]

Because immigrants predominated, who they were determined much about the character of Maryland society. The best information so far available comes from lists of indentured servants who left the ports of London, Bristol, and Liverpool. These lists vary in quality, but at the very least they distinguish immigrants by sex and general destination. A place of residence in England is usually given, although it may not represent the emigrant's place of origin; and age and occupation are often noted. These lists reveal several characteristics of immigrants to the Chesapeake and, by inference, to Maryland.[4]

Servants who arrived under indenture included yeomen, husband-

---

[2] Menard, "Immigrants and Their Increase," Fig. 1; William Hand Browne *et al.*, eds., *Archives of Maryland* (Baltimore, 1883–   ), XXV, 256, hereafter cited as *Maryland Archives.*

[3] Court proceedings for St. Mary's and Calvert counties have not survived.

[4] The lists of immigrants are found in John Camden Hotten, ed., *The Original Lists of Persons of Quality; Emigrants; Religious Exiles; Political Rebels; . . . and Others Who Went from Great Britain to the American Plantations, 1600–1700* (London, 1874); William Dodgson Bowman, ed., *Bristol and America: A Record of the First Settlers in the Colonies of North America, 1654–1685* (Baltimore, 1967) [orig. publ. London, 1929]; [C. D. P. Nicholson, comp., *Some Early Emigrants to America* (Baltimore, 1965)]; Michael Ghirelli, ed., *A List of Emigrants to America, 1682–1692* (Baltimore, 1968); and Elizabeth French, ed., *List of Emigrants to America from Liverpool, 1697–1707* (Baltimore, 1962) [orig. publ. Boston, 1913]. Folger Shakespeare Library, MS, V.B. 16 (Washington, D.C.), consists of 66 additional indentures that were originally part of the London records. For studies

men, farm laborers, artisans, and small tradesmen, as well as many un-
trained to any special skill. They were young: over half of the men on
the London lists of 1683–1684 were aged eighteen to twenty-two.
They were seldom under seventeen or over twenty-eight. The women
were a little older; the great majority were between eighteen and
twenty-five, and half were aged twenty to twenty-two. Most servants
contracted for four or five years of service, although those under fifteen were to serve at least seven years.[5] These youthful immigrants
represented a wide range of English society. All were seeking opportunities they had not found at home.

However, many immigrants—perhaps about half[6]—did not leave
England with indentures but paid for their passage by serving according to the custom of the country. Less is known about their social
characteristics, but some inferences are possible. From 1661, customary service was set by Maryland laws that required four-year (later five-
year) terms for men and women who were twenty-two years or over at
arrival and longer terms for those who were younger. A requirement of
these laws enables us to determine something about age at arrival of
servants who came without indentures. A planter who wished to obtain
more than four or five years of service had to take his servant before
the county court to have his or her age judged and a written record
made. Servants aged over twenty-one were not often registered, there
being no incentive for a master to pay court fees for those who would
serve the minimum term. Nevertheless, a comparison of the ages of
servants under twenty-two recorded in Charles County, 1658–1689,
with those under twenty-two on the London list is revealing. Of
Charles County male servants (N = 363), 77.1 percent were aged seventeen or under, whereas on the London list (N = 196), 77.6 percent
were eighteen or over. Women registered in Charles County court

---

of these lists see Mildred Campbell, "Social Origins of Some Early Americans," in James
Morton Smith, ed., *Seventeenth-Century America: Essays in Colonial History* (Chapel Hill,
N.C., 1959), 63–89; David W. Galenson, " 'Middling People' or 'Common Sort'?: The
Social Origins of Some Early Americans Reexamined," *William and Mary Quarterly*
(forthcoming). See also Menard, "Immigrants and Their Increase," Table 4.1, and
"Economy and Society," Table VIII–6; and Lorena S. Walsh, "Servitude and Opportu-
nity in Charles County," in Land, Carr, and Papenfuse, eds., *Law, Society and Politics in
Early Maryland*, 112–114, hereafter cited as Walsh, "Servitude and Opportunity."

[5] Campbell, "Social Origins of Some Early Americans," in Smith, ed., *Seventeenth-
Century America*, 74–77; Galenson, " 'Middling People' or 'Common Sort'?" *WMQ*
(forthcoming). When the ages recorded in the London list (Nicholson, comp., *Some
Early Emigrants*) and on the Folger Library indentures for servants bound for Maryland
and Virginia are combined, 84.5% of the men (N = 354) are found to have been aged 17
to 30, and 54.9% were 18 through 22. Of the women (N = 119), 81.4% were 18 through
25; 10% were older, 8.3% younger, and half (51.2%) immigrated between ages 20 and
22. Russell Menard has generously lent us his abstracts of the London list.

[6] This assumption is defended in Walsh, "Servitude and Opportunity," 129.

were somewhat older than the men, but among those under twenty-two (N = 107), 5.5 percent were aged twenty-one, whereas on the London list (N = 69), 46.4 percent had reached this age. Evidently, some immigrants who served by custom were younger than those who came indentured, and this age difference probably characterized the two groups as a whole. Servants who were not only very young but had arrived without the protection of a written contract were possibly of lower social origins than were servants who came under indenture. The absence of skills among Charles County servants who served by custom supports this supposition.[7]

Whatever their status, one fact about immigrant women is certain: many fewer came than men. Immigrant lists, headright lists, and itemizations of servants in inventories show severe imbalance. On a London immigrant list of 1634–1635 men outnumbered women six to one. From the 1650s at least until the 1680s most sources show a ratio of three to one. From then on, all sources show some, but not great, improvement. Among immigrants from Liverpool over the years 1697–1707 the ratio was just under two and one half to one.[8]

Why did not more women come? Presumably, fewer wished to leave family and community to venture into a wilderness. But perhaps more important, women were not as desirable as men to merchants and planters who were making fortunes raising and marketing tobacco, a crop that requires large amounts of labor. The gradual improvement in the sex ratio among servants toward the end of the century may have been the result of a change in recruiting the needed labor. In the late 1660s the supply of young men willing to emigrate stopped increasing sufficiently to meet the labor demands of a growing Chesapeake population. Merchants who recruited servants for planters turned to other sources, and among these sources were women. They did not crowd the ships arriving in the Chesapeake, but their numbers did increase.[9]

To ask the question another way, why did women come? Doubtless, most came to get a husband, an objective virtually certain of success in a land where women were so far outnumbered. The promotional literature, furthermore, painted bright pictures of the life that awaited men and women once out of their time; and various studies suggest that for

---

[7] *Ibid.*, 112–114, describes the legislation and the Charles County data base. There is some reason to believe that by 1700, young servants had contracts more often than earlier. Figures from the London list include the Folger Library indentures.

[8] Menard, "Immigrants and Their Increase," Table I.

[9] Menard, "Economy and Society," 336–356; Lois Green Carr and Russell R. Menard, "Servants and Freedmen in Early Colonial Maryland," in Thad W. Tate and David A. Ammerman, eds., *Essays on the Chesapeake in the Seventeenth Century* (Chapel Hill, N.C., forthcoming); E. A. Wrigley, "Family Limitation in Pre-Industrial England," *Economic History Review*, 2d Ser., XIX (1966), 82–109; Michael Drake, "An Elementary Exercise in Parish Register Demography," *ibid.*, XIV (1962), 427–445; J. D. Chambers, *Population, Economy, and Society in Pre-Industrial England* (London, 1972).

a while, at least, the promoters were not being entirely fanciful. Until the 1660s, and to a less degree the 1680s, the expanding economy of Maryland and Virginia offered opportunities well beyond those available in England to men without capital and to the women who became their wives.[10]

Nevertheless, the hazards were also great, and the greatest was untimely death. Newcomers promptly became ill, probably with malaria, and many died. What proportion survived is unclear; so far no one has devised a way of measuring it. Recurrent malaria made the woman who survived seasoning less able to withstand other diseases, especially dysentery and influenza. She was especially vulnerable when pregnant. Expectation of life for everyone was low in the Chesapeake, but especially so for women.[11] A woman who had immigrated to Maryland took an extra risk, though perhaps a risk not greater than she might have suffered by moving from her village to London instead.[12]

The majority of women who survived seasoning paid their transportation costs by working for a four- or five-year term of service. The kind of work depended on the status of the family they served. A female servant of a small planter—who through about the 1670s might have had a servant[13]—probably worked at the hoe. Such a man could not afford to buy labor that would not help with the cash crop. In wealthy families women probably were household servants, although some are occasionally listed in inventories of well-to-do planters as living on the quarters—that is, on plantations other than the dwelling plantation. Such women saved men the jobs of preparing food and washing linen but doubtless also worked in the fields.[14] In middling households experience must have varied. Where the number of people to feed and wash for was large, female servants would have had little time to tend the crops.

[10] John Hammond, *Leah and Rachel, or, the Two Fruitfull Sisters Virginia and Maryland* . . . , and George Alsop, *A Character of the Province of Mary-land* . . . , in Clayton Colman Hall, ed., *Narratives of Early Maryland, 1633–1684*, Original Narratives of Early American History (New York, 1910), 281–308, 340–387; Russell R. Menard, P. M. G. Harris, and Lois Green Carr, "Opportunity and Inequality: The Distribution of Wealth on the Lower Western Shore of Maryland, 1638–1705," *Md. Hist. Mag.*, LXIX (1974), 169–184; Russell R. Menard, "From Servant to Freeholder: Status Mobility and Property Accumulation in Seventeenth-Century Maryland," *WMQ*, 3d Ser., XXX (1973), 37–64; Carr and Menard, "Servants and Freedmen," in Tate and Ammerman, eds., *Essays on the Chesapeake*; Walsh, "Servitude and Opportunity," 111–133.

[11] Walsh and Menard, "Death in the Chesapeake," *Md. Hist. Mag.*, LXIX (1974), 211–227; Darrett B. and Anita H. Rutman, "Of Agues and Fevers: Malaria in the Early Chesapeake," *WMQ*, 3d Ser., XXXIII (1976), 31–60.

[12] E. A. Wrigley, *Population and History* (New York, 1969), 96–100.

[13] Menard, "Economy and Society," Table VII-5.

[14] Lorena S. Walsh, "Charles County, Maryland, 1658–1705: A Study in Chesapeake Political and Social Structure" (Ph.D. diss., Michigan State University, 1977), chap. 4.

Tracts that promoted immigration to the Chesapeake region asserted that female servants did not labor in the fields, except "nasty" wenches not fit for other tasks. This implies that most immigrant women expected, or at least hoped, to avoid heavy field work, which English women—at least those above the cottager's status—did not do.[15] What proportion of female servants in Maryland found themselves demeaned by this unaccustomed labor is impossible to say, but this must have been the fate of some. A study of the distribution of female servants among wealth groups in Maryland might shed some light on this question. Nevertheless, we still would not know whether those purchased by the poor or sent to work on a quarter were women whose previous experience suited them for field labor.

An additional risk for the woman who came as a servant was the possibility of bearing a bastard. At least 20 percent of the female servants who came to Charles County between 1658 and 1705 were presented to the county court for this cause.[16] A servant woman could not marry unless someone was willing to pay her master for the term she had left to serve.[17] If a man made her pregnant, she could not marry him unless he could buy her time. Once a woman became free, however, marriage was clearly the usual solution. Only a handful of free women were presented in Charles County for bastardy between 1658 and 1705. Since few free women remained either single or widowed for long, not many were subject to the risk. The hazard of bearing a bastard was a hazard of being a servant.[18]

This high rate of illegitimate pregnancies among servants raises lurid questions. Did men import women for sexual exploitation? Does John Barth's Whore of Dorset have a basis outside his fertile imagination?[19] In our opinion, the answers are clearly No. Servants were economic investments on the part of planters who needed labor. A female servant in a household where there were unmarried men must have both provided and faced temptation, for the pressures were great in a

---

[15] Hammond, *Leah and Rachel*, and Alsop, *Character of the Province*, in Hall, ed., *Narratives of Maryland*, 281–308, 340–387; Mildred Campbell, *The English Yeoman Under Elizabeth and the Early Stuarts*, Yale Historical Publications (New Haven, Conn., 1942), 255–261; Alan Everitt, "Farm Labourers," in Joan Thirsk, ed., *The Agrarian History of England and Wales*, 1540–1640 (Cambridge, 1967), 432.

[16] Lorena S. Walsh and Russell R. Menard are preparing an article on the history of illegitimacy in Charles and Somerset counties, 1658–1776.

[17] Abbot Emerson Smith, *Colonists in Bondage: White Servitude and Convict Labor in America, 1607–1776* (Chapel Hill, N.C., 1947), 271–273. Marriage was in effect a breach of contract.

[18] Lois Green Carr, "County Government in Maryland, 1689–1709" (Ph.D. diss., Harvard University, 1968), text, 267–269, 363. The courts pursued bastardy offenses regardless of the social status of the culprits in order to ensure that the children would not become public charges. Free single women were not being overlooked.

[19] John Barth, *The Sot-Weed Factor* (New York, 1960), 429.

society in which men outnumbered women by three to one. Nevertheless, the servant woman was in the household to work—to help feed and clothe the family and make tobacco. She was not primarily a concubine.

This point could be established more firmly if we knew more about the fathers of the bastards. Often the culprits were fellow servants or men recently freed but too poor to purchase the woman's remaining time. Sometimes the master was clearly at fault. But often the father is not identified. Some masters surely did exploit their female servants sexually. Nevertheless, masters were infrequently accused of fathering their servants' bastards, and those found guilty were punished as severely as were other men. Community mores did not sanction their misconduct.[20]

A female servant paid dearly for the fault of unmarried pregnancy. She was heavily fined and if no one would pay her fine, she was whipped. Furthermore, she served an extra twelve to twenty-four months to repay her master for the "trouble of his house" and labor lost, and the fathers often did not share in this payment of damages. On top of all, she might lose the child after weaning unless by then she had become free, for the courts bound out bastard children at very early ages.[21]

English life probably did not offer a comparable hazard to young unmarried female servants. No figures are available to show rates of illegitimacy among those who were subject to the risk,[22] but the female servant was less restricted in England than in the Chesapeake. She did not owe anyone for passage across the Atlantic; hence it was easier for

[20] This impression is based on Walsh's close reading of Charles County records, Carr's close reading of Prince George's County records, and less detailed examination by both of all other 17th century Maryland court records.

[21] Walsh, "Charles County, Maryland," chap. 4; Carr, "County Government in Maryland," chap. 4, n. 269. Carr summarizes the evidence from Charles, Prince George's, Baltimore, Talbot, and Somerset counties, 1689–1709, for comparing punishment of fathers and mothers of bastards. Leniency toward fathers varied from county to county and time to time. The length of time served for restitution also varied over place and time, increasing as the century progressed. See Charles County Court and Land Records, MS, L#1, ff. 276–277, Hall of Records, Annapolis, Md. Unless otherwise indicated, all manuscripts cited are at the Hall of Records.

[22] Peter Laslett and Karla Osterveen have calculated illegitimacy ratios—the percentage of bastard births among all births registered—in 24 English parishes, 1581–1810. The highest ratio over the period 1630–1710 was 2.4. Laslett and Osterveen, "Long Term Trends in Bastardy in England: A Study of the Illegitimacy Figures in the Parish Registers and in the Reports of the Registrar General, 1561–1960," *Population Studies*, XXVII (1973), 267. In Somerset County, Maryland, 1666–1694, the illegitimacy ratio ranged from 6.3 to 11.8. Russell R. Menard, "The Demography of Somerset County, Maryland: A Preliminary Report" (paper presented to the Stony Brook Conference on Social History, State University of New York at Stony Brook, June 1975), Table XVI. The absence of figures for the number of women in these places of childbearing age but with no living husband prevents construction of illegitimacy rates.

her to marry, supposing she happened to become pregnant while in service. Perhaps, furthermore, her temptations were fewer. She was not 3,000 miles from home and friends, and she lived in a society in which there was no shortage of women. Bastards were born in England in the seventeenth century, but surely not to as many as one-fifth of the female servants.

Some women escaped all or part of their servitude because prospective husbands purchased the remainder of their time. At least one promotional pamphlet published in the 1660s described such purchases as likely, but how often they actually occurred is difficult to determine.[23] Suggestive is a 20 percent difference between the sex ratios found in a Maryland headright sample, 1658–1681, and among servants listed in lower Western Shore inventories for 1658–1679.[24] Some of the discrepancy must reflect the fact that male servants were younger than female servants and therefore served longer terms; hence they had a greater chance of appearing in an inventory. But part of the discrepancy doubtless follows from the purchase of women for wives. Before 1660, when sex ratios were even more unbalanced and the expanding economy enabled men to establish themselves more quickly, even more women may have married before their terms were finished.[25]

Were women sold for wives against their wills? No record says so, but nothing restricted a man from selling his servant to whomever he wished. Perhaps some women were forced into such marriages or accepted them as the least evil. But the man who could afford to purchase a wife—especially a new arrival—was usually already an established landowner.[26] Probably most servant women saw an opportunity in such a marriage. In addition, the shortage of labor gave women some bargaining power. Many masters must have been ready to refuse to sell a woman who was unwilling to marry a would-be purchaser.

If a woman's time was not purchased by a prospective husband, she was virtually certain to find a husband once she was free. Those fa-

---

[23] Alsop, *Character of the Province*, in Hall, ed., *Narratives of Maryland*, 358.

[24] Maryland Headright Sample, 1658–1681 (N = 625); 257.1 men per 100 women; Maryland Inventories, 1658–1679 (N = 584): 320.1 men per 100 women. Menard, "Immigrants and Their Increase," Table I.

[25] A comparison of a Virginia Headright Sample, 1648–1666 (N = 4,272) with inventories from York and Lower Norfolk counties, 1637–1675 (N = 168) shows less, rather than more, imbalance in inventories as compared to headrights. This indicates fewer purchases of wives than we have suggested for the period after 1660. However, the inventory sample is small.

[26] Only 8% of the tenant farmers who left inventories in four Maryland counties of the lower Western Shore owned labor, 1658–1705. St. Mary's City Commission Inventory Project, "Social Stratification in Maryland, 1658–1705" (National Science Foundation Grant GS-32272), hereafter cited as "Social Stratification." This is an analysis of 1,735 inventories recorded from 1658 to 1705 in St. Mary's, Calvert, Charles, and Prince George's counties, which together constitute most of the lower Western Shore of Maryland.

mous spinsters, Margaret and Mary Brent, were probably almost unique in seventeenth-century Maryland. In the four counties of the lower Western Shore only two of the women who left a probate inventory before the eighteenth century are known to have died single.[27] Comely or homely, strong or weak, any young woman was too valuable to be overlooked, and most could find a man with prospects.

The woman who immigrated to Maryland, survived seasoning and service, and gained her freedom became a planter's wife. She had considerable liberty in making her choice. There were men aplenty, and no fathers or brothers were hovering to monitor her behavior or disapprove her preference. This is the modern way of looking at her situation, of course. Perhaps she missed the protection of a father, a guardian, or kinfolk, and the participation in her decision of a community to which she felt ties. There is some evidence that the absence of kin and the pressures of the sex ratio created conditions of sexual freedom in courtship that were not customary in England. A register of marriages and births for seventeenth-century Somerset County shows that about one-third of the immigrant women whose marriages are recorded were pregnant at the time of the ceremony—nearly twice the rate in English parishes.[28] There is no indication of community objection to this freedom so long as marriage took place. No presentments for bridal pregnancy were made in any of the Maryland courts.[29]

The planter's wife was likely to be in her mid-twenties at marriage. An estimate of minimum age at marriage for servant women can be made from lists of indentured servants who left London over the years 1683–1684 and from age judgments in Maryland county court records. If we assume that the 112 female indentured servants going to Maryland and Virginia whose ages are given in the London lists served full four-year terms, then only 1.8 percent married before age twenty, but 68 percent after age twenty-four.[30] Similarly, if the 141 women whose ages were judged in Charles County between 1666 and 1705 served out their terms according to the custom of the country, none married

[27] Sixty women left inventories. The status of five is unknown. The two who died single died in 1698. Menard, "Immigrants and Their Increase," Table I.

[28] Menard, "Demography of Somerset County," Table XVII; Daniel Scott Smith and Michael S. Hindus, "Premarital Pregnancy in America, 1640–1971: An Overview," *Journal of Interdisciplinary History*, V (1975), 541. It was also two to three times the rate found in New England in the late 17th century.

[29] In Maryland any proceedings against pregnant brides could have been brought only in the civil courts. No vestries were established until 1693, and their jurisdiction was confined to the admonishment of men and women suspected of fornication unproved by the conception of a child. Churchwardens were to inform the county court of bastardies. Carr, "County Government in Maryland," text, 148–149, 221–223.

[30] The data are from Nicholson, comp., *Some Early Emigrants*.

before age twenty-two, and half were twenty-five or over.[31] When adjustments are made for the ages at which wives may have been purchased, the figures drop, but even so the majority of women waited until at least age twenty-four to marry.[32] Actual age at marriage in Maryland can be found for few seventeenth-century female immigrants, but observations for Charles and Somerset counties place the mean age at about twenty-five.[33]

Because of the age at which an immigrant woman married, the number of children she would bear her husband was small. She had lost up to ten years of her childbearing life [34]—the possibility of perhaps four or five children, given the usual rhythm of childbearing.[35] At the same time, high mortality would reduce both the number of children she would bear over the rest of her life and the number who would live. One partner to a marriage was likely to die within seven years, and the chances were only one in three that a marriage would last ten years.[36]

[31] Charles County Court and Land Records, MSS, C #1 through B #2.

[32] Available ages at arrival are as follows:

Age	under 12	13	14	15	16	17	18	19	20	21	22	23	24	25	26	27	28	29	30
Indentured (1682–1687)			1		1	6	2	9	9	8	29	19	6	5	6	2	3	1	2	3
Unindentured (1666–1705)	8	5	12	4	7	18	16	13	34	9	11	2	1	1					

Terms of service for women without indentures from 1666 on were 5 years if they were aged 22 at arrival; 6 years if 18–21; 7 years if 15–17; and until 22 if under 15. From 1661 to 1665 these terms were shorter by a year, and women under 15 served until age 21. If we assume that (1) indentured women served 4 years; (2) they constituted half the servant women; (3) women under age 12 were not purchased as wives; (4) 20% of women aged 12 or older were purchased; and (5) purchases were spread evenly over the possible years of service, then from 1666, 73.9% were 23 or older at marriage, and 66.0% were 24 or older; 70.8% were 23 or older from 1661 to 1665, and 55.5% were 24 or older. Mean ages at eligibility for marriage, as calculated by dividing person-years by the number of women, were 24.37 from 1666 on and 23.42 from 1661 to 1665. All assumptions except (3) and (5) are discussed above. The third is made on the basis that native girls married as young as age 12.

[33] Walsh, "Charles County, Maryland," chap. 2; Menard, "Demography of Somerset County," Tables XI, XII.

[34] The impact of later marriages is best demonstrated with age-specific marital fertility statistics. Susan L. Norton reports that women in colonial Ipswich, Massachusetts, bore an average of 7.5 children if they married between ages 15 and 19; 7.1 if they married between 20 and 24; and 4.5 if they married after 24. Norton, "Population Growth in Colonial America: A Study of Ipswich, Massachusetts," *Pop. Studies*, XXV (1971), 444. Cf. Wrigley, "Family Limitation in Pre-Industrial England," *Econ. Hist. Rev.*, 2nd Ser., XIX (1966), 82–109.

[35] In Charles County the mean interval between first and second and subsequent births was 30.8, and the median was 27.3 months. Walsh, "Charles County, Maryland," chap. 2. Menard has found that in Somerset County, Maryland, the median birth intervals for immigrant women between child 1 and child 2, child 2 and child 3, child 3 and child 4, and child 4 and child 5 were 26, 26, 30, 27 months, respectively ("Demography of Somerset County," Table XX).

[36] Walsh, "Charles County, Maryland," chap. 2.

In these circumstances, most women would not bear more than three or four children—not counting those stillborn—to any one husband, plus a posthumous child were she the survivor. The best estimates suggest that nearly a quarter, perhaps more, of the children born alive died during their first year and that 40 to 55 percent would not live to see age twenty.[37] Consequently, one of her children would probably die in infancy, and another one or two would fail to reach adulthood. Wills left in St. Mary's County during the seventeenth century show the results. In 105 families over the years 1660 to 1680 only twelve parents left more than three children behind them, including those conceived but not yet born. The average number was 2.3, nearly always minors, some of whom might die before reaching adulthood.[38]

For the immigrant woman, then, one of the major facts of life was that although she might bear a child about every two years, nearly half would not reach maturity. The social implications of this fact are far-reaching. Because she married late in her childbearing years and because so many of her children would die young, the number who would reach marriageable age might not replace, or might only barely replace, her and her husband or husbands as child-producing members of the society. Consequently, so long as immigrants were heavily predominant in the adult female population, Maryland could not grow much by natural increase.[39] It remained a land of newcomers.

This fact was fundamental to the character of seventeenth-century Maryland society, although its implications have yet to be fully explored. Settlers came from all parts of England and hence from differing traditions—in types of agriculture, forms of landholding and estate management, kinds of building construction, customary contributions to community needs, and family arrangements, including the role of women. The necessities of life in the Chesapeake required all immigrants to make adaptations. But until the native-born became predominant, a securely established Maryland tradition would not guide or restrict the newcomers.

If the immigrant woman had remained in England, she would prob-

[37] Walsh and Menard, "Death in the Chesapeake," *Md. Hist. Mag.*, LXIX (1974), 222.

[38] Menard, using all Maryland wills, found a considerably lower number of children per family in a similar period: 1.83 in wills probated 1660–1665; 2.20 in wills probated 1680–1684 ("Economy and Society," 198). Family reconstitution not surprisingly produces slightly higher figures, since daughters are often underrecorded in wills but are recorded as frequently as sons in birth registers. In 17th-century Charles County the mean size of all reconstituted families was 2.75. For marriages contracted in the years 1658–1669 (N = 118), 1670–1679 (N = 79), and 1680–1689 (N = 95), family size was 3.15, 2.58, and 2.86 respectively. In Somerset County, family size for immigrant marriages formed between 1665 and 1695 (N = 41) was 3.9. Walsh, "Charles County, Maryland," chap. 2; Menard, "Demography of Somerset County," Table XXI.

[39] For fuller exposition of the process see Menard, "Immigrants and Their Increase."

ably have married at about the same age or perhaps a little later.[40] But the social consequences of marriage at these ages in most parts of England were probably different. More children may have lived to maturity, and even where mortality was as high newcomers are not likely to have been the main source of population growth.[41] The locally born would still dominate the community, its social organization, and its traditions. However, where there were exceptions, as perhaps in London, late age at marriage, combined with high mortality and heavy immigration, may have had consequences in some ways similar to those we have found in Maryland.

A hazard of marriage for seventeenth-century women everywhere was death in childbirth, but this hazard may have been greater than usual in the Chesapeake. Whereas in most societies women tend to outlive men, in this malaria-ridden area it is probable that men outlived women. Hazards of childbirth provide the likely reason that Chesapeake women died so young. Once a woman in the Chesapeake reached forty-five, she tended to outlive men who reached the same age. Darrett and Anita Rutman have found malaria a probable cause of an exceptionally high death rate among pregnant women, who are, it appears, peculiarly vulnerable to that disease.[42]

This argument, however, suggests that immigrant women may have lived longer than their native-born daughters, although among men the opposite was true. Life tables created for men in Maryland show that those native-born who survived to age twenty could expect a life span three to ten years longer than that of immigrants, depending upon the region where they lived. The reason for the improvement was doubtless immunities to local diseases developed in childhood.[43] A native woman developed these immunities, but, as we shall see, she

---

[40] P. E. Razell, "Population Change in Eighteenth-Century England. A Reinterpretation," *Econ. Hist. Rev.*, 2nd Ser., XVIII (1965), 315, cites mean age at marriage as 23.76 years for 7,242 women in Yorkshire, 1662–1714, and 24.6 years for 280 women of Wiltshire, Berkshire, Hampshire, and Dorset, 1615–1621. Peter Laslett, *The World We Have Lost: England before the Industrial Age*, 2nd ed. (London, 1971), 86, shows a mean age of 23.58 for 1,007 women in the Diocese of Canterbury, 1619–1690. Wrigley, "Family Limitation in Pre-Industrial England," *Econ. Hist. Rev.*, 2nd Ser., XIX (1966), 87, shows mean ages at marriage for 259 women in Colyton, Devon, ranging from 26.15 to 30.0 years, 1600–1699.

[41] For a brief discussion of Chesapeake and English mortality see Walsh and Menard, "Death in the Chesapeake," *Md. Hist. Mag.*, LXIX (1974), 224–225.

[42] George W. Barclay, *Techniques of Population Analysis* (New York, 1958), 136n; Darrett B. and Anita H. Rutman, " 'Now-Wives and Sons-in-Law': Parental Death in a Seventeenth-Century Virginia County," in Tate and Ammerman, eds., *Essays on the Chesapeake*; Rutman and Rutman, "Of Agues and Fevers," *WMQ*, 3d Ser., XXXIII (1976), 31–60. Cf. Peter H. Wood, *Black Majority: Negroes in Colonial South Carolina from 1670 through the Stono Rebellion* (New York, 1974), chap. 3.

[43] Walsh and Menard, "Death in the Chesapeake," *Md. Hist. Mag.*, LXIX (1974), 211–227; Menard, "Demography of Somerset County."

also married earlier than immigrant women usually could and hence had more children.[44] Thus she was more exposed to the hazards of childbirth and may have died a little sooner. Unfortunately, the life tables for immigrant women that would settle this question have so far proved impossible to construct.

However long they lived, immigrant women in Maryland tended to outlive their husbands—in Charles County, for example, by a ratio of two to one. This was possible, despite the fact that women were younger than men at death, because women were also younger than men at marriage. Some women were widowed with no living children, but most were left responsible for two or three. These were often tiny, and nearly always not yet sixteen.[45]

This fact had drastic consequences, given the physical circumstances of life. People lived at a distance from one another, not even in villages, much less towns. The widow had left her kin 3,000 miles across an ocean, and her husband's family was also there. She would have to feed her children and make her own tobacco crop. Though neighbors might help, heavy labor would be required of her if she had no servants, until—what admittedly was usually not difficult—she acquired a new husband.

In this situation dying husbands were understandably anxious about the welfare of their families. Their wills reflected their feelings and tell something of how they regarded their wives. In St. Mary's and Charles counties during the seventeenth century, little more than one-quarter of the men left their widows with no more than the dower the law required—one-third of his land for her life, plus outright ownership of one-third of his personal property. (See Table 1.) If there were no children, a man almost always left his widow his whole estate. Otherwise there were a variety of arrangements. (See Table 2.)

During the 1660s, when testators begin to appear in quantity, nearly a fifth of the men who had children left all to their wives, trusting them to see that the children received fair portions. Thus in 1663 John Shircliffe willed his whole estate to his wife "towards the maintenance of herself and my children into whose tender care I do Commend them Desireing to see them brought up in the fear of God and the

---

[44] In Charles County immigrant women who ended childbearing years or died before 1705 bore a mean of 3.5 children (N = 59); the mean for natives was 5.1 (N = 42). Mean completed family size in Somerset County for marriages contracted between 1665 and 1695 was higher, but the immigrant-native differential remains. Immigrant women (N = 17) bore 6.1 children, while native women (N = 16) bore 9.4. Walsh, "Charles County, Maryland," chap. 2; Menard, "Demography of Somerset County," Table XXI.

[45] Among 1735 decedents who left inventories on Maryland's lower Western Shore, 1658–1705, 72% died without children or with children not yet of age. Only 16% could be proved to have a child of age. "Social Stratification."

TABLE 1

Bequests of Husbands to Wives, St. Mary's and Charles Counties, Maryland, 1640 to 1710

	N	Dower or less N	%
1640s	6	2	34
1650s	24	7	29
1660s	65	18	28
1670s	86	21	24
1680s	64	17	27
1690s	83	23	28
1700s	74	25	34
Totals	402	113	28

Source: Wills, I–XIV, Hall of Records, Annapolis, Md.

TABLE 2

Bequests of Husbands to Wives with Children, St. Mary's and Charles Counties, Maryland, 1640 to 1710

	N	All estate		All or dwelling plantation for life		All or dwelling plantation for widowhood		All or dwelling plantation for minority of child		More than dower in other form		Dower or less or unknown	
		N	%	N	%	N	%	N	%	N	%	N	%
1640s	3	1	33									2	67
1650s	16	1	6	2	13	1	6	1	6	4	25	7	44
1660s	45	8	18	8	18	2	4	3	7	9	20	15	33
1670s	61	4	7	21	34	2	3	3	5	13	21	18	30
1680s	52	5	10	19	37	2	4	2	4	11	21	13	25
1690s	69	1	1	31	45	7	10	2	3	10	14	18	26
1700s	62			20	32	6	10	2	3	14	23	20	32
Totals	308	20	6	101	33	20	6	13	4	61	20	93	30

Source: Wills, I–XIV.

Catholick Religion and Chargeing them to be Dutiful and obedient to her." [46] As the century progressed, husbands tended instead to give the wife all or a major part of the estate for her life, and to designate how it should be distributed after her death. Either way, the husband put great trust in his widow, considering that he knew she was bound to

[46] Wills, I, 172.

remarry. Only a handful of men left estates to their wives only for their term of widowhood or until the children came of age. When a man did not leave his wife a life estate, he often gave her land outright or more than her dower third of his movable property. Such bequests were at the expense of his children and showed his concern that his widow should have a maintenance which young children could not supply.

A husband usually made his wife his executor and thus responsible for paying his debts and preserving the estate. Only 11 percent deprived their wives of such powers.[47] In many instances, however, men also appointed overseers to assist their wives and to see that their children were not abused or their property embezzled. Danger lay in the fact that a second husband acquired control of all his wife's property, including her life estate in the property of his predecessor. Over half of the husbands who died in the 1650s and 1660s appointed overseers to ensure that their wills were followed. Some trusted to the overseers' "Care and good Conscience for the good of my widow and fatherless children." Others more explicitly made overseers responsible for seeing that "my said child . . . and the other [expected child] (when pleases God to send it) may have their right Proportion of my Said Estate and that the said Children may be bred up Chiefly in the fear of God."[48] A few men—but remarkably few—authorized overseers to remove children from households of stepfathers who abused them or wasted their property.[49] On the whole, the absence of such provisions for the protection of the children points to the husband's overriding concern for the welfare of his widow and to his confidence in her management, regardless of the certainty of her remarriage. Evidently, in the politics of family life women enjoyed great respect.[50]

We have implied that this respect was a product of the experience of immigrants in the Chesapeake. Might it have been instead a reflection of English culture? Little work is yet in print that allows comparison of the provisions for Maryland widows with those made for the widows of English farmers. Possibly, Maryland husbands were making traditional wills which could have been written in the communities they left behind. However, Margaret Spufford's recent study of three Cambridgeshire villages in the late sixteenth century and early seventeenth

[47] From 1640 to 1710, 17% of the married men named no executor. In such cases, the probate court automatically gave executorship to the wife unless she requested someone else to act.

[48] Wills, I, 96, 69.

[49] Ibid., 193–194, 167, V, 82. The practice of appointing overseers ceased around the end of the century. From 1690 to 1710, only 13% of testators who made their wives executors appointed overseers.

[50] We divided wills according to whether decedents were immigrant, native born, or of unknown origins, and found no differences in patterns of bequests, choice of executors, or tendency to appoint overseers. No change occurred in 17th-century Maryland in these respects as a native-born population began to appear.

century suggests a different pattern. In one of these villages, Chippenham, women usually did receive a life interest in the property, but in
the other two they did not. If the children were all minors, the widow
controlled the property until the oldest son came of age, and then only
if she did not remarry. In the majority of cases adult sons were given
control of the property with instructions for the support of their
mothers. Spufford suggests that the pattern found in Chippenham
must have been very exceptional. On the basis of village censuses in six
other counties, dating from 1624 to 1724, which show only 3 percent
of widowed people heading households that included a married child,
she argues that if widows commonly controlled the farm, a higher proportion should have headed such households. However, she also argues
that widows with an interest in land would not long remain unmarried.[51] If so, the low percentage may be deceptive. More direct work
with wills needs to be done before we can be sure that Maryland husbands and fathers gave their widows greater control of property and
family than did their English counterparts.

   Maryland men trusted their widows, but this is not to say that many
did not express great anxiety about the future of their children. They
asked both wives and overseers to see that the children received "some
learning." Robert Sly made his wife sole guardian of his children but
admonished her "to take due Care that they be brought up in the true
fear of God and instructed in such Literature as may tend to their improvement." Widowers, whose children would be left without any parent, were often the most explicit in prescribing their upbringing.
Robert Cole, a middling planter, directed that his children "have such
Education in Learning as [to] write and read and Cast accompt I mean
my three Sonnes my two daughters to learn to read and sew with their
needle and all of them to be keept from Idleness but not to be keept as
Comon Servants." John Lawson required his executors to see that his
two daughters be reared together, receive learning and sewing instruction, and be "brought up to huswifery."[52] Often present was the fear
that orphaned children would be treated as servants and trained only
to work in the fields.[53] With stepfathers in mind, many fathers provided that their sons should be independent before the usual age of
majority, which for girls was sixteen but for men twenty-one. Sometimes fathers willed that their sons should inherit when they were as
young as sixteen, though more often eighteen. The sons could then escape an incompatible stepfather, who could no longer exploit their labor or property. If a son was already close to age sixteen, the father
might bind him to his mother until he reached majority or his mother

---

[51] Margaret Spufford, *Contrasting Communities: English Villagers in the Sixteenth and
Seventeenth Centuries* (Cambridge, 1974), 85–90, 111–118, 161–164.
[52] Wills, I, 422, 182, 321.
[53] For example, *ibid.*, 172, 182.

died, whichever came first. If she lived, she could watch out for his welfare, and his labor could contribute to her support. If she died, he and his property would be free from a stepfather's control.[54]

What happened to widows and children if a man died without leaving a will? There was great need for some community institution that could protect children left fatherless or parentless in a society where they usually had no other kin. By the 1660s the probate court and county orphans' courts were supplying this need.[55] If a man left a widow, the probate court—in Maryland a central government agency —usually appointed her or her new husband administrator of the estate with power to pay its creditors under court supervision. Probate procedures provided a large measure of protection. These required an inventory of the movable property and careful accounting of all disbursements, whether or not a man had left a will. William Hollis of Baltimore County, for example, had three stepfathers in seven years, and only the care of the judge of probate prevented the third stepfather from paying the debts of the second with goods that had belonged to William's father. As the judge remarked, William had "an uncareful mother."[56]

Once the property of an intestate had been fully accounted and creditors paid, the county courts appointed a guardian who took charge of the property and gave bond to the children with sureties that he or she would not waste it. If the mother were living, she could be the guardian, or if she had remarried, her new husband would act. Through most of the century bond was waived in these circumstances, but from the 1690s security was required of all guardians, even of mothers. Thereafter the courts might actually take away an orphan's property from a widow or stepfather if she or he could not find sureties—that is, neighbors who judged the parent responsible and hence were willing to risk their own property as security. Children without any parents were assigned new families, who at all times found surety if there were property to manage. If the orphans inherited land, English common law allowed them to choose guardians for themselves at age fourteen—another escape hatch for children in conflict with stepparents. Orphans who had no property, or whose property was insufficient to provide an income that could maintain them, were expected to work for their guardians in return for their maintenance. Every year the county courts were expected to check on the welfare of orphans of intestate parents and remove them or their property from

[54] Lorena S. Walsh, " 'Till Death Do Us Part': Marriage and Family in Charles County, Maryland, 1658–1705," in Tate and Ammerman, eds., *Essays on the Chesapeake.*

[55] The following discussion of the orphans' court is based on Lois Green Carr, "The Development of the Maryland Orphans' Court, 1654–1715," in Land, Carr, and Papenfuse, eds., *Law, Society, and Politics in Early Maryland,* 41–61.

[56] Baltimore County Court Proceedings, D, ff. 385–386.

guardians who abused them or misused their estates. From 1681, Maryland law required that a special jury be impaneled once a year to report neighborhood knowledge of mistreatment of orphans and hear complaints.

This form of community surveillance of widows and orphans proved quite effective. In 1696 the assembly declared that orphans of intestates were often better cared for than orphans of testators. From that time forward, orphans' courts were charged with supervision of all orphans and were soon given powers to remove any guardians who were shown false to their trusts, regardless of the arrangements laid down in a will. The assumption was that the deceased parent's main concern was the welfare of the child, and that the orphans' court, as "father to us poor orphans," should implement the parent's intent. In actual fact, the courts never removed children—as opposed to their property—from a household in which the mother was living, except to apprentice them at the mother's request. These powers were mainly exercised over guardians of orphans both of whose parents were dead. The community as well as the husband believed the mother most capable of nurturing his children.

Remarriage was the usual and often the immediate solution for a woman who had lost her husband.[57] The shortage of women made any woman eligible to marry again, and the difficulties of raising a family while running a plantation must have made remarriage necessary for widows who had no son old enough to make tobacco. One indication of the high incidence of remarriage is the fact that there were only sixty women, almost all of them widows, among the 1,735 people who left probate inventories in four southern Maryland counties over the second half of the century.[58] Most other women must have died while married and therefore legally without property to put through probate.

One result of remarriage was the development of complex family structures. Men found themselves responsible for stepchildren as well as their own offspring, and children acquired half-sisters and half-brothers. Sometimes a woman married a second husband who himself had been previously married, and both brought children of former spouses to the new marriage. They then produced children of their own. The possibilities for conflict over the upbringing of children are evident, and crowded living conditions, found even in the households of the wealthy, must have added to family tensions. Luckily, the children of the family very often had the same mother. In Charles County, at least, widows took new husbands three times more often than wid-

---

[57] In 17th-century Charles County two-thirds of surviving partners remarried within a year of their spouse's death. Walsh, "Charles County, Maryland," chap. 2.

[58] See n. 26.

owers took new wives.[59] The role of the mother in managing the relationships of half-brothers and half-sisters or stepfathers and stepchildren must have been critical to family harmony.

Early death in this immigrant population thus had broad effects on Maryland society in the seventeenth century. It produced what we might call a pattern of serial polyandry, which enabled more men to marry and to father families than the sex ratios otherwise would have permitted. It produced thousands of orphaned children who had no kin to maintain them or preserve their property, and thus gave rise to an institution almost unknown in England, the orphans' court, which was charged with their protection. And early death, by creating families in which the mother was the unifying element, may have increased her authority within the household.

When the immigrant woman married her first husband, there was usually no property settlement involved, since she was unlikely to have any dowry. But her remarriage was another matter. At the very least, she owned or had a life interest in a third of her former husband's estate. She needed also to think of her children's interests. If she remarried, she would lose control of the property. Consequently, property settlements occasionally appear in the seventeenth-century court records between widows and their future husbands. Sometimes she and her intended signed an agreement whereby he relinquished his rights to the use of her children's portions. Sometimes he deeded to her property which she could dispose of at her pleasure.[60] Whether any of these agreements or gifts would have survived a test in court is unknown. We have not yet found any challenged. Generally speaking, the formal marriage settlements of English law, which bypassed the legal difficulties of the married woman's inability to make a contract with her husband, were not adopted by immigrants, most of whom probably came from levels of English society that did not use these legal formalities.

The wife's dower rights in her husband's estate were a recognition of her role in contributing to his prosperity, whether by the property she had brought to the marriage or by the labor she performed in his household. A woman newly freed from servitude would not bring property, but the benefits of her labor would be great. A man not yet prosperous enough to own a servant might need his wife's help in the fields as well as in the house, especially if he were paying rent or still paying for land. Moreover, food preparation was so time-consuming that even if she worked only at household duties, she saved him time he needed for making tobacco and corn. The corn, for example, had to

---

[59] Walsh, " 'Till Death Do Us Part,' " in Tate and Ammerman, eds., *Essays on the Chesapeake.*
[60] *Ibid.*

be pounded in the mortar or ground in a handmill before it could be used to make bread, for there were very few water mills in seventeenth-century Maryland. The wife probably raised vegetables in a kitchen garden; she also milked the cows and made butter and cheese, which might produce a salable surplus. She washed the clothes, and made them if she had the skill. When there were servants to do field work, the wife undoubtedly spent her time entirely in such household tasks. A contract of 1681 expressed such a division of labor. Nicholas Maniere agreed to live on a plantation with his wife and child and a servant. Nicholas and the servant were to work the land; his wife was to "Dresse the Victualls milk the Cowes wash for the servants and Doe allthings necessary for a woman to doe upon the s[ai]d plantation."[61]

We have suggested that wives did field work; the suggestion is supported by occasional direct references in the court records. Mary Castleton, for example, told the judge of probate that "her husband late Deceased in his Life time had Little to sustaine himselfe and Children but what was produced out of ye ground by ye hard Labour of her the said Mary."[62] Household inventories provide indirect evidence. Before about 1680 those of poor men and even middling planters on Maryland's lower Western Shore—the bottom two-thirds of the married decedents—[63] show few signs of household industry, such as appear in equivalent English estates.[64] Sheep and woolcards, flax and hackles, and spinning wheels all were a rarity, and such things as candle molds were nonexistent. Women in these households must have been busy at other work. In households with bound labor the wife doubtless was fully occupied preparing food and washing clothes for family and hands. But the wife in a household too poor to afford bound labor— the bottom fifth of the married decedent group—might well tend tobacco when she could.[65] Eventually, the profits of her labor might en-

[61] *Maryland Archives*, LXX, 87. See also *ibid.*, XLI, 210, 474, 598, for examples of allusions to washing clothes and dairying activities. Water mills were so scarce that in 1669 the Maryland assembly passed an act permitting land to be condemned for the use of anyone willing to build and operate a water mill. *Ibid.*, II, 211–214. In the whole colony only four condemnations were carried out over the next 10 years. *Ibid.*, LI, 25, 57, 86, 381. Probate inventories show that most households had a mortar and pestle or a hand mill.

[62] Testamentary Proceedings, X, 184–185. Cf. Charles County Court and Land Records, MS, I #1, ff. 9–10, 259.

[63] Among married decedents before 1680 (N = 308), the bottom two-thirds (N = 212) were those worth less than £150. Among all decedents worth less than £150 (N = 451), only 12 (about 3%) had sheep or yarn-making equipment. "Social Stratification."

[64] See Everitt, "Farm Labourers," in Thirsk, ed., *Agrarian History of England and Wales*, 422–426, and W. G. Hoskins, *Essays in Leicestershire History* (Liverpool, 1950), 134.

[65] Among married decedents, the bottom fifth were approximately those worth less than £30. Before 1680 these were 17% of the married decedents. By the end of the period, from 1700 to 1705, they were 22%. Before 1680, 92% had no bound labor. From 1700 to 1705, 95% had none. Less than 1% of all estates in this wealth group had sheep or yarn-making equipment before 1681. "Social Stratification."

able the family to buy a servant, making greater profits possible. From such beginnings many families climbed the economic ladder in seventeenth-century Maryland.[66]

The proportion of servantless households must have been larger than is suggested by the inventories of the dead, since young men were less likely to die than old men and had had less time to accumulate property. Well over a fifth of the households of married men on the lower Western Shore may have had no bound labor. Not every wife in such households would necessarily work at the hoe—saved from it by upbringing, ill-health, or the presence of small children who needed her care—but many women performed such work. A lease of 1691, for example, specified that the lessee could farm the amount of land which "he his wife and children can tend." [67]

Stagnation of the tobacco economy, beginning about 1680, produced changes that had some effect on women's economic role.[68] As shown by inventories of the lower Western Shore, home industry increased, especially at the upper ranges of the economic spectrum. In these households women were spinning yarn and knitting it into clothing.[69] The increase in such activity was far less in the households of the bottom fifth, where changes of a different kind may have increased the pressures to grow tobacco. Fewer men at this level could now purchase land, and a portion of their crop went for rent.[70] At this level, more

[66] On opportunity to raise from the bottom to the middle see Menard, "From Servant to Freeholder," *WMQ*, 3d Ser., XXX (1973), 37–64; Walsh, "Servitude and Opportunity," 111–133; and Menard, Harris, and Carr, "Opportunity and Inequality," *Md. Hist. Mag.*, LXIX (1974), 169–184.

[67] Charles County Court and Land Records, MS, R #1, f. 193.

[68] For 17th-century economic development see Menard, Harris, and Carr, "Opportunity and Inequality," *Md. Hist. Mag.*, LXIX (1974), 169–184.

[69] Among estates worth £150 or more, signs of diversification in this form appeared in 22% before 1681 and in 67% after 1680. Over the years 1700–1705, the figure was 62%. Only 6% of estates worth less than £40 had such signs of diversification after 1680 or over the period 1700–1705. Knitting rather than weaving is assumed because looms were very rare. These figures are for all estates. "Social Stratification."

[70] After the mid-1670s information about landholdings of decedents becomes decreasingly available, making firm estimates of the increase in tenancy difficult. However, for householders in life cycle 2 (married or widowed decedents who died without children of age) the following table is suggestive. Householding decedents in life cycle 2 worth less than £40 (N = 255) were 21% of all decedents in this category (N = 1,218).

| | £0–19 | | | £20–39 | | |
	DECED- ENTS N	LAND UNKN. N	WITH LAND N	WITH LAND %	DECED- ENTS N	LAND UNKN. N	WITH LAND N	WITH LAND %
To 1675	10	0	7	70	34	2	29	91
1675 on	98	22	40	53	113	16	64	66

In computing percentages, unknowns have been distributed according to knowns.

A man who died with a child of age was almost always a landowner, but these were a small proportion of all decedents (see n. 45).

wives than before may have been helping to produce tobacco when they could. And by this time they were often helping as a matter of survival, not as a means of improving the family position.

So far we have considered primarily the experience of immigrant women. What of their daughters? How were their lives affected by the demographic stresses of Chesapeake society?

One of the most important points in which the experience of daughters differed from that of their mothers was the age at which they married. In this woman-short world, the mothers had married as soon as they were eligible, but they had not usually become eligible until they were mature women in their middle twenties. Their daughters were much younger at marriage. A vital register kept in Somerset County shows that some girls married at age twelve and that the mean age at marriage for those born before 1670 was sixteen and a half years.

Were some of these girls actually child brides? It seems unlikely that girls were married before they had become capable of bearing children. Culturally, such a practice would fly in the face of English, indeed Western European, precedent, nobility excepted. Nevertheless, the number of girls who married before age sixteen, the legal age of inheritance for girls, is astonishing. Their English counterparts ordinarily did not marry until their mid- to late twenties or early thirties. In other parts of the Chesapeake, historians have found somewhat higher ages at marriage than appear in Somerset, but everywhere in seventeenth-century Maryland and Virginia most native-born women married before they reached age twenty-one.[71] Were such early marriages a result of the absence of fathers? Evidently not. In Somerset County, the fathers of very young brides—those under sixteen—were usually living.[72] Evidently, guardians were unlikely to allow such marriages, and this fact suggests that they were not entirely approved. But the shortage of women imposed strong pressures to marry as early as possible.

Not only did native girls marry early, but many of them were pregnant before the ceremony. Bridal pregnancy among native-born women was not as common as among immigrants. Nevertheless, in

---

Several studies provide indisputable evidence of an increase in tenancy on the lower Western Shore over the period 1660–1706. These compare heads of households with lists of landowners compiled from rent rolls made in 1659 and 1704–1706. Tenancy in St. Mary's and Charles counties in 1660 was about 10%. In St. Mary's, Charles, and Prince George's counties, 1704–1706, 30–35% of householders were tenants. Russell R. Menard, "Population Growth and Land Distribution in St. Mary's County, 1634–1710" (ms. report, St. Mary's City Commission, 1971, copy on file at the Hall of Records); Menard, "Economy and Society," 423; Carr, "County Government in Maryland," text, 605.

[71] Menard, "Immigrants and Their Increase," Table III; n. 40 above.

[72] Menard, "Demography of Somerset County," Table XIII.

seventeenth-century Somerset County 20 percent of native brides bore children within eight and one-half months of marriage. This was a somewhat higher percentage than has been reported from seventeenth-century English parishes.[73]

These facts suggest considerable freedom for girls in selecting a husband. Almost any girl must have had more than one suitor, and evidently many had freedom to spend time with a suitor in a fashion that allowed her to become pregnant. We might suppose that such pregnancies were not incurred until after the couple had become betrothed, and that they were consequently an allowable part of courtship, were it not that girls whose fathers were living were usually not the culprits. In Somerset, at least, only 10 percent of the brides with fathers living were pregnant, in contrast to 30 percent of those who were orphans.[74] Since there was only about one year's difference between the mean ages at which orphan and non-orphan girls married, parental supervision rather than age seems to have been the main factor in the differing bridal pregnancy rates.[75]

Native girls married young and bore children young; hence they had more children than immigrant women. This fact ultimately changed the composition of the Maryland population. Native-born females began to have enough children to enable couples to replace themselves. These children, furthermore, were divided about evenly between males and females. By the mid-1680s, in all probability, the population thus began to grow through reproductive increase, and sexual imbalance began to decline. In 1704 the native-born preponderated in the Maryland assembly for the first time and by then were becoming predominant in the adult population as a whole.[76]

This appearance of a native population was bringing alterations in family life, especially for widows and orphaned minors. They were acquiring kin. St. Mary's and Charles counties wills demonstrate the change.[77] (See Table 3.) Before 1680, when nearly all those who died

[73] *Ibid.*, Table XVII; P. E. H. Hair, "Bridal Pregnancy in Rural England in Earlier Centuries," *Pop. Studies*, XX (1966), 237; Chambers, *Population, Economy, and Society in England*, 75; Smith and Hindus, "Premarital Pregnancy in America," *Jour. Interdisciplinary Hist.*, V (1975), 537–570.

[74] Menard, "Demography of Somerset County," Table XVIII.

[75] Adolescent subfecundity might also partly explain lower bridal pregnancy rates among very young brides.

[76] Menard develops this argument in detail in "Immigrants and Their Increase." For the assembly see David W. Jordan, "Political Stability and the Emergence of a Native Elite in Maryland, 1660–1715," in Tate and Ammerman, eds., *Essays on the Chesapeake*. In Charles County, Maryland, by 1705 at least half of all resident landowners were native born. Walsh, "Charles County, Maryland," chaps. 1, 7.

[77] The proportion of wills mentioning non-nuclear kin can, of course, prove only a proxy of the actual existence of these kin in Maryland. The reliability of such a measure may vary greatly from area to area and over time, depending on the character of the

TABLE 3

*Resident Kin of Testate Men
and Women Who Left Minor
Children, St. Mary's and Charles
Counties, 1640 to 1710*

A.

	FAMILIES N	NO KIN % FAMILIES	ONLY WIFE % FAMILIES	GROWN CHILD % FAMILIES	OTHER KIN % FAMILIES
1640–1669	95	23	43	11	23
1670–1679	76	17	50	7	26
1700–1710	71	6	35[a]	25	34[b]

B.

1700–1710					
Immigrant	41	10	37	37	17
Native	30		33[c]	10	57[d]

Notes: [a] If information found in other records is included, the percentage is 30.
[b] If information found in other records is included, the percentage is 39.
[c] If information found in other records is included, the percentage is 20.
[d] If information found in other records is included, the percentage is 70.
For a discussion of wills as a reliable source for discovery of kin see n. 78. Only 8 testators were natives of Maryland before 1680s; hence no effort has been made to distinguish them from immigrants.
Source: Wills, I–XIV.

and left families had been immigrants, three-quarters of the men and women who left widows and/or minor children made no mention in their wills of any other kin in Maryland. In the first decade of the eighteenth century, among native-born testators, nearly three-fifths mention other kin, and if we add information from sources other than wills—other probate records, land records, vital registers, and so on—at least 70 percent are found to have had such local connections. This

---

population and on local inheritance customs. To test the reliability of the will data, we compared them with data from reconstituted families in 17th-century Charles County.

These reconstitution data draw on a much broader variety of sources and include many men who did not leave wills. Because of insufficient information for female lines, we could trace only the male lines. The procedure compared the names of all married men against a file of all known county residents, asking how many kin in the male line might have been present in the county at the time of the married man's death. The proportions for immigrants were in most cases not markedly different from those found in wills. For native men, however, wills were somewhat less reliable indicators of the presence of such kin; when non-nuclear kin mentioned by testate natives were compared with kin found by reconstitution, 29% of the native testators had non-nuclear kin present in the county who were not mentioned in their wills.

development of local family ties must have been one of the most important events of early Maryland history.[78]

Historians have only recently begun to explore the consequences of the shift from an immigrant to a predominantly native population.[79] We would like to suggest some changes in the position of women that may have resulted from this transition. It is already known that as sexual imbalance disappeared, age at first marriage rose, but it remained lower than it had been for immigrants over the second half of the seventeenth century. At the same time, life expectancy improved, at least for men. The results were longer marriages and more children who reached maturity.[80] In St. Mary's County after 1700, dying men far more often than earlier left children of age to maintain their widows, and widows may have felt less inclination and had less opportunity to remarry.[81]

We may speculate on the social consequences of such changes. More

[78] Not surprisingly, wills of immigrants show no increase in family ties, but these wills mention adult children far more often than earlier. Before 1680, only 11% of immigrant testators in St. Mary's and Charles counties mention adult children in their wills; from 1700 to 1710, 37% left adult children to help the family. Two facts help account for this change. First, survivors of early immigration were dying in old age. Second, proportionately fewer young immigrants with families were dying, not because life expectancy had improved, but because there were proportionately fewer of them than earlier. A long stagnation in the tobacco economy that began about 1680 had diminished opportunities for freed servants to form households and families. Hence, among immigrants the proportion of young fathers at risk to die was smaller than in earlier years.

In the larger population of men who left inventories, 18.2% had adult children before 1681, but in the years 1700–1709, 50% had adult children. "Social Stratification."

[79] Examples of some recent studies are Carole Shammas, "English-Born and Creole Elites in Turn-of-the-Century Virginia," in Tate and Ammerman, eds., *Essays on the Chesapeake*; Jordan, "Political Stability and the Emergence of a Native Elite in Maryland," *ibid.*; Lois Green Carr, "The Foundations of Social Order: Local Government in Colonial Maryland," in Bruce C. Daniels, ed., *Town and Country: Essays on the Structure of Local Government in the American Colonies* (Middletown, Conn., forthcoming); Menard, "Economy and Society," 396–440.

[80] Allan Kulikoff has found that in Prince George's County the white adult sex ratio dropped significantly before the age of marriage rose. Women born in the 1720s were the first to marry at a mean age above 20, while those born in the 1740s and marrying in the 1760s, after the sex ratio neared equality, married at a mean age of 22. Marriages lasted longer because the rise in the mean age at which men married—from 23 to 27 between 1700 and 1740—was more than offset by gains in life expectancy. Kulikoff, "Tobacco and Slaves: Population, Economy, and Society in Eighteenth-Century Prince George's County, Maryland" (Ph.D. diss., Brandeis University, 1976), chap. 3; Menard, "Immigrants and Their Increase."

[81] Inventories and related biographical data have been analyzed by the St. Mary's City Commission under a grant from the National Endowment for the Humanities, "The Making of a Plantation Society in Maryland" (R 010585-74-267). From 1700 through 1776 the percentage of men known to have had children, and who had an adult child at death, ranged from a low of 32.8% in the years 1736–1738 to a high of 61.3% in the years 1707–1709. The figure was over 50% for 13 out of 23 year-groups of three to four years each. For the high in 1707–1709 see comments in n. 78.

fathers were still alive when their daughters married, and hence would have been able to exercise control over the selection of their sons-in-law. What in the seventeenth century may have been a period of comparative independence for women, both immigrant and native, may have given way to a return to more traditional European social controls over the creation of new families. If so, we might see the results in a decline in bridal pregnancy and perhaps a decline in bastardy.[82]

We may also find the wife losing ground in the household polity, although her economic importance probably remained unimpaired. Indeed, she must have been far more likely than a seventeenth-century immigrant woman to bring property to her marriage. But several changes may have caused women to play a smaller role than before in household decisionmaking.[83] Women became proportionately more numerous and may have lost bargaining power.[84] Furthermore, as marriages lasted longer, the proportion of households full of stepchildren and half-brothers and half-sisters united primarily by the mother must have diminished. Finally, when husbands died, more widows would have had children old enough to maintain them and any minor brothers and sisters. There would be less need for women to play a controlling role, as well as less incentive for their husbands to grant it. The provincial marriage of the eighteenth century may have more closely resembled that of England than did the immigrant marriage of the seventeenth century.

If this change occurred, we should find symptoms to measure. There should be fewer gifts from husbands to wives of property put at the wife's disposal. Husbands should less frequently make bequests to wives that provided them with property beyond their dower. A wife might even be restricted to less than her dower, although the law allowed her to choose her dower instead of a bequest.[85] At the same time, children should be commanded to maintain their mothers.

[82] On the other hand, these rates may show little change. The restraining effect of increased parental control may have been offset by a trend toward increased sexual activity that appears to have become general throughout Western Europe and the United States by the mid-18th century. Smith and Hindus, "Premarital Pregnancy in America," *Jour. Interdisciplinary Hist.*, V (1975), 537–570; Edward Shorter, "Female Emancipation, Birth Control, and Fertility in European History," *American Historical Review*, LXXVIII (1973), 605–640.

[83] Page Smith has suggested that such a decline in the wife's household authority had occurred in the American family by—at the latest—the beginning of the 19th century (*Daughters of the Promised Land: Women in American History* [Boston, 1970], chaps. 3, 4).

[84] There is little doubt that extreme scarcity in the early years of Chesapeake history enhanced the worth of women in the eyes of men. However, as Smith has observed, "the functioning of the law of supply and demand could not in itself have guaranteed status for colonial women. Without an ideological basis, their privileges could not have been initially established or subsequently maintained" (*ibid.*, 38–39). In a culture where women were seriously undervalued, a shortage of women would not necessarily improve their status.

[85] Acts 1699, chap. 41, *Maryland Archives*, XXII, 542.

However, St. Mary's County wills do not show these symptoms. (See Table 4.) True, wives occasionally were willed less than their dower, an arrangement that was rare in the wills examined for the period before 1710. But there was no overall decrease in bequests to wives of property beyond their dower, nor was there a tendency to confine the wife's interest to the term of her widowhood or the minority of the oldest son. Children were not exhorted to help their mothers or give them living space. Widows evidently received at least enough property to maintain themselves, and husbands saw no need to ensure the help of children in managing it. Possibly, then, women did not lose ground, or at least not all ground, within the family polity. The demographic disruption of New World settlement may have given women power which they were able to keep even after sex ratios became balanced and traditional family networks appeared. Immigrant mothers may have bequeathed their daughters a legacy of independence which they in turn handed down, despite pressures toward more traditional behavior.

It is time to issue a warning. Whether or not Maryland women in a creole society lost ground, the argument hinges on an interpretation of English behavior that also requires testing. Either position supposes that women in seventeenth-century Maryland obtained power in the household which wives of English farmers did not enjoy. Much of the evidence for Maryland is drawn from the disposition of property in wills. If English wills show a similar pattern, similar inferences might be drawn about English women. We have already discussed evidence from English wills that supports the view that women in Maryland were favored; but the position of seventeenth-century English women—especially those not of gentle status—has been little explored.[86] A finding of little difference between bequests to women in England and in Maryland would greatly weaken the argument that demographic stress created peculiar conditions especially favorable to Maryland women.

If the demography of Maryland produced the effects here described, such effects should also be evident elsewhere in the Chesapeake. The four characteristics of the seventeenth-century Maryland population—immigrant predominance, early death, late marriage, and sexual imbal-

[86] Essays by Cicely Howell and Barbara Todd, printed or made available to the authors since this article was written, point out that customary as opposed to freehold tenures in England usually gave the widow the use of the land for life, but that remarriage often cost the widow this right. The degree to which this was true requires investigation. Howell, "Peasant Inheritance in the Midlands, 1280–1700," in Jack Goody, Joan Thirsk, and E. P. Thompson, eds., *Family and Inheritance: Rural Society in Western Europe, 1200–1800* (Cambridge, 1976), 112–155; Todd, " 'In Her Free Widowhood': Succession to Property and Remarriage in Rural England, 1540–1800" (paper delivered to the Third Berkshire Conference of Women Historians, June 1976).

TABLE 4

Bequests of Husbands to Wives with Children, St. Mary's County, Maryland, 1710 to 1776

	N	All estate %	All or dwelling plantation for life %	All or dwelling plantation for widowhood %	All or dwelling plantation for minority of child %	More than dower in other form %	Dower or less or unknown %	Maintenance or house room %
1710–1714	13	0	46	0	0	23	31	0
1715–1719	25	4	24	4	0	28	36	4
1720–1724	31	10	42	0	0	28	23	3
1725–1729	34	3	29	0	0	24	41	3
1730–1734	31	6	16	13	0	29	35	0
1735–1739	27	0	37	4	4	19	37	0
1740–1744	35	0	40	0	3	23	34	0
1745–1749	39	3	31	8	0	31	28	0
1750–1754	43	2	35	7	0	16	40	0
1755–1759	34	3	41	3	0	41	12	0
1760–1764	48	2	46	10	2	13	27	0
1765–1769	45	4	27	11	2	18	33	4
1770–1774	46	4	26	7	0	37	26	0
1775–1776	19	5	32	26	0	5	32	0
Totals	470	3	33	7	1	24	31	1

Source: Wills, XIV–XLI.

ance—are to be found everywhere in the region, at least at first. The timing of the disappearance of these peculiarities may have varied from place to place, depending on date of settlement or rapidity of development, but the effect of their existence upon the experience of women should be clear. Should research in other areas of the Chesapeake fail to find women enjoying the status they achieved on the lower Western Shore of Maryland, then our arguments would have to be revised.[87]

Work is also needed that will enable historians to compare conditions in Maryland with those in other colonies. Richard S. Dunn's study of the British West Indies also shows demographic disruption.[88] When the status of wives is studied, it should prove similar to that of Maryland women. In contrast were demographic conditions in New England, where immigrants came in family groups, major immigration had ceased by the mid-seventeenth century, sex ratios balanced early, and mortality was low.[89] Under these conditions, demographic disruption must have been both less severe and less prolonged. If New England women achieved status similar to that suggested for women in the Chesapeake, that fact will have to be explained. The dynamics might prove to have been different[90]; or a dynamic we have not identified, common to both areas, might turn out to have been the primary engine of change. And, if women in England shared the status—which we doubt—conditions in the New World may have had secondary importance. The Maryland data establish persuasive grounds for a hypothesis, but the evidence is not all in.

[87] James W. Deen, Jr., "Patterns of Testation: Four Tidewater Counties in Colonial Virginia," *American Journal of Legal History*, XVI (1972), 154–176, finds a life interest in property for the wife the predominant pattern before 1720. However, he includes an interest for widowhood in life interest and does not distinguish a dower interest from more than dower.

[88] Richard S. Dunn, *Sugar and Slaves: The Rise of the Planter Class in the English West Indies*, 1624–1713 (Chapel Hill, N.C., 1972), 326–334. Dunn finds sex ratios surprisingly balanced, but he also finds very high mortality, short marriages, and many orphans.

[89] For a short discussion of this comparison see Menard, "Immigrants and Their Increase."

[90] James K. Somerville has used Salem, Massachusetts, wills from 1660 to 1770 to examine women's status and importance within the home ("The Salem [Mass.] Woman in the Home, 1660–1770," *Eighteenth-Century Life*, I [1974], 11–14). See also Alexander Keyssar, "Widowhood in Eighteenth-Century Massachusetts: A Problem in the History of the Family," *Perspectives in American History*, VIII (1974), 83–119, which discusses provisions for 22 widows in 18th-century Woburn, Massachusetts. Both men find provisions for houseroom and care of the widow's property enjoined upon children proportionately far more often than we have found in St. Mary's County, Maryland, where we found only five instances over 136 years. However, part of this difference may be a function of the differences in age at widowhood in the two regions. Neither Somerville nor Keyssar gives the percentage of widows who received a life interest in property, but their discussions imply a much higher proportion than we have found of women whose interest ended at remarriage or the majority of the oldest son.

Migrants and Motives: Religion and the Settlement of New England, 1630–1640

VIRGINIA DEJOHN ANDERSON

In all of the Atlantic empires before 1630, the typical voluntary emigres were young men who hoped to achieve material success by engaging in some activity in the Americas that they could not pursue in Europe. Spanish conquistadors conquered and looted Mexico and Peru, and many of their descendants acquired large haciendas or lavish town houses. West Indian settlers grew sugar. The Chesapeake colonists raised tobacco. Only in New England (and later in Pennsylvania) did the first settlers liquidate large amounts of property in England to finance the move to America, travel in family groups, and then try to reestablish almost the same economic activities that they had pursued in Europe. Merchants from London or other English ports moved to Boston or Salem to carry on their oceanic trade. Most artisans looked for ways to pursue the same crafts in New England. Most farmers, while willing to add such New World crops as maize and beans, raised grain and livestock in familiar ways. Indeed only in New England did many towns retain open field agriculture, as against independent farms, at least for the first generation.

Several recent historians believe that these activities uncover an underlying materialist thrust behind the settlement of New England, and they point to the depression in the English cloth trade in the 1620s, for example, to explain why men and women engaged in making textiles (usually in their homes) might wish to relocate somewhere else. Virginia Anderson sees quite a different pattern. Although the first settlers knew that they had to engage in some productive activity in the New World, that prospect did not draw them across the ocean. Basically she is returning the argument to what the settlers themselves said they were doing, creating a godly society in the wilderness. Is her case persuasive? What sort of economic activity should we expect a committed Puritan to engage in? What, if anything, can it tell us about that person's motives?

No man, perhaps, would seem to have been an unlikelier candidate for transatlantic migration than John Bent. He had never shown any particular interest in moving; indeed, in 1638, at the age of forty-one,

Reprinted by permission from Virginia Dejohn Anderson, "Migrants and Motives: Religion and the Settlement of New England," *New England Quarterly*, 58 (1985), 339–383.

Bent still lived in Weyhill, Hampshire, where both he and his father before him had been born. Having prospered in the village of his birth, John Bent held enough land to distinguish himself as one of Weyhill's wealthiest inhabitants. One might reasonably expect that Bent's substantial economic stake, combined with his growing familial responsibilities—which by 1638 included a wife and five children—would have provided him with ample incentive to stay put. By embarking on a transatlantic voyage—moving for the first time in his life and over a vast distance—Bent would exchange an economically secure present for a highly uncertain future and venture his family's lives and fortunes no less than his own. Yet in the spring of 1638, Bent returned his Weyhill land to the lord of the manor, gathered his family and possessions, and traveled twenty-five miles to the port of Southampton. There, he and his family boarded the *Confidence*, bound for Massachusetts Bay.[1]

In doing so, the Bent family joined thousands of other men, women, and children who left for New England between 1630 and 1642.[2] We know more about John Bent than about the vast majority of these other emigrants because certain information has fortuitously survived. Bent's name appears on one of the few extant ship passenger lists of the Great Migration, and genealogists and local historians have compiled enough additional data to sketch in the outlines of his life in Old and New England. Yet despite this rare abundance of information, John Bent's reasons for moving to Massachusetts remain obscure. In fact, the surviving biographical details render the question of motivation all the more tantalizing because they provide no identifiable economic reason for leaving but rather depict a man firmly rooted in his English homeland.

Most accounts of early New England include a general discussion of the emigrants' motivations, but none has dealt with the issue systematically. If we are ever to comprehend the nature and significance of the Great Migration, however, we must understand why men like John Bent left their homes. The Great Migration to New England, unlike

---

[1] Allen H. Bent, "The Bent Family," *New England Historical and Genealogical Register* (hereafter *NEHGR*) 47 (1894): 288–96; E. C. Felton, "The English Ancestors of John Bent, of Sudbury," *NEHGR* 48 (1895): 66; Sumner Chilton Powell, *Puritan Village: The Formation of a New England Town* (Middletown, Conn.: Wesleyan University Press, 1963), p. 8. The passenger list for the *Confidence* is printed by Henry Stevens, in "Passengers for New England, 1638," *NEHGR* 2 (1848): 108–10, with corrections by H. G. Somerby in *NEHGR* 5 (1851): 440.

[2] Estimates of the total number of emigrants vary. In 1651 Edward Johnson, a participant in the Great Migration, calculated a total of 21,200 persons. Recent research, however, suggests that Johnson's figure may be as much as a third too large. See J. Franklin Jameson, ed., [*Edward*] *Johnson's Wonder-Working Providence, 1628–1651* (New York: Charles Scribner's Sons, 1910), p. 58; Henry A. Gemery, "Emigration from the British Isles to the New World, 1630–1700: Inferences from Colonial Populations," *Research in Economic History* 5 (1980): 180, 197–98, 212.

the simultaneous outpouring of Englishmen to other New World colonies, was a voluntary exodus of families and included relatively few indentured servants. The movement, which began around 1630, effectively ceased a dozen years later with the outbreak of the English Civil War, further distinguishing it from the more extended period of emigration to other colonies.

These two factors—the emigrants' voluntary departure and the movement's short duration—suggest that the Great Migration resulted from a common, reasoned response to a highly specific set of circumstances. Such circumstances must have been compelling indeed to dislodge a man like John Bent from a comfortable niche in his community. And while Bent and his fellows could not have known it, their reasons for embarking for New England would not only change their own lives but also powerfully shape the society they would create in their new home.

I

Although modern commentators have disagreed over why New England's settlers left the mother country, none of the original chroniclers ever suggested that motivation was an open question. Edward Johnson, for example, knew exactly why the Great Migration occurred. The author of *The Wonder-Working Providence of Sion's Saviour in New England*, who first sailed to Massachusetts in 1630, announced that he and his fellow emigrants left England to escape the evils generated by "the multitude of irreligious lascivious and popish affected persons" who had spread "like Grashoppers" throughout the land. As England strayed from the paths of righteousness, the Lord had sought to preserve a saving remnant of His church by transferring it to an untainted refuge. Johnson adopted a military metaphor to describe the process: the decision to emigrate constituted a voluntary enlistment in Christ's Army, the instrument with which He would "create a new Heaven, and a new Earth in, new Churches, and a new Commonwealth together." [3] Other writers concurred with Johnson's providentialist interpretation. Nathaniel Morton and William Hubbard, both of whom emigrated as children, likewise believed the founding of Massachusetts to be the centerpiece of a divine plan to preserve the Gospel and proper forms of worship.[4] The most emphatic explication of the settlers' religious motivation, however, came not from a participant in the Great Migration but from a descendant of emigrants. Cotton Mather never doubted that the Lord "carried some Thousands of *Re-*

---

[3] *Johnson's Wonder-Working Providence*, pp. 23, 25.
[4] Nathaniel Morton, *New-Englands Memoriall* (originally published 1669, facsimile ed., Boston: Club of Odd Volumes, 1903), p. 83; Rev. William Hubbard, *A General History of New England, from the Discovery to MDCLXXX*, 2d ed. (Boston, 1680), reprinted in *Massachusetts Historical Society Collections*, 2d ser. 5 (1848): 109.

formers into the Retirements of an *American Desart,* on purpose," that
"He might there, *To* them first, and then *By* them, give a *Specimen* of
many Good Things, which He would have His Churches elsewhere
aspire and arise unto." [5]

Few modern scholars have shared the steadfast conviction of Mather
and his predecessors, but it was not until 1921 that the emigrants' religious motivation was seriously questioned. In that year, James Truslow
Adams suggested that most New England settlers—if not their leaders—emigrated "for the simple reason that they wanted to better their
condition." By leaving England, colonists escaped "the growing and
incalculable exactions of government" while at the same time they enjoyed unprecedented opportunities for freeholdership. Adams felt
compelled to discount the colonists' religious motivation because so
few became members of New England churches. His thesis soon provoked a spirited response from Samuel Eliot Morison, who questioned
Adams's statistics on church membership and pointed out that conversion was no easy process. An excess of piety, rather than a lack of it,
might as readily dissuade individuals from claiming fellowship with a
church's "visible saints." [6]

For some time the work of Adams and Morison defined the terms of
the historical debate as other scholars weighed in with arguments supporting either economics or religion as the principal force propelling
Englishmen from the Old World to the New.[7] More recent writers,
however, have woven a more complex web of causality. In his extensive
discussion of the background of the emigration from East Anglia,
N. C. P. Tyack concluded that economic, religious, and political factors all influenced individual decisions to move.[8] Timothy Breen,
Stephen Foster, and David Grayson Allen have likewise suggested that
the time has come to cease attempting to "separate the historically inseparable" and to begin examining the interrelationships of various
motives. It is quite possible, they have argued, that the emigrants
themselves would not have been able to distinguish among a variety of

[5] Cotton Mather, *Magnalia Christi Americana* (1702), ed. Kenneth B. Murdock, books
I and II (Cambridge: Harvard University Press, 1977), p. 93.

[6] James Truslow Adams, *The Founding of New England* (Boston: Atlantic Monthly
Press, 1921), pp. 121–22; Samuel Eliot Morison, *Builders of the Bay Colony* (Boston:
Houghton Mifflin Co., 1930; pbk. ed., 1958), pp. 379–86.

[7] See, e.g., Charles E. Banks, "Religious 'Persecution' as a Factor in Emigration to
New England, 1630–1640," *Massachusetts Historical Society Proceedings* 43 (1930): 136–51,
with a comment by Samuel Eliot Morison on pp. 151–54; Nellis M. Crouse, "Causes of
the Great Migration, 1630–1640," *New England Quarterly* 5 (1932): 3–36.

[8] N. C. P. Tyack, "Migration from East Anglia to New England before 1660" (Ph.D.
diss., University of London, 1951). In a recent article, Tyack argues that religion may
well have been the primary cause of the emigration of the "humbler folk" from one English region; see his "The Humbler Puritans of East Anglia and the New England
Movement: Evidence from the Court Records of the 1630s," *NEHGR* 138 (1984):
79–106.

highly localized factors—such as economic distress, religious persecution, the exhortations of a charismatic Puritan leader, or even an outbreak of the plague—and choose the single reason that convinced
them to leave their homes.[9]

These scholars have applied a much-needed corrective to what had
become a rather stale debate by reminding us that deciding to emigrate was a complicated and highly individualistic affair. But their conclusions are, in the end, disappointing, for they suggest that we must
accept the notion that the motives for emigration were so complex as
to be irrecoverable. If we examine more closely the lives of the emigrants themselves, we may yet find clues that reveal a common incentive underlying the Great Migration.

In seeking to identify emigrants and explore their motives for moving, historians have received invaluable assistance from none other
than Charles I. Not long after the exodus to Massachusetts began, the
king and his archbishop of Canterbury became increasingly concerned
about the departure of so many English folk for wilderness homes
across the seas. On 21 July 1635, in an attempt to keep track of the
movement, Charles I issued a proclamation requiring all those who
wished to leave the realm to obtain a special license from the Privy
Council. Customs officers were instructed to obtain certain information from prospective emigrants aboard each ship, including name,
residence, occupation, age, and destination.[10] Although the royal edict
was loosely enforced and the passage of more than three centuries has
inevitably reduced the amount of extant information, several of these
ship passenger lists do survive, and they provide a unique opportunity
to examine the lives of ordinary emigrants.

Seven ship passenger lists, which together include the names of 693
colonists, provide the information upon which this essay is based.
These appear to be the only lists that have been published in their en-
tirety from surviving documents.[11] All the lists contain the names of

[9] T. H. Breen and Stephen Foster, "Moving to the New World: The Character of
Early Massachusetts Immigration," *William and Mary Quarterly*, 3d ser., 30 (1973):
189–220; David Grayson Allen, *In English Ways: The Movement of Societies and the Transferal of English Local Law and Custom to Massachusetts Bay in the Seventeenth Century*
(Chapel Hill: University of North Carolina Press, 1981), pp. 163–204.

[10] Charles Boardman Jewson, ed., *Transcript of Three Registers of Passengers from Great
Yarmouth to Holland and New England*, Norfolk Record Society Publications 25 (1954): 6–7.
See also Ann N. Hansen, "Ships of the Puritan Migration to Massachusetts Bay," *Ameri-
can Neptune* 23 (1963): 62–66.

[11] All of the lists used here, along with many others, appear in Charles Edward Banks,
The Planters of the Commonwealth (Boston: Houghton Mifflin Co., 1930). Banks's work,
however, is not particularly reliable because he usually reordered the lists and often
omitted certain information, such as servant status or birthplace, mixed up family or
household groups, or added persons whom he thought belonged to a particular ship
even though the names were not listed. I have chosen, therefore, to obtain lists from the
following sources:

The *Hercules* (Sandwich, 1635) and a Sandwich ship of 1637: Eben Putnam, "Two

emigrants; most also include occupation (for adult males), residence, age, and evidence of family structure. In other words, each list provides sufficiently specific information to permit accurate tracing of individual passengers in the New World. The lists themselves, of course, can only tell us about the emigrants at one moment in time, the date of registration for the voyage, but an astonishingly large amount of additional information can be found in genealogies and local histories. Using these materials, it has been possible to reconstruct the New England careers of 578 emigrants, or 83.4 percent of those included on the lists.

Since no comprehensive record of the total emigrant population exists, one cannot determine the "representativeness" of these seven lists. Certain evidence, however, does suggest their reliability. According to John Winthrop's record of arriving ships, the three busiest years of the migration were 1634, 1635, and 1638; four of the emigrant groups examined here arrived in those years.[12] Both Winthrop's account and the research of Charles E. Banks, one of New England's most productive genealogists, indicate that most ships sailed from ports in southern and eastern England. The ships included here also came from this general area: two each sailed from Great Yarmouth in Norfolk, Sandwich in Kent, and Southampton in Hampshire, while the other left from Weymouth in Dorset. In addition, although information on numbers of passengers is incomplete, it seems that these ships, which carried between 75 and 119 emigrants, were typical. Winthrop noted the arrivals of 47 ships carrying between 80 and 150 people, with an average of about 110 passengers. In numbers of passengers, as well as in ports of origin and timing of departure, then, the ships examined here do reflect the patterns established by other sources.

Early Passenger Lists, 1635–1637," *NEHGR* 75 (1921): 217–27, with corrections by Elizabeth French Bartlett in *NEHGR* 79 (1925): 107–9.

Weymouth ship, 1635: William S. Appleton, "More Passengers for New-England," *NEHGR* 25 (1871): 13–15.

The *James* (Southampton, 1635): Louise Brownell Clarke, *The Greenes of Rhode Island, with Historical Records of English Ancestry, 1534–1902* (New York: Knickerbocker Press, 1903), pp. 768–69.

The *Rose* and the *Mary Anne* (Great Yarmouth, 1637): *Transcript of Three Registers*, pp. 21–23, 29–30.

The *Confidence* (Southampton, 1638): see n. 1.

The two Yarmouth lists and the Sandwich list of 1637 were examined by Breen and Foster in "Moving to the New World," pp. 189–220. All seven ships sailed to Massachusetts Bay; although the exact ports of arrival are not known, Salem or Boston are likeliest.

[12] Of 106 ships mentioned by Winthrop, 27 came in 1634, 21 in 1638, and 17 in 1635; see John Winthrop, *The History of New England from 1630 to 1649*, ed. James Savage, 2 vols. (Boston, 1825), vol. 1, passim. The other three ships in this study sailed in 1637. Because Winthrop's record of arrivals was not systematic, 1637 may have been either a year of lighter traffic or simply one of lighter documentation.

Evidence from these lists suggests that although few emigrants left explicit records of their reasons for moving, the motives of the majority need not remain a mystery. Analyzing the lists in light of supporting genealogical materials enables us to construct a social profile of the emigrants, which can then be compared with that of the English population at large. This comparison in turn suggests that once we know who the emigrants were we can begin to understand why they came.

II

The New England settlers more closely resembled the nonmigrating English population than they did other English colonists in the New World. The implications of this fact for the development of colonial societies can scarcely be overstated. While the composition of the emigrant populations in the Chesapeake and the Caribbean hindered the successful transfer of familiar patterns of social relationships, the character of the New England colonial population ensured it. The prospect of colonizing distant lands stirred the imaginations of young people all over England but most of these young adults made their way to the tobacco and sugar plantations of the South. Nearly half of a sample of Virginia residents in 1625 were between the ages of twenty and twenty-nine, and groups of emigrants to the Chesapeake in the seventeenth century consistently included a majority of people in their twenties.[13] In contrast, only a quarter of the New England settlers belonged to this age group (table 1).[14]

The age structure of New England's emigrant population virtually mirrored that of the country they had left (table 2). Both infancy and old age were represented: the *Rose* of Great Yarmouth carried one-year-old Thomas Baker as well as Katherine Rabey, a widow of sixty-eight. The proportion of people over the age of sixty was, not surprisingly, somewhat higher in the general English population than among the emigrants. Although Thomas Welde reported in 1632 that he traveled with "very aged" passengers, "twelve persons being all able to make well nigh one thousand years," a transatlantic voyage of three months' duration was an ordeal not easily undertaken, and the hard-

---

[13] James Horn, "Servant Emigration to the Chesapeake in the Seventeenth Century," in *The Chesapeake in the Seventeenth Century: Essays on Anglo-American Society and Politics*, ed. Thad W. Tate and David L. Ammerman (New York: W. W. Norton & Co., 1979), pp. 61–62; Edmund S. Morgan, *American Slavery, American Freedom: The Ordeal of Colonial Virginia* (New York: W. W. Norton & Co., 1975), p. 408. See also Richard S. Dunn, *Sugar and Slaves: The Rise of the Planter Class in the English West Indies, 1624–1713* (Chapel Hill: University of North Carolina Press, 1972), p. 53.

[14] All the aggregate information is derived from a computer-aided analysis (using the Statistical Package for the Social Sciences) of 693 emigrants. Although some information was available for nearly every emigrant, the mix of data varied for each individual; therefore, the totals will vary in different tables. The coverage for some major variables is as follows: sex, 97.9% (679/693); age at migration, 59.6% (413/693); English town or parish of residence, 85.1% (590/693); occupation [for adult males], 77.7% (139/179).

	TABLE 1	*Distribution of Ages of of New England Emigrants*

AGE (IN YEARS)	N	%
0–10	98	23.7
11–20	102	24.7
21–30	102	24.7
31–40	71	17.2
41–50	29	7.0
51–60	10	2.5
61–70	1	0.2
Total	413	100.0

TABLE 2 — *Age Structure of the Emigrant Population and England's Population in 1636*

AGE (IN YEARS)	New England emigrants		English population, 1636
	N	%	%
0–4	48	11.62	12.40
5–14	81	19.61	19.73
15–24	108	26.15	17.72
25–59	172	41.65	42.03
60+	4	00.97	08.12
Total	413	100.00	100.00

Source: For English figures, see table A3.1, Wrigley and Schofield, *Population History of England*, p. 528.

ships involved in settling the wilderness surely daunted prospective emigrants of advanced years.[15] On the whole, however, New England attracted people of all ages and thus preserved a normal pattern of intergenerational contact.

Similarly, the sex ratio of the New England emigrant group resembled that of England's population. If women were as scarce in the Chesapeake as good English beer, they were comparatively abundant in the northern colonies. In the second decade of Virginia's settlement, there were four or five men for each woman; by the end of the century, there were still about three men for every two women.[16] Among the emigrants studied here, however, nearly half were women and girls.

[15] Thomas Welde to his former parishioners at Tarling, June/July 1632, in *Letters from New England: The Massachusetts Bay Colony, 1629–1638*, ed. Everett Emerson (Amherst: University of Massachusetts Press, 1976), p. 95. Welde also mentioned that several other passengers were infants.

[16] Morgan, *American Slavery, American Freedom*, p. 111 n. 16, p. 336. See also Russell R. Menard, "Immigrants and Their Increase: The Process of Population Growth in Early Colonial Maryland," in *Law, Society, and Politics in Early Maryland*, ed. Aubrey C. Land, Lois Green Carr, and Edward C. Papenfuse (Baltimore: Johns Hopkins University Press, 1977), p. 96.

		Sex Ratio for New England Emigrants
TABLE 3		
	N	%
Male	386	56.8
Female	293	43.2
Total	679	100.0

Note: Sex ratio = 132

Such a high proportion of females in the population assured the young men of New England greater success than their southern counterparts in finding spouses (table 3).[17]

These demographic characteristics derive directly from the fact that the migration to New England was primarily a transplantation of families. Fully 87.8 percent (597 out of 680) of the emigrants traveled with relatives of one sort or another (table 4). Nearly three-quarters (498 out of 680) came in nuclear family units, with or without children. Occasionally, single spouses migrated with their children, either to meet a partner already in the New World or to wait for his or her arrival on a later ship. Grandparents comprised a relatively inconspicuous part of the migration, but a few hardy elders did make the trip. In 1637, Margaret Neave sailed to Massachusetts with her granddaughter Rachel Dixson, who was probably an orphan. In the following year, Alice Stephens joined her sons William and John and their families for the voyage to New England. More frequently, emigrant family structure extended horizontally, within a generation, rather than vertically, across three generations. Several groups of brothers made the trip together, and when the three Goodenow brothers decided to leave the West Country, they convinced their unmarried sister Ursula to come with them as well.

Thus, for the majority of these New England settlers, transatlantic migration did not lead to permanent separation from close relatives. Some unscrupulous men and women apparently migrated in order to flee unhappy marriages, but most nuclear family units arrived intact. When close kin were left behind, they usually joined their families within a year or so.[18] Samuel Lincoln, for instance, who traveled

---

[17] The ratio varied somewhat among individual ships. The *Rose* was the only vessel carrying a majority of women (sex ratio = 84), while the *James*, with nearly two men for every woman, had the most unbalanced ratio, 184.

[18] In about 80 percent of the cases for which there is information (61 of 77), nuclear families moving to New England brought all of their members along. Only eight families—about 10 percent—are known for certain to have left members behind in England. Seventeenth-century court records are interspersed with orders for husbands and wives to rejoin their spouses either in England or New England; see, e.g., George Francis Dow, ed., *Records and Files of the Quarterly Courts of Essex County, Massachusetts*, 8 vols. (Salem: Essex Institute, 1911–75), 1:123–24, 137, 159, 160, 166, 208, 228, 229, 231, 244, 245, 274, 275, 306, 360.

TABLE 4

The Structure of Household Groups among New England Emigrants

CATEGORIES	CLASSES	WITHOUT SERVANTS	WITH SERVANTS	TOTAL	%	NO. OF EMIGRANTS IN EACH GROUP	CATEGORY
Solitaries	(a) Widowed	2	0	2		2	
	(b) Single/unknown marital status	56	5	61	38.0	73	11.0%
No family	(a) Co-resident siblings	3	0	3		6	
	(b) Co-resident relatives of other kinds	1	0	1	2.4	2	1.2%
Simple family households	(a) Married couples, alone	4	6	10		36	
	(b) Married couples, with children	32	42	74		462	
	(c) Husband with children	1	3	4	54.8	28	
	(d) Wife with children	0	1	1		8	
	(e) Widow with children	2	0	2		6	79.4%
Extended family households	(a) Extended laterally						
	(1) Brothers	2	1	3		18	
	(2) Other kin	2	0	2		16	
	(b) Combinations						
	(1) Nuclear family and servant's family	0	1	1	4.8	7	8.4%
	(2) Nuclear family with others of unknown relationship	1	0	1		10	
	(3) Brothers and families with mother	0	1	1		6	
Total number of groups:				166	100.0		
Total number of emigrants in all groups:						680	100.0%

Note: This table is modeled on that in Laslett, Family life and illicit love, pp. 96–97.

aboard the *Rose* in 1637, soon joined his brother Thomas, who had settled in Hingham in 1633. Another brother, Stephen, arrived in the following year with both his family and his mother. Edward Johnson, who had first crossed the ocean with the Winthrop fleet in 1630, returned to England in 1637 to fetch his wife and seven children. For Thomas Starr, who left Sandwich in 1637, migration meant a reunion with his older brother Comfort, a passenger on the *Hercules* two years earlier. Although some disruption of kin ties was unavoidable, it was by no means the rule.

The average size of migrating households was 4.07 persons, which again resembled conditions in the mother country; mean household size in a sample of 33 seventeenth-century English parishes was 4.60 persons.[19] The proportion of single people aboard the ships was, however, higher than that in the English population at large, a fact that substantially reduced the mean household size. The four-person mean therefore tends to obscure the fact that fully 20 percent of the emigrants traveled in family groups of six persons and over 10 percent in groups of eight or more (table 5). The "mean experienced household size"—that is, the household size familiar to the average individual— was a considerably larger 6.31 persons.

Further exploration of demographic patterns reveals other subtle but significant differences between the migrating population and that of England. These differences illustrate the important fact that migration was a selective process; not all people were equally suited to or interested in the rigors of New World settlement. Since the movement to New England was a voluntary, self-selective affair, most of this winnowing-out process occurred before the hearths of English homes, as individuals and families discussed whether or not to leave.

Although family groups predominated within the emigrant population, many individuals came to New England on their own.[20] The vast majority of these solitary travelers were male—men outnumbered women by a factor of ten to one—and together they constituted 38 percent of the emigrant households (table 4). This figure stands in sharp contrast to England's population, where only about 5 percent of all households were composed of one individual.[21] About one in six emigrants aged twenty-one to thirty sailed independently, perhaps drawn to New England by hopes of employment or freeholdership.

---

[19] Peter Laslett, "Mean household size in England since the sixteenth century," in *Household and Family in Past Time: Comparative studies in the size and structure of the domestic group over the last three centuries in England, France, Serbia, Japan and colonial North America, with further materials from Western Europe*, ed. Peter Laslett and Richard Wall (Cambridge: Cambridge University Press, 1972), p. 130.

[20] Servants are not included in this category; they are included in the household with which they traveled.

[21] The figure is based on Laslett's calculations for 100 English communities for the period 1574–1821; see table 4.8 in his "Mean household size," p. 146.

TABLE 5

Size of Emigrant Groups Traveling to New England

SIZE OF GROUP	N OF GROUPS	% OF GROUPS	N OF PEOPLE IN GROUPS OF THIS SIZE	% OF PEOPLE IN GROUPS OF THIS SIZE
1	56	33.5	56	8.2
2	13	7.8	26	3.8
3	9	5.4	27	4.0
4	16	9.6	64	9.4
5	18	10.8	90	13.3
6	23	13.8	138	20.3
7	13	7.8	91	13.4
8	7	4.2	56	8.2
9	3	1.8	27	4.0
10	4	2.4	40	5.9
11	1	0.6	11	1.6
12	2	1.2	24	3.5
13	1	0.6	13	1.9
16	1	0.6	16	2.4
Total	167	100.1	679	99.9

These men were hardly freewheeling adventurers; instead, they provided the new settlements with skilled labor. The unaccompanied travelers included shoemakers, a carpenter, butcher, tanner, hempdresser, weaver, cutler, physician, fuller, tailor, mercer, and skinner. Some were already married at the time of the voyage, and those who were single seldom remained so for more than a couple of years after their arrival. Through marriage, the men became members of family networks within their communities. Within a few years of his arrival in 1635, for instance, Henry Ewell, a young shoemaker from Sandwich in Kent, joined the church in Scituate and married the daughter of a prominent local family. William Paddy, a London skinner, managed to obtain land, find a wife, and get elected to Plymouth's first general court of deputies within four years of his voyage.[22]

Analysis of the composition of migrating families reveals other important differences between the colonizing population and that of England. Children were a less ubiquitous component of emigrating household groups than they were in the general English population.

[22] For Henry Ewell, see James Savage, *A Genealogical Dictionary of the First Settlers of New England, Showing Three Generations of Those Who Came before May, 1692, . . .* , 4 vols. (Boston, 1860–62), 2:132; C. F. Swift, *Genealogical Notes of Barnstable Families, Being a Reprint of the Amos Otis Papers, Originally Published in the Barnstable Patriot*, 2 vols. (Barnstable, Mass., 1888), 1:359. For William Paddy, see Savage, *Genealogical Dictionary*, 3:328–29; Charles Henry Pope, *The Pioneers of Massachusetts, A Descriptive List, Drawn From Records of Colonies, Towns, and Churches, and Other Contemporary Documents* (Boston: the author, 1900), p. 338.

			Distribution of Households in		
TABLE 6			*England and New England*		

| No. of children | *Groups with this number of children* | | *Number of children in groups of this size* | | |
| | New England | | New England | | Sample of 100 English parishes |
	N	%	N	%	%
1	14	16.1	14	5.2	11.2
2	25	28.7	50	18.7	18.4
3	17	19.5	51	19.0	23.1
4	13	14.9	52	19.4	18.1
5	12	13.8	60	22.4	13.4
6	2	2.3	12	4.5	7.7
7+	4	4.7	29	10.8	7.2
Total	87	100.0	268	100.0	99.1

Source: For English figures, see Laslett, "Mean household size," p. 148.

Between 1574 and 1821, for example, it seems that not less than three-quarters of English households included children. For the New England emigrants at the time of their departure, the figure was just over half of all households (90 of 166). Yet 90 out of 99 emigrating *families* had children, and within these families, children were a conspicuous presence indeed. Most emigrant families that had children had three or more (table 6). The average number of children per family was 3.08, compared to an average of 2.76 for a sample of 100 English communities.[23] Emigrating children did not suffer for lack of playmates aboard ship or in the New World; over half of them came in groups including four or more children.

New England clearly attracted a special group of families. The average age of emigrant husbands was 37.4 years (N = 81); for their wives the average was 33.8 (N = 55). The westward-bound ships carried couples who were mature, who had probably been married for nearly a decade, and who had established themselves firmly within their communities. The typical migrating family was complete—composed of husband, wife, and three or four children—but was not yet completed. They were families in process, with parents who were at most halfway through their reproductive cycle and who would continue to produce children in New England. They would be responsible for the rapid population growth that New England experienced in its first decades of settlement. Moreover, the numerous children who emigrated with their parents contributed their efforts to a primitive economy sorely lacking in labor.

[23] Figures for English households are from Laslett, "Mean household size," p. 148.

The task of transforming wilderness into farmland, however, demanded more labor than parents and their children alone could supply, and more than half of the emigrating families responded to this challenge by bringing servants with them to the New World (table 4). Perhaps some had read William Wood's advice in *New England's Prospect* and learned that "men of good estates may do well there, always provided that they go well accommodated with servants." In any case, servants formed an integral part, just over 17 percent, of the colonizing population and in fact were at first somewhat more commonplace in New England than in England.[24] Most were males (80 of 114) and labored alongside their masters, clearing land, planting corn, and building houses and barns. Their presence substantially increased the ratio of producers to consumers in the newly settled towns.[25]

Household heads, however, knew that servants might easily become a drain on family resources in the critical early months of settlement. Their passages had to be paid and food and shelter provided at a time when those commodities were at a premium. Hence, when arranging for a suitable labor supply, masters heeded the advice of writers like William Wood, who emphasized that emigrants should not take too many servants and should choose men and women of good character. "It is not the multiplicity of many bad servants (which presently eats a man out of house and harbor, as lamentable experience hath made manifest)," he warned, "but the industry of the faithful and diligent laborer that enricheth the careful master; so that he that hath many dronish servants shall soon be poor and he that hath an industrious family shall as soon be rich."[26] Most families attempted to strike a balance between their need for labor and available resources by transporting

[24] William Wood, *New England's Prospect*, ed. Alden T. Vaughan (Amherst: University of Massachusetts Press, 1977), p. 70; Laslett, "Mean household size," p. 152. Ann Kussmaul, in examining the prevalence of servants in husbandry (not domestic servants) found that they comprised 1 to 13 percent of the population in a sample of six seventeenth-century parishes; see her *Servants in Husbandry in Early Modern England* (Cambridge: Cambridge University Press, 1981), p. 12. Peter Laslett calculated that in Clayworth in 1676, servants were present in 31 percent of the households, and comprised 16.7 percent of the parish's population, see Peter Laslett, *Family life and illicit love in earlier generations* (Cambridge: Cambridge University Press, 1977), p. 90. Since the vast majority of New England servants were male, Kussmaul's figures may provide the more relevant comparison here, that comparison indicates that servants in early New England may have been up to twice as common as in England.

[25] Wrigley and Schofield calculated the "dependency ratio" for England over five-year intervals for the period from 1541 to 1871. This ratio measures the numbers of persons aged 0 to 14 years and over 60 years—presumably those too young or too old to provide much productive labor—as a proportion of every 1,000 persons in the general population. In England in 1636, the dependency ratio was 674 per 1,000; among the New England emigrants studied here, the comparable figure was a considerably lower 475 per 1,000. See E. A. Wrigley and R. S. Schofield, *The Population History of England, 1541–1871: A Reconstruction* (Cambridge: Harvard University Press, 1981), p. 528.

[26] Wood, *New England's Prospect*, pp. 70–71.

Figure 1 English Origins of Passengers on Seven Ships to Massachusetts, 1635–1638

The numbers of passengers from each county (and London) are as follows—Berkshire: 6, Dorset: 18, Hampshire: 54, Kent: 182, London: 3, Middlesex: 1, Norfolk: 152, Oxford: 20, Somerset: 33, Suffolk: 36, Wiltshire: 86, Worcestershire: 1. English residences were unknown for 101 passengers. After a map of Richard Stinely in David Grayson Allen, *In English Ways: The Movement of Societies and the Tranferal of English Local Law and Custom to Massachusetts Bay in the Seventeenth Century* (Chapel Hill: University of North Carolina Press, 1981), p. 17. Published for the Institute of Early American History and Culture. Used with permission.

only a few servants. Nearly half of the families brought just one and another quarter of them brought only two.

III

Before departing for New England, the emigrants had called a wide variety of English towns and villages their homes (see fig. 1). Most lived in the lowland area of England, a region that extends south and east of a line drawn diagonally from Teesmouth in the northeast to the port of Weymouth on the Dorset coast. The lowlands in general enjoyed a more even topography, drier climate, and richer soil than did the highlands to the north and supported the bulk of the country's population.[27] Within this expanse of southeastern England, those who chose to emigrate had known many different forms of social organization, agricultural practice, industrial development, and local government. At one end of the spectrum, Parnell Harris, William Paddy, and Edmund Hawes all left the burgeoning metropolis of London, which was about to overtake Paris as the largest city of Europe; at the other, the widow Emme Mason left the tiny Kentish parish of Eastwell, which was "not more than a mile across each way," and whose church in 1640 counted just 55 communicants.[28]

A relatively large proportion of the New England settlers dwelled in urban areas prior to their emigration. In addition to London, substantial towns such as Norwich in Norfolk, Canterbury in Kent, and Salisbury in Wiltshire were residences for scores of prospective colonists. In the mid-seventeenth century, only about one out of five Englishmen was a town-dweller, whereas at least one of three emigrants had lived in a community with three thousand or more inhabitants. Fully 60 percent of the future New Englanders came from market towns. Although these communities were not "urban" on the same scale as a large provincial capital like Norwich or Canterbury, they differed qualitatively from their neighboring communities. Each served as a focus for networks of trade and distribution, and often for the social life, of its surrounding region.[29]

[27] Joan Thirsk, "The Farming Regions of England," in *The Agrarian History of England and Wales*, vol. 4, 1500–1640, ed. Joan Thirsk (Cambridge: Cambridge University Press, 1967), pp. 2–15.

[28] E. A. Wrigley, "A Simple Model of London's Importance in Changing English Society and Economy, 1650–1750," *Past and Present* 37 (1967): 44; Edward Hasted, *The History and Topographical Survey of the County of Kent*, 2d ed., 12 vols. (Canterbury, 1797–1801), 7:399, 411. For the most recent discussion of the diversity of New Englanders' origins, see Allen, *In English Ways*; see also Powell, *Puritan Village*.

[29] Two hundred emigrants, out of 590 with known English residences, came from the seven towns of Canterbury, Dover, Great Yarmouth, London, Maidstone, Norwich, and Salisbury. Population figures for these towns are in John Patten, *English Towns, 1500–1700* (Folkestone: Dawson, 1978), pp. 106, 111–12, 251; Wrigley, "A Simple Model," p. 44; C. W. Chalklin, *Seventeenth-Century Kent: A Social and Economic History* (London: Longmans, 1965), pp. 30–31. For market towns, see Alan Everitt, "The Marketing of Agricultural Produce," in *Agrarian History*, 4:470–75, 488–90.

New England would never offer its first generation of settlers anything approaching the bustle and complexity of the urban centers they
had abandoned. But large towns best furnished prospective emigrants
like the locksmith William Ludkin or the cutler Edmund Hawes with
markets for their specialized skills. Emigrants involved in trade resided
in sizable towns like Norwich, Romsey, or Sandwich, which provided
access to important commercial networks. Likewise, prospective settlers who made their livings in the cloth industry frequently depended
on the manufacturing and marketing amenities of large towns such as
Norwich, Salisbury, Canterbury, and Sandwich. Weavers from these
towns acquired yarn from local spinners, produced a multitude of different fabrics, and often sold them as well.[30]

Town life also equipped future emigrants with complex and region-
ally distinctive experiences of local government. Most incorporated
boroughs were run by an annually elected mayor, but the numbers and
duties of subsidiary officeholders varied widely.[31] Admission to a
town's body of freemen—which often brought enfranchisement and eligibility for officeholding—was based on different criteria in different
places. In Norwich, Nicholas Busby and William Nickerson probably
achieved freeman status by completing seven-year apprenticeships and
proving competence in their craft as weavers. Henry Bachelor and
Nathaniel Ovell, two emigrants from Dover, however, would have had
to demonstrate that their lands were worth at least five pounds a
year.[32] Electoral practices also varied. In Reading, home of the emigrant Augustine Clement, the town's aldermen selected the mayor; in
Salisbury, the mayor was chosen by the common council. In Norwich,
freemen voted in both municipal and parliamentary contests.[33] Each

---

[30] K. J. Allison, "The Norfolk Worsted Industry in the Sixteenth and Seventeenth
Centuries [Part I]," *Yorkshire Bulletin of Economic and Social Research* 12 (1960): 73–78;
G. D. Ramsay, *The Wiltshire Woollen Industry in the Sixteenth and Seventeenth Centuries*, 2d
ed. (London: Oxford University Press, 1965), pp. 2–19; Chalklin, *Seventeenth-Century
Kent*, pp. 123–26.

[31] In addition to a mayor, Dover had 12 *jurats* and a 36-member common council.
Southampton had 9 justices, a sheriff, 2 bailiffs, and 24 common councilmen, plus an
equal number of burgesses, while Newbury had a high steward, a recorder, 6 aldermen,
and 24 capital burgesses, and Canterbury had a recorder, 12 aldermen, and 24 common
councilmen. See Rev. John Lyon, *The History of the Town and Port of Dover, and of Dover
Castle; with a Short Account of the Cinque Ports*, 2 vols. (Dover, 1813–14), 1:218; Richard
Warner, *Collections for the History of Hampshire, and the Bishopric of Winchester . . .* , 5
vols. (London, 1795), 1:179; anon., *The History and Antiquities of Newbury and Its Environs, Including Twenty-Eight Parishes, Situate in the County of Berks . . .* (Speenhamland,
1839), p. 129; Hasted, *History and Topographical Survey . . . of Kent*, 11:28.

[32] Both Busby and Nickerson were freemen, whether Bachelor and Ovell were also is
unknown. See Jewson, *Transcript of Three Registers*, pp. 21–22; John Evans, *Seventeenth-
Century Norwich: Politics, Religion, and Government, 1620–1690* (Oxford: Clarendon Press,
1979), p. 8; Lyon, *History of the Town and Port of Dover*, 1:22.

[33] Rev. Charles Coates, *The History and Antiquities of Reading* (London, 1802), p. 65;
Mary E. Ransome, "City Government, 1612–1835," in *A History of Wiltshire*, ed. R. B.

borough had its own distinct political calendar regulating its citizens' participation in local affairs, often in accordance with liturgical cycles inherited from pre-Reformation days. Mayors were chosen on the Feast of the Nativity of Our Lady (2 February) in Dover, on the first of May in Norwich, on St. Matthew's Day (21 September) in Newbury, All Souls' (2 November) in Maidstone, and on the Monday after St. Andrew's Day (30 November) in Sandwich.[34]

In addition, seventeenth-century English towns, especially the larger ones, often encompassed a multiplicity of civil and ecclesiastical jurisdictions. If Edmund Batter, Michael Shafflin, or any of the other emigrants from Salisbury lived in the cathedral close, their neighborhood was administered by the diocesan dean and chapter, who clashed at times with the municipal government.[35] Provincial centers such as Canterbury and Norwich were divided into several parishes; the Kentish city had at least eight in 1640, while the East Anglian capital boasted thirty-four parishes.[36] Moreover, town-dwellers lived in the midst of a more heterogeneous population than did persons who resided in the countryside. Major textile manufacturing centers received an influx of foreign artisans in the late sixteenth and early seventeenth centuries. The newcomers, mainly Dutch and Walloon tradesmen, settled primarily in Kent and East Anglia and helped to revitalize the depressed cloth industry in those areas. Their congregations grew rapidly and often gained important concessions from local authorities—such as permission to worship separately—which helped both to maintain their sense of identity and to impart a more cosmopolitan flavor to the towns in which they lived.[37]

In the countryside, although the contrasts were perhaps less striking, villages also differed significantly from one another. Much of seventeenth-century England was an intricate patchwork of parishes with particular local customs dating from time out of mind. Ancient practice often dictated the shape of the landscape, patterns of settlement,

---

Pugh and Elizabeth Crittall, 12 vols., *The Victoria History of the Counties of England* (London: Oxford University Press, for the University of London Institute of History, 1956–75), 6:105; Evans, *Seventeenth-Century Norwich*, p. 7.

[34] Lyon, *History of the Town and Port of Dover*, 2:267, 287; Evans, *Seventeenth-Century Norwich*, p. 57; *History and Antiquities of Newbury*, p. 129; William Newton, *The History and Antiquities of Maidstone, the County-Town of Kent* (London, 1741), p. 27.

[35] Paul Slack, "Poverty and Politics in Salisbury, 1597–1666," in *Crisis and Order in English Towns, 1500–1700: Essays in Urban History*, ed. Peter Clark and Paul Slack (London: Routledge and Kegan Paul, 1972), pp. 187–88.

[36] Hasted, *History and Topographical Survey . . . of Kent*, 11:214–86. Breen and Foster, "Moving to the New World," p. 199 n. 27.

[37] K. J. Allison, "The Norfolk Worsted Industry in the Sixteenth and Seventeenth Centuries [Part 2]," *Yorkshire Bulletin of Economic and Social Research* 13 (1961): 61–69; Dorothy Gardiner, *Historic Haven: The Story of Sandwich* (Derby: Pilgrim Press, 1954), pp. 182–85; Chalklin, *Seventeenth-Century Kent*, pp. 123–24.

modes of landholding, and rituals of agrarian activity. Even within a single county, substantial variation was evident. The emigrant Nathaniel Tilden's home in Tenterden lay in the densely wooded Wealden region of southern Kent, where most of the land was devoted to pasture. He probably spent much of his time tending cattle and perhaps a few sheep and pigs. Many Wealden farms contained dairy houses and cheese chambers; Lydia Tilden and her daughters may have supplemented the family's diet and income by converting some of their herd's milk into cheese and butter. In addition, the Tildens and their servants, like other Wealden farmers, probably cultivated a dozen or so acres of wheat, oats, and peas for domestic use. Since mixed farming of this sort left farmers and their families with spare time at certain periods of the year, some Tildens may have turned to by-employments, like spinning for local cloth producers, to keep themselves busy and to earn a few shillings during the slack months.[38]

Thomas Call and his family, who sailed to New England in 1637, lived only twenty-odd miles north of the Tildens, but their agricultural routine would have been quite different. The Calls lived in Faversham, a village of about a thousand inhabitants located in the northern part of the county near the coast. Here, unlike the region around Tenterden, the country was "a fine extended level, the fields of a considerable size, and most unincumbered with trees or hedgerows."[39] Because of its fertile soil and easy access by water to London, north Kent had become an important supplier of the city's food. Thomas Call's neighbors concentrated on the production of wheat and, to a lesser extent, barley. Much of the grain harvested from their fields was shipped either to the metropolis or, if of lower quality, sent along the coast to other parts of the country. In addition, Call probably grew a crop of beans or peas as fodder for his animals. Since north Kentish farms tended to be larger than those in the Weald, Call was likely to have owned more land than Nathaniel Tilden did in Tenterden. Perhaps he used some of his acreage to plant an orchard; by the middle of the seventeenth century, farmers in his neighborhood had begun to produce large quantities of cherries for market.[40]

Agricultural diversity likewise prevailed in the county of Norfolk, where Henry and Elizabeth Smith of New Buckenham lived with their two sons. Norfolk's wood pasture region, like the Kentish Weald, supported a considerable population of small farmers engaged in stock

[38] Thirsk, "Farming Regions of England," pp. 57–59; Chalklin, *Seventeenth-Century Kent,* pp. 75–82.

[39] Hasted, *History and Topographical Survey . . . of Kent,* 6:319.

[40] F. J. Fisher, "The Development of the London Food Market, 1540–1640," in *Essays in Economic History,* ed. E. M. Carus-Wilson, 3 vols. (London: E. Arnold, 1954–62), 1:136, 138–42; Chalklin, *Seventeenth-Century Kent,* pp. 74–82, 90; Thirsk, "Farming Regions of England," pp. 56–57, 62.

rearing and dairying. Large hedges marked the boundaries of enclosed fields where cattle grazed and farmers cultivated small plots of barley, wheat, and rye, and perhaps some oats and peas, for household consumption. In these wooded regions in both counties, manorial organization was weak, its function reduced to intermittent financial and legal administration which intruded only sporadically into inhabitants' daily lives. The Smiths, like the Tildens, may also have engaged in byemployments, such as combing wool or weaving flax, during the winter months.

But the Moulton, Page, and Dow families, who emigrated from the small coastal village of Ormsby, knew a different Norfolk. They lived and worked in a district devoted to the twin agricultural pursuits of grain cultivation and sheep rearing. Barley, rye, and wheat were again the main crops but here were grown for market. Sheep provided fertilizer as they were bred and fattened for sale. Manorial structure maintained its hold; inhabitants lived in nucleated villages and often farmed cooperatively in open fields. The lords of the manors, who stood at the apex of society in this sheep-corn region, grazed their flocks on tenants' harvested and fallow fields and dominated the local sheep market. As husbandmen, John Moulton, Robert Page, and Henry Dow may not have owned any sheep themselves but might have preferred instead to leave that enterprise to the local gentry while they concentrated on planting cereals. Although arable regions did not generally sustain much local industry, northern Norfolk was unusual in that several of its villages supported worsted cloth manufacture. The three Ormsby families who emigrated may well have spun yarn or have woven fabric in addition to farming.[41]

Other rural routines regulated the lives of emigrants from southwestern counties. Peter Noyes and John Bent followed ancient custom when they returned their lands to the lord of the manor in the openfield parish of Penton in Hampshire before embarking for New England. Property-holding in this grain-growing and sheep-rearing downland enmeshed farmers in a network of feudal dues and practices.[42] Dorsetshire farmers such as Edmund and William Kerley labored in a pastoral region of dairying and pig raising dominated by the local manor, while across the border in southern Wiltshire, Edmund and John Goodenow farmed in another commonfield district devoted to sheep-and-corn husbandry. To the west, Robert and Joan Martin worked in Batcombe, Somerset, a small village where the "lands are all enclosed, but not crouded with wood; and there is a

---

[41] Thirsk, "Farming Regions of England," pp. 46–49, 42–46; K. J. Allison, "The Sheep-Corn Husbandry of Norfolk in the Sixteenth and Seventeenth Centuries," *Agricultural History Review* 5 (1957): 12–30.

[42] Powell, *Puritan Village*, pp. 3, 7–10.

greater proportion of pasture than tillage." [43] In the migration to New England, then, not only would villagers and townsfolk intermingle but farmers would also encounter other countrymen with very different experiences of rural life.

IV

The diversity of the emigrants' English backgrounds—and their urban origins in particular—influenced the distribution of their occupations. Virtually the same number of men were engaged in farming and in artisanal trades not involved with cloth manufacture; slightly fewer earned their livings in the textile industry (table 7).[44] Most of the cloth workers emigrated from cities well known for their textile manufacture; half of the fourteen weavers left Norwich, while five of the sixteen tailors had lived in Salisbury. The geographical distribution of the other artisans was more even, yet many also had congregated in urban areas. Ten of the eleven shoemakers came from Norwich, Great Yarmouth, Sandwich, and Marlborough, while the only two joiners had lived in Canterbury and Norwich. Nearly all of the men with highly specialized skills lived in large towns; the locksmith William Ludkin in Norwich, the cutler Edmund Hawes in London, the surgeon John Greene (who appears to have been a physician, not a barber-surgeon) in Salisbury. Artisans, both in the cloth trades and in other pursuits, formed a greater proportion of the emigrant population than tradesmen did in the English population as a whole. In 1696, Gregory King estimated that "freeholders" and "farmers" outnumbered "artizans and handicrafts" by a factor of more than seven to one;

---

[43] Thirsk, "Farming Regions of England," p. 4; Powell, *Puritan Village*, fig. 2; Eric Kerridge, "Agriculture *c.* 1500–*c.* 1793," in the Victoria *History of Wiltshire*, 4:43–45; quotation from John Collinson, *The History and Antiquities of the County of Somerset . . .*, 3 vols. (Bath, 1791), 3:466; Thomas G. Barnes, *Somerset 1625–1640: A County's Government During the "Personal Rule"* (Cambridge, Mass.: Harvard University Press, 1961), p. 4.

[44] In the category "agriculture" (33.8% of the total of men with listed occupations), I have included 30 husbandmen, 5 yeomen, 6 laborers, and 6 men called "husbandmen or laborers," a dual label retained in the coding. "Cloth trades" includes 1 clothier, 14 weavers, 16 tailors, 2 mercers, a calenderer, and a fuller (25.2%). "Other artisans" consists of 1 hempdresser, 13 shoemakers, 2 tanners, 1 skinner, 12 carpenters, 1 sawyer, 3 joiners, 3 coopers, 1 "moulter," 2 butchers, a brewer, a painter, a cutler, 2 ropers, a chandler, and a locksmith (33.1%). "Trade" includes 2 merchants and a grocer (2.2%); "Maritime" includes 2 mariners and a fisherman (2.2%); and "professional" includes 2 surgeons, 2 ministers, and a schoolmaster (3.6%). This occupational distribution is roughly similar to that obtained by N. C. P. Tyack for 147 East Anglian emigrants. He found 16.3% of his sample in agriculture, 23.1% in cloth trades, 26.5% in other artisanal trades, 3.4% each in trade and maritime occupations, and 27.2% in the professions. This last figure includes a large number of ministers leaving East Anglia in the early 1630s. See Tyack, "Migration from East Anglia," appendix 3.

TABLE 7	*Occupational Distribution of Adult Male Emigrants*	
CATEGORY	*N*	%
Agriculture	47	33.8
Cloth trades	35	25.2
Other artisans	46	33.1
Trade	3	2.2
Maritime	3	2.2
Professional	5	3.6
Total	139	100.1

among the emigrants to New England, however, artisans predominated by a ratio of nearly two to one.[45]

The occupational spectrum of future New Englanders placed them at the more prosperous end of English society. As farmers and artisans, prospective emigrants belonged to that part of the population that—according to Gregory King—"increased the wealth of the kingdom." Yet in striking contrast to Virginia, where, at least initially, the population included "about six times as large a proportion of gentlemen as England had," New England attracted very few members of the upper class.[46] Sir Henry Vane and Sir Richard Saltonstall were unique among the leaders of the migration, and for the most part even they submitted to government by such gentle but untitled figures as John Winthrop and Thomas Dudley. On the whole, emigrants were neither very high nor very low in social and economic status. Husbandmen predominated among the farmers who came to Massachusetts; thirty of them emigrated compared to just five yeomen.[47] By the seventeenth century, the legal distinctions between the status of yeoman and that of husbandman had largely eroded and evidence indicates that the labels generally denoted relative position on the economic and social ladder. Both groups primarily made their livings from the land, but yeomen were generally better off. New England, however, was peopled by less affluent—but not necessarily poor—husbandmen.[48]

[45] Charles Wilson, *England's Apprenticeship, 1603–1763* (London: Longmans, 1965), p. 239.

[46] Wilson, *England's Apprenticeship*, p. 239; Morgan, *American Slavery, American Freedom*, p. 84.

[47] Tyack found a similar result: twenty-two husbandmen, one yeoman, and one "farmer"; see "Migration from East Anglia," pp. 54–56, and appendix 3, vi–via.

[48] Mildred Campbell, *The English Yeoman in the Tudor and Early Stuart Age* (New Haven: Yale University Press, 1942), pp. 11–13, 23–33; Gordon Batho, "Noblemen, Gentlemen, and Yeomen," in *Agrarian History*, 4:301–6; Margaret Spufford, *Contrasting Communities: English Villagers in the Sixteenth and Seventeenth Centuries* (Cambridge: Cambridge University Press, 1974), pp. 37–39. Husbandmen could, in fact, be quite

Emigrant clothworkers practiced trades that also placed them on the middle rungs of the economic ladder. Textile manufacturing in the early seventeenth century employed the skills of dozens of different craftsmen, from the shearmen, carders, and combers who prepared wool for spinning to the wealthy clothiers who sold the finished product. But the emigrant clothworkers did not represent the entire spectrum of skills; most were weavers and tailors who made a modest living at their trade. While it is true that, during his impeachment trial, the former bishop of Norwich was accused of harrying some of the city's most important and prosperous tradesmen—including the weavers Nicholas Busby, Francis Lawes, and Michael Metcalf—out of the land, these emigrants' economic status was probably exaggerated.[49] Most urban weavers from Norfolk in this period had goods worth no more than £100, and one out of five did not even own his own loom.[50] Among the non-clothworking artisans, shoemakers and carpenters predominated, and they too worked in trades that would bring comfort, if not riches. All in all, the New England-bound ships transported a population characterized by a greater degree of social homogeneity than existed in the mother country. Despite Winthrop's reminder to his fellow passengers on the *Arbella* that "some must be rich some poor, some highe and eminent in power and dignitie; others meane and in subieccion," New Englanders would discover that the process of migration effectively reduced the distance between the top and the bottom of their social hierarchy.[51]

V

In a letter to England written in 1632, Richard Saltonstall commented on the social origins of New England's inhabitants. "It is strange," he wrote, "the meaner sort of people should be so backward [in migrating], having assurance that they may live plentifully by their neighbors." At the same time, he expressed the hope that more "gentlemen of ability would transplant themselves," for they too might prosper both spiritually and materially in the new land. For young Richard, the

---

well-off. Benjamin Cooper, a husbandman who sailed on the *Mary Anne*, died during the voyage in 1637. An inventory of his estate, recorded in Massachusetts that September, amounted to £1,278.12.00; Probate docket no. 4, Suffolk County Registry of Probate, Boston, Mass.

[49] John Browne, *History of Congregationalism and Memorials of the Churches in Norfolk and Suffolk* (London, 1877), p. 89.

[50] Allison, "Norfolk Worsted Industry [Part I]," pp. 76–77. Lack of suitable records makes it nearly impossible to assess the emigrants' economic positions prior to their voyages; even the few extant tax lists are inaccurate measures of total wealth. See Breen and Foster, "Moving to the New World," pp. 198–99 n. 27.

[51] "A Modell of Christian Charitie," *Winthrop Papers*, 5 vols. (Boston: Massachusetts Historical Society, 1929–47), 2:282.

twenty-one-year-old son of Sir Richard Saltonstall, New England promised much but as yet lacked the proper balance of social groups within its population that would ensure its success. The migration of the "meaner sort" would help lower the cost of labor, while richer emigrants would "supply the want we labor under of men fitted by their estates to bear common burdens." Such wealthy men would invest in the colony's future even as they enhanced their own spiritual welfare by becoming "worthy instruments of propagating the Gospel" to New England's natives.[52]

Saltonstall wrote early in the migration decade, but the succeeding years did little to redress the social imbalance he perceived in Massachusetts. Two years later, William Wood could still write that "none of such great estate went over yet."[53] Throughout the decade of the 1630s, New England continued to attract colonists who were overwhelmingly ordinary. Demographically they presented a mirror image of the society they had left behind, and socially and economically they fairly represented England's relatively prosperous middle class. The question is inescapable: why did so many average English men and women pass beyond the seas to Massachusetts' shores?

Whether or not they have assigned it primary importance, most historians of the period have noted that economic distress in England in the early seventeenth century must have been causally related to the Great Migration. These were years of agricultural and industrial depression, and farmers and weavers were conspicuous passengers on the transatlantic voyages. A closer examination of the connections between economic crisis and the movement to New England, however, indicates that the links were not as close as they have been assumed to be.

Agriculture—especially in the early modern period—was a notoriously risky business. Success depended heavily upon variables beyond human control. A dry summer or an unusually wet season rendered futile the labor of even the most diligent husbandman, and English farmers in the early seventeenth century had to endure more than their share of adversity. While the decade of the 1620s began propitiously, with excellent harvests in 1619 and 1620, the farmers' luck did not hold. The next three years brought one disastrous harvest after another; improvement in 1624 was followed by dearth in 1625. The beginning of the 1630s, especially in the eastern counties, was marked by further distress; in 1630, the mayor of Norwich complained that "scarcity and dearth of corn and other victuals have so increased the number and misery of the poor in this city" that civic taxes had to be boosted to unprecedented heights and the city's stock of grain dwin-

---

[52] Richard Saltonstall to Emmanuel Downing, 4 February 1631/2, in *Letters from New England*, p. 92.
[53] Wood, *New England's Prospect*, p. 68.

dled dangerously. In 1637, a severe drought spawned further hardship.[54]

Although this period of agricultural depression undoubtedly touched the lives of many English families, it did not necessarily compel them to emigrate. The worst sustained period of scarcity occurred in the early 1620s, a decade or so before the Great Migration began; if agrarian distress was a "push" factor, it produced a curiously delayed reaction. Furthermore, annual fluctuations were endemic in early modern agriculture. Englishmen knew from experience that times would eventually improve, even if that day were unpleasantly distant; moreover, they had no reason to suppose that farmers in New England would somehow lead charmed lives, exempt from similar variations in the weather. In addition, dearth was not an unmitigated disaster for families engaged in husbandry: as supplies of grain and other products shrank, prices rose. In 1630, a year with one of the worst harvests in the first half of the seventeenth century, the price of grain was twice what it had been in the more plentiful years of 1619 and 1620. Thus for farmers involved in market agriculture, a bad year, with half the yield of a good one, could still bring the same income.[55] As the Norwich mayor's lament amply demonstrates, the people really hurt in times of scarcity were city-dwellers dependent on the countryside for their food. That urban dwellers left for New England to assure themselves of a steady food supply, however, is highly unlikely. Emigrants would surely have anticipated the primitive state of the region's agriculture; reports of scarcity at Plymouth and the early Massachusetts Bay settlements had quickly filtered back to England. Moreover, emigrating urban artisans certainly understood that, in the New World, responsibility for feeding their families would lie in their own hands—hands more accustomed to the loom or the last than the plow.

The slump in England's textile industry has also been accounted an incentive for emigration. The industry was indeed mired in a severe depression in the early seventeenth century; it is true as well that a quarter of the adult male emigrants were employed in a trade related to cloth manufacture. The weavers Nicholas Busby, Francis Lawes, and Michael Metcalf of Norwich all completed their apprenticeships at a time when the textile trade "like the moon [was] on the want," and the future of Norfolk's preeminent industry was growing dimmer each

---

[54] B. E. Supple, *Commercial Crisis and Change in England, 1600–1642: A Study in the Instability of a Mercantile Economy* (Cambridge: Cambridge University Press, 1959), pp. 55, 57, 101, 110–11; Peter Bowden, "Agricultural Prices, Farm Profits, and Rents," *Agrarian History*, 4:623–32; Tyack, "Migration from East Anglia," pp. 124–37; and "Grain Shortages in 1630–31 and the Measures Taken in Somerset, Derbyshire, Nottinghamshire, and Norwich," in *Seventeenth-Century Economic Documents*, ed. Joan Thirsk and J. P. Cooper (Oxford: Clarendon Press, 1972), pp. 37–38.

[55] Thirsk, *Agrarian History*, vol. 4, Statistical Appendix, table 6, pp. 849–50.

year.[56] Throughout the sixteenth century, the county's traditional worsted manufacture had steadily lost ground in its European markets to a developing continental industry. In southern England and the West Country, broadcloth producers suffered reverses as well. In 1631, the clothiers of Basingstoke, Hampshire—a town about fifteen miles southwest of the home of the emigrant weaver Thomas Smith of Romsey—informed the county's justices that the "poor do daily increase, for there are in the said town 60 householders, whose families do amount to 300 persons and upwards being weavers, spinners, and clothworkers, the most of them being heretofore rated towards the relief of the poor, do now many of them depend upon the alms of the parish" and begged for some kind of relief.[57]

The decline in sales of the white, undressed fabric that had been the mainstay of English clothiers proved to be irreversible. At the same time, however, certain sectors in the textile industry recovered by switching over to the production of "new draperies." These fabrics, lighter in weight and brighter in color than the traditional English product, were made from a coarser—and therefore cheaper—type of wool. They were introduced in England largely by immigrant Dutch and Walloon artisans, who were frequently encouraged by local authorities to take up residence in England. East Anglia and Kent became centers of the revitalized industry; the cities of Norwich, Canterbury, and Sandwich counted scores of these north European "strangers" among their inhabitants. With the end of hostilities between England and Spain in 1604, trade expanded, and the new fabrics found ready markets in the Mediterranean and the Levant. By the mid-seventeenth century, the production of Norwich stuffs—new versions of worsted wool—had "probably raised the prosperity of the industry to an unprecedented level" and brought renewed prosperity to a number of beleaguered artisans as well.[58]

We cannot know whether worsted weavers like Nicholas Busby, William Nickerson, or Francis Lawes adapted to prevailing trends in their trade, but they seem not to have been in serious economic straits at the time they decided to go to Massachusetts. The identification of

---

[56] The quotation is from a parliamentary debate of 1621, in Supple, *Commercial Crisis and Change*, p. 54.

[57] Allison, "Norfolk Worsted Industry [Part I]," pp. 73, 78–80; Chalklin, *Seventeenth-Century Kent*, pp. 121–22; Peter Clark, *English Provincial Society from the Reformation to the Revolution: Religion, Politics, and Society in Kent, 1500–1640* (Hassocks, Sussex: Harvester Press, 1977), p. 356, quotation from "Depression in the Hampshire Cloth Industry, 1631," in *Seventeenth-Century Economic Documents*, pp. 38–39.

[58] Allison, "Norfolk Worsted Industry [Part 2]," pp. 61–77, quotation from p. 77; Supple, *Commercial Crisis and Change*, pp. 136–62; Chalklin, *Seventeenth-Century Kent*, pp. 123–36; Evans, *Seventeenth-Century Norwich*, p. 16; Ramsay, *Wiltshire Woollen Industry*, 2d ed., pp. 65–84, 101–21.

Busby, Lawes, and Michael Metcalf among Norwich's most important tradesmen at Bishop Wren's impeachment trial, even if those claims were somewhat exaggerated, attested to their standing in the community. Busby's service as a *jurat* responsible for checking the quality of worsted wool produced in the city certainly indicated that he had achieved considerable status in his profession. Economic advancement attended professional prominence: before their departure for the New World, Busby and his wife owned a houselot in a prospering parish in the northern part of the city. In the countryside as well, some cloth workers managed to make a good living in hard times. Thomas Payne, a weaver from the village of Wrentham in Suffolk, emigrated to Salem in 1637 but died soon thereafter. His will, written in April 1638, not only listed property recently acquired in Salem, but also mentioned his share in the ship *Mary Anne*, on which he had sailed to Massachusetts. At the time of the departure from Suffolk, then, Payne could not only afford his family's transportation costs but also had funds to invest in the New England enterprise.[59]

Even if evidence did suggest that emigrant weavers were compelled by economic adversity to leave their homeland, Massachusetts would not have been a wise choice of destination if they hoped to continue in their trade. Flight to the Netherlands, a place with a well-developed textile industry, would have been a more rational choice for artisans worried about the fate of their trade in England and anxious to persist in its practice. Massachusetts lacked both the wool supply and the intricate network of auxiliary tradesmen—such as combers, carders, calenderers, fullers, dyers, etc.—upon which England's weavers depended. Several of the emigrants packed up their looms along with their other belongings, but there is little evidence that they were able to earn their livings in Massachusetts solely by weaving.[60]

Arguments linking the Great Migration to economic hardship in England all share an important weakness. Although historians have discovered that many *places* from which emigrants came suffered from agricultural or industrial depression, they have had little success in connecting those unfavorable economic circumstances to the fortunes of individual emigrants. On the contrary, it appears that the families that went to New England had largely avoided the serious setbacks that afflicted many of their countrymen during those years.

[59] Evans, *Seventeenth-Century Norwich*, pp. 18, 21–22; William L. Sachse, ed., *Minutes of the Norwich Court of Mayoralty, Norfolk Record Society Publications* 15 (1942): 68; Anna C. Kingsbury, *A Historical Sketch of Nicholas Busby the Emigrant* (n.p., 1924), pp. 5–8; Nathaniel E. Paine, *Thomas Payne of Salem and His Descendants: The Salem Branch of the Paine Family* (Haverhill, Mass.: Record Publishing Co., 1928), p. 16.

[60] Jewson, *Transcript of Three Registers*, contains lists of East Anglians heading for Holland. Most appear to have been going for short periods of time—to visit friends or to enter military service—and not to pursue their trade.

An alternative interpretation of the colonists' economic motivation has recently been proposed by Peter Clark, who discovered similarities between the New England settlers and "betterment migrants" traveling within the county of Kent during the decades preceding the English Civil War. Betterment migrants, like the New England colonists, were persons of solid means who, Clark argues, sought further to improve their economic positions. Most betterment migrants traveled only a short distance, usually to a nearby town; the New Englanders differed from them primarily through the immense length of their transatlantic journeys. On the whole, betterment migrants were not especially mobile; in their search for opportunity, they generally moved just once in their lives. New England emigrants like John Bent, while they lived in England, also tended to be geographically stable. In addition, betterment migrants shared with the Massachusetts settlers a tendency to rely on kin connections in their choice of destinations.[61]

Clark's model of betterment migration fits the New England movement in certain particulars, but it makes little sense within the larger context of the transatlantic transplantation. If migration to New England was not a sensible economic decision for farmers or weavers hurt by hard times in England, it was even less sensible for people doing well. Most emigrants exchanged an economically viable present for a very uncertain future. As we have seen, nearly one in ten was over forty years old at the time of the migration and had little reason to expect to live long enough to enjoy whatever prosperity the New World might bring. The emigrant groups studied here all left England five or more years after the Great Migration had begun and a decade and a half after the landing at Plymouth; they surely heard from earlier arrivals that New England was no land of milk and honey. If any had a chance to read Edward Winslow's *Good Newes from New England,* published in 1624, he or she would have learned that the "vain expectation of present profit" was the "overthrow and bane" of plantations. People might prosper through "good labor and diligence," but in the absence of a cash crop, great wealth was not to be expected. The message of William Wood's *New England's Prospect,* published a decade later, was similar. Some colonists were lured westward by descriptions of plenty, Wood acknowledged, but they soon fell to criticizing the new society, "saying a man cannot live without labor." These disgruntled settlers "more discredit and disparage themselves in giving the world occasion to take notice of their dronish disposition that would live off the sweat of another man's brows. Surely they were much deceived, or else ill informed, that ventured thither in hope to live in plenty and idleness, both at a time." Letters as well as published reports informed would-

---

[61] Clark, *English Provincial Society,* pp. 372–73, and "The migrant in Kentish towns 1580–1640," in *Crisis and Order in English Towns,* pp. 134–38.

be settlers that New England was not a particularly fertile field for
profit. In 1631, one young colonist wrote to his father in Suffolk, England, that "the cuntrey is not so as we ded expecte it." Far from bringing riches, New England could not even provide essentials; the disillusioned settler begged his father to send provisions, for "we do
not know how longe we may subeseiste" without supplies from
home.[62]

If prospective emigrants were not hearing that New England offered
ample opportunities for economic betterment, they *were* informed that
life in Massachusetts could bring betterment of another sort. When
Governor Thomas Dudley provided the countess of Lincoln with an
account of his first nine months in New England, he announced that
"if any come hether to plant for worldly ends that canne live well at
home hee comits an errour of which he will soon repent him. But if for
spirituall [ends] and that noe particular obstacle hinder his removeall,
he may finde here what may well content him." Dudley worried that
some might be drawn to Massachusetts by exaggerations of the land's
bounty and wanted to make clear who would benefit most from emigration. "If any godly men out of religious ends will come over to
helpe vs in the good worke wee are about," the governor wrote, "I
think they cannot dispose of themselves nor of their estates more to
God's glory and the furtherance of their owne reckoninge."[63] New
England promised its settlers *spiritual* advantages only; men merely in
search of wealth could go elsewhere. Emmanuel Downing, in a letter
to Sir John Coke, clarified the important difference between New
England and other colonial ventures. "This plantation and that of Virginia went not forth upon the same reasons nor for the same end.
Those of Virginia," he explained, "went forth for profit. . . . These
went upon two other designs, some to satisfy their own curiosity in
point of conscience, others . . . to transport the Gospel to those heathen that never heard thereof."[64]

Both published tracts and private correspondence advertised New
England's religious mission. In *The Planter's Plea*, Rev. John White
proclaimed that "the most eminent and desirable end of planting
Colonies, is the propagation of Religion." Prospective emigrants

[62] Edward Winslow, *Good Newes from New England: or a true Relation of things very remarkable at the Plantation of Plimoth in New-England* (London, 1624), reprinted in *Chronicles of the Pilgrim Fathers of the Colony of Plymouth, from 1602 to 1625*, 2d ed., ed. Alexander Young (Boston, 1844), pp. 272–73, 370–71; Wood, *New England's Prospect*, p. 68; [?]
Pond to William Pond, *Winthrop Papers*, 3:18.

[63] "Gov. Thomas Dudley's Letter to the Countess of Lincoln, March, 1631," in *Tracts
and Other Papers Relating Principally to the Origin, Settlement, and Progress of the Colonies in
North America, From the Discovery of the Country to the Year 1776*, ed. Peter Force, 4 vols.
(Washington, D.C., 1836–46), 2:12.

[64] This letter is quoted in *Letters from New England*, p. 93. For a similar statement, see
John Winthrop's "General Observations: Autograph Draft," *Winthrop Papers*, 2:117.

learned from the Rev. Francis Higginson's *New-England's Plantation*, published in 1630, that "that which is our greatest comfort . . . is, that we haue here the true Religion and holy Ordinances of Almightie God taught amongst us: Thankes be to God, we haue here plentie of Preaching, and diligent Catechizing, with strickt and carefull exercise, and good and commendable orders to bring our People into a Christian conuersation with whom we haue to doe withall."[65] Indeed, New England's Puritan predilections were so well known that colonial leaders feared retribution from the Anglican establishment in England. *The Planter's Plea* specifically sought to dispel rumors that Massachusetts was overrun with Separatists, and, during the early 1630s, Edward Howes maintained a steady correspondence with John Winthrop, Jr. concerning similar allegations of New England radicalism. In 1631, Howes reported that "heare is a mutteringe of a too palpable seperation of your people from our church gouernment." The following year, he again informed Winthrop of claims that "you neuer vse the Lords prayer, that your ministers marrie none, that fellowes which keepe hogges all the weeke preach on the Saboth, that euery towne in your plantation is of a seuerall religion; that you count all men in England, yea all out of your church, and in the state of damnacion." Howes knew such rumors were false but feared that many other Englishmen believed them. The spread of such lies endangered not only the colony's reputation but perhaps its very survival as well.[66]

Prospective emigrants, then, could hardly have been unaware of the peculiar religious character of New England society. Accounts of the region's commitment to Puritanism were too numerous to be overlooked; those who made the voyage had to know what they were getting into. Adherence to Puritan principles, therefore, became the common thread that stitched individual emigrants together into a larger movement. As John White declared, "Necessitie may presse some; Noveltie draw on others; hopes of gaine in time to come may prevaile with a third sort: but that the most and most sincere and godly part have the advancement of the *Gospel* for their maine scope I am co[n]fident."[67]

White's confidence was by no means misplaced. The roster of passengers to New England contains the names of scores of otherwise ordinary English men and women whose lives were distinguished by

[65] John White, *The Planter's Plea* (London, 1630), reprinted in *Tracts and Other Papers*, 2:12; Rev. Francis Higginson, *New-England's Plantation with The Sea Journal and Other Writings* (facsimile, Salem: Essex Book and Print Company, 1908), p. 108. See also the letter from Edward Trelawney to his brother Robert in *Letters from New England*, pp. 175–78.

[66] White, *Planter's Plea*, pp. 33–36; Edward Howes to John Winthrop, Jr., 9 November 1631 and 28 November 1632, *Winthrop Papers*, 3:54, 100–101.

[67] White, *Planter's Plea*, p. 36.

their steadfast commitment to nonconformity, even in the face of official harassment. The *Hercules* left Sandwich in 1635 with William Witherell and Comfort Starr aboard; both men had been in trouble with local ecclesiastical authorities. Anthony Thacher, a nonconformist who had been living in Holland for two decades, returned to Southampton that same year to embark for New England on the *James*. Two years later, the *Rose* carried Michael Metcalf away from the clutches of Norwich diocesan officials. Metcalf had appeared before ecclesiastical courts in 1633 and again in 1636 for refusing to bow at the name of Jesus or to adhere to the "stinking tenets of Arminius" adopted by the established Church. Before his departure, Metcalf composed a letter "to all the true professors of Christs gospel within the city of Norwich" that chronicled his troubled encounters with church officials and explained his exclusively religious reasons for emigration. Thomas and Mary Oliver, Metcalf's fellow parishioners at St. Edmund's in Norwich, had also been cited before the archepiscopal court in 1633 and set sail for Massachusetts the same year as Metcalf. Other emigrants leaving in 1637 were John Pers and John Baker, two Norwich residents evidently also in trouble with church officials; Joan Ames, the widow of the revered Puritan divine William Ames, who had only recently returned from a lengthy stay in Rotterdam; and Margaret Neave and Adam Goodens, whose names appeared on Separatist lists in Great Yarmouth. Peter Noyes, who emigrated in 1638, came from a family long involved in nonconformist activities in England's southwest.[68]

Although New England was not populated solely by unsuccessful defendants in ecclesiastical court proceedings, the nonconformist beliefs of other emigrants should not be underestimated merely because they avoided direct conflict with bishops and deacons. John Winthrop's religious motivation has never been in doubt even though he was never convicted of a Puritan offense. Winthrop's "General Observations for the Plantation of New England," like Metcalf's letter to the citizens of Norwich, emphasized the corrupt state of England's ecclesiastical affairs and concluded that emigration "wilbe a service to the church of great consequens" redounding to the spiritual benefit of emigrants and Indians alike. Those few men who recorded their own reasons for removal likewise stressed the role of religion. Roger Clap, who sailed in 1630, recalled in his memoirs that "I never so much as

[68] Clark, *English Provincial Society*, p. 372; Savage, *Genealogical Dictionary*, 4: 270–71; Breen and Foster, "Moving to the New World," pp. 202–3, 207 n. 37; Jewson, *Transcript of Three Registers*, p. 8; Champlin Burrage, *The Early English Dissenters in the Light of Recent Research, 1550–1641*, 2 vols. (Cambridge: Cambridge University Press, 1912), 2:309; Powell, *Puritan Village*, p. 4; "Michael Metcalfe," *NEHGR* 16(1862):279–84. The incomplete survival of ecclesiastical records in England makes it impossible to discover the full extent of colonists' troubles with the authorities.

heard of *New-England* until I heard of many godly Persons that were going there" and firmly believed that "God put it into my Heart to incline to Live abroad" in Massachusetts. John Dane, who seems to have spent most of his youth fighting off his evil inclinations, "bent myself to cum to nu ingland, thinking that I should be more fre here then thare from temptations." Arriving in Roxbury in the mid-1630s, Dane soon discovered that relocation would not end his struggle with sinfulness; the devil sought him out as readily in the New World as in the Old.[69]

To declare that most emigrants were prompted by radical religious sentiment to sail to the New World, however, does not mean that these settlers resembled Hawthorne's memorable "stern and black-browed Puritans" in single-minded pursuit of salvation. The decision to cross the seas indelibly marked the lives of those who made it. Even the most pious wrestled with the implications of removal from family, friends, and familiar surroundings. Parents often objected to the departure of their children; a son following the dictates of his conscience might risk the estrangement of a disappointed father.[70] Although religious motivation is the only factor with sufficient power to explain the departure of so many otherwise ordinary families, the New England Puritans should not be seen as utopians caught up in a movement whose purpose totally transcended the concerns of daily life.

Solitary ascetics can afford to reject the things of this world in order to contemplate the glories of the next; family men cannot. Even as prospective settlers discussed the spiritual benefits that might accompany a move to New England, they worried about what they would eat, where they would sleep, and how they would make a living. In the spring of 1631, Emmanuel Downing wrote with considerable relief to John Winthrop that the governor's encouraging letters "haue much refreshed my hart and the myndes of manic others" for "yt was the Iudgement of most men here, that your Colonye would be dissolved partly by death through want of Food, howsing and rayment, and the rest to retorne or to flee for refuge to other plantacions."[71] Other leaders and publicists of the migration continued both to recognize and to sympathize with the concerns of families struggling with the decision of whether or not to move, and they sought to reassure prospective settlers that a decision in favor of emigration would not

---

[69] *Winthrop Papers*, 2:111; "Memoirs of Roger Clap," *Dorchester Antiquarian and Historical Society Collections* 1 (1844): 18–19; "John Dane's Narrative, 1682," *NEHGR* 8 (1854): 154.

[70] See, e.g., the story of Samuel Rogers in Kenneth W. Shipps, "The Puritan Emigration to New England: A New Source on Motivation," *NEHGR* 135 (1981): 83–97. Both Roger Clap and John Dane noted that their fathers, at least initially, protested their emigration, see "Memoirs of Roger Clap," p. 18; "John Dane's Narrative," p. 154.

[71] Edward Downing to John Winthrop, 30 April [1631], *Winthrop Papers*, 3:30.

doom their families to cold and starvation in the wilderness. At the same time, the way in which these writers composed their comforting messages to would-be emigrants underscored the settlers' understanding of the larger meaning of their mission.

Although several of the tracts and letters publicizing the migration contained favorable descriptions of the new land, they were never intended to be advertisements designed to capture the interest of profit-seekers. When John White, Thomas Dudley, and others wrote about the blessings of New England's climate, topography, and flora and fauna, they simply hoped to assure godly English men and women that a move to the New World would not engender poverty as well as piety. In *The Planter's Plea*, John White succinctly answered objections that New England lacked "meanes if wealth." "An unanswerable argument," White replied, "to such as make the advancement of their estates, the scope of their undertaking." But, he added, New England's modest resources were in "no way a discouragement to such as aime at the propagation of the Gospell, which can never bee advanced but by the preservation of Piety in those that carry it to strangers." For, White concluded, "nothing sorts better with Piety than Compete[n]cy." He referred his readers to Proverbs 30:8—"Remove far from me vanity and lies: give me neither poverty nor riches; feed me with food convenient for me." Thomas Dudley in effect explicated the meaning of "competency" in a New England context when he listed such goods as "may well content" a righteous colonist. In Massachusetts, Dudley noted, settlers could expect to have "materialls to build, fewell to burn, ground to plant, seas and rivers to fish in, a pure ayer to breath in, good water to drinke till wine or beare canne be made, which togeather with the cowes, hoggs, and goates brought hether allready may suffice for food." Such were the amenities that emigrants not only could but should aspire to enjoy.[72]

John White repeatedly assured his readers that "all Gods directions"—including the divine imperative to settle New England—"have a double scope, mans good and Gods honour." "That this commandement of God is directed unto mans good *temporall and spirituall*," he went on, "is as cleere as the light."[73] The Lord, in other words, would take care of His own. To providentialists steeped in the conviction that God intervened directly in human lives, that divine pleasure or disapproval could be perceived in the progress of daily events, White's statement made eminent sense. If emigrant families embarked on their voyages with the purpose of abandoning England's corruption in order to worship God according to biblical precepts in their new homes, and if

---

[72] White, *Planter's Plea*, p. 18; "Dudleys Letter to the Countess of Lincoln," p. 12. See also Wood, *New England's Prospect*, p. 68.

[73] White, *Planter's Plea*, p. 2; italics added.

they adhered to this purpose, they might expect as a sign of divine favor to achieve a competency, if not riches. Thus John Winthrop could assert that "such thinges as we stand in neede of are vsually supplied by Gods blessing vpon the wisdome and industry of man." The governor's firm belief in the connection between divine favor and human well-being explains why in his "Particular Considerations" concerning his own removal out of England, he admitted that "my meanes heere [in England] are so shortned (now my 3 eldest sonnes are come to age) as I shall not be able to continue in this place and imployment where I now am." If he went to Massachusetts, Winthrop anticipated an improvement in his fortunes, noting that "I [can] live with 7. or 8: servants in that place and condition where for many years I have spent 3: or 400 *li.* per an[num]." Winthrop, despite these musings on his worldly estate, did not emigrate in order to better his economic condition. Rather, he removed in order to undertake the "publike service" that God had "bestowed" on him and hoped that God might reward him if his efforts were successful. In similar fashion, thousands of other emigrants could justify their decisions to move to New England. They believed that, by emigrating, they followed the will of God and that their obedience would not escape divine notice. In return for their submission to His will, the emigrants sincerely hoped that God might allow them—through their own labor—to enjoy a competency of this world's goods.[74]

Historians have generally agreed that early New England displayed a distinctive social character. The first colonists, after all, succeeded in creating a remarkably stable society on the edge of a vast wilderness. But stability alone does not sum up the New Englanders' achievement, for colonists who went to other parts of North America also established lasting settlements. What set New England society apart was its Puritan heritage. Religious and social ideals became inextricably intertwined as settlers applied the Puritan concept of the covenantal relationship between God and man to their temporal as well as religious affairs. When New Englanders pledged themselves to God in their churches and to each other in their towns, they imbued their society with a deeply spiritual significance. Other British colonists would also strive to create social harmony, but none would do so with the same intensity of religious purpose as New England's founding generation.[75]

[74] *Winthrop Papers*, 2:143–44, 126.
[75] Some of the major works on New England Puritanism and its relationship to social stability include Perry Miller, *Errand into the Wilderness* (Cambridge: Harvard University Press, 1956); Kenneth Lockridge, *A New England Town: The First Hundred Years* (New York: W. W. Norton and Co., 1970); Timothy Breen and Stephen Foster, "The Puritans' Greatest Achievement: A Study of Social Cohesion in Seventeenth-Century Massachusetts," *Journal of American History* 60 (1973): 5–22. In their recent work on early Virginia, Darrett and Anita Rutman have argued that communalism also characterized

Ironically, the scholarly portrait of New England society has largely been drawn without reference to the identity of the emigrant population. Historians have instead turned to the writings of religious leaders and to the formulaic language of town covenants in order to explicate the meaning of the New England experiment. And while their efforts have produced a most coherent and convincing analysis of that society and culture, their conclusions are rendered even more compelling when the character and motivation of the emigrants themselves are also taken into account. For then it becomes clear that the predilections of the emigrants were just as important as the prescriptions of the clergy in shaping New England society.

At the heart of the colonists' achievement lies an apparent paradox. Settlers in Massachusetts, Plymouth, and Connecticut created a remarkably unified culture and a homogeneous society in a setting where the power of central authorities was exceedingly weak. Preachers and magistrates could have expended every effort extolling the virtues of communal and spiritual harmony and yet failed miserably had not their audience shared in their aspirations. But since the majority of emigrants responded to a common spiritual impulse in moving to New England, they readily accepted the idea of the covenant as the proper model for their social as well as spiritual relationships. Indeed, covenants, because of their voluntary nature, provided the only truly effective means of maintaining social cohesion where coercive power was limited. The social homogeneity of the emigrant population—the absence of both rich and poor folk—unintentionally reinforced covenantal ideals by reducing the differences in status among partners. In this way, social fact joined with communal ideals to create a society of comparative equals pledged to one another's support. At the same time, social and religious covenants helped settlers from diverse geographical and occupational backgrounds to come to terms with their new common enterprise. Emigrants concerned solely with their own material improvement would scarcely have acceded so readily to an ideal of mutual cooperation. It is only because most colonists (at least initially) placed the good of their souls above all else and trusted in the Lord to provide for them that the story of New England's origins occupies a unique place in American history.

English colonies in the Chesapeake region and was not specifically a function of religious belief. David Allen has also suggested that much of what we have assumed to be distinctively Puritan in Massachusetts in fact represents transplanted local English customs. Yet for reasons that I hope are clear from this essay, I believe that New England culture was indeed distinguished by its Puritan character and that its pervasive Puritanism resulted from the shared beliefs of the emigrants themselves. See Rutman and Rutman, *A Place in Time: Middlesex County, Virginia, 1650–1750* (New York: W. W. Norton & Co., 1984); Allen, *In English Ways.*

Family Structure in Seventeenth-Century Andover, Massachusetts

PHILIP J. GREVEN, JR.

Philip Greven is another of the prominent demographic historians of colonial America. He applies the same quantitative and conceptual analysis to the study of life in Andover that Demos does in regard to Plymouth, and yet his results are sharply divergent. Greven's Andover was a very static community in which children married late, lived close to the homes of their parents, and were quite mature before they owned farms of their own. It was a patriarchal society in which first-generation males held onto control of their families, lands, and town government, and in which continuity was fostered by a self-conscious system of arranged marriages. There seems to have been little immigration into Andover or emigration from the town.

"Family structure" is a relatively novel concept in historical analysis, but Greven uses it to show how sociological categories can provide fresh historical insights. His implicit contention is that until we understand precisely how men behaved, we shall not be able to find out why they acted as they did. His essay attempts to demonstrate how very broad conclusions can be drawn from masses of very minute bits of evidence, however, and he suggests that many questions about the New England town remain unanswered. One obvious problem is why Andover should have been so different from Plymouth. Might the answers lie outside the scope of demographic inquiry?

Surprisingly little is known at present about family life and family structure in the seventeenth-century American colonies. The generalizations about colonial family life embedded in textbooks are seldom the result of studies of the extant source materials, which historians until recently have tended to ignore.[1] Genealogists long have been using records preserved in county archives, town halls, churches, and graveyards as well as personal documents to compile detailed informa-

---

[1] Two notable exceptions to this generalization are Edmund S. Morgan, *The Puritan Family . . .* (Boston, 1956), and John Demos, "Notes on Life in Plymouth Colony," *William and Mary Quarterly*, 3d Ser., XXII (1965), 264–286.

Reprinted by permission from Philip J. Greven, "Family Structure in Seventeenth-Century Andover, Massachusetts," *William and Mary Quarterly*, 3d Ser., XXIII (1966), 234–256. A revised version of this article is included in Philip J. Greven, *Four Generations: Population, Land and Family in Colonial Andover, Massachusetts* (Ithaca, 1970).

tion on successive generations of early American families. In addition to the work of local genealogists, many communities possess probate records and deeds for the colonial period. A study of these last testaments and deeds together with the vital statistics of family genealogies can provide the answers to such questions as how many children people had, how long people lived, at what ages did they marry, how much control did fathers have over their children, and to what extent and under what conditions did children remain in their parents' community. The answers to such questions enable an historian to reconstruct to some extent the basic characteristics of family life for specific families in specific communities. This essay is a study of a single seventeenth-century New England town, Andover, Massachusetts, during the lifetimes of its first and second generations—the pioneers who carved the community out of the wilderness, and their children who settled upon the lands which their fathers had acquired. A consideration of their births, marriages, and deaths, together with the disposition of land and property within the town from one generation to the next reveals some of the most important aspects of family life and family structure in early Andover.

The development of a particular type of family structure in seventeenth-century Andover was dependent in part upon the economic development of the community during the same period. Andover, settled by a group of about eighteen men during the early 1640's and incorporated in 1646, was patterned at the outset after the English open field villages familiar to many of the early settlers. The inhabitants resided on house lots adjacent to each other in the village center, with their individual holdings of land being distributed in small plots within two large fields beyond the village center. House lots ranged in size from four to twenty acres, and subsequent divisions of land within the town were proportionate to the size of the house lots. By the early 1660's, about forty-two men had arrived to settle in Andover, of whom thirty-six became permanent residents. During the first decade and a half, four major divisions of the arable land in the town were granted. The first two divisions established two open fields, in which land was granted to the inhabitants on the basis of one acre of land for each acre of house lot. The third division, which provided four acres of land for each acre of house lot, evidently did not form another open field, but was scattered about the town. The fourth and final division of land during the seventeenth century occurred in 1662, and gave land to the householders at the rate of twenty acres for each acre of their house lots. Each householder thus obtained a minimum division allotment of about eighty acres and a maximum allotment of about four hundred acres. Cumulatively, these four successive divisions of town land, together with additional divisions of meadow and swampland, provided each of the inhabitants with at least one hundred acres of land for farming, and as much as six hundred acres. During the years following

these substantial grants of land, many of the families in the town removed their habitations from the house lots in the town center onto
their distant, and extensive, farm lands, thus altering the character of
the community through the establishment of independent family farms
and scattered residences. By the 1680's, more than half the families in
Andover lived outside the original center of the town on their own ample farms. The transformation of the earlier open field village effectively recast the basis for family life within the community.[2]

An examination of the number of children whose births are recorded in the Andover town records between 1651 and 1699 reveals a
steady increase in the number of children being born throughout the
period. (See Table 1.[3]) Between 1651 and 1654, 28 births are recorded,
followed by 32 between 1655 and 1659, 43 between 1660 and 1664, 44
between 1665 and 1669, 78 between 1670 and 1674, and 90 between
1675 and 1679. After 1680, the figures rise to more than one hundred
births every five years. The entire picture of population growth in Andover, however, cannot be formed from a study of the town records
alone since these records do not reflect the pattern of generations
within the town. Looked at from the point of view of the births of the
children of the first generation of settlers who arrived in Andover between the first settlement in the mid-1640's and 1660, a very different
picture emerges, hidden within the entries of the town records and genealogies.[4] The majority of the second-generation children were born
during the two decades of the 1650's and the 1660's. The births of 159
second-generation children were distributed in decades as follows: 10
were born during the 1630's, either in England or in the towns along
the Massachusetts coast where their parents first settled; 28 were born
during the 1640's; 49 were born during the 1650's; 43 were born during the 1660's; declining to 21 during the 1670's, and falling to only 8
during the 1680's. Because of this pattern of births, the second generation of Andover children, born largely during the 1650's and the

[2] For a full discussion of the transformation of 17th-century Andover, see my article,
"Old Patterns in the New World: The Distribution of Land in 17th Century Andover,"
Essex Institute Historical Collections, CI (April 1965), 133–148. See also the study of Sud-
bury, Mass., in Sumner Chilton Powell, *Puritan Village: The Formation of a New England
Town* (Middletown, Conn., 1963).

[3] The figures in Table 1 were compiled from the first MS book of Andover vital
records. A Record of Births, Deaths, and Marriages, Begun 1651 Ended 1700, located in
the vault of the Town Clerk's office, Town Hall, Andover, Mass. For a suggestive comparison of population growth in a small village, see W. G. Hoskins, "The Population of
an English Village, 1086–1801: A Study of Wigston Magna," *Provincial England: Essays in
Social and Economic History* (London, 1963), 195–200.

[4] The most important collection of unpublished genealogies of early Andover families
are the typed MSS of Charlotte Helen Abbott, which are located in the Memorial Library, Andover. The two vols. of *Vital Records of Andover, Massachusetts, to the End of the
Year 1849* (Topsfield, Mass., 1912) provide an invaluable and exceptionally reliable reference for vital statistics of births, marriages, and deaths.

The Number of Sons and Daughters
Living at the Age of 21 in
TABLE 1   *Twenty-nine First-Generation Families*

Sons	0	1	2	3	4	5	6	7	8	9	10
Families	1	2	7	1	6	6	3	3	0	0	0
Daughters	0	1	2	3	4	5	6	7	8	9	10
Families	0	2	7	6	11	2	0	0	0	1	0

1660's, would mature during the late 1670's and the 1680's. Many of the developments of the second half of the seventeenth century in Andover, both within the town itself and within the families residing there, were the result of the problems posed by a maturing second generation.

From the records which remain, it is not possible to determine the size of the first-generation family with complete accuracy, since a number of children were undoubtedly stillborn, or died almost immediately after birth without ever being recorded in the town records. It is possible, however, to determine the number of children surviving childhood and adolescence with considerable accuracy, in part because of the greater likelihood of their names being recorded among the children born in the town, and in part because other records, such as church records, marriage records, tax lists, and wills, also note their presence. Evidence from all of these sources indicates that the families of Andover's first settlers were large, even without taking into account the numbers of children who may have been born but died unrecorded. An examination of the families of twenty-nine men who settled in Andover between 1645 and 1660 reveals that a total of 247 children are known to have been born to these particular families. Of these 247 children whose births may be ascertained, thirty-nine, or 15.7 per cent, are known to have died before reaching the age of 21 years.[5] A total of 208 children or 84.3 per cent of the number of children known to be born thus reached the age of 21 years, having survived the hazards both of infancy and of adolescence. This suggests that the number of deaths among children and adolescents during the middle of the seventeenth century in Andover was lower than might have been expected.

In terms of their actual sizes, the twenty-nine first-generation families varied considerably, as one might expect. Eleven of these twenty-

---

[5] While this figure is low, it should not be discounted entirely. Thomas Jefferson Wertenbaker, *The First Americans, 1607–1690* (New York, 1929), 185–186, found that, "Of the eight hundred and eight children of Harvard graduates for the years from 1658 to 1690, one hundred and sixty-two died before maturity. This gives a recorded child mortality among this selected group of *twenty* per cent." Italics added.

nine families had between 0 and 3 sons who survived to the age of 21 years; twelve families had either 4 or 5 sons surviving, and six families had either 6 or 7 sons living to be 21. Eighteen of these families thus had four or more sons to provide with land or a trade when they reached maturity and wished to marry, a fact of considerable significance in terms of the development of family life in Andover during the years prior to 1690. Fewer of these twenty-nine families had large numbers of daughters. Fifteen families had between 0 and 3 daughters who reached adulthood, eleven families had 4 daughters surviving, and three families had 5 or more daughters reaching the age of 21. In terms of the total number of their children born and surviving to the age of 21 or more, four of these twenty-nine first-generation families had between 2 and 4 children (13.8 per cent), eleven families had between 5 and 7 children (37.9 per cent), and fourteen families had between 8 and 11 children (48.3 per cent). Well over half of the first-generation families thus had 6 or more children who are known to have survived adolescence and to have reached the age of 21. The average number of children known to have been born to these twenty-nine first-generation families was 8.5, with an average of 7.2 children in these families being known to have reached the age of 21 years.[6] The size of the family, and particularly the number of sons who survived adolescence, was a matter of great importance in terms of the problems which would arise later over the settlement of the second generation upon land in Andover and the division of the estates of the first generation among their surviving children. The development of a particular type of family structure within Andover during the first two generations depended in part upon the number of children born and surviving in particular families.

Longevity was a second factor of considerable importance in the development of the family in Andover. For the first forty years following the settlement of the town in 1645, relatively few deaths were recorded among the inhabitants of the town. Unlike Boston, which evidently suffered from smallpox epidemics throughout the seventeenth century, there is no evidence to suggest the presence of smallpox or other epidemical diseases in Andover prior to 1690. With relatively few people, many of whom by the 1670's were scattered about the town upon their own farms, Andover appears to have been a remarkably healthy community during its early years. Lacking virulent epidemics, the principal

[6] Comparative figures for the size of families in other rural New England villages are very rare. Wertenbaker, *First Americans*, 182–185, suggested that families were extremely large, with 10 to 20 children being common, but his data for Hingham, Mass., where he found that 105 women had "five or more children," with a total of 818 children "giving an average of 7.8 for each family," is in line with the data for Andover. The figures for seventeenth-century Plymouth are also remarkably similar. See Demos, "Notes on Life in Plymouth Colony," 270–271.

hazards to health and to life were birth, accidents, non-epidemical diseases, and Indians. Death, consequently, visited relatively few of Andover's inhabitants during the first four decades following its settlement. This is evident in the fact that the first generation of Andover's
settlers was very long lived. Prior to 1680, only five of the original settlers who came to Andover before 1660 and established permanent
residence there had died; in 1690, fifteen of the first settlers (more
than half of the original group) were still alive, forty-five years after
the establishment of their town. The age at death of thirty men who
settled in Andover prior to 1660 can be determined with a relative degree of accuracy. Their average age at the time of their deaths was 71.8
years. Six of the thirty settlers died while in their fifties, 11 in their six-
ties, 3 in their seventies, 6 in their eighties, 3 in their nineties, and 1 at
the advanced age of 106 years.[7] The longevity of the first-generation
fathers was to have great influence on the lives of their children, for
the authority of the first generation was maintained far longer than
would have been possible if death had struck them down at an early
age. The second generation, in turn, was almost as long lived as the
first generation had been. The average age of 138 second-generation
men at the time of their deaths was 65.2 years, and the average age of
sixty-six second-generation women at the time of their deaths was 64.0
years. (See Table 2.[8]) Of the 138 second-generation men who reached
the age of 21 years and whose lifespan is known, only twenty-five or
18.1 per cent, died between the ages of 20 and 49. Forty-two (30.3 per
cent) of these 138 men died between the ages of 50 and 69; seventy-
one (51.6 per cent) died after reaching the age of 70. Twenty-five second-generation men died in their eighties, and four died in their
nineties. Longevity was characteristic of men living in seventeenth-
century Andover.

---

[7] The town of Hingham, according to the evidence in Wertenbaker, *First Americans*,
181–186, was remarkably similar to Andover, since the life expectancy of its inhabitants
during the 17th century was very high. "Of the eight hundred and twenty-seven persons
mentioned as belonging to this period [17th century] and whose length of life is
recorded, one hundred and five reached the age of eighty or over, nineteen lived to be
ninety or over and three . . . attained the century mark."

[8] Since the size of the sample for the age of women at the time of their death is only
half that of the sample for men, the average age of 64.0 may not be too reliable. However, the evidence for Hingham does suggest that the figures for Andover ought not to
be dismissed too lightly. "The average life of the married women of Hingham during the
seventeenth century," Wertenbaker noted, "seems to have been 61.4 years." He also
found that for their 818 children, the average age at the time of death was 65.5 years.
"These figures," he added, "apply to one little town only, and cannot be accepted as con-
clusive for conditions throughout the colonies, yet they permit of the strong presumption that much which has been written concerning the short expectation of life for
women of large families is based upon insufficient evidence." *Ibid.*, 184. The observation
remains cogent. For the longevity of Plymouth's settlers, see Demos, "Notes on Life in
Plymouth Colony," 271.

TABLE 2   *Second-Generation Ages at Death*

	Males		Females	
AGES	NUMBERS	PERCENTAGES	NUMBERS	PERCENTAGES
20–29	10	7.3	4	6.1
30–39	9	6.5	4	6.1
40–49	6	4.3	6	9.1
50–59	16	11.5	10	15.2
60–69	26	18.8	13	19.7
70–79	42	30.4	16	24.2
80–89	25	18.1	8	12.1
90–99	4	3.1	5	7.5
Total	138	100.0%	66	100.0%

The age of marriage often provides significant clues to circumstances affecting family life and to patterns of family relationships which might otherwise remain elusive.[9] Since marriages throughout the seventeenth century and the early part of the eighteenth century were rarely fortuitous, parental authority and concern, family interests, and economic considerations played into the decisions determining when particular men and women could and would marry for the first time. And during the seventeenth century in Andover, factors such as these frequently dictated delays of appreciable duration before young men, especially, might marry. The age of marriage both of men and of women in the second generation proved to be much higher than most historians hitherto have suspected.[10]

Traditionally in America women have married younger than men, and this was generally true for the second generation in Andover. Although the assertion is sometimes made that daughters of colonial families frequently married while in their early teens, the average age

[9] The most sophisticated analyses of marriage ages and their relationship to the social structure, family life, and economic conditions of various communities have been made by sociologists. Two exceptionally useful models are the studies of two contemporary English villages by W. M. Williams: *Goeforth: The Sociology of an English Village* (Glencoe, Ill., 1956), esp. pp. 45–49, and *A West Country Village, Ashworthy: Family, Kinship, and Land* (London, 1963), esp. pp. 85–91. Another useful study is Conrad M. Arensberg and Solon T. Kimball, *Family and Community in Ireland* (Cambridge, Mass., 1940). For the fullest statistical and historiographical account of marriage ages in the United States, see Thomas P. Monahan, *The Pattern of Age at Marriage in the United States*, 2 vols. (Philadelphia, 1951).

[10] In Plymouth colony during the seventeenth century, the age of marriage also was higher than expected. See Demos, "Notes on Life in Plymouth Colony," 275. For a discussion of various historians' views on marriage ages during the colonial period, see Monahan, *Pattern of Age at Marriage*, I, 99–104.

TABLE 3		*Second-Generation Female Marriage Ages*

AGE	NUMBERS	PERCENTAGES	
Under 21	22	33.3	24 & under = 69.7%
21–24	24	36.4	25 & over = 30.3%
25–29	14	21.2	29 & under = 90.9%
30–34	4	6.1	30 & over = 9.1%
35–39	1	1.5	
40 & over	1	1.5	
			Average age = 22.8 years
	66	100.0%	

of sixty-six second-generation daughters of Andover families at the time of their first marriage was 22.8 years. (See Table 3.) Only two girls are known to have married at 14 years, none at 15, and two more at 16. Four married at the age of 17, with a total of twenty-two of the sixty-six girls marrying before attaining the age of 21 years (33.3 per cent). The largest percentage of women married between the ages of 21 and 24, with twenty-four or 36.4 per cent being married during these years, making a total of 69.7 per cent of the second-generation daughters married before reaching the age of 25. Between the ages of 25 and 29 years, fourteen women (21.2 per cent) married, with six others marrying at the age of 30 or more (9.1 per cent). Relatively few second-generation women thus married before the age of 17, and nearly 70 per cent married before the age of 25. They were not as young in most instances as one might have expected if very early marriages had prevailed, but they were relatively young nonetheless.

The age of marriage for second-generation men reveals a very different picture, for instead of marrying young, as they so often are said to have done, they frequently married quite late. (See Table 4.) The average age for ninety-four second-generation sons of Andover families at the time of their first marriages was 27.1 years. No son is known to have married before the age of 18, and only one actually married then. None of the ninety-four second-generation men whose marriage ages could be determined married at the age of 19, and only three married at the age of 20. The contrast with the marriages of the women of the same generation is evident, since only 4.3 per cent of the men married before the age of 21 compared to 33.3 per cent of the women. The majority of second-generation men married while in their twenties, with thirty-three of the ninety-four men marrying between the ages of 21 and 24 (35.1 per cent), and thirty-four men marrying between the ages of 25 and 29 (36.2 per cent). Nearly one quarter of the second-generation men married at the age of 30 or later, however, since twenty-three men or 24.4 per cent delayed their mar-

TABLE 4   *Second-Generation Male Marriage Ages*

AGE	NUMBERS	PERCENTAGES		
Under 21	4	4.3	24 & under	= 39.4%
21–24	33	35.1	25 & over	= 60.6%
25–29	34	36.2	29 & under	= 75.6%
30–34	16	17.2	30 & over	= 24.4%
35–39	4	4.3		
40 & over	3	2.9		
			Average age	= 27.1 years
	94	100.0%		

riages until after their thirtieth year. In sharp contrast with the women of this generation, an appreciable majority of the second-generation men married at the age of 25 or more, with 60.6 per cent marrying after that age. This tendency to delay marriages by men until after the age of 25, with the average age being about 27 years, proved to be characteristic of male marriage ages in Andover throughout the seventeenth century.

Averages can sometimes obscure significant variations in patterns of behavior, and it is worth noting that in the second generation the age at which particular sons might marry depended in part upon which son was being married. Eldest sons tended to marry earlier than younger sons in many families, which suggests variations in their roles within their families, and differences in the attitudes of their fathers towards them compared to their younger brothers. For twenty-six eldest second-generation sons, the average age at their first marriage was 25.6 years. Second sons in the family often met with greater difficulties and married at an average age of 27.5 years, roughly two years later than their elder brothers. Youngest sons tended to marry later still, with the average of twenty-two youngest sons being 27.9 years. In their marriages as in their inheritances, eldest sons often proved to be favored by their families; and family interests and paternal wishes were major factors in deciding which son should marry and when. More often than not, a son's marriage depended upon the willingness of his father to allow it and the ability of his father to provide the means for the couple's economic independence. Until a second-generation son had been given the means to support a wife—which in Andover during the seventeenth century generally meant land—marriage was virtually impossible.

Marriage negotiations between the parents of couples proposing marriage and the frequent agreement by the father of a suitor to provide a house and land for the settlement of his son and new bride are familiar facts.[11] But the significance of this seventeenth-century custom is much greater than is sometimes realized. It generally meant that the marriages of the second generation were dependent upon their fathers' willingness to let them leave their families and to establish themselves in separate households elsewhere. The late age at which so many sons married during this period indicates that the majority of first-generation parents were unwilling to see their sons married and settled in their own families until long after they had passed the age of 21. The usual age of adulthood, marked by marriage and the establishment of another family, was often 24 or later. Since 60 per cent of the second-generation sons were 25 or over at the time of their marriage and nearly one quarter of them were 30 or over, one wonders what made the first generation so reluctant to part with its sons?

At least part of the answer seems to lie in the fact that Andover was largely a farming community during the seventeenth century, structured, by the time that the second generation was maturing, around the family farm which stood isolated from its neighbors and which functioned independently. The family farm required all the labor it could obtain from its own members, and the sons evidently were expected to assist their fathers on their family farms as long as their fathers felt that it was necessary for them to provide their labor. In return for this essential, but prolonged, contribution to their family's economic security, the sons must have been promised land by their fathers when they married, established their own families, and wished to begin their own farms. But this meant that the sons were fully dependent upon their fathers as long as they remained at home. Even if they wanted to leave, they still needed paternal assistance and money in order to purchase land elsewhere. The delayed marriages of second-generation men thus indicate their prolonged attachment to their families, and the continuation of paternal authority over second-generation sons until they had reached their mid-twenties, at least. In effect, it appears, the maturity of this generation was appreciably later than has been suspected hitherto. The psychological consequences of this prolonged dependence of sons are difficult to assess, but they must have been significant.

Even more significant of the type of family relationships emerging with the maturing of the second generation than their late age of marriage is the fact that paternal authority over sons did not cease with

[11] See especially Morgan, *Puritan Family*, 39–44. For one example of marriage negotiations in Andover during this period, see the agreement between widow Hannah Osgood of Andover and Samuel Archard, Sr., of Salem, about 1660 in the *Records and Files of the Quarterly Courts of Essex County, Massachusetts* (Salem, 1912–21), III, 463, cited hereafter as *Essex Quarterly Court*. Also see the negotiations of Simon Bradstreet of Andover and Nathaniel Wade of Ipswich, *New England Historical and Genealogical Register*, XIII, 204, quoted in Morgan, *Puritan Family*, 41.

marriage. In this community, at least, paternal authority was exercised by the first generation not only prior to their sons' marriages, while the second generation continued to reside under the same roof with their parents and to work on the family farm, and not only at the time of marriage, when fathers generally provided the economic means for their sons' establishment in separate households, but also *after* marriage, by the further step of the father's withholding legal control of the land from the sons who had settled upon it.[12] The majority of first-generation fathers continued to own the land which they settled their sons upon from the time the older men received it from the town to the day of their deaths. All of the first-generation fathers were willing to allow their sons to build houses upon their land, and to live apart from the paternal house after their marriage, but few were willing to permit their sons to become fully independent as long as they were still alive. By withholding deeds to the land which they had settled their sons upon, and which presumably would be theirs to inherit someday, the first generation successfully assured the continuity of their authority over their families long after their sons had become adults and had gained a nominal independence.[13] Since the second generation, with a few exceptions, lacked clear legal titles to the land which they lived upon and farmed, they were prohibited from selling the land which their fathers had settled them upon, or from alienating the land in any other way without the consent of their fathers, who continued to own it. Being unable to sell the land which they expected to inherit, second-generation sons could not even depart from Andover without their fathers' consent, since few had sufficient capital of their own with which to purchase land for themselves outside of Andover. The family thus was held together not only by settling sons

---

[12] Similar delays in the handing over of control of the land from one generation to the next are discussed by W. M. Williams in his study of Ashworthy, *West Country Village*, 84–98. Williams noted (p. 91) that "the length of time which the transference of control takes is broadly a reflection of the degree of patriarchalism within the family: the more authoritarian the father, the longer the son has to wait to become master."

[13] The use of inheritances as a covert threat by the older generation to control the younger generation is revealed only occasionally in their wills, but must have been a factor in their authority over their sons. One suggestive example of a threat to cut off children from their anticipated inheritances is to be found in the will of George Abbot, Sr., who died in 1681, about 64 years old. Prior to his death, his two eldest sons and one daughter had married, leaving at home five unmarried sons and two unmarried daughters with his widow after his death. Abbot left his entire estate to his wife except for the land which he had already given to his eldest son. At her death, he instructed, his wife was to divide the estate with the advice of her sons and friends, and all the children, except the eldest, who had already received a double portion, were to be treated equally unless "by their disobedient carige" towards her "there be rasen to cut them short." Widow Abbot thus had an effective means for controlling her children, the oldest of whom was 24 in 1681. George Abbot, MS will, Dec. 12, 1681, Probate File 43, Probate Record Office, Registry of Deeds and Probate Court Building, Salem, Mass.

upon family land in Andover, but also by refusing to relinquish control of the land until long after the second generation had established its nominal independence following their marriages and the establishment of separate households. In a majority of cases, the dependence of the second-generation sons continued until the deaths of their fathers. And most of the first generation of settlers was very long lived.

The first generation's reluctance to hand over the control of their property to their second-generation sons is evident in their actions.[14] Only three first-generation fathers divided their land among all of their sons before their deaths and gave them deeds of gift for their portions of the paternal estate. All three, however, waited until late in their lives to give their sons legal title to their portions of the family lands. Eleven first-generation fathers settled all of their sons upon their family estates in Andover, but gave a deed of gift for the land to only one of their sons; the rest of their sons had to await their fathers' deaths before inheriting the land which they had been settled upon. Ten of the settlers retained the title to all of their land until their deaths, handing over control to their sons only by means of their last wills and testaments. For the great majority of the second generation, inheritances constituted the principal means of transferring the ownership of land from one generation to the next.[15] The use of partible inheritances in Andover is evident in the division of the estates of the first generation.[16] Twenty-one of twenty-two first-generation families

[14] For deeds of gift of first-generation Andover fathers to their second-generation sons, see the following deeds, located in the MSS volumes of Essex Deeds, Registry of Deeds and Probate Court Building, Salem, Mass.: Richard Barker, v. 29, pp. 115–116; Hannah Dane (widow of George Abbot), v. 94, pp. 140–141; Edmund Faulkner, v. 39, p. 250; John Frye, v. 9, pp. 287–288; Nicholas Holt, v. 6, pp. 722–723, 814–821; v. 7, pp. 292–296; v. 9, p. 12; v. 32, pp. 130–131; v. 34, pp. 255–256; Henry Ingalls, v. 14, pp. 40–41; John Lovejoy, v. 33, pp. 40–41.

[15] The intimate relationship between inheritance patterns and family structure has been noted and examined by several historians and numerous sociologists. George C. Homans, in his study of *English Villagers of the Thirteenth Century* (New York, 1960), 26, pointed out that "differences in customs of inheritance are sensitive signs of differences in traditional types of family organization." See Homans' discussions of inheritance in England, chs. VIII and IX. H. J. Habakkuk, in his article, "Family Structure and Economic Change in Nineteenth-Century Europe," *The Journal of Economic History*, XV (1955), 4, wrote that "inheritance systems exerted an influence on the structure of the family, that is, on the size of the family, on the relations of parents to children and between the children. . . ." Very little, however, has been written about the role of inheritance in American life, or of its impact upon the development of the American family. One of the few observers to perceive the importance and impact of inheritance customs upon American family life was the shrewd visitor, Alexis de Tocqueville. See, for instance, his discussion of partible inheritance in *Democracy in America*, ed. Phillips Bradley (New York, 1956), I, 47–51.

[16] For further details, see the following wills: George Abbot, Probate File 43; Andrew Allen, Probate File 370; John Aslett, *Essex Quarterly Court*, IV, 409; William Ballard, Administration of Estate, Probate Record, Old Series, Book 4, vol. 304, pp. 388–389;

which had two or more sons divided all of their land among all of their surviving sons. Out of seventy-seven sons who were alive at the time their fathers either wrote their wills or gave them deeds to the land, seventy-two sons received some land from their fathers. Out of a total of sixty-six sons whose inheritances can be determined from their fathers' wills, sixty-one or 92.4 per cent received land from their fathers' estates in Andover. Often the land bequeathed to them by will was already in their possession, but without legal conveyances having been given. Thus although the great majority of second-generation sons were settled upon their fathers' lands while their fathers were still alive, few actually owned the land which they lived upon until after their fathers' deaths. With their inheritances came ownership; and with ownership came independence. Many waited a long time.

The characteristic delays in the handing over of control of the land from the first to the second generation may be illustrated by the lives and actions of several Andover families. Like most of the men who wrested their farms and their community from the wilderness, William Ballard was reluctant to part with the control over his land. When Ballard died intestate in 1689, aged about 72 years, his three sons, Joseph, William, and John, agreed to divide their father's estate among themselves "as Equally as they could." [17] They also agreed to give their elderly mother, Grace Ballard, a room in their father's house and to care for her as long as she remained a widow, thus adhering voluntarily to a common practice for the provision of the widow. The eldest son, Joseph, had married in 1665/6, almost certainly a rather young man, whereas his two brothers did not marry until the early 1680's, when their father was in his mid-sixties. William, Jr., must have been well over 30 by then, and John was 28. Both Joseph and William received as part of their division of their father's estate in Andover the land where their houses already stood, as well as more than 75 acres of land

---

Richard Barker, Probate File 1708; Samuel Blanchard, Probate File 2612; William Blunt, Probate File 2658; Thomas Chandler, Probate File 4974; William Chandler, Probate File 4979; Rev. Francis Dane, Probate File 7086; John Farnum, Probate File 9244; Thomas Farnum, Probate File 9254; Edmund Faulkner, Probate File 9305; Andrew Foster, Probate Record, Old Series, Book 2, vol. 302, pp. 136–137 (photostat copy); John Frye, Probate File 10301; Henry Ingalls, Probate File 14505; John Lovejoy, Probate File 17068; John Marston, Probate File 17847; Joseph Parker, *Essex Quarterly Court*, VII, 142–144; Andrew Peters, Probate File 21550; Daniel Poor, Probate Record, vol. 302, pp. 196–197; John Russ, Probate File 24365; John Stevens, *Essex Quarterly Court*, II, 414–416; and Walter Wright, Probate File 30733. The Probate Files of manuscript wills, inventories, and administrations of estates, and the bound Probate Records, are located in the Probate Record Office, Registry of Deeds and Probate Court Building, Salem, Mass.

[17] MS Articles of Agreement, Oct. 23, 1689, Probate Records, Old Series, Book 4, vol. 304, pp. 388–389 (photostat copy). For genealogical details of the Ballard family, see Abbott's Ballard genealogy, typed MSS, in the Memorial Library, Andover.

apiece. The youngest son, John, got all the housing, land, and meadow "his father lived upon except the land and meadow his father gave William Blunt upon the marriage with his daughter," which had taken place in 1668. It is unclear whether John lived with his wife and their four children in the same house as his parents, but there is a strong likelihood that this was the case in view of his assuming control of it after his father's death. His two older brothers had been given land to build upon by their father before his death, but no deeds of gift had been granted to them, thus preventing their full independence so long as he remained alive. Their family remained closely knit both by their establishment of residences near their paternal home on family land and by the prolonged control by William Ballard over the land he had received as one of the first settlers in Andover. It was a pattern repeated in many families.

There were variations, however, such as those exemplified by the Holt family, one of the most prominent in Andover during the seventeenth century. Nicholas Holt, originally a tanner by trade, had settled in Newbury, Massachusetts, for nearly a decade before joining the group of men planting the new town of Andover during the 1640's. Once established in the wilderness community, Holt ranked third among the householders, with an estate which eventually included at least 400 acres of land in Andover as a result of successive divisions of the common land.[18] At some time prior to 1675, he removed his family from the village, where all the original house lots had been located, and built a dwelling house on his third division of land. Although a small portion of his land still lay to the north and west of the old village center, the greatest part of his estate lay in a reasonably compact farm south of his new house. Holt owned no land outside of Andover, and he acquired very little besides the original division grants from the town. It was upon this land that he eventually settled all his sons. In 1662, however, when Nicholas Holt received the fourth division grant of 300 acres from the town, his eldest son, Samuel, was 21 years old, and his three other sons were 18, 15, and 11. The fifth son was yet unborn. His four sons were thus still adolescents, and at ages at which they could provide the physical labor needed to cultivate the land already cleared about the house, and to clear and break up the land which their father had just received. The family probably provided most of the labor, since there is no evidence to indicate that servants or hired laborers were numerous in Andover at the time. With the exception of two daughters who married in the late 1650's, the Holt family

---

[18] For Nicholas Holt's land grants in Andover, see the MS volume, A Record of Town Roads and Town Bounds, 18–19, located in the vault of the Town Clerk's office, Andover, Mass. For genealogical information on the Holt family, see Daniel S. Durrie, *A Genealogical History of the Holt Family in the United States . . .* (Albany, N.Y., 1864), 9–16.

remained together on their farm until 1669, when the two oldest sons and the eldest daughter married.

By 1669, when Holt's eldest son, Samuel, finally married at the age of 28, the only possible means of obtaining land to settle upon from the town was to purchase one of the twenty-acre lots which were offered for sale. House-lot grants with accommodation land had long since been abandoned by the town, and Samuel's marriage and independence therefore depended upon his father's willingness to provide him with sufficient land to build upon and to farm for himself. Evidently his father had proved unwilling for many years, but when Samuel did at last marry, he was allowed to build a house for himself and his wife upon his father's "Three-score Acres of upland," known otherwise as his third division.[19] Soon afterwards, his second brother, Henry, married and also was given land to build upon in the third division. Neither Samuel nor Henry was given a deed to his land by their father at the time he settled upon it. Their marriages and their establishment of separate households left their three younger brothers still living with their aging father and step-mother. Five years passed before the next son married. James, the fourth of the five sons, married in 1675, at the age of 24, whereupon he, too, was provided with a part of his father's farm to build a house upon.[20] The third son, Nicholas, Jr., continued to live with his father, waiting until 1680 to marry at the late age of 32. His willingness to delay even a token independence so long suggests that personal factors must have played an important part in his continued assistance to his father, who was then about 77 years old.[21] John Holt, the youngest of the sons, married at the age of 21, shortly before his father's death.

For Nicholas Holt's four oldest sons, full economic independence was delayed for many years. Although all had withdrawn from their father's house and had established separate residences of their own, they nonetheless were settled upon their father's land not too far distant from their family homestead, and none had yet been given a legal title to the land where he lived. Until Nicholas Holt was willing to give his sons deeds of gift for the lands where he had allowed them to build and to farm, he retained all legal rights to his estate and could still dispose of it in any way he chose. Without his consent, therefore, none of his sons could sell or mortgage the land where he lived since none of them owned it. In the Holt family, paternal authority rested upon firm economic foundations, a situation characteristic of the majority of Andover families of this period and these two generations.

[19] Essex Deeds, v. 32, p. 130.
[20] Ibid., v. 7, pp. 292–296.
[21] See ibid., v. 6, pp. 814–815.

Eventually, Nicholas Holt decided to relinquish his control over his Andover property by giving to his sons, after many years, legal titles to the lands which they lived upon. In a deed of gift, dated February 14, 1680/1, he conveyed to his eldest son, Samuel, who had been married almost twelve years, one half of his third division land, "the Said land on which the said Samuels House now Stands," which had the land of his brother, Henry, adjoining on the west, as well as an additional 130 acres of upland from the fourth division of land, several parcels of meadow, and all privileges accompanying these grants of land.[22] In return for this gift, Samuel, then forty years old, promised to pay his father for his maintenance so long as his "naturall life Shall Continue," the sum of twenty shillings a year. Ten months later, December 15, 1681, Nicholas Holt conveyed almost exactly the same amount of land to his second son, Henry, and also obligated him to pay twenty shillings yearly for his maintenance.[23] Prior to this gift, Nicholas had given his fourth son, James, his portion, which consisted of one-third part of "my farme" including "the land where his house now stands," some upland, a third of the great meadow, and other small parcels. In return, James promised to pay his father three pounds a year for life (three times the sum his two elder brothers were to pay), and to pay his mother-in-law forty shillings a year when she should become a widow.[24] The farm which James received was shared by his two other brothers, Nicholas and John, as well. Nicholas, in a deed of June 16, 1682, received "one third part of the farme where he now dwells," some meadow, and, most importantly, his father's own dwelling house, including the cellar, orchard, and barn, which constituted the principal homestead and house of Nicholas Holt, Sr.[25] In "consideration of this my fathers gift . . . to me his sone," Nicholas, Junior, wrote, "I doe promise and engage to pay yearly" the sum of three pounds for his father's maintenance. Thus Nicholas, Junior, in return for his labors and sacrifices as a son who stayed with his father until the age of 32, received not only a share in the family farm equal to that of his two younger brothers, but in addition received the paternal house and homestead. The youngest of the five Holt sons, John, was the only one to receive his inheritance from his father by deed prior to his marriage. On June 19, 1685, Nicholas Holt, Sr., at the age of 83, gave his "Lovinge" son a parcel of land lying on the easterly side of "my now Dwelling house," some meadow, and fifteen acres of upland "as yett unlaid out."[26] One month later, John married, having already built

---

[22] *Ibid.,* v. 32, pp. 130–131.
[23] *Ibid.,* v. 34, pp. 255–256.
[24] *Ibid.,* v. 7, pp. 292–296.
[25] *Ibid.,* v. 6, pp. 814–816.
[26] *Ibid.,* v. 9, p. 12.

himself a house upon the land which his father promised to give him. Unlike his older brothers, John Holt thus gained his complete independence as an exceptionally young man. His brothers, however, still were not completely free from obligations to their father since each had agreed to the yearly payment of money to their father in return for full ownership of their farms. Not until Nicholas Holt's death at the end of January 1685/6 could his sons consider themselves fully independent of their aged father. He must have died content in the knowledge that all of his sons had been established on farms fashioned out of his own ample estate in Andover, all enjoying as a result of his patriarchal hand the rewards of his venture into the wilderness.[27]

Some Andover families were less reluctant than Nicholas Holt to let their sons marry early and to establish separate households, although the control of the land in most instances still rested in the father's hands. The Lovejoy family, with seven sons, enabled the four oldest sons to marry at the ages of 22 and 23. John Lovejoy, Sr., who originally emigrated from England as a young indentured servant, acquired a seven-acre house lot after his settlement in Andover during the mid-1640's, and eventually possessed an estate of over 200 acres in the town.[28] At his death in 1690, at the age of 68, he left an estate worth a total of £327.11.6, with housing and land valued at £260.00.0, a substantial sum at the time.[29] Although he himself had waited until the age of 29 to marry, his sons married earlier. His eldest son, John, Jr., married on March 23, 1677/8, aged 22, and built a house and began to raise crops on land which his father gave him for that purpose. He did not receive a deed of gift for his land, however; his inventory, taken in 1680 after his premature death, showed his major possessions to consist of "one house and a crope of corn" worth only twenty pounds. His entire estate, both real and personal, was valued at only £45.15.0, and was encumbered with £29.14.7 in debts.[30] Three years later, on April 6, 1683, the land which he had farmed without owning was given to his three-year-old son by his father, John Lovejoy, Sr. In a deed of gift, the elder Lovejoy gave his grandson, as a token of the love and affection he felt for his deceased son, the land which John, Junior, had had, consisting of fifty acres of upland, a piece of meadow, and a small par-

---

[27] For an example of a first-generation father who gave a deed of gift to his eldest son only, letting his five younger sons inherit their land, see the MS will of Richard Barker, dated Apr. 27, 1688, Probate File 1708. The deed to his eldest son is found in the Essex Deeds, v. 29, pp. 115–116. All of Barker's sons married late (27, 31, 35, 28, 28, and 25), and all but the eldest continued to be under the control of their father during his long life.

[28] For John Lovejoy's Andover land grants, see the MS volume, A Record of Town Roads and Town Bounds, 96–98.

[29] See John Lovejoy's MS inventory in Probate File 17068.

[30] For the inventory of the estate of John Lovejoy, Jr., see Essex Quarterly Court, VIII, 56.

cel of another meadow, all of which lay in Andover.[31] Of the surviving
Lovejoy sons only the second, William, received a deed of gift from
the elder Lovejoy for the land which he had given them.[32] The others
had to await their inheritances to come into full possession of their
land. In his will dated September 1, 1690, shortly before his death,
Lovejoy distributed his estate among his five surviving sons: Christopher received thirty acres together with other unstated amounts of
land, and Nathaniel received the land which his father had originally
intended to give to his brother, Benjamin, who had been killed in
1689. Benjamin was 25 years old and unmarried at the time of his
death, and left an estate worth only £1.02.8, his wages as a soldier.[33]
Without their father's land, sons were penniless. The youngest of the
Lovejoy sons, Ebenezer, received his father's homestead, with the
house and lands, in return for fulfilling his father's wish that his
mother should "be made comfortable while she Continues in this
world."[34] His mother inherited the east end of the house, and elaborate provisions in the will ensured her comfort. With all the surviving
sons settled upon their father's land in Andover, with the residence of
the widow in the son's house, and with the fact that only one of the
sons actually received a deed for his land during their father's life-time,
the Lovejoys also epitomized some of the principal characteristics of
family life in seventeenth-century Andover.

Exceptions to the general pattern of prolonged paternal control over
sons were rare. The actions taken by Edmund Faulkner to settle his eldest son in Andover are instructive precisely because they were so exceptional. The first sign that Faulkner was planning ahead for his son
came with his purchase of a twenty-acre lot from the town at the annual town meeting of March 22, 1669/70.[35] He was the only first-gen-

[31] Essex Deeds, v. 33, pp. 40–41.

[32] This deed from John Lovejoy, Sr., to his son, William, is not recorded in the Essex
Deeds at the Registry of Deeds, Salem, Mass. The deed, however, is mentioned in his
will, Probate File 17068, wherein he bequeathed to William the lands which he already
had conveyed to his son by deed. It was customary for such deeds to be mentioned in
wills, since they usually represented much or all of a son's portion of a father's estate.

[33] For the inventory to Benjamin Lovejoy's estate, see the Probate File 17048.

[34] *Ibid.*, 17068. Provision for the widow was customary, and is to be found in all the
wills of first-generation settlers who left their wives still alive. Generally, the son who inherited the paternal homestead was obligated to fulfill most of the necessary services for
his mother, usually including the provision of firewood and other essentials of daily living. Provision also was made in most instances for the mother to reside in one or two
rooms of the paternal house, or to have one end of the house, sometimes with a garden
attached. Accommodations thus were written into wills to ensure that the mother would
be cared for in her old age and would retain legal grounds for demanding such provisions.

[35] Andover, MS volume of Ancient Town Records, located in the Town Clerk's office,
Andover.

eration settler to purchase such a lot, all of the other purchasers being either second-generation sons or newcomers, and it was evident that he did not buy it for himself since he already had a six-acre house lot and more than one hundred acres of land in Andover.[36] The town voted that "in case the said Edmond shall at any time put such to live upon it as the town shall approve, or have no just matter against them, he is to be admitted to be a townsman." The eldest of his two sons, Francis, was then a youth of about nineteen years. Five years later, January 4, 1674/5, Francis was admitted as a townsman of Andover "upon the account of the land he now enjoyeth," almost certainly his father's twenty acres.[37] The following October, aged about 24, Francis married the minister's daughter. A year and a half later, in a deed dated February 1, 1676/7, Edmund Faulkner freely gave his eldest son "one halfe of my Living here at home" to be "Equally Divided between us both."[38] Francis was to pay the town rates on his half, and was to have half the barn, half the orchard, and half the land about his father's house, and both he and his father were to divide the meadows. Significantly, Edmund added that "all my Sixscore acres over Shawshinne river I wholly give unto him," thus handing over, at the relatively young age of 52, most of his upland and half of the remainder of his estate to his eldest son. The control of most of his estate thereby was transferred legally and completely from the first to the second generation. Edmund's second and youngest son, John, was still unmarried at the time Francis received his gift, and waited until 1682 before marrying at the age of 28. Eventually he received some land by his father's will, but his inheritance was small compared to his brother's. Edmund Faulkner's eagerness to hand over the control of his estate to his eldest son is notable for its rarity and accentuates the fact that almost none of his friends and neighbors chose to do likewise.[39] It is just possible that Faulkner, himself a younger son of an English gentry family, sought to preserve most of his Andover estate intact by giving it to his eldest son. If so, it would only emphasize his distinctiveness from his neighbors. For the great majority of the first-generation settlers in Andover, partible inheritances and delayed control by the first generation over the land were the rule. Faulkner was the exception which proved it.

[36] For Edmund Faulkner's land grants in Andover, see the MS Record of Town Roads and Town Bounds, 52–53.

[37] Town meeting of Jan. 4, 1674/5, Andover, Ancient Town Records.

[38] Essex Deeds, v. 39, p. 250. Only one other instance of the co-partnership of father and son is to be found in the wills of seventeenth-century Andover, but not among the men who founded the town. See the MS will of Andrew Peters, Probate File 21550.

[39] The only instance of impartible inheritance, or primogeniture, to be found in the first generation of Andover's settlers occurred within the first decade of its settlement, before the extensive land grants of 1662 had been voted by the town. See John Osgood's will, dated Apr. 12, 1650, in *Essex Quarterly Court*, I, 239. Osgood left his entire Andover estate to the eldest of his two sons.

Embedded in the reconstructions of particular family histories is a general pattern of family structure unlike any which are known or suspected to have existed either in England or its American colonies during the seventeenth century. It is evident that the family structure which developed during the lifetimes of the first two generations in Andover cannot be classified satisfactorily according to any of the more recent definitions applied to types of family life in the seventeenth century. It was not simply a "patrilineal group of extended kinship gathered into a single household,"[40] nor was it simply a "nuclear independent family, that is man, wife, and children living apart from relatives."[41] The characteristic family structure which emerged in Andover with the maturing of the second generation during the 1670's and 1680's was a combination of both the classical extended family and the nuclear family. This distinctive form of family structure is best described as a *modified extended family*—defined as a kinship group of two or more generations living within a single community in which the dependence of the children upon their parents continues after the children have married and are living under a separate roof. This family structure is a *modified* extended family because all members of the family are not "gathered into a single household," but it is still an *extended* family because the newly created conjugal unit of husband and wife live in separate households in close proximity to their parents and siblings and continue to be economically dependent in some respects upon their parents. And because of the continuing dependence of the second generation upon their first-generation fathers, who continued to own most of the family land throughout the better part of their lives, the family in seventeenth-century Andover was *patriarchal* as well. The men who first settled the town long remained the dominant

[40] Bernard Bailyn, *Education in the Forming of American Society: Needs and Opportunities for Study* (Chapel Hill, 1960), 15–16. "Besides children, who often remained in the home well into maturity," Bailyn adds, the family "included a wide range of other dependents: nieces and nephews, cousins, and, except for families at the lowest rung of society, servants in filial discipline. In the Elizabethan family the conjugal unit was only the nucleus of a broad kinship community whose outer edges merged almost imperceptibly into the society at large." For further discussions of the extended family in England, see Peter Laslett, "The Gentry of Kent in 1640," *Cambridge Historical Journal*, IX (1948), 148–164; and Peter Laslett's introduction to his edition of *Patriarcha and Other Political Works of Sir Robert Filmer* (Oxford, 1949), esp. 22–26.

[41] Peter Laslett and John Harrison, "Clayworth and Cogenhoe," in H. E. Bell and R. L. Ollard, eds., *Historical Essays, 1660–1750, Presented to David Ogg* (London, 1963), 168. See also H. J. Habakkuk, "Population Growth and Economic Development," in *Lectures on Economic Development* (Istanbul, 1958), 23, who asserts that "from very early in European history, the social unit was the nuclear family—the husband and wife and their children—as opposed to the extended family or kinship group." See also Robin M. Williams, Jr., *American Society: A Sociological Interpretation*, 2d ed. rev. (New York, 1963), 50–57. For a contrasting interpretation of family structure in other 17th-century New England towns, see Demos, "Notes on Life in Plymouth Colony," 279–280.

figures both in their families and their community. It was their decisions and their actions which produced the family characteristic of seventeenth-century Andover.

One of the most significant consequences of the development of the
modified extended family characteristic of Andover during this period
was the fact that remarkably few second-generation sons moved away
from their families and their community. More than four fifths of the
second-generation sons lived their entire lives in the town which their
fathers had wrested from the wilderness.[42] The first generation evidently was intent upon guaranteeing the future of the community and
of their families within it through the settlement of all of their sons
upon the lands originally granted to them by the town. Since it was
quite true that the second generation could not expect to acquire as
much land by staying in Andover as their fathers had by undergoing
the perils of founding a new town on the frontier, it is quite possible
that their reluctance to hand over the control of the land to their sons
when young is not only a reflection of their patriarchalism, justified
both by custom and by theology, but also of the fact that they could
not be sure that their sons would stay, given a free choice. Through a
series of delays, however, particularly those involving marriages and
economic independence, the second generation continued to be
closely tied to their paternal families. By keeping their sons in positions of prolonged dependence, the first generation successfully managed to keep them in Andover during those years in which their youth
and energy might have led them to seek their fortunes elsewhere.
Later generations achieved their independence earlier and moved
more. It remains to be seen to what extent the family life characteristic
of seventeenth-century Andover was the exception or the rule in the
American colonies.

[42] Out of a total of 103 second-generation sons whose residences are known, only seventeen or 16.5 per cent, departed from Andover. Five left before 1690, and twelve left
after 1690. The majority of families in 17th-century Andover remained closely knit and
remarkably immobile.

"Tender Plants": Quaker Farmers and Children in the Delaware Valley, 1681–1735

BARRY J. LEVY

The social history of the Middle Colonies has lagged behind studies of New England and the Chesapeake, but Barry Levy has done much to narrow this gap. His study of Quaker families in southeastern Pennsylvania is all the more useful for the direct comparisons he makes with Philip Greven's Andover. Quaker parents accumulated far more land for their offspring than Puritans did, kept their children at home longer, treated them with greater affection, and granted them much fuller autonomy at marriage. As Levy shows, "holy conversation," or disciplined Quaker behavior, required a considerable base in material possessions to perpetuate itself from one generation to the next. Poor Quakers often could not meet these standards.

Can we explain these different patterns of behavior in material terms alone, or must we first understand the unique religious dynamic that distinguished Quakers from Puritans? Puritans saw their children as sinners who had to be converted or suffer inevitable damnation. Quakers regarded their offspring as innocents who had to be shielded from the corruptions of a hostile world. How important were these underlying religious attitudes in shaping such apparently unrelated matters as landholding patterns? Why should parents who believed their children innocent acquire more land than parents who saw children as sinners? What is "modern" about Quaker families, and what is not?

"And whoso shall receive one such little child in my name, receiveth me. But whoso shall offend one of these little ones which believe in me, it were better for him that a millstone were hanged about his neck, and that he were drowned in the depth of the sea" (Matthew 18:5–6).

I

In the late seventeenth and early eighteenth centuries, the settlers of Chester and the Welsh Tract, bordering Philadelphia, devoted themselves to their children, and the results were economically impressive but socially ambiguous. The settlers were under the influence of a difficult religious doctrine, which can be called "holy conversation," insti-

Reprinted from Barry J. Levy, " 'Tender Plants': Quaker Farmers and Children in the Delaware Valley, 1681–1735," *Journal of Family History*, 3 (1978), 116–135, by permission of JAI Press, Greenwich, Conn.

tutionalized in their Monthly Meetings and practiced in their households. "Holy conversation" dictated that implicit instruction by loving parents, not coercion or stern discipline, would lead to the child's salvation. The farmers thus used the resources of the Delaware Valley to create environments for children and young adults, accumulating vast amounts of land, limiting the type of labor they brought into their households, and devising intricate, demanding strategies to hand out land and money to children. They directed intense attention to marriage and the conjugal household and spoke endlessly in their Meetings about "tenderness" and "love." These families, however, were religious, not affectionate, sentimental, or isolated. It was their religious conception of the child that both inspired and clearly limited the development of these adults and their society forming in the Delaware Valley.

The settlers were able, middling people from remote parts of Great Britain. The Welsh came from varying social backgrounds; they included eight gentlemen (the Welsh gentry was not wealthy as a rule) and twenty-five yeomen and husbandmen. The Chester settlers were mostly yeomen and artisans from Cheshire and surrounding counties in northwest England. Most settlers in both groups arrived in nuclear families having two or more children. Approximately seventy-five such Welsh Quaker and seventy-eight Cheshire Quaker families settled between 1681 and 1690 along the Schuylkill and Delaware Rivers near Philadelphia (Browning, 1912:1–29; Glenn, 1970:1–72).

The farmers clearly thought the spiritual fate of their children a vital reason for their coming to Pennsylvania. Each settler carried a removal certificate of about two hundred words describing his or her character. Much of the discussion in these documents concerned children and parenthood. One Welsh Meeting, for example, wrote of David Powell that "he hath hopeful children, several of them having behaved themselves well in Friends' services where they lived and we hope and desire the Lords presence may go along with them" [Friends Historical Library, Radnor Monthly Meeting Records (henceforth RMMR), 3/23/1690]. The only thing said of Griffith John, a poor farmer, was that "all his endeavor hath been to bring up his children in the fear of the Lord according to the order of Truth" (RMMR 4/22/1690). Sina Pugh was a "good, careful, industrious woman in things relating to her poor small children" (RMMR 2/5/1684). The Welsh Meetings acted *in loco parentis* for children left without parents and sent the orphans to Pennsylvania: the Tuddr orphans, for example, "were under the tuition of Friends since their parents deceased and we found them living and honest children; and we did what we could to keep them out of the wicked way and to preserve their small estate from waste and confiscation" (RMMR 2/3/1689). Meetings often referred to children as "tender," "sweet," and "loving," virtues which typified the descriptions of adult Friends with the most praised behavior. The metaphor most often used by the Welsh farmers when describing children was "tender plants growing in the Truth."

Two Welsh Tract leaders, John Bevan and Thomas Ellis, thought that the need to protect children from corruption explained the Quakers' emigration to Pennsylvania. Barbara Bevan persuaded her husband John Bevan to come to Pennsylvania for the sake of their children. "Some time before the year 1683," he later wrote, "I had heard that our esteemed Friend William Penn had a patent from King Charles the Second for the Province in America called Pennsylvania, and my wife had a great inclination to go thither and thought it might be a good place to train up children amongst sober people and to prevent the corruption of them here by the loose behavior of youthes and the bad example of too many of riper years." Bevan did not want to go, "but I was sensible her aim was an upright one, on account of our children, I was willing to weigh the matter in a true balance." He found that he could keep his three Welsh farms and still buy land in Pennsylvania (a member of the gentry in Treverig, near Cardiff, Bevan was the only settler not to sell his British property). Bevan returned to Wales in 1704 with his wife and favorite daughter because "we stayed there (Pennsylvania) many years, and had four of our children married with our consent, and they had several children, and the aim intended by my wife was in good measure answered" (Bevan, 1709). Bevan clearly saw Pennsylvania as a place best suited for rearing children.

In 1684 on arrival in Haverford, Thomas Ellis, a Welsh Quaker minister, prayed in a poem, "Song of Rejoicing," that "In our bounds, true love and peace from age to age may never cease" . . . when "trees and fields increase" and "heaven and earth proclaim thy peace" (Smith, 1862:492). Children were implicit in his vision. When on a return trip to England in 1685, after he noted that many English Quakers were suspicious of the large emigration of Friends to Pennsylvania, he wrote to George Fox stressing the relationship between children and wealth: "I wish those that have estates of their own and to leave fullness in their posterity may not be offended at the Lord's opening a door of mercy to thousands in England especially in Wales who have no estates either for themselves or children . . . nor any visible ground of hope for a better condition for children or children's children when they were gone hence." Ellis's argument rested on the promise of Quaker life in the new world. In Pennsylvania, Ellis showed, land could combine fruitfully with community life:

> About fifteen families of us have taken our land together and there are to be eight more that have not yet come, who took (to begin) 30 acres apiece with which we build upon and do improve, and the other land we have to range for our cattle, we have our

> burying place where we intend our Meeting House, as near as we can to the center, our men and women's Meeting and other Monthly Meetings in both week dayes unto which four townships at least belongs. And precious do we find other opportunities that are given as free will offering unto the Lord in evenings, some time which not intended but Friends coming simply to one another and setting together the Lord appears to his name be the Glory (Ellis, June 13, 1685).

With land broadly distributed for children to inherit, settlers like Ellis could hope to permanently realize their goals.

The attention and worry that the Welsh Meetings, John Bevan, and Thomas Ellis directed to children stemmed from the Quakers' world view which made child-rearing difficult and important. By dividing the human behavior into two "languages"—"holy conversation" leading to salvation, and "carnal talk" leading to corruption and death—Quakers had no choice but to secure environments of "holy conversation" for their children. Quakers thought that the Word was communicated only spontaneously in human relations, that all set forms of speech were ineffective. They thus challenged the Puritan view that God's reality was set forth solely in the Bible and that grace could only be received by listening and responding to ministers' explications of the Biblical text. In his *Journal* George Fox always called the Puritans "professors" in order to stigmatize them as people who only professed their faith in response to sermons they had heard. Quakers, on the other hand, lived their faith, they claimed, becoming virtually embodiments of the Word. Quakers found appropriate means of expressing the Word in their communities. In the worship meeting, after a period of silence, the Word was communicated through a "minister's" words, he or she being a conduit of the Word, or by spontaneous, nonverbal communication between attenders. In society the Word was to be communicated almost all the time by a man or woman's "conversation" (Haller, 1957; Hill, 1967; Nuttal, 1946; Kibbey, 1973; Bauman, 1974).

"Conversation" was defined in the seventeenth century, according to the *Oxford English Dictionary*, as the "manner of conducting oneself in the world or in society." The Quakers' concept of "conversation" included the idea that it was reflective of a person's inner being and that it communicated meaning, as suggested in the King James and Geneva Bibles ["Only let your conversation be as becometh Gospel" (Phil. 1:27), "Be an example of believers in conversation in purity" (1 Tim. 4:12), "they may also be won by the conversation of their wives" (1 Pet. 3:1)]. "Conversation" thus included not only speech but also behavior and non-verbal communication. Human communication, as Dell Hymes has argued, includes not just written and spoken words, but all "speech events," events that a culture regards as having a clear human message (Hymes, 1972; Hymes, 1974). Quakers posited in effect two "languages" * underlying all formal languages and gesture: "holy conversation," the language of the Word, and "carnal conversation," the language of pride and of the world.

The emigrants' removal certificates into Pennsylvania described the settlers' "conversation" and give some idea of the qualities that made up the charismatic presence of the converted Friend. Thirty-six different adjectives or adjectival phrases described the adults in these sixty-two certificates. The adjectives most often used were "honest" (thirty-three), "blameless" (fourteen), "loving" (thirteen), "tender" (nine), "savory" (nine), "serviceable" (nine), "civil" (eight), "plain" (seven), and "modest" (five). Except for three cases—two cases of "industriousness," and one case of "punctual"—the adjectives related to Christlike qualities.

Almost all the adjectives had Biblical origins. "Holy conversation" was the language and behavior of both the Apostles and of the Quakers, who both claimed direct knowledge of Christ. All Quaker testimonies and practices were defended by Biblical reference. Fox, Barclay, Pennington, Naylor, and other Quaker ministers had interlarded their texts with Biblical quotation. Friends used "thee and thou" instead of "you" because it was the pronoun which Quaker ministers thought Christ and the Apostles used. As was the case in the Genevan Bible, Quakers avoided the use of pagan names for months and days, and refused to use titles, even Mr. and Mrs. Refusal to give that honor, refusal to take oaths, pacifism, non-violence, and special dress were all vocabulary in "holy conversation." The Bible (as well as the leadership of the Monthly, Quarterly and Yearly Meetings), though not the source of Truth for Friends, provided an anchor against what easily could become the anarchy of revelation (Levy, 1976:35–45).

The removal certificates discussed the relationship between "holy conversation" and children's spiritual development. Children were born with both Adam's sin and Christ's redeeming Seed. Which developed as the major principle in their lives depended greatly on the environment in which they grew, and particularly important was the character of their parents (Frost, 1973). The Merionth Meeting said of William Powell, for example:

> His conversation since [his conversion] hath been honest and savory in so much that his wife came soon to be affected with the Truth, and became a good example to her children by which means they also became affected with Truth, innocency, and an innocent conversation to this day (RMMR, 1686).

The Tyddyn Gareg Meeting said of the children of Griffith John: "As for their honesty and civility and good behavior we have not anything

---

* "Language" is used here metaphorically to represent a whole communicative system. The Quakers, particularly George Fox, were hostile to "language" in its usual sense.

to say to the contrary but they behaved themselves very well as they come from a very honest family" (RMMR, 1686). Virtually all the children were discussed in these terms. Bachelors and spinsters, moreover, were also "hopeful" when like Elizabeth Owen, they came from "good and honest parentage" (RMMR, 1686). No belief developed in these Meetings similar to the idea which Edmund Morgan has shown developed among Massachusetts' ministers in the late seventeenth century who believed that the children of church members, being part of Abraham's Seed, were virtually assured justification (Morgan, 1966:161–186). Quaker members were known only by their "conversation" and children were only "hopeful" because of their parents' conversation.

By 1680 the guiding institution of Quaker life was the Monthly Meeting, whose purpose was, as George Fox said, "that all order their conversation aright, that they may see the salvation of God; they may all see and know, possess and partake of, the government of Christ, of the increase of which there is no end" (Fox, 1963:152). The men's and women's Monthly Meetings in Chester and the Welsh Tract, like those elsewhere, encouraged "holy conversation" by identifying and disowning carnal talk and by organizing life for the rule of the Word. Their aim was, in a sense, to construct an ideal speech community, where the Word would constantly be exchanged in human relations. Newcomers would not be recognized as members unless they presented a removal certificate, an informed discussion of their spiritual personality, vouching for the high quality of their "conversation." The term is centrally mentioned in ninety-five percent of all the Welsh certificates from 1680 to 1694 (65) and eighty-seven percent of those fully recorded for Quakers within the jurisdiction of the Chester Monthly Meeting (22). When Friends got married in Chester and the Welsh Tract they had their "clearness and conversation" inspected, and when disowned, they were denounced for "scandelous," "disorderly," "indecent," or "worldly" "conversation."

The primary support of the Quakers' social design was their elaborate marriage discipline, which controlled the establishment of new households. Most of the business that came before the Welsh Tract and Chester Men's and Women's Meetings directly concerned marriage. In the Welsh Tract, in the Men's Monthly Meeting (1683–1709) forty-six percent of the business dealt with marriages; the next largest category of business, administrative concerns, like building burial grounds and arranging worship meetings, included only seventeen percent of the itemized business. In the Women's Monthly Meeting marriages took fifty-four percent of the business and charity nineteen percent. In Chester the Men's and Women's Meeting sat together until 1705. Between 1681 and 1705, forty-three percent of the business concerned marriages; the next largest category, discipline, accounted for fourteen percent of the business. These figures do not account for the fact that marriage infractions composed the majority of discipline cases. In the Welsh Tract between 1684 and 1725, eighty-two percent of all condemnations involved young men and women and seventy-eight percent marriage or fornication (fornication without marriage was rare, involving only four percent of the cases). Jack Marietta found similar figures for a number of other Pennsylvania Monthly Meetings, and Susan Forbes found that over seventy-five percent of the disownments in another Chester County meeting, New Garden, related to marriage (Marietta, 1968; Forbes, 1972; Radnor Men's and Women's Monthly Meeting Minutes, 1684–1725; Chester Men's and Women's Monthly Meeting Minutes, 1681–1725).

The Quaker marriage procedure was time-consuming, thorough, and intrusive. A prospective marriage couple had first to obtain permission for both courtship and then marriage from all the parents or closest relatives involved. They then had to announce their intention of marriage before both the Men's and Women's Monthly Meetings. After hearing the announcement, the Meetings appointed two committees, each composed of two well established Friends, in order to investigate the "clearness" from prior ties and particularly the "conversation" of the man and woman (two women investigated the woman, two men the man). The man and woman would appear at the next Monthly Meeting to hear the verdict, which was usually favorable, since the Meetings warned off Friends with problems. After the second visit to the Monthly Meetings the marriage ceremony took place usually in the Meeting house of the woman's family. The Quakers married directly before God, the guests and attendants served as witnesses, signing the marriage certificate. The precedent for this type of ceremony was, according to George Fox, the marriage of Adam and Eve in the Garden. The couple had thus to be restored to the sinless state of Adam and Eve before the Fall in order for the ceremony to be meaningful (Fox, 1663; Fox, 1911:II, 154; Braithwaite, 1919:262). Not all Pennsylvania Friends conformed to Fox's spiritually pure concept of marriage. Both Meetings allowed a few questionable men and women to marry "out of tenderness to them" if they sincerely promised to reform and live as Friends. Two officials from the Monthly Meeting closely watched the ceremony to assure that it was conducted accordingly to "Gospel Order." A committee of "weighty" Friends also visited the new couple (along with other families in these communities) at least four times a year in order to see that they were living according to the standards of "holy conversation." The Quaker marriage discipline and ritual aimed to insure that every Quaker spouse was sustained by another Quaker and that every Quaker child grew up under converted parents in a sustaining, religious environment.

In order to enhance the religious tone of the family, despite the control exercised by parents and Meetings, Friends wanted couples to love one another before they wed. Quaker writers stressed that this was to be a virtuous, Christian love, not romantic lust. It is of course impossible to know what quality of love these Friends expected, demanded, or actually received. Nevertheless, the idea was taken seriously; the Monthly Meetings record a number of Friends, mostly women, rejecting their male Friends at the last minute before the ceremony. After laboriously inspecting and approving one marriage in 1728, for example, the men of Chester were surprised to discover that the marriage had not taken place. The investigating committee reported "that the said Jane Kendal signified to them that she doth not love him well enough to marry him." Similarly in 1705 at Chester, Thomas Martin gained approval to marry Jane Hent, but next month "the above marriage not being accomplished, two Friends—Alice Simcock and Rebecca Faucit—spoke to Jane Hent to know the reason thereof and her answer was that she could not love him well enough to be her husband." Two other cases of this type occurred in Chester and the Welsh Tract between 1681 and 1750. The annoyed Meetings always deferred to the young people (Friends Historical Library, Chester Men's Monthly Meeting Minutes, 10/30/1728, 5/30/1705, 9/6/1705, 4/9/1730, 4/10/1708).

The marriage discipline, despite such responsiveness, was an obstacle to many Quaker children. Many went to a "priest" or magistrate in Philadelphia to marry. Sometimes they had married a non-Quaker, but more often Quaker children would avoid the marriage procedure and their parents' approval by eloping to Philadelphia, often after sexual intimacy. Over one half of the offenders were disowned. The rest "acknowledged" their sin and after a period of spiritual probation were accepted fully as Friends.

Institutional surveillance could only go so far; Quaker families also needed wealth to assure that their children would live their lives among people of "holy conversation." In England and Wales farms were typically from forty to forty-five acres; farmers could rarely keep their children from service or from leaving for the city, particularly London (Hoskins, 1963:151–160; Campbell, 1942:chap. 3,4). For this reason William Penn wanted Pennsylvania settlers to form townships, "for the more convenient bringing up of youth . . . ," of 5000 acres with each farmer having ample, contiguous holdings of from one hundred to five hundred acres. The Quaker proprietor believed that farming was the least corrupting employment and that in England parents were too "addicted to put their children into Gentlemen's service or send them to towns to learn trades, that husbandry is neglected; and after a soft and delicate usage there, they are unfitted for the labor of farming life" (Penn, 1681, Lemon, 1972:98–99). An analysis of removal certificates and tax lists from Chester and Radnor indeed shows that youth did live and work at home.

Welsh Tract and Chester Settlers'
Land Held at Death or Distributed
to Their Children Before Death,
TABLE 1   *1681–1735*

ACRES	PERCENTAGES OF SETTLERS (N)
50–199	9% (5)
200–399	19 (10)
400–599	21 (11)
600–799	21 (11)
800–999	15 (8)
1000+	15 (8)
	100% (53)

Source: Philadelphia City Hall, Philadelphia County Deeds, Philadelphia County Wills and Inventories; Chester County Court House, Chester County Deeds, Chester County Wills and Inventories.

The Welsh Tract and Chester settlers accumulated more land than William Penn proposed. By the late 1690s the mean holding of the seventy resident families in the Welsh Tract was 332 acres. In the towns comprising the Chester Monthly Meeting, the mean holding of seventy-six families was 337 acres. Only six men had holdings of under one hundred acres, and eighty percent held over 150 acres. The Chester and Welsh settlers continued to buy land after 1699 as appears from a comparison of the landholdings of fifty-three Chester and Welsh Quaker settlers in 1699 and the land which they distributed to their children or sold at death. In the 1690s these men had an average of 386 acres, about the same average as the general population of landowners. They gave or sold to their children, however, an average of 701 acres, an average increase of 315 acres from 1690. Seventy percent of the settlers gave 400 acres or more (see Table 1) (Land Bureau, Harrisburg, Land Commissioner's Minutes of the Welsh Tract, 1702; Chester County Historical Society, Chester County Treasurer's Book, 1685–1716). The settlers bought land as their families grew. A correlation exists between the number of sons families had and the amount of land they held. Between the 1690s and the end of their lives, the three men without sons did not increase their acreage; those with one son increased their acreage an average of 135 acres; those with two sons increased their acreage an average of 242 acres; those with three an average of 309 acres; and those with four or more an average of 361 acres. Sons received over two hundred acres on an average, and daughters received the equivalent in Pennsylvania currency.

The settlers bought land almost exclusively for their children. The fifty-three men gave away or sold a total of 160 parcels during their lives, a third of these to their children. Six men engaged in forty-six percent of the sales, however. These men were land speculators, though this role combined with serving as middle men between William Penn and arriving colonists. They were active members of their Monthly Meetings, acquaintances of William Penn, and first purchasers. Most settlers did not engage in land speculation. Thirty-nine of the forty-one wills existing for the fifty-three settlers show large quantities of unused land which was later bequeathed to children. Joseph Baker, for example, besides his plantation in Edgemount, bequeathed a 200 acre tract in Thornberry to his son. Francis Yarnell, beside his plantation in Willistown, bequeathed a 120 acre tract in Springfield. Only three men worked their additional land and only two men had tenants (Chester County Court House, Chester County Deeds, 1681–1790; Philadelphia City Hall, Philadelphia County Deeds, 1681–1790; Chester County Court House, Chester County Wills, August 25, 1724: A-155, 6/6/1721:A-124).

A study of these families' inventories confirms the child-centered use of land. Of the forty-one inventories, twenty-seven of these men at the time of their death already portioned at least two of their children. Seven of these men were nearly retired, though they still used their farms. The rest (fourteen) had portioned only one child or none at the time of their death, so they were probably near the height of productivity. The average farmer had a small herd of animals (six cows, four steers, six horses, fourteen sheep, and eight pigs) and was cultivating between forty and fifty acres for wheat, barley, and corn. The rule of thumb in eighteenth-century farming was three acres for one cow (this was the practice in Cheshire), so the cows and steers would require at least thirty acres. The six horses would need about six acres and grain, and the thirteen sheep about two acres a year. This gives a figure of, at least, eighty acres in use for the average farmer who had about 700 acres. The additional 620 acres awaited children (Chester County Court House, Chester County Inventories, 1681–1790; Philadelphia City Hall Annex, Philadelphia County Inventories, 1681–1776).

The land use pattern of Edmund Cartledge was typical, although he used more land than most. He had a personal estate of £377, including £63 worth of crops, mostly wheat, and £90 worth of livestock. In the "house chamber" and "in the barn" Cartledge had about 115 bushels of wheat, which was the harvest of about ten to fifteen acres. "In the field" he had twenty acres of wheat and rye (worth about £30) and ten acres of summer corn, barley, and oats (£18). He had in all at least forty to fifty acres under cultivation. "In the yard" were a large number of cows, pigs, and horses and in the field a flock of sheep. According to the usual feed requirements, he used from fifty to fifty-five acres for these animals. For both livestock and crops, he used about one hundred acres. His inventory describes his farm as "250 acres of land, buildings, orchards, garden, fences, wood, and meadows," evaluated at £400. From 1690 to 1710 ten inventories show the evaluation of improved land was £2:3:6 per acre and unimproved land was at £0:6:7 per acre. A comparison of his evaluation with the general evaluations of improved and unimproved lands tends to confirm that he used about one-half to two-thirds of his plantation. At his death, he also had 100 acres in Springfield and 1,107 acres in Plymouth at a low evaluation of £300, indicating that they were unimproved. Like the other Quaker farmers, Cartledge bought land to farm and more land to settle his children upon (Chester County Court House, Chester County Inventories, 2/2/1703:143).

Although individual farmers and planters in early America had more land than the average Quaker in the Delaware Valley, few seventeenth- or early eighteenth-century communities appear collectively to have had such a high mean acreage, such a broad distribution of land, or a land distribution so generously devoted to children. James Henretta has argued that northern farmers accumulated land to pay off their sons' and daughters' labor and to secure their aid when old (Henretta, 1978:3–32). These Quaker accumulations roughly fit such an economic model, though they exceed the average needs of a young farmer. An average young man might need forty to one hundred acres of land to begin a family, not two or three hundred acres. Most fathers, moreover, did not need their sons' economic assistance in old age. A large percentage of sons bought their land from their fathers, who retired on interest from bonds.* To a large degree, the Quaker farmers were responding to the requirements, as they perceived them, of "holy conversation." Three hundred acres could seem to insure a new household's protection from the world.

II

In order to buy land Quaker farmers often needed to take "strangers" into their household as laborers. However, laborers brought into the household who fostered ungodly relationships could ruin the whole purpose of insulating the family from evil influences. These rural Quakers had few slaves or servants. Of the forty-one men who left inventories, among those families that were reconstructed, only nine recorded servants or slaves (twenty-five percent) and four had slaves (five percent) or about one in every twenty families. The fertile but inexpensive land of the Valley allowed rural Friends—unlike those in the city—to keep the use of servants to a minimum. At the same time, the wealth derived from the Valley allowed many Friends to afford slaves.

* The economy of these farmers was relatively sophisticated. Over fifty percent of the farmers, according to their inventories, held bonds of over £100. The money was lent to other farmers. Older men had the most bonds and were clearly living on the income (Levy, 1976:145–150).

The restriction of slavery was therefore partly the response to an explicitly expressed self-conscious policy.

Chester County Friends clearly remained sensitive to evidence of carnal talk or exotic people in their households. Robert Pyle, a prosperous Concord farmer writing in 1698, testified that he bought a slave because of the scarcity of white domestic labor. Pyle, however, felt the threat of contamination and had bad dreams:

> I was myself and a Friend going on a road, and by the roadside I saw a black pot, I took it up, the Friend said give me part, I said not, I went a little further and I saw a great ladder standing exact upright, reaching up to heaven, up which I must go to heaven with the pot in my hand intending to carry the black pot with me, but the ladder standing so upright, and seeing no man holding of it up, it seemed it would fall upon me; at which I stepped down, laid the pot at the foot of the ladder, and said them that take it might, for I found work enough for both hands to take hold of this ladder (Cadbury, ed., 1937:492–493).

Pyle concluded that "self must be left behind, and to let black Negroes or pots alone." To purify his household and himself, Pyle manumitted his black slave. Cadwallader Morgan of the Welsh Tract bought a Negro in 1698 so he could have more time to go to Meetings. But Morgan realized that greed was his real aim, that the slave symbolized the rule of the self over the Word. Pyle and Morgan also worried over the social and familial problems attending slavery. Pyle projected that Quakers might be forced to take up arms, if Negroes became too numerous in their communities. Morgan saw a host of problems for Quaker families. "What," Morgan asked, "if I should have a bad one of them, that must be corrected, or would run away, or when I went from home and leave him with a woman or maid, and he should desire to committ wickedness." Fearing many varieties of corruption, Morgan manumitted his slave and testified against slavery (Cadbury, ed., 1942:213; Drake, 1941:575–576).

Such fears were widespread. The Chester Quarterly and Monthly Meetings issued five letters or messages to the Philadelphia Yearly Meeting between 1690 and 1720, requesting a testimony against buying or importing slaves. The Chester Monthly Meeting in 1715 recorded that "it is the unanimous sense of this Meeting that Friends should not be concerned hereafter in the importation thereof nor buy any, and we request the concurrence of the Quarterly Meeting." The Philadelphia Quarterly Meeting in the same year chided Chester Friends for acting prejudicially against slave owners in their Meeting by excluding them from positions of authority (Turner, 1911:60–75; Davis, 1966:315).

Holy conversation and child-centeredness also brought these Friends using white, indentured servants problems. Friendly "conversation" conflicted with the need of keeping servants diligently at work. The Chester Meeting called John Worral before them in 1693 for whipping one of his male servants. He condemned his act "for the reputation of Truth" but said the fellow was "worthless" and "deserved to be beaten" (Historical Society of Pennsylvania, Chester Monthly Meeting Acknowledgments, 10/2/1693). By placing a lazy woman servant in a "noxious hole," Thomas Smedley thought he had found the alternative to whipping and beating, but the Chester Monthly Meeting thought his solution unseemly, and he had to condemn it (Historical Society of Pennsylvania, Chester Monthly Meeting Acknowledgments, 1/3/1740). In 1700 the Welsh Tract Monthly Meeting established a "committee to maintain good order," which recommended "that Friends be watchful over their families and that they should be careful what persons they brought or admitted to their families, whether servants or others, lest they should be hurt by them." The committee devised techniques for disciplining servants without flogging them. When their terms expired, masters were to write "certificates . . . concerning their behavior according to their deserts." No credit or jobs were to be extended to ex-servants unless they had such references. The Meeting established a public committee to "deal hard with servants" and to hear their complaints about their masters. No evidence exists as to what techniques the committee used to handle unruly servants, but they were probably non-violent. Because of their ideas about purified households, these rural Friends discouraged bringing blacks into the house and invented gentler ways of disciplining labor.

III

Controlling their children as they passed from youth to adulthood presented the final challenge for Chester and Welsh Tract parents. Quaker doctrine demanded that children be guided, not coerced into Quakerism. The choice to preserve the Light had to be a free one. There was very little evidence of disinheritance among Chester and Welsh Tract families.* The choosing of a mate involved parental approval and direction, but also courtship and free choice. The Meetings asked couples when announcing their proposed marriage to face both the Men's and Women's Meeting alone. A youth, as it has been seen, could call off his or her marriage at any time before the ceremony. Parents, however, still had to make new households Quakerly and sub-

---

* A collation of wills and deeds of families whose children married out shows that there was seldom any economic penalty. Male children who married out were often not deeded land. They got land when their father died (Levy, 1976:121–123).

stantial. For Quaker parents "holy conversation" meant establishing all their children on decently wealthy farms, married to Friends of their own choosing, with parental approval—a difficult job.

In Andover, Massachusetts in the seventeenth and early eighteenth centuries, parents had more implements to accomplish a similar task. Puritan parents shared responsibility with the local minister for their children's conversions, they had baptism, an intellectual regimen (sermons and Bible reading) and by the 1690s a general belief that the children of church members were likely to be justified (Morgan, 1966: 65–86; Axtell, 1976:160–200). They also had power. Quaker parents had environments, wealth, and their own example. As Philip Greven has shown, during the seventeenth and early eighteenth century in Andover, Massachusetts, it was common for parents to allow sons to marry, live on their fathers' land and yet not own the land until their fathers died. According to Greven's description, "although the great majority of second generation sons were settled upon their father's land while their fathers were still alive, only about a quarter of them actually owned the land they lived upon until after their father's death." The proximity of the father to the households of his married sons reinforced this pattern of economic dependency and patriarchy. Seventy-five percent of the sons of the first generation settled in the closely packed township of Andover. Well into the middle of the eighteenth century, "many members of families lived within reasonably short distances of each other," as Greven describes it, "with family groups often concentrated together in particular areas of the town." This strong system of parental power, as Greven argued, changed only slowly during the eighteenth century in the town (Greven, 1970: 72–99, 139).

Delaware Valley families were similar in structure to those in Andover. Because Quaker birth and death records were poorly kept, it is possible only to estimate what health conditions were like in the seventeenth century along the Schuylkill and Delaware Rivers. Twenty-five Quaker settlers, traced through the Quaker registers in England and America, had an average age at death of sixty-seven years, with only four men dying in their forties, and four in their fifties. The survival rate of children also supports the view that conditions were fairly healthy. Based on a total of seventy-two reconstructed families in the first generation, the average number of children per family to reach twenty-one years of age was 4.73 in the Welsh Tract and 5.65 in Chester. In the Welsh Tract and Chester, based on ninety-three reconstructions of second generation families, the average number of children to reach twenty-one was 5.53. These families were smaller than those of 7.2 children to reach twenty-one which Greven found for early eighteenth-century Andover families whose children were born in the 1680s and 1690s (Greven, 1970:111).

TABLE 2

Land Distribution of Chester, Welsh Tract, and Andover Settlers

ACRES	Welsh Tract and Chester first generation percent settlers (*N*)		Andover first generation percent settlers (*N*)	
0–99	0%	(0)	0%	(0)
100–199	10	(5)	67	(27)
200–299	15	(8)	18	(7)
300–399	2	(1)	8	(3)
400–499	6	(3)	2.5	(1)
500–599	15	(8)	2.5	(1)
600–699	10	(5)	0	(0)
700+	42	(22)	2.5	(1)
	100%	(53)	100.5%	(40)

Source: Philadelphia City Hall, Philadelphia County Deeds, Philadelphia County Wills and Inventories; Chester County Court House, Chester County Deeds, Chester County Wills and Inventories. Greven, 1970:58.

Compared to the Andover settlers and descendants, the Delaware Valley settlers consistently had more land (see Table 2). Andover, moreover, began in a remote wilderness where it took many years to develop a cash economy. Throughout much of the lives of the founding generation, as Greven noted, both grain and livestock were being used in lieu of cash in exchange for hard goods from Salem merchants. A lack of specie, cash, or credit is suggested by the fact that sons did not regularly purchase land from their fathers until after 1720, eighty years after settlement. The fertile land of the Delaware Valley was more conducive to lucrative farming than the rocky soil of Andover. The settlers enjoyed the fast growing market in Philadelphia under the control of able Quaker merchants with connections in the West Indies. One thousand Finnish and Swedish farmers, who had been living modestly along the Delaware River for over fifty years, helped provide the settling Quakers with provisions. Cash and credit existed in Pennsylvania, as attested by the frequent and early purchasing of estates by sons. As early as 1707, twenty-six years after settlement, Ralph Lewis sold over one hundred acres to his son Abraham for £60, and after 1709 deeds of purchase were more frequently given than deeds of gift (Bridenbaugh, 1976:170; Chester County Court House, Chester County Deeds, April 15, 1707:B-86; Greven, 1970:68).

Begging the question of the typicality of Andover as a New England town, it is clear that the road to an independent household (independent from kin, not from community) was smoother in the Welsh Tract and Chester communities than it was in Andover. The economy of the

Delaware Valley was more conducive to the setting up of independent households than that of Andover. Quaker families were also smaller. The older marriage ages of the Quakers strongly suggests, however, that religious community also played some role in creating a different pattern in Pennsylvania. The settlers in the Welsh Tract and Chester carefully helped establish their childrens' new households by providing sufficient material wealth, even if it meant making children wait a long time before marriage. The community closely watched new households. Yet, in contrast to Andover, Quaker parents tended to make their children financially independent at marriage or soon after marriage. They also set up their sons further from home.

Fifty-four of the settlers' sons received deeds in Chester and the Welsh Tract; and seventy-three percent (40) received them either before marriage or in one year after marriage. Fifty-nine of the eighty-four sons who received land from wills also received their land before marriage. Among all the second generation sons in the Delaware Valley whose inheritance, deeds of gift and purchase, and date of marriage can be known (139), seventy-one percent received land before, at, or within two years of marriage without restrictions. In Andover when a father gave a deed to a son he usually placed restrictions upon the gift. Most sons shared the experience of Stephen Barker, who received a deed of gift from his father for a homestead and land, provided "that he carefully and faithfully manure and carry on my whole living yearly." His father also retained the right to any part of his son's land "for my comfortable maintenance." Thomas Abbot of Andover sold his homestead, land, and buildings to the eldest of his three sons in 1723 for £20, but reserved for himself the right to improve half the land and to use half the buildings during his lifetime (Greven, 1970: 144, 145). Only one Welsh Tract or Chester deed from the first to second generations contained a restrictive clause, and no Quaker deeds from the second to third generations contained such clauses. Once established, three quarters of the new households in the Welsh Tract and Chester were independent.*

Typical of the Quaker father was Thomas Minshall, whose son Isaac married Rebecca Owen in 1707. That same year, three months after the marriage, Thomas Minshall "for natural love and affection" gave Isaac gratis the "380 acres in Neither Providence where he now dwelleth." A younger son, Jacob, married at the age of twenty-one in 1706 to Sarah Owen and that year received gratis five hundred acres of land and a stone dwelling house. The Minshalls were among the wealthiest families in Chester and Radnor Meetings. Poorer families also granted independence to their married children. Ralph Lewis,

---

* John Waters found differences between inheritance patterns of Quakers and Puritans in seventeenth-century Barnstable similar to the differing patterns between Andover and Delaware Valley families (Waters, 1976).

who came over as a servant to John Bevan, gave deeds to three of his sons before or just after marriage. In 1707 he sold to his son Abraham at marriage a 200 acre tract for £60. Samuel Lewis, another son, bought 250 acres from his father for £60 in 1709. A deed three years later, shows that his debt to his father was paid off in 1712, the year he married (Philadelphia City Hall, Philadelphia County Deeds, 2/3/1706:A-203, 8/23/1707:A-172; Chester County Court House, Chester County Deeds, October 6, 1709:B-342, 3/2/1712:C-326).

In contrast to the situation in Andover, moreover, most second generation Delaware Valley sons did not live in the same townships as their fathers. Forty-five percent of the sons (71) of the first generation Welsh Tract and Chester families settled in the same township as their fathers, but a majority fifty-five percent (88) did not. Most sons (65) lived in other townships because their fathers bought land for them there. Francis Yarnell of Willistown, for example, found land for five of his sons in Willistown (his own town) and one in Springfield and one in Middletown. Andrew Job bought two of his sons land in Virginia. Indeed eleven of the second generation Delaware Valley sons moved outside southeastern Pennsylvania to Maryland, Virginia, North Carolina, and Long Island onto land purchased by their fathers. John Bevan who moved to Wales never saw his American sons again. Quaker fathers often sacrificed control for "holy conversation" and land.

The tendency of fathers to give away land to their sons and money to their daughters, when they married, left many of these fathers bereft of power. Quaker fathers took to giving exhortations, some of which have survived. Edward Foulke, the richest Quaker farmer in Gwynedd, left an exhortation to his children written just before his death in 1741. He gave all four of his sons land near the time of their marriages. Evan Foulke, for example, received 250 acres in Gwynedd at his marriage in 1725 (Philadelphia City Hall, Philadelphia County Deeds, December 15, 1725:I-14-248). But Foulke worried. He urged his children and grandchildren not to let business take priority over attending week-day Meetings. He noted that business carried out at such a time "did not answer my expectation of it in the morning." He worried also about his child-rearing practices: "It had been better for me, if I had been more careful, in sitting with my family at meals with a sober countenance because children, and servants have their eyes and observations on those who have command and government over them." This, he wrote, "has a great influence on the life and manners of youth" (Historical Society of Pennsylvania, Cope Collection, 1740:F-190). Another exhortation was left by Walter Faucit of Chester in 1704 who was nervous about his wealthy grown son's spiritual and economic future, "If thou refuse to be obedient to God's teachings and do thy own will and not His than thou will be a fool and a vagabound" (Historical

Society of Pennsylvania, Cope Collection, 1704:F-23). Greven found no exhortations in Andover and most likely they did not exist. Seventeenth- and early eighteenth-century rural Puritan fathers left land, not advice, to obedient, married sons.

The mutual obligations in the Quaker family system show that the Welsh Tract and Chester families were nonetheless both well organized and demanding. The case of a family of comfortable means gives an idea of how independent households in the Delaware Valley were created. In the family of Philip Yarnell, almost all the sons received land for a price, and the time between marriage and receiving a deed was a time for sons to work the land in order to pay off their father. The purchase price would be returned to the family kitty in order to help portion the other children. Among the Yarnells' nine children, six sons and three daughters, their eldest son married at the age of twenty-six in 1719 and completed purchase of the land in 1725, when he received 200 acres and a farm house for £60 Pennsylvania currency from his father. Their second son also married in 1719 and bought his land from his father in 1724, a year earlier than his brother. He received a similar amount of land and also paid £60. The purchase price was about half the actual market value of the land. Yarnell's fifth son, Nathan, married in 1731 at the age of twenty-four and three years later received his land free in Philip Yarnell's will. Yarnell's third, unmarried son, Job, had a different role. In Philip's will he received "all my land in Ridley township," but had to pay £80 to daughter Mary Yarnell, half at eighteen and half at the age of twenty. Mary was then only ten years old, so Job had eight years to raise the first payment. He never married. Though the Yarnells were one of the wealthiest families in the Chester Meeting, they managed a vulnerable economic unit. Their children tended to marry by inclination, not in rank order. When a son or daughter married, his or her work and the land given was lost to the other children. Like most Quaker families, the Yarnells made the family into a revolving fund; new households became independent relatively soon after marriage, and with the returned money the other children became attractive marriage partners, and the parents bought bonds for their retirement (Chester County Court House, the Chester County Deeds, December 8, 1724: f-43, February 27, 1725:E-513; Chester County Court House, Chester County Wills, 6/14/1733:A-414).*

This demanding family system explains why the settlers' children married relatively late in life, despite the settlers' large landholdings. Although the Quaker families had fewer children and over twice the farm land, their children married later than the Andover settlers' chil-

---

* The "revolving fund" method was used by all but the wealthiest and poorest Quaker families. For other examples see (Levy, 1976:210–214).

dren and also later than the third generation in Andover, who matured between 1705 and 1735, coeval to the second generation in Chester and the Welsh Tract. The marriage ages of Quaker men were older than those of men in Andover in both the second and third generations, and the marriage ages of Quaker women were older than those of Andover women in the second generation, though slightly lower than Andover women in the third generation (see Table 3). While bachelors and spinsters were rare in New England towns, at least 14.4 percent of the Chester and Welsh Tract youth did not marry (see Table 4).

Another symptom of economic pressure upon families was a competitive marriage market in which poorer Friends and their children tended to fail as Quakers. In Chester and the Welsh Tract poorer children had to control (or appear to control) their sexual impulses longer than wealthier children. Among the poorer families the mean marriage age was seven years older for men and almost six years older for women than for the children of the wealthiest families. The children of Ellis Ellis, for example, a relatively poor Welsh Tract farmer, all married in the Radnor Meeting, but his two sons married at the ages of forty and thirty-four, and his three daughters at the ages of twenty-nine, thirty-three, and thirty-one. John Bevan's son Evan, on the other hand, who inherited over one thousand acres, married at nineteen years of age and John Bevan's three daughters married at the ages of twenty, twenty, and eighteen. Poorer Friends also married out more often. Only fifteen percent of the children of the first generation in Chester and the Welsh Tract married out of discipline, and virtually all of these came from the poorer families (see Tables 4 and 5). The wealthiest families like the Simcocks, Bevans, Worrals, and Owens had among one hundred and one children only three children who married out of discipline. Two of the nineteen wealthiest families had children who broke the discipline, compared to fourteen of thirty-four families evaluated at £30 and £40 in Philadelphia and Chester County tax assessments.

IV

The distribution of prestige confirmed and reinforced the economic and religious pressures on parents to perform their tasks well. In these communities successful parents received not only Quakerly children but also religious status and self-assurance. Participation in the Monthly Meeting was broad, but not all Friends participated equally. In the Welsh Tract (1683–1689, 1693–1695) twenty men and women, for example, shared a majority of the tasks of the Monthly Meetings. These Friends dominated virtually all the differing categories of tasks assigned to the Meeting, including the arbitration of disputes, disci-

TABLE 3

Age at Marriage: Delaware Valley
Quakers and Andover

AGE AT MARRIAGE	Quakers (Chester, Welsh Tract)		Andover (second generation)		Andover (third generation)	
	N	PERCENT	N	PERCENT	N	PERCENT
Men						
Under 21	5	5	5	5	6	3
21–24	35	32	36	35	72	32
25–29	30	27	39	38	87	39
30–34	26	23	17	16	39	17
35–39	9	8	4	4	12	5
40 and over	6	5	3	3	8	4
	111	100	104	101	224	100
29 and under	70	63	80	77	165	74
30 and over	41	37	24	23	59	26
Women						
Under 21	7	37	29	36	58	28
21–24	22	30	32	40	74	35
25–29	15	20	14	17	48	23
30–34	5	7	3	4	12	6
35–39	2	3	2	3	10	5
40 and over	3	4	1	1	8	4
	74	101	81	101	210	101
24 and under	49	66	61	75	132	63
25 and over	25	34	20	25	78	37

Source: Friends Historical Library, Radnor Monthly Meeting Records, Chester Monthly Meeting Records; Greven, 1970:31–37, 119, 121.

TABLE 4

Wealth, Marriage and Discipline

Average rate in pounds	Number of families	Number of children	Number married out	Number and (percent) disowned	Number single	Mean marriage age—men	Mean marriage age—women
90–100	19	101	3	1 (1%)	15	23	23
70–89	12	76	5	2 (3%)	5	27	24
50–69	11	45	3	2 (4%)	5	27	23
40–49	12	58	15	12 (20%)	9	26	23
30–39	18	81	21	17 (20%)	18	30	28
	72	341	47	34	47		

Source: Friends Historical Library, Radnor Men's and Women's Monthly Meeting Minutes, 1681–1745, Chester Men's and Women's Monthly Meeting Minutes, 1681–1745; Historical Society of Pennsylvania, Chester County Tax Lists, 1715–1765.

TABLE 5   *Marriage Portions and Discipline*

Women

POUNDS (PENNSYLVANIA)	MARRIED IN	SPINSTER	MARRIED OUT
80–150	10	1	0
40–79	9	1	1
20–39	30	0	1
0–19	7	9	12

Men

LAND		BACHELOR	
300 acres+	17	3	1
200 acres+	40	0	3
100 acres+	4	3	13

Source: Philadelphia City Hall, Philadelphia County Wills, 1681–1776, Philadelphia County Deeds, 1681–1776; Chester County Court House, Chester County Wills, 1681–1765, Chester County Deeds, 1681–1765.

pline, marriage investigations, and visiting families. Quakers described their leaders in terms of spiritual achievement: honorific terms included "elder," "ancient Friend"; or they were familial: John and Barbara Bevan were a "nursing father and mother to some weak and young amongst us." The Meetings expected leaders, more than others, to express "holy conversation." An elder in Radnor in 1694 allowed his daughter to marry a first cousin, an act against the discipline. It is a "scandal upon the Truth and Friends," the Meeting decided, "that he being looked upon as an elder should set such a bad example" (Friends Historical Library, Radnor Men's Monthly Meeting Minutes, 2/3/1694). These men and women were supposed to provide the same charismatic, loving authority for Quaker adults as Quaker parents provided for their children.

Approximately seventy percent of the Welsh leaders came from gentry families, but so did eighteen percent of the less active, and thirty percent of the leaders were yeomen and artisans. Although some significant correlation existed between land and leadership (see Table 6), the high standard deviations show that wealth was not the sole determinant of leadership. Among the men in the fifty-three reconstructed families, those who were leaders were in fact more distinguished by their Quakerly children than by their wealth. Though above average in wealth, the leaders were not consistently the wealthiest men. On the other hand, their families were twice as well disciplined as the remaining families (see Table 7).

The religious standing of the men in Chester and the Welsh Tract clearly hinged on family events. Those who could not control their

| | | *Real Property and Meeting Influence* | |
| TABLE 6 | | *Among Welsh Tract Men, 1683–1695* | |
PERCENTILE MEN	PERCENT POSITIONS	MEAN ACREAGE	STANDARD DEVIATION
10	45	745	25
20	67	356	189
30	78	395	570
40	86	312	240
50	91	227	119
60	94	280	482
70	97	233	60
80	98	160	34
90	99	212	32
100 (87)	100	325	211

Kendat Tau Beta: +.486

Source: Friends Historical Library, Radnor Men's Monthly Meeting Minutes, 1683–1689, 1693–1695; Bureau of Land Records, Harrisburg, Pennsylvania, Land Commissioner's Minutes of the Welsh Tract, 1702.

own family had no claim to honor. The Meetings did not usually penalize a parent if only one child married out. Randal Malin, for example, held ninety-eight positions in the Chester Meeting between 1681 and 1721, more than the other Friends studied, despite his daughter marrying out in 1717 (as did another in 1721, after Malin's death) (Friends Historical Society, Chester Women's Monthly Meeting Minutes, 2/30/1716, Chester Men's Monthly Meeting Minutes, 10/29/1717, 3/29/1721). Richard Ormes, however, stumbled from leadership when his pregnant daughter got married in Meeting in 1715 after fooling the female inspectors. Ormes had been a fully recognized minister, sent by the Meeting on trips to Maryland, and an Elder, holding about five Meeting positions a year. Between 1693 and 1715 the Radnor Monthly Meeting sent him to the Quarterly Meeting five times. After his daughter's case, however, Ormes did not serve the Meeting again until 1720, five years later (Friends Historical Library, Radnor Men's Monthly Meeting Minutes, 9/3/1701, 7/2/1716). Neither Ormes nor Malin cooperated with their wayward children. If a father did cooperate, he was disciplined and dropped from leadership instantly. Howell James held four positions between 1693 and 1697, but in the latter year went to his son's Keithian wedding. He acknowledged his mistake but never served the Meeting again (Friends Historical Library, Radnor Men's Monthly Meeting Minutes, 6/27/1716).

When more than one child married out, even if a father did not cooperate, the man lost prestige and often was subjected to the attention of the Meeting. Edward Kinneson held twenty-four Meeting positions

TABLE 7

Meeting Positions, Wealth, and Children's Behavior

	N	N jobs	Percentage jobs	Average acreage	Percent of children who married out
			WELSH TRACT		
Top quartile	6	178	64%	750	1 of 17 (5%)
2nd quartile	6	66	87%	829	4 of 29 (13%)
3rd quartile	6	26	97%	555	4 of 40 (10%)
4th quartile	6	4	100%	327	6 of 24 (25%)
	24	274			
			CHESTER TRACT		
Top quartile	6	408	67%	585	5 of 47 (11%)
2nd quartile	6	146	91%	553	10 of 40 (25%)
3rd quartile	6	50	99%	600	8 of 40 (20%)
4th quartile	5	3	100%	435	6 of 32 (18%)

Source: Friends Historical Society, Radnor Men's Monthly Meeting Minutes, 1681–1715, Chester Men's Monthly Meeting Minutes, 1681–1715.

in Chester and Goshen between 1709 and 1721, when his daughter
Mary married out. He continued to be appointed at nearly the same
rate until 1726, when his son Edward married out, and then he was
dropped from leadership. Although he did nothing to encourage the
marriage or cooperate with his son, the Meeting decided to "treat with
his father Edward who appears to have been remiss in endeavoring to
prevent the marriage." When his daughter Hannah married out in
1732, the Meeting decided that "her father has been more indulgent
therein than is agreeable with the testimony of Truth." In 1733, James
Kinneson, Edward's last son, married out. The Meeting treated Kinneson gently: "Considering his age and weakness [we are] willing to
pass by his infirmity." Though he remained a Friend until he died in
1734, his wife Mary responded to his humiliation. In 1741 the Goshen
Meeting got the word "that Mary Kinneson, widow of Edward, who
some time since removed herself into the colony of Virginia hath forsaken our Society and joined herself to the Church of England"
(Friends Historical Library, Goshen Men's Monthly Meeting Minutes,
3/21/1733, 6/21/1732, 9/4/1726, 8/19/1741). A source of Kinneson's
problem was clearly his relative poverty. He had only two hundred
acres of land. His children all married in their early twenties; they
most likely would have waited to marry or might not have married at
all, if they had confined themselves to the Quaker marriage market.

In these communities the assessment of spiritual and social honor
depended heavily then on having a successful Quaker household, and
wealth helped to achieve this standard. Wealth reduced marriage ages
and helped keep sons and daughters isolated from the world. Insufficient wealth increased the age at marriage and increased the contacts
likely between Quaker children and carnal talkers. Wealth was not monopolized nor simply emblematic of a social or political upper class. It
was regarded as necessary for full participation in the Quaker community. The cheap land of the Delaware Valley helped create this situation, but it was legitimized and partly formed by "holy conversation"
and the settlers' Quakerly devotion to their children.

Religious ideas about children, not pure affection, dominated the
families of the Welsh Tract and Chester Quaker communities in the
late seventeenth and early eighteenth centuries. Though many Quaker
doctrines approached those of the sentimental, domesticated family,
doctrines such as the emphasis on household environments, childrens'
rights to choose their own marriage partners, and the independence of
conjugal units, Quaker doctrine often strongly directed families away
from affection, emotion, and eroticism. Late marriage ages and
celibacy among poorer families—"poor" relative only to other Quakers—show the constraints on emotion imposed by the Quakers' discipline. The intense "holy watching" in both Chester and the Welsh
Tract shows clearly that Quaker families were subordinated to de-

manding communal ideals of "holy conversation." Only on the fringes of these communities, among the children who married out and the disowned and humiliated fathers and mothers who cooperated with them, does the isolated affectionate nuclear family appear. Such families may have been as numerous as those who retained full loyalty to the Quakers' world view, but they could not match the organization, power, or authority of the Quaker tribe in the Delaware Valley.

V

For the Quakers, their religious view of the world was crucial and demanding. Their impulse originated in the 1650s in England and Wales. The First Publishers of Truth (the original core of Quaker ministers), revitalized by their conversions in the 1650s, had become like joyous, unpredictable, fearless children themselves; but by the 1680s the Quaker farmers of Chester and the Welsh Tract had real children of their own. No longer joyous children themselves, beset with responsibilities and exhausted by persecution and poverty, the Quaker settlers became responsible, hard-working adults sustained by their belief that, if protected and nurtured with "holy conversation" in the rich, isolated lands of Pennsylvania, the innocent child would spring to life among their own children. In this way they began the development of what would become a privatistic, middle-class social order in the Delaware Valley.

BIBLIOGRAPHY

Axtell, James (1974). The School Upon a Hill: Education and Society in Colonial New England. New Haven: Yale University Press.

Bauman, Richard (1974). "Speaking in the Light: the Role of the Quaker Minister." In Richard Bauman and Joel Sherzer, eds., Explorations in the Ethnography of Speaking. New York: Cambridge University Press.

Bevan, John (1709). "John Bevan's Narrative." In James Levick, ed., Pennsylvania Magazine of History and Biography. XVII: 235–245.

Braithwaite, William Charles (1919). The Second Period of Quakerism. Cambridge, England: Cambridge University Press.

Bridenbaugh, Carl (1976). "The Old and New Societies of the Delaware Valley in the Seventeenth Century." Pennsylvania Magazine of History and Biography. 2:143–172.

Browning, Charles (1912). Welsh Settlement of Pennsylvania. Philadelphia: William Campbell.

Bureau of Land Record, Harrisburg, Pennsylvania Land Commissioner's Minutes of the Welsh Tract, 1702.

Campbell, Mildred (1942). The English Yeomen under Elizabeth and the Early Stuarts. New Haven: Yale University Press.

Chester County Court House, West Chester, Pennsylvania
   Chester County Deeds, 1681–1776. Chester County Wills and Inventories 1681–1776.
Chester County Historical Society, West Chester, Pennsylvania
   Chester County Treasurer's Book, 1681–1760.
Davis, David Brion (1966). The Problem of Slavery in Western Culture. Ithaca, New York: Cornell University Press.
Drake, Thomas (1950). Quakers and Slavery. New Haven: Yale University Press.
Ellis, Thomas (1685). "Thomas Ellis to George Fox, 13 June, 1685." Journal of Friends Historical Society. 6:173–175.
Forbes, Susan (1972). "Twelve Candles Lighted." Ph.d. dissertation: University of Pennsylvania.
Fox, George (1911). The Journal of George Fox. ed. Norman Penny. Cambridge, England: Cambridge University Press.
   (1663). Concerning Marriage. London: n.p.
Friends Historical Library, Swarthmore, Pennsylvania
   Chester Men's Monthly Meeting Minutes, 1681–1760.
   Chester Monthly Meeting Records: Births, Deaths, Removals, 1681–1760.
   Chester Women's Monthly Meeting Minutes, 1705–1760.
   Radnor Men's Monthly Meeting Minutes, 1681–1778.
   Radnor Monthly Meeting Records (RMMR): Births, Deaths, Removals, 1681–1770.
   Radnor Women's Monthly Meeting Minutes, 1683–1765.
Frost, J. William (1973). The Quaker Family in Colonial America. New York: St. Martin's Press.
Glenn, Thomas Allen (1970). Merion in the Welsh Tract. Baltimore: Genealogical Publishing Company.
Greven, Philip J. (1970). Four Generations: Population, Land, and Family in Colonial Andover, Massachusetts. Ithaca, New York: Cornell University Press.
Haller, William (1957). The Rise of Puritanism. New York: Harper and Row.
Henretta, James (1978). "Families and Farms: *Mentalité* in Pre-Industrial America." William and Mary Quarterly. 1:3–32.
Hill, Christopher (1967). Society and Puritanism in Pre-Revolutionary England. New York: Schocken.
Historical Society of Pennsylvania
   Chester County Tax Lists, 1715–1776.
   Cope Collection, Volumes 1–95, 1681–1790.
Hoskins, W. G. (1963). Provincial England: Essays in Social and Economic History. London: Cromwell.
Hymes, Dell (1972). "Toward Ethnographies of Communication: The Analysis of Communicative Events." In Peter Paolo Giglioni, ed., Language and Social Context. London: Penguin.
   (1974). Foundations in Sociolinguistics: An Ethnographic Approach. Philadelphia: University of Pennsylvania Press.
Kibbey, Ann (1973). "Puritan Beliefs about Language and Speech." Paper given before the American Anthropological Association, New Orleans, 30 Dec., 1973.

Marietta, Jack B. (1968). "Ecclesiastical Discipline in the Society of Friends, 1685–1776." Ph.d. dissertation: Stanford University.

Morgan, Cadwallader (1700). "Morgan's Testimony." In Henry Cadbury, ed., "Another Early Quaker Anti-Slavery Document." Journal of Negro History. 27:213.

Morgan, Edmund S. (1966). The Puritan Family: Religion and Domestic Relations in Seventeenth Century New England. New York: Harper and Row.

Nuttal, Geoffrey (1946). The Holy Spirit in Puritan Faith Experience. Oxford, England: Blackwell.

Penn, William (1681). "Some Account of the Province of Pennsylvania." In Albert Cook Meyers, ed., Narratives of Early Pennsylvania, West New Jersey and Delaware 1630–1707. New York: Barnes and Noble.

Philadelphia City Hall
    Philadelphia County Deeds 1681–1776. Philadelphia County Wills and Inventories 1681–1765.

Pyle, Robert (1698). "Robert Pyle's Testimony." In Henry J. Cadbury, ed., "An Early Quaker Anti-Slavery Statement." Journal of Negro History. 22:492–493.

Smith, George (1862). History of Delaware County. Philadelphia: Ashmead.

Turner, Edward (1911). The Negro in Pennsylvania: Slavery, Freedom 1639–1861. New York: Arno Press.

Vann, Richard (1969). The Social Development of English Quakerism, 1655–1755. Cambridge: Harvard University Press.

Warner, Sam Bass (1968). The Private City: Philadelphia in Three Periods of Its Growth. Philadelphia: University of Pennsylvania Press.

Waters, John (1976). "The Traditional World of the New England Peasants: A View From Seventeenth Century Barnstable." The New England Historical and Genealogical Register. 130:19.

Wolf, Stephanie (1976). Urban Village: Population, Community, and Family Structure in Germantown, Pennsylvania 1683–1800. Princeton: Princeton University Press.

Colonial South Carolina and the Caribbean Connection

JACK P. GREENE

The American Revolution and the creation of the United States have frequently colored historians' interpretations of the British Empire of the seventeenth and eighteenth centuries. Until the period of the Revolution, for example, Britain's overseas empire in

Reprinted by permission from Jack P. Greene, "Colonial South Carolina and the Caribbean Connection," *South Carolina Historical Magazine*, 88 (1987), 192–210.

the Western Hemisphere really cannot be properly understood by exclusive reference to the thirteen colonies that eventually became the United States.

Canada and Britain's Caribbean island colonies became integral parts of the imperial system, and it was not at all obvious until the Revolution that South Carolina was more appropriately grouped with its northern neighbors in the Chesapeake than its island neighbors in the West Indies. Likewise, however obvious it may seem to us today that Canada is a distinctly different sort of place than its neighbors south of the St. Lawrence, such a view would have seemed no more peculiar to New Englanders than the notion that they shared something in common with Virginians of the same period.

Jack P. Greene, a leading interpreter of social and political experience in the British American colonies of the period, chooses in this essay to focus upon the connection between South Carolina and Barbados. Noting that South Carolina was originally settled by immigrants from Barbados, he goes on to insist that the connection between the two colonies was persistent and that, moreover, patterns of social, economic, and political development were quite similar as well. Furthermore, Greene argues persuasively that by almost every conceivable measure South Carolina was far more like Barbados and other colonies of Barbadian origin than it was like any of the mainland colonies.

The implications of this interpretation deserve exploration. In some ways, it is more an argument for the significance of Barbados in the British Empire than it is an interpretation of South Carolina, but it raises important questions for the study of the mainland colonies. If Greene is correct, at what point and for what reasons did South Carolina's experience diverge sufficiently from Barbados to permit it to join the revolutionary movement of the 1760s and 1770s while Barbados and the other island colonies remained loyal? Another way of asking the same question is to inquire about the differences between South Carolina and Barbados as well as about the similarities. From what forces might such differences have emerged?

Greene's interpretation is, in any event, a challenging one that urges us to be cautious about reading what we know of the eighteenth-century history of British North America backwards into the seventeenth century. Further, it reminds us that the social and cultural origins of American institutions are complex, arising not only from aboriginal, European, and African sources, but also from creole societies like the one in Barbados from which South Carolina grew.

Within the leavings of the Hispanic and Portuguese American Empires during the first half of the seventeenth century, English adventurers established viable settlements in four separate areas: the Chesapeake, Bermuda, New England, and Barbados. Notwithstanding the fact that they all shared a common English heritage, no two of the new societies that emerged out of these settlements were alike, and three of them—those in the Chesapeake, New England, and Barbados—became what some cultural geographers refer to as culture hearths. That is, they became sites for the creation of powerful local cultures, including social institutions and ways of manipulating a particular kind of environment, that proved to be remarkably capable of recreation and, with appropriate modifications, transferable to other areas in the Anglo-American world.

Historians have long been familiar with the processes by which the tobacco and mixed farming culture of Virginia spread north into Maryland, Delaware, and parts of Pennsylvania and south into North Carolina and by which the mixed-farming and fishing culture of Puritan Massachusetts Bay extended itself into offshoot societies in Connecticut, Rhode Island, New Haven, New Hampshire, Long Island, New Jersey, and Maine. Until recently, they have paid far less attention to the equally fecund staple agricultural culture of Barbados.

During the last half of the seventeenth century, the culture first articulated in Barbados slowly spread to the nearby Leeward Islands in the eastern Caribbean and, after its capture from the Spaniards in 1655, to the large island of Jamaica in the central Caribbean. After 1750, a variant strain of that culture, developed—within the English-world, in the Leeward Island colonies of St. Kitts, Antigua, Nevis, and Montserrat—found a congenial setting in the new British West Indian island colonies of the Virgin Islands, Grenada, St. Vincent, Dominica, and Tobago.

As most South Carolinians familiar with their early history will know, however, the extension of Barbadian culture went beyond the West Indies to the North American mainland. Established in 1670 with some small settlements near the confluence of the Ashley and Cooper Rivers, South Carolina and the Lower South culture that developed out of those small beginnings and gradually spread north to the Cape Fear region of North Carolina and south into Georgia and East and West Florida, was as much the offspring of Barbados as was Jamaica or the other English Caribbean colonies.

Although scholars have long appreciated the role of Barbados in the origins of the Lower South, the sudden and artificial separation of the North American continental colonies from the West Indian colonies as a result of the American Revolution and the simultaneous incorporation of South Carolina and Georgia into the larger American culture of the United States have tended to focus attention away from the continuing vibrancy of South Carolina's Caribbean connection throughout the colonial period. The same developments have also tended to obscure the related fact that, for much of its colonial existence, South Carolina exhibited socio-economic and cultural patterns that, in many important respects, corresponded more closely to those in the Caribbean colonies than to those in the mainland colonies to the north. Though it is still far from complete, new work over the past fifteen years on the social history of Britain's early modern colonies now makes it more possible than ever before to analyze the developmental parallels and contrasts among the several colonies that trace their origins in some major part to the Barbados culture hearth.

This essay will explore three themes: first, South Carolina's Caribbean roots; second, its continuing connection with the Caribbean colonies during the colonial period; and third, the developmental parallels between it and the other colonies—the Leeward Islands and Jamaica—that emerged out of the Barbadian culture hearth during the seventeenth and early eighteenth centuries.

II

Why Barbados became a base and a prototype for the establishment of so many other colonies in the Caribbean and in the Lower South can only be explained by an examination of its early history. For ten years after its initial settlement in 1627, Barbados, like earlier English colonies in Virginia and Bermuda, concentrated very largely on tobacco culture, though it also began producing considerable quantities of cotton and indigo during the late 1630s. From the beginning, Barbados was a reasonably successful producer of staples for the English market, and this success drew large numbers of English immigrants to it and set off a feverish rush for land that, within a decade, had resulted in the occupation of virtually all of the arable land both in Barbados, which covered an area of only 166 square miles and in the nearby Leeward Islands, all four of which covered an area of only 251 square miles.[1]

As had been the case in early Virginia, the entire society was organized for profit. A few people from English gentry and commercial families, mostly younger sons, came to make their fortunes, but most

[1] F. C. Innes, "The Pre-Sugar Era of European Settlement in Barbados," *Journal of Caribbean History* I (1970): 1–22; Richard S. Dunn, *Sugar and Slaves: The Rise of the Planter Class in the English West Indies, 1624–1713* (Chapel Hill, 1972), pp. 46–59, and "Experiments Holy and Unholy, 1630–1," in K. R. Andrews, N. P. Canny, and P. E. H. Hair, eds., *The Westward Enterprise: English Activities in Ireland, the Atlantic, and America 1480–1650* (Detroit, 1979), pp. 272–75; Richard B. Sheridan, *Sugar and Slavery: Economic History of the British West Indies 1623–1775* (Baltimore, 1974), pp. 75–96, 123; Richard Pares, *Merchants and Planters* (Cambridge, 1960), pp. 1–25.

immigrants were single male dependent indentured servants imported to labor in the cultivation and processing of tobacco, cotton, and indigo. Every bit as competitive, exploitative, and materialistic as early Virginia, Barbados experienced a rapid concentration of wealth, as the society polarized into small groups of proprietors and a mass of dependent indentured servants or mobile free laborers. Paying but scant attention to religion or other social and cultural institutions, Barbados and the Leeward Islands were notorious for their riotous and abandoned styles of life, while high mortality among new immigrants and the imbalance of women in the population contributed to the slow process of family development.[2]

Most of these early tendencies were even further enhanced by the gradual substitution of sugar for minor staple cultivation beginning in Barbados in the mid-1640s and gradually extending to the Leeward Islands and Jamaica in subsequent decades. This capital and labor intensive crop led to the further concentration of property into the hands of the few people who could command the capital to purchase the labor and equipment necessary to produce sugar competitively. At the same time they were amassing larger and larger estates for themselves, these plantation owners were replacing white servants and free white laborers with African slaves, who seem to have been both a more economical and a more reliable source of labor. Like their counterparts in Virginia, Barbadian planters had, from the beginning of settlement, shown no reluctance to treat white servant labor as a disposable commodity, and the wholesale importation of African slaves into Barbados and the Leeward Islands represented both a logical extension of that impulse and the first large-scale use of slavery and non-European labor in any of the English colonies.

By the early 1650s, as a result of the sugar revolution, Barbados had achieved a population density greater than any comparable area in the English-speaking world, except London. But the introduction of black slaves into Barbados contributed to a rapid decline of white population, as many whites migrated to other colonies where there were greater opportunities to acquire land or returned to England. From a high of about 30,000 in 1650, the number of whites fell to about 20,000 in 1680 and 15,500 in 1700. Despite the fall in numbers of white settlers, Barbados, in 1670, was certainly, as Richard S. Dunn has written, "the richest, most highly developed, most populous, and most congested English colony in America, with a thriving sugar industry and 50,000 inhabitants, including 30,000 Negroes."

As Barbados and its neighboring colonies in the Leeward Islands be-

[2] Dunn, *Sugar and Slaves*, pp. 263–334; Babette M. Levy, "Early Puritanism in the Southern and Island Colonies," *American Antiquarian Society Proceedings* LXX (1961): 278–307.

came more black and the concentration on sugar production became ever more intensive, profits soared and wealth accumulation among the possessing classes was phenomenal. By 1660, the wealth of Barbados, the earliest and best developed of the island colonies, exceeded that of any other contemporary English overseas possession. But the rapid rise of a wealthy and conspicuous elite did not immediately give either much cohesion or stability to Barbadian society. Indeed, many of those wealthy few proprietors who could afford it began to flee the tropical sugar factories they had established for the more settled and, especially after 1680, healthier world of England.[3]

That the socio-economic model first successfully articulated in Barbados with its exploitative and materialistic orientation, concentration on sugar production, a slave-powered plantation system, a highly stratified social structure, great disparities in wealth and styles of life, a high ratio of blacks to whites, little attention to the development of family life and other traditional social institutions and cultural amenities, high levels of absenteeism among the wealthy, a rapid turnover among the elite, and heavy mortality—that Barbadian cultural system also came to characterize the four neighboring Leeward Island colonies is scarcely surprising. In part because of the concentration of capital and labor in Barbados and in part because rivalries with the Dutch and French prevented English settlers from securing uncontested control over most of them until 1713, however, the Leeward Island colonies developed far more slowly than did Barbados and never attracted such a large white immigration. By the 1720s and 1730s, however, they had successfully emulated the experience of Barbados in the previous century.[4]

But the Barbadian model also proved capable of transfer beyond the Lesser Antilles in the eastern Caribbean to much larger physical entities in Jamaica and South Carolina. Settled by the English in the second half of the seventeenth century, these two colonies, like the Leeward Islands, also developed far more slowly than Barbados. But they eventually became highly successful plantation colonies on the Barba-

---

[3] Carl and Roberta Bridenbaugh, *No Peace Beyond the Line: The English in the Caribbean, 1624–1690* (New York, 1972), pp. 165–305; Dunn, *Sugar and Slaves*, pp. 59–83, 117–26, 188–264, "Experiments Holy and Unholy," pp. 285–89, and "The English Sugar Islands and the Founding of South Carolina," this *Magazine* LXXII (1971): 82; Sheridan, *Sugar and Slavery*, pp. 128–40; Hilary McD. Beckles, "Rebels and Reactionaries: The Political Response of White Labourers to Planter-Class Hegemony in Seventeenth-Century Barbados," *Journal of Caribbean History* XV (1981): 1–19, and "The Economic Origins of Black Slavery in the British West Indies, 1640–1680: A Tentative Analysis of the Barbados Model," *Journal of Caribbean History* XVI (1982): 36–56; John J. McCusker and Russell R. Menard, *The Economy of British America 1607–1789* (Chapel Hill, 1985), pp. 151–53.

[4] Sheridan, *Sugar and Slavery*, pp. 148–207.

dian model. Indeed, by the mid-eighteenth century, they had become two of the three wealthiest and economically most important British-American colonies, with only Virginia—and not even Barbados—approaching them in this regard.

Continuously occupied by Spaniards since the early sixteenth century, Jamaica, prior to the English conquest in 1655, had been primarily a producer of livestock and minor staples, especially cocoa, and had never been an important part of the Hispanic American empire. With 4,411 square miles of territory, more than twenty-six and a half times that of Barbados and approximately the same size as the area that would later comprise the South Carolina lowcountry, Jamaica was first settled by disbanded English soldiers and the flow of excess population from England's eastern Caribbean colonies. This flow included many planters who, having made considerable fortunes in Barbados or the Leeward Islands, migrated with their slaves to Jamaica, where they hoped to establish a new, and infinitely more expandable, sugar colony that would have land enough to enable them to provide for their younger sons. This migration began in earnest in 1664 when one of Jamaica's first governors, Sir Thomas Modyford, and some 700 other Barbadian planters arrived in the colony with their slaves.

Jamaica soon rivaled Barbados in riches. But in the early decades its wealth came more from the activities of its freebooting buccaneers, who used its strategic position in the central Caribbean to tap the vast wealth of the Hispanic American empire. Through a combination of trade and raids, they converted their Jamaica base at Port Royal into the richest spot in English America. Primarily because it did not for many decades have access to a plentiful slave supply, however, Jamaica was slow to develop as a sugar-producing staple colony. Following the example of the Spaniards, all of whom had fled the colony within three or four years after the English conquest, leaving their large stocks of cattle behind, many of Jamaica's new proprietors raised cattle and other livestock for food consumption in Jamaica and elsewhere in the Caribbean, while others produced minor staples, including cocoa, indigo, and provisions. Not until the beginning of the eighteenth century did Jamaica export as much sugar as tiny Barbados.[5]

No less than the Leeward Islands and Jamaica, South Carolina also represented a successful extension of the Barbados culture hearth. As more and more of its arable land was converted to sugar and foodstuffs and other supplies had to be imported from elsewhere, Barbadian leaders began to look to the unoccupied portions of the southeastern mainland of North America as a potential site for new settlements that

[5] Dunn, *Sugar and Slaves*, pp. 149–87; Sheridan, *Sugar and Slavery*, pp. 92–96, 208–16; Orlando Patterson, *The Sociology of Slavery: An Analysis of the Origins, Development and Structure of Negro Slave Society in Jamaica* (Rutherford, N.J., 1969), pp. 15–69.

would be able to supply the provisions and other necessities required to sustain the island's sugar economy. With approval of the Lords Proprietors to whom, following his Restoration to the English throne in 1660, Charles II had granted authority to colonize Carolina and the Bahamas, a group of Barbadians, including the same Sir Thomas Modyford who settled in Jamaica in 1664, had unsuccessfully sought to establish settlements at Cape Fear and Port Royal in the mid-1660s.

As several historians have recently emphasized, Barbadians also played an extensive role in the first successful settlement in 1670. Almost half of the whites and considerably more than half of the blacks who came to the new settlement during the first two years were from Barbados, and this distribution continued for at least two decades. The most thorough and authoritative study we have of the origins of the 1,343 white settlers who immigrated to South Carolina between 1670 and 1690 indicates that more than 54 percent were probably from Barbados. They included people from all social classes. The great majority were from the small planter and freeman classes of families, a small planter owning at least ten acres but fewer than twenty slaves and a freeman owning less than ten acres. Some of these simply sold out and used the proceeds to transport themselves and their families and slaves to Carolina, while others came as indentured servants.

But South Carolina's Barbadian immigrants also included a few members of the island's elite. According to Dunn, representatives of eighteen of those 175 big Barbadian sugar planting families which had at least sixty slaves apiece, "held the best land, sold the most sugar, and monopolized the chief offices on the island" obtained land in South Carolina. Not all of these families actually settled in the colony. But a significant number, including, among the earlier immigrants, Edward and Arthur Middleton, James Colleton, and Robert and Thomas Gibbes, did. Further research by Richard Waterhouse has shown that, in addition, "representatives of as many as thirty-three 'middling' [Barbadian] planter families settled in Carolina between 1670 and 1690," middling planters being those who owned between twenty and fifty-nine slaves. Finally, a number of Barbadian merchants acquired land in South Carolina. Although many of them used agents to manage their plantations, several, including John Ladson, Benjamin Quelch, and Bernard Schenckingh, actually moved to the colony.

Not only did these Barbadians bring "energy, experience, and wealth" to South Carolina. They also brought the social and cultural system that had been so fully articulated in the island over the previous four decades. The only mainland English colony that began its existence with a preference for African slave labor and a significant number of African slaves among its original settlers, South Carolina early revealed that strong commercial, materialistic, and exploitative mentality that had found such a ready field for action in the Caribbean. For at least a generation, the colony functioned effectively as its West Indian proponents had initially intended, as an adjunct to the Barbadian economy. South Carolina developed a vigorous grazing economy that in size rivaled that of Jamaica, and, in return for sugar products and black slaves, it sent large quantities of beef, pork, corn, lumber, naval stores, and Indian slaves to Barbados, the Leeward Islands, and Jamaica.

Even in its earliest days, however, the South Carolina economy was never wholly dependent on trade to the Caribbean. Provisioning privateers and pirates and, even more important, trading with the large number of Indians residing in the southeastern part of the North American continent for great quantities of deerskins for export to England were also lucrative activities. No less than early Barbadians, however, early South Carolinians were avid in their search for a profitable agricultural staple that would do for their colony what sugar had done for Barbados. Early experiments with tobacco and indigo were reasonably successful, but it was not until the successful experimentation with rice in the 1690s that the colony's planters found a staple that was sufficiently profitable to provide the basis for a viable plantation system on the Barbadian model. Over the next three decades, rice, naval stores, provisions, and deerskins brought in the capital necessary to acquire the almost wholly African slave labor force that helped to give South Carolina such a close resemblance to its West Indian progenitors. Already by 1710 there were more blacks than whites in South Carolina. By 1720, blacks outnumbered whites by almost two to one, a far higher ratio than would ever be exhibited by any other English mainland colony.[6]

III

If, especially in recent decades, historians have tended to emphasize the extent to which, "more than any mainland colony," South Carolina's "roots and early commercial ties stretched toward Barbados and other islands of the English Caribbean," they have paid far less atten-

---

[6] South Carolina's early development, including its relations with Barbados and the Leeward Islands, may be followed in John P. Thomas, Jr., "The Barbadians in Early South Carolina," this *Magazine* XXXI (1930): 75–92; M. Eugene Sirmans, *Colonial South Carolina, 1663–1763* (Chapel Hill, 1966), pp. 1–100; Dunn, "English Sugar Islands and the Founding of South Carolina," pp. 81–93; Richard Waterhouse, "England, the Caribbean, and the Settlement of Carolina," *Journal of American Studies* IX (1975): 259–81; Converse D. Clowse, *Economic Beginnings in Colonial South Carolina* (Columbia, 1971); Peter H. Wood, *Black Majority: Negroes in Colonial South Carolina from 1670 through the Stono Rebellion* (New York, 1974), pp. 3–194; Clarence L. Ver Steeg, *Origins of a Southern Mosaic: Studies of Early Carolina and Georgia* (Athens, 1975), pp. 103–32; Philip M. Brown, "Early Indian Trade in the Development of South Carolina: Politics, Economics, and Social Mobility during the Proprietary Period, 1670–1719," this *Magazine* LXXVI (1975): 118–28.

tion to the continuing vitality of that connection. Within the early modern British Empire, such connections were maintained through flows of people, goods, and ideas along the major arteries of trade. Of these various flows, that of people probably dropped to quite low levels during the eighteenth century. A small number of wealthy planters and merchants fled the island colonies throughout the eighteenth century. Though most of them went to Britain or to one of the more northerly colonies, especially Rhode Island and New York, a few came to South Carolina. The families of Rawlins Lowndes, which came from St. Kitts in 1730, and Eliza Lucas Pinckney, which came from Antigua in 1738, are conspicuous examples.[7]

But the fact was that few of the island colonies had an exportable population in the eighteenth century. Neither the Leeward Island colonies nor Jamaica ever seem to have had more than a few whites to spare, while Barbados experienced a reversal in its long-term decline of white population after 1710. Perhaps the result of improving health conditions, the number of whites in Barbados rose by almost 50 percent from a low of 13,000 in 1710 to around 18,500 in 1773. Although it had a rising, rather than a falling, white population, Barbados probably sent few of its whites to other colonies after 1710. With regard to the black population, all of the West Indian colonies, including Barbados, experienced high slave mortality of from 2 percent to 6 percent annually throughout the eighteenth century and had to maintain imports at that level just to keep the slave population from declining in absolute numbers.[8]

Although the stream of immigrants from the West Indies to South Carolina all but dried up in the eighteenth century, the flow of goods remained strong. In addition to small quantities of wine, limes, lime juice, cocoa, coffee, and sugar, South Carolina imported directly from the West Indies between 70 percent and 85 percent of the roughly 1,000 hogsheads each of sugar and molasses and 4,000 hogsheads of rum it consumed each year. Down through the 1730s, Barbados was the primary source of these sugar products, but both the Leeward Islands and Jamaica surpassed Barbados in the 1750s and 1760s.

In return, South Carolina shipped a variety of products to all of the West Indian colonies. Exports of naval stores were high early in the century but diminished over time; beef and pork, corn and peas, and leather remained fairly steady over the whole period, with Jamaica,

---

[7] Wood, *Black Majority*, p. 55; Elise Pinckney, *The Letterbook of Eliza Lucas Pinckney 1739–1762* (Chapel Hill, 1972), pp. xv–xxvi.

[8] McCusker and Menard, *Economy of British America*, pp. 153–54; Sheridan, *Sugar and Slavery*, pp. 123, 502–6; Robert V. Wells, *The Population of the British Colonies in America before 1776: A Survey of Census Data* (Princeton, 1975), pp. 194–251.

Barbados, and the Leeward Islands continuing to be the leading importers of each down into the 1760s. Exports of lumber, barrel staves, and shingles increased dramatically after 1750, with Jamaica usually taking the largest quantities followed by Barbados, Antigua, and St. Kitts. To the West Indies, as to Europe, South Carolina's leading export was rice. The island colonies took about 10 percent of South Carolina's total rice exports in 1717–20 and around 20 percent in the 1760s. Barbados was the largest market through the 1730s, but it had fallen to third place behind Jamaica and the Leeward Islands by the late 1750s.

Altogether, in most years during the eighteenth century, about a fourth to a third of the total tonnage entering Charleston came from or via the West Indies, while between 15 percent to 25 percent of the ships cleared from Charleston traded to the West Indies. This disparity can be partly explained by contemporary shipping routes. Prevailing wind patterns dictated that many vessels from Britain came via the West Indies, while return voyages usually proceeded directly back to Britain. Although more ships entered Charleston from the West Indies than returned, by the 1760s, nearly forty ships based in the West Indies annually cleared the port of Charleston with return cargoes of rice and other commodities for Jamaica, Barbados, the Leeward Islands, and the Bahamas.[9]

This steady flow of goods back and forth between South Carolina and the West Indies brought news, ideas, even architectural innovations. The published business correspondence of Robert Pringle and Henry Laurens contained frequent correspondence with trading partners in Bridgetown, Barbados, and elsewhere in the West Indies, and the *South Carolina Gazette* often reprinted items from island newspapers, and vice versa. Especially interesting to South Carolina readers was news of the frequent slave uprisings in Jamaica and other sugar islands. As a recent architectural historian has shown, the verandah or front porch, first developed in the West Indies, appeared almost simultaneously about 1735 in most of the North American colonies engaged in the West Indian trade, including South Carolina.

IV

For South Carolina, these continuing connections were made more palpable by the obvious similarities between its own social development and that of the major West Indian colonies of Barbados, the Leeward Islands, and Jamaica. During the eighteenth century, however, no

---

[9] The figures are derived from Converse D. Clowse, *Measuring Charleston's Overseas Commerce, 1717–1767: Statistics from the Port's Naval Lists* (Washington, D.C., 1981).

two of these products of the Barbados culture hearth followed precisely the same culture.

As declining soil fertility and higher processing costs required more and more capital and labor to yield ever-diminishing rates of return, Barbados continued its inexorable movement toward "a capital-intensive, power-intensive system of agriculture conducted on a sustain-yield basis." But the drive toward intensive sugar monoculture and many of the tendencies associated with that drive either lost vigor or changed in character between 1700 and 1775. By the 1730s, Barbados exhibited an actual turning away from sugar to livestock, and the movement towards property consolidation had leveled off by 1750, with roughly a third of the proprietors owning somewhat more than half of the estates and sugar mills. By mid-century, the colony, once again exhibiting a spirit of innovation of the kind it had demonstrated a century earlier during the sugar revolution, was responding to its increasingly unfavorable place in the Atlantic sugar market by successfully developing methods to produce more sugar by-products, methods that yielded almost 50 percent more rum than the British West Indian average.

Despite these innovations, neither the size of estates nor the rate of profit was high enough to support much absenteeism among the large planter families, who exhibited a persistence and a commitment to the colony that defied the stereotype of early modern West Indian planter society. Nor were more than 20 percent to 25 percent of the island's whites members of the large estate owning class. About a quarter belonged to an intermediate class of officeholders, small merchants, professionals, estate managers, and small estate owners who produced cotton and foodstuffs on less than 100 acres. The rest consisted of a numerous class of poor whites, families with ten acres or less who lived largely on the margins of the plantation system, many in considerable poverty. After 1710, all classes of whites in Barbados enjoyed more favorable health conditions than did settlers elsewhere in the Caribbean, on the southern North American mainland, or even in continental cities such as Boston and Philadelphia.

Along with the steady growth in white population between 1710 and 1775, the slave population continued to rise, increasing by nearly three-fourths over the same period to over 68,500. Slave imports remained fairly high, but they accounted for a declining proportion of the slave population. With falling profits, planters found it more economical to provide better diet and health care in an effort to breed slaves locally and so save the costs of high annual replacements. Better living conditions and a growing ratio of seasoned creoles to the total number of slaves combined to lower annual mortality rates among Barbadian slaves from about 6 percent during the first quarter of the century to 3.8 percent during the third quarter. The ratio of blacks to whites leveled off at around four to one between 1750 and 1780.[10]

By contrast, the Leeward Islands showed no tendency to turn away from the drive toward sugar monoculture and no reversal in the decline of white settlers. In Nevis and Montserrat, the smallest of those islands, there was a steady loss of whites from the 1670s to a low point in 1745, followed by a slight rise over the next decade and a continuing downward trend thereafter. In St. Kitts and Antigua, which developed later, white population continued to climb into the 1720s and then dropped slowly thereafter.

Because the black populations tripled in all four islands between 1710 and 1780 and a substantial number of proprietors were absentees, perhaps as many as half in St. Kitts, the ratio of blacks to whites was much higher than in Barbados—15 to 1 in Antigua, 12 to 1 in St. Kitts, 11 to 1 in Nevis, and 7.5 to 1 in Montserrat. The result was that all four of the Leeward Islands were little more than a congeries of sugar factories with large concentrations of black slaves and quite small white populations that consisted of little more than a handful of white settler families, a few plantation managers, and a small intermediate class of merchants, lawyers, and doctors. The Leeward Islands thus represented an extreme version of the Barbadian model that perhaps more closely resembled a nineteenth-century industrial enterprise than the settler societies developing elsewhere in British America. Far more than Barbados, they were being transformed by the 1770s from colonies of settlement to colonies of exploitation with the impoverished cultural and political life usually associated with colonies of that category. The new colonies begun by the British in the West Indies after 1750 all tended to follow the Leeward Island example.[11]

Despite many similarities, Jamaica diverged considerably from the patterns exhibited by the smaller islands. Its sugar industry continued to grow slowly during the first four decades of the eighteenth century because of a variety of factors, including the secular decline of the British sugar market, the engrossment of some of the best sugar lands by large landholders who did not have the labor to exploit them, an inadequate slave supply, and the fierce opposition of the Maroons, bands of runaway slaves who lived in the inaccessible interior and terrorized outlying areas of the colony, especially between 1725 and 1739.

[10] Sheridan, *Sugar and Slavery*, pp. 124–47; McCusker and Menard, *Economy of British America*, pp. 165–66; Karl Watson, *The Civilized Island Barbados: A Social History 1750–1816* (Bridgetown, 1979), pp. 30–125; Wells, *Population of the British Colonies*, pp. 236–51; Gary A. Puckrein, *Little England: Plantation Society and Anglo-Barbadian Politics, 1627–1700* (New York, 1984), pp. 181–94; Hilary Beckles, *Black Rebellion in Barbados: The Struggle Against Slavery, 1627–1838* (Bridgetown, 1984), pp. 52–85.

[11] Sheridan, *Sugar and Slavery*, pp. 148–207; Wells, *Population of the British Colonies*, pp. 207–36; Margaret Deane Rouse-Jones, "St. Kitts, 1713–1763: A Study of the Development of a Plantation Society" (Ph.D. Diss., Johns Hopkins University, 1977).

After the cessation of hostilities with the Maroons in 1739 and in response to a rising sugar market, Jamaica experienced spectacular economic growth from 1740 to 1775. The number of slaves and sugar estates doubled. By 1775, Jamaica was exporting ten times as many sugar products as Barbados and had three times as many slaves. Over the same period, the aggregate value of the colony's economy increased almost five times, from just over £3.5 million to over £15.1 million. It was far and away Britain's most valuable American colony. Its net worth per free white person was an astonishing £1,200 in 1775, more than nine times that found in the richest continental colonies in the upper and lower South.

But this rapid expansion produced significantly different results from those arising from the similar development of Barbados a century earlier or of the Leeward Islands a half century before. Jamaica never approached becoming a sugar monoculture. Four out of ten slaves were in nonsugar production, and more than half of the plantations were devoted to livestock, provisions, and minor staples. Also, slave mortality was considerably lower than in the Leeward Islands, ranging from 4 percent down to 2 percent annually, the probable result of better dietary standards deriving from the local custom of allowing each slave a small plot of provision ground and one and one-half days per week for his or her own activities. From the produce grown on these provision grounds, Jamaican slaves developed a vigorous internal marketing system. The growing size of the free black and colored population, which exceeded that of Barbados by ten to one, suggests that the slave system in the island, though it was both harsh and given to frequent revolts, was more easily escaped than elsewhere in the British Caribbean. Finally, there was much uncultivated land and considerable land wastage in Jamaica, where the plantation economy was more land-intensive and less labor- and capital-intensive.

Nor did Jamaica experience a loss of white population. Notwithstanding the facts that as high as 30 percent of the sugar plantation may have belonged to absentees by the mid-eighteenth century and that the ratio of blacks to whites climbed steadily from about 6.5 to 1 in 1703 to slightly more than 11 to 1 in 1775, white population increased slowly but steadily from 7,000 in 1703 to 18,000 in 1774. In contrast to that of the Leeward Islands, this population was not limited to a handful of resident managers of large sugar estates and a few professionals and local factors of London merchants. As in Barbados, as many as a fifth of island whites were from large landholding or wealthy and substantial mercantile or professional families, and there were many small planters, estate managers, urban artisans, clerks, and shopkeepers, many of whom lived in Kingston or Spanish Town, respectively Jamaica's chief port and capital. In the mid-1770s, Kingston, by far the largest urban place in the British West Indies, numbered over

11,000 inhabitants, including 5,000 whites, 1,200 free blacks and mulattoes, and 5,000 slaves.

Unlike the Leeward Islands but like Barbados, Jamaica managed, despite some absenteeism, to sustain a "self-conscious, articulate, cohesive social class of proprietor-administrators" well into the later eighteenth century. Like the large estate owners in Barbados, there were "committed settlers" who, especially after 1750, constructed grand houses in an emergent Jamaican vernacular style; supported an active press; built churches, schools, and hospitals; and exerted political and social control through dynamic and self-conscious local political institutions.[12]

In many ways, South Carolina's eighteenth-century development paralleled that of Jamaica. Its economic welfare was also closely tied to the fortunes of an external market for its principal staple. What sugar was for the West Indian colonies, rice became for South Carolina. Following its emergence in the 1690s, rice production as measured by exports grew steadily during the first three decades of the eighteenth century from 1.5 million pounds in 1710 to nearly 20 million by 1730. By the 1720s, it had become South Carolina's most valuable export, a position it held throughout the colonial period. Between 1730 and 1750, the rice market was erratic, and exports increased slowly, except for a brief period in the late 1730s. But starting in the early 1750s exports once again began to surge steadily upward. In terms of total value, rice, by the early 1770s, ranked fourth among exports from Britain's American colonies behind sugar, tobacco, and wheat.[13]

Like Jamaica, South Carolina never became monocultural, however. Throughout the colonial period, it continued to export most of its earliest products: deerskins, naval stores, lumber and barrel staves, grains, and meat. Beginning in the 1740s, the reintroduction of indigo by Eliza Lucas Pinckney and others and its successful production provided South Carolina with a second highly profitable staple, albeit one whose quality was not sufficiently high to sustain it following the withdrawal of a British bounty after the American Revolution. Around 1770, rice accounted for about 55 percent of the value of all exports,

[12] Sheridan, *Sugar and Slavery*, pp. 208–33; McCusker and Menard, *Economy of British America*, p. 61; Wells, *Population of the British Colonies*, pp. 194–207; Edward Brathwaite, *The Development of Creole Society in Jamaica 1770–1820* (Oxford, 1971), pp. xiv, 8–175; Edward Long, *The History of Jamaica* (3 vols., London, 1774), II, p. 103.

[13] McCusker and Menard, *Economy of British America*, pp. 175–80, 186–87; Daniel C. Littlefield, *Rice and Slaves: Ethnicity and the Slave Trade in Colonial South Carolina* (Baton Rouge, 1981), pp. 74–114; James M. Clifton, "The Rice Industry in Colonial America," *Agricultural History* LV (1981): 266–83; Henry C. Dethloff, "The Colonial Rice Trade," *Agricultural History* LVI (1982): 231–43; Peter A. Coclanis, "Rice Prices in the 1720s and the Evolution of the South Carolina Economy," *Journal of Southern History* XLVIII (1982): 531–44.

indigo for 20 percent, deerskins, naval stores and lumber products each for between 5 percent and 7 percent, and grain and meat products each for about 2 percent. The diversity of the South Carolina economy is illustrated by Robert M. Weir's calculation that the record rice crop of 1770 was grown by less than 50% of the slave population on no more than 3 percent of the land in private hands, while the largest harvest of indigo was grown by only about 13% of the slaves on less than 0.5 percent of such land.[14]

Also like Jamaica, staple agriculture brought South Carolina masses of black slaves, a precarious racial balance in the population, and enormous wealth. The black population rose dramatically from about 2,500 in 1700 to 5,000 in 1710, 39,000 in 1730, and 75,000 in 1770. Before 1720, South Carolina's black population seems to have been able to generate a natural increase. But with the intensification of staple agriculture in the 1720s and 1730s and, probably much more important, the importation of large numbers of new slaves from Africa, it began, like its counterparts in the West Indian colonies, to experience a net annual decrease. Though the slave population seems to have again become self-sustaining after 1750, most of the enormous increase in slaves was, throughout the colonial period, the result of large imports, which, except for the decade of the 1740s, remained high.[15]

Though it was greater by far than any other contemporary British continental colony, the ratio of blacks to whites for South Carolina as a whole never approached that in the Caribbean colonies. For most of the period after 1720, it seems to have remained roughly at 2 to 2.5 to 1. But these figures are deceptive. In some lowcountry parishes, the importation of blacks and the emigration of whites had, by the 1750s, raised the ratio as high as nine to one, a figure well beyond that found in Barbados and only slightly below that found in Jamaica. Such a racial distribution indeed made those parts of the lowcountry seem, in the words of one contemporary, "more like a Negro country" than a settlement of people of European descent.[16]

Because of the proximity of the Spanish in Florida, the French in Louisiana, and many powerful Indian tribes, South Carolina, like the Caribbean colonies, already lived in persistent danger of external at-

---

[14] G. Terry Sharrer, "The Indigo Bonanza in South Carolina, 1740–1790," *Technology and Culture* XII (1971): 447–55, and "Indigo in Carolina, 1671–1796," this *Magazine* LXXII (1971): 94–103; David L. Coon, "Eliza Pinckney and the Reintroduction of Indigo Culture in South Carolina," this *Magazine* LXXX (1979): 61–76; McCusker and Menard, *Economy of British America*, p. 174; Robert M. Weir, *Colonial South Carolina: A History* (Millwood, N.Y., 1983), p. 172.

[15] Wood, *Black Majority*, pp. 131–66; "Estimated Population of the American Colonies: 1610–1780," in Jack P. Greene, ed., *Settlements to Society, 1584–1763: A Documentary History of the American Colonies* (New York, 1966), pp. 238–39.

[16] Wood, *Black Majority*, pp. 131–66.

tack, and the large disproportion of blacks in the rural rice-growing areas gave the colony, again like those in the Caribbean, a potentially powerful domestic enemy. Based on that of Barbados, South Carolina's slave code was the most draconian on the continent, though some of the harshness that characterized Jamaican slavery may have been mitigated in South Carolina by the task system. Most South Carolina slaves worked not in gangs, like the sugar slaves of the Caribbean or the tobacco slaves of the Chesapeake, but by tasks, an arrangement that permitted the more industrious to grow their own produce and raise their own animals for sale to whites in a domestic marketing system that in its extent and economic importance probably approached that of Jamaica. For whatever reasons, South Carolina, in contrast to seventeenth-century Barbados and to Jamaica throughout the colonial period, both of which were riven by slave revolts, had only one major slave uprising, the Stono Rebellion of 1739. But the specter of slave revolt always lurked in the background. Also like the situation in the Caribbean colonies, South Carolina seems to have had a higher incidence of interracial sexual unions than any other colony on the continent.[17]

If staple agriculture and slavery brought South Carolina danger for whites and degradation for blacks, it also, by the middle of the eighteenth century brought whites wealth that, while considerably less than that enjoyed by their counterparts in Jamaica, far exceeded that of any other settler population in British North America. Per capita wealth in the Charleston District of South Carolina in 1774 was an astonishing £2,337.7, more than four times that of people living in the tobacco areas of the Chesapeake and nearly six times greater than that of people living in the towns of New York and Philadelphia.

This wealth enabled South Carolina's richest planters and merchants to live a luxurious life comparable to that of similar groups in seventeenth-century Barbados and eighteenth-century Jamaica. Beginning in the 1740s, members of this group built, usually in the English style but sometimes with some West Indian modifications, several expensive public buildings and many sumptuous private houses. Most wealthy rice planters chose Charleston as the site for their most elegant resi-

[17] M. Eugene Sirmans, "The Legal Status of the Slave in South Carolina, 1670–1740," *Journal of Southern History* XXVIII (1962): 462–73; Philip D. Morgan, "Work and Culture: The Task System and the World of Lowcountry Blacks, 1700 to 1880," *William & Mary Quarterly*, 3d ser., XXXIX (1982): 563–99; Michael Craton, *Testing the Chains: Resistance to Slavery in the British West Indies* (Ithaca, 1982), pp. 67–96, 105–79; David Barry Gaspar, *Bondmen and Rebels: A Study of Master-Slave Relations in Antigua with Implications of Colonial British America* (Baltimore, 1985); Beckles, *Black Rebellion in Barbados*, pp. 25–51; Wood, *Black Majority*, pp. 308–26; Winthrop D. Jordan, "American Chiaroscuro: The Status and Definition of Mulattoes in the British Colonies," *William & Mary Quarterly*, 3d ser., XIX (1962): 183–200.

dence, and, with this large absentee planter class resident for much of
the year, Charleston, a city of 11,000 by the 1770s, was a lively cultural
center with a library company, concerts, theatre, horse races, and a variety of benevolent organizations, fraternal groups, and social clubs. By
the 1770s, some South Carolina families had become sufficiently
wealthy that they were even following the example of the West Indians
and abandoning the colony altogether. In the early 1770s, as many as
fifty absentee South Carolina proprietors were living in London.[18]

An important reason why England appealed to both West Indians
and South Carolinians was the appalling health conditions that obtained in their home colonies. Life expectancy in South Carolina
seems to have been slightly better than that in either Jamaica or the
Leeward Islands, both of which were notorious for their high mortality
among both whites and blacks. But both Charleston and lowcountry
South Carolina suffered from a disease environment that was far more
malignant than that of any other British continental colony. Crude
death rates recently calculated for Charleston in the 1720s show that
they were almost twice as high as those in contemporary Philadelphia
or England and Wales.[19]

V

South Carolina had begun in the late seventeenth century as an offshoot of the prolific Barbadian culture hearth; although it lagged
somewhat behind, in its subsequent demographic, socio-economic,
and cultural development it thus closely paralleled that of Jamaica,
Barbados's other principal seventeenth-century colony. Both South
Carolina and Jamaica were heavily involved in the production of agricultural staples and both imported extraordinarily high numbers of
African slaves that resulted in a population in which the numerical preponderance of blacks was overwhelming. As a result, both had a harsh
system of labor discipline and lived in fear of slave revolt. Elites in
both colonies enjoyed phenomenal wealth that enabled them to live
splendidly in the English manner and to build elaborate public build-

[18] Alice Hanson Jones, *Wealth of a Nation To Be: The American Colonies on the Eve of the Revolution* (New York, 1980), p. 357; Richard Waterhouse, "The Development of Elite Culture in the Colonial American South: A Study of Charles Town, 1670–1770," *Australian Journal of Politics and History* XXVIII (1982): 391–404; Lewis P. Frisch, "The Fra- ternal and Charitable Societies of Colonial South Carolina" (B.A. Thesis, Johns Hopkins University, 1969); Diane Sydenham, " 'Going Home': South Carolinians in England, 1745–1775" (unpublished seminar paper, Johns Hopkins University, 1975).

[19] Peter A. Coclanis, "Death in Early Charleston: An Estimate of the Crude Death Rate for the White Population of Charleston, 1722–1732," this *Magazine* LXXXV (1984): 280–91; H. Roy Merrens and George D. Terry, "Dying in Paradise: Malaria, Mortality, and the Perceptual Environment in Colonial South Carolina," *Journal of Southern History* L (1984): 533–50.

ings, private houses, and showy cultural institutions, while at least the wealthiest among them even managed altogether to escape the unhealthy disease environment that characterized both colonies.

If, however, the parallels were so striking, how do we explain why in the American Revolution Jamaica stayed within the British Empire, while South Carolina joined the other continental colonies in revolt? This question becomes more salient when we realize that the Jamaican Assembly in 1774 petitioned the Crown endorsing the American arguments against the Coercive Acts and other measures that led directly to the Revolution but indicating that its enormous population of slaves made it too weak to offer any physical resistance.[20]

We may search for the answers to this puzzle in South Carolina's continental situation or in the many ways it had fallen short of Jamaica in realizing the full potential of the Barbados model in a larger physical setting. South Carolina did not have such a large or disproportionately black and slave population as did Jamaica, it had not had nearly so much overt slave unrest, and it had far less absenteeism and, perhaps, a white settler elite that was considerably more committed to maintaining its ties with the colony. Notwithstanding these important differences, however, South Carolina did have a lot of slaves, and in 1775–76 it was, in fact, nearly paralyzed by the fear that if it carried resistance against Britain too far political chaos and slave revolt might follow.[21]

John Drayton, one of South Carolina's earliest social analysts, had, perhaps, a better answer to this question. During the twenty years before the Revolution, Drayton observed in his *View of South Carolina*, published in 1802, the wholesale influx of white settlers into the backcountry of South Carolina "added thousands to her domestic strength." That influx, which raised the colony's white population from 25,000 in 1750 to 87,000 in 1780, was by the mid-1770s slowly altering South Carolina's racial composition. Instead of 2 to 1, the proportion of black slaves to white free people was falling to 1.1 to 1, almost to parity. Only with the augmentation of her "domestic strength" in the form of growing numbers of whites, Drayton implied, did South Carolina have the wherewithal even to begin "collecting and preparing against a revolution." Without that vast immigration, Drayton thus suggested, South Carolina would have found it impossible to revolt—for the very same reason that deterred Jamaica. According to Drayton,

---

[20] Jamaica Assembly's Petition to the King, Dec. 28, 1774, in Peter Force, ed., *American Archives* (Washington, D.C., 1837–53), 4th ser., I, pp. 1072–74; George Metcalf, *Royal Government and Political Conflict in Jamaica 1729–1783* (London, 1965), pp. 167–91; Richard B. Sheridan, "The Jamaican Slave Insurrection Scare of 1776 and the American Revolution," *Journal of Negro History* LXI (1976): 199–301.

[21] See Robert Olwell, " 'Domestick Enemies': Slavery and Political Independence in South Carolina" (unpublished seminar paper, Johns Hopkins University, 1985).

this was the critical social fact that gave lowcountry South Carolina leaders the nerve to revolt.[22]

Of course, it was a social fact that obtained only temporarily. As soon as backcountry planters could secure the capital to buy slaves, they did so, and the successful introduction of cotton culture into the area in the 1780s and 1790s greatly accelerated the process. In a very real sense, the spread of cotton and slavery across the Lower South over the next half century testified to the continuing viability and adaptability of the Barbadian social model.

That model had not, in any case, ever been confined by national boundaries. Already by the late seventeenth century, it was being successfully adapted by the French in the small islands of Guadeloupe and Martinique. During the following century, it would be established, again by the French, in the large island colony of St. Domingue. In the nineteenth century, it was extended to the Spanish islands of Cuba and Puerto Rico. In the 1790s, the continuing affinity of lowcountry South Carolina with the West Indies was pointedly underlined by the ease with which the many refugees from the St. Domingue revolt, the only genuine social revolution to take place during the so-called era of democratic revolutions, were first welcomed by and then settled happily into lowcountry society.

---

[22] John Drayton, *View of South Carolina* (Charleston, 1802), pp. 102–03.

CRISIS
AND
TRANSITION

III

War and Culture:
The Iroquois Experience

DANIEL K. RICHTER

*Settlers, Africans, and Indians all faced major crises and trans-
formations in the last three decades of the seventeenth century.
The expansion of the colonies led to brutal wars with Indians in
New England and the Chesapeake in 1675–1976, and this
struggle touched off Bacon's Rebellion in Virginia, a major theme
in Edmund S. Morgan's essay in this section. All colonies faced
new pressures from the growing imperial demands of the English
state, as Adrian Howe's essay on New York makes clear. Africans,
as Winthrop Jordan shows, learned that their ambiguous status
in the colonies, somewhere between servitude and slavery, was
rapidly becoming hereditary slavery. Yet Indians faced the most
appalling menace of all, the very real possibility of utter extinction through exposure to European diseases.*

*Daniel K. Richter studies the response of the Iroquois Five Na-
tions (Mohawks, Oneidas, Onondagas, Cayugas, and Senecas) to
this danger. The Confederation survived the threat of depopulation by drastically intensifying the traditional institution of the
"mourning war," through which one or more nations would replace a dead person by capturing and adopting someone else. At
first firearms gave the Iroquois a decisive advantage over their
Indian neighbors, but as these tribes also acquired such weapons
and proved able to fight back, often with French assistance, the
Five Nations began to lose rather than gain population through
these military efforts. In response to this crisis, the Confederation
in 1701 chose neutrality with its immediate neighbors (French,
English, and Indian), an arrangement that English officials usually tried to construe as an alliance. The Confederation continued
to wage mourning wars against more distant enemies to the
south and west, such as the Catawbas who are discussed in the
following essay.*

*As Richter's essay and other studies show, Indians made war
from motives quite different from those that drove Europeans
into armed conflict. Even the Iroquois, who often did act as middlemen in the beaver trade, seldom fought for territory or com-*

Reprinted from Daniel K. Richter, "War and Culture: The Iroquois Experience,"
William and Mary Quarterly, XL (1983), 528–559. © 1983 by Daniel K. Richter.

> *merce. Most of the time they accepted combat to gain live captives, some of whom were tortured to death while others were adopted (or, later, ransomed). How likely were settlers to appreciate Indian motives for conflict, or Indians to understand why settlers, when they went to war, preferred to kill large numbers of people, often including women and children as* preferred *targets, at a single battle site, such as an Indian village whose warriors were off campaigning somewhere else?*

"The character of all these [Iroquois] Nations is warlike and cruel," wrote Jesuit missionary Paul Le Jeune in 1657. "The chief virtue of these poor Pagans being cruelty, just as mildness is that of Christians, they teach it to their children from their very cradles, and accustom them to the most atrocious carnage and the most barbarous spectacles."[1] Like most Europeans of his day, Le Jeune ignored his own countrymen's capacity for bloodlust and attributed the supposedly unique bellicosity of the Iroquois to their irreligion and uncivilized condition. Still, his observations contain a kernel of truth often overlooked by our more sympathetic eyes: in ways quite unfamiliar and largely unfathomable to Europeans, warfare was vitally important in the cultures of the seventeenth-century Iroquois and their neighbors. For generations of Euro-Americans, the significance that Indians attached to warfare seemed to substantiate images of bloodthirsty savages who waged war for mere sport. Only in recent decades have ethnohistorians discarded such shibboleths and begun to study Indian wars in the same economic and diplomatic frameworks long used by students of European conflicts. Almost necessarily, given the weight of past prejudice, their work has stressed similarities between Indian and European warfare.[2] Thus neither commonplace stereotypes nor scholarly efforts to combat them have left much room for serious consideration of the possibility that the non-state societies of aboriginal North America may have waged war for different—but no less rational and no more savage—purposes than did the nation-states of Europe.[3] This

[1] Reuben Gold Thwaites, ed., *The Jesuit Relations and Allied Documents: Travels and Explorations of the Jesuit Missionaries in New France, 1610–1791* (Cleveland, Ohio, 1896–1901), XLIII, 263, hereafter cited as *Jesuit Relations.*

[2] See, for example, George T. Hunt, *The Wars of the Iroquois: A Study in Intertribal Trade Relations* (Madison, Wis., 1940); W. W. Newcomb, Jr., "A Re-Examination of the Causes of Plains Warfare," *American Anthropologist*, N.S., LII (1950), 317–330; and Francis Jennings, *The Invasion of America: Indians, Colonialism, and the Cant of Conquest* (Chapel Hill, N.C., 1975), 146–170.

[3] While anthropologists disagree about the precise distinctions between the wars of state-organized and non-state societies, they generally agree that battles for territorial conquest, economic monopoly, and subjugation or enslavement of conquered peoples

article explores that possibility through an analysis of the changing role of warfare in Iroquois culture during the first century after European contact.

The Iroquois Confederacy (composed, from west to east, of the Five Nations of the Seneca, Cayuga, Onondaga, Oneida, and Mohawk) frequently went to war for reasons rooted as much in internal social demands as in external disputes with their neighbors. The same observation could be made about countless European states, but the particular internal motives that often propelled the Iroquois and other northeastern Indians to make war have few parallels in Euro-American experience. In many Indian cultures a pattern known as the "mourning-war" was one means of restoring lost population, ensuring social continuity, and dealing with death.[4] A grasp of the changing role of this pattern in Iroquois culture is essential if the seventeenth- and early eighteenth-century campaigns of the Five Nations—and a vital aspect of the contact situation—are to be understood. "War is a necessary exercise for the Iroquois," explained missionary and ethnologist Joseph François Lafitau, "for, besides the usual motives which people have in declaring it against troublesome neighbours . . . , it is indispensable to them also because of one of their fundamental laws of being."[5]

I

Euro-Americans often noted that martial skills were highly valued in Indian societies and that, for young men, exploits on the warpath were important determinants of personal prestige. This was, some hyperbolized, particularly true of the Iroquois. "It is not for the Sake of Tribute . . . that they make War," Cadwallader Colden observed of the Five Nations, "but from the Notions of Glory, which they have

---

are the product of the technological and organizational capacities of the state. For overviews of the literature see C. R. Hallpike, "Functionalist Interpretations of Primitive Warfare," *Man*, N.S., VIII (1973), 451–470, and Andrew Vayda, "Warfare in Ecological Perspective," *Annual Review of Ecology and Systematics*, V (1974), 183–193.

[4] My use of the term *mourning-war* differs from that of Marian W. Smith in "American Indian Warfare," New York Academy of Sciences, *Transactions*, 2d Ser., XIII (1951), 348–365, which stresses the psychological and emotional functions of the mourning-war. As the following paragraphs seek to show, the psychology of the mourning-war was deeply rooted in Iroquois demography and social structure; my use of the term accordingly reflects a more holistic view of the cultural role of the mourning-war than does Smith's. On the dangers of an excessively psychological explanation of Indian warfare see Jennings, *Invasion of America*, 159; but see also the convincing defense of Smith in Richard Drinnon, "Ravished Land," *Indian Historian*, IX (Fall 1976), 24–26.

[5] Joseph François Lafitau, *Customs of the American Indians Compared with the Customs of Primitive Times*, ed. and trans. William N. Fenton and Elizabeth L. Moore (Toronto, 1974, 1977 [orig. publ. Paris, 1724]), II, 98–99.

ever most strongly imprinted on their Minds." [6] Participation in a war party was a benchmark episode in an Iroquois youth's development, and later success in battle increased the young man's stature in his clan and village. His prospects for an advantageous marriage, his chances for recognition as a village leader, and his hopes for eventual selection to a sachemship depended largely—though by no means entirely—on his skill on the warpath, his munificence in giving war feasts, and his ability to attract followers when organizing a raid.[7] Missionary-explorer Louis Hennepin exaggerated when he claimed that "those amongst the *Iroquoise* who are not given to War, are had in great Contempt, and pass for Lazy and Effeminate People," but warriors did in fact reap great social rewards.[8]

The plaudits offered to successful warriors suggest a deep cultural significance; societies usually reward warlike behavior not for its own sake but for the useful functions it performs.[9] Among the functions postulated in recent studies of non-state warfare is the maintenance of stable population levels. Usually this involves—in more or less obvious ways—a check on excessive population growth, but in some instances warfare can be, for the victors, a means to increase the group's numbers.[10] The traditional wars of the Five Nations served the latter purpose. The Iroquois conceptualized the process of population maintenance in terms of individual and collective spiritual power. When a person died, the power of his or her lineage, clan, and nation was diminished in proportion to his or her individual spiritual strength.[11] To replenish the depleted power the Iroquois conducted "requickening"

[6] Cadwallader Colden, *The History of the Five Indian Nations of Canada, Which Are Dependent on the Province of New-York in America, and Are the Barrier between the English and French in That Part of the World* (London, 1747), 4, hereafter cited as Colden, *History* (1747).

[7] Gabriel Sagard, *The Long Journey to the Country of the Hurons,* ed. George M. Wrong and trans. H. H. Langton (Toronto, 1939 [orig. publ. Paris, 1632]), 151–152; *Jesuit Relations,* XLII, 139; William N. Fenton, ed., "The Hyde Manuscript: Captain William Hyde's Observations of the 5 Nations of Indians at New York, 1698," *American Scene Magazine,* VI (1965), [9]; Bruce G. Trigger, *The Children of Aataentsic: A History of the Huron People to 1660* (Montreal, 1976), I, 68–69, 145–147.

[8] Hennepin, *A New Discovery of a Vast Country in America . . . ,* 1st English ed. (London, 1698), II, 88.

[9] Newcomb, "Re-Examination of Plains Warfare," *Am. Anthro.,* N.S., LII (1950), 320.

[10] Andrew P. Vayda, "Expansion and Warfare among Swidden Agriculturalists," *Am. Anthro.,* N.S., LXIII (1961), 346–358; Anthony Leeds, "The Functions of War," in Jules Masserman, ed., *Violence and War, with Clinical Studies* (New York, 1963), 69–82; William Tulio Divale and Marvin Harris, "Population, Warfare, and the Male Supremacist Complex," *Am. Anthro.,* N.S., LXXVIII (1976), 521–538.

[11] J. N. B. Hewitt, "Orenda and a Definition of Religion," *Am. Anthro.,* N.S., IV (1902), 33–46; Morris Wolf, *Iroquois Religion and Its Relation to Their Morals* (New York, 1919), 25–26; Alvin M. Josephy, Jr., *The Indian Heritage of America* (New York, 1968), 94; Åke Hultkrantz, *The Religions of the American Indians,* trans. Monica Setterwall (Berkeley, Calif., 1979), 12.

ceremonies at which the deceased's name—and with it the social role and duties it represented—was transferred to a successor. Vacant positions in Iroquois families and villages were thus both literally and symbolically filled, and the continuity of Iroquois society was confirmed, while survivors were assured that the social role and spiritual strength embodied in the departed's name had not been lost.[12] Warfare was crucial to these customs, for when the deceased was a person of ordinary status and little authority the beneficiary of the requickening was often a war captive, who would be adopted "to help strengthen the familye in lew of their deceased Freind." [13] "A father who has lost his son adopts a young prisoner in his place," explained an eighteenth-century commentator on Indian customs. "An orphan takes a father or mother; a widow a husband; one man takes a sister and another a brother." [14]

On a societal level, then, warfare helped the Iroquois to deal with deaths in their ranks. On a personal, emotional level it performed similar functions. The Iroquois believed that the grief inspired by a relative's death could, if uncontrolled, plunge survivors into depths of despair that robbed them of their reason and disposed them to fits of rage potentially harmful to themselves and the community. Accordingly, Iroquois culture directed mourners' emotions into ritualized channels. Members of the deceased's household, "after having the hair cut, smearing the face with earth or charcoal and gotten themselves up in the most frightful negligence," embarked on ten days of "deep mourning," during which "they remain at the back of their bunk, their face against the ground or turned towards the back of the platform, their head enveloped in their blanket which is the dirtiest and least clean rag that they have. They do not look at or speak to anyone except through necessity and in a low voice. They hold themselves excused from every duty of civility and courtesy." [15] For the next year the survivors engaged in less intense formalized grieving, beginning to resume their daily habits but continuing to disregard their personal appearance and many social amenities. While mourners thus channeled their emotions, others hastened to "cover up" the grief of the bereaved

[12] *Jesuit Relations*, XXIII, 165–169; Lafitau, *Customs of American Indians*, ed. and trans. Fenton and Moore, I, 71; B. H. Quain, "The Iroquois," in Margaret Mead, ed., *Cooperation and Competition among Primitive Peoples* (New York, 1937), 276–277.

[13] Fenton, ed., "Hyde Manuscript," *Am. Scene Mag.*, VI (1965), [16].

[14] Philip Mazzei, *Researches on the United States*, ed. and trans. Constance B. Sherman (Charlottesville, Va., 1976 [orig. publ. Paris, 1788]), 349. See also P[ierre] de Charlevoix, *Journal of a Voyage to North-America . . .* (London, 1761 [orig. publ. Paris, 1744]), I, 370–373, II, 33–34, and George S. Snyderman, "Behind the Tree of Peace: A Sociological Analysis of Iroquois Warfare," *Pennsylvania Archaeologist*, XVIII, nos. 3–4 (1948), 13–15.

[15] Lafitau, *Customs of American Indians*, ed. and trans. Fenton and Moore, II, 241–245, quotation on p. 242.

with condolence rituals, feasts, and presents (including the special variety of condolence gift often somewhat misleadingly described as *wergild*). These were designed to cleanse sorrowing hearts and to ease the return to normal life. Social and personal needs converged at the culmination of these ceremonies, the "requickening" of the deceased.[16]

But if the mourners' grief remained unassuaged, the ultimate socially sanctioned channel for their violent impulses was a raid to seek captives who, it was hoped, would ease their pain. The target of the mourning-war was usually a people traditionally defined as enemies; neither they nor anyone else need necessarily be held directly responsible for the death that provoked the attack, though most often the foe could be made to bear the blame.[17] Raids for captives could be either large-scale efforts organized on village, nation, or confederacy levels or, more often, attacks by small parties raised at the behest of female kin of the deceased. Members of the dead person's household—presumably lost in grief—did not usually participate directly. Instead, young men who were related by marriage to the bereaved women but who lived in other longhouses were obliged to form a raiding party or face the matrons' accusations of cowardice.[18] When the warriors re-

---

[16] *Jesuit Relations*, X, 273–275, XIX, 91, XLIII, 267–271, LX, 35–41. On *wergild* see Lewis H. Morgan, *League of the Ho-dé-no-sau-nee, or Iroquois* (Rochester, N.Y., 1851), 331–333, and Jennings, *Invasion of America*, 148–149. The parallel between Iroquois practice and the Germanic tradition of blood payments should not be stretched too far; Iroquois condolence presents were an integral part of the broader condolence process.

[17] Smith, "American Indian Warfare," N.Y. Acad. Sci., *Trans.*, 2d Ser., XIII (1951), 352–354; Anthony F. C. Wallace, *The Death and Rebirth of the Seneca* (New York, 1970), 101. It is within the context of the mourning-war that what are usually described as Indian wars for revenge or blood feuds should be understood. The revenge motive—no doubt strong in Iroquois warfare—was only part of the larger complex of behavior and belief comprehended in the mourning-war. It should also be noted that raids might be inspired by *any* death, not just those attributable to murder or warfare and for which revenge or other atonement, such as the giving of condolence presents, was necessary. Among Euro-American observers, only the perceptive Lafitau seems to have been aware of this possibility (*Customs of American Indians*, ed. and trans. Fenton and Moore, II, 98–102, 154). I have found no other explicit contemporary discussion of this phenomenon, but several accounts indicate the formation of war parties in response to deaths from disease or other nonviolent causes. See H. P. Biggar *et al.*, eds. and trans., *The Works of Samuel de Champlain* (Toronto, 1922–1936), II, 206–208, hereafter cited as *Works of Champlain*; *Jesuit Relations*, LXIV, 91; Jasper Dankers [Danckaerts] and Peter-Sluyter, *Journal of a Voyage to New York and a Tour in Several of the American Colonies in 1679–80*, trans. and ed. Henry C. Murphy (Long Island Historical Society, *Memoirs*, I [Brooklyn, N.Y., 1867]), 277; and William M. Beauchamp, ed., *Moravian Journals Relating to Central New York, 1745–66* (Syracuse, N.Y., 1916), 125–126, 183–186.

[18] *Jesuit Relations*, X, 225–227; E. B. O'Callaghan *et al.*, eds., *Documents Relative to the Colonial History of the State of New-York . . .* (Albany, N.Y., 1856–1887), IV, 22, hereafter cited as *N.-Y. Col. Docs.*; Lafitau, *Customs of American Indians*, ed. and trans. Fenton and Moore, II, 99–103; Snyderman, "Behind the Tree of Peace," *Pa. Archaeol.*, XVIII, nos. 3–4 (1948), 15–20.

turned with captured men, women, and children, mourners could select a prisoner for adoption in the place of the deceased or they could vent their rage in rituals of torture and execution.[19]

The rituals began with the return of the war party, which had sent word ahead of the number of captives seized. Most of the villagers, holding clubs, sticks, and other weapons, stood in two rows outside the village entrance to meet the prisoners. Men—but usually not women or young children—received heavy blows designed to inflict pain without serious injury. Then they were stripped and led to a raised platform in an open space inside the village, where old women led the community in further physical abuse, tearing out fingernails and poking sensitive body parts with sticks and firebrands.[20] After several hours, prisoners were allowed to rest and eat, and later they were made to dance for their captors while their fate was decided. Headmen apportioned them to grieving families, whose matrons then chose either to adopt or to execute them.[21] If those who were adopted made a sincere effort to please their new relatives and to assimilate into village society, they could expect a long life; if they displeased, they were quietly and unceremoniously killed.

A captive slated for ritual execution was usually also adopted and subsequently addressed appropriately as "uncle" or "nephew," but his status was marked by a distinctive red and black pattern of facial paint. During the next few days the doomed man gave his death feast, where his executioners saluted him and allowed him to recite his war honors.

---

[19] The following composite account is based on numerous contemporaneous reports of Iroquois treatment of captives. Among the more complete are *Jesuit Relations*, XXII, 251–267, XXXIX, 57–77, L, 59–63, LIV, 23–35; Gideon D. Scull, ed., *Voyages of Peter Esprit Radisson: Being an Account of His Travels and Experiences among the North American Indians, from 1652 to 1684* (Boston, 1885), 28–60; and James H. Coyne, ed. and trans., "Exploration of the Great Lakes, 1660–1670, by Dollier de Casson and de Bréhant de Galinée," Ontario Historical Society, *Papers and Records*, IV (1903), 31–35. See also the many other portrayals in *Jesuit Relations;* the discussions in Lafitau, *Customs of American Indians*, ed. and trans. Fenton and Moore, II, 148–172; Nathaniel Knowles, "The Torture of Captives by the Indians of Eastern North America," American Philosophical Society, *Proceedings*, LXXXII (1940), 181–190; and Wallace, *Death and Rebirth of the Seneca*, 103–107.

[20] The gauntlet and the public humiliation and physical abuse of captives also served as initiation rites for prospective adoptees; see John Heckewelder, "An Account of the History, Manners, and Customs of the Indian Nations Who Once Inhabited Pennsylvania and the Neighbouring States," Am. Phil. Soc., *Transactions of the Historical and Literary Committee*, I (1819), 211–213. For a fuller discussion of Indian methods of indoctrinating adoptees see James Axtell, "The White Indians of Colonial America," *William and Mary Quarterly*, 3d Ser., XXXII (1975), 55–88.

[21] Usually only adult male captives were executed, and most women and children seem to have escaped physical abuse. Occasionally, however, the Iroquois did torture and execute women and children. See Scull, ed., *Voyages of Radisson*, 56, and *Jesuit Relations*, XXXIX, 219–221, XLII, 97–99, LI, 213, 231–233, LII, 79, 157–159, LIII, 253, LXII, 59, LXIV, 127–129, LXV, 33–39.

On the appointed day he was tied with a short rope to a stake, and villagers of both sexes and all ages took turns wielding firebrands and various red-hot objects to burn him systematically from the feet up. The tormentors behaved with religious solemnity and spoke in symbolic language of "caressing" their adopted relative with their firebrands. The victim was expected to endure his sufferings stoically and even to encourage his torturers, but this seems to have been ideal rather than typical behavior. If he too quickly began to swoon, his ordeal briefly ceased and he received food and drink and time to recover somewhat before the burning resumed. At length, before he expired, someone scalped him, another threw hot sand on his exposed skull, and finally a warrior dispatched him with a knife to the chest or a hatchet to the neck. Then the victim's flesh was stripped from his bones and thrown into cooking kettles, and the whole village feasted on his remains. This feast carried great religious significance for the Iroquois, but its full meaning is irretrievable; most European observers were too shocked to probe its implications.[22]

Mourners were not the only ones to benefit from the ceremonial torture and execution of captives. While grieving relatives vented their emotions, all of the villagers, by partaking in the humiliation of every prisoner and the torture of some, were able to participate directly in the defeat of their foes. Warfare thus dramatically promoted group cohesion and demonstrated to the Iroquois their superiority over their enemies. At the same time, youths learned valuable lessons in the behavior expected of warriors and in the way to die bravely should they ever be captured. Le Jeune's "barbarous spectacles" were a vital element in the ceremonial life of Iroquois communities.[23]

The social demands of the mourning-war shaped strategy and tactics in at least two ways. First, the essential measure of a war party's success was its ability to seize prisoners and bring them home alive. Capturing of enemies was preferred to killing them on the spot and taking their scalps, while none of the benefits European combatants derived from

[22] Several authors—from James Adair and Philip Mazzei in the 18th century to W. Arens in 1979—have denied that the Iroquois engaged in cannibalism (Adair, *The History of the American Indians . . .* [London, 1775], 209; Mazzei, *Researches*, ed. and trans. Sherman, 359; Arens, *The Man-Eating Myth: Anthropology & Anthropophagy* [New York, 1979] 127–129). Arens is simply wrong, as Thomas S. Abler has shown in "Iroquois Cannibalism: Fact Not Fiction," *Ethnohistory*, XXVII (1980), 309–316. Adair and Mazzei, from the perspective of the late 18th century, were on firmer ground; by then the Five Nations apparently had abandoned anthropophagy. See Adolph B. Benson, ed., *Peter Kalm's Travels in North America* (New York, 1937), 694.

[23] Robert L. Rands and Carroll L. Riley, "Diffusion and Discontinuous Distribution," *Am. Anthro.*, N.S., LX (1958), 284–289; Maurice R. Davie, *The Evolution of War: A Study of Its Role in Early Societies* (New Haven, Conn., 1929), 36–38; Hennepin, *New Discovery*, II, 92.

war—territorial expansion, economic gain, plunder of the defeated—outranked the seizure of prisoners.[24] When missionary Jérôme Lalemant disparaged Iroquoian warfare as "consisting of a few broken heads along the highways, or of some captives brought into the country to be burned and eaten there," he was more accurate than he knew.[25] The overriding importance of captive taking set Iroquois warfare dramatically apart from the Euro-American military experience. "We are not like you CHRISTIANS for when you have taken Prisoners of one another you send them home, by such means you can never rout one another," explained the Onondaga orator Teganissorens to Gov. Robert Hunter of New York in 1711.[26]

The centrality of captives to the business of war was clear in pre-combat rituals: imagery centered on a boiling war kettle; the war feast presaged the future cannibalistic rite; mourning women urged warriors to bring them prisoners to assuage their grief; and, if more than one village participated in the campaign, leaders agreed in advance on the share of captives that each town would receive.[27] As Iroquois warriors saw it, to forget the importance of captive taking or to ignore the rituals associated with it was to invite defeat. In 1642 missionary Isaac Jogues observed a ceremony he believed to be a sacrifice to Areskoui, the deity who presided over Iroquois wars. "At a solemn feast which they had made of two Bears, which they had offered to their demon, they had used this form of words: 'Aireskoi, thou dost right to punish us, and to give us no more captives' (they were speaking of the Algonquins, of whom that year they had not taken one . . .) 'because we have sinned by not eating the bodies of those whom thou last gavest us; but we promise thee to eat the first ones whom thou shalt give us, as we now do with these two Bears.' "[28]

A second tactical reflection of the social functions of warfare was a strong sanction against the loss of Iroquois lives in battle. A war party that, by European standards, seemed on the brink of triumph could be expected to retreat sorrowfully homeward if it suffered a few fatalities. For the Indians, such a campaign was no victory; casualties would subvert the purpose of warfare as a means of restocking the population.[29] In contrast to European beliefs that to perish in combat was acceptable and even honorable, Iroquois beliefs made death in battle a frightful prospect, though one that must be faced bravely if necessary. Slain warriors, like all who died violent deaths, were said to be excluded

[24] *Jesuit Relations*, LXII, 85–87, LXVII, 173; Knowles, "Torture of Captives," Am. Phil. Soc., *Procs.*, LXXXII (1940), 210–211.

[25] *Jesuit Relations*, XIX, 81.

[26] *N.-Y. Col. Docs.*, V, 274.

[27] *Works of Champlain*, IV, 330; Charlevoix, *Voyage to North-America*, I, 316–333.

[28] *Jesuit Relations*, XXXIX, 221.

[29] *Works of Champlain*, III, 73–74; *Jesuit Relations*, XXXII, 159.

from the villages of the dead, doomed to spend a roving eternity seeking vengeance. As a result, their bodies were not interred in village cemeteries, lest their angry souls disturb the repose of others. Both in burial and in the afterlife, a warrior who fell in combat faced separation from his family and friends.[30]

Efforts to minimize fatalities accordingly underlay several tactics that contemporary Euro-Americans considered cowardly: fondness for ambushes and surprise attacks; unwillingness to fight when outnumbered; and avoidance of frontal assaults on fortified places. Defensive tactics showed a similar emphasis on precluding loss of life. Spies in enemy villages and an extensive network of scouts warned of invading war parties before they could harm Iroquois villagers. If intruders did enter Iroquoia, defenders attacked from ambush, but only if they felt confident of repulsing the enemy without too many losses of their own. The people retreated behind palisades or, if the enemy appeared too strong to resist, burned their own villages and fled—warriors included—into the woods or to neighboring villages. Houses and corn supplies thus might temporarily be lost, but unless the invaders achieved complete surprise, the lives and spiritual power of the people remained intact. In general, when the Iroquois were at a disadvantage, they preferred flight or an insincerely negotiated truce to the costly last stands that earned glory for European warriors.[31]

That kind of glory, and the warlike way of life it reflected, were not Iroquois ideals. Warfare was a specific response to the death of specific individuals at specific times, a sporadic affair characterized by seizing from traditional enemies a few captives who would replace the dead, literally or symbolically, and ease the pain of those who mourned. While war was not to be undertaken gladly or lightly, it was still "a necessary exercise for the Iroquois," [32] for it was an integral part of individual and social mourning practices. When the Iroquois envisioned a day of no more wars, with their Great League of Peace extended to all peoples, they also envisioned an alternative to the mourning functions of warfare. That alternative was embodied in the proceedings of league councils and Iroquois peace negotiations with other peoples, which began with—and frequently consisted entirely of—condolence ceremonies and exchanges of presents designed to dry the tears, unstop the mouths, and cleanse the hearts of bereaved participants.[33]

---

[30] *Jesuit Relations*, X, 145, XXXIX, 29–31; J. N. B. Hewitt, "The Iroquoian Concept of the Soul," *Journal of American Folk-Lore*, VIII (1895), 107–116.

[31] Sagard, *Long Journey*, ed. Wrong and trans. Langton, 152–156; *Jesuit Relations*, XXII, 309–311, XXXII, 173–175, XXXIV, 197, LV, 79, LXVI, 273; Hennepin, *New Discovery*, II, 86–94; Patrick Mitchell Malone, "Indian and English Military Systems in New England in the Seventeenth Century" (Ph.D. diss., Brown University, 1971), 33–38.

[32] Lafitau, *Customs of American Indians*, ed. and trans. Fenton and Moore, II, 98.

[33] Paul A. W. Wallace, *The White Roots of Peace* (Philadelphia, 1946); A. F. C. Wallace, *Death and Rebirth of the Seneca*, 39–48, 93–98; William M. Beauchamp, *Civil, Religious*

Only when grief was forgotten could war end and peace begin. In the century following the arrival of Europeans, grief could seldom be forgotten.

II

After the 1620s, when the Five Nations first made sustained contact with Europeans, the role of warfare in Iroquois culture changed dramatically. By 1675, European diseases, firearms, and trade had produced dangerous new patterns of conflict that threatened to derange the traditional functions of the mourning-war.

Before most Iroquois had ever seen a Dutchman or a Frenchman, they had felt the impact of the maladies the invaders inadvertently brought with them.[34] By the 1640s the number of Iroquois (and of their Indian neighbors) had probably already been halved by epidemics of smallpox, measles, and other European "childhood diseases," to which Indian populations had no immunity.[35] The devastation continued through the century. A partial list of plagues that struck the Five Nations includes "a general malady" among the Mohawk in 1647; "a great mortality" among the Onondaga in 1656–1657; a smallpox epidemic among the Oneida, Onondaga, Cayuga, and Seneca in 1661–1663; "a kind of contagion" among the Seneca in 1668; "a fever of . . . malignant character" among the Mohawk in 1673; and "a general Influenza" among the Seneca in 1676.[36] As thousands died, ever-growing numbers of captive adoptees would be necessary if the Iroquois were even to begin to replace their losses; mourning-wars of unprecedented scale loomed ahead. Warfare would cease to be a sporadic and specific response to individual deaths and would become in-

---

and Mourning Councils and Ceremonies of Adoption of the New York Indians, New York State Museum Bulletin 113 (Albany, N.Y., 1907). For a suggestive discussion of Indian definitions of peace see John Phillip Reid, *A Better Kind of Hatchet: Law, Trade, and Diplomacy in the Cherokee Nation during the Early Years of European Contact* (University Park, Pa., 1976), 9–17.

[34] On the devastating impact of European diseases—some Indian populations may have declined by a factor of 20 to 1 within a century or so of contact—see the works surveyed in Russell Thornton, "American Indian Historical Demography: A Review Essay with Suggestions for Future Research," *American Indian Culture and Research Journal,* III, No. 1 (1979), 69–74.

[35] Trigger, *Children of Aataentsic,* II, 602; Cornelius J. Jaenen, *Friend and Foe: Aspects of French Amerindian Cultural Contact in the Sixteenth and Seventeenth Centuries* (New York, 1976), 100. Most of the early Iroquois epidemics went unrecorded by Europeans, but major smallpox epidemics are documented for the Mohawk in 1634 and the Seneca in 1640–1641; see [Harmen Meyndertsz van den Bogaert], "Narrative of a Journey into the Mohawk and Oneida Country, 1634–1635," in J. Franklin Jameson, ed., *Narratives of New Netherland, 1609–1664* (New York, 1909), 140–141, and *Jesuit Relations,* XXI, 211.

[36] *Jesuit Relations,* XXX, 273, XLIV, 43, XLVII, 193, 205, XLVIII, 79–83, L, 63, LIV, 79–81, LVII, 81–83, LX, 175.

stead a constant and increasingly undifferentiated symptom of societies in demographic crisis.

At the same time, European firearms would make warfare unprecedentedly dangerous for both the Iroquois and their foes, and would undermine traditional Indian sanctions against battle fatalities. The introduction of guns, together with the replacement of flint arrowheads by more efficient iron, copper, and brass ones that could pierce traditional Indian wooden armor, greatly increased the chances of death in combat and led to major changes in Iroquois tactics. In the early seventeenth century Champlain had observed mostly ceremonial and relatively bloodless confrontations between large Indian armies, but with the advent of muskets—which Europeans had designed to be fired in volleys during just such battles—massed confrontations became, from the Indian perspective, suicidal folly. They were quickly abandoned in favor of a redoubled emphasis on small-scale raids and ambushes, in which Indians learned far sooner than Euro-Americans how to aim cumbersome muskets accurately at individual targets.[37] By the early 1640s the Mohawk were honing such skills with approximately three hundred guns acquired from the Dutch of Albany and from English sources. Soon the rest of the Five Nations followed the Mohawk example.[38]

Temporarily, the Iroquois' plentiful supply and skillful use of firearms gave them a considerable advantage over their Indian enemies: during the 1640s and 1650s the less well armed Huron and the poorly armed Neutral and Khionontateronon (Petun or Tobacco Nation) succumbed to Iroquois firepower. That advantage had largely disappeared by the 1660s and 1670s, however, as the Five Nations learned in their battles with such heavily armed foes as the Susquehannock. Once muskets came into general use in Indian warfare, several drawbacks became apparent: they were more sluggish than arrows to fire and much slower to reload; their noise lessened the capacity for surprise; and reliance on them left Indians dependent on Euro-Americans for ammunition, repairs, and replacements. But there could be no

[37] *Works of Champlain*, II, 95–100; Malone, "Indian and English Military Systems," 179–200; Jennings, *Invasion of America*, 165–166. After the introduction of firearms the Iroquois continued to raise armies of several hundred to a thousand men, but they almost never engaged them in set battles. Large armies ensured safe travel to distant battlegrounds and occasionally intimidated outnumbered opponents, but when they neared their objective they usually broke into small raiding parties. See Daniel Gookin, "Historical Collections of the Indians in New England" (1674), Massachusetts Historical Society, *Collections*, I (1792), 162, and Cadwallader Colden, *The History of the Five Indian Nations Depending on the Province of New-York in America* (New York, 1727), 8–10, hereafter cited as Colden, *History* (1727).

[38] *N.-Y. Col. Docs.*, I, 150; "Journal of New Netherland, 1647," in Jameson, ed., *Narratives of New Netherland*, 274; *Jesuit Relations*, XXIV, 295; Carl P. Russell, *Guns on the Early Frontiers: A History of Firearms from Colonial Times through the Years of the Western Fur Trade* (Berkeley, Calif., 1957), 11–15, 62–66.

return to the days of bows and arrows and wooden armor. Few Iroquois war parties could now expect to escape mortal casualties.[39]

While European diseases and firearms intensified Indian conflicts and stretched the mourning-war tradition beyond previous limits, a third major aspect of European contact pushed Iroquois warfare in novel directions. Trade with Europeans made economic motives central to American Indian conflicts for the first time. Because iron tools, firearms, and other trade goods so quickly became essential to Indian economies, struggles for those items and for furs to barter for them lay behind numerous seventeenth-century wars. Between 1624 and 1628 the Iroquois gained unimpeded access to European commodities when Mohawk warriors drove the Mahican to the east of the Hudson River and secured an open route to the Dutch traders of Albany.[40] But obtaining the furs to exchange for the goods of Albany was a problem not so easily solved. By about 1640 the Five Nations perhaps had exhausted the beaver stock of their home hunting territories; more important, they could not find in relatively temperate Iroquoia the thick northern pelts prized by Euro-American traders.[41] A long, far-flung series of "beaver wars" ensued, in which the Five Nations battled the Algonquian nations of the Saint Lawrence River region, the Huron, the Khionontateronon, the Neutral, the Erie, and other western and northern peoples in a constant struggle over fur supplies. In those wars the Iroquois more frequently sought dead beavers than live ones: most of their raids were not part of a strategic plan to seize new hunting grounds but piratical attacks on enemy canoes carrying pelts to Montreal and Trois-Rivières.[42]

[39] *Jesuit Relations*, XXVII, 71, XLV, 205–207; Elisabeth Tooker, "The Iroquois Defeat of the Huron: A Review of Causes," *Pa. Archaeol.*, XXXIII (1963), 115–123; Keith F. Otterbein, "Why the Iroquois Won: An Analysis of Iroquois Military Tactics," *Ethnohistory*, XI (1964), 56–63; John K. Mahon, "Anglo-American Methods of Indian Warfare, 1676–1794," *Mississippi Valley Historical Review*, XLV (1958), 255.

[40] Bruce G. Trigger, "The Mohawk-Mahican War (1624–28): The Establishment of a Pattern," *Canadian Historical Review*, LII (1971), 276–286.

[41] Harold A. Innis, *The Fur Trade in Canada: An Introduction to Canadian Economic History* (New Haven, Conn., 1930), 1–4, 32–33; Hunt, *Wars of the Iroquois*, 33–37; John Witthoft, "Ancestry of the Susquehannocks," in John Witthoft and W. Fred Kinsey III, eds., *Susquehannock Miscellany* (Harrisburg, Pa., 1959), 34–35; Thomas Elliot Norton, *The Fur Trade in Colonial New York, 1686–1776* (Madison, Wis., 1974), 9–15.

[42] The classic account of the beaver wars is Hunt, *Wars of the Iroquois*, but three decades of subsequent scholarship have overturned many of that work's interpretations. See Allen W. Trelease, "The Iroquois and the Western Fur Trade: A Problem in Interpretation," *MVHR*, XLIX (1962), 32–51; Raoul Naroll, "The Causes of the Fourth Iroquois War," *Ethnohistory*, XVI (1969), 51–81; Allan Forbes, Jr., "Two and a Half Centuries of Conflict: The Iroquois and the Laurentian Wars," *Pa. Archaeol.*, XL, nos. 3–4 (1970), 1–20; William N. Fenton, "The Iroquois in History," in Eleanor Burke Leacock and Nancy Oestreich Lurie, eds., *North American Indians in Historical Perspective* (New York, 1971), 139–145; Karl H. Schlesier, "Epidemics and Indian Middlemen: Rethinking the Wars of the Iroquois, 1609–1653," *Ethnohistory*, XXIII (1976), 129–145; and Trigger, *Children of Aataentsic*, esp. II, 617–664.

The beaver wars inexorably embroiled the Iroquois in conflict with the French of Canada. Franco-Iroquois hostilities dated from the era of Champlain, who consistently based his relations with Canada's natives upon promises to aid them in their traditional raids against the Five Nations. "I came to the conclusion," wrote Champlain in 1619, "that it was very necessary to assist them, both to engage them the more to love us, and also to provide the means of furthering my enterprises and explorations which apparently could only be carried out with their help." [43] The French commander and a few of his men participated in Indian campaigns against the Five Nations in 1609, 1610, and 1615, and encouraged countless other raids.[44] From the 1630s to the 1660s, conflict between the Five Nations and Canadian Indians intensified, and Iroquois war parties armed with guns frequently blockaded the Saint Lawrence and stopped the flow of furs to the French settlements. A state of open war, punctuated by short truces, consequently prevailed between New France and various members of the Five Nations, particularly the Mohawk. The battles were almost exclusively economic and geopolitical—the Iroquois were not much interested in French captives—and in general the French suffered more than the Iroquois from the fighting.[45] Finally, in 1666, a French army invaded Iroquoia and burned the Mohawks' fortified villages, from which all had fled to safety except a few old men who chose to stay and die. In 1667, the Five Nations and the French made a peace that lasted for over a decade.[46]

While the fur trade introduced new economic goals, additional foes, and wider scope to Iroquois warfare, it did not crowd out older cultural motives. Instead, the mourning-war tradition, deaths from disease, dependence on firearms, and the trade in furs combined to produce a dangerous spiral: epidemics led to deadlier mourning-wars fought with firearms; the need for guns increased the demand for pelts to trade for them; the quest for furs provoked wars with other nations;

[43] *Works of Champlain*, III, 31–32; see also II, 118–119, 186–191, 246–285, III, 207–228.

[44] *Ibid.* II, 65–107, 120–138, III, 48–81.

[45] *Jesuit Relations*, XXI–L, *passim*; Robert A. Goldstein, *French-Iroquois Diplomatic and Military Relations, 1609–1701* (The Hague, 1969), 62–99. The actual Canadian death toll in wars with the Iroquois before 1666 has recently been shown to have been quite low. Only 153 French were killed in raids while 143 were taken prisoner (perhaps 38 of those died in captivity); John A. Dickinson, "La guerre iroquoise et la mortalité en Nouvelle-France, 1608–1666," *Revue d'histoire de l'amérique française*, XXXVI (1982), 31–54. On 17th-century French captives of the Iroquois see Daniel K. Richter, "The Iroquois Melting Pot: Seventeenth-Century War Captives of the Five Nations" (paper presented at the Shelby Cullom Davis Center Conference on War and Society in Early America, Princeton University, March 11–12, 1983), 18–19.

[46] *Jesuit Relations*, L, 127–147, 239; *N.-Y. Col. Docs.*, III, 121–127; A. J. F. van Laer, trans. and ed., *Correspondence of Jeremias van Rensselaer, 1651–1674* (Albany, N.Y., 1932), 388.

and deaths in those conflicts began the mourning-war cycle anew. At each turn, fresh economic and demographic motives fed the spiral.

Accordingly, in the mid-seventeenth-century Iroquois wars, the quest for captives was at least as important as the quest for furs. Even in the archetypal beaver war, the Five Nations–Huron conflict, only an overriding—even desperate—demand for prisoners can explain much of Iroquois behavior. For nearly a decade after the dispersal of the Huron Confederacy in 1649, Iroquois war parties killed or took captive every starving (and certainly peltry-less) group of Huron refugees they could find. Meanwhile, Iroquois ambassadors and warriors alternately negotiated with, cajoled, and threatened the Huron remnants living at Quebec to make them join their captive relatives in Iroquoia. Through all this, Mohawks, Senecas, and Onondagas occasionally shed each other's blood in arguments over the human spoils. Ultimately, in 1657, with French acquiescence, most of the Huron refugees filed away from Quebec—the Arendaronon nation to the Onondaga country and the Attignawantan nation to the Mohawk country.[47]

Judging by the number of prisoners taken during the Five Nations' wars from the 1640s to the 1670s with their other Iroquoian neighbors—the Neutral, Khionontateronon, Erie, and Susquehannock—these conflicts stemmed from a similar mingling of captive-taking and fur trade motives. Like the Huron, each of those peoples shared with the Iroquois mixed horticultural and hunting and fishing economies, related languages, and similar beliefs, making them ideal candidates for adoption. But they could not satisfy the spiraling Iroquois demand for furs and captives; war parties from the Five Nations had to range ever farther in their quest. In a not atypical series of raids in 1661–1662, they struck the Abenaki of the New England region, the Algonquians of the subarctic, the Siouans of the Upper Mississippi area, and various Indians near Virginia, while continuing the struggle with enemies closer to home.[48] The results of the mid-century campaigns are recorded in the *Jesuit Relations*, whose pages are filled with descriptions of Iroquois torture and execution of captives and note enormous numbers of adoptions. The Five Nations had absorbed so many prisoners that in 1657 Le Jeune believed that "more Foreigners than natives of the country" resided in Iroquoia.[49] By the mid-1660s several mission-

[47] *Jesuit Relations*, XXXV, 183–205, XXXVI, 177–191, XLI, 43–65, XLIII, 115–125, 187–207, XLIV, 69–77, 165–167, 187–191; A. J. F. van Laer, trans. and ed., *Minutes of the Court of Fort Orange and Beverwyck, 1657–1660*, II (Albany, N.Y., 1923), 45–48; Scull, ed., *Voyages of Radisson*, 93–119; Nicholas Perrot, "Memoir on the Manners, Customs, and Religion of the Savages of North America" (c. 1680–1718), in Emma Helen Blair, ed. and trans., *The Indian Tribes of the Upper Mississippi Valley and Region of the Great Lakes* . . . (Cleveland, Ohio, 1911), I, 148–193.

[48] *Jesuit Relations*, XLVII, 139–153.

[49] *Ibid.*, XLIII, 265.

aries estimated that two-thirds or more of the people in many Iroquois villages were adoptees.[50]

By 1675 a half-century of constantly escalating warfare had at best enabled the Iroquois to hold their own. Despite the beaver wars, the Five Nations still had few dependable sources of furs. In the early 1670s they hunted primarily on lands north of Lake Ontario, where armed clashes with Algonquian foes were likely, opportunities to steal peltries from them were abundant, and conflict with the French who claimed the territory was always possible.[51] Ironically, even the Franco-Iroquois peace of 1667 proved a mixed blessing for the Five Nations. Under the provisions of the treaty, Jesuit priests, who had hitherto labored in Iroquois villages only sporadically and at the risk of their lives, established missions in each of the Five Nations.[52] The Jesuits not only created Catholic converts but also generated strong Christian and traditionalist factions that brought unprecedented disquiet to Iroquois communities. Among the Onondaga, for example, the Christian sachem Garakontié's refusal to perform his duties in the traditional manner disrupted such important ceremonies as dream guessings, the roll call of the chiefs, and healing rituals.[53] And in 1671, traditionalist Mohawk women excluded at least one Catholic convert from her rightful seat on the council of matrons because of her faith.[54] Moreover, beginning in the late 1660s, missionaries encouraged increasing numbers of Catholic Iroquois—particularly Mohawks and Oneidas—to desert their homes for the mission villages of Canada; by the mid-1670s well over two hundred had departed.[55] A large proportion of those who left, however, were members of the Five Nations in name only. Many—perhaps most—were recently adopted Huron and other prisoners, an indication that the Iroquois were unable to assimilate effectively the mass of newcomers their mid-century wars had brought them.[56]

Problems in incorporating adoptees reflected a broader dilemma: by the late 1670s the mourning-war complex was crumbling. Warfare was failing to maintain a stable population; despite torrents of prisoners, gains from adoption were exceeded by losses from disease, combat, and migrations to Canada. Among the Mohawk—for whom more frequent contemporary population estimates exist than for the other na-

---

[50] *Ibid.*: XLV, 207, LI, 123, 187.

[51] *N.-Y. Col. Docs.*, IX, 80; Victor Konrad, "An Iroquois Frontier: The North Shore of Lake Ontario during the Late Seventeenth Century," *Journal of Historical Geography*, VII (1981), 129–144.

[52] *Jesuit Relations*, LI, 81–85, 167–257, LII, 53–55.

[53] *Ibid.*, LV, 61–63, LVII, 133–141, LVIII, 211, LX, 187–195.

[54] *Ibid.*, LIV, 281–283.

[55] *Ibid.*, LVI, 29, LVIII, 247–253, LX, 145–147, LXI, 195–199, LXIII, 141–189.

[56] *Ibid.*, LV, 33–37, LVIII, 75–77.

tions of the confederacy—the number of warriors declined from 700 or 800 in the 1640s to approximately 300 in the late 1670s. Those figures imply that, even with a constant infusion of captive adoptees, Mohawk population fell by half during that period.[57] The Five Nations as a whole fared only slightly better. In the 1640s the confederacy, already drastically reduced in numbers, had counted over 10,000 people. By the 1670s there were perhaps only 8,600.[58] The mourning-war, then, was not discharging one of its primary functions.

Meanwhile, ancient customs regarding the treatment of prisoners were decaying as rituals degenerated into chaotic violence and sheer murderous rage displaced the orderly adoption of captives that the logic of the mourning-war demanded. In 1682 missionary Jean de Lamberville asserted that Iroquois warriors "killed and ate . . . on the spot" over six hundred enemies in a campaign in the Illinois country; if he was even half right, it is clear that something had gone horribly wrong in the practice of the mourning-war. The decay of important customs associated with traditional warfare is further indicated by Lamberville's account of the return of that war party with its surviving prisoners. A gauntlet ceremony at the main Onondaga village turned into a deadly attack, forcing headmen to struggle to protect the lives of

---

[57] E. B. O'Callaghan, ed., *The Documentary History of the State of New-York*, octavo ed. (Albany, N.Y., 1849–1851), I, 12–14; *Jesuit Relations*, XXIV, 295. Reflecting the purposes of most Euro-Americans who made estimates of Indian population, figures are usually given in terms of the number of available fighting men. The limited data available for direct comparisons of estimates of Iroquois fighting strength with estimates of total population indicate that the ratio of one warrior for every four people proposed in Sherburne F. Cook, "Interracial Warfare and Population Decline among the New England Indians," *Ethnohistory*, XX (1973), 13, applies to the Five Nations. Compare the estimates of a total Mohawk population of 560–580 in William Andrews to the Secretary of the Society for the Propagation of the Gospel in Foreign Parts, Sept. 7, 1713, Oct. 17, 1715, Records of the Society for the Propagation of the Gospel, Letterbooks, Ser. A, VIII, 186, XI, 268–269, S.P.G. Archives, London (microfilm ed.), with the concurrent estimates of approximately 150 Mohawk warriors in Bernardus Freeman to the Secretary of S.P.G., May 28, 1712, *ibid.*, VII, 203; Peter Wraxall, *An Abridgement of the Indian Affairs . . . Transacted in the Colony of New York, from the Year 1678 to the Year 1751*, ed. Charles Howard McIlwain (Cambridge, Mass., 1915), 69; *N.-Y. Col. Docs.*, V, 272; and Lawrence H. Leder, ed., *The Livingston Indian Records, 1666–1723* (Gettysburg, Pa., 1956), 220.

[58] The estimate of 10,000 for the 1640s is from Trigger, *Children of Aataentsic*, I, 98; the figure of 8,600 for the 1670s is calculated from Wentworth Greenhalgh's 1677 estimate of 2,150 Iroquois warriors, in O'Callaghan, ed., *Documentary History*, I, 12–14. Compare the late 1670s estimate in Hennepin, *New Discovery*, II, 92–93, and see the tables of 17th- and 18th-century Iroquois warrior population in Snyderman, "Behind the Tree of Peace," *Pa. Archaeol.*, XVIII, nos. 3–4 (1948), 42; Bruce G. Trigger, ed., *Northeast*, in William C. Sturtevant, ed., *Handbook of North American Indians*, XV (Washington, D.C., 1978), 421; and Gunther Michelson, "Iroquois Population Statistics," *Man in the Northeast*, No. 14 (1977), 3–17. William Starna has recently suggested that all previous estimates for 1635 and earlier of Mohawk—and by implication Five Nations—population are drastically understated ("Mohawk Iroquois Populations: A Revision," *Ethnohistory*, XXVII [1980], 371–382).

the captives. A few hours later, drunken young men, "who observe[d] no usages or customs," broke into longhouses and tried to kill the prisoners whom the headmen had rescued. In vain leaders pleaded with their people to remember "that it was contrary to custom to ill-treat prisoners on their arrival, when They had not yet been given in the place of any person . . . and when their fate had been left Undecided by the victors."[59]

Nevertheless, despite the weakening of traditional restraints, in the 1670s Iroquois warfare still performed useful functions. It maintained a tenuous supply of furs to trade for essential European goods; it provided frequent campaigns to allow young men to show their valor; and it secured numerous captives to participate in the continual mourning rituals that the many Iroquois deaths demanded (though there could never be enough to restock the population absolutely). In the quarter-century after 1675, however, the scales would tip: by 1700 the Anglo-French struggle for control of the continent would make warfare as the Five Nations were practicing it dangerously dysfunctional for their societies.

III

During the mid-1670s the Five Nations' relations with their Indian and European neighbors were shifting. In 1675 the Mohawk and the Mahican made peace under pressure from Albany and ended—except for a few subsequent skirmishes—over a decade of conflict that had cost each side heavily.[60] In the same year the long and destructive war of the Oneida, Onondaga, Cayuga, and Seneca against the Susquehannock concluded as the latter withdrew from Pennsylvania to Maryland. The end of hostilities with the Mahican and Susquehannock allowed the Iroquois to refocus westward their quest for furs and captives. In the late 1670s and early 1680s conflicts with the Illinois, Miami, and other western peoples intensified, while relations with the Wyandot (composed of remnants of the Huron and other Iroquoian groups forced to the west in earlier wars with the Five Nations) and with various elements of the Ottawa alternated between skirmishes and efforts to cement military alliances against other enemies of the Iroquois.[61] As the Onondaga orator Otreouti (whom the French called *La Grande*

[59] *Jesuit Relations*, LXII, 71–95, quotation on p. 83.

[60] Leder, ed., *Livingston Indian Records*, 35–38; Allen W. Trelease, *Indian Affairs in Colonial New York: The Seventeenth Century* (Ithaca, N.Y., 1960), 229–230; Francis Jennings, "Glory, Death, and Transfiguration: The Susquehannock Indians in the Seventeenth Century," Am. Phil. Soc., *Procs.*, CXII (1968), 15–53.

[61] *Jesuit Relations*, LVI, 43–45, LIX, 251, LX, 211, LXII, 185; Hennepin, *New Discovery*, I, 100–295. Although the western nations had been included in the Franco-Iroquois peace of 1667, skirmishing in the west had never totally ceased; see *Jesuit Relations*, LIII, 39–51, LIV, 219–227, and *N.-Y. Col. Docs.*, IX, 79–80.

Gueule, "Big Mouth") explained in 1684, the Five Nations "fell upon the *Illinese* and the *Oumamies* [Miami], because they cut down the trees of Peace that serv'd for limits or boundaries to our Frontiers. They came to hunt Beavers upon our Lands; and contrary to the custom of all the Savages, have carried off whole Stocks, both Male and Female." [62] Whether those hunting grounds actually belonged to the Five Nations is questionable, but the importance of furs as an Iroquois war aim is not. And captives were also a lucrative prize, as the arrival in 1682 of several hundred Illinois prisoners demonstrated.[63] But this last of the beaver wars—which would melt into the American phase of the War of the League of Augsburg (King William's War)—was to differ devastatingly from earlier Iroquois conflicts. At the same time that the Five Nations began their fresh series of western campaigns the English and French empires were also beginning to compete seriously for the furs and lands of that region. The Iroquois would inevitably be caught in the Europeans' conflicts.[64]

Until the mid-1670s the Five Nations had only to deal, for all practical purposes, with the imperial policies of one European Power, France. The vital Iroquois connection with the Dutch of New Netherland and, after the 1664 conquest, with the English of New York had rested almost solely on trade. But when the English took possession of the province for the second time in 1674, the new governor, Sir Edmund Andros, had more grandiose designs for the Iroquois in the British American empire. He saw the Five Nations as the linchpin in his plans to pacify the other Indian neighbors of the English colonies; he hoped to make the Five Nations a tool in his dealings with the Calverts of Maryland; and he sought an opportunity to annex land to New York from Connecticut by encouraging the Iroquois to fight alongside New England in its 1675–1676 war on the Wampanoag Metacom ("King Philip") and his allies.[65] After Andros, New York–Iroquois relations would never be the same, as successors in the governor's chair attempted to use the Five Nations for imperial purposes. Thomas Dongan, who assumed the governorship in 1683, tried to

[62] Baron [de] Lahontan, *New Voyages to North-America* . . . (London, 1703), I, 41.

[63] *Jesuit Relations*, LXII, 71.

[64] For fuller accounts of the complex diplomacy, intrigue, trade wars, and military conflicts concerning the west between 1675 and 1689 touched on in the following paragraphs see, from a Canadian perspective, W. J. Eccles, *Frontenac: The Courtier Governor* (Toronto, 1959), 99–229, and, from a New York perspective, Trelease, *Indian Affairs in Colonial New York*, 204–301. A brief discussion of the Iroquois role is Richard Aquila, "The Iroquois Restoration: A Study of Iroquois Power, Politics, and Relations with Indians and Whites, 1700–1744" (Ph.D. diss., Ohio State University, 1977), 16–29.

[65] *N.-Y. Col. Docs.*, III, 254–259; Francis Paul Jennings, "Miquon's Passing: Indian-European Relations in Colonial Pennsylvania, 1674 to 1755" (Ph.D. diss., University of Pennsylvania, 1965), 10–50; Douglas Edward Leach, *Flintlock and Tomahawk: New England in King Philip's War* (New York, 1958), 59–60, 176–177.

strengthen New York's tenuous claims to suzerainty over the Five Nations—in 1684 he ceremoniously distributed the duke of York's coat of arms to be hung in their villages—and he directly challenged French claims in the west by sending trading parties into the region.[66]

Meanwhile the French had begun their own new westward thrust. In 1676 Canadian governor Louis de Buade de Frontenac established a post at Niagara and a few years later René-Robert Cavelier de La Salle began to construct a series of forts in the Illinois country. The French had long trodden a fine line in western policy. On the one hand, Iroquois raids in the west could not be allowed to destroy Indian allies of New France or to disrupt the fur trade, but, on the other hand, some hostility between the Iroquois and the western Indians helped prevent the latter from taking their furs to Albany markets. In the late 1670s and the 1680s Frontenac, and especially the governors during the interval between his two tenures, Joseph-Antoine Le Febvre de La Barre and Jacques-René de Brisay de Denonville, watched that policy unravel as they noted with alarm New York trading expeditions in the west, Iroquois raids on Indian hunters and *coureurs de bois*, Iroquois negotiations with the Wyandot and Ottawa, and the continual flow of firearms from Albany to the Five Nations.[67] As Iroquois spokesmen concisely explained to Dongan in 1684, "The French will have all the Bevers, and are angry with us for bringing any to you." [68]

French officials, faced with the potential ruin of their western fur trade, determined to humble the Five Nations. For over a decade, Canadian armies repeatedly invaded Iroquoia to burn villages, fields, and corn supplies. Although the first French attempt, led by La Barre against the Seneca in 1684, ended in ignoble failure for the French and diplomatic triumph for the Iroquois, later invasions sent the Five Nations to the brink of disaster. In 1687 La Barre's successor, Denonville, marched against Iroquoia with an army of over 2,000 French regulars, Canadian militia, and Indian warriors. Near Fort Frontenac his troops kidnapped an Iroquois peace delegation and captured the residents of two small villages of Iroquois who had lived on the north shore of Lake Ontario for nearly two decades. Denonville sent over thirty of

[66] O'Callaghan, ed., *Documentary History*, I, 391–420; Wraxall, *Abridgement of Indian Affairs*, ed. McIlwain, 10; Helen Broshar, "The First Push Westward of the Albany Traders," *MVHR*, VII (1920), 228–241; Henry Allain St. Paul, "Governor Thomas Dongan's Expansion Policy," *Mid-America*, XVII (1935), 172–184, 236–272; Gary B. Nash, "The Quest for the Susquehanna Valley: New York, Pennsylvania, and the Seventeenth-Century Fur Trade," *New York History*, XLVIII (1967), 3–27; Daniel K. Richter, "Rediscovered Links in the Covenant Chain: Previously Unpublished Transcripts of New York Indian Treaty Minutes, 1677–1691," American Antiquarian Society, *Proceedings*, XCII (1982), 63–66.

[67] Hennepin, *New Discovery*, I, 20–144; Lahontan, *New Voyages*, I, 269–274; *Jesuit Relations*, LXII, 151–165; *N.-Y. Col. Docs.*, IX, 296–303.

[68] *N.-Y. Col. Docs.*, III, 417.

the prisoners to France as slaves for the royal galleys, and then proceeded toward the Seneca country. After a brief but costly skirmish with Seneca defenders who hid in ambush, the invaders destroyed what was left of the Seneca villages, most of which the inhabitants had burned before fleeing to safety. Six years later, after war had been declared between France and England, the Canadians struck again. In January 1693, 625 regulars, militia, and Indians surprised the four Mohawk villages, captured their residents, and burned longhouses and stores of food as they retreated. Then, in 1696, the aged Frontenac—again governor and now carried into the field on a chair by his retainers—led at least 2,000 men to Onondaga, which he found destroyed by the retreating villagers. While his troops razed the ripening Onondaga corn, he received a plea for negotiation from the nearby Oneida village. The governor despatched Philippe de Rigaud de Vaudreuil and a detachment of 600 men, who extracted from the few Oneida who remained at home a promise that their people would soon move to a Canadian mission. Vaudreuil burned the village anyway.[69]

The repeated French invasions of Iroquoia took few lives directly—only in the campaign against the Mohawk in 1693 did the invaders attack fully occupied villages—but their cumulative effect was severe. One village or nation left homeless and deprived of food supplies could not depend on aid from the others, who faced similar plights. And as the Five Nations struggled to avoid starvation and to rebuild their villages, frequent raids by the Indian allies of the French levied a heavy toll in lives. In December 1691 a Mohawk–Oneida war party sustained fifteen deaths in an encounter on Lake George—losses significant beyond their numbers because they included all of the two nations' war chiefs and contributed to a total of 90 Mohawk and Oneida warriors killed since 1689. The Mohawk, who in the late 1670s had fielded approximately 300 warriors, in 1691 could muster only 130.[70] Combat fatalities, the continued exodus of Catholic converts to Canada, and the invasion of 1693 had, lamented a Mohawk orator, left his nation "a mean poor people," who had "lost all by the Enemy." [71] Fighting in the early 1690s had considerably weakened the three western Iroquois nations as well. In February 1692, for example, 50 Iroquois encountered a much larger French and Indian force above Montreal, and 40 suffered death or capture; a month later, 200 met disaster farther up the Saint Lawrence, when many were "captured, killed and

[69] N.-Y. Col. Docs., IX, 234–248, 358–369, 550–561, 639–656; Jesuit Relations, LXIII, 269–281, LXIV, 239–259, LXV, 25–29; Lahontan, New Voyages, I, 29–45, 68–80; Francis Parkman, Count Frontenac and New France under Louis XIV (Boston, 1877), 89–115, 139–157, 309–316, 410–417.
[70] N.-Y. Col. Docs., III, 814–816.
[71] Ibid., IV, 38–39.

defeated with loss of their principal chiefs." [72] Through the mid-1690s sporadic raids in and around Iroquoia by Canada's Indian allies kept the Five Nations on the defensive. [73]

The Five Nations did not meekly succumb. In 1687, soon after Denonville's capture of the Iroquois settled near Fort Frontenac and his invasion of the Seneca country, a Mohawk orator declared to Governor Dongan his people's intention to strike back at the French in the tradition of the mourning-war. "The Governor of Canada," he proclaimed, "has started an unjust war against all the [Five] nations. The Maquase [Mohawk] doe not yet have any prisoners, but that Governor has taken a hundred prisoners from all the nations to the West. . . . Therefore the nations have desired to revenge the unjust attacks." [74] Iroquois raids for captives kept New France in an uproar through the early 1690s. [75] The warriors' greatest successes occurred during the summer of 1689. That June a Mohawk orator, speaking for all Five Nations, vowed "that the Place where the French Stole their Indians two years ago should soon be cut off (meaning Fort Frontenac) for to steal people in a time of Peace is an Inconsiderate work." [76] Within two months the Iroquois had forced the temporary abandonment of Frontenac and other French western posts, and, in an assault at Lachine on Montreal Island, had killed twenty-four French and taken seventy to ninety prisoners. [77]

Later in the 1690s, however, as the Five Nations' losses mounted, their capacity to resist steadily diminished. They repeatedly sought military support from governors of New York, but little was forthcoming. "Since you are a Great People & we but a small, *you will protect us from the French,*" an Iroquois orator told Dongan in 1684. "We have put *all our Lands & ourselves,* under the Protection of the Great Duke of york." [78] Yet as long as the crowns of England and France remained at peace, the duke's governors largely ignored their end of the bargain. England's subsequent declaration of war against France coincided with

---

[72] *Ibid.,* IX, 531–535, quotation on p. 531.

[73] Leder, ed., *Livingston Indian Records,* 172–174; *N.-Y. Col. Docs.,* IX, 599–632; Colden, *History* (1747), 180–181.

[74] Leder, ed., *Livingston Indian Records,* 136–137.

[75] *Ibid.,* 139–140; *Jesuit Relations,* LXIII, 279, 287–289, LXIV, 249–259, LXV, 29; *N.-Y. Col. Docs.,* IX, 503–504, 538, 554–555.

[76] Treaty Minutes, June 17, 1689, untitled notebook, Indians of North America, Miscellaneous Papers, 1620–1895, Manuscript Collections, American Antiquarian Society, Worcester, Mass.

[77] Richard A. Preston, trans., and Leopold Lamontagne, ed., *Royal Fort Frontenac* (Toronto, 1958), 175–180; Lahontan, *New Voyages,* I, 98–102, 147–151; *N.-Y. Col. Docs.,* IX, 434–438; Eccles, *Frontenac,* 186–197. English sources claimed 200 French deaths and 120 captures at Lachine (Trelease, *Indian Affairs in Colonial New York,* 297–298).

[78] Treaty Minutes, Aug. 2, 1684, untitled notebook, Indians of North America, Miscellaneous Papers, 1620–1895, Manuscript Collections, AAS.

the Glorious Revolution of 1688, which unleashed in New York the period of political chaos known as Leisler's Rebellion. In 1689 Mohawks visiting Albany witnessed firsthand the turmoil between Leislerians and anti-Leislerians, and soon the Iroquois observed the resulting English military impotence. In February 1690, a few miles from the easternmost Mohawk village, a party of French and their Indian allies destroyed the sleeping town of Schenectady, whose Leislerian inhabitants had ignored warnings from anti-Leislerian authorities at Albany to be on guard.[79] Soon after the attack, the Mohawk headmen visited Albany to perform a condolence ceremony for their neighbors' losses at Schenectady. When they finished, they urged prompt New York action against the French. But neither then nor during the rest of the war did the Iroquois receive a satisfactory response. New York's offensive war consisted of two ill-fated and poorly supported invasions of Canada: the first, in 1690, was a dismal failure, and the second, in 1691, cost nearly as many English casualties as it inflicted on the enemy.[80] After 1691 New York factional strife, lack of aid from England, and the preoccupation of other colonies with their own defense prevented further commitments of English manpower to support the Iroquois struggle with the French. The Five Nations received arms and ammunition from Albany—never as much or as cheap as they desired—and little else.[81]

What to the Five Nations must have seemed the most typical of English responses to their plight followed the French invasion of the Mohawk country in 1693. Though local officials at Albany and Schenectady learned in advance of the Canadian army's approach and provided for their own defense, they neglected to inform the Mohawk. In the wake of the attack, as approximately 300 Mohawk prisoners trooped toward Canada, Peter Schuyler assembled at Schenectady a force of 250 New Yorkers and some Mohawks who had escaped capture, but he was restrained from immediate pursuit by his vacillating commander, Richard Ingoldsby. At length Schuyler moved on his own initiative and, reinforced by war parties from the western Iroquois nations, overtook the French army and inflicted enough damage to force the release of most of the captive Mohawk. Meanwhile, when word of the invasion reached Manhattan, Gov. Benjamin Fletcher mustered 150 militia and sailed to Albany in the unprecedented time of less than three days; nevertheless, the fighting was already over. At a conference with Iro-

[79] O'Callaghan, ed., *Documentary History*, I, 284–319, II, 130–132; Leder, ed., *Livingston Indian Records*, 158–160.

[80] O'Callaghan, ed., *Documentary History*, II, 164–290; *N.-Y. Col. Docs.*, III, 800–805, IV, 193–196, IX, 513–515, 520–524.

[81] *N.-Y. Col. Docs.*, III, 836–844; Leder, ed., *Livingston Indian Records*, 165–166; O'Callaghan, ed., *Documentary History*, I, 323–325, 341–345; Herbert L. Osgood, *The American Colonies in the Eighteenth Century*, I (New York, 1924), 228–265.

quois headmen a few days later, Fletcher's rush upriver earned him the title by which he would henceforth be known to the Five Nations: Cayenquiragoe, or "Great Swift Arrow." Fletcher took the name—chosen when the Iroquois learned that the word *fletcher* meant arrow-maker—as a supreme compliment. But, in view of the Mohawk's recent experience with the English—receiving no warning of the impending invasion, having to cool their heels at Schenectady while the enemy got away and Schuyler waited for marching orders, and listening to Fletcher rebuke them for their lax scouting and defense—the governor's political opponent Peter De La Noy may have been right to claim that Cayenquiragoe was a "sarcasticall pun" on Fletcher's name, bestowed for a showy effort that yielded no practical results.[82]

Yet if the English had been unable—or, as the Iroquois undoubtedly saw it, unwilling—to give meaningful military aid to the Five Nations, they were able to keep the Indians from negotiating a separate peace with the French that might leave New York exposed alone to attack. Although after 1688 ambassadors from several Iroquois nations periodically treated with the Canadians, New Yorkers maintained enough influence with factions among the Five Nations to sabotage all negotiations.[83] New York authorities repeatedly reminded their friends among the Iroquois of past French treacheries. At Albany in 1692, for example, Commander-in-Chief Ingoldsby warned the ambassadors of the Five Nations "that the Enemy has not forgot their old tricks." The French hoped "to lull the Brethren asleep and to ruine and distroy them at once, when they have peace in their mouths they have warr in their hearts."[84] Many Iroquois heeded the message. Lamberville complained in 1694 that "the english of those quarters have so intrigued that they have ruined all the hopes for peace that we had entertained."[85] The repeated failure of negotiations reinforced Canadian mistrust of the Iroquois and led French authorities to prosecute the war with more vigor. By the mid-1690s, with talks stymied, all the Five Nations could do was to accept English arms and ammunition and continue minor raids on their enemies while awaiting a general peace.[86]

For the Iroquois that peace did not come with the Treaty of Ryswick in 1697. At Ryswick, the European powers settled none of the issues that had provoked the conflict, yet they gained a respite that allowed each side to regroup. Paradoxically, however, a truce between the em-

---

[82] *N.-Y. Col. Docs.*, IV, 6–7, 14–24, 222; Colden, *History* (1747), 142–150.

[83] *N.-Y. Col. Docs.*, IX, 384–393, 515–517, 565–572, 596–599; *Jesuit Relations*, LXIV, 143–145.

[84] *N.-Y. Col. Docs.*, III, 841–844; see also *ibid.*, IV, 77–98, 279–282.

[85] *Jesuit Relations*, LXIV, 259.

[86] *N.-Y. Col. Docs.*, IX, 601–671.

pires precluded an end to conflict between the French and the Five Nations; jurisdiction over the Iroquois and their territory was one of the sticking points left unsettled. Accordingly, Frontenac and his successor, Louis-Hector de Callière, refused to consider the Iroquois—whom they called unruly French subjects—to be included in the treaty with England and insisted that they make a separate peace with New France. Fletcher and his successor, Richard Coote, earl of Bellomont, argued equally strenuously that the Iroquois were comprehended in the treaty as English subjects. Thus they tried to forbid direct Franco-Iroquois negotiations and continued to pressure their friends among the Five Nations to prevent serious talks from occurring.[87] While Iroquois leaders struggled to escape the diplomatic bind, the Indian allies of New France continued their war against their ancient Iroquois enemies. In the late 1690s the Ojibwa led a major western Indian offensive that, according to Ojibwa tradition, killed enormous numbers of Seneca and other Iroquois. Euro-American sources document more moderate, yet still devastating, fatalities: the Onondaga lost over ninety men within a year of the signing of the Treaty of Ryswick, and the Seneca perhaps as many. Such defeats continued into 1700, when the Seneca suffered over fifty deaths in battles with the Ottawa and Illinois. All along at Albany, authorities counseled the Five Nations not to strike back, but to allow Bellomont time to negotiate with Callière on their behalf.[88]

IV

By 1700 Iroquois warfare and culture had reached a turning point. Up to about 1675, despite the impact of disease, firearms, and the fur trade, warfare still performed functions that outweighed its costs. But thereafter the Anglo-French struggle for control of North America made war disastrous for the Five Nations. Conflict in the west, instead of securing fur supplies, was cutting them off, while lack of pelts to trade and wartime shortages of goods at Albany created serious economic hardship in Iroquoia.[89] Those problems paled, however, in comparison with the physical toll. All of the Iroquois nations except the Cayuga had seen their villages and crops destroyed by invading armies, and all five nations were greatly weakened by loss of members to captivity, to death in combat, or to famine and disease. By some es-

---

[87] Trelease, *Indian Affairs in Colonial New York*, 323–342; *N.-Y. Col. Docs.*, IV, 367–374, 402–409.

[88] Leroy V. Eid, "The Ojibwa–Iroquois War: The War the Five Nations Did Not Win," *Ethnohistory*, XXVI (1979), 297–324; Wraxall, *Abridgement of Indian Affairs*, ed. McIlwain, 29–30; *N.-Y. Col. Docs.*, IX, 681–688, 708–709.

[89] Aquila, "Iroquois Restoration," 71–79.

timates, between 1689 and 1698 the Iroquois lost half of their fighting strength. That figure is probably an exaggeration, but by 1700 perhaps 500 of the 2,000 warriors the Five Nations fielded in 1689 had been killed or captured or had deserted to the French missions and had not been replaced by younger warriors. A loss of well over 1,600 from a total population of approximately 8,600 seems a conservative esti- mate.[90]

At the turn of the century, therefore, the mourning-war was no longer even symbolically restocking the population. And, far from be- ing socially integrative, the Five Nations' current war was splitting their communities asunder. The heavy death toll of previous decades had robbed them of many respected headmen and clan matrons to whom the people had looked for guidance and arbitration of disputes. As a group of young Mohawk warriors lamented in 1691 when they came to parley with the Catholic Iroquois settled near Montreal, "all those . . . who had sense are dead." [91] The power vacuum, war weari- ness, and the pressures of the imperial struggle combined to place at each other's throats those who believed that the Iroquois' best chance lay in a separate peace with the French and those who continued to rely on the English alliance. "The [Five] Nations are full of faction, the French having got a great interest among them," reported the Al- bany Commissioners for Indian Affairs in July 1700. At Onondaga, where, according to Governor Bellomont, the French had "full as many friends" as the English, the situation was particularly severe. Some sachems found themselves excluded from councils, and factions charged one another with using poison to remove adversaries from the scene. One pro-English Onondaga headman, Aquendero, had to take refuge near Albany, leaving his son near death and supposedly be- witched by opponents.[92] Their politics being ordered by an interlock- ing structure of lineages, clans, and moieties, the Iroquois found such factions, which cut across kinship lines, difficult if not impossible to handle. In the 1630s the Huron, whose political structure was similar, never could manage the novel factional alignments that resulted from the introduction of Christianity. That failure perhaps contributed to

[90] A 1698 report on New York's suffering during the War of the League of Augsburg states that there were 2,550 Iroquois warriors in 1689 and only 1,230 in 1698. The re- port probably contains some polemical overstatement: the first figure seems too high and the second too low. By comparison, 2,050 Iroquois warriors were estimated by De- nonville in 1685, 1,400 by Bellomont in 1691, 1,750 by Bernardus Freeman in 1700, and 1,200 by a French cabinet paper in 1701 (*N.-Y. Col. Docs.*, IV, 337, 768, IX, 281, 725; Freeman to the Secretary, May 28, 1712, Records of S.P.G., Letterbooks, Ser. A, VII, 203). If the figure of 1,750 warriors cited by Freeman—a minister who worked with the Mohawk—is correct, the total Iroquois population in 1700 was approximately 7,000, cal- culated by the ratio in note 57.

[91] *Jesuit Relations*, LXIV, 59–61.

[92] *N.-Y. Col. Docs.*, IV, 648–661, 689–690.

their demise at the hands of the Five Nations.[93] Now the Iroquois found themselves at a similar pass.

As the new century opened, however, Iroquois headmen were beginning to construct solutions to some of the problems facing their people. From 1699 to 1701 Iroquois ambassadors—in particular the influential Onondaga Teganissorens—threaded the thickets of domestic factionalism and shuttled between their country and the Euro-American colonies to negotiate what one scholar has termed "The Grand Settlement of 1701." [94] On August 4, 1701, at an immense gathering at Montreal, representatives of the Seneca, Cayuga, Onondaga, and Oneida, also speaking for the Mohawk, met Governor Callière and headmen of the Wyandot, Algonquin, Abenaki, Nipissing, Ottawa, Ojibwa, Sauk, Fox, Miami, Potawatomi, and other French allies. The participants ratified arrangements made during the previous year that provided for a general peace, established vague boundaries for western hunting territories (the Iroquois basically consented to remain east of Detroit), and eschewed armed conflict in favor of arbitration by the governor of New France. A few days later, the Iroquois and Callière reached more specific understandings concerning Iroquois access to Detroit and other French western trading posts. Most important from the French standpoint, the Iroquois promised neutrality in future Anglo-French wars.[95]

A delegation of Mohawks arrived late at the Montreal conference; they, along with ambassadors from the western Iroquois, had been at Albany negotiating with Lt. Gov. John Nanfan, who had replaced the deceased Bellomont. The Five Nations' spokesmen had first assured Nanfan of their fidelity and told him that the simultaneous negotiations at Montreal were of no significance. Then they had agreed equivocally to perpetuate their military alliance with the English, reiterated that trade lay at the heart of Iroquois–New York relations, consented to the passage through Iroquoia of western Indians going to trade at Albany, and granted the English crown a "deed" to the same western hunting territories assured to the Five Nations in the Mon-

---

[93] Trigger, *Children of Aataentsic*, II, 709–724. See also the discussions of Indian factionalism in Robert F. Berkhofer, Jr., "The Political Context of a New Indian History," *Pacific Historical Review*, XL (1971), 373–380; and Edward H. Spicer, *Cycles of Conquest: The Impact of Spain, Mexico, and the United States on the Indians of the Southwest, 1533–1960* (Tucson, Ariz., 1962), 491–501.

[94] Anthony F. C. Wallace, "Origins of Iroquois Neutrality: The Grand Settlement of 1701," *Pennsylvania History*, XXIV (1957), 223–235. The best reconstruction of the Iroquois diplomacy that led to the Grand Settlement is Richard L. Haan, "The Covenant Chain: Iroquois Diplomacy on the Niagara Frontier, 1697–1730" (Ph.D. diss., University of California, Santa Barbara, 1976), 64–147.

[95] Bacqueville de La Potherie, *Histoire de l'Amérique Septentrionale*, IV (Paris, 1722), *passim*; *N.-Y. Col. Docs.*, IX, 715–725.

treal treaty. In return, Nanfan promised English defense of Iroquois hunting rights in those lands. Meanwhile, at Philadelphia, yet a third series of negotiations had begun, which, while not usually considered part of the Grand Settlement, reflected the same Iroquois diplomatic thrust; by 1704 those talks would produce an informal trade agreement between the Five Nations and Pennsylvania.[96]

On one level, this series of treaties represented an Iroquois defeat. The Five Nations had lost the war and, in agreeing to peace on terms largely dictated by Callière, had acknowledged their inability to prevail militarily over their French, and especially their Indian, enemies.[97] Nevertheless, the Grand Settlement did secure for the Iroquois five important ends: escape from the devastating warfare of the 1690s; rights to hunting in the west; potentially profitable trade with western Indians passing through Iroquoia to sell furs at Albany; access to markets in New France and Pennsylvania as well as in New York; and the promise of noninvolvement in future imperial wars. The Grand Settlement thus brought to the Five Nations not only peace on their northern and western flanks but also a more stable economy based on guaranteed western hunting territories and access to multiple Euro-American markets. Henceforth, self-destructive warfare need no longer be the only means of ensuring Iroquois economic survival, and neither need inter-Indian beaver wars necessarily entrap the Five Nations in struggles between Euro-Americans.[98] In 1724, nearly a generation after the negotiation of the Grand Settlement, an Iroquois spokesman explained to a delegation from Massachusetts how the treaties, while limiting Iroquois diplomatic and military options, nevertheless proved beneficial. "Tho' the Hatchett lays by our side yet the way is open between this Place and Canada, and trade is free both going and coming," he answered when the New Englanders urged the Iroquois to attack New France. "If a War should break out and we should use the Hatchett that lays by our Side, those Paths which are now open wo[u]ld be stopped, and if we should make war it would not end in a few days as yours doth but it must last till one nation or the other is destroyed as it has been heretofore with us[.] . . . [W]e know what whipping and scourging is from the Governor of Canada." [99]

After the Grand Settlement, then, Iroquois leaders tried to abandon warfare as a means of dealing with the diplomatic problems generated

[96] *N.-Y. Col. Docs.*, IV, 889–911; *Minutes of the Provincial Council of Pennsylvania*, II (Harrisburg, Pa., 1838), 142–143; William M. Beauchamp, *A History of the New York Iroquois, Now Commonly Called the Six Nations*, New York State Museum Bulletin 78 (Albany, N.Y., 1905), 256; Jennings, "Miquon's Passing," 118–121.

[97] Eid, "Ojibwa–Iroquois War," *Ethnohistory*, XXVI (1979), 297–324.

[98] Aquila, "Iroquois Restoration," 109–171; Richard Haan, "The Problem of Iroquois Neutrality: Suggestions for Revision," *Ethnohistory*, XXVII (1980), 317–330.

[99] *N.-Y. Col. Docs.*, V, 724–725.

by the Anglo-French imperial rivalry and the economic dilemmas of
the fur trade. Through most of the first half of the eighteenth century
the headmen pursued a policy of neutrality between the empires with a
dexterity that the English almost never, and the French only seldom,
comprehended. At the same time the Iroquois began to cement peaceful trading relationships with the western nations. Sporadic fighting
continued in the western hunting grounds through the first decade and
a half of the eighteenth century, as the parties to the 1701 Montreal
treaty sorted out the boundaries of their territories and engaged in reciprocal raids for captives that were provoked by contact between Iroquois and western Indian hunters near French posts. Iroquois headmen quickly took advantage of Canadian arbitration when such
quarrels arose, however, and they struggled to restrain young warriors
from campaigning in the west.[100] As peace took hold, Alexander Montour, the son of a French man and an Iroquois woman, worked to build
for the Iroquois a thriving trade between the western nations and Albany.[101]

The new diplomatic direction was tested between 1702 and 1713,
when the imperial conflict resumed in the War of the Spanish Succession (Queen Anne's War). Through crafty Iroquois diplomacy, and
thanks to the only halfhearted effort each European side devoted to
the western theater, the Five Nations were able to maintain their neutrality and avoid heavy combat losses. Only between 1709 and 1711
did the imperial struggle again threaten to engulf the Five Nations. In
1709 Vaudreuil, now governor of New France, ordered the murder of
Montour to prevent further diversion of French western trade to the
Iroquois and the English. As a result, many formerly pro-French Iroquois turned against the Canadians, and most Mohawk and Oneida
warriors, with many Onondagas and Cayugas, joined in the plans of
Samuel Vetch and Francis Nicholson for an intercolonial invasion of
Canada. Only the Senecas, who were most exposed to attack by Indian
allies of the French, refused to participate.[102] The army of colonists
and Iroquois, however, never set foot in Canada because Whitehall re-
neged on its promise of a fleet that would simultaneously attack
Canada from the east. After the 1709 fiasco, Iroquois–French relations
continued to deteriorate. The Seneca determined on war with the

---

[100] Leder, ed., *Livingston Indian Records*, 192–200; *N.-Y. Col. Docs.*, IX, 759–765,
848–849, 876–878; Yves F. Zoltvany, "New France and the West, 1701–1713," *Can. Hist.
Rev.*, XLVI (1965), 315–321.

[101] Wraxall, *Abridgement of Indian Affairs*, ed. McIlwain, 44–67; "Continuation of
Colden's History of the Five Indian Nations, for the Years 1707 through 1720," New-
York Historical Society, *Collections*, LXVIII (1935), 360–367, hereafter cited as Colden,
"Continuation"; Haan, "Covenant Chain," 152–153.

[102] Wraxall, *Abridgement of Indian Affairs*, ed. McIlwain, 64–69; *N.-Y. Col. Docs.*, IX,
902; Leder, ed., *Livingston Indian Records*, 207–210; Colden, "Continuation," 370–380.

French in 1710, when they were attacked by western Indians apparently instigated by the Canadians. Then, in the spring of 1711, a party of French came to Onondaga and, spouting threats about the consequences of further Iroquois hostility, attempted to build a blockhouse in the village. When Vetch and Nicholson planned a second assault on Canada in the summer of 1711, large war parties from all Five Nations eagerly enlisted. Once more, however, the seaborne wing of the expedition failed, and the land army returned home without seeing the enemy.[103] The debacles of 1709 and 1711 confirmed the Iroquois in their opinion of English military impotence and contributed to a chill in Anglo-Iroquois relations that lasted for the rest of the decade.[104] Iroquois leaders once again steered a course of neutrality between the empires, and after the peace of Utrecht trade once again flourished with the western Indians.[105]

In addition to its diplomatic benefits, the Grand Settlement of 1701 provided a partial solution to Iroquois factionalism. Iroquoian non-state political structures could not suppress factional cleavages entirely, and in the years after 1701 differences over relations with the French and the English still divided Iroquois communities, as each European power continued to encourage its friends. Interpreters such as the Canadian Louis-Thomas Chabert de Joncaire and the New Yorker Lawrence Claeson (or Claes) struggled to win the hearts of Iroquois villagers; each side gave presents to its supporters; and on several occasions English officials interfered with the selection of sachems in order to strengthen pro-English factions. As a result, fratricidal disputes still occasionally threatened to tear villages apart.[106] Still, in general, avoidance of exclusive alliances or major military conflict with either European power allowed Iroquois councils to keep factional strife within bounds. A new generation of headmen learned to maintain a rough equilibrium between pro-French and pro-English factions at home, as well as peaceful relations with French and English abroad. Central to that strategy was an intricate policy that tried to balance French against English fortified trading posts, Canadian against New York

---

[103] Colden, "Continuation," 398–409; *N.-Y. Col. Docs.*, V, 242–249, 267–277; G. M. Waller, "New York's Role in Queen Anne's War, 1702–1713," *New York History*, XXXIII (1952), 40–53; Bruce T. McCully, "Catastrophe in the Wilderness: New Light on the Canada Expedition of 1709," *WMQ*, 3d Ser., XI (1954), 441–456; Haan, "Covenant Chain," 148–198.

[104] *N.-Y. Col. Docs.*, V, 372–376, 382–388, 437, 484–487; Wraxall, *Abridgement of Indian Affairs*, ed. McIlwain, 98–105.

[105] *N.-Y. Col. Docs.*, V, 445–446, 584; Colden, "Continuation," 414–432; Haan, "Problem of Iroquois Neutrality," *Ethnohistory*, XXVII (1980), 324.

[106] *N.-Y. Col. Docs.*, V, 545, 569, 632, IX, 816; Thomas Barclay to Robert Hunter, Jan. 26, 1713 (extract), Records of S.P.G., Letterbooks, Ser. A, VIII, 251–252. For examples of Claeson's and Joncaire's activities see Colden, "Continuation," 360–363, 432–434, and *N.-Y. Col. Docs.*, V, 538, 562–569, IX, 759–765, 814, 876–903.

blacksmiths, and Jesuit against Anglican missionaries. Each supplied the Iroquois with coveted aspects of Euro-American culture—trade goods, technology, and spiritual power, respectively—but each also could be a focus of factional leadership and a tool of Euro-American domination. The Grand Settlement provided a way to lessen, though hardly eliminate, those dangers.[107]

The Iroquois balancing act was severely tested beginning in 1719, when Joncaire persuaded pro-French elements of the Seneca to let him build a French trading house at Niagara. Neither confederacy leaders nor Senecas opposed to the French encroachment attempted to dislodge the intruders forcibly, as they had done in the previous century at Fort Frontenac. Instead, Iroquois headmen unsuccessfully urged New York authorities to send troops to destroy the post, thus hoping to place the onus on the British while avoiding an open breach between pro-French and pro-English Iroquois. But New York Gov. William Burnet had other plans. In 1724 he announced his intention to build an English counterpart to Niagara at Oswego. With the French beginning to fortify Niagara, league headmen reluctantly agreed to the English proposals. In acquiescing to both forts, the Iroquois yielded a measure of sovereignty as Europeans defined the term; yet they dampened internal strife, avoided exclusive dependence on either European power, and maintained both factional and diplomatic balance.[108]

The years following the Grand Settlement also witnessed the stabilization of Iroquois population. Though the numbers of the Iroquois continued to decline gradually, the forces that had so dramatically reduced them in the seventeenth century abated markedly after 1701. The first two decades of the seventeenth century brought only one major epidemic—smallpox in 1716—[109] while the flow of Catholic converts to Canadian missions also slowed. The missions near Montreal had lost much of the utopian character that had previously attracted so many Iroquois converts. By the early eighteenth century, drunkenness, crushing debts to traders, and insults from Euro-American neighbors were no less characteristic of Iroquois life in Canada than in Iroquoia, and the Jesuit priests serving the Canadian missions had become old, worn-out men who had long since abandoned dreams of turning Indians into Frenchmen.[110]

---

[107] *N. Y. Col. Docs.*, V, 217–227; Colden, "Continuation," 408–409; Wraxall, *Abridgement of Indian Affairs*, ed. McIlwain, 79n–80n.

[108] The evolution of Iroquois, French, and English policies concerning Niagara and Oswego may be followed in *N.-Y. Col. Docs.*, V, *passim*, IX, 897–1016; Jennings, "Miquon's Passing," 256–274; and Haan, "Covenant Chain," 199–237.

[109] Andrews to the Secretary, Oct. 11, 1716, Records of S.P.G., Letterbooks, Ser. A, XII, 241; *N.-Y. Col. Docs.*, V, 484–487, IX, 878.

[110] *Jesuit Relations*, LXVI, 203–207, LXVII, 39–41; *N.-Y. Col. Docs.*, IX, 882–884;

As the population drain from warfare, disease, and migration to mission villages moderated, peaceful assimilation of refugees from neighboring nations helped to replace those Iroquois who were lost. One French source even claimed, in 1716, that "the five Iroquois nations . . . are becoming more and more formidable through their great numbers." [111] Most notable among the newcomers were some 1,500 Tuscaroras who, after their defeat by the English and allied Indians of the Carolinas in 1713, migrated north to settle on lands located between the Onondaga and Oneida villages. They were adopted as the sixth nation of the Iroquois Confederacy about 1722. There are indications that the Tuscarora—who, according to William Andrews, Anglican missionary to the Mohawk, possessed "an Implacable hatred against Christians at Carolina"—contributed greatly to the spirit of independence and distrust of Europeans that guided the Six Nations on their middle course between the imperial powers. The Tuscarora, concluded Andrews, were "a great Occasion of Our Indians becoming so bad as they are, they now take all Occasions to find fault and quarrel, wanting to revolt." [112]

V

The first two decades of the eighteenth century brought a shift away from those aspects of Iroquois warfare that had been most socially disruptive. As the Iroquois freed themselves of many, though by no means all, of the demographic, economic, and diplomatic pressures that had made seventeenth-century warfare so devastating, the mourning-war began to resume some of its traditional functions in Iroquois culture.

As the Five Nations made peace with their old western and northern foes, Iroquois mourning-war raids came to focus on enemies the Iroquois called "Flatheads"—a vague epithet for the Catawba and other tribes on the frontiers of Virginia and the Carolinas. [113] Iroquois and Flathead war parties had traded blows during the 1670s and 1680s, conflict had resumed about 1707, and after the arrival of the Tuscarora

---

George F. G. Stanley, "The Policy of 'Francisation' as Applied to the Indians during the Ancien Regime," *Revue d'histoire de l'amérique française*, III (1949–1950), 333–348; Cornelius J. Jaenen, "The Frenchification and Evangelization of the Amerindians in the Seventeenth Century New France" (*sic*), Canadian Catholic Historical Association, *Study Sessions*, XXXV (1969), 57–71.

[111] *Jesuit Relations*, LXVII, 27.

[112] Andrews to the Secretary, Apr. 20, 1716, Apr. 23, 1717, Records of S.P.G., Letterbooks, Ser. A, XI, 319–320, XII, 310–312.

[113] Henry R. Schoolcraft, *Notes on the Iroquois: Or, Contributions to the Statistics, Aboriginal History, Antiquities and General Ethnology of Western New York* (New York, 1846), 148–149; Fenton, "Iroquois in History," in Leacock and Lurie, eds., *North American Indians*, 147–148; Beauchamp, *History of New York Iroquois*, 139.

in the 1710s Iroquois raiding parties attacked the Flatheads regularly and almost exclusively.[114] The Catawba and other southeastern Indians sided with the Carolinians in the Tuscarora War of 1711–1713, bringing them into further conflict with warriors from the Five Nations, who fought alongside the Tuscarora.[115] After the Tuscarora moved north, Iroquois–Flathead warfare increased in intensity and lasted—despite several peace treaties—until the era of the American Revolution. This series of mourning-wars exasperated English officials from New York to the Carolinas, who could conceive no rational explanation for the conflicts except the intrigues of French envoys who delighted in stirring up trouble on English frontiers.[116]

Canadian authorities did indeed encourage Iroquois warriors with arms and presents. The French were happy for the chance to harass British settlements and to strike blows against Indians who troubled French inhabitants of New Orleans and the Mississippi Valley.[117] Yet the impetus for raiding the Flatheads lay with the Iroquois, not the French. At Onondaga in 1710, when emissaries from New York blamed French influence for the campaigns and presented a wampum belt calling for a halt to hostilities, a Seneca orator dismissed their arguments: "When I think of the Brave Warriours that hav[e] been slain by the Flatheads I can Govern my self no longer. . . . I reject your Belt for the Hatred I bear to the Flatheads can never be forgotten." [118] The Flatheads were an ideal target for the mourning-wars demanded by Iroquois women and warriors, for with conflict channeled southward, warfare with northern and western nations that, in the past, had brought disaster could be avoided. In addition, war with the Flatheads placated both Canadian authorities and pro-French Iroquois factions, since the raids countered a pro-English trade policy with a military policy useful to the French. And, from the perspective of Iroquois–English relations, the southern campaigns posed few risks. New York officials alternately forbade and countenanced raids against southern Indians as the fortunes of frontier war in the Carolinas and the intrigues of intercolonial politics shifted. But even when the governors of the Carolinas, Virginia, Pennsylvania, and New York did agree on

---

[114] On Iroquois–Flathead conflicts before 1710 see Colden, *History* (1727), 30–71, and "Continuation," 361–363, and Wraxall, *Abridgement of Indian Affairs*, ed. McIlwain, 50–61. References to raids after 1710 in Colden, *N.-Y. Col. Docs.*, and other sources are too numerous to cite here; a useful discussion is Aquila, "Iroquois Restoration," 294–346.

[115] Wraxall, *Abridgement of Indian Affairs*, ed. McIlwain, 94–96; *N.-Y. Col. Docs.*, V, 372–376, 382–388, 484–493; Verner W. Crane, *The Southern Frontier, 1670–1732* (Durham, N.C., 1928), 158–161.

[116] *N.-Y. Col. Docs.*, V, 542–545, 562–569, 635–640.

[117] *Ibid.*, IX, 876–878, 884–885, 1085, 1097–1098.

[118] Colden, "Continuation," 382–383, brackets in original.

schemes to impose peace, experience with English military impotence had taught the Iroquois that the governors could do little to stop the conflict.[119]

While the diplomatic advantages were many, perhaps the most important aspect of the Iroquois–Flathead conflicts was the partial return they allowed to the traditional ways of the mourning-war. By the 1720s the Five Nations had not undone the ravages of the preceding century, yet they had largely extricated themselves from the socially disastrous wars of the fur trade and of the European empires. And though prisoners no longer flowed into Iroquois villages in the floods of the seventeenth century, the southern raids provided enough captives for occasional mourning and condolence rituals that dried Iroquois tears and reminded the Five Nations of their superiority over their enemies. In the same letter of 1716 in which missionary Andrews noted the growing independence of the Iroquois since the Tuscarora had settled among them and the southern wars had intensified, he also vividly described the reception recently given to captives of the Onondaga and Oneida.[120] Iroquois warfare was again binding Iroquois families and villages together.

The Indians' New World: The Catawba Experience

JAMES H. MERRELL

The Indians whom British voyagers to the Americas encountered have always been important players in the drama of early American history. For as long as scholars have been writing on the subject, they have acknowledged that the first Europeans to arrive in any part of the hemisphere had to confront the natives and deal

---

[119] For examples of shifting New York policies regarding the Iroquois southern campaigns see *N.-Y. Col. Docs.*, V, 446–464, 542–545, and Wraxall, *Abridgement of Indian Affairs*, ed. McIlwain, 123.

[120] Andrews to the Secretary, Apr. 20, 1716, Records of S.P.G., Letterbooks, Ser. A., XI, 320.

Reprinted by permission from James H. Merrell, "The Indians' New World: The Catawba Experience," *William and Mary Quarterly*, XLI (1984), 537–565.

with them. As the Crosby essay observes, from the European point of view this confrontation was often made easier by epidemic disease. Despite this longstanding awareness of the presence of other people on the land that the British soldiers and settlers wished to conquer and exploit, however, a sensitive history of relationships between the arriving Europeans and particular Indian cultural groups has only recently begun to emerge in the historical literature. In part, this failing can be explained by the difficulty involved in identifying appropriate sources, and in part it can be attributed to ethnocentrism and insensitivity.

Whatever the cause, the absence of genuinely bilateral histories of Indian-white encounters is now being brilliantly corrected by a younger generation of scholars of whom James H. Merrell is one of the most talented. Merrell's basic insight—that the arrival of Europeans marked the emergence of a "new" world for Indians as well as for whites—may seem so obvious as barely to merit notice. Yet it is a point that turns out to have startling explanatory power since it redirects the focus of research and interpretation in a way that grants to Indians (in this case the Catawbas) a distinctive historical experience that previous historians had unthinkingly denied them.

Merrell's interpretation should be compared with Daniel Richter's essay on the Iroquois since they exhibit many of the same virtues. Both the Iroquois and the Catawbas survived the perils of contact by aggressively incorporating neighboring peoples, a common experience that did not prevent them from hating each other. In addition, Merrell's focus on matters of trade and economic relations should remind us that in many respects Indians and British settlers found ways to accommodate themselves to each other's presence and even to gain from the connection.

At the same time, Merrell does not allow us to forget that Indian life was unalterably transformed by the arrival of white men and that, although gradual, change inevitably came to Catawba life. Has Merrell added an important new dimension to our understanding of early American history, or has he merely added detail to a story whose tragic conclusion was foreordained? Were the Catawbas really the formidable force he portrays them to be, or has he inflated their role in order to make a point?

In August 1608 John Smith and his band of explorers captured an Indian named Amoroleck during a skirmish along the Rappahannock River. Asked why his men—a hunting party from towns upstream—had attacked the English, Amoroleck replied that they had heard the strangers "were a people come from under the world, to take their world from them." [1] Smith's prisoner grasped a simple yet important truth that students of colonial America have overlooked: after 1492 native Americans lived in a world every bit as new as that confronting transplanted Africans or Europeans.

The failure to explore the Indians' new world helps explain why, despite many excellent studies of the native American past,[2] colonial history often remains "a history of those men and women—English, European, and African—who transformed America from a geographical expression into a new nation." [3] One reason Indians generally are left out may be the apparent inability to fit them into the new world theme, a theme that exerts a powerful hold on our historical imagination and runs throughout our efforts to interpret American development. From Frederick Jackson Turner to David Grayson Allen, from Melville J. Herskovits to Daniel C. Littlefield, scholars have analyzed encounters between peoples from the Old World and conditions in the New, studying the complex interplay between Europeans or African cultural patterns and the American environment.[4] Indians crossed no ocean, peopled no faraway land. It might seem logical to exclude them.

The natives' segregation persists, in no small degree, because historians still tend to think only of the new world as the New World, a geographic entity bounded by the Atlantic Ocean on the one side and the Pacific on the other. Recent research suggests that process was as important as place. Many settlers in New England recreated familiar forms with such success that they did not really face an alien environ-

---

[1] Edward Arber and A. G. Bradley, eds., *Travels and Works of Captain John Smith . . .* , II (Edinburgh, 1910), 427.

[2] Bernard W. Sheehan, "Indian-White Relations in Early America: A Review Essay," *William and Mary Quarterly*, 3d Ser., XXVI (1969), 267–286; James Axtell, "The Ethnohistory of Early America: A Review Essay," *ibid.*, XXXV (1978), 110–144.

[3] Benjamin W. Labaree, *America's Nation-Time: 1607–1789* (New York, 1976), cover, see also xi. Two exceptions are Gary B. Nash, *Red, White, and Black: The Peoples of Early America* (Englewood Cliffs, N.J., 1974), and Mary Beth Norton *et al.*, *A People and a Nation: A History of the United States* (Boston, 1982), I. For analyses of the scholarly neglect of Indians in colonial America see Thad W. Tate, "The Seventeenth-Century Chesapeake and Its Modern Historians," in Tate and David L. Ammerman, eds., *The Chesapeake in the Seventeenth Century: Essays on Anglo-American Society* (Chapel Hill, N.C., 1979), 30–32; Douglas Greenberg, "The Middle Colonies in Recent American Historiography," *WMQ*, 3d Ser., XXXVI (1979), 415–416; and Neal Salisbury, *Manitou and Providence: Indians, Europeans, and the Making of New England, 1500–1643* (New York, 1982), 3–7.

[4] Turner, "The Significance of the Frontier in American History," American Historical Association, *Annual Report for the Year 1893* (Washington, D.C., 1894), 199–227; Allen, *In English Ways: The Movement of Societies and the Transferal of English Local Law and Custom to Massachusetts Bay in the Seventeenth Century* (Chapel Hill, N.C., 1981); Herskovits, *The Myth of the Negro Past* (New York, 1941); Littlefield, *Rice and Slaves: Ethnicity and the Slave Trade in Colonial South Carolina* (Baton Rouge, La., 1981).

ment until long after their arrival.[5] Africans, on the other hand, were struck by the shock of the new at the moment of their enslavement, well before they stepped on board ship or set foot on American soil.[6] If the Atlantic was not a barrier between one world and another, if what happened to people was more a matter of subtle cultural processes than mere physical displacements, perhaps we should set aside the maps and think instead of a "world" as the physical and cultural milieu within which people live and a "new world" as a dramatically different milieu demanding basic changes in ways of life.[7] Considered in these terms, the experience of natives was more closely akin to that of immigrants and slaves, and the idea of an encounter between worlds can—indeed, must—include the aboriginal inhabitants of America.

For American Indians a new order arrived in three distinct yet overlapping stages.[8] First, alien microbes killed vast numbers of natives, sometimes before the victims had seen a white or black face. Next came traders who exchanged European technology for Indian products and brought natives into the developing world market. In time traders gave way to settlers eager to develop the land according to their own lights.[9] These three intrusions combined to transform native existence, disrupting established cultural habits and requiring creative responses to drastically altered conditions. Like their new neighbors, then, Indians were forced to blend old and new in ways that would permit them to survive in the present without forsaking their past. By the close of the colonial era, native Americans as well as whites and blacks had cre-

---

[5] Allen, *In English Ways*; T. H. Breen, "Persistent Localism: English Social Change and the Shaping of New England Institutions," *WMQ*, 3d Ser., XXXII (1975), 3–28, and "Transfer of Culture: Chance and Design in Shaping Massachusetts Bay, 1630–1660," *New England Historical and Genealogical Register*, CXXXII (1978), 3–17.

More generally, others have argued that the European settlement of America marked an expansion of the Old World rather than a separation from it, "an extension of Europe rather than a wholly new world" (G. R. Elton, "Contentment and Discontent on the Eve of Colonization," in David B. Quinn, ed., *Early Maryland in a Wider World* [Detroit, Mich., 1982], 117–118; quotation from Quinn, "Why They Came," *ibid.*, 143).

[6] Sidney W. Mintz and Richard Price, *An Anthropological Approach to the Afro-American Past: A Caribbean Perspective* (Philadelphia, 1976), 22; Nathan Irvin Huggins, *Black Odyssey: The Afro-American Ordeal in Slavery* (New York, 1977), 25–34.

[7] While never thoroughly examined, the term has often been used this way by students of Indian history and others. For example, see Elizabeth A. H. John, *Storms Brewed in Other Men's Worlds: The Confrontation of Indians, Spanish, and French in the Southwest, 1540–1795* (College Station, Tex., 1975); Carolyn Gilman, *Where Two Worlds Meet: The Great Lakes Fur Trade* (St. Paul, Minn., 1982); Peter Laslett, *The World We Have Lost*, 2d ed. (New York, 1973); Edgar P. Richardson, Brooke Hindle, and Lillian B. Miller, *Charles Willson Peale and His World* (New York, 1982); and Irving Howe, *World of Our Fathers* (New York, 1976).

[8] See T. J. C. Brasser, "Group Identification along a Moving Frontier," *Verhandlungen des XXXVIII Internationalen Amerikanistenkongresses*, II (Munich, 1970), 261–262.

[9] Salisbury divides the course of events into two phases, the first including diseases and trade goods, the second encompassing settlement (*Manitou and Providence*, 12).

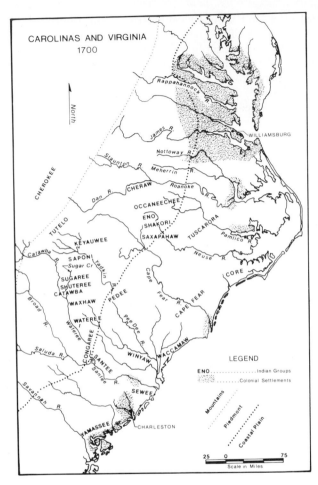

CAROLINAS AND VIRGINIA
1700

North

Rappahannock
James R.
WILLIAMSBURG
Staunton R.
Nottoway R.
Meherrin
CHEROKEE
Dan R.
CHERAW
Roanoke R.
OCCANEECHEE
ENO
SHAKORI
SAXAPAHAW
TUSCARORA
Pamlico
TUTELO
KEYAUWEE
Catawba
Neuse R.
SAPONI
Sugar Cr.
Yadkin
Cape Fear R.
CORE
SUGAREE
SHUTEREE
CATAWBA
WAXHAW
PEDEE
CAPE FEAR
Broad R.
WATEREE
Wateree
Pee Dee R.
Saluda R.
CONGAREE
SANTEE
WINYAW
WACCAMAW
LEGEND
Savannah R.
Santee R.
ENO . . . . Indian Groups
. . . . Colonial Settlements
SEWEE
Mountains
Piedmont
Coastal Plain
YAMASSEE
CHARLESTON
25   0   75
Scale in Miles

ated new societies, each similar to, yet very different from, its parent culture.

The range of native societies produced by this mingling of ingredients probably exceeded the variety of social forms Europeans and Africans developed.[10] Rather than survey the broad spectrum of Indian adaptations, this article considers in some depth the response of natives in one area, the southern piedmont (see map). Avoiding extinc-

[10] For the societies created by Europeans and Africans see James A. Henretta, *The Evolution of American Society, 1700–1815: An Interdisciplinary Analysis* (Lexington, Mass., 1973), esp. 112–116; Jack P. Greene, "Society and Economy in the British Caribbean during the Seventeenth and Eighteenth Centuries," *American Historical Review*, LXXIX (1974), 1515–1517; and Ira Berlin, "Time, Space, and the Evolution of Afro-American Society on British Mainland North America," *ibid.*, LXXXV (1980), 44–78.

tion and eschewing retreat, the Indians of the piedmont have been in continuous contact with the invaders from across the sea almost since the beginning of the colonial period, thus permitting a thorough analysis of cultural intercourse.[11] Moreover, a regional approach embracing groups from South Carolina to Virginia can transcend narrow (and still poorly understood) ethnic or "tribal" boundaries without sacrificing the richness of detail a focused study provides.

Indeed, piedmont peoples had so much in common that a regional perspective is almost imperative. No formal political ties bound them at the onset of European contact, but a similar environment shaped their lives, and their adjustment to this environment fostered cultural uniformity. Perhaps even more important, these groups shared a single history once Europeans and Africans arrived on the scene. Drawn together by their cultural affinities and their common plight, after 1700 they migrated to the Catawba Nation, a cluster of villages along the border between the Carolinas that became the focus of native life in the region. Tracing the experience of these upland communities both before and after they joined the Catawbas can illustrate the consequences of contact and illuminate the process by which natives learned to survive in their own new world.[12]

[11] Among some Indian peoples a fourth stage, missionaries, could be added to the three outlined above. These agents did not, however, play an important part in the piedmont (or in most other areas of the southeast) during the colonial period. Lack of evidence precludes discussion of native religion among upland communities or the changes in belief and ceremony that occurred after contact. It is clear, however, that Indians there opposed any systematic efforts to convert them to Christianity. See Hugh Jones, *The Present State of Virginia: From Whence Is Inferred a Short View of Maryland and North Carolina*, ed. Richard L. Morton (Chapel Hill, N.C., 1956), 59.

[12] Catawbas and their Indian neighbors have been objects of much study and considerable disagreement. Because these peoples lived away from areas of initial European settlement, detailed records are scarce, and archaeologists are only beginning to help fill the gaps in the evidence. Important questions—the linguistic and political affiliations of some groups, their social structures, the degree of influence exerted by powerful societies to the east, west, and south, even their population—remain unanswered. But there are many reasons to argue for a fundamental cultural uniformity in this area beyond a common environment, hints of similar cultural traits, and the shared destiny of the region's inhabitants. Although these scattered villages fought with outsiders from the coast and the mountains, the north and the south, there is a distinct lack of recorded conflict among peoples in the piedmont itself. Peaceful relations may have been reinforced by a sense of common origin, for some (if not all) of these groups—including Saponis, Tutelos, Occaneechees, Catawbas, and Cheraws—spoke variant forms of the Siouan language and were descended from migrants who entered the area some seven centuries before Columbus arrived in America. Finally, other natives were cognizant of connections among these far-flung towns. The Iroquois, for example, called natives from the Catawbas to the Tutelos by the collective name "Toderichroone." For studies of these peoples see James Mooney, *The Siouan Tribes of the East*, Smithsonian Institution, Bureau of American Ethnology, Bulletin 22 (Washington, D.C., 1894); Joffre Lanning Coe, "The Cultural Sequence of the Carolina Piedmont," in James B. Griffin, ed., *Archeology of Eastern United States* (Chicago, 1952), 301–311; Douglas Summers Brown, *The Catawba Indians: The People of the River* (Columbia, S.C., 1966); Charles M. Hudson, *The Catawba*

For centuries, ancestors of the Catawbas had lived astride important aboriginal trade routes and straddled the boundary between two cultural traditions, a position that involved them in a far-flung network of contacts and affected everything from potting techniques to burial practices.[13] Nonetheless, Africans and Europeans were utterly unlike any earlier foreign visitors to the piedmont. Their arrival meant more than merely another encounter with outsiders; it marked an important turning point in Indian history. Once these newcomers disembarked and began to feel their way across the continent, they forever altered the course and pace of native development.

Bacteria brought the most profound disturbances to upcountry villages. When Hernando de Soto led the first Europeans into the area in 1540, he found large towns already "grown up in grass" because "there had been a pest in the land" two years before, a malady probably brought inland by natives who had visited distant Spanish posts.[14] The sources are silent about other "pests" over the next century, but soon after the English began colonizing Carolina in 1670 the disease pattern became all too clear. Major epidemics struck the region at least once every generation—in 1698, 1718, 1738, and 1759—and a variety of less virulent illnesses almost never left native settlements.[15]

Indians were not the only inhabitants of colonial America living—

Nation (Athens, Ga., 1970); and James H. Merrell, "Natives in a New World: The Catawba Indians of Carolina, 1650–1800" (Ph.D. diss., The Johns Hopkins University, 1982).

[13] Coe, "Cultural Sequence," in Griffin, ed., *Archeology of Eastern U.S.*, 301–311; Hudson, *Catawba Nation*, 11–17; William E. Myer, "Indian Trails of the Southeast," Bureau of American Ethnology, *Forty-Second Annual Report* (Washington, D.C., 1928), plate 15.

[14] "True Relation of the Vicissitudes That Attended the Governor Don Hernando De Soto and Some Nobles of Portugal in the Discovery of the Province of Florida Now Just Given by a Fidalgo of Elvas," in Edward Gaylord Bourne, ed., *Narratives of the Career of Hernando de Soto . . .*, I(New York, 1904), 66. See also John Grier Varner and Jeannette Johnson Varner, trans. and eds., *The Florida of the Inca . . .* (Austin, Tex., 1951), 298, 315, and Henry F. Dobyns, *Their Number Become Thinned: Native American Population Dynamics in Eastern North America* (Knoxville, Tenn., 1983), 262–264.

[15] South Carolina Council to Lords Proprietors, Apr. 23, 1698, in Alexander S. Salley, ed., *Commissions and Instructions from the Lords Proprietors of Carolina to Public Officials of South Carolina, 1685–1715* (Columbia, S.C., 1916), 105; Alexander Spotswood to the Board of Trade, Dec. 22, 1718, C.O. 5/1318, 590, Public Record Office (Library of Congress transcripts, 488); *South Carolina Gazette* (Charleston), May 4, 11, 25, June 29, Oct. 5, 1738. Catawba losses in this epidemic were never tabulated, but fully half of the Cherokees may have died (see John Duffy, *Epidemics in Colonial America* [Baton Rouge, La., 1953], 82–83; Catawbas to the governor of South Carolina, Oct. 1759, William Henry Lyttelton Papers, William L. Clements Library, Ann Arbor, Mich.; and *S.C. Gaz.*, Dec. 15, 1759). Dobyns constructs epidemic profiles for the continent and for Florida that offer a sense of the prevalence of disease (*Their Number Become Thinned*, essays, 1, 6).

and dying—in a new disease environment. The swamps and lowlands of the Chesapeake were a deathtrap for Europeans, and sickness obliged colonists to discard or rearrange many of the social forms brought from England.[16] Among native peoples long isolated from the rest of the world and therefore lacking immunity to pathogens introduced by the intruders, the devastation was even more severe. John Lawson, who visited the Carolina upcountry in 1701, when perhaps ten thousand Indians were still there, estimated that "there is not the sixth Savage living within two hundred Miles of all our Settlements, as there were fifty Years ago." The recent smallpox epidemic "destroy'd whole Towns," he remarked, "without leaving one *Indian* alive in the Village." [17] Resistance to disease developed with painful slowness; colonists reported that the outbreak of smallpox in 1759 wiped out 60 percent of the natives, and, according to one source, "the woods were offensive with the dead bodies of the Indians; and dogs, wolves, and vultures were . . . busy for months in banqueting on them." [18]

Survivors of these horrors were thrust into a situation no less alien than what European immigrants and African slaves found. The collected wisdom of generations could vanish in a matter of days if sickness struck older members of a community who kept sacred traditions and taught special skills. When many of the elders succumbed at once, the deep pools of collective memory grew shallow, and some dried up altogether. In 1710, Indians near Charleston told a settler that "they have forgot most of their traditions since the Establishment of this Colony, they keep their Festivals and can tell but little of the reasons: their Old Men are dead." [19] Impoverishment of a rich cultural heritage followed the spread of disease. Nearly a century later, a South Carolinian exaggerated but captured the general trend when he noted that

[16] See Edmund S. Morgan, *American Slavery, American Freedom: The Ordeal of Colonial Virginia* (New York, 1975), chaps. 8–9; Darrett B. Rutman and Anita H. Rutman, "Of Agues and Fevers: Malaria in the Early Chesapeake," *WMQ*, 3d Ser., XXXIII (1976), 31–60; and several of the essays in Tate and Ammerman, eds., *Seventeenth-Century Chesapeake*.

[17] Lawson, *A New Voyage to Carolina*, ed. Hugh Talmage Lefler (Chapel Hill, N.C., 1967), 232. See also 17, 34. The population figure given here is a very rough estimate. Lawson reckoned that Saponis, Tutelos, Keyauwees, Occaneechees, and Shakoris numbered 750 and that Catawbas (he called them "Esaws") were "a very large Nation containing many thousand People" (pp. 242, 46). Totals for other groups in the piedmont are almost nonexistent.

[18] Philip E. Pearson, "Memoir of the Catawbas, furnished Gov. Hammond," MS (1842?), Wilberforce Eames Indian Collection, New York Public Library (typescript copy in the York County Public Library, Rock Hill, S.C.). For estimates of population losses see *S.C. Gaz.*, Dec. 15, 1759; Arthur Dobbs to the secretary of the Society for the Propagation of the Gospel in Foreign Parts, Apr. 15, 1760, in William L. Saunders, ed., *The Colonial Records of North Carolina*, 10 vols. (Raleigh, N.C., 1886–1890), VI, 235, hereafter cited as *N.C. Col. Recs.*

[19] Francis Le Jau to the secretary, June 13, 1710, in Frank J. Klingberg, ed., *The Carolina Chronicle of Dr. Francis Le Jau, 1706–1717* (Berkeley, Calif., 1956), 78.

Catawbas "have forgotten their ancient rites, ceremonies, and manufactures." [20]

The same diseases that robbed a piedmont town of some of its most precious resources also stripped it of the population necessary to maintain an independent existence. In order to survive, groups were compelled to construct new societies from the splintered remnants of the old. The result was a kaleidoscopic array of migrations from ancient territories and mergers with nearby peoples. While such behavior was not unheard of in aboriginal times, population levels fell so precipitously after contact that survivors endured disruptions unlike anything previously known.

The dislocations of the Saponi Indians illustrate the common course of events. In 1670 they lived on the Staunton River in Virginia and were closely affiliated with a group called Nahyssans. A decade later Saponis moved toward the coast and built a town near the Occaneechees. When John Lawson came upon them along the Yadkin River in 1701, they were on the verge of banding together in a single village with Tutelos and Keyauwees. Soon thereafter Saponis applied to Virginia officials for permission to move to the Meherrin River, where Occaneechees, Tutelos, and others joined them. In 1714, at the urging of Virginia's Lt. Gov. Alexander Spotswood, these groups settled at Fort Christanna farther up the Meherrin. Their friendship with Virginia soured during the 1720s, and most of the "Christanna Indians" moved to the Catawba Nation. For some reason this arrangement did not satisfy them, and many returned to Virginia in 1732, remaining there for a decade before choosing to migrate north and accept the protection of the Iroquois.[21]

Saponis were unusual only in their decision to leave the Catawbas. Enos, Occaneechees, Waterees, Keyauwees, Cheraws, and others have their own stories to tell, similar in outline if not in detail. With the exception of the towns near the confluence of Sugar Creek and the Catawba River that composed the heart of the Catawba Nation, piedmont communities decimated by disease lived through a common

---

[20] John Drayton to Dr. Benjamin Smith Barton, Sept. 9, 1803, Correspondence and Papers of Benjamin S. Barton, Historical Society of Pennsylvania, Philadelphia. I am indebted to Maurice Bric for this reference.

[21] Christian F. Feest, "Notes on Saponi Settlements in Virginia Prior to 1714," Archaeological Society of Virginia, *Quarterly Bulletin*, XXVIII (1974), 152–155; William Byrd, "The History of the Dividing Line betwixt Virginia and North Carolina Run in the Year of Our Lord 1728," in Louis B. Wright, ed., *The Prose Works of William Byrd of Westover: Narratives of a Colonial Virginian* (Cambridge, Mass., 1966), 315; H. R. McIlwaine *et al.*, eds., *Executive Journals of the Council of Colonial Virginia*, 6 vols. (Richmond, Va., 1925–1966), IV, 269, hereafter cited as *Va. Council Jours.*; "A List of all the Indian names present at the Treaty held in Lancaster in June 1744," in Samuel Hazard, ed., *Pennsylvania Archives Selected and Arranged from Original Documents . . .* , 1st Ser., I (Philadelphia, 1852), 657.

round of catastrophes, shifting from place to place and group to group in search of a safe haven. Most eventually ended up in the Nation, and during the opening decades of the eighteenth century the villages scattered across the southern upcountry were abandoned as people drifted into the Catawba orbit.

No mere catalog of migrations and mergers can begin to convey how profoundly unsettling this experience was for those swept up in it. While upcountry Indians did not sail away to some distant land, they, too, were among the uprooted, leaving their ancestral homes to try to make a new life elsewhere. The peripatetic existence of Saponis and others proved deeply disruptive. A village and its surrounding territory were important elements of personal and collective identity, physical links in a chain binding a group to its past and making a locality sacred. Colonists, convinced that Indians were by nature "a shifting, wandring People," were oblivious to this, but Lawson offered a glimpse of the reasons for native attachment to a particular locale. "In our way," he wrote on leaving an Eno-Shakori town in 1701, "there stood a great Stone about the Size of a large Oven, and hollow; this the *Indians* took great Notice of, putting some Tobacco into the Concavity, and spitting after it. I ask'd them the Reason of their so doing, but they made me no Answer." [22] Natives throughout the interior honored similar places—graves of ancestors, monuments of stones commemorating important events—that could not be left behind without some cost.[23]

The toll could be physical as well as spiritual, for even the most uneventful of moves interrupted the established cycle of subsistence. Belongings had to be packed and unpacked, dwellings constructed, palisades raised. Once migrants had completed the business of settling in, the still more arduous task of exploiting new terrain awaited them. Living in one place year after year endowed a people with intimate knowledge of the area. The richest soils, the best hunting grounds, the choicest sites for gathering nuts or berries—none could be learned without years of experience, tested by time and passed down from one generation to the next. Small wonder that Carolina Indians worried

[22] Lawson, *New Voyage*, ed. Lefler, 173, 63.

[23] Edward Bland, "The Discovery of New Brittaine, 1650," in Alexander S. Salley, ed., *Narratives of Early Carolina, 1650–1708* (New York, 1911), 13–14; William P. Cumming, ed., *The Discoveries of John Lederer* . . . (Charlottesville, Va., 1958), 12, 17, 19–20; John Banister, "Of the Natives," in Joseph Ewan and Nesta Ewan, eds., *John Banister and His Natural History of Virginia, 1678–1692* (Urbana, Ill., 1970), 377; William J. Hinke, trans. and ed., "Report of the Journey of Francis Louis Michel from Berne, Switzerland, to Virginia, October 2, 1701—December 1, 1702," *Virginia Magazine of History and Biography*, XXIV (1916), 29; Lawson, *New Voyage*, ed. Lefler, 50; David I. Bushnell, Jr., " 'The Indian Grave'—a Monacan Site in Albemarle County, Virginia," *WMQ*, 1st Ser., XXIII (1914), 106–112.

about being "driven to some unknown Country, to live, hunt, and get
our Bread in." [24]

Some displaced groups tried to leave "unknown Country" behind
and make their way back home. In 1716 Enos asked Virginia's permission to settle at "Enoe Town" on the North Carolina frontier, their location in Lawson's day.[25] Seventeen years later William Byrd II came
upon an abandoned Cheraw village on a tributary of the upper
Roanoke River and remarked how "it must have been a great misfortune to them to be obliged to abandon so beautiful a dwelling." The
Indians apparently agreed: in 1717 the Virginia Council received
"Divers applications" from the Cheraws (now living along the Pee
Dee River) "for Liberty to Seat themselves on the head of Roanoke
River." [26] Few natives managed to return permanently to their home-
lands. But their efforts to retrace their steps hint at a profound sense of
loss and testify to the powerful hold of ancient sites.

Compounding the trauma of leaving familiar territories was the necessity of abandoning customary relationships. Casting their lot with
others traditionally considered foreign compelled Indians to rearrange
basic ways of ordering their existence. Despite frequent contacts
among peoples, native life had always centered in kin and town. The
consequences of this deep-seated localism were evident even to a newcomer like John Lawson, who in 1701 found striking differences in
language, dress, and physical appearance among Carolina Indians living only a few miles apart.[27] Rules governing behavior also drew sharp
distinctions between outsiders and one's own "Country-Folks." Indians
were "very kind, and charitable to one another," Lawson reported,
"but more especially to those of their own Nation." [28] A visitor desiring a liaison with a local woman was required to approach her relatives
and the village headman. On the other hand, "if it be an *Indian* of their
own Town or Neighbourhood, that wants a Mistress, he comes to
none but the Girl." [29] Lawson seemed unperturbed by this barrier until he discovered that a "Thief [is] held in Disgrace, that steals from
any of his Country-Folks," "but to steal from the *English* [or any other
foreigners] they reckon no Harm." [30]

Communities unable to continue on their own had to revise these
rules and reweave the social fabric into new designs. What language
would be spoken? How would fields be laid out, hunting territories divided, houses built? How would decisions be reached, offenders punished, ceremonies performed? When Lawson remarked that "now

[24] Lawson, *New Voyage*, ed. Lefler, 214.

[25] Council Journals, Aug. 4, 1716, *N.C. Col. Recs.*, II, 242–243.

[26] William Byrd, "Journey to the Land of Eden, Anno 1733," in Wright, ed., *Prose Works*, 398; *Va. Council Jours.*, III, 440.

[27] Lawson, *New Voyage*, ed. Lefler, 35, 233.

[28] *Ibid.*, 184.

[29] *Ibid.*, 190.

[30] *Ibid.*, 184, 212, 24.

adays" the Indians must seek mates "amongst Strangers," he unwittingly characterized life in native Carolina.[31] Those who managed to withstand the ravages of disease had to redefine the meaning of the term *stranger* and transform outsiders into insiders.

The need to harmonize discordant peoples, an unpleasant fact of life for all native Americans, was no less common among black and white inhabitants of America during these years. Africans from a host of different groups were thrown into slavery together and forced to seek some common cultural ground, to blend or set aside clashing habits and beliefs. Europeans who came to America also met unexpected and unwelcome ethnic, religious, and linguistic diversity. The roots of the problem were quite different; the problem itself was much the same. In each case people from different backgrounds had to forge a common culture and a common future.

Indians in the southern uplands customarily combined with others like themselves in an attempt to solve the dilemma. Following the "principle of least effort," shattered communities cushioned the blows inflicted by disease and depopulation by joining a kindred society known through generations of trade and alliances.[32] Thus Saponis coalesced with Occaneechees and Tutelos—nearby groups "speaking much the same language"[33]—and Catawbas became a sanctuary for culturally related refugees from throughout the region. Even after moving in with friends and neighbors, however, natives tended to cling to ethnic boundaries in order to ease the transition. In 1715 Spotswood noticed that the Saponis and others gathered at Fort Christanna were "confederated together, tho' still preserving their different Rules."[34] Indians entering the Catawba Nation were equally conservative. As late as 1743 a visitor could hear more than twenty different dialects spoken by peoples living there, and some bands continued to reside in separate towns under their own leaders.[35]

[31] *Ibid.*, 193.

[32] Robert A. LeVine and Donald T. Campbell, *Ethnocentrism: Theories of Conflict, Ethnic Attitudes, and Group Behavior* (New York, 1972), 108.

[33] Spotswood to the bishop of London, Jan. 27, 1715, in R. A. Brock, ed., *The Official Letters of Alexander Spotswood, Lieutenant-Governor of the Colony of Virginia, 1710–1722* (Virginia Historical Society, *Collections*, N.S., II [Richmond, Va., 1885]), 88, hereafter cited as Brock, ed., *Spotswood Letters*. See also Byrd, "History," in Wright, ed., *Prose Works*, 314.

[34] Brock, ed., *Spotswood Letters*, 88.

[35] Samuel Cole Williams, ed., *Adair's History of the American Indians* (Johnson City, Tenn., 1930), 236; The Public Accounts of John Hammerton, Esq., Secretary of the Province, in Inventories, LL, 1744–1746, 29, 47, 51, South Carolina Department of Archives and History, Columbia, hereafter cited as Hammerton, Public Accounts; "Sketch Map of the Rivers Santee, Congaree, Wateree, Saludee, &c., with the Road to the Cuttauboes [1750?]," Colonial Office Library, Carolina 16, P.R.O. (copy in Brown, *Catawba Indians*, plate 6, between pp. 32–33); "Cuttahbaws Nation, men fit for warr 204 In the year 1756," Dalhousie Muniments, General John Forbes Papers, Document #2/104 (copy in S.C. Dept. Archs. and Hist.).

Time inevitably sapped the strength of ethnic feeling, allowing a more unified Nation to emerge from the collection of Indian communities that occupied the valleys of the Catawba River and its tributaries. By the mid-eighteenth century, the authority of village headmen was waning and leaders from the host population had begun to take responsibility for the actions of constituent groups.[36] The babel of different tongues fell silent as *"Kàtahba,"* the Nation's "standard, or court-dialect," slowly drowned out all others.[37] Eventually, entire peoples followed their languages and their leaders into oblivion, leaving only personal names like Santee Jemmy, Cheraw George, Congaree Jamie, Saponey Johnny, and Eno Jemmy as reminders of the Nation's diverse heritage.[38]

No European observer recorded the means by which nations became mere names and a congeries of groups forged itself into one people. No doubt the colonists' habit of ignoring ethnic distinctions and lumping confederated entities together under the Catawba rubric encouraged amalgamation. But Anglo-American efforts to create a society by proclamation were invariably unsuccessful [39]; consolidation had to come from within. In the absence of evidence, it seem reasonable to conclude that years of contacts paved the way for a closer relationship. Once a group moved to the Nation, intermarriages blurred ancient kinship networks, joint war parties or hunting expeditions brought young men together, and elders met in a council that gave everyone some say by including "all the Indian Chiefs or Head Men of that [Catawba] Nation and the several Tribes amongst them together." [40] The concentration of settlements within a day's walk of one another facilitated contact and communication. From their close proximity, common experience, and shared concerns, people developed ceremonies and myths that compensated for those lost to disease and gave

---

[36] J. H. Easterby, ed., *The Colonial Records of South Carolina: The Journal of the Commons House of Assembly, November 10, 1736–June 7, 1739* (Columbia, S.C., 1951), 481–482. Compare this to the Catawbas' failure to control Waccamaws living in the Nation a decade before (Journals of the Upper House of Assembly, Sept. 13, 1727, C.O. 5/429, 176–177 [microfilm, British Manuscripts Project, D 491]).

[37] Williams, ed., *Adair's History*, 236.

[38] Catawba Indians to Gov. Lyttelton, June 16, 1757, Lyttelton Papers (Santee Jemmy); Rev. William Richardson, "An Account of My Proceedings since I accepted the Indian mission in October 2d 1758 . . . ," Wilberforce Eames Indian Collection, entry of Nov. 8, 1758 (Cheraw George). South Carolina Council Journals (hereafter cited as S.C. Council Jours.), May 5, 1760, in William S. Jenkins, comp., Records of the States of the United States, microfilm ed. (Washington, D.C., 1950) (hereafter cited as Records of States), SC E.1p, Reel 8, Unit 3, 119 (Congaree Jamie); John Evans to Gov. James Glen, Apr. 18, 1748, in S.C. Council Jours., Apr. 27, 1748, Records of States, SC E.1p, 3/4 233 (Saponey Johnny); Hammerton, Public Accounts, 29, 51 (Eno Jemmy).

[39] See, for example, Spotswood's efforts to persuade some tributary groups to join the piedmont Indians at Fort Christanna. *Va. Council Jours.*, III, 367; Spotswood to bishop of London, Jan. 27, 1715, in Brock, ed., *Spotswood Letters*, II, 88.

[40] Easterby, ed., *Journal of the Commons House, 1736–1739*, 487.

the Nation a stronger collective consciousness.[41] Associations evolved that balanced traditional narrow ethnic allegiance with a new, broader, "national" identity, a balance that tilted steadily toward the latter. Ethnic differences died hard, but the peoples of the Catawba Nation learned to speak with a single voice.

Muskets and kettles came to the piedmont more slowly than smallpox and measles. Spanish explorers distributed a few gifts to local headmen, but inhabitants of the interior did not enjoy their first real taste of the fruits of European technology until Englishmen began venturing inland after 1650. Indians these traders met in upcountry towns were glad to barter for the more efficient tools, more lethal weapons, and more durable clothing that colonists offered. Spurred on by eager natives, men from Virginia and Carolina quickly flooded the region with the material trappings of European culture. In 1701 John Lawson considered the Wateree Chickanees "very poor in *English* Effects" because a few of them lacked muskets.[42]

Slower to arrive, trade goods were also less obvious agents of change. The Indians' ability to absorb foreign artifacts into established modes of existence hid the revolutionary consequences of trade for some time. Natives leaped the technological gulf with ease in part because they were discriminating shoppers. If hoes were too small, beads too large, or cloth the wrong color, Indian traders refused them.[43] Items they did select fit smoothly into existing ways. Waxhaws tied horse bells around their ankles at ceremonial dances, and some of the traditional stone pipes passed among the spectators at these dances had been shaped by metal files.[44] Those who could not afford a European weapon fashioned arrows from broken glass. Those who could went to great lengths to "set [a new musket] streight, sometimes shooting away above 100 Loads of Ammunition, before they bring the Gun to shoot according to their Mind." [45]

Not every piece of merchandise hauled into the upcountry on a trader's packhorse could be "set streight" so easily. Liquor, for example, proved both impossible to resist and extraordinarily destructive. Indians "have no Power to refrain this Enemy," Lawson observed,

[41] See Brasser, "Group Identification," *Verhandlungen*, II (1970), 261–265.

[42] Lawson, *New Voyage*, ed. Lefler, 38.

[43] William Byrd to [Arthur North?], Mar. 8, 1685/6, in Marion Tinling, ed., *The Correspondence of the Three William Byrds of Westover, Virginia, 1684–1776*, I (Charlottesville, Va., 1977), 57, Byrd to Perry and Lane, July 8, 1686, 64, Byrd to [Perry and Lane?], Mar. 20, 1685, 30, Byrd to North, Mar. 29, 1685, 31.

[44] Lawson, *New Voyage*, ed. Lefler, 44–45; George Edwin Stuart, "The Post-Archaic Occupation of Central South Carolina" (Ph.D. diss., University of North Carolina, 1975), 133, fig. 72, B.

[45] Lawson, *New Voyage*, ed. Lefler, 33, 63. Archaeologists have uncovered these arrowheads. See Tommy Charles, "Thoughts and Records from the Survey of Private Collections of Prehistoric Artifacts: A Second Report," Institute of Archeology and Anthropology, University of South Carolina, *Notebook*, XV (1983), 31.

"though sensible how many of them (are by it) hurry'd into the other World before their Time." [46] And yet even here, natives aware of the risks sought to control alcohol by incorporating it into their ceremonial life as a device for achieving a different level of consciousness. Consumption was usually restricted to men, who "go as solemnly about it, as if it were part of their Religion," preferring to drink only at night and only in quantities sufficient to stupefy them.[47] When ritual could not confine liquor to safe channels, Indians went still further and excused the excesses of overindulgence by refusing to hold an intoxicated person responsible for his actions. "They never call any Man to account for what he did, when he was drunk," wrote Lawson, "but say, it was the Drink that caused his Misbehaviour, therefore he ought to be forgiven." [48]

Working to absorb even the most dangerous commodities acquired from their new neighbors, aboriginal inhabitants of the uplands, like African slaves in the lowlands, made themselves at home in a different technological environment. Indians became convinced that "Guns, and Ammunition, besides a great many other Necessaries, . . . are helpful to Man" [49] and eagerly searched for the key that would unlock the secret of their production. At first many were confident that the "*Quera*, or good Spirit," would teach them to make these commodities "when that good Spirit sees fit." [50] Later they decided to help their deity along by approaching the colonists. In 1757, Catawbas asked Gov. Arthur Dobbs of North Carolina "to send us Smiths and other Tradesmen to teach our Children." [51]

It was not the new products themselves but the Indians' failure to learn the mysteries of manufacture from either Dobbs or the *Quera* that marked the real revolution wrought by trade. During the seventeenth and eighteenth centuries, everyone in eastern North America—masters and slaves, farmers near the coast and Indians near the mountains—became producers of raw materials for foreign markets and found themselves caught up in an international economic network.[52] Piedmont natives were part of this larger process, but their adjustment

[46] Lawson, *New Voyage*, ed. Lefler, 211, 18.

[47] *Ibid.*, 211; Robert Beverley, *The History and Present State of Virginia*, ed. Louis B. Wright (Chapel Hill, N.C., 1947), 182.

[48] Lawson, *New Voyage*, ed. Lefler, 210. See also Craig MacAndrew and Robert B. Edgerton, *Drunken Comportment: A Social Explanation* (New York, 1969), chap. 5.

[49] Lawson, *New Voyage*, ed. Lefler, 220.

[50] *Ibid.* One Santee priest claimed he had already been given this power by "the white Man above, (meaning God Almighty)" (*ibid.*, 26–27).

[51] Catawba Nation to Gov. Dobbs, Oct. 5, 1757, encl. in Dobbs to Lyttelton, Oct. 24, 1757, Lyttelton Papers.

[52] Immanuel Wallerstein, *The Modern World-System: Capitalist Agriculture and the Origins of the European World-Economy in the Sixteenth Century* (New York, 1974), esp. chap. 6.

was more difficult because the contrast with previous ways was so pronounced. Before European contact, the localism characteristic of life in the uplands had been sustained by a remarkable degree of self-sufficiency. Trade among peoples, while common, was conducted primarily in commodities such as copper, mica, and shells, items that, exchanged with the appropriate ceremony, initiated or confirmed friendships among groups. Few, if any, villages relied on outsiders for goods essential to daily life.[53]

Intercultural exchange eroded this traditional independence and entangled natives in a web of commercial relations few of them understood and none controlled. In 1670 the explorer John Lederer observed a striking disparity in the trading habits of Indians living near Virginia and those deep in the interior. The "remoter Indians," still operating within a precontact framework, were content with ornamental items such as mirrors, beads, "and all manner of gaudy toys and knacks for children." "Neighbour-Indians," on the other hand, habitually traded with colonists for cloth, metal tools, and weapons.[54] Before long, towns near and far were demanding the entire range of European wares and were growing accustomed—even addicted—to them. "They say we English are fools for . . . not always going with a gun," one Virginia colonist familiar with piedmont Indians wrote in the early 1690s, "for they think themselves undrest and not fit to walk abroad, unless they have their gun on their shoulder, and their shot-bag by their side." [55] Such an enthusiastic conversion to the new technology eroded ancient craft skills and hastened complete dependence on substitutes only colonists could supply.

By forcing Indians to look beyond their own territories for certain indispensable products, Anglo-American traders inserted new variables into the aboriginal equation of exchange. Colonists sought two commodities from Indians—human beings and deerskins—and both undermined established relationships among native groups. While the demand for slaves encouraged piedmont peoples to expand their traditional warfare, the demand for peltry may have fostered conflicts over

[53] Harold Hickerson, "Fur Trade Colonialism and the North American Indians," *Journal of Ethnic Studies*, I (1973), 18–22; Charles Hudson, *The Southeastern Indians* (Knoxville, Tenn., 1976), 65–66, 316. Salt may have been an exception to this aboriginal self-sufficiency. Even here, however, Indians might have been able to get along without it or find acceptable substitutes. See Gloria J. Wentowski, "Salt as an Ecological Factor in the Prehistory of the Southeastern United States" (M.A. thesis, University of North Carolina, 1970). For substitutes see Lawson, *New Voyage*, ed. Lefler, 89; Banister, "Of the Natives," in Ewan and Ewan, eds., *Banister and His History*, 376; Beverley, *History*, ed. Wright, 180.

[54] Cumming, ed., *Discoveries of Lederer*, 41–42.

[55] Banister, "Of the Natives," in Ewan and Ewan, eds., *Banister and His History*, 382.

hunting territories.[56] Those who did not fight each other for slaves or deerskins fought each other for the European products these could bring. As firearms, cloth, and other items became increasingly important to native existence, competition replaced comity at the foundation of trade encounters as villages scrambled for the cargoes of merchandise. Some were in a better position to profit than others. In the early 1670s Occaneechees living on an island in the Roanoke River enjoyed power out of all proportion to their numbers because they controlled an important ford on the trading path from Virginia to the interior, and they resorted to threats, and even to force, to retain their advantage.[57] In Lawson's day Tuscaroras did the same, "hating that any of these Westward *Indians* should have any Commerce with the *English*, which would prove a Hinderance to their Gains." [58]

Competition among native groups was only the beginning of the transformation brought about by new forms of exchange. Inhabitants of the piedmont might bypass the native middleman, but they could not break free from a perilous dependence on colonial sources of supply. The danger may not have been immediately apparent to Indians caught up in the excitement of acquiring new and wonderful things. For years they managed to dictate the terms of trade, compelling visitors from Carolina and Virginia to abide by aboriginal codes of con-

[56] "It is certain the Indians are very cruel to one another," Rev. Francis Le Jau wrote his superiors in England in April 1708, "but is it not to be feared some white men living or trading among them do foment and increase that Bloody Inclination in order to get Slaves?" (Le Jau to the secretary, Apr. 22, 1708, in Klingberg, ed., *Carolina Chronicle*, 39). Over the summer his worst fears were confirmed: "It is reported by some of our Inhabitants lately gone on Indian Trading that [Carolina traders] excite them to make War amongst themselves to get Slaves which they give for our European Goods" (Le Jau to the secretary, Sept. 15, 1708, *ibid.*, 41). For an analysis of the Indian slave trade see J. Leitch Wright, Jr., *The Only Land They Knew: The Tragic Story of the American Indians in the Old South* (New York, 1981), chap. 6. General studies of Indian warfare in the Southeast are John R. Swanton, *The Indians of the Southeastern United States*, Smithsonian Institution, Bureau of American Ethnology, Bulletin 137 (Washington, D.C., 1946), 686–701, and Hudson, *Southeastern Indians*, 239–257.

Evidence of an escalation in competition for hunting territories is sparse. But in 1702, only a year after Lawson noted that deer were scarce among the Tuscaroras, Indians in Virginia complained that Tuscarora hunting parties were crossing into the colony in search of game and ruining the hunting grounds of local groups. See Lawson, *New Voyage*, ed. Lefler, 65, and *Va. Council Jours.*, II, 275. It seems likely that this became more common as pressure on available supplies of game intensified.

[57] "Letter of Abraham Wood to John Richards, August 22, 1674," in Clarence Walworth Alvord and Lee Bidgood [eds.], *First Explorations of the Trans-Allegheny Region by the Virginians, 1650–1674* (Cleveland, Ohio, 1912), 211, 215–217, 223–225; "Virginias Deploured Condition: Or an Impartiall Narrative of the Murders comitted by the Indians there, and of the Sufferings of his Maties. Loyall Subjects under the Rebellious outrages of Mr. Nathaniell Bacon Junr. to the tenth day of August A. o Dom 1676," Massachusetts Historical Society, *Collections*, 4th Ser., IX (Boston, 1871), 167.

[58] Lawson, *New Voyage*, ed. Lefler, 64.

duct and playing one colony's traders against the other to ensure an abundance of goods at favorable rates.[59] But the natives' influence over the protocol of exchange combined with their skill at incorporating alien products to mask a loss of control over their own destiny. The mask came off when, in 1715, the traders—and the trade goods—suddenly disappeared during the Yamassee War.

The conflict's origins lay in a growing colonial awareness of the Indians' need for regular supplies of European merchandise. In 1701 Lawson pronounced the Santees "very tractable" because of their close connections with South Carolina. Eight years later he was convinced that the colonial officials in Charleston "are absolute Masters over the Indians . . . within the Circle of their Trade." [60] Carolina traders who shared this conviction quite naturally felt less and less constrained to obey native rules governing proper behavior. Abuses against Indians mounted until some men were literally getting away with murder. When repeated appeals to colonial officials failed, natives throughout Carolina began to consider war. Persuaded by Yamassee ambassadors that the conspiracy was widespread and convinced by years of ruthless commercial competition between Virginia and Carolina that an attack on one colony would not affect relations with the other, in the spring of 1715 Catawbas and their neighbors joined the invasion of South Carolina.[61]

The decision to fight was disastrous. Colonists everywhere shut off the flow of goods to the interior, and after some initial successes Carolina's native enemies soon plumbed the depths of their dependence. In a matter of months, refugees holed up in Charleston noticed that "the Indians want ammunition and are not able to mend their Arms." [62] The peace negotiations that ensued revealed a desperate thirst for fresh supplies of European wares. Ambassadors from piedmont towns invariably spoke in a single breath of restoring "a Peace and a free Trade," and one delegation even admitted that its people "cannot live without the assistance of the English." [63]

[59] See Cumming, ed., *Discoveries of Lederer*, 41; Lawson, *New Voyage*, ed. Lefler, 210; and Merrell, "Natives in a New World," 74–77. For the competition between colonies see Verner W. Crane, *The Southern Frontier, 1670–1732* (New York, 1981 [orig. publ. Durham, N.C., 1928]), 153–157, and Merrell, "Natives in a New World," 136–147.

[60] Lawson, *New Voyage*, ed. Lefler, 23, 10.

[61] The best studies of this conflict are Crane, *Southern Frontier*, chap. 7; John Phillip Reid, *A Better Kind of Hatchet: Law, Trade, and Diplomacy in the Cherokee Nation during the Early Years of European Contact* (University Park, Pa., 1976), chaps. 5–7; and Richard L. Haan, "The 'Trade Do's Not Flourish as Formerly': The Ecological Origins of the Yamassee War of 1715," *Ethnohistory*, XXVIII (1981), 341–358. The Catawbas' role in the war is detailed in Merrell, "Natives in a New World," chap. 4.

[62] Le Jau to [John Chamberlain?], Aug. 22, 1715, in Klingberg, ed., *Carolina Chronicle*, 162.

[63] *Va. Council Jours.*, III, 406, 412, 422.

Natives unable to live without the English henceforth tried to live with them. No upcountry group mounted a direct challenge to Anglo-America after 1715. Trade quickly resumed, and the piedmont Indians, now concentrated almost exclusively in the Catawba valley, briefly enjoyed a regular supply of necessary products sold by men willing once again to deal according to the old rules. By mid-century, however, deer were scarce and fresh sources of slaves almost impossible to find. Anglo-American traders took their business elsewhere, leaving inhabitants of the Nation with another material crisis of different but equally dangerous dimensions.[64]

Indians casting about for an alternative means of procuring the commodities they craved looked to imperial officials. During the 1740s and 1750s native dependence shifted from colonial traders to colonial authorities as Catawba leaders repeatedly visited provincial capitals to request goods. These delegations came not to beg but to bargain. Catawbas were still of enormous value to the English as allies and frontier guards, especially at a time when Anglo-America felt threatened by the French and their Indian auxiliaries. The Nation's position within reach of Virginia and both Carolinas enhanced its value by enabling headmen to approach all three colonies and offer their people's services to the highest bidder.

The strategy yielded Indians an arsenal of ammunition and a variety of other merchandise that helped offset the declining trade.[65] Crown officials were especially generous when the Nation managed to play one colony off against another. In 1746 a rumor that the Catawbas were about to move to Virginia was enough to garner them a large shipment of powder and lead from officials in Charleston concerned about losing this "valuable people." [66] A decade later, while the two Carolinas fought for the honor of constructing a fort in the Nation, the Indians encouraged (and received) gifts symbolizing good will from both colonies without reaching an agreement with either. Surveying the tangled thicket of promises and presents, the Crown's superintendent of Indian affairs, Edmond Atkin, ruefully admitted that "the People of both Provinces . . . have I beleive [*sic*] tampered too

---

[64] Merrell, "Natives in a New World," 280–300, 358–359.

[65] For an example of the gifts received by Catawbas see the list of goods delivered to the Catawba Indians at the Congaree Fort, Feb. 14, 1752, in William L. McDowell, ed., *The Colonial Records of South Carolina: Documents Relating to Indian Affairs, May 21, 1750–August 7, 1754*, Ser. 2, *The Indian Books* (Columbia, S.C., 1958), 217–218, hereafter cited as *Indian Affairs Docs.*

[66] J. H. Easterby, ed., *The Colonial Records of South Carolina: Journals of the Commons House of Assembly, September 10, 1745–June 17, 1746* (Columbia, S.C., 1956), 132, 141, 173; George Haig to Gov. James Glen, Mar. 21, 1746, S.C. Council Jours., Mar. 27, 1746, Records of States, SC E.1p, 3/2, 74–75.

much on both sides with those Indians, who seem to understand well how to make their Advantage of it." [67]

By the end of the colonial period delicate negotiations across cultural boundaries were as familiar to Catawbas as the strouds they wore and the muskets they carried. But no matter how shrewdly the headmen loosened provincial purse strings to extract vital merchandise, they could not escape the simple fact that they no longer held the purse containing everything needed for their daily existence. In the space of a century the Indians had become thoroughly embedded in an alien economy, denizens of a new material world. The ancient self-sufficiency was only a dim memory in the minds of the Nation's elders.[68]

The Catawba peoples were veterans of countless campaigns against disease and masters of the arts of trade long before the third major element of their new world, white planters, became an integral part of their life. Settlement of the Carolina uplands did not begin until the 1730s, but once underway it spread with frightening speed. In November 1752, concerned Catawbas reminded South Carolina governor James Glen how they had "complained already . . . that the white People were settled too near us." [69] Two years later five hundred families lived within thirty miles of the Nation and surveyors were running their lines into the middle of native towns. [70] "[T]hose Indians are now in a fair way to be surrounded by White People," one observer concluded.[71]

Settlers' attitudes were as alarming as their numbers. Unlike traders who profited from them or colonial officials who deployed them as allies, ordinary colonists had little use for Indians. Natives made poor servants and worse slaves; they obstructed settlement; they attracted enemy warriors to the area. Even men who respected Indians and earned a living by trading with them admitted that they made unpleasant neighbors. "We may observe of them as of the fire," wrote the South Carolina trader James Adair after considering the Catawbas' situation on the eve of the American Revolution, " 'it is safe and useful, cherished at proper distance; but if too near us, it becomes dangerous, and will scorch if not consume us.' " [72]

---

[67] Atkin to Gov. William Henry Lyttelton, Nov. 23, 1757, Lyttelton Papers.

[68] Treaty between North Carolina Commissioners and the Catawba Indians, Aug. 29, 1754, *N.C. Col. Recs.*, V, 144a.

[69] Catawba King and Others to Gov. Glen, Nov. 21, 1752, *Indian Affairs Docs.*, 361.

[70] Mathew Rowan to the Board of Trade, June 3, 1754, *N.C. Col. Recs.*, V, 124; Samuel Wyly to clerk of Council, Mar. 2, 1754, in S.C. Council Jours., Mar. 13, 1754, Records of States, SC E.1p, 6/1, 140.

[71] Wilbur R. Jacobs, ed., *Indians of the Southern Colonial Frontier: The Edmond Atkin Report and Plan of 1755* (Columbia, S.C., 1954), 46.

[72] Williams, ed., *Adair's History*, 235.

A common fondness for alcohol increased the likelihood of intercultural hostilities. Catawba leaders acknowledged that the Indians "get very Drunk with [liquor] this is the Very Cause that they oftentimes Commit those Crimes that is offencive to You and us." [73] Colonists were equally prone to bouts of drunkenness. In the 1760s the itinerant Anglican minister, Charles Woodmason, was shocked to find the citizens of one South Carolina upcountry community "continually drunk." More appalling still, after attending church services "one half of them got drunk before they went home." [74] Indians sometimes suffered at the hands of intoxicated farmers. In 1760 a Catawba woman was murdered when she happened by a tavern shortly after four of its patrons "swore they would kill the first Indian they should meet with." [75]

Even when sober, natives and newcomers found many reasons to quarrel. Catawbas were outraged if colonists built farms on the Indians' doorstep or tramped across ancient burial grounds. [76] Planters, ignorant of (or indifferent to) native rules of hospitality, considered Indians who requested food nothing more than beggars and angrily drove them away. [77] Other disputes arose when the Nation's young men went looking for trouble. As hunting, warfare, and other traditional avenues for achieving status narrowed, Catawba youths transferred older patterns of behavior into a new arena by raiding nearby farms and hunting cattle or horses. [78]

Contrasting images of the piedmont landscape quite unintentionally generated still more friction. Colonists determined to tame what they considered a wilderness were in fact erasing a native signature on the land and scrawling their own. Bridges, buildings, fences, roads, crops, and other "improvements" made the area comfortable and familiar to

[73] Treaty between North Carolina and the Catawbas, Aug. 29, 1754, *N.C. Col. Recs.*, V, 143. See also conference held with the Catawbas by Mr. Chief Justice Henley at Salisbury, May 1756, *ibid.*, 581, 583; Matthew Toole to Glen, Oct. 28, 1752, *Indian Affairs Docs.*, 359; Catawbas to Lyttelton, June 16, 1757, Lyttelton Papers; and James Adamson to Lyttelton, June 12, 1759, *ibid.*

[74] Richard J. Hooker, ed., *The Carolina Backcountry on the Eve of the Revolution: The Journal and Other Writings of Charles Woodmason, Anglican Itinerant* (Chapel Hill, N.C., 1953), 7, 12. See also 30, 39, 53, 56, 97–99, 128–129.

[75] S.C. Council Jours., May 5, 1760, Records of States, SC E.1p, 8/3, 119.

[76] Robert Stiell to Gov. Glen, Mar. 11, 1753, *Indian Affairs Docs.*, 371; Gov. Thomas Boone to the Lords Commissioners of Trade and Plantations, Oct. 9, 1762, in W. Noel Sainsbury, comp., Records in the British Public Record Office Relating to South Carolina, 1663–1782, 36 vols., microfilm ed. (Columbia, S.C., 1955), XXIX, 245–246, hereafter cited as Brit. Public Recs., S.C.

[77] Treaty between North Carolina and the Catawbas, Aug. 29, 1754, *N.C. Col. Recs.*, V, 142–143; Council Journal, Mar. 18, 1756, *ibid.*, 655; Samuel Wyly to Lyttelton, Feb. 9, 1759, Lyttelton Papers.

[78] See, for example, Treaty between North Carolina and the Catawbas, Aug. 29, 1754, *N.C. Col. Recs.*, V, 142–143, and Catawbas to Lyttelton, June 16, 1757, Lyttelton Papers.

colonists but uncomfortable and unfamiliar to Indians. "The Country side wear[s] a New face," proclaimed Woodmason proudly [79]; to the original inhabitants, it was a grim face indeed. "His Land was spoiled," one Catawba headman told British officials in 1763. "They have spoiled him 100 Miles every way." [80] Under these circumstances, even a settler with no wish to fight Indians met opposition to his fences, his outbuildings, his very presence. Similarly, a Catawba on a routine foray into traditional hunting territories had his weapon destroyed, his goods confiscated, his life threatened by men with different notions of the proper use of the land.[81]

To make matters worse, the importance both cultures attached to personal independence hampered efforts by authorities on either side to resolve conflicts. Piedmont settlers along the border between the Carolinas were "people of desperate fortune," a frightened North Carolina official reported after visiting the area. "[N]o officer of Justice from either Province dare meddle with them." [82] Woodmason, who spent even more time in the region, came to the same conclusion. "We are without any Law, or Order," he complained; the inhabitants' "Impudence is so very high, as to be past bearing." [83] Catawba leaders could have sympathized. Headmen informed colonists that the Nation's people "are oftentimes Cautioned from . . . ill Doings altho' to no purpose for we Cannot be present at all times to Look after them." "What they have done I could not prevent," one chief explained.[84]

Unruly, angry, intoxicated—Catawbas and Carolinians were constantly at odds during the middle decades of the eighteenth century. Planters who considered Indians "proud and deveilish" were themselves accused by natives of being "very bad and quarrelsome." [85] Warriors made a habit of "going into the Settlements, robbing and stealing where ever they get an Oppertunity." [86] Complaints generally brought

[79] Hooker, ed., *Carolina Backcountry*, 63.

[80] Augusta Congress, Nov. 1763, in Brit. Public Recs., S.C., XXX, 84.

[81] Robert Stiell to Gov. Glen, Mar. 11, 1753, *Indian Affairs Docs.*, 371; Inhabitants of the Waxhaws to Samuel Wyly, Apr. 15, 1759, encl. in Wyly to Lyttelton, Apr. 26, 1759, Lyttelton Papers (colonists attacked). S.C. Council Jours., Feb. 6, 1769, Records of States, SC E.1p, 10/3, 9; King Frow to the governor, Mar. 15, 1770, in S.C. Council Jours., Mar. 27, 1770, *ibid.*, SC E.1p, 10/4, 56; "At a Meeting Held with the Catabaws," Mar. 26, 1771, Joseph Kershaw Papers, South Caroliniana Library, University of South Carolina, Columbia (Indians attacked).

[82] Information of John Frohock and others, Oct. 10, 1762, *N.C. Col. Recs.*, VI, 794–795.

[83] Hooker, ed., *Carolina Backcountry*, 45, 52.

[84] Treaty between North Carolina and the Catawbas, Aug. 29, 1754, *N.C. Col. Recs.*, V, 143; Catawbas to Glen, Nov. 21, 1752, *Indian Affairs Docs.*, 361.

[85] Waxhaw inhabitants to Wyly, Apr. 15, 1759, encl. in Wyly to Lyttelton, Apr. 26, 1759, Lyttelton Papers; Meeting between the Catawbas and Henley, May 1756, *N.C. Col. Recs.*, V, 581.

[86] Toole to Glen, Oct. 28, 1752, *Indian Affairs Docs.*, 358.

no satisfaction—"they laugh and makes their Game of it, and says it is what they will"—leading some settlers to "whip [Indians] about the head, beat and abuse them." [87] "The white People . . . and the Cut-tahbaws, are Continually at varience," a visitor to the Nation fretted in June 1759, "and Dayly New Animositys Doth a rise Between them which In my Humble oppion will be of Bad Consequence In a Short time, Both Partys Being obstinate." [88]

The litany of intercultural crimes committed by each side disguised a fundamental shift in the balance of physical and cultural power. In the early years of colonization of the interior the least disturbance by Indians sent scattered planters into a panic. Soon, however, Catawbas were few, colonists many, and it was the natives who now lived in fear. "[T]he white men [who] Lives Near the Neation is Contenuely asembleing and goes In the [Indian] towns In Bodys . . . ," worried another observer during the tense summer of 1759. "[T]he[y] tretton the[y] will Kill all the Cattabues." [89]

The Indians would have to find some way to get along with these unpleasant neighbors if the Nation was to survive. As Catawba population fell below five hundred after the smallpox epidemic of 1759 and the number of colonists continued to climb, natives gradually came to recognize the futility of violent resistance. During the last decades of the eighteenth century they drew on years of experience in dealing with Europeans at a distance and sought to overturn the common conviction that Indian neighbors were frightening and useless.

This process was not the result of some clever plan; Catawbas had no strategy for survival. A headman could warn them that "the White people were now seated all round them and by that means had them entirely in their power." [90] He could not command them to submit peacefully to the invasion of their homeland. The Nation's continued existence required countless individual decisions, made in a host of diverse circumstances, to complain rather than retaliate, to accept a subordinate place in a land that once was theirs. Few of the choices made survive in the record. But it is clear that, like the response to disease and to technology, the adaptation to white settlement was both painful and prolonged.

Catawbas took one of the first steps along the road to accommodation in the early 1760s, when they used their influence with colonial officials to acquire a reservation encompassing the heart of their an-

---

[87] *Ibid.*, 359; Meeting between the Catawbas and Henley, May 1756, *N.C. Col. Recs.*, V, 581.

[88] John Evans to Lyttelton, June 20, 1759, Lyttelton Papers.

[89] Adamson to Lyttelton, June 12, 1759, *ibid.*

[90] Meeting between the Catawbas and Henley, May 1756, *N.C. Col. Recs.*, V, 582.

cient territories.[91] This grant gave the Indians a land base, grounded in Anglo-American law, that prevented farmers from shouldering them aside. Equally important, Catawbas now had a commodity to exchange with nearby settlers. These men wanted land, the natives had plenty, and shortly before the Revolution the Nation was renting tracts to planters for cash, livestock, and manufactured goods.[92]

Important as it was, land was not the only item Catawbas began trading to their neighbors. Some Indians put their skills as hunters and woodsmen to a different use, picking up stray horses and escaped slaves for a reward.[93] Others bartered their pottery, baskets, and table mats.[94] Still others traveled through the upcountry, demonstrating their prowess with the bow and arrow before appreciative audiences.[95]

[91] The Indians lobbied for this land beginning in 1757. Crown officials finally reserved it to them in Nov. 1763 and surveyed it in Feb. 1764. See Catawbas to Lyttelton, June 16, 1757, Lyttelton Papers; *S.C. Gaz.*, Aug. 9, 1760; S.C. Council Jours., May 15, 1762, Records of States, SC E.1p, 8/6, 497; Augusta Congress, Nov. 1763, Brit. Public Recs., S.C., XXX, 84, 104–106, 112–113; and "A Map of the Catawba Indians Surveyed agreeable to a Treaty Entered into with Them At Augusta in Georgia on the tenth Day of November 1763 . . . Executed, Certified and Signed by me the 22nd Day of February Anno Domini 1764, Sam[ue]l Wyly D[eputy] S[urveyo]r," Miscellaneous Records, H, 460, S.C. Dept. Archs. and Hist.

[92] Brown, *Catawba Indians*, 283–284. For contemporary accounts, see Thomas Coke, *Extracts of the Journals of the Rev. Dr. Coke's Five Visits to America* (London, 1793), 148–149; "Travel Diary of Marshall and Benzien from Salem to South Carolina, 1790 . . . ," in Adelaide L. Fries et al., eds., *Records of the Moravians in North Carolina*, 11 vols. (Raleigh, N.C., 1922–1969), V, 1997; David Hutchison, "The Catawba Indians. By Request," *Palmetto State Banner* (Columbia), Aug. 30, 1849 (copy in the Draper Manuscript Collection, Ser. U, vol. 10, Doc. #100 [Wisconsin State Historical Society, Madison]), hereafter cited as Hutchison, "Catawba Indians."
This land system broke down in 1840 when the Catawbas ceded their lands to South Carolina in exchange for promises of money and land to be purchased for them in North Carolina. By that time, the Nation's place in South Carolina society was secure enough to survive the economic and social shock of losing its land base. When plans to live in North Carolina fell through and the Indians drifted back to their ancient territory, no one forced them to leave. Instead, the state of South Carolina purchased a small reservation for them, a tract of land that has been the core of Catawba life ever since. See Brown, *Catawba Indians*, chaps. 13–14.

[93] Affidavit of John Evans, S.C. Council Jours., Nov. 6, 1755, Records of States, SC E.1p, 7/2, 439; Affidavit of Liddy, Jan. 1, 1784, Kershaw Papers (horses). Report of the South Carolina Committee of Council, Apr. 19, 1769, Brit. Public Recs., S.C., XXX, 145–146; Hutchison, "Catawba Indians" (slaves).

[94] John F. D. Smyth, *A Tour in the United States of America . . .* , I (London, 1784), 193–194; Lucius Verus Bierce, "The Piedmont Frontier, 1822–23," in Thomas D. Clark, ed., *South Carolina: The Grand Tour, 1780–1865* (Columbia, S.C., 1973), 64; William Gilmore Simms, "Caloya; Or, The Loves of the Driver," in his *The Wigwam and the Cabin* (New York, 1856), 361–363.

[95] Frank G. Speck, *Catawba Hunting, Trapping, and Fishing*, Joint Publications, Museum of The University of Pennsylvania and The Philadelphia Anthropological Society, No. 2 (Philadelphia, 1946), 10; Thomas J. Kirkland and Robert M. Kennedy, *Historic Camden*, I: *Colonial and Revolutionary* (Columbia, S.C., 1905), 58–59.

The exchange of these goods and services for European merchandise marked an important adjustment to the settlers' arrival. In the past, natives had acquired essential items by trading peltry and slaves or requesting gifts from representatives of the Crown. But piedmont planters frowned on hunting and warfare, while provincial authorities—finding Catawbas less useful as the Nation's population declined and the French threat disappeared—discouraged formal visits and handed out fewer presents. Hence the Indians had to develop new avenues of exchange that would enable them to obtain goods in ways less objectionable to their neighbors. Pots, baskets, and acres proved harmless substitutes for earlier methods of earning an income.

Quite apart from its economic benefits, trade had a profound impact on the character of Catawba-settler relations. Through countless repetitions of the same simple procedure at homesteads scattered across the Carolinas, a new form of intercourse arose, based not on suspicion and an expectation of conflict but on trust and a measure of friendship. When a farmer looked out his window and saw Indians approaching, his reaction more commonly became to pick up money or a jug of whiskey rather than a musket or an axe. The natives now appeared, the settler knew, not to plunder or kill but to peddle their wares or collect their rents.[96]

The development of new trade forms could not bury all of the differences between Catawba and colonist overnight.[97] But in the latter half of the eighteenth century the beleaguered Indians learned to rely on peaceful means of resolving intercultural conflicts that did arise. Drawing a sharp distinction between "the good men that have rented Lands from us" and "the bad People [who] has frequently imposed upon us," Catawbas called on the former to protect the Nation from the latter.[98] In 1771 they met with the prominent Camden storekeeper, Joseph Kershaw, to request that he "represent us when [we are] a grieved." [99] After the Revolution the position became more formal. Catawbas informed the South Carolina government that, being "destitute of a man to take care of, and assist us in our affairs," they had cho-

---

[96] Compare, for example, the bitterness whites expressed to Adair before the Revolution (Williams, ed., *Adair's History*, 234) with the bemused tolerance in Simms's 19th-century fictional account of Catawbas and planters ("Caloya," in his *Wigwam and Cabin*, 361–429).

[97] Besides the conflicts over hunting noted above, see Hooker, ed., *Carolina Backcountry*, 20; Lark E. Adams, ed., *The State Records of South Carolina: Journals of the House of Representatives, 1785–1786* (Columbia, S.C., 1979), 511–512; Journals of the House of Representatives, Dec. 5, 1792, Records of States, SC A.1b, 23/1, 83.

[98] Catawba petition "To the Honourable the Legislature of the State of South Carolina now assembled at Charlestown," Feb. 13, 1784(?), Kershaw Papers. The Indians had made this distinction earlier. See S.C. Council Jours., Oct. 8, 1760, Records of States, SC E.1p, 8/5, 36.

[99] "At a Meeting Held with the Catabaws," Mar. 26, 1771, Kershaw Papers.

sen one Robert Patten "to take charge of our affairs, and to act and do for us." [100]

Neither Patten nor any other intermediary could have protected the Nation had it not joined the patriot side during the Revolutionary War. Though one scholar has termed the Indians' contribution to the cause "rather negligible," [101] they fought in battles throughout the southeast and supplied rebel forces with food from time to time.[102] These actions made the Catawbas heroes and laid a foundation for their popular renown as staunch patriots. In 1781 their old friend Kershaw told Catawba leaders how he welcomed the end of "this Long and Bloody War, in which You have taken so Noble a part and have fought and Bled with your white Brothers of America." [103] Grateful Carolinians would not soon forget the Nation's service. Shortly after the Civil War an elderly settler whose father had served with the Indians in the Revolution echoed Kershaw's sentiments, recalling that "his father never communicated much to him [about the Catawbas], except that all the tribe . . . served the entire war . . . and fought most heroically." [104]

Catawbas rose even higher in their neighbors' esteem when they began calling their chiefs "General" instead of "King" and stressed that these men were elected by the people.[105] The change reflected little if any real shift in the Nation's political forms,[106] but it delighted the victorious Revolutionaries. In 1794 the Charleston *City Gazette* reported that during the war "King" Frow had abdicated and the Indians chose "General" New River in his stead. "What a pity," the paper concluded, "certain people on a certain island have not as good optics as the Catawbas!" In the same year the citizens of Camden celebrated the anniversary of the fall of the Bastille by raising their glasses to toast "King Prow [*sic*]—may all kings who will not follow his example follow

[100] Catawba Petition to S.C. Legislature, Feb. 13, 1784(?), *ibid.*

[101] Hudson, *Catawba Nation*, 51.

[102] The story of the Indians' service is summarized in Brown, *Catawba Indians*, 260–271.

[103] "To the Brave Genl New River and the rest of the Headmen Warrieurs of the Catawba Nation," 1771 (misdated), Kershaw Papers.

[104] A. Q. Bradley to Lyman C. Draper, May 31, 1873, Draper MSS, 14VV, 260. For other expressions of this attitude see J. F. White to Draper, n.d., *ibid.*, 15VV, 96; T. D. Spratt to Draper, May 7, 1873, *ibid.*, 107–108; Ezekiel Fewell to Draper, n.d., *ibid.*, 318–319; and David Hutchison, "Catawba Indians."

[105] Brown, *Catawba Indians*, 276.

[106] The Nation's council "elected" headmen both before and after 1776, and kinship connections to former rulers continued to be important. For elections see S.C. Council Jours., Feb. 20, 1764, Records of States, SC E.1p, 9/2, 40–41; Nov. 9, 1764, *ibid.*, 354; Feb. 12, 1765, *ibid.*, 9/3, 442–443; S.C. Commons House Jours., Jan. 27, 1767, *ibid.*, SC A.1b, 8/1, n. p. For later hereditary links to former chiefs see John Drayton, *A View of South Carolina As Respects Her Natural and Civil Concerns* (Spartanburg, S.C., 1972 [orig. publ., 1802]), 98; Spratt to Draper, Jan. 12, 1871, Draper MSS, 15VV, 99–100.

that of Louis XVI." [107] Like tales of Indian patriots, the story proved durable. Nearly a century after the Revolution one nearby planter wrote that "the Catawbas, emulating the examples of their white brethren, threw off regal government." [108]

The Indians' new image as republicans and patriots, added to their trade with whites and their willingness to resolve conflicts peacefully, brought settlers to view Catawbas in a different light. By 1800 the natives were no longer violent and dangerous strangers but what one visitor termed an "inoffensive" people and one group of planters called "harmless and friendly" neighbors. [109] They had become traders of pottery but not deerskins, experts with a bow and arrow but not hunters, ferocious warriors against runaway slaves or tories but not against settlers. In these ways Catawbas could be distinctively Indian yet reassuringly harmless at the same time.

The Nation's separate identity rested on such obvious aboriginal traits. But its survival ultimately depended on a more general conformity with the surrounding society. During the nineteenth century both settlers and Indians owned or rented land. Both spoke proudly of their Revolutionary heritage and their republican forms of government. Both drank to excess. [110] Even the fact that Catawbas were not Christians failed to differentiate them sharply from nearby white settlements, where, one visitor noted in 1822, "little attention is paid to the sabbath, or religeon." [111]

In retrospect it is clear that these similarities were as superficial as they were essential. For all the changes generated by contacts with vital Euro-American and Afro-American cultures, the Nation was never torn loose from its cultural moorings. Well after the Revolution, Indians maintained a distinctive way of life rich in tradition and meaningful to those it embraced. Ceremonies conducted by headmen and folk tales told by relatives continued to transmit traditional values and skills from one generation to the next. Catawba children grew up speaking the native language, making bows and arrows or pottery, and otherwise

[107] *City Gazette* (Charleston), Aug. 14, 1794, quoted in Kirkland and Kennedy, *Historic Camden*, 320, 319.

[108] Spratt to Draper, Jan. 12, 1871, Draper MSS, 15VV, 99. See also Hutchison, "Catawba Indians."

[109] Smyth, *Tour*, I, 192; Report of the Commissioners Appointed to Treat with the Catawba Indians, Apr. 3, 1840, in A. F. Whyte, "Account of the Catawba Indians," Draper MSS, 1OU, 112.

[110] W. J. Rorabaugh, *The Alcoholic Republic: An American Tradition* (New York, 1979), chap. 1. For reports of excessive drinking by whites along the Catawba River see Records of the General Assembly, Petitions, N.D. (#1916), 1798 (#139), S.C. Dept. Archs. and Hist.; Journals of the Senate, Dec. 11, 1819, Records of States, SC A.1a, 25/3, 57; Journals of the House of Representatives, Nov. 23, 1819, Nov. 21, 1827, Records of States, SC A.1b, 28/1, 8, 29/5, 15, 24.

[111] Bierce, "Piedmont Frontier," in Clark, ed., *Grand Tour*, 66.

following patterns of belief and behavior derived from the past. The Indians' physical appearance and the meandering paths that set Catawba settlements off from neighboring communities served to reinforce this cultural isolation.[112]

The natives' utter indifference to missionary efforts after 1800 testified to the enduring power of established ways. Several clergymen stopped at the reservation in the first years of the nineteenth century; some stayed a year or two; none enjoyed any success.[113] As one white South Carolinian noted in 1826, Catawbas were "Indians still." [114] Outward conformity made it easier for them to blend into the changed landscape. Beneath the surface lay a more complex story.

Those few outsiders who tried to piece together that story generally found it difficult to learn much from the Indians. A people shrewd enough to discard the title of "King" was shrewd enough to understand that some things were better left unsaid and unseen. Catawbas kept their Indian names, and sometimes their language, a secret from prying visitors.[115] They echoed the racist attitudes of their white neighbors and even owned a few slaves, all the time trading with blacks and hiring them to work in the Nation, where the laborers "enjoyed considerable freedom" among the natives.[116] Like Afro-Americans on the plantation who adopted a happy, childlike demeanor to placate suspicious whites, Indians on the reservation learned that a "harmless and friendly" posture revealing little of life in the Nation was best suited to conditions in post-Revolutionary South Carolina.

Success in clinging to their cultural identity and at least a fraction of their ancient lands cannot obscure the cost Catawba peoples paid. From the time the first European arrived, the deck was stacked against them. They played the hand dealt them well enough to survive, but they could never win. An incident that took place at the end of the

---

[112] The story of the Catawbas' cultural persistence may be found in Merrell, "Natives in a New World," chap. 9, and "Reading 'an almost erased page': A Reassessment of Frank G. Speck's Catawba Studies," American Philosophical Society, *Proceedings*, CXXVII (1983), 248–262. For an interesting comparison of cultural independence in the slave quarter and the Indian reservation see Thomas L. Webber, *Deep Like the Rivers: Education in the Slave Quarter Community, 1831–1865* (New York, 1978), chap. 18.

[113] Hutchison, "Catawba Indians"; Daniel G. Stinson to Draper, July 4, 1873, Draper MSS, 9VV, 274–277.

[114] Robert Mills, *Statistics of South Carolina* . . . (Charleston, S.C., 1826), 773. See also the annual reports of the Catawba Agent to the Governor and State Legislature of South Carolina, 1841, 1842, 1848, 1849, 1860–1864, in Legislative Papers, Indian Affairs, Governors' Correspondence, S.C. Dept. Archs. and Hist.

[115] See Merrell, "Reading 'an almost erased page,' " Am. Phil. Soc., *Procs.*, CXXVII (1983), 256 (names). Smyth, *Tour*, I, 185; Coke, *Extracts*, 149; "Letter from the Country Landsford, S.C., September 6, 1867," in *Courier* (Charleston), Sept. 12, 1867, 3 (language).

[116] Catawba-black relations are analyzed in Merrell, "The Racial Education of the Catawba Indians," *Journal of Southern History*, L (1984), 363–384.

eighteenth century helps shed light on the consequences of compromise. When the Catawba headman, General New River, accidentally injured the horse he had borrowed from a nearby planter named Thomas Spratt, Spratt responded by "banging old New River with a pole all over the yard." This episode provided the settler with a colorful tale for his grandchildren; its effect on New River and his descendants can only be imagined.[117] Catawbas did succeed in the sense that they adjusted to a hostile and different world, becoming trusted friends instead of feared enemies. Had they been any less successful they would not have survived the eighteenth century. But poverty and oppression have plagued the Nation from New River's day to our own.[118] For a people who had once been proprietors of the piedmont, the pain of learning new rules was very great, the price of success very high.

On that August day in 1608 when Amoroleck feared the loss of his world, John Smith assured him that the English "came to them in peace, and to seeke their loves." [119] Events soon proved Amoroleck right and his captor wrong. Over the course of the next three centuries not only Amoroleck and other piedmont Indians but natives throughout North America had their world stolen and another put in its place. Though this occurred at different times and in different ways, no Indians escaped the explosive mixture of deadly bacteria, material riches, and alien peoples that was the invasion of America. Those in the southern piedmont who survived the onslaught were ensconced in their new world by the end of the eighteenth century. Population levels stabilized as the Catawba peoples developed immunities to once-lethal diseases. Rents, sales of pottery, and other economic activities proved adequate to support the Nation at a stable (if low) level of material life. Finally, the Indians' image as "inoffensive" neighbors gave them a place in South Carolina society and continues to sustain them today.

Vast differences separated Catawbas and other natives from their colonial contemporaries. Europeans were the colonizers, Africans the enslaved, Indians the dispossessed: from these distinct positions came distinct histories. Yet once we acknowledge the differences, instructive similarities remain that help to integrate natives more thoroughly into the story of early America. By carving a niche for themselves in response to drastically different conditions, the peoples who composed the Catawba Nation shared in the most fundamental of American experiences. Like Afro-Americans, these Indians were compelled to ac-

---

[117] Thomas Dryden Spratt, "Recollections of His Family, July 1875," unpubl. MS, South Caroliniana Lib., 62.

[118] See H. Lewis Scaife, *History and Condition of the Catawba Indians of South Carolina* (Philadelphia, 1896), 16–23, and Hudson, *Catawba Nation*, chaps. 4–6.

[119] Arber and Bradley, eds., *Works of Smith*, II, 427.

cept a subordinate position in American life yet did not altogether lose their cultural integrity. Like settlers of the Chesapeake, aboriginal inhabitants of the uplands adjusted to appalling mortality rates and wrestled with the difficult task of "living with death." [120] Like inhabitants of the Middle Colonies, piedmont groups learned to cope with unprecedented ethnic diversity by balancing the pull of traditional loyalties with the demands of a new social order. Like Puritans in New England, Catawbas found that a new world did not arrive all at once and that localism, self-sufficiency, and the power of old ways were only gradually eroded by conditions in colonial America. More hints of a comparable heritage could be added to this list, but by now it should be clear that Indians belong on the colonial stage as important actors in the unfolding American drama rather than bit players, props, or spectators. For they, too, lived in a new world.

Slavery and Freedom: The American Paradox

EDMUND S. MORGAN

In this presidential address to the Organization of American Historians, Edmund Morgan confronts the central paradox of our history: Americans have created the freest society the modern world has known, and yet they have also constructed a massive slave labor system which has left behind it a heritage of racial prejudice. For two centuries historians have tried either to justify or to explain the coexistence of these seemingly incompatible social systems. Morgan's provocative answer is that American freedom could not have existed without American slavery; the two systems were symbiotic rather than antagonistic.

Part of the argument is easy to understand. It has become almost commonplace to argue that the existence of black servitude helped to placate the underclass of propertyless whites, for whom racial status was arguably more significant than economic status. So long as poor whites could lord it over black slaves, the expected status anxiety of the poor was supplanted by identification with the plantation-owning elite.

[120] Morgan, *American Slavery, American Freedom*, chap. 8.

Reprinted by permission from Edmund S. Morgan, "Slavery and Freedom: The American Paradox," *Journal of American History*, 59 (June 1972), 5–29. Copyright Organization of American Historians, 1972.

Morgan thinks that it was precisely the reverse sort of status anxiety that encouraged the creation of the slave labor system. The colonists had emigrated from Elizabethan England at a time when the principal fear was that overpopulation would lead to a rootless, propertyless class of vagabonds who might undermine the social fabric. One solution was to send the poor to the colonies, where they might prosper or at least be removed as a threat to social order in the mother country. As life expectancy in the Tidewater South increased, and as land prices rose while tobacco prices fell, the southern colonies came, by the late seventeenth century, to resemble the perilous condition of pre-emigration England. This evoked comparable fears of social unrest, which were confirmed by the violence of Bacon's Rebellion and other disruptions. The answer (which Morgan thinks unconscious) was to supplant the white laboring force with an enslaved black labor force. This not only provided a more easily controlled labor supply, but it also created the economic conditions in which poor whites could improve themselves and, for the most part, exist on the fringe of the slave-owning class. It created a situation in which certain aspects of Virginia government were conceded to yeomen farmers. With slavery, that is, came freedom and republican government for all whites.

Morgan's thesis is elegantly argued, and it certainly provides a satisfying answer to the paradox of the coexistence of slavery and freedom. It does, however, raise some difficult questions. Does this argument account for the existence of slavery in the northern colonies? If not, can it be considered an explanation of "American" freedom? More narrowly, why should the emergence of the slave system have improved the lot of propertyless whites in the seventeenth century? What has slavery to do with Jeffersonian fears of an urban proletariat? You might consider some of these questions in the light of the demographic evidence presented by Russell Menard. Would you expect Menard to agree with Morgan? Most important, if the creation of slavery was not a conscious response to the fears of wealthy Southerners for the security of their society, should we consider their republican ideas more than a rationalization for the cultivation of an evil social system?

American historians interested in tracing the rise of liberty, democracy, and the common man have been challenged in the past two decades by other historians, interested in tracing the history of oppression, exploitation, and racism. The challenge has been salutary, because it has made us examine more directly than historians have hitherto been willing to do, the role of slavery in our early history. Colonial historians, in particular, when writing about the origin and development of American institutions have found it possible until recently to deal with slavery as an exception to everything they had to say. I am speaking about myself but also about most of my generation. We owe a debt of gratitude to those who have insisted that slavery was something more than an exception, that one fifth of the American population at the time of the Revolution is too many people to be treated as an exception.[1]

We shall not have met the challenge simply by studying the history of that one fifth, fruitful as such studies may be, urgent as they may be. Nor shall we have met the challenge if we merely execute the familiar maneuver of turning our old interpretations on their heads. The temptation is already apparent to argue that slavery and oppression were the dominant features of American history and that efforts to advance liberty and equality were the exception, indeed no more than a device to divert the masses while their chains were being fastened. To dismiss the rise of liberty and equality in American history as a mere sham is not only to ignore hard facts, it is also to evade the problem presented by those facts. The rise of liberty and equality in this country was accompanied by the rise of slavery. That two such contradictory developments were taking place simultaneously over a long period of our history, from the seventeenth century to the nineteenth, is the central paradox of American history.

The challenge, for a colonial historian at least, is to explain how a people could have developed the dedication to human liberty and dignity exhibited by the leaders of the American Revolution and at the same time have developed and maintained a system of labor that denied human liberty and dignity every hour of the day.

The paradox is evident at many levels if we care to see it. Think, for a moment, of the traditional American insistence on freedom of the seas. "Free ships make free goods" was the cardinal doctrine of American foreign policy in the Revolutionary era. But the goods for which the United States demanded freedom were produced in very large measure by slave labor. The irony is more than semantic. American reliance on slave labor must be viewed in the context of the American struggle for a separate and equal station among the nations of the earth. At the time the colonists announced their claim to that station they had neither the arms nor the ships to make the claim good. They desperately needed the assistance of other countries, especially France, and their single most valuable product with which to purchase assistance was tobacco, produced mainly by slave labor. So largely did that crop figure in American foreign relations that one historian has referred to the activities of France in supporting the Americans as "King

---

[1] Particularly Staughton Lynd, *Class Conflict, Slavery, and the United States Constitution: Ten Essays* (Indianapolis, 1967).

Tobacco Diplomacy," a reminder that the position of the United States in the world depended not only in 1776 but during the span of a long lifetime thereafter on slave labor.[2] To a very large degree it may be said that Americans bought their independence with slave labor.

The paradox is sharpened if we think of the state where most of the tobacco came from. Virginia at the time of the first United States census in 1790 had 40 percent of the slaves in the entire United States. And Virginia produced the most eloquent spokesmen for freedom and equality in the entire United States: George Washington, James Madison, and above all, Thomas Jefferson. They were all slaveholders and remained so throughout their lives. In recent years we have been shown in painful detail the contrast between Jefferson's pronouncements in favor of republican liberty and his complicity in denying the benefits of that liberty to blacks.[3] It has been tempting to dismiss Jefferson and the whole Virginia dynasty as hypocrites. But to do so is to deprive the term "hypocrisy" of useful meaning. If hypocrisy means, as I think it does, deliberately to affirm a principle without believing it, then hypocrisy requires a rare clarity of mind combined with an unscrupulous intention to deceive. To attribute such an intention, even to attribute such clarity of mind in the matter, to Jefferson, Madison, or Washington is once again to evade the challenge. What we need to explain is how such men could have arrived at beliefs and actions so full of contradiction.

Put the challenge another way: how did England, a country priding itself on the liberty of its citizens, produce colonies where most of the inhabitants enjoyed still greater liberty, greater opportunities, greater control over their own lives than most men in the mother country, while the remainder, one fifth of the total, were deprived of virtually all liberty, all opportunities, all control over their own lives? We may admit that the Englishmen who colonized America and their revolutionary descendants were racists, that consciously or unconsciously they believed liberties and rights should be confined to persons of a light complexion. When we have said as much, even when we have probed the depths of racial prejudice, we will not have fully accounted for the paradox. Racism was surely an essential element in it, but I should like to suggest another element, that I believe to have influenced the development of both slavery and freedom as we have known them in the United States.

---

[2] Curtis P. Nettels, *The Emergence of a National Economy 1775–1815* (New York, 1962), 19. See also Merrill Jensen, "The American Revolution and American Agriculture," *Agricultural History*, XLIII (Jan. 1969), 107–24.

[3] William Cohen, "Thomas Jefferson and the Problem of Slavery," *Journal of American History*, LVI (Dec. 1969), 503–26; D. B. Davis, *Was Thomas Jefferson An Authentic Enemy of Slavery?* (Oxford, 1970); Winthrop D. Jordan, *White over Black: American Attitudes Toward the Negro, 1550–1812* (Chapel Hill, 1968), 429–81.

Let us begin with Jefferson, this slaveholding spokesman of freedom. Could there have been anything in the kind of freedom he cherished that would have made him acquiesce, however reluctantly, in the slavery of so many Americans? The answer, I think, is yes. The freedom that Jefferson spoke for was not a gift to be conferred by governments, which he mistrusted at best. It was a freedom that sprang from the independence of the individual. The man who depended on another for his living could never be truly free. We may seek a clue to Jefferson's enigmatic posture toward slavery in his attitude toward those who enjoyed a seeming freedom without the independence needed to sustain it. For such persons Jefferson harbored a profound distrust, which found expression in two phobias that crop up from time to time in his writings.

The first was a passionate aversion to debt. Although the entire colonial economy of Virginia depended on the willingness of planters to go into debt and of British merchants to extend credit, although Jefferson himself was a debtor all his adult life—or perhaps because he was a debtor—he hated debt and hated anything that made him a debtor. He hated it because it limited his freedom of action. He could not, for example, have freed his slaves so long as he was in debt. Or so at least he told himself. But it was the impediment not simply to their freedom but to his own that bothered him. "I am miserable," he wrote, "till I shall owe not a shilling. . . ." [4]

The fact that he had so much company in his misery only added to it. His Declaration of Independence for the United States was mocked by the hold that British merchants retained over American debtors, including himself.[5] His hostility to Alexander Hamilton was rooted in his recognition that Hamilton's pro-British foreign policy would tighten the hold of British creditors, while his domestic policy would place the government in the debt of a class of native American creditors, whose power might become equally pernicious.

Though Jefferson's concern with the perniciousness of debt was almost obsessive, it was nevertheless altogether in keeping with the ideas of republican liberty that he shared with his countrymen. The trouble with debt was that by undermining the independence of the debtor it threatened republican liberty. Whenever debt brought a man under another's power, he lost more than his own freedom of action. He also weakened the capacity of his country to survive as a republic. It was an axiom of current political thought that republican government re-

---

[4] Julian P. Boyd, ed., *The Papers of Thomas Jefferson* (18 vols., Princeton, 1950–), X, 615. For other expressions of Thomas Jefferson's aversion to debt and distrust of credit both private and public, see *ibid.*, II, 275–76, VIII, 398–99, 632–33, IX, 217–18, 472–73, X, 304–05, XI, 472, 633, 636, 640, XII, 385–86.

[5] Jefferson's career as an ambassador to France was occupied very largely by unsuccessful efforts to break the hold of British creditors on American commerce.

quired a body of free, independent, property-owning citizens.[6] A nation of men, each of whom owned enough property to support his family, could be a republic. It would follow that a nation of debtors, who had lost their property or mortgaged it to creditors, was ripe for tyranny. Jefferson accordingly favored every means of keeping men out of debt and keeping property widely distributed. He insisted on the abolition of primogeniture and entail; he declared that the earth belonged to the living and should not be kept from them by the debts or credits of the dead; he would have given fifty acres of land to every American who did not have it—all because he believed the citizens of a republic must be free from the control of other men and that they could be free only if they were economically free by virtue of owning land on which to support themselves.[7]

If Jefferson felt so passionately about the bondage of the debtor, it is not surprising that he should also have sensed a danger to the republic from another class of men who, like debtors, were nominally free but whose independence was illusory. Jefferson's second phobia was his distrust of the landless urban workman who labored in manufactures. In Jefferson's view, he was a free man in name only. Jefferson's hostility to artificers is well known and is generally attributed to his romantic preference for the rural life. But both his distrust for artificers and his idealization of small landholders as "the most precious part of a state" rested on his concern for individual independence as the basis of freedom. Farmers made the best citizens because they were "the most vigorous, the most independant, the most virtuous. . . ." Artificers, on the other hand, were dependent on "the casualties and caprice of customers." If work was scarce, they had no land to fall back on for a living. In their dependence lay the danger. "Dependance," Jefferson argued, "begets subservience and venality, suffocates the germ of virtue, and prepares fit tools for the designs of ambition." Because artificers could lay claim to freedom without the independence to go with it, they were "the instruments by which the liberties of a country are generally overturned." [8]

In Jefferson's distrust of artificers we begin to get a glimpse of the limits—and limits not dictated by racism—that defined the republican vision of the eighteenth century. For Jefferson was by no means unique

---

[6] See Caroline Robbins, *The Eighteenth-Century Commonwealthman: Studies in the Transmission, Development and Circumstance of English Liberal Thought from the Restoration of Charles II until the War with the Thirteen Colonies* (Cambridge, Mass., 1959); J. G. A. Pocock, "Machiavelli, Harrington, and English Political Ideologies in the Eighteenth Century," *William and Mary Quarterly*, XXII (Oct. 1965), 549–83.

[7] Boyd, ed., *Papers of Thomas Jefferson*, I, 344, 352, 362, 560, VIII, 681–82.

[8] *Ibid.*, VIII, 426, 682; Thomas Jefferson, *Notes on the State of Virginia*, William Peden, ed. (Chapel Hill, 1955), 165. Jefferson seems to have overlooked the dependence of Virginia's farmers on the casualties and caprice of the tobacco market.

among republicans in his distrust of the landless laborer. Such a distrust was a necessary corollary of the widespread eighteenth-century insistence on the independent, property-holding individual as the only bulwark of liberty, an insistence originating in James Harrington's republican political philosophy and a guiding principle of American colonial politics, whether in the aristocratic South Carolina assembly or in the democratic New England town.[9] Americans both before and after 1776 learned their republican lessons from the seventeenth- and eighteenth-century British commonwealthmen; and the commonwealthmen were uninhibited in their contempt for the masses who did not have the propertied independence required of proper republicans.

John Locke, the classic explicator of the right of revolution for the protection of liberty, did not think about extending that right to the landless poor. Instead, he concocted a scheme of compulsory labor for them and their children. The children were to begin at the age of three in public institutions, called working schools because the only subject taught would be work (spinning and knitting). They would be paid in bread and water and grow up "inured to work." Meanwhile the mothers, thus relieved of the care of their offspring, could go to work beside their fathers and husbands. If they could not find regular employment, then they too could be sent to the working school.[10]

It requires some refinement of mind to discern precisely how this version of women's liberation from child care differed from outright slavery. And many of Locke's intellectual successors, while denouncing slavery in the abstract, openly preferred slavery to freedom for the lower ranks of laborers. Adam Ferguson, whose works were widely read in America, attributed the overthrow of the Roman republic, in part at least, to the emancipation of slaves, who "increased, by their numbers and their vices, the weight of that dreg, which, in great and prosperous cities, ever sinks, by the tendency of vice and misconduct to the lowest condition." [11]

That people in the lowest condition, the dregs of society, generally arrived at that position through their own vice and misconduct, whether in ancient Rome or modern Britain, was an unexamined article of faith among eighteenth-century republicans. And the vice that was thought to afflict the lower ranks most severely was idleness. The

---

[9] See Robbins, *The Eighteenth-Century Commonwealthmen;* Pocock, "Machiavelli, Harrington, and English Political Ideologies," 549–83; Michael Zuckerman, "The Social Context of Democracy in Massachusetts," *William and Mary Quarterly,* XXV (Oct. 1968), 523–44, Robert M. Weir, " 'The Harmony We Were Famous For': An Interpretation of Pre-Revolutionary South Carolina Politics," *ibid.,* XXVI (Oct. 1969), 473–501.

[10] C. B. Macpherson, *The Political Theory of Possessive Individualism* (Oxford, 1962), 221–24; H. R. Fox Bourne, *The Life of John Locke* (2 vols., London, 1876), II, 377–90.

[11] Adam Ferguson, *The History of the Progress and Termination of the Roman Republic* (5 vols., Edinburgh, 1799), I, 384. See also Adam Ferguson, *An Essay on the History of Civil Society* (London, 1768), 309–11.

eighteenth-century's preferred cure for idleness lay in the religious and ethical doctrines which R. H. Tawney described as the New Medicine for Poverty, the doctrines in which Max Weber discerned the origins of the spirit of capitalism. But in every society a stubborn mass of men and women refused the medicine. For such persons the commonwealthmen did not hesitate to prescribe slavery. Thus Francis Hutcheson, who could argue eloquently against the enslavement of Africans, also argued that perpetual slavery should be "the ordinary punishment of such idle vagrants as, after proper admonitions and tryals of temporary servitude, cannot be engaged to support themselves and their families by any useful labours." [12] James Burgh, whose *Political Disquisitions* earned the praises of many American revolutionists, proposed a set of press gangs "to seize all idle and disorderly persons, who have been three times complained of before a magistrate, and to set them to work during a certain time, for the benefit of great trading, or manufacturing companies, &c." [13]

The most comprehensive proposal came from Andrew Fletcher of Saltoun. Jefferson hailed in Fletcher a patriot whose political principles were those "in vigour at the epoch of the American emigration [from England]. Our ancestors brought them here and they needed little strengthening to make us what we are. . . ." [14] Fletcher, like other commonwealthmen, was a champion of liberty, but he was also a champion of slavery. He attacked the Christian church not only for having promoted the abolition of slavery in ancient times but also for having perpetuated the idleness of the freedmen thus turned loose on society. The church by setting up hospitals and almshouses had enabled men through the succeeding centuries to live without work. As a result, Fletcher argued, his native Scotland was burdened with 200,000 idle rogues, who roamed the country, drinking, cursing, fighting, robbing, and murdering. For a remedy he proposed that they all be made slaves to men of property. To the argument that their masters might abuse them, he answered in words which might have come a century and a half later from a George Fitzhugh: that this would be against the master's own interest, "That the most brutal man will not use his beast ill only out of a humour; and that if such Inconveniences do sometimes

---

[12] Francis Hutcheson, *A System of Moral Philosophy* (2 vols., London, 1755), II, 202; David B. Davis, *The Problem of Slavery in Western Culture* (Ithaca, 1966), 374–78. I am indebted to David B. Davis for several valuable suggestions.

[13] James Burgh, *Political Disquisitions: Or, An ENQUIRY into public Errors, Defects, and Abuses* . . . (3 vols., London, 1774–1775), III, 220–21. See the proposal of Bishop George Berkeley that "sturdy beggars should . . . be seized and made slaves to the public for a certain term of years." Quoted in R. H. Tawney, *Religion and the Rise of Capitalism: A Historical Essay* (New York, 1926), 270.

[14] E. Millicent Sowerby, ed., *Catalogue of the Library of Thomas Jefferson* (5 vols., Washington, 1952–1959), I, 192.

fall out, it proceeds, for the most part, from the perverseness of the Servant." [15]

In spite of Jefferson's tribute to Fletcher, there is no reason to suppose that he endorsed Fletcher's proposal. But he did share Fletcher's distrust of men who were free in name while their empty bellies made them thieves, threatening the property of honest men, or else made them slaves in fact to anyone who would feed them. Jefferson's own solution for the kind of situation described by Fletcher was given in a famous letter to Madison, prompted by the spectacle Jefferson encountered in France in the 1780s, where a handful of noblemen had engrossed huge tracts of land on which to hunt game, while hordes of the poor went without work and without bread. Jefferson's proposal, characteristically phrased in terms of natural right, was for the poor to appropriate the uncultivated lands of the nobility. And he drew for the United States his usual lesson of the need to keep land widely distributed among the people.[16]

Madison's answer, which is less well known than Jefferson's letter, raised the question whether it was possible to eliminate the idle poor in any country as fully populated as France. Spread the land among them in good republican fashion and there would still be, Madison thought, "a great surplus of inhabitants, a greater by far than will be employed in cloathing both themselves and those who feed them. . . ." In spite of those occupied in trades and as mariners, soldiers, and so on, there would remain a mass of men without work. "A certain degree of misery," Madison concluded, "seems inseparable from a high degree of populousness." [17] He did not, however, go on to propose, as Fletcher had done, that the miserable and idle poor be reduced to slavery.

The situation contemplated by Madison and confronted by Fletcher was not irrelevant to those who were planning the future of the American republic. In a country where population grew by geometric progression, it was not too early to think about a time when there might be vast numbers of landless poor, when there might be those mobs in great cities that Jefferson feared as sores on the body politic. In the United States as Jefferson and Madison knew it, the urban labor force as yet posed no threat, because it was small; and the agricultural labor force was, for the most part, already enslaved. In Revolutionary America, among men who spent their lives working for other men rather than working for themselves, slaves probably constituted a majority.[18]

[15] Andrew Fletcher, *Two Discourses Concerning the Affairs in Scotland; Written in the Year 1698* (Edinburgh, 1698). See second discourse (separately paged), 1–33, especially 16.

[16] Boyd, ed., *Papers of Thomas Jefferson*, VIII, 681–83.

[17] *Ibid.*, IX, 659–60.

[18] Jackson Turner Main, *The Social Structure of Revolutionary America* (Princeton, 1965), 271.

In Virginia they constituted a large majority.[19] If Jefferson and Madison, not to mention Washington, were unhappy about that fact and yet did nothing to alter it, they may have been restrained, in part at least, by thoughts of the role that might be played in the United States by a large mass of free laborers.

When Jefferson contemplated the abolition of slavery, he found it inconceivable that the freed slaves should be allowed to remain in the country.[20] In this attitude he was probably moved by his or his countrymen's racial prejudice. But he may also have had in mind the possibility that when slaves ceased to be slaves, they would become instead a half million idle poor, who would create the same problems for the United States that the idle poor of Europe did for their states. The slave, accustomed to compulsory labor, would not work to support himself when the compulsion was removed. This was a commonplace among Virginia planters before the creation of the republic and long after. "If you free the slaves," wrote Landon Carter, two days after the Declaration of Independence, "you must send them out of the country or they must steal for their support." [21]

Jefferson's plan for freeing his own slaves (never carried out) included an interim education period in which they would have been half-taught, half-compelled to support themselves on rented land; for without guidance and preparation for self support, he believed, slaves could not be expected to become fit members of a republican society.[22] And St. George Tucker, who drafted detailed plans for freeing Virginia's slaves, worried about "the possibility of their becoming idle, dissipated, and finally a numerous banditti, instead of turning their attention to industry and labour." He therefore included in his plans a provision for compelling the labor of the freedmen on an annual basis. "For we must not lose sight of this important consideration," he said, "that these people must be *bound* to labour, if they do not *voluntarily* engage therein. . . . In absolving them from the yoke of slavery, we must not forget the interests of society. Those interests require the exertions of every individual in some mode or other; and those who have not wherewith to support themselves honestly without corporal labour, whatever be their complexion, ought to be compelled to labour." [23]

---

[19] In 1755, Virginia had 43,329 white tithables and 60,078 black. Tithables included white men over sixteen years of age and black men and women over sixteen. In the census of 1790, Virginia had 292,717 slaves and 110,936 white males over sixteen, out of a total population of 747,680. Evarts B. Greene and Virginia D. Harrington, *American Population before the Federal Census of 1790* (New York, 1932), 150–55.

[20] Jefferson, *Notes on the State of Virginia*, 138.

[21] Jack P. Greene, ed., *The Diary of Colonel Landon Carter of Sabine Hall, 1752–1778* (2 vols., Charlottesville, 1965), II, 1055.

[22] Boyd, ed., *Papers of Thomas Jefferson*, XIV, 492–93.

[23] St. George Tucker, *A Dissertation on Slavery with a Proposal for the Gradual Abolition of It, in the State of Virginia* (Philadelphia, 1796). See also Jordan, *White over Black*, 555–60.

It is plain that Tucker, the would-be emancipator, distrusted the idle poor regardless of color. And it seems probable that the Revolutionary champions of liberty who acquiesced in the continued slavery of black labor did so not only because of racial prejudice but also because they shared with Tucker a distrust of the poor that was inherent in eighteenth-century conceptions of republican liberty. Their historical guidebooks had made them fear to enlarge the free labor force.

That fear, I believe, had a second point of origin in the experience of the American colonists, and especially of Virginians, during the preceding century and a half. If we turn now to the previous history of Virginia's labor force, we may find, I think, some further clues to the distrust of free labor among Revolutionary republicans and to the paradoxical rise of slavery and freedom together in colonial America.

The story properly begins in England with the burst of population growth there that sent the number of Englishmen from perhaps three million in 1500 to four-and-one-half million by 1650.[24] The increase did not occur in response to any corresponding growth in the capacity of the island's economy to support its people. And the result was precisely that misery which Madison pointed out to Jefferson as the consequence of "a high degree of populousness." Sixteenth-century England knew the same kind of unemployment and poverty that Jefferson witnessed in eighteenth-century France and Fletcher in seventeenth-century Scotland. Alarming numbers of idle and hungry men drifted about the country looking for work or plunder. The government did what it could to make men of means hire them, but it also adopted increasingly severe measures against their wandering, their thieving, their roistering, and indeed their very existence. Whom the workhouses and prisons could not swallow the gallows would have to, or perhaps the army. When England had military expeditions to conduct abroad, every parish packed off its most unwanted inhabitants to the almost certain death that awaited them from the diseases of the camp.[25]

As the mass of idle rogues and beggars grew and increasingly threatened the peace of England, the efforts to cope with them increasingly threatened the liberties of Englishmen. Englishmen prided themselves on a "gentle government," [26] a government that had been releasing its subjects from old forms of bondage and endowing them with new liberties, making the "rights of Englishmen" a phrase to conjure with. But there was nothing gentle about the government's treatment of the poor; and as more Englishmen became poor, other Englishmen had

[24] Joan Thrisk, ed., *The Agrarian History of England and Wales,* Vol. IV: *1500–1640* (Cambridge, England, 1967), 531.
[25] See Edmund S. Morgan, "The Labor Problem at Jamestown, 1607–18," *American Historical Review,* 76 (June 1971), 595–611, especially 600–06.
[26] This is Richard Hakluyt's phrase. See E. G. R. Taylor, ed., *The Original Writings & Correspondence of the Two Richard Hakluyts* (2 vols., London, 1935), I, 142.

less to be proud of. Thoughtful men could see an obvious solution: get the surplus Englishmen out of England. Send them to the New World, where there were limitless opportunities for work. There they would redeem themselves, enrich the mother country, and spread English liberty abroad.

The great publicist for this program was Richard Hakluyt. His *Principall Navigations, Voiages and Discoveries of the English nation* [27] was not merely the narrative of voyages by Englishmen around the globe, but a powerful suggestion that the world ought to be English or at least ought to be ruled by Englishmen. Hakluyt's was a dream of empire, but of benevolent empire, in which England would confer the blessings of her own free government on the less fortunate peoples of the world. It is doubtless true that Englishmen, along with other Europeans, were already imbued with prejudice against men of darker complexions than their own. And it is also true that the principal beneficiaries of Hakluyt's empire would be Englishmen. But Hakluyt's dream cannot be dismissed as mere hypocrisy any more than Jefferson's affirmation of human equality can be so dismissed. Hakluyt's compassion for the poor and oppressed was not confined to the English poor, and in Francis Drake's exploits in the Caribbean Hakluyt saw, not a thinly disguised form of piracy, but a model for English liberation of men of all colors who labored under the tyranny of the Spaniard.

Drake had gone ashore at Panama in 1572 and made friends with an extraordinary band of runaway Negro slaves. "Cimarrons" they were called, and they lived a free and hardy life in the wilderness, periodically raiding the Spanish settlements to carry off more of their people. They discovered in Drake a man who hated the Spanish as much as they did and who had the arms and men to mount a stronger attack than they could manage by themselves. Drake wanted Spanish gold, and the Cimarrons wanted Spanish iron for tools. They both wanted Spanish deaths. The alliance was a natural one and apparently untroubled by racial prejudice. Together the English and the Cimarrons robbed the mule train carrying the annual supply of Peruvian treasure across the isthmus. And before Drake sailed for England with his loot, he arranged for future meetings.[28] When Hakluyt heard of this alliance, he concocted his first colonizing proposal, a scheme for seizing the Straits of Magellan and transporting Cimarrons there, along with surplus Englishmen. The straits would be a strategic strong point for England's world empire, since they controlled the route from Atlantic to Pacific. Despite the severe climate of the place, the Cimarrons and their English friends would all live warmly together, clad in English

---

[27] Richard Hakluyt, *The Principall Navigations, Voiages and Discoveries of the English nation . . .* (London, 1589).

[28] The whole story of this extraordinary episode is to be found in I. A. Wright, ed., *Documents Concerning English Voyages to the Spanish Main 1569–1580* (London, 1932).

woolens, "well lodged and by our nation made free from the tyrannous Spanyard, and quietly and courteously governed by our nation." [29]

The scheme for a colony in the Straits of Magellan never worked out, but Hakluyt's vision endured, of liberated natives and surplus Englishmen, courteously governed in English colonies around the world. Sir Walter Raleigh caught the vision. He dreamt of wresting the treasure of the Incas from the Spaniard by allying with the Indians of Guiana and sending Englishmen to live with them, lead them in rebellion against Spain, and govern them in the English manner.[30] Raleigh also dreamt of a similar colony in the country he named Virginia. Hakluyt helped him plan it.[31] And Drake stood ready to supply Negroes and Indians, liberated from Spanish tyranny in the Caribbean, to help the enterprise.[32]

Virginia from the beginning was conceived not only as a haven for England's suffering poor, but as a spearhead of English liberty in an oppressed world. That was the dream; but when it began to materialize at Roanoke Island in 1585, something went wrong. Drake did his part by liberating Spanish Caribbean slaves, and carrying to Roanoke those who wished to join him.[33] But the English settlers whom Raleigh sent there proved unworthy of the role assigned them. By the time Drake arrived they had shown themselves less than courteous to the Indians on whose assistance they depended. The first group of settlers murdered the chief who befriended them, and then gave up and ran for home aboard Drake's returning ships. The second group simply disappeared, presumably killed by the Indians.[34]

What was lost in this famous lost colony was more than the band of colonists who have never been traced. What was also lost and never quite recovered in subsequent ventures was the dream of the Englishman and Indian living side by side in peace and liberty. When the English finally planted a permanent colony at Jamestown they came as conquerors, and their government was far from gentle. The Indians

[29] Taylor, ed., *Original Writings & Correspondence*, I, 139–46.

[30] Walter Raleigh, *The Discoverie of the large and bewtiful Empire of Guiana*, V. T. Harlow, ed. (London, 1928), 138–49; V. T. Harlow, ed., *Ralegh's Last Voyage: Being an account drawn out of contemporary letters and relations . . .* (London, 1932), 44–45.

[31] Taylor, ed., *Original Writings & Correspondence*, II, 211–377, especially 318.

[32] Irene A. Wright, trans. and ed., *Further English Voyages to Spanish America, 1583–1594: Documents from the Archives of the Indies at Seville . . .* (London, 1951), lviii, lxiii, lxiv, 37, 52, 54, 55, 159, 172, 173, 181, 188–89, 204–06.

[33] The Spanish reported that "Although their masters were willing to ransom them the English would not give them up except when the slaves themselves desired to go." *Ibid.*, 159. On Walter Raleigh's later expedition to Guiana, the Spanish noted that the English told the natives "that they did not desire to make them slaves, but only to be their friends; promising to bring them great quantities of hatchets and knives, and especially if they drove the Spaniards out of their territories." Harlow, ed., *Ralegh's Last Voyage*, 179.

[34] David Beers Quinn, ed., *The Roanoke Voyages 1584–1590* (2 vols., London, 1955).

willing to endure it were too few in numbers and too broken in spirit to play a significant part in the settlement.

Without their help, Virginia offered a bleak alternative to the workhouse or the gallows for the first English poor who were transported there. During the first two decades of the colony's existence, most of the arriving immigrants found precious little English liberty in Virginia.[35] But by the 1630s the colony seemed to be working out, at least in part, as its first planners had hoped. Impoverished Englishmen were arriving every year in large numbers, engaged to serve the existing planters for a term of years, with the prospect of setting up their own households a few years later. The settlers were spreading up Virginia's great rivers, carving out plantations, living comfortably from their corn fields and from the cattle they ranged in the forests, and at the same time earning perhaps ten or twelve pounds a year per man from the tobacco they planted. A representative legislative assembly secured the traditional liberties of Englishmen and enabled a larger proportion of the population to participate in their own government than had ever been the case in England. The colony even began to look a little like the cosmopolitan haven of liberty that Hakluyt had first envisaged. Men of all countries appeared there: French, Spanish, Dutch, Turkish, Portuguese, and African.[36] Virginia took them in and began to make Englishmen out of them.

It seems clear that most of the Africans, perhaps all of them, came as slaves, a status that had become obsolete in England, while it was becoming the expected condition of Africans outside Africa and of a good many inside.[37] It is equally clear that a substantial number of Virginia's Negroes were free or became free. And all of them, whether servant, slave, or free, enjoyed most of the same rights and duties as other Virginians. There is no evidence during the period before 1660 that they were subjected to a more severe discipline than other servants. They could sue and be sued in court. They did penance in the parish church for having illegitimate children. They earned money of their own,

[35] Morgan, "The Labor Problem at Jamestown, 1607–18," pp. 595–611; Edmund S. Morgan, "The First American Boom: Virginia 1618 to 1630," *William and Mary Quarterly*, XXVIII (April 1971), 169–98.

[36] There are no reliable records of immigration, but the presence of persons of these nationalities is evident from county court records, where all but the Dutch are commonly identified by name, such as "James the Scotchman," or "Cursory the Turk." The Dutch seem to have anglicized their names at once and are difficult to identify except where the records disclose their naturalization. The two counties for which the most complete records survive for the 1640s and 1650s are Accomack-Northampton and Lower Norfolk. Microfilms are in the Virginia State Library, Richmond.

[37] Because the surviving records are so fragmentary, there has been a great deal of controversy about the status of the first Negroes in Virginia. What the records do make clear is that not all were slaves and that not all were free. See Jordan, *White over Black*, 71–82.

bought and sold and raised cattle of their own. Sometimes they bought their own freedom. In other cases, masters bequeathed them not only freedom but land, cattle, and houses.[38] Northampton, the only county for which full records exist, had at least ten free Negro households by 1668.[39]

As Negroes took their place in the community, they learned English ways, including even the truculence toward authority that has always been associated with the rights of Englishmen. Tony Longo, a free Negro of Northampton, when served a warrant to appear as a witness in court, responded with a scatological opinion of warrants, called the man who served it an idle rascal, and told him to go about his business. The man offered to go with him at any time before a justice of the peace so that his evidence could be recorded. He would go with him at night, tomorrow, the next day, next week, any time. But Longo was busy getting in his corn. He dismissed all pleas with a "Well, well, Ile goe when my Corne is in," and refused to receive the warrant.[40]

The judges understandably found this to be contempt of court; but it was the kind of contempt that free Englishmen often showed to authority, and it was combined with a devotion to work that English moralists were doing their best to inculcate more widely in England. As England had absorbed people of every nationality over the centuries and turned them into Englishmen, Virginia's Englishmen were absorbing their own share of foreigners, including Negroes, and seemed to be successfully moulding a New World community on the English model.

But a closer look will show that the situation was not quite so promising as at first it seems. It is well known that Virginia in its first fifteen or twenty years killed off most of the men who went there. It is less well known that it continued to do so. If my estimate of the volume of immigration is anywhere near correct, Virginia must have been a death trap for at least another fifteen years and probably for twenty

---

[38] For examples, see Northampton County Court Records, Deeds, Wills, etc., Book III, f. 83, Book V, ff. 38, 54, 60, 102, 117–19; York County Court Records, Deeds, Orders, Wills, etc., no. 1, ff. 232–34; Surry County Records, Deeds, Wills, etc., no. 1, f. 349; Henrico County Court Records, Deeds and Wills 1677–1692, f. 139.

[39] This fact has been arrived at by comparing the names of householders on the annual list of tithables with casual identifications of persons as Negroes in the court records. The names of householders so identified for 1668, the peak year during the period for which the lists survive (1662–1677) were: Bastian Cane, Bashaw Ferdinando, John Francisco, Susan Grace, William Harman, Philip Mongum, Francis Pane, Manuel Rodriggus, Thomas Rodriggus, and King Tony. The total number of households in the county in 1668 was 172; total number of tithables 435; total number of tithable free Negroes 17; total number of tithable unfree Negroes 42. Thus nearly 29 percent of tithable Negroes and probably of all Negroes were free; and about 13.5 percent of all tithables were Negroes.

[40] Northampton Deeds, Wills, etc., Book V, 54–60 (Nov. 1, 1654).

or twenty-five. In 1625 the population stood at 1,300 or 1,400; in 1640 it was about 8,000.[41] In the fifteen years between those dates at least 15,000 persons must have come to the colony.[42] If so, 15,000 immigrants increased the population by less than 7,000. There is no evidence of a large return migration. It seems probable that the death rate throughout this period was comparable only to that found in Europe during the peak years of a plague. Virginia, in other words, was absorbing England's surplus laborers mainly by killing them. The success of those who survived and rose from servant to planter must be attributed partly to the fact that so few did survive.

After 1640, when the diseases responsible for the high death rate began to decline and the population began a quick rise, it became increasingly difficult for an indigent immigrant to pull himself up in the world. The population probably passed 25,000 by 1662,[43] hardly what Madison would have called a high degree of populousness. Yet the rapid rise brought serious trouble for Virginia. It brought the engrossment of tidewater land in thousands and tens of thousands of acres by

[41] The figure for 1625 derives from the census for that year, which gives 1,210 persons, but probably missed about 10 percent of the population. Morgan, "The First American Boom," 170n–71n. The figure for 1640 is derived from legislation limiting tobacco production per person in 1639–1640. The legislation is summarized in a manuscript belonging to Jefferson, printed in William Waller Hening, *The Statutes at Large; Being a Collection of All the Laws of Virginia, from the First Session of the Legislature, in the Year 1619* (13 vols., New York, 1823), I, 224–25, 228. The full text is in "Acts of the General Assembly, Jan. 6, 1639–40," *William and Mary Quarterly*, IV (Jan. 1924), 17–35, and "Acts of the General Assembly, Jan. 6, 1639–40," *ibid.* (July 1924), 159–62. The assembly calculated that a levy of four pounds of tobacco per tithable would yield 18,584 pounds, implying 4,646 tithables (men over sixteen). It also calculated that a limitation of planting to 170 pounds per poll would yield 1,300,000, implying 7,647 polls. Evidently the latter figure is for the whole population, as is evident also from Hening, *Statutes*, I, 228.

[42] In the year 1635, the only year for which such records exist, 2,010 persons embarked for Virginia from London alone. See John Camden Hotten, ed., *The Original Lists of Persons of Quality . . .* (London, 1874), 35–145. For other years casual estimates survive. In February 1627/8 Francis West said that 1,000 had been "lately received." Colonial Office Group, Class 1, Piece 4, folio 109 (Public Record Office, London). Hereafter cited CO 1/4, f. 109. In February 1633/4 Governor John Harvey said that "this yeares newcomers" had arrived "this yeare." Yong to Sir Tobie Matthew, July 13, 1634, "Aspinwall Papers," *Massachusetts Historical Society Collections*, IX (1871), 110. In May 1635, Samuel Mathews said that 2,000 had arrived "this yeare." Mathews to ? , May 25, 1635, "The Mutiny in Virginia, 1635," *Virginia Magazine of History and Biography*, I (April 1894), 417. And in March 1636, John West said that 1,606 persons had arrived "this yeare." West to Commissioners for Plantations, March 28, 1636, "Virginia in 1636," *ibid.*, IX (July 1901), 37.

[43] The official count of tithables for 1662 was 11,838. Clarendon Papers, 82 (Bodleian Library, Oxford). The ratio of tithables to total population by this time was probably about one to two. (In 1625 it was 1 to 1.5; in 1699 it was 1 to 2.7.) Since the official count was almost certainly below the actuality, a total population of roughly 25,000 seems probable. All population figures for seventeenth-century Virginia should be treated as rough estimates.

speculators, who recognized that the demand would rise.[44] It brought a huge expansion of tobacco production, which helped to depress the price of tobacco and the earnings of the men who planted it.[45] It brought efforts by planters to prolong the terms of servants, since they were now living longer and therefore had a longer expectancy of usefulness.[46]

It would, in fact, be difficult to assess all the consequences of the increased longevity; but for our purposes one development was crucial, and that was the appearance in Virginia of a growing number of freemen who had served their terms but who were now unable to afford land of their own except on the frontiers or in the interior. In years when tobacco prices were especially low or crops especially poor, men who had been just scraping by were obliged to go back to work for their larger neighbors simply in order to stay alive. By 1676 it was estimated that one fourth of Virginia's freemen were without land of their own.[47] And in the same year Francis Moryson, a member of the governor's council, explained the term "freedmen" as used in Virginia to mean "persons without house and land," implying that this was now the normal condition of servants who had attained freedom.[48]

Some of them resigned themselves to working for wages; others preferred a meager living on dangerous frontier land or a hand-to-mouth existence, roaming from one county to another, renting a bit of land here, squatting on some there, dodging the tax collector, drinking, quarreling, stealing hogs, and enticing servants to run away with them.

The presence of this growing class of poverty-stricken Virginians was not a little frightening to the planters who had made it to the top

---

[44] Evidence of the engrossment of lands after 1660 will be found in CO 1/39, f. 196; CO 1/40, f. 23; CO 1/48, f. 48; CO 5/1309, numbers 5, 9, and 23; Sloane Papers, 1008, ff. 334–35 (British Museum, London). A recent count of headrights in patents issued for land in Virginia shows 82,000 headrights claimed in the years from 1635 to 1700. Of these nearly 47,000 or 57 percent (equivalent to 2,350,000 acres) were claimed in the twenty-five years after 1650. W. F. Craven, *White, Red, and Black: The Seventeenth-Century Virginian* (Charlottesville, 1971), 14–16.

[45] No continuous set of figures for Virginia's tobacco exports in the seventeenth century can now be obtained. The available figures for English imports of American tobacco (which was mostly Virginian) are in United States Bureau of the Census, *Historical Statistics of the United States, Colonial Times to 1957* (Washington, D.C., 1960), series Z 238–240, p. 766. They show for 1672 a total of 17,559,000 pounds. In 1631 the figure had been 272,300 pounds. Tobacco crops varied heavily from year to year. Prices are almost as difficult to obtain now as volume. Those for 1667–1675 are estimated from London prices current in Warren Billings, "Virginia's Deploured Condition, 1660–1676: The Coming of Bacon's Rebellion" (doctoral dissertation, Northern Illinois University, 1969), 155–59.

[46] See below.

[47] Thomas Ludwell and Robert Smith to the king, June 18, 1676, vol. LXXVII, f. 128, Coventry Papers Longleat House, American Council of Learned Societies British Mss. project, reel 63 (Library of Congress).

[48] *Ibid.*, 204–05.

or who had arrived in the colony already at the top, with ample supplies of servants and capital. They were caught in a dilemma. They wanted the immigrants who kept pouring in every year. Indeed they needed them and prized them the more as they lived longer. But as more and more turned free each year, Virginia seemed to have inherited the problem that she was helping England to solve. Virginia, complained Nicholas Spencer, secretary of the colony, was "a sinke to drayen England of her filth and scum." [49]

The men who worried the uppercrust looked even more dangerous in Virginia than they had in England. They were, to begin with, young, because it was young persons that the planters wanted for work in the fields; and the young have always seemed impatient of control by their elders and superiors, if not downright rebellious. They were also predominantly single men. Because the planters did not think women, or at least English women, fit for work in the fields, men outnumbered women among immigrants by three or four to one throughout the century.[50] Consequently most of the freedmen had no wife or family to tame their wilder impulses and serve as hostages to the respectable world.

Finally, what made these wild young men particularly dangerous was that they were armed and had to be armed. Life in Virginia required guns. The plantations were exposed to attack from Indians by land and from privateers and petty-thieving pirates by sea.[51] Whenever England was at war with the French or the Dutch, the settlers had to be ready to defend themselves. In 1667 the Dutch in a single raid captured twenty merchant ships in the James River, together with the English warship that was supposed to be defending them; and in 1673 they captured eleven more. On these occasions Governor William Berkeley gathered the planters in arms and at least prevented the enemy from making a landing. But while he stood off the Dutch he worried about the ragged crew at his back. Of the able-bodied men in the colony he estimated that "at least one third are Single freedmen (whose Labour will hardly maintaine them) or men much in debt, both which wee may reasonably expect upon any Small advantage the Enemy may

---

[49] Nicholas Spencer to Lord Culpeper, Aug. 6, 1676, *ibid.*, 170. See also CO 1/49, f 107.

[50] The figures are derived from a sampling of the names of persons for whom headrights were claimed in land patents. Patent Books I–IX (Virginia State Library, Richmond). Wyndham B. Blanton found 17,350 women and 75,884 men in "a prolonged search of the patent books and other records of the times . . . ," a ratio of 1 woman to 4.4 men. Wyndham B. Blanton "Epidemics, Real and Imaginary, and other Factors Influencing Seventeenth Century Virginia's Population," *Bulletin of the History of Medicine*, XXXI (Sept.–Oct. 1957), 462. See also Craven, *White, Red, and Black*, 26–27.

[51] Pirates were particularly troublesome in the 1680s and 1690s. See CO 1/48, f. 71; CO 1/51, f. 340; CO 1/52, f. 54; CO 1/55, ff. 105–106; CO 1/57, f. 300; CO 5/1311, no. 10.

gaine upon us, wold revolt to them in hopes of bettering their Condicion by Shareing the Plunder of the Country with them." [52]

Berkeley's fears were justified. Three years later, sparked not by a Dutch invasion but by an Indian attack, rebellion swept Virginia. It began almost as Berkeley had predicted, when a group of volunteer Indian fighters turned from a fruitless expedition against the Indians to attack their rulers. Bacon's Rebellion was the largest popular rising in the colonies before the American Revolution. Sooner or later nearly everyone in Virginia got in on it, but it began in the frontier counties of Henrico and New Kent, among men whom the governor and his friends consistently characterized as rabble.[53] As it spread eastward, it turned out that there were rabble everywhere, and Berkeley understandably raised his estimate of their numbers. "How miserable that man is," he exclaimed, "that Governes a People wher six parts of seaven at least are Poore Endebted Discontented and Armed." [54]

Virginia's poor had reason to be envious and angry against the men who owned the land and imported the servants and ran the government. But the rebellion produced no real program of reform, no ideology, not even any revolutionary slogans. It was a search for plunder, not for principles. And when the rebels had redistributed whatever wealth they could lay their hands on, the rebellion subsided almost as quickly as it had begun.

It had been a shattering experience, however, for Virginia's first families. They had seen each other fall in with the rebels in order to save their skins or their possessions or even to share in the plunder. When it was over, they eyed one another distrustfully, on the lookout for any new Bacons in their midst, who might be tempted to lead the still restive rabble on more plundering expeditions. When William Byrd and Laurence Smith proposed to solve the problems of defense against the Indians by establishing semi-independent buffer settlements on the upper reaches of the rivers, in each of which they would engage to keep fifty men in arms, the assembly at first reacted favorably. But it quickly occurred to the governor and council that this would in fact mean gathering a crowd of Virginia's wild bachelors and furnishing them with an abundant supply of arms and ammunition. Byrd had himself led such a crowd in at least one plundering foray during the rebellion. To put him or anyone else in charge of a large and permanent gang of armed men was to invite them to descend again on the people whom they were supposed to be protecting.[55]

[52] CO 1/30, ff. 114–115.

[53] CO 1/37, ff. 35–40.

[54] Vol. LXXVII, 144–46, Coventry Papers.

[55] Hening, *Statutes*, II, 448–54; CO 1/42, f. 178; CO 1/43, f. 29; CO 1/44, f. 398; CO 1/47, ff. 258–260, 267; CO 1/48, f. 46; vol. LXXVIII, 378–81, 386–87, 398–99, Coventry Papers.

The nervousness of those who had property worth plundering continued throughout the century, spurred in 1682 by the tobacco-cutting riots in which men roved about destroying crops in the fields, in the desperate hope of producing a shortage that would raise the price of the leaf.[56] And periodically in nearby Maryland and North Carolina, where the same conditions existed as in Virginia, there were tumults that threatened to spread to Virginia.[57]

As Virginia thus acquired a social problem analogous to England's own, the colony began to deal with it as England had done, by restricting the liberties of those who did not have the proper badge of freedom, namely the property that government was supposed to protect. One way was to extend the terms of service for servants entering the colony without indentures. Formerly they had served until twenty-one; now the age was advanced to twenty-four.[58] There had always been laws requiring them to serve extra time for running away; now the laws added corporal punishment and, in order to make habitual offenders more readily recognizable, specified that their hair be cropped.[59] New laws restricted the movement of servants on the highways and also increased the amount of extra time to be served for running away. In addition to serving two days for every day's absence, the captured runaway was now frequently required to compensate by labor for the loss to the crop that he had failed to tend and for the cost of his apprehension, including rewards paid for his capture.[60] A three week's holiday might result in a year's extra service.[61] If a servant struck his master, he was to serve another year.[62] For killing a hog he had to serve the owner a year and the informer another year. Since the owner of the hog, and the owner of the servant, and the informer were frequently the same man, and since a hog was worth at best less than one tenth the hire of a servant for a year, the law was very profitable to masters. One Lancaster master was awarded six years extra service from a servant who killed three of his hogs, worth about thirty shillings.[63]

The effect of these measures was to keep servants for as long as possible from gaining their freedom, especially the kind of servants who were most likely to cause trouble. At the same time the engrossment of land was driving many back to servitude after a brief taste of freedom.

[56] CO 1/48 *passim.*
[57] CO 1/43, ff. 359–365; CO 1/44, ff. 10–62; CO 1/47, f. 261; CO 1/48, ff. 87–96, 100–102, 185; CO 5/1305, no. 43; CO 5/1309, no. 74.
[58] Hening, *Statutes,* II, 113–14, 240.
[59] *Ibid.,* II, 266, 278.
[60] *Ibid.,* II, 116–17, 273–74, 277–78.
[61] For example, James Gray, absent twenty-two days, was required to serve fifteen months extra. Order Book 1666–1680, p. 163, Lancaster County Court Records.
[62] Hening, *Statutes,* II, 118.
[63] Order Book 1666–1680, p. 142, Lancaster County Court Records.

Freedmen who engaged to work for wages by so doing became servants again, subject to most of the same restrictions as other servants.

Nevertheless, in spite of all the legal and economic pressures to keep men in service, the ranks of the freedmen grew, and so did poverty and discontent. To prevent the wild bachelors from gaining an influence in the government, the assembly in 1670 limited voting to landholders and householders.[64] But to disfranchise the growing mass of single freemen was not to deprive them of the weapons they had wielded so effectively under Nathaniel Bacon. It is questionable how far Virginia could safely have continued along this course, meeting discontent with repression and manning her plantations with annual importations of servants who would later add to the unruly ranks of the free. To be sure, the men at the bottom might have had both land and liberty, as the settlers of some other colonies did, if Virginia's frontier had been safe from Indians, or if the men at the top had been willing to forego some of their profits and to give up some of the lands they had engrossed. The English government itself made efforts to break up the great holdings that had helped to create the problem.[65] But it is unlikely that the policy makers in Whitehall would have contended long against the successful.

In any case they did not have to. There was another solution, which allowed Virginia's magnates to keep their lands, yet arrested the discontent and the repression of other Englishmen, a solution which strengthened the rights of Englishmen and nourished their attachment to liberty which came to fruition in the Revolutionary generation of Virginia statesmen. But the solution put an end to the process of turning Africans into Englishmen. The rights of Englishmen were preserved by destroying the rights of Africans.

I do not mean to argue that Virginians deliberately turned to African Negro slavery as a means of preserving and extending the rights of Englishmen. Winthrop Jordan has suggested that slavery came to Virginia as an unthinking decision.[66] We might go further and say that it came without a decision. It came automatically as Virginians bought the cheapest labor they could get. Once Virginia's heavy mortality ceased, an investment in slave labor was much more profitable than an investment in free labor; and the planters bought slaves as rapidly as traders made them available. In the last years of the seventeenth century they bought them in such numbers that slaves probably already

---

[64] Hening, *Statutes,* II, 280. It had been found, the preamble to the law said, that such persons "haveing little interest in the country doe oftner make tumults at the election to the disturbance of his majesties peace, then by their discretions in their votes provide for the conservasion thereof, by makeing choyce of persons fitly qualifyed for the discharge of soe greate a trust. . . ."

[65] CO 1/39, f. 196; CO 1/48, f. 48; CO 5/1309, nos. 5, 9, 23; CO 5/1310, no. 83.

[66] Jordan, *White over Black,* 44–98.

constituted a majority or nearly a majority of the labor force by 1700.[67] The demand was so great that traders for a time found a better market in Virginia than in Jamaica or Barbados.[68] But the social benefits of an enslaved labor force, even if not consciously sought or recognized at the time by the men who bought the slaves, were larger than the economic benefits. The increase in the importation of slaves was matched by a decrease in the importation of indentured servants and consequently a decrease in the dangerous number of new freedmen who annually emerged seeking a place in society that they would be unable to achieve.[69]

If Africans had been unavailable, it would probably have proved impossible to devise a way to keep a continuing supply of English immigrants in their place. There was a limit beyond which the abridgement of English liberties would have resulted not merely in rebellion but in protests from England and in the cutting off of the supply of further servants. At the time of Bacon's Rebellion the English commission of investigation had shown more sympathy with the rebels than with the well-to-do planters who had engrossed Virginia's lands. To have attempted the enslavement of English-born laborers would have caused more disorder than it cured. But to keep as slaves black men who arrived in that condition *was* possible and apparently regarded as plain common sense.

The attitude of English officials was well expressed by the attorney who reviewed for the Privy Council the slave codes established in Barbados in 1679. He found the laws of Barbados to be well designed for the good of his majesty's subjects there, for, he said, "although Negros in that Island are punishable in a different and more severe manner than other Subjects are for Offences of the like nature; yet I humbly conceive that the Laws there concerning Negros are reasonable Laws, for by reason of their numbers they become dangerous, and being a brutish sort of People and reckoned as goods and chattels in that Island, it is of necessity or at least convenient to have Laws for the Government of them different from the Laws of England, to prevent the

---

[67] In 1700 they constituted half of the labor force (persons working for other men) in Surry County, the only county in which it is possible to ascertain the numbers. Robert Wheeler, "Social Transition in the Virginia Tidewater, 1650–1720: The Laboring Households as an Index," paper delivered at the Organization of American Historians' meeting, New Orleans, April 15, 1971. Surry County was on the south side of the James, one of the least wealthy regions of Virginia.

[68] See the letters of the Royal African Company to its ship captains, Oct. 23, 1701; Dec. 2, 1701; Dec. 7, 1704; Dec. 21, 1704; Jan. 25, 1704/5, T70 58 (Public Record Office, London).

[69] Abbot Emerson Smith, *Colonists in Bondage: White Servitude and Convict Labor in America 1607–1776* (Chapel Hill, 1947), 335. See also Thomas J. Wertenbaker, *The Planters of Colonial Virginia* (Princeton, 1922), 130–31, 134–35; Craven, *White, Red, and Black*, 17.

great mischief that otherwise may happen to the Planters and Inhabitants in that Island." [70] In Virginia too it seemed convenient and reasonable to have different laws for black and white. As the number of slaves increased, the assembly passed laws that carried forward with much greater severity the trend already under way in the colony's labor laws. But the new severity was reserved for people without white skin. The laws specifically exonerated the master who accidentally beat his slave to death, but they placed new limitations on his punishment of "Christian white servants." [71]

Virginians worried about the risk of having in their midst a body of men who had every reason to hate them.[72] The fear of a slave insurrection hung over them for nearly two centuries. But the danger from slaves actually proved to be less than that which the colony had faced from its restive and armed freedmen. Slaves had none of the rising expectations that so often produce human discontent. No one had told them that they had rights. They had been nurtured in heathen societies where they had lost their freedom; their children would be nurtured in a Christian society and never know freedom.

Moreover, slaves were less troubled by the sexual imbalance that helped to make Virginia's free laborers so restless. In an enslaved labor force women could be required to make tobacco just as the men did; and they also made children, who in a few years would be an asset to their master. From the beginning, therefore, traders imported women in a much higher ratio to men than was the case among English servants,[73] and the level of discontent was correspondingly reduced. Vir-

---

[70] CO 1/45, f. 138.

[71] Hening, *Statutes*, II, 481–82, 492–93; III, 86 88, 102–03, 179–80, 333–35, 447–62.

[72] For example, see William Byrd II to the Earl of Egmont, July 12, 1736, in Elizabeth Donnan, ed., *Documents Illustrative of the History of the Slave Trade to America* (4 vols., Washington, 1930–1935), IV, 131–32. But compare Byrd's letter to Peter Beckford, Dec. 6, 1735, "Letters of the Byrd Family," *Virginia Magazine of History and Biography*, XXXVI (April 1928), 121–23, in which he specifically denies any danger. The Virginia assembly at various times laid duties on the importation of slaves. See Donnan, ed., *Documents Illustrative of the History of the Slave Trade*, IV, 66–67, 86–88, 91–94, 102–17, 121–31, 132–42. The purpose of some of the acts was to discourage imports, but apparently the motive was to redress the colony's balance of trade after a period during which the planters had purchased far more than they could pay for. See also Wertenbaker, *The Planters of Colonial Virginia*, 129.

[73] The Swiss traveler Francis Ludwig Michel noted in 1702 that "Both sexes are usually bought, which increase afterwards." William J. Hinke, trans. and ed., "Report of the Journey of Francis Louis Michel from Berne Switzerland to Virginia, October 2, (1) 1701–December 1, 1702: Part II," *Virginia Magazine of History and Biography*, XXIV (April 1916), 116. A sampling of the names identifiable by sex, for whom headrights were claimed in land patents in the 1680s and 1690s shows a much higher ratio of women to men among blacks than among whites. For example, in the years 1695–1699 (Patent Book 9) I count 818 white men and 276 white women, 376 black men and 220 black women (but compare Craven, *White, Red, and Black*, 99–100). In Northampton County in 1677, among seventy-five black tithables there were thirty-six men, thirty-

ginians did not doubt that discontent would remain, but it could be repressed by methods that would not have been considered reasonable, convenient, or even safe, if applied to Englishmen. Slaves could be deprived of opportunities for association and rebellion. They could be kept unarmed and unorganized. They could be subjected to savage punishments by their owners without fear of legal reprisals. And since their color disclosed their probable status, the rest of society could keep close watch on them. It is scarcely surprising that no slave insurrection in American history approached Bacon's Rebellion in its extent or in its success.

Nor is it surprising that Virginia's freedmen never again posed a threat to society. Though in later years slavery was condemned because it was thought to compete with free labor, in the beginning it reduced by so much the number of freedmen who would otherwise have competed with each other. When the annual increment of freedmen fell off, the number that remained could more easily find an independent place in society, especially as the danger of Indian attack diminished and made settlement safer at the heads of the rivers or on the Carolina frontier. There might still remain a number of irredeemable, idle, and unruly freedmen, particularly among the convicts whom England exported to the colonies. But the numbers were small enough, so that they could be dealt with by the old expedient of drafting them for military expeditions.[74] The way was thus made easier for the remaining freedmen to acquire property, maybe acquire a slave or two of their own, and join with their superiors in the enjoyment of those English liberties that differentiated them from their black laborers.

---

eight women, and one person whose sex cannot be determined. In Surry County in 1703, among 211 black tithables there were 132 men, seventy-four women, and five persons whose sex cannot be determined. These are the only counties where the records yield such information. Northampton County Court Records, Order Book 10, 189–91; Surry County Court Records, Deeds, Wills, etc., No. 5, part 2, 287–90.

[74] Virginia disposed of so many this way in the campaign against Cartagena in 1741 that a few years later the colony was unable to scrape up any more for another expedition. Fairfax Harrison, "When the Convicts Came," *Virginia Magazine of History and Biography,* XXX (July 1922), 250–60, especially 256–57; John W. Shy, "A New Look at Colonial Militia," *William and Mary Quarterly,* XX (April 1963), 175–85. In 1736, Virginia had shipped another batch of unwanted freedmen to Georgia because of a rumored attack by the Spanish. Byrd II to Lord Egmont, July 1736, "Letters of the Byrd Family," *Virginia Magazine of History and Biography,* XXXVI (July 1928), 216–17. Observations by an English traveler who embarked on the same ship suggest that they did not go willingly: "our Lading consisted of all the Scum of Virginia, who had been recruited for the Service of Georgia, and who were ready at every Turn to mutiny, whilst they belch'd out the most shocking Oaths, wishing Destruction to the Vessel and every Thing in her." "Observations in Several Voyages and Travels in America in the Year 1736," *William and Mary Quarterly,* XV (April 1907), 224.

A free society divided between large landholders and small was much less riven by antagonisms than one divided between landholders and landless, masterless men. With the freedman's expectations, sobriety, and status restored, he was no longer a man to be feared. That fact, together with the presence of a growing mass of alien slaves, tended to draw the white settlers closer together and to reduce the importance of the class difference between yeoman farmer and large plantation owner.[75]

The seventeenth century has sometimes been thought of as the day of the yeoman farmer in Virginia; but in many ways a stronger case can be made for the eighteenth century as the time when the yeoman farmer came into his own, because slavery relieved the small man of the pressures that had been reducing him to continued servitude. Such an interpretation conforms to the political development of the colony. During the seventeenth century the royally appointed governor's council, composed of the largest property-owners in the colony, had been the most powerful governing body. But as the tide of slavery rose between 1680 and 1720 Virginia moved toward a government in which the yeoman farmer had a larger share. In spite of the rise of Virginia's great families on the black tide, the power of the council declined; and the elective House of Burgesses became the dominant organ of government. Its members nurtured a closer relationship with their yeoman constituency than had earlier been the case.[76] And in its chambers Virginians developed the ideas they so fervently asserted in the Revolution: ideas about taxation, representation, and the rights of Englishmen, and ideas about the prerogatives and powers and sacred calling of the independent, property-holding yeoman farmer—commonwealth ideas.

In the eighteenth century, because they were no longer threatened by a dangerous free laboring class, Virginians could afford these ideas, whereas in Berkeley's time they could not. Berkeley himself was obsessed with the experience of the English civil wars and the danger of rebellion. He despised and feared the New Englanders for their association with the Puritans who had made England, however briefly, a commonwealth.[77] He was proud that Virginia, unlike New England, had no free schools and no printing press, because books and schools bred heresy and sedition.[78] He must have taken satisfaction in the fact

[75] Compare Lyon G. Tyler, "Virginians Voting in the Colonial Period," *William and Mary Quarterly*, VI (July 1897), 7–13.

[76] John C. Rainbolt, "The Alteration in the Relationship between Leadership and Constituents in Virginia, 1660 to 1720," *William and Mary Quarterly*, XXVII (July 1970), 411–34.

[77] William Berkeley to Richard Nicholls, May 20, 1666, May 4, 1667, Additional Mss. 28, 218, ff. 14–17 (British Museum, London).

[78] Hening, *Statutes*, II, 517.

that when his people did rebel against him under Bacon, they generated no republican ideas, no philosophy of rebellion or of human rights. Yet a century later, without benefit of rebellions, Virginians had learned republican lessons, had introduced schools and printing presses, and were as ready as New Englanders to recite the aphorisms of the commonwealthmen.

It was slavery, I suggest, more than any other single factor, that had made the difference, slavery that enabled Virginia to nourish representative government in a plantation society, slavery that transformed the Virginia of Governor Berkeley to the Virginia of Jefferson, slavery that made the Virginians dare to speak a political language that magnified the rights of freemen, and slavery, therefore, that brought Virginians into the same commonwealth political tradition with New Englanders. The very institution that was to divide North and South after the Revolution may have made possible their union in a republican government.

Thus began the American paradox of slavery and freedom, intertwined and interdependent, the rights of Englishmen supported on the wrongs of Africans. The American Revolution only made the contradictions more glaring, as the slaveholding colonists proclaimed to a candid world the rights not simply of Englishmen but of all men. To explain the origin of the contradictions, if the explanation I have suggested is valid, does not eliminate them or make them less ugly. But it may enable us to understand a little better the strength of the ties that bound freedom to slavery, even in so noble a mind as Jefferson's. And it may perhaps make us wonder about the ties that bind more devious tyrannies to our own freedoms and give us still today our own American paradox.

Enslavement of Negroes in America to 1700

WINTHROP D. JORDAN

Winthrop Jordan casts his net widely in search of the origins of Negro slavery in seventeenth-century America. While he admits that there was no such legal status in England, he argues that Englishmen were familiar with the conception of slavery as a

Reprinted, by permission of the author and the publisher, from *White over Black: American Attitudes Toward the Negro, 1550–1812* by Winthrop Jordan. Published for the Institute of Early American History and Culture, Williamsburg, Va., Copyright 1968 The University of North Carolina Press.

condition of perpetual, absolute unfreedom and that contempo-
rary Europe provided them with real examples of the practice.
Jordan notes that slavery came into existence before the end of the
seventeenth century everywhere in British North America, al-
though the process varied greatly from the West Indian islands to
New England to Virginia and Maryland. Unhindered by Puri-
tan ideology or the "captivity" analogy, the Southern colonies
provide an example of the gradual creation of a full-blown slave
system. Southern blacks were treated differently from the start
(and some may have served for life almost as soon), but by 1640
there is clear evidence of total enslavement and by the end of the
century slaves were already treated more like property than men.
Slave status and racial distaste worked together to create the "pe-
culiar institution." Thus for Jordan, slavery resulted from social
conditions in Europe and in the colonies, from the attitudes of the
colonists, and from the experience of settling the New World. He
believes that the legal structure of slavery did not reflect the con-
ditions of its growth, since law so often lags behind social reality.

From the vantage point of the late eighteenth century, the
question of the origins of slavery does not make very much differ-
ence, since on any account the results were the same. But for the
historian of the colonial period the differences in interpretation
are critical, for they reflect dramatically opposed views of social
organization and human behavior in the first century of Ameri-
can life. To discover how men developed such a labor system is
therefore to find out what is most basic about the way in which
they lived.

At the start of English settlement in America, no one had in mind to
establish the institution of Negro slavery. Yet in less than a century the
foundations of a peculiar institution had been laid. The first Negroes
landed in Virginia in 1619, though very, very little is known about
their precise status during the next twenty years. Between 1640 and
1660 there is evidence of enslavement, and after 1660 slavery crystal-
lized on the statute books of Maryland, Virginia, and other colonies.
By 1700 when African Negroes began flooding into English America
they were treated as somehow deserving a life and status radically different from English and other European settlers. . . . Englishmen in
America had created a legal status [for Negroes] which ran counter to
English law.

Unfortunately the details of this process can never be completely reconstructed; there is simply not enough evidence (and very little
chance of more to come) to show precisely when and how and why
Negroes came to be treated so differently from white men, though
there is just enough to make historians differ as to its meaning. Con-

cerning the first years of contact especially we have very little information as to what impression Negroes made upon English settlers: accordingly, we are left knowing less about the formative years than about later periods of American slavery. That those early years were crucial ones is obvious, for it was then that the cycle of Negro debasement began; once the Negro became fully the slave it is not hard to see why white men looked down upon him. Yet precisely because understanding the dynamics of these early years is so important to understanding the centuries which followed, it is necessary to bear with the less than satisfactory data and to attempt to reconstruct the course of debasement undergone by Negroes in seventeenth-century America. In order to comprehend it, we need first of all to examine certain social pressures generated by the American environment and how these pressures interacted with certain qualities of English social thought and law that existed on the eve of settlement, qualities that even then were being modified by examples set by England's rivals for empire in the New World.

1. The Necessities of a New World

When Englishmen crossed the Atlantic to settle in America, they were immediately subject to novel strains. In some settlements, notably Jamestown and Plymouth, the survival of the community was in question. An appalling proportion of people were dead within a year, from malnutrition, starvation, unconquerable diseases, bitter cold, oppressive heat, Indian attacks, murder, and suicide. The survivors were isolated from the world as they had known it, cut off from friends and family and the familiar sights and sounds and smells which have always told men who and where they are. A similar sense of isolation and disorientation was inevitable even in the settlements that did not suffer through a starving time. English settlers were surrounded by savages. They had to perform a round of daily tasks to which most were unaccustomed. They had undergone the shock of detachment from home in order to set forth upon a dangerous voyage of from ten to thirteen weeks that ranged from unpleasant to fatal and that seared into every passenger's memory the ceaselessly tossing distance that separated him from his old way of life.[1]

Life in America put great pressure upon the traditional social and economic controls that Englishmen assumed were to be exercised by civil and often ecclesiastical authority. Somehow the empty woods seemed to lead much more toward license than restraint. At the same time, by reaction, this unfettering resulted in an almost pathetic social conservatism, a yearning for the forms and symbols of the old familiar social order. When in 1618, for example, the Virginia Company wan-

[1] There is an eloquent revivification by William Bradford, *Of Plymouth Plantation, 1620–1647*, ed. Samuel Eliot Morison (N.Y., 1952), 61–63.

gled a knighthood for a newly appointed governor of the colony the objection from the settlers was not that this artificial elevation was inappropriate to wilderness conditions but that it did not go far enough to meet them; several planters petitioned that a governor of higher rank be sent. . . . English social forms were transplanted to America not simply because they were nice to have around but because without them the new settlement would have fallen apart and English settlers would have become men of the forest, savage men devoid of civilization.

For the same reason, the communal goals that animated the settlement of the colonies acquired great functional importance in the wilderness; they served as antidotes to social and individual disintegration. The physical hardships of settlement could never have been surmounted without the stiffened nerve and will engendered by commonly recognized if sometimes unarticulated purposes. . . . For Englishmen planting in America . . . it was of the utmost importance to know that they were Englishmen, which was to say that they were educated (to a degree suitable to their station), Christian (of an appropriate Protestant variety), civilized, and (again to an appropriate degree) free men.

It was with personal freedom, of course, that wilderness conditions most suddenly reshaped English laws, assumptions, and practices. In America land was plentiful, labor scarce, and, as in all new colonies, a cash crop desperately needed. These economic conditions were to remain important for centuries; in general they tended to encourage greater geographical mobility, less specialization, higher rewards, and fewer restraints on the processes and products of labor. Supporting traditional assumptions and practices, however, was the need to retain them simply because they were familiar and because they served the vital function of maintaining and advancing orderly settlement. Throughout the seventeenth century there were pressures on traditional practices which similarly told in opposite directions.

In general men who invested capital in agriculture in America came under fewer customary and legal restraints than in England concerning what they did with their land and with the people who worked on it. On the other hand their activities were constrained by the economic necessity of producing cash crops for export, which narrowed their choice of how they could treat it. Men without capital could obtain land relatively easily: hence the shortage of labor and the notably blurred line between men who had capital and men who did not. Men and women in England faced a different situation. A significant amount of capital was required in order to get to America, and the greatest barrier to material advancement in America was the Atlantic Ocean.

Three major systems of labor emerged amid the interplay of these social and economic conditions in America. One, which was present from the beginning, was free wage labor, in which contractual arrangements rested upon a monetary nexus. Another, which was the last to appear, was chattel slavery, in which there were no contractual arrangements (except among owners). The third, which virtually coincided with first settlement in America, was temporary servitude, in which complex contractual arrangements gave shape to the entire system. It was this third system, indentured servitude, which permitted so many English settlers to cross the Atlantic barrier. Indentured servitude was linked to the development of chattel slavery in America, and its operation deserves closer examination.

A very sizable proportion of settlers in the English colonies came as indentured servants bound by contract to serve a master for a specified number of years, usually from four to seven or until age twenty-one, as repayment for their ocean passage. The time of service to which the servant bound himself was negotiable property, and he might be sold or conveyed from one master to another at any time up to the expiration of his indenture, at which point he became a free man. (Actually it was his *labor* which was owned and sold, not his *person*, though this distinction was neither important nor obvious at the time.) Custom and statute law regulated the relationship between servant and master. Obligation was reciprocal: the master undertook to feed and clothe and sometimes to educate his servant and to refrain from abusing him, while the servant was obliged to perform such work as his master set him and to obey his master in all things. This typical pattern, with a multitude of variations, was firmly established by mid-seventeenth century. In Virginia and Maryland, both the legal and actual conditions of servants seem to have improved considerably from the early years when servants had often been outrageously abused and sometimes forced to serve long terms. Beginning about 1640 the legislative assemblies of the two colonies passed numerous acts prescribing maximum terms of service and requiring masters to pay the customary "freedom dues" (clothing, provisions, and so forth) at the end of the servant's time.[2] This legislation may have been actuated partly by the need to attract more immigrants with guarantees of good treatment, in which case underpopulation in relation to level of technology and to natural resources in the English colonies may be said to have made for greater personal freedom. On the other hand, it may also have been a matter of protecting traditional freedoms threatened by this same fact of underpopulation which generated so powerful a need for labor which would not be transient and temporary. In this instance, very clearly, the imperatives enjoined by settlement in the wilderness inter-

---

[2] William Waller Hening, ed., *The Statutes at Large Being a Collection of All the Laws of Virginia*, 13 vols. (Richmond, N.Y., and Phila., 1809–23), I, 257, 435, 439–42, II, 113–14, 240, 388, III, 447–62; *Archives of Maryland*, 69 vols. (Baltimore, 1883–), I, 53, 80, 352–53, 409–10, 428, 443–44, 453–54, 464, 469, II, 147–48, 335–36, 527.

acted with previously acquired ideas concerning personal freedom. Indeed without some inquiry into Elizabethan thinking on that subject, it will remain impossible to comprehend why Englishmen became servants in the plantations, and Negroes slaves.

2. Freedom and Bondage in the English Tradition

Thinking about freedom and bondage in Tudor England was confused and self-contradictory. In a period of social dislocation there was considerable disagreement among contemporary observers as to what actually was going on and even as to what ought to be. Ideas about personal freedom tended to run both ahead of and behind actual social conditions. Both statute and common law were sometimes considerably more than a century out of phase with actual practice and with commonly held notions about servitude. Finally, ideas and practices were changing rapidly. It is possible, however, to identify certain important tenets of social thought that served as anchor points amid this chaos.

Englishmen lacked accurate methods of ascertaining what actually was happening to their social institutions, but they were not wrong in supposing that villenage, or "bondage" as they more often called it, had virtually disappeared in England. William Harrison put the matter most strenuously in 1577: "As for slaves and bondmen we have none, naie such is the privilege of our countrie by the especiall grace of God, and bountie of our princes, that if anie come hither from other realms, so soone as they set foot on land they become so free of condition as their masters, whereby all note of servile bondage is utterlie remooved from them." [3] Other observers were of the (correct) opinion that a few lingering vestiges—bondmen whom the progress of freedom had passed by—might still be found in the crannies of the decayed manorial system, but everyone agreed that such vestiges were anachronistic. In fact there were English men and women who were still "bond" in the mid-sixteenth century, but they were few in number and their status was much more a technicality than a condition. In the middle ages, being a villein had meant dependence upon the will of a feudal lord but by no means deprivation of all social and legal rights. In the thirteenth and fourteenth centuries villenage had decayed markedly, and it may be said not to have existed as a viable social institution in the second half of the sixteenth century.[4] Personal freedom had become the

---

[3] [Harrison], *Historicall Description of Britaine*, in *Holinshed's Chronicles*, I, 275.

[4] The best place to start on this complicated subject is Paul Vinagradof, *Villainage in England: Essays in English Mediaeval History* (Oxford, 1892). The least unsatisfactory studies of vestiges seem to be Alexander Savine, "Bondmen under the Tudors," Royal Historical Society, *Transactions*, 2d Ser., 17 (1903), 235–89; I. S. Leadam, "The Last Days of Bondage in England," *Law Quarterly Review*, 9 (1893), 348–65. William S. Holdsworth, *A History of English Law*, 3d ed., 12 vols. (Boston, 1923), III, 491–510, explodes the supposed distinction between villeins *regardant* and *gross*.

normal status of Englishmen. Most contemporaries welcomed this fact; indeed it was after about 1550 that there began to develop in England that preening consciousness of the peculiar glories of English liberties.

How had it all happened? Among those observers who tried to explain, there was agreement that Christianity was primarily responsible. They thought of villenage as a mitigation of ancient bond slavery and that the continuing trend to liberty was animated, as Sir Thomas Smith said in a famous passage, by the "perswasion . . . of Christians not to make nor keepe his brother in Christ, servile, bond and under-ling for ever unto him, as a beast rather than as a man." [5] They agreed also that the trend had been forwarded by the common law, in which the disposition was always, as the phrase went, *in favorem libertatis*, "in favor of liberty." Probably they were correct in both these suppositions, but the common law harbored certain inconsistencies as to freedom which may have had an important though imponderable effect upon the reappearance of slavery in English communities in the seventeenth century.

The accreted structure of the common law somtimes resulted in imperviousness to changing conditions. The first book of Lord Coke's great *Institutes of the Laws of England* (1628), for example, was an extended gloss upon Littleton's fifteenth-century treatise on *Tenures* and it repeatedly quoted the opinions of such famous authorities as Bracton, who had died in 1268. When Bracton had described villenage, English law had not yet fully diverged from the civil or Roman law, and villenage actually existed. Almost four hundred years later some legal authorities were still citing Bracton on villenage without even alluding to the fact that villenage no longer existed. The widely used legal dictionary, Cowell's *Interpreter* (1607 and later editions), quoted Bracton at length and declared that his words "express the nature of our villenage something aptly." [6] Anyone relying solely on Cowell's *Interpreter* would suppose that some Englishmen in the early seventeenth century were hereditary serfs. Thus while villenage was actually extinct, it lay unmistakably fossilized in the common law. Its survival in that rigid form must have reminded Englishmen that there existed a sharply differing alternative to personal liberty. It was in this vague way that villenage seems to have been related to the development of chattel slavery in America. Certainly villenage was not the forerunner of slavery, but its survival in the law books meant that a possibility which might have been foreclosed was not. Later, after Negro slavery had clearly emerged, English lawyers were inclined to think of slavery

    [5] Thomas Smith, *De Republica Anglorum: A Discourse on the Commonwealth of England*, ed. L. Alston (Cambridge, Eng., 1906), 133.
    [6] Coke's section on villenage is Lib. II, cap. XI; see John Cowell, *The Interpreter: Or Booke Containing the Signification of Words* . . . (Cambridge, Eng., 1607), "villein."

as being a New World version of the ancient tenure described by Bracton and Cowell and Coke.

That the common law was running centuries behind social practice was only one of several important factors complicating Tudor thought about the proper status of individuals in society. The social ferment of the sixteenth century resulted not only in the impalpable mood of control and subordination which seems to have affected English perception of Africans but also in the well-known strenuous efforts of Tudor governments to lay restrictions on elements in English society which seemed badly out of control. From at least the 1530's the countryside swarmed with vagrants, sturdy beggars, rogues, and vagabonds, with men who could but would not work. They committed all manner of crimes, the worst of which was remaining idle. It was an article of faith among Tudor commentators (before there were "Puritans" to help propound it) that idleness was the mother of all vice and the chief danger to a well-ordered state. Tudor statesmen valiantly attempted to suppress idleness by means of the famous vagrancy laws. . . . They assumed that everyone belonged in a specific social niche and that anyone failing to labor in the niche assigned to him by Providence must be compelled to do so by authority. . . .

. . . Tudor authorities gradually hammered out the legal framework of a labor system which permitted compulsion but which did not permit so total a loss of freedom as lifetime hereditary slavery. Apprenticeship seemed to them the ideal status, for apprenticeship provided a means of regulating the economy and of guiding youth into acceptable paths of honest industry. By 1600, many writers had come to think of other kinds of bound labor as inferior forms of apprenticeship, involving less of an educative function, less permanence, and a less rigidly contractual basis. This tendency to reason from apprenticeship downward, rather than from penal service up, had the important effect of imparting some of the very strong contractualism in the master-apprentice relationship to less formal varieties of servitude. There were "indentured" servants in England prior to English settlement in America. Their written "indentures" gave visible evidence of the strong element of mutual obligation between master and servant: each retained a copy of the contract which was "indented" at the top so as to match the other.

As things turned out, it was indentured servitude which best met the requirements for settling in America. Of course there were other forms of bound labor which contributed to the process of settlement: many convicts were sent and many children abducted.[7] Yet among all the numerous varieties and degrees of non-freedom which existed in

[7] The "standard" work on this subject unfortunately does not address itself to the problem of origins. Abbot Emerson Smith, *Colonists in Bondage: White Servitude and Convict Labor in America, 1607–1776* (Chapel Hill, 1947).

England, there was none which could have served as a well-formed model for the chattel slavery which developed in America. This is not to say, though, that slavery was an unheard-of novelty in Tudor England. On the contrary, "bond slavery" was a memory trace of long standing. Vague and confused as the concept of slavery was in the minds of Englishmen, it possessed certain fairly consistent connotations which were to help shape English perceptions of the way Europeans should properly treat the newly discovered peoples overseas.

3. The Concept of Slavery

At first glance, one is likely to see merely a fog of inconsistency and vagueness enveloping the terms *servant* and *slave* as they were used both in England and in seventeenth-century America. When Hamlet declaims "O what a rogue and peasant slave am I," the term seems to have a certain elasticity. When Peter Heylyn defines it in 1627 as "that ignominious word, *slave;* whereby we use to call ignoble fellowes, and the more base sort of people," [8] the term seems useless as a key to a specific social status. And when we find in the American colonies a reference in 1665 to "Jacob a negro slave and servant to Nathaniel Utye," [9] it is tempting to regard slavery as having been in the first half of the seventeenth century merely a not very elevated sort of servitude.

In one sense it was, since the concept embodied in the terms *servitude, service,* and *servant* was widely embracive. *Servant* was more a generic term than *slave.* Slaves could be "servants"—as they were eventually and ironically to become in the ante-bellum South—but servants *should not* be "slaves." This injunction, which was common in England, suggests a measure of precision in the concept of slavery. In fact there was a large measure which merits closer inspection.

First of all, the "slave's" loss of freedom was complete. "Of all men which be destitute of libertie or freedome," explained Henry Swinburne in his *Briefe Treatise of Testaments and Last Willes* (1590), "the slave is in greatest subjection, for a slave is that person which is in servitude or bondage to an other, even against nature." "Even his children," moreover, . . . are infected with the Leprosie of his father's bondage." . . . At law, much more clearly than in literary usage, "bond slavery" implied utter deprivation of liberty.

Slavery was also thought of as a perpetual condition. While it had not yet come invariably to mean lifetime labor, it was frequently thought of in those terms. Except sometimes in instances of punishment for crime, slavery was open ended; in contrast to servitude, it did not involve a definite term of years. Slavery was perpetual also in

---

[8] *Hamlet,* II, ii; Heylyn, ΜΙΚΡΌΚΟΣΜΟΣ, 175.
[9] *Archives of Maryland,* XLIX, 489.

the sense that it was often thought of as hereditary. It was these dual aspects of perpetuity which were to assume such importance in America.

So much was slavery a complete loss of liberty that it seemed to Englishmen somehow akin to loss of humanity. No theme was more persistent than the claim that to treat a man as a slave was to treat him as a beast. Almost half a century after Sir Thomas Smith had made this connection a Puritan divine was condemning masters who used "their servants as slaves, or rather as beasts" while Captain John Smith was moaning about being captured by the Turks and "all sold for slaves, like beasts in a marketplace." [10] No analogy could have better demonstrated how strongly Englishmen felt about total loss of personal freedom.

Certain prevalent assumptions about the origins of slavery paralleled this analogy at a different level of intellectual construction. Lawyers and divines alike assumed that slavery was impossible before the Fall, that it violated natural law, that it was instituted by positive human laws, and, more generally, that in various ways it was connected with sin. These ideas were as old as the church fathers and the Roman writers on natural law. In the social atmosphere of pre-Restoration England it was virtually inevitable that they should have been capsulated in the story of Ham. . . . Sir Edward Coke (himself scarcely a Puritan) declared, "This is assured, That Bondage or Servitude was first inflicted for dishonouring of Parents: For Cham the Father of Canaan . . . seeing the Nakedness of his Father Noah, and shewing it in Derision to his Brethren, was therefore punished in his Son Canaan with Bondage." [11]

The great jurist wrote this in earnest, but at least he did offer another description of slavery's genesis. In it he established what was perhaps the most important and widely acknowledged attribute of slavery: at the time of the Flood "all Things were common to all," but afterward, with the emergence of private property, there "arose battles"; "then it was ordained by Constitution of Nations . . . that he that was taken in Battle should remain Bond to his taker for ever, and he to do with him, all that should come of him, his Will and Pleasure, as with his Beast, or any other Cattle, to give, or to sell, or to kill." This final power, Coke noted, had since been taken away (owing to "the Cruelty

[10] William Gouge, *Of Domesticall Duties Eight Treatises* (London, 1622), 690; Edward Arber, ed., *Travels and Works of Captain John Smith* . . . , 2 vols. (Edinburgh, 1910), II, 853.

[11] *The Whole Works of the Right Rev. Jeremy Taylor* . . . , 10 vols. (London, 1850–54), X, 453; Sir Edward Coke, *The First Part of the Institutes of the Laws of England: or, a Commentary upon Littleton* . . . , 12th ed. (London, 1738), Lib. II, Cap. XI. For the long-standing assumption that slavery was brought about by man's sinfulness see R. W. and A. J. Carlyle, *A History of Medieval Political Theory in the West*, 6 vols. (Edinburgh and London, 1903–36), I, 116–24, II, 119–20.

of some Lords") and placed in the hands only of kings.[12] The animating rationale here was that captivity in war meant an end to a person's claim to life as a human being; by sparing the captive's life, the captor acquired virtually absolute power over the life of the man who had lost the power to control his own.

More than any other single quality, *captivity* differentiated slavery from servitude. Although there were other, subsidiary ways of becoming a slave, such as being born of slave parents, selling oneself into slavery, or being adjudged to slavery for crime, none of these were considered to explain the way slavery had originated. Slavery was a power relationship; servitude was a relationship of service. Men were "slaves" to the devil but "servants" of God. Men were "galley-slaves," not galley servants. Bondage had never existed in the county of Kent because Kent was "never vanquished by [William] the Conquerour, but yeelded it selfe by composition." [13]

This tendency to equate slavery with captivity had important ramifications. Warfare was usually waged against another people; captives were usually foreigners—"strangers" as they were termed. Until the emergence of nation-states in Europe, by far the most important category of strangers was the non-Christian. International warfare seemed above all a ceaseless struggle between Christians and Turks. Slavery, therefore, frequently appeared to rest upon the "perpetual enmity" which existed between Christians on the one hand and "infidels" and "pagans" on the other.[14] In the sixteenth and seventeenth centuries Englishmen at home could read scores of accounts concerning the miserable fate of Englishmen and other Christians taken into "captivity" by Turks and Moors and oppressed by the "verie worst manner of bondmanship and slaverie." [15] Clearly slavery was tinged by the religious disjunction.

Just as many commentators thought that the spirit of Christianity was responsible for the demise of bondage in England, many divines distinguished between ownership of Christian and of non-Christian servants. The Reverend William Gouge referred to "such servants as being strangers were bond-slaves, over whom masters had a more absolute power than others." The Reverend Henry Smith declared, "He

[12] Coke, *Institutes*, Lib. II, Cap. XI.

[13] William Lambard[e], *A Perambulation of Kent* . . . (London, 1576), II. The notion of selling oneself into slavery was very much subsidiary and probably derived from the Old Testament. Isaac Mendelsohn, *Slavery in the Ancient Near East* . . . (N.Y., 1949), 18, points out that the Old Testament was the only ancient law code to mention voluntary slavery and self-sale.

[14] The phrases are from Michael Dalton, *The Countrey Justice* . . . (London, 1655), 191.

[15] *The Estate of Christians, Living under the Subjection of the Turke* . . . (London, 1595), 5.

which counteth his servant a slave, is in error: for there is difference
betweene beleeving servants and infidell servants." [16] Implicit in every
clerical discourse was the assumption that common brotherhood in
Christ imparted a special quality to the master-servant relationship.

Slavery did not possess that quality, which made it fortunate that
Englishmen did not enslave one another. As we have seen, however,
Englishmen did possess a *concept* of slavery, formed by the clustering of
several rough but not illogical equations. The slave was treated like a
beast. Slavery was inseparable from the evil in men; it was God's punishment upon Ham's prurient disobedience. Enslavement was captivity,
the loser's lot in a contest of power. Slaves were infidels or heathens.

On every count, Negroes qualified.

4. The Practices of Portingals and Spanyards

Which is not to say that Englishmen were casting about for a people
to enslave. What happened was that they found thrust before them not
only instances of Negroes being taken into slavery but attractive opportunities for joining in that business. Englishmen actually were
rather slow to seize these opportunities; on most of the sixteenth-century English voyages to West Africa there was no dealing in slaves.
The notion that it was appropriate to do so seems to have been drawn
chiefly from the example set by the Spanish and Portuguese.

Without inquiring into the reasons, it can be said that slavery had
persisted since ancient times in the Iberian peninsula, that prior to the
discoveries it was primarily a function of the religious wars against the
Moors,[17] that Portuguese explorers pressing down the coast in the fif-
teenth century captured thousands of Negroes whom they carried back
to Portugal as slaves, and that after 1500, Portuguese ships began supplying the Spanish and Portuguese settlements in America with Negro
slaves. By 1550 European enslavement of Negroes was more than a
century old, and Negro slavery had become a fixture of the New
World.

For present purposes there is no need to inquire into the precise nature of this slavery except to point out that in actual practice it did fit
the English concept of bond slavery. The question which needs answering pertains to contemporary English knowledge of what was going on. And the answer may be given concisely: Englishmen had easily
at hand a great deal of not very precise information.

[16] Gouge, *Domesticall Duties*, 663; *The Sermons of Master Henry Smith* . . . (London,
1607), 40.

[17] The complex situation is set forth by Charles Verlinden, *L'Esclavage dans L'Europe
Médiévale. Vol. I, Péninsule Ibérique-France* (Brugge, 1955). The still prevalent state of enmity becomes clear in Franklin L. Baumer, "England, the Turk, and the Common Corps
of Christendom," *American Historical Review*, 50 (1944–45), 26–48; Chew, *The Crescent
and the Rose*.

The news that Negroes were being carried off to forced labor in America was broadcast across the pages of the Hakluyt and Purchas collections. While only one account stated explicitly that Negroes "be their slaves during their life," it was clear that the Portuguese and Spaniards treated Negroes and frequently the Indians as "slaves." [18] This was the term customarily used by English voyagers and by translators of foreign . . . documents. Readers of a lament about the treatment of Indians in Brazil by an unnamed Portuguese could hardly mistake learning that slavery there was a clearly defined condition: Indians held "a title of free" but were treated as "slaves, all their lives," and when masters died the poor Indians "remaine in their wils with the name of free, but bound to serve their children perpetually . . . as if they were lawful slaves." . . . Repeatedly the language employed in these widely read books gave clear indication of how the Negro was involved. William Towrson was told by a Negro in 1556 "that the Portingals were bad men, and that they made them slaves, if they could take them, and would put yrons upon their legges." There were "rich trades" on that coast in Negroes "which be caried continually to the West Indies." The Portuguese in the Congo "have divers rich Commodities from this Kingdome, but the most important is every yeere about five thousand Slaves, which they transport from thence, and sell them at good round prices in . . . the West Indies." In the New World the Spaniards "buy many slaves to follow their husbandry" and had "Negros to worke in the mynes.". . .

Some Englishmen decided that there might be profit in supplying the Spanish with Negroes, despite the somewhat theoretical prohibition of foreigners from the Spanish dominions in the New World. John Hawkins was first; in the 1560's he made three voyages to Africa, the islands, and home. The first two were very successful; the third met disaster at San Juan de Ulua when the Spanish attacked his ships, took most of them, and turned the captured English seamen over to the Inquisition.[19] This famous incident . . . may have done something to discourage English slave trading in favor of other maritime activities. English vessels were not again active frequently in the slave trade until the next century.

As assiduously collected by Richard Hakluyt, the various accounts of the Hawkins voyages did not state explicitly that English seamen were making "slaves" of Negroes. They scarcely needed to do so. On the

---

[18] Hakluyt, *Principall Navigations* (1589), 572; see also the comment, "It is good traffiking with the people of Guinea, specialy with such as are not over ruled and opprest by the Portingales, which take the people, and make them slaves, for which they are hated," in *John Huigen van Linschoten. His Discours of Voyages into the Easte and West Indies . . . ,* trans. William Phillip (London, [1598]), 198.

[19] Well told by Rayner Unwin, *The Defeat of John Hawkins: A Biography of His Third Slaving Voyage* (N.Y., 1960).

first voyage in 1562 Hawkins learned at the Canary Islands "that Negroes were very good merchandise in Hispaniola, and that store of Negroes might easily be had upon the coast of Guinea." At Sierra Leone Hawkins "got into his possession, partly by the sword, and partly by other meanes . . . 300. Negroes at the least." Thereupon, "with this praye" he sailed westwards where he "made vent of" the Negroes to the Spaniards. On his second voyage he was able to get hold of Negroes from one tribe which another tribe "tooke in the warres, as their slaves," and he attacked the town of Bymba where the "Portingals" told him, "hee might gette a hundreth slaves." On the third voyage, in 1567, Hawkins agreed with an African chief to join in attacking another town "with promise, that as many Negroes as by these warres might be obtained, as well of his part as ours, should be at our pleasure." . . .

By the end of the first quarter of the seventeenth century it had become abundantly evident in England that Negroes were being enslaved on an international scale. A century before, Leo Africanus had referred frequently to "Negro-slaves" in North Africa. By 1589 Negroes had become so preeminently "slaves" that Richard Hakluyt gratuitously referred to five Africans brought temporarily to England as "black slaves." [20] Readers of Hakluyt, Purchas, and other popular accounts were informed that the Dutch had "Blacks (which are Slaves)" in the East Indies; that Greeks ventured "into Arabia to steale Negroes"; that the "blacks of Mozambique" were frequently taken as "slaves" to India, and, according to George Sandys, that near Cairo merchants purchased "Negroes" (for "slavery") who came from the upper Nile and were "descended of *Chus*, the Sonne of cursed *Cham;* as are all of that complexion." [21]

As suggested by Sandys's remark, an equation had developed between African Negroes and slavery. Primarily, the associations were with the Portuguese and Spanish, with captivity, with buying and selling in Guinea and in America. . . . [Yet] there is no reason to suppose Englishmen eager to enslave Negroes, nor even to regard Richard Jobson eccentric in his response to a chief's offer to buy some "slaves": "I made answer, We were a people, who did not deale in any such commodities, neither did wee buy or sell one another, or any that had our owne shapes." [22] By the seventeenth century, after all, English prejudices as well as English law were *in favorem libertatis.*

[20] Leo Africanus, *The History and Description of Africa,* trans. Pory, ed. Brown, I, 76–77, II, 309, 482, III, 724, 780, 791, 835; Hakluyt, *Principall Navigations* (1589), 97.

[21] Purchas, *Purchas His Pilgrimes,* IV, 519; Hakluyt, *Principall Navigations,* V, 301–2; Burnell and Tiele, *Voyage of Linschoten,* I, 275; [George Sandys], *A Relation of a Journey Begun An: Dom: 1610 . . .* , 2d ed. (London, 1621), 136, which was reprinted by Purchas, *Purchas His Pilgrimes,* VI, 213.

[22] Jobson, *The Golden Trade,* ed. Kingsley, 112.

When they came to settle in America, Englishmen found that things happened to liberty, some favorable, some not. Negroes became slaves, partly because there were social and economic necessities in America which called for some sort of bound, controlled labor. The Portuguese and Spanish had set an example, which, however rough in outline, proved to be, at very least, suggestive to Englishmen. It would be surprising if there had been a clear-cut line of influence from Latin to English slavery.[23] Elizabethans were not in the business of modeling themselves after Spaniards. Yet from about 1550, Englishmen were in such continual contact with the Spanish that they could hardly have failed to acquire the notion that Negroes could be enslaved. Precisely what slavery *meant*, of course, was a matter of English preconceptions patterning the information from overseas, but from the first, Englishmen tended to associate, in a diffuse way, Negroes with the Portuguese and Spanish. The term *negro* itself was incorporated into English from the Hispanic languages in mid-sixteenth century and *mulatto* a half century later. This is the more striking because a perfectly adequate term, identical in meaning to *negro*, already existed in English; of course *black* was used also, though not so commonly in the sixteenth century as later. . . .

By 1640 it was becoming apparent that in many of the new colonies overseas the English settlers had obtained Negroes and were holding them, frequently, as hereditary slaves for life. In considering the development of slavery in various groups of colonies [it is important to remember that the slave] status was at first distinguished from servitude more by duration than by onerousness; the key term in . . . many . . . early descriptions of the Negro's condition was *perpetual*. Negroes served "for ever" and so would their children. Englishmen did not do so. . . . Servitude, no matter how long, brutal, and involuntary, was not the same thing as perpetual slavery. Servitude comprehended alike the young apprentice, the orphan, the indentured servant, the redemptioner, the convicted debtor or criminal, the political prisoner, and, even, the Scottish and Irish captive of war who was sold as a "slave" to New England or Barbados. Yet none of these persons, no matter how miserably treated, served for life in the colonies, though of course many died before their term ended.[24] Hereditary lifetime service was

---

[23] The *clearest* instance of *direct* influence in America is probably the experience of Christopher Newport who was in Virginia five times between 1607 and 1611 and who had commanded a voyage in 1591 to the West Indies on which, as a member of his company reported, "wee tooke a Portugall ship . . . from Gunie . . . bound for Cartagena, wherein were 300. Negros young and olde." The English mariners took the prize to Puerto Rico and sent a Portuguese merchant ashore because "he hoped to help us to some money for his Negros there." Hakluyt, *Principall Navigations*, X, 184–85.

[24] Smith, *Colonists in Bondage*, 171, said flatly that "there was never any such thing as perpetual slavery for any white man in any English colony." To my knowledge, he was correct.

restricted to Indians and Negroes. Among the various English colonies in the New World, this service known as "slavery" seems first to have developed in the international cockpit known as the Caribbean.

5. Enslavement: The West Indies

The Englishmen who settled the Caribbean colonies were not very different from those who went to Virginia, Bermuda, Maryland, or even New England. Their experience in the islands, however, was very different indeed. By 1640 there were roughly as many English in the little islands as on the American continent. A half century after the first settlements were established in the 1620's, the major islands—Barbados, St. Kitts and the other Leeward Islands—were overcrowded. Thousands of whites who had been squeezed off the land by burgeoning sugar plantations migrated to other English colonies, including much larger Jamaica which had been captured from the Spanish in 1655. Their places were taken by Negro slaves who had been shipped to the islands, particularly after 1640, to meet an insatiable demand for labor which was cheap to maintain, easy to dragoon, and simple to replace when worked to death. Negroes outnumbered whites in Barbados as early as 1660. This rapid and thorough commitment to slavery placed white settlers under an ever-present danger of slave rebellion (the first rising came in 1638 on Providence Island), and whereas in the very early years authorities had rightly been fearful of white servant revolt, by the 1670's they were casting about desperately for means to attract white servants as protection against foreign and servile attack. Negro slavery matured hothouse fashion in the islands.

This compression of development was most clearly evident in the Puritan colony on the tiny island of Providence 150 miles off the coast of Central America, first settled in 1629 though not a going concern for several years. During the brief period before the Spanish snuffed out the colony in 1641 the settlers bought so many Negroes that white men were nearly outnumbered, and in England the Providence Company, apprehensive over possible Negro uprisings (with good reason as it turned out), drew up regulations for restricting the ratio of slaves to white men, "well knowing that if all men be left at Libty to buy as they please no man will take of English servants." [25] Not only were Ne-

---

[25] Earl of Holland, John Pym, Robert Warwick, and others to Governor and Council, London, July 3, 1638, Box 9, bundle: 2d and last portion of List no. 3, *re* Royal African Co. and Slavery Matters, 17. Parish Transcripts, New-York Historical Society, New York City. For Providence, see Arthur P. Newton, *The Colonising Activities of the English Puritans: The Last Phase of the Elizabethan Struggle with Spain* (New Haven, 1914); for further details on early slavery in the English West Indies and New England, Winthrop D. Jordan, "The Influence of the West Indies on the Origins of New England Slavery," *William and Mary Quarterly*, 3d Ser., 18 (1961), 243–50.

groes cheaper to maintain but it was felt that they could legitimately be treated in a different way from Englishmen—they could be held to service for life. At least this was the impression prevailing among officials of the Providence Company in London, for in 1638 they wrote Governor Nathaniel Butler and the Council, "We also think it reasonable that wheras the English servants are to answer XX [pounds of tobacco] per head the Negros being procured at Cheaper rates more easily kept as perpetuall servants should answer 40 [pounds of tobacco] per head. And the rather that the desire of English bodyes may be kept, we are depending upon them for the defence of the Island. We shall also expect that Negroes perform service in the publique works in double proporcon to the English." [26]

In Barbados this helpful idea that Negroes served for life seems to have existed even before they were purchased in large numbers. In 1627 the ship bearing the first eighty settlers captured a prize from which ten Negroes were seized, so white men and Negroes settled the island together.[27] Any doubt which may have existed as to the appropriate status of Negroes was dispelled in 1636 when Governor Henry Hawley and the Council resolved "that *Negroes* and *Indians*, that came here to be sold, should serve for Life, unless a Contract was before made to the contrary." [28] Europeans were not treated in this manner: in 1643 Governor Philip Bell set at liberty fifty Portuguese who had been captured in Brazil and then offered for sale to Barbadians by a Dutch ship. The Governor seems to have been shocked by the proposed sale of Christian white men.[29] In the 1650's several observers referred to the lifetime slavery of Negroes as if it were a matter of common knowledge. "Its the Custome for a Christian servant to serve foure yeares," one wrote at the beginning of the decade, "and then enjoy his freedome; and (which hee hath dearly earned) 10£ Ster. or the value of it in goods if his Master bee soe honest as to pay it; the Negros and Indians (of which latter there are but few here) they and the generation are Slaves to their owners to perpetuity." The widely read Richard Ligon wrote in 1657: "The Iland is divided into three sorts of men, *viz.* Masters, Servants, and slaves. The slaves and their posterity, being subject to their Masters for ever, are kept and preserv'd with greater care then the servants, who are theirs but for five yeers, ac-

---

[26] Earl of Holland and others to Governor and Council, July 3, 1638, Box 9, bundle: 2d and last portion of List no. 3, *re* Royal African Co. and Slavery Matters, 17, Parish Transcripts, N.-Y. Hist. Soc.

[27] Vincent T. Harlow, *A History of Barbados, 1625–1685* (Oxford, 1926), 4.

[28] [William Duke], *Memoirs of the First Settlement of the Island of Barbados and Other the Carribee Islands, with the Succession of the Governors and Commanders in Chief of Barbados to the Year 1742 . . .* (London, 1743), 20.

[29] Alan Burns, *History of the British West Indies* (London, 1954), 232*n*.

cording to the law of the Iland." [30] Finally, one Henry Whistler described the people of the island delightfully in 1655:

> The genterey heare doth live far better than ours doue in England: thay have most of them 100 or 2 or 3 of slaves apes whou they command as they pleas: hear they may say what they have is thayer oune: and they have that Libertie of contienc which wee soe long have in England foght for: But they doue abus it. This Island is inhabited with all sortes: with English, french, Duch, Scotes, Irish, Spaniards thay being Jues: with Ingones and miserabell Negors borne to perpetuall slavery thay and thayer seed: these Negors they doue alow as many wifes as thay will have, sume will have 3 or 4, according as they find thayer bodie abell: our English heare doth think a negor child the first day it is born to be worth 05^{li}, they cost them noething the bringing up, they goe all ways naked: some planters will have 30 more or les about 4 or 5 years ould: they sele them from one to the other as we doue shepe. This Illand is the Dunghill wharone England doth cast forth its rubidg: Rodgs and hors and such like peopcl are those which are gennerally Broght heare. [31]

Dunghill or no dunghill, Barbados was treating her Negroes as slaves for life.

The rapid introduction of Negro slavery into the English islands was accomplished without leaving any permanent trace of hesitation or misgivings. This was not the case in many of the continental colonies, both because different geographic and economic conditions prevailed there and because these conditions permitted a more complete and successful transplantation of English ways and values. This difference was particularly pronounced in New England, and it was therefore particularly ironic that the treatment accorded Negroes in New England seems to have been directly influenced by the West Indian model.

6. Enslavement: New England

. . . The question with New England slavery is not why it was weakly rooted, but why it existed at all. No staple crop demanded regiments of raw labor. That there was no compelling economic demand for Ne-

[30] "A Breife Description of the Ilande of Barbados," Vincent T. Harlow, ed., *Colonising Expeditions to the West Indies and Guiana, 1623–1667* (*Works Issued by the Hakluyt Soc.*, 2d Ser., 56 [1925]), 44–45; Richard Ligon, *A True and Exact History of the Island of Barbadoes* . . . (London, 1657), 43.

[31] "Extracts from Henry Whistler's Journal of the West India Expedition," Charles H. Firth, ed., *The Narrative of General Venables, with an Appendix of Papers Relating to the Expedition to the West Indies and the Conquest of Jamaica, 1654–1655* (London, 1900), 146.

groes is evident in the numbers actually imported: economic exigencies scarcely required establishment of a distinct status for only 3 per cent of the labor force. Indentured servitude was adequate to New England's needs, and in fact some Negroes became free servants rather than slaves. Why, then, did New Englanders enslave Negroes, probably as early as 1638? Why was it that the Puritans rather mindlessly (which was not their way) accepted slavery for Negroes and Indians but not for white men?

The early appearance of slavery in New England may in part be explained by the provenance of the first Negroes imported. They were brought by Captain William Peirce of the Salem ship *Desire* in 1638 from the Providence Island colony where Negroes were already being kept as perpetual servants.[32] A minor traffic in Negroes and other products developed between the two Puritan colonies, though evidently some of the Negroes proved less than satisfactory, for Governor Butler was cautioned by the Providence Company to take special care of "the cannibal negroes brought from New England." [33] After 1640 a brisk trade got under way between New England and the other English islands, and Massachusetts vessels sometimes touched upon the West African coast before heading for the Caribbean. Trade with Barbados was particularly lively, and Massachusetts vessels carried Negroes to that bustling colony from Africa and the Cape Verde Islands. As John Winthrop gratefully described the salvation of New England's economy, "it pleased the Lord to open to us a trade with Barbados and other Islands in the West Indies." [34] These strange Negroes from the West Indies must surely have been accompanied by prevailing notions about their usual status. Ship masters who purchased perpetual service in Barbados would not have been likely to sell service for term in Boston. Then too, white settlers from the crowded islands migrated to New England, 1,200 from Barbados alone in the years 1643–47.[35]

No amount of contact with the West Indies could have by itself created Negro slavery in New England; settlers there had to be willing to accept the proposition. Because they were Englishmen, they were so prepared—and at the same time they were not. Characteristically, as Puritans, they officially codified this ambivalence in 1641 as follows: "there shall never be any bond-slavery, villenage or captivitie amongst us; unlesse it be lawful captives taken in just warrs, and such strangers as willingly sell themselves, or are solde to us: and such shall have the libertyes and christian usages which the law of God established in Is-

[32] John Winthrop, *Winthrop's Journal: "History of New England," 1634–1649*, ed. James K. Hosmer, 2 vols. (N.Y., 1908), I, 260.

[33] Newton, *Colonising Activities of the English Puritans*, 260–61.

[34] Winthrop, *Journal*, ed. Hosmer, II, 73–74, 328; Donnan, ed., *Documents of the Slave Trade*, III, 4–5, 6, 9, 10, 11–14.

[35] Harlow, *Barbados*, 340.

raell concerning such persons doth morally require, provided, this exempts none from servitude who shall be judged thereto by Authoritie." [36] Here were the wishes of the General Court as expressed in the Massachusetts Body of Liberties, which is to say that as early as 1641 the Puritan settlers were seeking to guarantee in writing their own liberty without closing off the opportunity of taking it from others whom they identified with the Biblical term, "strangers." It was under the aegis of this concept that Theophilus Eaton, one of the founders of New Haven, seems to have owned Negroes before 1658 who were "servants forever or during his pleasure, according to Leviticus, 25:45 and 46." [37] . . . Apart from this implication that bond slavery was reserved to those not partaking of true religion nor possessing proper nationality, the Body of Liberties expressly reserved the colony's right to enslave convicted criminals. For reasons not clear, this endorsement of an existing practice was followed almost immediately by discontinuance of its application to white men. The first instance of penal "slavery" in Massachusetts came in 1636, when an Indian was sentenced to "bee kept as a slave for life to worke, unles wee see further cause." Then in December 1638, ten months after the first Negroes arrived, the Quarter Court for the first time sentenced three white offenders to be "slaves"—a suggestive but perhaps meaningless coincidence. Having by June 1642 sentenced altogether some half dozen white men to "slavery" (and explicitly releasing several after less than a year) the Court stopped.[38] Slavery, as had been announced in the Body of Liberties, was to be only for "strangers."

The Body of Liberties made equally clear that captivity in a just war constituted legitimate grounds for slavery. The practice had begun during the first major conflict with the Indians, the Pequot War of 1637. Some of the Pequot captives had been shipped aboard the *Desire*, to Providence Island; accordingly, the first Negroes in New England arrived in exchange for men taken captive in a just war! That this provenance played an important role in shaping views about Negroes is suggested by the first recorded plea by an Englishman on the North American continent for the establishment of an African slave trade. Emanuel Downing, in a letter to his brother-in-law John Winthrop in 1645, described the advantages: "If upon a Just warre [with the Narra-

---

[36] Max Farrand, ed., *The Laws and Liberties of Massachusetts* (Cambridge, Mass., 1929), 4. See the very good discussion in George H. Moore, *Notes on the History of Slavery in Massachusetts* (N.Y., 1866).

[37] Simeon E. Baldwin, "Theophilus Eaton, First Governor of the Colony of New Haven," New Haven Colony Historical Society, *Papers*, 7 (1908), 31.

[38] Nathaniel B. Shurtleff, ed., *Records of the Governor and Company of the Massachusetts Bay in New England*, 5 vols. in 6 (Boston, 1853–54), I, 181, 246; John Noble and John F. Cronin, eds., *Records of the Court of Assistants of the Colony of the Massachusetts Bay, 1630–1692*, 3 vols. (Boston, 1901–28), II, 78–79, 86, 90, 94, 97, 118.

gansett Indians] the Lord should deliver them into our hands, wee
might easily have men woemen and children enough to exchange for
Moores, which wilbe more gaynefull pilladge for us then wee conceive,
for I doe not see how wee can thrive untill wee get into a stock of
slaves sufficient to doe all our business, for our children's children will
hardly see this great Continent filled with people, soe that our servants
will still desire freedome to plant for themselves, and not stay but for
verie great wages. And I suppose you know verie well how wee shall
mayneteyne 20 Moores cheaper than one Englishe servant." [39]

These two facets of justifiable enslavement—punishment for crime
and captivity in war—were closely related. Slavery as punishment
probably derived from analogy with captivity, since presumably a king
or magistrates could mercifully spare and enslave a man whose crime
had forfeited his right to life. The analogy had not been worked out by
commentators in England, but a fairly clear linkage between crime and
captivity seems to have existed in the minds of New Englanders concerning Indian slavery. In 1644 the commissioners of the United
Colonies meeting at New Haven decided, in light of the Indians'
"proud affronts," "hostile practices," and "protectinge or rescuinge of
offenders," that magistrates might "send some convenient strength of
English and, . . . seise and bring away" Indians from any "plantation
of Indians" which persisted in this practice and, if no satisfaction was
forthcoming, could deliver the "Indians seased . . . either to serve or
be shipped out and exchanged for Negroes." [40] Captivity and criminal
justice seemed to mean the same thing, slavery.

It would be wrong to suppose that all the Puritans' preconceived
ideas about freedom and bondage worked in the same direction. While
the concepts of difference in religion and of captivity worked against
Indians and Negroes, certain Scriptural injunctions and English pride
in liberty told in the opposite direction. In Massachusetts the magistrates demonstrated that they were not about to tolerate glaring
breaches of "the Law of God established in Israel" even when the victims were Negroes. In 1646 the authorities arrested two mariners,
James Smith and Thomas Keyser, who had carried two Negroes directly from Africa and sold them in Massachusetts. What distressed
the General Court was that the Negroes had been obtained during a
raid on an African village and that this "haynos and crying sinn of man
stealing" had transpired on the Lord's Day. The General Court decided to free the unfortunate victims and ship them back to Africa,

[39] Donnan, ed., *Documents of the Slave Trade*, III, 8.

[40] Nathaniel B. Shurtleff and David Pulsifer, eds., *Records of the Colony of New Plymouth
in New England*, 12 vols. (Boston, 1855–61), IX, 70–71. See also Ebenezer Hazard,
comp., *Historica Collections; Consisting of State Papers, and Other Authentic Documents* . . . ,
2 vols. (Phila., 1792–94), II, 63–64.

though the death penalty for the crime (clearly mandatory in Scripture) was not imposed.[41] More quietly than in this dramatic incident, Puritan authorities extended the same protections against maltreatment to Negroes and Indians as to white servants. . . .

. . . From the first, however, there were scattered signs that Negroes were regarded as different from English people not merely in their status as slaves. In 1639 Samuel Maverick of Noddles Island attempted, apparently rather clumsily, to breed two of his Negroes, or so an English visitor reported: "*Mr. Maverick* was desirous to have a breed of Negroes, and therefore seeing [that his "Negro woman"] would not yield by persuasions to company with a Negro young man he had in his house; he commanded him will'd she nill'd she to go to bed to her which was no sooner done but she kickt him out again, this she took in high disdain beyond her slavery." In 1652 the Massachusetts General Court ordered that Scotsmen, Indians, and Negroes should train with the English in the militia, but four years later abruptly excluded Negroes, as did Connecticut in 1660.[42] Evidently Negroes, even free Negroes, were regarded as distinct from the English. They were, in New England where economic necessities were not sufficiently pressing to determine the decision, treated differently from other men.

7. Enslavement: Virginia and Maryland

In Virginia and Maryland the development of Negro slavery followed a very different course, for several reasons. Most obviously, geographic conditions and the intentions of the settlers quickly combined to produce a successful agricultural staple. The deep tidal rivers, the long growing season, the fertile soil, and the absence of strong communal spirit among the settlers opened the way. Ten years after settlers first landed at Jamestown they were on the way to proving, in the face of assertions to the contrary, that it was possible "to found an empire upon smoke." More than the miscellaneous productions of New England, tobacco required labor which was cheap but not temporary, mobile but not independent, and tireless rather than skilled. In the Chesapeake area more than anywhere to the northward, the shortage of labor and the abundance of land—the "frontier"—placed a premium on involuntary labor.

[41] Donnan, ed., *Documents of the Slave Trade*, III, 6–9. Exodus 21:16: "And he that stealeth a man, and selleth him, or if he be found in his hand, he shall surely be put to death." Compare with Deuteronomy 24:7: "If a man be found stealing any of his brethren of the children of Israel, and maketh merchandise of him, or selleth him; then that thief shall die; and thou shalt put evil away from among you."

[42] John Josselyn, *An Account of Two Voyages to New-England* . . . , 2d ed. (London, 1675), reprinted in Massachusetts Historical Society, *Collections*, 3d Ser., 3 (1833), 231; Shurtleff, ed., *Records of Massachusetts Bay*, III, 268, 397, IV, Pt. i, 86, 257; *Acts and Resolves Mass.*, I, 130; Trumbull and Hoadly, eds., *Recs. Col. Conn.*, I, 349.

This need for labor played more directly upon these settlers' ideas about freedom and bondage than it did either in the West Indies or in New England. Perhaps it would be more accurate to say that settlers in Virginia (and in Maryland after settlement in 1634) made their decisions concerning Negroes while relatively virginal, relatively free from external influences and from firm preconceptions. Of all the important early English settlements, Virginia had the least contact with the Spanish, Portuguese, Dutch, and other English colonies. At the same time, the settlers of Virginia did not possess either the legal or Scriptural learning of the New England Puritans whose conception of the just war had opened the way to the enslavement of Indians. Slavery in the tobacco colonies did not begin as an adjunct of captivity; in marked contrast to the Puritan response to the Pequot War the settlers of Virginia did *not* generally react to the Indian massacre of 1622 with propositions for taking captives and selling them as "slaves." It was perhaps a correct measure of the conceptual atmosphere in Virginia that there was only one such proposition after the 1622 disaster and that that one was defective in precision as to how exactly one treated captive Indians.[43]

In the absence, then, of these influences which obtained in other English colonies, slavery as it developed in Virginia and Maryland assumes a special interest and importance over and above the fact that Negro slavery was to become a vitally important institution there and, later, to the southwards. In the tobacco colonies it is possible to watch Negro slavery *develop*, not pop up full-grown overnight, and it is therefore possible to trace, very imperfectly, the development of the shadowy, unexamined rationale which supported it. The concept of Negro slavery there was neither borrowed from foreigners, nor extracted from books, nor invented out of whole cloth, nor extrapolated from servitude, not generated by English reaction to Negroes as such, nor necessitated by the exigencies of the New World. Not any one of these made the Negro a slave, but all.

In rough outline, slavery's development in the tobacco colonies seems to have undergone three stages. Negroes first arrived in 1619, only a few days late for the meeting of the first representative assembly in America. John Rolfe described the event with the utmost unconcern: "About the last of August came in a dutch man of warre that sold us twenty Negars." [44]

Negroes continued to trickle in slowly for the next half century; one report in 1649 estimated that there were three hundred among Virginia's population of fifteen thousand—about 2 per cent.[45] Long be-

[43] Kingsbury, ed., *Recs. Virginia Company*, III, 672–73, 704–7.

[44] Arber, ed., *Travels of John Smith*, II, 541.

[45] *A Perfect Description of Virginia* . . . (London, 1649), reprinted in Peter Force, ed., *Tracts* . . . , 4 vols. (N.Y., 1947), II, no. 8.

fore there were more appreciable numbers, the development of slavery had, so far as we can tell, shifted gears. Prior to about 1640, there is very little evidence to show how Negroes were treated—though we will need to return to those first twenty years in a moment. After 1640 there is mounting eidence that some Negroes were in fact being treated as slaves, at least they they were being held in hereditary lifetime service. This is to say that the twin essences of slavery—the two kinds of perpetuity—first become evident during the twenty years prior to the beginning of legal formulation. After 1660 slavery was written into statute law. Negroes began to flood into the two colonies at the end of the seventeenth century. In 1705 Virginia produced a codification of laws applying to slaves.

Concerning the first of these stages, there is only one major historical certainty, and unfortunately it is the sort which historians find hardest to bear. There simply is not enough evidence to indicate with any certainty whether Negroes were treated like white servants or not. At least we can be confident, therefore, that the two most common assertions about the first Negroes—that they were slaves and that they were servants—are *unfounded*, though not necessarily incorrect. And what of the positive evidence?

Some of the first group bore Spanish names and presumably had been baptized, which would mean they were at least nominally Christian, though of the Papist sort. They had been "sold" to the English; so had other Englishmen but not by the Dutch. Certainly these Negroes were not fully free, but many Englishmen were not. It can be said, though, that from the first in Virginia Negroes were set apart from white men by the word *Negroes*. The earliest Virginia census reports plainly distinguished Negroes from white men, often giving Negroes no personal name; in 1629 every commander of the several plantations was ordered to "take a gcnerall muster of all the inhabitants men woemen and Children as well *Englishe* as Negroes." [46] A distinct name is not attached to a group unless it is regarded as distinct. It seems logical to suppose that this perception of the Negro as being distinct from the Englishman must have operated to debase his status rather than to raise it, for in the absence of countervailing social factors, the need for labor in the colonies usually told in the direction of non-freedom. There were few countervailing factors present, surely, in such instances as in 1629 when a group of Negroes were brought to Virginia freshly captured from a Portuguese vessel which had snatched them from Angola a few weeks earlier.[47] Given the context of English

[46] Henry R. McIlwaine, ed., *Minutes of the Council and General Court of Colonial Virginia, 1622–1632, 1670–1676* (Richmond, 1924), 196. Lists and musters of 1624 and 1625 are in John C. Hotten, ed., *The Original Lists of Persons of Quality . . .* (N.Y., 1880), 169–265.

[47] Philip A. Bruce, *Economic History of Virginia in the Seventeenth Century . . .* , 2 vols. (N.Y., 1896), II, 73.

thought and experience sketched in this chapter, it seems probable that the Negro's status was not ever the same as that accorded the white servant. But we do not know for sure.

When the first fragmentary evidence appears about 1640 it becomes clear that *some* Negroes in both Virginia and Maryland were serving for life and some Negro children inheriting the same obligation.[48] Not all Negroes, certainly, for Nathaniel Littleton had released a Negro named Anthony Longoe from all service whatsoever in 1635, and after the mid-1640's the court records show that other Negroes were incontestably free and were accumulating property of their own. At least one Negro freeman, Anthony Johnson, himself owned a Negro. Some Negroes served only terms of usual length, but others were held for terms far longer than custom and statute permitted with white servants.[49] The first fairly clear indication that slavery was practiced in the tobacco colonies appears in 1639, when a Maryland statute declared that "all the Inhabitants of this Province being Christians (Slaves excepted) Shall have and enjoy all such rights liberties immunities priviledges and free customs within this Province as any naturall born subject of England." Another Maryland law passed the same year provided that "all persons being Christians (Slaves excepted)" over eighteen who were imported without indentures would serve for four years.[50] These laws make very little sense unless the term *slaves* meant Negroes and perhaps Indians.

The next year, 1640, the first definite indication of outright enslavement appears in Virginia. The General Court pronounced sentence on three servants who had been retaken after absconding to Maryland. Two of them, a Dutchman and a Scot, were ordered to serve their masters for one additional year and then the colony for three more, but "the third being a negro named John Punch shall serve his said master or his assigns for the time of his natural life here or else where." No white servant in any English colony, so far as is known, ever received a like sentence. Later the same month a Negro (possibly the same enterprising fellow) was again singled out from a group of recaptured runaways; six of the seven culprits were assigned additional time while the Negro was given none, presumably because he was already serving for life.[51]

After 1640, when surviving Virginia county court records began to mention Negroes, sales for life, often including any future progeny,

---

[48] Further details are in Winthrop D. Jordan, "Modern Tensions and the Origins of American Slavery," *Journal of Southern History*, 28 (1962), 18–30.

[49] Susie M. Ames, *Studies of the Virginia Eastern Shore in the Seventeenth Century* (Richmond, 1940), 99; John H. Russell, *The Free Negro in Virginia, 1619–1865* (Baltimore, 1913), 23–39; and his "Colored Freemen As Slave Owners in Virginia," *Journal of Negro History*, 1 (1916), 234–37.

[50] *Archives Md.*, I, 41, 80, also 409, 453–54.

[51] "Decisions of the General Court," *Virginia Magazine of History and Biography*, 5 (1898), 236–37.

were recorded in unmistakable language. In 1646 Francis Pott sold a Negro woman and boy to Stephen Charlton "to the use of him . . . forever." Similarly, six years later William Whittington sold to John Pott" one Negro girle named Jowan; aged about Ten yeares and with her Issue and produce duringe her (or either of them) for their Life tyme. And their Successors forever"; and a Maryland man in 1649 deeded two Negro men and a woman "and all their issue both male and Female." The executors of a York County estate in 1647 disposed of eight Negroes—four men, two women, and two children—to Captain John Chisman "to have hold occupy posesse and injoy and every one of the afforementioned Negroes forever." [52] The will of Rowland Burnham of "Rapahanocke," made in 1657, dispensed his considerable number of Negroes and white servants in language which clearly differentiated between the two by specifying that the whites were to serve for their "full terme of tyme" and the Negroes "for ever." [53] Nothing in the will indicated that this distinction was exceptional or novel.

Further evidence that some Negroes were serving for life in this period lies in the prices paid for them. In many instances the valuations placed on Negroes (in estate inventories and bills of sale) were far higher than for white servants, even those servants with full terms yet to serve. Higher prices must have meant that Negroes were more highly valued because of their greater length of service. Negro women may have been especially prized, moreover, because their progeny could also be held perpetually. In 1643, for example, William Burdett's inventory listed eight servants, with the time each had still to serve, at valuations ranging from 400 to 1,100 pounds of tobacco, while a "very anntient" Negro was valued at 3,000 and an eight-year-old Negro girl at 2,000 pounds, with no time remaining indicated for either. . . . Similarly, the labor owned by James Stone in 1648 was evaluated as follows:

	lb tobo
Thomas Groves, 4 yeares to serve	1300
Francis Bomley for 6 yeares	1500
John Thackstone for 3 yeares	1300
Susan Davis for 3 yeares	1000
Emaniell a Negro man	2000
Roger Stone 3 yeares	1300
Mingo a Negro man	2000 [54]

[52] For these four cases, Northampton County Deeds, Wills, etc., no. 4 (1651–54), 28 (misnumbered 29), 124, Virginia State Library, Richmond; *Archives Md.*, XLI, 261–62; York County Records, no. 2 (transcribed Wills and Deeds, 1645–49), 256–57, Va. State Lib.

[53] Lancaster County Loose Papers, Box of Wills, 1650–1719, Folder 1656–1659, Va. State Lib.

[54] York County Records, no. 2, 390, Va. State Lib.

. . . Besides setting a higher value on Negroes, these inventories failed to indicate the number of years they had still to serve, presumably because their service was for an unlimited time.

Where Negro women were involved, higher valuations probably reflected the facts that their issues were valuable and that they could be used for field work while white women generally were not. This latter discrimination between Negro and white women did not necessarily involve perpetual service, but it meant that Negroes were set apart in a way clearly not to their advantage. This was not the only instance in which Negroes were subjected to degrading distinctions not immediately and necessarily attached to the concept of slavery. Negroes were singled out for special treatment in several ways which suggest a generalized debasement of Negroes as a group. Significantly, the first indications of this debasement appeared at about the same time as the first indications of actual enslavement.

The distinction concerning field work is a case in point. It first appears on the written record in 1643, when Virginia almost pointedly endorsed it in a tax law. Previously, in 1629, tithable persons had been defined as "all those that worke in the ground of what qualitie or condition soever." The new law provided that *all* adult men were tithable and, in addition, *Negro* women. The same distinction was made twice again before 1660. Maryland adopted a similar policy beginning in 1654.[55] This official discrimination between Negro and other women was made by men who were accustomed to thinking of field work as being ordinarily the work of men rather than women. As John Hammond wrote in a 1656 tract defending the tobacco colonies, servant women were not put to work in the fields but in domestic employments, "yet som wenches that are nasty, and beastly and not fit to be so employed are put into the ground." [56] The essentially racial character of this discrimination stood out clearly in a law passed in 1668 at the time slavery was taking shape in the statute books:

> Whereas some doubts, have arisen whether negro women set free were still to be accompted tithable according to a former act, *It is declared by this grand assembly* that negro women, though permitted to enjoy their Freedome yet ought not in all respects to be admitted to a full fruition of the exemptions and impunities of the English, and are still lyable to payment of taxes.[57]

---

[55] Hening, ed., *Statutes Va.*, I, 144, 242, 292, 454; *Archives Md.*, I, 342, II, 136, 399, 538–39, XIII, 538–39.

[56] John Hammond, *Leah and Rachel, or, the Two Fruitfull Sisters Virginia, and Maryland: Their Present Condition, Impartially Stated and Related . . .* (London, 1656), 9.

[57] Hening, ed., *Statutes Va.*, II, 267.

Virginia law set Negroes apart from all other groups in a second way by denying them the important right and obligation to bear arms. Few restraints could indicate more clearly the denial to Negroes of membership in the white community. This first foreshadowing of the slave codes came in 1640, at just the time when other indications first appeared that Negroes were subject to special treatment.[58]

Finally, an even more compelling sense of the separateness of Negroes was revealed in early reactions to sexual union between the races. Prior to 1660 the evidence concerning these reactions is equivocal, and it is not possible to tell whether repugnance for intermixture preceded legislative enactment of slavery. In 1630 an angry Virginia court sentenced "Hugh Davis to be soundly whipped, before an assembly of Negroes and others for abusing himself to the dishonor of God and shame of Christians, by defiling his body in lying with a negro," but it is possible that the "negro" may not have been female. With other instances of punishment for interracial union in the ensuing years, fornication rather than miscegenation may well have been the primary offense, though in 1651 a Maryland man sued someone who he claimed had said "that he had a black bastard in Virginia." . . . There may have been no racial feeling involved when in 1640 Robert Sweet, a gentleman, was compelled "to do penance in church according to laws of England, for getting a negroe woman with child and the woman whipt." [59] About 1650 a white man and a Negro woman were required to stand clad in white sheets before a congregation in lower Norfolk County for having had relations, but this punishment was sometimes used in cases of fornication between two whites.[60] A quarter century

---

[58] *Ibid.*, I, 226; for the same act in more detail, "Acts of General Assembly, Jan. 6, 1639–40," *Wm. and Mary Qtly.*, 2d Ser., 4 (1924), 147. In Bermuda, always closely connected with Virginia, the first prohibition of weapons to Negroes came in 1623, only seven years after the first Negro landed. The 1623 law was the first law anywhere in English specifically dealing with Negroes. After stressing the insolence of Negroes secretly carrying "cudgells and other weapons and working tools, very dangerous and not meete to be suffered to be carried by such vassalls," it prohibited (in addition to arms) Negroes going abroad at night, trespassing on other people's lands, and trading in tobacco without permission of their masters. Unfortunately the evidence concerning lifetime service for Negroes is much less definite in the scanty Bermuda sources than in those for Maryland and Virginia; the first known incident suggestive of the practice might reasonably be placed anywhere from 1631 to 1656. Later evidence shows Bermuda's slavery and proportion of Negroes similar to Virginia's, and it seems unlikely that the two colonies' early experience was radically different. Henry C. Wilkinson, *The Adventurers of Bermuda: A History of the Island from Its Discovery until the Dissolution of the Somers Island Company in 1684* (London, 1933), 114; J. H. Lefroy, comp., *Memorials of the Discovery and Early Settlement of the Bermudas or Somers Islands, 1515–1685* . . . , 2 vols. (London, 1877–79), I, 308–9, 505, 526–27, 633, 645, II, 34–35, 70. But Negroes were to be armed at times of alarm (*ibid.*, II, 242, 366, 380 [1666–73]): Bermuda was exposed to foreign attack.

[59] Hening, ed., *Statutes Va.*, I, 552; McIlwaine, ed., *Minutes Council Va.*, 477.

[60] Bruce, *Economic History of Va.*, II, 110.

later in 1676, however, the emergence of distaste for racial intermixture was unmistakable. A contemporary account of Bacon's Rebellion caustically described one of the ringleaders, Richard Lawrence, as a person who had eclipsed his learning and abilities "in the darke imbraces of a Blackamoore, his slave: And that in so fond a Maner, . . . to the noe meane Scandle and affrunt of all the Vottrisses in or about towne." [61]

Such condemnation was not confined to polemics. In the early 1660's when slavery was gaining statutory recognition, the assemblies acted with full-throated indignation against miscegenation. These acts aimed at more than merely avoiding confusion of status. In 1662 Virginia declared that "if any christian shall committ Fornication with a negro man or woman, hee or shee soe offending" should pay double the usual fine. (The next year Bermuda prohibited all sexual relations between whites and Negroes.) Two years later Maryland banned interracial marriages: "forasmuch as divers freeborne English women forgettfull of their free Condicion and to the disgrace of our Nation doe intermarry with Negro Slaves by which alsoe divers suites may arise touching the Issue of such woemen and a great damage doth befall the Masters of such Negros for prevention whereof for deterring such freeborne women from such shamefull Matches," strong language indeed if "divers suites" had been the only problem. A Maryland act of 1681 described marriages of white women with Negroes as, among other things, "always to the Satisfaccion of theire Lascivious and Lustfull desires, and to the disgrace not only of the English butt allso of many other Christian Nations." When Virginia finally prohibited all interracial liaisons in 1691, the Assembly vigorously denounced miscegenation and its fruits as "that abominable mixture and spurious issue." [62]

From the surviving evidence, it appears that outright enslavement and these other forms of debasement appeared at about the same time in Maryland and Virginia. Indications of perpetual service, the very nub of slavery, coincided with indications that English settlers discriminated against Negro women, withheld arms from Negroes, and—though the timing is far less certain—reacted unfavorably to interracial

---

[61] "The History of Bacon's and Ingram's Rebellion, 1676," in Charles M. Andrews, ed., *Narratives of the Insurrections, 1675–1690* (N.Y., 1915), 96. Cf. the will of John Fenwick (1683), *Documents Relating to the Colonial, Revolutionary and Post-Revolutionary History of the State of New Jersey* . . . [New Jersey Archives], 1st Ser. (Newark, etc., 1880–1949), XXIII, 162.

[62] Hening, ed., *Statutes Va.*, II, 170, III, 86–87; *Archives Md.*, I, 533–34, VII, 204; Lefroy, comp., *Memorials Bermudas*, II, 190 (a resolution, not a statute). Some evidence suggests miscegenation was not taken as seriously in 17th-century Bermuda as on the mainland: *ibid.*, I, 550, II, 30, 103, 141, 161, 228, 314.

sexual union. The coincidence suggests a mutual relationship between slavery and unfavorable assessment of Negroes. Rather than slavery causing "prejudice," or vice versa, they seem rather to have generated each other. Both were, after all, twin aspects of a general debasement of the Negro. Slavery and "prejudice," may have been equally cause and effect, continuously reacting upon each other, dynamically joining hands to hustle the Negro down the road to complete degradation. Much more than with the other English colonies, where the enslavement of Negroes was to some extent a borrowed practice, the available evidence for Maryland and Virginia points to less borrowing and to this kind of process: a mutually interactive growth of slavery and unfavorable assessment, with no cause for either which did not cause the other as well. If slavery caused prejudice, then invidious distinctions concerning working in the fields, bearing arms, and sexual union should have appeared *after* slavery's firm establishment. If prejudice caused slavery, then one would expect to find these lesser discriminations preceding the greater discrimination of outright enslavement. Taken as a whole, the evidence reveals a process of debasement of which hereditary lifetime service was an important but not the only part.

White servants did not suffer this debasement. Rather, their position improved, partly for the reason that they were not Negroes. By the early 1660's white men were loudly protesting against being made "slaves" in terms which strongly suggest that they considered slavery not as wrong but as inapplicable to themselves. The father of a Maryland apprentice petitioned in 1663 that "he Craves that his daughter may not be made a Slave a tearme soe Scandalous that if admitted to be the Condicon or tytle of the Apprentices in this Province will be soe distructive as noe free borne Christians will ever be induced to come over servants." [63] An Irish youth complained to a Maryland court in 1661 that he had been kidnapped and forced to sign for fifteen years, that he had already served six and a half years and was now twenty-one, and that eight and a half more years of service was "contrary to the lawes of God and man that a Christian Subject should be made a Slave." (The jury blandly compromised the dispute by deciding that he should serve only until age twenty-one, but that he was now only nineteen.) Free Negro servants were generally increasingly less able to defend themselves against this insidious kind of encroachment.[64] Increasingly, white men were more clearly free because Negroes had become so clearly slave.

[63] *Archives Md.*, I, 464.
[64] *Ibid.*, XLI, 476–78, XLIX, 123–24. Compare the contemporary difficulties of a Negro servant: William P. Palmer *et al.*, eds., *Calendar of Virginia State Papers* . . . , 11 vols. (Richmond, 1875–93), I, 9–10.

Certainly it was the case in Maryland and Virginia that the legal enactment of Negro slavery followed social practice, rather than vice versa, and also that the assemblies were slower than in other English colonies to declare how Negroes could or should be treated. These two patterns in themselves suggest that slavery was less a matter of previous conception or external example in Maryland and Virginia than elsewhere.

The Virginia Assembly first showed itself incontrovertibly aware that Negroes were not serving in the same manner as English servants in 1660 when it declared "that for the future no servant comeing into the country without indentures, of what christian nation soever, shall serve longer then those of our own country, of the like age." In 1661 the Assembly indirectly provided statutory recognition that some Negroes served for life: "That in case any English servant shall run away in company with any negroes who are incapable of makeing satisfaction by addition of time," he must serve for the Negroes' lost time as well as his own. Maryland enacted a closely similar law in 1663 (possibly modeled on Virginia's) and in the following year, on the initiative of the lower house, came out with the categorical declaration that Negroes were to serve "Durante Vita." [65] During the next twenty-odd years a succession of acts in both colonies defined with increasing precision what sorts of persons might be treated as slaves.[66] Other acts dealt with the growing problem of slave control, and especially after 1690 slavery began to assume its now familiar character as a complete deprivation of all rights.[67] As early as 1669 the Virginia Assembly unabashedly enacted a brutal law which showed where the logic of perpetual servitude was inevitably tending. Unruly servants could be chastened by sentences to additional terms, but "WHEREAS the only law in force for the punishment of refractory servants resisting their master, mistris or overseer cannot be inflicted upon negroes, nor the obstinacy of many of them by other then violent meanes supprest," if a slave "by the extremity of the correction should chance to die" his master was not to be adjudged guilty of felony "since it cannot be presumed that prepensed malice (which alone makes murther Felony) should induce any man to destroy his owne estate." [68] Virginia planters

[65] Hening, ed., *Statutes Va.*, I, 539, II, 26; *Archives Md.*, I, 449, 489, 526, 533–34. The "any negroes who are incapable" suggests explicit recognition that some were free, but in several sources the law as re-enacted the next year included a comma between "negroes" and "who," as did the Maryland act of 1663. See *The Lawes of Virginia Now in Force: Collected out of the Assembly Records . . .* (London, 1662), 59.

[66] Hening, ed., *Statutes Va.*, II, 170, 270, 283, 490–91, III, 137–40, 447–48; *Archives Md.*, VII, 203–5, XIII, 546–49, XXII, 551–52.

[67] Especially Hening, ed., *Statutes Va.*, II, 270–71, 481–82, 493, III, 86, 102–3; *Archives Md.*, XIII, 451–53, XIX, 167, 193, XXII, 546–48, XXVI, 254–56.

[68] Hening, ed., *Statutes Va.*, II, 270; compare law for servants, I, 538, II, 118.

felt they acted out of mounting necessity: there were disturbances among slaves in several areas in the early 1670's.[69]

By about 1700 the slave ships began spilling forth their black cargoes in greater and greater numbers. By that time, racial slavery and the necessary police powers had been written into law. By that time, too, slavery had lost all resemblance to a perpetual and hereditary version of English servitude, though service for life still seemed to contemporaries its most essential feature.[70] In the last quarter of the seventeenth century the trend was to treat Negroes more like property and less like men, to send them to the fields at younger ages, to deny them automatic existence as inherent members of the community, to tighten the bonds on their personal and civil freedom, and correspondingly to loosen the traditional restraints on the master's freedom to deal with his human property as he saw fit.[71] In 1705 Virginia gathered up the random statutes of a whole generation and baled them into a "slave code" which would not have been out of place in the nineteenth century. . . .[72]

8. The Un-English: Scots, Irish, and Indians

In the minds of overseas Englishmen, slavery, the new tyranny, did not apply to any Europeans. Something about Negroes, and to a lesser extent Indians, set them apart for drastic exploitation, oppression, and degradation. In order to discover why, it is useful to turn the problem inside out, to inquire why Englishmen in America did not treat any other peoples like Negroes. It is especially revealing to see how English settlers looked upon the Scotch (as they frequently called them) and the Irish, whom they often had opportunity and "reason" to enslave, and upon the Indians, whom they enslaved, though only, as it were, casually.

In the early years Englishmen treated the increasingly numerous settlers from other European countries, especially Scottish and Irish servants, with condescension and frequently with exploitive brutality. Englishmen seemed to regard their colonies as exclusively *English* preserves and to wish to protect English persons especially from the exploitation which inevitably accompanied settlement in the New World. In Barbados, for example, the assembly in 1661 denounced the

[69] *Ibid.*, II, 299.

[70] Robert Beverley, *The History and Present State of Virginia*, ed. Louis B. Wright (Chapel Hill, 1947), 271–72.

[71] For illustration, Hening, ed., *Statutes Va.*, II, 288, 479–80 (Negro *children* taxed from age 12, white *boys* from 14), III, 102–3; *Archives Md.*, VII, 76 (county courts required to register births, marriages, burials of all "Except Negroes Indians and Molottos").

[72] Hening, ed., *Statutes Va.*, III, 447–62.

kidnapping of youngsters for service in the colony in a law which applied only to "Children of the *English* Nation." [73] In 1650 Connecticut provided that debtors were not to "bee sould to any but of the English Nation." [74]

While Englishmen distinguished themselves from other peoples, they also distinguished *among* those different peoples who failed to be English. It seems almost as if Englishmen possessed a view of other peoples which placed the English nation at the center of widening concentric circles each of which contained a people more alien than the one inside it. On occasion these social distances left by Englishmen may be gauged with considerable precision, as in the sequence employed by the Committee for Trade and Foreign Plantations in a query to the governor of Connecticut in 1680: "What number of English, Scotch, Irish or Forreigners have . . . come yearly to . . . your Corporation. And also, what Blacks and Slaves have been brought in." Sometimes the English sense of distance seems to have been based upon a scale of values which would be thought of today in terms of nationality. When the Leeward Islands encouraged immigration of foreign Protestants the Assembly stipulated that the number of such aliens "shall not exceed the One Fourth of *English, Scotch, Irish, and Cariole* [Creole] Subjects." . . . Maryland placed a discriminatory duty on Irish servants while Virginia did the same with all servants not born in England or Wales.[75]

At other times, though, the sense of foreignness seems to have been explicitly religious, as instanced by Lord William Willoughby's letter from Barbados in 1667: "We have more than a good many Irish amongst us, therefore I am for the down right Scott, who I am certain will fight without a crucifix about his neck." [76] It is scarcely surprising that hostility toward the numerous Irish servants should have been especially strong, for they were doubly damned as foreign and Papist. Already, for Englishmen in the seventeenth century, the Irish were a special case, and it required more than an ocean voyage to alter this perception. . . .

---

[73] Hening, ed., *Statutes Va.*, I, 161; *Acts of Assembly, Passed in the Island of Barbadoes, from 1648, to 1718* (London, 1721), 22.

[74] Trumbull and Hoadly, eds., *Recs. Col. Conn.*, I, 510.

[75] *Ibid.*, III, 293 (an inquiry also sent other governors); *Acts of Assembly, Passed in the Charibbee Leeward Islands, from 1690 to 1730* (London, 1734), 127; *Acts of Assembly, Passed in the Island of Jamaica; From 1681, to 1737, Inclusive* (London, 1738), 100; also *Montserrat Code of Laws: From 1668, to 1788* (London, 1790), 19; Hening, ed., *Statutes Va.*, III, 193; Thomas Bacon, ed., *Laws of Maryland at Large, 1637–1763* (Annapolis, 1765), 1715, chap. xxxvi, 1717, chap. x, 1732, chap. xxii. The Maryland laws aimed at Irish Papists.

[76] Willoughby quoted in C. S. S. Higham, *The Development of the Leeward Islands under the Restoration, 1660–1688; A Study of the Foundation of the Old Colonial System* (Cambridge, Eng., 1921), 170*n*.

As time went on Englishmen began to absorb the idea that their set-tlements in America were not going to remain exclusively English pre-serves. In 1671 Virginia began encouraging naturalization of legal aliens, so that they might enjoy "all such liberties, priviledges, immu-nities whatsoever, as a naturall borne Englishman is capable of," and Maryland accomplished the same end with private naturalization acts that frequently included a potpourri of French, Dutch, Swiss, Swedes, and so forth.[77]

The necessity of peopling the colonies transformed the long-stand-ing urge to discriminate among non-English peoples into a necessity. Which of the non-English were sufficiently different and foreign to warrant treating as "perpetual servants"? The need to answer this question did not mean, of course, that upon arrival in America the colonists immediately jettisoned their sense of distance from those persons they did not actually enslave. They discriminated against Welshmen and Scotsmen who, while admittedly "the best servants," were typically the servants of Englishmen. There was a considerably stronger tendency to discriminate against Papist Irishmen, those "worst" servants, but never to make slaves of them.[78] And here lay the crucial difference. Even the Scottish prisoners taken by Cromwell at Worcester and Dunbar—captives in a just war!—were never treated as slaves in England or the colonies. Certainly the lot of those sent to Barbados was miserable, but it was a different lot from the African slave's. In New England they were quickly accommodated to the pre-vailing labor system, which was servitude. . . .

Indians too seemed radically different from Englishmen, far more so than any Europeans. They were enslaved, like Negroes, and so fell on the losing side of a crucial dividing line. It is easy to see why: whether considered in terms of complexion, religion, nationality, savagery, bes-tiality, or geographical location, Indians were more like Negroes than like Englishmen. Given this resemblance the essential problem be-comes why Indian slavery never became an important institution in the colonies. Why did Indian slavery remain numerically insignificant and typically incidental in character? Why were Indian slaves valued at much lower prices than Negroes? Why were Indians, as a kind of peo-ple, treated like Negroes and yet at the same time very differently?

Certain obvious factors made for important differentiations in the minds of the English colonists. As was the case with first confronta-

---

[77] Hening, ed., *Statutes Va.*, II, 289–90, 464–65; for one of many in Maryland, *Archives Md.*, II, 205–6.

[78] The designations are a prominent planter's, quoted in Higham, *Development of the Leeward Islands*, 169, also 170n.

tions in America and Africa, the different contexts of confrontation made Englishmen more interested in converting and civilizing Indians than Negroes. That this campaign in America too frequently degenerated into military campaigns of extermination did nothing to eradicate the initial distinction. Entirely apart from English intentions, the culture of the American Indians probably meant that they were less readily enslavable than Africans. By comparison, they were less used to settled agriculture, and their own variety of slavery was probably even less similar to the chattel slavery which Englishmen practiced in America than was the domestic and political slavery of the West African cultures. But it was the transformation of English intentions in the wilderness which counted most heavily in the long run. The Bible and the treaty so often gave way to the clash of flintlock and tomahawk. The colonists' perceptions of the Indians came to be organized not only in pulpits and printshops but at the bloody cutting edge of the English thrust into the Indians' lands. Thus the most pressing and mundane circumstances worked to make Indians seem very different from Negroes. In the early years especially, Indians were in a position to mount murderous reprisals upon the English settlers, while the few scattered Negroes were not. When English-Indian relations did not turn upon sheer power they rested on diplomacy. In many instances the colonists took assiduous precautions to prevent abuse of Indians belonging to friendly tribes. Most of the Indians enslaved by the English had their own tribal enemies to thank. It became a common practice to ship Indian slaves to the West Indies where they could be exchanged for slaves who had no compatriots lurking on the outskirts of English settlements.[79] In contrast, Negroes presented much less of a threat—at first.

Equally important, Negroes had to be dealt with as individuals— with supremely impartial anonymity, to be sure—rather than as nations. Englishmen wanted and had to live with their Negroes, as it were, side by side. Accordingly their impressions of Negroes were forged in the heat of continual, inescapable personal contacts. There were few pressures urging Englishmen to treat Indians as integral constituents in their society, which Negroes were whether Englishmen liked or not. At a distance the Indian could be viewed with greater detachment and his characteristics acknowledged and approached more coolly and more rationally. At a distance too, Indians could retain the

---

[79] Hening, ed., *Statutes Va.*, II, 299. A good study of Indian slavery is needed, but see Almon Wheeler Lauber, *Indian Slavery in Colonial Times within the Present Limits of the United States* (N.Y., 1913). In 1627 some imported Carib Indians proved unsalable in Virginia and were turned over to the colony; the General Court decided that, since the Caribs had stolen goods, attempted murder, tried to run away to the Virginia Indians, and might prove the downfall of the whole colony, the best way to dispose of the problem was to hang them: McIlwaine, ed., *Minutes Council Va.*, 155.

quality of nationality, a quality which Englishmen admired in themselves and expected in other peoples. Under contrasting circumstances in America, the Negro nations tended to become Negro people.

Here lay the rudiments of certain shadowy but persistent themes in what turned out to be a multi-racial nation. Americans came to impute to the braves of the Indian "nations" an ungovernable individuality (which was perhaps not merited in such exaggerated degree) and at the same time to impart to Negroes all the qualities of an eminently governable sub-nation, in which African tribal distinctions were assumed to be of no consequence and individuality unaspired to. More immediately, the two more primitive peoples rapidly came to serve as two fixed points from which English settlers could triangulate their own position in America; the separate meanings of *Indian* and *Negro* helped define the meaning of living in America. The Indian became for Americans a symbol of their American experience; it was no mere luck of the toss that placed the profile of an American Indian rather than an American Negro on the famous old five-cent piece. Confronting the Indian in America was a testing experience, common to all the colonies. Conquering the Indian symbolized and personified the conquest of the American difficulties, the surmounting of the wilderness. To push back the Indian was to prove the worth of one's own mission, to make straight in the desert a highway for civilization. With the Negro it was utterly different.

9. Racial Slavery: From Reasons to Rationale

And *difference*, surely, was the indispensable key to the degradation of Negroes in English America. In scanning the problem of *why* Negroes were enslaved in America, certain constant elements in a complex situation can be readily, if roughly, identified. It may be taken as given that there would have been no enslavement without economic need, that is, without persistent demand for labor in underpopulated colonies. Of crucial importance, too, was the fact that for cultural reasons Negroes were relatively helpless in the face of European aggressiveness and technology. In themselves, however, these two elements will not explain the enslavement of Indians and Negroes. The pressing exigency in America was labor, and Irish and English servants were available. Most of them would have been helpless to ward off outright enslavement if their masters had thought themselves privileged and able to enslave them. As a group, though, masters did not think themselves so empowered. Only with Indians and Negroes did Englishmen attempt so radical a deprivation of liberty—which brings the matter abruptly to the most difficult and imponderable question of all: what was it about Indians and Negroes which set them apart, which rendered them *different* from Englishmen, which made them special candidates for degradation?

To ask such questions is to inquire into the *content* of English attitudes, and unfortunately there is little evidence with which to build an
answer. It may be said, however, that the heathen condition of the Negroes seemed of considerable importance to English settlers in America—more so than to English voyagers upon the coasts of Africa—and
that heathenism was associated in some settlers' minds with the condition of slavery.[80] This is not to say that the colonists enslaved Negroes
because they were heathens. . . .

The importance and persistence of the tradition which attached
slavery to heathenism did not become evident in any positive assertions that heathens might be enslaved. It was not until the period of legal establishment of slavery after 1660 that the tradition became manifest at all, and even then there was no effort to place heathenism and
slavery on a one-for-one relationship. Virginia's second statutory definition of a slave (1682), for example, awkwardly attempted to rest enslavement on religious difference while excluding from possible enslavement all heathens who were not Indian or Negro.[81] Despite such
logical difficulties, the old European equation of slavery and religious
difference did not rapidly vanish in America, for it cropped up repeatedly after 1660 in assertions that slaves by becoming Christian did not
automatically become free. By about the end of the seventeenth century, Maryland, New York, Virginia, North and South Carolina, and
New Jersey had all passed laws reassuring masters that conversion of
their slaves did not necessitate manumission.[82] These acts were passed

---

[80] . . . Also John C. Hurd, *The Law of Freedom and Bondage in the United States*, 2
vols. (Boston, 1858–62), I, 159–60; Horne, *The Mirror of Justices*, ed. Robinson, 124;
Marcus W. Jernegan, *Laboring and Dependent Classes in Colonial America, 1607–1783;
Studies of the Economic, Educational, and Social Significance of Slaves, Servants, Apprentices,
and Poor Folk* (Chicago, 1931), 24–26; Helen T. Catterall, ed., *Judicial Cases Concerning
American Slavery and the Negro*, 5 vols. (Washington, 1926–37), I, 55*n*. Data in the following pages suggest this. The implication that slavery could last only during the heathen state is in Providence Company to Gov. Philip Bell, London, Apr. 20, 1635, Box 9,
bundle: List no. 7, 2d portion, MS. relating to the Royal African Co. and Slavery matters, 43, Parish Transcripts, N.-Y. Hist. Soc.: ". . . a Groundless opinion that Christians may not lawfully keepe such persons in a state of Servitude during their strangeness
from Christianity." In 1695 Gov. John Archdale of South Carolina prohibited sale of
some Indians, captured by his own Indian allies, as slaves to the West Indies and freed
them because they were Christians: John Archdale, *A New Description of That Fertile and
Pleasant Province of Carolina* . . . (London, 1707), in Alexander S. Salley, Jr., ed., *Narratives of Early Carolina, 1650–1708* (N.Y., 1911), 300.

[81] Hening, ed., *Statutes Va.*, II, 490–92.

[82] *Archives Md.*, I, 526, 533 (1664), II, 272; "Duke's Laws," C. O. 5/1142, f. 33v.,
P.R.O., a portion of the section of "Bondslavery" omitted from the standard New York
printed sources which reads "And also provided that This Law shall not extend to sett at
Liberty Any Negroe or Indian Servant who shall turne Christian after he shall have been
bought by Any Person." (This unpublished Crown Copyright material is reproduced by
permission of the Controller of H. M. Stationery Office.) *The Colonial Laws of New York
from the Year 1664 to the Revolution* . . . , 5 vols. (Albany, 1894–96), I, 597–98 (1706);

in response to occasional pleas that Christianity created a claim to freedom and to much more frequent assertions by men interested in converting Negroes that nothing could be accomplished if masters thought their slaves were about to be snatched from them by meddling missionaries.[83] This decision that the slave's religious condition had no relevance to his status as a slave (the only one possible if an already valuable economic institution was to be retained) strongly suggests that heathenism was an important component in the colonists' initial reaction to Negroes early in the century.

Yet its importance can easily be overstressed. For one thing, some of the first Negroes in Virginia had been baptized before arrival. In the early years others were baptized in various colonies and became more than nominally Christian; a Negro woman joined the church in Dorchester, Massachusetts, as a full member in 1641.[84] With some Negroes becoming Christian and others not, there might have developed a caste differentiation along religious lines, yet there is no evidence to suggest that the colonists distinguished consistently between the Negroes they converted and those they did not. It was racial, not religious, slavery which developed in America.

Still, in the early years, the English settlers most frequently contrasted themselves with Negroes by the term *Christian*, though they also sometimes described themselves as *English*; [85] here the explicit religious distinction would seem to have lain at the core of English reaction. Yet the concept embodied by the term *Christian* embraced so much more meaning than was contained in specific doctrinal affirmations that it is scarcely possible to assume on the basis of this linguistic contrast that the colonists set Negroes apart because they were heathen. The historical experience of the English people in the sixteenth century had made for fusion of religion and nationality; the qualities of being English and Christian had become so inseparably blended that it seemed perfectly consistent to the Virginia Assembly in 1670 to declare that "noe negroe or Indian though baptised and enjoyned their

---

Hening, ed., *Statutes Va.*, II, 260 (1667); Saunders, ed., *Col. Recs. N.C.*, I, 204 (1670), II, 857; Cooper and McCord, eds., *Statutes S.C.*, VII, 343 (1691), 364–65; *Anno Regni Reginae Annae . . . Tertio; [The Acts Passed by the Second Assembly of New Jersey in December, 1704* ([N.Y., 1704]), 20, an act which was disallowed for other reasons.

[83] For example, in 1652 a mulatto girl pleaded Christianity as the reason why she should not be "a perpetuall slave" (Lefroy, comp., *Memorials Bermudas*, II, 34–35, also 293–94), and in 1694 some Massachusetts ministers asked the governor and legislature to remove that "wel-knowne Discouragement" to conversion of slaves with a law denying that baptism necessitated freedom (*Acts and Resolves Mass.*, VII, 537).

[84] Winthrop, *Journal*, ed. Hosmer, II, 26.

[85] These statements on prevailing word usage are based on a wide variety of sources, many of them cited in this chapter; some passages already quoted may serve to amplify the illustrations in the following paragraphs.

owne Freedome shall be capable of any such purchase of christians, but yet not debarred from buying any of their owne nation." . . .

From the first, then, vis-à-vis the Negro the concept embedded in the term *Christian* seems to have conveyed much of the idea and feeling of *we* as against *they:* to be Christian was to be civilized rather than barbarous, English rather than African, white rather than black. The term *Christian* itself proved to have remarkable elasticity, for by the end of the seventeenth century it was being used to define a species of slavery which had altogether lost any connection with explicit religious difference. In the Virginia code of 1705, for example, the term sounded much more like a definition of race than of religion: "And for a further christian care and usage of all christian servants, *Be it also enacted* . . . That no negroes, mulattos, or Indians, although christians, or Jews, Moors, Mahometans, or other infidels, shall, at any time, purchase any christian servant, nor any other, except of their own complexion, or such as are declared slaves by this act." By this time "Christianity" had somehow become intimately and explicitly linked with "complexion." The 1705 statute declared "That all servants imported and brought into this country, by sea or land, who were not christians in their native country, (except Turks and Moors in amity with her majesty, and others that can make due proof of their being free in England, or any other christian country, before they were shipped, in order to transportation hither) shall be accounted and be slaves, and as such be here bought and sold notwithstanding a conversion to christianity afterwards." [86] As late as 1753 the Virginia slave code anachronistically defined slavery in terms of religion when everyone knew that slavery had for generations been based on the racial and not the religious difference. [87]

It is worth making still closer scrutiny of the terminology which Englishmen employed when referring both to themselves and to the two peoples they enslaved, for this terminology affords the best single means of probing the content of their sense of difference. The terms *Indian* and *Negro* were both borrowed from the Hispanic languages, the one originally deriving from (mistaken) geographical locality and the other from human complexion. When referring to the Indians the English colonists either used that proper name or called them *savages*, a term which reflected primarily their view of Indians as uncivilized, or occasionally (in Maryland especially) *pagans*, which gave more explicit expression to the missionary urge. When they had reference to Indians

[86] *Ibid.*, III, 447–48 (1705), also 283, V, 547–48, VI, 356–57. Lingering aftereffects of the old concept cropped up as late as 1791, when *Negro* was still contradistinguished by *Christian:* Certificate of Character of Negro Phill, Feb. 20, 1791, Character Certificates of Negroes, Papers of the Pennsylvania Abolition Society, Historical Society of Pennsylvania, Philadelphia.

[87] Hening, ed., *Statutes Va.*, VI, 356–57.

the colonists occasionally spoke of themselves as *Christians* but after the early years almost always as *English*.

In significant contrast, the colonists referred to *Negroes* and by the eighteenth century to *blacks* and to *Africans*, but almost never to Negro *heathens* or *pagans* or *savages*. Most suggestive of all, there seems to have been something of a shift during the seventeenth century in the terminology which Englishmen in the colonies applied to themselves. From the initially most common term *Christian*, at mid-century there was a marked drift toward *English* and *free*. After about 1680, taking the colonies as a whole, a new term appeared—*white*.

So far as the weight of analysis may be imposed upon such terms, diminishing reliance upon *Christian* suggests a gradual muting of the specifically religious element in the Christian-Negro disjunction in favor of secular nationality: Negroes were, in 1667, "not in all respects to be admitted to a full fruition of the exemptions and impunities of the English." [88] As time went on, as some Negroes became assimilated to the English colonial culture, as more "raw Africans" arrived, and as increasing numbers of non-English Europeans were attracted to the colonies, the colonists turned increasingly to the striking physiognomic difference. By 1676 it was possible in Virginia to assail a man for "eclipsing" himself in the "darke imbraces of a Blackamoore" as if "Buty consisted all together in the Antiphety of Complections." In Maryland a revised law prohibiting miscegenation (1692) retained *white* and *English* but dropped the term *Christian*—a symptomatic modification. As early as 1664 a Bermuda statute (aimed, ironically, at protecting Negroes from brutal abandonment) required that the "last Master" of senile Negroes "provide for them such accomodations as shall be convenient for Creatures of that hue and colour untill their death." By the end of the seventeenth century dark complexion had become an independent rationale for enslavement: in 1709 Samuel Sewall noted in his diary that a "Spaniard" had petitioned the Massachusetts Council for freedom but that "Capt. Teat alledg's that all of that Color were Slaves." [89] Here was a barrier between "we" and

---

[88] *Ibid.*, II, 267.

[89] "History of Bacon's and Ingram's Rebellion," Andrews, ed., *Narratives of the Insurrections*, 96; *Archives Md.*, XIII, 546–49; Lefroy, comp., *Memorials Bermudas*, II, 216; *Diary of Samuel Sewall, 1674–1729* (Mass. Hist. Soc., *Collections*, 5th Ser. 5–7 [1878–82]), II, 248. In 1698 Gov. Francis Nicholson informed the Board of Trade that the "major part" of Negroes in Maryland spoke English: *Archives Md.*, XXIII, 499. For first use of "white" in statutes of various colonies, Bartlett, ed., *Recs. Col. R.I.*, I, 243 (1652); *Archives Md.*, VII, 204–5 (1681); Aaron Leaming and Jacob Spicer, eds., *The Grants, Concessions, and Original Constitutions of the Province of New Jersey* . . . , 2d ed. (Somerville, N.J., 1881), 236 (1683); *Col. Laws N.Y.*, I, 148 (1684); Cooper and McCord, eds., *Statutes S.C.*, VII, 343 (1691); Hening, ed., *Statutes Va.*, III, 86–87 (1691); *Acts of Assembly, Made and Enacted in the Bermuda or Summer-Islands, from 1690, to 1713–14* (London, 1719), 12–13 (1690 or 1691). West Indian assemblies used the term in the 1680's and 1690's, possibly

"they" which was visible and permanent: the Negro could not become a white man. Not, at least, as yet.

What had occurred was not a change in the justification of slavery from religion to race. No such justifications were made. There seems to have been, within the unarticulated concept of the Negro as a different sort of person, a subtle but highly significant shift in emphasis. Consciousness of Negro's heathenism remained through the eighteenth and into the nineteenth and even the twentieth century, and an awareness, at very least, of his different appearance was present from the beginning. The shift was an alteration in emphasis within a single concept of difference rather than a development of a novel conceptualization. . . . Throughout the colonies the terms *Christian, free, English,* and *white* were for many years employed indiscriminately as metonyms. A Maryland law of 1681 used all four terms in one short paragraph! [90]

Whatever the limitations of terminology as an index to thought and feeling, it seems likely that the colonists' initial sense of difference from the Negro was founded not on a single characteristic but on a congeries of qualities which, taken as a whole, seemed to set the Negro apart. Virtually every quality in the Negro invited pejorative feelings. What may have been his two most striking characteristics, his heathenism and his appearance, were probably prerequisite to his complete debasement. His heathenism alone could never have led to permanent enslavement since conversion easily wiped out that failing. If his appearance, his racial characteristics, meant nothing to the English settlers, it is difficult to see how slavery based on race ever emerged, how the concept of complexion as the mark of slavery ever entered the colonists' minds. Even if the colonists were most unfavorably struck by the Negro's color, though, blackness itself did not urge the complete debasement of slavery. Other qualities—the utter strangeness of his language, gestures, eating habits, and so on—certainly must have contributed to the colonists' sense that he was very different, perhaps disturbingly so. In Africa these qualities had for Englishmen added up to *savagery;* they were major components in that sense of *difference* which provided the mental margin absolutely requisite for placing the European on the deck of the slave ship and the Negro in the hold.

The available evidence (what little there is) suggests that for Englishmen settling in America, the specific religious difference was initially of greater importance than color, certainly of much greater relative importance than for the Englishmen who confronted Negroes in

---

earlier. Officials in England were using "whites" and "blacks" as early as 1670 in questionnaires to colonial governors: Hening, ed., *Statutes Va.,* II, 515; Trumbull and Hoadly, eds., *Recs. Col. Conn.,* III, 293.

[90] *Archives Md.,* VII, 204.

their African homeland. Perhaps Englishmen in Virginia, living uncomfortably close to nature under a hot sun and in almost daily contact with tawny Indians, found the Negro's color less arresting than they might have in other circumstances. Perhaps, too, these first Virginians sensed how inadequately they had reconstructed the institutions and practices of Christian piety in the wilderness; they would perhaps appear less as failures to themselves in this respect if compared to persons who as Christians were *totally* defective. In this connection they may be compared to their brethren in New England, where godliness appeared (at first) triumphantly to hold full sway; in New England there was distinctly less contrasting of Negroes on the basis of the religious disjunction and much more militant discussion of just wars. Perhaps, though, the Jamestown settlers were told in 1619 by the Dutch shipmaster that these "negars" were heathens and could be treated as such. We do not know. The available data will not bear all the weight that the really crucial questions impose.

Of course once the cycle of degradation was fully under way, once slavery and racial discrimination were completely linked together, once the engine of oppression was in full operation, then there is no need to plead *ignoramus*. By the end of the seventeenth century in all the colonies of the English empire there was chattel racial slavery of a kind which would have seemed familiar to men living in the nineteenth century. No Elizabethan Englishman would have found it familiar, though certain strands of thought and feeling in Elizabethan England had intertwined with reports about the Spanish and Portuguese to engender a willingness on the part of English settlers in the New World to treat some men as suitable for private exploitation. During the seventeenth century New World conditions had exploited this predisposition and vastly enlarged it, so much so that English colonials of the eighteenth century were faced with full-blown slavery.

The Bayard Treason Trial: Dramatizing Anglo-Dutch Politics in Early Eighteenth-Century New York City

ADRIAN HOWE

The Middle Colonies were undeniably among the most heterogeneous societies in the Western world. Royal governors and proprietors alike had frequent cause to bemoan the social conflict and confusion that such diversity tended to inspire. Historians, in turn, have often repeated this description, but they have only recently attempted to portray ethnic relations and their consequences in precise terms. Just as recent attention has focused upon the previously unacknowledged roles of Indians, Africans, women, and other groups, so too has a creative group of scholars begun to sketch the outlines of a new interpretation of ethnicity in early America.

In New York, where claims of the corrosive effects of ethnic diversity were most frequently made, intergroup antagonism found a political lightning rod in a largely Dutch rebellion led by Jacob Leisler from 1689 to 1691, when he was executed by English imperial authorities. A decade later, however, the issues raised by the rebellion remained (at least on their face) unsettled. In the following essay, Adrian Howe uses the 1702 treason trial of Nicholas Bayard as a window on New York's political and social situation during the period that preceded as well as the period that followed the trial.

In an unusually subtle and nuanced interpretation, Howe is able to demonstrate that ethnic identity—conflict between Dutch and English cultures within the same provincial government— was a very complex matter in colonial New York and that much of this complexity lay beneath the surface of events. Moreover, Howe simultaneously offers a fascinating insight into the social and political function that legal institutions acquired in the culturally unstable environment of early New York.

Is Howe's view one with broader applicability either to other colonies or to other periods in American history? The conse-

Reprinted from Adrian Howe, "The Bayard Treason Trial: Dramatizing Anglo-Dutch Politics in Early Eighteenth-Century New York City," *William and Mary Quarterly*, 3d ser. XLVII (1990), 57–89, by permission of Dr. Adrian Howe, lecturer in criminology, Legal Studies Department, La Trobe University, Bundoora, Victoria, Australia 3083.

quences of demographic complexity and ethnic diversity have frequently been regarded as distinctively American social phenomenon. Do Howe's views on late seventeenth-century New York provide interpretive insights that can be applied to nineteenth-century American history or even to contemporary American life?

In June 1776 John Adams, frustrated by New York's dilatory response to the Revolutionary crisis, puzzled over that colony's hesitation in voting for Independence from Great Britain. "What is the Reason," he asked, "that New York is still asleep or dead, in Politicks and War?" Did the New Yorkers have "no sense, no Feeling? No sentiment? No Passions?" While all the other colonies were "rapidly advancing," New York's "Motions" seemed to Adams to be "rather retrograde." Was there something "in the Air, or Soil of New York, unfriendly to the Spirit of Liberty?" Or was it "Simple Dulness in the People of that Colony" that accounted for "their excentric and retrograde Politicks?" Whatever the reason, New York was "likely to have the Honour of being the very last of all in imbibing the genuine Principles and the true system of American Policy." [1] Adams should not have been surprised by New York's eccentricity. Just two years earlier he had described that colony's politics as "the devil's own incomprehensibles." [2]

No one who has explored colonial New York's immensely convoluted and factionalized politics would dispute John Adams's claim that it defies comprehension. Furthermore, New York's most ardent defenders agree that it was one of the "least militant and most hesitant" of the colonies to declare for Independence: its response to the Revolutionary crisis, they concede, was indeed "sluggish." [3] But, paradoxically, while Adams condemned New York politics as "retrograde," historians currently acclaim its political system as surprisingly sophisticated and essentially "modern." For Patricia U. Bonomi, for example, the eighteenth-century New Yorkers' unashamedly interest-oriented politics was their peculiar "contribution to modernity." In her view, their legitimization of self-interest as a public concept may have been "the sharpest single innovation of colonial politics." Furthermore, their techniques of political management and party building en-

---

[1] Adams to William Tudor, June 24, 1776, in Robert J. Taylor *et al.*, eds., *Papers of John Adams* (Cambridge, Mass., 1977–), IV, 335–336; Adams to John Sullivan, June 23, 1776, *ibid.*, 330–331; Adams to Samuel Holden Parsons, June 22, 1776, *ibid.*, 327–328.

[2] Quoted in Michael Kammen, *Colonial New York: A History* (New York, 1975), 341.

[3] Milton M. Klein, *The Politics of Diversity: Essays in the History of Colonial New York* (Port Washington, N.Y., 1974), 185; Patricia U. Bonomi, *A Factious People: Politics and Society in Colonial New York* (New York, 1971), 17.

sured them a "leading and innovative role . . . in the coming national era." [4]

There are, however, considerable problems associated with the development of a conceptual model emphasizing the modernity of colonial New York politics. The main difficulty is that such an emphasis creates the erroneous impression that in the six decades preceding the Stamp Act riots, New York politics, far from being "retrograde" as Adams thought, moved relentlessly forward toward the Revolution and the modern era. According to Bonomi, for example, eighteenth-century New York politics exhibited "a steadily rising intensity of competition among concerted factions" and drew in "ever larger numbers of people as time went on." Yet if, as she claims, the evidence for an "evolutionary view" of political development is convincing at the provincial level, such evidence simply does not exist for New York City, where popular political involvement was minimal and sporadic in the period 1700–1760. Aside from an uprising of black slaves in 1712, there were no insurrections; aside from a bakers' strike in 1741, scarcely any collective action was taken by artisan groups; aside from a few mass demonstrations and an election-day riot in the mid-1730s, conflict involving large numbers of people was notably absent. Thus, if eighteenth-century politicians were "excessively factious," as Bonomi claims, the populace of New York City was politically passive—asleep or dead—for most of the colonial period. [5]

The crucial question, then, is not why disputes occasionally erupted into open conflict, but why the populace was so notably quiescent. Answering this question necessitates shifting the focus to an analysis of the social basis of the town's elite-dominated politics and of the factors inhibiting the development of popular politics there. [6] We also need to dispense with an analytical framework that directs attention to the putatively "democratic" or "modern" aspects of New York's political system. Accordingly, this article opens a new line of inquiry, one that addresses the society and politics of colonial New York City on their own

[4] Bonomi, "The Middle Colonies: Embryo of the New Political Order," in Alden T. Vaughan and George Athan Billias, eds., *Perspectives on Early American History: Essays in Honor of Richard B. Morris* (New York, 1973), 91–92, and *Factious People*, 282–286. See also Klein, *Politics of Diversity*, 37, and Thomas J. Archdeacon, *New York City, 1664–1710: Conquest and Change* (Ithaca, N.Y., 1976), 155–157.

[5] Bonomi, *Factious People*, 16, 280. In another version of the "evolutionary" thesis Archdeacon maintains that the ethnic heterogeneity of the town's population helped "transform deferential politics into democratic politics" there. He claims, too, that the political involvement of a wide cross section of the populace in the last decade of the 17th century had "important implications for the study of democratically-orientated politics in the eighteenth century" (*New York City*, 30–31, 156).

[6] Gary B. Nash, a leading exponent of the "evolutionary" paradigm, has claimed that "new techniques of political management" introduced to New York City at the turn of the 18th century transformed and radicalized the town's politics and that the "technique

terms and analyzes conflict as it was experienced and perceived by the townsfolk who lived through it. The assumption of this inquiry is that if New York City, unlike Boston, was quiescent, the essential explanation must be sought in the town's social structure and ethnic cultural traditions.

I

In January 1701 Gov. Richard Coote, earl of Bellomont, boasted that New York City was the "growingest town in America." Since his arrival nearly three years earlier, "not fewer than a hundred fair brick houses" and "a very noble Town-house" had been built.[7] Bellomont's impression notwithstanding, New York was not the fastest growing town in northern America. Still, it did experience accelerated growth in the late 1690s, and by 1700 its area extended well beyond the wall built by the Dutch to fortify New Amsterdam. Inside the wall—now Wall Street—crowded conditions in the oldest section of town at the southeastern tip of the island had precipitated an uptown movement. Wealthy citizens were building mansions on Broadway near the fort, and the municipal government had begun developing the town's western side along the Hudson River. By this time, too, the new city hall mentioned by Governor Bellomont was under construction on Wall Street at the upper end of Broad Street.[8]

This new seat of local government contained the courtroom that was to be the scene of an extraordinary treason trial in 1702. To situate

of mobilizing the politically inert" became "increasingly important" in 18th-century New York City. Yet importantly, he has admitted that the evidence for the radicalization of New York City's politics is far less "compelling" than for Philadelphia or Boston. In New York, "attempts to mobilize a broad-based electorate were not as continuous." Nash concedes, too, that "the devices of popular politics were less in evidence" in New York, which did not have annual assembly elections or even a written ballot (*The Urban Crucible: Social Change, Political Consciousness, and the Origins of the American Revolution* [Cambridge, Mass., 1979], 90, 165, and "The Transformation of Urban Politics, 1700–1765," *Journal of American History*, LX [1973], 607–609). Even so, he underestimates the singularity of the situation in New York City, where for 60 years after the hotly contested 1701 municipal elections there is very little evidence of widespread participation in electoral politics. Occasionally, dissident members of the ruling elite set up slates of candidates and reached down into the community for support, but with few exceptions elections between 1700 and 1760 were dull affairs in which incumbents were routinely returned to office by an inert electorate.

[7] Bellomont to the Lords of Trade, Jan. 2, 1701, in E. B. O'Callaghan and Berthold Fernow, eds., *Documents Relative to the Colonial History of the State of New-York . . .* (Albany, N.Y., 1853–1887), IV, 826, hereafter cited as *N.-Y. Col. Docs.*

[8] The layout of the town is displayed, not altogether accurately, on the Miller Plan, the only extant map for this period. Drawn from memory by John Miller, chaplain of the garrison between 1692 and 1695, the plan gives us some idea of how far the town had sprawled beyond the walled boundaries of New Amsterdam. See I. N. Phelps Stokes, *The Iconography of Manhattan Island, 1498–1909* (New York, 1915–1928) I, 234–235. For building developments in the town at the turn of the century see *ibid.*, IV, 413–422.

that dramatic event in the context of the changing townscape, we note that City Hall replaced the Stadt Huys that had accommodated New Amsterdam's burgomasters. The demolition of the older building and the use of stones from the Dutch town wall in building City Hall signified the transformation of New York into an English town.[9] Yet in 1700, thirty-six years after New Amsterdam became New York, the English were still a minority—probably not much more than 25 percent—of the white population.[10] The Dutch Reformed congregation, composed of about 450 families, was about five times the size of the Anglican congregation,[11] and until Trinity Church, the town's first Anglican church, opened in 1698, Anglicans held their services in the Dutch chapel in the fort. This experience left them with the impression that New York was more like "a conquered Foreign Province held by the terrour of a Garrison" than an English colony.[12] In their eyes, New York was far from adequately anglicized at the turn of the eighteenth century.

This point is crucial to an understanding of early eighteenth-century New York City politics: the English and English-identified men who organized themselves into the English Party in opposition to Governor Bellomont perceived themselves to be an embattled minority liv-

[9] *Minutes of the Common Council of the City of New York, 1675–1776* (New York, 1905), II, 82; Stokes, *Iconography*, IV, 417. For the "anglicization" thesis see Archdeacon, *New York City*, 128–129.

[10] Determining the size of the English community in relation to the Dutch and French communities is not easy. While the census records show that the white population was about 4,300 in 1700, they do not break down the population according to national background. Another problem is determining just who were Dutch. On the one hand, there were townsfolk of Dutch descent who had anglicized to the point of becoming English by this time; on the other, there was probably a greater number of "Batavianizing" men of English or French descent who had become Dutch by marrying into the Dutch Reformed community and joining the Dutch church. But we do know that contemporary observers placed the English at no more than 25% of the town's population in the 1690s. In 1696, for example, the townfolk were reported to be "one half Dutch, a quarter part French Protestants, and a quarter part English" (Chidley Brooke and William Nicoll's memorial to the Lords of Trade, in *N.-Y. Col. Docs.*, IV, 181–182). The influx of migrants over the next five years may have changed the balance in favor of the English, but not markedly, as many of the newcomers were Dutch families from outlying rural areas. The English, then, were clearly a minority in 1700. For the concept of "Batavianization" see John M. Murrin, "English Rights as Ethnic Aggression: The English Conquest, the Charter of Liberties of 1683, and Leisler's Rebellion in New York" (paper presented at the meeting of the American Historical Association, San Francisco, 1973, 7–8).

[11] In 1695 the Anglican chaplain, John Miller, counted 450 Dutch Reformed families and only 90 Anglican families (*New York Considered and Improved, 1695*, ed. V. H. Paltsits [Cleveland, Ohio, 1903], 54). Miller's table showing the religious distribution of the town's families is transcribed incorrectly in Ira Rosenwaike, *Population History of New York City* (Syracuse, N.Y., 1972), 10.

[12] Trinity Church vestry to Archbishop Thomas Tenison, May 22, 1699, *N.-Y. Col. Docs.*, IV, 526–528.

ing in a town in which the Dutch still had too much power. They re-acted by accusing the governor of bringing Dutch-English antagonism to the forefront of politics. He had, they said, appointed Dutchmen over Englishmen to important government posts, thereby setting up a Dutch against an English interest, and these same Dutchmen, domi-nating the municipal and provincial governments, were oppressing the English and French inhabitants.[13]

Bellomont's death in March 1701 did not improve the perceived predicament of the English Party. According to Nicholas Bayard, the party's principal spokesman, "those of the English nation" in New York were still "opprest" by the governor's Dutch appointees.[14] In-deed, if Bayard can be believed, Dutch-English tensions had never been more pronounced. This, at least, is the impression left by English Party commentators. A report filed in September 1701 by the newly arrived attorney general, Samuel Shelton Broughton, is a case in point. According to Broughton, who was to side with the English Party, there were "two very opposite parties" in New York; although many allega-tions were made on both sides, he could not discern a "more material ground" for their differences than that they "want to be distinguished for nation sake." [15] The realities, however, were far more complicated. As will be demonstrated in the trial of Nicholas Bayard, English Party observers tended to obscure rather than clarify the sources of political conflict in the town. As for Broughton, a newcomer, he would soon learn that New York politics at the turn of the eighteenth century could only be understood against the background of political violence that had exploded in Leisler's Rebellion a decade earlier.

II

Leisler's Rebellion is a misnomer for the uprising of townsmen—the only popular uprising in the history of New York City before the Stamp Act riots—that occurred in the wake of the Glorious Revolu-tion. The insurrection took place in May 1689, when the militia and townsfolk, frustrated by the reluctance of the ruling elite to declare for William of Orange, seized the fort and held it in the name of the new

[13] The English Party is first mentioned in the records in a report filed by Bellomont concerning the 1699 General Assembly election: in order to win the vote of the English townsmen, his opponents called themselves the English Party. This electioneering tactic struck Bellomont as ludicrous because three of the four English Party candidates were "as meer Dutch as any are in this town." Their names were Dutch and the men, he said, could scarcely speak English. Bellomont claimed that he was doing all he could to dis-courage "these distinctions of Dutch and English which is set on foot by the factious people of this town." Bellomont to the Lords of Trade, Apr. 27, 1699, *N.-Y. Col. Docs.*, IV, 507–508.

[14] "Heads of Accusation against the Earl of Bellomont," Mar. 11, 1700, *ibid.*, 620–621. Bayard to Meadows, Mar. 8, 1701, *ibid.*, 848.

[15] Broughton to the Lords of Trade, Sept. 3, 1701, *ibid.*, 913.

king of England. The displaced ruling elite accused Jacob Leisler, a captain of one of the dissident militia companies, of instigating the revolt, but eyewitness reports confirm the claims of the Leislerians, as the rebels came to be called, that Leisler, who assumed the title of lieutenant governor, took command of the insurgents only when Nicholas Bayard, the colonel of the militia, refused to lead them.[16]

Leisler's Rebellion was one of several in the American colonies during the crisis of authority created by the Glorious Revolution. It has been interpreted as an urban democratic movement, a "nativistic conflict," a "collective outburst of anxiety and anti-authoritarianism," [17] "an ethnic Dutch reaction to the English Conquest," and "a movement of displaced Dutchmen." [18] There is no space here to assess these interpretations,[19] but the evidence clearly establishes that Leisler's Rebellion was primarily a Dutch revolt—one made, moreover, in the name of a Dutch leader who had ascended the English throne. According to Bayard, for example, the insurgents acted on rumors that William would restore New York to Dutch rule. Bayard is not always a reliable witness, but, significantly, when the Leislerians came to ex-

---

[16] Bayard accused Leisler of instigating the rebellion in "Colonel Bayard's Narrative of Occurences in New-York, from April to December, 1689," *ibid.*, III, 637. Compare the view of Stephen Van Cortlandt, another prominent Anti-Leislerian, in Van Cortlandt to Edmund Andros, July 9, 1689, *ibid.*, 594–595. For the Leislerian version see Members of the Dutch Church of New York to the Classis of Amsterdam, Oct. 21, 1698, in Edward T. Corwin, ed., *Ecclesiastical Records of the State of New York* (Albany, N.Y., 1901–1916) II, 1249–1250, hereafter cited as *Ecc. Recs.* See also "Documents Relating to the Administration of Leisler," New-York Historical Society, *Collections*, I (New York, 1868), 268–269, 288–289, 345–346.

[17] Jerome R. Reich, *Leisler's Rebellion: A Study of Democracy in New York, 1664–1720* (Chicago, 1953), *passim*; Beverly McAnear, "Politics in Provincial New York, 1689–1761" (Ph.D. diss., Stanford University, 1935), 199–200; Kammen, *Colonial New York*, 118.

[18] Murrin, "English Rights as Ethnic Aggression," 2; Thomas J. Archdeacon, "The Age of Leisler—New York City, 1689–1710: A Social and Demographic Interpretation," in Jacob Judd and Irwin H. Polishook, eds., *Aspects of Early New York Society and Politics* (Tarrytown, N.Y., 1974), 73, 79. Generalizing from the case of Jacob Leisler, a wealthy merchant of German descent who may well have resented being on "the periphery" rather than at "the center of . . . power," Archdeacon claims that the rank-and-file insurgents had grievances that were "congruent" with those of their leaders. But he produces no evidence to show that they shared Leisler's enmity toward the "Anglo-French" mercantile elite that controlled the government at the time of the revolt (*New York City*, 109–113). See also Robert C. Ritchie, *The Duke's Province: A Study of New York Politics and Society, 1664–1691* (Chapel Hill, N.C., 1977), chap. 9.

[19] For an assessment of the evidence that concludes that the Dutch were more firmly entrenched in the town's economic structure than has previously been recognized see Adrian Howe, "Accommodation and Retreat: Politics in Anglo-Dutch New York City, 1700–1760" (Ph.D. diss., University of Melbourne, 1982), 115–120. See also Joyce D. Goodfriend, " 'Too Great a Mixture of Nations': The Development of New York City Society in the Seventeenth Century" (Ph.D. diss., University of California, Los Angeles, 1975), 141–163.

plain the nature of the rebellion, they claimed that they had been hold-ing the town for a Dutch prince who had come to liberate England and its American colonies just as his ancestors had delivered the Netherlands from "the Spanish Yoke." Significantly, too, they claimed to have acted out of an affection for the royal house of Nassau "which was natural to the Dutch nation—for thus are we designated here." [20]

The second point that can be established about Leisler's Rebellion is that New York's Dutch were divided in their response: while the large artisan community seems to have supported Leisler almost unani-mously, most of the merchants sided against him. So, too, did the min-ister of the Dutch Reformed church, who denounced Leisler from the pulpit. A third and related point is that the anti-insurgents rarely re-sorted to ethnic slurs to vilify members of Leisler's administration.[21] For example, when some of Leisler's enemies attempted to discredit his administration as a "Dutch plott," more astute observers among them pointed out that "the notion of the Dutch plott" was wrong inas-much as the Dutch townsmen "of best repute" had always opposed Leisler: the Leislerians were better described "the meanest and most abject common people." Ten years later, however, the Anti-Leislerians would consistently denigrate the Leislerians who returned to power under Bellomont as Dutchmen—"mean" and "indigent" Dutchmen, to be sure—but Dutchmen nevertheless.[22] In this important respect, the propaganda put out by the English Party against the Leislerian Dutch at the turn of the century was substantially different from that put out during Leisler's administration. Then his opponents consistently main-tained that political divisions in New York followed class rather than ethnic lines; now they emphasized a Dutch-English split.

Leisler's rule ended when he surrendered the fort to Gov. Henry Sloughter in March 1691. Two months later, he and his second-in-command, Jacob Milborne, were executed for treason. Another six men prominent in his administration received death sentences, and several others were indicted for riot. Leisler's execution created deep resentment among many of his followers, which, significantly, they di-rected less at Sloughter—whose name they pointedly misspelled "Slaughter"—than at the Anti-Leislerians whom he restored to power

[20] "Colonel Bayard's Narrative," in *N.-Y. Col. Docs.*, III, 639; Members of the Dutch Church to the Classis of Amsterdam, Oct. 21, 1698, *Ecc. Recs.*, II, 1248.

[21] Ritchie, *Duke's Province*, 220. For his part, Leisler occasionally made threats against "English rogues" but far more frequently he denounced his enemies as papists or "Popish Doggs" (Murrin, "English Rights as Ethnic Aggression," 19). For the most re-cent assessment of Leisler see David William Voorhees, " 'In Behalf of the true Protes-tant religion': The Glorious Revolution in New York" (Ph.D. diss., New York Univer-sity, 1988). Voorhees argues that religious and not ethnic considerations prevailed.

[22] "A Memorial of what has occurred in New-York," in *N.-Y. Col. Docs.*, III, 738–739; "Answer to the Memorial of Captain Benjamin Blagg to the King," *ibid.*, 763–766; "Heads of Accusation against the Earl of Bellomont," Mar. 11, 1700, *ibid.*, IV, 620–623.

and whom they knew had persuaded him to sign the death warrants.
The man they singled out in this regard was Nicholas Bayard. Eight
years after Leisler's execution, his followers still remembered Bayard's
"mortal grudge" against their leader for having imprisoned him during
the rebellion. They recalled, too, that Leisler had been condemned as
a traitor at a trial "mannag'd" by Bayard and other "a Vowed Enemies." It was Bayard who had lodged Governor Sloughter at his house
in order to persuade him to sign Leisler's death warrant. More provok-
ing still, Bayard had gone so far as to hang a flag from his window to
celebrate his success in dispatching Leisler to the gallows.[23]

Four years after the execution, the Anglican chaplain, John Miller,
observed that Leisler and Milborne had been hanged "to the great sorrow & regret of their whole party," which, he was credibly informed,
had "vowed revenge" and were waiting for an opportunity to "effect
their purpose." As will be seen, only a very small minority of Leisler's
followers were prepared to seize that occasion when it arose, but
Miller was right when he predicted that the "most unhappy division
and breach" resulting from "injuries" sustained during Leisler's rule
would take a long time to heal. In January 1702 Nicholas Bayard,
awaiting trial on a charge of high treason, observed from his prison
cell that the town's "former unhappy Breaches and Divisions" had broken out "to a more Violent Degree and Flame than ever." [24] Bayard
had good cause to dread his fate. A petition campaign that he and his
English Party colleagues had organized in the fall of 1701 had finally
provided his Leislerian enemies, who now controlled the government,
with the opportunity to turn the tables on the man they held primarily
responsible for Leisler's death.

III

On January 16, 1702, the Provincial Council opened an inquiry into
allegations that papers criticizing the government had been circulated
in the town. According to information received by Lt. Gov. John Nanfan, most of the soldiers garrisoned at Fort William Henry had signed
these papers. Judging this to be a matter of "dangerous Consequence,"
the Council learned by questioning officers and troops that the papers
were petitions to the king, the House of Commons, and Lord Cornbury, the governor-designate, complaining of oppressive government
in New York. The soldiers testified that the "Chief Actors" were

---

[23] "Petition and Remonstrance of the New York House of Representatives," May 15,
1699, N.-Y. Hist. Soc., *Colls.*, I (New York, 1868), 413–414. Bayard's role in Leisler's execution is well established. See Reich, *Leisler's Rebellion*, 120, and Mariana Van Rensselaer, *History of the City of New York in the Seventeenth Century* (New York, 1909), II,
549–560.

[24] Miller, *New York Considered and Improved*, ed. Paltsits, 68–69; Bayard to Henry
Adderly and Charles Lodwick, Jan. 28, 1702, in *N.-Y. Col. Docs.*, IV, 946.

Nicholas Bayard and his son Samuel, that the Bayards had persuaded people to sign the petitions in the town's coffeehouse, and that the West Ward alderman, John Hutchins, had invited the troops to his tavern near the fort, where, after drinking free beer, almost the entire garrison had signed the petitions on being promised that they would be made freemen of the town.[25]

The Council summoned the Bayards and ordered them to produce the petitions signed at the coffeehouse. When the Bayards refused, they were placed on bonds to appear before the Supreme Court. Hutchins, too, was taken into custody for refusing to hand over the petitions signed at his tavern. Then, on January 20, the council received an address from Nicholas Bayard, Philip French, Thomas Wenham, and Rip Van Dam demanding Hutchins's release on the ground that they had custody of the petitions, the legality of which they intended to prove.[26]

The petitions were never produced at the Council's inquiry. (Nor were they produced at the subsequent trials.) But by January 21, the Council had established that they were signed by French townsmen, several of whom were aliens (persons not subjects of the king of England), by "strangers" (men passing through the town), and by teenage boys. Most of the witnesses claimed not to have read the petitions, but those who admitted reading them testified that they set out a list of allegations: first, that the Speaker of the Provincial Assembly was an alien; second, that the assembly had passed several laws "to the prejudice of the country"; third, that Lieutenant Governor Nanfan had been bribed to assent to these laws; fourth, that the chief justice had also received bribes; fifth, that Bellomont had dismissed from office "the most Ingenious and sensible men" and replaced them with "the Scum of the people"; and last, that Nanfan had continued this "Scum" in office, thereby making the government "vile and cheap in the eyes of the people." [27]

The Council concluded its inquiry on January 21 by ordering the arrest of Nicholas Bayard. The warrant charged him with violating a law passed by the General Assembly in 1691 that made it high treason to "endeavour by force of arms or other ways to disturb the peace, good and quiet" of the government. Specifically, he had conspired with Hutchins and other "disaffected persons" to draw in soldiers and others to sign "Scandalous Libells whereby they have endeavoured to render the past and present Administration vile and cheap in the eyes of the people." In effect, he had "invited the people to disown" the king's

[25] New York Council Manuscript Minutes, 1668–1783, VIII, 297–298, New York State Library, Albany.

[26] Ibid., 299–301.

[27] Ibid., 302.

government in New York.[28] Yet if the conspicuous issue was loyalty to
the crown, the reality to the townsfolk was that the treason trial of
Nicholas Bayard was a political trial, and no attempt was made to disguise that fact. The arrest warrant was signed by the lieutenant governor and the five Council members who effectively controlled the government. All five—Abraham De Peyster, Samuel Staats, Robert
Walters, Thomas Weaver, and William Atwood—were Leislerians.
Anxious to try Bayard before the new governor arrived, the Council
decided not to wait until the April sitting of the Supreme Court but to
convene a special court of oyer and terminer. This court was called to
order on February 19 with Chief Justice William Atwood, Robert
Walters, and Abraham De Peyster on the bench; Thomas Weaver, in
the specially created post of solicitor general, presented the government's case, because the attorney general refused to prosecute.[29]

According to an account of the trial published in 1702 by Bayard
and David Jamison, a lawyer present at the proceedings, Weaver
opened with a long "harangue" designed to "incense and inflame the
jury," in which he vilified Bayard as the head of a "malignant party"
opposed to Leisler, made "scandalous" reflections on the Anglican
minister, William Vesey, and concluded by announcing himself a
member of the Leislerian party, saying he would "stand or fall by it."
The Bayard-Jamison version of the trial does not purport to be verba-
tim; it claims only to present "the substance of what passed." [30] But in
a defense of the proceedings published in London in 1703, Atwood
confirmed that Weaver did make remarks to this effect. Furthermore,
while Atwood dismissed the Bayard-Jamison account as a libel contain-

---

[28] *Ibid.*, 303. More elaborate language was used in the indictment read at Bayard's
subsequent trial. Bayard, according to the indictment, had been "moved and seduced by
the instigation of the devil as a rebel and traitor" to withdraw the "cordial love, due obedience fidelity and allegiance" which every subject owed the king. Thomas B. Howell, *A
Complete Collection of State Trials and Proceedings for High Treason* (London, 1816), XIV,
476.

[29] Howell, *State Trials*, XIV, 482–483.

[30] The Bayard-Jamison account, entitled *An Account of the Illegal Prosecution and Tryal
of Coll. Nicholas Bayard . . .* (New York, 1702), was published in London as *An Account of
the Commitment, Arraignment, Tryal and Condemnation of Nicholas Bayard for High Treason
. . .* (1703). This publication is reproduced in Howell, *State Trials*, XIV, 471–516. The
original is preserved as No. 1038 in Charles Evans, comp., *American Bibliography . . .*
(Chicago, New York, and Worcester, Mass., 1903–1959). The preface states that the account "comprehends the substance of what passed, as well as many of the Auditors could
bring away in their Memory, compared and assisted with such Notes, as privately (unknown to the Court) were taken" (*ibid.*, 1–2). This account also claimed that the bench
had "strictly prohibited" the taking of notes during the trial. But in fact the judge allowed a solicitor to take notes, and this solicitor, Paroculus Parmyter, later affirmed that
the Bayard-Jamison version of the proceedings was a "just and true relation of the most
material part and Substance thereof" (New York Colonial Manuscripts, XLVI, 156, N.Y.
State Lib.).

ing many "gross Falsehoods," his rebuttals were for the most part against inconsequential omissions rather than major misrepresentations. Thus the Bayard-Jamison account, the only detailed one we have, provides the basis for the following summary of the Bayard treason trial.[31]

IV

From the start, Bayard and his lawyers gave notice that the partisan composition of the bench would not keep them from protesting against injustices in the proceedings. Accordingly, even before the grand jury was sworn in, the defense objected that jurors had been heard to say that "if Bayard's neck was made of gold he should be hanged." Two days later, when the foreman, Johannes De Peyster, declared that the jury had found the bill of indictment to be sustained by the evidence, the defense promptly moved that the indictment be quashed on the ground that it had not been found by twelve jurors as the law required. But notwithstanding the fact that eight of the nineteen men who composed the "rump" jury protested in court that they had not found the bill against Bayard, Atwood ordered that Bayard be sent to trial.[32]

When the court reconvened on March 2, Bayard pled not guilty of conspiring to promote mutiny and desertion among the soldiers by enticing them and others to sign "false and scandalous" papers libeling the government as oppressive. The court then adjourned to March 6. On that day, about eighty men who had been impaneled as petit jurors appeared. The following day, Bayard protested the composition of this panel. He had, he said, frequently asked to be tried by Englishmen, but he had not been allowed one English grand juror. They had all been Dutchmen, some of whom could not understand the English language. Now he found that the impaneled petit jurors were also nearly all "of Dutch extraction and education" and "extreme ignorant in the English language." Moreover, most of them were laboring men, few of whom had served on a jury. Atwood responded by reprimanding Bayard for "indiscreetly" questioning the court's impartiality.[33] A twelve-

---

[31] "The Case of William Atwood, Esq.," N.-Y. Hist. Soc., *Colls.*, XIII (New York, 1880), 279, 299–302, hereafter cited as "Case of William Atwood." Note also that the minutes of the trial, which provide only a skeleton outline of the proceedings, coincide in almost every detail with the Bayard-Jamison account (Paul M. Hamlin and Charles E. Baker, *Supreme Court of Judicature of the Province of New York, 1691–1704* [New York, 1952–1959], II, 79–87). For a discussion of the accounts of the trial see Julius Goebel, Jr., and T. Raymond Naughton, *Law Enforcement in Colonial New York: A Study in Criminal Procedure, 1664–1776* (New York, 1944), 85.

[32] Howell, *State Trials*, XIV, 477–478. Twenty-four men were impaneled for the grand jury, but one, Johannes Hardenbroek, did not attend. Atwood dismissed four of the remaining twenty-three. See Table 1.

[33] *Ibid.*, 484–485.

man jury was sworn in, and Weaver opened the prosecution case, as we have seen, by denouncing Bayard as the head of the Anti-Leislerian party. He then called the witnesses for the crown.[34]

The prosecution established without difficulty that papers had been signed at the coffeehouse, at Hutchins's tavern, and, in addition, at Bayard's house. But proving that Bayard had solicited signatures or that the papers contained treasonous material was another matter entirely. Professing to have forgotten the contents of the addresses, witnesses for the crown would now admit only that they had signed them. Some claimed not to have read them. Only Samuel Clowes testified more fully. He told the court that he had called on Bayard about a business matter some three weeks before the latter's arrest. In the course of their discussion, Bayard had shown him three addresses. One, Clowes recalled, declared that "the hottest and ignorantest of the people were put into places of trust" by Governor Bellomont and alleged that the assembly had bribed Nanfan and Atwood. But Clowes could not be induced to testify that Bayard had pressed him to sign; he was adamant that he had done so voluntarily. The next witness, Peter Odyre, who did not speak English, told the court through an interpreter that "Mr Bodinot"—Elias Boudinot, an elder in the French church—had asked him to step into Bayard's house to sign an address to the king. Bayard had shown him the addresses, telling him they were "for the good of the country." But Odyre, like Clowes, insisted that he had signed of his own accord.[35]

Witnesses called to testify about the signing of addresses at the coffeehouse also refused to implicate Bayard. One, who admitted having gone to the coffeehouse where he saw about a hundred people and where he had signed three addresses without reading them, declared that Bayard was "no more acting or concerned than any other." As to Bayard's involvement in the signing of papers at Hutchins's tavern, Weaver again met with little success.[36] Several of the witnesses were soldiers. One, John Buckley, testified that he had refused Hutchins's request to sign the addresses on the ground that he was an officer of the garrison. The other soldiers all admitted to having signed at Hutchins's instigation. One testified that Hutchins had told him that the addresses were for the "good of the country and the English." He and others also testified that they had signed in the expectation of be-

---

[34] *Ibid.*, 486–487.

[35] On several occasions Weaver and Atwood suggested to witnesses that they had divulged more information at the Council inquiry (*ibid.*, 487–490).

[36] Hutchins's wife, Hannah, testified that Bayard had delivered certain papers to their tavern, where they had remained for three days, but she insisted that Bayard had not visited the tavern during that time. John Read, who admitted to being only 17 years of age, testified that he had signed papers at Hutchins's tavern, but while he had seen about 200 names on the papers, he had not seen Bayard at the tavern. *Ibid.*, 490–492.

ing made freemen of the town. Another soldier told the court that "a great many soldiers of the garrison" had signed when promised that they would be made freemen. One even admitted signing his own name and putting down the names of others on blank rolls, and an illiterate soldier admitted to having put his mark to one of the papers. But none had seen Bayard at the tavern.[37]

Weaver concluded by claiming to have proved the government's case. It was now the turn of the defense. Bayard's barristers, William Nicholls and James Emott, denied that the evidence proved that Bayard had played a pivotal role in the petition-signing activities. But they were not primarily concerned to dispute the prosecution's evidence. Instead, Nicholls began by defending the right of aggrieved subjects to petition the king. He then presented the key defense argument, namely, that even if the acts were proved, they were not treasonable. Emott, New York's leading criminal barrister, elaborated on this point of law. In a lengthy submission he argued that the New York law on which Bayard's indictment was laid contravened English common law governing cases of treason. Furthermore, the New York law, entitled "An Act for the quieting and settling the Disorders that have lately happened within this Province," was not relevant to the case. In a provocative reference to Leisler's administration, Emott argued that this law had been enacted for a specific purpose: to prevent the setting up of an "arbitrary power" such as the one that had been "of such fatal consequence in the late unhappy disorders in this province." It followed that the assembly's intention had been to prosecute as traitors only those who illegally took over the government. By no "legal, genuine construction" of this act could Bayard's actions be considered treasonable.[38] To bolster the case, the defense called two character witnesses on Bayard's behalf.

In his charge to the jury Atwood gave short shrift to the defense's points of law. He ruled that the indictment was not laid on English law but properly on the New York act that made it high treason to disturb the peace and quiet of the government. By signing libels against the government and by drawing in soldiers to sign them, Bayard, in Atwood's view, had violated this law. Moreover, by taking the papers to

---

[37] *Ibid.*, 492–494.

[38] *Ibid.*, 495–503. Nicolls, who had been imprisoned during Leisler's Rebellion, and Emott served as prosecutors in the court of oyer and terminer set up to try the Leislerians in 1691. For their biographies see Hamlin and Baker, *Supreme Court*, Vol. III: *Biographical Dictionary*, 74–78, 148–151. The law on which the indictment was laid was passed by the Anti-Leislerians in May 1691. It provided that any persons who should "Endeavour by force of arms or otherwise to disturb the peace good and quiet" of the government were to be "Deemed and Esteemed as Rebells and Traitors." *The Colonial Laws of New York from the Year 1664 to the Revolution* . . . (Albany, N.Y., 1894–1896), I, 224.

Hutchins's house, Bayard had "made himself guilty of all that was done there." The jury, Atwood concluded, could not do otherwise than find the prisoner guilty.[39] According to the Bayard-Jamison account, Atwood then adjourned the court until the evening of Saturday, March 7. When the jury failed to agree on that day, he adjourned again until March 9. But the jurors were still not agreed on Monday morning, at which time they requested direction from the bench on points of law. Atwood, who had already sent them written instructions on matters of law, told them to decide only on the facts of the case, thereby relieving them of the responsibility for deciding whether the facts constituted treason. Then, ignoring Emott's objection that jurors were judges of both fact and law, Atwood renewed his charge to the jury. That afternoon, the jury brought in a verdict of guilty. A week later, Atwood sentenced Bayard to death after peremptorily overruling all the pleas to arrest judgment offered by the defense.[40]

The center of action now shifted from the courtroom to the town's taverns, where Bayard's friends met to plan their strategy. Their immediate concern was to obtain a reprieve. To this end, they interceded with Lieutenant Governor Nanfan. Meanwhile, Bayard drafted petition after petition to Nanfan requesting a reprieve. All were rejected because Bayard had refused to confess. According to his account, Nanfan was under the influence of a conspiracy of jurors and others. Bayard had been told that his Leislerian enemies were entertaining Nanfan at Gabriel Thompson's Wall Street tavern with the aim of getting him drunk enough to sign the death warrant. But if there were such conspirators among the Leislerians, they failed in their purpose, for Nanfan granted Bayard a reprieve on March 30, the day fixed for his execution, Bayard having finally apologized for his offense to the satisfaction of the Council.[41]

V

The Bayard treason trial, a fascinating yet neglected episode, is a puzzling affair, made so by frustratingly incomplete documentation. We shall probably never be able to answer some of the questions it raises. Did the prosecution's witnesses, as Atwood alleged, testify more fully against Bayard than the Bayard-Jamison account discloses? Why did

---

[39] Howell, *State Trials*, XIV, 503–504.

[40] *Ibid.*, 504–516.

[41] "Case of William Atwood," 281–282; *A Narrative of the Treatment Coll. Bayard Received* . . . (New York, 1702), Evans No. 1079, *passim*. Bayard, "with much regrett and being extreamly disturbed and almost distracted in my scenes," finally confessed and asked pardon for the offense "which by the said sentence he finds and is convinced he has committed." He refused to erase the words "by the said sentence" on the ground that "if it was not for the said sentence," he was not "sensible" of having committed any crime. Bayard to the Lords of Trade, Apr. 24, 1702, *N.-Y. Col. Docs.*, IV, 953.

Atwood and prosecutor Weaver, neither of whom had known Leisler, display such vindictiveness toward Bayard? Why did the townsmen who had sided with Leisler leave it to two British placemen to conduct almost single-handedly proceedings that Bayard, for one, had expected would release the pent-up loathing for him in the predominantly Dutch Leislerian community?[42]

The Leislerians had waited eleven years to avenge their leader. Now, at last, the arrest of Bayard provided the opportunity. Yet Bayard escaped the gallows, and it is even possible that the Leislerian-controlled government had intended to reprieve him all along. By Bayard's account, two of the judges, Walters and De Peyster, refused to consent to the death sentence until Nanfan promised to grant a reprieve if Bayard confessed.[43] Furthermore, very few of the Leislerian jurymen appear to have appreciated the irony of turning the law condemning Leisler's Rebellion against one of the leading Anti-Leislerians.[44]

It is, however, precisely the enigmatic nature of the proceedings against Bayard that makes them valuable as a point of entry into the complex configurations of early eighteenth-century New York City politics. This becomes apparent when we interpret the trial as a drama highlighting the very different political orientations of Dutch and English townsmen. In this paradigm, the courtroom becomes a theater and the trial a play in which some of the participants, notably Bayard, Atwood, Weaver, and the foremen of the grand and petit juries, act out Leislerian versus Anti-Leislerian antagonisms, while the supporting cast of Dutch Leislerian townsmen refuse to play the roles assigned them in the drama directed by the Leislerian councillors. The drama stopped short of execution, leaving the impression that the Leislerians were simply play-acting—putting on a show in order to frighten Bayard into confessing in order to triumph symbolically. If it was all a game, however, the Leislerian jurymen seem not to have wanted to play, perhaps because they might have to endure the consequences, as

---

[42] "Case of William Atwood," 300. Weaver arrived in New York in 1698. Atwood did not arrive until July 1701. See the biographical accounts in Hamlin and Baker, *Supreme Court*, III, 11–18, 200–213. The Anti-Leislerians later claimed that Atwood "of his own meer violent humour and causeless malice, without any just reason or color of right," had "laboured to procure" indictments against Bayard and Hutchins ("Articles exhibited by the principal Merchants, Freeholders, and Inhabitants of the City of New York against W. Atwood, Chief Justice," Sept. 5, 1702, in W. Noël Sainsbury *et al.*, eds., *Calendar of State Papers, Colonial Series. America and West Indies* (London, 1860–1963), (*Jan.–Dec. 1, 1702,* 757).

[43] *Narrative of the Treatment Coll. Bayard Received,* Mar. 17, 1702.

[44] This irony has not been lost on historians. See Lawrence H. Leder, *Robert Livingston, 1654–1728, and the Politics of Colonial New York* (Chapel Hill, N.C., 1961) 177; Hamlin and Baker, *Supreme Court,* I, 303–304; and Van Rensselaer, *History of New York,* 11, 552. Van Rensselaer points out that Bayard was tried for "acts defined as treason by the statute which in 1691 he himself had induced the legislature to enact" (*ibid.,* 565).

they had in 1691. But leaving speculation aside, let us keep the spot-
light on the involuntary leading actor, Nicholas Bayard, who by making such an issue of Dutch and English distinctions in the courtroom
dramatized the ethnic hostilities that he and his English Party cohorts
claimed existed in the town.[45]

When he came to trial, Bayard could have boasted a Dutch pedigree
equal if not superior to that of any other New Yorker. He was the Hol-
land-born nephew of Peter Stuyvesant, the last Dutch governor of
New Netherland and the most famous personality of Dutch New
York.[46] He could have pointed to a record eight terms as elder in the
Dutch Reformed church. His name was enshrined in the church's
charter as one of its "first and present elders," and as late as 1698 he
was praised by the dominie for his "unwearied labors and great zeal"
on behalf of the Dutch congregation.[47] But by the time he came to
trial in 1702, Bayard was no longer Dutch. He had become English.
He was still, apparently, receiving communion in the Dutch church at
the time of his arrest, but he had also begun attending Anglican services at Trinity.[48] By transferring his affiliation from the "Church of

[45] For another reading of a colonial American trial as drama and, more generally, for
an explication of the possibilities of "dramaturgical analysis" of colonial American culture see Rhys-Isaac, "Dramatizing the Ideology of Revolution: Popular Mobilization in
Virginia, 1774 to 1776," *William and Mary Quarterly*, 3d Ser., XXXIII (1976), 357–371.
For a convincing case for insights gained from "reviewing the interaction of past people
as though the episodes considered were displayed in a theater" see Isaac, *The Transformation of Virginia, 1740–1790* (Chapel Hill, N.C., 1982), 325–326. For his elaboration of
an ethnographic methodology that applies a "theater model" to colonial American history see his "discourse on method," *ibid.*, esp. 350–357. If my dramaturgical reading of
colonial New York City politics seems to be unduly negative, it is interesting to note that
Milton Klein, reflecting on the enigmatic and much-debated nature of colonial New
York's political structure, asserted that "a number of conclusions seem acceptable even to
the most contentious historians." Significantly, the conclusions he arrived at were *all
negative:* "There was no simple oligarchy of home-grown aristocrats; no politically mute
masses; no clearly discernible clash between democrats and aristocrats, conservatives and
radicals" (*Politics of Diversity,* 198–199).

[46] Genealogists have disputed the pre-American ancestry of the Bayard family. By
family tradition, Nicholas Bayard's grandfather was Balthazar Bayard, a French Protestant divine who fled to Holland after the St. Bartholomew's Day massacre. Skeptics have
suggested that the grandfather was either one Capt. Martin Bayard of Ghent or Lazare
Bayard, a Walloon divine. Mrs. Anson Phelps Atterbury, *The Bayard Family . . .* (Baltimore, 1928); "Contributions to the History of the Ancient Families of New York," *New
York Genealogical and Biographical Record,* IX (1878), 54–55; *ibid.,* X (1879), 36–38; *ibid.,*
XVI (1885), 49–52; *ibid.,* LXV (1934), 345–348. See also the sketch of Bayard's life in
Dictionary of American Biography.

[47] *Ecc. Recs.,* II, 1148, 1243–1244.

[48] Atwood supplied this information. To Atwood, a man who conversed in the "Dutch
dialect" and who required assistance to "dress" his prose in an "*English* Stile," as he
claimed Bayard did, was a Dutchman. He therefore ridiculed Bayard's English preten-
sions and dismissed his attendance at the Anglican church as politically motivated: in Atwood's view it helped promote Bayard's "Ambition of being *Head of a pretended English*

the Fatherland," Bayard entered the final stage of his transformation into an Englishman. Moreover, at the trial he became assertively English, demanding an all-English jury and calling two English townsmen to testify on his behalf. One, William Vesey, minister of Trinity, said that he had been "personally acquainted" with Bayard for six years and knew him to be "an exemplary Christian." The other, Capt. John Tudor, a leading New York lawyer and a Trinity vestryman, testified that in the twenty-six years he had known him, Bayard had been a "moderate, civil, good man" who had never been "disaffected." [49]

It is interesting that Tudor dated his friendship with Bayard from 1676. We cannot know whether he did so pointedly, realizing that he could not vouch for Bayard's loyalty before that year without perjuring himself. In October 1675, Nicholas Bayard, described as "disaffected," was imprisoned for refusing to take the oath of allegiance after the transfer of New Netherland to the English for the second and last time. Together with seven other leading Dutch burghers, he had petitioned the new English governor, Edmund Andros, to guarantee the privileges of the "Dutch Nation in New-York" before imposing the oath. Their petition, the most militant nationalist statement to have come down to us from the New York Dutch, promised "full obedience" as long as the liberty of their church was guaranteed and they were not forced to take up arms against "any native Dutch nation." So strong indeed was their objection to "swearing lightly what nature and love for our own nation forbid," that the petitioners wished to leave New York if their demands were rejected. Instead, they were arrested, sent to trial, found guilty of promoting rebellion, and sentenced to forfeit their goods and chattels. The convicted Dutch leaders protested the sentence, which was later reduced to a third of their estates, but only Bayard, evidently the most recalcitrant, was imprisoned in the "Hole" following their conviction. [50]

---

and Church Party" ("Case of William Atwood," 275, 293, 302). Atwood's allegations about Bayard can be corroborated. In 1698 Bayard concluded a petition by apologizing that he had drawn it up "for want of assistance in the best forme and English I could" ("The Answer of Nicholas Bayard to the Reasons Exhibited by the Earle of Bellomont for Suspending him from the Council," Oct. 17, 1698, Bayard Papers, 1698–1710, New-York Historical Society). Though the Anglican church membership lists have not survived for this period, we know that Bayard was a Trinity vestryman from 1705 to 1711 ("Rectors, Church Wardens and Vestrymen of the Corporation of Trinity Church," Trinity Church, Box 29, N.-Y. Hist. Soc.).

[49] Howell, *State Trials*, XIV, 503.

[50] "Petition of the Dutch Nation in New-York, heretofore called New Netherland," Mar. 16, 1675, *N.-Y. Col. Docs.*, II, 740–743; E. B. O'Callaghan, ed., *Calendar of Historical Manuscripts in the Office of the Secretary of State, Albany, N.Y.* (Albany, N.Y., 1866), XI, *English Manuscripts*, XXIV, 72–84, 186, 196; *ibid.*, XXV, 1–2, 14–15. For an account of the loyalty oath crisis see Ritchie, *Duke's Province*, 140–142.

While it is difficult to gauge the effect of this loyalty oath controversy on the Dutch community, the effect on Bayard is easy to measure: he adjusted to English rule by taking the oath of allegiance and
becoming English himself. It took him ten years to win office in the
English administration, but on the eve of Leisler's Rebellion, few, if
any, of the other prominent anglicizing Dutch merchants who collabo-
rated with Andros's Dominion government were as fully integrated
into the new order as this former belligerent Dutch nationalist.[51]

When in January 1702 the Leislerian councillors reported to the
London colonial office that the leader of the "factious party" in New
York was one Colonel Bayard, "of foreign birth a man never easy under an English Government," they were probably not referring to his
long-forgotten stand on behalf of the "Dutch Nation" in 1675 but to
his refusal to lead the "true English subjects" who in 1689 had held the
town for William of Orange. In Leislerian eyes, Bayard had been doubly traitorous: as a Dutchman to the prince of Orange and as an Englishman to the king of England. Worse, he had betrayed his own people. Asked in the name of the militia to declare allegiance to William,
Bayard, the commanding officer, had refused, even though he knew
that all would have followed his example. Leislerian townsmen listening to Captain Tudor's testimony on Bayard's behalf therefore had
good reason to scoff at his statement that Bayard had always "stood up
for" King William. They knew him to have been one of "the last and
backwardest" to acknowledge the monarch's sovereignty.[52]

Now, in 1702, Bayard had much more to answer for—his role in the
execution of Leisler, the man who, in the eyes of his followers, had
filled the leadership vacuum that Bayard himself had created. As he
awaited trial, Bayard contemplated "the envy of the Leislerian party
. . . against mee" and despaired of his fate. As he well knew, he had
been all along "the principal object of their Malice and chiefly markt
out by them for destruction." He felt sure he would be sacrificed to
their "canckered envy and hatred." [53] The selection of jurors confirmed his worst expectations. Not only were they all "ignorant"
Dutchmen, but most of the men impaneled for the grand jury were, he

[51] Ritchie, *Duke's Province*, 143; Murrin, "English Rights as Ethnic Aggression," 5–6.

[52] Council of New York to the Lords of Trade, Jan. 20, 1702, in *N.-Y. Col. Docs.*, IV,
942–943; Members of the Dutch Church to the Classis of Amsterdam, Oct. 21, 1698, in
Ecc. Recs., II, 1249–1250; "Loyalty Vindicated . . . ," N.-Y. Hist. Soc., *Colls.*, I (New
York, 1868), 375.

[53] Bayard to Adderly and Lodwick, Jan. 28, 1702, in *N.-Y. Col. Docs.*, IV, 947. Early in
Bellomont's administration Bayard had fled to England believing that it would not be
safe to return to New York unless he could obtain from the English colonial office
"something to be my protection" (quoted in Leder, *Robert Livingston*, 144). Bayard knew
he had been the "Chief Ey sore" of the Leislerians during the rebellion ("Colonel Bayard's Narrative," *N.-Y. Col. Docs.*, III, 645).

protested, his "mortal enemies," and all twelve members of the trial jury were "parties concerned against" him "in the very matter he was tried for." [54] And yet at the trial they failed to act decisively against him. To discover why, we need to shift our focus to the townsmen who performed as jurors in the courtroom drama.

VI

Consider the grand jury (Table 1). To begin with, the twenty-three impaneled men were not all Dutchmen, as Bayard claimed: John Corbett, a Trinity vestryman, and Caleb Cooper were English; William Jackson was born in Edinburgh. The remaining twenty, however, were Dutch, and, except for Burger Myndertse, a Lutheran, they were all members of the Dutch Reformed church. Most were second- or third-generation descendants of the original settlers of New Amsterdam, but four had migrated from the Netherlands: Jacob Boelen, Leendert Huygen De Cleyn, and Johannes Outman from Holland, and Jan Van Giesen from Utrecht.[55] Bayard maintained that several grand jurors were aliens who should therefore have been disqualified from jury service. This was true in three cases, but whether these Dutch grand jurors did not understand English, as Bayard also claimed, cannot be determined.[56]

Second, positive identification of the political allegiance of twenty-one grand jurors establishes that they were not all Leislerians, as Bayard implied when he described them as "parties concerned against"

[54] Howell, *State Trials*, XIV, 485, 511–512. Bayard repeated these accusations against the jurors in a report sent to the London colonial office after his trial. He had, he said, "put upon me both a grand and Petty Jury, some of [th]em Aliens, and the rest of them either very ignorant in the English language or my implacable enemies . . . and very many of them a party concerned against me, in relation to the Grievances complained of in the Addresses" (Bayard to the Lords of Trade, Apr. 24, 1702, *N.-Y. Col. Docs.*, IV, 952).

[55] Boelen and Huygen De Cleyn arrived in New Amsterdam with their parents. Outman migrated in the 1680s. For the Boelen and Huygen De Cleyn family genealogies see *N.Y. Gen. and Bio. Record*, VII (1876), 148, and *ibid.*, LXXII (1941), 265–268. The backgrounds of Outman and Van Giesen have been identified from marriage and membership records of the Dutch Reformed church. For details on sources identifying the jurymen see below, n. 58.

[56] Boelen, Huygen De Cleyn, and Outman were not naturalized until 1715 ("The Oath of Abjuration, 1715–1716," New-York Historical Society, *Quarterly Bulletin*, III [1919], 35–40, hereafter cited as "Oath of Abjuration"). We know that Huygen De Cleyn's first language was Dutch because the year he was elected as church warden on the civil vestry (in 1714), the church wardens' accounts were kept in Dutch (Accounts of the Church Wardens, New York City Box 50, N.-Y. Hist. Soc.). It is possible that even the foreman of the grand jury, Johannes De Peyster, a third-generation Dutch New Yorker, was less than fluent in English. A few months after the trial, he wrote a letter—in Dutch—from Boston in which he informed his brother that "I *now* [my emphasis] know the way and understand the speech" (Johannes De Peyster to Abraham De Peyster, Nov. 19, 1702, De Peyster Papers, 1695–1710, N.-Y. Hist. Soc.).

TABLE 1   *Bayard Treason Trial: Grand Jury*

	POLITICAL ALLEGIANCE	OCCUPATION	1702 TAX ASSESSMENT (£)
Jacob Boelen P	L	goldsmith	70
Martin Clock	L	cordwainer	110
Caleb Cooper D	AL	merchant	180
John Corbett D	AL	mariner	30
Jacob De Key D	AL	bolter	150
Johannes De Peyster	L	merchant	210
Adrian Hooglandt	L	merchant	110
Leendert Huygen De Cleyn	L	baker	260
William Jackson P	AL	cordwainer	70
Hendrick Jellisse	L	cordwainer	100
Abraham Keteltas	unknown	blacksmith	50
Abraham Kip P	AL	brewer	100
Burger Myndertse P	AL	blacksmith	30
Johannes Outman	unknown	merchant	160
David Provoost	L	merchant	200
Barent Rynders	L	merchant	100
Johannes Van Cortlandt D	AL	merchant	100
Johannes Vander Spiegel P	L	bolter	40
Jan Van Giesen	L	shopkeeper	75
John Van Horne P	AL	bolter	100
Gerrit Van Horne P	AL	bolter	110
Peter Van Tilburgh	L	bolter	120
Johannes Van Zandt P	AL	blockmaker	20

P = Protested in court that he did not find the bill of indictment against Bayard.
D = Dismissed for refusing to observe Atwood's charge.
L = Leislerian.
AL = Anti-Leislerian.
Source: Hamlin and Baker, *Supreme Court*, II, 79–80.
Occupations: "The Burghers of New Amsterdam and the Freeman of New York," New-York Historical Society, *Collections*, XVIII (New York, 1885); "Indentures of Apprenticeship, 1695–1708," *ibid.*, "Abstracts of Wills," *ibid.*, XXV (1892), XXVI (1893), XXVII (1894)
Assessment: New York City assessment roll, April 1702, microfilm, Historical Documents Collection, Paul Klapper Library, Queens College, City University of New York.

him. No fewer than ten were Anti-Leislerians—that is, men who were aligned with Bayard's English party. One, Jacob De Key, had been arrested by Leisler during the uprising of 1689. Several others, notably Johannes Van Cortlandt and John and Gerrit Van Horne, were members of leading Anti-Leislerian families who had actually signed Bayard's allegedly treasonable addresses.[57] The positions taken by these ten Anti-Leislerian grand jurors were predictable enough: four were dismissed for having refused to observe Atwood's charge and for having "clamorously insisted upon *hearing Witnesses*" for Bayard. The other six protested in court that they had not found the bill of indictment against Bayard.[58]

This is puzzling. Why did the Leislerian sheriff, Isaac De Riemer, select ten Anti-Leislerians as grand jurors? [59] Why did two of the Leislerian grand jurors—Jacob Boelen and Johannes Vander Spiegel, who had voted for the Leislerians at the municipal elections in 1701—join the dissenting Anti-Leislerian jurors when the foreman brought in the indictment endorsed "Billa Vera"? This left only eleven grand jurors—one fewer than the law required—who agreed to find the bill against Bayard.[60] Bayard, then, did the grand jurors an injustice when he dismissed them all indiscriminately as his "implacable enemies." Nearly half were Anti-Leislerians, and the affidavit filed by the grand jury at the later inquiry reveals that several men positively identified as Leislerians were not prepared to indict Bayard for treason. Jacob Boelen explained why he, for one, had reservations. While he found the bill according to the evidence—which was for signing the addresses—he was not prepared to indict Bayard for treason as he did not understand the

[57] The others were identified as Anti-Leislerians from the poll lists for the municipal election held six months before the trial (*Minutes of the Common Council*, II, 163–178).

[58] "Case of William Atwood," 278; Hamlin and Baker, *Supreme Court*, II, 80; Howell, *State Trials*, XIV, 478. William Jackson's Anti-Leislerian allegiance is established by the fact that he served on several of the stacked juries in the Leislerian trials of 1691 (Lawrence H. Leder, ed., "Records of the Trials of Jacob Leisler and His Associates," *New-York Historical Society Quarterly*, XXXVI [1952], 441–446). Data on ethnicity have been drawn from church and marriage records, wills, and genealogies. For genealogies of Dutch New York families see *N.Y. Gen. and Bio. Record, passim*, and Jonathan Pearson, *Contributions for the Genealogies of the First Settlers of the Ancient County of Albany, from 1630 to 1800* (Albany, N.Y., 1872).

[59] For an account of Isaac De Riemer's Leislerian politics see Hamlin and Baker, *Supreme Court*, III, 64–69.

[60] Atwood, however, wrote that fourteen grand jurors agreed in finding the bill. The matter was clarified at a later inquiry into the proceedings against Bayard. According to the grand jurors who testified before the commission set up in Nov. 1702 to collect evidence relating to Bayard's trial, only a few grand jurors had agreed to indict Bayard for treason. Five others, including the Leislerian Johannes Vander Spiegel, had voted against finding any bill. Several others, including three Leislerians—Boelen, Hendrick Jellise and Peter Van Tilburgh—had "found the bill according to the evidence . . . but not the treason." As Abraham Kipp explained, these men had found Bayard guilty of signing the addresses and "promoting" others to sign them. But they had not found that this was an indictable offense. The foreman, Johannes De Peyster, had ignored this important distinction when he counted the votes for finding the bill against Bayard. "Case of William Atwood," 302; N.Y. Colonial MSS, XLVI, 147, 161–172.

law on which the indictment was laid.[61] Eliminating Boelen and the other men who testified that they had not agreed to indict Bayard, we are left with a core group of only eight of the original twenty-three who, as far as the records show, at no time expressed misgivings about the propriety of the proceedings. These eight were the only men on the panel prepared to play the role of Bayard's "mortal enemies" in the courtroom drama.

Four of these eight were principals in the Leislerian Party. Johannes De Peyster, David Provoost, and Martin Clock had stood for alderman in the recent municipal election. All three were captains of militia companies. The fourth, Jacob Boelen, was a leading member of the Dutch church. The remaining four were rank-and-file Leislerians.[62] One, Jan Van Giesen, had a personal score to settle with Bayard: he was one of the rebels sued by Bayard in 1692 for damaging his house during the uprising. Yet there is no evidence that Van Giesen played an aggressive role during the trial. He was not, for example, one of the jurors whom Bayard later sued for damages for having falsely indicted him.[63] Nor was he one of the men named by Bayard as having "conspired" to get him executed. In his account of his efforts for a reprieve, Bayard named only two "Chief Conspirators" in what he described as a plot against his life. They were De Peyster, foreman of the grand jury, and Provoost, who, Bayard was informed, had taken Nanfan to a tavern with the aim of pressing him to sign Bayard's death warrant.[64]

That De Peyster fled from New York shortly after the arrival of Governor Cornbury in May 1702 suggests that he may have been implicated in a plot to dispose of Bayard, but Bayard's allegations against him cannot be verified.[65] The evidence does show, however, that if De

[61] "Case of William Atwood," 162.

[62] De Peyster and Provoost, who received their commissions from Jacob Leisler in 1689, were also members of the General Assembly. Sources used to identify Leislerians include the poll lists for the 1701 election, *Minutes of the Common Council*, II, 163–178; "List of the Commissions issued by Lieutenant-Governor Jacob Leisler," in Edmund B. O'Callaghan, ed., *The Documentary History of the State of New-York* (Albany, N.Y., 1849–1851), III, 347–354; and "Documents Relating to the Administration of Leisler," N.-Y. Hist. Soc., *Colls.*, I, 324–348.

[63] O'Callaghan, ed., *Documentary History*, II, 393–394. The other three Leislerians were Leendert Huygen De Cleyn, Adrian Hooglandt and Abraham Keteltas. In Apr. 1702 Bayard brought actions against two of the judges in his trial—Robert Walters and Abraham De Peyster—and three of the grand jurors—Barent Rynders, David Provoost and Leendert Huygen De Cleyn. Hamlin and Baker, *Supreme Court*, I, "Introduction," 174. (Note that Hamlin and Baker confuse Abraham De Peyster, whom Atwood names as one of the men sued by Bayard, with his brother, Johannes De Peyster. "Case of William Atwood," 297.)

[64] *Narrative of the Treatment Coll. Bayard Received*, Mar. 26, 29, 1702.

[65] Johannes De Peyster arrived in Boston in July 1702. He received legal advice there to "take care not to be outlawed," but he remained confident. He even hoped that Bayard "would enter an action before the Court" because the governor of Massachusetts

Peyster did actively "conspire" against Bayard, he failed to persuade some of the Leislerians on the grand jury to agree to a true bill.[66] Furthermore, if De Peyster called for Bayard's blood and maneuvered to get Nanfan to sign the death warrant, his eldest brother, Col. Abraham De Peyster, one of the judges in the treason trial, effectively canceled his actions.

Four days before he was sentenced to death, Bayard wrote Abraham De Peyster a letter protesting his innocence. The letter, which Atwood read out in court when he passed sentence, singled out the De Peyster family as the "likely chief instruments of the total destruction both of myself and all my family and posterity." Bayard did not elaborate on "all the plots, contrivances and intrigues used in this Matter," except to say that Johannes De Peyster and David Provoost had made threats against his life. In particular, Bayard failed to clarify Abraham De Peyster's role in what he called a "conspiracy" to "cut me off." Instead, he employed a biblical analogy to insinuate that Abraham De Peyster acted out of resentment because his ambition had in some way been thwarted—how, we are not told. Yet by Bayard's own account, Abraham De Peyster would not consent to the death sentence until Nanfan promised to grant a reprieve if Bayard applied for one. Then, when Bayard refused to draw up his petition for a reprieve in the form of a full confession, Abraham De Peyster and other members of the Leislerian Council solicited the aid of the dominie of the Dutch church to inform Bayard that if he confessed his crime "in general terms" he would be reprieved. These backstage dealings, which Bayard wrongly dismissed as "all Trick and Fraud," [67] may well have puzzled Atwood, who had resided in New York for less than a year. But they would have been recognized as familiarly Dutch by seasoned observers of New York City's highly personalized and labyrinthine politics, who would probably not have been surprised to learn that while one member of a leading Dutch family appeared to be working for Bayard's execution, another member of the same family was working for a reprieve. Quite possibly, they were both working, in fact, to get the confession. The Dutch frequently acted in such puzzling ways.

A study of the grand jury, then, introduces us to the enigmatic behavior of the Dutch. The conflicting actions of the De Peyster brothers are a case in point. Another is the fact that the Dutch Leislerian sheriff unaccountably returned as many as ten Anti-Leislerian grand

---

told him "they could not harm me." Johannes to Abraham De Peyster, Aug. 3, 1702, De Peyster Papers.

[66] For example, Peter Van Tilburgh, who had voted for De Peyster in the 1701 municipal election, claimed after the trial that he was against finding Bayard guilty of treason. N.Y. Colonial MSS, XLIV, 169.

[67] Howell, State Trials, XIV, 510–511; Narrative of the Treatment Coll. Bayard Received, Mar. 17, 28, 1702.

jurors, who, predictably, balked at indicting Bayard for treason. As demonstrated, the Dutch Leislerian members of the panel, whom Bayard expected to avenge Leisler's death, divided among themselves. Moreover, they divided in other ways that also highlight the complex nature of Leislerian/Anti-Leislerian conflict, which, contrary to Bayard's claims, was not straightforwardly Dutch versus English. While the grand jurors identified as Leislerians were all Dutchmen, so, too, were all but three of the Anti-Leislerians. Furthermore, political divisions did not follow economic lines. Ordinarily, grand jurors were chosen from among the more substantial freeholders, and the men selected for Bayard's trial, notwithstanding his insinuation that they were not men of the best "estates," were no exception to the rule.[68] The taxable wealth of the grand jurors recorded on the tax roll drawn up a few weeks after the trial reveals that all but two were freeholders and most were men of means. Three of the Leislerians—Johannes De Peyster, David Provoost, and Leendert Huygen De Cleyn—had taxable assets valued at £200 or more, placing them in a higher bracket than any of the Anti-Leislerian grand jurors. At the other end of the scale, Johannes Vander Spiegel, a bolter, was assessed at only £40. Vander Spiegel was a Leislerian. But Johannes Van Zandt, a blockmaker by trade who was not a freeholder and who possessed a personal estate valued at only £20, was an Anti-Leislerian. (See Table 1). Tax rolls are not a reliable guide to real wealth, but the evidence they give of the status of the grand jurors supports Thomas J. Archdeacon's claim that "wealth did not significantly affect political affiliation" in early eighteenth-century New York politics.[69]

All this raises more questions about the political allegiance and commitment of New Yorkers than can be addressed here. But before turning to our main question—the reluctance of the Dutch Leislerian jurors to act against Bayard—let us identify the members of the trial jury (Table 2). Contrary to Bayard's allegations, all except one were freeholders.[70] But only the foreman, Jacobus Goelet, and Coenraet Ten Eyck were substantial freeholders, and with the exception of Barent Kool, a moderately wealthy merchant, all were artisans—"labouring men," in Bayard's eyes.[71] Furthermore, eleven were Dutch and the

---

[68] Goebel and Naughton, *Law Enforcement in New York*, 466–467. On Mar. 6 Bayard complained to the court that he had wanted to be tried by men "of the best character for knowledge, integrity, justice, conscience, and estates" (Howell, *State Trials*, XIV, 485).

[69] Archdeacon, *New York City*, 141.

[70] When the Leislerians came to reply to the allegation that the Bayard jury had been selected from "the meanest and ignorantest of the People," they denied that the jurors were as "ignorant and mean" as Bayard claimed: every one, they insisted, "was a good and Substantiall freeholder of the City" ("Petition of Severall of the Principall Freeholders . . . to the Queen," Misc. MSS "Atwood," N.-Y. Hist. Soc.).

[71] Yet only one, Garret Viele, a brazier who had come from Albany in the 1690s, did not own his home. Two weeks after the trial, his personal estate was valued at only £10— £40 below that required by law of jurors who were not freeholders. The real and per-

TABLE 2   *Bayard Treason Trial: Petit Jury*

	POLITICAL ALLEGIANCE	OCCUPATION	1702 TAX ASSESSMENT (£)
Samuel Beekman	Leislerian	cordwainer	40
Cornelius Clopper	Leislerian	cordwainer	30
Jacobus Cornelissen	—	farmer	20
Jacobus Goelet	Leislerian	bricklayer	100
Barent Kool	—	merchant	70
Andries Maerschalk	—	bolter	60
Saert Olpherts	Leislerian	bricklayer	75
Thomas Sanders	—	baker	35
Issac Stoutenburgh	—	carpenter	15
Coenraet Ten Eyck	—	cordwainer	120
Jacobus Vander Spiegel	Leislerian	silversmith	50
Garret Viele	—	brazier	10

Sources: Hamlin and Baker, *Supreme Court*, II, 83, and sources cited in Table 1.

twelfth, Thomas Sanders, who married into the Dutch Reformed community, was a Dutch-identified man.[72] Three had migrated from the Netherlands.[73] Two of these three, Andries Maerschalk and Goelet, were aliens and as such should have been disqualified from

---

sonal estates of five of the other jurors were assessed at below £50. They were to this extent "mean," but they were hardly men "of mean capacities to an extreme degree," as Bayard claimed. For the genealogy of the Viele family see *N.Y. Gen. and Bio. Record*, XLIV (1913), 232–236. The Jury Act passed by the Leislerian assembly in 1699 required jurors to be men of property owning "one dwelling house free from all Incumbrances or a personall Estate to the value of fifty pounds." "A Bill for the Regulating and returning of able and Sufficient Jurors in Tryalls at Law," May 16, 1699, *N.Y. Colonial Laws*, I, 387–388. Archdeacon erroneously claims that jurors had to own a £60 estate (*New York City*, 126). For a discussion of the jury law see Hamlin and Baker, *Supreme Court*, I, 177–183.

[72] Thomas Sanders (Sanderszen in the Dutch records) married Aeltie Santvoort in the New York Dutch church in 1696. Jonathan Pearson describes his father as an "Amsterdam smith" who migrated to New Netherland before 1640. He and his wife, Sara Thomas, had settled in Albany (then Beverwyck) by the 1650s (*Contributions for the Genealogies of the First Settlers of Albany*). Murrin includes the Sanders family in his list of "Batavianizing" English families ("English Rights as Ethnic Aggression," 23). But note that when Jasper Danckaerts visited Albany in 1680 his interpreter was Robert Sanders (Thomas Sanders's oldest brother), whom he described as a "good Englishman" (Bartlett Burleigh James and J. Franklin Jameson, eds., *Journal of Jasper Danckaerts, 1679–1680* [New York, 1913], 216).

[73] Jacob Goelet arrived from Holland in 1678. Maerschalk, who was born in Vlissingen in Zeeland, arrived a few years later. Saert (or Sioert or Shuart) Olpherts arrived in New Amsterdam from Friesland in 1663. He was listed as Schout Olferts on the New Amsterdam passenger lists. See "A List of Early Immigrants to New Netherland,"

jury service as the defense insisted.[74] Were the trial jurors prejudiced against Bayard—"parties against" him—as he alleged? The five whose political allegiance can be determined were all Leislerians. While the political sympathies of the remaining seven are not recorded, it can be presumed that they were also Leislerians since they lived in the North Ward, a Leislerian stronghold and the only ward that the Leislerians won outright in 1701.[75] We cannot, however, assume that men with Leislerian sympathies were automatically "parties" against Bayard: the hesitation of the trial jury to find him guilty has already made that clear.

What can be gleaned from the records about the jury's attitude toward the proceedings against Bayard? We recall that, according to the Bayard-Jamison account, Atwood found it necessary to send the jurors written instructions explaining the law of treason when they failed to follow his charge to "bring in the prisoner guilty." [76] Two of the jurors, Thomas Sanders and Isaac Stoutenburgh, who later testified that the jurymen were all "ignorant of the Laws of England at that time not knowing what was High Treason," confirmed the allegation. They also testified that as many as eight or nine of the jurors had wanted to return a verdict of not guilty, but had been persuaded to change their minds by the foreman, who convinced them that it was treason "by the Law of this Province" to disturb the peace as Bayard had done by signing and encouraging others to sign the addresses. But some of the jurors were apparently still unsure of the law and requested further direction from the bench. Only after Atwood had sent the jury written replies and renewed his charge to them did Sanders and Stoutenburgh "yield and submit to find the prisoner guilty." Even then they did so

---

N.Y. Gen. and Bio. Record, XV (1884), 37. The Goelets were a Huguenot family that settled in Amsterdam in the 1620s. Jacobus Goelet was born in Buiksloot, a small village near Amsterdam, in 1665. Goelet Family Papers, Holland Society, New York City. Andries Maerschalk, whose time of arrival is unknown, married Elisabeth Van Gelder in the Dutch church in 1690.

[74] If Goelet had, as Emott claimed, "lately sent to England for to procure a denization," the application must have been unsuccessful as he did not become naturalized until 1715 (Howell, *State Trials*, XIV, 509; "Oath of Abjuration," 37–38).

[75] For sources identifying the trial jurors as Leislerians see O'Callaghan, ed., *Documentary History*, III, 347, and *Minutes of the Common Council*, II, 150, 163–178. Evidence from a later period indicates that Coenraet Ten Eyck, a Dock Ward resident, was also a Leislerian. In November 1702 he, Jacobus Vander Spiegel, and three members of the grand jury—Adrian Hooglandt, Leendert Huygen De Cleyn, and Martin Clock—"behaved with much Insolence and ill Manners" when they appeared before an assembly committee that was preparing a bill declaring the illegality of the proceedings against Bayard. Vander Spiegel, Hooglandt, and Clock were found guilty of "contempt towards the House" and taken into custody. *Journal of the Votes and Proceedings of the General Assembly of the Colony of New York, from 1766 to 1776 . . .* (Albany, N.Y., 1820), I, 153.

[76] Howell, *State Trials*, XIV, 503–505.

"with much regret and trouble of mind." Unfortunately, there is no way to check the authenticity of this testimony that took the form of an unsworn statement submitted to a Council inquiry set up several months after the trial.[77] Yet, even if this statement is dismissed as fabrication, a question remains: why did the jurors, most of whom were Leislerians, have to be pressured into returning a guilty verdict against the man they surely recognized as Leisler's nemesis? Why, even if they were all "ignorant" of the law of treason, did they not simply seize this opportunity to follow Atwood's clear instruction to find him guilty and so see him hanged as Leisler and Milborne had been?

VII

These questions are not easy to answer. Aside from the unsworn statement of the two trial jurors and the affidavits filed by the grand jurors several months after the trial, we have no statements from the Leislerians who took part in the trial explaining their attitude. However, two related considerations may help to make their hesitations intelligible. First, there was prudence born of experience. Leislerians had been ruthlessly repressed in 1691, when their opponents returned to power under Governor Sloughter. Two of their leaders had been executed. Six others, sentenced to death for murder or treason, lived under threat of execution for several years. As many as thirty supporters were exempted from the general pardon act of 1691 and had to wait until 1699 to be indemnified for their "actings in the late happy Revolution." [78] Now, in 1702, the imminent arrival of a new governor—correctly thought to be sympathetic to the Anti-Leislerians—made it unwise to act precipitously.[79] Thus fear of being called to account, as they had been in 1691, may well have inhibited the Leislerian jurors from acting out the antagonism felt toward Bayard in the Leislerian com-

---

[77] Sanders and Stoutenburgh "owned and said" it was true, but they refused to swear to it or sign their deposition. *Calendar of Historical Manuscripts*, II, 152. Many documents and depositions referred to in this calendar were destroyed or badly obliterated by the New York State capitol fire of 1911. Fortunately, several depositions relating to the Bayard treason trial were transcribed in the 19th century. They are filed as "Transcripts of Manuscripts . . . Relating to the trial of Nicholas Bayard for Treason . . . ," Misc: Bayard, N.-Y. Hist. Soc. The depositions of Sanders and Stoutenburgh are in this collection.

[78] "A Bill for the Indemnifieying of all Such Persons as were Excepted out of the Generall pardon," May 16, 1699, *N.Y. Colonial Laws*, I, 384–385. The jurors may also have taken into consideration the fact that in 1691 Bayard had sued 20 Leislerians for imprisoning him and another 13 Leislerians for "Wrongs Spoils and Injuries," committed to his house during the uprising. O'Callaghan, ed., *Documentary History*, II, 393–394. See Reich's account of the Anti-Leislerian "policy of repression" (*Leisler's Rebellion*, 120–130).

[79] The Anti-Leislerians were informed that Cornbury would be sympathetic to their cause as early as Nov. 1701 (Leder, *Robert Livingston*, 174–175).

munity. This could also explain why such leading Leislerians as Abraham De Peyster adopted a low profile during the trial. As far as the extant records show, he refrained from displaying any overt hostility toward Bayard. He did pass Bayard's letter on to the chief justice, but when Atwood read parts of the letter in court, De Peyster, as far as we know, was mute and impassive. In all probability, this demeanor was adopted with a view to self-preservation. This, however, is speculation. Still, pragmatism characterized the response of the Dutch to crises in New York City politics, and in this respect Abraham De Peyster, who survived the political vicissitudes of the Leislerian era better than any other townsman, was an archetypical New York Dutch politician.[80]

The reluctance of the Dutch Leislerians to act against Bayard may also have been a matter of temperament and tradition. Evidence suggests that something of what Johannes Huizinga calls "the humane tenor of Dutch life" in the seventeenth century carried over to the Dutch community of New Netherland.[81] Unlike Puritan New England, for example, the Dutch colony did not enact laws against witchcraft. Indeed, prosecutions for capital crimes of any kind were rare, and death sentences were "virtually never carried out" in New Netherland, where administrators preferred to pardon offenders.[82] By the time Bayard came to trial in 1702, the Dutch community had seen the establishment of a precedent for executing a traitor: the 1691 executions of Leisler and Milborne. Some of their followers apparently

[80] Howell, *State Trials*, XIV, 510. In 1689 Capt. Abraham De Peyster sided with the insurgents against his commanding officer, Nicholas Bayard. But he was never a warm Leislerian partisan, and within a year he was denouncing Leisler as an "Insolent Alien," "Address of New York Merchants to the King and Queen," May 19, 1690, *N.-Y. Col. Docs.*, III, 748–749. Thereafter he never allowed his decidedly murky Leislerian leanings to interfere with a political career that he pursued with extraordinary success under every administration, Leislerian and Anti-Leislerian alike, between 1689 and 1702. As a member of the Council, a Supreme Court judge, deputy auditor general, and colonel of the New York County militia, he was at the pinnacle of his career when Bayard came to trial. See Hamlin and Baker, *Supreme Court*, III, 56–63.

[81] Huizinga boasts that the Dutch "gave up the atrocities of witch-hunting more than a century earlier than our neighbours" ("Dutch Civilisation in the Seventeenth Century," in Pieter Geyl and F.W.N. Hugenholtz, eds., Arnold J. Pomerans, trans., *Dutch Civilisation in the Seventeenth Century and Other Essays* [London, 1968], 59–60).

[82] Philip English Mackey, "Capital Punishment in New Netherland," *de halve maen*, XLVII (July 1972), 7–8. See also Earle H. Houghtaling, "Administration of Justice in New Amsterdam," *ibid.*, XLIII (Oct. 1968), 18–19. He claims that compared with the New England Puritans, the New Amsterdam Dutch "exhibited a remarkable spirit of tolerance and magnanimity." For example, they prosecuted criminals infrequently (and witches not at all), and they interfered minimally with religious freedom. In his view, this constitutes important evidence of "the humaneness" of the Dutch. It is interesting to note that a gallows is not even mentioned in the early New Amsterdam records. The structure dominating the view made of the town in the 1750s, which was once thought to be a gibbet, has since been identified as a beam for weighing merchandise. See frontispiece: "Nieuw Amsterdam Ofte Nue Nieuw Iorx Opt T Eylant Man," Stokes, *Iconography*, I, 122–123.

vowed revenge, and some, according to Bayard, pressed the acting governor to sign his death warrant. And yet the demeanor of most of the Dutch Leislerian jurymen suggests that if they did feel vindictive toward Bayard, they were not prepared to participate actively in what he later described as a "Conspiracy of Blood-thirsty Men." [83]

As the Dutch rarely articulated their views, it is difficult to prove that the Leislerians were inhibited, either by cultural traditions or by memories of their bitter political experience in 1691, from hounding Bayard to the gallows. One important statement, however, reveals that they felt alienated by the politics of reprisal at which Anti-Leislerians appeared to excel. On October 21, 1698—the day after Leisler's and Milborne's remains were exhumed from the grave and reinterred in the Dutch Reformed churchyard—five leading Leislerian members of the Dutch congregation wrote to the Classis of Amsterdam to request that an "impartial" minister be sent from Holland to assist their "partisan" dominie, Henricus Selyns. Four of these five spokesmen for the Leislerian community—Johannes De Peyster, David Provoost, Jan Van Giesen, and Jacobus Goelet—served as jurors in the Bayard trial.[84] Their letter warrants a close reading, for it provides a rare insight into the elusive Leislerian psyche.

Dominie Selyns, they complained to the Amsterdam divines, had been a virulent opponent of Leisler. By denouncing him from the pulpit and demanding that an example be made of him, Selyns had intensified the hatred felt by Leisler's followers against those who had instigated his "murder." Selyns also defended the vindictive politics of Leisler's enemies and announced that unless the Leislerian members of his congregation "confessed their faults there could be no pardon." He had thus become a mouthpiece for those "bitter men"—many of whom were members of the Dutch church—who were bent on retaliation and who would have executed hundreds of Leisler's supporters. Some of these "bitter men"—their "fellow believers"—had boasted that they "wanted to take their full revenge," by which they meant that "if they could not have the blood of their victims they would have their goods." The Leislerian correspondents felt that the Amsterdam divines had only to be reminded how draconian the law of confiscation was in England to realize what the "bitter men" would have done in New York had not "the fear of being called to account held them back." [85]

[83] "Case of William Atwood," 305.

[84] Members of the Dutch Church of New York to the Classis of Amsterdam, Oct. 21, 1868, *Ecc. Recs.*, II, 1246–1261. An older and slightly different translation of this letter can be found in "Documents Relating to the Administration of Leisler," N.-Y. Hist. Soc., *Colls.*, I, 398–411.

[85] *Ecc. Recs.*, II, 1250–1251, 1257–1259. Bayard was one of the "bitter" (but unnamed) Anti-Leislerian church officials referred to in the Leislerians' letter to the Classis of Amsterdam (*ibid.*, 1258).

What is most significant about this rare Dutch Leislerian description of the Anti-Leislerians' politics of revenge is that the Leislerian correspondents saw that politics as intrinsically English. Indeed, they pointedly contrasted the English law of confiscation with the generous Dutch method of dealing with conquered towns. The custom in the Netherlands, as they recalled, was to punish the "principals" but to pardon the rest, "especially when the offenders are numerous." How different had been the experience of the Dutch of New York City when Leisler surrendered the fort in 1691.[86] Significantly, too, this policy of granting "a perfect pardon and amnesty to all the rest" was put into practice by the Leislerian government. On January 24, 1702, two days after Bayard's arrest, the Leislerian Provincial Council issued a proclamation denying rumors that "Severity and the utmost Rigour of the Law" would be used against Bayard's adherents. The Council disclaimed any intention to punish those who had been "deluded": only the "chief Promoters" of the "conspiracy" would be prosecuted. Accordingly, an amnesty was granted on March 10—the day after Bayard had been found guilty of treason—to "all persons concerned in libeling the government." Those persons who had been "Wholly drawn in and no ways Instrumental in drawing in the Souldery" were reassured that the government intended to prosecute only two men—Bayard and Hutchins—"so far as to the loss of either Life or Limb," and only three—Philip French, Thomas Wenham, and Rip Van Dam—for misdemeanor. Moreover, Van Dam, who was believed to have been "wrought upon and seduced" to sign Bayard's addresses and the petition defending the addresses, could escape prosecution by admitting his offense.[87] The Leislerian councillors must have been relieved when Van Dam cooperated: to have prosecuted him might have provoked a backlash among Dutch townsfolk whose tradition called for the pardoning of all but the "principal" offenders.[88]

Bayard, by contrast, was a "principal" offender in the eyes of the Leislerians. He had not only refused to lead the people in promptly declaring allegiance to King William but had played a leading role in repressing the Leislerians. In the process he had become English, and aggressively English at that. To Atwood, Bayard was a Dutchman, but

[86] *Ibid.*, 1259.

[87] N.Y. Colonial MSS, XLV, 57–58 (transcript in Misc. Bayard, N.-Y. Hist. Soc.), 76. Together with Bayard, these three had petitioned the Council to release John Hutchins on the grounds that they had custody of the controversial addresses. When they refused to produce the addresses the Council ordered that they be bound over for misdemeanor. N.Y. Council Minutes, VIII, 303–304. See also Hamlin and Baker, *Supreme Court*, II, 351–352. John Hutchins was convicted of treason and sentenced to death on Apr. 6, 1702, by the same court of oyer and terminer that tried Bayard (*ibid.*, 88–91).

[88] The Leislerians did not regard Van Dam as a "chief promoter" of the conspiracy against the government: even Atwood acknowledged that Van Dam had been "halled along" by those demanding Hutchins's release. "Case of William Atwood," 270–271.

the Leislerian townsmen knew better. Were he Dutch, he would not have hesitated to declare for William. Nor would he have become vindictively English or moved to the English church. For having thus betrayed in so many ways his Dutch heritage, Bayard was faced with having to pay a very high price: he was tried, condemned, and threatened with hanging as a traitor to the English king.

That, however, was the only price he had to pay. In a report written to convince the Board of Trade of the leniency of the Leislerian administration, Atwood later claimed that the only intention of the government had been to pressure Bayard into signing a confession. Self-justifying though his report was, Atwood may well have been telling the truth. Furthermore, that Bayard escaped the gallows suggests a lack of support for the proceedings against him within the Leislerian community. Still, the public mood is difficult to gauge. After the death sentence was passed, the sheriff told Bayard that the chief justice believed that "the people in town were hot to have him executed," but this was only hearsay that Bayard dismissed as a ruse to frighten him into confessing. Again, if there was a "conspiracy" against Bayard's life, the "chief conspirators" failed to whip up agitation outside the courtroom for his blood; there is no evidence of a public uproar against him. While Bayard's supporters were openly critical of the trial proceedings, the Leislerians were apparently content with the government's decision to reprieve him.[89] None, as far as the records show, protested.

VIII

In conclusion, the Bayard treason trial, interpreted as a drama, provides a new perspective on the complexities of Dutch-English politics in early eighteenth-century New York City. When Nicholas Bayard, the principal actor in the play, identified the jurors as Dutchmen and as political enemies, he suggested that the courtroom confrontation was a straightforward one between Dutch Leislerians and Anti-Leislerians. Yet Bayard, by self-definition English, had been a leading member of the Dutch Reformed community until the turn of the century, when he helped form the English Party, which several of the Dutch members of the grand jury supported. Equally significant, some of the Leislerian Dutch participants refused to play their designated roles of Bayard's "mortal enemies." The Dutch sheriff did not stack the grand jury with Leislerians; the grand jury hesitated to indict Bayard; the

[89] "The humble Memorial of William Atwood," n.d., N.-Y. Col. Docs., IV, 106; Narrative of the Treatment Coll. Bayard Received, Mar. 21, 1702. Atwood wrote that he found it necessary to silence critics of the proceedings against Bayard by threatening them with prosecution, but he did not mention any agitation in the town against Bayard ("Case of William Atwood," 281).

trial jury of Dutchmen did not in the first instance find Bayard guilty; and the Leislerian government, which according to English Party propaganda represented a Dutch interest in New York politics, did not carry out the death sentence. In short, the Dutch townsmen taking part in the drama did not perform as Bayard's allegations suggested. They either failed to act out the Dutch-English antagonisms that he claimed determined political alignments in the town, or they acted them out in characteristically enigmatic fashion.

In the final analysis, then, the Bayard trial is most rewardingly interpreted as a drama highlighting the different political orientations of Dutch-identified and English-identified townsmen in eighteenth-century New York City. For the most part, the Dutch participants in the trial played low-keyed, even passive, roles and refrained from displaying overt hostility. Indeed, the demeanor of the majority of Dutch jurors suggests that they would have preferred not to have been thrust into the limelight of a political trial. The behavior of two of the judges—Abraham De Peyster and the Dutch-identified Englishman Robert Walters—is another case in point.[90] They spoke only once during the proceedings and then simply to concur with the judgment handed down by the chief justice. After the trial, Atwood and Weaver hurriedly left New York. But aside from Johannes De Peyster—who allegedly plotted Bayard's execution and who later fled New York fearing reprisals for his part in the proceedings—no Dutch Leislerians, as far as is known, felt the need to leave. Having played such passive roles in the English-run vendetta against Bayard, they had reason to feel secure against being called to account.

In contrast, the English and English-identified participants played aggressive roles in the trial drama. It was Atwood and Weaver, the two English placemen conducting the proceedings, who were later singled out as the "Chief contrivers and managers" of the prosecution; the other members of the Leislerian government were merely "willing instruments."[91] For their part, Atwood and Weaver singled out another Englishman, William Vesey, the minister of the Anglican church, as the most outspoken critic of the proceedings. Vesey had condemned the trial and on one occasion "passionately" interrupted the prosecution. While the Dutch participants watched quietly from the sidelines, the English judge, Atwood, silenced Vesey in such a menacing way that

---

[90] English-born Walters married into the Leisler family and sided with Leisler in 1689. Murrin identifies him as a "Batavianizing" Englishman in "English Rights as Ethnic Aggression," 23. See also Hamlin and Baker, *Supreme Court*, III, 196–199.

[91] "The Address of Several of the Inhabitants of New York against Mr Atwood and Mr Weaver," Sept. 5, 1702, Colonial Office, American and West Indies, Original Correspondence, 1606–1807, 5: 1047, 588, Public Record Office (microfilm, N.-Y. Hist. Soc.); Lord Cornbury to Lords of Trade, Sept. 27, 1702, in Sainsbury *et al.*, eds., *Calendar of State Papers, Jan. 1702–Dec. 1, 1702*, 611.

he fled New York, according to Atwood, in fear of his life.[92] Finally, there was Bayard, who defiantly demanded an English jury, vilified his jurors as "ignorant" Dutchmen, and later brought actions against his judges and some of the grand jurors. He also sought passage of a law disabling the judges and jurors from ever being judges, jurors, witnesses, executors, or administrators, thereby providing yet another example of the contrasting political styles of English- and Dutch-identified men.[93]

While positive proofs that the Dutch and Dutch-identified townsmen had a fundamentally different political orientation from the English are hard to come by, negative evidence such as their failure to act decisively against Bayard suggests strongly that they were disinclined to become actively involved in the politics of reprisal at which the English-identified townsmen excelled, and that they had their own ways of pursuing vendettas. This disinclination was based in experience. Leading members of the Dutch community had learned during the 1675 loyalty oath crisis that confronting the English did not pay political dividends. Dutch merchants accordingly accommodated to the reality of English conquest by becoming English, like Nicholas Bayard, or by becoming consummately pragmatic in politics, like Abraham De Peyster. The political orientation of the Dutch artisans was also accommodative. They retreated from politics, at least from the politics of confrontation. This too was experimentially based: in 1691 they had learned what kind of repercussions to expect if they became militant as they had during Leisler's Rebellion.

The lesson learned by rank-and-file Dutch Leislerians in 1691, reinforcing strong traditions in their culture, had long-term consequences for the evolution of colonial New York City politics. In 1698, 1,500 men, mostly Dutchmen—"scum," in the eyes of English Party observers—turned out for the special funeral service held for Leisler and Milborne in the Dutch Reformed church, but very few of these men were prepared to translate their lingering loyalty to Leisler into the politics of reprisal when his nemesis, Nicholas Bayard, was tried for his life four years later.[94] Indeed, for seventy years after Leisler's Rebellion, Dutch-identified artisans seldom played active or initiating roles in oppositional politics. Consequently, popular political activity peaked in eighteenth-century New York City only when aggressive English and English-identified men became intensely involved in organizing broad-based opposition parties, as they did at the turn of the century

---

[92] Howell, *State Trials*, XIV, 484, 487; "Case of William Atwood," 279.

[93] Goebel and Naughton, *Law Enforcement in New York*, 719.

[94] "Heads of Accusation against the Earl of Bellomont," Mar. 11, 1700, *N.-Y. Col. Docs.*, IV, 620.

and again in the 1730s and 1760s. In the intervals, the Dutch towns-men's politics of accommodation and retreat muted conflict by inhibit-ing confrontations. In effect, the failure of the Leislerian Dutch to act decisively against Nicholas Bayard manifested a pattern that was fol-lowed by the Dutch in New York City for the duration of the colonial period.

SOCIAL AND POLITICAL CHANGE IN THE 18TH CENTURY

IV

An Empire of Goods: The Anglicization
of Colonial America, 1690–1776

T. H. BREEN

*Timothy H. Breen reminds us that the colonies were very much a
part of an Atlantic empire held together, not just by governmental edicts that regulated political life and the movement of trade,
but by the commerce itself, the goods that continually flowed in
both directions across the ocean. He shifts the emphasis from the
formal institutions of control and even from the production of
staple crops to the dynamically expanding consumption of British
manufactures in colonial America, especially after 1740. In the
process he also tries to destroy the very notion of the "subsistence
farmer" in the colonies. The settlers craved British goods and, argues Breen, willingly participated in market relations to get
them. Consumer behavior, he insists, was making the colonists
more British—and thus more like one another—with particular
intensity in the four decades that preceded the Declaration of Independence. He even suggests that the anxieties aroused by this
process helped to trigger the Revolution.*

*How does Breen's pattern of consumer behavior fit with what
Michael Zuckerman describes in another essay in this section as
perhaps the central political value of eighteenth-century New
England, the need to maintain the autonomy or independence of
the individual household? How could farmers in particular be
both "independent" and heavily involved in market relations,
both as producers and consumers?*

Just before Christmas 1721 William Moore, described in court records
as "a Pedler or Petty Chapman," arrived in the frontier community of
Berwick, Maine. Had Moore bothered to purchase a peddler's license,
we would probably know nothing of his visit. He was undone by success. His illicit sales drew the attention of local authorities, and they
confiscated Moore's "bagg or pack of goods." From various witnesses
the magistrates learned that the man came to Berwick with "sundry
goods and Merchandizes for Saile & that he has Travelled from town

Reprinted from T. H. Breen, "An Empire of Goods: The Anglicization of Colonial
America," *Journal of British Studies*, 25 (1986), 467–499. Copyrighted 1986 by The
North American Conference on British Studies.

to town Exposeing said Goods to Sale and has Sold to Sundry persons."

The people of Berwick welcomed Moore to their isolated community. One can almost imagine the villagers, most of them humble farmers, rushing to Phillip Hubbard's house to examine the manufactured goods that the peddler had transported from Boston. Daniel Goodwin, for example, purchased "a yard and halfe of Stuff for handcarchiefs." Sarah Gooding could not forgo the opportunity to buy some muslin, fine thread, and black silk. She also bought "a yard and Quarter of Lase for a Cap." Patience Hubbard saw many things that she wanted, but in the end she settled for a "pare of garters." Her neighbor, Sarah Stone, took home a bundle of "smole trifles." None of the purchases amounted to more than a few pennies.[1]

I

Colonial American historians have understandably overlooked such trifling transactions. They have concentrated instead on the structure of specific communities, and though they have taught us much about the people who lived in villages such as Berwick, they have generally ignored the social and economic ties that connected colonists to men and women who happened to dwell in other places. But Moore's visit reminds us that Berwick was part of an empire—an empire of goods. This unfortunate peddler brought the settlers into contact with a vast market economy that linked them to the merchants of Boston and London, to the manufacturers of England, to an exploding Atlantic economy that was changing the material culture not only of the well-to-do but also of average folk like Sarah Stone and Patience Hubbard.

For more than a generation, eighteenth-century American historians have taken the mother country for granted. Charles McLean Andrews, who died in 1943, was one of the last scholars to offer a broad interpretation of the empire. He rejected the strident parochialism of earlier writers, insisting instead that the colonial historian should bring "the mother country into the forefront of the picture as the central figure, the authoritative and guiding force, the influence of which did more than anything else to shape the course of colonial achievement." Even those who question various tenets of what has come to be known as the Imperial School admire Andrews's stunning achievement. He wrote on a large canvas, tracing the early development of the mainland as well as the Caribbean colonies. He made sense out of the confusing evolution of British commercial policy. Andrews's four-volume *The Colonial Period of American History*, published between 1934 and 1938,

[1] Neal W. Allen, Jr., ed., *Province and Court Records of Maine*, 6 vols. (Portland, Maine, 1975), 6:72–73, 76.

is a brilliant example of a kind of institutional history no longer in vogue.[2]

Andrews did not live to complete his monumental study. The first three volumes of *The Colonial Period of American History* provided a narrative of the founding of the seventeenth-century colonies. The fourth volume focused on the passage and enforcement of the Navigation Acts. As Andrews neared the eighteenth century, however, he sensed that his project was in jeopardy. The organizing themes that had worked so well for the seventeenth century threatened to come unraveled. It was tempting, of course, to view the colonists as patriots in the making, as people preparing for independence. Andrews would have none of that. He well understood the danger of interpreting the events of the early eighteenth century as a rehearsal for revolution. "One period of our history, that from 1690 to 1750, has long been recognized as a neglected period," he explained in 1914, "and it will continue to be neglected as long as we treat colonial history merely as a time of incubation." [3]

The problem was how to make sense out of so many separate polities, so many people of different races and ethnic backgrounds moving over such a vast territory. Andrews despaired of ever telling the colonial side of the story, let alone relating it to events in the mother country. "The task which up to this time has been relatively simple, because the issues have been clear and the direction forward and without detours or complications, now becomes entangled and obscured," he confessed just before his death. "We are called upon to deal with aspects of colonial life no longer mainly institutional, but social, economic, educational, domestic, and religious, and in some respects political. Just here, then, arises the problem of how to write a volume on colonial life in the eighteenth century." [4]

Though Lawrence Henry Gipson took up the challenge, he never quite fulfilled Andrews's dream of placing "our colonial history in the larger history of the world of its time." [5] Younger scholars who were sympathetic with the "imperial" approach redefined the task and, instead of looking to the "larger history of the world," focused on the

[2] Charles McLean Andrews, *The Colonial Period of American History*, 4 vols. (New Haven, Conn., 1934–38), I:xi. See also Leonard Woods Labaree's introduction to C. M. Andrews, *The Colonial Background of the American Revolution* (1924; reprint, New Haven, Conn., 1961), p. ix; and Lawrence Henry Gipson, "The Imperial Approach to Early American History," in *The Reinterpretation of Early American History: Essays in Honor of John Edwin Pomfret*, ed. Ray Allen Billington (San Marino, Calif., 1966), pp. 185–200.

[3] C. M. Andrews, "Colonial Commerce," *American Historical Review* 20 (1914): 47.

[4] C. M. Andrews, "On the Writing of Colonial History," *William and Mary Quarterly*, 3d ser., 1 (1944): 31.

[5] Ibid., p. 27. L. H. Gipson, *The British Empire before the American Revolution*, 15 vols. (Caldwell, Idaho, and New York, 1936–70); Leonard W. Labaree, *Royal Government in America* (New Haven, Conn., 1930).

development of royal government in a specific colony or region. Stanley N. Katz, James A. Henretta, Alison G. Olson, William Pencak, Jack P. Greene, John A. Schutz, and William W. Abbot provided insights into how decisions made—or not made—in England affected the political character of the various eighteenth-century colonies. They help us to comprehend the extraordinary power that a man like the duke of Newcastle exercised over American appointments.[6] But however valuable these works may be, they do not provide much evidence that the average American cared one way or another about the empire. The institutional ties between England and America were fragile. Few royal officials resided in the colonies. The Americans obeyed the Navigation Acts because it was convenient and profitable for them to do so, not because they were coerced. It may be—as Richard L. Bushman suggests in his study of the political culture of eighteenth-century Massachusetts—that membership in the empire involved no more to most colonists than sharing common political symbols with people who happened to live in England.[7] They all professed to love the king, at least so long as he kept away from their pocketbooks, and when he did not, the symbolic ties quickly dissolved.

Failure of nerve alone cannot explain the sudden demise of the Imperial School. After World War II the entire discipline fragmented, and, as it did so, colonial historians turned their attention increasingly to local studies. They adopted quantitative methodologies, and by far the most impressive scholarship produced during this period concentrated on seventeenth-century New England villages. In recent years historians of the Chesapeake have published work of equally high quality. For the most part, these investigations simply ignore the mother country. They depict white colonists busily establishing families, setting up churches, and dividing the land. England was a country left behind, an Old World whose relevance was becoming increasingly tenuous in the lives of eighteenth-century Americans.[8]

[6] Stanley N. Katz, *Newcastle's New York: Anglo-American Politics, 1732–1753* (Cambridge, Mass., 1968); James A. Henretta, *"Salutary Neglect": Colonial Administration under the Duke of Newcastle* (Princeton, N.J., 1972); Alison G. Olson, *Anglo-American Politics, 1660–1775* (New York, 1973); William Pencak, *War, Politics, and Revolution in Provincial Massachusetts* (Boston, 1981); Jack P. Greene, *The Quest for Power: The Lower Houses of Assembly in the Southern Royal Colonies, 1689–1776* (Chapel Hill, N.C., 1963); John A. Schutz, *William Shirley: King's Governor of Massachusetts* (Chapel Hill, N.C., 1961); and William Wright Abbot, *The Royal Governors of Georgia, 1754–1775* (Chapel Hill, N.C., 1959).

[7] Richard L. Bushman, *King and People in Provincial Massachusetts* (Chapel Hill, N.C., 1985).

[8] An excellent review of these historiographic trends is I. K. Steele, "The Empire and the Provincial Elites: An Interpretation of Some Recent Writings on the English Atlantic, 1675–1740," *Journal of Imperial and Commonwealth History* 8 (1980): 2–32. Some historians have recently expressed considerable concern over the alleged fragmentation of early American history. They note that the people working in this field have aban-

Richard Hofstadter's *America at 1750*, published in 1971, reflected this historiographic development. Hofstadter provided a thorough analysis of demographic and religious trends in eighteenth-century America, but nowhere in this valuable little book can the reader find a sustained discussion of the links that bound the colonists to the mother country, indeed of what it meant to them to be members of a transatlantic empire.[9] It is perhaps not surprising that John M. Murrin admonished—no doubt, tongue in cheek—that any American historian who ventured into eighteenth-century studies "risks condemnation as an antiquarian, a pedant, a bore, or all three." [10]

Despite such warnings, the empire refused to disappear. Over the last several years, in fact, historians have begun to address some of the very questions that perplexed Charles McLean Andrews, and though their approach is quite different from his, they certainly share his broad vision. In a series of provocative articles, J. G. A. Pocock called for a "new" British history, one that would not concern itself exclusively with how England came to dominate other cultures throughout the world. Rather he urged historians to think of the British empire not as an institutional structure but as a process that brought people of different cultures and backgrounds into contact. In other words, Pocock adopted a complex interactionist model. The new British history, he explained, "must be a plural history, tracing the processes by which a diversity of societies, nationalities, and political structures came into being and situating in the history of each and in the history of their interactions the processes that have led them to whatever

---

not only the "imperial" approach but also other frameworks capable of incorporating these proliferating local studies into a larger, coherent interpretation of colonial society. In an attempt to promote at least middle-level generalizations, Jack P. Greene and Jack Pole sponsored in 1981 an international conference of early American historians. In a planning document for this meeting, they observed, "For some time now, it has been clear that the wealth of new information generated annually by students of colonial history has given rise to a severe case of intellectual indigestion. . . . As scholars have concentrated more and more upon smaller and smaller units in their laudable efforts to recover the context and texture of colonial life in as much detail as the sources and scholarly ingenuity will permit, there has been surprisingly little effort to relate their findings to the larger picture of British-American development over the whole period" (Jack P. Greene and Jack Pole, eds., *Colonial British America: Essays in the New History of the Early Modern Era* [Baltimore, 1984], p. 7). Other conferences have challenged historians in Great Britain and the United States who work in this period to think in more broadly comparative terms, to relate, e.g., social, economic, and demographic trends in the mother country to those in mainland colonies. It is premature to assess what effect these meetings will have on the study of Anglo-American history, but to date few eighteenth-century scholars have shown much interest in producing the kind of grand synthesis that the conference planners apparently envisioned.

[9] Richard Hofstadter, *America at 1750: A Social Portrait* (New York, 1971).

[10] John M. Murrin, "The Myths of Colonial Democracy and Royal Decline in Eighteenth-Century America: A Review Essay," *Cithara* 5 (1965): 52–69, 53–54.

forms of association or unity exist in the present or have existed in the past." Pocock admitted that the task would not be easy. He envisioned a kind of Braudelian history of the British empire, and though historians of eighteenth-century America may not be quite up to the challenge of *histoire totale*, they can at least thank Pocock for suggesting a way out of the morass of local and regional studies that, however eloquently presented, seem of late to be yielding less and less interesting results.[11]

Bernard Bailyn placed the problem of empire in an even broader perspective. In an essay published in 1976, he argued that the most significant element of the eighteenth century was the vast movement of peoples. Everywhere Bailyn looked, he found men and women shifting about, from country to country and, in colonial America, from colony to colony, from seacoast to frontier. Government officials in England and America were simply overwhelmed by the dimensions of the challenge. For one thing the British empire was grossly understaffed. "Before 1768," Bailyn observed, "the minister in official charge of American affairs was the Secretary of State for the Southern Department, a post that was held in the seven years between 1761 and 1768 by no fewer than six individuals, appointed and dismissed in rapid succession for reasons that had nothing to do with American land policy, or with American affairs at all." [12]

Even if these men had been better trained, even if there had been a huge bureaucracy, it is doubtful that British officials could have brought order out of a situation that seemed to them so chaotic. As Bailyn noted, "All of this frantic peopling of half a continent . . . was beyond the control, indeed the comprehension, of those who managed the British government." [13] In other words, this was an empire not of formal institutions but of common men and women making decisions about the quality of their lives, of thousands of people on the move, a human network so large that one wonders how even a historian armed with computers and supported by legions of graduate students could possibly make more sense out of the story than did the poor, beleaguered administrators of the eighteenth century.

---

[11] J. G. A. Pocock, "The Limits and Divisions of British History: In Search of the Unknown Subject," *American Historical Review* 87 (1982): 311–36, and "British History: A Plea for a New Subject," *New Zealand Historical Journal* 8 (1974): 3–21 (reprinted in *Journal of Modern History* 47 [1975]: 601–21).

[12] Bernard Bailyn, "1776: A Year of Challenge—a World Transformed," *Journal of Law and Economics* 19 (1976): 437–66, 456.

[13] Ibid., p. 456. An interesting attempt to trace one strand of this vast eighteenth-century migration to America is Ned C. Landsman, *Scotland and Its First American Colony, 1683–1765* (Princeton, N.J., 1985). See also T. H. Breen, "Creative Adaptations: Peoples and Cultures," in Greene and Pole, eds., pp. 195–232.

Charles McLean Andrews, no doubt, would have welcomed these essays.[14] Both Bailyn and Pocock—as did Andrews himself—force colonial American historians to think of the empire in the broadest possible terms, and even if the promise of this *histoire totale* so far remains unfulfilled, these preliminary statements suggest that the new imperial history will focus on the movement of peoples and the clash of cultures, on common folk rather than on colonial administrators, on processes rather than on institutions, on aspects of daily life that one would not regard as narrowly political. It will be an integrated story, neither American nor English, but an investigation of the many links that connected men and women living on both sides of the Atlantic Ocean. It will anticipate neither the coming of the Revolution nor the rise of industrial society. Rather the new imperial history must interpret people within a context that they themselves would have understood.

II

John J. McCusker and Russell R. Menard suggest yet another way to reintegrate the American colonies into the history of the British empire. The goals that these two economic historians set for themselves in their new book, *The Economy of British America*, seem modest.[15] They intend to produce a comprehensive assessment of the economic literature of the prerevolutionary period and, where appropriate, to indicate fruitful questions for future research. If McCusker and Menard had provided no more than a review of recent economic scholarship, much of it quite technical and published in journals unfamiliar to many cultural and political historians, they would deserve our gratitude. After all, anyone who helps bridge the gaps separating various subfields in the discipline is performing an important service. But McCusker and Menard have achieved much more. Not only do they synthesize this vast literature in clear, jargon-free prose, but they also present a powerful case for their own interpretation of the economic development of the American colonies, those of the Caribbean as well

[14] One should note that two historians have launched multivolume studies of the British empire in America. Both works concentrate on economic and political development, and though the authors are often provocative, they have not as yet had much to say about the eighteenth century. See Stephen Saunders Webb, *The Governors-General: The English Army and the Definition of the Empire, 1569–1681* (Chapel Hill, N.C., 1979); and J. M. Sosin, *English America and the Restoration Monarchy of Charles II: Transatlantic Politics, Commerce, and Kinship* (Lincoln, Nebr., 1980), and *English America and the Revolution of 1688: Royal Administration and the Structure of Provincial Government* (Lincoln, Nebr., 1982).

[15] John J. McCusker and Russell R. Menard, *The Economy of British America, 1607–1789* (Chapel Hill, N.C., 1985).

as of the mainland. This essay will concentrate on their analysis of the eighteenth century, but for the reader interested in the story of the founding of the various colonies, especially in how demographic experience affected economic growth in the seventeenth century, *The Economy of British America* has a great deal to offer.

Throughout their book, McCusker and Menard insist that an interpretative framework called the staple thesis best explains the character and pace of colonial economic development. As with other analytic models, this one makes assumptions about human behavior, especially about *homo economicus*, and it is to the authors' credit that they spell out these assumptions clearly. "Advocates of the staple thesis," explains one economic historian, "maintain that although commercial agriculture was limited by geography, technology, and economic factors, most farmers, attuned to the potentials of the market, were motivated by liberal, entrepreneurial, individualistic, or capitalistic values, seeking to maximize income and profits and willing to take risks and accept innovation." [16] In other words, the Europeans who settled in North America wanted to improve their material lot and were quite willing, indeed eager, to exploit the human and physical resources they found there to gain prosperity.

However commonplace this proposition may sound, the staple theorists treat it with awe. Indeed, from this initial entrepreneurial premise flow complex explanations about the character of the American labor systems, both free and unfree, the dispersion of people across the landscape, the growth of population, and the distribution of wealth. According to McCusker and Menard, the key is exports. In each region the colonists discovered a different way to make money. The Chesapeake planters cultivated tobacco. The Carolinians relied on rice and indigo. The farmers of the Middle Colonies grew rich selling wheat and flour, while New Englanders peddled fish, whale products, and timber throughout the Atlantic world. In each case, Americans sought to maximize income. Sometimes that desire meant purchasing additional slaves; sometimes it persuaded men to invest in sailing vessels. An expanding market linked frontiersmen to city dwellers, colonists living on the periphery of empire to the great merchants of the metropolis. Even slight changes in the prices offered for American goods called forth adjustments throughout the system. As McCusker and Menard observe, the staple thesis "argues that the export sector played a leading role in the economy of British America and maintains

---

[16] Richard B. Sheridan, "The Domestic Economy," in Greene and Pole, eds., p. 67. See also Daniel Scott Smith, "Early American Historiography and Social Science History," *Social Science History* 6 (1982): 267–91; and David W. Galenson and Russell R. Menard, "Approaches to the Analysis of Economic Growth in Colonial British America," *Historical Methods* 13 (1980): 3–18.

that the specific character of those exports shaped the process of colonial development." [17]

For the purposes of this essay, there is no need to recount the examples that McCusker and Menard offer in support of their interpretation. Suffice it to say that this is a superbly researched volume, one that compels historians who possess no particular interest in the marketing of American exports to think seriously about the significance of an expanding Atlantic market for the development of colonial society and culture in the eighteenth century. These authors remind us of the complex commercial ties that connected even humble American producers to European consumers. This was an impressively sophisticated economic system, constantly changing, always calling forth adjustments. Moreover, proponents of the staple thesis successfully avoid crude forms of teleological argumentation. One can certainly tell the story of the export sector without anticipating the Battle of Bunker Hill or glancing ahead to the Industrial Revolution. The approach that McCusker and Menard adopt is one that might well have pleased Charles McLean Andrews.[18] To be sure, they do not have much to say about political institutions, but, like Andrews, they insist on analyzing colonial economic behavior within a broad imperial context.

Though this is a fine book, one cannot help but wish that McCusker and Menard had pushed their analysis further, that they had explored more fully the implications of their own insights into the workings of the Atlantic economy. The staple thesis may be the source of the problem. These authors are so concerned with the production of American crops that they fail to pay proper attention to the extraordinary growth of manufacturing in eighteenth-century England. After all, the colonists raised staple exports only to exchange them for other goods they wanted more. The mother country had not yet entered the Industrial Revolution, but throughout the kingdom sharp-eyed businessmen were mastering the techniques necessary to turn out small consumer goods on an unprecedented scale. Indeed, the flood of these items onto the domestic market was responsible for what some historians have termed the "birth of a consumer society." As Neil McKendrick re-

---

[17] McCusker and Menard, p. 18.

[18] Some recent studies that attempt to tie colonial economic development to an expanding world market for American staples are Jacob M. Price, *France and the Chesapeake: A History of the French Tobacco Monopoly, 1674–1791, and Its Relationship to the British and American Tobacco Trades*, 2 vols. (Ann Arbor, Mich., 1973). *Capital and Credit in British Overseas Trade: The View from the Chesapeake, 1700–1776* (Cambridge, Mass., 1980), "Economic Function and the Growth of American Port Towns in the Eighteenth Century," *Perspectives in American History* 8 (1974): 121–86, and "The Economic Growth of the Chesapeake and the European Market, 1697–1775," *Journal of Economic History* 24 (1964): 496–511; and Paul G. Clemens, *The Atlantic Economy and Colonial Maryland's Eastern Shore: From Tobacco to Grain* (Ithaca, N.Y., 1980).

minds us, "It is often forgotten that industrial revolution was, to a large extent, founded on the sales of humble products to very large markets—the beer of London, the buckles and buttons of Birmingham, the knives and forks of Sheffield, the cups and saucers of Staffordshire, the cheap cottons of Lancashire." [19] The list of goods could easily be extended. Moreover, this was a period of general prosperity. Because real wages rose as food prices declined, Englishmen of all classes found that they could afford the new manufactures. In addition, the cost of producing many common household items gradually fell. In little more than a generation—sometimes less—shoppers transformed former luxuries into necessities. Even contemporaries were amazed. Some observers condemned the trend as immoral; others like Daniel Defoe celebrated it. But whatever position one took, it was clear that the explosion of consumption was changing the face of English society. [20]

Consumer demand was the driving engine of economic change. Knowledge of the availability of these goods sparked desire, and though humble buyers obviously could not afford quality items, they purchased what they could. Sometimes they aped their betters, drinking tea, for example, instead of beer. They also read of the new goods in country newspapers and smart magazines. Advertising became part of everyday life. Josiah Wedgwood mastered these merchandising techniques, but others knew how to inflame consumer desire. Impatient buyers brought about a total restructuring of the marketplace. Country fairs and occasional hawkers were replaced by commercial travelers and, more significant, by stores equipped with "bow-windows" in which local entrepreneurs displayed colorful goods. [21] Shopping became a year-round activity, and the pressure to supply the village merchants with goods forced the business community to develop

[19] Neil McKendrick, "The Commercialization of Fashion," in *The Birth of a Consumer Society: The Commercialization of Eighteenth-Century England*, by Neil McKendrick, John Brewer, and J. H. Plumb (Bloomington, Ind., 1982), p. 53.

[20] Some titles that have been most helpful in understanding the transformation of the eighteenth-century British economy are Charles H. Wilson, *England's Apprenticeship, 1603–1763* (Cambridge, 1965); Ralph Davis, *A Commercial Revolution: English Overseas Trade in the Seventeenth and Eighteenth Centuries* (London, 1967). *The Rise of the Atlantic Economies* (Ithaca, N.Y., 1973), and "English Foreign Trade, 1700–1774," *Economic History Review* 15 (1962): 285–303; T. S. Ashton, *An Economic History of England: The Eighteenth Century* (London, 1955); Leslie A. Clarkson, *The Pre-industrial Economy in England, 1500–1750* (London, 1971); Roy Porter, *English Society in the Eighteenth Century* (Harmondsworth, 1982); Harold Perkin, *Origins of Modern English Society* (London, 1969); D. A. Farnie, "The Commercial Empire of the Atlantic, 1607–1783," *Economic History Review* 15 (1962): 205–18; J. V. Beckett, "The Eighteenth-Century Origins of the Factory System: A Case Study from the 1740s," *Business History* 19 (1977): 55–67; and Jacob Price, "The Transatlantic Economy," in Greene and Pole, eds., pp. 18–42.

[21] J. H. Plumb, "Commercialization of Leisure," in McKendrick et al., p. 273.

more efficient communication and transportation. As A. H. John observed, "The growth of a steadier demand for goods, both by consumers and manufacturers, had its repercussions on the manner in which the wholesale market was organized." The great London wholesalers linked producers to scattered retailers, and along the entire chain flowed unprecedented amounts of credit, usually in the form of bills of exchange.[22]

American historians have been slow to appreciate how the creation of this "consumer society" affected the character of the entire British empire. In the volume prepared by McCusker and Menard, for example, colonial consumption rated only a single chapter. The authors apologize for this seeming imbalance, noting that "we have paid more attention to the production of goods and services, to the earning and the distribution of income and wealth, than to spending. We have talked about supply, but not much about demand. This reflects the state of the discipline: colonial economic historians have paid more attention to production than they have to consumption." [23] Their assessment is accurate. The literature dealing with colonial consumption is surprisingly thin.

The problem is not simply lack of statistical evidence. Studies frequently take note of the spectacular American demand for English goods during the eighteenth century. "England's exports to North America," reported Bernard Bailyn, "increased almost eightfold from 1700 to 1773; between 1750 and 1773 it rose 120 percent; and in the five years from 1768 to 1772 it rose 43 percent." [24] However impressive these figures appeared to Bailyn and others, they have not generated much scholarly curiosity.

The explanation for this apparent indifference is obvious. Historians have long favored the analysis of production over that of consumption. This bias, no doubt, could be traced back to the whole Classical School of economics. Marx and other critics of the capitalist system later picked up this emphasis on production, significantly because by that time demand could be taken for granted.[25] For some political economists of the eighteenth century, mass consumption seemed to threaten the traditional social order. As Albert O. Hirschman recently noted, "a *nouveau riche*, that agent of social disintegration, is typically

[22] A. H. John, "Aspects of English Economic Growth in the First Half of the Eighteenth Century," in *Growth of the British Overseas Trade in the Seventeenth and Eighteenth Centuries*, ed. W. E. Minchinton (London, 1969), p. 178; and B. A. Holderness, "Credit in a Rural Community," *Midland History* 3 (1975): 93–115.

[23] McCusker and Menard, p. 277; Price, "The Transatlantic Economy," pp. 34–35.

[24] Bailyn (n. 12 above), p. 447.

[25] I am grateful to Harold Perkin for bringing the role of "demand" in the writings of late eighteenth- and early nineteenth-century economists to my attention.

someone who is decked out in all kinds of novelties." No wonder that
shrill criticism of "luxury" accompanied the spread of prosperity.[26]
Easy access to manufactured goods confused social boundaries, and the
very wealthy found that they had to spend ever greater amounts of income just to distinguish themselves from middling consumers.

III

In the historiography of colonial America the aversion to consumption
runs particularly deep. Indeed, the subject sometimes evoked moral
comment, as if the colonists' desire to purchase pretty ribbons or
printed cloth revealed weakness in their character. As in England,
these judgments considerably increased in the eighteenth century.
Members of the colonial elite condemned what seemed to them the
improvident expenditures of the lower orders. In 1762 a wealthy New
Yorker clucked, "Our people, both in town and country, are shamefully
gone into the habit of tea-drinking." Another gentleman traveling
through the American countryside some years earlier was horrified to
discover that a young family living in a "cottage" had indulged in "superfluous things which showed an inclination to finery . . . such as a
looking glass with a painted frame, half a dozen pewter spoons and as
many plates . . . a set of stone tea dishes, and a tea pot." Such hardy
farmers, the visitor exclaimed, should have purchased "wool to make
yarn." They should have realized that "a little water in a wooden pail
might serve for a looking glass, and wooden plates and spoons would
be as good for use and, when clean almost as ornamental."[27] The
point is not to document the condescension of the rich. Rather it is to
remind modern historians how easy it was to slip into this pattern of
rhetoric.

But moral judgments—often embedded in liberal economic theory—are only part of the problem. Another major obstacle to fresh
analysis of the Anglo-American empire of the eighteenth century is the
almost unshakable conviction that the colonists were economically
self-sufficient. Modern historians who do not agree on other points of

[26] Albert O. Hirschman, *Shifting Involvements: Private Interest and Public Action*
(Princeton, N.J., 1982), pp. 49–57. For a comparative perspective, see Jan de Vries,
"Peasant Demand Patterns and Economic Development: Friesland, 1550–1750," in *Eu-
ropean Peasants and Their Markets: Essays in Agrarian Economic History*, ed. William N.
Parker and Eric L. Jones (Princeton, N.J., 1975), pp. 168–205. The moral implications
of popular consumption are discussed in John Sekora, *Luxury: The Concept in Western
Thought, Eden to Smollett* (Baltimore, 1977).

[27] Alexander Hamilton, *Gentleman's Progress: Itinerarium of Dr. Alexander Hamilton*, ed.
Carl Bridenbaugh (Chapel Hill, N.C., 1948), p. 55. On the danger of forcing people in
the past to conform to modern economy theory, see Sharon V. Salinger and Charles
Wetherell, "Wealth and Renting in Prerevolutionary Philadelphia," *Journal of American
History* 71 (1985): 826–40; and Eugene D. Genovese, "Yeomen Farmers in a Slavehold-
ers' Democracy," *Agricultural History* 49 (1975): 331–43.

interpretation have found themselves defending this hardy perennial. Before World War II, it was common to encounter in the scholarly literature the resourceful yeoman, an independent, Jeffersonian figure who carved a farm out of the wilderness and managed by the sweat of his brow to feed and clothe his family. This is the theme of patriotic mythology. These were men and women who possessed the "right stuff." [28]

In recent years this self-sufficient yeoman has recruited some enthusiastic new support. James A. Henretta, in an influential essay entitled "Families and Farms," offered perhaps the most coherent argument for this position.[29] These colonial farmers, he insisted, were not agrarian entrepreneurs who focused their energies on maximizing profit. To the contrary, they represented a "precapitalist" way of life. They saw themselves not so much as individuals as members of lineal families or of little communities. Since their primary goals were to provide for the welfare of dependents, to pass productive land on to future generations, and to achieve economic security, these colonial farmers studiously avoided the risks associated with the market economy. They rejected innovation in favor of tradition. They were deaf to market incentives. Within their households they attempted to satisfy as many of their material needs as possible, and when they required something they could not produce, they preferred to deal with neighbors rather than outside merchants. In other words, from this perspective, subsistence was not the result of personal failure or physical isolation. It was a positive expression of precapitalist values, a *mentalité*, that was slowly and painfully being eroded by the advance of commercial capitalism. If this is correct, we might as well forget about the consumer society. It hardly seems likely that a few imported English baubles would have turned the heads of such militantly self-sufficient farmers.

This thesis struck a responsive chord among some American historians. They saw the essay as an important statement in a much larger critique of capitalism in the United States, and they claim to have discovered this precapitalist mentality throughout American history, in urban as well as rural situations, in the South as well as the North.[30]

---

[28] This historiography is discussed in Carole Shammas, "How Self-sufficient Was Early America?" *Journal of Interdisciplinary History* 13 (1982): 247–72. The fullest early statement of this position was Percy Wells Bidwell and John I. Falconer, *History of Agriculture in the Northern United States, 1620–1860* (Washington, D.C., 1925).

[29] James A. Henretta, "Families and Farms: *Mentalité* in Pre-industrial America," *William and Mary Quarterly*, 3d ser., 35 (1978): 3–32.

[30] For example, Robert E. Mutch, "Yeoman and Merchant in Pre-industrial America: Eighteenth-Century Massachusetts as a Case Study," *Societas* 7 (1977): 282, and "The Cutting Edge: Colonial America and the Debate about the Transition to Capitalism," *Theory and Society* 9 (1980): 847–63; Michael Merrill, "Cash Is Good to Eat: Self-Sufficiency and Exchange in the Rural Economy of the United States." *Radical History Review* 4 (1977): 42–72; James Henretta, "Reply to James Lemon," *William and Mary Quarterly*,

For them, colonial yeomen become "cultural heroes," warriors in what James T. Lemon has ironically termed "a desperate rear-guard action" against the encroachment of capitalism.[31] One review article noted, for example, that "the incursion of an external market-oriented world onto the traditional communities of the yeomen farmer" has become the explanation for just about every incident of rural unrest from seventeenth-century Salem Village to nineteenth-century populist Georgia.[32] From this perspective consumption is transformed into the handmaiden of capitalism and American history into a tedious jeremiad against commercialism.

Though these embattled precapitalist farmers flourish in the pages of learned journals, they have proved remarkably difficult to find in the historical record. Colonial historians who have gone in search of precapitalist colonial America have discovered instead entrepreneurial types, men and women shamelessly thrusting themselves into the market economy. Joyce Appleby reviewed this literature and announced that "evidence mounts that prerevolutionary America witnessed a steady commercialization of economic life: trades of all kinds increased; frontier communities quickly integrated themselves into market networks; large and small farmers changed crops in response to commercial incentives; new consuming tastes and borrowing practices proliferated."[33] James T. Lemon experienced no better luck than did Appleby in discovering a precapitalist mentality. This careful student of Pennsylvania agriculture stated that, "far from being opposed to the market, 'independent' farmers eagerly sought English manufactured goods and in other ways acted as agents of capitalism."[34]

Common sense alone makes it difficult to imagine that these scholars could have reached any other conclusion. After all, the market was not an eighteenth-century invention. As Winifred B. Rothenberg reminds us, "Massachusetts did not begin as an experiment in self-suffi-

---

3d ser., 37 (1980): 696–700; Christopher Clark, "Household Economy, Market Exchange and the Rise of Capitalism in the Connecticut Valley, 1800–1860," *Journal of Social History* 13 (1979): 169–89. See also Richard L. Bushman, "Family Security in the Transition from Farm to City, 1750–1850," *Journal of Family History* 6 (1981): 238–43; Gregory A. Stiverson, "Early American Farming: A Comment," *Agricultural History* 50 (1976): 37–44.

[31] James T. Lemon, "Spatial Order: Households in Local Communities and Regions," in Greene and Pole, eds. (n. 8 above), p. 102.

[32] Harry L. Watson, "Conflict and Collaboration: Yeomen, Slaveholders, and Politics in the Antebellum South," *Social History* 10 (1985): 273–298, 285. See also Steven Hahn and Jonathan Prude, eds., *The Countryside in the Age of Capitalist Transformation: Essays in the Social History of Rural America* (Chapel Hill, N.C., 1985).

[33] Joyce Appleby, "Value and Society," in Greene and Pole, eds., p. 309.

[34] Lemon, p. 102. See Charles S. Grant, *Democracy in the Connecticut Frontier Town of Kent* (New York, 1961); Darrett B. Rutman and Anita H. Rutman, *A Place in Time: Middlesex County, Virginia, 1650–1750*, 2 vols. (New York, 1984), 1:204–5.

ciency."[35] The settlers who migrated to America had participated in local and regional markets. In fact, they were certainly familiar with something that looks remarkably like commercial agriculture. Perhaps the trip to the New World dulled the Puritans' entrepreneurial spirit—a doubtful proposition—but it surely did nothing to dampen the profit motive among those planters who colonized the Chesapeake, the Carolinas, and the Caribbean.[36] Even on the Shenandoah frontier of the eighteenth century, one encounters small farmers attempting "to obtain a variety of goods from the outside world, both necessities and luxuries."[37] As the evidence mounts, the "precapitalist" economy looks increasingly like Locke's state of nature: an Edenic society that apparently existed before the dawn of recorded history.

The argument for self-sufficiency encounters other problems as well. Henretta originally posed his interpretation as a dichotomous proposition: either colonial Americans toiled to preserve the "lineal family," or they strove to participate fully in the market economy. But, surely, there is some middle ground. No one seriously maintains that the people who settled New England and the Middle Colonies were unconcerned about the well-being of family members. They knew how difficult it was to survive a hard winter. They planned ahead as best they could. They also worried about their children's futures, about providing education, about dowries for daughters and land for sons. Such human concerns would hardly seem to be the monopoly of precapitalists. Love of family certainly did not cool the enthusiasm of Pennsylvania farmers for commercial agriculture, nor for that matter did the sale of wheat on the world market unloose an outpouring of corrosive economic individualism.[38]

But more is at stake here than family economics. Various historians have relied on the beleaguered subsistence farmer to explain the tensions allegedly connected with social change. The market economy, we learn, disrupted communal relations. The story follows a familiar pattern. The precapitalists resist, but in the end they are overwhelmed by the forces of economic individualism. It happened in Salem Village in

[35] Winifred B. Rothenberg, "The Market and Massachusetts Farmers, 1750–1855," *Journal of Economic History* 41 (1981): 283–314, 312.

[36] See T. H. Breen, "Back to Sweat and Toil: Suggestions for the Study of Agricultural Work in Early America," *Pennsylvania History* 49 (1982): 241–58; Clemens (n. 18 above), pp. 19–20.

[37] Robert D. Mitchell, *Commercialism and Frontier: Perspectives on the Early Shenandoah Valley* (Charlottesville, Va., 1977), p. 152.

[38] Breen, "Back to Sweat and Toil," p. 245; Joyce Appleby, "Commercial Farming and the 'Agrarian Myth' in the Early Republic," *Journal of American History* 68 (1982): 833–49; James T. Lemon, "Household Consumption in Eighteenth-Century America and Its Relationship to Production and Trade: The Situation in Southeastern Pennsylvania," *Agricultural History* 41 (1967): 59–70, and *The Best Poor Man's Country: A Geographical Study of Early Southeastern Pennsylvania* (Baltimore, 1972).

the 1690s. It divided the towns of New England during the Great Awakening. It accounts for the strains that set neighbor against neighbor on the eve of revolution. Everywhere the spirit of capitalism erodes the traditional community. What are we to make of this universal explanation? According to Gary Nash, not much. These interpretations, he notes, do not seem credible. Nash writes that, taken together, they "make it appear that the transition to mercantile capitalism was occurring—and causing social trauma—at widely spread points in time within a region smaller than the state of North Dakota." [39] This antimarket analysis reminds one of the old debate over the rising middle class. That group was always on the rise just as the precapitalists were always about to go down for the last time. Such generalized interpretations explain too little by attempting to explain too much.

One historian recently turned the antimarket model on its head. The results were fascinating. In *Commerce and Culture*, Christine Heyrman documented the development of two Massachusetts towns between 1690 and 1750. At the beginning of this period, Gloucester and Marblehead seemed remarkably un-Puritan. Indeed, the people who lived in these two villages often appeared downright nasty, showing more inclination to feud than to live in brotherly love. In time, however, Gloucester and Marblehead were drawn increasingly into the Atlantic economy. The townsfolk promoted commercial fishing. Merchants set up businesses. And as these changes occurred, Gloucester and Marblehead did not degenerate into Hobbesian nightmares. To the contrary, they took on the characteristics that one usually associates with traditional Puritan villages. Commerce stimulated a sense of community. It actually strengthened institutional religion. "By the middle of the eighteenth century," declares Heyrman, "the ethos prevailing in both towns, by that time important seaports, was remarkably similar to that in the surrounding agrarian villages. . . . Most people in Gloucester and Marblehead now relied for their livelihoods on trade and the maritime industries, but the drive for profit did not dominate social relationships or redefine attitudes governing economic behavior. Forbearance towards local creditors, a cautious approach to investment, limited aspirations for expansion and innovation, and a concern for communal welfare characterized the outlook of all participants in local commerce, even major merchants and entrepreneurs." [40] To be sure, one cannot be certain that these two towns were typical of the rest of New England society. What Heyrman does make clear, however, is that the spreading market economy did not necessarily destroy community. She provides a fresh perspective on the role of com-

---

[39] Gary B. Nash, "Social Development," in Greene and Pole, eds., p. 236.

[40] Christine Leigh Heyrman, *Commerce and Culture: The Maritime Communities of Colonial Massachusetts, 1690–1750* (New York, 1984), p. 19.

merce, on the production of exports as well as the consumption of imports.

Despite mounting criticism from many different quarters, the precapitalist, largely self-sufficient farmer somehow clung to life. But not for long. Carole Shammas and Bettye Hobbs Pruitt, two economic historians, soon administered the coup de grace to this mythic eighteenth-century figure. They asked the crucial questions, Did these colonists actually possess the means to be self-sufficient? If there had been no market, could these men and women have fed and clothed themselves?

The answer seems to be an emphatic no. Pruitt's careful research in the Massachusetts archives revealed that most colonists could not have provided for the basic needs of their own families. The problem was not a failure of will. Their farms simply lacked too many items essential to successful mixed husbandry. Some men did not own enough land; others did not possess oxen or plows. "What these statistics clearly indicate," Pruitt concluded, "is that many farms, especially the poorer ones, could not have been self-sufficient in food." The implications of her findings for the Henretta thesis were devastating. The colonists that Pruitt studied engaged in market activities because they had to. They had no choice. If they had stubbornly maintained a precapitalist mentality, the farmers of most Massachusetts communities would have starved. This discovery, Pruitt explained, "casts a somewhat different light on their motivations in marketing and exchange and, indeed, on all the internal commerce of the province. . . . Traditionally sharp distinctions between subsistence and commercial agriculture can be set aside as inapplicable to an agrarian economy in which production for home consumption and production for sale or exchange were complementary, not mutually exclusive, objectives." Of course, the farmers of this region did not starve. During the eighteenth century, no one worried much about the possibility of famine. According to Pruitt, the explanation for such complacency was "interdependence." [41] Individual farms might have been too small or too poor to support a family, but by trading for food and fodder with neighbors, by selling the labor of dependent sons to other villagers, these seemingly marginal farmers managed somehow to survive.

Shammas pushed this line of analysis even further. She observed that Pruitt had exchanged self-sufficient farmers for self-sufficient communities. But as Shammas sifted through the probate records, she came to

[41] Bettye Hobbs Pruitt, "Self-Sufficiency and the Agricultural Economy of Eighteenth-Century Massachusetts," *William and Mary Quarterly*, 3d ser., 41 (1984): 333–64, 338. See also Bettye Hobbs Pruitt, "Communications," *William and Mary Quarterly*, 3d ser., 41 (1985): 559–62; Mary Beth Norton, "The Evolution of White Women's Experience in Early America," *American Historical Review* 89 (1984): 604–5.

appreciate just how dependent these villagers had actually been on the external market. Few colonial women, for example, could possibly have clothed their families in homespun. The task would have taken more time than most young mothers had available. Moreover, it is doubtful that they would have possessed the tools necessary to spin yarn and then to weave it into cloth. Nor, for that matter, could most households have made beer. Glass and metal goods had to come from outside the rural community. So too ceramics. These farm families may have traded labor for food on the local market, but for the rest of their needs they looked to shopkeepers, to merchants, to manufacturers, to a chain of people that stretched from the rural countryside of Massachusetts all the way to Great Britain. Shammas estimated that nearly a quarter of all expenditures that these families made during a given year "went toward buying goods brought in from outside the province [Massachusetts]." [42] These were not precapitalist farmers sullenly submitting to the market. They welcomed economic change. Not only did the market provide them with goods that they could not produce themselves, but it also freed them—especially the women—from the backbreaking toil connected with subsistence. Shammas reminds readers who look back with nostalgia at a lost colonial world that self-sufficiency was never a very appealing goal.

IV

Having liberated ourselves from the myth of self-sufficiency, we can return with fresh appreciation to the world of consumption. Between 1700 and 1770, the population of the mainland colonies rose approximately eightfold, from roughly 275,000 to 2,210,000. During the decade of the 1760s, it jumped almost 40 percent. Such extraordinarily rapid growth must have strained economic and political institutions. At any given time the majority of this population consisted of young people, boys and girls who were consumers but not yet full producers in this agricultural economy. And yet, contrary to Malthusian expectations, the eighteenth-century colonists were remarkably prosperous. They managed to raise the value of their exports to the mother country by some 500 percent during this period. The importation of British

[42] Carole Shammas, "Consumer Behavior in Colonial America," *Social Science History* 6 (1982): 67–86, 81. In another essay, Shammas concludes that "the growth of the colonial population, European Atlantic ports, the British shipping industry, indentured servitude, and chattel slavery all stand as testimony to the voracious appetite of Western consumers for new market commodities, and there is no evidence that Americans did not fully participate in that commercial world" ("How Self-sufficient Was Early America?" [n. 28 above], p. 268). Even archaeologists affirm this argument (see Michael D. Coe, "The Line of Forts: Archeology of the Mid-Eighteenth Century on the Massachusetts Frontier," *Dublin Seminar for New England Folklife: Annual Proceedings* 2 [1977]: 44–56).

goods rose at an even faster rate. In 1700 the average American annually purchased British imports valued at just under a pound sterling. By 1770 the per capita figure had jumped to £1.20, a rise made all the more impressive when set against the population explosion. What this meant is each succeeding generation of colonial American farmers possessed more British imports than their fathers had. Gloria L. Main discovered that even in New England, the poorest region of the continent, "parents of each generation succeeded in raising their children in material circumstances no worse and possibly a little better than that enjoyed by themselves." [43]

These numbers alone reveal why British merchants and manufacturers were increasingly drawn to this robust American market. Over the course of the eighteenth century, the center of Britain's commercial gravity shifted west, away from traditional linkages to the Continent to new ports such as Liverpool and Glasgow that catered to the colonial consumer demand. In other words, as the American buyers became more dependent on British suppliers, the British business community became more dependent on the colonial market. "It was thus hard facts," explains Jacob M. Price, "and not imagination that made British manufacturers so sensitive to the opening and closing of the North American market at the time of the nonimportation agreements of the 1760's and 1770's." [44]

The Americans were only slowly integrated into the British consumer economy. The key decade in this commercial process appears to be the 1740s. Before that time, colonial demand for imports rose, but not very rapidly. Some manufactured items began to appear in inventories early in the century. The range and quality of these items, however, was not particularly impressive. Colonial newspapers carried few advertisements for "the latest goods imported from England," and though various urban merchants introduced new manufactures into the colonial market, the average American in 1720 probably experienced a material culture closer to that of the original settlers than of the revolutionary generation. According to Gloria Main, "wealthy colonials in New England as well as in the Chesapeake lived relatively

[43] Gloria L. Main, "The Standard of Living in Colonial Massachusetts," *Journal of Economic History* 43 (1983): 108; Bailyn (n. 12 above), pp. 446–48; McCusker and Menard (n. 15 above), chap. 13.

[44] Jacob M. Price, "Colonial Trade and British Economic Development, 1660–1775," in *La Revolution americaine et l'Europe*, ed. Claude Fohlen and Jacques Godechot (Paris, 1979), p. 225. See also David Ormrod, "English Re-exports and the Dutch Staplemarket in the Eighteenth Century," in *Enterprise and History: Essays in Honour of Charles Wilson*, ed. D. C. Coleman and Peter Mathias (Cambridge, 1984), p. 114; Davis, "English Foreign Trade" (n. 20 above), pp. 289–90, and *A Commercial Revolution* (n. 20 above), pp. 18–19; Wilson (n. 20 above); and W. E. Minchinton, introduction to Minchinton, ed. (n. 22 above), p. 40.

simply in the early part of the eighteenth century, compared with what was achieved in the half-century to follow." [45]

During the 1740s, the American market suddenly took off. British goods flooded the colonies, and though war occasionally disrupted trade, business always rebounded. Journals carried more and more advertisements for consumer goods. Stores popped up in little New England country villages and along the rivers of the Chesapeake. Carolinians demanded consumer goods; so too did the wheat farmers and the Indian traders of the Middle Colonies. Everywhere the pace of business picked up. By 1772 the Americans were importing British manufactures in record volume. As in the mother country, this market was driven largely by demand. To pay for these goods the colonists produced more and more tobacco, rice, indigo, wheat, fish, tar—indeed, anything that would supply the income necessary to purchase additional imports. The Staple Colonies maintained direct trade links with England and Scotland, but in New England and the Middle Colonies the consumer challenge forced merchants to peddle local products wherever there was a market. Pennsylvania merchants carried ever larger amounts of wheat and flour to southern Europe. New Englanders relied on the West Indian trade to help pay the bill for British manufactures. As one New Yorker explained in 1762, "Our importation of dry goods from England is so vastly great, that we are obliged to betake ourselves to all possible arts to make remittances to the British merchants. It is for this purpose we import cotton from St. Thomas's and Surinam; lime-juice and Nicaragua wood from Curacoa [*sic*]; and logwood from the bay, &c. and yet it drains us of all the silver and gold we can collect." [46]

This consumer revolution affected the lives of all Americans. To be sure, the social effect was uneven, and the British imports initially flowed into the households of the well-to-do. These are the goods that

[45] Gloria L. Main, *Tobacco Colony: Life in Early Maryland, 1650–1720* (Princeton, N.J., 1982), pp. 5–8, 239; Lorena S. Walsh, "Urban Amenities and Rural Sufficiency: Living Standards and Consumer Behavior in the Colonial Chesapeake, 1643–1777," *Journey of Economic History* 43 (1983), 110; Lois Green Carr and Lorena S. Walsh, "Changing Life Styles and Consumer Behavior in the Colonial Chesapeake" (paper presented at the Conference on Britain and America in the Early Modern Era, 1600–1820, Williamsburg, Va., September 5–7, 1985).

[46] William Smith, *The History of the Late Province of New York . . . 1762*. Collections of the New York Historical Society, vol. 4, pt. 2 (New York, 1829), p. 281. See also Marc M. Egnal and Joseph A. Ernst, "An Economic Interpretation of the American Revolution," *William and Mary Quarterly*, 3d ser., 29 (1972): 3–32; Jacob M. Price, "Buchanan & Simson, 1759–1763: A Different Kind of Glasgow Firm Trading to the Chesapeake," *William and Mary Quarterly*, 3d ser., 40 (1983): 3–41; Edward C. Papenfuse, *In Pursuit of Profit: The Annapolis Merchants in the Era of the American Revolution, 1763–1805* (Baltimore, 1975), p. 15; McCusker and Menard, pp. 268–70; Stephen Botein, "The Anglo-American Book Trade before 1776: Personnel and Strategies," in *Printing and Society in Early America*, ed. William I. Joyce et al. (Worcester, Mass., 1983), p. 80.

catch our eyes in modern museums and restored colonial homes. Not surprisingly, we know a good deal about the buying habits of the gentry. Their lives were often well documented, and the fine pieces of china and silver that came into their possession are more apt to have survived to the present than were the more ordinary items that found their way into modest households. The general pattern of cultural diffusion seems clear enough. Poorer colonists aped their social betters, just as wealthy Americans mimicked English gentlemen. However slowly these new tastes may have been communicated, they eventually reached even the lowest levels of society. In her study of colonial Maryland, for example, Lorena Walsh discovered that, "by the 1750s, even the poorer sorts were finding a wide variety of non-essentials increasingly desirable. At the lowest levels of wealth this meant acquiring more of the ordinary amenities families had so long foregone—tables, chairs, bed steads, individual knives and forks, bed and table linens, and now-inexpensive ceramic tableware." [47] A similar transformation of material culture was occurring in other regions.

Perhaps the central item in this rapidly changing consumer society was tea. In the early decades of the eighteenth century, tea began to appear in the homes of wealthier Americans. It may have replaced stronger drinks such as the popular rum punch, and by the 1740s proper ladies and gentlemen regularly socialized over tea. Taking tea became a recognized ritual requiring the correct cups and saucers, sugar bowls, and a collection of pots. By mid-century lesser sorts insisted on drinking tea, and though their tea services may not have been as costly as those of the local gentry, they performed the ritual as best they could. Even the poor wanted tea. One historian found that, during a confrontation with city officials that occurred in 1766, the residents of the Philadelphia poor house demanded Bohea tea. For all these Americans, drinking tea required cups that could hold extremely hot liquids and that, in turn, forced them to import the technically advanced ceramics that originated in Staffordshire. Not until well after the Revolution were American potters able to produce cups of such high quality at competitive prices.[48] What catches our attention is how colonial Americans were increasingly drawn into the marketplace. A

---

[47] Walsh, p. 111; Carole Shammas, "The Domestic Environment in Early Modern England and America," *Journal of Social History* 14 (1980): 3–24; Carr and Walsh: Rhys Isaac, "Radicalised Religion and Changing Lifestyles: Virginia in the Period of the American Revolution," in *The Origins of Anglo-American Radicalism*, ed. Margaret Jacob and H. James Jacob (London, 1984), pp. 257–67; Richard L. Bushman, "American High-Style and Vernacular Cultures," in Greene and Pole, eds. (n. 8 above), pp. 345–83.

[48] Main, *Tobacco Colony*, p. 247; Rodris Roth, "Tea Drinking in Eighteenth-Century America: Its Etiquette and Equipage," in *Contributions from the Museum of History and Technology*, U.S. National Museum Bulletin 225 (Washington, D.C., 1961), pp. 61–91. Billy Smith, "The Material Lives of Laboring Philadelphians, 1750 to 1800," *William and Mary Quarterly*, 3d ser., 38 (1981): 163–202.

decision to buy tea led to other purchases. English glasses held imported wines. English cloth fashioned into dresses and coats looked better with imported metal buttons. One had to serve imported sugar in the appropriate imported pewter or silver bowl.

The consumer revolution also introduced choice into the lives of many Americans. With each passing generation the number of imported goods available to the colonists expanded almost exponentially. In the 1720s, for example, the newspapers carried advertisements for at most a score of British manufactures. Usually, these were listed in general categories, such as dry goods, and one has the impression that even urban merchants carried a basic and familiar stock. But after the 1740s American shoppers came to expect a much larger selection, and merchants had to maintain ever larger inventories. When Gottlieb Mittelberger, a German minister, traveled through Pennsylvania in the early 1750s, he could not believe how many imported items he saw for sale: wine, spices, sugar, tea, coffee, rice, rum, fine china, Dutch and English cloth, leather, linen cloth, fabrics, silks, damask, and velvet. "Already," Mittelberger declared, "it is really possible to obtain all the things one can get in Europe in Pennsylvania, since so many merchant ships arrive there every year." [49] Individual merchants placed journal advertisements during the 1760s announcing the arrival from the mother country of hundreds of items. During some busy months, more than 4,000 separate goods appeared in the newspaper columns. Advertisers now broke down general merchandise groups by color and design. The consumer revolution exposed the colonists not only to a proliferation of goods but also to an ever escalating descriptive language. No doubt, as time passed, colonial buyers became more discerning, demanding increasingly better quality and wider variety.

For many consumers—particularly for women—the exercise of choice in the marketplace may have been a liberating experience, for with choice went a measure of economic power. One could literally take one's business elsewhere. We have come to think of consumerism as a negative term, as a kind of mindless mass behavior, but for the colonists of the mid-eighteenth century, shopping must have heightened their sense of self-importance. It was an arena in which they could ask questions, express individuality, and make demands. One could plausibly argue that, by exposing colonists to this world of consumer choice, the British reinforced the Americans' already strong conviction of their own personal independence.

The distribution of goods generated complex commercial networks. Merchants linked British manufacturers with American consumers, mediating misunderstandings, providing credit, and cutting through

---

[49] Gottlieb Mittelberger, *Journey to Pennsylvania* (Cambridge, Mass., 1960), pp. 37, 88–89; McCusker and Menard, p. 287; Walsh, p. 110.

bureaucratic regulation. During the eighteenth century, trade flowed through sophisticated channels, from the potters and weavers of England to the great Atlantic ports, from there to colonial cities or Chesapeake plantations, until, finally, they reached eager colonial buyers. The major merchants of Boston, New York, and Philadelphia occupied the central place in this process. They received imports in bulk from British suppliers. They then broke these cargoes down, sending smaller parcels of goods on coasters to the lesser colonial ports. One historian who studied the business records of the Hancock family waxed eloquent about these chains of commercial communication. Thomas Hancock spent much time arranging with the owners of "tiny coasters" to carry his freight to scattered destinations. "The skippers' receipts," reports W. T. Baxter, "show that the welcome parcels of clothes and hemp, powder and shot, glass and pepper were often bound for townships far up the rivers of Connecticut, and might sometimes be taken thence to western Massachusetts. In our mind's eye, then, we may watch cottons from India and nails from England creeping slowly round the coast and up the waterways, over packhorse trails, past the furthest villages, and so at last into the hands of frontiersmen." [50] Similar routes carried goods from New York to Albany and from there to the Iroquois, from Philadelphia west and then south all the way to North Carolina along the Great Wagon Road, from Charleston west to the upland plantations. As the colonial population grew and as the Americans became more prosperous, these networks became more elaborate.

The merchants of eighteenth-century America seldom complained about the Navigation Acts. To be sure, some mercantile constraints were simply ignored. New England traders did not bother to pay customs on West Indian molasses. Dutch tea somehow managed to appear on colonial tables. But on the whole, smuggling did not amount to much. Most merchants obeyed British trade restrictions. It made good business sense for them to do so. McCusker and Menard concluded that the costs of being in the empire "were largely offset by the benefits: naval protection; access to a large free-trading area; easy credit and cheap manufactures; and restricted competition." [51] To this

[50] William T. Baxter, *The House of Hancock: Business in Boston, 1724–1775* (Cambridge, Mass., 1945), p. 189. Other valuable studies of major American merchants are James B. Hedges, *The Browns of Providence Plantations*, 2 vols. (Cambridge, Mass., 1952–68); Philip L. White, *The Beekmans of New York in Politics and Commerce, 1647–1877* (New York, 1956); Arthur L. Jensen, *The Maritime Commerce of Colonial Philadelphia* (Madison, Wis., 1963); [Joshua Johnson], *Joshua Johnson's Letterbook, 1771–1774: Letters from a Merchant in London to His Partners in Maryland*, ed. Jacob M. Price, London Record Society, Publication 15 (London, 1979).

[51] McCusker and Menard, p. 354. See also Peter D. McClelland, "The Cost to America of British Imperial Policy," *American Economic Review* 59 (1969): 370–81; Gary M. Walton, "The New Economic History and the Burdens of the Navigation Acts," *Eco-*

list might be added the convenience and security of trading with familiar contacts in a familiar language. Over time the colonial merchants formed close friendships with British counterparts, and at mid-century the Americans had little incentive to challenge the mercantile system.

However obedient the colonists may have been, the structure of Atlantic trade changed substantially between 1690 and 1776. During the early decades of the eighteenth century, northern merchants usually acted as agents for larger British firms. Sometimes the Americans accepted goods on consignment. The situation in the South was not very different. The great tobacco planters of the Chesapeake sent their crops to Britain on consignment. English merchants sold the tobacco, filled orders for manufactured goods, and then credited the planters' accounts with whatever sums remained. The planters themselves often purchased items for their poorer neighbors. But in either case, the Americans worked through the British merchants. They seldom arranged for shipping; they did not enjoy direct contact with manufacturers.

As the colonial market expanded, especially after the 1740s, American merchants found this arrangement increasingly objectionable. They wanted to enlarge the scale of their operations, and though they were willing to work within the framework of the Navigation Acts, they sought a greater share of the profits. They began to dispatch their own vessels to the mother country. They tried to go around the British merchants and to negotiate with the men who actually produced goods for export. A similar restructuring occurred within the colonies. Merchants working out of smaller American ports broke with Boston and New York. Everywhere colonists were attempting to carve out profitable niches. In 1750, for example, Obadiah Brown, the wealthiest merchant of Providence, Rhode Island, decided that the time had come to strike out on his own. He sent the *Smithfield* to London carrying a three-folio-page order for British manufacturers. "With the sailing of this ship with this order," writes historian James B. Hedges, "Obadiah Brown was in a sense proclaiming the mercantile independence of Providence. He was by-passing the great men of Newport and Boston, from whom the Providence shopkeepers had largely purchased their English goods, and he was sending out a ship under his own direction to bring back his own supplies from London and Bristol." [52] In Virginia a few so-called cargo merchants tried shipping tobacco to Great Britain on American vessels.[53] All these efforts were

---

nomic History Review, 2d ser., 24 (1971): 533–42; Thomas C. Barrow, *Trade and Empire: The British Customs Service in Colonial America, 1660–1775* (Cambridge, Mass., 1967), chap. 7.

[52] Hedges, 1:8.

[53] Jacob M. Price, "The Last Phase of the Virginia-London Consignment Trade: James Buchanan & Co., 1758–1768," *William and Mary Quarterly*, 3d ser., 43 (1986): 64–98. See also Egnal and Ernst; McCusker and Menard, pp. 197–98.

tentative. They involved great risks and often ended in disappoint-
ment. Whatever the results of these experiments, however, they reveal
that the colonists wanted to compete with the British, to tap the lucrative commercial possibilities that the empire had suddenly created.

The large merchant houses of Great Britain did not welcome these
American initiatives. Indeed, they responded in ways that nearly
bankrupted some colonial traders. In the northern cities, the British
dumped goods in auction or vendue sales and, thereby, undercut established local merchants. As Marc Egnal and Joseph A. Ernst explain,
"These sales had been an integral part of colonial life before 1748, but
most often their role had been to aid in the disposal of damaged or
outmoded goods rather than to serve as a major wholesale outlet. Now
new merchants began importing directly for auctions to sell off large
quantities of goods with only fractional profits on each sale." Moreover, the British started selling goods directly to shopkeepers. "By the
1760s and 1770s," Egnal and Ernst report, "it was not uncommon to
find numerous English 'agents' in any colonial city drumming up business for their parent firms and seeking liaisons with the smallest shopkeepers along with the largest importers." [54]

In the Chesapeake, the Scots aggressively moved to capture a larger
share of the tobacco trade. Factors dispatched to the colonies by Glasgow firms set up scores of stores on the rivers and creeks of the region
and, thereby, freed the small planters from reliance on the local gentry
for goods and credit. The stores spread like wildfire. In 1743 Francis
Jerdone, a merchant in Hanover County, Virginia, announced, "There
are 25 stores within 18 miles round me which is 13 more than at Mr.
Johnson's death [in 1740] and 4 or 5 more expected next year from
some of the outports [of Great Britain]." [55] These structural shifts in
merchandising, in the northern as well as the southern colonies, may
have irritated Americans who dreamed of commercial fortunes, but
however angry they may have been, it seems apparent that this fierce
competition inevitably drew colonial consumers closer to the mother
country. More stores and lower prices translated into increasing sales.

These colonial stores, wherever they appeared, provided an important link between the common people of America and the mother
country. Unfortunately, we do not know much about these scattered
places of business. Most were probably small, no larger than a garage
in a home today. Such certainly was the store operated by Jonathan
Trumbull in rural Connecticut. But despite their modest size, these
buildings—sometimes a room in the merchant's home—held an amaz-
ing variety of goods. As Glenn Weaver, Trumbull's biographer, ex-

---

[54] Egnal and Ernst, pp. 15–16.

[55] Cited in Carr and Walsh, p. 31. Rutman and Rutman (n. 34 above), pp. 205–31;
Price, "Buchanan & Simson," pp. 4–33; Mitchell (n. 37 above), pp. 154–59; Walsh, p.
116.

plains, a sampling of the merchant's ledger books during the 1730s and 1740s reveals an amazingly full stock of imports: "Pepper, lace, gloves, gunpowder, flints, molasses, rum, *Watts' Psalms*, mohair, drugs, tiles, paper, garlix (a kind of cloth), pots, pans, 'manna,' cord, pails, needles, knives, indigo, logwood, earthenware, raisins, thimbles, buckles, all-spice, tea, buttons, mace, combs, butter, spectacles, soap, brimstone, nails, shot, sewing silk, sugar, wire, looking glasses, tape, 'Italian crape,' 'allam,' pewter dishes, etc." [56] One wonders what items were hidden in Weaver's "etc." He seems already to have listed just about everything that a Connecticut farm family might have desired.

The only unusual characteristic about Trumbull's store is that the records of his business have been so well preserved. But stores of similar description could have been found from Maine to Georgia. The stores that Jerdone described in Virginia, for example, carried the same range of goods. Moreover, all these mid-eighteenth-century businesses stayed open the full year, as earlier stores had not, and thus it was possible for the Connecticut farmer or the Virginia planter to shop whenever that activity fit into his busy schedule. As competition increased, colonial shopkeepers began to merchandise their wares more aggressively. When newspaper space was available, they placed advertisements. They also learned to display goods in more pleasing ways, to court customers. The eighteenth-century shopkeeper ignored women at his peril. In 1748 one Maryland factor informed a correspondent of what it took to succeed in this market: "You know the influence of the Wives upon their Husbands, & it is but a trifle that wins 'em over, they must be taken notice of or there will be nothing with them." [57] These pressures escalated. Chesapeake historians Lois G. Carr and Lorena Walsh claim that by the 1750s "some merchants would begin to build substantial brick store buildings equipped with more elaborate shelves and counters for display, and chairs, tables, glassware, and teaware for the genteel entertainment of customers." [58]

Along the roads of mid-eighteenth-century America also traveled the peddlers, the chapmen, and the hawkers, figures celebrated in folklore but ignored almost completely by serious historians. The failure to explore the world of these itinerant salesmen is unfortunate, for they seem to have accounted for a considerable volume of trade. The peddlers made up a sizable percentage of James Beckman's customers, and he was one of the most successful import merchants in New York City.[59] In Boston Thomas Hancock took good care of his "country

[56] Glenn Weaver, *Jonathan Trumbull: Connecticut's Merchant Magistrate (1710–1785)* (Hartford, Conn., 1956), p. 19.

[57] Cited in Carr and Walsh, p. 33. See also Harry D. Berg, "The Organization of Business in Colonial Philadelphia," *Pennsylvania History* 10 (1943): 157–77.

[58] Carr and Walsh, p. 33.

[59] White, pp. 390–91.

chaps," making certain British merchants and manufacturers supplied them with the items that the colonists actually wanted to buy.[60] These travelers seem to have hawked their goods along city streets as well as country highways. Men as well as women peddled their wares. A New York law setting conditions for this sort of business specifically mentioned "he" and "she," indicating that in this colony at least people of both sexes carried consumer goods from town to town.[61]

But whatever their gender, itinerants sometimes traveled far, popping up everywhere, ubiquitous denizens of village taverns. When Alexander Hamilton journeyed through the northern colonies in 1744, for example, he regularly encountered peddlers. "I dined att William's att Stonington, [Connecticut,] with a Boston merchant name Gardiner and one Boyd, a Scotch Irish pedlar," Hamilton scribbled. "The pedlar seemed to understand his business to a hair. He sold some dear bargains to Mrs. Williams, and while he smoothed her up with palaber, the Bostoner amused her with religious cant. This pedlar told me he had been some time agoe att Annapolis[, Maryland]." In Bristol, Rhode Island, Hamilton and his black servant were taken for peddlers because they carried large "portmanteaux," and the local residents rushed out into the street to inspect their goods.[62] The number of peddlers on the road appears to have been a function of the general prosperity of the colonial economy. In other words, they do not seem to have represented a crude or transitional form of merchandising. As the number of stores increased, so too did the number of peddlers. In fact, the two groups often came into conflict, for the peddlers operating with little overhead could easily undercut the established merchant's price. Shopkeepers petitioned the various colonial legislatures about this allegedly unfair competition. In turn, the lawmakers warned the peddlers to purchase licenses, some at substantial fees, but judging from the repetition of these regulations in the statutes, one concludes that the peddlers more than held their own against the rural merchants.

The mid-eighteenth century also witnessed a spectacular expansion of credit. Indeed, the entire chain of merchandising from British manufacturers to rural American consumers depended on liberal credit arrangements. Without such a system, the colonists could not have participated in the Atlantic economy. They never possessed an adequate

[60] Baxter (n. 50 above), p. 188.

[61] For example, *The Colonial Laws of New York from the Year 1664 to the Revolution,* 5 vols. (Albany, N.Y., 1894), 4:388–89. On women as traders in early America, see Laurel Thatcher Ulrich, *Good Wives: Image and Reality in the Lives of Women in Northern New England, 1650–1750* (New York, 1980), chap. 2; Linda K. Kerber, *Women of the Republic: Intellect and Ideology in Revolutionary America* (Chapel Hill, N.C., 1980), pp. 148–50.

[62] Hamilton (n. 27 above), pp. 150, 160. See Richard L. Bushman, *From Puritan to Yankee: Character and the Social Order in Connecticut, 1690–1765* (Cambridge, Mass., 1967), p. 113; Rutman and Rutman, p. 231.

money supply. Specie quickly drained back to the mother country, and though some colonies issued paper currency, these bills did not satisfy the requirements of long-distance trade. But convenience is only part of the story of credit. During this period, British merchants eager to increase business offered credit in larger amounts and on more generous terms than they had ever done before. This decision involved great risks. The British apparently concluded, however, that the profits from the American trade outweighed the bad debts, and they pumped credit through the system. It flowed from the major port cities to the little storekeepers like Jonathan Trumbull, from Glasgow to tobacco factors residing in the Chesapeake. Everywhere the historian encounters people accepting goods long before they had to pay for them.[63] The huge debts that the Chesapeake planters owed on the eve of revolution have attracted scholarly attention, but the character and function of credit relations in other regions have not been examined.[64] Since the loan of money or the issuance of credit raised profound questions about personal honor, it would be interesting to know who received it and under what circumstances it was given. Did credit follow bloodlines? Did credit sustain political networks in rural communities?

One can only speculate about the motivation of the colonial buyer. The psychology of eighteenth-century consumption was complex, and each person entered the market for slightly different reasons. Some men and women wanted to save money and time. After all, producing one's own garments—a linen shirt, for example—was a lengthy, tedious process, and the purchase of imported cloth may have been more cost effective than was turning out homespun. Beauty also figured into the calculus of consumption. An imported Staffordshire plate or a piece of ribbon brought color into an otherwise drab environment. Contemporary merchants certainly understood that aesthetics played a major role in winning customers. In 1756, for example, one frustrated English supplier wrote to the Philadelphia merchant John Reynall, "There is no way to send goods with any certainty of sale but by sending Patterns of the several colours in vogue with you." [65] No doubt, some Americans realized that ceramic plates and serving dishes were more sanitary to use than were the older wooden trenchers. In addition, consumer goods provided socially mobile Americans with boundary

[63] Wilbur C. Plummer, "Consumer Credit in Colonial Philadelphia," *Pennsylvania Magazine of History and Biography* 66 (1942): 385–409; White, pp. 335–485; Walsh, p. 116; Lois G. Carr and Lorena Walsh, "Inventories and the Analysis of Wealth and Consumption Patterns in St. Mary's County, Maryland, 1658–1777," *Historical Methods* 13 (1980): 81–104.

[64] On the size and meaning of debt, see T. H. Breen, *Tobacco Culture: The Mentality of the Great Tidewater Planters on the Eve of Revolution* (Princeton, N.J., 1985), chap. 4; Emory Evans, "Planter Indebtedness and the Coming of the Revolution in Virginia," *William and Mary Quarterly*, 3d ser., 19 (1962): 511–33.

[65] Cited in Berg, p. 171.

markers, an increasingly recognized way to distinguish betters from
their inferiors, for though the rural farmer may have owned a tea cup,
he could not often afford real china. In whatever group one traveled,
however, one knew that consumer goods mediated social status. Their
possession gave off messages full of meanings that modern historians
have been slow to comprehend. Finally, just as it is today, shopping in
colonial times was entertaining. Consumer goods became topics of
conversation, the source of a new vocabulary, the spark of a new kind
of social discourse.

V

This survey of the birth of an American consumer society returns to
the interpretative problems posed by Charles McLean Andrews, to a
reassessment of the meaning of empire in the eighteenth century. Even
at this preliminary stage of research, it can be appreciated that British
imports provided white Americans with a common framework of experience. Consumption drew the colonists together even when they
themselves were unaware of what was happening. Men and women living in different parts of the continent purchased a similar range of
goods. The items that appeared in New England households also
turned up in the Carolinas. The rice planters of Charleston probably
did not know that northern farmers demanded the same kinds of imports. They may not have even cared. But however tenuous communication between mid-eighteenth-century colonists may have been, there
could be no denying that British manufacturers were standardizing the
material culture of the American colonies. Without too much exaggeration, Staffordshire pottery might be seen as the Coca-Cola of the
eighteenth century. It was a product of the metropolitan economy that
touched the lives of people living on the frontier of settlement, erod-
ing seventeenth-century folkways and bringing scattered planters and
farmers into dependence on a vast world market that they did not yet
quite comprehend.

Herein lies a paradox that anthropologists and historians such as
John M. Murrin, Michael D. Coe, and James Deetz have brought to
our attention. The road to Americanization ran through Anglicization.[66] In other words, before these widely dispersed colonists could
develop a sense of their own common cultural identity, they had first

---

[66] The term "Anglicization" was originally employed by John M. Murrin ("Angliciz-
ing an American Colony: The Transformation of Provincial Massachusetts" [Ph.D. diss.,
Yale University, 1966]). James Deetz describes this cultural process as "re-Anglicization"
(*In Small Things Forgotten: The Archeology of Early American Life* [Garden City, N.Y.,
1977]), and Michael D. Coe writes of the "Georgianization" of eighteenth-century
American culture ([n. 42 above], pp. 53–54).

to be integrated fully into the British empire. Royal government in colonial America was never large enough to effect Anglicization. Nor could force of arms have brought about this cultural redefinition. Such a vast shift in how Americans viewed the mother country and each other required a flood of consumer goods, little manufactured items that found their way into gentry homes as well as frontier cabins. According to anthropologist James Deetz, this transformation of everyday material culture "meant that on the eve of the American Revolution, Americans were more English than they had been in the past since the first years of the colonies." [67]

The extent of this imperialism of goods amazed even contemporaries. In 1771, William Eddis, an Englishman living in Maryland, wrote home that "the quick importation of fashions from the mother country is really astonishing. I am almost inclined to believe that a new fashion is adopted earlier by the polished and affluent American than by many opulent persons in the great metropolis. . . . In short, very little difference is, in reality, observable in the manners of the wealthy colonist and the wealthy Briton." [68] Eddis may have exaggerated, but probably not much. Students of the book trade, for example, have discovered that the colonists demanded volumes printed in England. Indeed, so deep was the Anglicization of American readers that "a false London imprint could seem an effective way to sell a local publication." [69] Newspaper advertisements announced that merchants carried the "latest English goods." By the mid-eighteenth century, these imported items had clearly taken on symbolic value. Put simply, pride of ownership translated into pride of being part of the empire, a sentiment that was reinforced but not created by the victory of the British army over the French in the Seven Years' War.

So long as the king of England ruled over an empire of goods, his task was relatively easy. The spread of the consumer society, at least before the Stamp Act Crisis, tied the colonists ever closer to the mother country. This is what Benjamin Franklin tried to communicate to the House of Commons. He observed that before 1763 the Americans had "submitted willingly to the government of the Crown, and paid, in all their courts, obedience to acts of parliament." It cost Parliament almost nothing, Franklin explained, to maintain the loyalty of this rapidly growing population across the Atlantic. The colonists "were governed by this country at the expense only of a little pen, ink, and paper. They were led by a thread. They had not only a respect, but an affection, for Great Britain, for its laws, its customs and manners, and even a fondness for its fashions, that greatly increased the com-

[67] Deetz, p. 38.

[68] William Eddis, *Letters from America*, ed. Aubrey C. Land (Cambridge, Mass., 1969), pp. 57–58.

[69] Botein (n. 46 above), pp. 79, 80.

merce." [70] No American, of course, had a greater fondness for cosmopolitan fashion than did Franklin. And in 1763 he could not comprehend why anyone would want to upset a system that seemed to operate so well.

The Anglicization thesis obviously makes it hard to explain the American Revolution. The solution to this puzzle may be suggested, at least in part, by the complex character of nationalism itself. As J. G. A. Pocock noted in reference to another rebellious country, "It can be shown without much difficulty that Ireland became more nationalist and more revolutionary as it was increasingly assimilated to English-derived political and cultural norms, and that, in this case as in many others, revolutionary nationalism is less a means of resisting acculturation than a method of asserting one's own power over the process." [71] Pocock provides an important insight into the American situation. As their debts to the mother country mounted after 1750, the colonists began to fear for the loss of their own independence. "The goods always were most extravagantly dear," cried one Virginia planter to his sister in 1753, "but now [they] . . . got the parties so much in debt to the merchants [that] they might [not] be able to pay this money in years if ever yet." [72] This was not an unusual complaint. For many white Americans dependence meant slavery, the deprivation of freedom, a state that they could never tolerate.

The colonists responded to this unhappy state of affairs—one that Parliament exacerbated by taxing the colonists without their consent—by attempting to turn back the clock. They claimed that they wanted to reverse the consumer tide, and in a series of increasingly successful boycotts against British manufactures, they redefined the symbolic meaning of imported goods. In public discourse these items became politicized, badges of dependence. Or, to restate the proposition, during the decade preceding revolution, Americans communicated abstract notions about politics through consumer goods. One's attitude toward tea indicated where one stood on constitutional liberties. The process was slow, sometimes superficial, but it touched people of all classes. Charles Grahame, a respected Maryland leader, explained how goods mobilized public opinion in one colony. At a meeting held in Charles County, "I found our country people on Saturday almost unanimous against that part of the Annapolis Resolves which regarded nonexportation. . . . This point being settled . . . we had a wrangle about importation and though it was once agreed that we should have

---

[70] "The Examination of Benjamin Franklin in the House of Commons, February 13, 1766," in *Colonies to Nation: 1763–1789*, ed. Jack P. Greene (New York, 1975), pp. 72–77.
[71] Pocock, "British History" (n. 11 above), p. 610.
[72] Cited in Douglas Southall Freeman, *George Washington: A Biography*, 7 vols. (New York, 1948–57), 1:168–69. See Richard Pares, *Merchants and Planters*, Economic History Review Supplement no. 4 (Cambridge, 1960), p. 50; and Breen, *Tobacco Culture*, chap. 3.

a partial one of such goods as should be thought by the general meeting of the province proper, yet toward evening the people of the inferior class growing naturally a little tumultuous[,] the question was resumed and it was agreed we should have no importation at all." [73] The little farmers of this Chesapeake county declared their independence from consumer goods just as the working people of Boston did when they dumped the tea into the harbor. Once that symbolic link between England and America had been severed, once common men and women asserted their control over the process of acculturation, the political ties of empire quickly unraveled.[74]

Taking the Trade:
Abortion and Gender Relations in an
Eighteenth-Century New England Village

CORNELIA HUGHES DAYTON

Cornelia Hughes Dayton demonstrates the approach of recent social historians who ingeniously reconstruct the details of everyday, local life in early America. In this essay, she uses the remarkably ample records of an obscure mid-eighteenth-century Connecticut murder trial to recreate aspects of colonial human interactions

[73] Cited in Ronald Hoffman, *A Spirit of Dissension: Economics, Politics, and the Revolution in Maryland* (Baltimore, 1973), pp. 130–31. On the symbolic meaning of goods, see Mihaly Csikszentmihalyi and Eugene Rochberg-Halton, *The Meaning of Things: Domestic Symbols and the Self* (Cambridge, 1981); Mary Douglass and Baron Isherwood, *The World of Goods: Toward an Anthropology of Consumption* (New York, 1979), chap. 4; Chandra Mukerji, *From Graven Images: Patterns of Modern Materialism* (New York, 1983).

[74] The revolutionary implications of consumption are explored in Timothy H. Breen, "Baubles of Britain: The Meaning of Things" (paper presented to the United States Capitol Historical Society, March 20, 1986), which will appear in Ronald Hoffman and Cary Carson, eds., *Of Consuming Interests: The Style of Life in the Eighteenth Century* (in press).

previously obscure to historians, especially gender and sexual re-
lations. The vivid story of the liaison between Amasa Sessions
and Sarah Grosvenor is fascinating in its own right as an un-
usually detailed example of intimate personal relations. How-
ever, Dayton also insists upon its larger historical significance as
an indication of the emergence of the sexual double standard in
eighteenth-century New England, the gendering of family reac-
tions to Sarah Grosvenor's death, the possibility of the social ac-
ceptability of abortion that did not result in death to the mother,
and the ambivalent character of contemporary medical practice.

  Dayton's essay raises an important methodological question
about narrative local history: How far can one generalize upon
the basis of a unique example? Even if the Sessions-Grosvenor
episode is characteristic of Connecticut, what are its implications
for other regions in colonial America? What confidence can we
place in legal depositions taken from family members several
years after the incident in question? Above all, Dayton forces us
to confront the significance of gender relations in understanding
historical change. Until recently, historians ignored gender as an
historical factor. Were they wrong?

In 1742 in the village of Pomfret, perched in the hills of northeastern
Connecticut, nineteen-year-old Sarah Grosvenor and twenty-seven-
year-old Amasa Sessions became involved in a liaison that led to pregnancy, abortion, and death. Both were from prominent yeoman families, and neither a marriage between them nor an arrangement for the
support of their illegitimate child would have been an unusual event
for mid-eighteenth century New England. Amasa Sessions chose a
different course; in consultation with John Hallowell, a self-pro-
claimed "practitioner of physick," he coerced his lover into taking an
abortifacient. Within two months, Sarah fell ill. Unbeknownst to all
but Amasa, Sarah, Sarah's sister Zerviah, and her cousin Hannah, Hallowell made an attempt to "Remove her Conseption" by a "manual
opperation." Two days later Sarah miscarried, and her two young relatives secretly buried the fetus in the woods. Over the next month,
Sarah struggled against a "Malignant fever" and was attended by several physicians, but on September 14, 1742, she died.[1]

---

[1] The documentation is found in the record books and file papers of the Superior
Court of Connecticut: *Rex v. John Hallowell et al.*, Superior Court Records, Book 9, 113,
173, 175, and Windham County Superior Court Files, box 172, Connecticut State Library, Hartford. Hereafter all loose court papers cited are from *Rex v. Hallowell*, Windham County Superior Court Files, box 172, unless otherwise indicated. For the quotations see Security bond for John Hallowell, undated; Deposition of Ebenezer
Grosvenor, probably Apr. 1746; Indictment against John Hallowell and Amasa Sessions,
Sept. 20, 1746; Deposition of Parker Morse.

Most accounts of induced abortions among seventeenth- and eighteenth-century whites in the Old and New Worlds consist of only a few lines in a private letter or court record book; these typically refer to the taking of savin or pennyroyal—two common herbal abortifacients. While men and women in diverse cultures have known how to perform abortions by inserting an instrument into the uterus, actual descriptions of such operations are extremely rare for any time period. Few accounts of abortions by instrument have yet been uncovered for early modern England, and I know of no other for colonial North America.[2] Thus the historical fragments recording events in a small New England town in 1742 take on an unusual power to illustrate how an abortion was conducted, how it was talked about, and how it was punished.

We know about the Grosvenor-Sessions case because in 1745 two prominent Windham County magistrates opened an investigation into Sarah's death. Why there was a three-year gap between that event and legal proceedings, and why justices from outside Pomfret initiated the legal process, remain a mystery. In November 1745 the investigating magistrates offered their preliminary opinion that Hallowell, Amasa Sessions, Zerviah Grosvenor, and Hannah Grosvenor were guilty of Sarah's murder, the last three as accessories. From the outset, Connecticut legal officials concentrated not on the act of abortion per se, but on the fact that an abortion attempt had led to a young woman's death.[3]

---

[2] One such abortion was reported in *Gentleman's Magazine* (London), II, No. 20 (August 1732), 933–934; see Audrey Eccles, *Obstetrics and Gynaecology in Tudor and Stuart England* (London, 1982), 70. On the history of abortion practices see George Devereux, "A Typological Study of Abortion in 350 Primitive, Ancient, and Pre-Industrial Societies," in Harold Rosen, ed., *Abortion in America: Medical, Psychiatric, Legal, Anthropological, and Religious Considerations* (Boston, 1967), 97–152; Angus McLaren, *Reproductive Rituals: The Perception of Fertility in England from the Sixteenth Century to the Nineteenth Century* (London, 1984), chap. 4; Linda Gordon, *Woman's Body, Woman's Right: A Social History of Birth Control in America* (New York, 1976), 26–41, 49–60; and Edward Shorter, *A History of Women's Bodies* (New York, 1982), chap. 8.

For specific cases indicating use of herbal abortifacients in the North American colonies see Julia Cherry Spruill, *Women's Life and Work in the Southern Colonies* (New York, 1972; orig. pub. Chapel Hill, N. C., 1938), 325–326; Roger Thompson, *Sex in Middlesex: Popular Mores in a Massachusetts County, 1649–1699* (Amherst, Mass., 1986), II, 24–26, 107–108, 182–183; and Lyle Koehler, *A Search for Power: The "Weaker Sex" in Seventeenth-Century New England* (Urbana, Ill., 1980), 204–205. I have found two references to the use of an abortifacient in colonial Connecticut court files. Doubtless, other accounts of abortion attempts for the colonial period will be discovered.

[3] Abortion before quickening (defined in the early modern period as the moment when the mother first felt the fetus move) was not viewed by the English or colonial courts as criminal. No statute law on abortion existed in either Britain or the colonies. To my knowledge, no New England court before 1745 had attempted to prosecute a physician for carrying out an abortion.

On the history of the legal treatment of abortion in Europe and the United States see McLaren, *Reproductive Rituals*, chap. 5; Gordon, *Woman's Body, Woman's Right*, chap. 3;

The case went next to Joseph Fowler, king's attorney for Windham County. He dropped charges against the two Grosvenor women, probably because he needed them as key witnesses and because they had played cover-up roles rather than originating the scheme. A year and a half passed as Fowler's first attempts to get convictions against Hallowell and Sessions failed either before grand juries or before the Superior Court on technical grounds. Finally, in March 1747, Fowler presented Hallowell and Sessions separately for the "highhanded Misdemeanour" of attempting to destroy both Sarah Grosvenor's health and "the fruit of her womb." [4] A grand jury endorsed the bill against Hallowell but rejected a similarly worded presentment against Sessions. At Hallowell's trial before the Superior Court in Windham, the jury brought in a guilty verdict and the chief judge sentenced the physician to twenty-nine lashes and two hours of public humiliation standing at the town gallows. Before the sentence could be executed, Hallowell managed to break jail. He fled to Rhode Island; as far as records indicate, he never returned to Connecticut. Thus, in the end, both Amasa Sessions and John Hallowell escaped legal punishment for their actions, whereas Sarah Grosvenor paid for her sexual transgression with her life.

Nearly two years of hearings and trials before the Superior Court produced a file of ten depositions and twenty-four other legal documents. This cache of papers is extraordinarily rich, not alone for its unusual chronicle of an abortion attempt, but for its illumination of the fault lines in Pomfret dividing parents from grown children, men from women, and mid-eighteenth-century colonial culture from its seventeenth-century counterpart.

The depositions reveal that in 1742 the elders of Pomfret, men and women alike, failed to act as vigilant monitors of Sarah Grosvenor's courtship and illness. Instead, young, married householders—kin of Sarah and Amasa—pledged themselves in a conspiracy of silence to allow the abortion plot to unfold undetected. The one person who had the opportunity to play middleman between the generations was Hallowell. A man in his forties, dogged by a shady past and yet adept at acquiring respectable connections, Hallowell provides an intriguing

James C. Mohr, *Abortion in America: The Origins and Evolution of National Policy, 1800–1900* (New York, 1978); Michael Grossberg, *Governing the Hearth: Law and the Family in Nineteenth-Century America* (Chapel Hill, N. C., 1985), chap. 5; and Carroll Smith-Rosenberg, "The Abortion Movement and the AMA, 1850–1880," in *Disorderly Conduct: Visions of Gender in Victorian America* (New York, 1985), 217–244.

In 1683, a Newport, Rhode Island, woman was whipped for fornication and "Indeavouringe the distruction of the Child in her womb" (Supreme Court Records, Bk. A, 66, Supreme Court Judicial Records Center, Pawtucket; I thank Catherine Osborne DeCesare for alerting me to this case).

[4] Indictment against John Hallowell, Mar. 1746/ 47.

and rare portrait of a socially ambitious, rural medical practitioner. By siding with the young people of Pomfret and keeping their secret, Hallowell betrayed his peers and elders and thereby opened himself to severe censure and expulsion from the community.

Beyond depicting generational conflict, the Grosvenor-Sessions case dramatically highlights key changes in gender relations that reverberated through New England society in the eighteenth century. One of these changes involved the emergence of a marked sexual double standard. In the mid-seventeenth century, a young man like Amasa Sessions would have been pressured by parents, friends, or the courts to marry his lover. Had he resisted, he would most likely have been whipped or fined for the crime of fornication. By the late seventeenth century, New England judges gave up on enjoining sexually active couples to marry. In the 1740s, amid shifting standards of sexual behavior and growing concern over the evidentiary impossibility of establishing paternity, prosecutions of young men for premarital sex ceased. Thus fornication was decriminalized for men, but not for women. Many of Sarah Grosvenor's female peers continued to be prosecuted and fined for bearing illegitimate children. Through private arrangements, and occasionally through civil lawsuits, their male partners were sometimes cajoled or coerced into contributing to the child's upkeep.[5]

What is most striking about the Grosvenor-Sessions case is that an entire community apparently forgave Sessions for the extreme measures he took to avoid accountability for his bastard child. Although he initiated the actions that led to his lover's death, all charges against him were dropped. Moreover, the tragedy did not spur Sessions to leave town; instead, he spent the rest of his life in Pomfret as a respected citizen. Even more dramatically than excusing young men from the crime of fornication, the treatment of Amasa Sessions confirmed that the sexually irresponsible activities of men in their youth

---

[5] The story of the decriminalization of fornication for men in colonial New England is told most succinctly by Carol F. Karlsen, *The Devil in the Shape of a Woman: Witchcraft in Colonial New England* (New York, 1987), 194–196, 198–202, 255. Laurel Thatcher Ulrich describes a late eighteenth-century Massachusetts jurisdiction in *A Midwife's Tale: The Life of Martha Ballard, Based on Her Diary, 1785–1812* (New York, 1990), 147–160. For New Haven County see Cornelia Hughes Dayton, "Women Before the Bar: Gender, Law, and Society in Connecticut, 1710–1790" (Ph.D. diss., Princeton University, 1986), 151–186. See also Zephaniah Swift, *A System of Laws of the State of Connecticut*, 2 vols. (Windham, Conn., 1795–1796), I, 209. A partial survey of fornication prosecutions in the Windham County Court indicates that here, too, the local JPs and annually appointed grand jurymen stopped prosecuting men after the 1730s. The records for 1726–1731 show that 15 men were prosecuted to enjoin child support and 21 single women were charged with fornication and bastardy, while only 2 women brought civil suits for child maintenance. Nearly a decade ahead, in the 3-year period 1740–1742, *no* men were prosecuted while 23 single women were charged with fornication and 10 women initiated civil paternity suits.

would not be held against them as they reached for repute and prosperity in their prime.[6]

The documents allow us to listen in on the quite different responses of young men and women to the drama unfolding in Pomfret. Sarah Grosvenor's female kin and friends, as we shall see, became preoccupied with their guilt and with the inevitability of God's vengeance. Her male kin, on the other hand, reacted cautiously and legalistically, ferreting out information in order to assess how best to protect the Grosvenor family name. The contrast reminds us yet again of the complex and gendered ways in which we must rethink conventional interpretations of secularization in colonial New England.

Finally, the Grosvenor case raises more questions than it answers about New Englanders' access to and attitudes toward abortion. If Sarah had not died after miscarriage, it is doubtful that any word of Sessions's providing her with an abortifacient or Hallowell's operation would have survived into the twentieth century. Because it nearly went unrecorded and because it reveals that many Pomfret residents were familiar with the idea of abortion, the case supports historians' assumptions that abortion attempts were far from rare in colonial America.[7] We can also infer from the case that the most dangerous abortions before 1800 may have been those instigated by men and performed by surgeons with instruments.[8] But both abortion's frequency and the lineaments of its social context remain obscure. Did cases in which older women helped younger women to abort unwanted pregnancies far outnumber cases such as this one in which men initiated the process? Under what circumstances did family members and neighbors help married and unmarried women to hide abortion attempts?

Perhaps the most intriguing question centers on why women and men in early America acted *covertly* to effect abortions when abortion before quickening was legal. The Grosvenor case highlights the answer that applies to most known incidents from the period: abortion

---

[6] Such also was the message of many rape trials in the mid- and late 18th century. See Dayton, "Women Before the Bar," 112–143; trial of Frederick Calvert, Baron Baltimore, as reported in the *Connecticut Journal*, New Haven, June 10, 1768, and in other colonial newspapers and separate pamphlets; and the Bedlow-Sawyer trial discussed by Christine Stansell in *City of Women: Sex and Class in New York, 1789–1860* (New York, 1986), 23–30.

[7] For a recent summary of the literature see Brief for American Historians as *Amicus Curiae* Supporting the Appellees 5–7, *William L. Webster et al. v. Reproductive Health Services et al.*, 109 S.Ct. 3040 (1989).

[8] In none of the cases cited in n. 2 above did the woman ingesting an abortifacient die from it. If abortions directed by male physicians in the colonial period were more hazardous than those managed by midwives and lay women, then, in an inversion of the mid-20th-century situation, women from wealthy families with access to, and preferences for, male doctors were those most in jeopardy. For a general comparison of male and female medical practitioners see Ulrich, *A Midwife's Tale*, 48–66, esp. 54.

was understood as blameworthy because it was an extreme action designed to hide a prior sin, sex outside of marriage.[9] Reading the depositions, it is nearly impossible to disentangle the players' attitudes toward abortion itself from their expressions of censure or anxiety over
failed courtship, illegitimacy, and the dangers posed for a young
woman by a secret abortion. Strikingly absent from these eighteenth-
century documents, however, is either outrage over the destruction of
a fetus or denunciations of those who would arrest "nature's proper
course." Those absences are a telling measure of how the discourse
about abortion would change dramatically in later centuries.

The Narrative

Before delving into the response of the Pomfret community to Sarah
Grosvenor's abortion and death, we need to know just who participated in the conspiracy to cover up her pregnancy and how they managed it. The following paragraphs, based on the depositions, offer a
reconstruction of the events of 1742. A few caveats are in order. First,
precise dating of crucial incidents is impossible, since deponents did
not remember events in terms of days of the week (except for the Sabbath) but rather used phrases like "sometime in August." Second, the
testimony concentrated almost exclusively on events in the two
months preceding Sarah's death on September 14. Thus, we know
very little about Sarah and Amasa's courtship before July 1742.[10]
Third, while the depositions often indicate the motivations and feelings of the principals, these will be discussed in subsequent sections of
this article, where the characters' attitudes can be set in the context of
their social backgrounds, families, and community. This section essentially lays out a medical file for Sarah Grosvenor, a file that unfolds in
four parts: the taking of the abortifacient, Hallowell's operation, the
miscarriage, and Sarah's final illness.

The case reveals more about the use of an abortifacient than most
colonial court records in which abortion attempts are mentioned.
Here we learn not only the form in which Sarah received the dose but
also the special word that Pomfret residents applied to it. What the
documents do not disclose are either its ingredients[11] or the number
of times Sarah ingested it.

---

[9] Married women may have hidden their abortion attempts because the activity was
associated with lewd or dissident women.

[10] Conception must have occurred sometime in the months of January through
March, most probably in late January. Sarah had been pregnant nearly 7 months at her
delivery in early August, according to one version offered later by her sister.

[11] Hallowell's trade may have been an imported medicine or a powder he mixed himself, consisting chiefly of oil of savin, which could be extracted from juniper bushes
found throughout New England. For a thorough discussion of savin and other commonly used abortifacients see Shorter, *History of Women's Bodies*, 184–188.

The chronicle opens in late July 1742 when Zerviah Grosvenor, aged twenty-one, finally prevailed upon her younger sister to admit that she was pregnant. In tears, Sarah explained that she had not told Zerviah sooner because "she had been taking [the] trade to remove it." [12] "Trade" was used in this period to signify stuff or goods, often in the deprecatory sense of rubbish and trash. The *Oxford English Dictionary* confirms that in some parts of England and New England the word was used to refer to medicine. In Pomfret trade meant a particular type of medicine, an abortifacient, thus a substance that might be regarded as "bad" medicine, as rubbish, unsafe and associated with destruction. What is notable is that Sarah and Zerviah, and neighboring young people who also used the word, had no need to explain to one another the meaning of "taking the trade." Perhaps only a few New Englanders knew how to prepare an abortifacient or knew of books that would give them recipes, but many more, especially young women who lived with the fear of becoming pregnant before marriage, were familiar with at least the *idea* of taking an abortifacient.

Sarah probably began taking the trade in mid-May when she was already three-and-a-half-months pregnant.[13] It was brought to her in the form of a powder by Amasa.[14] Sarah understood clearly that her lover had obtained the concoction "from docter hollowel," who conveyed "directions" for her doses through Amasa. Zerviah deposed later that Sarah had been "loath to Take" the drug and "Thot it an Evil," probably because at three and a half months she anticipated quickening, the time from which she knew the law counted abortion an "unlawful measure." [15] At the outset, Sarah argued in vain with Amasa against his proposed "Method." Later, during June and July, she sometimes "neglected" to take the doses he left for her, but, with mounting urgency, Amasa and the doctor pressed her to comply. "It

[12] Deposition of Zerviah Grosvenor. In a second deposition Zerviah used the word "Medicines" instead of "trade"; Testimony of Zerviah Grosvenor in Multiple Deposition of Hannah Grosvenor et al.: hereafter cited as Testimony of Zerviah Grosvenor. Five times out of 8, deponents referred to "the trade," instead of simply "trade" or "some trade."

[13] So her sister Zerviah later estimated. Testimony of Rebecca Sharp in Multiple Deposition of Hannah Grosvenor et al.

[14] After she was let into the plot, Zerviah more than once watched Amasa take "a paper or powder out of his pockett" and insist that Sarah "take Some of it." Deposition of Zerviah Grosvenor.

[15] Deposition of John Grosvenor; Deposition of Zerviah Grosvenor; Testimony of Zerviah Grosvenor in Multiple Deposition of Hannah Grosvenor et al. "Unlawful measure" was Zerviah's phrase for Amasa's "Method." Concerned for Sarah's well-being, she pleaded with Hallowell not to give her sister "any thing that should harm her"; Deposition of Zerviah Grosvenor. At the same time, Sarah was thinking about the quickening issue. She confided to a friend that when Amasa first insisted she take the trade, "she [had] feared it was too late"; Deposition of Abigail Nightingale.

was necessary," Amasa explained in late July, that she take "more, or [else] they were afraid. She would be greatly hurt by what was already done." To calm her worries, he assured her that "there was no life [left] in the Child" and that the potion "would not hurt her." [16] Apparently, the men hoped that a few more doses would provoke a miscarriage, thereby expelling the dead fetus and restoring Sarah's body to its natural balance of humors.

Presumably, Hallowell decided to operate in early August because Sarah's pregnancy was increasingly visible, and he guessed that she was not going to miscarry. An operation in which the fetus would be removed or punctured was now the only certain way to terminate the pregnancy secretly.[17] To avoid the scrutiny of Sarah's parents, Hallowell resorted to a plan he had used once before in arranging a private examination of Sarah. Early one afternoon he arrived at the house of John Grosvenor and begged for a room as "he was weary and wanted Rest." [18] John, Sarah's thirty-one-year-old first cousin, lived with his wife, Hannah, and their young children in a homestead only a short walk down the hill but out of sight of Sarah's father's house. While John and Hannah were busy, the physician sent one of the little children to fetch Sarah.[19]

The narrative of Sarah's fateful meeting with Hallowell that August afternoon is best told in the words of one of the deponents. Abigail Nightingale had married and moved to Pomfret two years earlier, and by 1742 she had become Sarah's close friend.[20] Several weeks after the operation, Sarah attempted to relieve her own "Distress of mind" by confiding the details of her shocking experience to Abigail. Unconnected to the Grosvenor or Sessions families by kinship, and without

[16] Deposition of Zerviah Grosvenor; Testimony of Zerviah Grosvenor.

[17] Hallowell claimed that he proceeded with the abortion in order to save Sarah's life. If the powder had had little effect and he knew it, then this claim was a deliberate deception. On the other hand, he may have sincerely believed that the potion had poisoned the fetus and that infection of the uterine cavity had followed fetal death. Since healthy babies were thought at that time to help with their own deliveries, Hallowell may also have anticipated a complicated delivery if Sarah were allowed to go to full term—a delivery that might kill her. On the operation and variable potency of herbal abortifacients see Gordon, *Woman's Body, Woman's Right*, 37, 40; Shorter, *History of Women's Bodies*, 177–188; and Mohr, *Abortion in America*, 8–9.

[18] Testimony of Hannah Grosvenor in Multiple Deposition of Hannah Grosvenor et al. Hannah may have fabricated the account of Hallowell's deception to cover her own knowledge of and collusion in Hallowell and Sessions's scheme to conceal Sarah's pregnancy.

[19] Deposition of Zerviah Grosvenor. Hallowell attended Sarah overnight at John Grosvenor's house once in July; Multiple Deposition of Sarah and Silence Sessions.

[20] On Abigail's husband, Samuel, and his family see Clifford K. Shipton, *Biographical Sketches of Those Who Attended Harvard College in the Classes 1731–1735* (Boston, 1956), IX, 425–428; Pomfret Vital Records, Barbour Collection, Conn. State Lib. All vital and land records cited hereafter are found in the Barbour Collection.

any other apparent stake in the legal uses of her testimony, Abigail can probably be trusted as a fairly accurate paraphraser of Sarah's words.[21] If so, we have here an unparalleled eyewitness account of an eighteenth-century abortion attempt.

This is how Abigail recollected Sarah's deathbed story:

> On [Sarah's] going down [to her cousin John's], [Hallowell] said he wanted to Speake with her alone; and then they two went into a Room together; and then sd. Hallowell told her it was necessary that something more should be done or else she would Certainly die; to which she replyed that she was afraid they had done too much already, and then he told her that there was one thing more that could easily be done, and she asking him what it was; he said he could easily deliver her. but she said she was afraid there was life in the Child, then he asked her how long she had felt it; and she replyed about a fortnight; then he said that was impossible or could not be or ever would; for that the trade she had taken had or would prevent it: and that the alteration she felt Was owing to what she had taken. And he farther told her that he verily thought that the Child grew to her body to the Bigness of his hand, or else it would have Come away before that time. and that it would never Come away, but Certainly Kill her, unless other Means were used.[22] On which she yielded to his making an Attempt to take it away; charging him that if he could perceive that there was life in it he would not proceed on any Account. And then the Doctor openning his portmantua took an Instrument[23] out of it and Laid it on the Bed, and she asking him what it was for, he replyed that it was to make way; and that then he tryed to remove the Child for Some time in vain putting her to the Utmost Distress, and that at Last she observed he trembled and immediately perceived a Strange alteration in her body and thought a bone of the Child was broken; on which she desired him (as she said) to Call in some body, for that she feared she was a dying, and instantly swooned away.[24]

---

[21] Hearsay evidence was still accepted in many 18th-century Anglo-American courts; see J. M. Beattie, *Crime and the Courts in England, 1660–1800* (Princeton, N. J., 1986), 362–376. Sarah's reported words may have carried special weight because in early New England persons on their deathbeds were thought to speak the truth.

[22] Twentieth-century obstetrical studies show an average of 6 weeks between fetal death and spontaneous abortion; J. Robert Willson and Elsie Reid Carrington, eds., *Obstetrics and Gynecology*, 8th ed. (St. Louis, Mo., 1987), 212. Hallowell evidently grasped the link between the 2 events but felt he could not wait 6 weeks, either out of concern for Sarah's health or for fear their plot would be discovered.

[23] A 1746 indictment offered the only other point at which the "instrument" was mentioned in the documents. It claimed that Hallowell "with his own hands as [well as] with a certain Instrument of Iron [did] violently Lacerate and . . . wound the body of Sarah"; Indictment against John Hallowell, endorsed "Ignoramus," Sept. 4, 1746.

[24] Deposition of Abigail Nightingale.

With Sarah's faint, Abigail's account broke off, but within minutes others, who would testify later, stepped into the room. Hallowell reacted to Sarah's swoon by unfastening the door and calling in Hannah, the young mistress of the house, and Zerviah, who had followed her sister there. Cold water and "a bottle of drops" were brought to keep Sarah from fainting again, while Hallowell explained to the "much Surprized" women that "he had been making an Attempt" to deliver Sarah. Despite their protests, he then "used a further force upon her" but did not succeed in "Tak[ing] the Child . . . away." [25] Some days later Hallowell told a Pomfret man that in this effort "to distroy hir conception" he had "either knipt or Squeisd the head of the Conception." [26] At the time of the attempt, Hallowell explained to the women that he "had done so much to her, as would Cause the Birth of the Child in a Little time." Just before sunset, he packed up his portmanteau and went to a nearby tavern, where Amasa was waiting "to hear [the outcome of] the event." [27] Meanwhile, Sarah, weak-kneed and in pain, leaned on the arm of her sister as the young women managed to make their way home in the twilight.

After his attempted "force," Hallowell fades from the scene, while Zerviah and Hannah Grosvenor become the key figures. About two days after enduring the operation, Sarah began to experience contractions. Zerviah ran to get Hannah, telling her "she Tho't . . . Sarah would be quickly delivered." They returned to find Sarah, who was alone "in her Father's Chamber," just delivered and rising from the chamber pot. In the pot was "an Untimely birth"—a "Child [that] did not Appear to have any Life In it." To Hannah, it "Seemed by The Scent . . . That it had been hurt and was decaying," while Zerviah later remembered it as "a perfect Child," even "a pritty child." [28] Determined to keep the event "as private as they Could," the two women helped Sarah back to bed, and then "wr[ap]ed . . . up" the fetus, carried it to the woods on the edge of the farmstead, and there "Buried it in the Bushes." [29]

On learning that Sarah had finally miscarried and that the event had evidently been kept hidden from Sarah's parents, Amasa and Hallowell

[25] Joint Testimony of Hannah and Zerviah Grosvenor in Multiple Deposition of Hannah Grosvenor et al.; Deposition of Hannah Grosvenor; Deposition of Zerviah Grosvenor.

[26] Deposition of Ebenezer Grosvenor.

[27] Deposition of John Grosvenor; Deposition of Hannah Grosvenor; Deposition of Ebenezer Grosvenor.

[28] Testimony of Hannah Grosvenor, Alexander Sessions, and Rebecca Sharp in Multiple Deposition of Hannah Grosvenor et al. In a second statement Hannah said that "the head Seemed to be brused"; Deposition of Hannah Grosvenor.

[29] Testimony of Rebecca Sharp, Hannah Grosvenor, and Alexander Sessions in Multiple Deposition of Hannah Grosvenor et al.; Testimony of Silence Sessions in Multiple Deposition of Sarah and Silence Sessions.

may have congratulated themselves on the success of their operation. However, about ten days after the miscarriage, Sarah grew feverish and weak. Her parents consulted two college-educated physicians who hailed from outside the Pomfret area. Their visits did little good, nor were Sarah's symptoms—fever, delirium, convulsions—relieved by a visit from Hallowell, whom Amasa "fetcht" to Sarah's bedside.[30] In the end, Hallowell, who had decided to move from nearby Killingly to more distant Providence, washed his hands of the case. A few days before Sarah died, her cousin John "went after" Hallowell, whether to bring him back or to express his rage, we do not know. Hallowell predicted "that She woul[d] not live." [31]

Silence seems to have settled on the Grosvenor house and its neighborhood after Sarah's death on September 14. It was two and a half years later that rumors about a murderous abortion spread through and beyond Pomfret village, prompting legal investigation. The silence, the gap between event and prosecution, the passivity of Sarah's parents—all lend mystery to the narrative. But despite its ellipses, the Grosvenor case provides us with an unusual set of details about one young couple's extreme response to the common problem of failed courtship and illegitimacy. To gain insight into both the mysteries and the extremities of the Grosvenor-Sessions case, we need to look more closely at Pomfret, at the two families centrally involved, and at clues to the motivations of the principal participants. Our abortion tale, it turns out, holds beneath its surface a complex trail of evidence about generational conflict and troubled relations between men and women.

The Pomfret Players

In 1742 the town of Pomfret had been settled for just over forty years. Within its central neighborhood and in homesteads scattered over rugged, wooded hillsides lived probably no more than 270 men, women, and children.[32] During the founding decades, the fathers of

---

[30] Joint Testimony of Hannah and Zerviah Grosvenor in Multiple Deposition of Hannah Grosvenor et al.; Deposition of Parker Morse of Woodstock, Apr. 1746. Although Pomfret had had its own resident physician (Dr. Thomas Mather) since 1738, Sarah's family called in young Dr. Morse of Woodstock, who visited twice (he later admitted he was not much help), and a Dr. Coker of Providence (who I assume was Theodore Coker). On Mather see Ellen D. Larned, *History of Windham County, Connecticut* (Worcester, Mass., 1874), I, 354. On Morse: Shipton, *Biographical Sketches*, IX, 424. On Coker: ibid., VIII, 19, and Eric H. Christianson, "The Medical Practitioners of Massachusetts, 1630–1800: Patterns of Change and Continuity," in *Medicine in Colonial Massachusetts, 1620–1820*, Publications of the Colonial Society of Massachusetts, LVII (Boston, 1980), 123.

[31] Deposition of John Grosvenor.

[32] I am using a list of 40 heads of household in the Mashamoquet neighborhood of Pomfret in 1731, presuming 5 persons to a household, and assuming a 2.5% annual population growth. See Larned, *History of Windham County*, I, 342, and Bruce C. Daniels,

Sarah and Amasa ranked among the ten leading householders; Leicester Grosvenor and Nathaniel Sessions were chosen often to fill important local offices.

Grosvenor, the older of the two by seven years, had inherited standing and a choice farmstead from his father, one of the original six purchasers of the Pomfret territory.[33] When the town was incorporated in 1714, he was elected a militia officer and one of the first selectmen. He was returned to the latter post nineteen times and eventually rose to the highest elective position—that of captain—in the local trainband. Concurrently, he was appointed many times throughout the 1710s and 1720s to ad hoc town committees, often alongside Nathaniel Sessions. But unlike Sessions, Grosvenor went on to serve at the colony level. Pomfret freemen chose him to represent them at ten General Assembly sessions between 1726 and 1744. Finally, in the 1730s, when he was in his late fifties, the legislature appointed him a justice of the peace for Windham County. Thus, until his retirement in 1748 at age seventy-four, his house would have served as the venue for petty trials, hearings, and recordings of documents. After retiring from public office, Grosvenor lived another eleven years, leaving behind in 1759 an estate worth over £600.[34]

Nathaniel Sessions managed a sizable farm and ran one of Pomfret's taverns at the family homestead. Town meetings were sometimes held there. Sessions was chosen constable in 1714 and rose from ensign to lieutenant in the militia—always a step behind Leicester Grosvenor. He could take pride in one exceptional distinction redounding to the family honor: in 1737 his son Darius became only the second Pomfret resident to graduate from Yale College, and before Sessions died at

---

The Connecticut Town: Growth and Development, 1635–1790 (Middletown, Conn., 1979), 44–51. Pomfret village had no central green or cluster of shops and small house lots around its meetinghouse. No maps survive for early Pomfret apart from a 1719 survey of proprietors' tracts. See Larned, *History of Windham County* (1976 ed.), I, foldout at 185.

[33] Leicester's father, John Grosvenor, a tanner, had emigrated from England about 1670 and settled in Roxbury, Mass., whence the first proprietors of Pomfret hailed. John died in 1691 before he could resettle on his Connecticut tract, but his widow, Esther, moved her family to their initial allotment of 502 acres in Pomfret in 1701. There she lived until her death at 87 in 1738, known in the community as a woman of energy and "vigorous habits," "skillful in tending the sick," and habitual in "walking every Sunday to the distant meeting-house." See Daniel Kent, *The English Home and Ancestry of John Grosvenor of Roxbury, Mass.* (Boston, 1918), 10–13, and Larned, *History of Windham County*, I, 353–355.

[34] Kent, *The English Home of John Grosvenor*, 10–13; Larned, *History of Windham County*, I, 200–202, 204, 208–209, 269, 354, 343–344; Charles J. Hoadly and J. Hammond Trumbull, eds., *The Public Records of the Colony of Connecticut, 1636–1776*, 15 vols. (Hartford, Conn., 1850–1890), V–IX; Inventory of Leicester Grosvenor, Oct. 29, 1759, Pomfret District Probate Court Records, II, 260.

ninety-one he saw Darius elected assistant and then deputy governor of Rhode Island.[35]

The records are silent as to whether Sessions and his family resented the Grosvenors, who must have been perceived in town as more prominent, or whether the two families—who sat in adjoining private pews in the meetinghouse—enjoyed a close relationship that went sour for some reason *before* the affair between Sarah and Amasa. Instead, the signs (such as the cooperative public work) of the two fathers, the visits back and forth between the Grosvenor and Sessions girls) point to a long-standing friendship and dense web of interchanges between the families. Indeed, courtship and marriage between a Sessions son and a Grosvenor daughter would hardly have been surprising.

What went wrong in the affair between Sarah and Amasa is not clear. Sarah's sisters and cousins knew that "Amasy" "made Sute to" Sarah, and they gave no indication of disapproving. The few who guessed at Sarah's condition in the summer of 1742 were not so much surprised that she was pregnant as that the couple "did not marry." [36] It was evidently routine in this New England village, as in others, for courting couples to post banns for their nuptials soon after the woman discovered that she was pregnant.

Amasa offered different answers among his Pomfret peers to explain his failure to marry his lover. When Zerviah Grosvenor told Amasa that he and Sarah "had better Marry," he responded, "That would not do," for "he was afraid of his Parents . . . [who would] always make their lives [at home] uncomfortable." [37] Later, Abigail Nightingale heard rumors that Amasa was resorting to the standard excuse of men wishing to avoid a shotgun marriage—denying that the child was his.[38] Hallowell, with whom Amasa may have been honest, claimed "the Reason that they did not marry" was "that Sessions Did not Love her well a nough for [he] saith he did not believe it was his son and if he Could Cause her to gitt Red of it he would not Go near her

[35] Larned, *History of Windham County*, I, 201, 204, 206, 208–209, 344; Ellen D. Larned, *Historic Gleanings in Windham County, Connecticut* (Providence, R. I., 1899), 141, 148–149; Francis G. Sessions, comp., *Materials for a History of the Sessions Family in America; The Descendants of Alexander Sessions of Andover, Mass., 1669* (Albany, N. Y., 1890), 34–35, hereafter cited as Sessions, *Sessions Family*. Nathaniel's inheritance from his father Alexander of Andover (d. 1687) was a mere £2.14.5.

[36] Deposition of Hannah Grosvenor; Deposition of Ebenezer Grosvenor; Deposition of Anna Wheeler, Nov. 5, 1745; Deposition of Zerviah Grosvenor; Testimony of Zerviah Grosvenor.

[37] Deposition of Zerviah Grosvenor; Testimony of Zerviah Grosvenor.

[38] Deposition of Abigail Nightingale. Contradicting Amasa's attempt to disavow paternity were both his investment in Hallowell's efforts to get rid of the fetus and his own ready admission of paternity privately to Zerviah and Sarah.

again." [39] Showing yet another face to a Grosvenor kinsman after Sarah's death, Amasa repented his actions and extravagantly claimed he would "give All he had" to "bring Sarah . . . To life again . . . and have her as his wife." [40]

The unusual feature of Amasa's behavior was not his unwillingness to marry Sarah, but his determination to terminate her pregnancy before it showed. Increasing numbers of young men in eighteenth-century New England weathered the temporary obloquy of abandoning a pregnant lover in order to prolong their bachelorhood or marry someone else.[41] What drove Amasa, and an ostensibly reluctant Sarah, to resort to abortion? Was it fear of their fathers? Nathaniel Sessions had chosen Amasa as the son who would remain on the family farm and care for his parents in their old age. An ill-timed marriage could have disrupted these plans and threatened Amasa's inheritance.[42] For his part, Leicester Grosvenor may have made it clear to his daughter that he would be greatly displeased at her marrying before she reached a certain age or until her older sister wed. Rigid piety, an authoritarian nature, an intense concern with being seen as a good household governor—any of these traits in Leicester Grosvenor or Nathaniel Sessions could have colored Amasa's decisions.

Perhaps it was not family relations that proved the catalyst but Amasa's acquaintance with a medical man who boasted about a powder more effective than the herbal remedies that were part of women's lore. Hallowell himself had fathered an illegitimate child fifteen years earlier, and he may have encouraged a rakish attitude in Amasa, beguiling the younger man with the promise of dissociating sex from its possible consequences. Or the explanation may have been that classic one: another woman. Two years after Sarah's death, Amasa married Hannah Miller of Rehoboth, Massachusetts. Perhaps in early 1742 he

---

[39] Deposition of Ebenezer Grosvenor. Hallowell revealed this opinion in an Aug. 1742 conversation with Sarah's 28-year-old cousin Ebenezer at Ebenezer's house in Pomfret. In a study of 17th-century Massachusetts court records Roger Thompson finds evidence that when pregnancy failed to pressure a couple into marriage, it was often because love "had cooled"; Thompson, *Sex in Middlesex*, 69.

[40] Testimony of John Shaw in Multiple Deposition of Hannah Grosvenor et al.

[41] For one such case involving two propertied families see Kathryn Kish Sklar, "Culture Versus Economics: A Case of Fornication in Northampton in the 1740's," *The University of Michigan Papers in Women's Studies* (1978), 35–56. For the incidence of illegitimacy and premarital sex in families of respectable yeomen and town leaders see Dayton, "Women Before the Bar," 151–186, and Ulrich, *A Midwife's Tale*, 156.

[42] Two years later, in Feb. 1744 (9 months before Amasa married), the senior Sessions deeded to his son the north part of his own farm for a payment of £310. Amasa, in exchange for caring for his parents in their old age, came into the whole farm when his father died in 1771. Pomfret Land Records, III, 120; Estate Papers of Nathaniel Sessions, 1771, Pomfret Probate District. On the delay between marriage and "going to housekeeping" see Ulrich, *A Midwife's Tale*, 138–144.

was already making trips to the town just east of Providence to see his future wife.[43]

What should we make of Sarah's role in the scheme? It is possible that she no longer loved Amasa and was as eager as he to forestall external pressures toward a quick marriage. However, Zerviah swore that on one occasion before the operation Amasa reluctantly agreed to post banns for their nuptials and that Sarah did not object.[44] *If* Sarah was a willing and active participant in the abortion plot all along, then by 1745 her female kin and friends had fabricated and rehearsed a careful and seamless story to preserve the memory of the dead girl untarnished.

In the portrait drawn by her friends, Sarah reacted to her pregnancy and to Amasa's plan first by arguing and finally by doing her utmost to protect her lover. She may have wished to marry Amasa, yet she did not insist on it or bring in older family members to negotiate with him and his parents. Abigail Nightingale insisted that Sarah accepted Amasa's recalcitrance and only pleaded with him that they not "go on to add sin to sin." Privately, she urged Amasa that there was an alternative to taking the trade—a way that would enable him to keep his role hidden and prevent the couple from committing a "Last transgression [that] would be worse then the first." Sarah told him that "she was willing to take the sin and shame to her self, and to be obliged never to tell whose Child it was, and that she did not doubt but that if she humbled her self on her Knees to her Father he would take her and her Child home." Her lover, afraid that his identity would become known, vetoed her proposal.[45]

According to the Pomfret women's reconstruction, abortion was not a freely chosen and defiant act for Sarah. Against her own desires, she reluctantly consented in taking the trade only because Amasa "So very earnestly perswaided her." In fact, she had claimed to her friends that she was coerced; he "would take no denyal." [46] Sarah's confidantes presented her as being aware of her options, shrinking from abortion as an unnatural and immoral deed, and yet finally choosing the strat-

---

[43] Sessions, *Sessions Family*, 60; Pomfret Vit. Rec., I, 29.

[44] The banns never appeared on the meetinghouse door. Sarah may have believed in this overdue betrothal. She assured her anxious sister Anna that "thay designed to mary as soone as thay Could and that Sessions was as much Concarned as she." Deposition of Zerviah Grosvenor; Testimony of Zerviah Grosvenor; Deposition of Anna Wheeler.

[45] Deposition of Abigail Nightingale. I have argued elsewhere that this is what most young New England women in the 18th century did when faced with illegitimacy. Their parents did not throw them out of the house but instead paid the cost of the mother and child's upkeep until she managed to marry. Dayton, "Women Before the Bar," 163–180.

[46] Deposition of John Grosvenor; Deposition of Abigail Nightingale. Amasa Sessions, "in his prime," was described as "a very strong man," so it is possible that his physical presence played a role in intimidating Sarah. See Sessions, *Sessions Family*, 31.

egy consistent with her lover's vision of what would best protect their futures. Thus, if Amasa's hubris was extreme, so too was Sarah's internalization of those strains of thought in her culture that taught women to make themselves pleasing and obedient to men.

While we cannot be sure that the deponents' picture of Sarah's initial recoil and reluctant submission to the abortion plot was entirely accurate, it is clear that once she was caught up in the plan she extracted a pledge of silence from all her confidantes. Near her death, before telling Abigail about the operation, she "insist[ed] on . . . [her friend's] never discovering the Matter" to anyone.[47] Clearly, she had earlier bound Zerviah and Hannah on their honor not to tell their elders. Reluctant when faced with the abortionist's powder, Sarah became a leading co-conspirator when alone with her female friends.

One of the most remarkable aspects of the Grosvenor-Sessions case is Sarah and Amasa's success in keeping their parents in the dark, at least until her final illness. If by July Sarah's sisters grew suspicious that Sarah was "with child," what explains the failure of her parents to observe her pregnancy and to intervene and uncover the abortion scheme? Were they negligent, preoccupied with other matters, or willfully blind? [48] Most mysterious is the role of forty-eight-year-old Rebecca Grosvenor, Grosvenor's second wife and Sarah's stepmother since 1729. Rebecca is mentioned only once in the depositions,[49] and she was not summoned as a witness in the 1745–1747 investigations into Sarah's death. Even if some extraordinary circumstance—an invalid condition or an implacable hatred between Sarah and her stepmother—explains Rebecca's abdication of her role as guardian, Sarah had two widowed aunts living in or near her household. These matrons, experienced in childbirth matters and concerned for the family reputation, were just the sort of older women who traditionally watched and advised young women entering courtship.[50]

In terms of who knew what, the events of summer 1742 in Pomfret apparently unfolded in two stages. The first stretched from Sarah's discovery of her pregnancy by early May to some point in late August

[47] Deposition of Abigail Nightingale.

[48] Like his wife, Leicester was not summoned to testify in any of the proceedings against Hallowell and Sessions.

[49] Zerviah testified that, a day or two after Sarah fell sick for the first time in July, the family heard "that Doctor Hallowell was at one of our Neighbors [and] my Mother desired me to go and Call him." Deposition of Zerviah Grosvenor.

Sarah's mother had died in May 1724, when Sarah was 11 months old. Perhaps Sarah and Zerviah had a closer relationship with their grandmother Esther (see n. 33 above) than with their stepmother. Esther lived in their household until her death in 1738, when Zerviah was 17 and Sarah 15.

[50] Laurel Thatcher Ulrich, *Good Wives: Image and Reality in the Lives of Women in Northern New England, 1650–1750* (New York, 1982), chap. 5, esp. 98.

after her miscarriage. In this period a determined, collective effort by Sarah and Amasa and their friends kept their elders in the dark.[51] When Sarah fell seriously ill from the aftereffects of the abortion attempt and miscarriage, rumors of the young people's secret activities reached Leicester Grosvenor's neighbors and even one of the doctors he had called in.[52] It is difficult to escape the conclusion that by Sarah's death in mid-September her father and stepmother had learned of the steps that had precipitated her mortal condition and kept silent for reasons of their own.

Except for Hallowell, the circle of intimates entrusted by Amasa and Sarah with their scheme consisted of young adults ranging in age from nineteen to thirty-three.[53] Born between about 1710 and 1725, these young people had grown up just as the town attracted enough settlers to support a church, militia, and local market. They were second-generation Pomfret residents who shared the generational identity that came with sitting side by side through long worship services, attending school, playing, and working together at children's tasks. By 1740, these sisters, brothers, cousins, courting couples, and neighbors, in their visits from house to house—sometimes in their own households, sometimes at their parents'—had managed to create a world of talk and socializing that was largely exempt from parental supervision.[54] In Pomfret in 1742 it was this group of young people in their twenties and early thirties, *not* the cluster of Grosvenor matrons over forty-five, who monitored Sarah's courtship, attempted to get Amasa to marry his lover, privately investigated the activities and motives of

---

[51] In Larned's account, the oral legend insisted that Hallowell's "transaction" (meaning the abortion attempt) and the miscarriage were "utterly unsuspected by any . . . member of the household" other than Zerviah. *History of Windham County*, I, 363.

[52] Deposition of Parker Morse.

[53] Within days of Sarah's miscarriage, the initial conspirators disclosed their actions to others: Hallowell talked to 2 of Sarah's older male cousins, John (age 31) and Ebenezer (age 28), while Zerviah confessed to Amasa's brother Alexander (age 28) and his wife Silence. Anna Wheeler (age 33), Sarah's older sister, knew of Sarah's pregnancy before the abortion operation and thus must have guessed or secured information about the miscarriage. As we have seen, Sarah would soon confess privately to Abigail Nightingale, recently married and in her 20s. Others in the peer group may also have known. Court papers list 7 witnesses summoned to the trials for whom no written testimony survives. At least 4 of those witnesses were in their 20s or early 30s.

[54] The famous "bad books" incident that disrupted Jonathan Edwards's career in 1744 involved a similar group of unsupervised young adults ages 21 to 29. See Patricia J. Tracy, *Jonathan Edwards, Pastor: Religion and Society in Eighteenth-Century Northampton* (New York, 1980), 160–164. The best general investigation of youth culture in early New England is Thompson's *Sex in Middlesex*, 71–96. Thompson discusses the general ineffectiveness of parental supervision of courtship (pp. 52–53, 58–59, 69–70). Ellen Rothman concludes that in New England in the mid- to late 18th century "parents made little or no effort to oversee their children's courting behavior"; Rothman, *Hands and Hearts: A History of Courtship in America* (New York, 1984), 25.

Amasa and Hallowell, and, belatedly, spoke out publicly to help Connecticut juries decide who should be blamed for Sarah's death.

That Leicester Grosvenor made no public move to punish those around him and that he avoided giving testimony when legal proceedings commenced are intriguing clues to social changes underway in New England villages in the mid-eighteenth century. Local leaders like Grosvenor, along with the respectable yeomen whom he represented in public office, were increasingly withdrawing delicate family problems from the purview of their communities. Slander, illegitimacy, and feuds among neighbors came infrequently to local courts by mid-century, indicating male householders' growing preference for handling such matters privately.[55] Wealthy and ambitious families adopted this ethic of privacy at the same time that they became caught up in elaborating their material worlds by adding rooms and acquiring luxury goods. The "good feather bed" with all of its furniture that Grosvenor bequeathed to his one unmarried daughter was but one of many marks of status by which the Grosvenors differentiated themselves from their Pomfret neighbors.[56] But all the fine accoutrements in the world would not excuse Justice Grosvenor from his obligation to govern his household effectively. Mortified no doubt at his inability to monitor the young people in his extended family, he responded, ironically, by extending their conspiracy of silence. The best way for him to shield the family name from scandal and protect his political reputation in the county and colony was to keep the story of Sarah's abortion out of the courts.

The Doctor

John Hallowell's status as an outsider in Pomfret and his dangerous, secret alliance with the town's young adults may have shaped his destiny as the one conspirator sentenced to suffer at the whipping post. Although the physician had been involved in shady dealings before 1742, he had managed to win the trust of many patients and a respectable social standing. Tracking down his history in northeastern

---

[55] Helena M. Wall, *Fierce Communion: Family and Community in Early America* (Cambridge, Mass., 1990); Bruce H. Mann, *Neighbors and Strangers: Law and Community in Early Connecticut* (Chapel Hill, N. C., 1987).

[56] Leicester Grosvenor's Will, Jan. 23, 1754, Pomfret Dist. Prob. Ct. Rec., I, 146. For recent studies linking consumption patterns and class stratification see Richard L. Bushman, "American High-Style and Vernacular Cultures," in Jack P. Greene and J. R. Pole, eds., *Colonial British America: Essays in the New History of the Early Modern Era* (Baltimore, 1984), 345–383; T. H. Breen, " 'Baubles of Britain': The American and Consumer Revolutions of the Eighteenth Century," *Past and Present*, 119 (May 1988), 73–104; and Kevin M. Sweeney, "Furniture and the Domestic Environment in Wethersfield, Connecticut, 1639–1800," in Robert Blair St. George, ed., *Material Life in America, 1600–1860* (Boston, 1988), 261–290.

Connecticut tells us something of the uncertainty surrounding personal and professional identity before the advent of police records and medical licensing boards. It also gives us an all-too-rare glimpse into the fashion in which an eighteenth-century country doctor tried to make his way in the world.

Hallowell's earliest brushes with the law came in the 1720s. In 1725 he purchased land in Killingly, a Connecticut town just north of Pomfret and bordering both Massachusetts and Rhode Island. Newly married, he was probably in his twenties at the time. Seven months before his wife gave birth to their first child, a sixteen-year-old Killingly woman charged Hallowell with fathering her illegitimate child. Using the alias Nicholas Hallaway, he fled to southeastern Connecticut, where he lived as a "transient" for three months. He was arrested and settled the case by admitting to paternity and agreeing to contribute to the child's maintenance for four years.[57]

Hallowell resumed his life in Killingly. Two years later, now referred to as "Dr.," he was arrested again; this time the charge was counterfeiting. Hallowell and several confederates were hauled before the governor and council for questioning and then put on trial before the Superior Court. Although many Killingly witnesses testified to the team's suspect activities in a woodland shelter, the charges against Hallowell were dropped when a key informer failed to appear in court.[58]

Hallowell thus escaped conviction on a serious felony charge, but he had been tainted by stories linking him to the criminal subculture of transient, disorderly, greedy, and manually skilled men who typically made up gangs of counterfeiters in eighteenth-century New England.[59] After 1727 Hallowell may have given up dabbling in

---

[57] Killingly Land Records, II, 139; *Rex v. John Hallowell and Mehitable Morris*, Dec. 1726, Windham County Court Records, Book I, 43, and Windham County Court Files, box 363. Hallowell paid the £28 he owed Mehitable, but there is no evidence that he took any other role in bringing up his illegitimate namesake. Just before his death, Samuel Morris, the maternal grandfather of John Hallowell, Jr., out of "parentiall Love and Effections," deeded the young man a 300-acre farm "for his advancement and Settlement in the World"; Killingly Land Rec., IV, 261.

[58] Hallowell was clearly the mastermind of the scheme, and there is little doubt that he lied to the authorities when questioned. According to one witness, Hallowell had exclaimed that "If he knew who" had informed anonymously against him, "he would be the death of him tho he ware hanged for it the next minit"; Letter of Joseph Leavens, Sept. 1727, Windham Sup. Ct. Files, box 170. The case is found in ibid.; Sup. Ct. Rec., bk. 5, 297–298; and *Public Records Conn. Colony*, VII, 118. One associate Hallowell recruited was Ephraim Shevie, who had been banished from Connecticut for counterfeiting four years earlier. See Kenneth Scott, *Counterfeiting in Colonial America* (New York, 1957), 41–45.

[59] The authority on counterfeiting in the colonies is Kenneth Scott. His 1957 general book on the subject emphasizes several themes: the gangs at the heart of all counterfeiting schemes, the ease with which counterfeiters moved from colony to colony (especially

money-making schemes and turned to earning his livelihood chiefly from his medical practice. Like two-thirds of the male medical practitioners in colonial New England, he probably did not have college or apprentice training, but his skill, or charm, was not therefore necessarily less than that of any one of his peers who might have inherited a library of books and a fund of knowledge from a physician father. All colonial practitioners, as Richard D. Brown reminds us, mixed learned practices with home or folk remedies, and no doctor had access to safe reliable pharmacological preparations or antiseptic surgical procedures.[60]

In the years immediately following the counterfeiting charge, Hallowell appears to have made several deliberate moves to portray himself as a sober neighbor and reliable physician. At about the time of his second marriage, in 1729, he became a more frequent attendant at the Killingly meetinghouse, where he renewed his covenant and presented his first two children for baptism.[61] He also threw himself into the land and credit markets of northeastern Connecticut, establishing himself as a physician who was also an enterprising yeoman and a frequent litigant.[62]

---

between Connecticut and Rhode Island), "the widespread co-operation between" gangs, "the readiness of [men of all ranks] . . . to enter such schemes," the frequent use of aliases, the irresistible nature of the activity once entered into, and "the extreme difficulty of securing the conviction of a counterfeiter"; *Counterfeiting in Colonial America,* esp. 123, 35, 10, 36. See also Scott's more focused studies, *Counterfeiting in Colonial Connecticut* (New York, 1957), and *Counterfeiting in Colonial Rhode Island* (Providence, R. I., 1960).

For an illuminating social profile of thieves and burglars who often operated in small gangs see Daniel A. Cohen, "A Fellowship of Thieves: Property Criminals in Eighteenth-Century Massachusetts," *Journal of Social History,* XXII (1988), 65–92.

[60] Richard D. Brown, "The Healing Arts in Colonial and Revolutionary Massachusetts: The Context for Scientific Medicine," in Col. Soc. Mass., *Medicine in Colonial Massachusetts,* esp. 40–42. For detailed analysis of the backgrounds and training of one large sample of New England practitioners see Christianson, "Medical Practitioners of Massachusetts," in ibid., 49–67, and Eric H. Christianson, "Medicine in New England," in Ronald L. Numbers, ed., *Medicine in the New World: New Spain, New France, and New England* (Knoxville, Tenn., 1987), 101–153. That the majority of colonial physicians made "free use of the title 'doctor' " (ibid., 118) and simply "taught themselves medicine and set up as doctors" is reiterated in Whitfield J. Bell, Jr., "A Portrait of the Colonial Physician," *Bulletin of the History of Medicine,* XLIV (1970), 503–504.

[61] Hallowell's sons, baptized between 1730 and 1740, were named Theophilus, Bazaleel, Calvin, and Luther. Killingly Vital Records, I, 3, 24; Putnam First Congregational Church Records, I, 5–7, 14–15. Hallowell may have been one of the " 'horse-shed' Christians" whom David D. Hall describes as concerned to have their children baptized but more interested in the men's talk outside the meetinghouse than in the minister's exposition of the Word. Hall, *Worlds of Wonder, Days of Judgment: Popular Religious Belief in Early New England* (New York, 1989), 15–16.

[62] Between 1725 and 1742, Hallowell was a party to 20 land sales and purchases in Killingly; he also assumed 2 mortgages. During the same period he was involved in

These activities had dual implications. On the one hand, they suggest that Hallowell epitomized the eighteenth-century Yankee citizen—a man as comfortable in the courtroom and countinghouse as at a patient's bedside; a man of restless energy, not content to limit his scope to his fields and village; a practical, ambitious man with a shrewd eye for a good deal.[63] On the other hand, Hallowell's losses to Boston creditors, his constant efforts to collect debts, and his farflung practice raise questions about the nature of his activities and medical practice. He evidently had clients not just in towns across northeastern Connecticut but also in neighboring Massachusetts and Rhode Island. Perhaps rural practitioners normally traveled extensively, spending many nights away from their wives and children.[64] It is also possible, however, either that Hallowell was forced to travel because established doctors from leading families had monopolized the local practice or that he chose to recruit patients in Providence and other towns as a cover for illicit activities.[65] Despite his land speculations and his frequent resort to litigation, Hallowell was losing money. In the sixteen years before 1742, his creditors secured judgments against him for a total of £1,060, while he was able to collect only £700 in debts.[66] The disjunction between his ambition and actual material gains may have led Hallowell in middle age to renew his illicit moneymaking schemes. By supplying young men with potent abortifacients and dabbling in schemes to counterfeit New England's paper money, he betrayed the very gentlemen whose respect, credit, and society he sought.

What is most intriguing about Hallowell was his ability to ingratiate himself throughout his life with elite men whose reputations were unblemished by scandal. Despite the rumors that must have circulated about his early sexual dalliance, counterfeiting activities, suspect medi-

---

county court litigation an average of 3 times a year, more often as plaintiff than defendant, for a total of 46 suits.

[63] For example, in early 1735 Hallowell made a £170 profit from the sale of a 60-acre tract with mill and mansion house that he had purchased 2 months earlier. Killingly Land Rec., IV, 26, 36.

[64] Evidence of Hallowell's widespread clientele comes from his 1727–1746 suits for debt, from his traveling patterns as revealed in the depositions of the abortion case, and from a petition written in 1747 on his behalf by 14 male citizens of Providence. They claimed that "Numbers" in Rhode Island "as well as in the Neighbouring Colonies" had "happily experienc'd" Hallowell's medical care. Petition of Resolved Waterman et al., Oct. 1747, Connecticut Archives, Crimes and Misdemeanors, Series I, IV, 109.

[65] For a related hypothesis about the mobility of self-taught doctors in contrast to physicians from established medical families see Christianson, "Medical Practitioners of Massachusetts," in Col. Soc. Mass., *Medicine in Colonial Massachusetts*, 61.

[66] These figures apply to suits in the Windham County Court record books, 1727–1742. Hallowell may, of course, have prosecuted debtors in other jurisdictions.

cal remedies, heavy debts, and shady business transactions,[67] leading ministers, merchants, and magistrates welcomed him into their houses. In Pomfret such acceptance took its most dramatic form in September 1739 when Hallowell was admitted along with thirty-five other original covenanters to the first private library association in eastern Connecticut. Gathering in the house of Pomfret's respected, conservative minister, Ebenezer Williams, the members pledged sums for the purchase of "useful and profitable English books." In the company of the region's scholars, clergy, and "gentlemen," along with a few yeomen—all "warm friends of learning and literature"—Hallowell marked himself off from the more modest subscribers by joining with thirteen prominent and wealthy signers to pledge a sum exceeding £15.[68]

Lacking college degree and family pedigree, Hallowell traded on his profession and his charm to gain acceptability with the elite. In August 1742 he shrewdly removed himself from the Pomfret scene, just before Sarah Grosvenor's death. In that month he moved, without his wife and children, to Providence, where he had many connections. Within five years, Hallowell had so insinuated himself with town leaders such as Stephen Hopkins that fourteen of them petitioned for mitigation of what they saw as the misguided sentence imposed on him in the Grosvenor case.[69]

Hallowell's capacity for landing on his feet, despite persistent brushes with scandal, debt, and the law, suggests that we should look at the fluidity of New England's eighteenth-century elite in new ways.[70] What bound sons of old New England families, learned men, and upwardly mobile merchants and professionals in an expanded elite may partly have been a reshaped, largely unspoken set of values shared by men. We know that the archetype for white New England women as sexual beings was changing from carnal Eve to resisting Pamela and

---

[67] In Dec. 1749, Samuel Hunt, "Gentleman" of Worcester County, revoked the power of attorney he had extended to Hallowell for a Killingly land sale. Hunt claimed that the physician had "behaved greatly to my hindrance [and] Contrary to the trust and Confidence I Reposed in him." Killingly Land Rec., V, 151.

[68] Larned, *History of Windham County*, I, 356–359.

[69] The petition's signers included Hopkins, merchant, assembly speaker, and Superior Court justice, soon to become governor; Daniel Jencks, judge, assembly delegate, and prominent Baptist; Obadiah Brown, merchant and shopkeeper; and George Taylor, justice of the peace, town schoolmaster, and Anglican warden. Some of the signers stated that they had made a special trip to Windham to be "Earwitnesses" at Hallowell's trial. The petition is cited in n. 64 above.

[70] For discussions of the elite see Jackson Turner Main, *Society and Economy in Colonial Connecticut* (Princeton, N. J., 1985), esp. 317–366, and Joy B. and Robert R. Gilsdorf, "Elites and Electorates: Some Plain Truths for Historians of Colonial America," in David D. Hall, John M. Murrin, and Thad W. Tate, eds., *Saints and Revolutionaries: Essays on Early American History* (New York, 1984), 207–244.

that the calculus of accountability for seduction was shifting blame solely to women.[71] But the simultaneous metamorphosis in cultural images and values defining manhood in the early and mid-eighteenth century has not been studied. The scattered evidence we do have suggests that, increasingly, for men in the more secular and anglicized culture of New England, the lines between legitimate and illegitimate sexuality, between sanctioned and shady business dealings, and between speaking the truth and protecting family honor blurred. Hallowell's acceptability to men like minister Ebenezer Williams and merchant Stephen Hopkins hints at how changing sexual and moral standards shaped the economic and social alliances made by New England's male leadership in the 1700s.[72]

Women's Talk and Men's Talk

If age played a major role in determining who knew the truth about Sarah Grosvenor's illness, gender affected how the conspiring young adults responded to Sarah's impending death and how they weighed the issue of blame. Our last glimpse into the social world of eighteenth-century Pomfret looks at the different ways in which women and men reconstructed their roles in the events of 1742.

An inward gaze, a strong consciousness of sin and guilt, a desire to avoid conflict and achieve reconciliation, a need to confess—these are the impulses expressed in women's intimate talk in the weeks before Sarah died. The central female characters in the plot, Sarah and Zerviah Grosvenor, lived for six weeks with the daily fear that their parents or aunts might detect Sarah's condition or their covert comings and goings. Deposing three years later, Zerviah represented the sisters as suffering under an intensifying sense of complicity as they had passed through two stages of involvement in the concealment plan. At first, they were passive players, submitting to the hands of men. But once Hallowell declared that he had done all he could, they were left to salvage the conspiracy by enduring the terrors of a first delivery alone, knowing that their failure to call in the older women of the family resembled the decision made by women who committed in-

---

[71] Ulrich, *Good Wives*, 103–105, 113–117.

[72] Compare the 17th-century case of Stephen Batchelor (Charles E. Clark, *The Eastern Frontier: The Settlement of Northern New England, 1610–1763* [New York, 1970], 43–44) with 18th-century Cape Cod, where ministers retained their posts despite charges of sexual misconduct (J. M. Bumsted, "A Caution to Erring Christians: Ecclesiastical Disorder on Cape Cod, 1717 to 1738," *William and Mary Quarterly*, 3d Series, XXVIII [1971], 413–438). I am grateful to John Murrin for bringing these references to my attention. For a prominent Northampton, Mass., man (Joseph Hawley) who admitted to lying in civil and church hearings in the 1740s and yet who suffered no visible damage to his career see Sklar, "A Case of Fornication," *Mich. Papers in Women's Studies* (1978), 46–48, 51.

fanticide.[73] While the pain and shock of miscarrying a five-and-one-half-month fetus through a possibly lacerated vagina may have been the experience that later most grieved Sarah, Zerviah would be haunted particularly by her stealthy venture into the woods with Hannah to bury the shrouded evidence of miscarriage.[74]

The Grosvenor sisters later recalled that they had regarded the first stage of the scheme—taking the trade—as "a Sin" and "an Evil" not so much because it was intended to end the life of a fetus as because it entailed a protracted set of actions, worse than a single lie, to cover up an initial transgression: fornication.[75] According to their religion and the traditions of their New England culture, Sarah and Zerviah knew that the proper response to the sin of "uncleanness" (especially when it led to its visible manifestation, pregnancy) was to confess, seeking to allay God's wrath and cleanse oneself and one's community. Dire were the consequences of hiding a grave sin, so the logic and folklore of religion warned.[76] Having piled one covert act upon another, all in defiance of her parents, each sister wondered if she had not ventured beyond the pale, forsaking God and in turn being forsaken.

Within hours after the burial, Zerviah ran in a frenzy to Alexander Sessions's house and blurted out an account of her sister's "Untimely birth" and the burying of the fetus. While Alexander and Silence Sessions wondered if Zerviah was "in her right mind" and supposed she was having "a very bad fit," we might judge that she was in shock—horrified and confused by what she had done, fearful of retribution, and torn between the pragmatic strategy of silence and an intense spiritual longing to confess. Silence took her aside and demanded, "how could you do it?—I could not!" Zerviah, in despair, replied, "I don't Know; the Devil was in us." Hers was the characteristic refuge of the defiant sinner: Satan made her do it.[77]

[73] See Ulrich, *Good Wives*, 195–201, and Cornelia Hughes Dayton, "Infanticide in Early New England," unpub. paper presented to the Organization of American Historians, Reno, Nev., Mar. 1988.

[74] Burying the child was one of the key dramatic acts in infanticide episodes and tales, and popular beliefs in the inevitability that "murder will out" centered on the buried corpse. For two 18th-century Connecticut cases illustrating these themes see ibid., n. 31. For more on "murder will out" in New England culture see Hall, *Worlds of Wonder*, 176–178, and George Lyman Kittredge, *The Old Farmer and His Almanack . . .* (New York, 1920), 71–77.

[75] Testimony of Zerviah Grosvenor.

[76] Hall, *Worlds of Wonder*, 172–178.

[77] Testimony of Silence Sessions in Multiple Deposition of Sarah and Silence Sessions; Testimony of Alexander Sessions in Multiple Deposition of Hannah Grosvenor et al.; Testimony of Silence Sessions; Hall, *Worlds of Wonder*, 174. Alexander and Silence may have had in mind their brother Amasa's interests as a criminal defendant when they cast doubt on Zerviah's reliability as the star prosecution witness.

Sarah's descent into despondency, according to the portrait drawn in the women's depositions, was not so immediate. In the week following the miscarriage she recovered enough to be up and about the house. Then the fever came on. Bedridden for weeks, yet still lucid, she exhibited such "great Concern of mind" that Abigail, alone with her, felt compelled to ask her "what was the Matter." "Full of Sorrow" and "in a very affectionate Manner," Sarah replied by asking her friend "whether [she] thought her Sins would ever be pardoned?" Abigail's answer blended a reassuringly familiar exhortation to repent with an awareness that Sarah might have stepped beyond the possibility of salvation. "I answered that I hoped she had not Sinned the unpardonable Sin [that of renouncing Christ], but with true and hearty repentance hoped she would find forgiveness." On this occasion, and at least once more, Sarah responded to the call for repentance by pouring out her troubled heart to Abigail—as we have seen—confessing her version of the story in a torrent of words.[78]

Thus, visions of judgment and of their personal accountability to God haunted Sarah and Zerviah during the waning days of summer—or so their female friends later contended. Caught between the traditional religious ethic of confession, recently renewed in revivals across New England, and the newer, status-driven cultural pressure to keep moral missteps private, the Grosvenor women declined to take up roles as accusers. By focusing on their own actions, they rejected a portrait of themselves as helpless victims, yet they also ceded to their male kin responsibility for assessing blame and mediating between the public interest in seeing justice done and the private interests of the Grosvenor family. Finally, by trying to keep the conspiracy of silence intact and by allowing Amasa frequent visits to her bedside to lament his role and his delusion by Hallowell, Sarah at once endorsed a policy of private repentance and forgiveness *and* indicated that she wished her lover to be spared eventual public retribution for her death.

Talk among the men of Pomfret in the weeks preceding and following Sarah's death centered on more secular concerns than the preoccupation with sin and God's anger that ran through the women's conversations. Neither Hallowell nor Sessions expressed any guilt or sense of sin, as far as the record shows, *until* Sarah was diagnosed as mortally ill.[79] Indeed, their initial accounts of the plot took the form

[78] Deposition of Abigail Nightingale.
[79] Testimony of Zerviah Grosvenor; Deposition of John Grosvenor. Abigail Nightingale recalled a scene when Sarah "was just going out of the world." She and Amasa were sitting on Sarah's bed, and Amasa "endeavour[ed] to raise her up &c. He asked my thought of her state &c. and then leaning over her used these words: poor Creature, I have undone you[!]"; Deposition of Abigail Nightingale.

of braggadocio, with Amasa (according to Hallowell) casting himself as the rake who could "gitt Red" of his child and look elsewhere for female companionship, and Hallowell boasting of his abortionist's surgical technique to Sarah's cousin Ebenezer. Later, anticipating popular censure and possible prosecution, each man "Tried to Cast it" on the other. The physician insisted that "He did not do any thing but What Sessions Importuned him to Do," while Amasa exclaimed "That he could freely be Strip[p]ed naked provided he could bring Sarah . . . To life again . . . , but Doct Hollowell had Deluded him, and Destroyed her." [80] While this sort of denial and buck-passing seems very human, it was the antithesis of the New England way—a religious way of life that made confession its central motif. The Grosvenor-Sessions case is one illustration among many of how New England women continued to measure themselves by "the moral allegory of repentance and confession" while men, at least when presenting themselves before legal authorities, adopted secular voices and learned self-interested strategies.[81]

For the Grosvenor men—at least the cluster of Sarah's cousins living near her—the key issue was not exposing sin but protecting the family's reputation. In the weeks before Sarah died, her cousins John and Ebenezer each attempted to investigate and sort out the roles and motives of Amasa Sessions and John Hallowell in the scheme to conceal Sarah's pregnancy. Grilled in August by Ebenezer about Sarah's

[80] Deposition of Ebenezer Grosvenor; Testimony of John Shaw in Multiple Deposition of Hannah Grosvenor et al. See also Deposition of John Grosvenor. For discussions of male and female speech patterns and the distinctive narcissistic bravado of men's talk in early New England see Robert St. George, " 'Heated' Speech and Literacy in Seventeenth-Century New England," in David Grayson Allen and David D. Hall, eds., *Seventeenth-Century New England*, Publications of the Colonial Society of Massachusetts, LXIII (Boston, 1984), 305–315; Dayton, "Women Before the Bar," 248–251, 263–283, 338–341; and John Demos, "Shame and Guilt in Early New England," in Carol Z. Stearns and Peter N. Stearns, eds., *Emotion and Social Change: Toward a New Psychohistory* (New York, 1988), 74–75.

[81] On the centrality of confession see Hall, *Worlds of Wonder*, 173, 241. The near-universality of accused men and women confessing in court in the 17th century is documented by Gail Sussman Marcus in " 'Due Execution of the Generall Rules of Righteousnesse': Criminal Procedure in New Haven Town and Colony, 1638–1658," in Hall, Murrin, and Tate, eds., *Saints and Revolutionaries*, esp. 132–133. For discussions of the increasing refusal of men to plead guilty to fornication (the most frequently prosecuted crime) from the 1670s on see Thompson, *Sex in Middlesex*, 29–33; Karlsen, *Devil in the Shape of a Woman*, 194–196, 198–202; and Dayton, "Women Before the Bar," 168–169. On the growing gap between male and female piety in the eighteenth century see Mary Maples Dunn, "Saints and Sisters: Congregational and Quaker Women in the Early Colonial Period," *American Quarterly*, XXX (1978), 582–601. For the story of how the New England court system became more legalistic after 1690 and how lawyerly procedures subsequently began to affect religious practices and broader cultural styles see Mann, *Neighbors and Strangers*, and John M. Murrin, "Anglicizing an American Colony: The Transformation of Provincial Massachusetts" (Ph.D. diss., Yale University, 1966).

condition, Hallowell revealed that "Sessions had bin Interseeding with him to Remove her Conseption." On another occasion, when John Grosvenor demanded that he justify his actions, Hallowell was more specific. He "[did] with her [Sarah] as he did . . . because Sessions Came to him and was So very earnest . . . and offered him five pounds if he would do it." "But," Hallowell boasted, "he would have twenty of[f] of him before he had done." John persisted: did Amasa know that Hallowell was attempting a manual abortion at John's house on that day in early August? Hallowell replied that Amasa "knew before he did anything and was at Mr. Waldo's [a Pomfret tavernkeeper] to hear the event." [82]

John and Ebenezer, deposing three or four years after these events, did not mention having thrown questions at Amasa Sessions at the time, nor did they explain why they did not act immediately to have charges brought against the two conspirators. Perhaps these young householders were loath to move against a male peer and childhood friend. More likely, they kept their information to themselves to protect John's wife, Hannah, and their cousin Zerviah from prosecution as accessories. They may also have acted, in league with their uncle Leicester, out of a larger concern for keeping the family name out of the courts. Finally, it is probable that the male cousins, partly because of their own complicity and partly because they may have believed that Sarah had consented to the abortion, simply did not think that Amasa's and Hallowell's actions added up to the murder of their relative.

Three years later, yet another Grosvenor cousin intervened, expressing himself much more vehemently than John or Ebenezer ever had. In 1742, John Shaw at age thirty-eight may have been perceived by the younger Grosvenors as too old—too close to the age when men took public office and served as grand jurors—to be trusted with their secret. Shaw seems to have known nothing of Sarah's taking the trade or having a miscarriage until 1745 when "the Storys" suddenly surfaced. Then Hannah and Zerviah gave him a truncated account. Shaw reacted with rage, realizing that Sarah had died not of natural causes but from "what Hollowell had done," and he set out to wring the truth from the doctor. Several times he sought out Hallowell in Rhode Island to tell him that "I could not look upon him otherwise Than [as] a Bad man Since he had Destroyed my Kinswoman." When Hallowell countered that "Amasa Sessions . . . was the Occasion of it," Shaw's

---

[82] Deposition of Ebenezer Grosvenor; Deposition of John Grosvenor. Although a host of witnesses testified to the contrary, Hallowell on one occasion told Amasa's brother "That Sessions never applied to him for anything, to cause an abortion and that if She was with Child he did not Think Amasa knew it"; Testimony of Alexander Sessions in Multiple Deposition of Hannah Grosvenor et al.

fury grew. "I Told him he was like old Mother Eve When She said The Serpent beguild her; . . . [and] I Told him in my Mind he Deserved to dye for it." [83]

Questioning Amasa, Shaw was quick to accept his protestations of sincere regret and his insistence that Hallowell had "Deluded" him.[84] Shaw concluded that Amasa had never "Importuned [Hallowell] . . . to lay hands on her" (that is, to perform the manual abortion). Forged in the men's talk about the Grosvenor-Sessions case in 1745 and 1746 appears to have been a consensus that, while Amasa Sessions was somewhat blameworthy "as concerned in it," it was only Hallowell—the outsider, the man easily labeled a quack—who deserved to be branded "a Man of Death." Nevertheless, it was the stories of *both* men and women that ensured the fulfillment of a doctor's warning to Hallowell in the Leicester Grosvenor house just before Sarah died: "The Hand of Justice [will] Take hold of [you] sooner or Later." [85]

The Law

The hand of justice reached out to catch John Hallowell in November 1745. The warrants issued for the apprehension and examination of suspects that autumn gave no indication of a single informer or highly placed magistrate who had triggered the prosecution so long after the events. Witnesses referred to "those Stories Concerning Amasa Sessions and Sarah Grosvenor" that had begun to circulate beyond the inner circle of Pomfret initiates in the summer of 1745. *Something* had caused Zerviah and Hannah Grosvenor to break their silence.[86] Zerviah provided the key to the puzzle, as she alone had been present at the crucial series of incidents leading to Sarah's death. The only surviving account of Zerviah's belated conversion from silence to public confession comes from the stories told by Pomfret residents into the nineteenth century. In Ellen Larned's melodramatic prose, the "whispered" tale recounted Zerviah's increasing discomfort thus: "Night after night, in her solitary chamber, the surviving sister was awakened by the rattling of the rings on which her bed-curtains were suspended, a ghostly knell continuing and intensifying till she

[83] Testimony of John Shaw in Multiple Deposition of Hannah Grosvenor et al. One of these confrontations took place in the Providence jail, probably in late 1745 or early 1746.

[84] It is interesting to note that Sessions claimed to have other sources for strong medicines: he told Shaw that, had he known Sarah was in danger of dying, "he tho't he could have got Things that would have preserved her Life"; ibid.

[85] Ibid. Shaw here was reporting Dr. [Theodore?] Coker's account of his confrontation with Hallowell during Sarah's final illness. For biographical data on Coker, see n. 30 above.

[86] Testimony of Rebecca Sharp, Zebulon Dodge, and John Shaw in Multiple Deposition of Hannah Grosvenor et al.; Deposition of Ebenezer Grosvenor.

was convinced of its preternatural origin; and at length, in response to her agonized entreaties, the spirit of her dead sister made known to her, 'That she could not rest in her grave till her crime was made public.' " [87]

Embellished as this tale undoubtedly is, we should not dismiss it out of hand as a Victorian ghost story. In early modern English culture, belief persisted in both apparitions and the supernatural power of the guiltless victim to return and expose her murderer.[88] Zerviah in 1742 already fretted over her sin as an accomplice, yet she kept her pledge of silence to her sister. It is certainly conceivable that, after a lapse of three years, she could no longer bear the pressure of hiding the acts that she increasingly believed amounted to the murder of her sister and an unborn child. Whether Zerviah's sudden outburst of talk in 1745 came about at the urging of some Pomfret confidante, or perhaps under the influence of the revivals then sweeping Windham County churches, or indeed because of her belief in nightly visitations by her dead sister's spirit, we simply cannot know.[89]

The Pomfret meetinghouse was the site of the first public legal hearing into the facts behind Sarah Grosvenor's death. We can imagine that townsfolk crowded the pews over the course of two November days to watch two prominent county magistrates examine a string of witnesses before pronouncing their preliminary judgment.[90] The evidence, they concluded, was sufficient to bind four people over for trial at the Superior Court: Hallowell, who in their opinion was "Guilty of murdering Sarah," along with Amasa Sessions, Zerviah Grosvenor, and Hannah Grosvenor as accessories to that murder.[91]

[87] Larned reported that, according to "the legend," the ghostly visitations ceased when "Hallowell fled his country." *History of Windham County*, I, 363.

[88] For mid-18th-century Bristol residents who reported seeing apparitions and holding conversations with them see Jonathan Barry, "Piety and the Patient: Medicine and Religion in Eighteenth Century Bristol," in Roy Porter, ed., *Patients and Practitioners: Lay Perceptions of Medicine in Pre-Industrial Society* (Cambridge, 1985), 157.

[89] None of the depositions produced by Hallowell's trial offers any explanation of the 3-year gap between Sarah's death and legal proceedings. Between 1741 and 1747, revivals and schisms touched every Windham County parish except Pomfret's First Church, to which the Grosvenors belonged; see Larned, *History of Windham County*, I, 393–485, esp. 464.

[90] One of the magistrates, Ebenezer West, had been a justice of the county court since 1726. The other, Jonathan Trumbull, the future governor, was serving both as a county court justice and as an assistant. The fact that the 2 men made the 24-mile trip from their hometown of Lebanon to preside over this Inferior Court, rather than allow local magistrates to handle the hearing, may indicate that one or both of them had insisted the alleged crime be prosecuted.

[91] Record of the Inferior Court held at Pomfret, Nov. 5–6, 1745. Hallowell was the only one of the 4 persons charged who was not examined at this time. He was in jail in Providence for debt. Apprehended in Connecticut the following March, he was jailed

The inclusion of Zerviah and Hannah may have been a ploy to pressure these crucial, possibly still reluctant, witnesses to testify for the crown. When Joseph Fowler, the king's attorney, prepared a formal indictment in the case eleven months later, he dropped all charges against Zerviah and Hannah. Rather than stand trial, the two women traveled frequently during 1746 and 1747 to the county seat to give evidence against Sessions and Hallowell.

The criminal process recommenced in September 1746. A grand jury empaneled by the Superior Court as its Windham session first rejected a presentment against Hallowell for murdering Sarah "by his Wicked and Diabolical practice." Fowler, recognizing that the capital charges of murder and accessory to murder against Hallowell and Sessions were going to fail before jurors, changed his tack. He presented the grand jury with a joint indictment against the two men not for outright murder but for endangering Sarah's health by trying to "procure an Abortion" with medicines and "a violent manual opperation"; this time the jurors endorsed the bill. When the Superior Court trial opened in November, two attorneys for the defendants managed to persuade the judges that the indictment was faulty on technical grounds. However, upon the advice of the king's attorney that there "appear reasons vehemently to suspect" the two men "Guilty of Sundry Heinous Offenses" at Pomfret four years earlier, the justices agreed to bind them over to answer charges in March 1747.[92]

Fowler next moved to bring separate indictments against Hallowell and Sessions for the "highhanded misdemeanour" of endeavoring to destroy Sarah's health "and the fruit of her womb." This wording echoed the English common law designation of abortion as a misdemeanor, not a felony or capital crime. A newly empaneled grand jury of eighteen county yeomen made what turned out to be the pivotal decision in getting a conviction: they returned a true bill against Hallowell and rejected a similarly worded bill against Sessions.[93] Only Hallowell, "the notorious physician," would go to trial.[94]

---

until the Pomfret witnesses could travel to Windham for a hearing before Trumbull and West. At the second hearing, the magistrates charged Hallowell with "murdering Sarah . . . *and* A Bastard Female Child with which she was pregnant" (emphasis added). See Record of an Inferior Court held at Windham, Apr. 17, 1746.

[92] Indictment against Hallowell, Sept. 4, 1746; Indictment against Hallowell and Sessions, Sept. 20, 1746; Pleas of Hallowell and Sessions before the adjourned Windham Superior Court, Nov. [18], 1746; Sup. Ct. Rec., bk. 12, 112–117, 131–133.

[93] Sup. Ct. Rec., bk. 12, 173, 175; Indictment against John Hallowell, Mar. 1746/47; *Rex* v. *Amasa Sessions*, Indictment, Mar. 1746/47, Windham Sup. Ct. Files, box 172. See William Blackstone, *Commentaries on the Laws of England* (Facsimile of 1st ed. of 1765–69) (Chicago, 1979), I, 125–126, IV, 198.

[94] Larned, *History of Windham County*, I, 363.

On March 20, 1747, John Hallowell stepped before the bar for the final time to answer for the death of Sarah Grosvenor. He maintained his innocence, the case went to a trial jury of twelve men, and they returned with a guilty verdict. The Superior Court judges, who had discretion to choose any penalty less than death, pronounced a severe sentence of public shaming and corporal punishment. Hallowell was to be paraded to the town gallows, made to stand there before the public for two hours "with a rope visibly hanging about his neck," and then endure a public whipping of twenty-nine lashes "on the naked back." [95]

Before the authorities could carry out this sentence, Hallowell escaped and fled to Rhode Island. From Providence seven months after his trial, he audaciously petitioned the Connecticut General Assembly for a mitigated sentence, presenting himself as a destitute "Exile." As previously noted, fourteen respected male citizens of Providence took up his cause, arguing that this valued doctor had been convicted by prejudiced witnesses and hearsay evidence and asserting that corporal punishment was unwarranted in a misdemeanor case. While the Connecticut legislators rejected these petitions, the language used by Hallowell and his Rhode Island patrons is yet another marker of the distance separating many educated New England men at mid-century from their more God-fearing predecessors. Never mentioning the words "sin" or "repentance," the Providence men wrote that Hallowell was justified in escaping the lash since "every Person is prompted [by the natural Law of Self-Preservation] to avoid Pain and Misery." [96]

In the series of indictments against Hallowell and Sessions, the central legal question became who had directly caused Sarah's death. To the farmers in their forties and fifties who sat as jurors, Hallowell clearly deserved punishment. By recklessly endangering Sarah's life he

---

[95] Even in the context of the inflation of the 1740s, Hallowell's bill of costs was unusually high: £110.2s.6d. Sessions was hit hard in the pocketbook too; he was assessed £83.14s.2d. in costs.

[96] Petition of John Hallowell, Oct. 1747, Conn. Archives, Crimes and Misdemeanors, Ser. 1, IV, 108; Petition of Resolved Waterman et al., ibid., 109. Specifically, Hallowell and his supporters asked that his sentence be reduced to a fine in an amount "adequate to his reduced Circumstances." Such requests for reduced sentences were increasingly submitted by convicted felons in 18th-century Connecticut, and some were granted. See ibid., Ser. 1 and 2. Rumors of bankruptcy had haunted Hallowell since he moved to Providence in 1742. As a physician and shopkeeper, between 1742 and 1750 he won a net of £325 in frequent county court litigation (including two substantial executions against Dr. Theodore Coker). However, two 1743–1744 Superior Court judgments against him totalling over £4000 spelled financial ruin. His name last appears in Connecticut records in 1749, and in Rhode Island, as far as I can tell, in 1750. Three of his sons settled in Providence as mariners. These conclusions are based on an analysis of Rhode Island Census records, and the Record books and indices of the Providence County Court of Common Pleas and of the Supreme Court at the Judicial Records Center, Pawtucket.

had abused the trust that heads of household placed in him as a physician.[97] Moreover, he had conspired with the younger generation to keep their dangerous activities secret from their parents and elders.

Several rationales could have been behind the Windham jurors' conclusion that Amasa Sessions ought to be spared the lash. Legally, they could distinguish him from Hallowell as not being immediately responsible for Sarah's death. Along with Sarah's male kin, they dismissed the evidence that Amasa had instigated the scheme, employed Hallowell, and monitored all of his activities. Perhaps they saw him as a native son who deserved the chance to prove himself mature and responsible. They may have excused his actions as nothing more than a misguided effort to cast off an unwanted lover. Rather than acknowledge that a culture that excused male sexual irresponsibility was responsible for Sarah's death, the Grosvenor family, the Pomfret community, and the jury men of the county persuaded themselves that Sessions had been ignorant of the potentially deadly consequences of his actions.

Memory and History

No family feud, no endless round of recriminations followed the many months of deposing and attending trials that engaged the Grosvenor and Sessions clans in 1746 and 1747. Indeed, as Sarah and Amasa's generation matured, the ties between the two families thickened. In 1748 Zerviah married a man whose family homestead adjoined the farm of Amasa's father. Twenty years later, when the aging Sessions patriarch wrote his will, Zerviah and her husband were at his elbow to witness the solemn document. Amasa, who would inherit "the Whole of the Farm," was doubtless present also.[98] Within another decade, the third generation came of age, and despite the painful memories of Sarah's death that must have lingered in the minds of her now middle-aged siblings, a marriage directly joining the two families finally took place. In 1775 Amasa's third son, and namesake, married sixteen-year-old Esther Grosvenor, daughter of Sarah's brother, Leicester, Jr.[99]

It is clear that the Grosvenor clan was not willing to break ranks with their respectable yeoman neighbors and heap blame on the Sessions family for Sarah's death. It would, however, be fascinating to know what women in Pomfret and other Windham County towns had

---

[97] Note Blackstone's discussion of the liability of "a physician or surgeon who gives his patient a potion . . . to cure him, which contrary to expectation kills him." *Commentaries*, IV, 197.

[98] Killingly Land Rec., III, 99; Estate papers of Nathaniel Sessions, 1771, Pomfret Prob. Dist. Although Zerviah bore five daughters, she chose not to name any of them after the sister she had been so close to. In 1747, the final year of the trials, Sarah's much older sister, Anna, gave birth to a daughter whom she named Sarah.

[99] Pomfret Vit. Rec., II, 67.

to say about the outcome of the legal proceedings in 1747. Did they concur with the jurors that Hallowell was the prime culprit, or did they, unlike Sarah Grosvenor, direct their ire more concertedly at Amasa, insisting that he too was "a Bad man?" Several decades later, middle-class New England women would organize against the sexual double standard. However, Amasa's future career tells us that female piety in the 1740s did not instruct Windham County women to expel the newly married, thirty-two-year-old man from their homes.[100]

Amasa, as he grew into middle age in Pomfret, easily replicated his father's status. He served as militia captain in the Seven Years' War, prospered in farming, fathered ten children, and lived fifty-seven years beyond Sarah Grosvenor. His handsome gravestone, inscribed with a long verse, stands but twenty-five feet from the simpler stone erected in 1742 for Sarah.

After his death, male kin remembered Amasa fondly; nephews and grandsons recalled him as a "favorite" relative, "remarkably capable" in his prime and "very corpulent" in old age. Moreover, local story-telling tradition and the published history of the region, which made such a spectacular ghost story out of Sarah's abortion and death, preserved Amasa Sessions's reputation unsullied: the name of Sarah's lover was left out of the tale.[101]

If Sarah Grosvenor's life is a cautionary tale in any sense for us in the late twentieth century, it is as a reminder of the historically distinctive ways in which socialized gender roles, community and class solidarity, and legal culture combine in each set of generations to excuse or make invisible certain abuses and crimes against women. The form in which Sarah Grosvenor's death became local history reminds us of how the excuses and erasures of one generation not unwittingly become embedded in the narratives and memories of the next cultural era.

---

[100] Carroll Smith-Rosenberg, "Beauty, the Beast and the Militant Woman: A Case Study in Sex Roles and Social Stress in Jacksonian America," *American Quarterly*, XXIII (1971), 562–584. There were branches of the Female Moral Reform Society in several Connecticut towns.

[101] Sessions, *Sessions Family*, 31, 35; Larned, *History of Windham County*, I, 363–364. Indeed Larned referred to the Grosvenor and Sessions families only obliquely, characterizing them as among Pomfret's "proudest," "first and wealthiest families." The only principal in the case whom she identified directly was the culprit Hallowell.

The Social Context of Democracy
in Massachusetts

MICHAEL ZUCKERMAN

Michael Zuckerman attempts to characterize political behavior in eighteenth-century Massachusetts by relating politics to social organization. He argues that colonial authority was largely delegated to towns and that the towns operated by consensus rather than by the resolution of conflict. Since the legal powers of towns were not great, agreement on fundamental issues was a prerequisite of the maintenance of order. Successful consensual politics required a virtual homogeneity of interest among the inhabitants and forced the towns rigidly to exclude potential dissidents of all sorts. It was only through strict limitations on the possibility of disagreement that the towns were able to operate within what was formally a "democratic" political system.

Zuckerman's reinterpretation of the social context of New England politics necessitates reevaluation of some of our traditional assumptions about colonial political behavior in the eighteenth century. In particular, he denies that the recent demonstration of the broad scope of the electoral franchise proves anything about the nature of popular participation in government. The right to vote can be assessed only in conjunction with the meaning of voting in the political process, and if elections were not choices between alternative policies, many historians have badly misunderstood public life in provincial Massachusetts.

Zuckerman seems to imply that town government was always consensual, and he does not come to grips with the argument that the town meeting underwent an important evolution during the seventeenth century. Is it possible that Massachusetts politics underwent a transition from the free conflict of interests to a consensual basis? If Zuckerman's theory about the town meeting can be extended to the General Court, do we need an entirely different explanation for legislative behavior in the middle and southern colonies?

For at least a decade now, a debate has passed through these pages on the extent of democracy in the Old New England town. It began, of course, with Robert E. Brown, and it did not begin badly: Brown's

Reprinted by permission from Michael Zuckerman, "The Social Context of Democracy in Massachusetts," *William and Mary Quarterly*, 3d Ser., XXV (1968), 523–544.

work was a breath of fresh air in a stale discussion, substituting statistics for cynicism and adding figures to filiopietism. But what was begun decently has degenerated since, and findings that should have provoked larger questions have only produced quibbles and counter-quibbles over methodology and quantification. The discussion has not been entirely futile—few would now maintain the old claim that the franchise was very closely confined in provincial Massachusetts—but neither has its apparent potential been realized. We are, ultimately, as far from agreement as we ever were about whether eighteenth-century Massachusetts was democratic. Somehow, the discussion has stalled at the starting point; a promising avenue of inquiry has not developed beyond its initial promise.

Perhaps a part of that failure was implicit in Brown's initial formulation of the problem; but one man cannot do everything, and Brown did advance our consideration of the New England town as far as any one man ever has. If he did not answer, or even ask, all the questions which might have been raised, other students could have done so. Brown's work made that possible. But since *Middle-Class Democracy and the Revolution in Massachusetts* (Ithaca, 1955) no comparable advances have been made. Indeed, the discussion seems to have stopped conceptually where Brown stopped, and one is forced to wonder not merely whether the right questions are being asked but whether any significant questions at all are being asked, other than those of how better to compute voting percentages. Certainly the terms of the debate have been, and are, inadequate to its resolution. Most obviously, figures on the franchise simply cannot serve to establish democracy. In our own time we have seen too many travesties on universal suffrage in too many non-democratic regimes to continue to take seriously in and of itself such an abstract calculus. Yet on both sides the discussion of New England town-meeting democracy has often assumed that the franchise is a satisfactory index of democracy, and the recourse to the seeming solidity of the voting statistics has depended, if only implicitly, upon that dubious premise.

Even those few critics who have challenged the contention that the issue of eighteenth-century democracy could be settled by counting heads have generally acquiesced in the far more fundamental assumption that in one way or another the issue of the eighteenth century was what the Browns have declared it to be: "democracy or aristocracy?" But democracy and aristocracy are probably false alternatives in any case for provincial Massachusetts; and in this case they are surely so, because they have been made initial tools of inquiry instead of end terms.

Of course, the Browns have hardly been alone in their strategy of frontal assault. On the contrary, it is indicative of how thoroughly their work established the contours of subsequent study that others have also rushed right into the issue of democracy without even a pause to ponder whether that issue was quite so readily accessible. Yet it would be admitted on most sides that democracy was hardly a value of such supreme salience to the men of provincial Massachusetts that it governed their conscious motives and aspirations; nor, after all, did it provide the framework for social structure in the towns of the province. In application to such a society, then, a concept such as democracy must always be recognized for just that: a concept of our own devising. It is not a datum that can be directly apprehended in all its immediacy; it is an abstraction—a rather elevated abstraction— which represents a covering judgment of the general tenor or tendency of social relations and institutions. As such, it can carry its own assurance of validity only if it proceeds out of, rather than precedes, analysis of the society to which it is applied. To rip it out of its social context is to risk exactly the disembodied discussion of democracy we have witnessed over the past decade.

If we could study democracy in provincial Massachusetts, we cannot plunge headlong into that issue without sacrificing the context which conferred meaning on whatever degree of democracy did exist. Since democracy was incidental to the prime purposes of provincial society, we must first confront that society. Democracy, to the extent that it existed, was no isolated element in the organization of the political community, and problems of political participation and inclusion cannot be considered apart from the entire question of the nature of the provincial community. Even if most men in eighteenth-century Massachusetts could vote, that is only the beginning, not the end, of inquiry. What, then, was the *function* of a widely extended suffrage, and what was the function of voting itself in the conduct of the community? Who specifically was admitted to the franchise, and who was denied that privilege, and on what grounds? For ultimately, if we are to understand the towns that made the Revolution in Massachusetts, we must find out not only *whether* most men could vote but also *why*.

It is particularly imperative that we place provincial democracy in its social context because nothing else can plausibly account for its development. The founders of the settlement at Massachusetts Bay came with neither an inclusive ethos nor any larger notions of middle-class democracy. In 1630 a band of true believers had entered upon the wilderness, possessed of a conviction of absolute and invincible righteousness. Their leaders, in that first generation, proudly proclaimed that they "abhorred democracy," and, as Perry Miller maintained, "theirs was not an idle boast."[1] The spirit of the founders was set firmly against inclusion, with the very meaning of the migration dependent for many on an extension of the sphere of ecclesiastical exclusivity. The right of every church to keep out the unworthy was pre-

---

[1] Perry Miller, *Orthodoxy in Massachusetts* (Boston, 1959), 37.

cisely the point of the Congregationalists' difference with the established church, and it was a right which could not be realized in England.[2] Yet, without any English prodding and within about a decade of the first settlements, the original ideals of exclusion had begun to break down at the local level. Until 1692 the colonial suffrage extended only to freemen, but by that time non-freemen had been voting in town affairs for almost half a century.[3] The ability of the settlers to sustain suffrage restrictions at the colonial level so long after they were abandoned in the towns not only indicates the incomplete coincidence of intellectual currents and local conduct in early New England but also contradicts any contention that the pressures for democratic participation derived from Puritan theology or thought. The New England Puritans were pressed to the popularization of political authority only in grudging adjustment to the exigencies of their situation.

Their situation, quite simply, was one that left them stripped of any *other* sanctions than those of the group. The sea passage had cut the new settlement off from the full force of traditional authority, so that even the maintenance of law and order had to be managed in the absence of any customarily accepted agencies for its establishment or enforcement. Furthermore, as the seventeenth century waned and settlement dispersed, the preservation of public order devolved increasingly upon the local community. What was reluctantly admitted in the seventeenth century was openly acknowledged in the eighteenth, after the arrival of the new charter: the public peace could not be entrusted to Boston, but would have to be separately secured in each town in the province. And though this devolution of effective authority to the local level resolved other difficulties, it only aggravated the problem of order, because the towns even more than the central government were without institutions and authorities sanctioned by tradition. Moreover, the towns had relatively limited instruments of enforcement, and they were demonstrably loath to use the coercive power they did possess.[4]

---

[2] Edmund S. Morgan, *Visible Saints* (New York, 1963), esp. 10–12, 21.

[3] The first break occurred in 1641 when the Body of Liberties made all men free to attend town meetings; an enactment of 1647 allowed them to vote. On the other hand, some restrictions on non-freemen did remain. See Joel Parker, "The Origin, Organization, and Influence of the Towns of New England," Massachusetts Historical Society, *Proceedings*, IX (Boston, 1866), 46.

[4] Difficulties of enforcement are not easy to demonstrate in a few sentences, but they can be suggested, perhaps, by the ease of mob mobilization and by the extensive evasion of the office of constable, especially by the middling and upper classes of the community, which was both symptomatic of and contributory to the structural weakness of the constabulary. There was, in other words, a formal legal system in the province without an autonomous instrument for its own enforcement. A more elaborate development of the general theme is in Michael Zuckerman, The Massachusetts Town in the Eighteenth Century (unpubl. Ph.D. diss., Harvard University, 1967), esp. 118–126.

Nonetheless, order was obtained in the eighteenth-century town, and it was obtained by concord far more than by compulsion. Consensus governed the communities of provincial Massachusetts, and harmony and homogeneity were the regular—and required—realities of local life. Effective action necessitated a public opinion approaching if not attaining unanimity, and public policy was accordingly bent toward securing such unanimity. The result was, to be sure, a kind of government by common consent, but government by consent in eighteenth-century Massachusetts did not imply democracy in any more modern sense because it required far more than mere majoritarianism. Such majoritarianism implied a minority, and the towns could no more condone a competing minority by their norms and values than they could have constrained it by their police power. Neither conflict, dissent, nor any other structured pluralism ever obtained legitimacy in the towns of the Bay before the Revolution.[5]

Thus, authority found another form in provincial Massachusetts. Its instrument was the town meeting, which was no mere forum but the essential element in the delicate equipoise of peace and propriety which governed the New England town. In the absence of any satisfactory means of traditional or institutional coercion, the recalcitrant could not be compelled to adhere to the common course of action. Therefore, the common course of action had to be so shaped as to leave none recalcitrant—that was the vital function of the New England town meeting. To oversimplify perhaps, the town meeting solved the problem of enforcement by evading it. The meeting gave institutional expression to the imperatives of peace. In the meetings consensus was reached, and individual consent and group opinion were placed in the service of social conformity. There the men of the province established their agreements on policies and places, and there they legitimized those agreements so that subsequent deviation from those accords became socially illegitimate and personally immoral as well, meaning as it did the violation of a covenant or the breaking of a promise. In the town meetings men talked of politics, but ultimately they sought to establish moral community.

---

[5] The import of the argument sketched here and developed below must be understood. No full-scale defense of the consensus hypothesis will be attempted here, nor would one be possible in such a piece as this: an examination of such a narrow matter as electoral eligibility can hardly *prove* a set of propositions about so substantial a subject as the social organization of the New England town. A full-scale defense of the hypothesis assumed here is found in Zuckerman, Massachusetts Town in the Eighteenth Century. What is in fact claimed here is, first, that this hypothesis in particular does illuminate many aspects of political "democracy" in the Massachusetts town of the eighteenth century and, second, that whatever failings may be found in this particular hypothesis, *some* kind of hypothesis is surely necessary to ground the discussion of democracy in the colony and establish it in a social context.

In the context of such a community, the significance of an extended franchise becomes quite clear: governance by concord and concurrence required inclusiveness. In communities in which effective enforcement depended on the moral binding of decisions upon the men who made them, it was essential that most men be parties to such decisions. Not the principled notions of the New Englanders but the stern necessities of enforcement sustained town-meeting democracy in Massachusetts. The politics of consensus made a degree of democracy functional, even made it a functional imperative. Men were allowed to vote not out of any overweening attachment to democratic principles *per se* but simply because a wide canvass was convenient, if not indeed critical, in consolidating a consensus in the community.

Under this incentive to inclusion, most towns did set their suffrage almost as liberally as Brown claimed. To seek the social context of the suffrage, then, necessitates no major quarrel with Brown's figures on franchise democracy; what it may provide is an explanation for them. It also offers the possibility of accounting for more than just the figures. As soon as we see that the high degree of participation permitted in the politics of the provincial town was not an isolated phenomenon but rather an integral aspect of the conduct of the community, we are in a position to go beyond a disembodied study of electoral eligibility and a simple celebration of middle-class democracy in Massachusetts. We are in a position to convert polemics into problems, and to press for answers.

In many communities, for example, a substantial and sometimes an overwhelming proportion of the people were *not* technically entitled to vote. Brown did not discuss some of these places, and ones he did discuss were added to his evidence only with the special explanation that sometimes even the ineligible were admitted to the ballot box. But in the context of community such lapses would not necessarily invalidate his larger conclusions, nor would such *ad hoc* expedients be required; for the same imperatives impinged on towns where few were legally qualified as on the others, and the same results of wide political participation obtained because of the same sense that inclusiveness promoted peace while more rigorous methods threatened it. The town of Douglas, with only five qualified voters in its first years, flatly refused to be bound by a determination confined to those five, declaring its conviction "that the intent of no law can bind them to such ill consequences." Mendon, in its "infant state" in 1742, voted "to permit a considerable number of persons not qualified by law to vote . . . being induced thereto by an apprehension that it would be a means of preserving peace and unity amongst ourselves." Princeton, incorporated in 1760 with forty-three settlers but only fourteen eligible to vote according to provincial regulations, established a formal "agreement among themselves to overlook" those regulations, and the General Court upheld that agreement. "The poor freeholders" in the early days of Upton were also "allowed liberty to vote in town meeting," and it had produced "an encouraging harmony" in local affairs until 1746, when a few of the qualified voters, momentarily possessed of a majority of the ten in town, sought to upset the customary arrangements and limit the franchise as the law required. The rest of the town at once protested that "such a strenuous method of proceeding would endanger the peace of the town" and begged the General Court "to prevent the dismal damages that may follow" therefrom. The Court did exactly as it was asked, and at the new meeting the town reverted to its old form: "everyone was admitted to vote, qualified or not." [6]

The principle which governed such universalism was not deliberate democracy; it was merely a recognition that the community could not be governed solely by the qualified voters if they were too few in number. Such a situation was most likely to occur in new communities, but it was not limited to them. Middleton had been established for almost a quarter of a century when it was conceded that in the local elections of 1752 "there was double the number of votes to the lawful voters." In a variety of towns and at other times, requirements for the franchise were also ignored and admission of the unqualified acknowledged explicitly.[7] Thomas Hutchinson's wry lament that "anything with the appearance of a man" was allowed the vote may have been excessive, but it was not wholly fabricated.[8] And even towns whose political procedures were more regular resorted to universalism in cases of conflict or of major issues. Fitchburg, for instance, voted in 1767 that "every freholder be a votter in Chusing of a minestr," while twenty years earlier, in a bitterly contested election in Haverhill, "there was not any list of valuation read nor any list of non-voters nor any weighting of what name or nature whatsoever by which the selectman did pretend to show who was qualified to vote in town affairs." [9]

The question of inclusiveness itself sometimes came before a town, not always without challenge but generally with a democratic outcome. Dudley, more than a decade after the incorporation of the town, voted "that all the freeholder of sd town should be voters by a graet majorytie and all agreed to it." In Needham in 1750 it was also "put to vote whether it be the mind of the town to allow all freehold-

---

[6] Massachusetts Archives, CXV, 168, 169, 316–317, 319–320, 469–471, 864–865; CXVII, 647–649, 652; CXVIII, 734–735a, 762, State House, Boston; Francis E. Blake, *History of the Town of Princeton* (Princeton, Mass., 1915), I, 76–77.

[7] Mass. Archives, VIII, 279, for others see *ibid.*, 278; XLIX, 398–400; L, 20–22, 25–26, 85–88, 89–90; CXIII, 270; CXV, 36–37, 291; CXVI, 373–374; CXVII, 291–293, 302–305; CLXXXI, 23–24a.

[8] Brown, *Middle-Class Democracy*, 60.

[9] Walter A. Davis, comp., *The Old Records of the Town of Fitchburg Massachusetts 1764–1789* (Fitchburg, Mass., 1898), 39; Mass. Archives, VIII, 273.

ers in town to vote for a moderator," and there too the vote carried in the affirmative. And that verdict for inclusion was not even as revealing as the method by which that verdict was reached, for in voting *whether* to include all in the election, Needham *did* include all in the procedural issue. Every man did vote on the question of whether every man was to be allowed to vote.[10]

Of course, absolute inclusiveness never prevailed in provincial Massachusetts—women could not vote at all, and neither could anyone under 21—and property and residence qualifications, introduced in 1692, were probably adhered to as often as they were ignored, so that even the participation of adult males was something less than universal. It was an important part of Brown's achievement to show that, in general, it was not *very much* less than universal, but, by the nature of his research strategy, he could go no further than that. If we are to penetrate to particulars—if we are to ask who was excluded, and why, and why the suffrage standards were what they were—we must consider not only numbers but also the conditions of community.

The men who were not allowed legitimately to vote with their fellow townsmen were commonly tenants or the sons of voters; as Brown discovered, it was these two groups against which the property requirement primarily operated. But where the controversialists seek to *excuse* these exclusions, or to magnify them, a broader perspective allows one to *explain* them, for against these two groups sanctions were available that were far more effective than those of the generalized community. Stringent property qualifications were clearly self-defeating in a society where consensus was the engine of enforcement, but overly generous qualifications were equally unnecessary. Where some men, such as tenants and dependent sons, could be privately coerced, liberality on their behalf, from the standpoint of social control, would have meant the commission of a sin of superfluity.

Similarly, almost nothing but disadvantage could have accrued from a loose residence requirement enabling men not truly members of the community to participate in its decision-making process, since voting qualifications in provincial Massachusetts were connected to the concept of community, not the concept of democracy. The extensions and contractions of the franchise were significant to the townsmen of the eighteenth century primarily as a means of consolidating communal consensus. All those whose acquiescence in public action was necessary were included, and all those whose concurrence could be compelled otherwise or dispensed with were excluded, often very emphatically. Sixty-six citizens of Watertown, for example, petitioned against the allowance of a single unqualified voter in a 1757 election because

---

[10] *Town Records of Dudley, Massachusetts*, 1732–1754, I (Pawtucket, R.I., 1893), 106; Mass. Archives, CXV, 616–617.

he was "well known to belong to the town of Lincoln." In many towns such as Sudbury the town clerk "very carefully warned those that were not legally qualified not to vote and prayed the selectmen to be very careful and watchful that nobody voted that was not legally qualified." [11] Even in disputes over specific qualifications, both sides often agreed on the principle of exclusion of the unqualified; contention occurred only over the application of that principle.[12]

Consciousness of voting qualifications colored the conduct of other town affairs as well as elections, as indeed was natural since the meaning of the franchise went so far beyond mere electoral democracy. Protests by men recently arrived in a town could be discredited, as they were in Haverhill in 1748, without any reference to the justice of the protest itself, simply by stating that "many of their petitioners are not qualified to vote in town affairs as may be seen by the selectmen's list of voters, and some of them were never known to reside in town or did we ever hear of them before we saw their petition." Similarly, in the creation of new communities qualification for the franchise could be crucial. Inhabitants of Bridgewater resisted their own inclusion in a precinct proposed by thirty-seven men dwelling in their vicinity by pointing out that "there is not above eleven or twelve that are qualified to vote in town meetings as the law directs." Many towns in their corporate capacity made much the same plea when confronted with an appeal for separation from the community. As Worcester once noted in such a case, more than half the petitioners were "not voters and one is a single Indian." [13]

Such consciousness of qualifications sometimes appeared to be nothing more than an insistence on a "stake in society" in order to participate in the society's deliberations and decisions, but the stake-in-society concept, despite its popularity in the West and its convergence with certain conditions of public life in the province, was not precisely the notion which controlled those restrictions of the franchise which did persist after 1692. It was not out of any intrinsic attachment to that concept, but simply out of a fear that those without property were overly amenable to bribery or other such suasion, that the men of Massachusetts clung to their voting qualifications. As the Essex Result was to state the principle in 1778, "all the members of the state are qualified to make the election, unless they have not suffi-

---

[11] Mass. Archives, CXVII, 302–305; XLIX, 361–362; see also *ibid.*, CXVII, 300, 306–307, 647–649; Jeremiah L. Hanaford, *History of Princeton* (Worcester, Mass., 1852), 23.

[12] See for example, Mass. Archives, CXV, 412–413, 463.

[13] *Ibid.*, 305–308, 144; "Early Records of the Town of Worcester," Worcester Society of Antiquity, *Collections* (Worcester, 1881–1882), II, no. 8, 42–43. See also, Mass. Archives, CXV, 392.

cient discretion, or are so situated as to have no wills of their own." [14] Participation in community decisions was the prerogative of independent men, of *all* a town's independent men, but, ideally, *only* of those. Indeed, it was precisely because of their independence that they had to be accorded a vote, since only by their participation did they bind themselves to concur in the community's chosen course of action. The town meeting was an instrument for enforcement, not—at least not intentionally—a school for democracy.

This logic of competence governed the exclusion of women and children and also accounted for the antipathy to voting by tenants. The basis of the prohibitions which were insisted upon was never so much an objection to poverty *per se*—the stake-in-society argument— as to the tenant's concomitant status of dependence, the pervasive assumption of which emerged clearly in a contested election in Haverhill in 1748. There the petitioners charged that a man had been "refused as a voter under pretense that he was a tenant and so not qualified, when the full reason was that he was a tenant to one of their [the selectmen's] opposers and so at all hazards to be suppressed," while another man, a tenant to one of the selectmen themselves, had been received as a voter though "rated at much less in the last year's taxes than he whom they refused." The protest was thus directed primarily against the abuses of the selectmen: that tenants would do as their landlords desired was simply taken for granted.[15] And naturally the same sort of assumption controlled the exclusion of sons still living with their parents. The voting age of twenty-one was the most rudimentary expression of this requirement of a will of one's own, but the legal age was not very firm at the edges. Like other laws of the province, it could not stand when it came up against local desires, and the age qualifications were often abrogated when unusual dependence or independence was demonstrable, as in the case of the eighteen-year-old who voted in a Sheffield election of 1751 because his father had died and he had become head of his family. As the town's elected representative could declare on that occasion, quite ignoring the legal age requirement, the lad "had a good right to vote, for his estate rested in him and that he was a town-born child and so was an inhabitant." [16]

---

[14] [Theophilus Parsons], *Result of the Convention of Delegates Holden at Ipswich . . .* (Newburyport, 1778), 28–29.

[15] Mass. Archives, CXV, 330–334, 412–413; CXVI, 276–277; CXVII, 84–86, 306–307; "Early Records of Worcester," Worc. Soc. Ant., *Coll.*, II, no. 6, 63.

[16] Mass. Archives, VIII, 278; for a comparable case in the opposite direction see *ibid.*, CXVI, 668–669. Another basis for exclusion was insanity. For a revealing contretemps see *ibid.*, L, 85–88; CXVII, 295–297, 302–305.

Of course, the townsmen of the eighteenth century placed no premium on independence as such. Massachusetts townsmen were expected to be independent but not too independent; ultimately, they were supposed on their own to arrive at the same actions and commitments as their neighbors. Any *genuine* independence, excessive or insufficient, was denigrated if not altogether denied a place in the community. Thus, when a number of inhabitants of a gore of land near Charlton faced the threat of incorporation with the town, they submitted "one word of information" about the townsmen who had asked for that incorporation. The note said only:

Baptist signers	- 7
Churchmen	- 3
Tenants	- 4
Neither tenants nor freeholders but intruders upon other men's property	- 15
The whole of the petitioners in Charlton consisting of 35 in number	

In other words, tenants were tainted, but so too were all others who were their own men, such as squatters and those who dared to differ in religion. In denigrating them, the inhabitants of the gore drew no distinctions; tenant and Baptist were equally offensive because equally outside of orthodoxy, beyond the confines of consensus.[17]

Ultimately almost *any* taint on membership in the homogeneous community was a potential basis for derogation. Some inhabitants of Rutland once even attempted to deny the validity of a town decision merely because many of its supporters were "such as were and are dissenters from the public worship of God in the old meeting-house." And though Rutland's religious orthodoxy was a bit exquisite even for eighteenth-century New England, it was so only in degree. For example, when Sutton opposed the erection of a new district out of parts of itself and several other towns in 1772, the town actually deducted the Anabaptists from the number of signatories to the application—Baptists simply did not count as full citizens. Worcester did the same thing and indeed went even further. Several of the signers of the petition for separation were not heads of families but mere "single persons, some of them transient ones," and so, said the town, were not to be "accounted as part of the number of families the petitioners say are within the limits of the proposed district." Whereas excessively reli-

---

[17] *Ibid.*, CXVII, 86, and see 84–85.

able bonds confined the tenant, no reliable bonds at all attached a single man to the community, and either alternative evoked suspicion.[18]

Ultimately, however, the insistence on orthodoxy did not directly exclude any excessive number, and neither did the property and residence requirements disqualify any great proportion of the province's adult males. In the perspective of the English villages from which the New Englanders came, these very dimensions of disqualification may be better seen, in fact, as defining a broader qualification than had previously prevailed in English practice. Far more fundamentally, the criteria of exclusion were measures of the inclusiveness of the communities of early Massachusetts.

The most fundamental shift that had occurred was the one from property to residence as the irreducible basis of town citizenship. In England, several classes of property-holders were "technically termed inhabitants even though they dwelt in another town"; property defined political citizenship, and only those who held the requisite property in the community directed its affairs. In provincial Massachusetts such stake-in-society notions never prevailed for reasons that had little to do with any abstract attachment to democracy or antipathy to absentee ownership. They never prevailed because the point of the town meeting was not so much the raising of a revenue as it was political government, especially the maintenance of law and order. In Massachusetts it was necessary to act only on the individuals living in each town, and it was imperative to act upon all of them. Of course, taxation as well as residence provided the basis for the ballot in Massachusetts, but that was of a piece with the residence requirement. As early as 1638 "every inhabitant of a town was declared liable for his proportion of the town's charges," in sharp contrast to the towns of England where only a few were so taxed.[19]

The democracy of the Massachusetts towns was, then, a democracy despite itself, a democracy without democrats. But it was still, so far as anything yet said is concerned, a democracy, at least in the simple sense of a widely diffused franchise. Such democracy is admitted—indeed, required—in the analysis advanced above; the objection urged against the defenders of that democracy is not that they are wrong but that they are right for the wrong reasons, or for no reasons at all. When they examine electoral eligibility apart from its social setting

---

[18] *Ibid.*, CXV, 741–742; CXVIII, 613–616, 619; see also *ibid.*, CXVI, 276–277. And others found more reasons to discredit any who stood outside communal orthodoxy. See *ibid.*, CXV, 393–396, 412–413, 596.

[19] Edward Channing, "Town and County Government in the English Colonies of North America," *Johns Hopkins University Studies in Historical and Political Science*, 2d Ser., II, no. 10 (1884), 12, 32.

and when they place franchise democracy at the center of provincial social organization instead of in the peripheral position it actually occupied, they do not condemn their findings to invalidity, only to sterility. They may be correct about the degree of diffusion of the vote, but they can go no further. Within their original terms, they cannot systematically study the purposes of participation, the relative importance of inclusiveness when it confronted competing values, the limits of eligibility and the reasons for them, or, more broadly, the particular texture of the electorate as against abstract statistics.

But if the analysis urged thus far has basically buttressed Brown's position by extending and explaining his statistics, that analysis also has another side. For when we see franchise democracy as a mere incident in the central quest for concord and concurrence among neighbors, we must also observe that the same concern for consensus which promoted wide participation also imposed very significant limitations on the democracy of the provincial community, limitations sufficiently serious to suggest that the democratic appellation itself may be anachronistic when applied to such a society.

For one thing, the ideal of "townsmen together" [20] implied the power of each town to control its own affairs, and that control not only extended to but also depended upon communal control of its membership. From the founding of the first towns communities retained the right to accept only those whom they wished, and that right persisted without challenge to the time of the Revolution. "Such whose dispositions do not suit us, whose society will be hurtful to us," were simply refused admission as enemies of harmony and homogeneity. Dedham's first covenant, "to keepe of from us all such, as ar contrarye minded. And receave onely such unto us as be such as may be probably of one harte," was typical. For inhabitancy was a matter of public rather than private concern, and among the original settlers it scarcely had to be argued that "if the place of our cohabitation be our own, then no man hath right to come in to us without our consent." [21] Consent meant the formal vote of the town or its selectmen, and none were admitted without one or the other. Not even inhabitants themselves could entertain outsiders—"strangers," they were called—with-

---

[20] The phrase is from Conrad M. Arensberg, "American Communities," *American Anthropologist*, LVII (1955), 1150. For affirmations of that ideal as a consummatory value see Mass. Archives, CXIII, 616–617; CIV, 645; CXV, 282–283; CXVI, 527–528; CXVII, 563–565; CLXXXI, 122b–122d.

[21] Sumner C. Powell, *Puritan Village* (Middletown, Conn., 1963), xviii; George L. Haskins, *Law and Authority in Early Massachusetts* (New York, 1960), 70; Josiah Benton, *Warning Out in New England* (Boston, 1911), 8. The early towns also forbade inhabitants to "sell or let their land or houses to strangers without the consent of the town"; see *ibid.*, 18, 19, 23, 87, and William Weeden, *Economic and Social History of New England, 1620–1789* (Boston, 1891), 57.

out the permission of the town, and any who violated the rule were subject to penalties.[22] And of course the original thrust of congregational Puritanism to lodge disciplinary powers with the individual churches rather than with bishops also aimed at more local control of the membership of the local community.[23]

Most of these practices continued unabated into the eighteenth century. Swansea's "foundation settlement" of 1667 provided that "if any person denied any particular in the said agreement they should not be admitted an inhabitant in said town," and half a century later seventy-eight townsmen reaffirmed their commitment to the ancestral covenant. Cotton Mather's manual of 1726, *Ratio Disciplinae Fratrum Nov-Anglorum* (Boston, 1726), described a process of "mutual Conferences" by which men came to "a good understanding" which might be subscribed to by any applicant. And even in the crisis of the dissolution of a church, as at Bellingham in 1747, the congregation could not simply disperse to the nearest convenient towns. Each of the congregants, for all that he had already met the tests of church membership and partaken of communion, had to be accepted anew into the nearby churches and approved by their towns, and in 1754 Sunderland claimed that this right of prior approval was "always customary." [24]

Another customary instrument for the stringent control of access to the town which was also sustained throughout the provincial era was the practice of "warning out." Under this aegis, anyone who did secure entry to the town and was then deemed undesirable could be warned and, if necessary, lawfully ejected from the community. Such a policy was, in some part, a device to escape undue expenses in the support of paupers, but it was also, and more importantly, the product of the powerful communitarian assumptions of the early settlers, and those assumptions did not decline in the eighteenth century. William Weeden found the invocation of warning procedures so common that "the actual occurrences hardly need particular mention," and he concluded that "the old restrictions on the admission of freemen to the municipality, and on the sale of land to outsiders, do not appear to have been relaxed generally" as late as the era immediately preceding the imperial crisis. Town records such as Worcester's were studded with such warnings, from the time of the town's founding to the time

---

[22] Benton, *Warning Out*, 18, 33. And the fines were indeed established and enforced in the towns. See Myron Allen, *The History of Wenham* (Boston, 1860), 26, and Weeden, *Economic and Social History*, 79–80.

[23] Morgan, *Visible Saints*, 10–12, 21.

[24] Mass. Archives, CXIII, 613–615; CXV, 268, 272, 276; XLIX, 380–383; Mather, *Ratio Disciplinae*, Pt. iii, 2. See also Mass. Archives, CXVI, 392–393; CXVII, 15–16. In one case, that of Medway, *ibid.*, XLIX, 380–383, such consideration was not accorded.

of the Revolution itself. In other towns, too, penalties were still imposed for violation of the rules of inhabitancy.[25]

The result was that fundamental differences in values were rarely admitted within a town, while differences of race, nationality, or culture scarcely appeared east of the Hudson River before the Revolution. Massachusetts was more nearly restricted to white Anglo-Saxon Protestants than any other province in English America, with the possible exception of its New England neighbors, Connecticut and New Hampshire. Less than 1 per cent of the quarter of a million Germans who came to the English colonies between 1690 and 1770 came to New England, and the proportion of Irish, Scotch, and Scotch-Irish was little larger. There was no welcome whatsoever for French Catholics and very little encouragement, according to Governor Bellomont, even for the Huguenots.[26] Negroes never attained significant numbers at the Bay—by 1780 they accounted for only 2 per cent of the population of the province and a bare 1 per cent of all Negroes in the Confederation—and the Indians, who once were significant, were on their way to extinction well before the Revolution broke out.[27] Committed to a conception of the social order that precluded pluralism, the townsmen of Massachusetts never made a place for those who were not of their own kind. The community they desired was an enclave of common believers, and to the best of their ability they secured such a society, rooted not only in ethnic and cultural homogeneity but also in common moral and economic ideas and practices. Thus, the character of the community became a critical—and nondemocratic—condition of provincial democracy; for a wide franchise could be ventured only after a society that sought harmony had been made safe for such democracy. In that society it was possible to let men vote precisely because so many men were not allowed entry in the first place.

Thus we can maintain the appearance of democracy only so long as we dwell on elections and elections alone, instead of the entire electoral process. As soon as we depart from that focus, the town meetings of Massachusetts fall short of any decent democratic standard. Wide

---

[25] Weeden, *Economic and Social History*, 519, 673; "Early Records of Worcester," Worc. Soc. Ant., *Coll.*, II, no. 6, 22–23, 102, 122–123; II, no. 8, 19, 27, 57–58, 128; IV, 28, 47, 67, 85, 99, 137, 147, 148, 202, 223. For penalties in other towns, see *Town of Weston: Records of the First Precinct, 1746–1754 and of the Town, 1754–1803* (Boston, 1893), 61, 101, 108, 115, 126; Herman Mann, *Historical Annals of Dedham, from its Settlement in 1635 to 1847* (Dedham, Mass., 1847), 23, 25; Allen, *History of Wenham*, 26.

[26] On the Germans and Scotch-Irish see Clarence Ver Steeg, *The Formative Years, 1607–1763* (New York, 1964), 167–168. On the Huguenots see Charles W. Baird, *History of the Huguenot Emigration to America* (New York, 1885), II, 251–253; G. Elmore Reaman, *The Trail of the Huguenots . . .* (London, 1964), 129.

[27] On the Negro, Marvin Harris, *Patterns of Race in the Americas* (New York, 1964), 84. For some of the story of the extinction of the last Indian town in the province see Mass. Archives, CXVII, 690–691, 733–735.

participation did obtain, but it was premised on stringently controlled access to eligibility, so that open elections presupposed anterior constriction of the electorate. Similarly, most men could vote, but their voting was not designed to contribute to a decision among meaningful alternatives. The town meeting had one prime purpose, and it was not the provision of a neutral battleground for the clash of contending parties or interest groups. In fact, nothing could have been more remote from the minds of men who repeatedly affirmed, to the very end of the provincial period, that "harmony and unanimity" were what "they most heartily wish to enjoy in all their public concerns." Conflict occurred only rarely in these communities, where "prudent and amicable composition and agreement" were urged as preventives for "great and sharp disputes and contentions." When it did appear it was seen as an unnatural and undesirable deviation from the norm. Protests and contested elections almost invariably appealed to unity and concord as the values which had been violated; and in the absence of any socially sanctioned role for dissent, contention was generally surreptitious and scarcely ever sustained for long. The town meeting accordingly aimed at unanimity. Its function was the arrangement of agreement or, more often, the endorsement of agreements already arranged, and it existed for accommodation, not disputation.[28]

Yet democracy devoid of legitimate difference, dissent, and conflict is something less than democracy; and men who are finally to vote only as their neighbors vote have something less than the full range of democratic options. Government by mutual consent may have been a step in the direction of a deeper-going democracy, but it should not be confused with the real article. Democratic consent is predicated upon legitimate choice, while the town meetings of Massachusetts in the provincial era, called as they were to reach and register accords, were still in transition from assent to such consent. The evidence for such a conclusion exists in an abundance of votes from all over the province on all manner of matters "by the free and united consent of the whole" or "by a full and Unanimous Vote that they are Easie and satisfied With What they have Done." [29] Most men may have been eligible to vote, but their voting did not settle differences unless most men voted together. In fact, differences had no defined place in the society that voting could have settled, for that was not in the nature of town politics. Unanimity was expected ethically as well as empirically. Indeed, it was demanded as a matter of social decency, so that even the

---

[28] Mass. Archives, CXVIII, 707–712, 715–717. The theme is omnipresent in the records of the towns and of such conflicts as did occur. See Zuckerman, *Massachusetts Town in the Eighteenth Century,* especially chap. 3.

[29] Mass. Archives, CXVIII, 388–390; *Weston Records,* II. See also Mass. Archives CXVI, 446–447; CXVIII, 715–717; "Records of Worcester," Worc. Soc. Ant., *Coll.,* II, no. 8, 43, 75; IV, 18, 173, 264–266.

occasional cases of conflict were shaped by the canons of concord and consensus, with towns pleading for the preservation of "peace and unanimity" as "the only occasion of our petitioning." [30]

This demand for unanimity found its ultimate expression in rather frequent denials of one of the most elementary axioms of democratic theory, the principle of majority rule. A mere majority often commanded scant authority at the local level and scarcely even certified decisions as legitimate. In communities which provided no regular place for minorities a simple majority was not necessarily sufficient to dictate social policy, and many men such as the petitioners from the old part of Berwick were prepared to say so quite explicitly. Since its settlement some eighty or ninety years earlier, that town had grown until by 1748 the inhabitants of the newer parts easily outnumbered the "ancient settlers" and wished to establish a new meetinghouse in a place which the inhabitants of the older parts conceived injurious to their interest. Those who lived in the newer parts of town had the votes, but the "ancient settlers" were icily unimpressed nonetheless. Injury could not be justified "merely because a major vote of the town is or may be obtained to do it," the petitioners protested. They would suffer "great hurt and grievance," and "for no other reason than this: a major vote to do it, which is all the reason they have for the same." Equity, on the other hand, required a "just regard" for the old part of town and its inhabitants. They "ought"to retain their privileges despite their loss of numerical preponderance. And that principle was no mere moral fabrication of a desperate minority. Six years earlier the Massachusetts General Court had endorsed exactly the same position in a similar challenge to the prerogatives of numerical power by the "ancient part" of another town, and in the Berwick controversy the town majority itself tacitly conceded the principle upon which the old quarter depended. Accusing the old quarter of "gross mis-representation," the rest of the town now maintained that there had been a disingenuous confusion of geography and population. There could be no question as to the physical location of the old town, but, as to its inhabitants, "the greatest part of the ancient settlers and maintainers of the ministry do live to the northward of the old meetinghouse and have always kept the same in times of difficulty and danger." The newer townsmen, then, did not deny that ancient settlers were entitled to special consideration; they simply denied that the inhabitants of the old quarter were in fact the ancient settlers.[31]

Antiquity restricted majoritarianism elsewhere as well in demands of old settlers and in determinations of the General Court. In Lancaster as in Berwick, for example, a "standing part" could cite efforts

---

[30] Mass. Archives, L, 30–31; CXV, 479–480; CXVI, 709–710.
[31] *Ibid.,* CXV, 368–375, 377–378, 393–396.

to disrupt the old order which had been rejected by the Court as unreasonable, "and now though they have obtained a vote from the town the case still remains equally unreasonable." In other towns, too, a majority changed nothing.[32] Consensus comprehended justice and history as well as the counting of a vote. In such a society a case could not be considered solely in its present aspects, as the original inhabitants of Lunenburg made quite clear. "What great discouragement must it needs give to any new settler," those old ones inquired,

> to begin a settlement and go through the difficulties thereof, which are well known to such as have ever engaged in such service, if when, so soon as ever they shall through the blessing of heaven upon their diligence and industry have arrived to live in some measure peaceably and comfortably, if then, after all fatigues and hardships undergone, to be cut to pieces and deprived of charter privileges and rights, and instead of peace and good harmony, contention and confusion introduced, there will be no telling what to trust to.[33]

Nor was history the only resort for the repudiation of a majority. Other men offered other arguments, and some scarcely deigned to argue at all. In a contested election in Haverhill, for example, one side simply denied any authority at all to a majority of the moment. It was, they said, nothing but the creature of "a few designing men who have artfully drawn in the multitude and engaged them in their own cause." That, they argued, was simply "oppression." The merchants of Salem similarly refused to accept the hazards of populistic politics, though their refusal was rather more articulate. The town meeting had enacted a tax schedule more advantageous to the farmers than to themselves, and the merchants answered that they felt no force in that action, because "the major part of those who were present were [farmers], and the vote then passed was properly their vote and not the vote of the whole body of the town." That legitimacy and obligation attached only to a vote of the whole community was simply assumed by the merchants, as they sought a subtle separation of a town ballot—sheer majoritarianism—from a "vote of the whole body of the town"—a notion akin to the general will—for which the consent of every part of the population was requisite.[34]

---

[32] *Ibid.*, CXIV, 613–614; CXIII, 275–276; CXVI, 736–738.

[33] *Ibid.*, CXVII, 165–169. In this case, nonetheless, the general Court declined to accept the argument and thus afforded no special safeguard to the original settlers. For similar cases without the adverse action of the Court see *ibid.*, CXIV, 286–288; CXV, 729–730.

[34] *Ibid.*, 330–334, 596.

Disdain for direct democracy emerged even more explicitly and sweepingly in a petition from the west precinct of Bridgewater in 1738. The precinct faced the prospect of the loss of its northern part due to a town vote authorizing the northern inhabitants to seek separation as an independent town, and the precinct feared that the loss would be fatal. Accordingly, the parishioners prayed the General Court's intervention, and after briefly disputing the majority itself, the precinct allowed that, whether or not a majority in the town *had* been obtained, such a majority *could* be contrived. "We own it is easy for the two neighboring parishes joining with the petitioners to vote away our just rights and privileges and to lay heavy burdens upon us, which they would not be willing to touch with the ends of their fingers." Yet for all the formal validity of such a vote, the precinct would not have assented to it or felt it to be legitimate, "for we trust that your Excellency and Honors will not be governed by numbers but by reason and justice." Other men elsewhere urged the same argument; perhaps none caught the provincial paradox of legality without legitimacy any better than the precinct of Salem Village, soon to become the independent town of Danvers. After a recitation of the imposition it had suffered from the town of Salem for no reason but superior numbers, the village came to its indictment of the town: "we don't say but you have had a legal right to treat us so, but all judgment without mercy is tedious to the flesh." [35]

Typically in such cases, the defense against this indictment was not an invocation of majority rights but rather a denial of having employed them oppressively. Both sides, therefore, operated upon an identical assumption. One accused the other of taking advantage of its majority, the other retorted that it had done no such thing, but neither disputed the principle that majority disregard of a minority was indefensible. [36]

This principle was no mere pious protestation. In Kittery, for instance, the parent parish complained that the men who later became the third parish had "long kept us in very unhappy circumstances . . . counter-acting us in all our proceedings" until finally "we were obliged to come into an agreement with them for dividing the then-lower parish of Kittery into two separate parishes," yet it was conceded on both sides that the old inhabitants enjoyed an easy numerical supremacy. Had they been disposed to employ it, almost any amount of "counter-acting" could have been contained and ultimately quashed, so far as votes in public meeting were concerned. But the parish clearly did not rely upon simple majoritarian procedures. It was

[35] *Ibid.*, CXIV, 244–246, 244a, 786–788; also CXVII, 463–465.
[36] *Ibid.*, CXV, 866, 872–875; CXVIII, 388–390; CLXXXI, 133–134, 139.

more than morality that made consensus imperative; it was also the incapacity for coercion without widespread consent. It was the same incapacity which shaped a hundred other accomodations and abnega-
tions across the province, which enabled some "aggrieved brethern" in
Rehoboth to force the resignation of a minister, which paralyzed the
town of Upton in the relocation of its meetinghouse. "All are agreed
that it should be removed or a new one built," a town petition explained, "but cannot agree upon the place." In the absence of agreement they could see no way to act at all on their own account; there
was never any thought of constructing a coalition within the town or
contending for a majority.[37]

Ultimately almost every community in the province shared Upton's
determination "to unite the people." Disputes, when they arose at all,
were commonly concluded by "a full and amicable agreement" in
which all parties "were in peace and fully satisfied," and the conflicts
that did occur evoked no efforts at resolution in a majoritarian manner. "Mutual and general advantage" was the condition of town continuance in "one entire corporate body." [38] But that corporate ethos
was something distant indeed from democracy, and electoral eligibility
is, therefore, an unsatisfactory index even of political participation, let
alone of any more meaningful democracy. Most men may have been
able to vote in the eighteenth-century town, but the town's true politics were not transacted at the ballot box so much as at the tavern and
all the other places, including the meeting itself, where men met and
negotiated so that the vote might be a mere ratification, rather than a
decision among significant alternatives. Alternatives were antithetical
to the safe conduct of the community as it was conceived at the Bay,
and so to cast a vote was only to participate in the consolidation of
the community, not to make a choice among competing interests or
ideals.

Accordingly, the claim for middle-class democracy in provincial
Massachusetts simply cannot be sustained from the figures on electoral eligibility; relevant participation resided elsewhere than in the final, formal vote. And yet, ironically, local politics may have been
democratic indeed, at least in the limited terms of political participation, since a politics of consensus required consultation with most of
the inhabitants in order to assure accord. In little towns of two or
three hundred adult males living in close, continuing contact, men
may very well have shared widely a sense of the amenability of the po-

---

[37] *Ibid.*, CXV, 872–875; CXVI, 276–277; CXVIII, 207; George H. Tilton, *A History of Rehoboth, Massachusetts* (Boston, 1918), 106–107, 102.

[38] Mass. Archives, CXV, 461–462; CXVIII, 526, 707–712; see also Samuel A. Bates, ed., *Records of the Town of Braintree, 1640 to 1793* (Randolph, Mass., 1886), 69–70.

litical process to their own actions and attitudes, and the feeling of involvement may well have been quite general. But to find out we will have to go beyond counting heads or tallying the town treasurers' lists.

The Origins of Afro-American Society in Tidewater Maryland and Virginia, 1700 to 1790

ALLAN KULIKOFF

The history of slavery is a topic of perennial interest to U.S. historians. Only in very recent years, however, have scholars attempted to draw a complete picture of the institution from the inside by investigating the cultural and communal life of slaves and subjecting it to the same sort of searching analysis that they have brought to bear on the life of the Europeans who established the institution in the first place. In the next article by Allan Kulikoff and the following one by Philip D. Morgan, two ingenious historians offer their interpretation of black life in the Chesapeake Tidewater and South Carolina, respectively.

Kulikoff, who has been one of the leading social historians of the colonial South, takes on a complex set of issues with significant implications for all of American history. By undertaking a strategy that includes economic, political, and religious factors, as well as family history, Kulikoff offers a persuasive portrait of the

From Allan Kulikoff, "The Origins of Afro-American Society in Tidewater Maryland and Virginia, 1700–1790," *William and Mary Quarterly*, XXXV (1978), 226–259. Reprinted with permission of the author.

formative period in African American history. In addition, his research contains innovative approaches to the use of evidence that previous scholars either ignored or were unable to exploit to enhance understanding of black as well as white Southern culture.

At another level, of course, Kulikoff seeks to understand an even more profound and difficult issue: the relationship between race and culture. Kulikoff argues that African Americans were able to develop a remarkably independent communal and cultural life, even within the constraints that slavery imposed. He goes on to suggest that this independent cultural life has been remarkably enduring. What are the full implications of this argument? Are those critics correct who think that Kulikoff is asking the evidence to carry more explanatory weight than it can reasonably bear? Of the many factors he identifies as being crucial to black life in early America, which are most important and precisely what sort of impact did they have?

Although the eighteenth-century Chesapeake planter looked upon newly enslaved Africans as strange and barbaric folk, he knew that American-born slaves could be taught English customs. Hugh Jones, a Virginia cleric, commented in 1724 that "the languages of the new Negroes are various harsh jargons," but added that slaves born in Virginia "talk good English, and affect our language, habits, and customs." [1] How readily slaves in Maryland, Virginia, and other British colonies accepted English ways is currently a subject of controversy. Some scholars hold that the preponderance of whites in the population was so large, and the repressive power of whites over blacks so great, that slaves in the Chesapeake colonies were forced to accept Anglo-American beliefs, values, and skills. Other writers maintain that slave migrants and their descendents created indigenous social institutions within the framework of white rule.[2] This essay supports the second position by describing how slaves living in Maryland and Virginia during the eighteenth century developed their own community life.

---

[1] Hugh Jones, *The Present State of Virginia . . .*, ed. Richard L. Morton (Chapel Hill, N.C., 1956 [orig. publ. London, 1724]), 75–76. For other contemporary comparisons of African and native slaves see William Stevens Perry, *Papers Relating to the Church in Virginia, 1650–1776*, I (Geneva, N.Y., 1870), 264–265, 280, 293, 297.

[2] Gerald W. Mullin, *Flight and Rebellion: Slave Resistance in Eighteenth Century Virginia* (New York, 1972), chaps. 2–3, argues that native slaves in Virginia assimilated white norms. Herbert G. Gutman, *The Black Family in Slavery and Freedom, 1750–1925* (New York, 1976), chap. 8 and Allan Kulikoff, "The Beginnings of the Afro-American Family in Maryland," in Aubrey C. Land, *et al.*, eds., *Law, Society, and Politics in Early Maryland* (Baltimore, 1977), 171–196, hereafter cited as Kulikoff, "Beginnings of the Afro-American Family," maintains that slaves in the region developed their own society and culture.

The proponents of the idea that Afro-Americans developed a distinctive social structure and culture are divided over the extent of the survival of African forms and structures in the Americas. Sidney W. Mintz and Richard Price have recently published a provocative analysis of the process of slave acculturation in the New World. Blacks who were brought to the Americas, they argue, did not have a common culture. Their religious beliefs, kinship systems, and forms of social organization differed substantially. Nevertheless, Mintz and Price add, West Africans did share some values and experiences. For example, each West African group developed different kinship practices, but throughout the region each person located his place in society by his position in his kin group and lineage. When Africans arrived in the New World, their cultural differences were initially of greater significance than the values they shared. They were not *"communities* of people at first, and they could only become communities by processes of cultural change. What they shared at the outset was their enslavement; all—or nearly all—else had to be *created by them."* The features of the society they formed, Mintz and Price assert, depended upon the demands of the white masters, the characteristics of the economy, the demography of slave and white populations, and the extent of ethnic divisions among blacks. As they interacted daily among themselves, slaves learned to cope with ordinary problems of working, eating, marrying, and childrearing under the conditions of slavery. The social institutions they developed were neither imposed by Europeans nor directly taken from African communities, but were a unique combination of elements borrowed from the European enslavers and from various African societies that held common values. "Once effective slave institutions became operative among a miscellaneous aggregate of slaves, that aggregate . . . would begin to become a community. Thereupon, the more divisive or disruptive aspects of life could begin to work themselves out against the existing structure of behavioral patterns," and slaves could place their new, Afro-American structures in a settled social context.[3]

Mintz and Price describe a process of cultural change that may have been common in slave societies, but they do not adequately explain how specific social institutions and values emerged in particular areas

---

[3] Sidney W. Mintz and Richard Price, *An Anthropological Approach to the Afro-American Past: A Caribbean Perspective*, ISHI Occasional Papers in Social Change, No. 2 (Philadelphia, 1976), 1–21. Quotations are found on pp. 9 and 21. I am indebted to Mr. Mintz for permitting me to read versions of this essay before its publication. "Society," as used here, concerns social institutions and structures such as family, government, work groups, or churches; "culture" includes values and beliefs that motivate and justify behavior in a society. A belief that witches ought to suffer death is part of a group's culture, but the act of killing a witch takes place in the society's governmental or religious structures.

and they pass over lightly the specific ways in which the economic and demographic structures of a region limited the kind of culture and society that slaves were able to develop. Nor do Mintz and price suggest how the length of the process of slave acculturation might vary in places with differing economic and demographic structures.

The size of working units, the density of black population, the pattern of African immigration and the proportion of whites in the population greatly influenced the development of slave societies and cultures. Some crops required large plantations; others could be grown on small farms. Since large plantation areas needed more slaves than did small farm regions, they attracted greater numbers of slave immigrants and, consequently, major plantation regions often had greater concentrations of slaves and a larger proportion of immigrants in their slave population than areas dominated by small farms. Slaves who lived on a large plantation in a region where a substantial majority of the people were black and the density of the slave population was great probably had more opportunities to worship their gods, begin stable families, and develop their own communities than did slaves who lived on a small quarter in a preponderantly white country. A slave who lived with many Africans in a place where constant, heavy immigration of blacks kept the proportion of Africans high was more likely to adapt African customs than the slave who lived where migration was sporadic, the proportion of immigrants among adult blacks low, and the numbers of whites great.[4]

The slave economy and black population patterns found in the Chesapeake colonies can be adequately analyzed from existing sources, but the specific content of the culture and society slaves formed is far more difficult to determine. While probate inventories and wills, plantation accounts and vital registers, and British naval office records allow a detailed reconstruction of crop production, slave imports, the distribution of slaves on plantations, and the density, as well as the ethnic and demographic composition, of the black population, the exact connection between these variables and slave institutions, beliefs, and values cannot be precisely defined. However, occasional descriptions of slaves' reactions to their conditions, slave beliefs, and slave behavior can be found in planters' letters, plantation records,

---

[4] These comments are based upon my reading of Mintz and Price, *Anthropological Approach* and upon the following works: Richard S. Dunn, *Sugar and Slaves: The Rise of the Planter Class in the English West Indies, 1624–1715* (Chapel Hill, N.C., 1972); Orlando Patterson, *The Sociology of Slavery: An Analysis of the Origins, Development and Structure of Slave Society in Jamaica* (London, 1967), Peter H. Wood, *Black Majority: Negroes in Colonial South Carolina from 1677 through the Stono Rebellion* (New York, 1974); Mullin, *Flight and Rebellion;* and Russell R. Menard, "The Maryland Slave Population, 1658 to 1730: A Demographic Profile of Blacks in Four Counties," *William and Mary Quarterly*, 3d Ser., XXXII (1975), 29–54.

local court order books, and newspaper ads for runaways. These kinds of information are used here to suggest plausible connections between demographic structures and slave society, but the data are often fragmentary and much more must be found before firm statements can be made.

Data from tidewater Maryland and Virginia suggest that African and Afro-American slaves developed a settled community life very slowly. Three stages of community development can be discerned. From roughly 1650 to 1690, blacks assimilated the norms of white society, but the growth of the number of blacks also triggered white repression. The period from about 1690 to 1740 was an era of heavy black immigration, small plantation sizes, and social conflicts among blacks. The infusion of Africans often disrupted newly formed slave communities. Finally, from 1740 to 1790, immigration declined and then stopped, plantation sizes increased, the proportion of blacks in the population grew, and divisions among slaves disappeared; consequently, native blacks in the tidewater formed settled communities.

Between 1650 and 1690 two demographic patterns shaped black life. Tobacco was the region's cash crop, and most planters were men of moderate means who could afford few slaves. Therefore, blacks constituted a very small percentage of the Chesapeake population— only about 3 percent (or 1,700) of the people in 1650 and 15 percent in 1690 (or 11,500). Most slaves lived on small plantations of fewer than eleven blacks. Moreover, almost all slaves were immigrants, and most came to the Chesapeake from the West Indies. Some had recently arrived in the islands from Africa; others had lived there a long time or had been born there.[5]

These characteristics led blacks toward assimilation in the Chesapeake colonies. Natives of the islands and long-time residents knew English and were experienced in slavery; new African slaves soon learned English in order to communicate with masters and most other blacks. Blacks and whites worked together in the fields, and blacks learned to imitate the white servants by occasionally challenging the master's authority. Seventeenth-century Englishmen perceived Africans as an alien, evil, libidinous, and heathen people, but even they saw that their slaves did not fit this description, and whites treated many blacks as they did white servants. Some black residents became and remained free.[6]

---

[5] Wesley Frank Craven, *Red, White and Black: The Seventeenth-Century Virginian* (Charlottesville, 1971), 84, 93–95, 97; U.S. Bureau of the Census, *Historical Statistics of the United States, Colonial Times to 1970* (Washington, D.C., 1976), 1168, hereafter cited as *Historical Statistics*; Menard, "Md. Slave Population," *WMQ*, 3d Ser., XXXII (1975), 34–35.

[6] Edmund S. Morgan, *American Slavery—American Freedom: The Ordeal of Colonial Virginia* (New York, 1975), 154–156, 310–315; Winthrop D. Jordan, *White over Black:*

After 1660 the lot of blacks deteriorated; stringent racial laws were passed in Virginia each year between 1667 and 1672, and in 1680, 1682, and 1686.[7] The timing of these laws was due in part to the growth and changing composition of the black population. The number of blacks in the Chesapeake colonies doubled in every decade but one from 1650 to 1690, while white population grew more slowly. African slaves began to be imported directly from Africa for the first time around 1680; from 1679 to 1686, seven ships with about 1,450 slaves arrived in Virginia from Africa.[8] These blacks seemed to Englishmen to be the strange, libidinous, heathenish, and disobedient people they believed typical of Africans.

Africans continued to pour into the Chesapeake: from 1700 to 1740, roughly 43,000 blacks entered Virginia, about 39,000 of whom were Africans. The proportion of Africans among all slave immigrants rose from about 73 percent between 1710 and 1718 to 93 percent between 1727 and 1740.[9] Over half, and perhaps three-quarters, of the immigrant slaves went to a few lower tidewater counties, while some of the rest worked in the upper tidewater.[10] The proportion of recent immigrants among black slave adults fluctuated with trade cycles: about one-half in 1709, one-third in 1720, one-half in 1728, and one-third in 1740 had left Africa or the West Indies within ten years.[11]

American Attitudes toward the Negro, 1550–1812 (Chapel Hill, N.C., 1968), chap. I; Ross M. Kimmel, "Free Blacks in Seventeenth-Century Maryland," *Maryland Historical Magazine*, LXXI (1976), 19–25; Warren M. Billings, "The Case of Fernando and Elizabeth Key: A Note on the Status of Blacks in Seventeenth-Century Virginia," *WMQ*, 3d Ser., XXX (1973), 468–474; James H. Brewer, "Negro Property Holders in Seventeenth-Century Virginia," *Ibid.*, XII (1955), 575–580.

[7] Jordan, *White over Black*, 71–82. A useful compilation of Virginia's laws on slaves and servants can be found in Betty W. W. Coyle, "The Treatment of Slaves and Servants in Colonial Virginia" (M.A. thesis, College of William and Mary, 1974), 100–108.

[8] *Historical Statistics*, 756; Allan Kulikoff, "A 'Prolifick' People: Black Population Growth in the Chesapeake Colonies," *Southern Studies*, XVI (1977), 391–428.

[9] Elizabeth Donnan, ed., *Documents Illustrative of the Slave Trade to America* (Washington, D.C., 1931–1935), IV, 172–174, corrected with original Naval Officer Returns; Kulikoff, " 'Prolifick' Prople," *So. Studies*, XVI (1977), 391–428.

[10] This assertion is based upon an analysis of slave ages judged in the York and Lancaster counties Court Order Books, 1710–1740, found in the Virginia State Library, Richmond. From 1680 to the Revolution the name and age of every black immigrant under 16 had to be registered with the local court. William Waller Hening, ed., *The Statutes at Large, Being a Collection of All the Laws of Virginia* (Richmond, 1819–1823), II, 479–480, III, 258–259, VI, 40–41. I estimated the number of immigrants coming to tidewater by (1) multiplying the numbers of ages judged by four to estimate the number of adult immigrants; and (2) multiplied the resulting York total by 10 (York, Gloucester, James City, New Kent, Charles City, Elizabeth City, Warwick, Surry, Isle of Wright, and Accomac-Northampton equalled York's total) and the Lancaster figures by seven (Northumberland, Richmond, Middlesex, King and Queen, King William, and Westmoreland equalled Lancaster's totals). This procedure yielded the following tidewater shares of total Virginia black immigration: 41 to 75% in the 1720s (mean 56%), 41 to 95% in the 1730s (mean 59%), and 19 to 58% in the 1740s (mean 36%).

This immigration affected every facet of black life in tidewater, for every few years native blacks and earlier comers had to absorb many recently imported Africans into their ranks.

The demographic composition of slave cargoes suggests that Africans had a difficult time establishing a regular family life after their arrival in the Chesapeake. The slave ships usually carried two men for every woman. Children composed less than one-fifth of imported slaves, and there was a similar surplus of boys over girls. Very young children were infrequent in these cargoes; perhaps three-quarters of them were aged ten to fourteen, and nearly all the rest were eight or nine.[12]

Nonetheless, newly enslaved Africans possessed a few building blocks for a new social order under slavery. Many shared a similar ethnic identity. Data from Port York for two periods of heavy immigration show that about half the African migrants were Ibos from Nigeria, while another one-fifth came from Angola.[13] From 1718 to 1726, 60 percent came from Biafra; between 1728 and 1739, 85 percent migrated from Biafra or Angola.[14] (See Table I.) Most immigrants spoke similar languages, lived under the same climate, cultivated similar crops, and shared comparable kinship systems.[15] When they arrived in the Chesapeake, they may have been able to combine common threads in their societies and cultures into new Afro-American structures with some ease.

Before Africans could reconstruct their lives, they had to survive the middle passage, the demoralizing experience of being sold, and the stresses of their first year in the Chesapeake. The terrible hardships of the middle passage are well known. Africans were often packed naked

---

[12] *Ibid.*

[13] Most Africans from Biafra were Ibos. Philip D. Curtin, *The Atlantic Slave Trade: A Census* (Madison, Wis., 1969), 157–158, 161, 188, 245; Roger Anstey, *The Atlantic Slave Trade and British Abolition, 1760–1810* (Atlantic Highlands, N.J., 1975), 70–72. Other groups, especially Ibibio, Efkin, and "Mokos," also came from the region. Angola encompassed a larger area and no single group dominated the trade. *Ibid.*, 60.

[14] Curtin, *Atlantic Slave Trade*, 157–158, and Herbert S. Klein, "Slaves and Shipping in Eighteenth-Century Virginia," *Journal of Interdisciplinary History*, V (1975), 388–389, argue from this data that the distribution of Africans migrating to Virginia was relatively random. But both included all Africans who entered all Virginia ports for most of the 18th century. The York totals given in Table I include most of the slaves whose origins were recorded. For example, the 5,818 slaves reported for York, 1728–1739, constitute 46% of all those listed in Donnan, ed., *Documents of Slave Trade*, IV, 40, for the 1727–1769 period and 61% when the vague "Guinea" origin is eliminated.

[15] C. K. Meek, *Law and Authority in a Nigerian Tribe: A Study in Indirect Rule* (London, 1937), chap. 1; Ikenna Nzimiro, *Studies in Ibo Political Systems: Chieftancy and Politics in Four Niger States* (Berkeley and Los Angeles, 1972), 25–29; "The Early Travels of Olaudah Equiano" (1789), in Philip D. Curtin, *et al.*, eds., *Africa Remembered: Narratives by West Africans from the Era of the Slave Trade* (Madison, Wis., 1967), 69–88; Jan Vansina, *Kingdoms of the Savanna* (Madison, Wis., 1966), chap. 1 and 191–197.

	Geographic Origins of Africans Entering
TABLE I	Port York, Virginia, 1718 to 1739

PORT OF ORIGIN	Percentage of Slaves Entering York	
	1718–1726	1728–1739
Bight of Biafra	60	44
Angola	5	41
Gold Coast	13	5
Senegambia	4	10
Madagascar	9	
Windward Coast	7	
Sierra Leone	1	
Total	99	100
Number Known	8400	5818
Total Number	8613	8786
Percent Unknown	3	34

Source: Elizabeth Donnan, ed., *Documents Illustrative of the Slave Trade to America* (Washington, D.C., 1931–1935), IV, 183–185, 188–204. The categories are taken from Philip D. Curtin, *The Atlantic Slave Trade: A Census* (Madison, Wis., 1969), 128–130.

into crowded and unsanitary ships, coffled together much of the time, and fed a starchy diet. Perhaps one in five died en route. Although they sometimes managed to develop friendships with shipmates that mitigated their misery, these fragile connections were usually destroyed after the ships made port.[16] The survivors arrived tired, weak, and sick from their long voyage. Records from the period 1710 to 1718 indicate that about one-twentieth of them died before they could be sold.[17] The sales took place aboard ship, and the slaves were bought one by one, in pairs, or in larger groups over several afternoons. The buyers were strange white men and women, fully clothed and healthy and speaking an alien tongue, who peered and poked all over the Africans' bodies. After the sale, some shipmates left with different masters, while others were returned to their chains to be sold another day.[18]

Many slaves had to endure the indignity of slave sales many times before they were finally purchased. Early in the century, some slave

[16] Daniel P. Mannix and Malcolm Cowley, *Black Cargoes: A History of the Atlantic Slave Trade, 1518–1865* (New York, 1962), chap. 5; Mintz and Price, *Anthropological Approach*, 22–23. Curtin, *Atlantic Slave Trade*, 277, shows that Nantes traders between 1715 and 1741 lost about 19% of their slaves in transit (mean of five-year cohorts).

[17] Donnan, ed., *Documents of Slave Trade*, IV, 175–181.

[18] Robert Carter Diary, 1722–1727, Sept. 18, 20, 21, 27, 29, 1727, Alderman Library, University of Virginia, Charlottesville; Mullin, *Flight and Rebellion*, 14; Gregory A. Stiverson and Patrick H. Butler III, eds., "Virginia in 1732: *The Travel Journal of William Hugh Grove*," *Virginia Magazine of History and Biography*, LXXXV (1977), 31–32.

ships sold Africans in Barbados and then came to Yorktown; in the
1720s and 1730s, slavers went first to Yorktown and then upriver to
West Point or to ports on the Rappahannock River.[19] Once they arrived in Virginia, slaves were shown to customers for an average of
two to five days before being bought.[20] How often an African was
placed on sale depended upon the individual's age, sex, and health, and
the state of the market for slaves. Planters purchased healthy men
first; women and children were second and third choices; unhealthy
slaves were sold last. Women and children were sometimes bought by
middlemen who took them from the ship and sold them in the interior of the province.[21]

Despite the degradation of the slave sale, Africans made a small beginning toward a new community life as they traveled several days to
the masters' plantations. Although they had left most of their shipmates behind, they usually walked in groups and could use the trip to
renew old friendships or make new ones. Only about one-third of the
Africans in five samples drawn from the years 1689 to 1721 were pur-

[19] Between 1710 and 1718, 41% of all Africans stopped first in the Islands; 15% from
1732 to 1739 were displayed there first. Donnan, ed., *Documents of Slave Trade*, IV,
175–204, compared with *ibid.*, II, 299–300, 427–432; see also *Virginia Gazette* (Parks),
Apr. 21, 1738, and Aug. 10, 1739. Donnan, ed., *Documents of Slave Trade*, IV, 175–206,
shows that from 1710 to 1733 from 72 to 81% of African immigrants entered York and
17 to 20% came to Rappahannock (grouped years 1710–1718, 1718–1727, 1727–1733);
1735–1740, 58% York, 18% Rappahannock, 12% Upper James. For West Point, see
ibid., 101 (Greyhound, 1723) and *Va. Gaz.*, June 1, 1739. For Yorktown, see *ibid.*, Apr. 8,
1737, and June 8, 1739. For Yorktown and West Point see *ibid.*, Aug. 19, 1739. For Rappahannock (from York), see Augustus Moore to Isaac Hobhouse, May 3, 1723, in Walter
E. Minchinton, ed., "The Virginia Letters of Isaac Hobhouse, Merchant of Bristol,"
VMHB, LXVI (1958), 294.

[20] Data are from two ships consigned to Robert Carter: the *John and Betty*, the third
ship at Rappahannock in 1727 (2.2 days), and the *Rose*, the last ship at Rappahannock in
1727 (5.3 days). Both ships had high proportions of women and children. Robert Carter
Diary, July 17-Aug. 3 and Sept. 18-Oct. 5, 1727; Carter to John Pemberton, July 26,
1727 (added to June 28 letter), and Carter to George Eskridge, Sept. 21, 1727, Robert
Carter Letterbooks, 1727–1728, Virginia Historical Society, Richmond. There were
three slaves on the *Rose* unaccounted for.

[21] "Sale of the Charfield Slaves Begun July 23, 1717 Belonging to Samuel Jacobs and
Company, Bristol," Stephen Loyd-John Tayloe Account Book, Va. Hist. Soc.; John Baylor Account Book, 1719–1721, Baylor Papers, Alderman Lib., Univ. Va., 139, 162–164;
Robert Carter to Messrs. Francis Chamberlayne and Francis Sitwell, July 26, 1720, and
Sept. 27, 1727, in Louis B. Wright, ed., *Letters of Robert Carter, 1720–1727: The Commercial Interests of a Virginia Gentleman* (San Marino, Calif., 1940), 41–43, 52–53 (the date is
misprinted on the second letter). The 1717 *Charfield* sale record is listed in order of purchase but the day of sale is not indicated (compare Tayloe to Jacobs, July, 1719. Loyd-
Tayloe Account Book, where Tayloe relates that John Baylor sold the last slaves to Mr.
Robinson with the purchase of two slaves by William Robinson recorded as the next-to-
last entry in the sale record). Baylor sold the following slaves, page by page: (1) 17 men,
6 women, 4 boys, 1 girl; (2) 19 men, 9 women, 7 boys, 8 girls; (3) 16 men, 8 women, 5
boys, 1 girl; (4) 7 men, 8 women, 7 boys, 1 girl; (5) 12 men, 4 women, 5 boys, 1 girl.
Page 5 included 2 old men, 3 sick women, and a "bursten boy."

chased singly; about one-fourth left in pairs and the rest in larger groups. (See Table II.) Furthermore, slaves destined for different masters may have traveled together whenever a planter who lived more than a day's trip from the sale site asked a neighbor going to the sale to buy a slave for him.[22]

Once they entered the plantation world, African immigrants had to begin to cope with their status. The absolute distinction between slavery and freedom found in the Chesapeake colonies did not exist in West African societies. African communities and kin groups possessed a wide range of rights-in-persons. A captive in war might end up as anything from a chattel, who could be sold, to the wife of one of the victorious tribesmen; he might become a soldier, domestic servant, or agricultural laborer. At first, such outsiders would be strangers, but eventually they or their children could move from marginality to partial or full membership in a kin group or community.[23]

When they reached their new homes, Africans were immediately put to work making tobacco. Most were broken in on the most routine tasks of production. Nearly two-thirds of them arrived between June and August, when the tobacco plants had already been moved from seed beds and were growing rapidly. The new slaves' first task was weeding between the rows of plants with hands, axes, or hoes. These jobs were similar to those that Ibos and other Africans had used in growing other crops in their native lands. After a month or two of such labor, slaves could be instructed in the more difficult task of harvesting.[24] Some Africans refused to accept this new work discipline, either not understanding or pretending not to understand their mas-

---

[22] Even Robert Carter had slaves delivered to him on occasion. Carter to [??] [May 21, 1728], Carter Letterbooks, Va. Hist. Soc. I estimated distance of purchasers from the *Charfield*, which was berthed at Urbanna on the Rappahannock (John Tayloe to Samuel Jacobs and Co., July 1727, Loyd-Tayloe Account Book), from data in Clayton Torrence, comp., *Virginia Wills and Administrations, 1632–1800 . . .* (Richmond [1931]). Only purchasers who lived on the Middle Peninsula or the Northern Neck were included. A buyer was identified with a county if a man with the same name was listed in Torrence or if there were substantial numbers of decedents with his family name in only one county. This procedure is subject to errors of commission and omission. After identifying the purchasers, I assumed that masters lived in the middle of the county, measured mileage from Urbanna on a modern road map, and then multiplied the mileage by 1.25 because colonial roads were rarely direct. I identified the destinations of 75/128 slaves sold at this sale to planters (those probably resold were excluded), and the mean distance traveled was 37 miles, a trip of about two days. For travel times see Allan Kulikoff, "Tobacco and Slaves: Population, Economy, and Society in Eighteenth-Century Prince George's County, Maryland" (Ph.D. diss., Brandeis University, 1976), 338.

[23] Igor Kopytoff and Suzanne Miers, "African 'Slavery' as an Institution of Marginality," in Miers and Kopytoff, eds., *Slavery in Africa: Historical and Anthropological Perspectives* (Madison, Wis., 1977), 3–81.

[24] Donnan, ed., *Documents of Slave Trade*, IV, 188–243; Klein, "Slaves and Shipping," *Jour. Interdis. Hist.*, V (1975), 396–397. For the tobacco-growing cycle see Kulikoff, "Tobacco and Slaves," 354 and sources cited there.

TABLE II   *The Distribution of Africans Among*
                      Purchasers in Virginia, 1689 to 1721[a]

			Percentage of Slaves Bought			
NUMBER PURCHASED	ROYAL AFRICAN COMPANY 1689–1713[b]	AFRICA GALLEY 1702	CHARFIELD, 1717[c] ALL	WEIGHTED	JOHN BAYLOR'S SALES 1719–21	PRINCE EUGENE 1719 WOMEN & CHILDREN
1	38	11	25	30	41	52
2	25	49	27	32	31	17
3	14	11	4	5	4	5
4	9	8	3	3	10	14
5 and over	14	21	42	30	14	12
Total	100	100	101	100	100	100
Number Sold	217	53	150	124	83	58

Notes and Sources: [a] Charles Killinger, "The Royal African Company Slave Trade to Virginia, 1689–1713" (M.A. thesis, College of William and Mary, 1969), 137–148; Donnan, ed., *Documents of Slave Trade*, IV, 71–72; "Sale of the Charfield Slaves," Loyd-Tayloe Account Book, Virginia Historical Society, Richmond; John Baylor Account Book, 1719–1721, Alderman Library, University of Virginia, Charlottesville.

[b] These statistics are not based upon actual sales but on bills and bonds of planters to the Royal African Company. Killinger used the amount of the bond to determine the number of slaves purchased, a generally accurate method. I included only the numbers of slaves bought in contiguous years. (His data included all purchases of each planter over the entire period.)

[c] The "all" includes all sales; the weighted excludes 26 slaves probably destined to be resold: 7 men, 1 woman, and 2 boys to Christopher Robinson, an Urbanna merchant who died in 1727 with 2 women, 1 man, 4 old women, and 2 children; 7 men and 4 women to John Baylor for Beverly and Lyde (Baylor and Lyde were slavetraders). I also determined that 29 slaves sold in groups greater than 5 probably stayed with their purchasers. Then, using this data, I distributed the unknowns in large sales (over 5) in the same manner as the knowns. The Robinson inventory can be found in Middlesex Wills, 1713–1734, 317–320.

ters. Edward Kimber, a visitor to the Eastern Shore in 1747, wrote that "a new Negro" (a newly enslaved African) "must be broke. . . . You would be surpriz'd at their Perseverance; let an hundred Men shew him how to hoe, or drive a Wheelbarrow, he'll still take the one by the Bottom, and the Other by the Wheel." [25]

Under these conditions, Africans were often struck with loneliness and illness. For example, Ayuba (Job) Suleiman was brought to Maryland's Eastern Shore in 1730. He was "put . . . to work making tobacco" but "every day showed more and more uneasiness under this

[25] "Eighteenth-Century Maryland as Portrayed in the 'Itinerant Observations of Edward Kimber,'" *Md. Hist. Mag.*, LI (1956), 327–328.

exercise, and at last grew sick, being no way able to bear it; so that his master was obliged to find easier work for him, and therefore put him to tend the cattle." A new slave might become so ill that he could not work. Thomas Swan, a planter in Prince George's County, Maryland, bought two Africans in the summer of 1728; in November of that year he asked the county court to refund one poll tax because "one of them has been sick ever since he bought him and has done him little or no Service."[26]

One in four new Negroes died during their first year in the Chesapeake; in some years—1711, 1727, 1737, 1743—mortality seems to have been especially high. In 1727 Robert Carter lost at least seventy hands—perhaps a quarter of all his slaves born abroad and more than half his new Negroes. Because Africans possessed some native immunities against malaria, most survived the malarial attacks of their first summer in the region, but respiratory illnesses struck them hard the following winter and spring. Planters considered late spring "the best time of buying them by reason they will be well season'd before the winter."[27] Blacks living in New Kent County, Virginia, between 1714 and 1739 died infrequently in the summer, but deaths rose somewhat in the fall, increased from December to February, and peaked in March and April. The county undoubtedly included many Africans. Whites in the same parish died more frequently in autumn, and less often in spring, than their slaves.[28]

[26] Thomas Bluett, "The Capture and Travels of Ayuba Suleiman Ibrahims," in Curtin *et al.*, eds., *Africa Remembered*, 41; Prince George's Court Record, Liber O. fol. 335, Maryland Hall of Records, Annapolis.

[27] Robert Carter to William Dawkins, May 13, 1727, Carter Letterbooks, Va. Hist. Soc.; Carter to Dawkins, June 3, 1727, Carter Letterbooks, Univ. Va.; Conquest Wyatt to Richard Wyatt, June 1, 1737, and July 20, 1743, earl of Romney's Deposit, Loan 15, British Library; Robert Bristow to Thomas Booth, Oct. 30, 1710, and Sept. 15, 1711, Robert Bristow Letterbooks, Va. St. Lib.; Elizabeth Suttell, "The British Slave Trade to Virginia, 1698–1728" (M.A. thesis, College of William and Mary, 1965), 58–59; Robert Carter Inventory, 1733, Va. Hist. Soc. Carter owned 733 slaves when he died in 1732. Assume he owned 700 slaves in 1727, that the sex ratio of his native slaves was 100, and that he bought two men or boys (10 to 14) for every woman or girl. Then, he would have owned 222 immigrants. Assume further that the death rate of native workers was equal to West level 5, in Ansley J. Coale and Paul Demeny, *Regional Model Life Tables and Stable Populations* (Princeton, N.J., 1966), 34–35, 130–131. This would yield 10 to 15 deaths among the 248 working natives depending on the growth rate chosen. The remaining 55–60 deaths would yield a death rate of 250 to 270 per 1,000 for all immigrant slaves. If Carter bought 80 slaves in 1726, as he did in 1727, and the death rate of seasoned Africans followed West level 5, then 61 to 68% of the new Negroes would have died.

[28] See the death register printed in C. G. Chamberlayne, ed., *The Vestry Book and Register of St. Peter's Parish, New Kent and James City Counties, Virginia, 1684–1786* (Richmond, 1937). The presence of Africans is suggested by high black adult sex ratios in the register: the adult sex ratio was 151 men per 100 women (and 157 excluding mulattoes), the black child sex ratio was 100, and the white adult sex ratio was 115.

Despite disease and death, new Negroes soon began to develop friendships with other slaves, and to challenge the authority of their masters by attempting to make a new life for themselves off their quarters. They were able to oppose their masters because so many of their fellow workers were also recent immigrants who shared their new experiences under slavery. In the mid-1700s, late-1710s, mid-1720s, and mid-1730s, when unusually large numbers of blacks entered Virginia, these Africans, united by their common experiences and able to communicate through the heavily African pidgin they probably created, ran off to the woods together, formed temporary settlements in the wilderness, and several times conspired to overthrow their white masters.[29]

First, Africans had to find or create a common language because there were few speakers of any single African tongue in any neighborhood. Some new slaves may have devised nonoral means of communication soon after arrival, but the large concentration of Ibos and Angolans among the Africans suggests that many spoke similar languages and that others could have become bilingual. Others probably spoke some West African pidgin that they had learned in Africa in order to communicate with Europeans. A new creole language may have emerged in the Chesapeake region combining the vocabulary of several African languages common among the immigrants. African linguistic structures, and the few English words needed for communication with the master.[30]

Almost as soon as Africans landed, they attempted to run away together. Seven of Robert Carter's new Negroes did so on July 17, 1727. They took a canoe and may have crossed the Rappahannock River. Carter sent men "sev[era]l ways" for them, and on July 15 they were returned to him. Enough new Negroes ran away to convince the Virginia assembly to pass laws in 1705 and 1722 detailing procedures to follow when Africans who did not speak English and could not name their master were recaptured.[31]

---

[29] Kulikoff, " 'Prolifick' People," *So. Studies*, XVI (1977), 391–428.

[30] "Capture of Ayuba Suleiman," Curtin *et al.*, eds., *Africa Remembered*, 42–43; "Travels of Olaudah Equiano," *ibid.*, 88–89; Gov. Spotswood of Virginia feared slaves could rebel without speaking a common language: "freedom Wears a Cap which Can Without a Tongue, Call Together all Those who Long to Shake the Fetters of Slavery," he wrote in the 1710s. Quoted in Menard, "Md. Slave Population," *WMQ*, 3d Ser., XXXII (1975), 35. The problem of language was first discussed by Mullin, *Flight and Rebellion*, 44–47; for pidgins, see Wood, *Black-Majority*, chap. 6 and J. L. Dillard, *Black English: Its History and Usage in the United States* (New York, 1972), 73–93.

[31] Carter Diary, July 17, 24, 1727; Hening, ed., *Statutes at Large*, III, 456, IV. 168–175; Randolph W. Church, ed., *The Laws of Virginia, Being a Supplement to Hening's The Statutes at Large, 1700–1750*, comp. Waverly K. Winfree (Richmond, 1971), 212–222; Mullin, *Flight and Rebellion*, 40–45.

A few Africans formed communities in the wilderness in the 1720s, when black immigration was high and the frontier close to tidewater. In 1725 the Maryland assembly asserted that "sundry" slaves "have of late Years runaway into the Back-Woods, some of which have there perished, and others . . . have been entertained and encouraged to live and inhabit with the Shewan-Indians." Other slaves, who heard of their success, were "daily making Attempts to go the same Way." Any slave who ran beyond the Monocacy River, at the edge of white settlement, was to have an ear cut off and his chin branded with an "R." The assembly, recognizing that Africans habitually ran away, withheld this punishment for new Negroes during their first year in the colony.[32]

At least two outlying runaway communities were established during the 1720s. Fifteen slaves began a settlement in 1729 on the frontier near present-day Lexington, Virginia. They ran from "a new Plantation on the head of the James River," taking tools, arms, clothing, and food with them. When captured, "they had already begun to clear the ground." Another small community evidently developed on the Maryland frontier in 1728 and 1729. Early in 1729, Harry, one of the runaways, returned to southern Prince George's County to report on the place to his former shipmates. He told them that "there were many Negroes among the Indians at Monocosy" and tried to entice them to join the group by claiming that Indians were soon going to attack the whites.[33]

As soon as Africans arrived in the Cheaspeake colonies in large numbers, government officials began to complain about their clandestine meetings. In 1687 the Virginia Council asserted that masters allowed their blacks to go "on broad on Saturdays and Sundays . . . to meet in great Numbers in makeing and holding of Funneralls for Dead Negroes." Governor Francis Nicholson of Maryland wrote in 1698 that groups of six or seven slaves traveled thirty or forty miles on weekends to the sparsely inhabited falls of the Potomac.[34]

Whites suppressed clandestine meetings primarily because they feared slave rebellions. Africans pushed to suicidal actions might revolt against the slave system. Revolts were rare in the Chesapeake colonies, where whites heavily outnumbered slaves, but Africans apparently participated in conspiracies in Surry, James City, and Isle of

[32] William Hande Browne et al., eds., Archives of Maryland . . . (Baltimore, 1883–), XXXVI, 583–586, XXXV, 505–506, XXXVII, 211, XXV, 394–395 Prince George's Court Rec., L, 515.

[33] Mullin, Flight and Rebellion, 43–44; quotation is in Michael Mullin, ed., American Negro Slavery (New York, 1976), 83; Prince George's Court Rec., O, 414–415.

[34] H. R. McIlwaine, ed., Executive Journals, Council of Virginia, I (Richmond, 1925), 86–87; Md., Arch., XXIII, 498–499, also cited in Menard, "Md. Slave Population," WMQ, 3d Ser., XXXII (1975), 37–38; Hening, ed., Statutes at Large, IV, 128–129.

Wight counties in Virginia in 1710, and in Prince George's County, Maryland, in 1739 and 1740. The 1739–1740 conspiracy, which is the best documented, was organized by slaves who lived in St. Paul's Parish, an area of large plantations, where numerous slaveholders had recently bought Africans. The Negroes spent eight months in 1739 planning to seize their freedom by killing their masters and other white families in the neighborhood. Their leader, Jack Ransom, was probably a native, but most of the conspirators were Africans, for it is reported that the planning was done by slaves in "their country language." The revolt was postponed several times, and finally the white authorities got wind of it. Stephen Boardley, an Annapolis lawyer, reported that whites believed that two hundred slaves planned to kill all the white men, marry the white women, and then unite both shores of Maryland under their control. Ransom was tried and executed; four other slaves were acquitted; and the furor died down.[35]

Every attempt of Africans to establish an independent social life off the plantation failed because whites, who held the means of terror, insisted that their slaves remain at home. Running to the woods, founding outlying communities, or meeting in large groups challenged work discipline and cost the planter profits. Nevertheless, substantial numbers of Africans probably participated in activities away from the plantation. Slaves from many different African communities proved that they could unite and live together. Others, though unable to join them, must have heard of their exploits and discovered that a new social life might be possible. Sooner or later, however, Africans had to turn to their plantation to develop communities.

But as late as the 1730s, plantations were not very conducive places in which to create a settled social life. A major determinant was the small size of the slave populations of the plantation quarters. On quarters of fewer than ten slaves, completed families of husbands, wives, and children were uncommon and the slaves, who lived in outbuildings, did not control enough space of their own to run their own lives apart from the master. Table III shows how small the tidewater plantations were. Only 28 percent of the slaves on Maryland's lower Western Shore before 1711 lived on plantations of over twenty slaves, and some of these lived in quarters distant from the main plantation. The rest lived on smaller farms. Quarters were similarly small in York and Lancaster counties in the 1710s. From 1710 to 1740, plantation sizes

[35] Herbert Aptheker, *American Negro Slave Revolts* (New York, 1943), 169–170 and sources cited there (Aptheker calls one conspiracy two); Stephen Boardley Letter Books, 1738–1740, 55–58, Maryland Historical Society, Baltimore; *Md. Arch.*, XXVIII, 188–190, 230–232, XL, 425, 428, 457, 523; Prince George's Court Rec., X, 573–576; Chancery Records, VIII, 38–39, Md. Hall Recs. (shipment of 320 Africans in 1734 to Benedict near the site of the rebellion). I checked all of Aptheker's sources in *Slave Revolts*, chap. 8, and the 1710 conspiracy seemed to be the only one in Virginia that included Africans.

TABLE III — *Plantation Sizes in Tidewater Maryland and Virginia, 1658 to 1740*

	Proportion of Slaves Living on Units of				
	1–5	6–10	11–20	21+	NUMBER
PLACE AND TIME	SLAVES	SLAVES	SLAVES	SLAVES	OF SLAVES
Maryland Lower Western Shore[a]					
1658–1710	29	22	21	28	1618
1721–1730[c]	17	19	20	44	974
Prince George's, Maryland					
1731–1740	17	26	34	24	842
St. Mary's, Maryland					
1721–1730	26	21	25	28	484
1731–1740	32	22	35	11	524
York County, Virginia					
1711–1720	28	20	22	30	618
1721–1730	29	21	34	16	459
1731–1740	25	30	27	18	446
Lancaster County, Virginia[b]					
1711–1725	29	22	31	17	248
1726–1735[c]	14	18	24	45	322
1736–1745[c]	14	17	18	52	499
"King" Carter's Plantations					
1733	2	14	40	45	733

Note and Sources: Menard, "Maryland Slave Population," *William and Mary Quarterly*, 3d Ser., XXXI (1975), 32, 43; Kulikoff, "Tobacco and Slaves: Population, Economy, and Society in Eighteenth-Century Prince George's County, Maryland" (Ph.D. diss., Brandeis University, 1976), 185; St. Mary's City Commission data from St. Mary's Inventories; York County Orders, Wills, etc., collected by Edward Ayres; Lancaster County Wills (or Deeds, Wills) for years listed; Robert Carter Inventory, Va. Hist. Soc. Inventories tend to over represent the wealthier slave owners and to combine a master's slaves from several quarters in one place; therefore the proportions of slaves who lived on larger units is overestimated. Since the bias remains constant, the changes between periods are usually accurate.

[a] St. Mary's, Charles, Calvert, and Prince George's, 1658–1710; Prince George's and Charles, 1721–1730.

[b] Odd years chosen because the number of cases (slaves) in first period otherwise too low.

[c] Unusually large number of planters with major slave holdings (21+) died. Part of the change shown in the table is due to this fact.

in Prince George's and Lancaster counties increased, while those in York and St. Mary's stayed the same. If these four counties were typical of tidewater in the 1730s, then 46 percent of the slaves lived on quarters of ten or fewer and only 25 percent resided on units of over twenty (but usually under thirty).[36]

[36] The figures are means of the entries of Table III, with each county equaling one observation. Only 9% of Carter's slaves lived on units of over 30 in 1733. See n. 56.

African social structures centered on the family, but slaves in the Chesapeake had difficulty maintaining family life. Men who lived on small quarters often had to find wives elsewhere, a task made more difficult by the high ratio of men to women in much of tidewater. As long as adult sex ratios remained high, men had to postpone marriage, while women might be forced to marry early. Along the lower Western Shore of Maryland, the sex ratio was about 150 in the 1690s and 1700s, but by the 1710s it was under 150 in York County and under 120 in Lancaster County, remaining at those levels until 1740. Even on large plantations men could not count on living in family units, for sex ratios there were higher than on small quarters. During the 1730s the adult sex ratio in Prince George's was 187, but on nine large plantations in that county, each having ten or more adult slaves, it stood at 249. A similar pattern has been found in both York and Lancaster counties at times between 1710 and 1740.[37]

Since most slaves lived on small plantations, the development of settled black community life required visiting between quarters. Sometimes slaves met on larger plantations, getting "drunke on the Lords Day beating their Negro Drums by which they call considerable Numbers of Negroes together." On one Sunday in 1735, Edward Pearson's Negroes with some of his "Neighbours Negroes was Beating a Drum and Danceing but by my Consent" in Prince George's.[38] Slaves probably did not regularly visit friends on nearby plantations, however. Visiting networks could develop only where blacks were densely settled and constituted a large part of the population. The population in tidewater was never over half slave except in a few counties between the James and York rivers before 1740. Only 16 percent of the people in the Chesapeake colonies were black in 1690, but this proportion grew to 25 percent in 1710 and 28 percent in 1740.[39]

The large plantations in tidewater housed masters, overseers, native blacks, new Negroes, and less recent immigrants, while smaller units, with only a few natives or immigrants, tended to be more homogeneous. The concentration of men on large plantations suggests that

---

[37] Kulikoff, " 'Prolifick' People," *So. Studies,* XVI (1977), 391–428; Kulikoff, "Tobacco and Slaves," 77; York County Wills and Orders, XIV-XVIII, Va. St. Lib.; Lancaster County Wills, X-XIII, Va. St. Lib. York adult sex ratios were, in 1711–1720, 126 and 145 on large plantations (numbering five) with 10 or more adult slaves, and the sex ratio on Robert Carter's plantations in 1733 (Carter Inventory, Va. Hist. Soc.) was 153, while the sex ratio in Lancaster inventories, 1726–1735, was 113 Lancaster and York counties inventories in the 1720s and 1730s show large plantation sex ratios about the same or even lower than all plantations, but the number of observations is too small to be certain.

[38] Menard, "Md. Slave Population," *WMQ,* 3d Ser., XXXII (1975), 37; Prince George's Court Rec., V, 618, 630.

[39] *Historical Statistics,* 1168; Menard, "Economy and Society," 412; Menard, "Md. Slave Population," *WMQ,* 3d Ser., XXXII (1975), 35. The statement about the James-York region is based upon later data found in Evarts B. Greene and Virginia D. Harrington, *American Population before the Federal Census of 1790* (New York, 1932), 150–151.

most African adults were bought by the gentry—a pattern documented by the composition of John Mercer's and Robert Carter's plantations. Mercer bought sixty-nine slaves between 1731 and 1746. These purchases included six seasoned Africans or natives in 1731 and 1732, twenty-five new Negroes from 1733 to 1739, and twenty new Negroes and fifteen seasoned slaves in the 1740s. By 1740 Mercer owned a mixed group of new Negroes, seasoned immigrants, and native children and adults. The composition of Carter's quarters in 1733 shows the culmination of this process. Over half of Carter's 734 slaves lived on plantations where one-fifth to one-half were recent immigrants, and another third resided on quarters composed predominantly of natives or older immigrants. Only one-seventh of his slaves lived on quarters dominated by new Negroes. About one-half (6/13) of the quarters of over twenty slaves, and natives formed a majority of the rest. Most of the farms (11/18) with eleven to twenty slaves included Africans and natives, but five others were peopled by natives. Nine of the eleven quarters where new Negroes formed a majority were small units of fewer than ten slaves.[40]

Most new Negroes learned to be slaves on such diversified plantations. Nearly two-thirds (64 percent) of Carter's recent immigrant slaves lived on plantations with numerous native adults and children, and white overseers resided at almost every quarter. Africans had to learn some English in order to communicate with masters, overseers, and native slaves, and they were put into the fields with other slaves who had already learned that they had to work to avoid punishment and that resistance had to be indirect. Africans saw that a few slaves were given responsibility—and power—over other slaves or were taught new skills. Slaves born in Africa apparently were well acculturated on Robert Carter's quarters. While the great majority of his adult slaves were agricultural laborers, some Africans (who had probably been in the country for a number of years) joined their native friends as foremen who worked under white overseers. Perhaps nineteen of the thirty-three foremen on these plantations were born in Africa. Four other men—possibly Africans—became sloopers (boatmen) on Carter's main plantation.[41]

Nevertheless, Africans and native slaves quarrelled on occasion because of the great differences between their respective experiences. Natives had not been herded into ships and sold into bondage. They

[40] John Mercer's Ledger B, Buck's County Historical Society, 12 (film copy at Colonial Williamsburg Research Dept.); Carter Inventory, Va. Hist. Soc. I identified as immigrants all men, women, and children 10–14 who did not live in a family and all husband-wife households. Of course, some immigrants had children, and some of the adults living in sex-segregated households were teenagers not yet married, but this method gives a plausible estimate.

[41] Carter Inventory, Va. Hist. Soc. There were resident overseers on all but two quarters with 9 slaves (of 734). Two overseers supervised two quarters; 63 slaves lived on these four farms.

were probably healthier than immigrants. Many of them were baptized Christians, and some became believers. To immigrants, by contrast, Christianity was an alien creed, and they sometimes tried to maintain their own Islamic or African religions in opposition to it. Ben, for example, was brought from Africa to Charles County, Maryland, about 1730. According to his grandson, Charles Ball, Ben "always expressed great contempt for his fellow slaves, they being . . . a mean and vulgar race, quite beneath his rank, and the dignity of his former station." Ben never attended a Christian service but held that Christianity was "altogether false, and indeed no religion at all."[42]

The most significant difference between recent immigrants and native blacks can be seen in their family life. A native-born slave on Robert Carter's plantations in 1733 usually lived in a family composed of husband, wife, and children, whereas new Negroes were placed in sex-segregated barracks, and seasoned immigrants often lived in conjugal units without children. Though polygamy was common in some African societies, only one of Carter's slaves managed to keep two wives.[43] Conditions at Carter's plantations were optimal; elsewhere, high sex ratios severely limited the marriage opportunities of African men. At first, older slaves could become "uncles" to younger Africans, and Africans of the same age could act as brothers, but African men had to find wives in order to begin a Chesapeake genealogy.[44] They had to compete with natives for the available women; native women may well have preferred native men, who were healthy, spoke English, and knew how to act in a white world, to unhealthy or unseasoned Africans. Furthermore, newly enslaved African women often waited two or three years before taking a husband, thereby reducing the supply of prospective wives even further. The reluctance of Afro-American women to marry Africans may have been one of the grievances of the Prince George's conspirators in 1739–1740.[45]

Several incidents on Edmund Jenings's plantations in King William County, Virginia, in 1712–1713, suggest that Africans competed among themselves for wives, sometimes with tragic results. George,

---

[42] Kulikoff, " 'Prolifick' People," *So. Studies*, XVI (1977), 391–428; Charles Ball, *Fifty Years in Chains*, ed. Philip Foner (New York, 1970 [orig. publ. 1837]), 21–22; "Capture of Ayuba Suleiman," Curtin *et al.*, eds., *Africa Remembered*, 42.

[43] Carter Inventory, Va. Hist. Soc. One can identify those who had been in the country a number of years by the ages of their children. Husband-wife households were rare on Charles Carroll of Carrollton's holdings (386 slaves) in 1773–1774; almost all households included children. Husband-wife households are therefore probably immigrant households. For Carroll see Kulikoff, "Beginnings of Afro-American Family," 178–183. Children 10–14 on Carter's plantations are usually listed with parents; where they are not, I assumed that they were immigrants.

[44] Mintz and Price, *Afro-American Anthropology*, 34–35.

[45] Kulikoff, " 'Prolifick' People," *So. Studies*, XVI (1977), 391–428; Stephen Boardley thought the conspirators planned to kill black women as well as white men. Boardly Letter Books, 55–58.

who lived at Beaverdam Quarter, complained in November 1712 that "his country men had poysened him for his wife," and he died the following February from the poison. Roger, of Silsdon Quarter, apparently wanted more than one wife. In December 1712 or January 1713, he "hanged himselfe in ye old 40 foot Tob house not any reason he being hindred from keeping other negroes men wifes besides his owne." The overseer "had his head cutt off and stuck on a pole to be a terror to the others." [46]

Slaves in the Chesapeake colonies failed to establish a settled community life in the times of heavy immigrations in the 1710s, 1720s, and 1730s. Conflicts among Africans and between African and native slaves could never be fully resolved as long as substantial numbers of Africans were forced into slavery in the two colonies. On the other hand, the rate of immigration, the proportion of Africans in the slave population, and the percentage of blacks in the population were never great enough to permit successful communities based mostly upon African institutions and values to develop either on the plantation or away from it.

The demographic conditions that prevented blacks from developing a cohesive social life before 1740 changed during the quarter century before the Revolution, as the immigration of Africans to tidewater Maryland and Virginia declined sharply. Only 17 percent of Virginia's adult black population in 1750 and 15 percent in 1755 had arrived within the previous ten years, and these newcomers went in relatively greater numbers to newer piedmont counties than had their predecessors.[47] The proportion of adult blacks in 1755 who had entered Virginia since 1750 ranged from 4 percent in Lancaster County and 8 percent in York County in tidewater Virginia to 15 percent in Caroline County and 21 percent in Fairfax County, both near the fall line.[48] After 1755, almost all of Virginia's black immigrants went to piedmont counties.[49]

---

[46] "Inventories of the Negroes etc. on the Estate of Edmund Jenings Esqr, 1712–13." Francis Porteus Corbin Papers, Duke University, Durham, N.C. (film at Colonial Williamsburg).

[47] Kulikoff, " 'Prolifick' People," *So. Studies*, XVI (1977), 391–428; Donnan, ed., *Documents of Slave Trade*, IV, 204–224, shows that in the 1740s, York remained the major slave port, but Upper James (where most new settlement occurred) became the second port: 22% entered Upper James, 53% York, and 11% Rappahannock.

[48] Ages of slaves judged found in Lancaster Orders, IX-X, York Judgments and Orders, 1746–1752 and 1752–1754, Fairfax Orders, 1749–1754 and 1754–1756, all are in Va. St. Lib.; and T. E. Campbell, *Colonial Caroline: A History of Caroline County, Virginia* (Richmond, 1954), 331. I used the Fairfax index to orders located at the Fairfax County Municipal Building, courtesy of Donald Sweig of that county's bicentennial commission. The method of calculating the proportion of immigrants is described in n. 10 above.

[49] The redistribution of African immigrants to piedmont after 1750 can be seen in two ways. First, Upper James became the dominant slave port (50% of slaves in 1750–1754, 62% in 1760–1764), while York fades into insignificance (42%, 1750–54 and 46%, 1760–1764). Until the early 1770s, almost all ships on the Upper James went to

As the number of African immigrants in tidewater declined, the internal division among blacks diminished. These immigrants were under greater pressure than their predecessors to acquire the language, values, and beliefs of the dominant native majority. Like new Negroes before them, they sometimes ran away but with less success. On arrival, they found themselves isolated and alone. Olaudah Equiano, for example, was brought to Virginia in 1757 at age twelve. "I was now exceedingly miserable," he wrote, "and thought myself worse off than any . . . of my companions; for they could talk to each other, but I had no person to speak to that I could understand. In this state I was constantly grieving and pining, and wishing for death." But once slaves like Equiano learned English, they became part of the Afro-American community. Bob, twenty-nine, and Turkey Tom, thirty-eight, were new Negroes who lived on the home plantation of Charles Carroll of Carrollton in 1773. Since Bob and Tom were apparently the only two recent immigrant slaves on any of Carroll's many plantations, they both could participate fully in plantation life. Bob was a smith, a position usually reserved for natives; he married the daughter of a carpenter, and lived with her and their two children. Tom, a laborer, also found a place in the plantation's kinship networks: his wife was at least a third-generation Marylander.[50] Very few Africans probably ever became artisans, but most lived on plantations where they could find wives among the native majority.

The size of quarters increased after 1740 throughout tidewater, providing greater opportunities for slaves to develop a social life of their own. The proportion who lived on units of over twenty slaves doubled in St. Mary's County, increased by half in York County, and grew, though more slowly, in Prince George's. In the 1780s one-third to two-thirds of the slaves in nine tidewater counties lived on farms of more than twenty slaves, and only a sixth to a tenth lived on units of fewer than six. If these counties were typical, 43 percent of tidewater's

---

Bermuda Hundred, a small settlement at the convergence of the Appomatox and James rivers, near present-day Petersburg, and close to the expanding Southside. Donnan, ed., *Documents of Slave Trade*, IV, 219–231; *Va. Gaz.* (Hunter), Sept. 12, 1751, July 10, 30, 1752, Aug. 12, 1752; *ibid.* (Royle), Nov. 4, 1763; *ibid.* (Purdie and Dixon), June 27, Aug. 1, and Sept. 5, 1766, Aug. 11, 1768, May 18, 1769—all are ads for slave ships about to enter the Upper James and bound for Bermuda Hundred. Secondly, ages judged disappear from tidewater court records: from 1755 to 1770, there were 6 ages judged in York (1755–1758 missing), 3 in Lancaster, 15 in Caroline, 41 in Fairfax, and 46 in Prince Edward (1754–1758 and 1765–1769) on the Southside frontier. York Judgments and Orders, 1759–1763, 1763–1765, 1765–1768, and 1768–1770; Lancaster Orders 10–14; Fairfax Orders (from index cited in n. 48) 1754–1756, and Minutes 1756–1763; Campbell, *Caroline County*, 331.

[50] John Blassingame, *The Slave Community: Plantation Life in the Antebellum South* (New York, 1972), 16; "A List of Negroes on Doohoregan Manor taken in Familys with their Ages Decr. 1, 1773," Charles Carroll (of Carrollton) Account Book, Md. Hist. Soc.

blacks lived on farms of over twenty slaves, and another 25 percent lived on medium-sized units of eleven to twenty. (See Table IV.[51]) The number of very large quarters also grew. Before 1740 few quarters housed over thirty slaves, but by the 1770s and 1780s the wealthiest gentlemen ran home plantations with over one hundred slaves and quarters with thirty to fifty.[52]

Because plantation sizes increased, more Afro-Americans lived on quarters away from the master's house and his direct supervision. On small plantations the quarter could be located in an outbuilding or in a single dwelling. On large plantations "a Negro Quarter, is a Number of Huts or Hovels, built some Distance from the Mansion-House; where the Negroes reside with their Wives and Families, and cultivate at vacant Times the little Spots allow'd them." Slave houses and the yards surrounding them were centers of domestic activity. The houses were furnished with straw bedding, barrels for seats, pots, pans, and usually a grindstone or handmill for beating corn into meal. Agricultural tools and livestock were scattered outside the house, and the quarter was surrounded by plots of corn and tobacco cultivated by the slaves.[53]

[51] Figures are means with the proportion in each county equaling one observation.

[52] The change in the size of the largest plantations cannot be traced through inventories because they often do not properly divide a decedent's slaves among his quarters. Quarter-by-quarter lists of the slaves of Robert Carter in 1733 (Carter Inventory, Va. Hist. Soc.), Charles Carroll (of Carrollton) in 1773 ("Negroes on Doohoregan Manor"), and the manumission record of Robert Carter of Nomini in 1791 (Louis Morton, *Robert Carter of Nomini Hall: A Virginia Tobacco Planter of the Eighteenth Century* [Williamsburg, 1941], Table 9 in the appendix, 284) suggest, however, the dimensions of the change:

NUMBER OF SLAVES	*Percent Living on Quarters of Various Sizes on*		
	R. CARTER 1733	C. CARROLL 1773	R. CARTER 1791
1–10	16	2	5
11–20	40	18	9
21–30	35	37	33
31–40	9	10	14
41–50	0	0	17
101+	0	34	22
Total Number of Slaves	733	386	509

[53] "Eighteenth-Century Maryland," *Md. Hist. Mag.*, LI (1956), 327. A plat of a quarter, surrounded by fields, can be found in Moore V. Meek, Ejectment Papers, Box 30. A quarter located in a kitchen is described in Provincial Court Judgments, EI #4, 110–112, Md. Hall Recs. The furnishing and implements at quarters are listed in Prince George's Inventories, TB#1, 93–94 (1726), 32–38, 64–68 (1727); PD#1, 6–10, 26–28 (1729), 247–248 (1734), 426 (1738); DD#1, 56–58; 82–83 (1741), 363 (1744); DD#2, 128–129, 219, 322 (1752); GS#1, 245–246 (1758); and GS#2, 257–258 (1772), 357–359 (1775)—all in Md. Hall Recs.

TABLE **IV**

Sizes of Plantations in Maryland and Virginia, 1741 to 1790[a]

	Proportion of Slaves Living on Units of				
	1–5	6–10	11–20	21+	NUMBER
COUNTY AND YEAR	SLAVES	SLAVES	SLAVES	SLAVES	OF CASES
Prince George's					
1741–1750	14	18	22	48	1,090
1751–1760	11	17	28	44	1,126
1761–1770	13	22	31	35	1,144
1771–1779	10	17	18	55	1,099
1790	11	13	23	52	11,176
St. Mary's					
1741–1750	39	24	27	11	580
1751–1760	21	27	30	23	892
1761–1770[b]	15	20	28	37	1,453
1771–1777	16	26	31	26	831
1790	16	21	25	37	6,985
Anne Arundel[c]					
1783	12	17	29	41	5,855
York[d]					
1741–1750	19	24	36	22	689
1751–1760[b]	12	13	26	49	803
1761–1770	7	17	40	37	663
1771–1780	12	17	33	39	788
1785	16	20	30	33	2,190
James City					
1783	12	22	28	38	2,039
Warwick					
1783	18	26	24	33	897
Charles City					
1784	11	16	26	47	2,808
Middlesex					
1783	10	12	15	63	2,277
Lancaster					
1783	9	20	28	42	3,024

Sources: [a] Kulikoff, "Tobacco and Slaves," 185; St. Mary's Inventories collected by the St. Mary's City Commission; Anne Arundel County Tax lists, Maryland Historical Society, Baltimore; Bureau of the Census, *Heads of Families at the First Census of the United States Taken in the Year 1790: Maryland* (Washington, D.C., 1907), 92–98, 104–109; York County Wills and Inventories, 19–22, Virginia State Library, Richmond; personal property tax lists for York, 1785, James City, 1783, Warwick, 1783, Charles City, 1783—all at Va. St. Lib.; Nancy Lous Oberseider, "A Socio-Demographic Study of the Family as a Social Unit in Tidewater Virginia 1660–1776" (Ph.D. diss., University of Maryland, 1975), 202–203 for Middlesex. Bureau of the Census, *Heads of Families at the First Census of the United States Taken in the Year 1790: Records of the State Enumerations: 1782 to 1785, Virginia* (Washington, D.C., 1908), 55–56, for Lancaster.

(Notes continue at top of facing page)

Notes: The data in the 1780s and 1790 is not comparable with the earlier data for it covers *all* planters listed in tax records and censuses and not a biased inventory sample. The inventory will be biased upward, for more wealthy than poor planters had inventories taken. Nor are the data for Prince George's and St. Mary's in 1790 and Lancaster in 1783 comparable to the other lists from the 1780s, for data from these three counties include all a planter's holdings taken together while the other data are divided into precincts and a planter's holdings in each precinct is separately enumerated.

  b Greater than usual number of planters died.

  c Not entire county. Excludes Annapolis, but includes 12 hundreds of the remaining 18 or 63% of the slaves excluding those in Annapolis. Hundreds from all parts of the county were chosen.

  d In these inventories, but not in any others, I separated the quarters of one planter into separate observations and excluded from the table all slaves on plantations in piedmont. In general, the numbers on large plantations are still far too large.

Afro-Americans made the quarters into little communities, usually organized around families. Because African immigration largely ceased, the adult sex ratio decreased throughout tidewater until it reached about one hundred by the time of the Revolution.[54] Almost all men and women could marry, and by the 1770s many slaves had native grandparents and great-grandparents. Smaller quarters contained a family or two, and larger quarters were populated by extended families in which most residents were kinfolk. Domestic activities such as eating, playing in the yard, or tending the garden were organized by families, and each family member had a part in them. The quarter was the center of family activity every evening and on Sundays and holidays, for except during the harvest, slaves had these times to themselves. Nonresident fathers visited their wives and children, runaways stayed with friends or kinfolk. In the evenings native men sometimes traveled to other quarters where they passed the night talking, singing, smoking, and drinking. On occasional Sundays they held celebrations at which they danced to the banjo and sang bitter songs about their treatment by the master.[55]

The economy of the quarters was partially controlled by the slaves, since distance from the master allowed them a certain autonomy in small matters. Slaves occasionally slaughtered stock without permission, ate some of the meat, and traded the surplus. Chickens, sheep,

---

[54] For details, see Kulikoff, " 'Prolifick' People," *So. Studies*, XVI (1977).

[55] Kulikoff, "Beginnings of Afro-American Family," 180–183; *The Journal of Nicholas Cresswell, 1774–1777* (New York, 1924), 18–19; *Md. Arch.*, XLIV, 647–648; Ferdinand M. Bayard, *Travels of a Frenchman in Maryland and Virginia . . . in 1791 . . .* , ed. Ben C. McCary (Williamsburg, 1950), 96; Thomas Bacon, *Four Sermons Preached at the Parish Church of St. Peter, in Talbot County, . . .* (Bath, 1783 [orig. publ. London, 1753]), 56–58; Carville Earle, *The Evolution of a Tidewater Settlement: All Hallow's Parish, Maryland, 1650–1783* (University of Chicago, Geography Research Paper No. 170, 1975), 160–161.

and swine were traded to fellow slaves, as well as to peddlers, merchants, and other whites. The danger and excitement of stealing the master's livestock were shared by all the quarter's families. This illegal activity was apparently widespread. A Prince George's planter complained in 1770 that "in the Neighbourhood where I live, it is almost impossible to raise a stock of Sheep or Hogs, the Negroes are constantly killing them to sell to some white people who are little better than themselves." [56]

After 1740, the density of the black population and the proportion of slaves in the population of tidewater both increased, and as a result, the area's slave society gradually spread out to embrace many neighboring plantations in a single network. Ironically, masters provided slaves with several tools they could use to extend these cross-quarter networks. As masters sold and transferred their slaves, more and more kinfolk lived on neighboring quarters, and naturally they retained ties of affection after they were separated. Whites built numerous roads and paths to connect their farms and villages, and their slaves used these byways to visit friends or run away and evade recapture. By the 1770s and 1780s, Afro-Americans numerically dominated many neighborhoods and created many cross-plantation social networks.

The density of black population and the proportion of slaves in the population increased in both Chesapeake colonies. The number of slaves per square mile increased by more than one-third between 1755 and the early 1780s in three tidewater areas. Slaves composed 26 percent of the population of the lower Western Shore of Maryland in 1710, 38 percent in 1755, and 46 percent in 1782. A similar change occurred on the Eastern Shore, and by 1775, the results were visible in tidewater Virginia. In that year, nearly every county between the Rappahannock and the James rivers as far west as the heads of navigation was more than one-half black; over half of Virginia's slaves lived in these counties. Between 40 and 50 percent of the people were black in 1775 in the Northern Neck and in piedmont counties adjacent to tidewater. [57]

Quarters were connected by extensive networks of roads and paths,

[56] Mullin, *Flight and Rebellion*, 60–62; *Md. Arch.*, XXIV, 732–733, XXVII, 155–158, L, 436; *Maryland Gazette* (Annapolis), Oct. 12, 1758, Oct. 18, 1770, Mar 13, 1777; *Va. Gaz.* (Rind), Mar. 17, 1768; Dunlop's *Md. Gaz.* (Baltimore), Nov. 4, 1772; Prince George's Court Rec., EE#2, 99, 543 (1778).

[57] "Number of Inhabitants in Maryland," *Gentleman's Magazine; and Historical Chronical*, XXIV (1764), 261; Greene and Harrington, *American Population*, 154–155; Kulikoff, "Tobacco and Slaves," 202–203, 323, 428–432; Bureau of the Census, *Heads of Families at the First Census of the United States . . . Records of the State Enumerations: 1782–1785, Virginia* (Washington, D.C., 1908), 9–10; Lester J. Cappon *et al.*, eds. *Atlas of Early American History: The Revolutionary Era, 1760–1790* (Princeton, N.J., 1976), 24, 67, 100, 102. The number of slaves per square mile on Maryland's lower Western Shore (Prince

which grew remarkably complex during the eighteenth century. For example, Prince George's County had about 50 miles of public roads in 1700, but 295 in 1739, and 478 in 1762. In 1762 there was one mile of public road for every square mile of taxed land in the county. This elaboration of roads made it easier for slaves to visit nearby plantations. Whites could not patrol all these roads, let alone private paths not maintained by the county, without a general mobilization of the white population.[58]

Two Maryland examples from the 1770s and 1780s illustrate the demographic characteristics of places where Afro-American slaves were able to develop cross-plantation social networks. The area around Upper Marlborough, Prince George's county seat, was over six-tenths black and had over twenty-five slaves per square mile in 1783. The region, which covered about 130 square miles, extended to the Patuxent River and included an adjacent area across the river in Anne Arundel County. Perhaps half the blacks in this region lived on quarters of over twenty slaves and another fourth on farms of eleven to twenty. The road network here was the most developed in the county. Elk Ridge was located near Baltimore town. In 1783 its population was about half black, with fourteen slaves per square mile. About six-tenths of the Elk Ridge slaves lived on farms of over twenty blacks, and another one-fifth on units between eleven and twenty. One neighborhood in this area was very heavily black. In 1774, 330 of Charles Carroll's slaves lived at Doohregan Manor on the main plantation and at nine other quarters spread over the 10,000-acre tract. Many social activities could occur in the village of 130 slaves on the main plantation, and a somewhat smaller number among the 143 who lived on farms of 21 to 40 slaves. The rest of Carroll's slaves resided on small quarters of under twenty-one people. Visiting among slaves on Carroll's various quarters must have been common, however, because slaves on one quarter were frequently related by blood and marriage to those on another.[59]

George's, Charles, Calvert, and St. Mary's counties) was 12 in 1755 and 18 in 1782; in York, Charles City, James City, and New Kent, 15 in 1755 and 18 in 1790; in Lancaster, Middlesex, Richmond, and Essex counties, 14 in 1755 and 21 in 1790. I multiplied 1755 Virginia tithables by two and divided by square miles. Blacks accounted for roughly 57% of the population in both 1755 and 1790 in York, Charles City, James City, and New Kent and 51% in 1755 and 59% in 1790 of the population in Lancaster, Middlesex, Richmond, and Essex. I multiplied white tithables by two for 1755 and determined the rough proportion of blacks in adult population.

[58] Kulikoff, "Tobacco and Slaves," 327–339; Earle, *Tidewater Settlement System*, 154–157.

[59] Kulikoff, "Tobacco and Slaves," 205, 532–536; Anne Arundel Summary of 1783 Tax Lists, Executive Papers, Md. Hall Recs.; Lyons Creek and Elk Ridge Hundred 1783

These ideal conditions could not be found everywhere in tidewater. From just north of the Patuxent to just south of the James, plantations were large, black population density was high, few whites were present, and road networks were well developed. Slaves in these areas could create a rudimentary cross-plantation society. By contrast, in other regions on the Eastern Shore and upper Western Shore of Maryland, blacks were a minority, and small planters tilled the soil with their sons and perhaps several slaves. Here whites controlled the environment, and slaves had fewer opportunities to pursue their own activities.[60]

Even within areas of high black populations and large plantations, the opportunities of slaves for social life outside their own plantations varied from place to place. In twenty-eight taxing districts of Anne Arundel and Prince George's counties in 1783, the black population ranged from 27 to 66 percent. Large plantations tended to be located where the population was predominantly Afro-American, but the relationship was not exact: in Anne Arundel in 1783, 18 to 58 percent of the blacks in eight "hundreds" whose population was over half black lived on quarters of over twenty slaves.[61] Neighborhoods close to each other could have very different racial compositions. Taxing districts along the Potomac River in Prince George's, about fifteen miles from Upper Marlborough, were only four-tenths black, and around Oxon Creek, where most of the householders were white tenants, only 30 percent of the people were slaves. Only one-third of the slaves along the Potomac lived on farms with over twenty of their fellows. In Virginia, both James City and York counties were over 60 percent black in the 1780s. Most of the large plantations in these counties were located in upper Yorkhampton Parish, where over half the blacks lived on quarters of over twenty slaves. Only one-third to one-fourth of the slaves lived on big quarters in the remainder of these counties.[62]

Even on large plantations, social life was often insecure. Some slaves were sold or forced to accompany their masters to the piedmont, far away from family and friends: about 20 percent of all slaves in southern Maryland left the region between 1755 and 1782. Even

---

Tax List, Md. Hist. Soc.; "Negroes on Doohregan Manor," Carroll Account Book, Md. Hist. Soc. The distribution of slaves on plantations for the region around Upper Marlborough is based upon Lyons Creek Hundred in Anne Arundel and on work in Prince George's inventories. Individual 1783 tax lists do not survive for Prince George's.

[60] These generalizations are based upon study of tax lists cited in Table IV and summaries of 1783 tax lists, Executive Papers for all Maryland Counties, Md. Hall Rec.

[61] The Pearson Product Moment Correlation between percent black and percent living on farms of more than 20 slaves for 12 hundreds (27–61% black) was .744.

[62] Kulikoff, "Tobacco and Slaves," 205; James City Personal Property Tax List, 1783, and York County Personal Property Tax List, 1785, Va. St. Lib. I am indebted to Edward Ayres for helping me with the geography of James City and York.

when a slave remained the property of the same white family, he might not live on the same farm for more than a few years. For example, after the Revolution large planters in Elizabeth City County, Virginia, tended to hire out their slaves to tenants and small landowners. A slave might live on a different plantation every year, suffering separation from spouse, children, and friends.[63]

Nevertheless, one-half to three-quarters of the Afro-Americans who lived in tidewater in the 1780s enjoyed some sort of social life not controlled by their masters. Perhaps 43 percent lived on large quarters, and another 4 percent were men who lived in the neighborhoods with many large quarters and could visit nearby farms. Another 25 percent lived on farms of eleven to twenty blacks and could participate in the family and community activities of their quarters. The remaining one-fourth of the slaves were women and children who lived on small plantations. They usually did not travel from quarter to quarter but waited for husbands and fathers to visit them.

The Afro-Americans made good use of these opportunities to create their own society. In the years before the Revolution, they developed a sense of community with other slaves both on their own plantations and in the neighborhood. This social solidarity was shown in several ways. In the first place, Afro-Americans often concealed slaves from the neighborhood on their quarters. Since masters searched the neighborhood for runaways and placed notices on local public buildings before advertising in a newspaper, many runaways were not so advertised. The increasing appearance of such advertisements in the *Maryland Gazette* during the thirty years before the Revolution suggests that slaves were becoming more successful in evading easy recapture. The number of runaways in southern Maryland rose in each five-year period between 1745 and 1779, except the years 1765 and 1769, and the increase was especially great during the Revolution, when some escaped slaves were able to reach British troops.[64]

Most runaways required help from other blacks. Only a small minority were helped by whites, and about three-quarters (22/29) of those so helped in southern Maryland were artisans, mulattoes, or women. Women infrequently ran away, and there were few slave mulattoes and artisans.[65] The majority of runaways traveled from plantation to plantation through a quarter underground. Some joined family members or friends on nearby or even distant plantations; others

[63] Kulikoff, "Tobacco and Slaves," 84–88; Sarah Shaver Hughes, "Slaves for Hire: The Annual Allocation of Black Labor in Elizabeth City County, Virginia, 1782 to 1810," *WMQ*, 3d Ser., XXXV (1978), 260–286.

[64] See Table V; *Md. Gaz.*, Mar. 9, 1758 (notices put up for runaway); Benjamin Quarles, *The Negro in the American Revolution* (Chapel Hill, N.C., 1961), chap. 2.

[65] Mullin, *Flight and Rebellion*, 112–116; *Md. Gaz.*, Apr. 9, 1772, Jan. 29, 1767, Feb. 14, 1771.

TABLE V — *Motives of Runaway Slaves in Southern Maryland, 1745 to 1779*[a]

MOTIVE	Percentage of Runaways by Years			Totals	
	1745–1759	1760s	1770s	PERCENT	NUMBER
To Visit	60	30	58	54	63
To Pass as Free; to Work	20	45	21	25	29
To Escape Maryland	20	25	21	21	25
Number	25	20	72	100	117
Number of Unknowns	35	33	59		127
Total Number of Runaways	60	53	131		244
Percent Unknown	58	62	45	52	

Notes and Sources: [a] All runaway ads published in the *Maryland Gazette* (Annapolis), 1745–1779, the *Maryland Journal* (Baltimore), 1773–1779, and Dunlop's *Maryland Gazette* (Baltimore), 1775–1779, from Prince George's, Charles, Calvert, Frederick (south of Monocacy River), and Anne Arundel counties and any slave born or traveling to those areas. Each slave runaway equals a single observation, but when a slave ran away twice in a five-year period, he was counted only once. Every motive in each ad is counted. If the ad states, for example, that a slave will both visit and try to pass as free, then it is counted in both places. The "to pass as free" column includes all slaves whose masters believed they would attempt to pass for free in Maryland or search for work in the province. The "to escape Maryland" column includes all those headed for Virginia or Pennsylvania and all those attempting to join either Revolutionary or British armies.

attempted to pass as free in small port towns, find employment, or leave the region. About one-half of southern Maryland runaways (see Table V) and nearly one-third (29 percent) of Virginia's advertised runaways before 1775 stayed with friends or kinfolk. They hid on quarters or in surrounding woods for a few days or weeks, and then returned voluntarily or were recaptured. Many of the other slaves, who wanted to pass as free, also had to use the plantation underground to reach their destinations, and at least half of them stayed within visiting distance of their family and friends. Only one runaway in four in southern Maryland and one in three in Virginia before 1775 left his home province and tried to begin a new life as a free person.[66]

The slave community, of course, had its share of conflicts, and on occasion a slave assaulted or stole from another slave. Nevertheless, several accounts of these incidents suggest that the rest of the slave community united against the transgressors. Slaves usually refused to

[66] Table V; Mullin, *Flight and Rebellion*, 108, 129. Since the number of unknowns is so large, it is difficult to be more precise. If one eliminates "acculturated" slaves (by Mullin's difinition), then the Maryland and Virginia data become very similar.

testify in court against their fellows, especially when blacks stole goods from whites, but when a member of the black community was hurt, slaves testified against the guilty person to protect themselves or their property. In May 1763 Jack poisoned Clear with a mixture of rum and henbane; she became ill and died the following February. Six slaves who belonged to Clear's master informed him of the act and testified against Jack in Prince George's court. They were joined by three slaves who lived on nearby plantations. The jury found Jack guilty, and he was sentenced to hang. Similarly, when Tom broke into Weems's quarter in Anne Arundel County and took goods belonging to Weems's slaves, six men and women owned by James and David Weems testified against him. He was found guilty and was hanged.[67]

Afro-American slaves had developed strong community institutions on their quarters and in their families and kin groups by the 1760s and 1770s, but the values and beliefs held by members of this community are difficult to determine. Since blacks in the Chesapeake region did not achieve a settled social life until after heavy African immigration stopped and since whites continued to live in even the most densely black areas, one would expect slave culture in the region to reflect white values and beliefs. Even native-born slaves had little choice either about their work or about the people who lived with them in their quarters. Nevertheless, they had a measure of self-determination in their family life, in their religion, and in the ways they celebrated or mourned. The skimpy surviving evidence suggests that when they could choose, tidewater Afro-Americans simultaneously borrowed from whites and drew on the values and beliefs their ancestors brought from West Africa to form a culture not only significantly different from that of Anglo-Americans but also different from the culture of any West African group or any other group of North American slaves.

The way Afro-Americans organized their family life indicates most clearly how they used both African and Euro-American forms to create a new institution compatible with their life under slavery. By the time of the Revolution, most slaves lived in families, and slave households were similar to those of their white masters. About as many Afro-Americans as whites lived in two-parent and extended households. Whites all lived in monogamous families, and only scattered examples of the African custom of polygamy can be found among blacks. Slavery forced the kinfolk of extended families to live very close to one another on large plantations where they played and worked together. By contrast, whites only occasionally visited their extended kinfolk

    [67] Prince George's Court Rec., XXVI, 343, 357; Anne Arundel Judgments, 1B#6, 347–348, 355; *Md. Gaz.*, Dec. 14, 1774.

and worked their fields only with their children, not with adult brothers and sisters. This closeness fostered a sense of kin solidarity among Afro-Americans. They named their children after both sides of the family (but interestingly enough, daughters were not often named for their mothers). And they sometimes refused to marry within the plantation even when sex ratios were equal: many of the available potential partners were first cousins, and blacks refused to marry first cousins. This may have represented a transformation of African marriage taboos that differed from tribe to tribe but tended to be stricter than those of Chesapeake whites, who frequently married first cousins.[68]

Native slaves occasionally accepted the outward signs of Christian belief. Their children were baptized and sometimes received religious instruction. All three Anglican clergymen of Prince George's County reported in 1724 that they baptized slave children and adults and preached to those who would listen. In 1731 one Prince George's minister baptized blacks "where perfect in their Catechism" and "visit[ed] them in their sickness and married them when called upon." Similar work continued in both Maryland and Virginia in the generation before the Revolution.[69]

Afro-Americans may have superimposed Christianity upon the beliefs, values, and ceremonies learned from African forebears and from each other. Thomas Bacon, a Maryland cleric and publisher of a compendium of the colony's laws, preached to blacks on Maryland's Eastern Shore in the 1740s at services they directed, "at their *funerals* (several of which I have attended)—and to such small congregations as their *marriages* have brought together." Bacon felt that the slaves he saw were "living in as profound Ignorance of what Christianity really is, (except as to a few outward Ordinances) as if they had remained in the midst of those barbarous Heathen Countries from whence their parents had been first imported." [70]

---

[68] Kulikoff, "Tobacco and Slaves," chap. 10, and "Beginnings of Afro-American Family," 175–185; Gutman, *Black Family*, 88–90, chaps. 3–5. Gutman, along with Ira Berlin and Mary Beth Norton, have found extensive kin naming on the plantations of Charles Carroll and Thomas Jefferson during the 18th century. I am indebted to Mr. Gutman for sharing this unpublished data with me.

[69] William Stevens Perry, *Historical Collections Relating to the American Colonial Church*, IV (Davenport, Iowa, 1878), 201, 206, 304, 306–307; Bacon, *Four Sermons Preached*, 4; Thad W. Tate, *The Negro in Eighteenth-Century Williamsburg* (Charlottesville, Va., 1972), 65–75. Prince George's responses in the 1720s and 1730s seem typical of those from other parishes on Maryland's lower Western Shore, but those returns are scattered in Perry, *Historical Collections*, IV.

[70] Thomas Bacon, *Four Sermons upon the Great and Indispensible Duty of All Christian Masters and Mistresses to Bring Up Their Negro Slaves in the Knowledge and Fear of God* (London, 1749), v, vii. Eugene D. Genovese, *Roll, Jordan, Roll. The World the Slaves Made* (New York, 1975), Book 2, Pt. 1, describes how slaves transformed Protestant religion in the antebellum period and how it differed from white religion.

Native slaves retained folk beliefs that may have come from Africa. Some African medicine men, magicians, and witches migrated and passed on their skills to other slaves. Medicine men and magicians were spiritual leaders in many African communities, including those of the Ibos, and they continued to practice among Afro-Americans who still believed in their powers. William Grimes was born in King George County, Virginia, in 1784; his narrative of his life as a runaway suggests that he was terrified of a woman he thought was a witch, that he feared sleeping in the bed of a dead man, and that he consulted fortune tellers.[71]

Slave music and dance displayed a distinctly African character. In 1774 Nicholas Cresswell, a British visitor, described slave celebrations in Charles County, Maryland. On Sundays, he wrote, the blacks "generally meet together and amuse themselves with Dancing to the Banjo. This musical instrument . . . is made of a Gourd something in imitation of a Guitar, with only four strings." "Their poetry," Cresswell reported, "is like the music—Rude and uncultivated. Their Dancing is most violent exercise, but so irregular and grotesque. I am not able to describe it." The banjo was probably of African origin, and Cresswell's reaction to the dancing suggests that it contained African rhythms unknown in European dance. If the form was African, it was placed in an American context: the slave songs Cresswell heard "generally relate the usage they have received from their Masters and Mistresses in a very satirical stile and manner."[72]

Although these little pieces of data do not add up to a complete description of slave culture in the Chesapeake on the eve of the Revolution, some tentative conclusions can nonetheless be drawn. In several areas, where slaves could choose how to behave, they did not follow white norms but combined African memories with fragments of white culture. The result, however, does not seem to have been heavily African, at least on the surface, and blacks in Maryland and Virginia preserved far less African content in their culture than did slaves in the British West Indies.

African and Afro-American slaves developed their own social institutions in the generations preceding the Revolution, and probably formed their own indigenous culture as well. A period of great disruption among blacks early in the century was followed in the pre-Revolutionary years by a time of settled communities. Newly enslaved Africans came to the Chesapeake colonies in large enough numbers to

---

[71] Charles H. Nichols, Jr., "The Case of William Grimes, the Runaway Slave," *WMQ*, 3d Ser., VIII (1951), 556–558. Grimes was in Georgia when he encountered the witch, but his training in Virginia obviously influenced his belief.

[72] *Journal of Cresswell*, 18–19. Blassingame, *Slave Community*, 27–32.

cause conflicts between native slaves and new Negroes, but the migration was too small to allow Africans to develop syncretistic African communities successfully. Africans were forced by their masters to stay on the quarter, where natives also lived and where unit sizes were small and sex ratios high. As a result, slaves could not transform individual friendships into community institutions. It was only when native adults began to predominate that the earlier conflicts among blacks were contained, and families and quarter communities began to emerge through out tidewater. At the same time as immigration of Africans declined, the proportion of natives among blacks grew, the sex ratio declined, and the number of slaves per unit increased. These demographic changes made the development of communal institutions easier.

As slaves responded to the demographic and economic environment of the Chesapeake colonies, they developed indigenous institutions. This essay confirms the overall argument made by Mintz and Price, but further suggests the crucial importance of slave immigration, the density of slave population, the size of units, and the adult sex ratio in the development of slave communities in the Chesapeake colonies. Because demographic and economic conditions in the Chesapeake were not favorable to black cultural autonomy until nearly the middle of the eighteenth century, the development of distinctive social institutions among the slaves of the region was a long process, much slower than Mintz and Price suggest for the West Indies. Detailed study of slave demography and the economics of slavery in various colonies might well show why Afro-American communities and cultures developed at different rates and possessed different characteristics in the Chesapeake, South Carolina, and the West Indies.

Much work remains to be done on slave society in the colonial Chesapeake and in other mainland colonies. Three areas especially require research. First, we need to know a great deal about the internal life of the slave quarters. The impact of Christianity on African and Afro-American beliefs and on slave family and community life needs much further exploration. Only with more details on slave culture in the Chesapeake colonies and elsewhere in the colonial South can the relationships between slave demography and slave culture suggested in this article be adequately tested.

Secondly, we should explore in detail the interaction between whites and Africans and whites and native slaves. Knowledge of which whites Africans saw every day and of the values and beliefs the whites followed will tell us how much Africans borrowed from whites and what ideas and structures may have come from African communities. Slaves obviously could form communities and extended families only if permitted by the masters, for whites could greatly disrupt slave life through the sale of slaves, the organization of work, and the punishment of their chattels. An investigation of the mundane attitudes of masters toward their slaves both in the fields and in the quarters would therefore be very useful.

Finally, this essay deals with only a portion of older settled tidewater areas. In the 1730s and 1740s proportionately more black immigrants went to the piedmont than to tidewater, and after 1755 nearly every African found his new home in a piedmont county. How much of the history of tidewater was repeated in the piedmont? If the population of the piedmont was heavily African, perhaps the characteristics of slave society in tidewater in the 1720s and 1730s were replicated in the piedmont in the 1750s and 1760s. But if enough black migrants from tidewater entered the piedmont, the story of the 1750s and 1760s may have been much the same in the two regions. Of course, it is possible that the relationships between slave demography and slave society documented here did not exist in the piedmont. If that is proven, then the basic patterns described here might be called into question.

To find the answers to these questions will be difficult, for whites in the Chesapeake showed little interest in the internal lives of their slaves. However, much remains to be collected from family papers, probate records, court order books, vestry books, parish registers, and even mercantile records. The search for answers may be difficult but it is certainly worth undertaking when the problems of race and culture that began in the colonial era are still with us.

Work and Culture: The Task System and the World of Lowcountry Blacks, 1700 to 1880

PHILIP D. MORGAN

In the next article, Philip D. Morgan approaches the internal history of slave life from a perspective quite different from Kulikoff's. Arguing that one factor above all—the task system—influenced the development of Afro-American culture in the earliest period, Morgan contends that the domestic economy and rhythms of daily life can be charted with surprising accuracy. Like Kulikoff, moreover, he is at pains to identify not merely the pattern of the early period but also to trace its effects into the national period of U.S. history. Indeed, he concludes his exploration not in 1780 but in 1880.

The article is a tour de force *of historical reconstruction exploiting as it does sources more often used for quite different purposes. In addition, it fits not merely into the "new" history of the colonial South and of slavery, but also into another larger trend in historical writing: labor history. Like many recent labor historians, Morgan finds ironic results growing from the efforts of those who controlled the labor system to engineer the social and cultural lives of workers. Just as labor historians of other times and places have found that attempts to elicit obedience and to enforce social control frequently permitted and even promoted the*

Reprinted by permission from Philip D. Morgan, "Work and Culture: The Task System and the World of Lowcountry Blacks, 1700 to 1880," *William and Mary Quarterly,* XXXIX (1982), 563–599.

emergence of independent cultural life among workers, so Morgan finds that the task system had a similar effect upon slaves.

Morgan's and Kulikoff's articles demand comparison. How different are their sources? How can the differences in their conclusions be explained? What sorts of assumptions do they bring to their writing and what effect do those assumptions appear to have on the final result? In addition, however, Morgan and Kulikoff's approach might also be compared to that used by Greven on the one hand and Soderlund on the other. In addition, Kulikoff and Menard as well as Carr and Walsh worked simultaneously on developing the study of the Chesapeake. Can their mutual influence be identified in their essays? How? At what sorts of problems are these historians (and others in this volume) aiming? Why has it taken so long for scholars to approach these issues with the originality and creativity that are exhibited here?

Within the realm of slavery studies there has been a pronounced preoccupation with the external or institutional aspects of the slave system. Despite repeated clarion calls for investigations of life in the slave quarters, little scholarly attention has been directed to the domestic economy of the slaves, their work routines, their attitudes toward resource allocation, their attempts to accumulate, and their patterns of consumption.[1] This academic shortsightedness is more easily identified than remedied. Attitudes toward work and patterns of work constitute an area of inquiry that sprawls awkwardly across academic demarcations: the subject is all too easily neglected.[2] In addition, the

---

[1] Comparative studies of slavery have been especially prone to the institutional or external perspective. Even one of the best studies of slave life—Eugene D. Genovese's *Roll, Jordan, Roll: The World the Slaves Made* (New York, 1974)—devotes only a few pages to the domestic economy of the slaves (pp. 535–540), although slave work routines (pp. 285–324) and aspects of consumption patterns (pp. 550–561) are explored sensitively and at length.

[2] Anthropologists, for example, have been criticized for neglecting the subject. See the introduction to Sandra Wallman, ed., *Social Anthropology of Work*, Association of Social Anthropologists, Monograph 19 (London, 1979).

genre to which this type of history is most akin, namely, labor history, often suffers from its own myopia: studies that begin by aiming to uncover the experience of workers can all too readily focus instead on management priorities.[3] Moreover, what has been said with respect to the English farm laborer applies even more forcefully to the Afro-American slave: "No one has written his signature more plainly across the countryside; but no one has left more scanty records of his achievements." [4]

Mindful of these pitfalls, this article attempts to bring history closer to the central concerns of ordinary people's lives—in this case, the lives of Afro-American slaves in the lowcountry region of South Carolina and Georgia. In this light, perhaps the most distinctive and central feature of lowcountry slave life was the task system. In Lewis Gray's words, "Under the task system the slave was assigned a certain amount of work for the day, and after completing the task he could use his time as he pleased," whereas under the gang system, prevalent in most Anglo-American plantation societies, "slaves were worked in groups under the control of a driver or leader . . . and the laborer was compelled to work the entire day." [5] While previous commentators have drawn attention to the task system, few have explored how this peculiarity arose and how it structured the world of those who labored under it. In order to shed light on the first matter, I shall open three windows onto different phases in the development of this labor arrangement: its origins in the first half of the eighteenth century, its routinization during the Revolutionary era, and its full flowering by the time of the Civil War. I shall also explore the ramifications of the task system for the slaves by analyzing its most distinctive feature so far as they were concerned: the opportunities it provided for working on their own behalf once the stipulated task had been completed.[6] I shall argue, then, that a particular mode of labor organization and a

---

[3] The labor history that is practiced in *History Workshop* and in the volumes published in the *History Workshop* series are the kind to which this article aspires. Also noteworthy is a recent trend in American labor history that treats the reality of work as the focus, or starting point, of investigation. See David Brody, "Labor History in the 1970s: Toward a History of the American Worker," in Michael Kammen, ed., *The Past before Us: Contemporary Historical Writing in the United States* (Ithaca, N.Y., 1980), 268.

[4] Alan Everitt, "Farm Labourers," in Joan Thirsk, ed., *The Agrarian History of England and Wales*, IV (Cambridge, 1967), 396.

[5] Lewis Cecil Gray, *History of Agriculture in the Southern United States to 1860* (Gloucester, Mass., 1958 [orig. publ. Washington, D.C., 1933]), I, 550–551.

[6] Equally, we could investigate more fully than will be possible here the special role of the black driver, the marketing opportunities, or the occupational structure that a rice tasking system produced.

particular domestic economy involved simultaneously in the colonial and antebellum lowcountry.[7]

This argument can best be secured by broadening our horizons to take in not only colonial and early national developments but also those of the antebellum and even postbellum years. On the one hand, such a strategy will show how colonial developments bore directly on nineteenth- and even twentieth-century realities. To take a minor example, the basic task unit still current in the minds of freedmen in the 1930s will be shown to have had a precise colonial origin. On the other hand, the opportunities that the task system presented slaves can be understood only in the light of mid-nineteenth-century experiences. To take a more significant example, the resemblance between the experiences of some lowcountry slaves and of the protopeasants found among the slaves of certain Caribbean plantation societies emerges most clearly from a glance at the behavior of slaves and freedmen in the years surrounding the Civil War.[8] In other words, to understand the evolution of the task system and its concomitant domestic economy, we shall need a telescope rather than a microscope.

I

> If the Negroes are skilful and industrious, they plant
> something for themselves after the day's work.
> Johann Bolzius, 1751

The earliest, fragmentary descriptions of work practices in the lowcountry rice economy indicate that a prominent characteristic of the task system—a sharp division between the master's "time" and the slave's "time"—was already in place. In the first decade of the eighteenth century the clergy of South Carolina complained that slaves were planting "for themselves as much as will cloath and subsist them and their famil[ies]." During the investigation of a suspected slave conspiracy in mid-century, a lowcountry planter readily acknowledged that one of his slaves had planted rice "in his own time" and could do

---

[7] The word *particular* is important here because I do not intend to suggest that the independent production of goods and the accumulation of property by slaves was necessarily predicated on a task system. From situations as diverse as a sugar plantation in Jamaica to an iron foundry in the United States, slaves were often able to control the accumulation and disposal of sizable earnings and possessions. Rather, in the lowcountry, a particular conjunction arose that probably led—but this would need much greater space for comparative presentation—to a distinctive internal economy among the slaves.

[8] In exploring these resemblances, I have found the work of Sidney W. Mintz to be particularly helpful. See "The Origins of Reconstituted Peasantries," in *Caribbean Transformations* (Chicago, 1974), 146–156, and "Slavery and the Rise of Peasantries," in Michael Craton, ed., *Roots and Branches: Current Directions in Slave Studies* (Toronto, 1979), 213–242.

with it as he wished.[9] The most acute observer of early work practices, Johann Bolzius, described how slaves, after "their required day's work," were "given as much land as they can handle" on which they planted corn, potatoes, tobacco, peanuts, sugar and water melons, and pumpkins and bottle pumpkins.[10] The opportunity to grow such a wide range of provisions on readily available land owed much to the early establishment and institutionalization of the daily work requirement. By mid-century the basic "task" unit had been set at a quarter of an acre. Moreover, other activities, outside of the rice field, were also tasked: in pounding the rice grain, slaves were "tasked at seven Mortars for one day," and in providing fences lowcountry slaves were expected to split 100 poles of about twelve feet in length (a daily "task" that remained unchanged throughout the slave era, as Table I indicates).[11] These tasks were not, of course, easily accomplished, and occasionally planters exacted even higher daily requirements; but, as Bolzius noted, the advantage to the slaves of having a daily goal was that they could, once it was met, "plant something for themselves." [12]

A tried and tested model of labor organization—the gang system practiced on both tobacco and sugar plantations—was available when lowcountry planters discovered their own plantation staple. In fact, many of the first immigrants were from Barbados, where they must have had direct experience of operating gangs of slaves.[13] Why did they and others decide to adopt a new system? U. B. Phillips claimed that temporary absenteeism was responsible: "The necessity of the master's moving away from his estate in the warm months, to escape the malaria, involved the adoption of some system of routine which would work with more or less automatic regularity without his own inspiring or impelling presence." However, while absenteeism may have contributed to the attractiveness of this system, it seems an insufficiently powerful agent to account for its inception. The example of Caribbean sugar production is pertinent here; if the withdrawal of an

---

[9] The Instructions of the Clergy of South Carolina given to Mr. Johnston, 1712, A8/429, Society of the Propagation of the Gospel, London; testimony of Thomas Akin and Ammon, Feb. 7, 1749, Council Journal, No. 17, Pt. I, 160, South Carolina Department of Archives and History, Columbia.

[10] "Johann Martin Bolzius Answers a Questionnaire on Carolina and Georgia," trans. and ed. Klaus G. Loewald *et al.*, *William and Mary Quarterly*, 3d Ser., XIV (1957), 259.

[11] Dr. Alexander Garden to the Royal Society, Apr. 20, 1755, Guard Book I, 36, Royal Society of Arts, London; "Bolzius Answers a Questionnaire," trans. and ed. Loewald *et al.*, *WMQ*, 3d Ser., XIV (1957), 258.

[12] "Bolzius Answers a Questionnaire," trans. and ed. Loewald *et al.*, *WMQ*, 3d Ser., XIV (1957), 256.

[13] Richard S. Dunn, "The English Sugar Islands and the Founding of South Carolina," *South Carolina Historical Magazine*, LXXII (1971), 81–93; Richard Waterhouse, "England, the Caribbean, and the Settlement of Carolina," *Journal of American Studies*, IX (1975), 259–281.

inspiring master encouraged the development of tasking, why did not sugar planters in the West Indies, where absenteeism began relatively early, adopt the system? [14]

The absence of masters may be an unconvincing explanation for the development of a task system, but perhaps the presence of particular slaves can serve in its place. Peter H. Wood and Daniel C. Littlefield have pointed out that some black immigrants to early South Carolina were already familiar with the techniques of rice cultivation.[15] These slaves' expertise, it might be argued, accounts for the evolution of a system that would operate more or less automatically. It has even been suggested, in this regard, that a work pattern of alternating bouts of intense labor and idleness tends to occur wherever men are to some degree in control of their own working lives (need one look any further than authors?).[16] By displaying their own understanding of the basic requirements of rice cultivation, lowcountry slaves might have gained a measure of control over their lives, at least to the extent of determining the length of their working days. While this is an attractive argument, it is not without problems. The coastal regions that seem to have supplied a majority of slaves to early South Carolina were not rice-producing areas; lowcountry whites have left no record of valuing the knowledge of rice planting that same slaves might have displayed; and familiarity with rice planting is hardly the same as familiarity with irrigated rice culture, practiced in South Carolina from early days.[17]

---

[14] Ulrich Bonnell Phillips, "The Slave Labor Problem in the Charleston District," in Elinor Miller and Eugene D. Genovese, eds., *Plantation, Town, and County: Essays on the Local History of American Slave Society* (Urbana, Ill., 1974), 9. For Caribbean absenteeism see Richard S. Dunn, *Sugar and Slaves: The Rise of the Planter Class in the English West Indies, 1624–1713* (Chapel Hill, N.C., 1972), 101–103, 161–163.

[15] Wood, *Black Majority: Negroes in Colonial South Carolina from 1670 through the Stono Rebellion* (New York, 1974), 56–62; Littlefield, *Rice and Slaves: Ethnicity and the Slave Trade in Colonial South Carolina* (Baton Rouge, La., 1981), 74–114.

[16] E. P. Thompson, "Time, Work-Discipline, and Industrial Capitalism," *Past and Present*, No. 38 (1967), 73.

[17] Of those slaves imported into South Carolina before 1740 and for whom an African coastal region of origin is known, I calculate that 15% were from rice-producing areas. Unfortunately, we know little or nothing about the regional origins of the earliest slave vessels to South Carolina. The first association between an African region and the cultivation of rice that I have found comes late in the day and may have been no more than a mercantile gambit. In 1758 the merchant firm Austin and Laurens described the origins of the slave ship *Betsey* as the "Windward and Rice Coast" (*South-Carolina Gazette* [Charleston], Aug. 11, 1758). Whites in other areas of North America are on record as valuing the familiarity with rice planting that some Africans displayed (see Henry P. Dart, "The First Cargo of African Slaves for Louisiana, 1718," *Louisiana Historical Quarterly*, XIV [1931], 176–177, as referred to in Joe Gray Taylor, *Negro Slavery in Louisiana* [Baton Rouge, La., 1963], 14). For the West Africans' widespread unfamiliarity with irrigation see Littlefield, *Rice and Slaves*, 86, and the issue of *Africa*, LI, No. 2 (1981), devoted to "Rice and Yams in West Africa." A fuller discussion of all these matters will be presented in my "Slave Counterpoint: Black Culture in the Eighteenth-Century Chesapeake and Lowcountry" (unpubl. MS).

TABLE I   *Tasking Requirements, c. 1750 to c. 1860*

Representative Tasks	1750s [1]	1770s [2]	1820s [3]
Rice			
Turning up land	¼a		¼a
Trenching/Covering	½a		¾a
First Hoeing	¼a		¼ – ½a
Second Hoeing			
Third Hoeing	½a		
Reaping			
Threshing			600s
Pounding	7m		
Ditching			600sf
Cotton			
Listing			¼a
Bedding			¼a
Hoeing			½a
Picking			90–100 lbs
Assorting			30– 50 lbs
Ginning			20– 30 lbs
Moting			30– 50 lbs
General			
Splitting rails	100	100	100
Squaring timber		100'	100'

a = acre   s = sheaves   m = mortars
c = compasses   sf = square feet

[1] "Bolzius Answers a Questionnaire," trans. and ed. Loewald *et al.*, *WMQ*, 3d Ser., XIV (1957), 258; Garden to the Royal Society, Apr. 20, 1755, Guard Book I, 36.
[2] John Gerar William De Brahm, *Report of the General Survey in the Southern District of North America*, ed. Louis De Vorsey, Jr. (Columbia, S.C., 1971), 94.
[3] "Estimate of the Daily Labour of Negroes," *American Farmer*, V (1823–1824), 319–320; [Edwin C. Holland], *A Refutation of the Calumnies Circulated against . . . Slavery . . .* (New York, 1969 [orig. publ. Charleston, S.C., 1822]), 53; Basil Hall, *Travels in North America in the Years 1827 and 1828*, III (London, 1829), 219–223.
[4] "A Memorandum of Tasks," *Southern Agriculturalist*, VII (1834), 297–299; W. H. Capers, "On the Culture of Sea-Island Cotton," *ibid.*, VIII (1835), 402–411.
[5] Edmund Ruffin, *Report of the Commencement and Progress of the Agricultural Survey of South-Carolina for 1843* (Columbia, S.C., 1843), 118; J. A. Turner, *The Cotton Planter's Manual* (New York, 1865), 285.

TABLE I (*Continued*)

Representative Tasks	*1830s*[4]	*1840s*[5]	*1850s–1860s*[6]
Rice			
Turning up land	¼a	¼ – ½a	¼a
Trenching/Covering	¾a	¾a	½a
First Hoeing	½a	½a	¼ – ½a
Second Hoeing	½a	½a	
Third Hoeing	¾a	20c	
Reaping		¾a	¾a
Threshing	600s	600s	600s
Pounding			
Ditching	700sf	500sf	600sf
Cotton			
Listing	¼a	½a	¼ – ½a
Bedding	¼a	⅜a	¼ – ½a
Hoeing	½a	½a	½a
Picking	70–100 lbs		
Assorting	60 lbs		
Ginning	30 lbs		20–30 lbs
Moting	30 lbs		
General			
Splitting rails	100		100–125
Squaring timber	100'		100'

a = acre s = sheaves m = mortars
c = compasses sf = square feet

[6] Frederick Law Olmsted, *A Journey in the Seabord Slave States* . . . (New York, 1968 [orig. publ. 1856]), 434–435; Francis S. Holmes, *Southern Farmer and Market Gardener* (Charleston, S.C., 1852), 234–236; Weehaw Plantation Book, 1855–1861, South Carolina Historical Society, Charleston; "Tasks for Negroes," *Southern Cultivator*, XVIII (1860), 247; Col. A. J. Willard to W. H. Smith, Nov. 13, 1865 (A7011); testimony of Harry McMillan, 1863 (K78) (see below, n. 81 for explanation of these notations); J. A. Turner, *The Cotton Planter's Manual*, 133–135. See also George P. Rawick, ed., *The American Slave: A Composite Autobiography* (Westport, Conn., 1972), II, Pt. ii, 302, III, Pt. iii, 92, Pt. iv, 117.

Slaves undoubtedly contributed a great deal to the development of South Carolina's rice economy; but, on present evidence, it would be rash to attribute the development of a task system to their prowess, especially when that prowess went largely unrecognized and may not have been significant.

A consideration of staple-crop requirements provides the most satisfactory, if not complete, answer to the question of the system's origins. The amount of direct supervision demanded by various crops offers at least one clue to the puzzle. Unlike tobacco, which involved scrupulous care in all phases of the production cycle and was therefore best cultivated by small gangs of closely attended laborers, rice was a hardy plant, requiring a few relatively straightforward operations for its successful cultivation.[18] The great expansion of rice culture in seventeenth-century Lombardy, for instance, was predicated not on a stable, sophisticated, and well-supervised labor force but on a pool of transient labor drawn from far afield.[19] Nor did rice production require the strict regimentation and "semi-industrialised" production techniques that attended the cultivation of sugar and necessitated gang labor.[20] However, the Caribbean plantation experience does offer parallels to the lowcountry rice economy: in the British West Indies, crops that required little supervision or regimentation—notably coffee and pimento—were, like rice, grown by a slave labor force organized by tasks rather than into gangs.[21]

In addition to the degree of direct supervision required by a crop, the facility with which the laborers' output could be measured also shaped different forms of labor organization. For example, the productivity of a single coffee and pimento worker could be measured accurately and cheaply, particularly in the harvesting cycle. It was easy to

---

[18] In 1830 one Cuban planter, with little historical sense, could even argue that the culture of the tobacco plant "properly belongs to a white population, for there are few plants requiring more attention and tender treatment than this does" (Joseph M. Hernandez, "On the Cultivation of the Cuba Tobacco Plant," *Southern Agriculturalist*, III [1830], 463).

[19] Domenico Sella, *Crisis and Continuity: The Economy of Spanish Lombardy in the Seventeenth Century* (Cambridge, Mass., 1979), 121–122.

[20] Dunn, *Sugar and Slaves*, 189–200. The connection between sugar cultivation and gang labor was not absolutely axiomatic, at least in the postemancipation era. See Douglas Hall, *Free Jamaica, 1838–1865: An Economic History* (New Haven, Conn., 1959), 44–45; Jerome Handler, "Some Aspects of Work Organization on Sugar Plantations in Barbados," *Ethnology*, IV (1965), 16–38; and James McNeill and Chimman Lal, *Report to the Government of India on the Conditions of Indian Immigrants in Four British Colonies and Surinam* in *British Parliamentary Papers*, 1915, Cd. 7744, 7745 (I am indebted to Stanley Engerman for the last reference).

[21] B. W. Higman, *Slave Population and Economy in Jamaica, 1807–1834* (Cambridge, 1976), 23–24, 220. A Jamaican bookkeeper reported that the only work on a coffee plantation *not* carried out by tasks was the drying of the berries, because "this required constant attention" (*ibid.*, 23).

weigh an individual's baskets of coffee or pimento berries, and tasking may have first developed in this stage of the respective crop cycles before being extended to other operations. Conversely, the much larger volumes involved in the cane harvest would have proved far less easy and much more expensive to measure on an individual "task" basis; not surprisingly, gang labor was employed at this and other stages of the sugar cycle.[22] In the case of rice, it was less the harvesting and more the cultivation of the crop that lent itself to inexpensive and efficient measurement. As Phillips pointed out, drainage ditches, which were necessary in lowcountry rice cultivation, provided convenient units by which the performance of tasks could be measured.[23] The ubiquity and long-standing history of the quarter-acre task suggest that the planting and weeding stages of the rice cycle provided the initial rationale for the task system; once tasking became firmly established, it was extended to a whole host of plantation operations.

Thus various staple-crop requirements seem to have served as the most important catalysts for the development of particular modes of labor organization. Undoubtedly other imperatives contributed to the attractiveness of one or the other labor arrangement: absenteeism and the ease with which slaves took to rice cultivation may well have encouraged a more widespread and rapid diffusion of the task system in the lowcountry than might otherwise have been the case. Moreover, once a task system had been tried, tested, and not found wanting, it could be extended to crops that were produced elsewhere by means of gang labor. In other words, once tasking became a way of life, means were found to circumvent the otherwise powerful dictates of the various staple crops.[24]

Whatever the origins of the task system, its consequences soon became apparent. Indeed, the way in which slaves chose to spend their own "time" created unease among ruling South Carolinians. One of the earliest laws relating to slaves, enacted in 1686, prohibited the exchange of goods between slaves or between slaves and freemen without their masters' consent. A decade later, slaves were expressly forbidden from felling and carrying away timber on lands other than their masters'. In 1714 the legislature enacted its stiffest prohibition; slaves were no longer to "plant for themselves any corn, peas or rice." [25] While this stark ban appears definitive, later legislation sug-

---

[22] Barry Higman suggested this to me in a personal communication.

[23] Ulrich Bonnell Phillips, *American Negro Slavery: A Survey of the Supply, Employment and Control of Negro Labor As Determined by the Plantation Regime* (Baton Rouge, La., 1966 [orig. publ. New York, 1918]), 247.

[24] See the relevant discussions, below, of how the task system was extended to the cultivation of cotton and even sugar in the late 18th- and early 19th-century lowcountry.

[25] Thomas Cooper and David J. McCord, eds., *The Statutes at Large of South Carolina* (Columbia, S.C., 1836–1841), II, 22–23, VII, II, 368.

gests its ineffectiveness. In 1734, for example, an act for the better regulation of patrols allowed patrollers to confiscate "all fowls and other provisions" found in the possession of "stragling negroes." That slaves produced provisions independently is further implied in a 1738 act for the licensing of hawkers and pedlars, which aimed to stamp out the illicit traffic in rice and provisions between slaves and itinerant traders. By 1751 the legislators bowed to the inevitable. By outlawing the sale of slaves' rice and corn to anybody other than their masters, they were implicitly recognizing the right of slaves to cultivate such crops.[26] The law of 1714 had thus died a natural death.

From the evidence of plantation account books and estate records, the act of 1751 simply brought the law closer into line with social practice. In 1728 Abraham, a Ball family slave, was paid £1 10s. for providing his master with eighteen fowls, while a female slave received £8 for supplying hogs. In 1736 twenty-two Ball family slaves were paid more than £50 for supplying varying amounts of rice to their master.[27] The extent of this trade in provisions was occasionally impressive; over the course of two years, the slaves belonging to James Hartley's estate were paid £124 for supplying 290 bushels of their corn.[28] Henry Ravenel not only purchased his slaves' provision goods, consisting of corn, fowls, hogs, and catfish, but also their canoes, baskets, and myrtle wax.[29]

Masters undoubtedly benefited from these exchanges while displaying their benevolence, but we should not assume that there was no bargaining, however unequal, between the parties. Henry Laurens, for example, advised one of his newly appointed overseers to "purchase of your own Negroes all [the provisions] that you know Lawfully belongs to themselves at the lowest price that they will sell it for."[30] If a master refused to give slaves a fair price for their produce, they could take it elsewhere. One of the most persistent complaints of lowcountry planters and legislators concerned illicit trading across plantation boundaries.[31] A slave who produced rice "in his own time" also traveled more than fifteen miles up the Cooper River to sell a barrel of his

[26] *Ibid.*, III, 398, 489, VII, 423.

[27] Ball Family Account Book, 174, 32, and unpaginated memorandum, Jan. 21, 1736, South Carolina Historical Society, Charleston.

[28] Administration of James Hartley's estate, Aug. 1758–July 1760, Inventory Book V, 160–175, S.C. Archs., Columbia.

[29] Henry Ravenel's Day Book, particularly for the years 1763–1767, S.C. Hist. Soc., Charleston.

[30] George C. Rogers *et al.*, eds., *The Papers of Henry Laurens*, V (Columbia, S.C., 1976), 41.

[31] Apart from the acts already mentioned, see Cooper and McCord, eds., *Statutes*, VII, 407–409, 434–435. See also Charlestown Grand Jury Presentments, *S.C. Gaz.*, Nov. 5, 1737.

crop to his brother, who resided on another plantation.[32] A white boatman, implicated in a slave conspiracy, openly acknowledged that he had exchanged his hog for a slave's deer skin.[33] The records of one lowcountry estate even register payments to a neighboring planter's slaves for their seed rice.[34] In other words, once slaves were allowed to produce provisions, they would always find ways to market them, be it to passing traders, neighboring whites, or fellow slaves.

Lowcountry slaves took the opportunity to raise a wide array of agricultural products, many of which reflected their African background. In the third decade of the eighteenth century Mark Catesby observed two African varieties of corn in the lowcountry but only among the "Plantations of *Negroes*." When William Bartram visited the lowcountry in the 1770s he noticed that the tania or tannier (a tuberous root found in the West Indies and tropical Africa) was "much cultivated and esteemed for food, particularly by the Negroes." [35] Bernard Romans claimed that slaves had introduced the groundnut into South Carolina; by the early nineteenth century, according to David Ramsay's informants on Edisto Island, groundnuts were "planted in small patches chiefly by the negroes, for market." [36] Romans also attributed the introduction of the "sesamen or oily grain" to lowcountry slaves; they used it, he maintained, "as a food either raw, toasted or boiled in their soups and are very fond of it, they call it *Benni*." Over one-and-a-half centuries later, a black sea islander was to be found planting what he called "bene." He used it in the same ways that his ancestors had done. Most significant, when asked where he acquired the seed, he said "his parents always had it and he was told "Dey brung it fum Africa.'" [37] Apparently peppers were also the preserve of slaves. Knowing that his slave old Tom "plants a good deal of pepper," Elias Ball desired him to send "sum Read pepper pounded

---

[32] Testimony of Thomas Akin and Ammon, Feb. 7, 1749, Council Journal, No. 17, Pt. I, 160.

[33] Testimony of Lawrence Kelly, Jan. 30, 1749, *ibid.*, 85.

[34] Administration of David Caw's estate, Oct. 20, 1761, Inventory Book V, 12–19.

[35] Mark Catesby, *The Natural History of Carolina, Florida and the Bahama Islands* . . . , II (London, 1743), xviii; Francis Harper, ed., *The Travels of William Bartram* (New Haven, Conn., 1958), 297.

[36] Romans, *A Concise Natural History of East and West Florida* . . . , I (New York, 1775), 131; Ramsay, *The History of South Carolina*, II (Charleston, S.C., 1808), 289. The groundnut is a South American cultivated plant which was disseminated so widely and rapidly within Africa that some have postulated an African origin. This is not the case, but Africans apparently introduced the plant into North America (A. Krapovickas, "The Origin, Variability and Spread of the Groundnut," in Peter J. Ucko and G. W. Dimbleby, eds., *The Domestication and Exploitation of Plants and Animals* [London, 1969], 427–441).

[37] Romans, *History of East and West Florida*, I, 130; Orrin Sage Wightman and Margaret Davis Cate, *Early Days of Coastal Georgia* (St. Simons Island, Ga., 1955), 163.

and corked up in a pint Bottle." In 1742, when Eliza Lucas sent her friend some of the same product, she referred to it, in revealing fashion, as "negroe pepper." [38] The only tobacco grown in early eighteenth-century South Carolina belonged to the slaves.[39] Janet Schaw was so impressed by the way in which Carolina slaves used their "little piece[s] of land" to grow vegetables, "rear hogs and poultry, sow calabashes, etc." that she thought they cultivated them "much better than their Master[s]." Furthermore, she believed that "the Negroes are the only people that seem to pay any attention to the various uses that the wild vegetables may be put to." [40]

The cultivation and subsequent exchange of provisions allowed some slaves to claim more substantial items of property. In 1714 the South Carolina legislature denied the slaves' claim to "any stock of hogs, cattle or horses." This directive apparently fell on deaf ears, for in 1722 it became lawful to seize any hogs, boats, or canoes belonging to slaves. Moreover, this later act referred to the "great inconveniences [that] do arise from negroes and other slaves keeping and breeding of horses"; not only were these horses (and cattle) to be seized, but the proceeds of their sale were to be put to the support of the parish poor. The irony of slave property sustaining white paupers was presumably lost on South Carolina legislators but perhaps not on the slaves. Once again, legislative intentions seem to have been thwarted, for in 1740 more complaints were to be heard about those "several owners of slaves [who] have permitted them to keep canoes, and to breed and raise horses, neat cattle and hogs, and to traffic and barter in several parts of this Province, for the particular and peculiar benefit of such slaves." [41] The most dramatic example of property ownership by a lowcountry slave in the first half of the eighteenth century involved not horses or canoes, but men. According to a deed of manumission, a slave named Sampson "by his Industry and the Assistance of Friends" had purchased and "procured in his owne Right and property and for his owne Use" another Negro slave named Tom.

[38] Elias Ball to Elias Ball, Feb. 26, 1786, Ball Family Papers, University of South Carolina, Columbia; Elise Pinckney, ed., *The Letterbook of Eliza Lucas Pinckney, 1739–1762* (Chapel Hill, N.C., 1972), 28.

[39] "Bolzius Answers a Questionnaire," trans. and ed. Loewald *et al.*, *WMQ*, 3d Ser., XIV (1957), 236; John Glen to the Board of Trade, Mar. 1753, C.O. 5/374, 147, Public Record Office; Bernhard A. Uhlendorf, trans. and ed., *The Siege of Charleston: With an Account of the Province of South Carolina . . .* (Ann Arbor, Mich., 1938), 353. The cultivation of tobacco spread rapidly through West Africa during the 17th century, so that 18th-century black immigrants to South Carolina might well have been familiar with the crop. See, for example, Jack R. Harlan *et al.*, eds., *Origins of African Plant Domestication* (The Hague, 1976), 296, 302, and Philip D. Curtin, *Economic Change in Precolonial Africa: Senegambia in the Era of the Slave Trade* (Madison, Wis., 1975), 230.

[40] Evangeline Walker Andrews and Charles McLean Andrews, eds., *Journal of a Lady of Quality . . .* (New Haven, Conn., 1923), 176–177.

[41] Cooper and McCord, eds., *Statutes*, VII, 368, 382, 409.

Sampson then exchanged his slave Tom for "fifty years of his [that is, Sampson's] Life time and Servitude (to come)." [42] If the task system had created the opportunities for Sampson's "Industry" to manifest itself in this way, it truly was a potent force.

II

Once a slave has completed his task, his
master feels no right to call on him.
Daniel Turner, 1806

By the late eighteenth century the task system had taken deep root in the lowcountry. Tasks were set for almost all operations—from clearing new ground (one-eighth of an acre) to the weekly task of a pair of sawyers (600 feet of pine or 780 feet of cypress).[43] However, the basic unit, a quarter-acre, was still the yardstick for virtually all rice-planting operations.[44] In recognition of this reality, one Georgia absentee in 1786 sent a chain "for running out the Tasks" to his plantation manager. "It is 105 feet long," he noted, "and will save a great deal of time in Laying out the field, and do it with more exactness." Henry Ferguson, an East Floridian who had spent seventeen years in South Carolina and Georgia, was able to specify precisely how much land his slaves had cleared "from the Tasks which he set to his Negroes having measured the Ground frequently for that purpose." He added that "a Task was a quarter of an Acre to weed p. day." [45] Even opponents of the task system testify to its pervasiveness. William Butler, a keen observer of rice culture, argued in 1786 that slaves "should always be Kept in Gangs or parcels and not scattered over a field in Tasks as is too generally done, for while in gangs they are more immediately under the Superintendants Eyes, [and] of course may be much better and more immediately inspected." [46]

---

[42] Mr. Isaac Bodett's Release to a Negro for Fifty Years, Nov. 13, 1728, Records of the Secretary of the Province, Book II, 42–43, S.C. Archs., Columbia.

[43] John Gerar William De Brahm, *Report of the General Survey in the Southern District of North America*, ed. Louis De Vorsey, Jr. (Columbia, S.C., 1971), 94.

[44] William Butler, "Observations on the Culture of Rice," 1786, S.C. Hist. Soc., Charleston. One plantation journal recorded completed daily tasks and acres planted: the quarter-acre task was uniformly applied throughout the planting season. See Plantation Journal, 1773, Wragg Papers, S.C. Hist. Soc.

[45] J. Channing to Edward Telfair, Aug. 10, 1786, Telfair Papers, Duke University, Durham, N.C.; Wilbur H. Siebert, ed., *Loyalists in East Florida, 1774 to 1785*, II (DeLand, Fla., 1929), 67.

[46] Butler, "Observations," 1786. There was a parallel debate in England at this time between the advocates of regularly employed wage-labor and the advocates of "taken-work." One of those who censured the recourse to taken-work made a similar point to that of Butler: people only agreed to tasking, this critic alleged, in order "to save themselves the trouble of watching their workmen" (Thompson, "Time, Work-Discipline," *Past and Present*, No. 38 [1967], 78–79).

The extension of the task system to the cultivation of sea island cotton confirms the failure of Butler's advice. Since both the long- and short-staple varieties of cotton required close attention, especially in the tedious hoeing and thinning phases of their cultivation, they were ideal candidates for gang labor. Most upcountry South Carolina planters adopted this arrangement from the first, and sea island planters were encouraged to do the same: one lowcountry planter from Georgia advised his South Carolina colleagues that "there is no possibility of tasking Negroes" in cotton culture. However, his peers proved him wrong. By the early nineteenth century the tasking requirements of all sea island cotton operations were well established. They remained substantially unchanged throughout the nineteenth century (see Table I).[47]

Perhaps the profits being generated under the existing task system discouraged lowcountry planters from adopting gang labor, for they were not likely to restructure an arrangement that was so patently successful. In 1751 James Glen reported that South Carolina planters expected a slave to pay for himself within four to five years. Dr. Alexander Garden calculated that in 1756 planters made between £15 to £30 sterling for every slave they employed in the field, which he noted was "indeed a great deal." At that rate, a slave would pay for himself in two to three years. In 1772 a visitor to South Carolina noted that indigo planters made from £35 to £45 sterling for every able Negro; in this case, a newly purchased slave paid for himself in less than two years.[48] The rate of return of a 200-acre rice plantation, employing forty slaves in the late colonial period, was estimated to be 25 percent, more than double the opportunity cost of capital.[49] And although the Revolutionary war was enormously disruptive of the lowcountry economy, the 1790s were boom years for planters, as they replaced one highly profitable secondary staple (indigo) with another (sea island cotton). So profitable was this second staple that planters on Edisto Island in

[47] Letter to printers, *City Gazette* (Charleston), Mar. 14, 1796. The readiness with which sea island planters extended the task system to sea island cotton planting suggests prior familiarity which, in turn, suggests that indigo planting had been subject to tasking. No direct evidence of this connection is available, so far as I am aware. Few upland cotton plantations employed a thoroughgoing task system. One that did—the Silver Bluff plantation belonging to Christopher Fitzsimmons, subsequently owned by James Henry Hammond—was run as an absentee property and was more than likely populated by slaves already inured to tasking when resident on Fitzsimmons's tidewater plantation (Drew Gilpin Faust, personal communication).

[48] James Glen to the Board of Trade, July 15, 1751, C.O. 5/373, 155–157, P.R.O.; Garden to the Royal Society, May 1, 1757, Guard Book III, 86; G. Moulton to [?], Dec. 20, 1772, Add. MSS 22677, 70, British Library.

[49] John Gerar William De Brahm, *History of the Province of Georgia . . .* (Wormsloe, Ga., 1849), 51; Ralph Gray and Betty Wood, "The Transition from Indentured to Involuntary Servitude in Colonial Georgia," *Explorations in Economic History*, XIII (1976), 361–364.

1808 averaged a return of between $170 and $260 for every field hand.[50]

Crucial to the continuing profitability of rice plantations was the wholesale transfer of production from inland to tidal swamps, a process that was well underway by the late eighteenth century. John Drayton, writing at the turn of the century, identified some of the advantages of this shift in location: "River swamp plantations, from the command of water, which at high tides can be introduced over the fields, have an undoubted preference to inland plantations; as the crop is more certain, and the work of the negroes less toilsome." Surely it was a tidewater rice plantation that a Virginian witnessed in 1780 when he observed that "after the ground is once well cleared little cultivation does the ground [need] being soft by continued moisture." [51] In short, the development of tidewater rice culture reduced the heavy hoeing formerly required of slaves in the summer months. As might be expected, the daily task unit expanded, and squares of 150 feet (approximately a half of an acre) appeared in tidewater rice fields.[52] The other side of this coin was the increase in heavy labor required of slaves in the winter months, for tidewater cultivation demanded an elaborate system of banks, dams, canals, and ditches. By the turn of the century, no doubt, lowcountry laborers were as familiar with the daily ditching requirement (about 600 to 700 square feet or ten compasses) as they had ever been with the quarter-acre task.[53]

Although the precise definition of daily tasks had advantages from the slaves' point of view, the potential conflict that stereotyped tasks and their careless assignment could engender should not be underestimated. Indeed, the evidence of conflict should alert us to a battle that undoubtedly was being waged but that rarely surfaces in the historical record; namely, the constant warring between taskmaster and laborer over what constituted a fair day's work. After one such altercation between a black driver and a group of slaves, the latter took their case to

[50] Ramsay, *History of South Carolina*, II, 278–280. High rates of profit continued to characterize the large rice plantations (see Dale Evans Swan, *The Structure and Profitability of the Antebellum Rice Industry, 1859* [New York, 1975]).

[51] John Drayton, *A View of South-Carolina as Respects Her Natural and Civil Concerns* (Spartanburg, S.C., 1972 [orig. publ. Charleston, S.C., 1802]), 116; James Parker's Journal of the Charlestown Expedition, Feb. 5, 1780, Parker Family Papers, 920 PAR I 13/2, Liverpool City Libraries, Liverpool, England.

[52] Timothy Ford speaks of half-acre tasks (Joseph W. Barnwell, ed., "Diary of Timothy Ford, 1785–1786," *S.C. Hist. Mag.*, XIII [1912], 182). However, the first specific reference that I have so far found to the 150-square-feet task is in Edmund Ruffin, *Report of the Commencement and Progress of the Agricultural Survey of South-Carolina for 1843* (Columbia, S.C., 1843), 104.

[53] See Table I. Time and space do not permit an investigation of the effect of developments in machinery on slave work routines. However, to give but one example, the pounding task of the early 18th century was, by the end of the century, redundant. Agricultural manuals in the 19th century do not set daily tasks for pounding.

their master in Charleston. When he asked them "why they could not do their Tasks as well as the rest," they answered that "their Tasks were harder." The master was sympathetic, knowing that "there is sometimes a great difference in Tasks, and Paul told me he remembered that Jimmy had a bad Task that Day. I was sorry to see poor Caesar amongst them for I knew him to be an honest, inoffensive fellow and tho't if any will do without severity, he will. I inquired his fault, & Paul told me . . . he had been 2 days in a Task." [54] Hoeing was at issue in this dispute; on another plantation, threshing became a source of conflict. Three slaves belonging to George Austin—Liverpool, Moosa, and Dutay—"ran off early in December, for being a little chastis'd on Account of not finishing the Task of Thrashing in due time." [55] By the early nineteenth century, a *modus vivendi* had apparently been reached on most lowcountry plantations. One South Carolina planter reckoned that the "daily task does not vary according to the arbitrary will and caprice of their owners, and although [it] is not fixed by law, it is so well settled by long usage, that upon every plantation it is the *same*. Should any owner increase the work beyond what is customary, he subjects himself to the reproach of his neighbors, and to such discontent amongst his slaves as to make them of but little use to him." [56] The task system's requirements were hammered out just as much in conflicts with the work force as in the supposedly inevitable march of technological progress.

However onerous tasking could become for some slaves, the system at least had the virtue of allowing the slave a certain latitude to apportion his own day, to work intensively in his task and then have the balance of his time. With the institutionalization of the task system, the slave's "time" became sacrosanct. The right not to be called on once the task had been completed was duly acknowledged by lowcountry

---

[54] Richard Hutson to Mr. Croll, Aug. 22, 1767, Charles Woodward Hutson Papers, University of North Carolina, Chapel Hill.

[55] Josiah Smith to George Austin, Jan. 31, 1774, Josiah Smith Letterbook, Univ. N.C., Chapel Hill.

[56] [Edwin C. Holland], *A Refutation of the Calumnies Circulated against . . . Slavery . . .* (New York, 1969 [orig. publ. Charleston, S.C., 1822]), 53. In the antebellum era, the role of the laborers continued to be significant in the evolution of the task system. For a particularly good example of the difficulty in modifying a long-established task (in this case, threshing), see James M. Clifton, ed., *Life and Labor on Argyle Island: Letters and Documents of a Savannah River Rice Plantation, 1833–1867* (Savannah, Ga., 1978), 8–9. Frederick Law Olmsted also noted that "in all ordinary work custom has settled the extent of the task, and it is difficult to increase it." If these customs were systematically ignored, Olmsted continued, the planter simply increased the likelihood of "a general stampede to the 'swamp' " (*A Journey in the Seabord Slave States* [New York, 1968 (orig. publ. 1856)], 435–436). James Henry Hammond waged what appears to have been an unsuccessful battle with his laborers when he tried to impose gang labor in place of the task system much preferred by his slaves (Drew Gilpin Faust, "Culture, Conflict, and Community: The Meaning of Power on an Ante-bellum Plantation," *Journal of Social History*, XIV [1980], 86).

masters.[57] One of the advantages of such a right is neatly illustrated in an incident that befell a Methodist circuit rider, Joseph Pilmore. On March 18, 1773—a Thursday—he arrived at the banks of the Santee River in the Georgetown district of South Carolina. After waiting in vain for the appearance of the regular ferry, he was met by a few Negroes. Presumably they told him that they "had finished their task," for that is how he explained their availability in his journal. He then hired their "time" so that he could be ferried across the river. The actual time was about three o'clock in the afternoon.[58] Slaves could not only complete their work by mid-afternoon; they might then earn money on their own account.

In the same year that Pilmore visited the Georgetown district, another observer of lowcountry society, "Scotus Americanus," testified more fully to the advantages that a fully institutionalized task system presented to slaves:

> Their work is performed by a daily task, allotted by their master or overseer, which they have generally done by one or two o'clock in the afternoon, and have the rest of the day for themselves, which they spend in working in their own private fields, consisting of 5 or 6 acres of ground, allowed them by their masters, for planting of rice, corn, potatoes, tobacco, &c. for their own use and profit, of which the industrious among them make a great deal. In some plantations, they have also the liberty to raise hogs and poultry, which, with the former articles, they are to dispose of to none but their masters (this is done to prevent bad consequences) for which, in exchange, when they do not chuse money, their masters give Osnaburgs, negro cloths, caps, hats, handkerchiefs, pipes, and knives. They do not plant in their fields for subsistence, but for amusement, pleasure, and profit, their masters giving them clothes, and sufficient provisions from their granaries.[59]

[57] Daniel Turner to his parents, Aug. 13, 1806, Daniel Turner Papers, Library of Congress (microfilm). Equally sacrosanct, at least to some slaves, was the product of their "time." Thus, in 1781, a set of plantation slaves attempted to kill their overseer because he tried to appropriate the corn that they were apparently planning to market (*South-Carolina and American General Gazette* [Charleston], Jan. 20, 1781).

[58] Frederick E. Maser and Howard T. Maag, eds., *The Journal of Joseph Pilmore, Methodist Itinerant: For the Years August 1, 1769 to January 2, 1774* (Philadelphia, 1969), 188.

[59] ["Scotus Americanus"], *Information Concerning the Province of North Carolina, Addressed to Emigrants from the Highlands and Western Isles of Scotland* (Glasgow, 1773), in William K. Boyd, "Some North Carolina Tracts of the Eighteenth Century," *North Carolina Historical Review*, III (1926), 616. This account almost certainly refers to the Cape Fear region of North Carolina. For slightly less-detailed accounts see François Alexandre Frédéric, duc de La Rochefoucauld-Liancourt, *Travels through the United States of North America* . . . , I (London, 1799), 599; Drayton, *View of South Carolina*, 145; and Edmund Botsford, *Sambo & Tony, a Dialogue in Three Parts* (Georgetown, S.C., 1808), 8, 13, 34.

As we shall see, planting for "amusement, pleasure, and profit" continued to be a prerogative of lowcountry slaves.

Pilmore and Scotus Americanus alert us to the ways in which lowcountry slaves continued to acquire money. It should hardly surprise us, then, that lowcountry bondmen still aspired to the ownership of more substantial items of property. In spite of the acts of 1714, 1722, and 1740, slaves remained singularly reluctant to relinquish their claims to horses. In 1772 the Charleston District Grand Jury was still objecting to "Negroes being allowed to keep horses . . . contrary to Law."[60] In a transaction that bore a remarkable similarity to the one effected by Sampson a half-century earlier, a slave named Will showed even less regard for the law by exchanging his horses for his freedom. A witness to the exchange heard Will's master, Lewis Dutarque, say to

> old fellow Will that he had been a faithful servant to him and if he had a mind to purchase his freedom he should obtain the same by paying him three hundred pounds old currency and says he Will you have two Horses which will nearly pay me. I will allow you hundred pounds old currency for a Roan Gelding and forty five currency for your Gray for which the fellow Will readily consented to the proposals and Mr. Dutarque took possession of the Horses and the fellow Will was to pay the Balance as soon as he could make it up. Mr. Dutarque also borrowed of the fellow Will a small Black mare which he lost and he said she was worth six Guineas and would allow him that price for her.[61]

One begins to wonder how many horses Will possessed. Horse trading may even have been possible within the slave community, if a notice placed in a South Carolina newspaper in 1793 is any indication: "On Sunday last was apprehended by the patrol in St. George's parish, a certain negro man who calls himself *Titus* and his son about 10 year who is called *Tom*; he was trading with the negroes in that neighbourhood, and he had in his possession 2 horses . . . one poultry cart, and several articles of merchandise, consisting of stripes, linens, and handkerchiefs."[62] Given these examples, one lowcountry master was perhaps right to be sanguine about an unsuccessful hunt that he had launched for a group of seven absentees. He was "convinced these runaways would not go far, being connected at home, and having too much property to leave."[63]

[60] Charlestown District Grand Jury Presentments, *S.C. Gaz.*, Jan. 25, 1772.

[61] Declaration of John Blake, Apr. 25, 1788, Miscellaneous Record Book VV, 473, S.C. Archs., Columbia.

[62] *State Gazette of South-Carolina* (Charleston), Oct. 26, 1793.

[63] William Read to Jacob Read, Mar. 22, 1800, Read Family Papers, S.C. Hist. Soc., Charleston. For another description of property owning by lowcountry slaves in the early 19th century, see Sidney Walter Martin, ed., "A New Englander's Impressions of Georgia in 1817–1818: Extracts from the Diary of Ebenezer Kellogg," *Journal of Southern History*, XII (1946), 259–260.

III

Q. You think that they have a love for property?
A. Yes, Sir; Very strong; they delight in accumulating.

Testimony of Rufus Saxton, 1863

By the middle of the nineteenth century the task system dominated agricultural life in the lowcountry. Indeed, the term so pervaded the region's agricultural terminology that its varied meanings have to be disentangled. For example, a lowcountry planter might say that he had planted "seven tasks (within one task of two acres, as a planter well knows)." At this time, a slave was expected to be able to sow two acres of rice a day; this is presumably what this planter had in mind when referring to the single task of two acres. And yet, the early eighteenth-century definition of a task as measuring one-quarter of an acre was still very much current. It was possible, therefore, to speak of seven units, measuring one-quarter of an acre each, within a larger unit measuring two acres.[64] Similarly, a planter might say that he had penned "thirty head of cattle on a task for one week" (the "task" here refers to one-quarter of an acre); or he might mention setting a "task" of three rice barrels a day for his cooper.[65] In other words, in common usage the term "task" not only referred to a unit of labor (a fixed or specified quantity of labor exacted from a person is the dictionary definition) but also to a unit of land measurement (almost invariably one-quarter of an acre or 105 square feet).

Slaves were completely conversant with this terminology, as the recollections of ex-slaves attest. Testifying before Southern Claims Commissioners in 1873, Peter Way knew precisely what constituted a "task" as a unit of land measurement. "Five poles make a task," he noted authoritatively, "and there is twenty-one feet in a pole."[66] Using the term in this sense, former slaves might say that "Mr. Mallard's house was about four or five tasks from Mr. Busby's house" (about 420 or 525 feet distant), or that Sherman's troops were "about three tasks off in the woods. I could see [them] from [my] house" (about 315 feet

---

[64] A Georgian, "Account of the Culture and Produce of the Bearded Rice," *South. Agric.*, III (1830), 292. For the evidence that about two acres was the sowing "task," see "A Memorandum of Tasks," *ibid.*, VII (1834), 297, and Ruffin, *Report*, 118.

[65] A Plain Farmer, "On the Culture of Sweet Potatoes," *South. Agric.*, V (1832), 120; for the cooper's task see the sources cited in the footnotes to Table I.

[66] Testimony of Peter Way, claim of William Roberts, July 4, 1873, Liberty County, Georgia, Case Files, Southern Claims Commission, Records of the 3d Auditor, Record Group 217, Records of the U.S. General Accounting Office, National Archives. Hereafter, only the name and date—county and state will be added whenever a claim originates from an area other than Liberty Co., Ga.—will be given, followed by the abbreviation, SCC.

away).[67] When Mason Crum interviewed an old Negro woman (a former slave) in the 1930s, she told him that she owned her land "and that she had in the tract t'ree acres and a tass'," by which she meant three-and-a-quarter acres.[68] When freedmen referred to the crops that they had produced for themselves in "slavery times," they used the units acres and "tasks" interchangeably (tasks here again refer to quarter-acre plots).[69] At the same time, ex-slaves used the term "task" to connote a unit of labor. A freedman, referring to the terms of the contract that he had signed with his employer, spoke of giving "five tasks, that is, I work five tasks for him and plant everything he has a mind to have it planted in for all the land myself and wife can cultivate."[70] The dual meaning of the term is nowhere better illustrated than in the words of one former slave, interviewed in the 1930s, who in one and the same breath recalled "de slave [having] but two taks ob land to cultivate for se'f" (by which he meant half an acre) and "in daytime [having] to do his task" (by which he meant a quantity of labor depending on the operation at hand).[71]

Tasking was so much a way of life in the antebellum lowcountry that virtually all crops and a whole host of plantation operations were subject to its dictates. The cultivation of corn was discussed in terms of the number of hills in a "task-row" and the number of "beds" in a task.[72] Sea island cotton had its own task-acre as distinct from the task-acre utilized in tidewater rice culture.[73] Even when lowcountry

[67] Testimony of Philip Campbell, claim of Windsor Stevens, July 12, 1873, SCC; claimant's deposition, claim of Diana Cummings, June 17, 1873, Chatham County, Ga.; see also testimony of Henry LeCount, claim of Marlborough Jones, July 30, 1873.

[68] Mason Crum, *Gullah: Negro Life in the Carolina Sea Islands* (Durham, N.C., 1940), 51; for a similar use of the term, but by a son of former slave parents, see Wightman and Cate, *Early Days of Coastal Georgia*, 81.

[69] For example, see the claim depositions of James Anderson, William Cassell, Prince Cumings, Hamlet Delegal, and Thomas Irving of Liberty Co., Ga., SCC.

[70] Claimant's deposition, claim of Marlborough Jones, July 30, 1873, SCC; see also claimant's deposition, claim of Somerset Stewart, July 30, 1873.

[71] George P. Rawick, ed., *The American Slave: A Composite Autobiography*, III (Westport, Conn., 1972), Pt. iii, 200–201. A black Edisto Islander, born in 1897, interviewed in 1970, was also conversant with the dual meaning of the term "task" (Nick Lindsay, transc., *An Oral History of Edisto Island: The Life and Times of Bubberson Brown* [Goshen, Ind., 1977], 27, 46–47, 50, 53).

[72] "Memoranda of a Crop of Corn Grown in St. Andrew's Parish," *South. Agric.*, III (1830), 77; "Account of the Mode of Culture Pursued in Cultivating Corn and Peas," *ibid.*, IV (1831), 236. An intensive application of tasking to operations that ranged from the construction of post and rail fences to the digging of groundnuts can be found in the Plantation Journal of Thomas W. Peyre, 1834–1851, esp. 259, 332, 365, S.C. Hist. Soc., Charleston. (I am grateful to Gene Waddell, Director of the Society, for bringing this to my attention.)

[73] Even Lewis Gray and U. B. Phillips, the two standard authorities on the task system, are confused on this issue. The task-acre in tidewater rice cultivation ideally took the form of a field 300' × 150', divided into two half-acre "tasks" of 150' square. The

planters experimented with sugar cultivation in the 1820s and 1830s, they attempted to retain the notion of a task: a hundred plants, according to one authority, were to be put in a task-row and two hands could then both plant and cut a task a day.[74] On Hopeton plantation, where sugar was grown on a large scale, task work was "resorted to whenever the nature of the work admits of it; and working in gangs as is practiced in the West Indies and the upper country, is avoided. The advantages of this system are encouragement to the labourers, by equalizing the work of each agreeably to strength, and the avoidance of watchful superintendance and incessant driving." [75] Whether this attempt to adapt sugar cultivation to the task system contributed to the failure of lowcountry sugar production is difficult to say; but it is possible that sugar, unlike cotton, just could not be successfully grown without gang labor.

Tasking was ubiquitous in another sense: those slaves not able to benefit from the system's opportunities had to be compensated in other ways. The proposition that drivers, as a group, suffered discrimination is barely credible, but in the lowcountry, at least, such was the case. As one ex-slave recalled, "I suppose the Foreman had advantages in some respects and in others not, for he had no task-work and had no time of his own, while the other slaves had the Evenings to themselves." The son of a Georgia planter remembered that his father's driver was "obliged to oversee all day," whereas the field hands "were allowed to work in any way they chose for themselves after the tasks were done." [76] By way of compensation, lowcountry drivers were entitled to receive a certain amount of help in tending their own crops. Thomas Mallard's driver "had the privilege of having hands to work one acre of corn and one acre of rice" on his behalf; the driver on Raymond Cay's plantation had Cay's field hands plant one acre of corn and three to five "tasks" in rice on his account.[77] One ex-slave recalled that "drivers had the privilege of planting two or three acres of rice and some corn and having it worked by the slaves"; and, in order to dispel any misimpressions, he emphasized that "these hands worked

---

task-acre on inland rice and sea island cotton plantations was ideally a square of 210', divided into four quarter-acre squares, each side 105' in length. See R. F. W. Allston, "Sea-Coast Crops of the South," *De Bow's Review*, XVI (1854), 596, 609; cf. Phillips, *Negro Slavery*, 247, 259, and Gray, *History of Agriculture*, I, 553.

[74] Jacob Wood, "Account of the Process of Cultivating, Harvesting and Manufacturing the Sugar Cane," *South. Agric.*, III (1830), 226.

[75] The Editor, "Account of an Agricultural Excursion Made into the South of Georgia in the Winter of 1832," *ibid.*, VI (1833), 576.

[76] Testimony of William Winn, claim of David Stevens, July 17, 1873, SCC; testimony of James Frazer, claim of John Bacon, July 7, 1873.

[77] Claimant's deposition, claim of Joseph Bacon, Aug. 12, 1873, SCC; testimony of Peter Way, claim of Silvia Baker, Aug. 9, 1873.

for [the drivers] in the White people's time." [78] Other occupational groups received different forms of compensation. A former slave plowman recalled that he "didn't work by the task but at the end of the year [his master] gave [him] 6 bushels of corn" by way of redress. A former slave carpenter recollected that "when [he] worked carpentering [his] master allowed [him] every other saturday and when [he] worked farming [his master] gave him tasks." [79] In this man's mind, apparently, these "privileges" were about equal.

The central role of the task system in lowcountry life can best be gauged by investigating its fate immediately after emancipation. Throughout the postwar cotton South freedmen firmly rejected most of the elements of their old system of labor: from the first, gang labor was anathema.[80] At the same time, however, freedmen in the lowcountry were tenaciously striving to retain—and even extend—the fundamentals of their former system. A Freedmen's Bureau official, resident in lowcountry Georgia in 1867, identified a basic response of the former slaves to their new work environment when he observed that they "usually stipulate to work by the task." [81] Lowcountry freedmen even demonstrated their attachment to the task system when they rejected one element of their former slave past by refusing to do the ditching and draining so necessary in rice and sea island cotton cultivation.[82] This work was arduous and disagreeable, of course, and since ditching was more amenable to gang labor than any other operation in lowcountry agriculture, blacks appropriately sought to avoid it at all costs. But in an 1865 petition a group of planters from Georgetown district touched on an even more compelling reason for the freedmen's refusal to perform this familiar task. They pointed out that "it is a work which, as it does not pertain to the present crop, the negroes are unwilling to perform." The recipient of this petition, Colonel Willard, was a sympathetic and sensitive observer, and his elaboration of this rationale penetrates to the heart of the issue. The freedmen's real fear, he explained, was that having prepared the ditches for the forthcoming crop, the planters would "insist on having them by the month." This arrangement would be absolutely unacceptable, because the

---

[78] Testimony of Tony Law, claim of Linda Roberts, July 19, 1873, SCC. See also D. E. Huger Smith, *A Charlestonian's Recollections, 1846–1913* (Charleston, S.C., 1950), 29.

[79] Claimant's deposition, claim of John Crawford, Mar. 3, 1874, SCC; claimant's deposition, claim of Frank James, Mar. 14, 1874.

[80] See, for example, Leon F. Litwack, *Been in the Storm So Long: The Aftermath of Slavery* (New York, 1980), 410.

[81] Lt. Douglas G. Risley to Col. C. C. Sibley, June 2, 1867 (A123), Freedman and Southern Society, files of documents in the Natl. Archs., University of Maryland, College Park. (Hereafter reference to documents read at the Society will be given in parentheses.) But cf. Litwack, *Been in the Storm*, 410.

[82] Bvt. Maj. Gen. Charles Devens to Bvt. Lt. Col. W. L. M. Burger, AAG, Oct. 29, 1865, and Nov. 13, 1865 (C1361, Pt. I, C4160, Pt. 1); Brig. Gen. W. T. Bennett to Bvt. Lt. Col. W. L. M. Burger, AAG, Oct. 11, 1865 (C1361, Pt. 1).

freedmen had "been accustomed to working by the task, which has always given them leisure to cultivate land for themselves, tend their
stock, and amuse themselves." If they gave way on this issue, he continued, "their privileges will go and their condition will be less to their
taste than it was when they were slaves."[83]

Precisely to avoid such a condition was the overriding imperative
governing the actions of lowcountry freedmen. Once this is understood, the multifarious and fluid labor arrangements that characterized the postwar lowcountry become comprehensible. In 1865 and
1866 two basic forms of labor contract (with many individual variations) were employed in the lowlands of South Carolina and Georgia.
Either the freedmen worked for a share of the crop (anywhere from
one-half to three-quarters, a higher share than found elsewhere in the
South), with the freedmen's share being divided among them on the
basis of tasks performed, or they hired themselves for the year, with
payment being made on the basis of the numbers of tasks completed
(usually fifty cents a task, although payment was by no means always
made in cash).[84] Whatever the mode of reimbursement, the task was
central to most early contracts.

In 1866 a third labor arrangement arose that soon became general
throughout the lowcountry. Known as the "two-day" or, less frequently, "three-day" system, it simply extended the concept of task labor, for it drew an even more rigid demarcation between the planters'
"time" and the laborers' "time." The Freedmen's Bureau agent for
eastern Liberty County, Georgia, observed as early as February 1867
that there were in his district no freedmen working by the month and
only a few for wages. Some were working for a share of the crop, but
most were employed by the "two-day" system, working a third of the
time on the employers' crop and receiving land to work on their own
account for the remainder of the time.[85] The agricultural census of

[83] Ben Allston et al., to Col. Willard, Oct. 30, 1865 (C1602, Pt. 2); Lt. Col. A. J.
Willard to Capt. G. W. Hooker, AAG, Nov. 7, 1865 (C1614, Pt. 2).

[84] This information was derived from Lt. Col. A. J. Willard to Capt. G. W. Hooker,
AAG, Nov. 7, 1865, and Dec. 6, 1865 (C1614, Pt. 2, C1503, Pt. 1); case #104, James
Geddes v. William B. Seabrook, Feb. 11, 1867 (C1534, Pt. 1); contract between William
H. Gibbons and 120 Freedmen, Chatham Co., Ga., Mar. 1, 1866 (A5798); Maj. Gen.
James B. Steedman and Bvt. Brig. Gen. J. S. Fullerton to E. M. Stanton, June 4, 1866
(A5829); Capt. Henry C. Brandt to Lt. Col. A. W. Smith, Jan. 12, 1867 (A5395). See
also John David Smith, "More than Slaves, Less than Freedmen: The 'Share Wages' Labor System During Reconstruction," Civil War History, XXVI (1980), 256–266, for the
example of a contract, not the analysis that accompanies it. A detailed analysis of the labor contracts in operation in these years would undoubtedly enrich, and perhaps modify,
this section.

[85] A. M. McIver to Lt. J. M. Hogg (SAC), Feb. 28, 1867 (A5769); see also Lt. W. M.
Wallace to Capt. E. W. H. Read, Jan. 8, 1867 (C1619); D. M. Burns to [?], Mar. 17,
1867 (A7188); and Joel Williamson, After Slavery: The Negro in South Carolina during Reconstruction, 1861–1877 (Chapel Hill, N.C., 1965), 135–136.

1880 reported that the "two-day" system was ubiquitous on the South Carolina sea islands. For ten months of the year, slaves worked two days in each week for their employers and received in return a house, fuel, and six acres of land for their own use, free of rent. Proprietors were said to dislike the system because their employees only cultivated about two acres in the owners' "time." However, the report continued, "the laborers themselves prefer this system, having four days out of the week for themselves." As a result, "they are more independent and can make any day they choose a holiday." [86]

The reasons for the slaves' (and the freedmen's) attachment to the task system should be readily apparent, but the subject is worth a moment's extra consideration because we are in the privileged and rare position of being able to listen to the participants themselves. The most obvious advantage of the task system was the flexibility it permitted slaves in determining the length of the working day. Working from sunup to sundown was the pervasive reality for most antebellum slaves; but ex-slaves from the lowcountry recall a different reality. Richard Cummings, a former field hand, recalled that "a good active industrious man would finish his task sometimes at 12, sometimes at 1 and 2 oclock and the rest of the time was his own to use as he pleased." Scipio King, another former field hand, reckoned, as he put it, that "I could save for myself sometimes a whole day if I could do 2 tasks in a day then I had the next day to myself. Some kind of work I could do 3 tasks in a day." [87] Exhausting as task labor undoubtedly was, its prime virtue was that it was not unremitting.

A second advantage concerned the relationship between the slaves' provisions and the planters' rations. Whatever slaves produced beyond the task was regarded as surplus to, not a substitute for, basic planter allocations of food and clothing. One former slave recalled that his master continued to dispense rations "no matter how much they [the slaves] made of their own . . . [which] they could sell . . . if they chose." July Roberts, another ex-slave, emphasized that "every week we drew our rations no matter what we raised." When one former slave claimed the loss of corn, rice, and clothing taken by Federal troops, an attempt was made to deny him his title because these represented rations and "so belonged to the master." The response of this

---

[86] Harry Hammond, "Report on the Cotton Production of the State of South Carolina," in U.S. Census Office, *Tenth Census, 1880* (Washington, D.C., 1884), VI, Pt. ii, 60–61.

[87] Testimony of Richard Cummings, claim of Lafayette Delegal, July 11, 1873, SCC; claimant's deposition, claim of Scipio King, July 9, 1873. A number of lowcountry freedmen made similar statements. For the general recollections of ex-slaves, see, obviously, George P. Rawick, *From Sundown to Sunup: The Making of the Black Community* (Westport, Conn., 1972), and Paul D. Escott, *Slavery Remembered: A Record of Twentieth-Century Slave Narratives* (Chapel Hill, N.C., 1979), 38.

freedman's attorneys no doubt reflected the prevailing attitude of former slaves: "It is obvious to remark that if these things had not been taken from the claimant by the army, he would have had them after 'freedom came' and were to all intents his property."[88] Not only did slaves plant in their own time for "amusement, pleasure, and profit," they claimed the master's rations as their own to do with as they wished.

In view of these advantages, we might expect the scale and range of property owning by slaves to have assumed significant dimensions by the middle of the nineteenth century. An analysis of the settled claims submitted by former slaves to the Southern Claims Commission for loss of property to Federal troops provides the best test of this hypothesis.[89] Taking the Liberty County, Georgia, claimants as a sample, former field hands outnumber all other occupational groups. While most were mature adults when their property was taken, 30 percent were under the age of thirty-five. In terms of occupation and age these claimants constitute a relatively broad cross section of the slave population. Moreover, whether field hands or artisans, young or old, virtually all of them had apparently been deprived of a number of hogs, and a substantial majority listed corn, rice, and fowls among their losses. In addition, a surprising number apparently possessed horses and cows, while buggies or wagons, beehives, peanuts, fodder, syrup, butter, sugar, and tea were, if these claims are to be believed, in the hands of at least some slaves. The average cash value (in 1864 dollars) claimed by Liberty County former slaves was $357.43, with the highest claim totaling $2,290 and the lowest $49.[90]

Some claims were spectacular. Paris James, a former slave driver, was described by a neighboring white planter as a "substantial man before the war [and] was more like a free man than any slave."[91] James claimed, among other things, a horse, eight cows, sixteen sheep,

---

[88] Testimony of Peter Stevens, claim of Toney Elliott, Aug. 8, 1873, SCC; testimony of July Roberts, claim of Nedger Frazer, Feb. 27, 1874; report of R. B. Avery and testimony of Gilmore and Co., attorneys for claimant, claim of Jacob Dryer, Nov. 1, 1873.

[89] The settled or allowed claims from ex-slaves for Liberty and Chatham counties, Ga., and Beaufort, Charleston, and Georgetown counties, S.C., were investigated. For a fuller presentation of my findings, see "The Ownership of Property by Slaves in the Mid-Nineteenth-Century Lowcountry," *Jour. So. Hist.* (forthcoming).

[90] The Liberty Co., Ga., claims are the most numerous and most detailed. They contain few urban claimants and form the ideal sample for the purposes of this study. Eighty-nine former slaves from this county submitted claims that were settled: 50 of the 89 were field hands and 25 of 86 were under the age of 35 when their property was taken. For a fuller discussion of the reliability of these claims and an analysis of the claimed property, see my article cited in n. 89.

[91] Testimony of Raymond Cay, Jr., claim of Paris James, June 2, 1874, SCC. Cay also said that he "looked upon [James] as one of the most thrifty slaves in Liberty County." His claim totaled $1,218.

twenty-six hogs, and a wagon. Another slave driver, according to one of his black witnesses, lived "just like a white man except his color. His credit was just as good as a white man's because he had the property to back it." Although the claims commissioners were skeptical about his alleged loss of twenty cows—as they explained, "twenty cows would make a good large dairy for a Northern farmer"—his two white and three black witnesses supported him in his claim.[92] Other blacks were considered to be "more than usually prosperous," "pretty well off," and "hardworking and moneysaving"—unremarkable characterizations, perhaps, but surprising when the individuals were also slaves.[93] Alexander Steele, a carpenter by trade and a former house servant of Chatham County, Georgia, submitted a claim for $2,205 based on the loss of his four horses, mule, silver watch, two cows, wagon, and large quantities of fodder, hay, and corn. He had been able to acquire these possessions by "tradeing" for himself for some thirty years; he had had "much time of [his] own" because his master "always went north" in the summer months. He took "a fancy [to] fine horses," a whim he was able to indulge when he purchased "a blooded mare," from which he raised three colts. He was resourceful enough to hide his livestock on Onslow Island when Sherman's army drew near, but some of the Federal troops secured boats and took off his prize possessions. Three white planters supported Steele in his claim; indeed, one of them recollected making an unsuccessful offer of $300 for one of Steele's colts before the war. Lewis Dutarque's Will, a horse owner of note in the late eighteenth century, had found a worthy successor in Alexander Steele.[94]

The ownership of horses was not, however, confined to a privileged minority of slaves. Among the Liberty County claimants, almost as many ex-field hands as former drivers and skilled slaves claimed horses. This evidence supplies a context for the exchange recorded by Frederick Law Olmsted when he was being shown around the plantation of Richard J. Arnold in Bryan County, Georgia. Olmsted noticed a horse drawing a wagon of "common fieldhand negroes" and asked his host

"[do you] usually let them have horses to go to Church?"
"Oh no; that horse belongs to the old man."
"Belongs to him! Why, do they own horses?"

---

[92] Testimony of W. A. Golding, claim of Linda (and Caesar) Roberts, July 19, 1873, SCC. His claim totaled $1,519.

[93] Report of R. B. Avery, claim of Jacob Quarterman, July 5, 1873, SCC; report of R. B. Avery, claim of Prince Stewart, July 29, 1873; report of the Commissioners of Claims, claim of James Stacy, Aug. 15, 1873.

[94] Claimant's deposition and testimony of John Fish, claim of Alexander Steele, Aug. 17, 1872, Chatham Co., Ga., SCC.

"Oh yes; William (the House Servant) owns
two, and Robert, I believe, has three now;
that was one of them he was riding."
"How do they get them?"
"Oh they buy them."[95]

Although a few freedmen recalled that former masters had either prohibited horse ownership or confined the practice to drivers, most
placed the proportion of horse owners on any single plantation at between 15 and 20 percent.[96] A former slave of George Washington
Walthour estimated that "in all my master's plantations there were
over 30 horses owned by slaves. . . . I think come to count up there
were as many as 45 that owned horses—he would let them own any
thing they could if they only did his work." [97] Nedger Frazer, a former
slave of the Reverend C. C. Jones, recalled that on one of his master's
plantations (obviously Arcadia, from Frazer's description) there were
forty working hands, of whom five owned horses; and on another (obviously Montevideo) another ten hands out of fifty owned horses.[98]
This, in turn, supplies a context for an interesting incident that occurred within the Jones's "family" in 1857. After much soul-searching,
Jones sold one of his slave families, headed by Cassius, a field hand. A
man of integrity, Jones then forwarded Cassius the balance of his account, which amounted to $85, a sum that included the proceeds from
the sale of Cassius's horse.[99] Perhaps one freedman was not exaggerat-
ing when he observed in 1873 that "there was more stock property
owned by slaves before the war than are owned now by both white
and black people together in this county." [100]

The spectacular claims and the widespread ownership of horses naturally catch the eye, but even the most humdrum claim has a story to
tell. Each claim contains, for instance, a description of how property
was accumulated. The narrative of John Bacon can stand as proxy for
many such accounts: "I had a little crop to sell and bought some

[95] Charles E. Beveridge et al., eds., The Papers of Frederick Law Olmsted, II (Baltimore,
1981), 182. Twenty-four field hands, out of a total of 53 slaves, claimed horses.

[96] Two Liberty Co. freedmen testified to a ban on horse ownership on their plantations; three recalled that only drivers had horses; and fourteen supply the proportions
mentioned here.

[97] Claimant's deposition, claim of Paris James, June 2, 1874, SCC.

[98] Claimant's deposition, claim of Nedger Frazer, Feb. 27, 1874, SCC. This is the
same Niger, as he was known as a slave, who objected to being hired out in 1864 because
he was unable, as he put it, to "make anything for himself," and who pretended to have
yellow fever so that Sherman's troops would not deprive him of his property (see Robert
Manson Myers, ed., The Children of Pride: A True Story of Georgia and the Civil War [New
Haven, Conn., 1972], 1162, 1237).

[99] Myers, ed., Children of Pride, 244, 306.

[100] Testimony of W. A. Golding, claim of Linda (and Caesar) Roberts, July 19, 1873,
SCC.

chickens and then I bought a fine large sow and gave $10.00 for her. This was about ten years before the war and then I raised hogs and sold them till I bought a horse. This was about eight years before freedom. This was a breeding mare and from this mare I raised this horse which the Yankees took from me." [101] This was not so much primitive as painstaking accumulation; no wonder one freedman referred to his former property as his "laborment." [102] And yet, occasionally, the mode of procurement assumed a slightly more sophisticated cast: some slaves recall purchasing horses by installment [103]; some hired additional labor to cultivate their crops [104]; two slaves (a mill engineer and a stockminder) went into partnership to raise livestock [105]; and a driver lent out money at interest. [106] Whatever the mode of accumulation, the ultimate source, as identified by virtually all the ex-slaves, was the task system. As Joseph James, a freedman, explained, "They all worked by tasks, and had a plenty of time to work for themselves and in that way all slaves who were industrious could get around them considerable property in a short time." [107]

By the middle of the nineteenth century, in sum, it is possible to speak of a significant internal economy operating within a more conventional lowcountry economy. According to the depositions of the freedmen, this internal economy rested on two major planks. The first concerns the degree to which some slaves engaged in stock raising. One white planter, testifying on behalf of a freedman, recalled that "a good many" slaves owned a number of animals; he then checked himself, perhaps realizing the impression that he was creating, and guardedly stated that "what I mean was they were not allowed to go generally into stock raising." [108] And yet some slaves seem to have been doing just that. One ex-slave spoke of raising "horses to sell"; another

[101] Claimant's deposition, claim of John Bacon, July 7, 1873, SCC.

[102] Report of R. B. Avery, claim of Robert Bryant, Oct. 6, 1877, Beaufort Co., S.C., SCC.

[103] Claimant's deposition, claim of William Drayton, Feb. 20, 1874, Beaufort Co., S.C., SCC; testimony of Sterling Jones, claim of Sandy Austin, July 21, 1873.

[104] James Miller, for example, recalled that "many times I would get some one to help me, and get along that way, I would pay them whatever they asked according to the time they worked" (report of R. B. Avery, claim of James Miller, July 29, 1873, SCC). See also claimant's deposition, claim of Pompey Bacon, Aug. 7, 1873.

[105] Claimant's deposition, claim of Edward Moddick and Jacob Hicks, Mar. 17, 1873, Chatham Co., Ga., SCC.

[106] Report of J. P. M. Epping, claim of Pompey Smith, n.d., Beaufort Co., S.C., SCC.

[107] Testimony of Joseph James, claim of Linda and Caesar Jones, Aug. 1, 1873, SCC.

[108] Testimony of T. Fleming before R. B. Avery, claim of Prince Wilson, Jr., July 28, 1873, Chatham Co., Ga., SCC. The widespread ownership of animals is also indicated in the records of one lowcountry plantation. In 1859 almost 40 slaves, over half the adult males on the plantation, owned at least one cow, cow and calf, steer or heifer. Only about 10 of the 40 held skilled or privileged positions (Weehaw Plantation Book, 1855–1861, 87, S.C. Hist. Soc., Charleston).

claimed to have raised fourteen horses over a twenty-five-to-thirty-year period, most of which he had sold; and one freedwoman named some of the purchasers, all of whom were slaves, of the nine horses that she had raised.[109] The other major foundation of this internal economy was the amount of crop production by slaves. Jeremiah Everts observed that the slaves in Chatham County, Georgia, had "as much land as they can till for their own use." [110] The freedmen's recollections from all over the lowcountry support this statement: a number of ex-slaves reckoned that they had more than ten acres under cultivation, while four or five acres was the norm.[111] The proprietorial attitude encouraged by this independent production is suggested in one freedman's passing comment that he worked in his "own field." [112] Through the raising of stock and the production of provisions (together with the sale of produce from woodworking, basketmaking, hunting, and fishing), slaves were able to attract money into their internal economy. Robert W. Gibbes knew of an individual slave who received $120 for his year's crop of corn and fodder; Richard Arnold owed his slaves $500 in 1853 when Olmsted visited him.[113] Thus, while produce and livestock were constantly being bartered by slaves—"swapping" was rife, according to the freedmen—one observer of the mid-nineteenth-century lowcountry was undoubtedly

[109] Testimony of Fortune James, claim of Charles Warner, Aug. 6, 1873, SCC; claimant's deposition, claim of Prince Wilson, Jr., July 28, 1873, Chatham Co., Ga.; claimant's deposition, claim of Jane Holmes, July 21, 1873.

[110] Jeremiah Evarts Diary, Apr. 5, 1822, Georgia Historical Society, Savannah, as quoted in Thomas F. Armstrong, "From Task Labor to Free Labor: The Transition along Georgia's Rice Coast, 1820–1880," *Georgia Historical Quarterly*, LXIV (1980), 436.

[111] The Liberty Co. claimants who mention such acreages include Daniel Bryant, William Cassell, Prince Cumings, George Gould, Ned Quarterman, Paris James, and Richard LeCounte. The Chatham Co. claimants include Dennis Smith and Alfred Barnard. The Beaufort Co. claimants include John Morree, Andrew Riley, Pompey Smith, Moses Washington, and Benjamin Platts. When James Miller's brother, Lawrence, a student at Howard University, was asked whether the hundred bushels of rice claimed by his brother was not excessive, he replied, "I should not think so—not in his condition." James's "condition" was only that of a field hand, but he was the "director" of the family, and the family planted five acres (testimony of Lawrence Miller, claim of James Miller, July 29, 1873, SCC).

[112] Claimant's deposition, claim of Adam LeCount, Feb. 26, 1874, SCC.

[113] Gibbes, "Southern Slave Life," *De Bow's Review*, XXIV (1858), 324; Olmsted, *Journey*, 443. Fanny Kemble noted that two carpenters on the Butler estate sold a canoe to a neighboring planter for $60 and that slaves could earn large sums by collecting Spanish moss (Frances Anne Kemble, *Journal of a Residence on a Georgian Plantation in 1838–1839*, ed. John A. Scott [New York, 1961], 62, 364). Unfortunately, there are no estimates of the proportion of money circulating among the slaves. The handling of money certainly gave rise to some discernment: one freedman remembered paying $60 in "good money" for a horse. He continued, "I call silver money good money, I call confederate money wasps' nests" (claimant's deposition, claim of Simon Middleton, June 2, 1873, Chatham Co., Ga., SCC).

correct when he noted that "in a small way a good deal of money circulated among the negroes, both in the country and in the towns." [114]

The autonomy of this internal economy is further indicated by the development of a highly significant practice. By the middle of the nineteenth century, if not before, slave property was not only being produced and exchanged but also inherited. The father of Joseph Bacon bequeathed him a mare and all his other children $50 each.[115] Samuel Elliot claimed a more substantial legacy, for his father "had 20 head of cattle, about 70 heads of hogs—Turkeys Geese Ducks and Chickens a Plenty—he was foreman for his master and had been raising such things for years. When he died the property was divided among his children and we continued to raise things just as he had been raising." [116] The role of less immediate kin was also not negligible. Two freedmen recalled receiving property from their grandfathers; another inherited a sow from his cousin; and William Drayton of Beaufort County, South Carolina, noted that when his father died he "left with his oldest brother, my uncle, the means or property he left for his children," and Drayton bought a mule "by the advice of my uncle who had the means belonging to me." [117] There were rules governing lines of descent. One female claimant emphasized that she had not inherited any of her first husband's property because she had borne him no children; rather, his son by a former marriage received the property.[118] The ability to bequeath wealth and to link patrimony to genealogy serves to indicate the extent to which slaves created a measure of autonomy.

The property rights of slaves were recognized across proprietorial boundaries as well as across generations. Slaves even employed guardians to facilitate the transfer of property from one plantation to another. Thus when Nancy Bacon, belonging to John Baker, inherited cattle from her deceased husband who belonged to Mr. Walthour, she employed her second cousin, Andrew Stacy, a slave on the Walthour plantation, to take charge of the cattle and drive them over to her plantation. According to Stacy, Mr. Walthour "didn't object to my taking them [and] never claimed them." [119] The way in which slave cou-

---

[114] Alice R. Huger Smith, *A Carolina Rice Plantation of the Fifties* (New York, 1936), 72.

[115] Claimant's deposition, claim of Joseph Bacon, Aug. 12, 1873, SCC.

[116] Claimant's deposition, claim of Samuel Elliott, July 17, 1873, SCC.

[117] Claimant's deposition, claim of York Stevens, Mar. 2, 1874, SCC; claimant's deposition, claim of Edward Brown, Feb. 20, 1874, Beaufort Co., S.C.; claimant's deposition, claim of William Roberts, July 4, 1873; claimant's deposition, claim of William Drayton, Feb. 20, 1874, Beaufort Co., S.C.

[118] Claimant's deposition, claim of Jane Holmes, July 21, 1873, SCC. Twenty-three Liberty Co. freedmen referred to inheriting property within the same plantation.

[119] Claimant's deposition and testimony of Andrew Stacy, claim of Nancy Bacon, Mar. 14, 1874, SCC; Stacy performed the same service for Clarinda Porter (claimant's deposition, claim of Clarinda Porter, Feb. 18, 1874). Nine Liberty Co. freedmen referred to inheriting property across plantation boundaries.

ples took advantage of their divided ownership is suggested by Diana Cummings of Chatham County, Georgia. Her husband's master, she explained, "allowed him to sell but mine didn't," so Diana marketed her crops and stock through her husband and received a part of the proceeds. On her husband's death, she received all his property for, as she put it, her "entitle" (surname) was then the same as her husband's. She had since changed it, through remarriage to Sydney Cummings, but she noted that Cummings had "no interest in [the] property [being claimed]." [120]

By the middle of the nineteenth century the ownership of property by lowcountry slaves had become extensive and had assumed relatively sophisticated dimensions. This, in turn, gives rise to an obvious question. What significance was attached to the practice by the slaves? What was the *mentalité*, the moral economy, of this property-owning group? Certainly some freedmen spoke of "getting ahead" and of "accumulating" under slavery.[121] Jacob Monroe, a freedman, admitted that as a slave under the task system he "could go and come when [he] pleased, work and play after [his] task was done," but he pointedly emphasized that "he chose to work." [122] Competitiveness was also not alien to the slave quarters. One freedman recalled how the young adults on one plantation "were jealous of one another and tried to see which would get their days work done first."[123] William Gilmore referred to the disparities in property ownership that characterized Raymond Cay's slaves; he likened them to the "five wise and five foolish" and disparaged those who "slept and slumbered the time away." [124] Similar impressions are derived from those Northerners who came into contact with sea island blacks in the early 1860s. B. K. Lee observed that "they are very acquisitive indeed"; Henry Judd described their "passion for ownership of horses or some animal"; and Rufus Saxton was impressed to find that "they regard the rights of property among themselves. If a man has a claim upon a horse or sow he maintains his right and his neighbours recognize it." [125]

Acquisitiveness and respect for property had other overtones, as Rufus Saxton's resonant phrase—"they delight in accumulating"—suggests.[126] Display and ostentation, while not on any grand scale, of

[120] Claimant's deposition, claim of Diana Cummings, June 17, 1873, Chatham Co., Ga., SCC.

[121] See, for example, claimant's deposition, claim of Silvia Baker, Aug. 9, 1873, SCC; claimant's deposition, claim of Hamlet Delegal, Mar. 7, 1874; and claimant's deposition, claim of William Golding, May 16, 1874.

[122] Claimant's deposition, claim of Jacob Monroe, July 18, 1873, SCC.

[123] Testimony of Joshua Cassell, claim of George Gould, Aug. 11, 1873, SCC.

[124] Testimony of William Gilmore, claim of York Stevens, Mar. 2, 1874, SCC.

[125] Testimony of B. K. Lee, 1863 (K72); testimony of Henry G. Judd, 1863 (K74); testimony of Brig. Gen. Rufus Saxton, 1863 (K70).

[126] Testimony of Saxton, 1863 (K70).

course, seem an accurate characterization of some slaves' behavior. The ownership of horses undoubtedly had practical purposes—one freedman explained that "some of the slaves had families a good ways off and they used their horses to visit them. The masters said it was for their interest to have us own horses so that we could get back home to work." [127] But the exhibition of status appears also to have been involved. William Golding's ownership of a horse and saddle was proved because "he was given to riding about on Sundays." Frederick Law Olmsted not only witnessed a head houseservant mount his horse after church service but, in true paternalistic fashion, slip a coin to the boy who had been holding its reins.[128] Ex-slaves commonly justified their ownership of a horse and wagon by their need to go to church on Sunday. This was not just a practical matter: Leah Wilson could not disguise the sense of status she derived from being able to drive "right along together with our master going to church." [129] A horse, as Edward Philbrick observed in 1862, was more than a means of transport; it was "a badge of power and caste." Sea island blacks had no respect for people who could not present themselves on a horse. "They will hardly lift their hats to a white man on foot," he noted, and viewed a "walking nigger" with contempt.[130]

Although we find elements of display, of accumulation for its own sake, and of "getting ahead," the *mentalité* of the slaves cannot be reduced to any one of these traits and was indeed much more. We can uncover better the meaning and limits of such behavior by exploring, once again, the slaves' immediate response to freedom. In terms of their attitude toward labor, the freedmen firmly resisted the overtures of northern reformers and proclaimed a resounding attachment to what may be resonantly characterized as a task-orientation. Employers and Freedmen's Bureau officials alike constantly bemoaned the impossibility of persuading the freedmen to "perform more than their allotted tasks." [131] In 1867 Frances Butler Leigh observed freedmen who begged "to be allowed to go back to the old task system" when the agent of the Freedmen's Bureau attempted to have them work by the day. "One man," she reported, "indignantly asked Major D—— what the use of being free was, if he had to work harder than when he was a

---

[127] Testimony of Lafayette Delegal, claim of Richard Cummings, Feb. 28, 1874, SCC.

[128] Report of R. B. Avery, claim of William Golding, May 16, 1874, SCC; Olmsted, *Journey*, 428.

[129] Testimony of Leah Wilson, claim of Prince Wilson, Jr., July 28, 1873, Chatham Co., Ga., SCC. See also the claim depositions of William Gilmore and Hamlet Delegal, and the testimony of Simon Cassell, Henry Stephens, and Fortune James in the claims of Jacob Monroe, Clarinda Porter, and Charles Warner respectively.

[130] Edward S. Philbrick to Pierce, Mar. 27, 1862 (Q12).

[131] Bvt. Lt. Col. R. F. Smith report in Bvt. Maj. Gen. R. K. Scott to O. O. Howard, July 9, 1866 (C1428, Pt. I). See also Bvt. Lt. Col. B. F. Smith to O. A. Hart, Apr. 25, 1866 (C1617).

slave."[132] Few freedmen would work a full day, a full week, "and very seldom a full month steady," complained one employer.[133] One Northerner advocated the confiscation of the freedmen's boats so that instead of continuing in their ways of "precarious living," they might develop "habits of steady industry."[134] The freedmen were said to work "when they please and do just as much as they please"; they then relied on hunting and fishing "to make up for what they lose in the field."[135]

This clash between the proponents of Northeastern business methods and a laboring population wedded to an alternative work ethic reverberated throughout the postwar lowcountry. The conflict is neatly illustrated in an exchange that occurred in 1865 between Colonel Willard, a man generally sympathetic to the freedmen's plight, and two ex-slaves who were sawmill workers. Willard was approached by the harassed owner of the mill, who was unable to impress his workers with the virtues of "steady" work: they claimed, for example, at least two hours of rest during their work day. From the standpoint of a Northern businessman, Willard's argument to the two representatives of the work force was impeccable: "Laborers at the North," he pointed out, "got less wages, and worked from sunrise to sunset, this season of the year, only having an hour at noon." The freedmen's reply was equally forceful: "We want," they emphasized, "to work just as we have always worked." Willard was left to expostulate that these former slaves "have no just sense of the importance of persistent labor."[136]

The freedmen's attitude toward the accumulation of property, much like their attitude toward work, was decisively shaped by their former experience under the task system. The argument that "the more they cultivate, the more they gain" had, as one Northern army officer discovered, no appeal. In 1868 Frances Butler Leigh made a similar discovery when she found that some freedmen refused wages and rations, preferring to "raise a little corn and sweet potatoes, and with their facilities for catching fish and oysters, and shooting wild game, they have as much to eat as they want, and now are quite satisfied with that."[137] In short, lowcountry freedmen apparently wished to avoid an unlimited involvement in the market, favoring production for sale only within the familiar context of an assured production for subsistence. This explains, in large measure, why the freedmen would not

[132] Leigh, *Ten Years on a Georgia Plantation* (London, 1883), 55.
[133] E. T. Wright to Lt. Col. H. B. Clitz, Oct. 6, 1865 (C1361, Pt. I).
[134] J. G. Foster to [?], Sept. 20, 1864 (C1334, Pt. I).
[135] Joseph D. Pope to Maj. Gen. Q. A. Gilmore, June 29, 1865 (C1472).
[136] Lt. Col. A. J. Willard to W. H. Smith, Nov. 13, 1865 (A7011).
[137] Smith report in Scott to Howard, July 9, 1866 (C1428, Pt. I); Leigh, *Ten Years on a Georgia Plantation*, 124.

forego their hunting and fishing activities for a greater concentration on cash crops, why they aspired to the ownership or rental of land, and why they refused to work for wages.[138] The degree to which subsistence (in this case, hunting) formed the priorities of one freedman is captured in a brief anecdote. A special agent, who toured the lowcountry in 1878 investigating disputed claims, visited the home of Samuel Maxwell, a former slave. He was not impressed with this particular claimant's adaptation to freedom and advised him to participate more fully in the wider society. For a start, he suggested, why not raise hogs rather than dogs? To which Maxwell replied: "A pig won't help us catch coons and rabbits." [139]

The preferences and ambitions of the freedmen reflected, above all, a desire for autonomy not only from the impersonal marketplace but also from individual whites. As one would-be employer found out in 1866, the freedmen who rejected wages and wanted to supply their own seed were expressing a fundamental desire to "be free from personal constraint." [140] They sought, in other words, to build upon a foundation that the task system had laid, consisting of that part of a day, that plot of land, or those few animals that they, as slaves, had been able to call their own. Thus for many, if not most, lowcountry freedmen, the central priorities of subsistence and autonomy shaped whatever propensity for material accumulation and for "getting ahead" they may have had. And what these goals of subsistence and autonomy signally call to mind, of course, are nothing more than the central priorities of peasants throughout the world.[141]

The freedman's quest for a measure of autonomy from individual whites should not be construed, however, as a desire for total disengagement from whites, particularly in the immediate postemancipation years. The moral universe of lowcountry slaves apparently contained notions of social equity and of reciprocal obligations between blacks and whites that were not jettisoned when freedom came.[142] Henry Ravenel's slaves, for example, voluntarily presented themselves before their master in March 1865 and "said they would be willing to take a certain piece of land which they would cultivate for old Master—that they would not want a driver or overseer, but would work

---

[138] I have been influenced by Eric Foner, *Politics and Ideology in the Age of the Civil War* (New York, 1980), 97–127; Willie Lee Rose, *Rehearsal for Reconstruction: The Port Royal Experiment* (New York, 1976 [orig. publ. Indianapolis, Ind., 1964]), 226, 303, 406; and the works by Mintz cited in n. 8.

[139] Report of R. B. Avery, claim of Samuel Maxwell, June 8, 1878, SCC.

[140] J. R. Cheves to A. P. Ketchum, Jan. 21, 1866 (A7058).

[141] Apart from the standard works on peasants by Wolf, Shanin, and Mintz, I found the general implications of James C. Scott, *The Moral Economy of the Peasant: Rebellion and Subsistence in Southeast Asia* (New Haven, Conn., 1976) particularly helpful.

[142] For antebellum slaves, and on a general level, this is the argument of Genovese, *Roll, Jordan, Roll*, esp. 133–149.

that faithfully for him—and that they would take another piece of land to work for their own use." Another set of plantation blacks dumbfounded their former owner in July 1865 when they told him that they now considered the land as their own; perhaps more striking, however, was their readiness to grant "Master" a portion of the crop as "a free gift from themselves." [143] When the promise of land dimmed, the freedmen could be expected to assume a more hostile posture. While evidence of such hostility exists, some sensitive observers were still aware of a basic and continuing paradox. Thus Joseph Le Conte, writing of Liberty County, Georgia, freedmen in the 1890s, noted their refusal to be tied to whites and their rejection of wage labor based, in his view, on their ability to "live almost without work on fish, crawfish, and oysters." At the same time, however, he referred to "the kindliest feelings" existing "among the blacks . . . toward their former masters." While Le Conte may have been guilty of some self-deception, similar observations from his fellow whites suggest the reality of this paradox.[144] Once again, this aspect of the freedmen's world view is strikingly reminiscent of a central feature of peasant life that, according to one authority, is permeated by the moral principle of reciprocity.[145]

The significance of the particular conjunction that this article set out to explore—the conjunction between a certain mode of labor organization and a particular domestic economy—can now be assessed. From the short-run perspective of masters, this conjunction had a number of benefits. They could escape their plantations in the summer months, they were supplied with additional provisions, and their slaves were *relatively* content, or so they believed. Oliver Bostick, a Beaufort County planter, explained that he "allowed [his] slaves to own and have their property and have little crops of their own for it Encouraged them to do well and be satisfied at home." Rufus King, another lowcountry master, was satisfied that "no Negro with a well-stocked poultry house, a small crop advancing, a canoe partly finished or a few tubs unsold, all of which he calculates soon to enjoy, will ever run away." [146] From the short-run perspective of the slaves, this con-

---

[143] Arney Robinson Childs, ed., *The Private Journal of Henry William Ravenel, 1859–1887* (Columbia, S.C., 1947), 216; Capt. H. A. Storey to C. B. Fillebrown, July 9, 1865 (C1468). Ravenel still considered his plantation hands to be slaves in Mar. 1865.

[144] William Dallam Armes, ed., *The Autobiography of Joseph Le Conte* (New York, 1903), 234. Long after emancipation, when he had ceased to be a landowner, Daniel Huger Smith still shared in "the same interchange of small gifts of eggs or a chicken or two on the one side and perhaps an article of clothing on the other" that had characterized master-slave relations many years before (*Recollections*, 127).

[145] Scott, *Moral Economy of the Peasant*, 157–192.

[146] Testimony of Oliver P. Bostick, claim of Andrew Jackson, Mar. 10, 1874, Beaufort Co., S.C., SCC; Rufus King, Jr., to William Washington, Sept. 13, 1828, in *American Farmer*, X (1828), 346.

junction increased their autonomy, allowed them to accumulate (and bequeath) wealth, fed individual initiative, sponsored collective discipline and esteem, and otherwise benefited them economically and socially.[147] In other words, on a much reduced scale, there were lowcountry slaves who resembled the protopeasants found among Caribbean slaves. This similarity was derived from very different origins: in the lowcountry, from a particular mode of labor organization; in the Caribbean, from the need for slaves to grow most of their own food and provision the free population. There was, in short, a much wider "peasant breach in the slave mode of production" in the Caribbean than in the lowcountry.[148]

Still, the parallel is suggestive, for in the same way that protopeasant adaptations had a comparable short-term significance for masters and slaves in both Caribbean and lowcountry, there were comparable long-term results. Wherever there were significant protopeasant activities among the slaves, there emerged after emancipation a class of people who had acquired the requisite skills that helped them escape, at least in part or temporarily, their dependence on the plantation.[149] In the lowcountry, the course of the war, the capital requirements of its major staple crop, and the development of phosphates production go some way toward explaining the particular shape of its postwar labor history.[150] But surely certain elements of this configuration had deeper roots, roots that without exaggeration can be traced all the way back to the early eighteenth century. The imperatives so dear to generations of lowcountry slaves achieved a measure of realization in the

[147] See Mintz, "Slavery and the Rise of Peasantries," in Craton, ed., *Roots and Branches*, 241.

[148] The phrase was coined by Tadeusz Lepkowski, referred to by Sidney W. Mintz, "Was the Plantation Slave a Proletarian?" *Review*, II (1978) 94. I would also suggest that there was a significantly wider peasant breach in the slave mode of production in the lowcountry than elsewhere in North America where "incentives," in the forms of garden plots, opportunities to earn money, etc., were accorded slaves. More comparative work is obviously needed, but evidence from one area of the antebellum South supports my supposition (Roderick A. McDonald, "The Internal Economies of Slaves on Sugar Plantations in Jamaica and Louisiana" [unpubl. paper, Southern Historical Association Meeting, 1981]). In any case, I am reluctant to describe the task system as an incentive system; it was more a way of life.

[149] Mintz, "Slavery and the Rise of Peasantries," in Craton, ed., *Roots and Branches*, esp. 226–233. In the same way that I consider there to have been a wider peasant breach in the slave mode of production in the lowcountry than elsewhere in North America (though it was certainly not absent elsewhere), I also believe—and this is almost a corollary—that the ability to escape the plantation, while not unique to the lowcountry, was more effectively secured here than elsewhere in North America.

[150] As we might expect, lowcountry freedmen, particularly sea islanders, proved an unreliable source of labor for the phosphate mines. Their plots of land took precedence, and their earnings from mining formed only a welcome supplement to the income derived from farming (Tom W. Schick and Don H. Doyle, "Labor, Capital, and Politics in South Carolina: The Low Country Phosphate Industry, 1867–1920" [unpubl. paper], 11).

more distinctive features of the region's postwar labor arrangements. By 1880 the percentage of farms sharecropped in the coastal districts of South Carolina and Georgia ranked among the lowest in the South; the proportion of rural black landowners was one of the highest in the South; it is possible to speak of a "black yeomanry" in the late nineteenth-century lowcountry; and by 1880 one observer in coastal Georgia could describe how most of the Negroes in his county had "bought a small tract of land, ten acres or more [on which they made] enough rice . . . to be perfectly independent of the white man." [151] To paraphrase Sidney Mintz, nothing else during the history of lowcountry slavery was as important as the task system and its concomitant domestic economy in making possible the freed person's adaptation to freedom without the blessings of the former masters.[152]

The Transformation of Urban Politics, 1700–1764

GARY B. NASH

Very few historians have been as important as Gary Nash in reshaping the agenda of early American history. Nash has consistently pushed forward both the methodological and substantive parameters of the field. Among many influential articles and books, the one reproduced here stands out for its originality and boldness of interpretation. Political history has largely gone out of fashion among early American historians, but Nash demonstrates that the exercise and distribution of political power cannot easily be ignored if scholars really wish to understand the dynamics of society in the years before the American Revolution.

This is an essay of great subtlety and complexity. In addition to attempting to address a complicated set of issues that bear upon

---

[151] Roger L. Ransom and Richard Sutch, *One Kind of Freedom: The Economic Consequences of Emancipation* (Cambridge, 1977), 91–93; Williamson, *After Slavery*, 155; W.E.B. DuBois, "The Negro Landholder of Georgia," *Bulletin of the United States Department of Labor*, VI, 35 (1901), 647–677; T. J. Woofter, *Black Yeomanry* (New York, 1930); *Morning News* (Savannah), Jan. 30, 1880, quoted in Armstrong, "From Task Labor to Free Labor," *Ga. Hist. Qtly.*, LXIV (1980), 443. This last-mentioned article makes a similar argument to the one here.

[152] Mintz, "Plantation Slave," *Review*, II (1978), 95.

Reprinted by permission from Gary B. Nash, "The Transformation of Urban Politics, 1700–1764," *Journal of American History*, 60 (Dec. 1973), 605–632. Copyright Organization of American Historians, 1973.

social and economic history as well as political history, Nash also compares the experiences of the major cities of early America to each other. To have undertaken the same sort of analysis for a single city would have been an accomplishment. To do so for Boston, New York, and Philadelphia was an even more important contribution.

The central conceptual category in the essay is "political mobilization." What precisely does Nash mean by the term? To whom does it refer and from what sorts of sources has he gathered the information that makes it possible for him to calibrate levels of mobilization across both time and space? What, in Nash's view, were the major mechanisms that permitted mobilization to occur as it did in a political world that feared "the democracy" and its prejudices? What role, for example, does Nash believe literacy had in the process and how persuasively does he make the case for the political significance of the ability to read?

Finally, compare Nash's early America to the early America portrayed by some of the other authors represented in this volume. Are Nash's New Yorkers like Howe's? Does the conflict-ridden urban society that Nash describes seem different from or similar to rural societies that other scholars have analyzed? Most early Americans did not live in cities and, moreover, New York, Philadelphia, and Boston were barely cities either by the standards of our time or those of eighteenth-century Europe. Why should we bother with them at all, accounting as they did for only about 5 percent of the population of British North America?

That colonial politics were highly factional and unstable is a familiar theme in early American history. Like pieces of colored glass in kaleidoscopic arrangement, it is said, factions came and went, shifting with time, place, circumstances, and the personalities of leaders. But rarely, according to the historical studies of recent decades, did these groupings develop the organizational machinery, the coherence, the continuity, or the political sophistication of the political parties which emerged in the aftermath of the American Revolution.[1]

Historians have attempted primarily to unravel the legislative history of these factional struggles, especially as they pitted representative assemblies against royal or proprietary governors and officeholders, and to invest these contests with either economic or ideological significance. Thus scholars know a great deal about struggles over

---

[1] Bernard Bailyn, *The Origins of American Politics* (New York, 1968); Jack P. Greene, "Changing Interpretations of Early American Politics," in Ray A. Billington, ed., *The Reinterpretation of Early American History: Essays in honor of John Edwin Pomfret* (New York, 1968), 151–84.

parliamentary privileges, the power of the purse, and control of the courts. Historians have passed through almost a century of argument which has cyclically explained political contention as a clashing of rival social and economic groups or, alternatively, as a Whiggish struggle against prerogative government. But for all of this investigation, little is known about the actual practice and style of electoral politics in the first two-thirds of the eighteenth century.

By taking political factionalism as given, playing down the issues dividing factions, and shifting the analysis from the motivations of political groups, it is possible to focus on the practice of factional politics and on the kind of political ethos or culture which was emerging in the period before 1765. An examination of three cities which would become instrumental in the coming of the Revolution—Boston, New York, and Philadelphia—yields compelling evidence that in the six decades before the Stamp Act crisis a "radical" mode of politics was evolving in the urban centers of colonial life.[2] This "transformation" involved activation of previously quiescent lower-class elements; the organization of political clubs, caucuses, and tickets; the employment of political literature and inflammatory rhetoric as never before; the involvement of the clergy and the churches in politics; and the organization of mobs and violence for political purposes. Although many of these innovations were managed by and for political elites and not intended to democratize colonial political life, the effect was to broaden the spectrum of individuals actively involved in public affairs and to produce a political culture that was far from deferential, increasingly antiauthoritarian, occasionally violent, and often destructive of the very values which the political elite wished to preserve.

At election time in 1726, a prominent Quaker merchant in Philadelphia wrote an English friend that "we have our Mobs, Bonfires, Gunns, Huzzas . . . Itinerations and processions too—Trains made up (as 'tis said) not of the Wise, the Rich or the Learned, for the Gentleman while he was Governour took care to discard all Such. . . ."[3] In this description Issac Norris expressed his dismay that Gov-

---

[2] Eighteenth-century writers employed the term "radical" only infrequently; and when they did, they meant "root" or "basic." Thus Samuel Davies looked for an "*outpouring of the Spirit*" as the "grand, radical, all-comprehensive blessing" in 1757; and "Plain Dealer," writing from Philadelphia in 1764, asserted that the cause of Pennsylvania's troubles "is radical, interwoven in the Constitution, and so become of the very Nature of Proprietary Governments." See Alan Heimert, *Religion and the American Mind from the Great Awakening to the Revolution* (Cambridge, Mass., 1966), 13; [Hugh Williamson], *Plain Dealer* #2 (Philadelphia, 1764), 7. The term is used here to mean not only basic but also basic in its tendency to shift power downward in a society where politics had heretofore been corporate and elitist in nature.

[3] Isaac Norris to Jonathan Scarth, Oct. 21, 1726, Letter Book, 1716–1730, Isaac Norris Papers (Historical Society of Pennsylvania, Philadelphia).

ernor William Keith, who no longer felt obliged to serve the interests of his employer, the widow of William Penn, had cultivated the support of a stratum of society that the "wise, Rich and Learned" believed had no place in the political process. Since 1723, in fact, Keith had been mobilizing support among lower-class workingmen in Philadelphia and newly arrived German and Scotch-Irish immigrants.

Elitist politicians and proprietary supporters complained bitterly of "Sir William's town Mob" and the governor's "sinister army," lamented that elections were "mobbish and carried by a levelling spirit," and charged that the "common People both in town & Country" were "blown up even to a degree of madness." [4] Of the 1726 elections Norris wrote that Keith had "perambulated" the city, "Popping into ye dramshops tiff & alehouses where he would find a great number of modern statesmen & some patriots settling affairs, cursing some, praising others, contriving laws & swearing they will have them enacted *cum multis aegis.*" Worse still, Keith's electoral victory was celebrated by an exuberant procession, "mostly made of Rabble Butchers porters & Tagrags—thus triumphantly has he made his Gradations Downward from a Government to an Equal with Every plain Country Member." [5]

Keith's attempt to build a broader political base in order to gain control of an assembly dominated by Quakers was not the first attempt in Philadelphia to develop new sources of political support to defeat an entrenched opponent. Two decades before, David Lloyd had accomplished a substantial shift of political power by expanding the politically relevant strata of Pennsylvania society and activating a part of the community that had played an insignificant role in politics. Though his real goal was to shield Pennsylvania from proprietary authority, not to shift the center of political gravity downward, Lloyd found that—given the power of the proprietary group—it was mandatory to establish a new base of political support.[6]

This technique of mobilizing the politically inert became increasingly more important to eighteenth-century political life. For the Pennsylvania Quakers, who had overcome earlier disunity and formed a strong anti-proprietary party, the problem was how to maintain in-

[4] Thomas Wendel, "The Keith-Lloyd Alliance: Factional and Coalition Politics in Colonial Pennsylvania," *Pennsylvania Magazine of History and Biography*, 92 (July 1968): 298, 296n, 301.

[5] Norris to Scarth, Oct. 21, 1728, Letter Book, 1716–1730, Norris Papers. Eight years later, commenting on the residual effects of William Keith's politics, Norris would write with displeasure that the "usual care was taken to bring in Crowds of Journeymen & such like in opposition." Norris to his son, Oct. 2, 1734, Copy Book of Letters, 1730–1735, ibid.

[6] Gary B. Nash, *Quakers and Politics, Pennsylvania, 1681–1726* (Princeton, 1968), 294–99.

fluence in a society where they were fast becoming a minority. For the proprietary party, the problem was how to develop popular sources of support in order to overcome Quaker domination of the assembly. Thus both factions, led by men of high position and reputation, nervously began to eye the Germans who were streaming into the colony after 1715. Neither the Quaker-dominated anti-proprietary or "Assembly" party nor the Anglican-based proprietary party welcomed the inundation of German immigrants who were regarded by Englishmen of both groups as crude, alien, and too numerous. But both factions cultivated their support. That the Quakers continued to control the assembly throughout the half-century preceding the Revolution, despite their fading numerical importance, was attributable largely to their success in politicizing the Germans, who were more interested in farming than legislative assemblies but found themselves dragged into the thicket of politics.[7]

With even greater misgivings, the proprietary party courted the German community, which by the 1750s represented about 40 percent of the population in Pennsylvania. In private discourse and correspondence its leaders continued to regard the Germans as "an uncultivated Race" of uncouth peasants, incapable, as one put it, "of using their own Judgment in matters of Government. . . ."[8] But political requirements conquered social and ethnic reservations, and, while proprietary leaders could describe the Germans in 1750 as "more licentious and impotent of a just government than any others" and "a body of ignorant, proud stubborn Clowns," they worked hard to split the German vote, as they had been doing since about 1740.[9] This drive for German support yielded only meager rewards in the political battles of the mid-1750s, but by 1764 the proprietary campaign was crowned with success. Benjamin Franklin and Joseph Galloway attributed their loss in the hotly contested election of that year to the

---

[7] Arthur D. Graeff, *The Relations Between The Pennsylvania Germans and The British Authorities (1750–1776)* (Philadelphia, 1939); Dietmar Rothermund, *The Layman's Progress: Religious and Political Experience in Colonial Pennsylvania, 1740–1770* (Philadelphia, 1961); Glenn Weaver, "Benjamin Franklin and the Pennsylvania Germans," *William and Mary Quarterly*, 14 (Oct. 1957): 536–59; John J. Zimmerman, "Benjamin Franklin and the Quaker Party, 1755–1756," ibid., 17 (July 1960): 291–313.

[8] Graeff, *Pennsylvania Germans*, 61–63.

[9] James Hamilton to Thomas Penn, Nov. 8, 1750, Official Correspondence, 5:88, Penn Family Papers (Historical Society of Pennsylvania, Philadelphia); [William Smith], *A Brief State of the Province of Pennsylvania*, . . . (London, 1755), 40. By 1764 William Smith would be defending the "industrious Germans" from what he claimed were Benjamin Franklin's reference to them—after they defected from Franklin's party in large numbers—as "a wretched rabble." Leonard W. Labaree and others, ed., *The Papers of Benjamin Franklin* (24 vols., New Haven, 1959–), 11:505. The attempts of the proprietary party to recruit the German vote in the early 1740s can be followed in the letters of the party leaders, James Allen and Richard Peters, to John Penn and Thomas Penn, Official Correspondence, 3, Penn Family Papers.

"Dutch vote" which had swung against them.[10] Proprietary leaders would have preferred to exert political leverage from power bases where men were appointed out of regard for their background, accomplishments, and standing in the community—the council, city corporation, College of Philadelphia, hospital, and Library Company.[11] But gradually—and reluctantly—proprietary politicians learned to seek support from groups which they would have preferred to regard as inadmissible to political life. The problem of challenging the legislative strength of their opponents could not otherwise be solved.

Just as members of the proprietary party learned to overcome their scruples with regard to involving Germans in the political process, they learned to swallow reservations about soliciting the support of lower-class mechanics and laborers. Galloway, a Quaker party stalwart, took great delight in pointing out that the "Gentlemen of the best fortune" in the proprietary party, who in their public statements spoke for hierarchy and order in all affairs, "thought it not mean or dishonourable to enter the Houses of the Lowest Mechanics to solicit their Opposition" to the Militia Act of 1756.[12] By 1764 these artisans would become all-important in the attempts of the proprietary party to defeat their opponents.

In New York a similar process was taking place, although attempts to mobilize a broad-based electorate were not as continuous. Jacob Leisler was perhaps the first to seek support among those whom by traditional thinking were better left outside the political arena. Leisler also relied upon the support of the Dutch who would continue to play a crucial role in electoral politics throughout the prerevolutionary period. Unlike the Germans in Philadelphia, however, the Dutch were well represented at all levels of the social structure and were well integrated into the social and economic fabric of New York City at the beginning of the eighteenth century.

Only a few years after Keith so effectively organized the artisanry of Philadelphia, the fires of political contention in New York, banked briefly after the Leislerian era by the adroit management of Governor Robert Hunter, grew hot enough to convince upper-class leaders that they must delve to deeper strata in society to develop political support.

---

[10] Labaree and others, eds., *Papers of Benjamin Franklin*, 11:397; Weaver, "Franklin and the Pennsylvanian Germans," 550.

[11] G. B. Warden, "The Proprietary Group in Pennsylvania, 1754–1764," *William and Mary Quarterly*, 21 (July 1964): 367–89.

[12] [Joseph Galloway], *A True and Impartial State of the Province of Pennsylvania: Containing an Exact Account of the Nature of Its Government, the Power of it Proprietaries, and Their Governors . . . also the Rights and Privileges of the Assembly and People . . .* (Philadelphia, 1759), 61.

The heavy-handed aggrandizement of power by Governor William Cosby and a decisive defeat in the assembly elections of 1727 were enough to convince the Morris party that they must play the game of tavern politics if they hoped to prevail. The city elections of 1733 and 1734, which among other things led to the trial of John Peter Zenger for seditious libel, reflected this new appeal to workingmen and the Dutch in the city. [13] That both sides could play the same game is evident in the attempts of Stephen De Lancey and Francis Harrison, members of the governor's inner circle, to carry the aldermanic election in the South Ward in 1734 by sending a troop of English soldiers from Fort George to the polls; and in the remarkable invitations of Governor Cosby himself, as Cadwallader Colden noted indignantly, to "many of low rank to dine with him such as had never pretended or expected so much respect." [14] These attempts at political mobilization were carried even further in 1737, if Colden can be believed. Describing the municipal elections he wrote: "The sick, the lame, and the blind were all carried to vote. They were carried out of Prison and out of the poor house to vote. Such a struggle I never saw and such a hurra[h]ing that above one half of the men in town are so hoarse that they cannot speak this day. The pole lasted from half an hour after nine in the morning till past nine at night." [15]

The ambition and energy of the De Lancey brothers, Stephen and Oliver, pushed the process a step further during the next decade. In their hatred of Governor George Clinton, who held office in New York from 1743 to 1753, the De Lanceys carefully cultivated the support of the large mechanic population in the city—an attempt, as Clinton complained, "to overturn his Majesty's Government by wresting the Power out of the Hands of His Officers, and placing it in a popular faction." [16] To the imperious Colden the sight of rich assembly candidates courting workingmen conjured up the remembrance that "true roman virtue was allmost totally extinguished before their great or rich men went about to court the common people for their votes." Colden hoped the "lower rank" in New York would not become "so low & weak as to take it as favour to be call'd by their names by rich men & to be shook by the hand," as had happened centuries ago while the Roman Empire was crumbling.[17]

[13] Stanley N. Katz, *Newcastle's New York: Anglo-American Politics, 1732–1753* (Cambridge, Mass., 1968), 68–70, 83–85; Bailyn, *Origins of American Politics*, 108–11.

[14] Nicholas, Varga, "New York Politics and Government in the Mid-Eighteenth Century," (doctoral dissertation, Fordham University, 1960), 397; *The Letters and Papers of Cadwallader Colden* (9 vols., New York, 1918–1937), 9:298.

[15] *Letters and Papers of Cadwallader Colden*, 2:179 (punctuation added).

[16] Quoted in Katz, *Newcastle's New York*, 175.

[17] *Letters and Papers of Cadwallader Colden*, 4:214; 3:313–14, 318–19.

Charges by elitists such as Colden and Clinton that opponents were attempting to rule by "meer popular influence" or were attempting "to instigate the passions of the lowest rank of people to the most wicked purposes" must be approached with caution.[18] But analysis of the three assembly elections of the 1760s indicates that the work of politicizing the laboring class had proceeded far enough to make it all but impossible to win electoral contests without the support not only of the skilled artificers, who often owned considerable property, but also the unskilled laborers, cartmen, mariners, and boatmen.[19] It is also important to note that the factional fighting that went on from the late 1720s through the 1760s sent all leaders scurrying after the Dutch vote. The Morris party did its best to cultivate the Dutch at the beginning of this period, as did the De Lancey faction at mid-century.[20] In the mid-1750s when New York was inflamed by the controversy over King's College, both sides recognized that the support of the Dutch was crucial and exhausted all means to obtain it. The inability of William Livingston and his partisans to win a large part of the Dutch vote explains more than anything else the shattered hopes of the Presbyterian faction in its attempt to prevent the Anglicans from obtaining a charter for the college.[21] The effect of this competition for Dutch support was to split an ethnic bloc which early in the century had been virtually unified at the polls.[22]

[18] Ibid., 3:390, 319. In 1740 Clinton accused Oliver De Lancey of working "openly and in all companyes, and among the lower rank of people" to defeat the governor's friends. Clinton to Duke of Bedford, June 12, 1750, in John R. Brodhead and others, eds., *Documents Relative to the Colonial History of the State of New York* (15 vols., Albany, 1853–87), 6:571.

[19] Roger J. Champagne, "Liberty Boys and Mechanics of New York City, 1764–1774," *Labor History*, 8 (Spring 1967): 124–31; Milton M. Klein, "Democracy and Politics in Colonial New York," *New York History*, 40 (July 1959): 238–39; Milton M. Klein, "Politics and Personalities in Colonial New York," ibid., 47 (Jan. 1966), 5–10.

[20] Katz, *Newcastle's New York*, 84; Milton M. Klein, "The American Whig: William Livingston of New York" (doctoral dissertation, Columbia University, 1954), 450. Historians have neglected the role of the Dutch in New York City politics, although they comprised about 35 percent of the electorate in the 1760s.

[21] Klein, "American Whig," 402. See also Beverly McAnear, "American Imprints Concerning King's College," *Papers of the Bibliographic Society of America*, 44 (Fourth Quarter 1950): 315.

[22] The extent to which ethnic bloc voting broke down in the eighteenth century is dramatically apparent in a comparison of surnames on the 1701 and 1761 poll lists that give the names of the electors for each candidate. All the percentages are higher on the 1761 breakdown because voters were choosing four representatives from a slate of six candidates whereas in the 1701 election (three wards only) voters were choosing one of two candidates. For the 1701 list, see *Minutes of the Common Council of the City of New York, 1675–1776* (8 vols., New York, 1905), 2:163–78. For the 1761 list, see *A Copy of the Poll List of the Election for Representatives for the City and County of New York which election began on Monday the 23rd day of January and ended on Friday the 27th day of the same month*

In Boston the process of activating the inactive proceeded along somewhat different lines but in the same direction. Unlike Philadelphia and New York, Boston had a population that was ethnically homogeneous. Throughout the colonial period factional leaders appealed for the support of a mass of English voters only lightly sprinkled with Scotch and Irish. Boston was also different in that ever since an armed crowd had mysteriously gathered in April 1689 to command the streets of Boston and force Edmund Andros into exile, its citizens, at all levels of society, had been far less quiescent than their counterparts in other urban centers. This may be partially explained by the effect on the political life of the city which the town meeting fostered.[23] In Boston, as in no other city, open debate was heard and decisions were made by majority vote on many issues, ranging from passing a bylaw "to prevent playing football in the streets" to voting £10 to Susana Striker for a kidney stone operation for her son, to taxing inhabitants for the erection of public buildings, poor relief, schoolteachers' salaries, and other expenses.[24] And whereas in New York and Philadelphia only a small number of municipal officers were elected, in Boston the voters installed not only selectmen, sheriffs, assessors, and constables, but surveyors of hemp, informers about deer, purchasers of grain, haywards, town criers, measurers of salt, scavengers, viewers of shingles, sheepreeves, hogreeves, sealers of leather, fenceviewers, firewards, cullers of stave hoops, auditors, and others.[25]

Thus in terms of a politically minded and active lower rank, Boston had already developed by the early eighteenth century what other urban centers haltingly and sporadically moved toward in the half-cen-

---

in the year of our Lord . . . (New York, 1880). The author is indebted to Joyce Goodfriend for an analysis of surnames.

	1701 Percentage of		1761 Percentage of	
	English Vote	Dutch Vote	English Vote	Dutch Vote
Candidate 1	73.7	11.5	83.1	85.0
Candidate 2	93.2	13.5	72.1	73.4
Candidate 3	94.1	24.4	59.0	76.1
Candidate 4	26.3	88.5	68.3	57.9
Candidate 5	6.8	86.5	60.4	55.7
Candidate 6	5.9	75.6	55.4	54.3

[23] See G. B. Warden, *Boston, 1689–1776* (Boston, 1970), 28–33.
[24] William H. Whitmore and others, eds., *Reports of the Record Commissioners of Boston* (39 vols., Boston, 1880–1902), 8:12, 33; 12:passim.
[25] In New York elections were held for the aldermen and assistants of the municipal corporation and for assessors, collectors, and constables. In Philadelphia the municipal corporation was self-perpetuating, but sheriffs, commissioners, assessors, and coroners were elected annually.

tury before 1765. Governor Cosby of New York pointed up this difference in 1735 when he charged the Morris faction, which was working the streets of New York to stir up opposition, with copying "the
example and spirit of the Boston people." [26]

But if the clay with which leaders of political factions worked was of
a somewhat different consistency in Boston, the problems of delving
deeper in society to ensure political victory were essentially the same.
Thus the "soft money" faction led by Elisha Cooke, Oliver Noyes,
Thomas Cushing, and William Clark "turned to the people as the
only possible base of political strength in Boston and took it upon
[themselves] to organize politics and elections in the town with unprecedented vigor and attention" in the 1720s.[27] In the following
decade, when a series of economic issues in Boston came to a head,
and in the 1740s, when the second currency crisis ripened, exceptional
measures were again taken to call upon those not included in the ranks
of respectability. "Interested Men," complained Peter Oliver in 1749,
had "set the Canaille to insult" Thomas Hutchinson for his leadership
of the conservative fiscal movement.[28] In this way political leaders recruited the support of lower-class artisans and mechanics whose bodies provided a new kind of political power, as demonstrated in three
mob actions of the 1740s in Boston directed by men of stature in the
community, and whose votes provided the margin of victory in the increasingly frequent contested elections.[29]

To engage in political mobilization, factional leaders found they had
to pursue a course which ran against the grain of their social philosophy. Given the widely shared belief in maintaining rank and order in
all human affairs and the rationalist view that only the cultivation of
the mind raised man above his naturally depraved state, it was to be

---

[26] Katz, *Newcastle's New York*, 83–84.

[27] Warden, *Boston*, 92.

[28] Douglas Adair and John A. Schutz, eds., *Peter Oliver's Origin & Progress of the American Revolution: A Tory View* (San Marino, Calif., 1961), 32.

[29] Eighteenth-century elections were by no means always contested. One measure of
politicization is the frequency of contested elections. A few preliminary statistics for
Boston may be illustrative. Defining a contested election as one in which the candidate
was opposed and lost at least 25 percent of the vote, one can trace a rise in oppositional
politics from the 1720s (when voting statistics for General Court elections are first regularly available) through the 1750s.

Boston Election Contests

Decade	Number of Contested Seats
1720–29	14/45 (31.1%)
1730–39	23/48 (47.9%)
1740–49	25/45 (55.0%)
1750–59	24/40 (60.0%)

expected that the gentility would look upon courting the favor of "the lesser sorts" or involving them in politics as a reckless policy containing the seeds of anarchy. To activate the multitude was to energize precisely that part of society which was ruled by passion—the baser impulses in human nature—rather than by reason. The letters and reports of leaders in Boston, New York, and Philadelphia are filled with allusions to "the rabble," "the unthinking multitude," and the dangers of exciting "the passions" of the populace. Although these fears resonated most strongly in conservative quarters, they were shared by popular leaders such as Livingston and Franklin, who were also concerned with preserving social hierarchy and respect for authority. It was more difficult, of course, for those with a more rigid and authoritarian outlook to reconcile the eighteenth-century rationalist philosophy with the necessity of campaigning for votes and adopting the techniques of popular politics. But when political necessity called, they too learned to set aside ingrained social principles. The best that could be hoped for was that somehow the support of unassimilated or lowerclass elements could be engaged without altering the structure of values by which such groups deferred to elitist politicians. Men at the top had embarked upon a radical course of political recruitment while hoping that these stratagems would not have radical effects.

Because all factions felt the necessity of broadening the political base, the dynamics of politics changed markedly. In a society in which the people at large acquiesced in the rule of the upper stratum, and in which social, economic, and political leadership were regarded as indivisible, political decisions could be made quietly and privately. Elites would be held in check, of course, by periodic tests of confidence administered by the propertied part of the community. But when the upper layer of society split into competing factions, which were obliged to recruit the support of those previously inert or outside the political process, then politics became open, abusive in tone, and sometimes violent.

New techniques of political organization were required. Men began to form political "tickets," as happened in Pennsylvania as early as 1705, in Boston at the end of the 1720s, and in New York as early as 1698. Leaders of the more conservative factions usually resisted this move in the direction of popular politics. Philadelphia conservatives James Logan and Norris, for example, decried the use of tickets that obliged the voter to "have eight men crammed down his throat at once." [30] The use of tickets was also accompanied by written balloting and the introduction of the caucus—closed at first—to nominate a slate of candidates. Thus Quaker leaders in the 1720s loudly de-

---

[30] Edward Armstrong, ed., *The Correspondence between William Penn and James Logan* (2 vols., Philadelphia, 1870–1872), 2:188, 336, 427.

claimed Keith's "Electing-Club" in Philadelphia.[31] But within a few decades the anti-Quaker proprietary leaders would be complaining bitterly that the Quakers used their yearly meeting, which met during the week before assembly elections, as a political caucus—a practice condemned in 1755 as "the finest Scheme that could possibly be projected for conducting political Intrigues, under the Mask of Religion."[32] Yielding to the realities of political life, the proprietary leaders in 1756 adopted the tactics of their opponents and even outdid the Quaker party by calling for open rather than private caucuses. A notice in the *Pennsylvania Gazette* summoned the electorate to the Philadelphia Academy for an open-air, on-the-spot primary election. Ideological consistency was abandoned as Quaker party writers condemned the innovation in the next issue of the newspaper, only to be attacked by the aristocratic proprietary spokesman who defended the rights of the freeholders "to meet in a peaceable Manner to chuse their Representatives."[33] Seeing a chance for electoral success in the Quaker opposition to war appropriations, the proprietary leaders put scruples aside and resorted to tactics that heretofore had offended their sense of political propriety.

In Boston popular politics came under the control of perhaps the best-organized caucus in the English colonial world. So far as the limited evidence indicates, the Boston caucus was organized about 1719 and functioned intermittently for about four decades before splitting into the North End Caucus and the South End Caucus. The Boston caucus nominated candidates for the city's four seats in the General Court and proposed selectmen and other town officials at the annual elections. Operating in the taverns, it perfected a network of political influence through affiliations with the independent fire companies, the Merchants' Club, and other social organizations.[34]

In New York the devices of popular politics were less in evidence than in Philadelphia or Boston because New York did not have annual assembly elections and employed viva-voce voting rather than the written ballot. Though a secret balloting law had been "long desired by . . . Friends to Liberty in this City," according to a political writer a few years before the Revolution, such a law had never

[31] Norris to Joseph Pike, Oct. 28, 1728, Letter Book, 1716–30, Norris Papers; *A Modest Apology for the Eight Members* . . . (Philadelphia, 1728).

[32] [William Smith], *A Brief State*, 26; Peters to Thomas Penn, Aug. 25, Nov. 17, 1742, Letter Book, 1737–50, Richard Peters Papers (Historical Society of Pennsylvania, Philadelphia).

[33] *Pennsylvania Gazette*, Sept. 12, 19, 1756. See also William R. Steckel, "Pietist in Colonial Pennsylvania: Christopher Sauer, Printer, 1738–1758" (doctoral dissertation, Stanford University, 1949), 233–44.

[34] G. B. Warden, "The Caucus and Democracy in Colonial Boston," *New England Quarterly*, 43 (March 1970): 19–33.

passed.[35] Nonetheless, popular politics took a long stride forward in 1739 with the replacement of the private nomination of assembly candidates by public nominating meetings. As Carl Becker noted more than half a century ago, this change constituted a recognition on the part of political leaders that "great numbers constituted as good a political asset as great names." [36] The origins of this innovation may be traced back to the work of the Morris-Alexander-Smith coalition against Governor Cosby in the early 1730s, although the first solid evidence of the open caucus is found in 1739 when the New York *Gazette* reported that "a great number of the freeholders and freemen of the . . . city have agreed and resolved to choose the following persons to represent them. . . ." [37]

An even more significant element in transforming politics from a private to a public affair was the use of the press. Although the political press had been used extensively in seventeenth-century England, it was not widely employed in colonial politics until the 1720s. Before that an occasional pamphlet had directed the attention of the public to a controversial issue. But such early polemical efforts as Joseph Palmer, *The Present State of New England* (Boston, 1689), or Thomas Lloyd, *A Seasonable Advertisement to the Freemen of this Province* . . . (Philadelphia, 1689), were beamed at the General Court or the assembly, though their authors probably hoped also to cultivate the support of the populace at large. "Campaign literature"—direct appeals to the freemen at election time—was rare in Boston before 1710, in Philadelphia before 1720, and in New York before 1730. But as issues became more heated and politicians discovered the need to reach a wider audience, the resort to the press became a fixed part of political culture. In Philadelphia, for example, where only five pieces of political literature had appeared in the first quarter of the century, the public was bombarded with forty-six pamphlets and broadsides between 1725 and 1728. Bostonians in 1721 and 1722 could spend their evenings in tavern discussions of any of the twenty-eight argumentative tracts on the currency crisis that appeared in those years. In New York, where the political press was somewhat more restrained in the

[35] New York *Gazette*, Jan. 8, 1770; Bernard Friedman, "The New York Assembly Elections of 1768 and 1769; The Disruption of Family Politics," *New York History*, 46 (Jan. 1965): 17–18.

[36] Carl L. Becker, "The History of Political Parties in the Province of New York, 1760–1776," *Bulletin of the University of Wisconsin*, 2 (1909–10): 18.

[37] Quoted in Carl L. Becker, "Nominations in Colonial New York," *American Historical Review*, 6 (Jan. 1901): 272. Another important aspect of popular politics was the proliferation of clubs which became both social and political organisms. These operated in all the cities from early in the eighteenth century and seem to have increased rapidly in the third quarter of the century. By the 1750s cultural and civic groups such as Franklin's Junto in Philadelphia, the Library Society in New York, and fire companies in all cities had also been highly politicized, much to the dismay of some of their founders.

prerevolutionary period than in Boston or Philadelphia, the Morris-Cosby struggle for power brought twenty-seven pamphlets from the presses between 1732 and 1734, when only an occasional piece had appeared before.[38]

By the 1740s the printed word had become an indispensable part of campaigning. In every contested election pamphleteers industriously alerted the public to the awful consequences that would attend a victory by the other side. When the excise bill was under consideration in 1754, seventeen pamphlets appeared in the streets of Boston to rally public support against it.[39] The King's College controversy in New York kept the city's two printers busy with the publication of several dozen efforts.[40] In Philadelphia the Paxton Massacre was argued pro-and-con in at least twenty-eight pamphlets, and in the election contest that followed in the fall of 1764 no less than forty-four pamphlets and broadsides were published, many with German editions.[41] A rise in polemical literature and election appeals is also evident in colonial newspapers which were increasing in number in the eighteenth century.[42]

This increase in the use of the press had important implications, not merely because of the quantity of political literature but also because the pamphlets and newspaper screeds were intended to make politics everyone's concern. The new political literature was distributed without reference to social standing or economic position and "accus-

---

[38] The pamphlets were identified in Charles Evans, *American Bibliography* (14 vols., Chicago and Worcester, Mass., 1903–59); and Clifford K. Shipton and James E. Mooney, *National Index of American Imprints Through 1800: The Short-Title Evans* (2 vols. [Worcester, Mass.], 1969).

[39] Paul S. Boyer, "Borrowed Rhetoric: The Massachusetts Excise Controversy of 1754," *William and Mary Quarterly*, 21 (July 1964): 328–51.

[40] See McAnear, "American Imprints Concerning King's College," 301–39.

[41] Many, although by no means all, of the pamphlets are reprinted in John R. Dunbar, ed., *The Paxton Papers* (The Hague, 1957), or discussed in J. Philip Gleason, "A Scurrilous Colonial Election and Franklin's Reputation," *William and Mary Quarterly*, 18 (Jan. 1961): 68–84.

[42] The sheer bulk of this literature grew rapidly in the second quarter of the century, though tapering off in New York and Boston thereafter. Election day sermons are not included in the figures for Boston.

Number of Pamphlets

Decade	Boston	New York	Philadelphia
1695–1704	6	5	2
1705–14	12	3	2
1715–24	40	0	2
1725–34	28	32	43
1735–44	37	13	15
1745–54	38	26	15
1755–64	26	19	109

tomed people of all classes, but especially of the middling and lower estates, to the examination and discussion of controversial issues of all sorts." [43] Thus, those whom even the most liberal politicians would not have formally admitted to the political arena were drawn into it informally.

The anguished cries of politicians about the dangerous effects of this new polemical literature give a clue to the ambivalent feelings which the elite held in regard to the use of the press. An optimist like Franklin looked upon fiery pamphlets and newspaper fusillades as instruments "to prepare the Minds of the Publick," [44] but most men assumed that man easily succumbed to his basest instincts and that the unthinking multitude, which included a vast majority of the population, was moved by passion rather than reason. Guided by these views, most leaders could not help but look upon exhortatory literature as a threat to the social order. Conservative politicians frequently attacked what they called irresponsible attempts "to inflame the minds of the people" or "to breed and nourish Discontent, and to foment Faction and Sedition." [45] And yet by the 1750s, and often before, even the most conservative leader could not resist the resort to the press, even though it might contradict his social philosophy. Men such as James De Lancey, who earlier had lamented its use, were eagerly employing the press by mid-century. Their opponents could only shake their heads in dismay—charging that attempts were being made to propagate "Clamour & Slander" and to turn the heads of "ignorant people & others who are not well acquainted with the publick affairs"—and then take up the pen themselves.[46] In Philadelphia it was the proprietary party, espousing social conservatism and constantly warning about the anarchic and leveling designs of Quaker politicians, that

---

[43] Carl Bridenbaugh, "The Press and the Book in Eighteenth-Century Philadelphia," *Pennsylvania Magazine of History and Biography*, 65 (Jan. 1941): 5. Although it is difficult to determine precisely who read—or was affected by—this literature, it is clear that for a few pounds an interested politician could supply every eligible voter in a city such as Philadelphia with a copy of an election polemic. One to three thousand copies of election pamphlets such as these were often printed in Philadelphia. Of equal significance, election pamphlets and broadsides were commonly read aloud at the polls.

[44] Labaree and others, eds., *The Papers of Benjamin Franklin*, 7:374. Franklin came close to changing his mind concerning the beneficial effects of the political press when he became the target of a savage pamphlet offensive in 1764.

[45] For example, see *A View of the Calumnies lately spread in some Scurrilous Prints against the Government of Pennsylvania* (Philadelphia, 1729).

[46] James De Lancey, *The Charge of the Honourable James De Lancey, Esqr. Chief Justice of the Province of New York, To the Gentlemen of the Grand-Jury for the City and County of New York, on Tuesday the 15th of October, 1734* (New York, 1734); James De Lancey, *The Charge of the Honourable James De Lancey Esq; Chief Justice of the Province of New York, to the Gentlemen of the Grand-Jury for the City and County of New York, on Tuesday the 15th Day of January, Annoq; Domini. 1733* (New York, 1734); *Letters and Papers of Cadwallader Colden*, 4:122, 161.

raised the art of pamphleteering to new levels of sophistication in the
1750s. No one in Philadelphia could quite match the imperious
William Smith for statements about the necessity of the ordered, deferential society; but no one did more to make the abusive pamphlet a
part of the eighteenth-century political arsenal.[47]

Given this increasing reliance upon the press, it was inevitable that
the professional pamphleteer would emerge as a new figure in politics.
Isaac Hunt, David James Dove, and Hugh Williamson of Philadelphia
were only three of a group of political writers who earned their pay by
devising new ways of touching the fears and aspirations of the electorate through deception, innuendo, and scurrility. The professional
pamphleteer, in the hire of elitist politicians, symbolized the contradiction between the new political strategems and the old social outlook.[48]

Not only a quantitative leap in political literature but also an escalation of rhetoric made the use of the press a particularly important part
of the new politics. As political literature became institutionalized, the
quality of language and the modes of argumentation changed
markedly. In the early eighteenth century pamphleteers exercised restraint, appealing to the public judgment and the "best interest of the
country." Perhaps mindful of the revolutionary potential of the
printed word, authors couched their arguments in legalistic terms. For
example, in Boston, during the exchange of pamphlets on the currency crisis in 1714, hundreds of pages were offered to the public, but
readers encountered nothing more virulent than charges that the opposition view was "strange and Unaccountable," "intolerable," "unreasonable and unjust," or that writers on the other side were guilty of
"bold and wilful Misrepresentation." But by 1754 the anti-excise pamphleteers were raising images in the public mind of "Little pestilent
Creature[s]," "dirty miscreants," and unspeakably horrible creatures
ready to "cram [their] . . . merciless and insatiable Maw[s] with our
very Blood, and bones, and Vitals" while making sexual advances on
wives and daughters.[49] In Philadelphia, Keith's political campaigns in
the 1720s introduced a genre of literature that for the first time di-

---

[47] Writing to the proprietor in 1755, Smith confessed that "The Appeal to the public
was against my Judgment." Another proprietary leader, Peters, had written earlier that "I
never knew any good come to the honest & right side of the Question in the Province
by Publick Papers." See Paul A. W. Wallace, *Conrad Weiser, 1696–1760, Friend of Colonist
and Mohawk* (Philadelphia, 1945), 115.

[48] Almost nothing has been written on the professional pamphlet writers of the colonial period, many of whom seem to have been schoolteachers. For a sketch of David
James Dove, which indicates how willingly he changed sides in the factional struggles in
Pennsylvania, see Joseph Jackson, "A Philadelphia Schoolmaster of the Eighteenth Century," *Pennsylvania Magazine of History and Biography*, 35 (No. 3, 1911): 315–32.

[49] Boyer, "Borrowed Rhetoric: The Massachusetts Excise Controversy of 1754,"
341–44.

rectly attacked men of wealth and learning. "According to my experience," wrote David Lloyd, "a mean Man, of small Interest, devoted to the faithful Discharge of his Trust and Duty to the Government, may do more good to the State than a Richer or more Learned Man, who by his ill Temper and aspiring Mind becomes an opposer of the Constitution by which he should act." [50] This was egalitarian rhetoric which inverted the social pyramid by rejecting the traditional notion that the maintenance of social order and political stability depended on vesting power in men of education and high status.

But this kind of language was a model of restraint compared to mid-century political vitriol. In newspapers and pamphlets, contending elites hurled insults at each other and charged their opponents, to cite one example from Philadelphia, with "Inveterate Calumny, foul-mouthed Aspersion, shameless Falsehood, and insatiate Malice. . . ." [51] New York also witnessed a change in rhetorical style as pamphleteers substituted slander and vituperation for reasoned discourse. The Anglican clergy was left no semblance of integrity in the attacks of the Livingston faction during the King's College controversy. In phrases that made Zenger's New York *Journal* seem polite by comparison, readers were told of the "ghastly juggling . . . and insatiate Lust of Power" of the Anglican clergymen and learned of "our intended Vassalage," the "Seduction of Priest-craft," and "clerical Rubbish and Villainy." [52]

In effect, the conservatives' worst fears concerning the use of the press were being confirmed as the tactics of printed political discourse changed from attacking the legality or wisdom of the opposition's policies or pleading for the election of public-minded men to assailing the character and motives of those on the other side. The effect of the new political rhetoric was self-intensifying as each increase in the brutality of language brought an equivalent or greater response from the opposition. Gradually the public was taught to suspect not simply the wisdom or constitutional right of one side or the other, but the motives, morality, and even sanity of its leaders. The very high-placed individuals to whom the rank-and-file were supposed to defer were being exposed as the most corrupt and loathsome members of society.

In mob activity and threats of violence the radicalization of politics can be seen in its most dramatic though not its most significant form. It is well to make a distinction between spontaneous disorders expressive of deeply felt lower-class grievances and mob activity arranged

---

[50] *A Vindication of the Legislative Power* (Philadelphia, 1725).

[51] *Pennsylvania Journal*, April 22, 1756. The charges were made against Smith in return for "the Vomitings of this infamous Hireling" whose attacks on Franklin "betoken that Redundancy of Rancour, and Rottiness of Heart which render him the most despicable of his Species." Ibid.

[52] Thomas Gordon, *The Craftsman* (New York, 1753), iii–xiii, xxv, xxvi.

and directed by political leaders to serve their own purposes. A connection existed between the two kinds of activity since political elites, witnessing random lower-class disorder, did not fail to note the effectiveness of collective force; and lower-class elements, encouraged or even rewarded by political leaders for participating in riotous activity, undoubtedly lost some of their awe and reverence for duly constituted authority, gaining a new sense of their own power.[53]

Mobs expressing class grievances were less common in the colonial cities than in rural areas, where land disputes and Indian policy were major sources of conflict throughout the eighteenth century.[54] The food rioting that was a persistent factor in the history of European cities of this period was almost unknown in Boston, New York, and Philadelphia.[55] Far more common was the sporadic violence directed at individuals identified with unpopular causes. Cotton Mather, who went unappreciated by a large part of Boston's population throughout his lifetime of religious and political eminence, had his house firebombed in 1721.[56] In 1749 Thomas Hutchinson, long identified with hard-money policies, watched ruefully as his house burned to the cheers of the mob while the fire company responded with a suspicious lack of speed.[57] James Logan and his wife spent a night under the bed when the mob bombarded their stately house with stones, convincing Logan that law and order in Philadelphia was as shattered as his window panes.[58] This kind of violence, along with unofficially sanctioned riots such as the annual Pope's Day battles between North End and

---

[53] Pauline Maier has shown that the prerevolutionary mob was usually anti-imperial or designed to extend rather than attack authority. See Pauline Maier, "Popular Uprisings and Civil Authority in Eighteenth-Century America," *William and Mary Quarterly*, 27 (Jan. 1970): 3–35. But she has ignored the role of the mob in provincial politics and, by focusing exclusively on the quasi-legal activity of mobs, overstates the acceptance of mob activity.

[54] There are few parallels in the history of the colonial cities to the forays of the White Pine rebels in Massachusetts, the land rioters in New York and New Jersey in the 1740s, and the Paxton Boys in Pennsylvania. For accounts of these movements, see Joseph J. Malone, *Pine Trees and Politics, The Naval Stores and Forest Policy in Colonial New England, 1691–1775* (Plymouth, England, 1964); Irving Mark, *Agrarian Conflicts in Colonial New York, 1711–1775* (New York, 1940); Donald L. Kemmerer, *Path to Freedom: The Struggle for Self-Government in New Jersey, 1703–1776* (Princeton, 1940); Theodore Thayer, *Pennsylvania Politics and the Growth of Democracy, 1740–1776* (Philadelphia, 1953); and Brooke Hindle, "The March of the Paxton Boys," *William and Mary Quarterly*, 3 (Oct. 1946): 461–86.

[55] For a comparative view of the mob, see Gordon S. Wood, "A Note on Mobs in the American Revolution," *William and Mary Quarterly*, 23 (Oct. 1966): 635–42; and William A. Smith, "Anglo-American Society and the Mob, 1740–1775" (doctoral dissertation, Claremont Graduate School, 1965).

[56] *The Diary of Cotton Mather, 1709–1724*, Massachusetts Historical Society Collections (8 vols., Boston, 1900–1912), 8:657–58.

[57] Warden, *Boston*, 140.

[58] James Logan to James Alexander, Oct. 23, 1749, Letter Book, 1748–50, James Logan Papers (Library Company of Philadelphia).

South End in Boston, reflected the general abrasiveness of life in the eighteenth century and the frailty of law enforcement in the cities.[59]

Far more significant was violence inspired and controlled by the elite. This was often directed at imperial officers charged with carrying out unpopular trade or military policies. Thus Boston was more or less in the hands of the mob for three days in 1747, after the commander of the British fleet in the harbor ordered his press gang to make a nocturnal sweep through the streets. The mob, wrote Governor William Shirley, "was secretly Contenanc'd and encourag'd by some ill minded Inhabitants and Persons of Influence in the Town. . . ."[60] The garrisoning of troops in New York City led to "constant violence" and the efforts of crown officials to block illegal trade with the enemy was forcibly resisted in 1759 by the city's merchants who employed waterfront mobs to do their work.[61] But mobs were also used in internal political struggles that did not involve imperial policy. In Boston in the 1730s, when the issue of a public market dominated municipal politics, a band of night raiders sawed through the supports of the market houses in the North End and later demolished another building. When Governor Jonathan Belcher vowed to see justice done, letters circulated in the town claiming that 500 men stood ready to oppose with force any attempt to intervene in the case.[62] In Philadelphia, Keith's "town mob," as his detractors called it, was sufficiently enlivened by their election victory in 1726 to burn the pillory and stocks—the symbols of authority and social control.[63] Two years later a dispute over a vacant assembly seat led to a campaign of intimidation and assault on Quaker members of the assembly by Keith's partisans. The Quakers complained that such "Indecensies [were] used towards the Members of Assembly attending the Service of the Country in *Philadelphia*, by rude and disorderly Persons," that it was unsafe to meet any longer in Philadelphia.[64] When the assembly met in the

[59] R. S. Longley, "Mob Activities in Revolutionary Massachusetts," *New England Quarterly*, 6 (Mar. 1933): 102–3.

[60] Maier, "Popular Uprisings," 4–15; Charles H. Lincoln, ed., *The Correspondence of William Shirley: Governor of Massachusetts and Military Commander in America, 1731–1760* (2 vols., New York, 1912), 1:406.

[61] Julius Goebel, Jr., and T. Raymond Naughton, *Law Enforcement in Colonial New York: A Study in Criminal Procedure (1664–1776)* (New York, 1944), 194; Milton M. Klein, "The Rise of the New York Bar: The Legal Career of William Livingston," *William and Mary Quarterly*, 15 (July 1958): 348.

[62] Warden, *Boston*, 121–24; Carl Bridenbaugh, *Cities in the Wilderness: The First Century of Urban Life in America, 1625–1742* (New York, 1938), 352.

[63] Patrick Gordon to John Penn, Oct. 17, 1726, Official Correspondence, 1, Penn Family Papers.

[64] Gertrude MacKenney, ed., *Votes and Proceedings of the House of Representatives of the Province of Pennsylvania, Pennsylvania Archives* (Eighth Series) (8 vols., Harrisburg, Pa., 1931–35), 3:1908. See also *The Proceedings of some Members of Assembly, at Philadelphia,* Apr. 1728 vindicated from the unfair *Reasoning* and unjust *Insinuations* of a certain *Remarker* (Philadelphia, 1728).

following spring, it faced an incipient insurrection. Keith's mob, according to James Logan, was to apply "first to the Assembly and then storm the Government," knocking heads, plundering estates, and putting houses to the torch, if necessary, to get what it wanted.[65] Only the hasty passage of an act authorizing the death penalty for riot and insurrection seems to have averted violence.

In 1742 Philadelphia was shaken by a bloody election-day riot. It was a prime example of the elite's willingness to employ the mob.[66] Even before election day, rumors circulated that the Quaker party intended to maintain its majority in the assembly by steering unnaturalized Germans to the polls and that the proprietary party meant to thwart this attempt by engaging a pack of toughs. The rumors had substance. When the leaders of the two political factions could not agree on procedures for supervising the election, heated words and curses were exchanged; and seventy sailors wielding clubs and shouting "down with the plain Coats & broad Brims" waded into the Quaker crowd assembled before the courthouse.[67] When the Quaker leaders retreated inside, the sailors filled the air with a hailstorm of bricks. A counterattack was launched by Germans and younger Quakers, who momentarily forgot their pacifist principles. "Blood flew plentifully around," the proprietary secretary reported.[68] Conducting investigations later, the Quaker assembly concluded that the riot had been engineered by the leaders of the proprietary party. Though some historians have disputed this, two of the proprietor's chief officials in Pennsylvania privately admitted as much.[69]

Although mob violence was probably not nearly so widespread in the colonial cities as in London, the leaders of all factions were sensitive to the power that the mob possessed. Few colonial leaders wanted to democratize society or shift political power downward in the social order. But locked in competition with other upper-class groups, they found it necessary to expand the politically relevant sector of society by encouraging the common people to participate in direct political action.

---

[65] Logan to John, Richard, and Thomas Penn, Apr. 24, 1729, Official Correspondence, 2:55, Penn Family Papers.

[66] For two interpretations of the riot, see Norman S. Cohen, "The Philadelphia Election Riot of 1742," *Pennsylvania Magazine of History and Biography*, 92 (July 1968): 306–19; and William T. Parsons, "The Bloody Election of 1742," *Pennsylvania History*, 36 (July 1969): 290–306.

[67] Richard Hockley to Thomas Penn, Nov. 1, 1742, Official Correspondence, 3, Penn Family Papers.

[68] Peters to the Proprietors, Nov. 17, 1742, Letter Book, 1737–50, Peters Papers.

[69] Hockley to Thomas Penn, Nov. 1 and Nov. 18, 1742, Official Correspondence, 3:241–43, Penn Family Papers; Peters to Thomas Penn, Nov. 17, 1742, Letter Book, 1737–50, Peters Papers.

It would be a mistake to believe that political mobs were passive instruments manipulated by the elite. Though lower-class economic and social grievances only rarely achieved ideological expression in this period, the men who worked by night in Boston or Philadelphia surely gained a new sense of their own power. The urban artisan or laborer discovered that he was not only a useful but also often an essential part of politics. As early as 1729, James Logan sensed the implications of deploying "the multitudes." "Sir William Keith," he wrote, "was so mad, as well as wicked, most industriously to sett up the lowest part of the People; through a vain expectation that he should always be able to steer and influence them as his own Will. But he weakly forgot how soon the minds of such People are changed by any new Accident and how licentious force, when the Awe of Government . . . is thrown off, has been turned against those who first taught them to throw it off." [70]

Another important facet of the "new politics" of the prerevolutionary decades was the growing involvement of religious leaders in politics, something nearly all leaders deplored but nonetheless exploited. Of course religious leaders had never been isolated from political life in the early history of the colonies; but such efforts as they made to influence public affairs were usually conducted discreetly and privately. When clergymen published pamphlets on political subjects, they did so anonymously. The common assumption that it was inappropriate for clergymen to mix religion and politics was clearly articulated in 1722 when Cotton Mather and John Wise were exposed as two of the principal controversialists in the heated currency debate in Massachusetts. "Some of our Ecclesiasticks of late," wrote an anonymous pampheleteer, "have been guilty of too officious a meddling with State Affairs. To see a Clergy-man (Commedian-like) stand belabouring his Cushion and intermixing his Harrangue with THUNDERBOLTS, while entertaining his peaceable Congregation with things whereof he is . . . Ignorant . . . how ridiculous is the Sight and the Sound." [71] Such attacks on clerical involvement in politics would continue throughout the prerevolutionary period. But by mid-century church leaders were beginning to shed their anonymity and to defend their right to engage in "preaching politics," as Jonathan Mayhew put it in Boston in 1750. [72]

To some extent this politicization of the clergy can be attributed to the Great Awakening, for amid the evangelical fervor of the early 1740s "religious controversies and political problems were blended in

[70] Logan to John, Richard, and Thomas Penn, Apr. 24, 1729, Official Correspondence, 2:55, Penn Family Papers.

[71] Andrew McF. Davis, *Colonial Currency Reprints, 1682–1751* (4 vols., Boston, 1910–11), 2:134.

[72] Quoted in Heimert, *Religion and the American Mind*, 15.

a unique pattern of interaction."[73] But perhaps more important was the fact that by the 1740s the fires of political contention were growing hotter, impelling factional leaders to enlist the services of religious leaders. In Philadelphia, the issue of war and defense appropriations in 1748, not the Great Awakening, brought the first full-scale exchange on a secular question between opposing denominational spokesmen. In a dozen signed pamphlets Presbyterian and Quaker leaders such as Gilbert Tennent and Samuel Smith carried out a public dialogue on the necessity of military defense—a battle of words that thrust the clergy into the political arena.[74]

No more dramatic representation of a politicized clergy can be imagined than the jailing of the Anglican ecclesiastic William Smith by the Pennsylvania assembly in 1758. Writing anonymously, Smith had published two open-handed attacks on the Quaker party in 1755 and 1756 as part of the proprietary party's offensive against the Quaker-dominated assembly. He continued his assaults in 1757 and 1758 in the *American Magazine* and the *Pennsylvania Journal*. Determined to halt these attacks, the assembly charged Smith and one of his fellow writes with libel. During the course of a long trial and subsequent appeals to England, Smith carried out his duties and political ambitions from the Philadelphia jail.[75]

The clergy's increasing involvement in politics had a second dimension which was closely related to the Great Awakening. One of the side effects of the revivalist movement was an expansion of political consciousness within the lower reaches of society. The average city dweller developed a new feeling of autonomy and importance as he partook of mass revivals, assumed a new power in ecclesiastical affairs, and was encouraged repeatedly from the pulpit to adopt an attitude of skepticism toward dogma and authority. Doctrinal controversy and attacks on religious and secular leaders became ritualized and accepted in the 1740s.[76] It was precisely this that caused high-placed individuals

[73] Rothermund, *Layman's Progress*, 82.

[74] The debate can be followed in a series of pamphlets published in 1748. See, for example, William Currie, *A Treatise on the Lawfulness of Defensive War* (Philadelphia, 1748); Gilbert Tennent, *The Late Association for Defence, Encourag'd, or the Lawfulness of a Defensive War* (Philadelphia, 1748); and John Smith, *The Doctrine of Christianity, As Held by the People Called Quakers, Vindicated: In Answer to Gilbert Tennent's Sermon on the Lawfulness of War* (Philadelphia, 1748).

[75] William Renwick Riddell, "Libel on the Assembly: a Prerevolutionary Episode," *Pennsylvania Magazine of History and Biography*, 52 (No. 2, 3, 4, 1928): 176–92, 249–79, 342–60; William S. Hanna, *Benjamin Franklin and Pennsylvania Politics* (Stanford, 1964), 134–37; Leonard W. Levy, *Freedom of Speech and Press in Early American History; Legacy of Suppression* (New York, 1963), 53–61.

[76] Rothermund, *Layman's Progress*, 55–60, 81–82; Heimert, *Religion and the American Mind*, 27–58, 239–93. The process was not confined to the cities. See Richard L. Bushman, *From Puritan to Yankee: Character and the Social Order in Connecticut, 1690–1765* (Cambridge, Mass., 1967).

to charge revivalists with preaching levelism and anarchy. "It is . . . an exceeding difficult gloomy time with us . . . ," wrote William Rand from Boston; "Such an enthusiastic, factious, censorious Spirit was never known here. . . . Every low-bred, illiterate Person can resolve Cases of Conscience, and settle the most difficult Points of Divinity, better than the most learned Divines."[77] Such charges were heard repeatedly during the Great Awakening, revealing the apprehension of those who trembled to see the "unthinking multitude" invested with a new dignity and importance. Nor could the passing of the Great Awakening reverse the tide, for this new sense of power did not atrophy with the decline of religious enthusiasm, but remained as a permanent part of the social outlook of the middle and lower strata of society.

The October 1764 elections in Philadelphia provide an opportunity to observe in microcosm all of the radicalizing tendencies of the previous three-quarters of a century. The city had already been badly shaken by the Paxton Boys, who descended on the capital to press demands for frontier defense and to take the lives of a group of Christian Indians, who were being sheltered by the government in barracks at Philadelphia. This exercise in vigilante government led to a Quaker-Presbyterian pamphlet war. Against this background the Quaker party decided to organize the October assembly elections around a campaign to replace proprietary with royal government.[78]

By the spring of 1764 the move to place Pennsylvania under royal government was underway, and political leaders in both camps were vying for popular support. Proprietary aristocrats, suppressing their contempt for the urban working class, made strenuous efforts to recruit artisan support and, for the first time, placed three ethnic candidates—two Germans and one Scotch-Irish—on their eight-man assembly slate. "The design," wrote a party organizer, "is by putting in two Germans to draw such a Party of them as will turn the scale in our Favor. . . ."[79] The success of these efforts can be measured by the conversion to the proprietary cause of Carl Wrangel and Henry Muhlenberg, the Lutheran church leaders in Philadelphia, and Christo-

---

[77] [William Rand], *The Late Religious Commotions in New England Considered . . .* (Boston, 1743), p. 18.

[78] Hindle, "The March of the Paxton Boys," 461–86; Hanna, *Benjamin Franklin and Pennsylvania Politics*, 154–68; James H. Hutson, "The Campaign to Make Pennsylvania a Royal Province, 1764–1770," *Pennsylvania Magazine of History and Biography*, 94 (Oct. 1970): 427–63; 95 (Jan. 1971): 28–49.

[79] Samuel Purviance, Jr., to James Burd, Sept. 10, 1764, Vol. 1, Shippen Family Papers (Historical Society of Pennsylvania, Philadelphia). James Pemberton, a Quaker leader, wrote that the proprietary leaders engaged in "unwearied Endeavors . . . to prejudice the minds of the lower class of the people" against Franklin. James Pemberton to John Fothergill, Oct. 11, 1764, James Pemberton Papers (Historical Society of Pennsylvania, Philadelphia).

pher Sauer, Jr., and Heinrich Miller, the German printers. By the end of the summer all of these men were writing or translating anti-Quaker pamphlets for distribution in the German community.[80]

The efforts of the proprietary party to search in the lower social strata for support drove Franklin and the assembly party to even greater lengths. In early April, Franklin called a mass meeting and sent messengers house-to-house to turn out the largest possible audience. The featured speaker was Galloway, who delivered an "inflammatory harangue" about the evils of proprietary government.[81] This was the opening shot in a campaign to gather signatures on a petition pleading for the institution of royal government. In the concerted drive to obtain signatures, according to one critic, "Taverns were engag'd, [and] many of the poorer and more dependent kind of labouring people in town were invited thither by night, the fear of being turn'd out of business and the eloquence of the punch bowl prevailed on many to sign. . . ." [82] The town was saturated with polemical literature, including 3,000 copies of the assembly's biting message to the proprietor and their resolves for obtaining royal government. Franklin and Galloway published pamphlets designed to stir unrest with proprietary government, and Quakers, according to one observer, went door-to-door in pairs soliciting signatures for the royal government petition.[83] John Penn, the nephew of the proprietor, was shocked that Franklin's party went "into all the houses in Town without distinction," and "by the assistance of Punch and Beer" were able to procure the signatures of "some of the lowest sort of people" in the city.[84]

It was only a matter of time before the proprietary party, using fire to fight fire, circulated a counter-petition and far outstripped the efforts of Franklin and Galloway to involve the populace in politics. Everyone in Philadelphia, regardless of religion, class, or ideological predisposition, found himself courted by the leaders of the two political factions.[85] Never in Pennsylvania's history had the few needed the many so much.

---

[80] Hutson, "Campaign to Make Pennsylvania a Royal Province," 452; Theodore Tappert and John W. Doberstein, trans. and eds., *The Journal of Henry Melchior Muhlenberg* (3 vols., Philadelphia, 1942–45), 2:91, 99–102, 106–7, 123.

[81] John Penn to Thomas Penn, May 5, 1764, Official Correspondence, 9:220, Penn Family Papers; John Dickinson, A *Reply to a Piece called the Speech of Joseph Galloway, Esquire* (Philadelphia, 1764), 32–33.

[82] Dunbar, ed., *Paxton Papers*, 369; Huston, "Campaign to Make Pennsylvania a Royal Province," 437–52.

[83] William Bingham to John Gibson, May 4, 1764, Shippen Papers.

[84] John Penn to Thomas Penn, May 5, 1764, Official Correspondence, 9:220, Penn Family Papers.

[85] Autograph Petitions, 1681–1764, Penn Family Papers.

As the battle thickened, pamphleteers reached new pinnacles of abusiveness and scurrility. Franklin was reviled as an intellectual charlatan who begged and bought honorary degrees, a corrupt politician intimately acquainted "with every Zig Zag Machination," a grasping, conniving, egotistical climber, and a lecherous old man who promoted royal government only for the purpose of installing himself in the governor's chair.[86] His friends responded by labeling an opposition pamphleteer "a Reptile" who "like a Toad, by the pestilential Fumes of his virulent Slabber" attempted "to blast the fame of a PATRIOT" and describing William Smith, leader of the opposition, as a "consumate Sycophant," an "indefatigable" liar, and an impudent knave with a heart "bloated with *infernal Malice*" and a head full of "*flatulent Preachments.*" [87] As for the Presbyterians, they were redesignated "Piss-Brute-arians (a bigoted, cruel and revengeful sect)" by a Franklin party pamphleteer who later reached the apogee of scatalogical polemics when he suggested that now was the time for Smith, president of the college and a director of the hospital, to consummate his alliance with the pamphleteer David Dove, who "will not only furnish you with that most agreeable of all Foods to your Taste, but after it has found a Passage through your Body . . . will greedily devour it, and, as soon as it is well digested, he will void it up for a Repast to the Proprietary Faction: they will as eagerly swallow it as the other had done before, and, when it has gone through their several Concoctions, they will discharge it in your Presence, that you may once more regale on it, thus refined." [88] One shocked outsider wrote to a friend in Philadelphia: "In the name of goodness stop your Pamphleteer's Mouths & shut up your presses. Such a torrent of low scurrility sure never came from any country as lately from Pennsylvan[i]a." [89]

Religious leaders were also drawn into the campaign. A rural clergyman related that the proprietary leaders had convinced Presbyterian and Anglican ministers in Philadelphia to distribute petitions requesting the preservation of proprietary government. "The Presbyterian ministers, with some others," he lamented, "held Synods about the

---

[86] Labaree and others, eds., *Papers of Benjamin Franklin*, 11:380–84.

[87] Quoted in ibid., 11:384; Gleason, "A Scurrilous Colonial Election and Franklin's Reputation," 82.

[88] [Isaac Hunt], *A Letter From a Gentleman in Transilvania To his Friend in* America *giving some Account of the late disturbances that happen'd in that Government, with some Remarks upon the political revolutions in the Magistracy, and the Debates that happened about the Change* (Philadelphia, 1764); [Isaac Hunt], *A Humble Attempt at Scurrility* (Philadelphia, 1765), 36–37.

[89] Quoted in Gleason, "A Scurrilous Colonial Election and Franklin's Reputation," 82n.

election, turned their pulpits into Ecclesiastical drums for politics and
told their people to vote according as they directed them at the peril
of their damnation. . . ." [90] Church leaders such as Tennent, Francis
Allison, and Muhlenberg wrote political pamphlets or sent circular
letters on the election to every congregation in the province. St. Peters and Christ Church were the scenes of pre-election rallies as denominational groups assumed an unprecedented role in politics.[91] A
"Gentlemen from Transylvania" charged that Philadelphia's Anglican
leaders had "prostituted their Temples . . . as an Amphitheatre for
the Rabbie to combat in. . . ." [92]

Inflammatory rhetoric, a large polemical literature, the participation of the churches in politics, mobilization of social layers previously
unsolicited and unwelcome in political affairs, all combined to produce an election in which almost everybody's integrity was questioned,
every public figure's use of power was attacked, and both sides paraded
themselves as true representatives of "the people." The effects were
dramatic: a record number of Philadelphians turned out for the election. The polls opened at 9 A.M. and remained open through the night
as party workers on both sides shepherded in the voters, including the
infirm and aged who were carried to the courthouse in litters and
chairs. By the next morning, party leaders were still seeking a few additional votes. Not until 3 P.M. on the second day were the polls
closed.[93] When the returns were counted, both Franklin and Galloway had lost their seats to men on the proprietary ticket.[94] Franklin
did not doubt that he had been defeated by defecting Germans and
propertyless laborers "brought to swear themselves intituled to a

[90]Quoted in Guy Soulliard Klett, *Presbyterians in Colonial Pennsylvania* (Philadelphia,
1937), 256.

[91] Thayer, *Pennsylvania Politics*, 97; Klett, *Presbyterians and Pennsylvania*, 256–57;
Rothermund, *Layman's Progress*, 126–30; Thomas Stewardson, contributor, "Extracts
from the Letter-Book of Benjamin Marshall 1763–1766," *Pennsylvania Magazine of History and Biography*, 20 (No. 2, 1896): 207–08.

[92] [Hunt], *A Letter from a Gentleman in Transilvania*, 10.

[93] Tappert and Doberstein, eds., *Journals of Henry Melchior Muhlenberg*, 2:122–23;
William B. Reed, *Life and Correspondence of Joseph Reed* (2 vols., Philadelphia, 1847), I,
36–37; William Logan to John Smith, Oct. 4, 1764, John Smith Papers (Historical Society of Pennsylvania, Philadelphia); Labaree and others, eds., *Papers of Benjamin Franklin*,
11:390–91. Benjamin Newcomb has studied the election and concluded that the Stamp
Act roiled Pennsylvania politics and consequently brought about a dramatic increase in
electoral participation. See Benjamin H. Newcomb, "Effects of the Stamp Act on Colonial Pennsylvania Politics," *William and Mary Quarterly*, 23 (Apr. 1966): 257–72. The
Stamp Act, however, was hardly mentioned in the outpouring of pamphlets accompanying the election of 1764, which revolved around the move for royal government.

[94] Tappert and Doberstein, eds., *Journals of Henry Melchior Muhlenberg*, 2:123; Reed,
ed., *Life and Correspondence of Joseph Reed*, 1:36–37. For the results of the city elections,
see Isaac Norris, "Journal, 1764" (Rosenbach Foundation, Philadelphia).

Vote" by the proprietary leaders.[95] A bit of post-election doggerel caught the spirit of the contest: "A Pleasant sight tis to Behold / The beggars hal'd from Hedges / The Deaf, the Blind, the Young, the Old: / T' Secure their priveledges / They're bundled up Steps, each sort Goes / A Very Pretty Farce Sir: / Some without Stockings, some no Shoes / Nor Breeches to their A—e Sir." [96]

Although the election represents an extreme case and was affected by factors unique to the politics of proprietary Pennsylvania, it reflected a trend in the political life of other cities as well. Political innovations, involving a new set of organizational and propagandistic techniques, a vocabulary of vituperation, resort to violence, attacks on authority and social position, and the politicization of layers and groups in society that had earlier been beyond the political pale, had transformed the political culture of each of these cities in the half-century before 1764.

The extent of these changes can be measured, though imperfectly, by charting electoral participation.[97] In Boston, where the population remained nearly static at about 15,000 from 1735 to 1764, and the number of eligible voters declined markedly between 1735 and 1750 before beginning a slow upward climb, the number of voters participating in General Court elections showed a significant rise.[98] Although voter turnouts fluctuated widely from year to year, a series of peaks in 1732, 1748, 1757, 1760, and 1763 brought the number of

[95] Labaree and others, eds., *Papers of Benjamin Franklin*, 11:434. The charge that "the riotous Presbyterians" had deprived Franklin of his seat in the assembly by "Illicit Arts and contrivances" was also communicated to the English ministry. Peter Collinson to Lord Hyde, Oct. 11, 1764, Peter Collinson-Bartram Papers (American Philosophical Society, Philadelphia).

[96] *The Election Medley* (Philadelphia, 1764).

[97] Despite the extensive literature on the subject, the extent of the franchise, particularly in the cities, is by no means certain. Robert E. Brown estimates that 56 percent of the adult males were eligible for the vote in Boston but later revises this upward to 75 percent or higher on the basis of literary evidence and inference. Robert E. Brown, *Middle-Class Democracy and the Revolution in Massachusetts, 1691–1780* (Ithaca, 1955), 50, 58, 96. For Philadelphia the estimate is 75 percent. Chilton Williamson, *American Suffrage from Property to Democracy, 1760–1860* (Princeton, 1960), 33–34. For New York, Milton Klein argues that "virtually all the white adult males" *could* obtain the franchise. Klein, "Democracy and Politics in New York," 235. Roger Champagne and Beverly McAnear show that about 65–70 percent of the adult males *were* qualified to vote. Champagne, "Liberty Boys and Mechanics of New York City," 125–29; and Beverly McAnear, "The Place of the Freeman in Old New York," *New York History*, 21 (Oct. 1940): 418–30. The number of eligible voters in the cities probably never exceeded 75 percent of the taxables, and this percentage seems to have been declining in the eighteenth century as urban poverty and propertylessness increased. Williamson indicates that in Philadelphia in 1774 only 1,423 of 3,124 adult males (about 45 percent) were taxed for real or personal property. Williamson, *American Suffrage*, 33. Of course it is possible that many who were ineligible still voted, as was almost certainly the case in Philadelphia.

voters from 650 in 1732 to 1,089 in 1763—a 66 percent increase during a period of population stagnation. It is also significant to note that from 1764 to 1775 the General Court elections in Boston never drew as many voters as in the years 1760 and 1763, or, for that matter, as in 1758.[98] These data throw doubt on traditional interpretations of the "democratization" of politics accompanying the Revolutionary movement, if we mean by that term the involvement of more people in the electoral process or the extension of the franchise.

In the city and county of Philadelphia a similar rise in political participation can be traced. Four years in which knowledgeable observers remarked on vigorous campaigning and heavy voter turnouts were 1728, 1742, 1754, and 1764.[100] Table I indicates the uneven but generally upward drift of political participation as the eighteenth century progressed. Extant voting statistics for the city of Philadelphia, exclusive of the surrounding areas of Philadelphia County, are obtainable for only a few scattered years, but a comparison of 1751 and 1764, both years of extensive political activity, shows a rise in voting participation from 40.9 to 54.5 percent of the taxable inhabitants.[101] In 1765, when the proprietary and anti-proprietary parties waged another fierce struggle around the issues raised in the campaign of 1764, the percentage of taxable inhabitants voting in the county and city of Philadelphia increased to 51.2 and 65.1 percent. Never again in the prerevolutionary decade would involvement in the electoral process be so widespread, not even in the hotly contested special assembly elections for the city of Philadelphia in April 1776.[102] These figures suggest that the barometric pressure of political culture was on the rise

[98] Precise population graphs for Boston cannot be devised, but the stagnant population level and the decrease in the number of taxables after 1735 seems firmly established by the scattered census materials and the references to the number of taxables for a number of years in the Selectmen's Records. See Warden, *Boston*, 127–29; Bridenbaugh, *Cities in the Wilderness*, 303n; Carl Bridenbaugh, *Cities in Revolt: Urban Life in America, 1743–1776* (New York, 1955), 5, 216; and *Boston Town Records*, 14:13, 100, 280.

[99] *Reports of the Record Commissioners of Boston*, vols. 8, 12, 16, 18. Scattered vote counts are available for the pre-1717 period for selectmen elections and town meetings.

[100] Voters in Philadelphia participated in two assembly elections each October, one for the eight representatives for Philadelphia County and one for two "burgesses" from the city. Thus they were doubly represented in the assembly. These elections were usually held on successive days. Voting statistics are from newspapers, private correspondence, and Isaac Norris, "Journals." The number of taxables for the four years has been extrapolated from the known number of taxables for the years 1720, 1734, 1740, 1741, 1760, and 1767.

[101] Isaac Norris, "Journals, 1764." For another set of totals for Philadelphia County, which vary slightly, see Benjamin Franklin Papers, 69:97 (American Philosophical Society, Philadelphia). The 1765 figures are from ibid., 98, and are reprinted in Labaree and others, eds., *Papers of Benjamin Franklin*, 12:290–91n.

[102] See David Hawke, *In the Midst of a Revolution* (Philadelphia, 1961), 13–31.

TABLE I

YEAR	TAXABLES	VOTERS	PERCENT OF TAXABLES VOTING
1728	2,963	971	32.8
1742	5,240	1,793	34.2
1754	6,908	2,173	31.4
1764	8,476	3,874	45.7

during the half-century preceding the Stamp Act crisis and may, in fact, have reached its pinnacle in the early 1760s.[103]

That an increasing percentage of qualified voters was participating in electoral politics not only by casting their votes but also by taking part in street demonstrations, rallies, and caucuses was emblematic of the changing political culture of the cities. Upper-class leaders, contending for political advantage, had mobilized the electorate and introduced new techniques and strategies for obtaining electoral majorities. Most of these leaders had little taste for the effects of this new kind of politics and perhaps none of them wished to bring political life to the kind of clamorous, unrestrained exercise in vitriol and slander that prevailed in Philadelphia in 1764 and 1765. But piecemeal they had contributed to a transformed political culture which by the 1760s they could only precariously control.

The transformation of politics was not restricted to the cities.[104] But it proceeded most rapidly in the urban centers of colonial life because it was in cities that men in power could influence large numbers of people; that printing presses were located and political literature was most widely distributed; that population density made possible the organization of clubs, mass meetings, and vociferous electioneering tactics; that numerous taverns provided natural nerve centers of feverish political activity; that disparities of wealth were growing most rapidly; and that new attitudes and behavioral patterns first found ideological expression. The countryside was far from immune to the new style of politics and a new political culture, but distances and popula-

[103] Voting statistics for New York City, where assembly elections were far less frequent, have been found for only two years in the period before 1765. But when combined with statistics for the elections of 1768 and 1769, it appears that in New York the peak of political participation before the Revolution may also have been reached in the early 1760s. See Klein, "Democracy and Politics in Colonial New York," 237.

[104] For example, see Kenneth A. Lockridge, *A New England Town, The First Hundred Years: Dedham, Massachusetts, 1636–1736* (New York, 1970), 93–164; and Edward M. Cook, Jr., "Social Behavior and Changing Values in Dedham, Massachusetts, 1700 to 1775," *William and Mary Quarterly*, 27 (Oct. 1970): 546–80.

tion dispersion created organizational and communication problems which were far harder to solve than in urban places.

But change occurred everywhere, rendering an older mode of politics obsolete. Internal, local, and intraclass as well as interclass struggles in colonial society had transfigured politics, creating almost by inadvertence a political culture which by 1764 already contained many of the changes in political style and behavior usually associated with the Revolutionary period.[105]

---

[105] For the view that the radicalization process should be associated with the post-1763 period, see Merrill Jensen, "The American People and the American Revolution," *Journal of American History*, 57 (June 1970): 5–35.

RELIGION, THE GREAT AWAKENING, AND SOCIAL CHANGE

V

A Transatlantic
Community of Saints:
The Great Awakening
and the First Evangelical
Network, 1735–1755

SUSAN O'BRIEN

Seen only from North America, as many have tried to do, the Great Awakening of the 1730s and 1740s appears to be a rather fitful and uncoordinated series of religious revivals, waxing in one place while waning in another. Viewed from the center of the empire, argues Susan O'Brien, these events acquire much greater coherence and direction. Jonathan Edwards's Connecticut Valley revivals of the mid-1730s probably aroused more interest in London than in Boston, which was not eager to receive its piety from the hinterland. His account of this extraordinary upheaval was first published in the capital of the empire, not in New England. Boston, in turn, was swept into the revivals only when the message of the new birth recrossed the Atlantic from London in the person of George Whitefield, a preacher of astonishing power who made seven trips to North America before his death in 1770. An ordained priest of the Church of England, Whitefield wore his surplice and carried the Book of Common Prayer with him during his public appearances.

Whitefield was also a Methodist; that is, he was part of an evangelical movement within the Church of England that was beginning to split into a Calvinist wing under his leadership and an Arminian (or anti-Calvinist) branch under John and Charles Wesley. Whitefield's primary impact fell upon dissenters, rather than Anglicans, and more outside England than inside. He and ministers who admired and corresponded with him won many thousands of converts in Scotland, New England, and the Middle Colonies, but never many in the Southern Colonies. The Wesleys made a tremendous impression within England and Ireland, but their followers began to achieve significant success in America only in the 1770s, and at first mostly in the Southern Colonies.

Reprinted by permission from Susan O'Brien, "A Transatlantic Community of Saints: The Great Awakening and the First Evangelical Network, 1735–1755," *American Historical Review*, 91 (1986), 811–832.

O'Brien's essay concentrates on Whitefield's circle of correspondents. She demonstrates the extraordinary ability of these men to incorporate their individual efforts into a transatlantic network of remarkable strength and effectiveness. So powerful was the demand for news of the revivals, for example, that some decidedly nonevangelical people, such as Benjamin Franklin, willingly cooperated in spreading the message. In the early 1740s about half of Franklin's business as a Philadelphia printer came directly from the revivals, and much of that from Whitefield, whom he always treated with great courtesy and respect.

The evangelicals themselves understood their activities in an imperial, not just an American context. As Nathan Hatch's essay in this section points out, Jonathan Edwards may have believed around 1740 that the millennium might actually begin in New England, but by the end of the decade he had become far more hopeful about Scotland than any part of America. He, Whitefield, and such Scots as John Erskine established a transatlantic Concert of Universal Prayer and kept in active touch with one another well into the 1750s, as O'Brien demonstrates.

ON NOVEMBER 8, 1742, SEVERAL HUNDRED MEN AND WOMEN packed into the London Spa Fields Tabernacle to celebrate the latest news of religious revival. The high point of the meeting came when letters from all over the revival world were read out loud, after which the congregation joined in a hymn specially written for the occasion:

> Great things in England, Wales and Scotland wrought,
> And in America to pass are brought,
> Awaken'd souls, warn'd of the wrath to come
> In Numbers flee to Jesus as their Home. . . .
> What is this News, that flies throughout our Land? [1]

This homespun hymn serves as a reminder that the events of the late 1730s and 1740s that historians have analyzed separately and severally as the American Great Awakening, the English Evangelical Revival, and the Scottish Cambuslang Wark, were perceived by many participants as parts of a single God-inspired phenomenon. Given the direction of the historiography during the past twenty years, the reminder is both timely and necessary.

The religious revivals of the period 1735 to 1750 have attracted the attention of an impressive number of historians, but few have made

---

[1] *Weekly History* (London), November 13, 1742, no. 84.

more than passing reference to their broad appeal. Rather, as the historical literature developed, the focus of inquiry narrowed from national and denominational levels of analysis to detailed studies of the regional and local settings. As a result, historians have gained new insights into the nature, causes, and meaning of the revivals, but our understanding of a revival in one country has remained isolated from our knowledge of a revival elsewhere.[2] This point can best be illustrated by reference to the most developed revival historiography—that on the American Great Awakening. Throughout the 1960s and 70s, scholars augmented the existing denominational and regional studies by a number of local studies, each seeking to bring out those characteristics of a particular environment that made it open to the revival impulse.[3] By the late 1970s, the weight of research and interpretation caused American historians to regard the Awakening as a peculiarly American phenomenon, central to the formation of a religious tradition whose hallmarks were millennial fervor, evangelicalism, and periodic schism.[4] Following this line of thought, some scholars described this very tradition as a distinguishing feature of American culture, and such an assessment, as Jon Butler recently pointed out, has become entrenched in American history survey texts.[5] Butler's critique of American "enthusiasm" for the Great Awakening, though contested, may well mark a turning point in our understanding. His stimulating essay argues that the Great Awakening was neither "great nor general," and its significance therefore cannot be as far reaching as historians have believed. Central to his case is the argument that American revival studies have unjustifiably centered on New England. Revivalism, in Butler's view,

---

[2] J. M. Bumsted used the phrase "splendid isolation" to describe the historiography of the Great Awakening. See Bumsted, " 'What must I do to be saved? A Consideration of Recent Writings on the Great Awakening in Colonial America," *Canadian Association for American Studies Bulletin*, 4 (1969): 50.

[3] See, for example, J. M. Bumsted, "Presbyterianism in Eighteenth Century Massachusetts: The Formation of a Church at Easton, 1752," *Journal of Presbyterian History*, 46 (1968): 243–53, and "Revivalism and Separatism in New England: The First Society of Norwich, Connecticut, as a Case Study," *William and Mary Quarterly*, 3d ser., 24 (1967): 588–612; Gerald F. Moran, "Conditions of Religious Conversion in the First Society of Norwich, Connecticut, 1718–1744," *Journal of Social History*, 5 (1972): 331–43; James Walsh, "The Great Awakening in the First Congregational Church of Woodbury, Connecticut," *William and Mary Quarterly*, 3d ser., 28 (1971): 543–62; and w. F. Willingham, "Religious Conversion in the Second Society of Windham, Connecticut, 1723–1743; A Case Study," *Societas*, 6 (1976): 109–19.

[4] For an expression of this position, see, among others, Sydney E. Ahlstrom, *A Religious History of the American People* (London, 1972): 280–94; and Timothy L. Smith, "Congregation, State and Denomination; The Formation of the American Religious Structure," *William and Mary Quarterly*, 3d ser., 25 (1968): 155–76.

[5] Jon Butler, "Enthusiasm Described and Decried: The Great Awakening as Interpretive Fiction," *Journal of American History*, 69 (1982): 305–25.

was both more than the Calvinist revival of New England and less than "the Key to the American Revolution." [6] Another look at the evidence suggests that a more serious recognition of revivals outside America could have provided Butler with a further angle from which to question the "American-ness" of the Awakening. This missed opportunity is characteristic of the historiography.

Given the predisposition to view the Great Awakening as American, the relatively slight interest in the comparative history of revivalism or in the possible connections and influences among revivalists is hardly surprising. For different but equally intelligible reasons, scholars have also viewed the history of the English revival in isolation.[7] In its broadest sense, revivalism in the mid-eighteenth century not only appeared in several places and involved a range of theologies and religious polities, including Anglican, Lutheran, and Pietist, as well as Calvinist, but these groupings also shared connections and influences.[8] Evidence

[6] William G. McLoughlin, " 'Enthusiasm for Liberty: The Great Awakening as the Key to the Revolution," in Jack P. Greene and William G. McLoughlin, eds., *Preachers and Politicians: Two Essays on the Origins of the American Revolution* (Worcester, Mass., 1977), 47–73. See also Alan Heimert, *Religion and the American Mind: From the Great Awakening to the Revolution* (Cambridge, Mass., 1966); Cedric B. Cowing, *The Great Awakening and the American Revolution* (Chicago, 1971); and Harry S. Stout, "Religion, Communications and the Ideological Origins of the American Revolution," *William and Mary Quarterly*, 3d ser., 34 (1977): 519–41.

[7] The religious history of mid-eighteenth-century England has been written almost exclusively by church historians and, because of the success of Wesleyanism, the Methodist perspective on the English revival has tended to swamp all others. Such concentration helps to explain the lack of attention paid to the transatlantic dimension of revivalism in this period, because the exchanges of ideas and literature did not involve Wesley or his followers. For a recognition of the interconnections between Whitefieldians, Wesleyans, and Dissenters in the 1740s, see Richard W. Evans, "The 18th Century Welsh Awakening with Its Relationship to the Contemporary English Evangelical Revival" (Ph.D. dissertation, Edinburgh University, 1955); Geoffrey Nuttall, *Philip Doddridge 1702–1751: His Contribution to English Religion* (London, 1951); John D. Walsh, "Origins of the Evangelical Revival," in Gareth V. Bennett and John D. Walsh, eds., *Essays in Modern English Church History* (London, 1966) and "The Cambridge Methodists," in Peter Brooks, ed., *Christian Spirituality: Essays in Honour of Gordon Rupp* (London, 1975), 251–83; Charles E. Watson, "Whitefield and Congregationalism," *Transactions of the Congregational Historical Society*, 8 (1920–23): 171–80, 273–345; Michael R. Watts, *The Dissenters: From the Reformation to the French Revolution* (Oxford, 1978), chap. 5.

[8] On connections involving pietists, for example, see Milton J. Coalter, "The Radical Pietism of Count Nicholas Zinzendorf as a Conservative Influence on the Awakener, Gilbert Tennent," *Church History*, 49 (1980): 35–46; John B. Frantz, "The Awakening of Religion among the German Settlers in the Middle Colonies," *William and Mary Quarterly*, 3d ser., 33 (1976): 266–88; Gillian L. Gollin, *Moravians in Two Worlds: A Study of Changing Communities* (New York, 1967); James E. Hutton, "The Moravian Contribution to the Evangelical Revival in England 1742–1745," in Thomas F. Tait and James Tout, eds., *Historical Essays* (Manchester, 1907); F. Ernest Stoeffler, *The Rise of Evangelical Pietism*, Studies in the History of Religions, 9 (Leiden, 1965); W. R. Ward, "The Relations of Enlightenment and Religious Revival in Central Europe and in the English Speaking World," in Derek Baker, ed., *Reform and Reformation: England and the Continent*

suggests that Calvinist evangelicals on both sides of the Atlantic were highly conscious of one another's activities. This transatlantic evangelical consciousness grew out of the isolated correspondence of individual ministers. Ministers and lay promoters extended the correspondence into a reliable, nonpersonal system of contacts, which they developed into a number of procedures for spreading the news from individuals to groups of committed laity and beyond to a wider lay audience. Because revival news was of great importance to Calvinist evangelicals, they had a strong motivation to create a relatively durable chain of correspondence. Once in place, the contacts proved useful to the ministers in other ways. Some uses were practical, for example, the circulation of devotional literature, recommendations for suitable reading, the collection of money for missionary work, and the provision of hospitality. On another level, ministers used transatlantic contacts for the discussion of theological questions, the nature of piety, and the practice of revivalism. It is not too much to say that through the exchange of ideas and materials Calvinist revivalists of the mid-eighteenth century built a "community of saints" that cut across physical barriers and, on occasion, theological divisions.

The significance of this community lies not in its novelty—there was nothing new about associations of ministers, or religious communication systems, even transatlantic ones—but rather in its effect on our understanding of eighteenth and nineteenth-century revivalism.[9] Although the historical literature is not devoid of references to "influence" and "cross-fertilization" between Britain, Northwest Europe, and the American colonies, recognition of these connections usually appeared in only two forms, neither of which has had much impact on interpretation.[10] In one, the focus of attention is George Whitefield,

---

c.1500–c.1750 (Oxford, 1979); and "Power and Piety: the Origins of Religious Revival in the Early Eighteenth Century," *Bulletin of the John Rylands University Library of Manchester,* 63 (1980): 231–52.

[9] There was a Puritan transatlantic network in existence between 1620 and 1730. As Cotton Mather wrote, "When the distance of the huge Atlantic separates Brethren from one another, one Method unto which we must resort for Maintaining the communion of saints is the epistolary." Carl Bridenbaugh, *Mitre and Sceptre: Transatlantic Faiths, Ideas, Personalities, and Politics, 1689–1775* (New York, 1962), 86. Also see Darrett B. Rutman, *American Puritanism: Faith and Practice* (New York, 1970), 16–21; and George Selement, *Keepers of the Vineyard: The Puritan Ministry and Collective Culture in Colonial New England* (Lanham, Md., 1984), 70. The Quakers developed their own transatlantic community in the early eighteenth century. See Frederick B. Tolles, "The Atlantic Community of the Early Friends," *Journal of the Friends Historical Society,* Supplement no. 24 (1952); and *Quakers and the Atlantic Culture* (New York, 1960).

[10] For a recognition of the transatlantic dimension, see John W. Raimo, "Spiritual Harvest: The Anglo-American Revival in Boston, Mass. and Bristol, England, 1735–1742" (Ph.D. dissertation, University of Wisconsin, 1974); and Watts, *Dissenters,* 394–406. Neither author, however, includes the Scottish revivalists, who were particularly active in the transatlantic network. In his discussion of enlightenment and religious

whose travels from England to Scotland and America are frequently mentioned. Scholars have traced revival connections between America and Britain and, in the process, reduced them to the activities of this wholly exceptional preacher.[11] The other type of recognition is of a different order. Historians working within a committed evangelical tradition have written of the revival much as the Spa Fields congregation saw it—as a widespread "stirring of dry bones," a movement of the Holy Spirit. Starting in 1754 with John Gillies' two-volume collection, Calvinist evangelical commentators have interpreted the eighteenth-century revival as broad and sweeping, careless of national and church boundaries, and evangelical in character.[12] Because of their commitment to a God-inspired explanation, historians in the evangelical tradition have not carefully examined the human causes and agencies of connection and influence and consequently have had little influence on secular historians. But the perception of the revival as international and evangelical is instructive, and evidence adduced by evangelical writers establishes that revivalists of the 1740s discussed the devices and methods for promoting and sustaining their work with colleagues all over the world. Indeed, their exchanges created an evangelical communications network long before the more widely recognized networks of the nineteenth century.

The major contrast that historians have drawn between the spontaneity of the mid-eighteenth-century revivals and the professionalism

---

revival, Ward did refer to "an international Calvinist network at the centre of which were ministers of the Church of Scotland," but it was not his concern to elaborate on the point. Ward, "Relations of Enlightenment and Religious Revival," 292.

[11] This is a position adopted, for example, by one of Whitefield's more recent biographers. Arnold Dallimore states that "Whitefield's ministry was the one human factor which bound this work together in the lands it reached." See Dallimore, *George Whitefield: The Life and Times of the Great Evangelist of the 18th Century Revival*, 2 vols. (London, 1970), 1: 14.

[12] John Gillies, *Historical Collections relating to remarkable periods of the success of the Gospel, and eminent Instruments employed in promoting it*, 2 vols. (Glasgow, 1754). The two volumes were revised and enlarged in 1845 by Horatius Bonar and a facsimile of this edition has been published (Fairfield, Pa., 1981). In addition to the *Historical Collections*, Gillies edited an *Appendix to the Historical Collections . . .* (Glasgow, 1761) and *A Supplement to the Historical Collections . . .* (Glasgow, 1796). Later Scottish evangelical historians writing in this tradition include John W. Couper, *Scottish Revivals* (Dundee, 1918); Duncan MacFarlan, *The Revivals of the Eighteenth Century, particularly at Cambuslang* (Edinburgh, 1847); and John MacInnes, *The Evangelical Movements in the Highlands of Scotland, 1688–1800* (Aberdeen, 1951). An important American text in the same tradition is Joseph Tracy, *The Great Awakening: A History of the Revival in the Time of Edwards and Whitefield* (Boston, 1842). More recently, but in the same tradition, Archibald Fawcett recognized the ties between Scotland and America. Even so, he concluded, "it is not easy to trace any definite connection between these movements and the little community at Cambuslang, and there is something infectious about such happenings." Fawcett, *The Cambuslang Revival: The Scottish Evangelical Revival of the Eighteenth Century* (London, 1971), 53.

of those in the nineteenth century is misleading.[13] Instead, the eighteenth-century revivals should take their place on a continuum of Protestant evangelical development, with its starting point in the seventeenth century. The real significance of the mid-eighteenth-century revivals was not their wondrous spontaneity or their primary role in the formation of national consciousness, but rather their combining of traditional Puritan practices with fresh evangelical techniques and attitudes. It was a combination that played a major part, and perhaps the most creative part, in the systematic development of evangelicalism.

IN 1736, NEWS OF THE RECENT REVIVALS IN Hampshire County, Massachusetts, crossed over to England in the letters of Boston minister Benjamin Colman to London Dissenting ministers John Guyse and Isaac Watts. These same men encouraged Jonathan Edwards to write an account of the awakening for publication. This was to become Edwards's famous *Narrative*, first published in London.[14] The correspondence between Colman, Watts, and Guyse that made this possible exemplified the Old Dissenting network—a network with its roots in the seventeenth-century Puritan "community of saints." By the mid-eighteenth century, Dissenters had not only developed informal contacts across the Atlantic, but had also established a formal machinery, the Dissenting Deputies, to protect their civil and legal welfare.[15] It would be misleading, therefore, to underestimate the extent of communication already in existence before the evangelical revival. Colman and Watts, for example, corresponded and exchanged books and pamphlets from the 1720s until a few months before Colman's death in 1747. Watts carried on an extensive correspondence with other New England religious leaders, including Samuel Mather, Thomas Prince, Sr., and Elisha Williams. Through his generous gifts of books to Harvard, Watts demonstrated his interest in and concern for the Dissenting

---

[13] For a classic expression of this distinction, see Calvin Colton, *The History and Character of American Revivals of Religion* (London, 1832). Most evangelical histories echo his view of eighteenth-century revivals. See also William G. McLoughlin, *Modern Revivalism* (New York, 1959), 11: "The difference between Edwards and Finney is essentially between the medieval and the modern tenure." This statement has been taken up more recently by John Kent in his discussion of the American revivalist tradition. See Kent, *Holding the Fort: Studies in Victorian Revivalism* (London, 1978), 24 and chap. 1.

[14] Jonathan Edwards, *A Faithful Narrative of the Surprising Work of God in the Conversion of Many Hundred Souls in Northampton, and the Neighbouring Towns and Villages of New Hampshire in New England in a letter to the Revd. Dr. Benjamin Colman of Boston. With a large preface by Dr. Watts and Dr. Guyse* (London, 1737). The exchange of correspondence involved in this first printing of the *Narrative* has been fully traced. See Clarence C. Goen, *The Great Awakening*, vol. 4 of *The Works of Jonathan Edwards*, John E. Smith, gen. ed. (New Haven and London, 1972), 32–46.

[15] Maurice W. Armstrong, "Dissenting Deputies and the American Colonies," *Church History*, 29 (1960): 298–320; Carl Bridenbaugh, *Mitre and Sceptre*, 44; and Bernard L. Manning, *The Protestant Dissenting Deputies* (Cambridge, 1952).

community abroad.[16] When the New England ministers wanted an English sponsor for Edwards's revival narrative, Watts was the obvious choice. But the colonial ministers were mistaken if they believed that the support they received from Watts, or from another interested correspondent, Philip Doddridge of Northampton (England), was similar to the response they could expect from English Dissenters.[17] Watts and Doddridge were attempting to occupy a middle ground between antinomianism and Arminianism and, as a result, remained relatively isolated among English Dissenters. Although colonial promoters of the revival narrative turned naturally to these two men, and, although both took part in the revival exchanges, they were not representative of English Dissent and of its response to the aims and style of revivalist religion.

For political, organizational, and theological reasons, the official channels of Dissent were not open to the revival of religion when it happened. Many Dissenters distrusted the tenets that became associated with revivalism: the emotionalism and even dogmatism of some of the converted, the new relationship proposed between clergy and laity, and the notion that an inspired preacher might be more efficacious than a trained minister would be. News of the New England conversions threatened to bring confrontation within both Nonconformism and Presbyterianism. The majority of English Nonconformist ministers, along with the spokesmen of the Assembly of the Church of Scotland, and of the Associate Presbytery, ultimately found they could not support the evangelicals. As a result, they lost their primacy in the transmission of revival news to a new grouping. The focus shifted from them to the Calvinist Methodists in England, to an active group of revivalists in the Church of Scotland, and to their kindred spirits in New England and the Middle Colonies. Because Anglican evangelicals, not Nonconformists, led the English revival, and because groups in Scotland, Wales, Holland, and America shared in the revival, a new religious community based on Calvinist evangelicalism came into existence.

This evangelical community was established through a network of correspondence that had George Whitefield at its center. Between 1739 and his death in 1770, in addition to his extensive preaching

---

[16] Massachusetts Historical Society (hereafter, MHS), Benjamin Colman Papers; "Letters of Dr. Watts," *Proceedings of the Massachusetts Historical Society*, 2d ser., 9 (Boston, 1895), 331–410; Thomas Milner, *The Life, Times and Correspondence of Rev. Isaac Watts, D.D.* (London, 1834); and Anne S. Pratt, *Isaac Watts and his Gifts of Books to Yale College* (New Haven, 1938).

[17] Nuttall, *Philip Doddridge*. Dr. Williams's Library, London, has the Doddridge MSS collection, and a calendar of his letters has been prepared. See Geoffrey F. Nuttall, *Calendar of the Correspondence of Philip Doddridge D.D.* (London, 1979), and John D. Humphreys, *The Correspondence and Diary of Philip Doddridge*, 5 vols. (London, 1829–31).

tours of England and Wales, Whitefield made seven journeys to America and fourteen to Scotland. His willingness to travel was only the most obvious expression of his eagerness to see the revival world as a single entity and to encourage others to do the same. His correspondence was as continuous and wide-ranging as his travels, and although we have no accurate figure of the number of people Whitefield wrote to, some impressions of the scale of his correspondence can be gained from his published letters and journals. He wrote regularly to all the main revival figures in Britain and America and to hundreds of other ministers and lay people. Gillies published nearly 1,500 of his letters in the early 1770s, and the evangelical magazines of the 1740s included many items from his correspondence. One unpublished collection contains letters from over fifty different correspondents.[18] When Whitefield sent letters from the colonies to London for distribution, he did so by the trunkload. He received so many letters himself that he was glad to accept the secretarial help of lay evangelicals, such as stockbroker William Seward and teacher John Syms, although the replies were nearly always Whitefield's own.[19] American correspondents received instructions through the *Pennsylvania Gazette* "to direct their letters [for Whitefield] to be left with Mr. James Hutton, Bookseller without Temple, London." [20] Many who wrote were ordinary men and women who sought spiritual advice from Whitefield, thanked him for preaching, or gave him local revival news. Their letters reflect their intense personal experiences and the importance of Whitefield as a focal point in the revival world. His centrality explains the exclusive emphasis that historians have placed on him, but Whitefield did not work alone, and the international dimension of the revival would not have had the same significance had it relied solely on the activities of one individual.

[18] *George Whitefield's Journals* (London, 1960); John Gillies, ed., *Works of George Whitefield*, 6 vols. (London, 1771–72), vols. 1 and 2. The unpublished collection cited here is Library of Congress MY–1–314, "Original Letters from various Persons in Great Britain and America to the Rev. George Whitefield from the Year 1738 to 1769. Collected by Thomas Raffles, Liverpool."

[19] William Seward (1711–40) described himself as a "Gentleman, Companion in Travel to the Reverend Mr. Whitefield." See Dallimore, *George Whitefield*, 1: 252. He had been brought up on the estate of a country squire near Bristol, where his father was a private secretary and had gone into stockbroking. Until his death, Seward was Whitefield's financial backer. See *Journal of the Calvinistic Methodist Historical Society*, 25 (1940), and 58 (1973). John Syms worked at the London Tabernacle where, at one time and another, he taught in the boys' school, dispatched letters, and kept the accounts for Whitefield's books. See Edwin Welch, ed., *Two Calvinistic Methodist Chapels 1743–1811: The London Tabernacle and Spa Fields Chapel* (London, 1975), 1: 5 7, 12; and Gomer M. Roberts, *Selected Trevecka Letters 1742–1747*, Trevecka Records Series no. 1 (Caernarvon, 1956), 215.

[20] *Pennsylvania Gazette*, December 4, 1740.

Within just seven years of the Northampton revival, an international epistolary circuit had developed. Although the emergence of the circuit owed a great deal to the common focus evangelicals had in Whitefield, it owed just as much to the meaning that many participants invested in the revival, and particularly in its widespread occurrence. Jonathan Edwards reflected on this meaning in a letter to James Robe of Edinburgh: "The Church of God, in all Parts of the World, is but one; the distant members are closely united in one Glorious Head. This Union is very much her Beauty; [as is] the mutual and friendly Correspondence of the various members in distant parts of the world." [21] Others perceived the conjunction of the Northampton revival with the conversions of Howell Harris, George Whitefield, and the Wesleys, as heralding a special work of God, perhaps even the beginning of the millennium. "The Lord seems to have some great Event upon the Wheel just now," wrote Hugh Kennedy of the Scottish Church in Rotterdam, "and I would fain hope, the Glory of the Latter days is not far off. The present convulsions and reelings among the nations, as well as the stirring of Dry Bones in Scotland, America and other places, confirms me more and more in this opinion." [22] Spurred on by this sense of the unique times in which they were living, ministers began to correspond with people they did not plan to visit. Initially, the desire to acknowledge and share a common experience was sufficient to prompt a letter between strangers. Ministers saw themselves as co-workers and "friends in God." They found one another's names in revival publications, Whitefield's published journals, the religious press, or through a friend: "It was a most pleasing surprise to me to receive your kind letter from New York," Colman wrote to Whitefield, "and the valuable Present of Journals, Sermons and Letters which accompanied it. I think myself under happy Direction of Providence in my writing to Mr. Pemberton since it has brought me into correspondence with you." [23] It was common to solicit a correspondence by referring to a mutual friend or a published work by the recipient. For example, Thomas Gillespie of Carnock in Scotland recommended himself to Edwards by praising Edwards's works: "The two

[21] James Robe, ed., *Christian Monthly History* (Edinburgh, 1745), vol. 2, no. 8, p. 235.

[22] William McCulloch, ed., *Glasgow Weekly History* (Glasgow, 1742), no. 43, p. 1. For another contemporary millennial view, see John Erskine, *The Signs of the Times Consider'd, or the high Probability that the present Appearances in New England, and the West of Scotland are a prelude of the Glorious Things promised to the Church in the Latter Ages* (Edinburgh, 1742).

[23] Colman to Whitefield, 1742, MHS, Benjamin Colman Papers. This letter has been dated 1742, but it is more likely to have been 1739 since it was printed in 1739 with two other of Whitefield's letters. George Whitefield, *Letter from New Brunswick and Letter in Answer to the Presbytery of Newcastle* (Philadelphia, 1739). Whitefield corresponded with Colman before 1742. See *Whitefield's Journals*, 457. He refers to Ebenezer Pemberton, at the time pastor of Wall Street Presbyterian Church, New York City.

performances you published on the subject of the late glorious work in New England, well adapted to that in Scotland, gave me great satisfaction. . . . I have many a time, for some years, designed to claim humbly the privilege of correspondence with you. . . . My friend and countryman Robert Abercrombie will inform you about me, if you have occasion to see him or hear from him." [24] In the case of John Hamilton of the Barony Parish in Glasgow, contact was made through a traveler and mutual friend: "This letter, I trust shall be deliver'd to you," he wrote to Thomas Prince, Sr., "by our Brother Mr. George Brown, Minister of St. James Island in South Carolina . . . , who is to go by way of Boston; which gives me the opportunity of sending my compliments to you and of introducing myself into your Acquaintance and favour." [25] Even printers were drawn into the epistolary circuit, for example, John Lewis of London, who worked for the revivalists, and whose print shop was often a useful clearing house for correspondence and revival literature.[26] Lewis felt honored to be recognized by Thomas Prince: "Who could ever imagine that such a poor insignificant creature as little I should ever have been thought of so many thousands of miles off. . . . I received your kind letter and . . . I shall be very glad to have a correspondence with you." [27]

These individual initiatives created a letter-writing network that had a core of ten leading ministers—Edwards, Colman, and Thomas Prince, Sr., of New England; James Robe, William McCulloch, John M'Laurin, and John Erskine of Scotland; and English ministers Watts, Whitefield, and Doddridge.[28] Their interlocking and overlapping connections made them a close-knit group. Whitefield was in contact with every member of this group, as was Edwards, while the rest corresponded with at least seven others. Colman, Watts, Doddridge, and Prince were simply continuing and extending their existing practice of communicating with like-minded ministers abroad. Prince, for example, was too elderly and infirm to take an active part in preaching the

[24] Gillespie to Edwards, November 24, 1747, in Sereno E. Dwight, *Life of President Edwards* (New York, 1830), 244. This is volume 1 of Dwight's ten-volume edition of Edwards's *Works*.

[25] Hamilton to Prince, Sr., March 3, 1739, MHS, Miscellaneous MSS Collection.

[26] John Lewis, who was originally from Monmouthshire, was a member of the London Tabernacle and the official printer to the Calvinist Methodists. See *Journal of Calvinist Methodist Historical Society*, 4 (1919): 84–92 and 5 (1920): 6–11.

[27] Lewis to Prince, Sr., August 20, 1743, MHS, Davis Papers. Dutton was an evangelical Baptist minister in Huntingdonshire, England, and the husband of writer and evangelical, Anne Dutton. See Stephen J. Stein, "A Note on Anne Dutton, Eighteenth Century Evangelical," *Church History*, 44 (1975): 485–91.

[28] The major manuscript, biographical, and periodical sources for this analysis are cited elsewhere in these notes. For a full discussion and citation, see Susan Durden, "Transatlantic Communications and Influence during the Great Awakening: A Comparative Study of British and American Revivalism, 1730–1760" (Ph.D. dissertation, Hull University, 1978).

American revival, but he was able to promote it and lend it his authority through his correspondence. In contrast to these "old hands," none of the Scottish ministers, with the exception of John M'Laurin, had initiated long-distance communications before the 1740s, but they soon became regular and conscientious correspondents. John Erskine, for example, visited Cambuslang as an undergraduate, and after talking to revival ministers, he actively pursued contacts in England, Scotland, and America. He was a young man of independent means who did not hesitate to use his wealth to supply books free of charge and to pay postage if he thought doing so would aid the cause. Later, Erskine became minister of Old Greyfriars Church in Edinburgh and a leader of the evangelical party in the Church of Scotland.[29] The contacts between the Scottish revivalists and their American counterparts are the most impressive set of bilateral relations in the revival, since they did not rely on any single figure and involved some relatively obscure individuals.[30]

Just beyond this inner core was another group of promoters who, though less closely connected, nonetheless had a broad range of revival correspondents. These ministers, lay evangelists, financial backers, and printers were all in touch with Whitefield and at least one other leading revival minister, with several of their own local revival ministers, and sometimes with one another. Included in their number were London printers John Lewis and Samuel Mason, Boston printer Daniel Henchman, and lay promoters such as Thomas Noble of New York, Samuel Hazard of Philadelphia, and Ann Dutton of Huntingdonshire, England.[31] The only revivalist who does not fit easily into either the inner core or this second grouping is the Welsh preacher Howell Harris. He wrote prolifically to his associates in England and Wales but as far as is known had no American correspondents.[32] This lack of Amer-

---

[29] Erskine to Hall, July 15, 1743, MHS, Erskine Papers, 28–37; and Erskine to Cooper, January 8, 1743, MHS, Erskine Papers, 8–14.

[30] There is an extensive literature on the economic, cultural, and religious links between Scotland and America. See, for example, John Clive and Bernard Bailyn, "England's Cultural Provinces: Scotland and America," *William and Mary Quarterly,* 3d ser., 11 (1954): 200–13; Andrew Hook, *Scotland and America; A Study of Cultural Relations 1750–1835* (Glasgow, 1975); and *Scottish Historical Review,* 63 (1984). The latter volume is entirely devoted to essays on Scottish-American connections.

[31] Daniel Henchman's Ledgers and Wastbook are part of the Hancock Collection, Harvard Business School, Boston. Thomas Noble was a merchant, one-time High Constable of New York, and a Moravian sympathizer who spent over £100 on revival texts from Henchman. He also commissioned Benjamin Franklin to print revival sermons and Whitefield's journals. See George S. Eddy, *Account Books Kept by Benjamin Franklin, Ledger 'D'* (New York, 1929): Samuel Hazard had many business and religious contacts in Britain and the colonies and acted as a clearinghouse for transatlantic correspondence and packages. See Historical Society of Pennsylvania, Hazard Collection.

[32] The Trevecka Collection, University Library of Wales, Aberystwyth, includes about 3,000 of Harris's letters. See Roberts, *Trevecka Letters* and Tom Benyon, ed., *How-*

ican contacts is surprising since Harris was more concerned than others were with maintaining the "catholic" or international spirit of the revival and, as one-time organizer at the London Tabernacle, was well placed to take part in a transatlantic network. Perhaps he failed to cultivate foreign correspondents because he felt his status as a mere "exhorter" was too lowly to warrant international attention. Even though he did not participate personally in the transatlantic communication network, his name was known abroad.[33]

THE NEW COMMUNITY CREATED BY INTERNATIONAL CORRESPONDENCE was, in part, a continuation of the seventeenth-century Puritan letter-writing community, but its spirit of evangelism marked a point of departure. Evidence suggests that revival correspondence was not only of personal significance to those involved but that it also served evangelical functions. Although letters between neighboring ministers were often of a practical nature—making arrangements for meetings and the exchange of pulpits, for example—those between distant and especially between international correspondents could be a means to convert the unconverted. In addition, because ministers discussed revival issues in their letters, their correspondence also helped to shape their attitudes to evangelism. These letters are a record of both the international workings of the revival and the issues that were of interest and concern to its leaders.

One of the primary and most straightforward purposes of letter writing was to describe the revival in one's own locality, and many of the revival letters were narrative and purely descriptive, particularly during the two years from 1740 to 1742 before the revival began to encounter opposition and internal disagreements. The same was true for correspondence within a region, but there was a heightened sense of excitement in writing to someone hundreds of miles away, and ministers were aware that news from afar could encourage the revival spirit in their own congregations: "In yours of Jan. 25 you acquainted me that what I wrote to Archibald Webster concerning the success of the Gospel in our American World, was most agreeable to you; and that it, with what was written by others, had refreshed many souls in my native country, Scotland, and filled their mouths with Praises."[34] Letters could be full of names of unknown ministers and places and details about individual converts, all written up in exuberant style: "I am now to inform you, that since my Last our exalted Saviour has been riding forth in his magnificence and Glory . . . , both Whites and Blacks,

---

ell Harris, Reformer and Soldier, 1714–1733, Trevecka Records Series, no. 2 (Caernarvon, 1958).

[33] Tom Benyon, ed., *Howell Harris's Visits to London* (Aberystwyth, 1960), 43.

[34] Abercrombie (New England) to Leslie (Scotland), May 25, 1742, *Glasgow Weekly History*, no. 34, pp. 1–4.

both Old and Young, both Prophane and Moral, awakened and made alive to God . . . at Taunton, Bridgewater, Abington, York, Ipswich, Rowley, Cape Ann." [35] Despite the distance between correspondents and their probable ignorance of the local geography, the letters contained catalogues of new revival areas, and ministers often requested such detail from one another. They attached great importance to explicitness, both because it helped to establish the authenticity of the revival and, they believed, "it had more influence because it came from a Foreigner." [36] Through narrative detail, correspondents were able to encourage one another and develop a sense of unity in a known and shared world.

As part of their descriptions, ministers included information about their own conduct and leadership. The exchange of information can be seen as an early development of revival techniques, because the communication of various methods and approaches and discussion of their effects encouraged a process of convergence within evangelicalism. Presbyterian minister John Moorhead of Boston was one of the many who gave information about the methods he used in his parish. He encouraged parishioners to examine their own thoughts and feelings, listen to itinerant preachers, organize fasts, and heed the reading by heads of families of the "most pungent Discourses they could find that treated on the Nature of Conversion and the New Birth." Although he emphasized the educative role of societies for prayer and instruction, he was concerned that these should be properly organized by the minister. [37]

Ministers who exchanged views in this way did not always find it easy to decide about the limits of their own role or the efficacy of human effort in bringing about conversion, but in spite of their qualms, they were influenced by the apparent success of this or that particular practice. They occasionally discussed the controversial issue of revivalistic "means to grace." "We ought not only to praise God for everything that appears favourable to the interests of religion, and to pray earnestly for a general revival, but also use means that are proper in order to it," Edwards wrote to Erskine. The practice under scrutiny here was weekly sacraments, which Edwards considered "a proper means," and which Erskine said he had been striving to establish in the face of "bigotry and prejudice." [38] Other revival means discussed regularly by correspondents included the use of prayer societies, the prac-

---

[35] Prince, Sr., to Whitefield, December 6, 1741, *Glasgow Weekly History*, no. 15, pp. 1–3.

[36] *Christian Monthly History*, vol. 1, no. 4, p. 5.

[37] Moorhead to a Gent. in N. Britain, June 14, 1743, *Christian Monthly History*, vol. 1, no. 2, pp. 11–23.

[38] Edwards to Erskine, November 15, 1750 and July 5, 1750; Dwight, *President Edwards*, 1: 417 and 407–09.

tice of itinerant preaching, and coordinated prayer days—all of which were recognized as potentially threatening to a minister's control. Besides offering practical advice, these epistolary exchanges were of more general significance, since they influenced the writing of revival tracts, devotional materials, and theological treatises of the revival. The writers formulated their opinions within a transatlantic context and those opinions in turn established a number of views and patterns of response within that same transatlantic world. A key example of this process was the conversion experience.

Although conversion was a personal experience, a matter between God and the individual, it was also of crucial interest to ministers. Perhaps because of the high regard in which New England was held by British revivalists, and certainly because of Edwards's writings on conversion, British ministers discussed features of the conversion experience with their American correspondents. In seeking to resurrect the centrality of individual conversion, revivalists drew on Puritan traditions, reprinting the works of seventeenth-century divines and recommending these to "seekers." [39] But the existence of a well-worked tradition did not obviate their own need to discuss contemporary conversions and their own particular experiences as the human promoters and arbiters of salvation and grace. Indeed, letters dealing with possible ways to distinguish a valid from a non-valid experience might be 5,000 words long and supported by specific instances and cases for discussion.[40] Ministers showed a desire to define and categorize the workings of grace, and, as their seventeenth-century counterparts had done, they provided models of the conversion experience that influenced the laity. A rare glimpse of this influence at work is afforded by Sarah Gill's diary entry for April 1742: "The next sabbath I heard dear Mr. Edwards," she wrote, "I trust I had the Presence of Christ with me, and *by the marks laid down* I concluded I had been drawn to Christ." [41] Ministers recommended to one another the practice of interviewing parishioners and questioning them closely on their spiritual life. John Moorhead explained how he made "each Person successively relate how far they had been acquainted with a work of conviction and Conversion upon their Souls." [42] This was also the practice at Cam-

---

[39] For a discussion of the literature of the revival, including both the reprinting of Puritan literature and the publication of new revival materials, see Susan Durden, "Transatlantic Communications," chap. 5.

[40] See, for example, Erskine to Prince, Sr., July 17, 1742, MHS, Erskine Papers.

[41] Boston Public Library, MS Religious Journal of Sarah Gill. The emphasis is mine. For another instance of ministerial influence, see Michael J. Crawford, ed., "The Spiritual Travels of Nathan Cole," *William and Mary Quarterly*, 3d ser., 33 (1976): 98. For a discussion of Edwards's influence on the morphology of conversion, see Goen, *Great Awakening*, 25–32.

[42] *Christian Monthly History*, vol. 1, no. 4, p. 14.

buslang, as the 110 conversion accounts taken down by McCulloch show.[43] The many marginal notes and comments made by these ministers throughout the Cambuslang conversion accounts being prepared for publication reflected their concern to sort out proper from improper experiences. James Robe of Kilsyth was happy to share his own method with others: "I have kept a book wherein from Day to Day, I wrote down whatever was most material in the Exercise of the Distrest. This may appear an unsupportable Labour at first view, especially where the Number of the Distrest is so many. Yet I found it to be very easy. . . . An Index I kept, brought me soon to the part of the Book, where the Person's case was recorded. . . . I saw what Progress their Convictions had made, and knew where I was to begin with them." Robe published many of these cases in his Kilsyth *Narrative*, which was reprinted in America and Holland and extracted in the Boston *Christian History*, where the editor recommended Robe's methods.[44]

Detecting a "defective" conversion was probably one of the most difficult and serious problems faced by a revival minister, but the heightened emotional tension so often inherent in a revival meeting could cause other problems. Were trances and dreams, for example, legitimized by Scripture? In New England, *Christian History* put across the view that "outcries" and excesses of expression were only to be expected but should not be taken as signifying conversion without other indicators. Aware that none of these experiences were new, the editor generally attempted to play down the emotionalism in the hope that people would thereby be discouraged from "indulging" themselves. As J. William T. Youngs has argued, many of these activities worried the very ministers who had encouraged the revival as a way to reunite and spiritualize the community, and who subsequently came to recognize that the same forces could impinge on their authority.[45] Troubled by these conflicting concerns, ministers could at least turn to a sympathetic community to voice their fears and obtain advice.

[43] New College Library, Edinburgh, MS. W. 13. b. 212, "Examination of Persons under Scriptural Concern at Cambuslang during the Revival in 1741–42 by the Revd. William MacCulloch, Minister at Cambulslang, with Marginal Notes by Dr. Webster and Other Ministers." The two volumes are paginated separately and individuals identified by a two-letter system. References here are to pages.

[44] James Robe, *A Faithful Narrative of the Extraordinary Work of One Spirit of God at Kilsyth and other Congregations in the Neighbourhood* (Glasgow, 1742), reprinted in Gillies, *Historicial Collections* (1754; reprint edn., 1981), 450. The *Narrative* was reprinted in *Christian History* (Boston, 1743), nos. 1–7 and went into three editions in Holland.

[45] J. William T. Youngs, Jr., *God's Messengers: Religious Leadership in Colonial New England 1700–1750* (Baltimore, 1976), 109–19. Robe and Edwards agreed that the people needed to be taught that "extraordinary joys and raptures" did not necessarily indicate a work of grace. Dwight, *President Edwards*, 1: 200–01.

BECAUSE PRIVATE CORRESPONDENCE INTENSIFIED their emotional identification with one another and reinforced a set of beliefs and practices, revival leaders soon realized that its usefulness could be multiplied if the news and information related in the letters were shared more widely. One simple and obvious method was to pass a letter around among friends. Another was to make a copy and pass the letter on, or to read it aloud to a congregation or prayer group. But the most sophisticated technique evolved by evangelicals was to found newspapers and magazines whose main content was revival letters. The first and most natural step was to use the ready-made networks of friends and colleagues among whom letters could be circulated. New England ministers, for example, circulated letters at their regular association meetings, which were neighborhood affairs, while others added new forms to achieve the same effect. Scottish ministers began a special "correspondent meeting," which reflected their desire to be more organized in their evangelism.[46] Originally, few of the letters read aloud at these meetings would have been written for such a purpose, but once ministers established the practice of public readings, it affected the style of the letters, making many of them more formal and impersonal. In England and Wales, where distances hindered meetings of like-minded ministers, workers at the London Tabernacle undertook a letter-transcribing service for revivalists outside London. Howell Harris provided this service for a time, as did John Syms, although they frequently complained that they lacked the work force to do the job thoroughly.[47] Instances of letter copying were to be found in Scotland and New England, too, but the practice was never as centralized or as systematic as it was in England and was likely to happen only if a letter were of exceptional interest. Daniel Wadsworth of Hartford, Connecticut, for example, recorded in his diary that he "saw a copy of a letter from Rowlands to Noble giving wonders wrought by his preaching" in Wales, and the same letter appears in the copybook of Ebenezer Parkman of Westborough, Massachusetts.[48] Even areas re-

[46] *Christian Monthly History* (Edinburgh), vol. 2, no. 8, p. 237. The English and Welsh Calvinist Methodists were organized through a monthly meeting of the whole society and weekly conferences of ministers and exhorters. In Cornwall, Anglican ministers held their own associations. See George C. B. Davies, *Early Cornish Evangelicals, 1735–1760: A Study of Walker of Truro and Others* (London, 1951). The development of ministers' associations in New England, and their role in the professionalization of the clergy has been well documented. See David D. hall, *Faithful Shepherd: A History of the New England Ministry in the Seventeenth Century* (Chapel Hill, N.C., 1972); Selement, *Keepers of the Vineyard*; and Youngs, *God's Messengers*.

[47] Roberts, *Selected Trevecka Letters*, 152.

[48] *Diary of Rev. Daniel Wadsworth* (Hartford, Conn., 1894), 55. Wadsworth had correspondence with Philip Doddridge, Benjamin Colman, and Jonathan Edwards and he subscribed to *Christian History* (Boston). MHS, Parkman MS, Copybook.

mote from the centers of communication could be brought in touch through the extension of local or internal networks. John Bonar of Torpichen wrote to McCulloch that he had heard of the revival in Cambuslang and other places in Britain and America and asked for "a particular account about this matter," which he received almost by return mail.[49] Henry Davidson of isolated Galashiels in Scotland cultivated fruitful exchanges with the Reverend Thomas Davidson of Braintree, Essex, England, and with the merchant William Hogg of Edinburgh, who in turn had contacts with the London Tabernacle and received American letters arriving in London and Edinburgh.[50] Similarly, Ebenezer Parkman conducted correspondence with Gilbert Tennant, Jonathan Edwards, and William Cooper, who were other colonials also involved in the transatlantic network, and with local ministers Andrew Eliot, John Webb, and Samuel Bliss.[51]

After circulating correspondence at their meetings and in private exchanges, ministers began to read letters, or at least some of the more stirring parts of them, to their congregations, in the hope that this experience would encourage people and communicate the idea of a special Providence from God. William McCulloch "frequently read to his hearers missives, attestations and journals which he had received from correspondents, giving an account of conversions which had taken place in different parts of the world, especially in New England."[52] One of his congregation, nineteen-year-old Elizabeth Jackson, included in her conversion account specific reference to the impact that McCulloch's readings had made on her: "Hearing a minister on a fast day, after a sermon, read some papers relating to the success of the Gospel abroad, I was greatly affected at the thought that so many were getting good, and I was getting none." Another, Margaret Richardson, "was very glad to hear that there was such a work of conversion in those distant places [New England] and was very busy from time to time contriving methods how [she] might get there."[53] By the late 1740s, Jonathan Edwards was able to reflect with some satisfaction on his own part in spreading the news. Implicit in his recollection is a sense of the processes and stages by which information moved outward: first, "by taking great pains to communicate to others" and, then, equal pains "to extract from all letters" received. He went on to

---

[49] *Edinburgh Christian Instructor*, September 1839, pp. 362–63, and 341n. "Among the Correspondents of Dr. Gillies, Mr. McCulloch and Rev. M'Laurin, we meet the names of Rev. James M'Lellan of Kirkowen, Thomas Forbe of Slains, James Smith of Kincardie, John Miller of Dunrossness, George Campbell of Botriphnie, W. Carlyle of Prestonpans, John Willison of Dundee and many more in Ross-shire."

[50] Henry Davidson, *Letters to Christian Friends* (Edinburgh, 1811), p. 43, *et passim*.

[51] Francis G. Walett, ed., "The Diary of Ebenezer Parkman," *Proceedings of the American Antiquarian Association*, 72 (April 1962): 31–233; and (October 1962): 329–481.

[52] John Sinclair, ed., *The Old Statistical Account* (Edinburgh, 1793), 267.

[53] "Examination of Persons under Spiritual Concern at Cambuslang, 1: 103, 2: 333.

make the contents of this correspondence public by readings to his congregation "and also to the association of ministers . . . and occasionally to many others." This work did not exhaust his evangelical outreach, for he copied sections of letters and sent them to other parts of Massachusetts and to Connecticut with advice to the recipient that he too should "communicate it to other ministers and . . . to his people." [54] It is difficult to imagine how any individual could have done more without intervening directly.

Public readings of foreign and domestic news known as Letter Days became institutionalized as a regular part of the society calendar in England and Wales, through the organization of the Calvinist Methodist Tabernacles. Limitation of the practice to these two countries may reflect the lower levels of literacy and stronger oral traditions in England and Wales as compared to New England and lowland Scotland, especially among those involved in the revival.[55] The English revivalists were also directly affected by the Church of the Brethren (the Moravians), a German pietist community that had been in England since 1735 under its leader Count Nikolaus Ludwig von Zinzendorf. The Moravian practice of *Gemeintag*, or mass meeting for the reading of missionary reports, impressed the new revival societies in England and Wales, which were particularly susceptible to Moravian influences. *Gemeintag* had been central to Moravian community life since 1728, and although it included ordinations, marriages, and prayer, the main feature was "the communication of the latest accounts from the churches and missions from all parts." [56]

The Moravians conducted their Letter Days wherever they went including the Fetter Lane Society in London, whose meetings Whitefield, the Wesleys, and other members of the Oxford Club attended. As early as 1739, English evangelicals had adopted the practice of Letter Days.[57] After separation from the Moravians in 1741, Whitefield and the Wesleys started their own Letter Day at the society in the Foundry in London, although they and their followers continued to attend the Moravian Letter Day, too. Howell Harris recorded in his diary that he "went to hear the letters read in the Foundry . . . then again to Fetter Lane to hear the Moravian letters." And in a letter to

[54] Edwards to McCulloch, May 23, 1749, Dwight, *President Edwards*, 1: 276–77.

[55] See T. C. Smout, "Born Again at Cambuslang: New Evidence on Popular Religion and Literacy in Eighteenth Century Scotland," *Past and Present*, 97 (1982): 114–27.

[56] John M. Levering, *A History of Bethlehem, Pennsylvania 1741–1892* (Bethlehem, Pa., 1903), 67; Walsh, "Cambridge Methodists," 263.

[57] From Bristol, Wesley wrote to London publisher and Methodist, James Sutton, "I wish you would constantly send me extracts of all your foreign letters, to be read out on Intercession Day." John Telford, ed., *Letters of John Wesley*, 8 vols. (London, 1960), 1: 314.

Daniel Rowlands, which reflected the early pluralism of the revival, Harris reported that "yesterday we Whitefield's Methodists had our monthly Day for reading letters about the Progress of the Gospel elsewhere—such accounts as we had from America and Scotland your ears never heard of. . . . Yesterday was the Letter Day with the Moravians where was glorious accounts from Pennsylvania." [58] The Calvinist Methodists established regular Letter Days as early as 1741, meeting in London on the second Monday of the month and in Bristol on the first Monday in the month.[59] These monthly readings continued for at least seven years as an important feature of the Whitefieldian movement.

A Letter Day assembly usually began with an exhortation followed by a reading of letters, each of which might be concluded by communal singing of a specially written verse. Another exhortation and prayer rounded off the service. The meeting lasted several hours and was an occasion of great excitement, "the Tabernacle being filled in all its Parts for Peoples sitting and many standing on the outsides of the seats." [60] Two sorts of letters were sent to the Tabernacle, one a personal letter donated by its recipient, the other a letter specially written to be read aloud and usually referred to as an "account" by the preachers who sent them in. Like the Epistles of Paul and the letters of George Fox to the Quakers, the second type of letter was consciously addressed to a large group of listeners and the style and content were adapted to that forum. Exhorters and superintendents of the societies were urged to send in a full account of their preaching, the persecutions they experienced, the new converts made, and new societies formed.

Letter Days, confined as they were to the centers of communication even in England, could not by themselves solve the problem of limited access to the news. From the outset, revivalists asked themselves how they could best multiply the effects they were achieving beyond their own immediate circles. The London printer John Lewis supplied the answer when, in September 1740, he began editing and printing a

---

[58] Harris's diary, October 4, 1742, Benyon, *Reformer and Soldier*, 26; and Harris to Rowlands, September 14, 1742, Roberts, *Selected Trevecka Letters*, 46.

[59] Luke Tyerman, *Life of the Rev. George Whitefield*, 2 vols. (London, 1876–77), 1: 542. Whitefield wrote to the Welsh evangelists, December 28, 1741: "I am about to settle a monthly meeting in Bristol and London where correspondents' letters are to be read." Also see Welch, *Two Calvinistic Methodist Chapels*, 19.

[60] *An Account of the Most Remarkable Particulars Relating to the Present Progress of the Gospel* (London, 1742), vol. 2, no. 2, p. 76.

[61] The sequence of publication was as follows: John Lewis, ed., *Christian's Amusement containing Letters Concerning the Progress of the Gospel both at Home and Abroad etc. together with an Account of the Waldenses and Albigenses* . . . (London, 1740), printed by John Lewis, September 1740-March 1741, 4 pp., price 1d. (hereafter, *CA*). Then: *Weekly History: Or, An Account of the Most Remarkable Particulars Relating to the Present Progress of the*

weekly revival newspaper.[61] His concern was with "the Progress of the Gospel both at Home and Abroad," and, from the first edition, he used letters as the main substance of the paper. Whitefield himself had seen the value of newspaper publicity, and, before Lewis's venture, had attempted to use the secular press to promote the revival. But he encountered too many obstacles to the success of this project, including a lack of interest by secular editors and difficulty in controlling his copy. He found an independent paper to be a more useful instrument. By April 1741, Whitefield had officially adopted Lewis's paper for publishing up-to-date revival news. From 1741 onward, the London paper became increasingly closely linked with Letter Day, eventually publishing little besides the letters read at the Tabernacle. Copyists transcribed letters received at the Tabernacle into books so that the leaders could make selections for publication and for public readings. Moreover, Lewis found imitators in Scotland and New England. William McCulloch of Glasgow, James Robe in Edinburgh, and Thomas Prince, Jr., of Boston took up Lewis's idea and edited revival papers or magazines. All of these ministers, as active members of the communications network, were well placed to take on this new role.[62] Even so, they relied heavily on one another to make a success of their papers. McCulloch drew on the *London Weekly History* for his *Glasgow Weekly History*, concentrating on reprinting letters to the near exclusion of other forms of literature. In his *Christian History*, Thomas Prince, Jr., aimed to print "extracts of written letters both from England, Scot-

---

Gospel. By the Encouragement of the Rev. Mr. Whitefield (London, 1741), vol. 1, printed by John Lewis, April 11, 1741–November 13, 1742, 4 pp., price 1d. (hereafter, *WH*). Then in Autumn 1742: *An Account of the Most Remarkable Particulars Relating to the Present Progress of the Gospel* (London, 1742), vols. 2, 3, and 4, printed by John Lewis, 84 pp., price 1/2 d. per week (hereafter, *Account*). Then in Autumn 1743, *Christian History or General Account of the Progress of the Gospel in England, Wales, Scotland and America as far as the Rev. Mr. Whitefield, his Fellow Labourers and Assistants are concerned* (London, 1743), vols. 5, 6, and 7, printed by John Lewis every seven weeks. Each volume was divided into four numbers of 84 pp. (hereafter, *CH*). Finally: *Christian History or General Account . . . of the Gospel . . .* (London, 1748), 1 volume printed by John Lewis containing letters June 1747–June 1748, 283 pp. (hereafter, *CH 1748*). The only complete collection is in the National Library of Wales, Aberystwyth. There is a discussion of these papers in Susan Durden, "A Study of the First Evangelical Magazines," *Journal of Ecclesiastical History*, 27 (1976): 255–75.

[62] William McCulloch, ed., *Glasgow-Weekly-History Relating to the Late Progress of the Gospel at Home and Abroad: Being a Collection of Letters partly reprinted from the London-Weekly-History . . .* (Glasgow, 1742), December 1741–December 1742, 8 pp., price 1d., bound with an index (hereafter, *GWH*); James Robe, ed., *Christian Monthly History or an Account of the Revival and Progress of Religion Abroad and at Home*, 2 vols. (Edinburgh, 1743), November 1743–January 1746 (hereafter, *CMH*); Thomas Prince, Jr., *Christian History, Containing Accounts of the Revival and Propagation of Religion in Great Britain and America . . . 1743 and 1744*, 2 vols. (Boston, Mass., 1743), March 5, 1743–February 23, 1745, 8 pp. (hereafter, *CH Boston*). See Durden, "First Evangelical Magazines."

land, New York, New Jersey, South Carolina and Georgia of a religious Nature as they shall be sent hither from creditable Persons and
communicated to us." James Robe, who put together the *Christian
Monthly History*, was aware that "a very extensive correspondence must
be established for the carrying on a Design of this sort to purpose."
Robe and Prince solicited letters for publication, but all the editors received unsolicited correspondence, including some from lay people.
Once the editors had made contact with one another and exchanged
complete sets of their own papers, coverage became as complete as was
possible.[63]

Only this inexpensive and full reprinting of letters overcame the
limitations of other methods of dissemination adopted in the early to
mid-eighteenth century. It gave each English-speaking revival country
its own newspaper or magazine that, for a few pence, brought the
reader current with all the latest revival news. Individuals could read
the newspapers privately or a minister could use them in many different ways. In the Ross-shire village of Nigg, for example, John Balfour
wrote to James Robe: "I procured most of your Narratives and Letters;
and this Post I commission for an entire set of them, and for Copies of
the *Christian Monthly History* . . . and have recommended to some
others to procure them and will to more. . . . The Design is very
laudable and has already been of great Use. It is a choice Means to
promote the Communion of Saints upon Earth." [64] Three thousand
miles away from Nigg, Nicholas Gilman of Durham, New Hampshire,
read to his parishioners from the *Glasgow Weekly History* and lent
copies out as part of his parish library scheme. From Somerset, England, Risdon Darracott, a Presbyterian minister, wrote thanking
Lewis for his good work, telling him that he had "distributed the
Weekly Papers among my People and they are much affected with
them." John Harrison, Nonconformist minister in Braintree, Essex,
thought the London papers particularly useful for keeping the young
people out of temptation's way, which he did for nearly three hours at a
time by reading "the substance of near 30 of Mr. Lewis's Papers." [65] All
the papers were miscellanies of news from Scotland, England, Wales,
the American colonies, and Holland, in the form of letters, narratives,
and extracts from printed works. Each paper reflected the views and
abilities of its editor. The Boston paper, for example, which came out
weekly for two years, was purposefully organized by Prince to "reaf-
firm the special covenant meaning of New England's past, by associat-

---

[63] Prince, Jr., to McCulloch, December 13, 1743, New York Public Library MSS letters, J. H. Benton sale, American Art Association 1920 catalogue, 3d session, March 13.

[64] *CMH*, vol. 1, no. 4.

[65] Nicholas Gilman MS Diary, New Hampshire Historical Society. See, for example,
the entry for October 19, 1742. Darracott's letter was printed in *WH*, no. 46; Harrison's
in *WH*, no. 52 and reprinted in *GWH*, no. 18, pp. 1–4.

ing the revival with Puritan traditions," but, even so, almost one-third of the paper contained news and articles from Scotland, with Prince drawing attention to the similarities between the two areas.[66]

Although evangelical papers and magazines were the most innovative and effective method for spreading the word, more traditional methods continued alongside them. Whitefield's correspondence, for example, found its way into print most commonly through his *Journals*, and he occasionally also had it printed on the back of sermons and pamphlets or used it to break up some longer and weighty piece of prose. Three American letters to Whitefield were bound between his own *Letter to New Brunswick* and *Letter in Answer to the Presbytery of Newcastle*. Whitefield and other revival leaders regarded these letters, and other personal correspondence, as general revival property that could be published for the edification of the community at large.[67] By combining their private networks for the dissemination of news and literature with their outlets for more general publication, revival leaders had an effective vehicle for launching specific projects or for conducting campaigns on an international level. In this way, they adopted and supported Whitefield's Georgia Orphan House, donated money to missionaries, and helped to establish the Presbyterian College of New Jersey.[68] Above all, they initiated and sustained the United Concert for Prayer, a parish-based international movement that became another of the major legacies bequeathed by the mid-eighteenth-century revivals to evanglical protestantism.

THE SUCCESSFUL ESTABLISHMENT OF COORDINATED PRAYER DAYS, organized as the United Concert for Prayer, is solid evidence for the effectiveness of the communication networks. Initially, revivalists simply

[66] Jan E. Van de Wetering, "The Christian History of the Great Awakening," *Journal of Presbyterian History*, 44 (1966): 124.

[67] See, for example, *Copy of Three Letters, the first written by Dr. John Nicol at New York, to Mr. William Wardrobe, Surgeon in the Grass-market of Edinburgh; the second by a dissenting minister in England to a Gentleman in Scotland; the third from a minister at Boston to his friend at Glasgow, Giving an Account of the Progress and Success of the Gospel in Foreign Parts* (Edinburgh, 1740). For another example, see Dwight, *President Edwards*, 1: 407.

[68] Collections were continually made for the Orphanage in Britain. See Welch, *Two C M Chapels*, xv, 8, 13. On missionary work, it is interesting to note that correspondence across the Atlantic continued through the 1750s and 1760s, as for example between Eleazor Wheelock, founder of an Indian Charity School at Dartmouth, New Hampshire, and his British patrons. Leon B. Richardson, *An Indian Preacher in England* (Hanover, N.H., 1933). William McCulloch himself spent £227 on missionary work; Fawcett, *Cambuslang Revival*, 216. British revivalists were also warm supporters of New Jersey College and the correspondence across the Atlantic about its foundation survives in the Burr MSS, Princeton University Library. Rev. Samuel Davies went on a fund-raising trip to Britain on behalf of the College, 1753–55. See George W. Pilcher, *The Rev. Samuel Davies Abroad: The Diary of a Journey to England and Scotland, 1753–55* (London, 1955).

adopted the Puritan tradition of days of prayer, and, by 1741, the practice of setting aside a named day for prayer and fasting for the general revival of religion was common among the various religious societies and meetings in Britain and America. At this date, each group acted independently of the others. Whitefield, for example, made his society's day the sixteenth of the month, and many Calvinist Methodist societies in England and Wales kept the same day. In Dundee, in March 1742, Church evangelicals "agreed to observe Thursday next for Thanksgiving to the Lord in all our prayer societies and others are invited to join in Praising the Lord." [69] Jonathan Edwards, too, recommended in *Some Thoughts Concerning the Present Revival*, published in 1742, that a shared day of prayer and fasting form the basis of a covenant between God and the converted. His *Thoughts* were widely read among Scottish revival activists and may have encouraged their own interest in shared prayer.[70] By 1743, the practice was well organized in Lowland Scotland: "There was a Proposal from the Praying Societies at Edinburgh transmitted in a short printed Memorial to us and other Places to set apart Friday the 18th now past for Thanksgiving . . . and Prayer. . . . There was a serious and apparent concern among the People." [71] In the space of two years, the prayer day had become increasingly organized. By 1744, these Scottish ministers were ready to take the concept a stage further. Their proposal in October for joint action with their English and American counterparts in a United Concert for Prayer created something new out of the old tradition. Societies and individuals would commit themselves to weekly and quarterly prayer times in which prayer would be offered for a universal revival of religion. The proposers drew societies in, partly by making use of the well-developed personal correspondence network and partly through the Edinburgh *Christian Monthly History*, which devoted a complete issue to the Concert.[72] The universal evangelism and catholic spirit of the Concert idea recommended it to the many shades of theological opinion within the revival movement,[73] and, when the two-year pledge period was over, a fresh Scottish proposal to continue for a further seven years was accepted. The new proposal, made in August 1746, took the form of a printed Memorial that could be circulated within the network. Edwards, as the main American supporter of the Concert, received 500 copies for distribution, which he seems to have redistributed using the "tree" method: "I have very lately received

[69] *GWH*, no. 26, p. 7.
[70] Fawcett, *Cambuslang Revival*, 225.
[71] *Account*, vol. 3, no. 1, p. 18.
[72] *CMH*, vol. 2, no. 1.
[73] John Wesley accepted an invitation to join, and himself suggested to Erskine that Edwards and Gilbert Tennent would probably agree to take part; Telford, *Letters of John Wesley*, 2: 33.

a Pacquet from Scotland," he wrote to Joseph Bellamy, "with several copies of a Memorial, for the continuing and propagating of an Agreement for joint Prayer, for the general Revival of religion, three of which I send to you, desiring you to dispose of two of 'em where they will be most serviceable." [74] When originally proposing the Concert, revivalists in Scotland had been hesitant about advertising it too publicly, possibly fearing that it might be regarded by some as "superstitious" and by others, especially employers, as "interfering with other duties." [75] By 1746, they were emboldened (perhaps because none of their fears were realized) to print and circulate the Memorial on the grounds that "notwithstanding of what may be done by private letters it is humbly expected that a Memorial . . . may reach where they will not." [76]

It is not easy to assess the number of societies and individuals associated with the Concert. Robe reported in 1749 that letters from New England told of the "great progress this Concert has made in these provinces. Many ministers, private Christians, yea congregations and churches, have entered into it and continue to enter." [77] But he gives no names or numbers. Certainly, the Concert received an additional boost from the publication by Edwards in 1747 of his *Humble Attempt to Promote Explicit Agreement and Visible Union of God's People in Extraordinary Prayers*, which gave the genesis and the history of the Concert and included the entire text of the 1746 Scottish Memorial. As late as 1754, revivalists maintained sufficient interest to ask for a second seven-year extension of the arrangement.

Evangelicals of the 1740s were eager to prove the existence of good Scriptural and Reformation precedents for the coordination of prayer, and they cited chapter and verse to support their case. [78] But their very strenuousness indicates an awareness that they were open to criticism for innovation. With benefit of hindsight, we can see that they had moved in the direction of a more instrumental approach to revivalism. Because it was planned on a large scale and was well organized and purposefully instrumental, the Concert, like the magazines, marked a shift in position by evangelicals. A number of them had constituted themselves into a group, with George Whitefield at its center, and created an evangelical community that consciously, if gradually, transformed revival practices.

---

[74] Frank B. Dexter, ed., *Manuscripts of Jonathan Edwards* (Cambridge, Mass., 1901), January 15, 1746.

[75] Gillies, *Historical Collections* (1754; reprint edn., 1981), 462–64.

[76] Jonathan Edwards, *An Humble Attempt to Promote Explicit Agreement and Visible Union of God's People in Extraordinary Prayer for the Revival of Religion and the Advancement of Christ's Kingdom on Earth* (Boston, 1747), 23.

[77] Gillies, *Historical Collections*, 464.

[78] *Ibid.*, 462–64.

The revival activities described here provided a link between eigh-teenth- and nineteenth-century revivalism. The Concert for Prayer, for example, was resuscitated in the 1780s by a group of Northamp-tonshire English Baptists. When this group, which included Pastor Andrew Fuller, received a copy of Jonathan Edwards's *Humble Attempt*, in a parcel of books sent by John Erskine, they agreed to try to pro-mote a revival of religion through a "prayer call." [79] In its turn, the prayer call was claimed by William Carey as the spiritual inspiration behind his founding of the Baptist Missionary Society (1792). These late eighteenth-century evangelicals were undoubtedly less hesitant about using these means for promoting revival than their original pro-ponents had been, and the confidence of later revivalists came in part from knowledge of precedent and example. The Concert came to them with a solid evangelical pedigree; they did not have to pioneer this form.

The mid-eighteenth-century revivalists had created the first evan-gelical magazines. Even if the appearance of these magazines accompa-nied a general expansion of periodical literature and of a magazine-reading public, the publication of evangelical magazines at this early date was not inevitable. Given the sheer effort required of amateurs to collect copy, print, distribute, and finance such a publication, it is hardly surprising that the magazines died when the revival impulse flagged. The absence of institutional support systems led in the 1750s to a lull in the publication of the magazines, despite their usefulness to evangelicals. By the last twenty years of the century, however, the mag-azines revived and became an integral and vital element in Christian outreach, so that in the nineteenth century, evangelicals often used the periodical press to promote and encourage revivals in ways reminiscent of the *Christian's Amusement* and its successors. These later publica-tions of course reflected the growth of denominationalism and the concomitant decline of ecumenical protestant evangelicalism. Histori-ans of nineteenth-century revivalism have not neglected these maga-zines as source material, or failed to see in them the mark of a more in-strumental revivalism.

THE HISTORY OF CONNECTION, interconnection, and direct assistance between evangelicals in different countries and across generations is understandably recounted with triumph by evangelical historians, even though they have shown less interest in the human agencies involved. Other historians of the same events have been well aware of this evan-gelical tradition, relying as they have on the materials collected by men such as Prince or Gillies, who recorded the details of chronology and

---

[79] These connections are traced in Fawcett, *Cambuslang Revival*, 223–33; Ernest A. Payne, *Prayer Call of 1784* (London, 1941), and Watts, *Dissenters*, 456–61.

location but did not regard them as significant. A familiar portrait of revival history has emerged from the evangelical tradition, painted with broad, bold strokes on a large canvas. In their turn, social historians have sought to get beyond these generalities to the particular nature of a revival in a specific place and at a specific period. By setting the religious behavior of mid-eighteenth-century men and women in the context of local social and political structures, they have rightly enmeshed the revival in community affairs. In their work, human activities and human emotions have replaced the hand of God as the focus of interest.

The evidence presented here shows that it is not necessary or helpful for historians to focus solely on local events. Revivals did indeed take place within particular communities, and we need to understand the complex relationships between revivalism and local religious and social groupings. But the international dimension of evangelicalism in the transatlantic world of the 1740s also needs to be recognized and understood. This dimension is as capable of explanation as the local context, and the human agencies are just as visible. The broad dissemination of news did not necessarily cause revivals, but the exciting knowledge that clergy and lay people acquired about events elsewhere shaped individual behavior and individual understanding of what the Lord had "upon the Wheel."

The Crisis of the Churches in the Middle Colonies, 1720–1750

MARTIN E. LODGE

The enormous mid-eighteenth-century upwelling of religious feeling that we call the Great Awakening was not only a phenomenon that touched all of the colonies; it was a transatlantic phenomenon as well. In no part of the Euro-American world, however, was the impact of the Awakening greater than it was in the Middle Colonies of New York, New Jersey, and Pennsylvania. In the valleys of the Hudson and the Delaware, evangelical religion found some of its most dedicated adherents. Martin Lodge tells the story of the Awakening in the Middle Colonies with great clarity and in relatively brief compass.

Reprinted by permission from Martin E. Lodge, "The Crisis of the Churches in the Middle Colonies, 1720–1750," *Pennsylvania Magazine of History and Biography*, 95 (1971), 195–220.

The main contention of Lodge's article is that the traditional churches of the Middle Colonies were in crisis by the 1720s and 1730s and that the revival, far from prompting their disintegration, was a response to an institutional decline that was already underway. Thus, Lodge aims not only to interpret the Awakening itself but the religious condition of the Middle Colonies before it began. In doing so, he reminds us of the social diversity of the Middle Colonies to which other authors in this volume also point. Howe and Nash particularly describe social processes much like those that Lodge seeks to analyze, and they place significant emphasis on similar explanatory factors; immigration is but one example.

Lodge makes another contribution as well. In addition to offering a creative approach to the origins of the Awakening, he also presents an interesting interpretive scheme for understanding its consequences. If the revival in Lodge's hands was a response to institutional decline, he also sees it as prompting a new set of organizing principles for the churches that eventually strengthened rather than weakened them. In that sense, his view of the Awakening shares something with Soderlund's interpretation of Quaker women. Just as Quaker men got both more and less than they bargained for in their attempts to limit the autonomy of Quaker women, the evangelicals of the Middle Colonies got both more and less than they bargained for with their aggressive attacks against church establishments. The truth of one of Charles Beard's dicta about the lessons of history—that the bee fertilizes the flower it robs—would seem to borne out by many of the essays in this volume.

Fifty years ago Herbert L. Osgood described the Great Awakening in America as "the first great and spontaneous movement in the history of the American people." [1] The profound significance that Osgood attached to the Great Awakening has spurred two generations of historians to explore in depth its impact upon the development of American life, institutions, and thought. In this preoccupation with the influence of the Awakening upon the later phases of American history, however, scholars have tended to overlook the origins of the upheaval. Nowhere is this hiatus more evident than in the historiography of the Middle Colonies. No one has ever attempted to explain why the Great Awak-

---

[1] Herbert L. Osgood, *The American Colonies in the Eighteenth Century* (New York, 1924; reprinted by Peter Smith, Gloucester, Mass., 1958), III, 409. I would like to thank Carl Bridenbaugh, Robert L. Middlekauff, and Russell F. Weigley for their criticism and their encouragement.

ening happened there, or why it was a "great and spontaneous" popular movement.[2]

The reason for this oversight, perhaps, has been the spell that the sectarians inhabiting the Middle Colonies have cast over modern historians. Their fascination with the Quakers and such German sects as the Mennonites seems to have blinded most students of the Middle Colonies to the significance of the denominations most affected by the revivals of the 1740s: the Presbyterian, Reformed, and Lutheran Churches.[3]

The Great Awakening in the Middle Colonies was almost exclusively a movement among the church people—those settlers whose religious heritage can be traced to the established churches of Europe. The Anglican George Whitefield and the New Brunswick party of the

---

[2] New England has been better served in this respect than have the rest of the colonies, particularly by Richard L. Bushman, *From Puritan to Yankee: Character and the Social Order in Connecticut, 1690–1765* (Cambridge, Mass., 1967), Chapters 9–12. Though Professor Bushman's book deals only with Connecticut, no other work discusses the background of the Awakening so comprehensively or with such insight. It should serve as a model for all future studies of the Great Awakening. The works of Perry Miller are invaluable for the intellectual origins of the revivals, especially his *The New England Mind; From Colony to Province* (Cambridge, Mass., 1953), and *Jonathan Edwards* (New York, 1949).

The only comprehensive study for the Middle Colonies is Charles Hartshorn Maxson, *The Great Awakening in the Middle Colonies* (Chicago, 1920; reprinted by Peter Smith, Gloucester, Mass., 1958), which is still a useful survey, particularly because it includes the German revivals. The most valuable study of the background of the Awakening, at least among the English speaking settlers, is Leonard J. Trinterud, *The Forming of an American Tradition: A Re-examination of Colonial Presbyterianism* (Philadelphia, 1949). Professor Trinterud examines Presbyterian evangelism in the light of the constitutional crises in the Presbyterian Church and he includes some useful information on the religious conditions among the clergy and the laity, information which should be supplemented by Guy Soulliard Klett, *Presbyterians in Colonial Pennsylvania* (Philadelphia, 1937), and Nelson R. Burr, *The Anglican Church in New Jersey* (Philadelphia, 1954). None of these books, however, though they contain much of the material used in this article, attempt to explain why the revivalists got such a tremendous response from the laymen.

The intellectual origins of the Great Awakening in the Middle Colonies will not be explored in this article. For German evangelism, the student should begin with the several studies of the Dunkers and especially the Moravians. Professor Trinterud's work is excellent for the intellectual background of the Tennent party, although his observations on the significance of pietism have been corrected by James Tanis, *Dutch Calvinistic Pietism in the Middle Colonies: A Study in the Life and Theology of Theodorus Jacobus Frelinghuysen* (The Hague, 1967).

[3] Throughout this article we will refer to "sect" and "sectarians," "church" and "church people." The term "sect" includes the Quakers, Mennonites, Schwenkfelders, Moravians, Dunkers, and such smaller groups as Conrad Beissel's Seventh Day Baptists encloistered at Ephrata, Pa. By the term "church" we mean the Church of England, the Presbyterians, the Congregationalists, and the various national branches of the Lutheran and Reformed Churches. For the difference between these two types of denominations, see footnote 9.

Presbyterian Church dominated the awakening of the English-speaking colonists. These evangelists drew their following either from settlers raised in the Calvinistic traditions of the churches of Scotland, Ireland, and New England or from previously "indifferent" people whose religious background was unknown [4] but who usually became Presbyterians as the result of their conversions. The Quakers, the principal English-speaking sect, were affected only superficially.[5]

The German Awakening was staged by the Dunkers and the Moravians, two pietistic sects recently organized in Germany out of separatists from the established churches.[6] Neither group had much impact upon the older Mennonite and Schwenkfelder sects; they soon found their appeal was infinitely greater among the Lutheran and Reformed laymen. Conrad Beissel, for instance, an erstwhile Dunker, who was the most successful German evangelist of the 1730s, was only an annoyance to the Mennonites, but he infuriated Reformed circles by his inroads on their congregations.[7] Similarly, the Moravian revivals of the following decade were confined to the church people after the Pennsylvania sects, led by the Schwenkfelders, thwarted Count Zinzendorf's design to create a "church of the spirit" embracing all denominations.[8]

In this essay we will attempt to show how the breakdown of church religion in the Middle Colonies created a situation which made the church people unusually susceptible to evangelism.[9] Our thesis, simply

---

[4] *The Querists, or An Extract of sundry Passages taken out of Mr. Whitefield's printed Sermons, Journals and Letters* (Philadelphia, 1740), 32; Samuel Blair, *A Particular Consideration of a Piece, Entitled, The Querists* (Philadelphia, 1741), 61–62; Thomas Prince, *The Christian History . . . For the Years 1744–5* (Boston, 1745), 295. There is good reason to believe that most of these "indifferent" people had once been affiliated with some church.

[5] Frederick B. Tolles, "Quietism versus Enthusiasm: The Philadelphia Quakers and the Great Awakening," *Pennsylvania Magazine of History and Biography*, LXIX (1945), 26–49.

[6] On Dunker origins see Donald F. Durnbaugh, *European Origins of the Brethren* (Elgin, Ill., 1958), Chapter 1. On the Moravians see John Jacob Sessler, *Communal Pietism among the Early American Moravians* (New York, 1933), 8–12.

[7] C. Henry Smith, *The Story of the Mennonites* (Newton, Kans., 1950), 547; John C. Wenger, *History of the Mennonites of the Franconia Conference* (Telford, Pa., 1937), 81; [John Peter Miller], *Chronicon Ephratense: A History of the Community of Seventh Day Baptists at Ephrata*, Translated by J. Max Hark (Lancaster, Pa., 1889), 70–73; William J. Hinke, ed., *Life and Letters of the Rev. John Philip Boehm, Founder of the Reformed Church in Pennsylvania 1683–1749* (Philadelphia, 1916), 200–203, 274–275, 353–355, hereinafter cited as Boehm.

[8] Sessler, 34–37; Smith, 547.

[9] To keep this article down to a reasonable length, we will not deal in detail with the accompanying question of why the older sects—especially the Quakers, Mennonites, and Schwenkfelders—failed to participate in the Great Awakening. It seems proper, however, to outline the answer to that question, particularly since it is implicit in the paragraphs that follow.

In general, the sects were more successful than the churches in establishing their religious institutions, thus avoiding the crisis that came to confront the struggling churches.

stated, is that the churches of the Middle Colonies failed to establish institutions capable of fulfilling the religious needs of a rapidly expanding population. Before the late 1740s, neither the Church of England nor the several national branches of the Lutheran and Reformed Churches founded any American institution above the level of the congregation. The Presbyterians managed, early in the century, to reproduce the ecclesiastical system of Scotland, but when this organization could not cope with the demands of its congregations, it fell apart in 1741. While the young churches were faltering in their struggle to gain an institutional foothold in the New World, they were swamped by the vast immigration of church people from the British Isles and Germany which flooded the Middle Colonies after 1718. Unprepared to offer the stability the new arrivals so desperately needed amidst the moral and social confusion attending their settlement, the churches stood helplessly by as hundreds of laymen turned away from their inherited faith, went over to the sects or lapsed into religious indifference. Organized religion seemed on the verge of collapse when the Great Awakening, though at first adding to the disorder, rescued the floundering churches. By 1750, the strength and effectiveness of every church was increasing rapidly.[10]

The first prerequisite of a thriving church is an effective ministry. A minister is essential to the functioning of every congregation because

---

two basic reasons for the greater ease the sects enjoyed in settling the Middle Colonies: (1) Almost without exception, the immigration of the sectarians was better planned, organized, and financed than was the migration of the church people; but more importantly, (2) sectarian institutions were better adapted to the primitive conditions of the New World than were church institutions. The essential difference between a church and a sect, in this context, lay in their different conceptions of the ministry. A church minister was distinctly set apart from the layman by education, by calling, and by a special ordination. Furthermore, his profession was considered so sacred that he was not supposed to labor in a secular occupation. The sectarians, on the other hand, held a less exalted view of the ministerial office. No special qualifications or training were required of a sectarian minister. He was chosen directly from the ranks of the lay membership, and he was expected to earn his livelihood in a secular calling. Because of this simplicity, sectarian institutions became fully effective as soon as a congregation banded together and elected its officers, but a church congregation was crippled until it could secure the services of a specially trained and lawfully ordained clergyman and find the means to support him.

[10] It should be pointed out that the generalizations we will develop in this article must be applied with some caution to the province of New York. First of all, the revivals on Long Island, and to some extent those among the New Englanders in northern New Jersey, follow the pattern of the New England Awakening rather than that of the Middle Colonies. New England revivalism grew out of the tensions that had arisen in an older, more homogeneous society, whose religious institutions were firmly established, while the Great Awakening in the Middle Colonies was largely a response to problems created by the process of settlement. Secondly, conditions in New York City and its immediate environs also varied in several respects from the rest of the Middle Colonies. The Church of England and the Dutch Reformed Church were more securely entrenched there, the sectarians were weaker, and the influx of immigrants much smaller.

only he can lawfully administer the sacraments and preach the Word of God. Furthermore, because of his specialized training in matters of the Spirit, the minister is the person best qualified to guide individual laymen in their private quest for righteousness and salvation. At the root of the institutional failure of the churches in the Middle Colonies, therefore, lay the churches' inability to establish a clergy numerous enough, or effective enough, to supply these elemental needs.

The most obvious symptom of the unhealthy condition of the churches in the Middle Colonies was the great disparity between the number of ministers and the number of congregations. The situation was particularly desperate in the German churches of Pennsylvania, where by 1740 there were but three German Reformed pastors for twenty-six congregations,[11] and only one clergyman for the twenty-seven German Lutheran congregations.[12] The Anglicans, the Dutch Reformed, and the Dutch and Swedish Lutherans were all better served than the Germans, although on any given Sabbath no more than half the pulpits of these denominations were ever occupied by ordained ministers.[13] The Presbyterian Church kept pace with the demands of its multiplying congregations throughout the 1720s.[14] During the following decade, however, the Church was overwhelmed by the influx of Scotch-Irish immigrants. By sending their younger mem-

[11] Boehm, 83, 88–89.

[12] *Ibid.*, 83; Henry Eyster Jacobs, *A History of the Evangelical Lutheran Church in the United States* (New York, 1893), 191.

[13] The Anglicans in New York were always well supplied, but in the other provinces the Church of England only managed to keep about half its parishes in ministers. In 1724, for example, all six parishes in New York had ministers. In Pennsylvania, New Jersey, and Delaware, however, there were eight ministers for sixteen parishes, two of which were considered too weak to support a minister. Fulham Papers, XXXVI, 54–57, Lambeth Palace Library. New Jersey had five ministers for ten parishes in 1740. Burr, 86, 113. For further data on Pennsylvania and Delaware see William Stevens Perry (ed.), *Historical Collections Relating to the American Colonial Church*, Volume 2: *Pennsylvania* (Hartford, 1871), 131–133, 145–146.

In 1737 the Dutch Reformed church, though it had had over a century to establish itself, could muster only nineteen ministers for sixty-five congregations. E. T. Corwin, J. H. Dubbs, and J. T. Hamilton, *A History of the Reformed Church, Dutch, the Reformed Church, German, and the Moravian Church in the United States* (New York, 1895), 136. There were usually one or two German clergymen in New York and another in New Jersey ministering to the scattered Dutch and German Lutherans in those provinces, Jacobs, 117–126.

The four congregations that made up the Swedish Lutheran Church were better off than any of the above denominations. During the first half of the eighteenth century the Wicacoa congregation near Philadelphia was vacant ten years, Racoon and Pennsneck in New Jersey twenty-one years each, and Christina, in what is now Wilmington, Del., just two years. Israel Acrelius, *A History of New Sweden* (Ann Arbor, 1966), 363. Besides their regular congregations, however, all the churches in the Middle Colonies had numerous out-parishes, or preaching stations, which were supplied haphazardly.

[14] Jedediah Andrews to Thomas Prince, Oct. 14, 1730, Samuel Hazard, *Register of Pennsylvania*, XV (March, 1835), 200–201.

bers on strenuous itinerations the presbyteries managed to bridge the widening gap between the supply of ministers and the number of congregations until the end of the 1730s, when it became impossible, even with some fifty clergymen enrolled in the American church, to honor every request for a preacher.[15]

The scarcity of ministers in the Middle Colonies stemmed ultimately from the churches' dependence upon Europe for their clergy. A church congregation could not simply appoint its minister from the ranks of the lay membership, as could a sectarian congregation. He had to be educated and ordained by institutions which were usually found only in the Old World. This reliance upon Europe (and upon New England, too, for the Presbyterians) was fatal because Europe could not begin to satisfy the colonial churches' demands for clergymen. Ministers were reluctant to emigrate to the New World. Unlike the Puritan hegira to New England or the immigration of the sects, the migration of church peoples to the Middle Colonies was not a movement of religious communities conducted by their religious leaders in pursuit of a religious ideal. Only the Scotch-Irish were driven at all by religious motives, and, partly for that reason, only Presbyterian ministers came to America in significant numbers.[16] Other denominations were reduced to cajoling clergymen into undertaking an American mission by offering them such worldly advantages as a handsome salary or preferment at home after a period of service abroad.[17]

Because the immigration of clergymen did not allow the American churches to prosper, their only alternative was to become self-sufficient. Self-sufficiency, unfortunately, required institutions that were beyond the capacity of most churches to create at so primitive a stage of their development. Each denomination had to set up an ecclesiastical organization, independent of Europe and invested with the power of ordination, and then found a college to train a native ministry.

Only the Presbyterian church attained self-sufficiency during the first half of the eighteenth century, reaching it at the very end of the period. With the founding of the Presbytery of Philadelphia in 1706, the authority to ordain and regulate the American clergy was perma-

---

[15] Presbytery of Philadelphia Minutes, 12–13, 48, 54, 56, 66 in Presbyterian Historical Society, hereinafter PHS; Presbytery of New Brunswick "Minutes," *Journal of the Presbyterian Historical Society*, VI, 230–232. Fifty-four ministers were members of the Synod of Philadelphia in 1739. *Records of the Presbyterian Church in the United States of America* (Philadelphia, 1841), 141.

[16] According to the most recent authority, religious persecution was only a secondary factor in prompting Presbyterian ministers to leave Ireland; they seem to have been driven chiefly by economic want. R. J. Dickson, *Ulster Emigration to Colonial America 1718–1775* (London, 1966), 27–28.

[17] Anglican ministers employed as missionaries by the Society for the Propagation of the Gospel were very well paid. See footnote 29. Swedish ministers were "provided with honorable situations" when they returned from an American mission. Acrelius, 369.

nently located in the New World. The development of educational institutions, however, was much slower. William Tennent's "Log College," established at Neshaminy, Pennsylvania, in 1727, did little before the Great Awakening to relieve the Presbyterians of their dependence upon New England and the British Isles for training their ministers. By 1738 Tennent had supplied just five men to the ministry, four of them his sons, and his seminary had become so entangled in the controversy over revivalism that its very existence was threatened.[18] Not until the Great Awakening saved Tennent's college and goaded the evangelical party to found the College of New Jersey in 1746 did the Presbyterian Church acquire an institution capable of preserving its independence.

The other churches lagged far behind the Presbyterians. None of them so much as attempted to found a college, and, until the late 1740s, their organization above the level of the congregations was rudimentary and dependent upon foreign authority. The episcopacy of the Church of England was represented in the Middle Colonies by two commissaries appointed by the Bishop of London, one at Philadelphia and the other in the city of New York. Their authority was small: they could hold visitations, call the clergy to informal meetings, report to the bishop on clerical conduct, and, in an emergency, temporarily suspend a wayward minister. Ordination and discipline, the two powers essential to ecclesiastical independence, remained the prerogative of the English hierarchy.[19]

At the beginning of the eighteenth century the Lutherans in the Middle Colonies—Dutch, Swedish, and German—were supervised by a provost, a deputy of the Archbishop of Sweden. With the exception of three occasions when the Archbishop permitted his agent to ordain a candidate for the ministry, the powers of this official were identical to those of an Anglican commissary. Sweden, however, thoughtlessly neglected to designate a provost between 1730 and 1748, leaving the American Lutherans with no government at all during the most crucial years of their growth.[20]

The Dutch and German Reformed ministers never had an overseeing official, such as a provost or a commissary. They were completely unorganized until after the Great Awakening, although the Dutch ministers in New York sometimes met informally to discuss matters of policy, as during the controversy over Frelinghuysen's revival in the 1720s. Twice the Classis of Amsterdam grudgingly granted the New York clergy the power to ordain a minister, but it was only in 1747, fol-

[18] Trinterud, 30, 71ff.
[19] Osgood, II, 23.
[20] Jacobs, 105–106; Acrelius, 364.

lowing a decade of petitioning, that the Classis permitted the Dutch and the German churches each to erect an independent Coetus.[21]

When the Lutherans established a synod the following year, all the churches in the Middle Colonies, except the Anglican, which did not receive a bishop until after the Revolution, were ecclesiastically independent of Europe. Only then, by ordaining and regulating their own clergy, did these churches begin to grapple effectively with the shortage of ministers.

Supplying their congregations with pastors was only the most immediate problem the churches faced in the Middle Colonies. An even greater obstacle was the difficulty every church experienced in preserving the authority of the clerical office. The social status of the American ministers, and especially their control over the congregations, had to be enforced if they were to perform effectively. But for reasons which were only partly understood at the time, respect for the cloth seemed to vanish in the free air of the New World.

This disregard for the status of the ministry was due in part, as many contemporaries perceived, to the fact that the young churches enjoyed none of the wealth and power of their established parents. In Europe the spiritual authority of the clerical office, imparted to it by the rite of ordination, was enforced by powerful ecclesiastical bodies which were financially secure and backed by the state. But in the Middle Colonies the Presbyterians alone had any ecclesiastical organization; only the Anglicans in the vicinity of New York City received encouragement from the civil authorities [22]; and, except for some individual congregations, all the churches were destitute. Stripped of the secular props that would have assured his authority, an American minister could count only on the sanctity of his office to command the respect and submission of the laity. In the words of Henry Melchior Muhlenberg: "A preacher must fight his way through with the sword of the Spirit alone . . . if he wants to be a preacher and proclaim the truth." [23]

The prestige of the clergy was eclipsed also by the influence the sectarians had attained in many parts of the Middle Colonies. The churches in Europe had cruelly persecuted the sects, but in America the shoe was often on the other foot, and the sects tormented their erstwhile oppressors by blackening the character of individual ministers and publicly denouncing them as "hireling preachers" who earned their bread by gulling the people. So low did the reputation of some clergymen sink under the brunt of this anticlericalism that parents dis-

[21] Boehm, 173; Corwin, 134, 136, 139.

[22] Osgood, II, 14–22; III, 117.

[23] Henry Melchior Muhlenberg, *The Journals of* . . . , Translated by Theodore G. Tappert and John W. Doberstein (Philadelphia, 1942), I, 67.

ciplined their children with stories of what the wicked parson would do if he caught them.[24]

The most ominous challenge to the ministers' authority, however, came not from the anticlericalism of the sects, nor even from the want of governmental support, but from the unruliness of their own congregations. Clergymen in the Middle Colonies found themselves at the mercy of the people they served. This perversion of the "normal" relationship between a pastor and his flock was intolerable to ministers who were accustomed to the freedom European clergymen enjoyed from the popular will of their parishioners. The withering of the clergy's control over the congregations seemed to poison the very roots of organized religion.

This displacement of pastoral power arose initially out of the circumstances surrounding the founding of congregations. Clergymen being so scarce in the Middle Colonies, particularly in the newer settlements, ministers were seldom present at the gathering of a congregation. Neighbors simply banded together, chose their officers, and, later on, at great sacrifice to themselves, bought a lot and erected a meetinghouse. All this was done without the authorization of the clergy; at most a minister would be called in to sanction the work of the laymen by installing church officers and celebrating communion.[25] By the time the laymen could afford to settle a minister permanently, they had secured an unbreakable hold over the affairs of the congregation. They owned the church property, they were liable for the debts incurred in purchasing a lot and building the meetinghouse, and, because of these responsibilities, they were unwilling to relinquish any of their control to the pastor.[26]

The minister's position in his congregation was further hampered by the control the laymen usually gained over his salary. No church in the Middle Colonies was independently wealthy: only in New York were tithes fixed by civil law[27]; the few congregations endowed with land often seem to have derived little income from it[28]; and only the Anglican missionaries employed by the Society for the Propagation of the

[24] *Ibid.*, I, 143, 221–222. For other examples of sectarian anticlericalism see *ibid.*, 96, 97, 122, 154, 204; John Holbrooke to Secretary S.P.G., Salem, N.J., Aug. 19, 1730, copy in H. F. Wallace Collection—New Jersey, Historical Society of Pennsylvania (HSP).

[25] For a particularly good description of the gathering of a congregation see Boehm, 157–158; also *Journal of the Presbyterian Historical Society*, III, 36, 86. For examples of the congregations' financial difficulties see Boehm, 241–242, 265–266, 281, 286, 413, 415–416, 457–458; Muhlenberg, *Journals*, I, 87, 94–95; William Becket Manuscript, 125, HSP.

[26] Boehm, 332.

[27] Osgood, II, 14–17.

[28] Perry, II, 223; Acrelius, 239–240, 253, 284, 289, 291–293, 297–298, 318, 328.

Gospel consistently received allowances from the mother country.[29] Nearly every congregation, therefore, supported its minister by a voluntary subscription to his salary, an arrangement irksome to layman and clergyman alike. Because most church people were poor, these salaries were small, difficult to collect, and the frequent cause of ill feeling between pastors and their flocks.[30]

Worst of all, the ministers' financial dependence crippled their authority over the congregations. Disciplining unruly parishioners could be costly because the chastened sometimes refused to pay their share of the pastor's salary. For the same reason, an entire congregation might be disrupted if some members took a dislike to the minister. His salary would diminish as his unpopularity spread until even the contented parishioners would turn against him for fear the burden of his support would fall upon them alone. Under these conditions, only a foolish minister, or an uncommonly courageous one, opposed the will of his people for long. Even preaching upon some unpleasant subject was risky: "I pay [the parson] by the year," explained one of Muhlenberg's parishioners, "but if his preaching does not please my taste, I'll go to another church where I can get it for nothing." The prevalence of such attitudes brought Muhlenberg to conclude, "it is easier to be a cowherd or a shepherd in many places in Germany than to be a preacher here, where every peasant wants to act the part of a patron of the parish, for which he has neither the intelligence nor the skill." [31]

The growth of popular control over the congregations was most noticeable in the German churches of Pennsylvania, where the clergy was too undermanned and too disorganized to offer much resistance. When Muhlenberg arrived in 1742, he immediately perceived how widely the American churches had deviated from the European norm: "In religious and church matters, each has the right to do what he pleases. . . . Everything depends on the vote of the majority." [32] The clergy was abashed by this drift toward lay rule. The one minister who

[29] Consequently, the Anglican clergy was the best paid ministry in the Middle Colonies. In 1724, for instance, the New York missionaries were given £50 sterling annually by the Society supplemented by a grant from the Assembly and voluntary contributions. The missionaries in New Jersey, Pennsylvania, and Delaware received between £60 and £70 sterling plus a small voluntary contribution from their congregations. Fulham Papers, XXXVI, 54–57. The Presbyterian ministers in Pennsylvania, by contrast, seem rarely to have received more than £60 local money from their congregations, often half of it in farm produce. Presbytery of Donegal Minutes, 128 129, 145, 181, PHS; Klett, 109.

[30] Salary squabbles are rife in the church records. For some examples see Presbytery of Donegal Minutes, 110–111, 141, 158–162, 164–165, 184, and Presbytery of Philadelphia Minutes, 59, 66, PHS; Perry, II, 152–153, 196, 217, 221–222; Acrelius, 257, 278.

[31] Muhlenberg, *Journals*, I, 100, 122, 251.

[32] *Ibid.*, I, 67.

dared to justify it, the Reformed pastor John Peter Miller, was scorned by his colleagues and took refuge in Conrad Beissel's cloister at Ephrata.[33] Other ministers fought stubbornly against the unruliness of their people, but they got nowhere until they organized themselves toward the end of the 1740s.[34]

Meanwhile the Presbyterian Church managed to keep its congregations under restraint by wielding the authority of the presbyteries. In 1737, for instance, when the vacant congregation at Paxton refused to receive Thomas Craighead, the supply sent by the Presbytery of Donegal, the Presbytery declared that the Paxton church had shown disrespect for the ministry and decreed that the congregation would receive no more supplies until it acknowledged its fault and promised "more kindly entertainment" to the ministers sent its way. The people yielded at once, and ministerial supplies were renewed.[35]

The restraining hand of the presbyteries, however, was lifted after Gilbert Tennent preached his famous Nottingham sermon in March, 1740. This utterance, the most significant of the Great Awakening in the Middle Colonies, justified, as never before, the popular tendencies within the congregations by defending the right of the layman to hear any minister he chose.[36] By accepting, rather than resisting, the increased independence of laymen in church affairs, Tennent unleashed a great popular upheaval. Responding to this passionate appeal, the laity revolted against their pastors and split their congregations, eventually rending the entire Presbyterian Church into Old and New Side.

The development of lay control in the Anglican congregations differed from the other churches in one significant respect. Because most Anglican clergymen in the Middle Colonies were missionaries employed by the Society for the Propagation of the Gospel, they received a handsome annuity from England, and consequently they were economically independent of their people. There were several instances of unpopular missionaries being hounded out of their pulpits by their congregations,[37] but, in general, clerical authority in the Church of England was somewhat better preserved than was the case elsewhere. Anglican ministers, for example, were able to preach against the Great Awakening, even while their people were swept up in it, without the dire consequences that overtook many Presbyterian opponents of the revival.[38]

[33] Boehm, 199–200, 254–256.

[34] For an example of one such struggle see *ibid.*, 198, 223–225, 281, 300–305, 324, 409–411, 430.

[35] Presbytery of Donegal Minutes, 137–138, 144, PHS.

[36] Gilbert Tennent, *The Danger of an Unconverted Ministry* (Philadelphia, 1740), 21.

[37] Perry, II, 217; Fulham Papers, VII, 174, 176.

[38] When the Presbyterian congregations split over the Great Awakening, some Old Side ministers asked to be dismissed chiefly because they could not subsist on their reduced salaries. This is clearly what happened in the case of John Elder and seems to have

Nevertheless, a minister who was not subsidized by the Society, such as the rector of Christ Church in Philadelphia, was vulnerable to the same popular pressures as the pastors of other denominations. In 1737, for example, a quarrel broke out in Christ Church which epitomizes the tensions existing in all the churches of the Middle Colonies. The vestry, representing the desires of a large part of the parish, tried to install Richard Peters as assistant to the pastor, Archibald Cummings. Cummings sternly opposed the vestry's wishes, but, seeking to avoid a bitter confrontation, he deferred the matter to the Bishop of London, arguing that the Bishop alone possessed the authority to nominate and appoint an American clergyman. The vestry then claimed the right to present candidates for the Bishop's licensing because the members of the parish had built the church themselves and supported its minister solely by their voluntary contributions. Some parishioners were even inclined to doubt whether the Bishop had any jurisdiction at all in the affair. Although the controversy ended with the vestry's complete submission to the authority of the hierarchy, Cummings' reflection on the Peters case echoed the misgivings of many ministers who had opposed the will of their people with less success:

> This and the like Disturbances might be prevented or easily cured had we a B[isho]p in these parts: Indeed in this Church 'tis no wonder Differences happen so often seeing there's no fixed Salary, but everything precarious, entirely at the will of the people; were it so in Old England I doubt not but in many parishes the like would frequently happen.[39]

There was a saying current in the middle of the eighteenth century which depicted Pennsylvania as a "hell for . . . preachers."[40] This description might well have included the Middle Colonies as a whole because everywhere the ministers worked under the severest handicaps. Their authority and social status had been drastically undermined by the lack of government support, by inadequate ecclesiastical organization, and, above all, by the unruliness of their own people, to say noth-

---

been the determining factor in the dismissals of Adam Boyd and John Thomson. Richard Webster, *A History of the Presbyterian Church in America* (Philadelphia, 1857), 454–455; Presbytery of Donegal Minutes, 230, 264, 286–289, PHS. This did not happen to the Anglican missionaries when many of their people abandoned them. Perry, II, 203–235 *passim*; Becket Manuscript, 101–112, 116–134, HSP.

[39] Fulham Papers, VII, 170, 175, 179, 189, 200, 201, 242; Hubertis Cummings, *Richard Peters: Provincial Secretary and Cleric 1704–1776* (Philadelphia, 1944), 13–23. An identical controversy arose in 1741 over establishing Peters as Cummings' successor. Fulham Papers, VII, 254, 291, 292, 300; Cummings, 42–70.

[40] "Pennsylvania is heaven for farmers, paradise for artisans, and hell for officials and preachers." Gottlieb Mittelberger, *Journey to Pennsylvania*, edited and translated by Oscar Handlin and John Clive (Cambridge, Mass., 1960), 48.

ing of the open contempt in which they were held by the sectarian population. At the same time, the scarcity of ministers, combined with the vastness of the country, greatly increased the physical burdens of their office. Most ministers traveled hundreds of miles through the wilderness every year preaching in vacant pulpits and administering to their own widely scattered flocks.[41]

When all these hardships are considered together, it is not surprising that the effectiveness of the ministry in the Middle Colonies was considerably reduced, and that a decline in religion among the churches inevitably resulted. Standards of religious observance suffered everywhere, in spite of the clergy's best efforts, and the religious needs of many church people went unfulfilled.

The journals of Henry Melchior Muhlenberg, written during his early ministry in Pennsylvania, illustrate how impossible it was to maintain European standards of worship. Because Muhlenberg's parishioners were so widely scattered over the countryside, his performance of routine duties, such as pastoral visits, inevitably fell short of standards set in Germany where congregations were huddled together in villages and the members could easily be visited several times a year. For similar reasons, Muhlenberg was forced to lower the requirements for confirmation. Children in Germany had to know their catechism by heart, but Muhlenberg could not supervise the instruction of the young so carefully, and he accepted them if they merely understood the most elementary doctrines. When ministering away from his own pulpit, Muhlenberg tailored his services to the ignorance of the people by shortening his sermons and spending the rest of the time catechizing his listeners. The celebration of communion in congregations where he did not personally know the qualifications of the members posed a particularly delicate problem of weeding out the ineligible. Muhlenberg's method was to cross-examine the deacons and elders about each applicant, hoping this would suffice, but he also soothed his ruffled conscience with the thought, "the Lord knoweth the heart." [42]

By these compromises with accepted standards, Muhlenberg actually made himself as effective as a clergyman could be in the Middle Colonies. Few ministers, however, possessed Muhlenberg's genius. They were generally men of only ordinary capacities, no better and no worse qualified than their European brethren.[43] But in America they

---

[41] For examples of the strenuousness and dangers of the clergy's peregrinations see William Becket Manuscript, 145, HSP; Perry, II, 126, 167, 179, 182; Muhlenberg, *Journals*, I, 183, 187–188, 210.

[42] *Ibid.*, I, 98, 118–120, 194–195, 235.

[43] The German churches were repeatedly scandalized by ministers fleeing an evil reputation in Europe, but the other churches seem to have done quite well in keeping unqualified men out of their pulpits. The Swedish Lutherans, Anglican, and Dutch Reformed ministries were selected with care by the European authorities, while the

faced extraordinary conditions which required unusual character, insight, and flexibility. Inevitably, many of them stumbled, and their blunders further impaired their effectiveness.

The most common kind of blunder, as one might expect, was the failure to adjust European usages to American conditions. Pastors who were unwilling to compromise with necessity risked destroying their usefulness altogether by alienating their congregations. Muhlenberg summarized their plight thus:

> Young beginners in this important office of the ministry do not have sufficient experience and possess more efficiency than insight. They start out vigorously and use European standards which do not always fit the complicated conditions in America. They usually stand alone without anyone with whom they might confer concerning the trials that occur. They are beset on every side by *spectateurs* and hostile lurkers who watch not only their whole work, but every little move they make, and treat even the smallest mistake as a criminal act.[44]

John Pugh, an Anglican missionary in Delaware, was such a stickler for European practices. In 1738 he wrote desperately to the Society for the Propagation of the Gospel asking whether he should adapt baptismal requirements to the demands of the settlers. He feared that his people, objecting to his rigid insistence upon qualified sponsors, would be driven over to the Presbyterians.[45] If a minister was to retain any effectiveness at all, therefore, he had to accept changes in religious observance.

It is not surprising that some ministers broke under the strain of such adjustments, while others became entangled in useless disputes with their parishioners, or, possessed by a sense of their inadequacy, fell into the dull, lifeless legalism which the revivalists were to exploit so pitilessly. Whatever the particular causes of individual failures, however, enough has been said to suggest that ministers in the Middle Colonies were considerably less effective than they probably would have been in Europe.

During the 1730s the impotence of the clergy brought organized religion to the brink of disintegration. When the ministry was unable to administer its office effectively, church institutions could no longer fulfill the religious needs of the laymen. This institutional breakdown be-

---

American presbyteries, though sometimes lax in disciplining their members, performed the same services for the Presbyterian church.

[44] Muhlenberg, *Journals*, I, 249.

[45] Perry, II, 201. The Anglican rite of baptism was a frequent source of difficulty for the missionaries. Burr, 173–174.

came ever more serious as immigration swelled the numbers of church people, thus multiplying the burdens of the undermanned ministry and resulting ultimately in widespread discontent. A spiritual crisis developed among the church people which enabled the revivalists to touch off the popular outbursts of the 1740s.

The breakdown of organized religion, by seeming to close off the normal approaches to heaven, was intolerable to most church people because they were still deeply concerned with the hereafter. Despite all that has been written about the secularization of thought during the early eighteenth century, salvation remained the ultimate goal in the lives of ordinary laymen.[46] Consequently, when church institutions failed, this fundamental religiosity was often deflected into unexpected channels, none of which were fully satisfying. Three such deflections were of especial importance in preparing the church people for the evangelical movements of the 1740s: a peculiar kind of religious indifference, legalism, and anticlericalism.

The most obvious symptom of religious malaise, to contemporaries of the Great Awakening, was the shocking growth of religious indifference. Although religious indifference assumed a variety of forms, ranging from hardened unbelief [47] to mere religious slothfulness,[48] there was one type of indifference which is considerably more important than the rest for understanding the mood of the church people before the Great Awakening. Many laymen no longer knew what religion to believe; they had come to doubt the validity of their own creed without having found a satisfying substitute. Such people were not indifferent in the strictest sense of the term because they were still spiritually concerned, and often deeply troubled, but in their uncertainty they frequently abandoned organized religion altogether and adopted a position indistinguishable, on the surface, from the slothfulness and hardened unbelief around them.

Among Muhlenberg's converts were several persons whose case histories illustrate this type of indifference in its purest form. The father of a young man in Muhlenberg's care, for example, told Muhlenberg that he had become skeptical of his Reformed beliefs and had allowed his children to grow up unbaptized because he was thoroughly confused by the multitude of denominations in Pennsylvania, each crying, "Here is Christ; we have the best medicine and the nearest road to heaven!" In spite of his own uncertainty, however, the father taught his children to read the Bible, hoping they would eventually be able to

---

[46] For a description of the religious conscience of the layman, see Ebenezer Pemberton, *Sermons on Several Subjects* (Boston, 1738), 17–19.

[47] For examples see Muhlenberg, *Journals*, I, 138; Perry, II, 161, 178.

[48] For example see John Pierson to Dr. Bearcroft, Salem, N.J., Oct. 30, 1744, copy in H. F. Wallace Collection—New Jersey, HSP.

choose for themselves the religion most in agreement with God's Word.[49]

This unwillingness to commit oneself to a denomination was frequently preceded by several changes in religion. Another of Muhlenberg's future parishioners, though raised in the Reformed Church, attended services with his Lutheran wife until he became disillusioned with the churches in general. He then tried some of the sects, but finding them equally unsatisfying, he resolved thereafter to hold aloof from all communions and seek peace only in Christ. The spiritual odyssey of Conrad Weiser, the famous Indian agent, followed a similar course. During the 1730s, Weiser progressed from Lutheranism, his ancestoral religion, through the Reformed faith to Conrad Beissel's monastery at Ephrata, which he later quit after a brief flirtation with the Moravians. Weiser no longer knew where to go when Muhlenberg met him in 1742, and for five years he lived in a religious limbo until Muhlenberg finally persuaded him again to receive communion in the Lutheran Church.[50]

In each case, the uncertainty which drove these men to adopt an attitude of outward indifference is closely related to the denominational heterogeneity of the Middle Colonies. The multiplicity of religions, more than any other single factor, appears to have provided the layman with the incentive to question his inherited faith. Opportunities for doubting one's beliefs were more limited in Europe and in New England where a dominant church either suppressed its rivals or relegated them to a distinctly inferior position. But in the Middle Colonies dozens of denominations competed on a more or less equal footing and the babble of creeds inevitably obscured the old certainties. Consequently, an unusually large number of settlers abandoned their beliefs and either joined another denomination or fell into a skeptical indifference.

Religious belief might have been better preserved had the Middle Colonies not been a veritable battleground of warring religions. All denominations were inflamed with a lust for proselytes. The Anglican missionaries, as instruments of their employers' grand design to bring the plantations under the sway of the Church of England,[51] were probably the most ambitious soul gatherers of any group of clergymen. Though their accomplishments fell far short of their objectives, they sustained their zeal and justified their salaries with glowing accounts of every little triumph over the "dissenters." [52] Nor were the Presbyteri-

[49] Muhlenberg, *Journals*, I, 236.

[50] *Ibid.*, I, 143–144, 102–103, 170, 172, 188–190.

[51] Carl Bridenbaugh, *Mitre and Sceptre; Transatlantic Faiths, Ideas, Personalities, and Politics 1689–1775* (New York, 1962), 26.

[52] For examples see Perry, II, 161–162, 170–171, 189–190, 194.

ans remiss in propagating their version of the Gospel. During the 1730s, for example, the Anglicans in the Pequea Valley of Pennsylvania pleaded desperately for a missionary to do battle with the Presbyterians who were leaving no stone unturned to draw them into their communion.[53]

The sects, rather than the churches, were the most successful proselytizers. Not only did the sectarians dominate many parts of the Middle Colonies in wealth and prestige, but the confused and disillusioned church people were unusually easy prey. Numerous immigrants from the British Isles quickly forsook their churches and joined the Quakers, while many Germans, impressed with the prestige of the Friends, became indolent in the practice of their own religion.[54] The greatest inroads among the German church people, however, were made by the pietistic sects, whose missionary efforts led directly to the German Awakening of the 1740's. The Mennonites too, though less zealous for converts than either the Quakers or the pietists, seldom shunned the opportunity to entangle an occasional stray in their nets.[55] Even unbelievers and "deists" joined the competition for proselytes, causing more than one Anglican priest to complain of "bad men" who promoted infidelity and profaneness throughout the country by sowing "loose and Atheistical" principles.[56]

It was difficult to avoid having one's religious beliefs challenged, because so many laymen, particularly from the sects, dabbled in missionary work among their neighbors. These zealots employed the crudest techniques, ridicule and insult, to destroy the faith of their victims. Typical of the heckling the church people endured was the scrape of an elderly Englishman with a local Quaker magnate: upon hearing his neighbor had just been baptized, the Friend jeered, "Why didn't thee desire the Minister rather to piss upon thy Head . . .; that would have been of more effect." Such an incident, though trivial in itself, could discourage even a devout person if it became an everyday experience. Muhlenberg tells of an old couple, staunch Lutherans in Germany, who were so ridiculed by their sectarian neighbors in Pennsylvania that by the time he found them "their candlewick scarcely glimmer[ed]." Not all laymen, of course, submitted to these attacks quietly. Whenever the sectarians challenged Frederick Stengel, one of Muhlenberg's most ardent parishioners, and provoked him to argument, he was so heated in the defense of his religion that they eventually learned to leave him alone. Disputatious fellows like Stengel lived dangerously, however, for, as Muhlenberg observed, if the sectarians

---

[53] *Ibid.*, II, 183.
[54] John Holbrook to Secretary S.P.G., Salem, N.J., Dec. 5, 1729, copy in H. E. Wallace Collection—New Jersey, HSP; Muhlenberg, *Journals*, I, 197.
[55] Smith, 547; Muhlenberg, *Journals*, I, 127–128, 144.
[56] Perry, II, 195–196, 177; William Becket Manuscript, 53, HSP.

found someone who was not solidly grounded in doctrine, they would relentlessly entangle him in his own arguments and lead him away from the church.[57]

Indentured servitude and religious intermarriage also encouraged lay proselytizing. An indentured servant, cut off from the fellowship of his co-religionists, was all but helpless before the indoctrination of his master. Such was the experience of the Lutheran, Michael Walker, for many years the servant of a prominent Friend. Walker was often tempted to join the Quakers and attended their meetings regularly, but eventually his earlier religious training prevailed, and, when freed, he became a Lutheran schoolmaster. Muhlenberg relates several other cases of Anglicans or Lutherans, indented to sectarians, who also survived to join his congregations.[58] One can presume, however, without stretching the imagination, that numerous church people succumbed to the propaganda of their employers and abandoned their original faith. Matrimonial converts were common, too, despite the strictures of every denomination against religious intermarriage. In 1741, for example, an Anglican missionary lamented the inroads the Presbyterians were making on his parish by marrying his young people, and Muhlenberg mentions several persons who married into the Lutheran Church.[59]

Religious intermarriage, indentured servitude, and the daily clashes with sectarians, therefore, all combined to undermine the religious beliefs of the church people. At the same time, the inefficacy of church institutions, and the economic burden of their support,[60] severely strained the layman's loyalty to his denomination. Unable to cope with such pressures, hundreds of people abandoned the churches. Many changed their beliefs and joined another communion, while countless others, hopelessly bewildered but still spiritually concerned, quit organized religion altogether.

Meanwhile, the laymen who remained steadfast in the practice of their religion were subjected to a legalism which was virtually a compromise with indifference. Many ministers, aware of the pressures driving the laymen away from the churches, sought to preserve the allegiance of their parishioners by easing the requirements for Christian fellowship. They made few demands upon the inward spirituality of their people, being content merely if their congregations attended worship regularly and were correct in doctrine and outward behavior.

This was the policy, for example, of Jedediah Andrews, pastor of the Presbyterian church in Philadelphia, whose legalistic preaching Benjamin Franklin immortalized in the pages of his *Autobiography*.

[57] Muhlenberg, *Journals*, I, 198, 151, 232.
[58] *Ibid.*, I, 202, 205, 213, 234.
[59] Perry, II, 215; Muhlenberg, *Journals*, I, 202, 241.
[60] Perry, II, 201. Presbytery of Donegal Minutes, 4, PHS.

Franklin, who at the time was nominally a Presbyterian, occasionally went to hear Andrews, though with growing reluctance because: "His discourses were chiefly either polemic arguments, or explications of the peculiar doctrines of our sect, and were all to me very dry, uninteresting, and unedifying, since not a single moral principle was inculcated or enforc'd, their aim seeming to be rather to make us good Presbyterians rather than good citizens." Eventually Andrews hit upon a text, which Franklin thought "could not miss of having some morality," but to his disgust Andrews confined the sermon to five points only: "1. Keeping holy the Sabbath day. 2. Being diligent in reading the holy Scriptures. 3. Attending duly the public worship. 4. Partaking of the Sacrament. 5. Paying due respect to God's ministry." This was not the useful, social morality Franklin had in mind, and he "attended his preaching no more." [61]

Though we may sympathize with Franklin's disillusionment, Andrews' legalistic preaching was, nevertheless, a necessary response to the plight of his people. His congregation, like many in the Middle Colonies, was a mixture of "divers Nations of different sentiments," [62] and it was forever threatened from within by the disintegration of religious belief and from without by sectarian criticism. Under these conditions, Andrews had little choice but to inculcate and defend the "peculiar doctrines" of Presbyterianism if he expected to hold such a group together and bolster its wavering faith. He had to insist, furthermore, that his people perform at least the minimum religious duties—read the Bible, attend church, etc.—if he was to prevent many of them from becoming outwardly indifferent.

Legalistic preaching, therefore, may not have been very inspired, but, because it dealt directly with many of the problems undermining church religion, it probably helped stave off a complete disintegration of religious belief. By preaching doctrine and good behavior, ministers, such as Andrews, instilled their congregations with a sense of denominational identity and pride. No doubt, too, the spiritual needs of some colonists were completely satisfied by this easy-going formalism, while others, inwardly shaken by the religious anarchy around them, suppressed their doubts and accepted legalism for want of anything better. Consequently, until the revivalists offered a more fulfilling alternative, legalism prevailed in congregations throughout the Middle Colonies.[63]

[61] Benjamin Franklin, *The Autobiography of . . .* (New York, 1950), 92.

[62] Jedediah Andrews to Benjamin Colman, Apr. 7, 1729, Ebenezer Hazard Manuscript Notes, I, PHS.

[63] For the prevalence of legalism in the Presbyterian Church see the testimonies of the antirevivalists against it: John Thomson, *The Government of the Church of Christ* (Philadelphia, 1741), 120–124; George Gillespie, *A Sermon against Divisions in Christ's Churches* (Philadelphia, 1740), Appendix, i–ii. In 1738 J. B. Boehm was accused of insufferable dullness by some of his people. Boehm, 261, 314.

Though some people found solace in legalism, other laymen were unhappy with its cold formalism, which could not satisfy the inward needs created by the spiritual crisis they were undergoing. Persons who were baffled by the variety of religions in the Middle Colonies, and had come to doubt their beliefs, could not be consoled by doctrines and rules. When their religion was reduced to a set of dogmas, it appeared to these troubled souls as just another creed, with only its familiarity to recommend it over the teachings of other denominations. Few settlers were qualified to undertake the comparative examination of theologies needed to decide whether their creed was the one most in accord with God's Word. Nor were they capable of making so weighty an intellectual decision without a deeper emotional affirmation. By failing to supply that emotional affirmation, legalism probably intensified the uncertainty of numerous laymen.

Because legalism was unable to mollify the spiritual confusion of the laity, there was nothing to prevent the discontent of the church people from spreading during the decade before the Great Awakening. John Peter Miller observed that by 1730 many church people in Pennsylvania were "so confused they no longer knew what to believe." [64] In a sermon in 1733, T. J. Frelinghuysen described the religious uncertainty he had detected among the settlers of New Jersey: "I would be religious, did I only know which religion is the true one; but how shall I who am young, arrive at a correct conclusion? One pursues this course, and another that—one professes this belief, and another that, and a third rejects both?" [65] The Anglican missionaries commented frequently, throughout these years, on the spiritual restlessness of the population. Robert Weyman, for example, noted with some surprise a "general disposition" of Pennsylvanians to hear him out, "notwithstanding the Prejudices they had been brought up in against the Church of England." Other missionaries in Pennsylvania and Delaware also reported "dissenters of all persuasions" flocking to their services.[66] More and more laymen, it seems, were ignoring denominational lines and looking for solace in any religion that was close at hand.

The ugliest symptom of the church people's uneasiness, however, was the growth of anticlericalism within the congregations. Reading through the church records of the 1730s, one becomes increasingly aware of a deep hostility on the part of many congregations toward their pastors, a hostility manifested in the readiness of laymen to exaggerate and denounce the pettiest professional and moral failures of the

[64] *Chronicon Ephratense*, 70.
[65] Theodorus Jacobus Frelinghuysen, *Sermons by . . .*, Translated by William Demarest (New York, 1856), 168–169.
[66] Perry, II, 162, 196, 197.

ministry.[67] The existence of this undercurrent of contempt for the clergy is confirmed by the Great Awakening itself, when one congregation after another openly aired its hatred, blackened its pastor's character, and tried to turn him out of his pulpit.[68] Historians have missed the full significance of this bitter censoriousness by attributing it simply to the barbarizing effect of the frontier or, in the case of the Scotch-Irish, to "racial" characteristics. But if we accept these denunciations of the clergy at face value, they are obviously an unequivocal expression of the laymen's profound discontent with their ministers.

That discontent can be traced ultimately to the inability of the clergy to deal with the needs of their people. In the eyes of ordinary laymen, the clergy had failed to provide the institutional stability they so desperately desired. Church members were disturbed by the puzzling weakness of clerical authority and distressed by the ineffectual performance of their pastors. Preaching seemed to have declined too, because doctrines which had been accepted as self-evident in the Old World, now often appeared to be no more worthy of belief than the creeds of the most fantastic sects. The clergy's insistence that their parishioners give them a comfortable maintenance, after the laymen had already sacrificed so much to establish the congregations, deepened popular resentment. Encouraged, perhaps, by the anticlericalism of the sects, the laity's frustration came to focus, half-consciously, upon the simplest possible explanation of these vexing conditions: their pastors were incompetent, avaricious, and morally degenerate.

Although the failures attributed to the clergy were exaggerated and often unavoidable, the latent hostility they engendered in the congregations provided much of the raw emotion necessary to the success of the Great Awakening as a popular movement. When revivalists, such as Gilbert Tennent and George Whitefield, publicly condemned their ministerial opponents as "unregenerate," blamed them for the languishing condition of the congregations, and urged the laity to abandon them,[69] hundreds of laymen thought they had found the answer to their religious predicament. "Unregenerate" ministers suddenly became the scapegoats for all the bitterness arising from the breakdown of religious institutions and beliefs. By striking down the "pharisee

---

[67] The Minutes of the Presbytery of Donegal are the best source for studying this phenomenon because they are the most thorough. See especially the disputes between William Orr and the Nottingham congregation, 13–22, 67–81, 85–96, 99–109, 112–115, 119–121. A similar hostility toward J. P. Boehm can be detected throughout his collected letters, but it is not very evident in Muhlenberg's *Journals*.

[68] See Presbytery of Donegal Minutes, 192ff, and Presbytery of Philadelphia Minutes, 78–80, 82–87, 97–99, PHS.

[69] Tennent, *Danger of an Unconverted Ministry*; George Whitefield, *Journals* (London, 1960), 345–346, 350–351.

preachers," many people felt they could free themselves from the unbearable psychological burden of their years in the Middle Colonies.[70]

The Great Awakening, however, was only incidentally a crusade against an unregenerate ministry. The central teaching of the revivalists, their doctrine of the New Birth, led them to a more enduring solution to the problems we have been discussing as constituting the "crisis of the churches" in the Middle Colonies. Their reinterpretation of conversion as an emotional experience provided the laity with an experimental basis for religious belief. A person experiencing the New Birth could know with some certainty that he was on the path to salvation, no matter what his denominational creed.[71] And when the New Birth was wedded to a specific set of doctrines, such as Calvinism, these doctrines, too, were empirically reaffirmed.[72] By resolving the layman's crisis of faith, the evangelists not only brought hundreds of people back into organized religion, but they also restored some of the prestige and moral authority the clergy had lacked before 1740. Pastors could once again minister to the innermost religious needs of their flocks, thus removing the most dangerous source of the tensions that had existed between ministers and their people. Once these tensions subsided, and the methods of the Great Awakening became common practice, the churches in the Middle Colonies could be rebuilt independent of the Old World and rooted in the peculiar conditions of America.

The Great Awakening in the Middle Colonies, therefore, was intimately bound up with the process of immigration and settlement. It arose out of the difficulties the churches experienced in establishing their religious institutions and maintaining their religious beliefs in a perplexing and often hostile environment. Before the 1740's the church people were confused Europeans, dependent upon the institutions and outlook they had left in the Old World. By 1750 this was, in

---

[70] Anticlericalism does not seem to have been a significant factor in the German Awakening, probably because there were so few ministers for the Moravian evangelists to oppose. Its importance for the Awakening among the Presbyterians, however, has been drastically underestimated. Condemning and overthrowing "unregenerate" ministers may have been more important than conversion to many laymen. Both conversion and anticlerical revolt served to remove the sense of guilt which had arisen among the church people as a result of the tensions we have been describing. Conversion purified the acknowledged sinner by giving him an experience of the grace of God. Anticlericalism operated more crudely, but it too relieved the individual of his burden of guilt by transferring it to the minister who was then denounced and, if possible, driven away. If this is an accurate interpretation of the significance of anticlericalism, the immediate emotional and psychological impact of the Great Awakening was broader and deeper than the rather small number of conversions would indicate.

[71] This was essentially the approach of Whitefield and Zinzendorf.

[72] Gilbert Tennent and the New Brunswick evangelists generally took this tack.

general, no longer true. The Great Awakening had provided them with a set of principles that could reconcile their Old World heritage with their New World experience.

"The Grand Prophet," Hugh Bryan: Early Evangelicalism's Challenge to the Establishment and Slavery in the Colonial South

LEIGH ERIC SCHMIDT

Whitefield's evangelical message sometimes carried radical implications that he never intended. Although he strongly favored the conversion of African slaves to Christianity, he also used the income from a slave plantation in America to help support his orphanage in Georgia, a colony that prohibited slavery for the first two decades after its founding in the early 1730s. In 1740–1741 he had a major impact on Charleston, South Carolina, but when his most ardent disciple, Hugh Bryan, began to transform that message into a call for the abolition of slavery, the planters overwhelmingly rejected this phase of the transatlantic revival.

Leigh Eric Schmidt recounts this dramatic story, which began to unfold shortly after the September 1739 Stono Rebellion, the most violent slave rising in the entire history of the mainland colonies before the nineteenth century. This upheaval reminded the planters just how brittle their society was. A devastating fire in Charleston in November 1740 convinced Bryan that the wrath of God was about to descend upon the land unless whites repented of their sins. He identified slavery as the province's most obvious form of turpitude. A man given to visions and prophecies, Bryan evidently believed that he was the new Moses sent to free God's most oppressed people. Apparently accompanied only by his brother, he hoped to prove that God had selected him for this role by trying to part the waters of an unnamed river, which refused to cooperate. He nearly drowned. Although his recantation readmitted him to polite society, he continued to believe in the conversion of slaves—without abolition. In many respects the origins of

Reprinted by permission from Leigh Eric Schmidt, " 'The Grand Prophet, Hugh Bryan: Early Evangelicalism's Challenge to the Establishment and Slavery in the Colonial South," *South Carolina Historical Magazine*, 87 (1986), 238–250.

African-American Christianity in the Lower South derived from the activities of the Bryan family. The slaves began to embrace a largely apolitical evangelicalism that was, however, quite distinct from the Low Church Anglican piety of most of their owners.

In the early 1740s those in authority in South Carolina, as elsewhere in the colonies, faced severe challenges. The troubles of the leading South Carolinians, however, were doubly acute. They faced both a dramatic upsurge in slave conspiracies and revolts as well as a growing group of awakened and disorderly dissenters. These domestic threats combined with the fear of foreign invasion, or at least subversion, from Spanish Florida to make civil and ecclesiastical authorities in South Carolina all the more uneasy and vulnerable. As Rhys Isaac has observed in connection with Virginia, so too it was with South Carolina: "a general crisis of authority" had come to pass.[1] Both religious and political establishments were cracking, if not yet crumbling. With the advent of the Awakening in the southern colonies these cracks within the colonial social structure were widened and deepened. By the 1740s two primary institutions of the colonial South—slavery and Anglicanism—were receiving their first concerted challenge. One early evangelical, planter, and prophet—Hugh Bryan—embodied this dual threat.

Few would argue that Hugh Bryan was a major evangelical figure or even an exemplary one. Indeed, not many would find reason to bother arguing about him one way or the other.[2] Though Bryan was confess-

---

[1] Rhys Isaac, "Religion and Authority: Problems of the Anglican Establishment in Virginia in the Era of the Great Awakening and the Parsons' Cause," *William and Mary Quarterly* 30 (1973):5. Isaac's work has been of primary importance in establishing the contours of the evangelical challenge to the Anglican social order. See also his "Evangelical Revolt: The Nature of the Baptists' Challenge to the Traditional Order in Virginia, 1765 to 1775," *William and Mary Quarterly* 31 (1974):345–368 and *The Transformation of Virginia, 1740–1790* (Chapel Hill, 1982).

[2] Bryan has received only cursory notice in the historiography. For nineteenth-century interpretations, see Joseph Tracy, *The Great Awakening* (Boston, 1845), pp. 240–241; Edward McCrady, *The History of South Carolina under the Royal Government, 1719–1776* (New York, 1879), pp. 238–243; and George Howe, *History of the Presbyterian Church in South Carolina*, 2 vols. (Columbia, 1870–1883), 1:238–246. This literature tends to view Bryan simply as "greatly excited and diseased" (McCrady, p. 241; Howe, p. 244). More recently Bryan has received notice in, for example, S. Charles Bolton, *Southern Anglicanism: The Church of England in Colonial South Carolina* (Westport, Conn., 1982), pp. 55, 117; Harvey H. Jackson, "The Carolina Connection: Jonathan Bryan, His Brothers, and the Founding of Georgia, 1733–1752," *Georgia Historical Quarterly* 68 (1984):147–172; David S. Lovejoy, *Religious Enthusiasm in the New World: Heresy to Revolution* (Cambridge, Mass., 1985), pp. 200–201; David T. Morgan, "The Great Awakening in South Carolina, 1740–1775" *South Atlantic Quarterly* 70 (1971):601; Robert M. Weir, *Colonial South Carolina: A History* (Millwood, N.Y., 1983), pp. 186–187; M. Eugene Sirmans, *Colonial South Carolina: A Political History, 1663–1773* (Chapel Hill, 1966), pp. 231–232; Herbert Aptheker, *American Negro Slave Revolts*, 5th ed. (New York, 1983), p. 190n; and William

edly a minor *persona* within the Awakening movement as a whole, his story is highly instructive, especially for the southern phase of the revival and particularly when examined in light of Rhys Isaac's ethnographic history. Isaac, in studying Virginian society of this period, has tried to grasp hold of figures in movement—what he describes simply as the exploration of *"people doing things."* He has sought to unravel "knots of dramatic encounter" and in doing so to explicate the meanings of various social actions and to discern the underlying patterns of social relations and authority that inhere in the drama.[3] Out of each knot Isaac weaves a subtly variegated and finely textured tapestry. Within this historiographical context, Hugh Bryan presents a possible node; his prophetic actions constitute a knot of dramatic encounter. Through him it should be possible to depict how early evangelicalism challenged the Anglican establishment and slavery in South Carolina particularly and in the southern colonies broadly.

In his second and most important trip to the American colonies the wayfaring evangelist George Whitefield arrived in South Carolina in January 1740. Among his early converts there was Hugh Bryan, a forty-one-year-old planter of considerable station and wealth and a colonel in the militia. With his wife Catherine and his brother Jonathan, Bryan was counted among the most zealous supporters and closest friends of the grand itinerant in the southern colonies. Though Catherine died later that year, the brothers kept in close contact with Whitefield and were among the most prominent backers of his orphanage, Bethesda, which soon became a notorious enclave of dissent on the outskirts of Savannah, Georgia. In fact, Hugh would even house the orphans for awhile when Georgia seemed endangered by the Spanish.[4] On the surface an orphanage would appear a benign and orderly institution, but Whitefield had brought in the New Englander Jonathan Barber, a renowned cohort of James Davenport, to provide ministerial leadership and inspiration at Bethesda. With Barber at its helm, the Bryans connected with it, and Whitefield collecting mone-

---

Howland Kenney, III, "Alexander Garden and George Whitefield: The Significance of Revivalism in South Carolina, 1738–1741," *this Magazine* 71 (1970):13–15. Of these, the Kenney article offers the best analysis of the challenge posed by evangelical revivalism to the Anglican establishment in S.C. Bryan's religious meetings with the slaves are not really assessed in any of them. Bryan and the evangelical community of which he was a part, however, are the focus of Harvey H. Jackson's forthcoming article "Hugh Bryan and the Evangelical Movement in Colonial South Carolina" in the *William and Mary Quarterly.* The analysis of Bryan offered by Jackson complements the discussion given here.

[3] Isaac, *Transformation of Virginia*, pp. 324, 332. "The storyteller's art, informed by ethnographic perspectives," Isaac further suggests, "must be developed as a vital part of social history" (p. 340). This is one tentative (and short) attempt at such a development.

[4] E. Merton Coulter, ed., *The Journal of William Stephens, 1741–1745*, 2 vols. (Athens, 1959), 1:116.

tary support and imposing a monastic discipline, the orphanage was a bastion of religious ecstacy, a center for the evangelical disruption of Anglicanism in Georgia and South Carolina. Bryan's involvement in an orphanage, which appeared to its critics to be in the hands of "a Parcell of Wild Enthusiasts," was only one early fruit of his conversion.[5]

In late November 1740 Bryan penned a controversial letter that made its way into the *South Carolina Gazette* after being edited by Whitefield. The letter lifted Bryan into the public eye and gained him with Whitefield and the printer warrants for their arrest: the charge, "libelling the king and . . . the clergy." [6] Inspired by a fire that destroyed much of Charlestown in November 1740, the letter warned of still more severe judgments to come and castigated the established clergy, those "negligent Watchmen," as corrupt and unconverted. Couched insistently in the phrases of Ezekiel and Jeremiah, Bryan's epistle urged all to repentance, but singled out especially the ecclesiastical and civil authorities—even the king—and enjoined them all to "humble themselves." "The Lord hath spoken," Bryan assured his fellow Carolinians, "His Drought hath spoken; His Diseases inflicted on us and our Cattle have spoken; the Insurrections of our Slaves have spoken . . . the yet later dreadful Fire of Charles-Town hath spoken Terror: And if we regard not this to lay it to Heart, humble ourselves, and repent truly of our Sins; the just God will yet pour out upon us more terrible Vials of his Wrath." [7] This prophetic stand was harsh and threatening. The Anglican Commissary Alexander Garden saw the missive as the latest Whitefieldian blast at the establishment and its clerics and denounced it as "a scurrilous Libel." Indeed, one Anglican, perhaps Garden, saw Bryan's letter as having the "malicious Intention to slander and defame the Clergy of this Province, and thereby prejudice their People against them, and defeat their Labours." [8] Garden and his fellows did what they could to curb Whitefield and his disciples, but arrest as a means evidently came to nought. The culprits were

[5] Ibid., 1:30. For the Bethesda group's badgering of one Anglican minister, Christopher Orton, see ibid., 1:29–34. They denounced him as unconverted and pronounced "Damnation" upon him for "preaching false Doctrine"—a censoriousness familiar to Barber from his days with Davenport and common to the extreme New Lights generally. For their pains Jonathan Barber and his compeer James Habersham were arrested and fined. On Bethesda, see also Neil J. O'Connell, "George Whitefield and Bethesda Orphan-House," *Georgia Historical Quarterly* 54 (1970):41–62.

[6] George Whitefield, *Letters of George Whitefield: For the Period 1734–1742* (Edinburgh, 1976), p. 231. See also pp. 229–230, 238–239, 414, 425–426 for other letters relating to the Bryans.

[7] *South Carolina Gazette*, Jan. 1, 1741. Whitefield and Bryan were not alone in their prophetic interpretation of the fire. Revival supporter and dissenting minister Josiah Smith expounded a similar view from his pulpit in Charlestown. See his *The Burning of Sodom, with its Moral Causes* (Boston, 1741).

[8] "Letters to the Bishop of London from the Commissaries in South Carolina," *South Carolina Historical Magazine* 78 (1977):300; *South Carolina Gazette*, Jan. 15, 1741.

released and no sentence is recorded. This initial intimidation was to little avail; Whitefield would return and Bryan's early jeremiad was mere prelude to grander revelations.

During the following year Bryan's new faith took another turn; he began to gather together "frequent and great Assemblies of Negroes . . . to the Terror of some, and to the Disturbance of many." [9] In his support for such religious meetings, Bryan revealed his deep concern for the enslaved. He himself had been taken captive by Native Americans in 1715 during the Yamassee War and had been "disposed of as a slave" for "near a year." [10] Perhaps these trials contributed to his unusual empathy for the slaves of his society. Yet not until the coming of the revival did Bryan's concern become a pressing desire for slave conversion. Again he found inspiration in Whitefield's preaching and writing. Particularly significant was a letter Whitefield published in 1740 addressed to "the Inhabitants of Maryland, Virginia, North and South-Carolina." In it Bryan's mentor proclaimed God's quarrel with the slaveholders of the South for their "abuse of and cruelty to the poor negroes." Whitefield even wondered aloud why the slaves had "not more frequently risen up in arms against their owners"—especially against those planters who were "monsters of barbarity." Whitefield's bewilderment must have been particularly exasperating to white South Carolinians, who, for the last five years, had already endured unusually frequent slave insurrections and conspiracies. While Whitefield did not support such rebellion—"I heartily pray GOD, they may never be permitted to get the upper hand"—he nonetheless concluded that if such insurrection came to pass "all good men must acknowledge the judgment would be just." On this and other points he waxed prophetic: the blood of slaves spilled by their owners "will ascend up to heaven against you," and damned souls, too, would cry out against the slaveholders who failed to bring the Gospel to the bondsmen.

This spiritual concern for the souls of the slaves was of preeminent importance to Whitefield. He informed the planters that Christianizing their slaves was their duty, but assured them that true Christianity would only make the blacks better slaves. "I challenge the world," he said, "to produce a single instance of a negroe's being made a thorough Christian, and thereby made a worse servant; it cannot be." [11] Hugh

---

[9] J. H. Easterby, ed., *The Colonial Records of South Carolina: The Journal of the Commons House of Assembly, 1736–1750,* 9 vols. (Columbia, 1951–1962), 3:381.

[10] On Bryan's own enslavement, see John Conder and Thomas Gibbons, eds., *Living Christianity delineated, in the Diaries and Letters of Two Eminently Pious Persons lately deceased; viz. Mr. Hugh Bryan and Mrs. Mary Hutson* (Boston, 1809), p. 2. This work was originally published in London in 1760 and contains valuable material on Bryan's conversion and spiritual life, though it breaks off in Oct. 1741 and only resumes in the year 1751. Hence it carefully excludes Bryan's most prophetic period.

[11] George Whitefield, "A Letter to the Inhabitants of Maryland, Virginia, North and South-Carolina" in *The Works of the Reverend George Whitefield,* 4 vols. (London, 1771)

Bryan was undoubtedly profoundly influenced by his teacher's view of slavery, especially Whitefield's prophetic statements and his call for slave conversion. But by 1742 Bryan seemed poised to confute the other side of Whitefield's conviction: that is, that evangelicalism would produce slave docility and actually strengthen the institution of slavery. By the same token Bryan appeared about to confirm Anglican and gentry fears of Awakening radicalism.

Bryan's "frequent and great Assemblies of Negroes" were indeed disturbing. They were also illegal and were quickly perceived as having "the most dangerous Consequence to the Peace and Safety of this Province." [12] To an anxious gentry, any such religious meetings among the slaves boded ill: as one South Carolinian described the fears of his countrymen, "Insurrection, Murder and Blood . . . This is what may be expected from converting Negroes!" [13] In the wake of the Stono Rebellion of 1739 South Carolina's white denizens were all the more wary of slave insurrection, and in 1740 the legislature tightened the laws constraining slave meetings and slave education. In this context Bryan's religious gatherings were easily transmuted from revival meetings into "Cabals of Negro's" in which "instead of teaching them the Principles of Christianity" he was "filling their Head with a Parcel of Cant-Phrases, Trances, Dreams, Visions, and Revelations, and something still worse, and which Prudence forbids me to name." [14] Bryan confirmed the fears of his fellows when his teachings became still more prophetic and apocalyptic. "The cry is, Repent, turn you, now is the accepted time," he insisted in October 1741, "now is the day of salvation." [15] Convinced of the imminence of judgment, his zeal was peaking. Evangelical fervor and, some of his contemporaries would add, bad fevers were about to give way to "enthusiastic Prophecies"; Bryan's "weak crazy tabernacle" was to rise a monument of prophetic strength. Soon "he went on," Eliza Lucas confided to a friend, "from one step to another till he came to working miracles and lived for several days in

---

4:37–41. Garden did not let this letter go unanswered. He thought Whitefield could well be "indicted for meddling" and for endangering "the Peace and Safety of the Community." He even gibed that the Carolinians' treatment of their slaves was more humane than Whitefield's "Abuse and Cruelty to the poor Orphans under your Care." See Garden, *Six Letters to the Rev. Mr. George Whitefield* (Boston, 1740), pp. 50–52. For a discussion of Whitefield's views about slavery, see Stephen J. Stein, "George Whitefield on Slavery: Some New Evidence," *Church History* 42 (1973):243–256.

[12] Easterby, *Records*, 3:381.

[13] *South Carolina Gazette*, July 23, 1737. The writer, however, believed that the right Christianity could still work as an agent of social control among the slaves. On the fears of the whites during the period, see Winthrop D. Jordan's chapter, "Anxious Oppressors," in *White Over Black: American Attitudes Toward the Negro, 1550–1812* (Chapel Hill, 1968).

[14] *South Carolina Gazette*, April 24, 1742.

[15] Conder and Gibbons, eds., *Living Christianity delineated*, p. 50.

the woods barefooted and alone and with his pen and Ink to write down his prophecies." [16]

Finally Bryan "sent a whole Volume of his Prophecies" that he had received in the wilderness from "an Angel of Light" to the Speaker of the Commons House of Assembly. The effect of his "horrid Blasphemy and Nonsense" upon the government was marked.[17] Officials took especial alarm at Bryan's vision of apocalypse in which he prophesied "the Destruction of Charles Town and Deliverance of the Negroes from their Servitude." [18] Destruction would come "by fire and sword" and was "to be executed by the Negroes before the first day of next month." Fear swept through the province as the white inhabitants "dreaded the consiquence of his prophecys coming to the ears of the African Hosts." [19] It was even rumored that he and his "African Hosts" were stockpiling munitions and were "encamp'd in the Wilderness" in preparation for this apocalyptic battle in which the slaves were to be God's forces avenging the wayward and in which they would set themselves at liberty. By February 1742 "the grand Prophet" had the province deeply disturbed and anxious.[20]

Yet Bryan's radicalism was short-lived and soon terror turned to relieved laughter. The South Carolina Assembly was quick to act in order to stop him. Once again Bryan's arrest was ordered and this time officers were sent after him. When they arrived to apprehend him and perhaps to disperse what they believed to be a slave encampment, instead of finding a pack of religious rebels, they discovered a solitary and defeated visionary. "A strange Revolution," they found, "had come over our Prophet." [21] Having earlier sent the Assembly prophecies of its doom and details of the impending judgment, "the grand Prophet" now begged forgiveness. He sought reintegration into white society before it was too late and confessed his former visions to have been "a Delusion of Satan," that "all his Prophecies had been inspired, not by

---

[16] Elise Pinckney, ed., *The Letterbook of Eliza Lucas Pinckney, 1739–1762* (Chapel Hill, 1972), p. 30; Easterby *Records*, 4:72; on Bryan's "flux and fever," see Conder and Gibbons, eds., *Living Christianity delineated*, pp. 49–50 and Whitefield, *Letters*, p. 239. In the Awakening as a whole a close connection was seen between bodily weakness—particularly fevers—and spiritual vision. This was the case with itinerants James Davenport, Andrew Croswell, Samuel Buell, and Whitefield as well as the Tennents. To opposers, this connection was one more sign that Awakening enthusiasm was disease and delusion.

[17] Easterby, *Records*, 3:461; *Boston Weekly Post-Boy*, May 3, 1742. The latter includes one of the more extensive accounts of Bryan's prophetic actions. Efforts to locate his volume of prophecies were unsuccessful. The journal may never have been saved in the first place for evidence by the Assembly, but destroyed expeditiously, since its contents were considered so dangerous.

[18] Easterby, *Records*, 4:72; also *South Carolina Gazette*, March 27, 1742.

[19] Pinckney, *Letterbook*, pp. 29–30.

[20] *Boston Weekly Post-Boy*, May 3, 1742.

[21] Ibid.

the Spirit of GOD, but by the Devil himself only." [22] His apocalyptic vision of liberation and destruction ended anti-climactically in his self-abasing confession of delusion.

More stood behind Bryan's "strange Revolution" than fear of arrest and confrontation. The true breaking-point had come, his brother would later suggest, when Hugh's prophetic powers failed him in his attempt to smite the waters of a river with a rod and then to "go over on dry Ground." This latter-day Moses had taken up his divinely-proportioned rod and away he had charged "full Tilt with it into the River" and there fell "a smiting, splashing and spluttering the Water about with it, till he was quite up to the Chinn." [23] The waters remained undivided. His brother barely saved him from drowning. "The grand Prophet" was wet and cold and highly disillusioned; "the Father of Lies" had tricked him.[24] He had to seek peace while there was still time. As James Davenport, New England's own grand prophet of the Awakening, would similarly learn, playing the prophet was a lonely and unrewarding enterprise. Davenport's cries of apocalypse in New England and his ritual enactment of the final conflagration in the bonfires in New London earned him, as with Bryan, only disillusionment and derision.[25]

As was the case with Davenport's downfall, Bryan's debacle, it was soon realized, was eminently suited for didacticism. When confessing his errors in March 1742, Bryan tentatively suggested the didactic import of his own delusion: "My Misfortune may caution others . . . to take Heed, lest they fall also." [26] What he suggested in ignominy, Anglican opposers, New England Old Lights, and evangelical moderates roundly seconded. Soon "the Carolina Story" was published throughout the colonies as a deterrent which it was hoped would prevent similar "tragical Events" in New England and elsewhere. Even opponents of the revivals in Scotland attempted to use the tale of Bryan's delusion as an antidote for enthusiasm.[27] Bryan, like Davenport, went along

[22] Ibid. and Easterby, *Records*, 3:461. On the patrols and the militia as systems of white control, see Peter H. Wood, *Black Majority: Negroes in Colonial South Carolina from 1670 through the Stono Rebellion* (New York, 1974), pp. 271–277.

[23] *Boston Weekly Post-Boy*, May 3, 1742.

[24] Ibid. and Easterby, *Records*, 3:461.

[25] On the extremists in New England, see Harry S. Stout and Peter Onuf, "James Davenport and the Great Awakening in New London," *Journal of American History* 71 (1983):556–578 and Leigh Eric Schmidt, " 'A Second and Glorious Reformation': The New Light Extremism of Andrew Croswell," *William and Mary Quarterly* 43 (1986):214–244. Bryan can be seen as the southern counterpart of such radicals as Davenport and Croswell in New England.

[26] Easterby, *Records*, 3:461.

[27] Ebenezer Turell, *A Dialogue between a Minister and His Neighbor about the Times* (Boston, 1742), p. 7; *Boston Weekly Post-Boy*, May 3, 1742; and *The State of Religion in New-England, since the Rev. Mr. George Whitefield's Arrival There* (Glasgow, 1743), pp. 70–74.

with his detractors as he found in confession and recantation a means of reintegration. Over the last several years of his life Bryan achieved successful readmission into the white society of the planters. He continued in his evangelicalism, became a worthy deacon in the Congregational Church at Stoney Creek, and received added attention as an examplar of enthusiasm bridled and radicalism chastened.[28] He also continued to own slaves and apparently never again returned to his prophecies of liberation and destruction.[29] His was a brief flaring of prophetic evangelicalism. Yet, his case is broadly instructive in its brevity and intensity.

Certainly one of the dominant features of Bryan's story is the early evangelical challenge to the Anglican establishment. These evangelicals introduced new forms of relegous authority that were set over against Anglican institutions, creeds, and clerics. Hugh Bryan's "many Days' intimate Converse with an invisible Spirit" was only an extreme example of how the awakened tapped sources of spiritual power and authority outside the establishment.[30] More common wasBryan's new birth—the experience of which helped mark off an enclosed and limited religious community within the putatively inclusive parishes of the establishment. Reborn, he was inbued with a "holy zeal for God" and drew a harsh line between himself and his former Anglican brethren. Simple observance of Anglican ordinances had become inadequate, or worse, damnable. Bryan epitomized the laity's assumption of a spiritual autonomy that distanced them from, or even made them hostile to, the institutionalized channels of grace. Further, his jeremiads against the sins of the existing social and religious order only added to this bifurcation of religious authority. In his prophetic lashings, Bryan, like Whitefield, singled out the Anglican clergy for abuse and helped fuel an anti-clericalism not only among the dissenters, but also among the Anglican gentry who began to blame their own clerics for the growth of religious unrest.[31] Even the evangelicals' orphanage, Bethesda, was a rebuke to Anglican authority as it set up a philanthropic institution

---

[28] See Conder and Gibbons, eds., *Living Christianity delineated*; "Register Kept By The Rev. Wm. Hutson," *South Carolina Historical Magazine* 38 (1937):21–36.

[29] He and his brother Jonathan continued their efforts to convert the slaves, but with little of their former radicalism. For example, his brother's slave, Andrew Bryan, would preside over one of the earliest independent black churches, the First African Church, organized in Savannah in 1788. Jonathan provided the land for the church. See Isabella Remshart Redding, *Life and Times of Jonathan Bryan, 1708–1788* (Savannah, 1901), pp. 43–44; Reba Carolyn Strickland, *Religion and the State in Georgia in the Eighteenth Century* (New York, 1939), pp. 131, 180–181; "Letters Showing The Rise and Progress of the Early Negro Churches of Georgia and the West Indies," *Journal of Negro History* 1 (1916):69–92.

[30] Easterby, *Records*, 3:461.

[31] Conder and Gibbons, eds., *Living Christianity delineated*, p. 40. On anti-clericalism, see Isaac, "Religion and Authority."

that was founded on an evangelical base and that assumed the inadequacy of Anglican benevolence and catechesis.

Bryan showed not only a disdain for Anglican authority, but also a disregard for the laws undergirding planter hegemony. To government officials he was disloyal—a traitor to his class, race, and religion. It was "public and notorious," the legislature said, that the slaves in their religious assemblies were "encouraged and countenanced by several white Persons residing in those Parts"—namely Bryan and his brother Jonathan.[32] The Bryans were clearly, the legislature said, "without Authority for so doing."[33] And yet they encouraged and countenanced anyway. In the topsy-turvy world of the prophet, Bryan in a sense underwent a reversal of status in which he temporarily allied himself with the slaves over against the civil and ecclesiastical powers of the colony. He soon realized the danger of such inverted loyalties, but he nonetheless revealed how the evangelicals in their intense concern for the salvation of the slaves could readily challenge authority. In short, Bryan embodied in extreme and dramatic form the tendencies of early evangelicalism to undermine the Anglican establishment in both its civil and ecclesiastical spheres. More broadly, he suggested the nature of the evangelical threat to any establishment whether in New England or the south.

Yet another feature of Bryan's story stands out in still bolder relief; namely, his close religious involvement with the enslaved and his auguries of freedom for the oppressed and destruction for the oppressors. His prophetic stature and his sizable following among the slaves are profoundly suggestive, especially when set within the larger context of slave religion and resistance. Gerald Mullin's conclusion, in discussing the intricate conspiracy of Gabriel Prosser in 1800, is particularly apposite in broaching Bryan's place within this broader framework: "Here is the source of Gabriel's failure: at a time when revivalism was a vital force among plantation slaves, those who would lead couched their appeal in political and secular terms. Unlike Nat Turner's magnificent Old Testament visions, which transfigured him and sustained his movement, Gabriel's Rebellion, lacking a sacred dimension, was without a Moses."[34] Hugh Bryan, it is clear, possessed this sacred dimension. He held the script of the Old Testament prophet; he could play the role of Moses. His actions suggest how thoroughly he had reentered the Biblical world of the prophets, how he was reenacting the Mosaic type, and how the prophetic role itself defined and delimited the kind of actions available to him and expected

---

[32] Easterby, *Records*, 3:381. Two other whites were also accused by name: William Gilbert and Robert Ogle.

[33] Ibid., 4:72.

[34] Gerald W. Mullin, *Flight and Rebellion: Slave Resistance in Eighteenth-Century Virginia* (New York, 1972), pp. 159–160.

of him. The sarcasm and disbelief of those who reported his actions did not obscure the prophetic script that underpinned—and shaped—his mission. Barefoot upon hold ground, divinely-led in the wilderness with sacred rod in hand, he would recreate the liberation of God's people.[35] Yet, he manipulated Biblical types and sacred symbols better than he did water and rivers. With the failure of his miraculous powers, his religious vision of liberation and apocalypse was dampened, if not washed away entirely.

Despite the shortness of Bryan's tenure as a latter-day Moses, his entry into this Biblical role remains provocative. Moses and the exodus were perhaps the most important Biblical archetypes informing the world view of the Christian slaves.[36] In a figure like Bryan one glimpses how the themes of liberation within the Bible could not be kept from the slaves. Even as the slaveholders wanted to circumscribe carefully what version of Christianity was presented to the slaves, it was altogether clear in the case of Bryan that the advent of the evangelicals would defeat their efforts. With preachers and teachers like Bryan—both black and white—the slaves could appropriate and re-fashion the evangelical strains of liberation and egalitarianism and incorporate them into their own distinctive Afro-American Christianity. The enslaved could readily re-mold Bryan's offer of escape "from the slavery of sin and death to liberty and eternal life" into a temporal and spiritual vision of deliverance.[37]

An early figure such as Hugh Bryan provided an important contact point between the evangelicalism of the whites and that burgeoning among the slaves. Bryan's frequent exhorting of "great Assemblies of Negroes" undoubtedly introduced many South Carolinian blacks for the first time to evangelical Christianity—to its distinctive piety, song, and fervor. A group of travellers near Bryan's plantation in December 1741 reported, for example, hearing "a Moorish slave woman . . . singing a spiritual near the water's edge." She evidently had been a part of those "great Bodies of Negroes" who assembled for "Religious Worship" at Bryan's and there "had attained a certain assurance of the forgiveness of sins." At one of the meetings, the travellers reported,

[35] His use of a magical divining rod and his intimate converse with spirits suggest Bryan's merger of popular religious beliefs with his Christianity. In his use of these alternative religious forms he was hardly eccentric, but apiece with much of his culture, black and white. See, for example, Jon Butler, "Magic, Astrology, and the Early American Religious Heritage, 1600–1760," *American Historical Review* 84 (1979):317–346.

[36] The work of Professor Albert J. Raboteau has particularly helped me interpret Bryan's prophetic actions within the context of slave religion. See, for example, his discussion of the exodus motif in *Slave Religion: The "Invisible Institution" in the Antebellum South* (New York, 1978), pp. 311–313. Fittingly, if ironically, in 1751—a decade after Bryan's prophecies—a child of one of his slaves would be baptized and christened Moses. See "Register," p. 29.

[37] Conder and Gibbons, eds., *Living Christianity delineated*, p. 39.

she "along with others who loved Christ, was shouting and jubilating because of this treasure" of salvation. Thus Bryan's evangelicalism could readily be appropriated by the slaves and transformed into their own Christianity.[38] More specifically, Bryan offered the slaves at these revivals—at least for a time—the dramatic visions of Christian apocalypticism.[39] Even after he stepped back into his role as planter and abandoned his prophetic character, lessons and visions like his lingered—and grew. With the memorable images of fire and judgment, liberation and destruction laid out before them, the slaves could create their own prophetic Christianity and their own forms of rebellion based in Biblical types.[40] They would often not suffer Bryan's weakness and disillusionment, but instead press their visions, as Nat Turner did, to bloody fulfillment and to crucifixion in their own Jerusalems.

In addition to serving as this contact point between two religious cultures, Bryan stands out as an early example of the contribution of white evangelicals to the assault on slavery. Bryan can be placed in a long line of white radicals who saw the liberation of the slaves and the destruction of their wayward captors as a divine cause. Here the "wild and visionary" and "very religious" George Boxley, who orchestrated a slave conspiracy in Virginia in 1816, would be in line with Bryan.[41] Or the white abolitionist Patrick Doyle, who helped lead a slave revolt in Kentucky in 1848, would be another exemplar.[42] And then, of course, there was John Brown. Bryan never went as far as Boxley or Doyle or Brown, but his aborted prophetic mission nonetheless portended their

[38] Easterby, *Records*, 4:72; George Fenwick Jones, ed. *Detailed Reports on the Salzburger Emigrants Who Settled in America*, 8 vols. (Athens, 1968–1985), 8:512, 569n. I am indebted to Professor Harvey H. Jackson for directing me to the latter source.

[39] That this sort of cultural interchange was already going on in South Carolina before Hugh Bryan and the rise of the evangelicals is clear. The S.P.G. missionary Francis Le Jau reported as early as 1710 that one black in his parish had embraced an apocalyptic creed and had informed his master that "there wou'd be a dismal time and the Moon wou'd be turned into Blood." His views caused a stir among the slaves and Anglicans alike. Le Jau was able to curb the excitement, or at least he thought so. See Frank J. Klingberg, ed., *The Carolina Chronicle of Dr. Francis Le Jau, 1706–1717* (Berkeley, 1956), p. 70. Hence Bryan and the evangelicals mark an expansion of the interchange, not its commencement.

[40] This is not to imply that Christianity was the only religious base for slave resistance and revolt. Islam, Vodun, and Obeah were also important, particularly outside the United States. Within the colonies traditional African religious beliefs served as a rallying point in the rebellion of 1712 in New York. In 1822 the conspiracy of Denmark Vesey and Gullah Jack Pritchard showed perhaps the most syncretic religious underpinning of any slave movement in North America. See Aptheker, *Slave Revolts*, and Eugene D. Genovese, *From Rebellion to Revolution: Afro-American Slave Revolts in the Making of the New World* (Baton Rouge, 1979).

[41] James Hugo Johnston, "The Participation of White Men in Virginia Negro Insurrections," *Journal of Negro History* 16 (1931):165–167; Aptheker, *Slave Revolts*, pp. 255–256.

[42] Aptheker, *Slave Revolts*, p. 338.

larger exploits. While he settled into a Whitefieldian accommodation-ism after 1742, his brief flaring of extremism throws light ahead onto a troop of radical antislavery evangelicals.

Unlike Whitefield's, however, Bryan's eventual accommodation to the slave system remained anxiety-ridden. Guilt from "overlooking . . . that justice which was due to my poor slaves, who were spending their strength and lives for me," would haunt him throughout his life. In a revealing passage recorded in his diary in 1751, Bryan suggested how his importunate sense of transgression was intimately linked with his need to minister to his slaves:

> Bathe my soul in the fountain of his blood, and take away all my guilt; so I shall rejoice in thee for ever. Was enabled, by the divine assistance, to speak with freedom to my poor negroes, and to pray with them, with some enlargement of heart. Blessed be God for the gift of his quickening spirit to some of them.[43]

He went on to pray that he would behold his servants in heaven with him, where their bonds would be broken. More than a perfunctory evangelical hope, the prospect of his slaves inheriting heaven helped him assuage his guilt over holding them as property in this world. Evangelicalism, as worked out by Bryan in his later years, offered an ambiguous legacy. At points, it continued to portend radicalism and did not lose completely its prophetic vision, but it also augered accommodation. His evangelical faith stimulated guilt and anxiety over enslaving his fellows, but offered, too, the means of relieving that uneasiness and concern.

Prophet and planter, Hugh Bryan was both. Yet he never reconciled these roles and in order to relieve the tension between them he had to stop playing Moses and act the part of the patriarch instead. Though still disquieted after 1742 by slaveholding and by Anglicanism, he nevertheless came to peace with his culture and accepted the role it meted out to him. As "the grand Prophet," Hugh Bryan had dramatized how early evangelicalism could threaten both the Anglican establishment and the slave system. As patriarch and planter, Colonel Bryan revealed how that challenge was circumscribed. Few figures suggest more vividly the radical potentialities of the evangelical movement in the colonial South; conversely, few suggest more starkly the limits of that radicalism.

---

[43] Conder and Gibbons, eds., *Living Christianity delineated*, pp. 6, 54–55. See also pp. 62, 88, 98–99.

The Origins of Civil Millennialism in America: New England Clergymen, War with France, and the Revolution

NATHAN O. HATCH

What was the political role of religion after the Great Awakening? Some historians have suggested a causal relationship between the Awakening and the Revolution, arguing that the New Light proponents of religious reform in the 1730s and 1740s became the Whig proponents of revolution in the 1760s and 1770s. Since the rhetoric of revolutionary America retained a high religious content, the question of the origins and nature of revolutionary religiosity remains one of the most important unresolved problems in colonial history.

Nathan Hatch suggests that the Great Awakening is the wrong place to search for the origins of what he terms "civil millennialism"—the notion that the triumph of American political values would hasten the coming of the kingdom of God. Hatch believes that, on the contrary, it was precisely the failure of the Awakening which turned clerical attention to the concerns of the here and now and accounted for the origins of a characteristically American "civil religion." The clergy, Hatch argues, found solace in the conquest of the French fortress at Louisbourg in Cape Breton and came to see the Anglo-French conflict of the 1740s and 1750s in apocalyptic terms. In particular, they conceptualized the war as the triumph of British liberty over Catholic ("Popish") tyranny. The clergy constructed a libertarian myth in which Great Britain represented the forces of good locked in struggle with the satanic forces of France. In so doing, ironically, they constructed a moral and behavioral model that can equally well be used to explain the triumph of American liberty over British tyranny in the years following 1763.

Hatch thus provides a way to explain what happened to Puritanism in the late eighteenth century, arguing that the salvation of self was transformed into national salvation. This seems an important contribution, if we are not to fall into the anachronism of treating revolutionary America as a modern, secular society. Hatch also leaves us with some difficult questions. Were there

Reprinted by permission from Nathan O. Hatch, "The Origins of Civil Millennialism in America: New England Clergymen, War with France, and the Revolution," *William and Mary Quarterly*, 3rd ser., XXXI (1974), 407–430.

analogies to this Puritan version of civil millennialism in the colonies to the south of Connecticut? How does the theory of civil millennialism relate to the country ideology described by Robert Weir in his study of South Carolina? How seriously is the religious content of this Puritan mythology to be taken—to what extent did the satanic imagery of France and England have persuasive emotional force for New Englanders? Whatever the answers given to these questions, Hatch performs an important service in reminding us that we cannot grasp eighteenth-century intellectual and political life in purely secular terms.

No doubts clouded the Reverend Samuel Sherwood's assessment of the impending war between Great Britain and the American colonies. "God Almighty, with all the powers of heaven, are on our side," he declared to his Connecticut audience early in 1776. "Great numbers of angels, no doubt, are encamping round our coast, for our defence and protection. Michael stands ready, with all the artillery of heaven, to encounter the dragon, and to vanquish this black host." With a confidence almost prophetic, Sherwood announced the coming defeat of the "antichristian tyranny" which the British government represented; because the king's chief ministers had sipped the golden cup of fornication with "the old mother of harlots," they faced the imminent doom reserved for the wicked, persecuting tyrants of the earth. In building the climax of his address, which translated the conflict into a struggle of cosmic significance, Sherwood predicted that the British attack on America was one "of the last efforts, and dying struggles of the man of sin." From this apocalyptic point of view America's victory would initiate Christ's millennial kingdom.[1]

Sherwood was by no means the only American minister whose millennial hopes were fired by the Revolutionary struggle. The cosmic interpretation of the conflict—God's elect versus antichrist—appeared as a significant pattern in the intricate tapestry of ideas used by New England clergymen to explain the war's purpose. Moreover, by the time American victory seemed assured, the rhetoric of New England sermons was brimming with euphoric images of America's role in hastening the kingdom. The prospects for this blessed age had not seemed so bright since the founding of New England. "Vice and immorality shall yet here, become . . . banished," proclaimed George Duffield, chaplain to the Continental Congress, "and the wilderness blossom as the rose." [2]

[1] Samuel Sherwood, *The Church's Flight into the Wilderness: An Address on the Times* (New York, 1776), 39–49, quotations on pp. 46, 15, 49.

[2] George Duffield, *A Sermon Preached in the Third Presbyterian Church* . . . (Philadelphia, 1784), 17.

Certainly the most striking feature of this millennial language in the Revolutionary era is the way it adapted the framework of apocalyptic history to commonly held political ideas. Sermons during the war stressed repeatedly that American liberty was God's cause, that British tyranny was antichrist's, and that sin was failure to fight the British. With the coming of peace many ministers envisioned Christ's thousand year reign on earth as an extension of the civil and religious liberty established in America.[3] This amalgam of traditional Puritan apocalyptic rhetoric and eighteenth-century political discourse I have chosen to call "civil millennialism," a term warranted by the extent to which these themes were directed by the society's political consciousness. Under the aegis of civil millennialism ministers of varying theological persuasions came to do homage at the same shrine, that of liberty, and expressed their allegiance in projections about the future which were as novel as they were pervasive.[4]

The language of civil millennialism has a strange ring to an ear accustomed to that of Puritan apocalyptic thought, but not because the political dimension of millennialism was itself a novelty. Englishmen since the Reformation had often been willing to oppose civil governments deemed to be under the control of antichristian power. They assumed that the frustration of French and Spanish hegemony abroad and Catholic political influence at home played a major role in realizing the day when swords would be beaten into plowshares. Across the Atlantic, New Englanders for a century also had watched political developments for signs of the coming times. What *does* give civil millennialism its distinctive quality is the new configuration of civil and religious priorities in the minds of the clergy. In a subtle but profound shift in emphasis the religious values that traditionally defined the ultimate goal of apocalyptic hope—the conversion of all nations to Christianity—became diluted with, and often subordinate to, the commit-

[3] For sermons that interpret the Revolution as the struggle of the elect versus antichrist see Abraham Keteltas, *God Arising and Pleading His People's Cause* . . . (Newburyport, Mass., 1777), and Samuel West, *A Sermon Preached before the Honorable Council* . . . (Boston, 1776). For good examples of ministers whose millennial hopes were aroused by American victory see Ezra Stiles, *The United States elevated to Glory and Honor* . . . (New Haven, Conn., 1783), and Benjamin Trumbull, *God is to be praised for the Glory of his Majesty* . . . (New Haven, Conn., 1784).

[4] I have described this apocalyptic orientation as "civil" rather than "civic" or "political" because this was the adjective most frequently used by ministers to define those privileges of citizenship which increasingly occupied their attention. Several scholars who have written about millennial interpretations of the Revolution have recognized a fundamental change from earlier apocalyptic understanding. See Ernest Lee Tuveson, *Redeemer Nation: The Idea of America's Millennial Role* (Chicago, 1968), 24; John G. Buchanan, "Puritan Philosophy of History from Restoration to Revolution," *Essex Institute Historical Collections*, CIV (1968), 342–343; and J. F. Maclear, "The Republic and the Millennium," in Elwyn A. Smith, ed., *The Religion of the Republic* (Philadelphia, 1971), 183–194.

ment to America as a new seat of liberty. Although its rhetoric was conventional, this new form of millennialism, channeled in the direction of prevailing political values, stood in marked contrast to traditional New England apocalyptic hopes.

Nothing makes this point clearer than the differences between civil millennialism and the apocalyptic expectations of the Great Awakening. Jonathan Edwards may have resembled Sherwood or Duffield in the application of apocalyptic ideas to his own times and in his postmillennial view of the future, but such similarities are less significant than the fundamental contrasts between the two perspectives. The New Light confidence in the progressive course of history was based on the spread of vital piety; Christ's kingdom advanced toward its completion by the effusion of God's spirit in widespread revivals. The Revolutionary millennialist, on the other hand, based his apocalyptic hopes on the civil and religious liberty that American victory over Britain would insure. His vision of the future inspired him to attempt to thwart the precipitate advance of power rather than to advocate the conversion of sinners. Edwards saw the Concert of Prayer as the primary institution for promoting the kingdom; praying bands of pious saints were the avant-garde who would drive back the forces of darkness. In contrast, ministers such as Abraham Keteltas or Samuel Langdon welcomed to the cause of God anyone who would take up the sword against the antichrist of British tyranny. The spontaneous defense of liberty in America encouraged them to interpret existing American society as the model upon which the millennial kingdom would be based. Inspired by the complex of ideas here called civil millennialism, New England ministers of the Revolutionary era resisted tyranny in God's name, hailed liberty as the virtue of the "New American Israel," and proclaimed that in sharing these values with all mankind America would become the principal seat of Christ's earthly rule.[5]

In view of the substantial differences between these two interpretations of prophecy it is necessary to reexamine the origins and development of civil millennialism in order to explain more adequately how it became so ingrained in the minds of New England ministers. Put another way, the intention is to rethink the assumption common in recent literature that the origins of civil millennialism can be traced directly to the piety of the Great Awakening. According to this interpretation, the revivals of the 1740s aroused a new, potent sense of

---

[5] For an excellent example of the striking contrast between the millennium of Edwards and that of the Revolution cf. Edwards, *Some Thoughts Concerning the Revival of Religion in New-England* . . . in C. C. Goen, ed., *The Works of Jonathan Edwards*, IV (New Haven, Conn., 1972), 348–370, with the sermon by Ebenezer Baldwin, *The Duty of Rejoicing under Calamities and Afflictions* . . . (New York, 1776).

American destiny—expressed by the millennialism of such New Lights as Edwards—which flowered into the intense religious patriotism of the young Republic. In his massive study of the mind of eighteenth-century New England Alan Heimert attributes the fervor of the Revolutionary clergy to an excited millennial expectancy that flowed from the Awakening.[6] Heimert recognizes certain characteristics of civil millennialism but sees them only as modifications of the dynamic post-millennialism of New Light ministers. In emphasizing the dominant imprint of the Awakening on the intellectual activity of the mid-eighteenth century, he not only dismisses the heritage of pre-Awakening Puritanism but also jumps quickly from the Awakening to the Revolution, assuming that the imperial wars of the period were "incidental, even irrelevant" to the clergy's definition of New England identity. Within this framework the ideas that developed before and after the Awakening had little bearing on the shifting patterns of religious patriotism. Edwards and his successors rekindled the torch of American mission and destiny lit by the founders of the "city on a hill" and passed it directly to the patriots who fought for a new republic.[7] Although not all scholars would accept Heimert's stress on the New Light origins of the Revolution, few would doubt that the piety of the Awakening was the main source of the civil millennialism of the Revolutionary period.[8]

This interpretation is open to serious question. In the first place, if the roots of civil millennialism are to be found primarily in New Light enthusiasm, it is strange that its rhetoric was employed by Old Lights such as Langdon, Jeremy Belknap, and Samuel West, as well as the rationalist John Adams. The prevalence of this way of thinking among men of contrasting theologies can hardly be explained simply by refer-

---

[6] Alan Heimert, *Religion and the American Mind: From the Great Awakening to the Revolution* (Cambridge, Mass., 1966), 59, 413–509.

[7] According to Heimert, the Awakening shattered "the social assumptions inherited from the seventeenth century [and] allowed the evangelical ministry to offer the American people new commitments, political as well as ethical." After 1740 little of intellectual significance remained outside of the issues posed by the "two parties" formed in the Awakening. *Ibid.*, 14, 3. For Heimert's discussion of the insignificance of developments between the Great Awakening and the Revolution, particularly the Anglo-French wars, see *ibid.*, 84–85.

[8] A complete historiographical essay could be written to explain the current scholarly paradigm of tracing the origins of American patriotism and nationalism primarily to the Great Awakening. See Sacvan Bercovitch, "Horologicals to Chronometricals: The Rhetoric of the Jeremiad," in Eric Rothstein, ed., *Literary Monographs*, III (Madison, Wis., 1970), 81; Darrett B. Rutman, ed., *The Great Awakening: Event and Exegesis* (New York, 1970), 4–5, 70; Conrad Cherry, ed., *God's New Israel: Religious Interpretations of American Destiny* (Englewood Cliffs, N.J., 1971), 29–30; and Cedric B. Cowing, *The Great Awakening and the American Revolution: Colonial Thought in the 18th Century* (Chicago, 1971), 203.

ence to the New Light intellectual tradition.[9] Secondly, while recent
scholarship has focused on the exultant hopes that characterized the
Awakening, it has conspicuously avoided the same careful analysis of
New Light thought in the years of the revival's demise. There has been
little effort to examine the influence of an increasingly secular society
upon the millennial perspective derived from the Awakening. Scholars
have not adequately considered the significance of the decline of apocalyptic hope in the later 1740s, when Americans concentrated on concerns other than vital religion.[10] The third and most basic flaw is the
almost total neglect of the apocalyptic categories used by the clergy to
explain their intense interest in the Anglo-French wars. Assuming that
after the Awakening the clergy's sense of history included a moral distinction between the Old World and America—an incipient American
nationalism—many scholars slight the importance of the conflict with
France for New England thought. Looking only for signposts pointing
in the direction of Americanization, they have made an easy detour
around many issues, significantly imperial in character and scope,
which profoundly influenced New England ministers in the two decades before the Stamp Act.[11]

In 1742 Edwards anticipated with excitement the dawning of the
millennium. In his defense of the Great Awakening, *Some Thoughts
Concerning the Revival of Religion*, he suggested that this "very great and

[9] When numerous opposers of enthusiastic religion discuss the Revolution using a
millennial paradigm, how can scholars assume that the Great Awakening was their common source? It would seem far more reasonable that a viewpoint prevalent among both
Old and New Lights would have its intellectual origins in their shared heritage and experience rather than in the source of their theological division.

[10] Few authors who discuss religion and its relation to the Revolution fathom the profound intellectual shift that Edmund S. Morgan has captured so poignantly in one sentence: "In 1740 America's leading intellectuals were clergymen and thought about theology; in 1790 they were statesmen and thought about politics." It is necessary to
reconsider what happens to New Light millennial confidence when society at large substitutes politics for religion "as the most challenging area of human thought and endeavor." "The American Revolution Considered as an Intellectual Movement," in
Arthur M. Schlesinger, Jr., and Morton White, eds., *Paths of American Thought* (Boston,
1963), 11.

[11] For Heimert nothing can be of real intellectual significance in 18th-century New
England unless it encouraged Americanization. The Awakening was "in a vital respect an
American declaration of independence from Europe." The "guiding light" of subsequent
Calvinism was "a delight in the New World itself." Thus New Lights found little to in-
terest them in the conflict with France because the drama of history no longer included
foreign characters. *Religion and the American Mind*, 14, 86–87, 98, 267–269. For a conflicting interpretation that sees New England intensely caught up in the French wars "as
another battle to make the world safe for Protestantism and purified of popery," see
Kerry A. Trask, "In the Pursuit of Shadows: A Study of Collective Hope and Despair in
Provincial Massachusetts during the Era of the Seven Years War, 1748 to 1764" (Ph.D.
diss., University of Minnesota, 1971), 223–286.

wonderful, and exceeding glorious work" surpassed any that had ever been seen in New England or in other lands. The great increase in seriousness, the new conviction of the truth of the gospel, and the unusual changes in young people throughout New England were convincing signs that God would soon transform the world into the "Latter-day Glory." Edwards was so encouraged by the progress of piety that he announced that the millennium would probably begin in America.[12]

Edwards did not stand alone in interpreting the renewal of vital religion as a foretaste of Christ's kingdom. *The Christian History*, published by Thomas Prince and his son to propagate the Awakening, reflected widespread assurance that the kingdom was making significant advances. Typical was the report of Peter Thacher, pastor at Middleborough, Massachusetts: "I desire to rejoice to hear that the Lord Christ is carrying on his own Work with such a mighty Arm in so many Places. . . . If it be the Dawn of the glorious Gospel-Day; I trust the whole earth shall soon be filled with the Knowledge of the *Saviour.*" [13] In the summer of 1743 almost seventy New England ministers signed *The Testimony and Advice of an Assembly of Pastors*, supporting the revivals and declaring that these effusions of the Spirit confirmed the expectations "of such as are *waiting for the Kingdom of God*, and the coming on of the . . . latter Days." [14]

These New Lights saw the millennium as a culmination of processes at work in the revival. They pictured the imminent age of peace in images that expressed the realization of revival hope. It would be a time of vital religion, when holiness of life rather than empty profession would prevail. Confident that these ends would be accomplished by a "wonderful *revival and propagation* of religion," Edwards identified the Awakening as "the earnest," "the dawning," "the prelude," "the forerunner" of that blissful age which was swiftly approaching.[15] In *The Christian History* Daniel Putnam made the connection between vital religion and the millennium even more explicit when he encouraged his fellow clergymen to pray for revival in order that "the *Kingdoms of this World* may become the *Kingdom* of OUR BLESSED LORD AND SAVIOUR JESUS CHRIST." [16]

For Edwards the revival impulse greatly overshadowed any political means of overthrowing antichrist and initiating the thousand years of

---

[12] Edwards, *Some Thoughts Concerning the Revival*, in Goen, ed., *Works*, IV, 343–344, 353.

[13] Thomas Prince, Jr., ed., *The Christian History* (Boston, 1743–1745), II, 95.

[14] *Ibid.*, I, 158, 163–164, 182.

[15] Jonathan Edwards, *The Works of President Edwards* (reprint ed., New York, 1968 [orig. publ. London, 1817]), V, 239; Edwards, *Some Thoughts Concerning the Revival*, in Goen, ed., *Works*, IV, 353–358.

[16] *The Christian History*, I, 182.

peace. "The authority of princes" could never accomplish the goal of
the Spirit, nor could political and military activities in themselves
sound the knell for Satan's empire. This could only be done by "multitudes flocking to Christ." [17] Later, during the French wars, Edwards
was often encouraged by God's providential defeat of the enemy, who
fought on the side of antichrist, but these defeats he interpreted as
"temporal mercies," incentives to the more important works of repentance and revival. Even in the political realm Edwards's primary vision
was of the day when "vital religion shall then take possession of kings
palaces and thrones; and those who are in highest advancement shall
be holy men.[18]

To their dismay Edwards and the other revivalists did not see their
dreams fulfilled in the immediate dawning of the new age. As early as
the summer of 1743 indications began to appear in *The Christian History* that all was not well with the revival. While the pastors explained
with a touch of nostalgia the earlier spiritual movings in their
churches, they wondered unhappily why the Spirit had withdrawn.
"*Manna* grows tasteless and insipid after a Year or two's Enjoyment,"
one minister lamented, "and too many are for making a Captain, and
returning to *Egypt*." [19] Throughout 1744 the clergy's dejection deepened. While not a single minister reported a fresh revival, many expressed anxiety at the "melancholy abatements" of divine grace. A letter signed by ten ministers in eastern Connecticut depicted the
situation with imagery drawn not from the hopeful visions of St. John's
Apocalypse but from the humble prayer of Isaiah that in the midst of
wrath God would remember mercy.[20] Even Edwards had to confess
that "the work is put to a stop every where, and it is a day of the Enemy's triumph." [21]

If the Great Awakening was the catalyst that transformed post-millennialism into a dynamic paradigm to explain current events, what
happened when the fires of the revival flickered and went out? How
did the New Lights respond to the increasingly difficult problem of relating millennial hope to historical reality? By the spring of 1745 this
problem had become acute. *The Christian History* collapsed early that

[17] Edwards, *Works*, V, 239, 241.
[18] *Ibid.*, II, 480; V, 253. In a letter to William M'Culloch, Sept. 23, 1747, Edwards re-
confirmed his subordination of political and military affairs to the issue of vital religion:
"New-England has had many other surprising deliverances from the French and Indians. . . . These deliverances are very wonderful . . . but there are no such effects of
these mercies upon us that are the subjects of them, as God requires, and most justly ex-
pects. The mercies are acknowledged in words, but we are not led to repentance by
them; there appears no such thing as any reformation or Revival of religion in the land."
S. E. Dwight, *The Life of President Edwards . . .* (New York, 1830), 243–244.
[19] *The Christian History*, I, 259.
[20] *Ibid.*, II, 114, 168, 311–312.
[21] Dwight, *Life of Edwards*, 212.

year for at least the obvious reason that there were simply no revivals to report. As New Englanders challenged the French at Louisbourg later that spring, their attention was further distracted from the concerns of vital piety. A new tour by George Whitefield went almost unnoticed amid the frenzied activity inspired by the "mad scheme" to seize Cape Breton Island.[22]

Several options, all rather unpleasant, faced the minister who had anticipated that the Awakening would issue directly into the millennium. The fact that the kingdom's advance was checked, at least temporarily, led to deferred hope among some and outright pessimism among others. The writings of Edwards, Aaron Burr, and Joseph Bellamy expressed three different responses to the pressing need to forge new links between an optimistic tradition of providential history and the discouraging facts of day-to-day experience in a society increasingly unsympathetic to the millennial message.

One solution was to take celebrational note of revivals wherever they might be found. The decline of piety in New England had no necessary counterpart in Europe or in other parts of the British Empire. In this context we can understand Edwards's increasing involvement in transatlantic affairs after 1745. His extensive correspondence with Scottish ministers reflected an interest in the success of awakened Protestantism that went far beyond any provincial commitment to New England or America. Never again did he assert that America would have a special role in the coming of the millennium. Thus in his *Humble Attempt* of 1747, written in response to a proposal by Scottish ministers for extensive networks of Christians who would pray regularly for new revivals, Edwards showed no inclination to draw a moral distinction between the Old World and the New. In lamenting the spiritual decadence of the whole British Empire he manifested a pessimism about America no less pronounced than for the British Isles.[23] On other occasions, in numerous letters to friends in Scotland, he contrasted the woeful decay of religion in America—"at present very sorrowful and dark"—with comforting evidences of divine activity elsewhere in the Empire. In one of these letters he expressed the hope that recent news from Britain would excite New Englanders to seek God's face, if they were not too far "buried in ignorance, or under the power of a lethargic stupor." Edwards could no longer find signs of the coming millennium exclusively in America; the decline of experimental religion there forced him to look beyond the Atlantic to see God at work.[24]

---

[22] John E. Van de Wetering, "The *Christian History* of the Great Awakening," *Journal of Presbyterian History*, XLIV (1966), 129; Edwin Scott Gaustad, *The Great Awakening in New England* (New York, 1957), 79.

[23] Edwards, *Works*, II, 476.

[24] Dwight, *Life of Edwards*, 262, 278, 287, 412.

Edwards's solution to the problem of relating history to millennial theory was at best a holding action that avoided the major question: How could one anticipate the millennium in a society unaffected by revivalism? What happened, for instance, when revival fires were extinguished not only in New England but also throughout the Empire? This was the problem that Edwards's son-in-law, Aaron Burr, faced in the 1750s. Finding that both England and America were afflicted by irreligion and infidelity, and fearing the spiritual destruction of the whole British people,[25] Burr maintained Edwards's postmillennialism but reshuffled his categories to develop a millennial vision that can only be called pessimistic.[26] Thus in his sermon *The Watchman's Answer*, Burr developed a view of history and the apocalypse that Edwards would hardly have recognized. According to Burr, the course of history since the Reformation had not progressed in a millennial direction. Not only had the initial break with Rome fallen far short of the hopes it had raised, but in more recent times the night of antichristian domination had continued and even deepened. Burr climaxed this pessimistic argument by disagreeing explicitly with Edwards's interpretation of the slaying of the witnesses in Revelation II. Whereas for Edwards this worst time of persecution for the church had already taken place, Burr confessed his belief that the "sorest Calamity and Distress" were yet to come. The church should prepare itself to suffer cheerfully in an era of "Heresy and Wickedness, Tumults and Corruptions." Instead of sounding a trumpet of hope, Burr issued an exhortation to endurance; instead of projecting a vision of progress, he renewed the jeremiad theme.[27] He saw the millennium as the ultimate extrication of the church from its plight of "Midnight Security." Like Cotton Mather, whose chiliasm envisioned no interruption of the downward course of the church until God supernaturally intervened, Burr articulated a post-millennialism in which only a cosmic reordering would defeat the evil forces rampant among men.[28]

[25] Aaron Burr, *A Discourse Delivered at New-Ark* . . . (New York, 1755), 23, 28. In his interpretation of this sermon Heimert singles out Burr's denunciations of Great Britain as an indication of the increasing American dissatisfaction with Old World Protestantism. Apparently he overlooks the fact that Burr directed this criticism as much to America as to England. *Religion and the American Mind*, 85–86.

[26] James W. Davidson has made the excellent point that postmillennialism was not a constant "which affected the behavior of people in different times and situations in any consistent manner." He effectively demonstrates that a postmillennial framework did not necessarily imply an imminent millennium, an unclouded optimism, or an intense activism to bring on the kingdom. "Searching for the Millennium: Problems for the 1790's and the 1970's," *New England Quarterly*, XLV (1972), 241–261, esp. 250–255, quotation on p. 255.

[27] Aaron Burr, *The Watchman's Answer* . . . (Boston, 1757), 19–22, 34–40, quotations on pp. 22, 39.

[28] For Cotton Mather's views on the second coming of Christ see Robert Middlekauff, *The Mathers: Three Generations of Puritan Intellectuals, 1596–1728* (New York, 1971), 320–349, esp. 335.

Both Edwards and Burr related their apocalyptic hopes to the events of contemporary history. The failure of the Awakening thus left them no choice but to alter their views of the future. Edwards maintained his optimism by broadening his vision to include the Empire; for Burr even that panorama failed to inspire hope. In contrast to both, another New Light leader, Joseph Bellamy, maintained his millennial expectations by disassociating the millennial future from contemporary history. He was thus able to speak optimistically of Christ's eventual kingdom without regard to its current record of success or lack thereof. His 1758 sermon *The Millennium*, without mentioning a single contemporary event, either religious or political, offered Christians only the timeless hope that someday Christ would prevail.[29]

The New Light millennial vision could never have provided the intellectual foundation for the historical optimism prevalent among ministers of the Revolutionary era. Based on the success of awakened piety, it could not sustain the interest of a generation whose infatuation with revivalism faded as quickly as it had flowered. When society ceased to march to the revival's cadence, the New Light drummers faced the necessity of developing a more compelling beat. The Anglo-French conflicts that claimed New England's attention after 1745 provided just such an opportunity. In the wars with France the New England clergy found a broader basis for a millennial hope that could encompass all of society.

In July 1745 the New England press reported what must have been for its readers the most astounding news story in memory: the French fortress of Louisbourg had been captured by New England arms! In reactions that were almost ecstatic, newspapers, firsthand accounts, and sermons told how four thousand undisciplined "Land-Men unused to War" had sailed to Cape Breton Island in a makeshift fleet without British naval support or heavy artillery and there had besieged and reduced the most awesome military bastion in North America. Poetic descriptions compared the feat to the greatest victories of Marlborough, and ministers were inspired to proclaim that God had "triumphed gloriously over his and our antichristian enemies." This mighty blow to the Man of Sin evoked numerous expressions of millennial hope from the clergy and pointed to the new concerns that would preoccupy them in the subsequent years of imperial war.[30]

---

[29] Joseph Bellamy, *The Millennium*, in Alan Heimert and Perry Miller, eds., *The Great Awakening: Documents Illustrating the Crisis and Its Consequences* (Indianapolis, Ind., 1967), 609–635. In other sermons Bellamy displays the same exclusively religious and apolitical concern. See *A Blow at the Root of the refined Antinomianism of the present Age* (Boston, 1763); *An Essay on the Nature and Glory of the Gospel of Jesus Christ . . .* (Boston, 1763); and *The Half-Way-Covenant* (New Haven, Conn., 1769).

[30] Thomas Prince, *Extraordinary Events the Doings of God . . .* (Boston, 1745), 20; Joseph Sewall, *The Lamb Slain . . .* (Boston, 1745), 29. There is no adequate analysis of

In the years between the "crusade" against Louisbourg in 1745 and the signing of the Peace of Paris in 1763 the conflict with France gripped New England society with an overriding intensity. Villages had to be defended against unpredictable attack and forces marshaled for offensive engagements. The urgency of other public affairs faded for those who experienced the anxiety of battle, the despair of defeat, the joy of victory.[31] New Englanders in general, and clergymen in particular, perceived the "Gallic peril" as a massive, insidious threat to their religion and liberties. John Mellen warned his countrymen in 1756: "Our enemies may yet triumph over us, and the gospel taken from us, instead of being by us transmitted to other nations. It is possible, our land may be given to the beast, the inhabitants to the sword, the righteous to the fire of martyrdom, our wives to ravishment, and our sons and our daughters to death and torture!"[32] Similarly, Ebenezer Pemberton declared that "the fires of *Smithfield*, which burnt with such *unrelenting* fury in the days of *Queen Mary*," should remind New England of the "*inhuman* barbarities" and the "methods of *torture* and *violence*" that characterized French rule.[33] Mellen and Pemberton joined a host of their colleagues who vented their anxiety by picturing the grim consequences of French victory. Images of enslavement, prisons, galleys, and horrible tortures expressed the clergy's fear that life under the yoke of France would be "lingering Death." To French tyranny, Solomon Williams preferred that New England be destroyed by an earthquake.[34]

The ministers' rhetoric associated France inseparably with "the merciless Rage of *Popish* power" and evoked images of the inquisition, the fury of Queen Mary, the schemes of the Stuarts, and the more recent suppression of Protestants in France. Roman Catholicism represented for New Englanders not only their ancestors' most hated foe but also an immediate conspiracy against the liberties of all mankind.[35]

---

the psychological impact of the Louisbourg campaign upon New Englanders. Francis Parkman, *A Half-Century of Conflict*, II (Boston, 1892), is as helpful as anyone.

[31] For discussions of New England's intense involvement in the French wars see John M. Murrin, "Anglicizing an American Colony: The Transformation of Provincial Massachusetts" (Ph.D. diss., Yale University, 1966), 118–119, and Trask, "In the Pursuit of Shadows," 13, 223–286.

[32] John Mellen, *The Duty of all to be ready for future impending Events* (Boston, 1756), 19–20.

[33] Ebenezer Pemberton, *A Sermon Delivered at the Presbyterian Church in New-York, July 31, 1746* (New York, 1746), 19.

[34] Gad Hitchcock, *A Sermon Preached in the 2d Precinct in Pembroke . . .* (Boston, 1757), 19; Solomon Williams, *The Duty of Christian Soldiers . . .* (New London, Conn., 1755), 33–34; Isaac Stiles, *The Character and Duty of Soldiers . . .* (New Haven, Conn., 1755), 2.

[35] William McClenachan, *The Christian Warrior* (Boston, 1745), 5; Thomas More Brown, "The Image of the Beast: Anti-Papal Rhetoric in Colonial America," in Richard

Typical of this mood was the fear expressed by Prince that "our inveterate and *popish* Enemies both without and within the Kingdom, are
restless to enslave and ruin us." If France won the struggle, "Cruel *Papists* would quickly fill the *British Colonies*, seize our Estates, abuse our
Wives and Daughters, and barbarously murder us; as they have done
the like in *France* and *Ireland*." [36]

These perceptions of a massive French-Catholic conspiracy were
linked directly to an apocalyptic interpretation of history in which the
French were accomplices in Satan's designs to subjugate God's elect in
New England. According to John Burt, the conduct of the French "be-
speaks them the Offspring of that *Scarlet Whore, that Mother of Harlots,*
who is justly the *Abomination of the Earth.*" [37] In the years of the French
wars the ministers' constant use of such highly charged images as "the
Man of Sin," "the North American Babylon," "the Mother of Harlots," and "the Romish Antichristian Power" expressed their sense of
the cosmic significance of the conflict and showed that the traditional
apocalyptic view of history retained great power.[38]

In delineating this moral dichotomy between themselves and the
French, New Englanders altered the patterns of apocalyptic thought.
Turning from spiritual introspection, they began to underscore their
collective role in the last decisive struggle with Satan. Rather than becoming "indifferent to and weary with" this interpretation of history,
clergymen at mid-century manifested an intensity of interest in antichrist's overthrow unknown since the time of John Cotton and Edward Johnson.[39] Vivid perceptions of an external foe confirmed their
sense of identity as God's elect people living in the end times and
linked their lives to the cosmic war between good and evil. In the
minds of Old Lights images of antichrist shifted from "enthusiasm" to
the French menace, and New Lights ceased to be preoccupied with the

---

O. Curry and Thomas More Brown, eds., *Conspiracy: The Fear Of Subversion in American
History* (New York. 1972), 1–20; Sister Mary Augustina Ray, *American Opinion of Roman
Catholicism in the Eighteenth Century* (New York, 1936).

[36] Thomas Prince, *A Sermon Delivered At the South Church in Boston . . .* (Boston,
1746), 12, 18.

[37] John Burt, *The Mercy of God to his People . . .* (Newport, R. I., 1759), 4.

[38] Nathaniel Appleton, *A Sermon Preached October 9 . . .* (Boston, 1760), 36; Williams,
Duty of Christian Soldiers, 26; Sewall, *The Lamb Slain,* 34.

[39] Heimert, *Religion and the American Mind,* 85. For a concise discussion of New England's collective introspection in the late 17th and early 18th centuries see Perry Miller,
"Errand into the Wilderness," in his *Errand into the Wilderness* (Cambridge, Mass.,
1956), 1–15. This literature of the jeremiad stands in marked contrast to the European
orientation of both New England's first settlers and that generation which after 1745
was preoccupied with imperial conflict. Aletha Joy Gilsdorf discusses the important role
that antichrist played in the thought of early New Englanders in "The Puritan Apocalypse: New England Eschatology in the Seventeenth Century" (Ph.D. diss., Yale University, 1965).

dangers of an unconverted ministry. More concerned with the common struggle than with divisive questions relating to the spread of vital piety, the clergy found remarkable solidarity in a renewed sense of apocalyptic history. [40]

The response of New England ministers to French defeat reveals the power of this apocalyptic perspective. Had the clergy, burdened by the anxiety of war, used the imagery of prophetic scripture as mere rhetoric to stir their countrymen to fight, one would expect this form of discourse to have ended with the cessation of conflict. Yet British victories, far from signaling the demise of the apocalyptic vision, gave rise to an unprecedented outpouring of hope that Christ's kingdom was imminent. When Louisbourg fell, ministers overcame their theological differences to join in a harmonious chorus of millennial rejoicing. Not only would the Man of Sin no longer rule as vice-regent in the area of Cape Breton, but the conquest of Louisbourg was a sign that the day was not far off when it would be proclaimed that "Babylon the Great is fallen." [41] Less than a year later the defeat of the Pretender at Culloden evoked even greater displays of millennial expectancy.[42] Not since the rousing times of the Awakening had the ministers been so sure that the new age was about to dawn.

For the duration of the French wars the apocalyptic dimensions of the conflict became even more pronounced in the minds of the clergy. By the mid-1750s references associating France with antichrist had increased significantly.[43] Nor was this perspective limited to New England. For the Virginian Samuel Davies the contest of an all-Catholic French alliance with an all-Protestant British coalition suggested nothing less than "the commencement of this grand decisive conflict between the Lamb and the beast." Without qualification he pictured the consequence of French victory as the slaying of the witnesses when antichrist would establish his reign. French defeat, on the other hand, would introduce the most significant revolution in history, namely, *"a new heaven and a new earth."* [44]

---

[40] The intensity of Old Light hatred of factionalism can be seen in Charles Chauncy, *Seasonable Thoughts on the State of Religion in New-England* (Boston, 1743), 175, and Isaac Stiles, *A Prospect of the City of Jerusalem* . . . (New London, Conn., 1742), 45. There was remarkable unanimity, for instance, in the Old and New Light reactions to the Louisbourg campaign. Cf. the thanksgiving sermons given on the same day by Prince, *Extraordinary Events*, and Charles Chauncy, *Marvellous Things done by the right Hand and holy Arm of God* . . . (Boston, 1745).

[41] Sewall, *The Lamb Slain*, 34; Chauncy, *Marvellous Things*, 21.

[42] Hull Abbot, *The Duty of God's People to pray for the Peace of Jerusalem* . . . (Boston, 1746), 25–26; Prince, *Sermon Delivered At the South Church*, 37.

[43] Trask notes that there were more publications with eschatological themes during the 1750s than in any other decade of the colonial period. "In the Pursuit of Shadows," 199.

[44] Davies presented this apocalyptic interpretation of the war in a fast sermon at Hanover, Va., in Oct. 1756. See Samuel Davies, *The Crisis: or, the Uncertain Doom of*

When the long-awaited news of French downfall in Canada reached New England millennial optimism knew no limits. In sermon after sermon ministers celebrated the removal of the last and greatest obstruction to the coming kingdom. Typical was the thanksgiving sermon of Nathaniel Appleton, who delighted in God's judgment upon the French—"a Vial of his Wrath [poured] upon this Part of Antichrist"—and anticipated the "greater and more marvellous Works" that God was about to accomplish. Samuel Langdon anticipated the "final ruin of that spiritual tyranny and *mystery of iniquity.*" The time was at hand for the shout of general joy: *"Babylon the great is fallen, is fallen!"* [45] Jonathan Mayhew, reversing his pessimistic estimation of the course of history prompted by the earthquake of 1755, expressed elation that God was revealing His purpose to destroy the Beast; in confounding the antichristian forces by a succession of judgments He would initiate "a most signal revolution in the civil and religious state of things in this world; and all the kingdoms thereof are to become the kingdoms of our Lord." [46] Only such acts of divine intervention as the Reformation, the defeat of the Armada, the overthrow of the Stuarts, the founding of New England, and the accession of the Hanoverians could be compared with the remarkable conquest of Canada, a victory that Solomon Williams declared to be "of more Importance than has ever been made by the *English,* since *England* was a Nation." [47]

In light of this rhetoric the suggestion that New England ministers had disengaged from the French and Indian War or saw it as "incidental, even irrelevant, to the central theme of history" seems as unbelievable as eighteenth-century Harvard College requesting the Pope to give the Dudleian Lecture. Far from withdrawing from the imperial conflict, New Englanders translated it into genuinely cosmic categories. Fighting the French became the cause of God; marching to battle hastened the destruction of antichrist; victory proclaimed a "Salvation, a Deliverance, by far superior to any—nay to all that *New-England* ever experienced." [48] If there were still some clergymen who in 1760 could not discern the progress of providential history in the French defeat and who still found their spirits uplifted solely by the

---

Kingdoms at Particular Times, in his *Sermons on Important Subjects,* V (Philadelphia, 1818), 239–266, quotations on pp. 257, 258.

[45] Appleton, *Sermon Preached October 9,* 1–6, 26, 36; Samuel Langdon, *Joy and Gratitude to God* . . . (Portsmouth, N. H., 1760), 42–43. See also Andrew Eliot, *A Sermon Preached October 25th 1759* . . . (Boston, 1759), 42.

[46] Jonathan Mayhew, *Two Discourses Delivered October 25th 1759* . . . (Boston, 1759), 49, 61.

[47] Solomon Williams, *The Relations of God's People to him* . . . (New London, Conn., 1760), 19. See also Thomas Barnard, *A Sermon Preached before his Excellency Francis Bernard.* . . (Boston, 1763), 36, 44.

[48] Heimert, *Religion and the American Mind,* 85; Eli Forbes, *God the Strength and Salvation of his People* . . . (Boston, 1761), 9.

Concert of Prayer, they were few and insignificant. With rare exceptions the clergy saw the war's end as unequivocal evidence that the
kingdom of darkness could no longer restrain the latter-day glory.
"What a Scene of Wonder opens to our View!" exclaimed Mather
Byles, almost breathless with anticipation. "Good God! what an astonishing Scene of Wonders! Methinks, a universal Transport animates
every Countenance, and sparkles in every Eye." [49]

By 1760 New England clergymen appear to have lost a clear distinction between the kingdom of God and the goals of their own political
community. Military victories of Protestants over Catholics, which for
earlier New Englanders had been means to the end of worldwide revival, now pointed toward a different end. The idea of a millennium of
liberty both civil and religious had captured the clergy's imagination.
During the two decades of war with France ministers had continued
the long-established practice of aligning their own cause with that of
God, but these years had worked a reordering of the clergy's values
and priorities. Yet because the French wars were not the only cause of
this pervasive shift, one must trace other, no less crucial intellectual
changes by which antichrist became much more a symbol of tyranny
than of heresy and the millennium much more an age of liberty than of
piety.

Rarely did New Englanders tire of building myths about the heroic
acts of the founders of "the city on a hill." For the historian these
myths are important because they reflect their authors' values and
were used by them to express their concerns.[50] In analyzing the
rhetoric of the jeremiad Perry Miller has shown how second- and
third-generation New England ministers reproached their contemporaries by constructing exalted myths of the early settlers. Similarly, by
tracing the formulation of myths during the two decades after 1740 we
can more easily grasp the changing values and interests of the eighteenth-century ministers who created them.[51]

Although the Great Awakening shattered the traditional language of
the jeremiad, it did not replace it with an alternative paradigm by
which ministers interpreted the mission of early New England. Rather,
it bisected the earlier myth so that each side in the dispute over enthusiastic religion inherited a facet of the older interpretation. In contrasting the exemplary first generation with the declension of their own

[49] Mather Byles, *A Sermon, Delivered March 6th 1760* . . . (New London, Conn.,
1760), 13.
[50] Wesley Frank Craven, *The Legend of the Founding Fathers* (New York, 1956), 1–65;
Carl Bridenbaugh, *Mitre and Sceptre: Transatlantic Faiths, Ideas, Personalities, and Politics,
1689–1775* (New York, 1962), 171–206.
[51] Perry Miller, *The New England Mind: From Colony to Province* (Cambridge, Mass.,
1953), 27–39.

age, both Old and New Lights focused on the particular characteristics of the founders that confirmed their points of view. While New Lights exalted the "Power of Religion among the primitive Planters" and lamented its subsequent decay, Old Lights dwelt upon the love and unity of the first settlers and bemoaned the "Unscriptural Separations and Disorderly Practices" that disturbed their own day.[52] Most important, neither of these myths about early New England differed in substance from the interpretation that characterized the traditional jeremiad. Both the New Light emphasis on vital religion and the Old Light stress on unity and charity were fragments of the same earlier myth that had honored the forefathers for both their piety and their harmony.[53]

During the French wars this religious mythology underwent a massive change. As early as 1736 Prince pointed in the new direction when he called for imitation of the "worthy Fathers" not only for their vital and pure Christianity, but also for their "LIBERTY both *Civil* and *Ecclesiastical*." [54] Reflecting the increasing concern of New Englanders for the privileges confirmed to them by the Glorious Revolution and the Massachusetts Charter of 1691, this new emphasis began to appear in numerous sermons on the nature of good government, but it was only after the Awakening that the myth of the forefathers as stalwarts of liberty became a dominant theme, revealing the clergy's changing concerns.

In 1754 Mayhew articulated the form of this myth, which would become standard for the following generation. "Our ancestors," he declared, "tho' not perfect and infallible in all respects, were a religious, brave and vertuous set of men, whose love of liberty, civil and religious, brought them from their native land, into the American deserts." [55] By the end of the French and Indian War this grafting of whig political values into the traditional conceptions of New England's collective identity was virtually complete. In his thanksgiving sermon for the victory at Quebec Samuel Cooper reflected on New England's

[52] *The Christian History*, I, 37; Stiles, *Prospect of Jerusalem*, 46. For New Light statements that idealized the power of vital religion among the first generation see *The Christian History*, I, 72, 98, 106. Old Light jeremiads, which emphasized the unity of New England's founders, are seen in William Worthington, *The Duty of Rulers and Teachers in Unitedly Leading God's People* . . . (New London, Conn., 1744), 23–24, and Nathaniel Appleton, *The Great Blessing of Good Rulers* . . . (Boston, 1742), 42.

[53] Both of these themes are evident in such earlier jeremiads as that of Samuel Danforth, *A Brief Recognition of New Englands Errand into the Wilderness* (1671), in A. W. Plumstead, ed., *The Wall and the Garden: Selected Massachusetts Election Sermons 1670–1772* (Minneapolis, Minn., 1968), 65–67.

[54] Thomas Prince, *A Chronological History of New England* (Boston, 1736), I, "Dedication," ii.

[55] Jonathan Mayhew, *A Sermon Preach'd in the Audience of His Excellency William Shirley* . . . (Boston, 1754), 28.

history and surmised that his progenitors had transplanted themselves into the wilds of America because they were "smitten with a Love of Liberty, and possessed with an uncommon Reverence to the Dictates of Conscience."[56] In repeating this interpretation of the myth New England ministers did not argue for a more secular interpretation of their own origins. Instead, they incorporated certain prevailing political values into a framework that still idealized the religious motivations of their ancestors. It was not piety alone but also the sacred cause of liberty that had inspired migration to the New World.[57]

The new terms of this myth indicate the evolution of the clergy's definition of their society's meaning and purpose as with greater frequency and intensity they attributed religious significance to commonly held political values. This quest for "civil and religious liberty" became the social ideal of clergymen who in many cases made a virtual identification of piety and whiggery. Benjamin Stevens expressed the sentiment of a growing number of ministers when he proposed that "liberty both civil and religious is the spirit and genius of the sacred writings."[58]

This new pattern of identity found expression in distinctly apocalyptic categories. The civil and religious liberty of British Protestants became the divine standard against the antichristian foe of French popery and slavery. In a sermon to soldiers in 1757 James Cogswell indicated the civil priorities that had come to evoke a religious reaction: "I would entreat you to see to it that *you engage in so noble a Cause for right Ends.* Let your principal Motives be the Honor of God, and the Defence of your Country. Fight for Liberty and against Slavery. Endeavour to stand the Guardians of the Religion and Liberties of *America*; to oppose Antichrist, and prevent the barbarous Butchering of your fellow Countrymen." Cogswell urged the troops to be "inspired with an unconquerable Aversion to Popery and Slavery and an ardent Love to Religion and Liberty." In this new eschatology the French were identified with cosmic evil as much for their civil tyranny as for any other reason, and, as Samuel Davies admitted, "the Art of War becomes a Part of our Religion."[59]

As the ministers more closely identified religion and liberty, it was not uncommon for them to attribute to antichrist a plot between "the

---

[56] Samuel Cooper, *A Sermon Preached before His Excellency Thomas Pownall . . .* (Boston, 1759), 28.

[57] Eliot, *Sermon Preached October 25th*, 17.

[58] Benjamin Stevens, *A Sermon Preached at Boston . . . , May 27, 1761 . . .* (Boston, 1761), 8.

[59] James Cogswell, *God, the pious Soldier's Strength and Instructor . . .* (Boston, 1757), 26, 11; Samuel Davies, *The Curse of Cowardice . . .* (Woodbridge, N. J., 1759), 2, 304. See also John Ballantine, *The Importance of God's Presence with an Army . . .* (Boston, 1756), 18–19.

scepter and the *surplice* for enslaving both the *bodies* and *souls* of men." [60] The civil dimension of Satan's designs became a major theme both in the development of myths about the past and in the depiction of the French threat. In this way New Englanders moved in the direction of equating the war of the dragon against the woman with the threat of "slavery" common to whig ideology.[61] Thus when John Adams in 1765 pictured the course of history as a progressive, if embattled, advance of civil and religious liberty against the tyranny of antichrist represented in the canon and feudal law, he was expressing a pattern of thought that was prevalent among New England intellectuals.[62]

Perceiving that popery and slavery had struck a bargain for their destruction, New Englanders grounded their collective identity solidly in the ideals of British Protestantism and the British constitution. Far from developing in the twenty years before the Stamp Act a sense of America's moral superiority to England, the clergy identified Great Britain as the bastion of freedom and the bulwark against antichrist. For most ministers the corollary of abhorring the superstition and idolatry of popish religion was "Loyalty to the Crown . . . Attachment to the Protestant Succession in the illustrious House of *Hanover* . . . and . . . Establishment in Protestant Principles." [63] New Englanders had never been more proud of their birthright as British subjects because increasingly the liberties they most valued were perceived as those of freeborn Britons. By the end of the French wars the preachers often referred to God's British Israel and included Britons among God's covenanted people.[64]

The clearest indication of the clergy's anglicization is the new dimension of their myth-building. During the two decades after the Great Awakening they not only altered the purposes for which their ancestors settled New England but enlarged their myths to include Great Britain. It is fair to say, in fact, that during the French wars New England ministers gave far more time to creating a usable British past than to formulating myths about the New World. Tracing providential history as the continuous battle of liberty versus tyranny, they centered their attention on the British constitution—"the admiration and Envy of the World." [65] In sermon after sermon they lifted up the standard of

---

[60] Jonathan Mayhew to Experience Mayhew, Oct. 1, 1747, Jonathan Mayhew Papers, Boston University Library, Boston.

[61] Charles W. Akers, *Called unto Liberty: A Life of Jonathan Mayhew, 1720–1766* (Cambridge, Mass., 1964), 81–97.

[62] John Adams, *A Dissertation on the Canon and Feudal Law*, in Charles Francis Adams, ed., *The Works of John Adams . . .* , III (Boston, 1851), 447–452.

[63] Abbot, *Duty of God's People*, 17–18.

[64] Thomas Foxcroft, *Grateful Reflections on the signal Appearances of Divine Providence . . .* (Boston, 1760), 10, 12; Langdon, *Joy and Gratitude*, 23–24.

[65] Barnard, *Sermon Preached before Bernard*, 37.

British liberty against the aggressive tyranny of Roman Catholicism. Assuming that popery and slavery were inseparably connected, they discovered that all Britain's past evils were attributable to Catholicism and France.[66] According to Thomas Prince, King Charles I "married a *French Papist*, Sister of King *Lewis* XIII of *France*, which was the pernicious Fountain of almost all the Miseries of the *British* Nations ever since." Similarly, the arbitrary government of James II could be linked to his "popish and despotic Principles," as could the futile designs of Charles the Pretender, whose outlook was characterized by *"Popish* Tyranny, Superstition, Bigotry, and cruel Principles." [67]

Although the ministers did include the founding of New England among the great acts by which providence had secured their rights as free men, they focused their myth-making on the Glorious Revolution and the accession of the Hanoverians. It was King William, "the Deliverer of the Nation, and the Shield of its Liberty," who more than anyone else protected succeeding generations from popish enslavement. Ministers repeatedly exalted the Glorious Revolution as the fountainhead of the privileges enjoyed by eighteenth-century Britons.[68] In similar fashion the standard myth portrayed the Hanoverians as preservers of liberty and Protestantism. According to Thomas Foxcroft, if George I had not come to the throne, events "might have involved *Britain*, and these Colonies with it, in Blood and Ruin, and might have entail'd Chains and Misery on the latest Posterity." [69] In another sermon Foxcroft summed up this myth of the British past:

> Now to single out a few very memorable Times, and not go back beyond the Memory of many yet alive:—Never to be forgotten is that glorious *Year* 1688, signalis'd as a *Year of the Right Hand of the most High*, by that most seasonable Interposition of Divine Providence in the wonderful REVOLUTION; delivering us from the Perils we were in of *Popery* and *Slavery*, two of the most comprehensive Mischiefs, and securing to us our invaluable Laws and Liberties, the Rights of Conscience, and the Religion of Protestants.—Again, Never to be forgotten is that glorious Year 1714, signalis'd as a *Year of the Right Hand of the most High*, by the happy and most seasonable *Accession* of the illustrious House of HANOVER to the *British* throne; Preventing that imminent Danger the *Protestant Succession* (in the Fate of which all our valuable Interests must be involv'd) was in at that Juncture, when

---

[66] Charles Chauncy, *The Counsel of two confederate Kings . . .* (Boston, 1746), 26; Foxcroft, *Grateful Reflections*, 12–20.

[67] Prince, *Sermon Delivered At the South Church*, 8, 12.

[68] Foxcroft, *Grateful Reflections*, 20. See also Chauncy, *Counsel of two confederate Kings*, 26, and Barnard, *Sermon preached before Bernard*, 38.

[69] Foxcroft, *Grateful Reflections*, 23.

deep-laid Plots of Papal Enemies and false Brethren threatened to subvert it.[70]

This idealization of British liberty, both civil and religious, came to maturity in the 1740s and 1750s. Although the Anglo-French wars were by no means the single determinant of this development, the conflict brought into the forefront of religious thinking certain whig political ideals which since the seventeenth century had been latent in New England thought. Against the onslaught of popery and slavery the sacred cause of liberty became the banner under which New Englanders rallied. The clergy expressed this new feeling of identity in the themes that reflected their sense of the past and view of the future. Not only had the course of providential history followed the rise of liberty, but the triumph of liberty would be realized in the coming of the millennium. Just as New Lights in the 1740s had seen the past and future in terms of the concerns of vital piety, so clergymen at war with France expressed their allegiance to liberty in the framework of civil millennialism.

Understandably exhilarated by the expulsion of France from North America, New Englanders anticipated the total destruction of the power of antichrist. They had scarcely savored victory, however, when the grasping hand of tyranny reappeared in a new and dangerous form. What is remarkable about the ministers' response both to the Stamp Act and to the attempt to create an American bishopric is their application of the compelling ideology of civil millennialism to these unexpected challenges.[71] Although the threats now came from England, they represented a continuation of the Man of Sin's assault on liberty. Thus when Sherwood attributed the Quebec Act to "the flood of the dragon that has been poured forth . . . for the establishment of popery," or when Langdon suspected that British taxation originated in popish religion, they were speaking from the same perspective of prov-

---

[70] Thomas Foxcroft, *A Seasonable Memento for New Year's Day* (Boston, 1747), 70.

[71] In his thanksgiving sermon on the repeal of the Stamp Act Joseph Emerson viewed this taxation in the same historical framework in which New Englanders had seen the threat of French oppression. It was another in a long succession of attempts by popery and slavery to subvert liberty. The purpose of the taxation was "to support the pride and vanity of diocesan Bishops, and it may be by and by making us tributary to the See of Rome." Emerson feared that the conflict between England and the American colonies would weaken both so that the French or the House of Stuart might come to power. *A Thanksgiving Sermon, Preach'd at Pepperell . . .* (Boston, 1760), 11–21. In similar fashion William Patten suggested that the sponsors of the Stamp Act were "perhaps no enemies to France, and not very friendly to Christian liberty," while Stephen Johnson feared the tyranny of "a corrupt, Frenchified party in the nation." *A Discourse Delivered at Hallifax . . .* (Boston, 1766), 21. See also Stephen Johnson, *Some Important Observations . . .* (Newport, R.I., 1766), 15.

idential history that had fired New England's opposition to French tyranny.[72] Attempting to identify the Image of the Beast (Rev. 13), Sherwood in the mid-1770s gave an illuminating demonstration of how civil millennialism could be mobilized against the British:

> Whether that persecuting power be intended, that has in years past, been so cruelly and barbarously exercised in France, and other popish countries, against the humble followers of Christ, to the massacre and destruction of so many thousands of protestants; or whether there be a reference to the corrupt system of tyranny and oppression, that has of late been fabricated and adopted by the ministry and parliament of Great-Britain, which appears so favourable to popery and the Roman catholic interest, aiming at the extension and establishment of it, and so awfully threatens the civil and religious liberties of all sound protestants; I cannot positively determine. But since the prophesies represent this wicked scheme of antichristian tyranny, as having such an extensive and universal spread over the earth . . . it need not appear strange or shocking to us, to find that our own nation has been, in some degree, infected and corrupted therewith.[73]

The civil millennialism of the Revolutionary era, expressed by rationalists as well as pietists, grew directly out of the politicizing of Puritan millennial history in the two decades before the Stamp Act crisis. In marked contrast to the apolitical millennial hopes of Jonathan Edwards, which had been based on the success of the revival, civil millennialism advanced freedom as the cause of God, defined the primary enemy as the antichrist of civil oppression rather than that of formal religion, traced the myths of its past through political developments rather than through the vital religion of the forefathers, and turned its vision toward the privileges of Britons rather than to a heritage exclusive to New England.

During the Revolutionary crisis, when ministers once again emphasized the moral distinction between the Old World and the New, ironically they did so because in the previous years their own identity had become shaped in the image of British culture.[74] The sacred cause of liberty of which the patriot clergy were so enamored was not the flowering of an incipient American nationalism planted by the Awakening, nor did the initial volley of American muskets transform the millennialism of Edwards into that of Sherwood or Langdon. Instead, the religious patriotism that animated the Revolution had intellectual roots

---

[72] Sherwood, *The Church's Flight*, 33; Samuel Langdon, *Government Corrupted by Vice* (Boston, 1755), 28–29.

[73] Sherwood, *The Church's Flight*, 14–15.

[74] For a full description of the British orientation of 18th-century American culture see Murrin, "Anglicizing an American Colony."

far more British than American. In the early 1770s, however, the intellectual and emotional force of civil millennialism, incorporating whig political values, was brought to bear against England itself, as ministers linked apocalyptic vision to the cause of American liberty, identified the "fixed plan to enslave the colonies" with Satan's continuing conspiracy against God's people, and detected in the growth of arbitrary power, the corruption of placemen, and the ominous threat of standing armies the unabated malice of the Man of Sin. It was this redefinition of the terms of providential history that constituted the distinctive contribution of the New England clergy to Revolutionary ideology. In picturing the struggle of liberty versus tyranny as nothing less than the conflict between heaven and hell, the clergy found their political commitments energized with the force of a divine imperative and their political goals translated into the very principles which would initiate the kingdom of God on earth.[75]

Evangelical Revolt: The Nature of the Baptists' Challenge to the Traditional Order in Virginia, 1765 to 1775

RHYS ISAAC

Having read Williams' account of the contentedness of Virginia's small farmers at mid-century, one might have asked whether social conflict played any part in the later colonial history of the Old Dominion. In this essay, Rhys Isaac (an Australian student of early American history) contends that Virginia's age of harmony was destroyed after 1765 by the delayed effects of the Great Awakening, in the form of the "New Light" Separate Baptists. The story of radical Protestant opposition to the established church in Virginia has usually been isolated as a chapter in the

[75] An adequate understanding of the clergy's role in the Revolution awaits a thorough analysis of the relationship between traditional ideas of providential history and the prevailing mood of "country" ideology. The most helpful work in this direction is Bernard Bailyn, "Religion and Revolution: Three Biographical Studies," *Perspectives in American History*, IV (1970), 85–169.

Reprinted by permission from Rhys Isaac, "Evangelical Revolt: The Nature of the Baptists' Challenge to the Traditional Order in Virginia, 1765 to 1775," *William and Mary Quarterly*, 3rd ser., XXXI (1974), 345–368.

*history of the emergence of religious freedom (that is, pluralism)
in the late eighteenth century. Without denying the validity of
that traditional account, Isaac suggests that the Baptist challenge
to the Church of England was symptomatic of a more profound
social conflict.*

*Isaac is a student of popular culture. He understands the cul-
ture of eighteenth-century Anglo-Virginians to have been a traditional one shared by all ranks, but dominated by the proud ruling gentry. The style of that culture was oriented to display,
public occasion, and individual self-assertion. It took its most
characteristic expression in entertainment, public display, and
gregariousness as evidenced on court days, in churches, and at
horse races. It was a style suited to the plantation house and was
only rudely adapted to the circumstances of smaller landholders.*

*In contrast, and emerging explicitly out of a challenge to the
gentry culture, Isaac describes a Baptist opposition culture which
systematically confronted the values of the gentry culture. The
Baptist culture flowed naturally from the evangelical springs of
Protestant sensibility, emphasizing sobriety, comradeship, and
egalitarianism. It was an austere, yet outward-reaching style
that was proffered even to the slave population and thus threatened the rigid notions of place that undergirded the superficially
expansive gentry culture. Baptist culture was thus an explicit
threat to traditional social organization in Virginia, and the belated gentry recognition of its subversive power resulted in an often violent conflict between the two competing models of life style.
Le style was, in other words, l'homme.*

*It is clear, then, that Isaac believes that the evangelical impact
in Virginia was profound because it tapped a subterranean vein
of social strain. Those small farmers who participated in a wa-
tered-down version of gentry culture were subconsciously poised to
accept a competing style of life, even one that was overtly con-
frontational to the dominant culture. This is, in other words, an
account of cultural politics in pre-revolutionary Virginia that
suggests a method of historical analysis of life outside the elite,
which has been the object of most historical inquiry.*

*Isaac is a historical anthropologist, but unlike the modern an-
thropologist, who can question his subjects, he must rely upon the
written and physical remains that constitute historical data. One
must examine the evidence he uses and the assumptions he makes
in order to understand the opportunities (and limits) for such
new forms of history. Might it be, for instance, that evangelical
behavior in other colonies is very similar to that in Virginia? If
those colonies have a dominant culture quite different from Virginia's, what could one say about Isaac's interpretation?*

An intense struggle for allegiance had developed in the Virginia countryside during the decade before the Revolution. Two eyewitness accounts may open to us the nature of the conflict.

First, a scene vividly remembered and described by the Reverend
James Ireland etches in sharp profile the postures of the forces in contest. As a young man Ireland, who was a propertyless schoolmaster of
genteel origin, had cut a considerable figure in Frederick County society. His success had arisen largely from his prowess at dancing and his
gay facility as a satiric wit. Then, like many other young men at this
time (ca. 1768), he came deeply "under conviction of sin" and withdrew from the convivialities of gentry society. When an older friend
and patron of Ireland heard that his young protégé could not be expected at a forthcoming assembly, this gentleman, a leader in county
society, sensed the challenge to his way of life that was implicit in Ireland's withdrawal. He swore instantly that "there could not be a dance
in the settlement without [Ireland] being there, and if they would leave
it to him, he would convert [him], and that to the dance, on Monday;
and they would see [Ireland] lead the ball that day." Frederick County,
for all its geographical spread, was a close community. Young James
learned that his patron would call, and dreaded the coming test of
strength:

> When I viewed him riding up, I never beheld such a display of
> pride arising from his deportment, attitude and jesture; he rode a
> lofty elegant horse, . . . his countenance appeared to me as bold
> and daring as satan himself, and with a commanding authority
> [he] called upon me, if I were there to come out, which I accord-
> ingly did, with a fearful and timorous heart. But O! how quickly
> can God level pride. . . . For no sooner did he behold my discon-
> solate looks, emaciated countenance and solemn aspect, than he
> . . . was riveted to the beast he rode on. . . . As soon as he could
> articulate a little his eyes fixed upon me, and his first address was
> this; "In the name of the Lord, what is the matter with you?" [1]

The evident overdramatization in this account is its most revealing
feature for it is eloquent concerning the tormented convert's heightened awareness of the contrast between the social world he was leaving
and the one he was entering.

The struggle for allegiance between these social worlds had begun
with the Great Awakening in the 1740s, but entered into its most
fierce and bitter phase with the incursions of the "New Light" Sepa-

---

[1] James Ireland, *The Life of the Reverend James Ireland* . . . (Winchester, Va., 1819),
83, 84–85.

rate Baptists into the older parts of Virginia in the years after 1765.[2] The social conflict was not over the distribution of political power or of economic wealth, but over the ways of men and the ways of God. By the figures in the encounter described we may begin to know the sides drawn: on the one hand, a mounted gentleman of the world with "commanding authority" responding to challenge; on the other, a guilt-humbled, God-possessed youth with "disconsolate looks . . . and solemn aspect."

A second scene—this time in the Tidewater—reveals through actions some characteristic responses of the forces arrayed. From a diary entry of 1771 we have a description of the disruption of a Baptist meeting by some gentlemen and their followers, intent on upholding the cause of the established Church:

> Brother Waller informed us . . . [that] about two weeks ago on the Sabbath Day down in Caroline County he introduced the worship of God by singing. . . . The Parson of the Parish [who had ridden up with his clerk, the sheriff, and some others] would keep running the end of his horsewhip in [Waller's] mouth, laying his whip across the hymn book, etc. When done singing [Waller] proceeded to prayer. In it he was violently jerked off the stage; they caught him by the back part of his neck, beat his head against the ground, sometimes up, sometimes down, they carried him through a gate that stood some considerable distance, where a gentleman [the sheriff] gave him . . . twenty lashes with his horsewhip. . . . Then Bro. Waller was released, went back singing praise to God, mounted the stage and preached with a great deal of liberty.[3]

Violence of this kind had become a recurrent feature of social-religious life in Tidewater and Piedmont. We must ask: What kind of conflict was this? What was it that aroused such antagonism? What manner of man, what manner of movement, was it that found liberty in endurance under the lash?

---

[2] For a valuable account of the triumph of evangelicalism in Virginia, 1740 to 1790, see Wesley M. Gewehr, *The Great Awakening in Virginia, 1740–1790* (Durham, N. C., 1930). The rate at which the Separate Baptists were spreading may be seen by the following summary: 1769—7 churches, 3 north of the James River; May 1771—14 churches (1,335 members); May–Oct. 1774—54 churches (4,004 members); 24 north of the James River. *Ibid.*, 117. In the manuscript notes of Morgan Edwards references to *at least* 31 disruptions of meetings, by riot and/or arrest, occuring before 1772 can be identified; 13 of these appear to have been plebeian affairs, 8 gentry-led, and 10 unspecified. Morgan Edwards, *Materials toward a History of the Baptists in the Province of Virginia*, 1772 *passim*, MS, Furman University Library, Greenville, S. C. (microfilm kindly supplied by the Historical Commission, Southern Baptist Convention, Nashville, Tenn.).

[3] John William's *Journal*, May 10, 1771, in Lewis Peyton Little, *Imprisoned Preachers and Religious Liberty in Virginia* (Lynchburg, Va., 1938), 230–231. A similar account by Morgan Edwards indicates that the men were mounted and mentions who the principals were. *Materials*, 75–76.

The continuation of the account gives fuller understanding of the meaning of this "liberty" and of the true character of this encounter. Asked "if his nature did not interfere in the time of violent persecution, when whipped, etc.," Waller "answered that the Lord stood by him . . . and poured his love into his soul without measure, and the brethren and sisters about him singing praises . . . so that he could scarcely feel the stripes . . . rejoicing . . . that he was worthy to suffer for his dear Lord and Master." [4]

Again we see contrasted postures: on the one hand, a forceful, indeed brutal, response to the implicit challenge of religious dissidence; on the other, an acceptance of suffering sustained by shared emotions that gave release—"liberty." Both sides were, of course, engaged in combat, yet their modes of conducting themselves were diametrically opposite. If we are to understand the struggle that had developed, we must look as deeply as possible into the divergent styles of life, at the conflicting visions of what life should be like, that are reflected in this episode.

Opposites are intimately linked not only by the societal context in which they occur but also by the very antagonism that orients them to each other. The strength of the fascination that existed in this case is evident from the recurrent accounts of men drawn to Baptist meetings to make violent opposition, who, at the time or later, came "under conviction" and experienced conversion.[5] The study of a polarity such as we find in the Virginia pre-Revolutionary religious scene should illuminate not only the conflict but also some of the fundamental structures of the society in which it occurred. A profile of the style of the gentry, and of those for whom they were a pattern, must be attempted. Their values, and the system by which these values were maintained, must be sketched. A somewhat fuller contrasting picture of the less familiar Virginia Baptist culture must then be offered, so that its character as a radical social movement is indicated.

The gentry style, of which we have seen glimpses in the confrontation with Baptists, is best understood in relation to the concept of honor—the proving of prowess.[6] A formality of manners barely concealed adversary relationships; the essence of social exchange was overt self-assertion.

---

[4] Williams's Journal, in Little, *Imprisoned Preachers*, 231.

[5] For examples see Edwards, Materials, 34, 54, 55, 73.

[6] For the sake of clarity a single "gentry style" is here characterized. Attention is focused on the forms that appear to have been most pervasive, perhaps because most adapted to the circumstances of common life. It is not, however, intended to obscure the fact that there were divergent and more refined gentry ways of life. The development within the genteel elite of styles formed in negation of the predominant mores will be the subject of a full separate analysis. I am indebted to Jack P. Greene for advice on this point.

Display and bearing were important aspects of this system. We can best get a sense of the self-images that underlay it from the symbolic importance of horses. The figure of the gentleman who came to call Ireland back to society was etched on his memory as mounted on a "lofty . . . elegant horse." It was noted repeatedly in the eighteenth century that Virginians would "go five miles to catch a horse, to ride only one mile upon afterwards." [7] This apparent absurdity had its logic in the necessity of being mounted when making an entrance on the social scene. The role of the steed as a valuable part of proud self-presentation is suggested by the intimate identification of the gentry with their horses that was constantly manifested through their conversation. Philip Fithian, the New Jersey tutor, sometimes felt that he heard nothing but "Loud disputes concerning the Excellence of each others Colts . . . their Fathers, Mothers (for so they call the Dams) Brothers, Sisters, Uncles, Aunts, Nephews, Nieces, and Cousins to the fourth Degree!" [8]

Where did the essential display and self-assertion take place? There were few towns in Virginia; the outstanding characteristic of settlement was its diffuseness. Population was rather thinly scattered in very small groupings throughout a forested, river-dissected landscape. If there is to be larger community in such circumstances, there must be centers of action and communication. Insofar as cohesion is important in such an agrarian society, considerable significance must attach to the occasions when, coming together for certain purposes, the community realizes itself. The principal public centers in traditional Virginia were the parish churches and the county courthouses, with lesser foci established in a scatter of inns or "ordinaries." The principal general gatherings apart from these centers were for gala events such as horse race meetings and cockfights. Although lacking a specifically community character, the great estate house was also undoubtedly a very significant locus of action. By the operation of mimetic process and by the reinforcement of expectations concerning conduct and relationships, such centers and occasions were integral parts of the system of social control. [9]

---

[7] J. F. D. Smyth, quoted in Jane Carson, *Colonial Virginians at Play* (Williamsburg, Va., 1965), 103–104. See also the comments of Hugh Jones and Edward Kimber, *ibid.*, 103.

[8] Hunter Dickinson Farish, ed., *Journal & Letters of Philip Vickers Fithian 1773–1774: A Plantation Tutor of the Old Dominion* (Williamsburg, Va., 1957), 177–178.

[9] I am unable to find a serviceable alternative for this much abused term. The concept has tended to be directed toward the operations of rules and sanctions, the restraint of the pursuit of self-interest, and the correction of deviant motivation. See *International Encyclopedia of the Social Sciences*, XIV (New York, 1968), 381–396. A different emphasis is adopted in this article, drawing attention to more fundamental aspects, namely, those processes by which cultural criteria of "proper" motivation and "true" self-interest are established and reinforced in a particular society. Closely related are the mechanisms whereby individuals' perceptions and valuations of their own and others' identities are

The most frequently held public gatherings at generally distributed centers were those for Sunday worship in the Anglican churches and chapels. An ideal identification of parish and community had been expressed in the law making persistent absence from church punishable. The continuance of this ideal is indicated by the fact that prosecutions under the law occurred right up to the time of the Revolution.[10]

Philip Fithian has left us a number of vivid sketches of the typical Sunday scene at a parish church, sketches that illuminate the social nature and function of this institution. It was an important center of communication, especially among the elite, for it was "a general custom on Sundays here, with Gentlemen to invite one another home to dine, after Church; and to consult about, determine their common business, either before or after Service," when they would engage in discussing "the price of Tobacco, Grain etc. and settling either the lineage, Age, or qualities of favourite Horses." The occasion also served to demonstrate to the community, by visual representation, the rank structure of society. Fithian's further description evokes a dramatic image of haughty squires trampling past seated hoi polloi to their pews in the front. He noted that it was "not the Custom for Gentlemen to go into Church til Service is beginning, when they enter in a Body, in the same manner as they come out." [11]

Similarly, vestry records show that fifty miles to the south of Fithian's Westmoreland County the front pews of a King and Queen County church were allocated to the gentry, but the pressure for place and precedence was such that only the greatest dignitaries (like the Corbins) could be accommodated together with their families; lesser gentlemen represented the honor of their houses in single places while their wives were seated farther back.[12]

The size and composition of the ordinary congregations in the midst of which these representations of social style and status took place is as yet uncertain, but Fithian's description of a high festival is very suggestive on two counts: "This being Easter-Sunday, all the Parish seem'd to meet together High, Low, black, White all come out." [13] We learn both that such general attendance was unusual, and that at least once a year full expression of ritual community was achieved. The whole society was then led to see itself in order.

shaped and maintained. My conceptualization derives from the ideas of "reality-maintenance" (almost of continuous socialization) which are fully developed in Peter L. Berger and Thomas Luckmann, *The Social Construction of Reality: A Treatise in the Sociology of Knowledge* (Garden City, N. J., 1966), 72–73, 84, 166–175, and *passim*.

[10] Little, *Imprisoned Preachers*, 265–266, 291.

[11] Farish, ed., *Journal of Fithian*, 29, 167.

[12] C. G. Chamberlayne, ed., *The Vestry Book of Stratton Major Parish, King and Queen County, Virginia, 1729–1783* (Richmond, Va., 1931), 167.

[13] Farish, ed., *Journal of Fithian*, 89. See also 137.

The county courthouse was a most important center of social action. Monthly court days were attended by great numbers, for these were also the times for markets and fairs. The facts of social dominance were there visibly represented by the bearing of the "gentlemen justices" and the respect they commanded. On court days economic exchange was openly merged with social exchange (both plentifully sealed by the taking of liquor) and also expressed in conventional forms of aggression—in banter, swearing and fighting.[14]

The ruling gentry, who set the tone in this society, lived scattered across broad counties in the midst of concentrations of slaves that often amounted to black villages. Clearly the great houses that they erected in these settings were important statements: they expressed a style, they asserted a claim to dominance. The lavish entertainments, often lasting days, which were held in these houses performed equally important social functions in maintaining this claim, and in establishing communication and control within the elite itself. Here the convivial contests that were so essential to traditional Virginia social culture would issue in their most elaborate and stylish performances.[15]

The importance of sporting occasions such as horse racing meets and cockfights for the maintenance of the values of self-assertion, in challenge and response, is strongly suggested by the comments of the marquis de Chastellux concerning cockfighting. His observations, dating from 1782, were that "when the principal promoters of this diversion [who were certainly gentry] propose to [match] their champions, they take great care to announce it to the public; and although there are neither posts, nor regular conveyances, this important news spreads with such facility, that the planters for thirty or forty miles round, attend, some with cocks, but all with money for betting, which is sometimes very considerable." [16] An intensely shared interest of this kind, crossing but not leveling social distinctions, has powerful effects in transmitting style and reinforcing the leadership of the elite that controls proceedings and excels in the display.

Discussion so far has focused on the gentry, for *there* was established in dominant form the way of life the Baptists appeared to challenge.

---

[14] Charles S. Sydnor, *American Revolutionaries in the Making: Political Practices in Washington's Virginia* (New York, 1965 [orig. publ. Chapel Hill, N. C., 1952]), 74–85. This is the incomparable authority for the nature and function of county court days, and for the rank, etc., of the justices. Chap. 4 makes clear the importance of liquor in social intercourse. That the custom of gentlemen establishing their "liberality" by "treating" their inferiors was not confined to the time of elections is suggested by Col. Wager's report "that he usually treated the members of his militia company with punch after the exercises were over." *Ibid.*, 58.

[15] Farish, ed., *Journal of Fithian, passim;* Carson, *Colonial Virginians at Play, passim.*

[16] Quoted in Carson, *Colonial Virginians at Play,* 160 and *passim.* For evidence of genteel patronage of the sport see *ibid.,* 156–157.

Yet this way was diffused throughout the society. All the forms of communication and exchange noted already had their popular acceptances with variations appropriate to the context, as can be seen in the recollections of the young Devereux Jarratt. The son of a middling farmer-artisan, Jarratt grew up totally intimidated by the proximity of gentlemen, yet his marked preference for engagement "in keeping and exercising race-horses for the turf . . . in taking care of and preparing game-cocks for a match and main" served to bind him nonetheless into the gentry social world, and would, had he persisted, have brought him into contact—gratifying contact—with gentlemen. The remembered images of his upbringing among the small farmers of Tidewater New Kent County are strongly evocative of the cultural continuum between his humble social world and that of the gentry. In addition to the absorbing contest pastimes mentioned, there were the card play, the gathering at farmhouses for drinking (cider not wine), violin playing, and dancing.[17]

The importance of pastime as a channel of communication, and even as a bond, between the ranks of a society such as this can hardly be too much stressed. People were drawn together by occasions such as horse races, cockfights, and dancing as by no other, because here men would become "known" to each other—"known" in the ways which the culture defined as "real." Skill and daring in that violent duel, the "quarter race"; coolness in the "deep play" of the betting that necessarily went with racing, cockfighting, and cards—these were means whereby Virginia males could prove themselves.[18] Conviviality was an essential part of the social exchange, but through its soft coating pressed a harder structure of contest, or "emulation" as the contemporary phrase had it. Even in dancing this was so. Observers noted not only the passion for dancing *"Virginians are of genuine Blood—They will dance or die!"*—but also the marked preference for the jig—in effect solo performances by partners of each sex, which were closely watched and were evidently competitive.[19] In such activities, in social contexts high or low, enhanced eligibility for marriage was established by young persons who emerged as virtuosos of the dominant style. Situations where so much could happen presented powerful images of the "good life" to traditional Virginians, especially young ones. It was

---

[17] Devereux Jarratt, *The Life of the Reverend Devereux Jarratt* . . . (Baltimore, 1806), 14, 19, 20, 23, 31, 42–44. It is interesting to note that although religious observance played a minimal part in Jarratt's early life, the Bible was the book from which he (and other small farmers' sons presumably) learned to read. A base was thereby prepared for evangelical culture. *Ibid.*, 20–21.

[18] Carson, *Colonial Virginians at Play, passim*. For an intensely illuminating discussion of the social significance of "deep play" in gambling see Clifford Geertz, "Deep Play: Notes on the Balinese Cockfight," *Daedalus*, CI (Winter, 1972), 1–37.

[19] Farish, ed., *Journal of Fithian*, 177; Carson, *Colonial Virginians at Play*, 21–35.

probably true, as alleged, that religious piety was generally considered appropriate only for the aged.[20]

When one turns to the social world of the Baptists, the picture that emerges is so striking a negative of the one that has just been sketched that it must be considered to have been structured to an important extent by processes of reaction to the dominant culture.

Contemporaries were struck by the contrast between the challenging gaiety of traditional Virginia formal exchange and the solemn fellowship of the Baptists, who addressed each other as "Brother" and "Sister" and were perceived as "the most melancholy people in the world"—people who "cannot meet a man upon the road, but they must ram a text of Scripture down his throat."[21] The finery of a gentleman who might ride forth in a gold-lace hat, sporting a gleaming Masonic medal, must be contrasted with the strict dress of the Separate Baptist, his hair "cut off" and such "superfluous forms and Modes of Dressing . . . as cock't hatts" explicitly renounced.[22]

Their appearance was austere, to be sure, but we shall not understand the deep appeal of the evangelical movement, or the nature and full extent of its challenging contrast to the style and vision of the gentry-oriented social world, unless we look into the rich offerings beneath this somber exterior. The converts were proffered some escape from the harsh realities of disease, debt, overindulgence and deprivation, violence and sudden death, which were the common lot of small farmers. They could seek refuge in a close, supportive, orderly community, "a congregation of faithful persons, called out of the world by divine grace, who mutually agree to live together, and execute gospel discipline among them."[23] Entrance into this community was attained by the relation of a personal experience of profound importance to the candidates, who would certainly be heard with respect, however hum-

[20] Jarratt wrote of "*Church people*, that generally speaking, none went to the *table* [for communion] except a few of the more aged," *Life*, 102; and Ireland, "I . . . determined to pursue the pleasures . . . until I arrived to such an advance in years, that my nature would . . . enjoy no further relish. . . . A merciful God . . . would accept of a few days or weeks of my sincere repenting," *Life*, 59. Likewise it may be noted that religiosity only enters markedly into the old-man phase of Landon Carter's diary. Jack P. Greene, ed., *The Diary of Colonel Landon Carter of Sabine Hall, 1752–1778*, 2 vols. (Charlottesville, Va., 1965), *passim*.

[21] David Thomas, *The Virginian Baptist* . . . (Baltimore, 1774), 59; Robert B. Semple, *A History of the Rise and Progress of the Baptists in Virginia*, ed. G. W. Beale (Richmond, Va., 1894), 30.

[22] Farish, ed., *Journal of Fithian*, 69; Upper King and Queen Baptist Church, King and Queen County, Records, 1774–1816, Sept. 16, 1780. (Microfilm of this and subsequently cited Baptist church books kindly provided by the Virginia Baptist Historical Society, Richmond.)

[23] John Leland, *The Virginia Chronicle* (Fredericksburg, Va., 1790), 27. See also Thomas, *The Virginian Baptist*, 24–25.

ble their station. There was a community resonance for deep feelings, since, despite their sober face to the outside world, the Baptists encouraged in their religious practice a sharing of emotion to an extent far beyond that which would elicit crushing ridicule in gentry-oriented society.[24] Personal testimonies of the experiences of simple folk have not come down to us from that time, but the central importance of the ritual of admission and its role in renewing the common experience of ecstatic conversion is powerfully evoked by such recurrent phrases in the church books as "and a dore was opened to experience." This search for deep fellow-feeling must be set in contrast to the formal distance and rivalry in the social exchanges of the traditional system.[25]

The warm supportive relationship that fellowship in faith and experience could engender appears to have played an important part in the spread of the movement. For example, about the year 1760 Peter Cornwell of Fauquier County sought out in the backcountry one Hays of pious repute, and settled him on his own land for the sake of godly companionship. "Interviews between these two families were frequent . . . their conversation religious . . . in so much that it began to be talked of abroad as a very strange thing. Many came to see them, to whom they related what God did for their souls . . . to the spreading of seriousness through the whole neighbourhood." [26]

A concomitant of fellowship in deep emotions was comparative equality. Democracy is an ideal, and there are no indications that the pre-Revolutionary Baptists espoused it as such, yet there can be no doubt that these men, calling each other brothers, who believed that the only authority in their church was the meeting of those in fellowship together, conducted their affairs on a footing of equality in sharp contrast to the explicit preoccupation with rank and precedence that characterized the world from which they had been called. Important Baptist church elections generally required unanimity and might be held up by the doubts of a few. The number of preachers who were raised from obscurity to play an epic role in the Virginia of their day is a clear indication of the opportunities for fulfillment that the movement opened up to men who would have found no other avenue for public achievement. There is no reason to doubt the contemporary reputation of the early Virginia Baptist movement as one of the poor

[24] The Baptists, it was sneered, were "always sighing, groaning, weeping." To which Thomas replied, "It is true lively Christians are apt to weep much, but that is often with joy instead of sorrow." *The Virginian Baptist*, 59.

[25] Chestnut Grove Baptist Church, or Albemarle-Buck Mountain Baptist Church, Records, 1773–1779, 1792–1811, *passim*. Ireland tells how, when he had given the company of travelers to the Sandy Creek Association of 1769 an account of "what the Lord had done for my soul. . . . They were very much affected . . . so much so that one of the ministers embraced me in his arms." *Life*, 141.

[26] Edwards, Materials, 25–26.

and unlearned. Only isolated converts were made among the gentry, but many among the slaves.[27]

The tight cohesive brotherhood of the Baptists must be understood as an explicit rejection of the formalism of traditional community organization. The antithesis is apparent in the contrast between Fithian's account of a parish congregation that dispersed without any act of worship when a storm prevented the attendance of both parson and clerk, and the report of the Baptist David Thomas that "when no minister . . . is expected, our people meet notwithstanding; and spend . . . time in praying, singing, reading, and in religious conversation." [28]

The popular style and appeal of the Baptist Church found its most powerful and visible expression in the richness of its rituals, again a total contrast to the "prayrs read over in haste" of the colonial Church of England, where even congregational singing appears to have been a rarity.[29] The most prominent and moving rite practiced by the sect was adult baptism, in which the candidates were publicly sealed into fellowship. A scrap of Daniel Fristoe's journal for June 15–16, 1771, survives as a unique contemporary description by a participant:

> (Being sunday) about 2000 people came together; after preaching [I] heard others that proposed to be baptized. . . . Then went to the water where I preached and baptized 29 persons. . . . When I had finished we went to a field and making a circle in the center, there laid hands on the persons baptized. The multitude stood round weeping, but when we sang *Come we that love the lord* and they were so affected that they lifted up their hands and faces towards heaven and discovered such chearful countenances in the midst of flowing tears as I had never seen before.[30]

The warm emotional appeal at a popular level can even now be felt in that account, but it must be noted that the scene was also a vivid enactment of *a* community within and apart from *the* community. We must try to see that closed circle for the laying on of hands through the eyes

---

[27] Thomas, *The Virginian Baptist*, 54. See also Semple, *History of the Baptists in Virginia*, 29, 270, and Leland, *Virginia Chronicle*, 23. I have not as yet been able to attempt wealth-status correlations for ministers, elders, deacons, and ordinary members of the churches. It must be noted that the role which the small group of gentry converts played (as one might expect from the history of other radical movements) assumed an importance out of all proportion to their numbers. See Morattico Baptist Church, Lancaster County, Records (1764), 1778–1814, *passim*, and Chesterfield Baptist Church, Lancaster County, Records, 1773–1788, for the role of the "rich" Eleazer Clay.

[28] Farish, ed., *Journal of Fithian*, 157; Thomas, *The Virginian Baptist*, 34.

[29] Farish, ed., *Journal of Fithian*, 167, 195.

[30] Morgan Edwards, Notes, in Little, *Imprisoned Preachers*, 243. See also Leland, *Virginia Chronicle*, 36: "At times appointed for baptism the people generally go singing to the water in grand procession: I have heard many souls declare they first were convicted or first found pardon going to, at, or coming from the water."

of those who had been raised in Tidewater or Piedmont Virginia with the expectation that they would always have a monistic parish community encompassing all the inhabitants within its measured liturgical celebrations. The antagonism and violence that the Baptists aroused then also become intelligible.

The celebration of the Lord's Supper frequently followed baptism, in which circumstances it was a further open enactment of closed community. We have some idea of the importance attached to this public display from David Thomas's justification:

> . . . should we forbid even the worst of men, from viewing the solemn representation of his [the LORD JESUS CHRIST's] dying agonies? May not the sight of this mournful tragedy, have a tendency to alarm stupid creatures . . . when GOD himself is held forth . . . trembling, falling, bleeding, yea, expiring under the intollerable pressure of that wrath due to [sin]. . . . And therefore, this ordinance should not be put under a bushel, but on a candlestick, that all may enjoy the illumination.[31]

We may see the potency attributed to the ordinances starkly through the eyes of the abashed young John Taylor who, hanging back from baptism, heard the professions of seven candidates surreptitiously, judged them not saved, and then watched them go "into the water, and from thence, as I thought, seal their own damnation at the Lord's table. I left the meeting with awful horror of mind." [32]

More intimate, yet evidently important for the close community, were the rites of fellowship. The forms are elusive, but an abundance of ritual is suggested by the simple entry of Morgan Edwards concerning Falls Creek: "In this church are admitted, Evangelists, Ruling Elders, deaconesses, laying on of hands, feasts of charity, anointing the sick, kiss of charity, washing feet, right hand of fellowship, and devoting children." Far from being mere formal observances, these and other rites, such as the ordaining of "apostles" to "pervade" the churches, were keenly experimented with to determine their efficacy.[33]

Aspects of preaching also ought to be understood as ritual rather than as formal instruction. It was common for persons to come under conviction or to obtain ecstatic release "under preaching," and this established a special relationship between the neophyte and his or her "father in the gospel." Nowhere was the ritual character of the preaching more apparent than in the great meetings of the Virginia Separate

---

[31] Thomas, *The Virginian Baptist*, 35–36; Albemarle Baptist Church Book, June 18, 1774.

[32] John Taylor, *A History of Ten Baptist Churches . . .* (Frankfort, Ky., 1823), 296.

[33] Edwards, Materials, 56; Albemarle Baptist Church Book, Aug. 1776; Semple, *History of the Baptists in Virginia*, 81.

Baptist Association. The messengers would preach to the people along the way to the meeting place and back; thousands would gather for the Sunday specially set aside for worship and preaching. There the close independent congregational communities found themselves merged in a great and swelling collective.[34] The varieties of physical manifestations such as crying out and falling down, which were frequently brought on by the ritualized emotionalism of such preaching, are too well known to require description.

Virginia Baptist sermons from the 1770s have not survived, perhaps another indication that their purely verbal content was not considered of the first importance. Ireland's account of his early ministry (he was ordained in 1769) reveals the ritual recurrence of the dominant themes expected to lead into repentance those who were not hardened: "I began first to preach . . . our awful apostacy by the fall; the necessity of repentance unto life, and of faith in the Lord Jesus Christ . . . our helpless incapacity to extricate ourselves therefrom I stated and urged." [35]

As "seriousness" spread, with fear of hell-fire and concern for salvation, it was small wonder that a gentleman of Loudoun County should find to his alarm "that the *Anabaptists* . . . growing very numerous . . . seem to be increasing in afluence [influence?]; and . . . quite destroying pleasure in the Country; for they encourage ardent Pray'r; strong and constant faith, and an intire Banishment of *Gaming, Dancing,* and Sabbath-Day Diversions." [36] That the Baptists were drawing away increasing numbers from the dominant to the insurgent culture was radical enough, but the implications of solemnity, austerity, and stern sobriety were more radical still, for they called into question the validity—indeed the propriety—of the occasions and modes of display and association so important in maintaining the bonds of Virginia's geographically diffuse society. Against the system in which proud men were joined in rivalry and convivial excess was set a reproachful model of an order in which God-humbled men would seek a deep sharing of emotion while repudiating indulgence of the flesh. Yet the Baptist movement, although it must be understood as a revolt against the traditional system, was not primarily negative. Behind it can be discerned

---

[34] Ireland, *Life*, 191; Taylor, *History of Ten Baptist Churches*, 7, 16; Semple, *History of the Baptists in Virginia*, 63; Garnett Ryland, *The Baptists of Virginia, 1699–1926* (Richmond, Va., 1955), 53–54.

[35] Ireland, *Life*, 185. Laboring day and night, "preaching three times a day very often, as well as once at night," he must have kept himself in an *exalté*, near trance-like condition. His instruction to those who came to him impressed with "their helpless condition" is also illuminating. "I would immediately direct them where their help was to be had, and that it was their duty to be as much engaged . . . as if they thought they could be saved by their own works, but not to rest upon such engagedness." *Ibid.*, 186.

[36] Farish, ed., *Journal of Fithian*, 72.

an impulse toward a tighter, more effective system of values and of exemplary conduct to be established and maintained within the ranks of the common folk.

In this aspect evangelicalism must be seen as a popular response to mounting social disorder. It would be difficult—perhaps even impossible—to establish an objective scale for measuring disorder in Virginia. What can be established is that during the 1760s and 1770s disorder was perceived by many as increasing. This has been argued for the gentry by Jack P. Greene and Gordon S. Wood, and need not be elaborated here. What does need to be reemphasized is that the gentry's growing perception of disorder was focused on those forms of activity which the Baptists denounced and which provided the main arenas for the challenge and response essential to the traditional "good life." It was coming to be felt that horse racing, cockfighting, and card play, with their concomitants of gambling and drinking, rather than serving to maintain the gentry's prowess, were destructive of it and of social order generally. Display might now be negatively perceived as "luxury." [37]

Given the absence of the restraints imposed by tight village community in traditional Virginia, disorder was probably an even more acute problem in the lower than in the upper echelons of society—more acute because it was compounded by the harshness and brutality of everyday life, and most acute in proportion to the social proximity of the lowest stratum, the enslaved. The last named sector of society, lacking sanctioned marriage and legitimated familial authority, was certainly disorderly by English Protestant standards, and must therefore have had a disturbing effect on the consciousness of the whole community.[38]

As the conversion experience was at the heart of the popular evangelical movement, so a sense of a great burden of guilt was at the heart of the conversion experience. An explanation in terms of social process must be sought for the sudden widespread intensification and vocal expression of such feelings, especially when this is found in areas of the Virginia Piedmont and Tidewater where no cultural tradition existed as preconditioning for the communal confession, remorse, and expiation that characterized the spread of the Baptist movement. The hypothesis here advanced is that the social process was one in which pop-

[37] Greene, ed., *Landon Carter Diary*, I, 14, 17–19, 21, 25, 33, 39, 44, 47, 52–53; Gordon S. Wood, "Rhetoric and Reality in the American Revolution," *William and Mary Quarterly*, 3d Ser., XXIII (1966), 27–31; Jack P. Greene, "Search for Identity: An Interpretation of the Meaning of Selected Patterns of Social Response in Eighteenth-Century America," *Journal of Social History*, III (1969–1970), 196–205.

[38] Gerald W. Mullin, *Flight and Rebellion: Slave Resistance in Eighteenth-Century Virginia* (New York, 1972), *passim*. This article owes an incalculable debt to Mullin's powerful and creative analysis of the dominant Virginia culture.

ular perceptions of disorder in society—and hence by individuals in themselves—came to be expressed in the metaphor of "sin." It is clear that the movement was largely spread by revolt from within, not by "agitators" from without. Commonly the first visit of itinerant preachers to a neighborhood was made by invitation of a group of penitents already formed and actively meeting together. Thus the "spread of seriousness" and alarm at the sinful disorder of the traditional world tended to precede the creation of an emotional mass movement "under preaching." [39] A further indication of the importance of order-disorder preoccupations for the spread of the new vision with its contrasted life style was the insistence on "works." Conversion could ultimately be validated among church members only by a radical reform of conduct. The Baptist church books reveal the close concern for the disciplinary supervision of such changes.[40]

Drunkenness was a persistent problem in Virginia society. There were frequent cases in the Baptist records where censure, ritual excommunication, and moving penitence were unable to effect a lasting cure. Quarreling, slandering, and disputes over property were other endemic disorders that the churches sought patiently and endlessly to control within their own communities.[41] With its base in slavery, this was a society in which contest readily turned into disorderly violence. Accounts of the occasion, manner, and frequency of wrestling furnish a horrifying testimony to the effects of combining a code of honor with the coarseness of life in the lower echelons of society. Hearing that "by appointment is to be fought this Day . . . two fist Battles between four young Fellows," Fithian noted the common causes of such conflicts, listing numbers of trivial affronts such as that one "has in a merry hour call'd [another] a *Lubber*, . . . or a *Buckskin*, or a *Scotchman*, . . . or offered him a dram without wiping the mouth of the Bottle." He noted also the savagery of the fighting, including "Kicking, Scratching, Biting, . . . Throtling, Gouging [the eyes], Dismembring [the private parts]. . . . This spectacle . . . generally is attended with a crowd of

[39] Edwards, Materials, 25, 69, 89, 90; Semple, *History of the Baptists in Virginia*, 19–20, 25, 26, 32, 33, 227, 431.

[40] I have closely read the following Baptist church records for the period up to 1790: Broad Run Baptist Church, Fauquier County, Records, 1762–1837; Chesterfield Baptist Church, Recs.; Chestnut Grove!Albemarle Church, Recs.; Hartwood-Potomac Baptist Church Book, Stafford County, 1771–1859; Mill Creek Baptist Church, Berkeley County, Records (1757), 1805–1928; Mill Swamp Baptist Church, Isle of Wight County, Records (1774), 1777–1790; Morattico Baptist Church, Recs.; Smith's Creek Baptist Church, Shenandoah and Rockingham counties, Records, 1779–1809 (1805); Upper King and Queen Baptist Church, Recs.

[41] Upper King and Queen Baptist Church, Recs., Jan. 20, 1781; Morattico Baptist Church, Recs., May 30, 1781, *et seq.*; Mill Swamp Baptist Church, Recs., Sept. 17, 1779; Broad Run Baptist Church, Recs., July 27, 1778.

People!" Such practices prevailed throughout the province.[42] An episode in the life of one of the great Baptist preachers, John, formerly "swearing Jack," Waller, illustrates both prevailing violence and something of the relationship between classes. Waller and some gentry companions were riding on the road when a drunken butcher addressed them in a manner they considered insolent. One of the gentlemen had a horse trained to rear and "paw what was before him," which he then had it do to frighten the butcher. The man was struck by the hooves and died soon after. Tried for manslaughter, the company of gentlemen were acquitted on a doubt as to whether the injury had indeed caused the butcher's death.[43] The episode may have helped prepare Waller for conversion into a radically opposed social world.

Nowhere does the radicalism of the evangelical reaction to the dominant values of self-assertion, challenge, and response of the gentry-oriented society reveal itself so clearly as in the treatment of physical aggression. In the Baptist community a man might come forward by way of confession with an accusation against himself for "Geting angry Tho in Just Defence of himself in Despute." The meeting of another church was informed that its clerk, Rawley Hazard, had been approached on his own land and addressed in "Very scurrilous language" and then assaulted, and that he then "did defend himself against this sd Violence, that both the Assailant and Defendent was much hurt." The members voted that the minister "do Admonish Brother Rawley . . . in the presents of the Church . . . saying that his defence was Irregular." [44]

A further mark of their radicalism, and without doubt the most significant aspect of the quest for a system of social control centered in the people, was the inclusion of slaves as "brothers" and "sisters" in their close community. When the Baptists sealed the slaves unto eternal life, leading them in white robes into the water and then back to receive the bread and wine, they were also laying upon them responsibility for godly conduct, demanding an internalization of strict Protestant Christian values and norms. They were seeking to create an orderly moral community where hitherto there had seemed to be none.

The slaves were members and therefore subject to church discipline. The incidence of excommunication of slaves, especially for the sin of adultery, points to the desire of the Baptists to introduce their own standards of conduct, including stable marital relationships, among

---

[42] Farish, ed., *Journal of Fithian*, 183; Carson, *Colonial Virginians at Play*, 164–168.

[43] Edwards, Materials, 72.

[44] Chestnut Grove!Albemarle Baptist Church, Recs., Dec. 1776; Morattico Baptist Church, Recs., Feb. 17, 1783.

slaves.[45] A revealing indication of the perception of the problem in this area is found in the recurrent phrase that was sometimes given as the sole reason for excommunication: "walking disorderly." Discipline was also clearly directed toward inculcating a sense of duty in the slaves, who could be excommunicated for "disobedience and Aggrevation to [a] master." [46]

The recurrent use of the words "order," "orderly," "disorderly" in the Baptist records reveals a preoccupation that lends further support to the hypothesis that concern for the establishment of a securer system of social control was a powerful impulse for the movement. "Is it orderly?" is the usual introduction to the queries concerning right conduct that were frequently brought forward for resolution at monthly meetings.[47]

With alarm at perceived disorder must also be associated the deep concern for Sabbath-day observance that is so strongly manifested in autobiographies, apologetics, and church books. It appears that the Virginia method of keeping the Sabbath "with sport, merriment, and dissipation" readily served to symbolize the disorder perceived in society. It was his observation of this that gave Ireland his first recorded shock. Conversely, cosmic order was affirmed and held up as a model for society in the setting aside on the Lord's Day of worldly pursuits, while men expressed their reverence for their Maker and Redeemer.[48]

When the Baptist movement is understood as a rejection of the style of life for which the gentry set the pattern and as a search for more powerful popular models of proper conduct, it can be seen why the

[45] Mill Swamp Baptist Church, Recs., Mar. 13, 1773.

[46] Morattico Baptist Church, Recs., Oct. 8, 1780. The role of the slaves in the 18th-century Baptist movement remains obscure. They always carried with them their slave identity, being designated "Gresham's Bob" or the like, or even "the property of." Yet it is reported that the slaves of William Byrd's great estates in Mecklenburg County were among the first proselytes to the Separate Baptists in Virginia. "Many of these poor slaves became bright and shining Christians. The breaking up of Byrd's quarters scattered these blacks into various parts. It did not rob them of their religion. It is said that through their labors in the different neighborhoods . . . many persons were brought to the knowledge of the truth, and some of them persons of distinction." Semple, *History of the Baptists in Virginia*, 291–292. The valuable researches of W. Harrison Daniel show that hearing of experience, baptism, and disciplining of whites and blacks took place in common. Black preachers were not uncommon and swayed mixed congregations. "In the 1780s one predominantly white congregation in Gloucester County chose William Lemon, a Negro, as its pastor." Segregation of the congregation does not begin to appear in the records until 1811. Daniel, "Virginia Baptists and the Negro in the Early Republic," *Virginia Magazine of History and Biography*, LXXX (1972), 62, 60–69.

[47] Mill Swamp Baptist Church, Recs., Mar. 13, June 9, 1778; Hartwood-Potomac Baptist Church, Recs., 1776, 9–10.

[48] Ireland, *Life*, 44; Thomas, *The Virginian Baptist*, 34–35.

ground on which the battle was mainly fought was not the estate or the great house, but the neighborhood, the farmstead, and the slave quarter. This was a contemporary perception, for it was generally charged that the Baptists were "continual fomenters of discord" who "not only divided good neighbours, but slaves and their masters; children and their parents . . . wives and their husbands." The only reported complaint against the first preachers to be imprisoned was of "their running into private houses and making dissensions." [49] The struggle for allegiance in the homesteads between a style of life modeled on that of the leisured gentry and that embodied in evangelicalism was intense. In humbler, more straitened circumstances a popular culture based on the code of honor and almost hedonist values was necessarily less securely established than among the more affluent gentry. Hence the anxious aggressiveness of popular anti-New Light feeling and action.[50]

The Baptists did not make a bid for control of the political system—still less did they seek a leveling or redistribution of worldly wealth. It was clearly a mark of the strength of gentry hegemony and of the rigidities of a social hierarchy with slavery at its base that the evangelical revolt should have been so closely restricted in scope. Yet the Baptists' salvationism and sabbatarianism effectively redefined morality and human relationships; their church leaders and organization established new and more popular foci of authority, and sought to impose a radically different and more inclusive model for the maintenance of order in society. Within the context of the traditional monistic, face-to-face, deferential society such a regrouping necessarily constituted a powerful challenge.

The beginnings of a cultural disjunction between gentry and sections of the lower orders, where hitherto there had been a continuum, posed a serious threat to the traditional leaders of the community; their response was characteristic. The popular emotional style, the encouragement given to men of little learning to "exercise their gifts" in preaching, and the preponderance of humble folk in the movement gave to the proud gentry their readiest defense—contempt and ridicule. The stereotype of the Baptists as "an ignorant . . . set . . . of . . . the contemptible class of the people," a "poor and illiterate sect" which "none of the rich or learned ever join," became generally established. References in the *Virginia Gazette* to "ignorant enthusiasts" were common, and there could appear in its columns without challenge a heartless satire detailing "A Receipt to make an Anabaptist

---

[49] Thomas, *The Virginian Baptist*, 57: John Blair to the King's Attorney in Spotsylvania County, July 16, 1768, in Little, *Imprisoned Preachers*, 100–101.

[50] Jarratt, *Life*, 23, 31, 38; Farish, ed., *Journal of Fithian*, 73; Semple, *History of the Baptists in Virginia, passim.*

Preacher": "Take the Herbes of Hypocrisy and Ambition, . . . of the Seed of Dissention and Discord one Ounce, . . . one Pint of the Spirit of Self-Conceitedness." [51]

An encounter with some gentlemen at an inn in Goochland County is recorded by Morgan Edwards, a college-educated Pennsylvania Baptist minister. He noted the moderation of the gentry in this area, yet their arrogant scorn for dissenters in general, and for Baptists in particular, is unmistakable from the dialogue reported. Since Edwards had just come from Georgia, they began with ribald jests about "mr Whitefield's children . . . by the squaw" and continued as follows:

Esq[uire] U: Pray are you not a clergyman? . . .
Capt. L: Of the church of England I presume?
N[orthern] M[inister]): No, Sir; I am a clergyman of a better church than that; for she is a persecutor.
Omnes: Ha! Ha! Ha! . . .
Esq. U: Then you are one of the fleabitten clergy?
N.M.: Are there fleas in this bed, Sir?
Esq. U: I ask, if you are a clergyman of the itchy true blue kirk of Scotland? . . .
Capt. L. (whispers): He is ashamed to own her for fear you should scratch him 'Squire.'. . .
[When they have discovered that this educated man, who shows such address in fencing with words, is a Baptist minister, they discuss the subject bibulously among themselves.]
Esq. U: He is no baptist . . . I take him to be one of the Georgia law[ye]rs.
Mr. G: For my part I believe him to be a baptist minister. There are some clever fellows among them. . . .
Major W: I confess they have often confounded me with their arguments and texts of Scripture; and if any other people but the baptists professed their religion I would make it my religion before tomorrow.[52]

The class of folk who filled the Baptist churches were a great obstacle to gentry participation. Behind the ridicule and contempt, of course, lay incomprehension, and behind that, fear of this menacing, unintelligible movement. The only firsthand account we have of a meeting broken up by the arrest of the preachers tells how they "were carried before the magistrate," who had them taken "one by one into a room and examined our pockets and wallets for firearms." He accused them of "carrying on a mutiny against the authority of the land." This sort of dark suspicion impelled David Thomas, in his printed defense of the Baptists, to reiterate several times that "We concern not our-

---

[51] Little, *Imprisoned Preachers*, 36; Thomas, *The Virginian Baptist*, 54. See also Semple, *History of the Baptists in Virginia*, 29; Leland, *Virginia Chronicle*, 23; *Virginia Gazette* (Purdie and Dixon), Oct. 31, 1771.
[52] Edwards, Materials, 86–88.

selves with the government . . . we form no intrigues . . . nor make any attempts to alter the constitution of the kingdom to which as men we belong." [53]

Fear breeds fantasy. So it was that alarmed observers put a very crude interpretation on the emotional and even physical intimacy of this intrusive new society. Its members were associated with German Anabaptists, and a "historical" account of the erotic indulgences of that sect was published on the front page of the *Virginia Gazette*. [54]

Driven by uneasiness, although toughened by their instinctive contempt, some members of the establishment made direct moves to assert proper social authority and to outface the upstarts. Denunciations from parish pulpits were frequent. Debates were not uncommon, being sought on both sides. Ireland recalled vividly an encounter that reveals the pride and presumption of the gentlemen who came forward in defense of the Church of England. Captain M'Clanagan's place was thronged with people, some of whom had come forty miles to hear John Pickett, a Baptist preacher of Fauquier County. The rector of a neighboring parish attended with some leading parishioners "who were as much prejudiced . . . as he was." "The parson had a chair brought for himself, which he placed three or four yards in front of Mr. Pickett . . . taking out his pen, ink and paper, to take down notes of what he conceived to be false doctrine." When Pickett had finished, "the Parson called him a schismatick, a broacher of false doctrines . . . [who] held up damnable errors that day." Pickett answered adequately (it appeared to Ireland), but "when contradicted it would in a measure confuse him." So Ireland, who had been raised a gentleman, took it on himself to sustain the Baptist cause. The parson immediately "wheeled about on his chair . . . and let out a broadside of his eloquence, with an expectation, no doubt, that he would confound me with the first fire." However, Ireland "gently laid hold of a chair, and placed . . . it close by him, determined to argue." The contest was long, and "both gentlemen and ladies," who had evidently seated themselves near the parson, "would repeatedly help him to scripture, in order to support his arguments." When the debate ended (as the narrator recalled) in the refutation of the clergyman, Ireland "addressed one of the gentle-

[53] John Waller to an unknown fellow Baptist, Aug. 12, 1771, in Little, *Imprisoned Preachers*, 276; Thomas, *The Virginian Baptist*, 33, 36.

[54] *Va. Gaz.* (Purdie and Dixon), Oct. 4, 1770. Thomas states that there is no evil which "has not been reported of us." *The Virginian Baptist*, 6. There is in a letter of James Madison a reference to the "Religion . . . of some enthusiasts, . . . of such a nature as to fan the amorous fire." Madison to William Bradford, Apr. 1, 1774, in William T. Hutchinson and William M. E. Rachal, eds., *The Papers of James Madison*, I (Chicago, 1962), 112. See also Richard J. Hooker, ed., *The Carolina Backcountry on the Eve of the Revolution* (Chapel Hill, N. C., 1953), 98, 100–104, 113–117, for more unrestrained fantasies concerning the emergent Southern Baptists.

men who had been so officious in helping his teacher; he was a magistrate . . . 'Sir, as the dispute between the Parson and myself is ended, if you are disposed to argue the subject over again, I am willing to enter upon it with you.' He stretched out his arm straight before him, at that instant, and declared that I should not come nigher than that length." Ireland "concluded what the consequence would be, therefore made a peaceable retreat." [55] Such scenes of action are the stuff of social structure, as of social conflict, and require no further comment.

Great popular movements are not quelled, however, by outfacing, nor are they stemmed by the ridicule, scorn, or scurrility of incomprehension. Moreover, they draw into themselves members of all sections of society. Although the social worlds most open to proselytizing by the Baptists were the neighborhoods and the slave quarters, there were converts from the great houses too. Some of the defectors, such as Samuel Harris, played a leading role in the movement.[56] The squirearchy was disturbed by the realization that the contemptible sect was reaching among themselves. The exchanges between Morgan Edwards and the gentlemen in the Goochland inn were confused by the breakdown of the stereotype of ignorance and poverty. Edwards's cultured facility reminded the squires that "there are some clever fellows among [the Baptists]. I heard one Jery Walker support a petition of theirs at the assembly in such a manner as surprised us all, and [made] our witts draw in their horns." [57] The pride and assurance of the gentry could be engaged by awareness that their own members might withdraw from their ranks and choose the other way. The vigorous response of Ireland's patron to the challenge implicit in his defection provides a striking example.

The intensity of the conflict for allegiance among the people and, increasingly, among the gentry, makes intelligible the growing frequency of violent clashes of the kind illustrated at the beginning of this article. The violence was, however, one-sided and self-defeating. The episode of April 1771 in which the parson brutally interfered with the devotions of the preacher, who was then horsewhipped by the sheriff, must have produced a shock of revulsion in many quarters. Those who engaged in such actions were not typical of either the Anglican clergy or the country gentlemen. The extreme responses of some, however, show the anxieties to which all were subject, and the excesses in question could only heighten the tension.

[55] Ireland, *Life*, 129–134.

[56] Although Samuel Harris, renouncing the world, gave up his newly built country seat to be a meetinghouse for his church, the role of patron died hard. He would kill cattle for love feasts that were held there. Edwards, Materials, 57.

[57] *Ibid.*, 88. The scene was concluded by the genteel Baptist being offered and accepting hospitality. He finally left the neighborhood with an assurance from his host "that he would never talk any more against the Baptists." *Ibid.*, 89.

Disquiet was further exacerbated by the fact that the law governing dissent, under which the repressive county benches were intent on acting, was of doubtful validity, and became the subject of public controversy in the fall of 1771.[58] This controversy, combined with the appalling scenes of disorder and the growing numbers of Separate Baptists, led the House of Burgesses to attempt action in its spring 1772 session. The Separates had shown renewed tendencies to intransigence as recently as May 1771, when a move was strongly supported to deny fellowship to all ministers who submitted to the secular authority by applying for permission to preach. The fact that eight months later the House of Burgesses received a petition for easier licensing conditions was a sign that a compromise was at last being sought. Nevertheless, prejudices were so strong that the bill that the Burgesses approved was considerably more restrictive than the English act that had hitherto been deemed law in the colony.[59]

The crisis of self-confidence which the evangelical challenges and the failure of forceful responses were inducing in the Virginia gentry was subtly revealed in March 1772 by the unprecedented decision of the House, ordinarily assertive of its authority, not to send the engrossed bill to the Council, but to have it printed and referred to the public for discussion. Nearly two years later, in January 1774, the young James Madison, exultant about the progress of the American cause in the aftermath of the Boston Tea Party, despaired of Virginia on account of religious intolerance. He wrote that he had "nothing to brag of as to the State and Liberty" of his "Country," where "Poverty and Luxury prevail among all sorts" and "that diabolical Hell conceived principle of persecution rages." In April of the same year he still had little hope that a bill would pass to ease the situation of dissenters. In the previous session "such incredible and extravagant stories" had been "told in the House of the monstrous effects of the Enthusiasm prevalent among the Sectaries and so greedily swallowed by their Enemies that . . . they lost footing by it." Burgesses "who pretend too much contempt to examine into their principles . . . and are too much devoted to the ecclesiastical establishment to hear of the Toleration of Dissentients" were likely to prevail once again.[60] Madison's foreboding was correct inasmuch as the old regime in Virginia never accomplished a legal resolution of the toleration problem.

The Revolution ultimately enshrined religious pluralism as a fundamental principle in Virginia. It rendered illegitimate the assumptions concerning the nature of community religious corporateness that un-

---

[58] *Va. Gaz.* (Purdie and Dixon), Aug. 15, 22, 1771; *Va. Gaz.* (Rind), Aug. 8, 1771.

[59] *Va. Gaz.* (Rind), Mar. 26, 1772. Especially severe were provisions designed to curb activities among the slaves.

[60] Madison to Bradford, Jan. 24, Apr. 1, 1774, in Hutchinson and Rachal, eds., *Madison Papers,* I, 106, 112.

derlay aggressive defense against the Baptists. It legitimated new forms of conflict, so that by the end of the century the popular evangelists were able to counterattack and symbolize social revolution in many localities by having the Episcopal Church's lands and even communion plate sold at auction. But to seek the conclusion to this study in such political-constitutional developments would be a deflection, for it has focused on a brief period of intense, yet deadlocked conflict in order to search out the social-cultural configurations of the forces that confronted each other. The diametrical opposition of the swelling Baptist movement to traditional mores shows it to have been indeed a radical social revolt, indicative of real strains within society.

Challenging questions remain. Can some of the appeal of the Revolution's republican ideology be understood in terms of its capacity to command the allegiance of both self-humbled evangelicals and honor-upholding gentry? What different meanings did the republican ideology assume within the mutually opposed systems of values and belief? And, looking forward to the post-Revolutionary period, what was the configuration—what the balance between antagonistic cultural elements—when confrontation within a monistic framework had given way to accommodation in a more pluralist republican society? These questions are closely related to the subject that this study has endeavored to illuminate—the forms and sources of popular culture in Virginia, and the relationship of popular culture to that of the gentry elite.